AMERICA VOTES 19

A HANDBOOK OF CONTEMPORARY
AMERICAN ELECTION STATISTICS

COMPILED AND EDITED BY

RICHARD M. SCAMMON

and

ALICE V. McGILLIVRAY

1990

ELECTIONS RESEARCH CENTER

CONGRESSIONAL QUARTERLY   WASHINGTON   1991

CONTENTS

Chicago, Detroit, Harris County (Texas), Los Angeles County, New York City and Philadelphia data will be found in the appropriate state sections.

INTRODUCTION

The nineteenth volume of AMERICA VOTES follows the general pattern used in previous editions of the handbook. Chapters are presented by state, with a profile sheet, map of the state by congressional district, tables of the voting data by county, past congressional election results for districts with unchanged boundaries, note section with general election information and primary elections data. Voting data, with voting division maps, are included for Chicago, Detroit, Harris county (Texas), New York City, Philadelphia and Los Angeles county. For the New England states, tables list the voting by larger cities and towns—except for Rhode Island, which lists all cities and towns.

Each chapter begins with tables of the post-World War II, state-wide vote for President, Governor and Senator. In the Presidential table, the plurality figures are calculated on a first-second party basis and are not limited to a Republican-Democratic plurality as in the Senator and Governor tables. This conforms with the data in the tables on the national state-by-state Presidential vote from 1920 through 1988. AMERICA VOTES 19 also contains voting information on the Presidential preference primaries from 1986 through 1988 by state or summary table or both.

Most states by the 1982 elections had their congressional district (CD) lines redrawn as a result of the 1980 Census. Ten states completed redistricting between 1982 and 1984 and one—Ohio—between 1984 and 1986. The CD maps for each state reflect the reapportionment changes. Because the voting data for each CD are only for the district with its present boundaries, data in the CD tables also are evidence of redistricting changes. For earlier election results (and earlier boundaries), readers should consult previous volumes of AMERICA VOTES. The 1990 Census population figures are carried in the county-by-county tables for each state.

Of particular importance is the note section at the close of each chapter, which sets out in detail many special situations that develop in the politics and elections of the various states. Included is information about the distribution of non-major party votes, recount tallies, withdrawals and substitutions, party nomenclature, boundary changes and discrepancies or corrections in the canvassed returns.

The AMERICA VOTES series draws from official state sources the raw material of American electoral behavior. From that raw material has been built a set of reference volumes on American politics. To make these volumes of the most use to readers, suggestions for additions, together with any corrections, are welcome.

For AMERICA VOTES 19, as for its predecessors, listing all those to whom acknowledgement is due would be impossible. The editors and the users of AMERICA VOTES 19 send their gratitude to those who helped prepare this volume for publication.

Richard M. Scammon
Alice V. McGillivray

Washington, D.C.
July, 1991

UNITED STATES

POST ELECTION CHANGES

Following the 1990 General Election, and prior to July 4, 1991 there were seven changes in the membership of the 102nd Congress.

SENATORS

California—Pete Wilson (R) resigned December 1990 upon being elected Governor of California in November 1990; John Seymour (R) was appointed December 1990 to fill the seat until a special election in November 1992 for the remaining two years of this term.

New Hampshire—Gordon J. Humphrey (R) resigned December 1990 to be sworn in as a state senator in New Hampshire; Senator-elect Robert F. Smith (R) was appointed in December 1990 to fill out the remaining weeks of this term.

Pennsylvania—H. John Heinz (R) died April 1991; Harris Wofford (D) was appointed May 1991 to fill the vacancy. As of publication, the date for a special election to fill the seat for the remaining years of this term had not been set.

REPRESENTATIVES

2nd CD Arizona—Morris K. Udall (D) resigned May 1991; this vacancy will be filled by a special election in September 1991.

15th CD Illinois—Edward R. Madigan (R) resigned March 1991 upon being sworn in as Secretary of Agriculture; Thomas Ewing (R) was elected July 1991 to succeed him.

1st CD Massachusetts—Silvio O. Conte (R) died February 1991; John Oliver (D) was elected June 1991 to succeed him.

3rd CD Texas—Steve Bartlett (R) resigned March 1991 to run for Mayor of Dallas; Sam Johnson (R) was elected May 1991 to succeed him.

UNITED STATES

SPECIAL ELECTIONS TO THE 101ST CONGRESS

Between the General Elections of 1988 and 1990, twelve special elections were held to fill vacancies in the 101st Congress. Details of these special elections are listed below.

REPRESENTATIVES

ALABAMA 3RD CD

Bill Nichols (D) died in December 1988; Glen Browder (D) was elected April 1989 to fill out the remaining term for the 101st Congress.

February 14, 1989 Republican Primary

11,487 John Rice; 4,729 Ray Robbins; 1,904 Mike James; 430 Jim W. Pace.

February 14, 1989 Democratic Primary

14,715 Glen Browder; 14,440 Johnny Ford; 10,184 Jim Preuitt; 9,851 Charles Adams; 5,882 Gerald Dial; 3,908 Donald Holmes; 291 Ted McLaughlin; 254 Mike Sprayberry; 108 Robert Emerson.

March 7, 1989 Democratic Run-Off Primary

44,647 Glen Browder; 26,318 Johnny Ford.

April 14, 1989 Special Election

47,294 Glen Browder (D); 25,142 John Rice (R); 1 scattered write-in.

CALIFORNIA 15TH CD

Tony Coelho (D) resigned in June 1989; Gary A. Condit (D) was elected in September 1989 to fill out the remaining term for the 101st Congress.

September 12, 1989 Special All-Party Election

51,543 Gary A. Condit (D); 31,592 Clare L. Berryhill (R); 2,939 Robert J. Weimer (R); 2,385 Cliff Burris (R); 781 Roy Shimp (Libertarian); 381 Dave Williams (R); 344 Chris Patterakis (R); 225 Jack E. McCoy (R).

FLORIDA 18TH CD

Claude Pepper (D) died in May 1989; Ileana Ros-Lehtinen (R) was elected in August 1989 to fill out the remaining term for the 101st Congress.

August 1, 1989 Republican Primary

16,873 Ileana Ros-Lehtinen; 2,251 Carlos Perez; 691 David M. Fleischer; 563 John M. Stembridge.

August 1, 1989 Democratic Primary

5,794 Gerald F. Richman; 5,635 Rosario Kennedy; 5,071 Jo Ann Pepper; 1,713 Marvin Dunn; 1,515 Sonny Wright; 703 Bernard Anscher; 280 John P. Rosser.

August 15, 1989 Democratic Run-Off Primary

14,414 Gerald F. Richman; 9,226 Rosario Kennedy.

UNITED STATES

August 29, 1989 Special Election

49,405 Ileana Ros-Lehtinen (R); 43,318 Gerald F. Richman (D); 5 scattered write-in.

HAWAII 2ND CD

Daniel A. Akaka (D) resigned May 1990 when appointed Senator upon the death of Senator Spark M. Matsunaga. Patsy T. Mink (D) was elected September 1990 to fill out the remaining months of the term for the 101st Congress.

September 22, 1990 Special All-Party Election

51,841 Patsy T. Mink (D); 50,164 Mufi Hannemann (D); 23,629 Ron Menor (D); 8,872 Andy Poepoe (R); 2,264 Stanley Monsef (R); 1,242 Duane A. Black (D); 791 Lloyd J. Mallan (Libertarian).

INDIANA 4TH CD

Daniel R. Coats (R) resigned in January 1989 when he was appointed to fill the Senate seat vacated by J. Danforth Quayle (R) who was elected Vice-President in November 1988; Jill L. Long (D) was elected in March 1989 to fill out the remaining term for the 101st Congress.

Candidates were nominated by local party committees.

March 28, 1989 Special Election

65,272 Jill L. Long (D); 63,494 Dan Heath (R).

MISSISSIPPI 5TH CD

Larkin Smith (R) died in August 1989; Gene Taylor (D) was elected in October 1989 to fill out the remaining term for the 101st Congress.

October 3, 1989 Special All-Party Primary

51,561 Gene Taylor (D); 45,727 Tom Anderson (R); 25,579 Mike Moore (D).

October 17, 1989 Special Run-Off Election

83,296 Gene Taylor (D); 44,494 Tom Anderson (R).

NEW JERSEY 1ST CD

James J. Florio (D) resigned in January 1990 upon being elected Governor in November 1989; Robert E. Andrews (D) was elected November 1990 to fill out the remaining months of the term for the 101st Congress.

June 5, 1990 Special Republican Primary

Daniel J. Mangini, unopposed.

June 5, 1990 Special Democratic Primary

15,786 Robert E. Andrews; 9,415 Linda Bowker.

November 6, 1990 Special Election

71,373 Robert E. Andrews (D); 58,087 Daniel J. Mangini (R).

UNITED STATES

NEW YORK 14TH CD

Guy V. Molinari (R) resigned in January 1990 upon being elected Staten Island borough president in November 1989; Susan Molinari (R) was elected in March 1990 to fill out the remaining term for the 101st Congress.

Candidates were nominated by local party committees.

March 20, 1990 Special Election

29,623 Susan Molinari (R-C); 17,396 Robert Gigante (D); 2,669 Barbara Bollaert (Right-to-Life); 429 Carl Grillo (Liberal); 5 scattered write-in.

NEW YORK 18TH CD

Robert Garcia (D) resigned in January 1990; Jose E. Serrano (D) was elected March 1990 to fill out the remaining term for the 101st Congress.

Candidates were nominated by local party committees.

March 20, 1990 Special Election

3,056 Jose E. Serrano (D); 1,468 Simeon Golar (R); 126 Kevin Brawley (Conservative); 1 scattered write-in.

TEXAS 12TH CD

James C. Wright (D) resigned in June 1989; Pete Geren (D) was elected September 1989 to fill out the remaining term for the 101st Congress.

August 12, 1989 Special All-Party Primary

21,978 Bob Lanier (R); 17,751 Pete Geren (D); 12,308 Jim Lane (D); 1,313 Laraine Bethke (R); 854 Bill Turner (D); 814 Jim Hunter (R); 475 Robert Buckingham (Libertarian); 217 George J. Petrovich (D); 78 scattered write-in.

September 12, 1989 Special Run-Off Election

40,210 Pete Geren (D); 38,590 Bob Lanier (R).

TEXAS 18TH CD

Mickey Leland (D) died in August 1989; Craig A. Washington (D) was elected December 1989 to fill out the remaining term for the 101st Congress.

November 7, 1989 Special All-Party Primary

27,367 Craig A. Washington (D); 22,797 Anthony Hall (D); 4,948 Ron Wilson (D); 3,095 Al Edwards (D); 2,123 Beverly A. Spencer (R); 1,315 Shirley Fobbs (D); 1,267 Timothy J. Hattenbach (D); 1,079 Manse R. Sharp (R); 1,058 Byron J. Johnson (R); 829 Gary Johnson (Libertarian); 342 Lee A. Demas (D); 38 scattered write-in.

December 9, 1989 Special Run-Off Election

24,140 Craig A. Washington (D); 18,484 Anthony Hall (D).

UNITED STATES

WYOMING AT-LARGE

Richard Cheney (R) resigned in March 1989 to become Secretary of Defense; Craig Thomas (R) was elected April 1989 to fill out the remaining term for the 101st Congress.

Candidates were nominated by the party state central committees.

April 26, 1989 Special Election

74,384 Craig Thomas (R); 60,845 John P. Vinich (D); 5,825 Craig McCune (Libertarian); 507 Daniel Johnson (Independent).

UNITED STATES

POPULAR VOTE FOR PRESIDENT 1920 TO 1988

Year	Total Vote	Republican Vote	Candidate	Democratic Vote	Candidate	Other Vote	Plurality	Percentage Total Vote Rep.	Dem.	Major Vote Rep.	Dem.
1988	91,594,809	48,886,097	Bush, George	41,809,074	Dukakis, Michael S.	899,638	7,077,023 R	53.4%	45.6%	53.9%	46.1%
1984	92,652,842	54,455,075	Reagan, Ronald	37,577,185	Mondale, Walter F.	620,582	16,877,890 R	58.8%	40.6%	59.2%	40.8%
1980	86,515,221	43,904,153	Reagan, Ronald	35,483,883	Carter, Jimmy	7,127,185	8,420,270 R	50.7%	41.0%	55.3%	44.7%
1976	81,555,889	39,147,793	Ford, Gerald R.	40,830,763	Carter, Jimmy	1,577,333	1,682,970 D	48.0%	50.1%	48.9%	51.1%
1972	77,718,554	47,169,911	Nixon, Richard M.	29,170,383	McGovern, George S.	1,378,260	17,999,528 R	60.7%	37.5%	61.8%	38.2%
1968	73,211,875	31,785,480	Nixon, Richard M.	31,275,166	Humphrey, Hubert H.	10,151,229	510,314 R	43.4%	42.7%	50.4%	49.6%
1964	70,644,592	27,178,188	Goldwater, Barry M.	43,129,566	Johnson, Lyndon B.	336,838	15,951,378 D	38.5%	61.1%	38.7%	61.3%
1960	68,838,219	34,108,157	Nixon, Richard M.	34,226,731	Kennedy, John F.	503,331	118,574 D	49.5%	49.7%	49.9%	50.1%
1956	62,026,908	35,590,472	Eisenhower, Dwight D.	26,022,752	Stevenson, Adlai E.	413,684	9,567,720 R	57.4%	42.0%	57.8%	42.2%
1952	61,550,918	33,936,234	Eisenhower, Dwight D.	27,314,992	Stevenson, Adlai E.	299,692	6,621,242 R	55.1%	44.4%	55.4%	44.6%
1948	48,793,826	21,991,291	Dewey, Thomas E.	24,179,345	Truman, Harry S.	2,623,190	2,188,054 D	45.1%	49.6%	47.6%	52.4%
1944	47,976,670	22,017,617	Dewey, Thomas E.	25,612,610	Roosevelt, Franklin D.	346,443	3,594,993 D	45.9%	53.4%	46.2%	53.8%
1940	49,900,418	22,348,480	Willkie, Wendell	27,313,041	Roosevelt, Franklin D.	238,897	4,964,561 D	44.8%	54.7%	45.0%	55.0%
1936	45,654,763	16,684,231	Landon, Alfred M.	27,757,333	Roosevelt, Franklin D.	1,213,199	11,073,102 D	36.5%	60.8%	37.5%	62.5%
1932	39,758,759	15,760,684	Hoover, Herbert C.	22,829,501	Roosevelt, Franklin D.	1,168,574	7,068,817 D	39.6%	57.4%	40.8%	59.2%
1928	36,805,951	21,437,277	Hoover, Herbert C.	15,007,698	Smith, Alfred E.	360,976	6,429,579 R	58.2%	40.8%	58.8%	41.2%
1924	29,095,023	15,719,921	Coolidge, Calvin	8,386,704	Davis, John W.	4,988,398	7,333,217 R	54.0%	28.8%	65.2%	34.8%
1920	26,768,613	16,153,115	Harding, Warren G.	9,133,092	Cox, James M.	1,482,406	7,020,023 R	60.3%	34.1%	63.9%	36.1%

For detail of other vote see note section included with each U.S. summary table that follows.

ELECTORAL COLLEGE VOTE 1920 TO 1988

Year	Total	Republican	Democratic	Other	
1988	538	426	111	1	BENTSEN
1984	538	525	13	—	
1980	538	489	49	—	
1976	538	240	297	1	REAGAN
1972	538	520	17	1	LIBERTARIAN
1968	538	301	191	46	AIP
1964	538	52	486	—	
1960	537	219	303	15	BYRD
1956	531	457	73	1	JONES
1952	531	442	89	—	
1948	531	189	303	39	SR
1944	531	99	432	—	
1940	531	82	449	—	
1936	531	8	523	—	
1932	531	59	472	—	
1928	531	444	87	—	
1924	531	382	136	13	PROGRESSIVE
1920	531	404	127	—	

PRESIDENT 1988

In West Virginia, one Democratic elector voted in the Electoral College for Lloyd Bentsen for President and Michael S. Dukakis for Vice-President.

In New York the Republican figures include Conservative votes and the Democratic figures include Liberal votes.

In Minnesota, the Republican candidates appear on the ballot as Independent-Republican, the Democratic as Democratic-Farmer-Labor. In many states various non-major party candidates appeared on the ballot with variations of the party designations given here, were listed as "Independent" or were carried with entirely different party labels.

In several states minor party Vice-Presidential candidates were different from those listed below.

The full list of candidates for President and Vice-President was:

48,886,097	George Bush and J. Danforth Quayle, *Republican.*
41,809,074	Michael S. Dukakis and Lloyd Bentsen, *Democratic.*
432,179	Ron Paul and Andre V. Marrou, *Libertarian.*
217,219	Lenora B. Fulani and Joyce Dattner, *New Alliance.*
47,047	David E. Duke and Floyd C. Parker, *Populist.*
30,905	Eugene J. McCarthy and Florence Rice, *Consumer.*
27,818	James C. Griffin and Charles J. Morsa, *American Independent.*
25,562	Lyndon H. LaRouche and Debra H. Freeman, *National Economic Recovery.*
20,504	William A. Marra and Joan Andrews, *Right to Life.*
18,693	Ed Winn and Barry Porster, *Workers League.*
15,604	James Warren and Kathleen Mickells, *Socialist Workers.*
10,370	Herbert Lewin and Vikki Murdock, *Peace and Freedom.*
8,002	Earl F. Dodge and George Ormsby, *Prohibition.*
7,846	Larry Holmes and Gloria LaRiva, *Workers World.*
3,882	Willa Kenoyer and Ron Ehrenreich, *Socialist.*
3,475	Delmar Dennis and Earl Jeppson, *American.*
1,949	Jack Herer and Dana Beal, *Grassroots.*
372	Louie G. Youngkeit with no Vice-Presidential candidate, *Independent.*
236	John G. Martin and Cleveland Sparrow, *Third World Assembly.*

The candidates listed above include all those who appeared on the ballot in at least one state. Republican, Democratic and New Alliance candidates appeared on the ballot in all fifty-one jurisdictions. The Libertarian nominees were on the ballot in all save four. Where identified by state authorities, write-in votes for minor party candidates are credited to their total above and listed in the individual state note sections. In addition to the votes listed, 21,041 scattered write-in votes were reported from various states and 6,934 votes were cast for "None of these Candidates" in Nevada.

UNITED STATES

PRESIDENT 1988

State	Electoral Vote Rep.	Dem.	Other	Total Vote	Republican	Democratic	Other	Plurality	Percentage Total Vote Rep.	Dem.	Major Vote Rep.	Dem
Alabama	9			1,378,476	815,576	549,506	13,394	266,070 R	59.2%	39.9%	59.7%	40.3%
Alaska	3			200,116	119,251	72,584	8,281	46,667 R	59.6%	36.3%	62.2%	37.8%
Arizona	7			1,171,873	702,541	454,029	15,303	248,512 R	60.0%	38.7%	60.7%	39.3%
Arkansas	6			827,738	466,578	349,237	11,923	117,341 R	56.4%	42.2%	57.2%	42.8%
California	47			9,887,065	5,054,917	4,702,233	129,915	352,684 R	51.1%	47.6%	51.8%	48.2%
Colorado	8			1,372,394	728,177	621,453	22,764	106,724 R	53.1%	45.3%	54.0%	46.0%
Connecticut	8			1,443,394	750,241	676,584	16,569	73,657 R	52.0%	46.9%	52.6%	47.4%
Delaware	3			249,891	139,639	108,647	1,605	30,992 R	55.9%	43.5%	56.2%	43.8%
Florida	21			4,302,313	2,618,885	1,656,701	26,727	962,184 R	60.9%	38.5%	61.3%	38.7%
Georgia	12			1,809,672	1,081,331	714,792	13,549	366,539 R	59.8%	39.5%	60.2%	39.8%
Hawaii		4		354,461	158,625	192,364	3,472	33,739 D	44.8%	54.3%	45.2%	54.8%
Idaho	4			408,968	253,881	147,272	7,815	106,609 R	62.1%	36.0%	63.3%	36.7%
Illinois	24			4,559,120	2,310,939	2,215,940	32,241	94,999 R	50.7%	48.6%	51.0%	49.0%
Indiana	12			2,168,621	1,297,763	860,643	10,215	437,120 R	59.8%	39.7%	60.1%	39.9%
Iowa		8		1,225,614	545,355	670,557	9,702	125,202 D	44.5%	54.7%	44.9%	55.1%
Kansas	7			993,044	554,049	422,636	16,359	131,413 R	55.8%	42.6%	56.7%	43.3%
Kentucky	9			1,322,517	734,281	580,368	7,868	153,913 R	55.5%	43.9%	55.9%	44.1%
Louisiana	10			1,628,202	883,702	717,460	27,040	166,242 R	54.3%	44.1%	55.2%	44.8%
Maine	4			555,035	307,131	243,569	4,335	63,562 R	55.3%	43.9%	55.8%	44.2%
Maryland	10			1,714,358	876,167	826,304	11,887	49,863 R	51.1%	48.2%	51.5%	48.5%
Massachusetts		13		2,632,805	1,194,635	1,401,415	36,755	206,780 D	45.4%	53.2%	46.0%	54.0%
Michigan	20			3,669,163	1,965,486	1,675,783	27,894	289,703 R	53.6%	45.7%	54.0%	46.0%
Minnesota		10		2,096,790	962,337	1,109,471	24,982	147,134 D	45.9%	52.9%	46.4%	53.6%
Mississippi	7			931,527	557,890	363,921	9,716	193,969 R	59.9%	39.1%	60.5%	39.5%
Missouri	11			2,093,713	1,084,953	1,001,619	7,141	83,334 R	51.8%	47.8%	52.0%	48.0%
Montana	4			365,674	190,412	168,936	6,326	21,476 R	52.1%	46.2%	53.0%	47.0%
Nebraska	5			661,465	397,956	259,235	4,274	138,721 R	60.2%	39.2%	60.6%	39.4%
Nevada	4			350,067	206,040	132,738	11,289	73,302 R	58.9%	37.9%	60.8%	39.2%
New Hampshire	4			451,074	281,537	163,696	5,841	117,841 R	62.4%	36.3%	63.2%	36.8%
New Jersey	16			3,099,553	1,743,192	1,320,352	36,009	422,840 R	56.2%	42.6%	56.9%	43.1%
New Mexico	5			521,287	270,341	244,497	6,449	25,844 R	51.9%	46.9%	52.5%	47.5%
New York		36		6,485,683	3,081,871	3,347,882	55,930	266,011 D	47.5%	51.6%	47.9%	52.1%
North Carolina	13			2,134,370	1,237,258	890,167	6,945	347,091 R	58.0%	41.7%	58.2%	41.8%
North Dakota	3			297,261	166,559	127,739	2,963	38,820 R	56.0%	43.0%	56.6%	43.4%
Ohio	23			4,393,699	2,416,549	1,939,629	37,521	476,920 R	55.0%	44.1%	55.5%	44.5%
Oklahoma	8			1,171,036	678,367	483,423	9,246	194,944 R	57.9%	41.3%	58.4%	41.6%
Oregon		7		1,201,694	560,126	616,206	25,362	56,080 D	46.6%	51.3%	47.6%	52.4%
Pennsylvania	25			4,536,251	2,300,087	2,194,944	41,220	105,143 R	50.7%	48.4%	51.2%	48.8%
Rhode Island		4		404,620	177,761	225,123	1,736	47,362 D	43.9%	55.6%	44.1%	55.9%
South Carolina	8			986,009	606,443	370,554	9,012	235,889 R	61.5%	37.6%	62.1%	37.9%
South Dakota	3			312,991	165,415	145,560	2,016	19,855 R	52.8%	46.5%	53.2%	46.8%
Tennessee	11			1,636,250	947,233	679,794	9,223	267,439 R	57.9%	41.5%	58.2%	41.8%
Texas	29			5,427,410	3,036,829	2,352,748	37,833	684,081 R	56.0%	43.3%	56.3%	43.7%
Utah	5			647,008	428,442	207,343	11,223	221,099 R	66.2%	32.0%	67.4%	32.6%
Vermont	3			243,328	124,331	115,775	3,222	8,556 R	51.1%	47.6%	51.8%	48.2%
Virginia	12			2,191,609	1,309,162	859,799	22,648	449,363 R	59.7%	39.2%	60.4%	39.6%
Washington		10		1,865,253	903,835	933,516	27,902	29,681 D	48.5%	50.0%	49.2%	50.8%
West Virginia		5	1	653,311	310,065	341,016	2,230	30,951 D	47.5%	52.2%	47.6%	52.4%
Wisconsin		11		2,191,608	1,047,499	1,126,794	17,315	79,295 D	47.8%	51.4%	48.2%	51.8%
Wyoming	3			176,551	106,867	67,113	2,571	39,754 R	60.5%	38.0%	61.4%	38.6%
Dist. of Col.		3		192,877	27,590	159,407	5,880	131,817 D	14.3%	82.6%	14.8%	85.2%
United States	426	111	1	91,594,809	48,886,097	41,809,074	899,638	7,077,023 R	53.4%	45.6%	53.9%	46.1%

PRESIDENT 1984

In New York the Republican figures include Conservative votes and the Democratic figures include Liberal votes.

In Minnesota, the Republican candidates appear on the ballot as Independent-Republican, the Democratic as Democratic-Farmer-Labor. In many states various non-major party candidates appeared on the ballot with variations of the party designations given here, were listed as "Independent" or "Non-Party", or were carried with entirely different party labels.

The Workers World candidate for President was Gavrielle Holmes in Ohio and Rhode Island; in several states minor party Vice-Presidential candidates were different from those listed below.

The full list of candidates for President and Vice-President was:

54,455,075	Ronald Reagan and George Bush, *Republican.*
37,577,185	Walter F. Mondale and Geraldine A. Ferraro, *Democratic.*
228,314	David Bergland and James A. Lewis, *Libertarian.*
78,807	Lyndon H. LaRouche and Billy M. Davis, *Independent.*
72,200	Sonia Johnson and Richard Walton, *Citizens.*
66,336	Bob Richards and Maureen Salaman, *Populist.*
46,868	Dennis L. Serrette and Nancy Ross, *Alliance.*
36,386	Gus Hall and Angela Davis, *Communist.*
24,706	Mel Mason and Matilde Zimmermann, *Socialist Workers.*
17,985	Larry Holmes and Gloria LaRiva, *Workers World.*
13,161	Delmar Dennis and Traves Brownlee, *American.*
10,801	Ed Winn and Helen Halyard, *Workers League.*
4,242	Earl F. Dodge and Warren C. Martin, *Prohibition.*
1,486	John B. Anderson and Grace Pierce, *National Unity.*
892	Gerald Baker and Ferris Alger, *Big Deal.*
825	Arthur J. Lowery and Raymond L. Garland, *United Sovreign Citizens.*

The candidates listed above are those who appeared on the ballot in at least one state. Where identified by state authorities, write-in votes for minor party candidates are credited to their total above and listed in the individual state note sections. In addition to the votes listed, 13,623 scattered write-in votes were reported from various states and 3,950 votes were cast for "None of these Candidates" in Nevada.

UNITED STATES

PRESIDENT 1984

State	Electoral Vote Rep.	Dem.	Other	Total Vote	Republican	Democratic	Other	Plurality	Pct Total Rep.	Dem.	Major Rep.	Dem.
Alabama	9			1,441,713	872,849	551,899	16,965	320,950 R	60.5%	38.3%	61.3%	38.7%
Alaska	3			207,605	138,377	62,007	7,221	76,370 R	66.7%	29.9%	69.1%	30.9%
Arizona	7			1,025,897	681,416	333,854	10,627	347,562 R	66.4%	32.5%	67.1%	32.9%
Arkansas	6			884,406	534,774	338,646	10,986	196,128 R	60.5%	38.3%	61.2%	38.8%
California	47			9,505,423	5,467,009	3,922,519	115,895	1,544,490 R	57.5%	41.3%	58.2%	41.8%
Colorado	8			1,295,380	821,817	454,975	18,588	366,842 R	63.4%	35.1%	64.4%	35.6%
Connecticut	8			1,466,900	890,877	569,597	6,426	321,280 R	60.7%	38.8%	61.0%	39.0%
Delaware	3			254,572	152,190	101,656	726	50,534 R	59.8%	39.9%	60.0%	40.0%
Florida	21			4,180,051	2,730,350	1,448,816	885	1,281,534 R	65.3%	34.7%	65.3%	34.7%
Georgia	12			1,776,120	1,068,722	706,628	770	362,094 R	60.2%	39.8%	60.2%	39.8%
Hawaii	4			335,846	185,050	147,154	3,642	37,896 R	55.1%	43.8%	55.7%	44.3%
Idaho	4			411,144	297,523	108,510	5,111	189,013 R	72.4%	26.4%	73.3%	26.7%
Illinois	24			4,819,088	2,707,103	2,086,499	25,486	620,604 R	56.2%	43.3%	56.5%	43.5%
Indiana	12			2,233,069	1,377,230	841,481	14,358	535,749 R	61.7%	37.7%	62.1%	37.9%
Iowa	8			1,319,805	703,088	605,620	11,097	97,468 R	53.3%	45.9%	53.7%	46.3%
Kansas	7			1,021,991	677,296	333,149	11,546	344,147 R	66.3%	32.6%	67.0%	33.0%
Kentucky	9			1,369,345	821,702	539,539	8,104	282,163 R	60.0%	39.4%	60.4%	39.6%
Louisiana	10			1,706,822	1,037,299	651,586	17,937	385,713 R	60.8%	38.2%	61.4%	38.6%
Maine	4			553,144	336,500	214,515	2,129	121,985 R	60.8%	38.8%	61.1%	38.9%
Maryland	10			1,675,873	879,918	787,935	8,020	91,983 R	52.5%	47.0%	52.8%	47.2%
Massachusetts	13			2,559,453	1,310,936	1,239,606	8,911	71,330 R	51.2%	48.4%	51.4%	48.6%
Michigan	20			3,801,658	2,251,571	1,529,638	20,449	721,933 R	59.2%	40.2%	59.5%	40.5%
Minnesota		10		2,084,449	1,032,603	1,036,364	15,482	3,761 D	49.5%	49.7%	49.9%	50.1%
Mississippi	7			941,104	582,377	352,192	6,535	230,185 R	61.9%	37.4%	62.3%	37.7%
Missouri	11			2,122,783	1,274,188	848,583	12	425,605 R	60.0%	40.0%	60.0%	40.0%
Montana	4			384,377	232,450	146,742	5,185	85,708 R	60.5%	38.2%	61.3%	38.7%
Nebraska	5			652,090	460,054	187,866	4,170	272,188 R	70.6%	28.8%	71.0%	29.0%
Nevada	4			286,667	188,770	91,655	6,242	97,115 R	65.8%	32.0%	67.3%	32.7%
New Hampshire	4			389,066	267,051	120,395	1,620	146,656 R	68.6%	30.9%	68.9%	31.1%
New Jersey	16			3,217,862	1,933,630	1,261,323	22,909	672,307 R	60.1%	39.2%	60.5%	39.5%
New Mexico	5			514,370	307,101	201,769	5,500	105,332 R	59.7%	39.2%	60.3%	39.7%
New York	36			6,806,810	3,664,763	3,119,609	22,438	545,154 R	53.8%	45.8%	54.0%	46.0%
North Carolina	13			2,175,361	1,346,481	824,287	4,593	522,194 R	61.9%	37.9%	62.0%	38.0%
North Dakota	3			308,971	200,336	104,429	4,206	95,907 R	64.8%	33.8%	65.7%	34.3%
Ohio	23			4,547,619	2,678,560	1,825,440	43,619	853,120 R	58.9%	40.1%	59.5%	40.5%
Oklahoma	8			1,255,676	861,530	385,080	9,066	476,450 R	68.6%	30.7%	69.1%	30.9%
Oregon	7			1,226,527	685,700	536,479	4,348	149,221 R	55.9%	43.7%	56.1%	43.9%
Pennsylvania	25			4,844,903	2,584,323	2,228,131	32,449	356,192 R	53.3%	46.0%	53.7%	46.3%
Rhode Island	4			410,492	212,080	197,106	1,306	14,974 R	51.7%	48.0%	51.8%	48.2%
South Carolina	8			968,529	615,539	344,459	8,531	271,080 R	63.6%	35.6%	64.1%	35.9%
South Dakota	3			317,867	200,267	116,113	1,487	84,154 R	63.0%	36.5%	63.3%	36.7%
Tennessee	11			1,711,994	990,212	711,714	10,068	278,498 R	57.8%	41.6%	58.2%	41.8%
Texas	29			5,397,571	3,433,428	1,949,276	14,867	1,484,152 R	63.6%	36.1%	63.8%	36.2%
Utah	5			629,656	469,105	155,369	5,182	313,736 R	74.5%	24.7%	75.1%	24.9%
Vermont	3			234,561	135,865	95,730	2,966	40,135 R	57.9%	40.8%	58.7%	41.3%
Virginia	12			2,146,635	1,337,078	796,250	13,307	540,828 R	62.3%	37.1%	62.7%	37.3%
Washington	10			1,883,910	1,051,670	807,352	24,888	244,318 R	55.8%	42.9%	56.6%	43.4%
West Virginia	6			735,742	405,483	328,125	2,134	77,358 R	55.1%	44.6%	55.3%	44.7%
Wisconsin	11			2,211,689	1,198,584	995,740	17,365	202,844 R	54.2%	45.0%	54.6%	45.4%
Wyoming	3			188,968	133,241	53,370	2,357	79,871 R	70.5%	28.2%	71.4%	28.6%
Dist. of Col.		3		211,288	29,009	180,408	1,871	151,399 D	13.7%	85.4%	13.9%	86.1%
United States	525	13	—	92,652,842	54,455,075	37,577,185	620,582	16,877,890 R	58.8%	40.6%	59.2%	40.8%

PRESIDENT 1980

In New York the Republican figures include Conservative votes and in a number of states candidates appeared on the ballot with variants of the party designations listed below, without any party designation, or with entirely different party names.

In several cases, Vice-Presidential nominees were different from those listed for most states and the Socialist Workers party nominee for President varied from state to state.

43,904,153	Ronald Reagan and George Bush, <u>Republican</u>.
35,483,883	Jimmy Carter and Walter F. Mondale, <u>Democratic</u>.
5,720,060	John B. Anderson and Patrick J. Lucey, <u>Independent</u>.
921,299	Edward E. Clark and David Koch, <u>Libertarian</u>.
234,294	Barry Commoner and LaDonna Harris, <u>Citizens</u>.
45,023	Gus Hall and Angela Davis, <u>Communist</u>.
41,268	John R. Rarick and Eileen M. Shearer, <u>American Independent</u>.
38,737	Clifton DeBerry and Matilde Zimmermann, <u>Socialist Workers</u>.
32,327	Ellen McCormack and Carroll Driscoll, <u>Right to Life</u>.
18,116	Maureen Smith and Elizabeth Barron, <u>Peace and Freedom</u>.
13,300	Deirdre Griswold and Larry Holmes, <u>Workers World</u>.
7,212	Benjamin C. Bubar and Earl F. Dodge, <u>Statesman</u>.
6,898	David McReynolds and Diane Drufenbrock, <u>Socialist</u>.
6,647	Percy L. Greaves and Frank L. Varnum, <u>American</u>.
6,272	Andrew Pulley and Matilde Zimmermann, <u>Socialist Workers</u>.
4,029	Richard Congress and Matilde Zimmermann, <u>Socialist Workers</u>.
3,694	Kurt Lynen and Harry Kieve, <u>Middle Class</u>.
1,718	Bill Gahres and J. F. Loughlin, <u>Down With Lawyers</u>.
1,555	Frank W. Shelton and George E. Jackson, <u>American</u>.
923	Martin E. Wendelken with no Vice-Presidential candidate, <u>Independent</u>.
296	Harley McLain and Jewelie Goeller, <u>Natural Peoples</u>.

In addition to these votes, 13,185 scattered write-in votes were reported from various states, 6,139 votes were cast in Minnesota for American party electors without designated national nominees, and 4,193 votes were cast for "None of these Candidates" in Nevada.

State-by-state vote details will be found in the individual state note sections and a supplementary state-by-state national table follows for all "other" candidates polling over 100,000 votes. An asterisk by the vote denotes write-in.

UNITED STATES

PRESIDENT 1980

State	Electoral Vote Rep.	Dem.	Other	Total Vote	Republican	Democratic	Other	Plurality	Total Vote Rep.	Dem.	Major Vote Rep.	Dem.
Alabama	9			1,341,929	654,192	636,730	51,007	17,462 R	48.8%	47.4%	50.7%	49.3%
Alaska	3			158,445	86,112	41,842	30,491	44,270 R	54.3%	26.4%	67.3%	32.7%
Arizona	6			873,945	529,688	246,843	97,414	282,845 R	60.6%	28.2%	68.2%	31.8%
Arkansas	6			837,582	403,164	398,041	36,377	5,123 R	48.1%	47.5%	50.3%	49.7%
California	45			8,587,063	4,524,858	3,083,661	978,544	1,441,197 R	52.7%	35.9%	59.5%	40.5%
Colorado	7			1,184,415	652,264	367,973	164,178	284,291 R	55.1%	31.1%	63.9%	36.1%
Connecticut	8			1,406,285	677,210	541,732	187,343	135,478 R	48.2%	38.5%	55.6%	44.4%
Delaware	3			235,900	111,252	105,754	18,894	5,498 R	47.2%	44.8%	51.3%	48.7%
Florida	17			3,686,930	2,046,951	1,419,475	220,504	627,476 R	55.5%	38.5%	59.1%	40.9%
Georgia		12		1,596,695	654,168	890,733	51,794	236,565 D	41.0%	55.8%	42.3%	57.7%
Hawaii		4		303,287	130,112	135,879	37,296	5,767 D	42.9%	44.8%	48.9%	51.1%
Idaho	4			437,431	290,699	110,192	36,540	180,507 R	66.5%	25.2%	72.5%	27.5%
Illinois	26			4,749,721	2,358,049	1,981,413	410,259	376,636 R	49.6%	41.7%	54.3%	45.7%
Indiana	13			2,242,033	1,255,656	844,197	142,180	411,459 R	56.0%	37.7%	59.8%	40.2%
Iowa	8			1,317,661	676,026	508,672	132,963	167,354 R	51.3%	38.6%	57.1%	42.9%
Kansas	7			979,795	566,812	326,150	86,833	240,662 R	57.9%	33.3%	63.5%	36.5%
Kentucky	9			1,294,627	635,274	616,417	42,936	18,857 R	49.1%	47.6%	50.8%	49.2%
Louisiana	10			1,548,591	792,853	708,453	47,285	84,400 R	51.2%	45.7%	52.8%	47.2%
Maine	4			523,011	238,522	220,974	63,515	17,548 R	45.6%	42.3%	51.9%	48.1%
Maryland		10		1,540,496	680,606	726,161	133,729	45,555 D	44.2%	47.1%	48.4%	51.6%
Massachusetts	14			2,524,298	1,057,631	1,053,802	412,865	3,829 R	41.9%	41.7%	50.1%	49.9%
Michigan	21			3,909,725	1,915,225	1,661,532	332,968	253,693 R	49.0%	42.5%	53.5%	46.5%
Minnesota		10		2,051,980	873,268	954,174	224,538	80,906 D	42.6%	46.5%	47.8%	52.2%
Mississippi	7			892,620	441,089	429,281	22,250	11,808 R	49.4%	48.1%	50.7%	49.3%
Missouri	12			2,099,824	1,074,181	931,182	94,461	142,999 R	51.2%	44.3%	53.6%	46.4%
Montana	4			363,952	206,814	118,032	39,106	88,782 R	56.8%	32.4%	63.7%	36.3%
Nebraska	5			640,854	419,937	166,851	54,066	253,086 R	65.5%	26.0%	71.6%	28.4%
Nevada	3			247,885	155,017	66,666	26,202	88,351 R	62.5%	26.9%	69.9%	30.1%
New Hampshire	4			383,990	221,705	108,864	53,421	112,841 R	57.7%	28.4%	67.1%	32.9%
New Jersey	17			2,975,684	1,546,557	1,147,364	281,763	399,193 R	52.0%	38.6%	57.4%	42.6%
New Mexico	4			456,971	250,779	167,826	38,366	82,953 R	54.9%	36.7%	59.9%	40.1%
New York	41			6,201,959	2,893,831	2,728,372	579,756	165,459 R	46.7%	44.0%	51.5%	48.5%
North Carolina	13			1,855,833	915,018	875,635	65,180	39,383 R	49.3%	47.2%	51.1%	48.9%
North Dakota	3			301,545	193,695	79,189	28,661	114,506 R	64.2%	26.3%	71.0%	29.0%
Ohio	25			4,283,603	2,206,545	1,752,414	324,644	454,131 R	51.5%	40.9%	55.7%	44.3%
Oklahoma	8			1,149,708	695,570	402,026	52,112	293,544 R	60.5%	35.0%	63.4%	36.6%
Oregon	6			1,181,516	571,044	456,890	153,582	114,154 R	48.3%	38.7%	55.6%	44.4%
Pennsylvania	27			4,561,501	2,261,872	1,937,540	362,089	324,332 R	49.6%	42.5%	53.9%	46.1%
Rhode Island		4		416,072	154,793	198,342	62,937	43,549 D	37.2%	47.7%	43.8%	56.2%
South Carolina	8			894,071	441,841	430,385	21,845	11,456 R	49.4%	48.1%	50.7%	49.3%
South Dakota	4			327,703	198,343	103,855	25,505	94,488 R	60.5%	31.7%	65.6%	34.4%
Tennessee	10			1,617,616	787,761	783,051	46,804	4,710 R	48.7%	48.4%	50.1%	49.9%
Texas	26			4,541,636	2,510,705	1,881,147	149,784	629,558 R	55.3%	41.4%	57.2%	42.8%
Utah	4			604,222	439,687	124,266	40,269	315,421 R	72.8%	20.6%	78.0%	22.0%
Vermont	3			213,299	94,628	81,952	36,719	12,676 R	44.4%	38.4%	53.6%	46.4%
Virginia	12			1,866,032	989,609	752,174	124,249	237,435 R	53.0%	40.3%	56.8%	43.2%
Washington	9			1,742,394	865,244	650,193	226,957	215,051 R	49.7%	37.3%	57.1%	42.9%
West Virginia		6		737,715	334,206	367,462	36,047	33,256 D	45.3%	49.8%	47.6%	52.4%
Wisconsin	11			2,273,221	1,088,845	981,584	202,792	107,261 R	47.9%	43.2%	52.6%	47.4%
Wyoming	3			176,713	110,700	49,427	16,586	61,273 R	62.6%	28.0%	69.1%	30.9%
Dist. of Col.		3		175,237	23,545	131,113	20,579	107,568 D	13.4%	74.8%	15.2%	84.8%
United States	489	49	—	86,515,221	43,904,153	35,483,883	7,127,185	8,420,270 R	50.7%	41.0%	55.3%	44.7%

PRESIDENT 1976

In Washington, one Republican elector voted in the Electoral College for Ronald Reagan for President and Robert Dole for Vice-President.

In New York the Republican figures include Conservative votes and the Democratic figures include Liberal votes; in Vermont the Democratic figures include votes cast on the Independent Vermonters party ticket.

In a number of states candidates appeared on the ballot with variants of the party designations listed below and in several cases with entirely different party names.

The ballot designations for electors for Eugene J. McCarthy for President varied from state to state, as did the names of Vice-Presidential candidates running with him. In New Jersey, the Maddox Vice-Presidential candidate was Edmund O. Matzal.

The full list of candidates for President and Vice-President was:

40,830,763	Jimmy Carter and Walter F. Mondale, Democratic.
39,147,793	Gerald R. Ford and Robert Dole, Republican.
756,691	Eugene J. McCarthy with various Vice-Presidential candidates, Independent.
173,011	Roger L. MacBride and David D. Bergland, Libertarian.
170,531	Lester G. Maddox and William D. Dyke, American Independent.
160,773	Thomas J. Anderson and Rufus Shackelford, American.
91,314	Peter Camejo and Willie Mae Reid, Socialist Workers.
58,992	Gus Hall and Jarvis Tyner, Communist.
49,024	Margaret Wright and Benjamin Spock, People's.
40,043	Lyndon H. LaRouche and R. W. Evans, United States Labor.
15,934	Benjamin C. Bubar and Earl F. Dodge, Prohibition.
9,616	Julius Levin and Constance Blomen, Socialist Labor.
6,038	Frank P. Zeidler and J. Q. Brisben, Socialist.
361	Ernest L. Miller and Roy N. Eddy, Restoration.
36	Frank Taylor and Henry Swan, United American.

In addition to these votes, 39,861 scattered write-in votes were reported from various states and 5,108 votes were cast for "None of these Candidates" in Nevada.

UNITED STATES

PRESIDENT 1976

State	Electoral Vote Rep.	Dem.	Other	Total Vote	Republican	Democratic	Other	Plurality	Total Vote Rep.	Dem.	Major Vote Rep.	Dem.
Alabama		9		1,182,850	504,070	659,170	19,610	155,100 D	42.6%	55.7%	43.3%	56.7%
Alaska	3			123,574	71,555	44,058	7,961	27,497 R	57.9%	35.7%	61.9%	38.1%
Arizona	6			742,719	418,642	295,602	28,475	123,040 R	56.4%	39.8%	58.6%	41.4%
Arkansas		6		767,535	267,903	498,604	1,028	230,701 D	34.9%	65.0%	35.0%	65.0%
California	45			7,867,117	3,882,244	3,742,284	242,589	139,960 R	49.3%	47.6%	50.9%	49.1%
Colorado	7			1,081,554	584,367	460,353	36,834	124,014 R	54.0%	42.6%	55.9%	44.1%
Connecticut	8			1,381,526	719,261	647,895	14,370	71,366 R	52.1%	46.9%	52.6%	47.4%
Delaware		3		235,834	109,831	122,596	3,407	12,765 D	46.6%	52.0%	47.3%	52.7%
Florida		17		3,150,631	1,469,531	1,636,000	45,100	166,469 D	46.6%	51.9%	47.3%	52.7%
Georgia		12		1,467,458	483,743	979,409	4,306	495,666 D	33.0%	66.7%	33.1%	66.9%
Hawaii		4		291,301	140,003	147,375	3,923	7,372 D	48.1%	50.6%	48.7%	51.3%
Idaho	4			344,071	204,151	126,549	13,371	77,602 R	59.3%	36.8%	61.7%	38.3%
Illinois	26			4,718,914	2,364,269	2,271,295	83,350	92,974 R	50.1%	48.1%	51.0%	49.0%
Indiana	13			2,220,362	1,183,958	1,014,714	21,690	169,244 R	53.3%	45.7%	53.8%	46.2%
Iowa	8			1,279,306	632,863	619,931	26,512	12,932 R	49.5%	48.5%	50.5%	49.5%
Kansas	7			957,845	502,752	430,421	24,672	72,331 R	52.5%	44.9%	53.9%	46.1%
Kentucky		9		1,167,142	531,852	615,717	19,573	83,865 D	45.6%	52.8%	46.3%	53.7%
Louisiana		10		1,278,439	587,446	661,365	29,628	73,919 D	46.0%	51.7%	47.0%	53.0%
Maine	4			483,216	236,320	232,279	14,617	4,041 R	48.9%	48.1%	50.4%	49.6%
Maryland		10		1,439,897	672,661	759,612	7,624	86,951 D	46.7%	52.8%	47.0%	53.0%
Massachusetts		14		2,547,558	1,030,276	1,429,475	87,807	399,199 D	40.4%	56.1%	41.9%	58.1%
Michigan	21			3,653,749	1,893,742	1,696,714	63,293	197,028 R	51.8%	46.4%	52.7%	47.3%
Minnesota		10		1,949,931	819,395	1,070,440	60,096	251,045 D	42.0%	54.9%	43.4%	56.6%
Mississippi		7		769,361	366,846	381,309	21,206	14,463 D	47.7%	49.6%	49.0%	51.0%
Missouri		12		1,953,600	927,443	998,387	27,770	70,944 D	47.5%	51.1%	48.2%	51.8%
Montana	4			328,734	173,703	149,259	5,772	24,444 R	52.8%	45.4%	53.8%	46.2%
Nebraska	5			607,668	359,705	233,692	14,271	126,013 R	59.2%	38.5%	60.6%	39.4%
Nevada	3			201,876	101,273	92,479	8,124	8,794 R	50.2%	45.8%	52.3%	47.7%
New Hampshire	4			339,618	185,935	147,635	6,048	38,300 R	54.7%	43.5%	55.7%	44.3%
New Jersey	17			3,014,472	1,509,688	1,444,653	60,131	65,035 R	50.1%	47.9%	51.1%	48.9%
New Mexico	4			418,409	211,419	201,148	5,842	10,271 R	50.5%	48.1%	51.2%	48.8%
New York		41		6,534,170	3,100,791	3,389,558	43,821	288,767 D	47.5%	51.9%	47.8%	52.2%
North Carolina		13		1,678,914	741,960	927,365	9,589	185,405 D	44.2%	55.2%	44.4%	55.6%
North Dakota	3			297,188	153,470	136,078	7,640	17,392 R	51.6%	45.8%	53.0%	47.0%
Ohio		25		4,111,873	2,000,505	2,011,621	99,747	11,116 D	48.7%	48.9%	49.9%	50.1%
Oklahoma	8			1,092,251	545,708	532,442	14,101	13,266 R	50.0%	48.7%	50.6%	49.4%
Oregon	6			1,029,876	492,120	490,407	47,349	1,713 R	47.8%	47.6%	50.1%	49.9%
Pennsylvania		27		4,620,787	2,205,604	2,328,677	86,506	123,073 D	47.7%	50.4%	48.6%	51.4%
Rhode Island		4		411,170	181,249	227,636	2,285	46,387 D	44.1%	55.4%	44.3%	55.7%
South Carolina		8		802,583	346,149	450,807	5,627	104,658 D	43.1%	56.2%	43.4%	56.6%
South Dakota	4			300,678	151,505	147,068	2,105	4,437 R	50.4%	48.9%	50.7%	49.3%
Tennessee		10		1,476,345	633,969	825,879	16,497	191,910 D	42.9%	55.9%	43.4%	56.6%
Texas		26		4,071,884	1,953,300	2,082,319	36,265	129,019 D	48.0%	51.1%	48.4%	51.6%
Utah	4			541,198	337,908	182,110	21,180	155,798 R	62.4%	33.6%	65.0%	35.0%
Vermont	3			187,765	102,085	80,954	4,726	21,131 R	54.4%	43.1%	55.8%	44.2%
Virginia	12			1,697,094	836,554	813,896	46,644	22,658 R	49.3%	48.0%	50.7%	49.3%
Washington	8		1	1,555,534	777,732	717,323	60,479	60,409 R	50.0%	46.1%	52.0%	48.0%
West Virginia		6		750,964	314,760	435,914	290	121,154 D	41.9%	58.0%	41.9%	58.1%
Wisconsin		11		2,104,175	1,004,987	1,040,232	58,956	35,245 D	47.8%	49.4%	49.1%	50.9%
Wyoming	3			156,343	92,717	62,239	1,387	30,478 R	59.3%	39.8%	59.8%	40.2%
Dist. of Col.		3		168,830	27,873	137,818	3,139	109,945 D	16.5%	81.6%	16.8%	83.2%
United States	240	297	1	81,555,889	39,147,793	40,830,763	1,577,333	1,682,970 D	48.0%	50.1%	48.9%	51.1%

PRESIDENT 1972

In Virginia one Republican elector voted in the Electoral College for the Libertarian candidates for President and Vice-President.

In New York the Republican figures include Conservative votes and the Democratic figures include Liberal votes. In Alabama the Democratic figures include votes cast on the National Democratic Party of Alabama ticket, and in South Carolina include United Citizens Party votes.

In certain states candidates appeared on the ballot under party names other than those used below; for the Socialist Workers party the votes listed for Jenness and Pulley were actually cast for substitute candidates (Reed and DeBerry) or without named candidates in several states.

The Democratic Vice-Presidential candidate originally was Senator Thomas F. Eagleton; on his withdrawal shortly after the party convention, R. Sargent Shriver was named by the Democratic National Committee as candidate.

The full list of candidates for President and Vice-President was:

47,169,911	Richard M. Nixon and Spiro T. Agnew, Republican.
29,170,383	George S. McGovern and R. Sargent Shriver, Democratic.
1,099,482	John G. Schmitz and Thomas J. Anderson, American.
78,756	Benjamin Spock and Julius Hobson, People's.
66,677	Linda Jenness and Andrew Pulley, Socialist Workers.
53,814	Louis Fisher and Genevieve Gunderson, Socialist Labor.
25,595	Gus Hall and Jarvis Tyner, Communist.
13,505	E. Harold Munn and Marshall E. Uncapher, Prohibition.
3,673	John Hospers and Theodora Nathan, Libertarian.
1,743	John V. Mahalchik and Irving Homer, America First.
220	Gabriel Green and Daniel Fry, Universal.

In addition to the above, 34,795 scattered votes were reported from various states.

Vice-President Agnew resigned in October 1973 and Representative Gerald R. Ford of Michigan was nominated by President Nixon to fill the vacancy. In November (Senate) and December (House of Representatives) this action was approved by Congress.

In August 1974 President Nixon resigned and was succeeded by Vice-President Ford. In the same month Nelson A. Rockefeller, former Governor of New York, was nominated to be Vice-President and was confirmed by Congress in December 1974.

UNITED STATES

PRESIDENT 1972

State	Electoral Vote Rep.	Dem.	Other	Total Vote	Republican	Democratic	Other	Plurality	Total Vote Rep.	Dem.	Major Vote Rep.	Dem.
Alabama	9			1,006,111	728,701	256,923	20,487	471,778 R	72.4%	25.5%	73.9%	26.1%
Alaska	3			95,219	55,349	32,967	6,903	22,382 R	58.1%	34.6%	62.7%	37.3%
Arizona	6			622,926	402,812	198,540	21,574	204,272 R	64.7%	31.9%	67.0%	33.0%
Arkansas	6			651,320	448,541	199,892	2,887	248,649 R	68.9%	30.7%	69.2%	30.8%
California	45			8,367,862	4,602,096	3,475,847	289,919	1,126,249 R	55.0%	41.5%	57.0%	43.0%
Colorado	7			953,884	597,189	329,980	26,715	267,209 R	62.6%	34.6%	64.4%	35.6%
Connecticut	8			1,384,277	810,763	555,498	18,016	255,265 R	58.6%	40.1%	59.3%	40.7%
Delaware	3			235,516	140,357	92,283	2,876	48,074 R	59.6%	39.2%	60.3%	39.7%
Florida	17			2,583,283	1,857,759	718,117	7,407	1,139,642 R	71.9%	27.8%	72.1%	27.9%
Georgia	12			1,174,772	881,496	289,529	3,747	591,967 R	75.0%	24.6%	75.3%	24.7%
Hawaii	4			270,274	168,865	101,409		67,456 R	62.5%	37.5%	62.5%	37.5%
Idaho	4			310,379	199,384	80,826	30,169	118,558 R	64.2%	26.0%	71.2%	28.8%
Illinois	26			4,723,236	2,788,179	1,913,472	21,585	874,707 R	59.0%	40.5%	59.3%	40.7%
Indiana	13			2,125,529	1,405,154	708,568	11,807	696,586 R	66.1%	33.3%	66.5%	33.5%
Iowa	8			1,225,944	706,207	496,206	23,531	210,001 R	57.6%	40.5%	58.7%	41.3%
Kansas	7			916,095	619,812	270,287	25,996	349,525 R	67.7%	29.5%	69.6%	30.4%
Kentucky	9			1,067,499	676,446	371,159	19,894	305,287 R	63.4%	34.8%	64.6%	35.4%
Louisiana	10			1,051,491	686,852	298,142	66,497	388,710 R	65.3%	28.4%	69.7%	30.3%
Maine	4			417,042	256,458	160,584		95,874 R	61.5%	38.5%	61.5%	38.5%
Maryland	10			1,353,812	829,305	505,781	18,726	323,524 R	61.3%	37.4%	62.1%	37.9%
Massachusetts		14		2,458,756	1,112,078	1,332,540	14,138	220,462 D	45.2%	54.2%	45.5%	54.5%
Michigan	21			3,489,727	1,961,721	1,459,435	68,571	502,286 R	56.2%	41.8%	57.3%	42.7%
Minnesota	10			1,741,652	898,269	802,346	41,037	95,923 R	51.6%	46.1%	52.8%	47.2%
Mississippi	7			645,963	505,125	126,782	14,056	378,343 R	78.2%	19.6%	79.9%	20.1%
Missouri	12			1,855,803	1,153,852	697,147	4,804	456,705 R	62.2%	37.6%	62.3%	37.7%
Montana	4			317,603	183,976	120,197	13,430	63,779 R	57.9%	37.8%	60.5%	39.5%
Nebraska	5			576,289	406,298	169,991		236,307 R	70.5%	29.5%	70.5%	29.5%
Nevada	3			181,766	115,750	66,016		49,734 R	63.7%	36.3%	63.7%	36.3%
New Hampshire	4			334,055	213,724	116,435	3,896	97,289 R	64.0%	34.9%	64.7%	35.3%
New Jersey	17			2,997,229	1,845,502	1,102,211	49,516	743,291 R	61.6%	36.8%	62.6%	37.4%
New Mexico	4			386,241	235,606	141,084	9,551	94,522 R	61.0%	36.5%	62.5%	37.5%
New York	41			7,165,919	4,192,778	2,951,084	22,057	1,241,694 R	58.5%	41.2%	58.7%	41.3%
North Carolina	13			1,518,612	1,054,889	438,705	25,018	616,184 R	69.5%	28.9%	70.6%	29.4%
North Dakota	3			280,514	174,109	100,384	6,021	73,725 R	62.1%	35.8%	63.4%	36.6%
Ohio	25			4,094,787	2,441,827	1,558,889	94,071	882,938 R	59.6%	38.1%	61.0%	39.0%
Oklahoma	8			1,029,900	759,025	247,147	23,728	511,878 R	73.7%	24.0%	75.4%	24.6%
Oregon	6			927,946	486,686	392,760	48,500	93,926 R	52.4%	42.3%	55.3%	44.7%
Pennsylvania	27			4,592,106	2,714,521	1,796,951	80,634	917,570 R	59.1%	39.1%	60.2%	39.8%
Rhode Island	4			415,808	220,383	194,645	780	25,738 R	53.0%	46.8%	53.1%	46.9%
South Carolina	8			673,960	477,044	186,824	10,092	290,220 R	70.8%	27.7%	71.9%	28.1%
South Dakota	4			307,415	166,476	139,945	994	26,531 R	54.2%	45.5%	54.3%	45.7%
Tennessee	10			1,201,182	813,147	357,293	30,742	455,854 R	67.7%	29.7%	69.5%	30.5%
Texas	26			3,471,281	2,298,896	1,154,289	18,096	1,144,607 R	66.2%	33.3%	66.6%	33.4%
Utah	4			478,476	323,643	126,284	28,549	197,359 R	67.6%	26.4%	71.9%	28.1%
Vermont	3			186,947	117,149	68,174	1,624	48,975 R	62.7%	36.5%	63.2%	36.8%
Virginia	11		1	1,457,019	988,493	438,887	29,639	549,606 R	67.8%	30.1%	69.3%	30.7%
Washington	9			1,470,847	837,135	568,334	65,378	268,801 R	56.9%	38.6%	59.6%	40.4%
West Virginia	6			762,399	484,964	277,435		207,529 R	63.6%	36.4%	63.6%	36.4%
Wisconsin	11			1,852,890	989,430	810,174	53,286	179,256 R	53.4%	43.7%	55.0%	45.0%
Wyoming	3			145,570	100,464	44,358	748	56,106 R	69.0%	30.5%	69.4%	30.6%
Dist. of Col.		3		163,421	35,226	127,627	568	92,401 D	21.6%	78.1%	21.6%	78.4%
United States	520	17	1	77,718,554	47,169,911	29,170,383	1,378,260	17,999,528 R	60.7%	37.5%	61.8%	38.2%

PRESIDENT 1968

In North Carolina one Republican elector voted in the Electoral College for the American Independent candidates for President and Vice-President.

In New York the Democratic figure includes Liberal votes and in Alabama the Democratic vote is the total of the Alabama Independent Democratic and National Democratic Party of Alabama vote. In certain states candidates appeared under variants of the party name used below and in most states the Vice-Presidential candidate of the American Independent party was listed as Marvin Griffin rather than Curtis E. LeMay.

The full list of candidates for President and Vice-President was:

31,785,480	Richard M. Nixon and Spiro T. Agnew, Republican.
31,275,166	Hubert H. Humphrey and Edmund S. Muskie, Democratic.
9,906,473	George C. Wallace and Curtis E. LeMay, American Independent.
52,588	Henning A. Blomen and George S. Taylor, Socialist Labor.
47,133	Dick Gregory, Peace and Freedom, with various Vice-Presidential candidates.
41,388	Fred Halstead and Paul Boutelle, Socialist Workers.
36,563	Eldridge Cleaver, Peace and Freedom, with various Vice-Presidential candidates.
25,552	Eugene J. McCarthy, under various titles and written-in, but without indication of Vice-Presidential candidates.
15,123	E. Harold Munn and Rolland E. Fisher, Prohibition.
1,519	Ventura Chavez and Adelicio Moya, People's Constitutional.
1,075	Charlene Mitchell and Michael Zagarell, Communist.
142	James Hensley and Roscoe B. MacKenna, Universal.
34	Richard K. Troxell and Merle Thayer, Constitution.
17	Kent M. Soeters and James P. Powers, Berkeley Defense Group.

In the vote listed above for Eldridge Cleaver, two states are included (California and Utah) in which only the party Vice-Presidential candidate appeared on the ballot.

In addition to these votes, 12,430 were cast for elector tickets for which there were no formal Presidential or Vice-Presidential candidates, and 11,192 scattered votes were reported from various states.

UNITED STATES

PRESIDENT 1968

State	Electoral Vote			Total Vote	Republican	Democratic	AIP	Other	Plurality	Percentage Total Vote		
	Rep.	Dem.	AIP							Rep.	Dem.	AIP
Alabama			10	1,049,922	146,923	196,579	691,425	14,995	494,846 A	14.0%	18.7%	65.9%
Alaska	3			83,035	37,600	35,411	10,024		2,189 R	45.3%	42.6%	12.1%
Arizona	5			486,936	266,721	170,514	46,573	3,128	96,207 R	54.8%	35.0%	9.6%
Arkansas			6	619,969	190,759	188,228	240,982		50,223 A	30.8%	30.4%	38.9%
California	40			7,251,587	3,467,664	3,244,318	487,270	52,335	223,346 R	47.8%	44.7%	6.7%
Colorado	6			811,199	409,345	335,174	60,813	5,867	74,171 R	50.5%	41.3%	7.5%
Connecticut		8		1,256,232	556,721	621,561	76,650	1,300	64,840 D	44.3%	49.5%	6.1%
Delaware	3			214,367	96,714	89,194	28,459		7,520 R	45.1%	41.6%	13.3%
Florida	14			2,187,805	886,804	676,794	624,207		210,010 R	40.5%	30.9%	28.5%
Georgia			12	1,250,266	380,111	334,440	535,550	165	155,439 A	30.4%	26.7%	42.8%
Hawaii		4		236,218	91,425	141,324	3,469		49,899 D	38.7%	59.8%	1.5%
Idaho	4			291,183	165,369	89,273	36,541		76,096 R	56.8%	30.7%	12.5%
Illinois	26			4,619,749	2,174,774	2,039,814	390,958	14,203	134,960 R	47.1%	44.2%	8.5%
Indiana	13			2,123,597	1,067,885	806,659	243,108	5,945	261,226 R	50.3%	38.0%	11.4%
Iowa	9			1,167,931	619,106	476,699	66,422	5,704	142,407 R	53.0%	40.8%	5.7%
Kansas	7			872,783	478,674	302,996	88,921	2,192	175,678 R	54.8%	34.7%	10.2%
Kentucky	9			1,055,893	462,411	397,541	193,098	2,843	64,870 R	43.8%	37.6%	18.3%
Louisiana			10	1,097,450	257,535	309,615	530,300		220,685 A	23.5%	28.2%	48.3%
Maine		4		392,936	169,254	217,312	6,370		48,058 D	43.1%	55.3%	1.6%
Maryland		10		1,235,039	517,995	538,310	178,734		20,315 D	41.9%	43.6%	14.5%
Massachusetts		14		2,331,752	766,844	1,469,218	87,088	8,602	702,374 D	32.9%	63.0%	3.7%
Michigan		21		3,306,250	1,370,665	1,593,082	331,968	10,535	222,417 D	41.5%	48.2%	10.0%
Minnesota		10		1,588,506	658,643	857,738	68,931	3,194	199,095 D	41.5%	54.0%	4.3%
Mississippi			7	654,509	88,516	150,644	415,349		264,705 A	13.5%	23.0%	63.5%
Missouri	12			1,809,502	811,932	791,444	206,126		20,488 R	44.9%	43.7%	11.4%
Montana	4			274,404	138,835	114,117	20,015	1,437	24,718 R	50.6%	41.6%	7.3%
Nebraska	5			536,851	321,163	170,784	44,904		150,379 R	59.8%	31.8%	8.4%
Nevada	3			154,218	73,188	60,598	20,432		12,590 R	47.5%	39.3%	13.2%
New Hampshire	4			297,298	154,903	130,589	11,173	633	24,314 R	52.1%	43.9%	3.8%
New Jersey	17			2,875,395	1,325,467	1,264,206	262,187	23,535	61,261 R	46.1%	44.0%	9.1%
New Mexico	4			327,350	169,692	130,081	25,737	1,840	39,611 R	51.8%	39.7%	7.9%
New York		43		6,791,688	3,007,932	3,378,470	358,864	46,422	370,538 D	44.3%	49.7%	5.3%
North Carolina	12		1	1,587,493	627,192	464,113	496,188		131,004 R	39.5%	29.2%	31.3%
North Dakota	4			247,882	138,669	94,769	14,244	200	43,900 R	55.9%	38.2%	5.7%
Ohio	26			3,959,698	1,791,014	1,700,586	467,495	603	90,428 R	45.2%	42.9%	11.8%
Oklahoma	8			943,086	449,697	301,658	191,731		148,039 R	47.7%	32.0%	20.3%
Oregon	6			819,622	408,433	358,866	49,683	2,640	49,567 R	49.8%	43.8%	6.1%
Pennsylvania		29		4,747,928	2,090,017	2,259,405	378,582	19,924	169,388 D	44.0%	47.6%	8.0%
Rhode Island		4		385,000	122,359	246,518	15,678	445	124,159 D	31.8%	64.0%	4.1%
South Carolina	8			666,978	254,062	197,486	215,430		38,632 R	38.1%	29.6%	32.3%
South Dakota	4			281,264	149,841	118,023	13,400		31,818 R	53.3%	42.0%	4.8%
Tennessee	11			1,248,617	472,592	351,233	424,792		47,800 R	37.8%	28.1%	34.0%
Texas		25		3,079,216	1,227,844	1,266,804	584,269	299	38,960 D	39.9%	41.1%	19.0%
Utah	4			422,568	238,728	156,665	26,906	269	82,063 R	56.5%	37.1%	6.4%
Vermont	3			161,404	85,142	70,255	5,104	903	14,887 R	52.8%	43.5%	3.2%
Virginia	12			1,361,491	590,319	442,387	321,833	6,952	147,932 R	43.4%	32.5%	23.6%
Washington		9		1,304,281	588,510	616,037	96,990	2,744	27,527 D	45.1%	47.2%	7.4%
West Virginia		7		754,206	307,555	374,091	72,560		66,536 D	40.8%	49.6%	9.6%
Wisconsin	12			1,691,538	809,997	748,804	127,835	4,902	61,193 R	47.9%	44.3%	7.6%
Wyoming	3			127,205	70,927	45,173	11,105		25,754 R	55.8%	35.5%	8.7%
Dist. of Col.		3		170,578	31,012	139,566			108,554 D	18.2%	81.8%	
United States	301	191	46	73,211,875	31,785,480	31,275,166	9,906,473	244,756	510,314 R	43.4%	42.7%	13.5%

PRESIDENT 1964

In New York the Democratic figure includes Liberal votes.

The full list of candidates for President and Vice-President was:

43,129,566	Lyndon B. Johnson and Hubert H. Humphrey, Democratic.
27,178,188	Barry M. Goldwater and William E. Miller, Republican.
45,219	Eric Hass and Henning A. Blomen, Socialist Labor.
32,720	Clifton DeBerry and Edward Shaw, Socialist Workers.
23,267	E. Harold Munn and Mark R. Shaw, Prohibition.
6,953	John Kasper and J. B. Stoner, National States Rights.
5,060	Joseph B. Lightburn and T. C. Billings, Constitution.
19	James Hensley and John O. Hopkins, Universal.

In addition, 210,732 votes were cast in Alabama for an unpledged Democratic elector ticket and 12,868 scattered votes were reported from various states.

UNITED STATES

PRESIDENT 1964

State	Electoral Vote Rep.	Electoral Vote Dem.	Electoral Vote Other	Total Vote	Republican	Democratic	Other	Plurality	Total Vote Rep.	Total Vote Dem.	Major Vote Rep.	Major Vote Dem.
Alabama	10			689,818	479,085		210,733	268,353 R	69.5%		100.0%	
Alaska		3		67,259	22,930	44,329		21,399 D	34.1%	65.9%	34.1%	65.9%
Arizona	5			480,770	242,535	237,753	482	4,782 R	50.4%	49.5%	50.5%	49.5%
Arkansas		6		560,426	243,264	314,197	2,965	70,933 D	43.4%	56.1%	43.6%	56.4%
California		40		7,057,586	2,879,108	4,171,877	6,601	1,292,769 D	40.8%	59.1%	40.8%	59.2%
Colorado		6		776,986	296,767	476,024	4,195	179,257 D	38.2%	61.3%	38.4%	61.6%
Connecticut		8		1,218,578	390,996	826,269	1,313	435,273 D	32.1%	67.8%	32.1%	67.9%
Delaware		3		201,320	78,078	122,704	538	44,626 D	38.8%	60.9%	38.9%	61.1%
Florida		14		1,854,481	905,941	948,540		42,599 D	48.9%	51.1%	48.9%	51.1%
Georgia	12			1,139,335	616,584	522,556	195	94,028 R	54.1%	45.9%	54.1%	45.9%
Hawaii		4		207,271	44,022	163,249		119,227 D	21.2%	78.8%	21.2%	78.8%
Idaho		4		292,477	143,557	148,920		5,363 D	49.1%	50.9%	49.1%	50.9%
Illinois		26		4,702,841	1,905,946	2,796,833	62	890,887 D	40.5%	59.5%	40.5%	59.5%
Indiana		13		2,091,606	911,118	1,170,848	9,640	259,730 D	43.6%	56.0%	43.8%	56.2%
Iowa		9		1,184,539	449,148	733,030	2,361	283,882 D	37.9%	61.9%	38.0%	62.0%
Kansas		7		857,901	386,579	464,028	7,294	77,449 D	45.1%	54.1%	45.4%	54.6%
Kentucky		9		1,046,105	372,977	669,659	3,469	296,682 D	35.7%	64.0%	35.8%	64.2%
Louisiana	10			896,293	509,225	387,068		122,157 R	56.8%	43.2%	56.8%	43.2%
Maine		4		380,965	118,701	262,264		143,563 D	31.2%	68.8%	31.2%	68.8%
Maryland		10		1,116,457	385,495	730,912	50	345,417 D	34.5%	65.5%	34.5%	65.5%
Massachusetts		14		2,344,798	549,727	1,786,422	8,649	1,236,695 D	23.4%	76.2%	23.5%	76.5%
Michigan		21		3,203,102	1,060,152	2,136,615	6,335	1,076,463 D	33.1%	66.7%	33.2%	66.8%
Minnesota		10		1,554,462	559,624	991,117	3,721	431,493 D	36.0%	63.8%	36.1%	63.9%
Mississippi	7			409,146	356,528	52,618		303,910 R	87.1%	12.9%	87.1%	12.9%
Missouri		12		1,817,879	653,535	1,164,344		510,809 D	36.0%	64.0%	36.0%	64.0%
Montana		4		278,628	113,032	164,246	1,350	51,214 D	40.6%	58.9%	40.8%	59.2%
Nebraska		5		584,154	276,847	307,307		30,460 D	47.4%	52.6%	47.4%	52.6%
Nevada		3		135,433	56,094	79,339		23,245 D	41.4%	58.6%	41.4%	58.6%
New Hampshire		4		288,093	104,029	184,064		80,035 D	36.1%	63.9%	36.1%	63.9%
New Jersey		17		2,847,663	964,174	1,868,231	15,258	904,057 D	33.9%	65.6%	34.0%	66.0%
New Mexico		4		328,645	132,838	194,015	1,792	61,177 D	40.4%	59.0%	40.6%	59.4%
New York		43		7,166,275	2,243,559	4,913,102	9,614	2,669,543 D	31.3%	68.6%	31.3%	68.7%
North Carolina		13		1,424,983	624,844	800,139		175,295 D	43.8%	56.2%	43.8%	56.2%
North Dakota		4		258,389	108,207	149,784	398	41,577 D	41.9%	58.0%	41.9%	58.1%
Ohio		26		3,969,196	1,470,865	2,498,331		1,027,466 D	37.1%	62.9%	37.1%	62.9%
Oklahoma		8		932,499	412,665	519,834		107,169 D	44.3%	55.7%	44.3%	55.7%
Oregon		6		786,305	282,779	501,017	2,509	218,238 D	36.0%	63.7%	36.1%	63.9%
Pennsylvania		29		4,822,690	1,673,657	3,130,954	18,079	1,457,297 D	34.7%	64.9%	34.8%	65.2%
Rhode Island		4		390,091	74,615	315,463	13	240,848 D	19.1%	80.9%	19.1%	80.9%
South Carolina	8			524,779	309,048	215,723	8	93,325 R	58.9%	41.1%	58.9%	41.1%
South Dakota		4		293,118	130,108	163,010		32,902 D	44.4%	55.6%	44.4%	55.6%
Tennessee		11		1,143,946	508,965	634,947	34	125,982 D	44.5%	55.5%	44.5%	55.5%
Texas		25		2,626,811	958,566	1,663,185	5,060	704,619 D	36.5%	63.3%	36.6%	63.4%
Utah		4		401,413	181,785	219,628		37,843 D	45.3%	54.7%	45.3%	54.7%
Vermont		3		163,089	54,942	108,127	20	53,185 D	33.7%	66.3%	33.7%	66.3%
Virginia		12		1,042,267	481,334	558,038	2,895	76,704 D	46.2%	53.5%	46.3%	53.7%
Washington		9		1,258,556	470,366	779,881	8,309	309,515 D	37.4%	62.0%	37.6%	62.4%
West Virginia		7		792,040	253,953	538,087		284,134 D	32.1%	67.9%	32.1%	67.9%
Wisconsin		12		1,691,815	638,495	1,050,424	2,896	411,929 D	37.7%	62.1%	37.8%	62.2%
Wyoming		3		142,716	61,998	80,718		18,720 D	43.4%	56.6%	43.4%	56.6%
Dist. of Col.		3		198,597	28,801	169,796		140,995 D	14.5%	85.5%	14.5%	85.5%
United States	52	486	—	70,644,592	27,178,188	43,129,566	336,838	15,951,378 D	38.5%	61.1%	38.7%	61.3%

PRESIDENT 1960

Senator Harry Flood Byrd received 15 votes for President in the Electoral College; these were the votes of 6 of the 11 Democratic electors in Alabama, all 8 unpledged Democratic electors in Mississippi, and one of the 8 Republican electors in Oklahoma. The Alabama and Mississippi electors also cast 14 votes for Senator Strom Thurmond for Vice-President; the single Oklahoma elector voted for Senator Barry M. Goldwater for Vice-President.

In New York the Democratic figure includes Liberal votes.

The full list of candidates for President and Vice-President was:

34,226,731	John F. Kennedy and Lyndon B. Johnson, Democratic.
34,108,157	Richard M. Nixon and Henry Cabot Lodge, Republican.
47,522	Eric Hass and Georgia Cozzini, Socialist Labor.
46,203	Rutherford L. Decker and E. Harold Munn, Prohibition.
44,977	Orval E. Faubus and John G. Crommelin, National States Rights.
40,165	Farrell Dobbs and Myra Tanner Weiss, Socialist Workers.
18,162	Charles L. Sullivan and Merritt B. Curtis, Constitution.
8,708	J. Bracken Lee and Kent H. Courtney, Conservative.
4,204	C. Benton Coiner and Edward J. Silverman, Conservative.
1,767	Lar Daly and B. M. Miller, Tax Cut.
1,485	Clennon King and Reginald Carter, Independent Afro-American.
1,401	Merritt B. Curtis and B. M. Miller, Constitution.

In addition, 169,572 votes were cast in Louisiana for Independent electors and 116,248 in Mississippi for an unpledged Democratic elector ticket. 539 votes were cast in Michigan for an Independent American ticket and 2,378 scattered votes were reported from various states.

23

UNITED STATES

PRESIDENT 1960

State	Electoral Vote Rep.	Electoral Vote Dem.	Electoral Vote Other	Total Vote	Republican	Democratic	Other	Plurality	Total Vote Rep.	Total Vote Dem.	Major Vote Rep.	Major Vote Dem.
Alabama		5	6	570,225	237,981	324,050	8,194	86,069 D	41.7%	56.8%	42.3%	57.7%
Alaska	3			60,762	30,953	29,809		1,144 R	50.9%	49.1%	50.9%	49.1%
Arizona	4			398,491	221,241	176,781	469	44,460 R	55.5%	44.4%	55.6%	44.4%
Arkansas		8		428,509	184,508	215,049	28,952	30,541 D	43.1%	50.2%	46.2%	53.8%
California	32			6,506,578	3,259,722	3,224,099	22,757	35,623 R	50.1%	49.6%	50.3%	49.7%
Colorado	6			736,236	402,242	330,629	3,365	71,613 R	54.6%	44.9%	54.9%	45.1%
Connecticut		8		1,222,883	565,813	657,055	15	91,242 D	46.3%	53.7%	46.3%	53.7%
Delaware		3		196,683	96,373	99,590	720	3,217 D	49.0%	50.6%	49.2%	50.8%
Florida	10			1,544,176	795,476	748,700		46,776 R	51.5%	48.5%	51.5%	48.5%
Georgia		12		733,349	274,472	458,638	239	184,166 D	37.4%	62.5%	37.4%	62.6%
Hawaii		3		184,705	92,295	92,410		115 D	50.0%	50.0%	50.0%	50.0%
Idaho	4			300,450	161,597	138,853		22,744 R	53.8%	46.2%	53.8%	46.2%
Illinois		27		4,757,409	2,368,988	2,377,846	10,575	8,858 D	49.8%	50.0%	49.9%	50.1%
Indiana	13			2,135,360	1,175,120	952,358	7,882	222,762 R	55.0%	44.6%	55.2%	44.8%
Iowa	10			1,273,810	722,381	550,565	864	171,816 R	56.7%	43.2%	56.7%	43.3%
Kansas	8			928,825	561,474	363,213	4,138	198,261 R	60.4%	39.1%	60.7%	39.3%
Kentucky	10			1,124,462	602,607	521,855		80,752 R	53.6%	46.4%	53.6%	46.4%
Louisiana		10		807,891	230,980	407,339	169,572	176,359 D	28.6%	50.4%	36.2%	63.8%
Maine	5			421,767	240,608	181,159		59,449 R	57.0%	43.0%	57.0%	43.0%
Maryland		9		1,055,349	489,538	565,808	3	76,270 D	46.4%	53.6%	46.4%	53.6%
Massachusetts		16		2,469,480	976,750	1,487,174	5,556	510,424 D	39.6%	60.2%	39.6%	60.4%
Michigan		20		3,318,097	1,620,428	1,687,269	10,400	66,841 D	48.8%	50.9%	49.0%	51.0%
Minnesota		11		1,541,887	757,915	779,933	4,039	22,018 D	49.2%	50.6%	49.3%	50.7%
Mississippi			8	298,171	73,561	108,362	116,248	7,886 U	24.7%	36.3%	40.4%	59.6%
Missouri		13		1,934,422	962,221	972,201		9,980 D	49.7%	50.3%	49.7%	50.3%
Montana	4			277,579	141,841	134,891	847	6,950 R	51.1%	48.6%	51.3%	48.7%
Nebraska	6			613,095	380,553	232,542		148,011 R	62.1%	37.9%	62.1%	37.9%
Nevada		3		107,267	52,387	54,880		2,493 D	48.8%	51.2%	48.8%	51.2%
New Hampshire	4			295,761	157,989	137,772		20,217 R	53.4%	46.6%	53.4%	46.6%
New Jersey		16		2,773,111	1,363,324	1,385,415	24,372	22,091 D	49.2%	50.0%	49.6%	50.4%
New Mexico		4		311,107	153,733	156,027	1,347	2,294 D	49.4%	50.2%	49.6%	50.4%
New York		45		7,291,079	3,446,419	3,830,085	14,575	383,666 D	47.3%	52.5%	47.4%	52.6%
North Carolina		14		1,368,556	655,420	713,136		57,716 D	47.9%	52.1%	47.9%	52.1%
North Dakota	4			278,431	154,310	123,963	158	30,347 R	55.4%	44.5%	55.5%	44.5%
Ohio	25			4,161,859	2,217,611	1,944,248		273,363 R	53.3%	46.7%	53.3%	46.7%
Oklahoma	7		1	903,150	533,039	370,111		162,928 R	59.0%	41.0%	59.0%	41.0%
Oregon	6			776,421	408,060	367,402	959	40,658 R	52.6%	47.3%	52.6%	47.4%
Pennsylvania		32		5,006,541	2,439,956	2,556,282	10,303	116,326 D	48.7%	51.1%	48.8%	51.2%
Rhode Island		4		405,535	147,502	258,032	1	110,530 D	36.4%	63.6%	36.4%	63.6%
South Carolina		8		386,688	188,558	198,129	1	9,571 D	48.8%	51.2%	48.8%	51.2%
South Dakota	4			306,487	178,417	128,070		50,347 R	58.2%	41.8%	58.2%	41.8%
Tennessee	11			1,051,792	556,577	481,453	13,762	75,124 R	52.9%	45.8%	53.6%	46.4%
Texas		24		2,311,084	1,121,310	1,167,567	22,207	46,257 D	48.5%	50.5%	49.0%	51.0%
Utah	4			374,709	205,361	169,248	100	36,113 R	54.8%	45.2%	54.8%	45.2%
Vermont	3			167,324	98,131	69,186	7	28,945 R	58.6%	41.3%	58.6%	41.4%
Virginia	12			771,449	404,521	362,327	4,601	42,194 R	52.4%	47.0%	52.8%	47.2%
Washington	9			1,241,572	629,273	599,298	13,001	29,975 R	50.7%	48.3%	51.2%	48.8%
West Virginia		8		837,781	395,995	441,786		45,791 D	47.3%	52.7%	47.3%	52.7%
Wisconsin	12			1,729,082	895,175	830,805	3,102	64,370 R	51.8%	48.0%	51.9%	48.1%
Wyoming	3			140,782	77,451	63,331		14,120 R	55.0%	45.0%	55.0%	45.0%
United States	219	303	15	68,838,219	34,108,157	34,226,731	503,331	118,574 D	49.5%	49.7%	49.9%	50.1%

24

PRESIDENT 1956

One of the 11 Democratic electors chosen in Alabama cast his Electoral College vote for Walter B. Jones and Herman Talmadge rather than for the national Democratic candidates.

The Republican figure in Mississippi includes votes cast for two elector tickets. In New York the Democratic figure includes Liberal votes.

The full list of candidates for President and Vice-President was:

35,590,472	Dwight D. Eisenhower and Richard M. Nixon, Republican.
26,022,752	Adlai E. Stevenson and Estes Kefauver, Democratic.
111,178	T. Coleman Andrews and Thomas H. Werdel, States Rights.
44,450	Eric Hass and Georgia Cozzini, Socialist Labor.
41,937	Enoch A. Holtwick and Edwin M. Cooper, Prohibition.
7,797	Farrell Dobbs and Myra Tanner Weiss, Socialist Workers.
2,657	Harry Flood Byrd and William E. Jenner, States Rights.
2,126	Darlington Hoopes and Samuel H. Friedman, Socialist.
1,829	Henry B. Krajewski and Anne Marie Yezo, American Third Party.
8	Gerald L. K. Smith and Charles F. Robertson, Christian Nationalist.

In addition, 196,318 votes were cast in Alabama, Louisiana, Mississippi, and South Carolina for Independent electors or for States Rights elector tickets not officially pledged to any candidate, and 5,384 scattered votes were reported from various states.

UNITED STATES

PRESIDENT 1956

State	Electoral Vote Rep.	Electoral Vote Dem.	Electoral Vote Other	Total Vote	Republican	Democratic	Other	Plurality	% Total Vote Rep.	% Total Vote Dem.	% Major Vote Rep.	% Major Vote Dem.
Alabama		10	1	496,861	195,694	280,844	20,323	85,150 D	39.4%	56.5%	41.1%	58.9%
Alaska												
Arizona	4			290,173	176,990	112,880	303	64,110 R	61.0%	38.9%	61.1%	38.9%
Arkansas		8		406,572	186,287	213,277	7,008	26,990 D	45.8%	52.5%	46.6%	53.4%
California	32			5,466,355	3,027,668	2,420,135	18,552	607,533 R	55.4%	44.3%	55.6%	44.4%
Colorado	6			657,074	394,479	257,997	4,598	136,482 R	60.0%	39.3%	60.5%	39.5%
Connecticut	8			1,117,121	711,837	405,079	205	306,758 R	63.7%	36.3%	63.7%	36.3%
Delaware	3			177,988	98,057	79,421	510	18,636 R	55.1%	44.6%	55.3%	44.7%
Florida	10			1,125,762	643,849	480,371	1,542	163,478 R	57.2%	42.7%	57.3%	42.7%
Georgia		12		669,655	222,778	444,688	2,189	221,910 D	33.3%	66.4%	33.4%	66.6%
Hawaii												
Idaho	4			272,989	166,979	105,868	142	61,111 R	61.2%	38.8%	61.2%	38.8%
Illinois	27			4,407,407	2,623,327	1,775,682	8,398	847,645 R	59.5%	40.3%	59.6%	40.4%
Indiana	13			1,974,607	1,182,811	783,908	7,888	398,903 R	59.9%	39.7%	60.1%	39.9%
Iowa	10			1,234,564	729,187	501,858	3,519	227,329 R	59.1%	40.7%	59.2%	40.8%
Kansas	8			866,243	566,878	296,317	3,048	270,561 R	65.4%	34.2%	65.7%	34.3%
Kentucky	10			1,053,805	572,192	476,453	5,160	95,739 R	54.3%	45.2%	54.6%	45.4%
Louisiana	10			617,544	329,047	243,977	44,520	85,070 R	53.3%	39.5%	57.4%	42.6%
Maine	5			351,706	249,238	102,468		146,770 R	70.9%	29.1%	70.9%	29.1%
Maryland	9			932,827	559,738	372,613	476	187,125 R	60.0%	39.9%	60.0%	40.0%
Massachusetts	16			2,348,506	1,393,197	948,190	7,119	445,007 R	59.3%	40.4%	59.5%	40.5%
Michigan	20			3,080,468	1,713,647	1,359,898	6,923	353,749 R	55.6%	44.1%	55.8%	44.2%
Minnesota	11			1,340,005	719,302	617,525	3,178	101,777 R	53.7%	46.1%	53.8%	46.2%
Mississippi		8		248,104	60,685	144,453	42,966	83,768 D	24.5%	58.2%	29.6%	70.4%
Missouri		13		1,832,562	914,289	918,273		3,984 D	49.9%	50.1%	49.9%	50.1%
Montana	4			271,171	154,933	116,238		38,695 R	57.1%	42.9%	57.1%	42.9%
Nebraska	6			577,137	378,108	199,029		179,079 R	65.5%	34.5%	65.5%	34.5%
Nevada	3			96,689	56,049	40,640		15,409 R	58.0%	42.0%	58.0%	42.0%
New Hampshire	4			266,994	176,519	90,364	111	86,155 R	66.1%	33.8%	66.1%	33.9%
New Jersey	16			2,484,312	1,606,942	850,337	27,033	756,605 R	64.7%	34.2%	65.4%	34.6%
New Mexico	4			253,926	146,788	106,098	1,040	40,690 R	57.8%	41.8%	58.0%	42.0%
New York	45			7,095,971	4,345,506	2,747,944	2,521	1,597,562 R	61.2%	38.4%	61.3%	38.7%
North Carolina		14		1,165,592	575,062	590,530		15,468 D	49.3%	50.7%	49.3%	50.7%
North Dakota	4			253,991	156,766	96,742	483	60,024 R	61.7%	38.1%	61.8%	38.2%
Ohio	25			3,702,265	2,262,610	1,439,655		822,955 R	61.1%	38.9%	61.1%	38.9%
Oklahoma	8			859,350	473,769	385,581		88,188 R	55.1%	44.9%	55.1%	44.9%
Oregon	6			736,132	406,393	329,204	535	77,189 R	55.2%	44.7%	55.2%	44.8%
Pennsylvania	32			4,576,503	2,585,252	1,981,769	9,482	603,483 R	56.5%	43.3%	56.6%	43.4%
Rhode Island	4			387,609	225,819	161,790		64,029 R	58.3%	41.7%	58.3%	41.7%
South Carolina		8		300,583	75,700	136,372	88,511	47,863 D	25.2%	45.4%	35.7%	64.3%
South Dakota	4			293,857	171,569	122,288		49,281 R	58.4%	41.6%	58.4%	41.6%
Tennessee	11			939,404	462,288	456,507	20,609	5,781 R	49.2%	48.6%	50.3%	49.7%
Texas	24			1,955,168	1,080,619	859,958	14,591	220,661 R	55.3%	44.0%	55.7%	44.3%
Utah	4			333,995	215,631	118,364		97,267 R	64.6%	35.4%	64.6%	35.4%
Vermont	3			152,978	110,390	42,549	39	67,841 R	72.2%	27.8%	72.2%	27.8%
Virginia	12			697,978	386,459	267,760	43,759	118,699 R	55.4%	38.4%	59.1%	40.9%
Washington	9			1,150,889	620,430	523,002	7,457	97,428 R	53.9%	45.4%	54.3%	45.7%
West Virginia	8			830,831	449,297	381,534		67,763 R	54.1%	45.9%	54.1%	45.9%
Wisconsin	12			1,550,558	954,844	586,768	8,946	368,076 R	61.6%	37.8%	61.9%	38.1%
Wyoming	3			124,127	74,573	49,554		25,019 R	60.1%	39.9%	60.1%	39.9%
United States	457	73	1	62,026,908	35,590,472	26,022,752	413,684	9,567,720 R	57.4%	42.0%	57.8%	42.2%

26

PRESIDENT 1952

The Republican figure in South Carolina includes votes cast for two elector tickets; in Mississippi the Republican total is the vote cast for an Independent elector ticket "pledged to vote for the nominees of the National Republican Party". In New York the Democratic figure includes Liberal votes.

The full list of candidates for President and Vice-President was:

33,936,234	Dwight D. Eisenhower and Richard M. Nixon, Republican.
27,314,992	Adlai E. Stevenson and John J. Sparkman, Democratic.
140,023	Vincent Hallinan and Charlotta Bass, Progressive.
72,949	Stuart Hamblen and Enoch A. Holtwick, Prohibition.
30,267	Eric Hass and Stephen Emery, Socialist Labor.
20,203	Darlington Hoopes and Samuel H. Friedman, Socialist.
10,312	Farrell Dobbs and Myra Tanner Weiss, Socialist Workers.
4,203	Henry B. Krajewski and Frank Jenkins, Poor Man's Party.

In addition, 17,205 votes were cast for various elector tickets filed on behalf of General Douglas MacArthur, including Christian Nationalist (with Jack B. Tenney as candidate for Vice-President), Constitution (with Vivien Kellems), and America First (with Senator Harry Flood Byrd). In California, Missouri, and Texas the MacArthur vote was cast for two elector tickets. 4,530 scattered votes were reported from various states.

UNITED STATES

PRESIDENT 1952

State	Electoral Vote Rep.	Dem.	Other	Total Vote	Republican	Democratic	Other	Plurality	Total Vote Rep.	Dem.	Major Vote Rep.	Dem.
Alabama		11		426,120	149,231	275,075	1,814	125,844 D	35.0%	64.6%	35.2%	64.8%
Alaska												
Arizona	4			260,570	152,042	108,528		43,514 R	58.3%	41.7%	58.3%	41.7%
Arkansas		8		404,800	177,155	226,300	1,345	49,145 D	43.8%	55.9%	43.9%	56.1%
California	32			5,141,849	2,897,310	2,197,548	46,991	699,762 R	56.3%	42.7%	56.9%	43.1%
Colorado	6			630,103	379,782	245,504	4,817	134,278 R	60.3%	39.0%	60.7%	39.3%
Connecticut	8			1,096,911	611,012	481,649	4,250	129,363 R	55.7%	43.9%	55.9%	44.1%
Delaware	3			174,025	90,059	83,315	651	6,744 R	51.8%	47.9%	51.9%	48.1%
Florida	10			989,337	544,036	444,950	351	99,086 R	55.0%	45.0%	55.0%	45.0%
Georgia		12		655,785	198,961	456,823	1	257,862 D	30.3%	69.7%	30.3%	69.7%
Hawaii												
Idaho	4			276,254	180,707	95,081	466	85,626 R	65.4%	34.4%	65.5%	34.5%
Illinois	27			4,481,058	2,457,327	2,013,920	9,811	443,407 R	54.8%	44.9%	55.0%	45.0%
Indiana	13			1,955,049	1,136,259	801,530	17,260	334,729 R	58.1%	41.0%	58.6%	41.4%
Iowa	10			1,268,773	808,906	451,513	8,354	357,393 R	63.8%	35.6%	64.2%	35.8%
Kansas	8			896,166	616,302	273,296	6,568	343,006 R	68.8%	30.5%	69.3%	30.7%
Kentucky		10		993,148	495,029	495,729	2,390	700 D	49.8%	49.9%	50.0%	50.0%
Louisiana		10		651,952	306,925	345,027		38,102 D	47.1%	52.9%	47.1%	52.9%
Maine	5			351,786	232,353	118,806	627	113,547 R	66.0%	33.8%	66.2%	33.8%
Maryland	9			902,074	499,424	395,337	7,313	104,087 R	55.4%	43.8%	55.8%	44.2%
Massachusetts	16			2,383,398	1,292,325	1,083,525	7,548	208,800 R	54.2%	45.5%	54.4%	45.6%
Michigan	20			2,798,592	1,551,529	1,230,657	16,406	320,872 R	55.4%	44.0%	55.8%	44.2%
Minnesota	11			1,379,483	763,211	608,458	7,814	154,753 R	55.3%	44.1%	55.6%	44.4%
Mississippi		8		285,532	112,966	172,566	•	59,600 D	39.6%	60.4%	39.6%	60.4%
Missouri	13			1,892,062	959,429	929,830	2,803	29,599 R	50.7%	49.1%	50.8%	49.2%
Montana	4			265,037	157,394	106,213	1,430	51,181 R	59.4%	40.1%	59.7%	40.3%
Nebraska	6			609,660	421,603	188,057		233,546 R	69.2%	30.8%	69.2%	30.8%
Nevada	3			82,190	50,502	31,688		18,814 R	61.4%	38.6%	61.4%	38.6%
New Hampshire	4			272,950	166,287	106,663		59,624 R	60.9%	39.1%	60.9%	39.1%
New Jersey	16			2,418,554	1,373,613	1,015,902	29,039	357,711 R	56.8%	42.0%	57.5%	42.5%
New Mexico	4			238,608	132,170	105,661	777	26,509 R	55.4%	44.3%	55.6%	44.4%
New York	45			7,128,239	3,952,813	3,104,601	70,825	848,212 R	55.5%	43.6%	56.0%	44.0%
North Carolina		14		1,210,910	558,107	652,803		94,696 D	46.1%	53.9%	46.1%	53.9%
North Dakota	4			270,127	191,712	76,694	1,721	115,018 R	71.0%	28.4%	71.4%	28.6%
Ohio	25			3,700,758	2,100,391	1,600,367		500,024 R	56.8%	43.2%	56.8%	43.2%
Oklahoma	8			948,984	518,045	430,939		87,106 R	54.6%	45.4%	54.6%	45.4%
Oregon	6			695,059	420,815	270,579	3,665	150,236 R	60.5%	38.9%	60.9%	39.1%
Pennsylvania	32			4,580,969	2,415,789	2,146,269	18,911	269,520 R	52.7%	46.9%	53.0%	47.0%
Rhode Island	4			414,498	210,935	203,293	270	7,642 R	50.9%	49.0%	50.9%	49.1%
South Carolina		8		341,087	168,082	173,004	1	4,922 D	49.3%	50.7%	49.3%	50.7%
South Dakota	4			294,283	203,857	90,426		113,431 R	69.3%	30.7%	69.3%	30.7%
Tennessee	11			892,553	446,147	443,710	2,696	2,437 R	50.0%	49.7%	50.1%	49.9%
Texas	24			2,075,946	1,102,878	969,228	3,840	133,650 R	53.1%	46.7%	53.2%	46.8%
Utah	4			329,554	194,190	135,364		58,826 R	58.9%	41.1%	58.9%	41.1%
Vermont	3			153,557	109,717	43,355	485	66,362 R	71.5%	28.2%	71.7%	28.3%
Virginia	12			619,689	349,037	268,677	1,975	80,360 R	56.3%	43.4%	56.5%	43.5%
Washington	9			1,102,708	599,107	492,845	10,756	106,262 R	54.3%	44.7%	54.9%	45.1%
West Virginia		8		873,548	419,970	453,578		33,608 D	48.1%	51.9%	48.1%	51.9%
Wisconsin	12			1,607,370	979,744	622,175	5,451	357,569 R	61.0%	38.7%	61.2%	38.8%
Wyoming	3			129,253	81,049	47,934	270	33,115 R	62.7%	37.1%	62.8%	37.2%
United States	442	89	—	61,550,918	33,936,234	27,314,992	299,692	6,621,242 R	55.1%	44.4%	55.4%	44.6%

28

PRESIDENT 1948

The electoral votes of Alabama, Louisiana, Mississippi, and South Carolina were cast for the States Rights nominees. In addition, one of the 12 Democratic electors chosen in Tennessee cast his Electoral College vote for the States Rights nominees rather than for the national Democratic candidates.

In Alabama the Democratic electors were pledged to the States Rights candidates. There were no national Democratic electors on the ballot in that state.

The Republican figure in Mississippi includes votes cast for two elector tickets. In New York the Democratic figure includes Liberal votes.

The full list of candidates for President and Vice-President was:

24,179,345	Harry S. Truman and Alben W. Barkley, Democratic.
21,991,291	Thomas E. Dewey and Earl Warren, Republican.
1,176,125	Strom Thurmond and Fielding L. Wright, States Rights.
1,157,326	Henry A. Wallace and Glen H. Taylor, Progressive.
139,572	Norman Thomas and Tucker P. Smith, Socialist.
103,900	Claude A. Watson and Dale H. Learn, Prohibition.
29,241	Edward A. Teichert and Stephen Emery, Socialist Labor.
13,614	Farrell Dobbs and Grace Carlson, Socialist Workers.

In addition, 3,412 scattered votes were reported from various states.

UNITED STATES

PRESIDENT 1948

State	Electoral Vote Rep.	Electoral Vote Dem.	Electoral Vote Other	Total Vote	Republican	Democratic	Other	Plurality	Percentage Total Vote Rep.	Percentage Total Vote Dem.	Percentage Major Vote Rep.	Percentage Major Vote Dem.
Alabama			11	214,980	40,930		174,050	130,513 SR	19.0%		100.0%	
Alaska												
Arizona		4		177,065	77,597	95,251	4,217	17,654 D	43.8%	53.8%	44.9%	55.1%
Arkansas		9		242,475	50,959	149,659	41,857	98,700 D	21.0%	61.7%	25.4%	74.6%
California		25		4,021,538	1,895,269	1,913,134	213,135	17,865 D	47.1%	47.6%	49.8%	50.2%
Colorado		6		515,237	239,714	267,288	8,235	27,574 D	46.5%	51.9%	47.3%	52.7%
Connecticut	8			883,518	437,754	423,297	22,467	14,457 R	49.5%	47.9%	50.8%	49.2%
Delaware	3			139,073	69,588	67,813	1,672	1,775 R	50.0%	48.8%	50.6%	49.4%
Florida		8		577,643	194,280	281,988	101,375	87,708 D	33.6%	48.8%	40.8%	59.2%
Georgia		12		418,844	76,691	254,646	87,507	169,511 D	18.3%	60.8%	23.1%	76.9%
Hawaii												
Idaho		4		214,816	101,514	107,370	5,932	5,856 D	47.3%	50.0%	48.6%	51.4%
Illinois		28		3,984,046	1,961,103	1,994,715	28,228	33,612 D	49.2%	50.1%	49.6%	50.4%
Indiana	13			1,656,212	821,079	807,831	27,302	13,248 R	49.6%	48.8%	50.4%	49.6%
Iowa		10		1,038,264	494,018	522,380	21,866	28,362 D	47.6%	50.3%	48.6%	51.4%
Kansas	8			788,819	423,039	351,902	13,878	71,137 R	53.6%	44.6%	54.6%	45.4%
Kentucky		11		822,658	341,210	466,756	14,692	125,546 D	41.5%	56.7%	42.2%	57.8%
Louisiana			10	416,336	72,657	136,344	207,335	67,946 SR	17.5%	32.7%	34.8%	65.2%
Maine	5			264,787	150,234	111,916	2,637	38,318 R	56.7%	42.3%	57.3%	42.7%
Maryland	8			596,748	294,814	286,521	15,413	8,293 R	49.4%	48.0%	50.7%	49.3%
Massachusetts		16		2,107,146	909,370	1,151,788	45,988	242,418 D	43.2%	54.7%	44.1%	55.9%
Michigan	19			2,109,609	1,038,595	1,003,448	67,566	35,147 R	49.2%	47.6%	50.9%	49.1%
Minnesota		11		1,212,226	483,617	692,966	35,643	209,349 D	39.9%	57.2%	41.1%	58.9%
Mississippi			9	192,190	5,043	19,384	167,763	148,154 SR	2.6%	10.1%	20.6%	79.4%
Missouri		15		1,578,628	655,039	917,315	6,274	262,276 D	41.5%	58.1%	41.7%	58.3%
Montana		4		224,278	96,770	119,071	8,437	22,301 D	43.1%	53.1%	44.8%	55.2%
Nebraska	6			488,940	264,774	224,165	1	40,609 R	54.2%	45.8%	54.2%	45.8%
Nevada		3		62,117	29,357	31,291	1,469	1,934 D	47.3%	50.4%	48.4%	51.6%
New Hampshire	4			231,440	121,299	107,995	2,146	13,304 R	52.4%	46.7%	52.9%	47.1%
New Jersey	16			1,949,555	981,124	895,455	72,976	85,669 R	50.3%	45.9%	52.3%	47.7%
New Mexico		4		187,063	80,303	105,464	1,296	25,161 D	42.9%	56.4%	43.2%	56.8%
New York	47			6,177,337	2,841,163	2,780,204	555,970	60,959 R	46.0%	45.0%	50.5%	49.5%
North Carolina		14		791,209	258,572	459,070	73,567	200,498 D	32.7%	58.0%	36.0%	64.0%
North Dakota	4			220,716	115,139	95,812	9,765	19,327 R	52.2%	43.4%	54.6%	45.4%
Ohio		25		2,936,071	1,445,684	1,452,791	37,596	7,107 D	49.2%	49.5%	49.9%	50.1%
Oklahoma		10		721,599	268,817	452,782		183,965 D	37.3%	62.7%	37.3%	62.7%
Oregon	6			524,080	260,904	243,147	20,029	17,757 R	49.8%	46.4%	51.8%	48.2%
Pennsylvania	35			3,735,348	1,902,197	1,752,426	80,725	149,771 R	50.9%	46.9%	52.0%	48.0%
Rhode Island		4		327,702	135,787	188,736	3,179	52,949 D	41.4%	57.6%	41.8%	58.2%
South Carolina			8	142,571	5,386	34,423	102,762	68,184 SR	3.8%	24.1%	13.5%	86.5%
South Dakota	4			250,105	129,651	117,653	2,801	11,998 R	51.8%	47.0%	52.4%	47.6%
Tennessee		11	1	550,283	202,914	270,402	76,967	67,488 D	36.9%	49.1%	42.9%	57.1%
Texas		23		1,249,577	303,467	824,235	121,875	520,768 D	24.3%	66.0%	26.9%	73.1%
Utah		4		276,306	124,402	149,151	2,753	24,749 D	45.0%	54.0%	45.5%	54.5%
Vermont	3			123,382	75,926	45,557	1,899	30,369 R	61.5%	36.9%	62.5%	37.5%
Virginia		11		419,256	172,070	200,786	46,400	28,716 D	41.0%	47.9%	46.1%	53.9%
Washington		8		905,058	386,314	476,165	42,579	89,851 D	42.7%	52.6%	44.8%	55.2%
West Virginia		8		748,750	316,251	429,188	3,311	112,937 D	42.2%	57.3%	42.4%	57.6%
Wisconsin		12		1,276,800	590,959	647,310	38,531	56,351 D	46.3%	50.7%	47.7%	52.3%
Wyoming		3		101,425	47,947	52,354	1,124	4,407 D	47.3%	51.6%	47.8%	52.2%
United States	189	303	39	48,793,826	21,991,291	24,179,345	2,623,190	2,188,054 D	45.1%	49.6%	47.6%	52.4%

PRESIDENT 1944

The Republican figures in Georgia, Mississippi and South Carolina include votes cast for two elector tickets. The Democratic figure in Mississippi includes votes cast for two elector tickets and in New York includes American Labor and Liberal votes.

In South Carolina an uncommitted Southern Democratic elector ticket ran in second place ahead of the Republican candidates.

The full list of candidates for President and Vice-President was:

25,612,610	Franklin D. Roosevelt and Harry S. Truman, <u>Democratic</u>.
22,017,617	Thomas E. Dewey and John W. Bricker, <u>Republican</u>.
79,003	Norman Thomas and Darlington Hoopes, <u>Socialist</u>.
74,799	Claude A. Watson and Andrew Johnson, <u>Prohibition</u>.
45,191	Edward A. Teichert and Arla A. Albaugh, <u>Socialist Labor</u>.
1,780	Gerald L. K. Smith and Harry Romer, <u>American First</u>.

In addition, 135,444 votes were cast in Texas for a Texas Regulars elector ticket and 7,799 in South Carolina for an uncommitted Southern Democratic elector ticket. There were 2,447 scattered votes reported from various states.

UNITED STATES

PRESIDENT 1944

State	Electoral Vote Rep.	Electoral Vote Dem.	Electoral Vote Other	Total Vote	Republican	Democratic	Other	Plurality	Percentage Total Vote Rep.	Percentage Total Vote Dem.	Percentage Major Vote Rep.	Percentage Major Vote Dem.
Alabama		11		244,743	44,540	198,918	1,285	154,378 D	18.2%	81.3%	18.3%	81.7%
Alaska												
Arizona		4		137,634	56,287	80,926	421	24,639 D	40.9%	58.8%	41.0%	59.0%
Arkansas		9		212,954	63,551	148,965	438	85,414 D	29.8%	70.0%	29.9%	70.1%
California		25		3,520,875	1,512,965	1,988,564	19,346	475,599 D	43.0%	56.5%	43.2%	56.8%
Colorado	6			505,039	268,731	234,331	1,977	34,400 R	53.2%	46.4%	53.4%	46.6%
Connecticut		8		831,990	390,527	435,146	6,317	44,619 D	46.9%	52.3%	47.3%	52.7%
Delaware		3		125,361	56,747	68,166	448	11,419 D	45.3%	54.4%	45.4%	54.6%
Florida		8		482,803	143,215	339,377	211	196,162 D	29.7%	70.3%	29.7%	70.3%
Georgia		12		328,129	59,900	268,187	42	208,287 D	18.3%	81.7%	18.3%	81.7%
Hawaii												
Idaho		4		208,321	100,137	107,399	785	7,262 D	48.1%	51.6%	48.3%	51.7%
Illinois		28		4,036,061	1,939,314	2,079,479	17,268	140,165 D	48.0%	51.5%	48.3%	51.7%
Indiana	13			1,672,091	875,891	781,403	14,797	94,488 R	52.4%	46.7%	52.9%	47.1%
Iowa	10			1,052,599	547,267	499,876	5,456	47,391 R	52.0%	47.5%	52.3%	47.7%
Kansas	8			733,776	442,096	287,458	4,222	154,638 R	60.2%	39.2%	60.6%	39.4%
Kentucky		11		867,924	392,448	472,589	2,887	80,141 D	45.2%	54.5%	45.4%	54.6%
Louisiana		10		349,383	67,750	281,564	69	213,814 D	19.4%	80.6%	19.4%	80.6%
Maine	5			296,400	155,434	140,631	335	14,803 R	52.4%	47.4%	52.5%	47.5%
Maryland		8		608,439	292,949	315,490		22,541 D	48.1%	51.9%	48.1%	51.9%
Massachusetts		16		1,960,665	921,350	1,035,296	4,019	113,946 D	47.0%	52.8%	47.1%	52.9%
Michigan		19		2,205,223	1,084,423	1,106,899	13,901	22,476 D	49.2%	50.2%	49.5%	50.5%
Minnesota		11		1,125,504	527,416	589,864	8,224	62,448 D	46.9%	52.4%	47.2%	52.8%
Mississippi		9		180,234	11,613	168,621		157,008 D	6.4%	93.6%	6.4%	93.6%
Missouri		15		1,571,697	761,175	807,356	3,166	46,181 D	48.4%	51.4%	48.5%	51.5%
Montana		4		207,355	93,163	112,556	1,636	19,393 D	44.9%	54.3%	45.3%	54.7%
Nebraska	6			563,126	329,880	233,246		96,634 R	58.6%	41.4%	58.6%	41.4%
Nevada		3		54,234	24,611	29,623		5,012 D	45.4%	54.6%	45.4%	54.6%
New Hampshire		4		229,625	109,916	119,663	46	9,747 D	47.9%	52.1%	47.9%	52.1%
New Jersey		16		1,963,761	961,335	987,874	14,552	26,539 D	49.0%	50.3%	49.3%	50.7%
New Mexico		4		152,225	70,688	81,389	148	10,701 D	46.4%	53.5%	46.5%	53.5%
New York		47		6,316,790	2,987,647	3,304,238	24,905	316,591 D	47.3%	52.3%	47.5%	52.5%
North Carolina		14		790,554	263,155	527,399		264,244 D	33.3%	66.7%	33.3%	66.7%
North Dakota	4			220,182	118,535	100,144	1,503	18,391 R	53.8%	45.5%	54.2%	45.8%
Ohio	25			3,153,056	1,582,293	1,570,763		11,530 R	50.2%	49.8%	50.2%	49.8%
Oklahoma		10		722,636	319,424	401,549	1,663	82,125 D	44.2%	55.6%	44.3%	55.7%
Oregon		6		480,147	225,365	248,635	6,147	23,270 D	46.9%	51.8%	47.5%	52.5%
Pennsylvania		35		3,794,793	1,835,054	1,940,479	19,260	105,425 D	48.4%	51.1%	48.6%	51.4%
Rhode Island		4		299,276	123,487	175,356	433	51,869 D	41.3%	58.6%	41.3%	58.7%
South Carolina		8		103,382	4,617	90,601	8,164	82,802 D	4.5%	87.6%	4.8%	95.2%
South Dakota	4			232,076	135,365	96,711		38,654 R	58.3%	41.7%	58.3%	41.7%
Tennessee		12		510,692	200,311	308,707	1,674	108,396 D	39.2%	60.4%	39.4%	60.6%
Texas		23		1,150,334	191,423	821,605	137,306	630,182 D	16.6%	71.4%	18.9%	81.1%
Utah		4		248,319	97,891	150,088	340	52,197 D	39.4%	60.4%	39.5%	60.5%
Vermont	3			125,361	71,527	53,820	14	17,707 R	57.1%	42.9%	57.1%	42.9%
Virginia		11		388,485	145,243	242,276	966	97,033 D	37.4%	62.4%	37.5%	62.5%
Washington		8		856,328	361,689	486,774	7,865	125,085 D	42.2%	56.8%	42.6%	57.4%
West Virginia		8		715,596	322,819	392,777		69,958 D	45.1%	54.9%	45.1%	54.9%
Wisconsin	12			1,339,152	674,532	650,413	14,207	24,119 R	50.4%	48.6%	50.9%	49.1%
Wyoming	3			101,340	51,921	49,419		2,502 R	51.2%	48.8%	51.2%	48.8%
United States	99	432	—	47,976,670	22,017,617	25,612,610	346,443	3,594,993 D	45.9%	53.4%	46.2%	53.8%

PRESIDENT 1940

The Republican figures in Connecticut, Georgia, Mississippi and South Carolina include votes cast for two or three elector tickets. In New York the Democratic figure includes American Labor votes.

The full list of candidates for President and Vice-President was:

27,313,041	Franklin D. Roosevelt and Henry A. Wallace, Democratic.
22,348,480	Wendell Willkie and Charles L. McNary, Republican.
116,410	Norman Thomas and Maynard C. Krueger, Socialist.
58,708	Roger Babson and Edgar V. Moorman, Prohibition.
46,259	Earl Browder and James W. Ford, Communist.
14,892	John W. Aiken and Aaron M. Orange, Socialist Labor.

In addition, 545 votes were cast in North Dakota for the individual candidacy of Alfred Knutson and 2,083 scattered votes were reported from various states.

UNITED STATES

PRESIDENT 1940

State	Electoral Vote Rep.	Dem.	Other	Total Vote	Republican	Democratic	Other	Plurality	Total Vote Rep.	Dem.	Major Vote Rep.	Dem.
Alabama		11		294,219	42,184	250,726	1,309	208,542 D	14.3%	85.2%	14.4%	85.6%
Alaska			·									
Arizona		3		150,039	54,030	95,267	742	41,237 D	36.0%	63.5%	36.2%	63.8%
Arkansas		9		200,429	42,122	157,213	1,094	115,091 D	21.0%	78.4%	21.1%	78.9%
California		22		3,268,791	1,351,419	1,877,618	39,754	526,199 D	41.3%	57.4%	41.9%	58.1%
Colorado	6			549,004	279,576	265,554	3,874	14,022 R	50.9%	48.4%	51.3%	48.7%
Connecticut		8		781,502	361,819	417,621	2,062	55,802 D	46.3%	53.4%	46.4%	53.6%
Delaware		3		136,374	61,440	74,599	335	13,159 D	45.1%	54.7%	45.2%	54.8%
Florida		7		485,640	126,158	359,334	148	233,176 D	26.0%	74.0%	26.0%	74.0%
Georgia		12		312,686	46,495	265,194	997	218,699 D	14.9%	84.8%	14.9%	85.1%
Hawaii												
Idaho		4		235,168	106,553	127,842	773	21,289 D	45.3%	54.4%	45.5%	54.5%
Illinois		29		4,217,935	2,047,240	2,149,934	20,761	102,694 D	48.5%	51.0%	48.8%	51.2%
Indiana	14			1,782,747	899,466	874,063	9,218	25,403 R	50.5%	49.0%	50.7%	49.3%
Iowa	11			1,215,432	632,370	578,802	4,260	53,568 R	52.0%	47.6%	52.2%	47.8%
Kansas	9			860,297	489,169	364,725	6,403	124,444 R	56.9%	42.4%	57.3%	42.7%
Kentucky		11		970,163	410,384	557,322	2,457	146,938 D	42.3%	57.4%	42.4%	57.6%
Louisiana		10		372,305	52,446	319,751	108	267,305 D	14.1%	85.9%	14.1%	85.9%
Maine	5			320,840	163,951	156,478	411	7,473 R	51.1%	48.8%	51.2%	48.8%
Maryland		8		660,104	269,534	384,546	6,024	115,012 D	40.8%	58.3%	41.2%	58.8%
Massachusetts		17		2,026,993	939,700	1,076,522	10,771	136,822 D	46.4%	53.1%	46.6%	53.4%
Michigan	19			2,085,929	1,039,917	1,032,991	13,021	6,926 R	49.9%	49.5%	50.2%	49.8%
Minnesota		11		1,251,188	596,274	644,196	10,718	47,922 D	47.7%	51.5%	48.1%	51.9%
Mississippi		9		175,824	7,364	168,267	193	160,903 D	4.2%	95.7%	4.2%	95.8%
Missouri		15		1,833,729	871,009	958,476	4,244	87,467 D	47.5%	52.3%	47.6%	52.4%
Montana		4		247,873	99,579	145,698	2,596	46,119 D	40.2%	58.8%	40.6%	59.4%
Nebraska	7			615,878	352,201	263,677		88,524 R	57.2%	42.8%	57.2%	42.8%
Nevada		3		53,174	21,229	31,945		10,716 D	39.9%	60.1%	39.9%	60.1%
New Hampshire		4		235,419	110,127	125,292		15,165 D	46.8%	53.2%	46.8%	53.2%
New Jersey		16		1,972,552	945,475	1,016,808	10,269	71,333 D	47.9%	51.5%	48.2%	51.8%
New Mexico		3		183,258	79,315	103,699	244	24,384 D	43.3%	56.6%	43.3%	56.7%
New York		47		6,301,596	3,027,478	3,251,918	22,200	224,440 D	48.0%	51.6%	48.2%	51.8%
North Carolina		13		822,648	213,633	609,015		395,382 D	26.0%	74.0%	26.0%	74.0%
North Dakota	4			280,775	154,590	124,036	2,149	30,554 R	55.1%	44.2%	55.5%	44.5%
Ohio		26		3,319,912	1,586,773	1,733,139		146,366 D	47.8%	52.2%	47.8%	52.2%
Oklahoma		11		826,212	348,872	474,313	3,027	125,441 D	42.2%	57.4%	42.4%	57.6%
Oregon		5		481,240	219,555	258,415	3,270	38,860 D	45.6%	53.7%	45.9%	54.1%
Pennsylvania		36		4,078,714	1,889,848	2,171,035	17,831	281,187 D	46.3%	53.2%	46.5%	53.5%
Rhode Island		4		321,152	138,654	182,181	317	43,527 D	43.2%	56.7%	43.2%	56.8%
South Carolina		8		99,830	4,360	95,470		91,110 D	4.4%	95.6%	4.4%	95.6%
South Dakota	4			308,427	177,065	131,362		45,703 R	57.4%	42.6%	57.4%	42.6%
Tennessee		11		522,823	169,153	351,601	2,069	182,448 D	32.4%	67.3%	32.5%	67.5%
Texas		23		1,124,437	212,692	909,974	1,771	697,282 D	18.9%	80.9%	18.9%	81.1%
Utah		4		247,819	93,151	154,277	391	61,126 D	37.6%	62.3%	37.6%	62.4%
Vermont	3			143,062	78,371	64,269	422	14,102 R	54.8%	44.9%	54.9%	45.1%
Virginia		11		346,608	109,363	235,961	1,284	126,598 D	31.6%	68.1%	31.7%	68.3%
Washington		8		793,833	322,123	462,145	9,565	140,022 D	40.6%	58.2%	41.1%	58.9%
West Virginia		8		868,076	372,414	495,662		123,248 D	42.9%	57.1%	42.9%	57.1%
Wisconsin		12		1,405,522	679,206	704,821	21,495	25,615 D	48.3%	50.1%	49.1%	50.9%
Wyoming		3		112,240	52,633	59,287	320	6,654 D	46.9%	52.8%	47.0%	53.0%
United States	82	449	—	49,900,418	22,348,480	27,313,041	238,897	4,964,561 D	44.8%	54.7%	45.0%	55.0%

PRESIDENT 1936

The Republican figures in Delaware, Mississippi, and South Carolina include votes cast for two elector tickets. In New York the Democratic figure includes American Labor votes.

The full list of candidates for President and Vice-President was:

27,757,333	Franklin D. Roosevelt and John N. Garner, <u>Democratic</u>.
16,684,231	Alfred M. Landon and Frank Knox, <u>Republican</u>.
892,267	William Lemke and Thomas C. O'Brien, <u>Union</u>.
187,833	Norman Thomas and George A. Nelson, <u>Socialist</u>.
80,171	Earl Browder and James W. Ford, <u>Communist</u>.
37,677	D. Leigh Colvin and Claude A. Watson, <u>Prohibition</u>.
12,829	John W. Aiken and Emil F. Teichert, <u>Socialist Labor</u>.
1,598	William Dudley Pelley and Willard W. Kemp, <u>Christian</u>.

In addition, 824 scattered votes were reported from various states.

UNITED STATES

PRESIDENT 1936

State	Electoral Vote Rep.	Dem.	Other	Total Vote	Republican	Democratic	Other	Plurality	Total Vote Rep.	Dem.	Major Vote Rep.	Dem.
Alabama		11		275,744	35,358	238,196	2,190	202,838 D	12.8%	86.4%	12.9%	87.1%
Alaska												
Arizona		3		124,163	33,433	86,722	4,008	53,289 D	26.9%	69.8%	27.8%	72.2%
Arkansas		9		179,431	32,049	146,765	617	114,716 D	17.9%	81.8%	17.9%	82.1%
California		22		2,638,882	836,431	1,766,836	35,615	930,405 D	31.7%	67.0%	32.1%	67.9%
Colorado		6		488,685	181,267	295,021	12,397	113,754 D	37.1%	60.4%	38.1%	61.9%
Connecticut		8		690,723	278,685	382,129	29,909	103,444 D	40.3%	55.3%	42.2%	57.8%
Delaware		3		127,603	57,236	69,702	665	12,466 D	44.9%	54.6%	45.1%	54.9%
Florida		7		327,436	78,248	249,117	71	170,869 D	23.9%	76.1%	23.9%	76.1%
Georgia		12		293,170	36,943	255,363	864	218,420 D	12.6%	87.1%	12.6%	87.4%
Hawaii												
Idaho		4		199,617	66,256	125,683	7,678	59,427 D	33.2%	63.0%	34.5%	65.5%
Illinois		29		3,956,522	1,570,393	2,282,999	103,130	712,606 D	39.7%	57.7%	40.8%	59.2%
Indiana		14		1,650,897	691,570	934,974	24,353	243,404 D	41.9%	56.6%	42.5%	57.5%
Iowa		11		1,142,737	487,977	621,756	33,004	133,779 D	42.7%	54.4%	44.0%	56.0%
Kansas		9		865,507	397,727	464,520	3,260	66,793 D	46.0%	53.7%	46.1%	53.9%
Kentucky		11		926,214	369,702	541,944	14,568	172,242 D	39.9%	58.5%	40.6%	59.4%
Louisiana		10		329,778	36,791	292,894	93	256,103 D	11.2%	88.8%	11.2%	88.8%
Maine	5			304,240	168,823	126,333	9,084	42,490 R	55.5%	41.5%	57.2%	42.8%
Maryland		8		624,896	231,435	389,612	3,849	158,177 D	37.0%	62.3%	37.3%	62.7%
Massachusetts		17		1,840,357	768,613	942,716	129,028	174,103 D	41.8%	51.2%	44.9%	55.1%
Michigan		19		1,805,098	699,733	1,016,794	88,571	317,061 D	38.8%	56.3%	40.8%	59.2%
Minnesota		11		1,129,975	350,461	698,811	80,703	348,350 D	31.0%	61.8%	33.4%	66.6%
Mississippi		9		162,142	4,467	157,333	342	152,866 D	2.8%	97.0%	2.8%	97.2%
Missouri		15		1,828,635	697,891	1,111,043	19,701	413,152 D	38.2%	60.8%	38.6%	61.4%
Montana		4		230,502	63,598	159,690	7,214	96,092 D	27.6%	69.3%	28.5%	71.5%
Nebraska		7		608,023	247,731	347,445	12,847	99,714 D	40.7%	57.1%	41.6%	58.4%
Nevada		3		43,848	11,923	31,925		20,002 D	27.2%	72.8%	27.2%	72.8%
New Hampshire		4		218,114	104,642	108,460	5,012	3,818 D	48.0%	49.7%	49.1%	50.9%
New Jersey		16		1,820,437	720,322	1,083,850	16,265	363,528 D	39.6%	59.5%	39.9%	60.1%
New Mexico		3		169,135	61,727	106,037	1,371	44,310 D	36.5%	62.7%	36.8%	63.2%
New York		47		5,596,398	2,180,670	3,293,222	122,506	1,112,552 D	39.0%	58.8%	39.8%	60.2%
North Carolina		13		839,475	223,294	616,141	40	392,847 D	26.6%	73.4%	26.6%	73.4%
North Dakota		4		273,716	72,751	163,148	37,817	90,397 D	26.6%	59.6%	30.8%	69.2%
Ohio		26		3,012,660	1,127,855	1,747,140	137,665	619,285 D	37.4%	58.0%	39.2%	60.8%
Oklahoma		11		749,740	245,122	501,069	3,549	255,947 D	32.7%	66.8%	32.8%	67.2%
Oregon		5		414,021	122,706	266,733	24,582	144,027 D	29.6%	64.4%	31.5%	68.5%
Pennsylvania		36		4,138,105	1,690,300	2,353,788	94,017	663,488 D	40.8%	56.9%	41.8%	58.2%
Rhode Island		4		310,278	125,031	164,338	20,909	39,307 D	40.3%	53.0%	43.2%	56.8%
South Carolina		8		115,437	1,646	113,791		112,145 D	1.4%	98.6%	1.4%	98.6%
South Dakota		4		296,452	125,977	160,137	10,338	34,160 D	42.5%	54.0%	44.0%	56.0%
Tennessee		11		477,086	147,055	328,083	1,948	181,028 D	30.8%	68.8%	30.9%	69.1%
Texas		23		849,701	104,661	739,952	5,088	635,291 D	12.3%	87.1%	12.4%	87.6%
Utah		4		216,679	64,555	150,248	1,876	85,693 D	29.8%	69.3%	30.1%	69.9%
Vermont	3			143,689	81,023	62,124	542	18,899 R	56.4%	43.2%	56.6%	43.4%
Virginia		11		334,590	98,336	234,980	1,274	136,644 D	29.4%	70.2%	29.5%	70.5%
Washington		8		692,338	206,892	459,579	25,867	252,687 D	29.9%	66.4%	31.0%	69.0%
West Virginia		8		829,945	325,358	502,582	2,005	177,224 D	39.2%	60.6%	39.3%	60.7%
Wisconsin		12		1,258,560	380,828	802,984	74,748	422,156 D	30.3%	63.8%	32.2%	67.8%
Wyoming		3		103,382	38,739	62,624	2,019	23,885 D	37.5%	60.6%	38.2%	61.8%
United States	8	523	—	45,654,763	16,684,231	27,757,333	1,213,199	11,073,102 D	36.5%	60.8%	37.5%	62.5%

PRESIDENT 1932

The Republican figure in Mississippi includes votes cast for two elector tickets.

The full list of candidates for President and Vice-President was:

22,829,501	Franklin D. Roosevelt and John N. Garner, Democratic.
15,760,684	Herbert C. Hoover and Charles Curtis, Republican.
884,649	Norman Thomas and James H. Maurer, Socialist.
103,253	William Z. Foster and James W. Ford, Communist.
81,872	William D. Upshaw and Frank S. Regan, Prohibition.
53,247	William H. Harvey and Frank Hemenway, Liberty.
34,043	Verne L. Reynolds and John W. Aiken, Socialist Labor.
7,431	Jacob S. Coxey and Julius J. Reiter, Farmer-Labor.
1,645	John Zahnd and Florence Garvin, National.
740	James R. Cox and Victor C. Tisdal, Jobless.

In addition, 157 votes were cast for a Jacksonian elector ticket in Texas and 9 in Arizona for an Arizona Progressive Democratic Ticket. There were 1,528 scattered votes reported from various states.

UNITED STATES

PRESIDENT 1932

State	Electoral Vote Rep.	Electoral Vote Dem.	Electoral Vote Other	Total Vote	Republican	Democratic	Other	Plurality	Percentage Total Vote Rep.	Percentage Total Vote Dem.	Percentage Major Vote Rep.	Percentage Major Vote Dem.
Alabama		11		245,303	34,675	207,910	2,718	173,235 D	14.1%	84.8%	14.3%	85.7%
Alaska												
Arizona		3		118,251	36,104	79,264	2,883	43,160 D	30.5%	67.0%	31.3%	68.7%
Arkansas		9		216,569	27,465	186,829	2,275	159,364 D	12.7%	86.3%	12.8%	87.2%
California		22		2,266,972	847,902	1,324,157	94,913	476,255 D	37.4%	58.4%	39.0%	61.0%
Colorado		6		457,696	189,617	250,877	17,202	61,260 D	41.4%	54.8%	43.0%	57.0%
Connecticut	8			594,183	288,420	281,632	24,131	6,788 R	48.5%	47.4%	50.6%	49.4%
Delaware	3			112,901	57,073	54,319	1,509	2,754 R	50.6%	48.1%	51.2%	48.8%
Florida		7		276,943	69,170	206,307	1,466	137,137 D	25.0%	74.5%	25.1%	74.9%
Georgia		12		255,590	19,863	234,118	1,609	214,255 D	7.8%	91.6%	7.8%	92.2%
Hawaii												
Idaho		4		186,520	71,312	109,479	5,729	38,167 D	38.2%	58.7%	39.4%	60.6%
Illinois		29		3,407,926	1,432,756	1,882,304	92,866	449,548 D	42.0%	55.2%	43.2%	56.8%
Indiana		14		1,576,927	677,184	862,054	37,689	184,870 D	42.9%	54.7%	44.0%	56.0%
Iowa		11		1,036,687	414,433	598,019	24,235	183,586 D	40.0%	57.7%	40.9%	59.1%
Kansas		9		791,978	349,498	424,204	18,276	74,706 D	44.1%	53.6%	45.2%	54.8%
Kentucky		11		983,059	394,716	580,574	7,769	185,858 D	40.2%	59.1%	40.5%	59.5%
Louisiana		10		268,804	18,853	249,418	533	230,565 D	7.0%	92.8%	7.0%	93.0%
Maine	5			298,444	166,631	128,907	2,906	37,724 R	55.8%	43.2%	56.4%	43.6%
Maryland		8		511,054	184,184	314,314	12,556	130,130 D	36.0%	61.5%	36.9%	63.1%
Massachusetts		17		1,580,114	736,959	800,148	43,007	63,189 D	46.6%	50.6%	47.9%	52.1%
Michigan		19		1,664,765	739,894	871,700	53,171	131,806 D	44.4%	52.4%	45.9%	54.1%
Minnesota		11		1,002,843	363,959	600,806	38,078	236,847 D	36.3%	59.9%	37.7%	62.3%
Mississippi		9		146,034	5,180	140,168	686	134,988 D	3.5%	96.0%	3.6%	96.4%
Missouri		15		1,609,894	564,713	1,025,406	19,775	460,693 D	35.1%	63.7%	35.5%	64.5%
Montana		4		216,479	78,078	127,286	11,115	49,208 D	36.1%	58.8%	38.0%	62.0%
Nebraska		7		570,135	201,177	359,082	9,876	157,905 D	35.3%	63.0%	35.9%	64.1%
Nevada		3		41,430	12,674	28,756		16,082 D	30.6%	69.4%	30.6%	69.4%
New Hampshire	4			205,520	103,629	100,680	1,211	2,949 R	50.4%	49.0%	50.7%	49.3%
New Jersey		16		1,630,063	775,684	806,630	47,749	30,946 D	47.6%	49.5%	49.0%	51.0%
New Mexico		3		151,606	54,217	95,089	2,300	40,872 D	35.8%	62.7%	36.3%	63.7%
New York		47		4,688,614	1,937,963	2,534,959	215,692	596,996 D	41.3%	54.1%	43.3%	56.7%
North Carolina		13		711,498	208,344	497,566	5,588	289,222 D	29.3%	69.9%	29.5%	70.5%
North Dakota		4		256,290	71,772	178,350	6,168	106,578 D	28.0%	69.6%	28.7%	71.3%
Ohio		26		2,609,728	1,227,319	1,301,695	80,714	74,376 D	47.0%	49.9%	48.5%	51.5%
Oklahoma		11		704,633	188,165	516,468		328,303 D	26.7%	73.3%	26.7%	73.3%
Oregon		5		368,751	136,019	213,871	18,861	77,852 D	36.9%	58.0%	38.9%	61.1%
Pennsylvania	36			2,859,021	1,453,540	1,295,948	109,533	157,592 R	50.8%	45.3%	52.9%	47.1%
Rhode Island		4		266,170	115,266	146,604	4,300	31,338 D	43.3%	55.1%	44.0%	56.0%
South Carolina		8		104,407	1,978	102,347	82	100,369 D	1.9%	98.0%	1.9%	98.1%
South Dakota		4		288,438	99,212	183,515	5,711	84,303 D	34.4%	63.6%	35.1%	64.9%
Tennessee		11		390,273	126,752	259,473	4,048	132,721 D	32.5%	66.5%	32.8%	67.2%
Texas		23		874,382	98,218	771,109	5,055	672,891 D	11.2%	88.2%	11.3%	88.7%
Utah		4		206,578	84,795	116,750	5,033	31,955 D	41.0%	56.5%	42.1%	57.9%
Vermont	3			136,980	78,984	56,266	1,730	22,718 R	57.7%	41.1%	58.4%	41.6%
Virginia		11		297,942	89,637	203,979	4,326	114,342 D	30.1%	68.5%	30.5%	69.5%
Washington		8		614,814	208,645	353,260	52,909	144,615 D	33.9%	57.5%	37.1%	62.9%
West Virginia		8		743,774	330,731	405,124	7,919	74,393 D	44.5%	54.5%	44.9%	55.1%
Wisconsin		12		1,114,814	347,741	707,410	59,663	359,669 D	31.2%	63.5%	33.0%	67.0%
Wyoming		3		96,962	39,583	54,370	3,009	14,787 D	40.8%	56.1%	42.1%	57.9%
United States	59	472	—	39,758,759	15,760,684	22,829,501	1,168,574	7,068,817 D	39.6%	57.4%	40.8%	59.2%

PRESIDENT 1928

The Republican figures in Georgia, Mississippi, and South Carolina include votes cast for two or three elector tickets; in Pennsylvania the Communist total includes votes cast for two elector tickets.

The full list of candidates for President and Vice-President was:

21,437,277	Herbert C. Hoover and Charles Curtis, <u>Republican</u>.
15,007,698	Alfred E. Smith and Joseph T. Robinson, <u>Democratic</u>.
265,583	Norman Thomas and James H. Maurer, <u>Socialist</u>.
46,896	William Z. Foster and Benjamin Gitlow, <u>Communist</u>.
21,586	Verne L. Reynolds and Jeremiah D. Crowley, <u>Socialist Labor</u>.
20,101	William F. Varney and James A. Edgerton, <u>Prohibition</u>.
6,390	Frank E. Webb and L. R. Tillman, <u>Farmer-Labor</u>.

In addition, 420 scattered votes were reported from various states.

UNITED STATES

PRESIDENT 1928

State	Electoral Vote Rep.	Electoral Vote Dem.	Electoral Vote Other	Total Vote	Republican	Democratic	Other	Plurality	Percentage Total Vote Rep.	Percentage Total Vote Dem.	Percentage Major Vote Rep.	Percentage Major Vote Dem.
Alabama		12		248,981	120,725	127,796	460	7,071 D	48.5%	51.3%	48.6%	51.4%
Alaska												
Arizona	3			91,254	52,533	38,537	184	13,996 R	57.6%	42.2%	57.7%	42.3%
Arkansas		9		197,726	77,784	119,196	746	41,412 D	39.3%	60.3%	39.5%	60.5%
California	13			1,796,656	1,162,323	614,365	19,968	547,958 R	64.7%	34.2%	65.4%	34.6%
Colorado	6			392,242	253,872	133,131	5,239	120,741 R	64.7%	33.9%	65.6%	34.4%
Connecticut	7			553,118	296,641	252,085	4,392	44,556 R	53.6%	45.6%	54.1%	45.9%
Delaware	3			104,602	68,860	35,354	388	33,506 R	65.8%	33.8%	66.1%	33.9%
Florida	6			252,068	145,860	101,764	4,444	44,096 R	57.9%	40.4%	58.9%	41.1%
Georgia		14		231,592	101,800	129,604	188	27,804 D	44.0%	56.0%	44.0%	56.0%
Hawaii												
Idaho	4			151,541	97,322	52,926	1,293	44,396 R	64.2%	34.9%	64.8%	35.2%
Illinois	29			3,107,489	1,769,141	1,313,817	24,531	455,324 R	56.9%	42.3%	57.4%	42.6%
Indiana	15			1,421,314	848,290	562,691	10,333	285,599 R	59.7%	39.6%	60.1%	39.9%
Iowa	13			1,009,189	623,570	379,011	6,608	244,559 R	61.8%	37.6%	62.2%	37.8%
Kansas	10			713,200	513,672	193,003	6,525	320,669 R	72.0%	27.1%	72.7%	27.3%
Kentucky	13			940,521	558,064	381,070	1,387	176,994 R	59.3%	40.5%	59.4%	40.6%
Louisiana		10		215,833	51,160	164,655	18	113,495 D	23.7%	76.3%	23.7%	76.3%
Maine	6			262,170	179,923	81,179	1,068	98,744 R	68.6%	31.0%	68.9%	31.1%
Maryland	8			528,348	301,479	223,626	3,243	77,853 R	57.1%	42.3%	57.4%	42.6%
Massachusetts		18		1,577,823	775,566	792,758	9,499	17,192 D	49.2%	50.2%	49.5%	50.5%
Michigan	15			1,372,082	965,396	396,762	9,924	568,634 R	70.4%	28.9%	70.9%	29.1%
Minnesota	12			970,976	560,977	396,451	13,548	164,526 R	57.8%	40.8%	58.6%	41.4%
Mississippi		10		151,568	27,030	124,538		97,508 D	17.8%	82.2%	17.8%	82.2%
Missouri	18			1,500,845	834,080	662,684	4,081	171,396 R	55.6%	44.2%	55.7%	44.3%
Montana	4			194,108	113,300	78,578	2,230	34,722 R	58.4%	40.5%	59.0%	41.0%
Nebraska	8			547,128	345,745	197,950	3,433	147,795 R	63.2%	36.2%	63.6%	36.4%
Nevada	3			32,417	18,327	14,090		4,237 R	56.5%	43.5%	56.5%	43.5%
New Hampshire	4			196,757	115,404	80,715	638	34,689 R	58.7%	41.0%	58.8%	41.2%
New Jersey	14			1,549,381	926,050	616,517	6,814	309,533 R	59.8%	39.8%	60.0%	40.0%
New Mexico	3			118,077	69,708	48,211	158	21,497 R	59.0%	40.8%	59.1%	40.9%
New York	45			4,405,626	2,193,344	2,089,863	122,419	103,481 R	49.8%	47.4%	51.2%	48.8%
North Carolina	12			635,150	348,923	286,227		62,696 R	54.9%	45.1%	54.9%	45.1%
North Dakota	5			239,845	131,419	106,648	1,778	24,771 R	54.8%	44.5%	55.2%	44.8%
Ohio	24			2,508,346	1,627,546	864,210	16,590	763,336 R	64.9%	34.5%	65.3%	34.7%
Oklahoma	10			618,427	394,046	219,174	5,207	174,872 R	63.7%	35.4%	64.3%	35.7%
Oregon	5			319,942	205,341	109,223	5,378	96,118 R	64.2%	34.1%	65.3%	34.7%
Pennsylvania	38			3,150,612	2,055,382	1,067,586	27,644	987,796 R	65.2%	33.9%	65.8%	34.2%
Rhode Island		5		237,194	117,522	118,973	699	1,451 D	49.5%	50.2%	49.7%	50.3%
South Carolina		9		68,605	5,858	62,700	47	56,842 D	8.5%	91.4%	8.5%	91.5%
South Dakota	5			261,857	157,603	102,660	1,594	54,943 R	60.2%	39.2%	60.6%	39.4%
Tennessee	12			353,192	195,388	157,143	661	38,245 R	55.3%	44.5%	55.4%	44.6%
Texas	20			717,733	372,324	344,542	867	27,782 R	51.9%	48.0%	51.9%	48.1%
Utah	4			176,603	94,618	80,985	1,000	13,633 R	53.6%	45.9%	53.9%	46.1%
Vermont	4			135,191	90,404	44,440	347	45,964 R	66.9%	32.9%	67.0%	33.0%
Virginia	12			305,364	164,609	140,146	609	24,463 R	53.9%	45.9%	54.0%	46.0%
Washington	7			500,840	335,844	156,772	8,224	179,072 R	67.1%	31.3%	68.2%	31.8%
West Virginia	8			642,752	375,551	263,784	3,417	111,767 R	58.4%	41.0%	58.7%	41.3%
Wisconsin	13			1,016,831	544,205	450,259	22,367	93,946 R	53.5%	44.3%	54.7%	45.3%
Wyoming	3			82,835	52,748	29,299	788	23,449 R	63.7%	35.4%	64.3%	35.7%
United States	444	87	—	36,805,951	21,437,277	15,007,698	360,976	6,429,579 R	58.2%	40.8%	58.8%	41.2%

PRESIDENT 1924

Wisconsin's 13 electoral votes were cast for the Progressive nominees, and in eleven other states in the Midwest and West the Progressive candidates ran second. In several states the Progressive total includes votes cast for two or three elector tickets.

The full list of candidates for President and Vice-President was:

15,719,921	Calvin Coolidge and Charles G. Dawes, Republican.
8,386,704	John W. Davis and Charles W. Bryan, Democratic.
4,832,532	Robert M. LaFollette and Burton K. Wheeler, Progressive.
56,292	Herman P. Faris and Marie Caroline Brehm, Prohibition.
34,174	Frank T. Johns and Verne L. Reynolds, Socialist Labor.
33,360	William Z. Foster and Benjamin Gitlow, Communist.
24,340	Gilbert O. Nations and Leander L. Pickett, American.
2,948	William J. Wallace and John C. Lincoln, Commonwealth Land.

In addition, 4,752 scattered votes were reported from various states.

UNITED STATES

PRESIDENT 1924

State	Electoral Vote Rep.	Dem.	Other	Total Vote	Republican	Democratic	Progressive	Other	Plurality	Pct Rep.	Dem.	Prog.
Alabama		12		164,563	42,823	113,138	8,040	562	70,315 D	26.0%	68.8%	4.9%
Alaska												
Arizona	3			73,961	30,516	26,235	17,210		4,281 R	41.3%	35.5%	23.3%
Arkansas		9		138,540	40,583	84,790	13,167		44,207 D	29.3%	61.2%	9.5%
California	13			1,281,778	733,250	105,514	424,649	18,365	308,601 R	57.2%	8.2%	33.1%
Colorado	6			342,261	195,171	75,238	69,946	1,906	119,933 R	57.0%	22.0%	20.4%
Connecticut	7			400,396	246,322	110,184	42,416	1,474	136,138 R	61.5%	27.5%	10.6%
Delaware	3			90,885	52,441	33,445	4,979	20	18,996 R	57.7%	36.8%	5.5%
Florida		6		109,158	30,633	62,083	8,625	7,817	31,450 D	28.1%	56.9%	7.9%
Georgia		14		166,635	30,300	123,262	12,687	386	92,962 D	18.2%	74.0%	7.6%
Hawaii												
Idaho	4			147,690	69,791	23,951	53,948		15,843 R	47.3%	16.2%	36.5%
Illinois	29			2,470,067	1,453,321	576,975	432,027	7,744	876,346 R	58.8%	23.4%	17.5%
Indiana	15			1,272,390	703,042	492,245	71,700	5,403	210,797 R	55.3%	38.7%	5.6%
Iowa	13			976,770	537,458	160,382	274,448	4,482	263,010 R	55.0%	16.4%	28.1%
Kansas	10			662,456	407,671	156,320	98,461	4	251,351 R	61.5%	23.6%	14.9%
Kentucky	13			813,843	396,758	375,593	38,465	3,027	21,165 R	48.8%	46.2%	4.7%
Louisiana		10		121,951	24,670	93,218		4,063	68,548 D	20.2%	76.4%	
Maine	6			192,192	138,440	41,964	11,382	406	96,476 R	72.0%	21.8%	5.9%
Maryland	8			358,630	162,414	148,072	47,157	987	14,342 R	45.3%	41.3%	13.1%
Massachusetts	18			1,129,837	703,476	280,831	141,225	4,305	422,645 R	62.3%	24.9%	12.5%
Michigan	15			1,160,419	874,631	152,359	122,014	11,415	722,272 R	75.4%	13.1%	10.5%
Minnesota	12			822,146	420,759	55,913	339,192	6,282	81,567 R	51.2%	6.8%	41.3%
Mississippi		10		112,442	8,494	100,474	3,474		91,980 D	7.6%	89.4%	3.1%
Missouri	18			1,310,095	648,488	574,962	83,996	2,649	73,526 R	49.5%	43.9%	6.4%
Montana	4			174,425	74,138	33,805	66,124	358	8,014 R	42.5%	19.4%	37.9%
Nebraska	8			463,559	218,985	137,299	105,681	1,594	81,686 R	47.2%	29.6%	22.8%
Nevada	3			26,921	11,243	5,909	9,769		1,474 R	41.8%	21.9%	36.3%
New Hampshire	4			164,769	98,575	57,201	8,993		41,374 R	59.8%	34.7%	5.5%
New Jersey	14			1,088,054	676,277	298,043	109,028	4,706	378,234 R	62.2%	27.4%	10.0%
New Mexico	3			112,830	54,745	48,542	9,543		6,203 R	48.5%	43.0%	8.5%
New York	45			3,263,939	1,820,058	950,796	474,913	18,172	869,262 R	55.8%	29.1%	14.6%
North Carolina		12		481,608	190,754	284,190	6,651	13	93,436 D	39.6%	59.0%	1.4%
North Dakota	5			199,081	94,931	13,858	89,922	370	5,009 R	47.7%	7.0%	45.2%
Ohio	24			2,016,296	1,176,130	477,887	358,008	4,271	698,243 R	58.3%	23.7%	17.8%
Oklahoma		10		527,828	225,756	255,798	46,274		30,042 D	42.8%	48.5%	8.8%
Oregon	5			279,488	142,579	67,589	68,403	917	74,176 R	51.0%	24.2%	24.5%
Pennsylvania	38			2,144,850	1,401,481	409,192	307,567	26,610	992,289 R	65.3%	19.1%	14.3%
Rhode Island	5			210,115	125,286	76,606	7,628	595	48,680 R	59.6%	36.5%	3.6%
South Carolina		9		50,755	1,123	49,008	623	1	47,885 D	2.2%	96.6%	1.2%
South Dakota	5			203,868	101,299	27,214	75,355		25,944 R	49.7%	13.3%	37.0%
Tennessee		12		301,030	130,831	159,339	10,666	194	28,508 D	43.5%	52.9%	3.5%
Texas		20		657,054	130,794	483,381	42,879		352,587 D	19.9%	73.6%	6.5%
Utah	4			156,990	77,327	47,001	32,662		30,326 R	49.3%	29.9%	20.8%
Vermont	4			102,917	80,498	16,124	5,964	331	64,374 R	78.2%	15.7%	5.8%
Virginia		12		223,603	73,328	139,717	10,369	189	66,389 D	32.8%	62.5%	4.6%
Washington	7			421,549	220,224	42,842	150,727	7,756	69,497 R	52.2%	10.2%	35.8%
West Virginia	8			583,662	288,635	257,232	36,723	1,072	31,403 R	49.5%	44.1%	6.3%
Wisconsin			13	840,827	311,614	68,115	453,678	7,420	142,064 P	37.1%	8.1%	54.0%
Wyoming	3			79,900	41,858	12,868	25,174		16,684 R	52.4%	16.1%	31.5%
United States	382	136	13	29,095,023	15,719,921	8,386,704	4,832,532	155,866	7,333,217 R	54.0%	28.8%	16.6%

PRESIDENT 1920

The Republican figure in South Carolina includes votes cast for two elector tickets; the figure in Florida is the vote cast for the one elector candidate who ran on both Republican tickets in that state. In Washington, the total vote for minor party candidates exceeded that for the Democratic candidates, but the Democratic total was greater than that for any one of the minor party nominees.

The full list of candidates for President and Vice-President was:

16,153,115	Warren G. Harding and Calvin Coolidge, <u>Republican</u>.
9,133,092	James M. Cox and Franklin D. Roosevelt, <u>Democratic</u>.
915,490	Eugene V. Debs and Seymour Stedman, <u>Socialist</u>.
265,229	Parley P. Christensen and Max S. Hayes, <u>Farmer-Labor</u>.
189,339	Aaron S. Watkins and D. Leigh Colvin, <u>Prohibition</u>.
48,098	James Ferguson and William J. Hough, <u>American</u>.
30,594	William W. Cox and August Gillhaus, <u>Socialist Labor</u>.
5,833	Robert C. Macauley and Richard C. Barnum, <u>Single Tax</u>.

In addition, 27,309 votes were cast in Texas for a Black-and-Tan Republican elector ticket and 514 scattered votes were reported from various states.

UNITED STATES

PRESIDENT 1920

State	Electoral Vote Rep.	Dem.	Other	Total Vote	Republican	Democratic	Other	Plurality	Percentage Total Vote Rep.	Dem.	Major Vote Rep.	Dem.
Alabama		12		233,951	74,719	156,064	3,168	81,345 D	31.9%	66.7%	32.4%	67.6%
Alaska												
Arizona	3			66,803	37,016	29,546	241	7,470 R	55.4%	44.2%	55.6%	44.4%
Arkansas		9		183,871	72,316	106,427	5,128	34,111 D	39.3%	57.9%	40.5%	59.5%
California	13			943,463	624,992	229,191	89,280	395,801 R	66.2%	24.3%	73.2%	26.8%
Colorado	6			292,053	173,248	104,936	13,869	68,312 R	59.3%	35.9%	62.3%	37.7%
Connecticut	7			365,518	229,238	120,721	15,559	108,517 R	62.7%	33.0%	65.5%	34.5%
Delaware	3			94,875	52,858	39,911	2,106	12,947 R	55.7%	42.1%	57.0%	43.0%
Florida		6		145,684	44,853	90,515	10,316	45,662 D	30.8%	62.1%	33.1%	66.9%
Georgia		14		149,558	42,981	106,112	465	63,131 D	28.7%	71.0%	28.8%	71.2%
Hawaii												
Idaho	4			138,281	91,351	46,930		44,421 R	66.1%	33.9%	66.1%	33.9%
Illinois	29			2,094,714	1,420,480	534,395	139,839	886,085 R	67.8%	25.5%	72.7%	27.3%
Indiana	15			1,262,974	696,370	511,364	55,240	185,006 R	55.1%	40.5%	57.7%	42.3%
Iowa	13			894,959	634,674	227,804	32,481	406,870 R	70.9%	25.5%	73.6%	26.4%
Kansas	10			570,243	369,268	185,464	15,511	183,804 R	64.8%	32.5%	66.6%	33.4%
Kentucky		13		918,636	452,480	456,497	9,659	4,017 D	49.3%	49.7%	49.8%	50.2%
Louisiana		10		126,397	38,539	87,519	339	48,980 D	30.5%	69.2%	30.6%	69.4%
Maine	6			197,840	136,355	58,961	2,524	77,394 R	68.9%	29.8%	69.8%	30.2%
Maryland	8			428,443	236,117	180,626	11,700	55,491 R	55.1%	42.2%	56.7%	43.3%
Massachusetts	18			993,718	681,153	276,691	35,874	404,462 R	68.5%	27.8%	71.1%	28.9%
Michigan	15			1,048,411	762,865	233,450	52,096	529,415 R	72.8%	22.3%	76.6%	23.4%
Minnesota	12			735,838	519,421	142,994	73,423	376,427 R	70.6%	19.4%	78.4%	21.6%
Mississippi		10		82,351	11,576	69,136	1,639	57,560 D	14.1%	84.0%	14.3%	85.7%
Missouri	18			1,332,140	727,252	574,699	30,189	152,553 R	54.6%	43.1%	55.9%	44.1%
Montana	4			179,006	109,430	57,372	12,204	52,058 R	61.1%	32.1%	65.6%	34.4%
Nebraska	8			382,743	247,498	119,608	15,637	127,890 R	64.7%	31.3%	67.4%	32.6%
Nevada	3			27,194	15,479	9,851	1,864	5,628 R	56.9%	36.2%	61.1%	38.9%
New Hampshire	4			159,092	95,196	62,662	1,234	32,534 R	59.8%	39.4%	60.3%	39.7%
New Jersey	14			910,251	615,333	258,761	36,157	356,572 R	67.6%	28.4%	70.4%	29.6%
New Mexico	3			105,412	57,634	46,668	1,110	10,966 R	54.7%	44.3%	55.3%	44.7%
New York	45			2,898,513	1,871,167	781,238	246,108	1,089,929 R	64.6%	27.0%	70.5%	29.5%
North Carolina		12		538,649	232,819	305,367	463	72,548 D	43.2%	56.7%	43.3%	56.7%
North Dakota	5			205,786	160,082	37,422	8,282	122,660 R	77.8%	18.2%	81.1%	18.9%
Ohio	24			2,021,653	1,182,022	780,037	59,594	401,985 R	58.5%	38.6%	60.2%	39.8%
Oklahoma	10			485,678	243,840	216,122	25,716	27,718 R	50.2%	44.5%	53.0%	47.0%
Oregon	5			238,522	143,592	80,019	14,911	63,573 R	60.2%	33.5%	64.2%	35.8%
Pennsylvania	38			1,851,248	1,218,215	503,202	129,831	715,013 R	65.8%	27.2%	70.8%	29.2%
Rhode Island	5			167,981	107,463	55,062	5,456	52,401 R	64.0%	32.8%	66.1%	33.9%
South Carolina		9		66,808	2,610	64,170	28	61,560 D	3.9%	96.1%	3.9%	96.1%
South Dakota	5			182,237	110,692	35,938	35,607	74,754 R	60.7%	19.7%	75.5%	24.5%
Tennessee	12			428,036	219,229	206,558	2,249	12,671 R	51.2%	48.3%	51.5%	48.5%
Texas		20		486,109	114,658	287,920	83,531	173,262 D	23.6%	59.2%	28.5%	71.5%
Utah	4			145,828	81,555	56,639	7,634	24,916 R	55.9%	38.8%	59.0%	41.0%
Vermont	4			89,961	68,212	20,919	830	47,293 R	75.8%	23.3%	76.5%	23.5%
Virginia		12		231,000	87,456	141,670	1,874	54,214 D	37.9%	61.3%	38.2%	61.8%
Washington	7			398,715	223,137	84,298	91,280	138,839 R	56.0%	21.1%	72.6%	27.4%
West Virginia	8			509,936	282,007	220,785	7,144	61,222 R	55.3%	43.3%	56.1%	43.9%
Wisconsin	13			701,281	498,576	113,422	89,283	385,154 R	71.1%	16.2%	81.5%	18.5%
Wyoming	3			56,253	35,091	17,429	3,733	17,662 R	62.4%	31.0%	66.8%	33.2%
United States	404	127	—	26,768,613	16,153,115	9,133,092	1,482,406	7,020,023 R	60.3%	34.1%	63.9%	36.1%

1988 PRESIDENTIAL PRIMARIES

In 1988 thirty-six states and the District of Columbia held Presidential primaries though there was no Republican voting in New York and no Democratic voting in South Carolina.

In some jurisdictions balloting was for delegate slates linked to specific Presidential candidates; in others, electors indicated only a personal preference as to their party's nominee.

The tables included here give the major party primary vote in each state for those candidates on the ballot in at least twenty states. An asterisk in the table indicates votes written-in for a candidate not on the ballot.

Republican candidates on the ballot in at least one state were George Bush, Paul B. Conley, Robert Dole, Robert F. Drucker, Pierre duPont, Alexander M. Haig, William Horrigan, Jack F. Kemp, Michael S. Levinson, Isabell Masters, Mary Jane Rachner, Pat Robertson and Harold E. Stassen.

Democratic candidates on the ballot in at least one state were Frank Ahern, Douglas Applegate, Bruce Babbitt, Norbert G. Dennerll, Florenzo DiDonato, Charles R. Doty, Michael S. Dukakis, David E. Duke, William J. duPont, Richard A. Gephardt, Albert Gore, Jr., Gary W. Hart, Jesse L. Jackson, Richard B. Kay, William King, Claude R. Kirk, Stephen A. Koczak, Lyndon H. LaRouche, Stanley Lock, Angus W. McDonald, William A. Marra, Anthony R. Martin-Trigona, Edward T. O'Donnell, Conrad W. Roy, Cyril E. Sagan, Paul Simon, Frank L. Thomas, Osie Thorpe, James A. Traficant, A. A. VanPetten, Jennifer Alden Wesner, W. A. Williams and Irwin Zucker.

ALABAMA MARCH 8

Republican   137,807 Bush; 34,733 Dole; 29,772 Robertson; 10,557 Kemp; 392 duPont; 300 Haig.

Democratic   176,764 Jackson; 151,739 Gore; 31,306 Dukakis; 30,214 Gephardt; 7,530 Hart; 3,063 Simon; 2,410 Babbitt; 1,771 Uncommitted; 845 LaRouche.

ARKANSAS MARCH 8

Republican   32,114 Bush, 17,667 Dole; 12,918 Robertson; 3,499 Kemp; 1,402 Uncommitted; 359 duPont; 346 Haig.

Democratic   185,758 Gore; 94,103 Dukakis; 85,003 Jackson; 59,711 Gephardt; 35,553 Uncommitted; 18,630 Hart; 9,020 Simon; 4,805 Duke; 2,614 Babbitt; 2,347 LaRouche.

CALIFORNIA JUNE 7

Republican   1,856,273 Bush; 289,220 Dole; 94,779 Robertson; 115 scattered write-in.

Democratic   1,910,808 Dukakis; 1,102,093 Jackson; 56,645 Gore; 43,771 Simon; 25,417 LaRouche.

American Independent   9,792 James C. Griffin; 5,401 James Gritz; 3 scattered write-in.

Peace & Freedom   2,117 Lenora B. Fulani; 1,222 Shirley Isaacson; 1,042 Larry Holmes; 778 Herb Lewin; 411 Willa Kenoyer; 353 Al Hamburg; 6 scattered write-in.

CONNECTICUT MARCH 29

Republican   73,501 Bush; 21,005 Dole; 3,281 Kemp; 3,193 Uncommitted; 3,191 Robertson.

Democratic   140,291 Dukakis; 68,372 Jackson; 18,501 Gore; 5,761 Hart; 3,140 Simon; 2,370 Babbitt; 1,951 Uncommitted; 1,009 Gephardt.

1988 PRESIDENTIAL PRIMARIES

FLORIDA MARCH 8

Republican 559,820 Bush; 191,197 Dole; 95,826 Robertson; 41,795 Kemp; 6,726 duPont; 5,858 Haig.

Democratic 521,041 Dukakis; 254,912 Jackson; 182,861 Gephardt; 161,165 Gore; 79,088 Undecided; 36,315 Hart; 27,620 Simon; 10,296 Babbitt.

GEORGIA MARCH 8

Republican 215,516 Bush; 94,749 Dole; 65,163 Robertson; 23,409 Kemp; 1,309 duPont; 782 Haig.

Democratic 247,831 Jackson; 201,490 Gore; 97,179 Dukakis; 41,489 Gephardt; 15,852 Hart; 8,388 Simon; 7,276 Uncommitted; 3,247 Babbitt.

IDAHO MAY 24

Republican 55,464 Bush; 6,935 None of the Names Shown; 5,876 Robertson.

Democratic 37,696 Dukakis; 8,066 Jackson; 2,308 "None of the Names Shown"; 1,891 Gore; 1,409 Simon.

ILLINOIS MARCH 15

Republican 469,151 Bush; 309,253 Dole; 59,087 Robertson; 12,687 Kemp; 4,653 duPont; 3,806 Haig.

Democratic 635,219 Simon; 484,233 Jackson; 245,289 Dukakis; 77,265 Gore; 35,108 Gephardt; 12,769 Hart; 6,094 LaRouche; 4,953 Babbitt.

Solidarity 170 Lenora B. Fulani.

INDIANA MAY 3

Republican 351,829 Bush; 42,878 Dole; 28,712 Robertson; 14,236 Kemp.

Democratic 449,495 Dukakis; 145,021 Jackson; 21,865 Gore; 16,777 Gephardt; 12,550 Simon.

KENTUCKY MARCH 8

Republican 72,020 Bush; 27,868 Dole; 13,526 Robertson; 4,020 Kemp; 2,245 Uncommitted; 844 Stassen; 457 duPont; 422 Haig.

Democratic 145,988 Gore; 59,433 Dukakis; 49,667 Jackson; 28,982 Gephardt; 11,798 Hart; 10,465 Uncommitted; 9,393 Simon; 1,290 Babbitt; 681 LaRouche; 537 Martin-Trigona; 487 Kay.

LOUISIANA MARCH 8

Republican 83,687 Bush; 26,295 Robertson; 25,626 Dole; 7,722 Kemp; 853 duPont; 598 Haig.

Democratic 221,532 Jackson; 174,974 Gore; 95,667 Dukakis; 66,434 Gephardt; 26,442 Hart; 23,390 Duke; 5,155 Simon; 3,701 Ahern; 3,076 Babbitt; 1,681 LaRouche; 1,575 Dennerll; 823 Kay.

MARYLAND MARCH 8

Republican 107,026 Bush; 64,987 Dole; 12,860 Robertson; 11,909 Kemp; 2,551 duPont; 1,421 Haig.

Democratic 242,479 Dukakis; 152,642 Jackson; 46,063 Gore; 42,059 Gephardt; 16,513 Simon; 14,948 Uncommitted; 9,732 Hart; 4,750 Babbitt; 2,149 LaRouche.

1988 PRESIDENTIAL PRIMARIES

MASSACHUSETTS MARCH 8

Republican   141,113 Bush; 63,392 Dole; 16,791 Kemp; 10,891 Robertson; 3,522 duPont; 3,416 No Preference; 1,705 Haig; 351 scattered write-in.

Democratic   418,256 Dukakis; 133,141 Jackson; 72,944 Gephardt; 31,631 Gore; 26,176 Simon; 11,866 No Preference; 10,837 Hart; 4,222 Babbitt; 1,971 DiDonato; 998 LaRouche; 1,405 scattered write-in.

MISSISSIPPI MARCH 8

Republican   104,814 Bush; 26,855 Dole; 21,378 Robertson; 5,479 Kemp.

Democratic   160,651 Jackson; 120,364 Gore; 29,941 Dukakis; 19,693 Gephardt; 13,934 Hart; 9,384 Uncommitted; 2,118 Simon; 2,037 Babbitt; 1,295 LaRouche. Data given are for the amended returns.

MISSOURI MARCH 8

Republican   168,812 Bush; 164,394 Dole; 44,705 Robertson; 14,180 Kemp; 5,563 Uncommitted; 1,788 duPont; 858 Haig.

Democratic   305,287 Gephardt; 106,386 Jackson; 61,303 Dukakis; 21,433 Simon; 14,549 Gore; 7,607 Hart; 6,635 Uncommitted; 1,760 Duke; 1,377 Babbitt; 664 LaRouche; 372 Kay; 241 Koczak; 191 Dennerll.

MONTANA JUNE 7

Republican   63,098 Bush; 16,762 Dole; 6,520 No Preference.

Democratic   83,684 Dukakis; 26,908 Jackson; 4,083 No Preference; 3,369 Gephardt; 2,261 Gore; 1,566 Simon.

NEBRASKA MAY 10

Republican   138,784 Bush; 45,572 Dole; 10,334 Robertson; 8,423 Kemp; 936 scattered write-in.

Democratic   106,334 Dukakis; 43,380 Jackson; 4,948 Gephardt; 4,763 Uncommitted; 4,220 Hart; 2,519 Gore; 2,104 Simon; 416 LaRouche; 324 scattered write-in.

New Alliance   10 Lenora B. Fulani.

NEW HAMPSHIRE FEBRUARY 16

Republican   59,290 Bush; 44,797 Dole; 20,114 Kemp; 15,885 duPont; 14,775 Robertson; 481 Haig; 130 Stassen; 107 Conley; 107 Rachner; 83 Drucker; 76 Horrigan; 43 Levinson; 1,756 scattered write-in.

Democratic   44,112 Dukakis; 24,513 Gephardt; 21,094 Simon; 9,615 Jackson; 8,400 Gore; 5,644 Babbitt; 4,888 Hart; 1,349 William J. duPont; 264 Duke; 188 LaRouche; 142 Marra; 122 Roy; 84 DiDonato; 61 Martin-Trigona; 47 Koczak; 36 King; 33 O'Donnell; 33 Sagan; 28 Thomas; 25 Kirk; 22 Zucker; 18 Dennerll; 16 Thorpe; 10 VanPetten; 9 Lock; 2,759 scattered write-in.

NEW JERSEY JUNE 7

Republican   241,033 Bush.

Democratic   414,829 Dukakis; 213,705 Jackson; 18,062 Gore; 2,621 LaRouche; 2,594 Marra; 2,491 Duke.

1988 PRESIDENTIAL PRIMARIES

NEW MEXICO JUNE 7

Republican   69,359 Bush; 9,305 Dole; 5,350 Robertson; 2,569 Uncommitted; 2,161 Haig.

Democratic   114,968 Dukakis; 52,988 Jackson; 6,898 Hart; 4,747 Gore; 3,275 Uncommitted; 2,913 Babbitt; 2,821 Simon.

NEW YORK APRIL 19

Republican   No Presidential primary held.

Democratic   801,457 Dukakis; 585,076 Jackson; 157,559 Gore; 17,011 Simon; 10,258 Uncommitted; 2,672 Gephardt; 1,153 LaRouche.

NORTH CAROLINA MARCH 8

Republican   124,260 Bush; 107,032 Dole; 26,861 Robertson; 11,361 Kemp; 2,797 No Preference; 944 duPont; 546 Haig.

Democratic   235,669 Gore; 224,177 Jackson; 137,993 Dukakis; 37,553 Gephardt; 16,381 Hart; 16,337 No Preference; 8,032 Simon; 3,816 Babbitt.

NORTH DAKOTA JUNE 14

Republican   37,062 Bush; 2,372 Rachner.

Democratic   No candidate names appeared on the ballot. Tallied write-in votes were 2,890 Dukakis; 515 Jackson.

Libertarian   985 Ron Paul.

OHIO MAY 3

Republican   643,907 Bush slate; 94,650 Dole slate; 56,347 Robertson slate. The data given here are for the state-wide at-large slates pledged to the candidates indicated.

Democratic   869,792 Dukakis slates; 378,866 Jackson slates; 29,931 Gore slates; 29,912 Traficant slates; 28,414 Hart slates; 25,068 Applegate slate; 15,524 Simon slates; 6,065 LaRouche slates. The data given here are the sum of the votes cast for delegate slates by Congressional District pledged to the candidates indicated. Only Dukakis and Gore had delegate slates in all twenty-one Congressional Districts.

OKLAHOMA MARCH 8

Republican   78,224 Bush; 73,016 Dole; 44,067 Robertson; 11,439 Kemp; 938 duPont; 715 Haig; 539 Masters.

Democratic   162,584 Gore; 82,596 Gephardt; 66,278 Dukakis; 52,417 Jackson; 14,336 Hart; 6,901 Simon; 2,388 Duke; 1,601 Babbitt; 1,078 LaRouche; 1,068 Koczak; 1,005 Doty; 475 Dennerll.

OREGON MAY 17

Republican   199,938 Bush; 49,128 Dole; 21,212 Robertson; 4,208 scattered write-in.

Democratic   221,048 Dukakis; 148,207 Jackson; 6,772 Gephardt; 5,445 Gore; 4,757 Simon; 1,562 LaRouche; 1,141 scattered write-in.

1988 PRESIDENTIAL PRIMARIES

PENNSYLVANIA APRIL 26

Republican   687,323 Bush; 103,763 Dole; 79,463 Robertson.

Democratic   1,002,480 Dukakis; 411,260 Jackson; 44,542 Gore; 20,473 Hart; 9,692 Simon; 7,546 Wesner; 7,254 Gephardt; 4,443 LaRouche.

RHODE ISLAND MARCH 8

Republican   10,401 Bush; 3,628 Dole; 911 Robertson; 792 Kemp; 174 Uncommitted; 80 duPont; 49 Haig.

Democratic   34,211 Dukakis; 7,445 Jackson; 2,028 Gephardt; 1,939 Gore; 1,395 Simon; 809 Uncommitted; 733 Hart; 469 Babbitt.

SOUTH CAROLINA MARCH 5

Republican   94,738 Bush; 40,265 Dole; 37,261 Robertson; 22,431 Kemp; 316 duPont; 177 Haig; 104 Stassen.

Democratic   No Presidential primary held.

SOUTH DAKOTA FEBRUARY 23

Republican   51,599 Dole slate; 18,310 Robertson slate; 17,404 Bush slate; 4,290 Kemp slate; 1,226 Uncommitted slate; 576 duPont slate.

Democratic   31,184 Gephardt; 22,349 Dukakis; 5,993 Gore; 3,992 Simon; 3,875 Hart; 3,867 Jackson; 346 Babbitt.

TENNESSEE MARCH 8

Republican   152,515 Bush; 55,027 Dole; 32,015 Robertson; 10,911 Kemp; 2,340 Uncommitted; 777 Haig; 646 duPont; 21 scattered write-in.

Democratic   416,861 Gore; 119,248 Jackson; 19,348 Dukakis; 8,470 Gephardt; 4,706 Hart; 3,032 Uncommitted; 2,647 Simon; 1,946 Babbitt; 56 scattered write-in.

TEXAS MARCH 8

Republican   648,178 Bush; 155,449 Robertson; 140,795 Dole; 50,586 Kemp; 12,563 Uncommitted; 4,245 duPont; 3,140 Haig.

Democratic   579,713 Dukakis; 433,335 Jackson; 357,764 Gore; 240,158 Gephardt; 82,199 Hart; 34,499 Simon; 11,618 Babbitt; 9,013 LaRouche; 8,808 Duke; 6,238 Williams; 3,700 Dennerll.

VERMONT MARCH 1

Republican   23,565 Bush; 18,655 Dole; 2,452 Robertson; 1,877 Kemp; 808 duPont; 324 Haig; 151 scattered write-in.

Democratic   28,353 Dukakis; 13,044 Jackson; 3,910 Gephardt; 2,620 Simon; 2,055 Hart; 809 scattered write-in.

Liberty Union   199 Willa Kenoyer; 65 Herb Lewin; 25 scattered write-in.

1988 PRESIDENTIAL PRIMARIES

VIRGINIA MARCH 8

Republican   124,738 Bush; 60,921 Dole; 32,173 Robertson; 10,809 Kemp; 3,675 Uncommitted; 1,229 duPont; 597 Haig.

Democratic   164,709 Jackson; 81,419 Gore; 80,183 Dukakis; 15,935 Gephardt; 7,045 Simon; 6,266 Hart; 6,142 Uncommitted; 2,454 Babbitt; 746 LaRouche.

WEST VIRGINIA MAY 10

Republican   110,705 Bush; 15,600 Dole; 10,417 Robertson; 3,820 Kemp; 1,604 Stassen; 994 Conley.

Democratic   254,289 Dukakis; 45,788 Jackson; 11,573 Gore; 9,284 Hart; 6,130 Gephardt; 3,604 McDonald; 2,280 Simon; 1,978 Babbitt; 1,482 LaRouche; 1,383 Duke; 1,339 Dennerll; 967 Traficant.

WISCONSIN APRIL 5

Republican   295,295 Bush; 28,460 Dole; 24,798 Robertson; 4,915 Kemp; 2,372 Uninstructed Delegation; 1,554 Haig; 1,504 duPont; 396 scattered write-in.

Democratic   483,172 Dukakis; 285,995 Jackson; 176,712 Gore; 48,419 Simon; 7,996 Gephardt; 7,068 Hart; 2,554 Uninstructed Delegation; 2,353 Babbitt; 513 scattered write-in.

DISTRICT OF COLUMBIA MAY 3

Republican   5,890 Bush; 469 Dole; 268 Robertson; 93 scattered write-in.

Democratic   68,840 Jackson; 15,415 Dukakis; 769 Simon; 648 Gore; 300 Gephardt; 80 Thorpe.

1988 REPUBLICAN PREFERENCE PRIMARIES

Date		State	Total Vote	Bush	Dole	duPont	Haig	Kemp	Robertson	Other
Feb.	16	New Hampshire	157,644	59,290	44,797	15,885	481	20,114	14,775	2,302
	23	South Dakota	93,405	17,404	51,599	576		4,290	18,310	1,226
Mar.	1	Vermont	47,832	23,565	18,655	808	324	1,877	2,452	151
	5	South Carolina	195,292	94,738	40,265	316	177	22,431	37,261	104
	8	Alabama	213,561	137,807	34,733	392	300	10,557	29,772	
	8	Arkansas	68,305	32,114	17,667	359	346	3,499	12,918	1,402
	8	Florida	901,222	559,820	191,197	6,726	5,858	41,795	95,826	
	8	Georgia	400,928	215,516	94,749	1,309	782	23,409	65,163	
	8	Kentucky	121,402	72,020	27,868	457	422	4,020	13,526	3,089
	8	Louisiana	144,781	83,687	25,626	853	598	7,722	26,295	
	8	Maryland	200,754	107,026	64,987	2,551	1,421	11,909	12,860	
	8	Massachusetts	241,181	141,113	63,392	3,522	1,705	16,791	10,891	3,767
	8	Mississippi	158,526	104,814	26,855			5,479	21,378	
	8	Missouri	400,300	168,812	164,394	1,788	858	14,180	44,705	5,563
	8	North Carolina	273,801	124,260	107,032	944	546	11,361	26,861	2,797
	8	Oklahoma	208,938	78,224	73,016	938	715	11,439	44,067	539
	8	Rhode Island	16,035	10,401	3,628	80	49	792	911	174
	8	Tennessee	254,252	152,515	55,027	646	777	10,911	32,015	2,361
	8	Texas	1,014,956	648,178	140,795	4,245	3,140	50,586	155,449	12,563
	8	Virginia	234,142	124,738	60,921	1,229	597	10,809	32,173	3,675
	15	Illinois	858,637	469,151	309,253	4,653	3,806	12,687	59,087	
	29	Connecticut	104,171	73,501	21,005			3,281	3,191	3,193
April	5	Wisconsin	359,294	295,295	28,460	1,504	1,554	4,915	24,798	2,768
	19	New York	No Primary held							
	26	Pennsylvania	870,549	687,323	103,763				79,463	.
May	3	Indiana	437,655	351,829	42,878			14,236	28,712	
	3	Ohio	794,904	643,907	94,650				56,347	
	3	District of Columbia	6,720	5,890	469				268	93
	10	Nebraska	204,049	138,784	45,572			8,423	10,334	936
	10	West Virginia	143,140	110,705	15,600			3,820	10,417	2,598
	17	Oregon	274,486	199,938	49,128				21,212	4,208
	24	Idaho	68,275	55,464					5,876	6,935
June	7	California	2,240,387	1,856,273	289,220				94,779	115
	7	Montana	86,380	63,098	16,762					6,520
	7	New Jersey	241,033	241,033						
	7	New Mexico	88,744	69,359	9,305		2,161		5,350	2,569
	14	North Dakota	39,434	37,062						2,372
			12,165,115	8,254,654	2,333,268	49,781	26,617	331,333	1,097,442	72,020

Other vote includes 34,950 Uncommitted; 12,733 No Preference; 6,935 "None of the Names Shown"; 2,682 Stassen; 2,479 Rachner; 2,372 Uninstructed Delegation; 1,101 Conley; 539 Masters; 83 Drucker; 76 Horrigan; 43 Levinson; 8,027 scattered.

1988 DEMOCRATIC PREFERENCE PRIMARIES

Date		State	Total Vote	Babbitt	Dukakis	Gephardt	Gore	Hart	Jackson	LaRouche	Simon	Other
Feb.	16	New Hampshire	123,512	5,644	44,112	24,513	8,400	4,888	9,615	188	21,094	5,058
	23	South Dakota	71,606	346	22,349	31,184	5,993	3,875	3,867		3,992	
Mar.	1	Vermont	50,791		28,353	3,910		2,055	13,044		2,620	809
	5	South Carolina	No Primary held									
	8	Alabama	405,642	2,410	31,306	30,214	151,739	7,530	176,764	845	3,063	1,771
	8	Arkansas	97,544	2,614	94,103	59,711	185,758	18,630	85,003	2,347	9,020	40,358
	8	Florida	1,273,298	10,296	521,041	182,861	161,165	36,315	254,912		27,620	79,088
	8	Georgia	622,752	3,247	97,179	41,489	201,490	15,852	247,831		8,388	7,276
	8	Kentucky	318,721	1,290	59,433	28,982	145,988	11,798	49,667	681	9,393	11,489
	8	Louisiana	624,450	3,076	95,667	66,434	174,974	26,442	221,532	1,681	5,155	29,489
	8	Maryland	531,335	4,750	242,479	42,059	46,063	9,732	152,642	2,149	16,513	14,948
	8	Massachusetts	713,447	4,222	418,256	72,944	31,631	10,837	133,141	998	26,176	15,242
	8	Mississippi	359,417	2,037	29,941	19,693	120,364	13,934	160,651	1,295	2,118	9,384
	8	Missouri	527,805	1,377	61,303	305,287	14,549	7,607	106,386	664	21,433	9,199
	8	North Carolina	679,958	3,816	137,993	37,553	235,669	16,381	224,177		8,032	16,337
	8	Oklahoma	392,727	1,601	66,278	82,596	162,584	14,336	52,417	1,078	6,901	4,936
	8	Rhode Island	49,029	469	34,211	2,028	1,939	733	7,445		1,395	809
	8	Tennessee	576,314	1,946	19,348	8,470	416,861	4,706	119,248		2,647	3,088
	8	Texas	1,767,045	11,618	579,713	240,158	357,764	82,199	433,335	9,013	34,499	18,746
	8	Virginia	364,899	2,454	80,183	15,935	81,419	6,266	164,709	746	7,045	6,142
	15	Illinois	1,500,930	4,953	245,289	35,108	77,265	12,769	484,233	6,094	635,219	
	29	Connecticut	241,395	2,370	140,291	1,009	18,501	5,761	68,372		3,140	1,951
April	5	Wisconsin	1,014,782	2,353	483,172	7,996	176,712	7,068	285,995		48,419	3,067
	19	New York	1,575,186		801,457	2,672	157,559		585,076	1,153	17,011	10,258
	26	Pennsylvania	1,507,690		1,002,480	7,254	44,542	20,473	411,260	4,443	9,692	7,546
May	3	Indiana	645,708		449,495	16,777	21,865		145,021		12,550	
	3	Ohio	1,383,572		869,792		29,931	28,414	378,866	6,065	15,524	54,980
	3	District of Columbia	86,052		15,415	300	648		68,840		769	80
	10	Nebraska	169,008		106,334	4,948	2,519	4,220	43,380	416	2,104	5,087
	10	West Virginia	340,097	1,978	254,289	6,130	11,573	9,284	45,788	1,482	2,280	7,293
	17	Oregon	388,932		221,048	6,772	5,445		148,207	1,562	4,757	1,141
	24	Idaho	51,370		37,696		1,891		8,066		1,409	2,308
June	7	California	3,138,734		1,910,808		56,645		1,102,093	25,417	43,771	
	7	Montana	121,871		83,684	3,369	2,261		26,908		1,566	4,083
	7	New Jersey	654,302		414,829		18,062		213,705	2,621		5,085
	7	New Mexico	188,610	2,913	114,968		4,747	6,898	52,988		2,821	3,275
	14	North Dakota	3,405		2,890				515			
			22,961,936	77,780	9,817,185	1,388,356	3,134,516	389,003	6,685,699	70,938	1,018,136	380,323

Other vote includes 116,262 Uncommitted; 79,088 Undecided; 45,289 Duke; 32,286 No Preference; 30,879 Traficant; 25,068 Applegate; 7,298 Dennerll; 7,546 Wesner; 6,238 Williams; 3,701 Ahern; 3,604 McDonald; 2,736 Marra; 2,554 Uninstructed Delegation; 2,308 "None of the Names Shown"; 2,055 DiDonato; 1,682 Kay; 1,356 Koczak; 1,349 duPont; 1,005 Doty; 598 Martin-Trigona; 122 Roy; 96 Thorpe; 36 King; 33 O'Donnell; 33 Sagan; 28 Thomas; 25 Kirk; 22 Zucker; 10 VanPetter; 9 Lock; 7,007 scattered.

1984 REPUBLICAN PREFERENCE PRIMARIES

Date		State	Total Vote	Reagan	Other
Feb.	28	New Hampshire	75,570	65,033	10,537
Mar.	6	Vermont	33,643	33,218	425
	13	Alabama	No Primary Held		
	13	Florida	344,150	344,150	—
	13	Georgia	50,793	50,793	—
	13	Massachusetts	65,937	58,996	6,941
	13	Rhode Island	2,235	2,028	207
	20	Illinois	595,078	594,742	336
	27	Connecticut	No Primary Held		
April	3	New York	No Primary Held		
	3	Wisconsin	294,813	280,608	14,205
	10	Pennsylvania	621,206	616,916	4,290
May	1	District of Columbia	5,692	5,692	—
	1	Tennessee	82,921	75,367	7,554
	5	Louisiana	16,687	14,964	1,723
	5	Texas	319,839	308,713	11,126
	8	Indiana	428,559	428,559	—
	8	Maryland	73,663	73,663	—
	8	North Carolina	No Primary Held		
	8	Ohio	658,169	658,169	—
	15	Nebraksa	146,648	145,245	1,403
	15	Oregon	243,346	238,594	4,752
	22	Idaho	105,687	97,450	8,237
June	5	California	1,874,975	1,874,897	78
	5	Montana	71,887	66,432	5,455
	5	New Jersey	240,054	240,054	—
	5	New Mexico	42,994	40,805	2,189
	5	South Dakota	No Primary Held		
	5	West Virginia	136,996	125,790	11,206
	12	North Dakota	44,109	44,109	
			6,575,651	6,484,987	90,664

Other vote includes 22,791 Uncommitted; 14,047 "Ronald Reagan No"; 12,749 Stassen; 10,383 No Preference; 8,23⁄ "None of the Names Shown"; 360 Kelley; 252 Arnold; 202 Fernandez; 21,643 scattered.

1984 DEMOCRATIC PREFERENCE PRIMARIES

Date		State	Total Vote	Glenn	Hart	Jackson	LaRouche	McGovern	Mondale	Other
Feb.	28	New Hampshire	101,131	12,088	37,702	5,311	—	5,217	28,173	12,640
Mar.	6	Vermont	74,059	—	51,873	5,761	—	—	14,834	1,591
	13	Alabama	428,283	89,286	88,465	83,787	—	—	148,165	18,580
	13	Florida	1,182,190	128,209	463,799	144,263	—	17,614	394,350	33,955
	13	Georgia	684,541	122,744	186,903	143,730	—	11,321	208,588	11,255
	13	Massachusetts	630,962	45,456	245,943	31,824	—	134,341	160,893	12,505
	13	Rhode Island	44,511	2,249	20,011	3,875	—	2,146	15,338	892
	20	Illinois	1,659,425	19,800	584,579	348,843	—	25,336	670,951	9,916
	27	Connecticut	220,842	955	116,286	26,395	—	2,426	64,230	10,550
April	3	New York	1,387,950	15,941	380,564	355,541	—	4,547	621,581	9,776
	3	Wisconsin	635,768	6,398	282,435	62,524	—	10,166	261,374	12,871
	10	Pennsylvania	1,656,294	22,605	551,335	264,463	19,180	13,139	747,267	38,305
May	1	District of Columbia	102,731	—	7,305	69,106	—	—	26,320	—
	1	Tennessee	322,063	4,198	93,710	81,418	—	3,824	132,201	6,712
	5	Louisiana	318,810	—	79,593	136,707	4,970	3,158	71,162	23,220
	5	Texas	No Primary held							
	8	Indiana	716,955	16,046	299,491	98,190	—	—	293,413	9,815
	8	Maryland	506,886	6,238	123,365	129,387	7,836	5,796	215,222	19,042
	8	North Carolina	960,857	17,659	289,877	243,945	—	10,149	342,324	56,903
	8	Ohio	1,447,236	—	608,528	237,133	4,336	8,991	583,595	4,653
	15	Nebraska	148,855	—	86,582	13,495	1,227	1,561	39,635	6,355
	15	Oregon	399,679	10,831	233,638	37,106	5,943	—	110,374	1,787
	22	Idaho	54,722	—	31,737	3,104	1,196	—	16,460	2,225
June	5	California	2,970,903	96,770	1,155,499	546,693	52,647	69,926	1,049,342	26
	5	Montana	34,214	—	3,080*	388*	—	—	2,026*	28,720
	5	New Jersey	676,561	—	200,948	159,788	10,309	—	305,516	—
	5	New Mexico	187,403	—	87,610	22,168	3,330	5,143	67,675	1,477
	5	South Dakota	52,561	—	26,641	2,738	1,383	—	20,495	1,304
	5	West Virginia	369,245	—	137,866	24,697	7,274	—	198,776	632
	12	North Dakota	33,555	—	28,603	—	4,018	—	934	—
			18,009,192	617,473	6,503,968	3,282,380	123,649	334,801	6,811,214	335,707

Other vote includes 77,697 No Preference; 59,254 Uncommitted; 52,759 Askew; 51,437 Cranston; 33,684 Hollings; 9,815 Brewster; 9,261 "None of the Names Shown"; 8,014 Griser; 7,957 Willis; 4,847 Williams; 2,699 Kay; 1,855 Koczak; 632 Timinski; 132 Buchanan; 127 Beckman; 74 O'Donnell; 34 King; 25 Kreml; 24 Bagley; 24 Kirk; 21 Rudnicki; 20 Clendenan; 20 Sagan; 19 Caplette; 15,276 scattered.

1980 REPUBLICAN PREFERENCE PRIMARIES

Date		State	Total Vote	Anderson	Baker	Bush	Connally	Crane	Reagan	Other
Feb.	26	New Hampshire	147,157	14,458	18,943	33,443	2,239	2,618	72,983	2,473
Mar.	4	Massachusetts	400,826	122,987	19,366	124,365	4,714	4,669	115,334	9,391
	4	Vermont	65,611	19,030	8,055	14,226	884	1,238	19,720	2,458
	8	South Carolina	145,501	—	773	21,569	43,113	—	79,549	497
	11	Alabama	211,353	—	1,963	54,730	1,077	5,099	147,352	1,132
	11	Florida	614,995	56,636	6,345	185,996	4,958	12,000	345,699	3,361
	11	Georgia	200,171	16,853	1,571	25,293	2,388	6,308	146,500	1,258
	18	Illinois	1,130,081	415,193	7,051	124,057	4,548	24,865	547,355	7,012
	25	Connecticut	182,284	40,354	2,446	70,367	598	1,887	61,735	4,897
	25	New York	No Primary Held							
April	1	Kansas	285,398	51,924	3,603	35,838	2,067	1,367	179,739	10,860
	1	Wisconsin	907,853	248,623	3,298	276,164	2,312	2,951	364,898	9,607
	5	Louisiana	41,683	—	—	7,818	—	—	31,212	2,653
	22	Pennsylvania	1,241,411	26,890	30,846	626,759	10,656	—	527,916	18,344
May	3	Texas	526,769	—	—	249,819	—	—	268,798	8,152
	6	Indiana	568,313	56,342	—	92,955	—	—	419,016	—
	6	North Carolina	168,391	8,542	2,543	36,631	1,107	547	113,854	5,167
	6	Tennessee	195,210	8,722	—	35,274	—	1,574	144,625	5,015
	6	District of Columbia	7,529	2,025	—	4,973	—	270	—	261
	13	Maryland	167,303	16,244	—	68,389	—	2,113	80,557	—
	13	Nebraska	205,203	11,879	—	31,380	—	1,062	155,995	4,887
	20	Michigan	595,176	48,947	—	341,998	—	—	189,184	15,047
	20	Oregon	315,366	32,118	—	109,210	—	2,324	170,449	1,265
	27	Arkansas	No Primary Held							
	27	Idaho	134,879	13,130	5,416	—	—	1,024	111,868	3,441
	27	Kentucky	94,795	4,791	—	6,861	—	—	78,072	5,071
	27	Nevada	47,395	—	—	3,078	—	—	39,352	4,965
June	3	California	2,564,072	349,315	—	125,113	—	21,465	2,057,923	10,256
	3	Mississippi	25,751	—	—	2,105	—	—	23,028	618
	3	Montana	79,423	—	—	7,665	—	—	68,744	3,014
	3	New Jersey	277,977	—	—	47,447	—	—	225,959	4,571
	3	New Mexico	59,546	7,171	—	5,892	—	4,412	37,982	4,089
	3	Ohio	856,773	—	—	164,485	—	—	692,288	—
	3	Rhode Island	5,335	—	—	993	—	—	3,839	503
	3	South Dakota	82,905	—	—	3,691	—	—	72,861	6,353
	3	West Virginia	138,016	—	—	19,509	—	—	115,407	3,100
			12,690,451	1,572,174	112,219	2,958,093	80,661	97,793	7,709,793	159,718

Other vote includes 38,708 Uncommitted; 24,753 Stassen; 23,423 Fernandez; 15,161 No Preference; 9,321 "None of the Names Shown"; 7,298 Dole; 4,965 "None of These Candidates"; 4,357 Jacobson; 3,757 Kelley; 1,063 Yeager; 483 Carris; 355 Belluso; 311 Carlson; 244 Badgley; 67 Pickett; 25,452 scattered.

1980 DEMOCRATIC PREFERENCE PRIMARIES

Date		State	Total Vote	Brown	Carter	Kennedy	LaRouche	Other
Feb.	26	New Hampshire	111,930	10,743	52,692	41,745	2,326	4,424
Mar.	4	Massachusetts	907,323	31,498	260,401	590,393	—	25,031
	4	Vermont	39,703	—	29,015	10,135	—	553
	8	South Carolina	No Primary Held					
	11	Alabama	237,464	9,529	193,734	31,382	—	2,819
	11	Florida	1,098,003	53,474	666,321	254,727	—	123,481
	11	Georgia	384,780	7,255	338,772	32,315	513	5,925
	18	Illinois	1,201,067	39,168	780,787	359,875	19,192	2,045
	25	Connecticut	210,275	5,386	87,207	98,662	5,617	13,403
	25	New York	989,062	—	406,305	582,757	—	—
April	1	Kansas	193,918	9,434	109,807	61,318	—	13,359
	1	Wisconsin	629,619	74,496	353,662	189,520	6,896	5,045
	5	Louisiana	358,741	16,774	199,956	80,797	—	61,214
	22	Pennsylvania	1,613,551	37,669	732,332	736,854	—	106,696
May	3	Texas	1,377,354	35,585	770,390	314,129	—	257,250
	6	Indiana	589,441	—	398,949	190,492	—	—
	6	North Carolina	737,262	21,420	516,778	130,684	—	68,380
	6	Tennessee	294,680	5,612	221,658	53,258	925	13,227
	6	District of Columbia	64,150	—	23,697	39,561	892	—
	13	Maryland	477,090	14,313	226,528	181,091	4,388	50,770
	13	Nebraska	153,881	5,478	72,120	57,826	1,169	17,288
	20	Michigan	78,424	23,043	—	—	8,948	46,433
	20	Oregon	368,322	34,409	208,693	114,651	—	10,569
	27	Arkansas	448,290	—	269,375	78,542	—	100,373
	27	Idaho	50,482	2,078	31,383	11,087	—	5,934
	27	Kentucky	240,331	—	160,819	55,167	—	24,345
	27	Nevada	66,948	—	25,159	19,296	—	22,493
June	3	California	3,363,969	135,962	1,266,276	1,507,142	71,779	382,810
	3	Mississippi	No Primary Held					
	3	Montana	130,059	—	66,922	47,671	—	15,466
	3	New Jersey	560,908	—	212,387	315,109	13,913	19,499
	3	New Mexico	159,364	—	66,621	73,721	4,798	14,224
	3	Ohio	1,186,410	—	605,744	523,874	35,268	21,524
	3	Rhode Island	38,327	310	9,907	26,179	1,160	771
	3	South Dakota	68,763	—	31,251	33,418	—	4,094
	3	West Virginia	317,934	—	197,687	120,247	—	—
			18,747,825	573,636	9,593,335	6,963,625	177,784	1,439,445

Other vote includes 950,378 Uncommitted; 301,695 No Preference; 48,061 Kay; 48,032 Finch; 22,493 "None of These Candidates"; 13,857 "None of the Names Shown"; 4,002 Maddox; 2,255 Reaux; 609 Nuckols; 571 Ahern; 364 Rollinson; 47,128 Scattered.

1976 REPUBLICAN PREFERENCE PRIMARIES

Date		State	Total Vote	Ford	Reagan	Other
February	24	New Hampshire	111,674	55,156	53,569	2,949
March	2	Massachusetts	188,449	115,375	63,555	9,519
	2	Vermont	32,157	27,014	4,892	251
	9	Florida	609,819	321,982	287,837	—
	16	Illinois	775,893	456,750	311,295	7,848
	23	North Carolina	193,727	88,897	101,468	3,362
April	6	Wisconsin	591,812	326,869	262,126	2,817
	27	Pennsylvania	796,660	733,472	40,510	22,678
May	4	District of Columbia	No Primary			
	4	Georgia	188,472	59,801	128,671	—
	4	Indiana	631,292	307,513	323,779	—
	11	Nebraska	208,414	94,542	113,493	379
	11	West Virginia	155,692	88,386	67,306	—
	18	Maryland	165,971	96,291	69,680	—
	18	Michigan	1,062,814	690,180	364,052	8,582
	25	Arkansas	32,541	11,430	20,628	483
	25	Idaho	89,793	22,323	66,743	727
	25	Kentucky	133,528	67,976	62,683	2,869
	25	Nevada	47,749	13,747	31,637	2,365
	25	Oregon	298,535	150,181	136,691	11,663
	25	Tennessee	242,535	120,685	118,997	2,853
June	1	Montana	89,779	31,100	56,683	1,996
	1	Rhode Island	14,352	9,365	4,480	507
	1	South Dakota	84,077	36,976	43,068	4,033
	8	California	2,450,511	845,655	1,604,836	20
	8	New Jersey	242,122	242,122	—	—
	8	Ohio	935,757	516,111	419,646	—
			10,374,125	5,529,899	4,758,325	85,901

Other vote includes 7,582 Daly; 1,088 Klein; 42,514 scattered write-ins; 15,391 No Preference; 14,727 Uncommitted; 2,365 "None of These Candidates"; 2,234 "None of the Names Shown".

1976 DEMOCRATIC PREFERENCE PRIMARIES

Date	State	Total Vote	Bayh	Brown	Byrd	Carter	Church	Harris	Jackson	McCormack	Shriver	Udall	Wallace	Other
February 24	New Hampshire	82,381	12,510	—	—	23,373	—	8,863	1,857	1,007	6,743	18,710	1,061	8,257
March 2	Massachusetts	735,821	34,963	—	—	101,948	—	55,701	164,393	25,772	53,252	130,440	123,112	46,240
2	Vermont	38,714	—	—	—	16,335	—	4,893	—	3,324	10,699	—	—	3,463
9	Florida	1,300,330	8,750	—	5,042	448,844	4,906	5,397	310,944	7,595	7,084	27,235	396,820	77,713
16	Illinois	1,311,914	—	—	—	630,915	—	98,862	—	—	214,024	—	361,798	6,315
23	North Carolina	604,832	—	—	—	324,437	—	5,923	25,749	—	—	14,032	210,166	24,525
April 6	Wisconsin	740,528	1,255	—	—	271,220	—	8,185	47,605	26,982	5,097	263,771	92,460	23,953
27	Pennsylvania	1,385,042	15,320	—	—	511,905	—	13,067	340,340	38,800	—	259,166	155,902	50,542
May 4	District of Columbia	33,291	—	—	—	10,521	—	461	—	—	—	6,999	—	15,310
4	Georgia	502,471	824	—	3,628	419,272	2,477	699	3,358	635	1,378	9,755	57,594	2,851
4	Indiana	614,389	—	—	—	417,480	—	—	72,080	31,708	—	—	93,121	—
11	Nebraska	175,013	407	—	—	65,833	67,297	811	2,642	6,033	384	4,688	5,567	21,351
11	West Virginia	372,577	—	—	331,639	—	—	—	—	—	—	—	40,938	—
18	Maryland	591,746	—	286,672	—	219,404	—	6,841	13,956	7,907	—	32,790	24,176	—
18	Michigan	708,666	—	—	—	307,559	—	4,081	10,332	7,623	5,738	305,134	49,204	18,995
25	Arkansas	501,800	—	—	—	314,306	—	—	9,554	—	—	37,783	83,005	57,152
25	Idaho	74,405	—	1,453	—	8,818	58,570	319	485	—	—	981	1,115	2,664
25	Kentucky	306,006	—	—	—	181,690	—	—	8,186	17,061	—	33,262	51,540	14,267
25	Nevada	75,242	—	39,671	—	17,567	6,778	—	1,896	—	—	2,237	2,490	4,603
25	Oregon	432,632	743	106,812	—	115,310	145,394	1,344	5,298	3,753	—	11,747	5,797	36,434
25	Tennessee	334,078	—	1,556	—	259,243	8,026	1,628	5,672	1,782	—	12,420	36,495	7,256
June 1	Montana	106,841	—	—	—	26,329	63,448	—	2,856	—	—	6,708	3,680	3,820
1	Rhode Island	60,348	247	—	—	18,237	16,423	—	756	2,468	—	2,543	507	19,167
1	South Dakota	58,671	—	—	—	24,186	—	573	558	4,561	—	19,510	1,412	7,871
8	California	3,409,701	11,419	2,013,210	—	697,092	250,581	16,920	38,634	29,242	—	171,501	102,292	78,810
8	New Jersey	360,839	—	—	—	210,655	49,034	—	31,820	21,774	—	—	31,183	16,373
8	Ohio	1,134,374	—	—	—	593,130	157,884	—	35,404	—	—	240,342	63,953	43,661
		16,052,652	86,438	2,449,374	340,309	6,235,609	830,818	234,568	1,134,375	238,027	304,399	1,611,754	1,995,388	591,593

Other vote includes 88,254 Shapp; 61,992 Humphrey; 43,661 Donahey; 19,805 Kennedy; 8,717 Blessitt; 4,046 Bentsen; 3,935 Lunger; 3,574 Gray; 3,555 Lomento; 3,021 Rollinson; 2,305 Fifi Rockefeller; 2,288 Gonas; 1,829 Kelleher; 1,487 Ahern; 404 Sanford; 398 Bone; 371 Arnold; 351 Eisenman; 174 Clegg; 153 Roden; 49 Loewenherz; 205,019 Uncommitted; 81,971 No Preference; 42,304 scattered write-ins; 7,154 "None of the Names Shown"; 4,603 "None of These Candidates".

1972 REPUBLICAN PREFERENCE PRIMARIES

Date	State	Total Vote	Ashbrook	McCloskey	Nixon	Other
March 7	New Hampshire	117,208	11,362	23,190	79,239	3,417
14	Florida	414,207	36,617	17,312	360,278	–
21	Illinois	33,569	170	47	32,550	802
April 4	Wisconsin	286,444	2,604	3,651	277,601	2,588
25	Massachusetts	122,139	4,864	16,435	99,150	1,690
25	Pennsylvania	184,801	–	–	153,886	30,915
May 2	District of Columbia	No Slates Entered				
2	Indiana	417,069	–	–	417,069	–
2	Ohio	692,828	–	–	692,828	–
4	Tennessee	114,489	2,419	2,370	109,696	4
6	North Carolina	167,899	–	8,732	159,167	–
9	Nebraska	194,272	4,996	9,011	179,464	801
9	West Virginia	No Candidates Entered				
16	Maryland	115,249	6,718	9,223	99,308	–
16	Michigan	336,743	–	9,691	321,652	5,400
23	Rhode Island	5,611	175	337	4,953	146
23	Oregon	282,010	16,696	29,365	231,151	4,798
June 6	California	2,283,922	224,922	–	2,058,825	175
6	New Jersey	No Candidates Entered				
6	New Mexico	55,469	–	3,367	49,067	3,035
6	South Dakota	52,820	–	–	52,820	–
		5,876,749	311,543	132,731	5,378,704	53,771

Other vote includes 1,211 Paulsen; 52,559 Uncommitted, None, and scattered.

1972 DEMOCRATIC PREFERENCE PRIMARIES

Date	State	Total Vote	Chisholm	Humphrey	Jackson	McCarthy	McGovern	Muskie	Wallace	Other
March 7	New Hampshire	88,854	–	348	197	–	33,007	41,235	175	13,892
14	Florida	1,264,554	43,989	234,658	170,156	5,847	78,232	112,523	526,651	92,498
21	Illinois	1,225,144	777	1,476	442	444,260	3,687	766,914	7,017	571
April 4	Wisconsin	1,128,584	9,198	233,748	88,068	15,543	333,528	115,811	248,676	84,012
25	Massachusetts	618,516	22,398	48,929	8,499	8,736	325,673	131,709	45,807	26,765
25	Pennsylvania	1,374,839	306	481,900	38,767	–	280,861	279,983	292,437	585
May 2	District of Columbia	29,560	–	–	–	–	–	–	–	29,560
2	Indiana	751,458	–	354,244	–	–	–	87,719	309,495	–
2	Ohio	1,212,330	–	499,680	98,498	26,026	480,320	107,806	–	–
4	Tennessee	492,721	18,809	78,350	5,896	2,267	35,551	9,634	335,858	6,356
6	North Carolina	821,410	61,723	–	9,416	–	–	30,739	413,518	306,014
9	Nebraska	192,137	1,763	65,968	5,276	3,194	79,309	6,886	23,912	5,829
9	West Virginia	368,484	–	246,596	–	–	–	–	121,888	–
16	Maryland	568,131	12,602	151,981	17,728	4,691	126,978	13,363	219,687	21,101
16	Michigan	1,588,073	44,090	249,798	6,938	–	425,694	38,701	809,239	13,613
23	Rhode Island	37,864	–	7,701	138	245	15,603	7,838	5,802	537
23	Oregon	408,644	2,975	51,163	22,042	8,943	205,328	10,244	81,868	26,081
June 6	California	3,564,518	157,435	1,375,064	28,901	34,203	1,550,652	72,701	268,551	77,011
6	New Jersey	76,834	51,433	–	–	–	–	–	–	25,401
6	New Mexico	153,293	3,205	39,768	4,236	–	51,011	6,411	44,843	3,819
6	South Dakota	28,017	–	–	–	–	28,017	–	–	–
		15,993,965	430,703	4,121,372	505,198	553,955	4,053,451	1,840,217	3,755,424	733,645

Other vote includes 331,415 Sanford; 196,406 Lindsay; 79,446 Yorty; 37,401 Mills; 21,217 Fauntroy; 16,693 Kennedy; 11,798 Hartke; 8,286 Mink; 869 Coll; 30,114 Uncommitted, None, and scattered.

58

1968 REPUBLICAN PREFERENCE PRIMARIES

Date		State	Total Vote	Nixon	Reagan	Other
March	12	New Hampshire	103,938	80,666	—	23,272
April	2	Wisconsin	489,853	390,368	50,727	48,758
	23	Pennsylvania	287,573	171,815	7,934	107,824
	30	Massachusetts	106,521	27,447	1,770	77,304
May	7	Indiana	508,362	508,362	—	—
	7	Ohio	614,492	—	—	614,492
	14	Nebraska	200,476	140,336	42,703	17,437
	28	Florida	51,509	—	—	51,509
	28	Oregon	312,159	203,037	63,707	45,415
June	4	California	1,525,091	—	1,525,091	—
	4	New Jersey	88,592	71,809	2,737	14,046
	4	South Dakota	68,113	68,113	—	—
	11	Illinois	22,403	17,490	1,601	3,312
			4,379,082	1,679,443	1,696,270	1,003,369

Other vote includes 614,492 Rhodes; 164,340 Rockefeller; 31,598 Stassen; 31,465 Volpe; 3,830 Romney; 1,302 Americus; 1,223 Shafer; 527 Stone; 247 Hoover; 161 Watumull; 151 Evans; 73 Coy; 39 DuMont; 58,272 No Preference and 95,649 scattered.

1968 DEMOCRATIC PREFERENCE PRIMARIES

Date		State	Total Vote	McCarthy	Kennedy	Johnson	Humphrey	Other
March	12	New Hampshire	55,464	23,263	—	27,520	—	4,681
April	2	Wisconsin	733,002	412,160	46,507	253,696	3,605	17,034
	23	Pennsylvania	597,089	428,259	65,430	21,265	51,998	30,137
	30	Massachusetts	248,903	122,697	68,604	6,890	44,156	6,556
May	7	Indiana	776,513	209,695	328,118	—	—	238,700
	7	Ohio	549,140	—	—	549,140		
	14	Nebraska	162,611	50,655	84,102	9,187	12,087	6,580
	28	Florida	512,357	147,216	—	—	—	365,141
	28	Oregon	373,070	163,990	141,631	45,174	12,421	9,854
June	4	California	3,181,753	1,329,301	1,472,166	—	—	380,286
	4	New Jersey	27,446	9,906	8,603	—	5,578	3,359
	4	South Dakota	64,287	13,145	31,826	19,316	—	—
	11	Illinois	12,038	4,646	—	—	2,059	5,333
			7,293,673	2,914,933	2,246,987	383,048	131,904	1,616,801

Other vote includes 549,140 Young; 238,700 Branigin; 236,242 Smathers; 33,520 Wallace; 4,052 Edward M. Kennedy; 186 Crommelin; 170 Lee; 77 Gordon; 521,046 No Preference and 33,668 scattered.

ALABAMA

GOVERNOR
Guy Hunt (R). Re-elected 1990 to a four-year term. Previously elected 1986.

SENATORS
Howell Heflin (D). Re-elected 1990 to a six-year term. Previously elected 1984, 1978.

Richard C. Shelby (D). Elected 1986 to a six-year term.

REPRESENTATIVES
1. H. L. Callahan (R)
2. William Dickinson (R)
3. Glen Browder (D)
4. Tom Bevill (D)
5. Bud Cramer (D)
6. Ben Erdreich (D)
7. Claude Harris (D)

POSTWAR VOTE FOR PRESIDENT

| | | Republican | | Democratic | | Other | | | Percentage | | | |
| | | | | | | | | Total Vote | | Major Vote | |
Year	Total Vote	Vote	Candidate	Vote	Candidate	Vote	Plurality	Rep.	Dem.	Rep.	Dem.
1988	1,378,476	815,576	Bush, George	549,506	Dukakis, Michael S.	13,394	266,070 R	59.2%	39.9%	59.7%	40.3%
1984	1,441,713	872,849	Reagan, Ronald	551,899	Mondale, Walter F.	16,965	320,950 R	60.5%	38.3%	61.3%	38.7%
1980	1,341,929	654,192	Reagan, Ronald	636,730	Carter, Jimmy	51,007	17,462 R	48.8%	47.4%	50.7%	49.3%
1976	1,182,850	504,070	Ford, Gerald R.	659,170	Carter, Jimmy	19,610	155,100 D	42.6%	55.7%	43.3%	56.7%
1972	1,006,111	728,701	Nixon, Richard M.	256,923	McGovern, George S.	20,487	471,778 R	72.4%	25.5%	73.9%	26.1%
1968 **	1,049,922	146,923	Nixon, Richard M.	196,579	Humphrey, Hubert H.	706,420	494,846 A	14.0%	18.7%	42.8%	57.2%
1964 **	689,818	479,085	Goldwater, Barry M.		Johnson, Lyndon B.	210,733	268,353 R	69.5%		100.0%	
1960	570,225	237,981	Nixon, Richard M.	324,050	Kennedy, John F.	8,194	86,069 D	41.7%	56.8%	42.3%	57.7%
1956	496,861	195,694	Eisenhower, Dwight D.	280,844	Stevenson, Adlai E.	20,323	85,150 D	39.4%	56.5%	41.1%	58.9%
1952	426,120	149,231	Eisenhower, Dwight D.	275,075	Stevenson, Adlai E.	1,814	125,844 D	35.0%	64.6%	35.2%	64.8%
1948 **	214,980	40,930	Dewey, Thomas E.		Truman, Harry S.	174,050	130,513 SR	19.0%		100.0%	

In 1968 other vote was 691,425 American Independent (Wallace); 10,960 American Independent of Alabama; 4,022 Prohibition and 13 scattered. In 1964 and 1948 the national Democratic candidates were not represented on the ballot. In 1964 other vote was 210,732 Unpledged Democratic and 1 scattered. In 1948 other vote was 171,443 States Rights; 1,522 Progressive and 1,085 Prohibition.

POSTWAR VOTE FOR GOVERNOR

| | | Republican | | Democratic | | Other | Rep.-Dem. | Percentage | | | |
| | | | | | | | | Total Vote | | Major Vote | |
Year	Total Vote	Vote	Candidate	Vote	Candidate	Vote	Plurality	Rep.	Dem.	Rep.	Dem.
1990	1,216,250	633,519	Hunt, Guy	582.106	Hubbert, Paul R.	625	51,413 R	52.1%	47.9%	52.1%	47.9%
1986	1,236,230	696,203	Hunt, Guy	537,163	Baxley, Bill	2,864	159,040 R	56.3%	43.5%	56.4%	43.6%
1982	1,128,725	440,815	Folmar, Emory	650,538	Wallace, George C.	37,372	209,723 D	39.1%	57.6%	40.4%	59.6%
1978	760,474	196,963	Hunt, Guy	551,886	James, Forrest H.	11,625	354,923 D	25.9%	72.6%	26.3%	73.7%
1974	598,305	88,381	McCary, Elvin	497,574	Wallace, George C.	12,350	409,193 D	14.8%	83.2%	15.1%	84.9%
1970 **	854,952		—	637,046	Wallace, George C.	217,906	637,046 D		74.5%		100.0%
1966	848,101	262,943	Martin, James D.	537,505	Wallace, Mrs. George C.	47,653	274,562 D	31.0%	63.4%	32.8%	67.2%
1962	315,776		—	303,987	Wallace, George C.	11,789	303,987 D		96.3%		100.0%
1958	270,952	30,415	Longshore, W. L.	239,633	Patterson, John	904	209,218 D	11.2%	88.4%	11.3%	88.7%
1954	333,090	88,688	Amernethy, Tom	244,401	Folsom, James E.	1	155,713 D	26.6%	73.4%	26.6%	73.4%
1950	170,541	15,127	Crowder, John S.	155,414	Persons, Gordon		140,287 D	8.9%	91.1%	8.9%	91.1%
1946	197,324	22,362	Ward, Lyman	174,962	Folsom, James E.		152,600 D	11.3%	88.7%	11.3%	88.7%

In 1970 other vote was 125,491 National Democratic Party of Alabama (Cashin); 75,679 Independent (Shelton); 9,705 Prohibition (Couch); 3,534 Independent (Walter) and 3,497 Whig (Watts).

ALABAMA

POSTWAR VOTE FOR SENATOR

Year	Total Vote	Republican Vote	Candidate	Democratic Vote	Candidate	Other Vote	Rep-Dem. Plurality	Percentage Total Vote Rep.	Dem.	Major Vote Rep.	Dem.
1990	1,185,563	467,190	Cabaniss, Bill	717,814	Heflin, Howell	559	250,624 D	39.4%	60.5%	39.4%	60.6%
1986	1,211,953	602,537	Denton, Jeremiah	609,360	Shelby, Richard C.	56	6,823 D	49.7%	50.3%	49.7%	50.3%
1984	1,371,238	498,508	Smith, Albert L.	860,535	Heflin, Howell	12,195	362,027 D	36.4%	62.8%	36.7%	63.3%
1980	1,296,757	650,362	Denton, Jeremiah	610,175	Folsom, James E., Jr.	36,220	40,187 R	50.2%	47.1%	51.6%	48.4%
1978	582,025		—	547,054	Heflin, Howell	34,971	547,054 D		94.0%		100.0%
1978 S	731,614	316,170	Martin, James D.	401,852	Stewart, Donald W.	13,592	85,682 D	43.2%	54.9%	44.0%	56.0%
1974	523,290		—	501,541	Allen, James B.	21,749	501,541 D		95.8%		100.0%
1972	1,051,099	347,523	Blount, Winston M.	654,491	Sparkman, John J.	49,085	306,968 D	33.1%	62.3%	34.7%	65.3%
1968	912,708	201,227	Hooper, Perry	638,774	Allen, James B.	72,707	437,547 D	22.0%	70.0%	24.0%	76.0%
1966	802,608	313,018	Grenier, John	482,138	Sparkman, John J.	7,452	169,120 D	39.0%	60.1%	39.4%	60.6%
1962	397,079	195,134	Martin, James D.	201,937	Hill, Lister	8	6,803 D	49.1%	50.9%	49.1%	50.9%
1960	554,081	164,868	Elgin, Julian	389,196	Sparkman, John J.	17	224,328 D	29.8%	70.2%	29.8%	70.2%
1956	330,191		—	330,182	Hill, Lister	9	330,182 D		100.0%		100.0%
1954	314,459	55,110	Guin, J. Foy	259,348	Sparkman, John J.	1	204,238 D	17.5%	82.5%	17.5%	82.5%
1950	164,011		—	125,534	Hill, Lister	38,477	125,534 D		76.5%		100.0%
1948	220,875	35,341	Parsons, Paul G.	185,534	Sparkman, John J.		150,193 D	16.0%	84.0%	16.0%	84.0%
1946 S	163,217		—	163,217	Sparkman, John J.		163,217 D		100.0%		100.0%

The 1946 election and one of the 1978 elections were for short terms to fill vacancies.

62

ALABAMA

Districts Established August 18, 1981

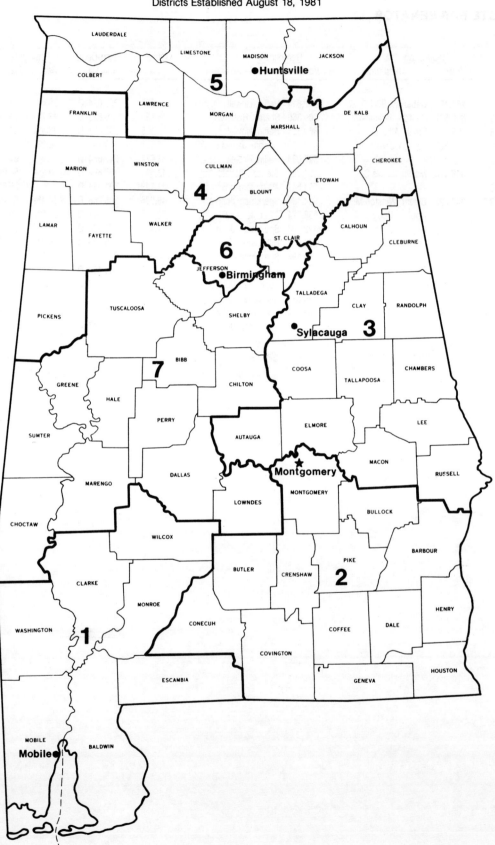

© ERC

ALABAMA

GOVERNOR 1990

1990 Census Population	County	Total Vote	Republican	Democratic	Other	Rep.-Dem. Plurality	Percentage Total Vote Rep.	Total Vote Dem.	Major Vote Rep.	Major Vote Dem.
34,222	AUTAUGA	11,354	6,833	4,521		2,312 R	60.2%	39.8%	60.2%	39.8%
98,280	BALDWIN	29,415	17,382	12,033		5,349 R	59.1%	40.9%	59.1%	40.9%
25,417	BARBOUR	7,963	3,100	4,863		1,763 D	38.9%	61.1%	38.9%	61.1%
16,576	BIBB	6,084	2,901	3,181	2	280 D	47.7%	52.3%	47.7%	52.3%
39,248	BLOUNT	12,981	8,457	4,524		3,933 R	65.1%	34.9%	65.1%	34.9%
11,042	BULLOCK	4,474	1,301	3,173		1,872 D	29.1%	70.9%	29.1%	70.9%
21,892	BUTLER	7,561	3,633	3,928		295 D	48.0%	52.0%	48.0%	52.0%
116,034	CALHOUN	28,988	15,097	13,891		1,206 R	52.1%	47.9%	52.1%	47.9%
36,876	CHAMBERS	9,995	4,045	5,950		1,905 D	40.5%	59.5%	40.5%	59.5%
19,543	CHEROKEE	5,382	2,188	3,193	1	1,005 D	40.7%	59.3%	40.7%	59.3%
32,458	CHILTON	12,442	7,286	5,155	1	2,131 R	58.6%	41.4%	58.6%	41.4%
16,018	CHOCTAW	6,209	2,067	4,142		2,075 D	33.3%	66.7%	33.3%	66.7%
27,240	CLARKE	9,444	4,543	4,900	1	357 D	48.1%	51.9%	48.1%	51.9%
13,252	CLAY	4,657	2,495	2,162		333 R	53.6%	46.4%	53.6%	46.4%
12,730	CLEBURNE	4,048	2,031	2,017		14 R	50.2%	49.8%	50.2%	49.8%
40,240	COFFEE	11,101	5,852	5,249		603 R	52.7%	47.3%	52.7%	47.3%
51,666	COLBERT	15,465	6,556	8,908	1	2,352 D	42.4%	57.6%	42.4%	57.6%
14,054	CONECUH	5,650	2,491	3,159		668 D	44.1%	55.9%	44.1%	55.9%
11,063	COOSA	3,912	1,761	2,149	2	388 D	45.0%	54.9%	45.0%	55.0%
36,478	COVINGTON	12,091	7,010	5,081		1,929 R	58.0%	42.0%	58.0%	42.0%
13,635	CRENSHAW	4,843	2,462	2,381		81 R	50.8%	49.2%	50.8%	49.2%
67,613	CULLMAN	23,453	14,139	9,314		4,825 R	60.3%	39.7%	60.3%	39.7%
49,633	DALE	10,753	6,247	4,506		1,741 R	58.1%	41.9%	58.1%	41.9%
48,130	DALLAS	15,554	6,660	8,894		2,234 D	42.8%	57.2%	42.8%	57.2%
54,651	DE KALB	17,138	9,110	8,017	11	1,093 R	53.2%	46.8%	53.2%	46.8%
49,210	ELMORE	15,845	9,692	6,152	1	3,540 R	61.2%	38.8%	61.2%	38.8%
35,518	ESCAMBIA	8,716	4,292	4,424		132 D	49.2%	50.8%	49.2%	50.8%
99,840	ETOWAH	32,400	15,992	16,408		416 D	49.4%	50.6%	49.4%	50.6%
17,962	FAYETTE	7,341	2,648	4,686	7	2,038 D	36.1%	63.8%	36.1%	63.9%
27,814	FRANKLIN	8,611	3,752	4,858	1	1,106 D	43.6%	56.4%	43.6%	56.4%
23,647	GENEVA	8,268	4,808	3,460		1,348 R	58.2%	41.8%	58.2%	41.8%
10,153	GREENE	4,102	963	3,138	1	2,175 D	23.5%	76.5%	23.5%	76.5%
15,498	HALE	5,602	2,121	3,481		1,360 D	37.9%	62.1%	37.9%	62.1%
15,374	HENRY	5,502	2,894	2,607	1	287 R	52.6%	47.4%	52.6%	47.4%
81,331	HOUSTON	22,128	14,177	7,945	6	6,232 R	64.1%	35.9%	64.1%	35.9%
47,796	JACKSON	10,236	4,371	5,865		1,494 D	42.7%	57.3%	42.7%	57.3%
651,525	JEFFERSON	211,683	116,034	95,287	362	20,747 R	54.8%	45.0%	54.9%	45.1%
15,715	LAMAR	5,437	2,271	3,163	3	892 D	41.8%	58.2%	41.8%	58.2%
79,661	LAUDERDALE	21,890	9,800	12,089	1	2,289 D	44.8%	55.2%	44.8%	55.2%
31,513	LAWRENCE	8,278	2,984	5,294		2,310 D	36.0%	64.0%	36.0%	64.0%
87,146	LEE	19,883	9,919	9,964		45 D	49.9%	50.1%	49.9%	50.1%
54,135	LIMESTONE	14,177	7,715	6,454	8	1,261 R	54.4%	45.5%	54.4%	45.6%
12,658	LOWNDES	4,528	1,243	3,284	1	2,041 D	27.5%	72.5%	27.5%	72.5%
24,928	MACON	7,332	1,202	6,130		4,928 D	16.4%	83.6%	16.4%	83.6%
238,912	MADISON	72,078	44,799	27,279		17,520 R	62.2%	37.8%	62.2%	37.8%
23,084	MARENGO	8,152	3,649	4,503		854 D	44.8%	55.2%	44.8%	55.2%
29,830	MARION	10,561	4,342	6,219		1,877 D	41.1%	58.9%	41.1%	58.9%
70,832	MARSHALL	18,280	11,140	7,138	2	4,002 R	60.9%	39.0%	60.9%	39.1%
378,643	MOBILE	96,841	48,132	48,633	76	501 D	49.7%	50.2%	49.7%	50.3%
23,968	MONROE	7,443	3,627	3,816		189 D	48.7%	51.3%	48.7%	51.3%
209,085	MONTGOMERY	69,795	34,223	35,509	63	1,286 D	49.0%	50.9%	49.1%	50.9%
100,043	MORGAN	29,647	17,707	11,930	10	5,777 R	59.7%	40.2%	59.7%	40.3%
12,759	PERRY	5,009	1,747	3,262		1,515 D	34.9%	65.1%	34.9%	65.1%
20,699	PICKENS	6,317	2,995	3,322		327 D	47.4%	52.6%	47.4%	52.6%
27,595	PIKE	9,729	4,901	4,827	1	74 R	50.4%	49.6%	50.4%	49.6%
19,881	RANDOLPH	6,134	2,969	3,165		196 D	48.4%	51.6%	48.4%	51.6%
46,860	RUSSELL	8,576	2,613	5,963		3,350 D	30.5%	69.5%	30.5%	69.5%
50,009	ST. CLAIR	14,222	9,053	5,169		3,884 R	63.7%	36.3%	63.7%	36.3%
99,358	SHELBY	30,241	22,006	8,186	49	13,820 R	72.8%	27.1%	72.9%	27.1%
16,174	SUMTER	5,399	1,386	4,007	6	2,621 D	25.7%	74.2%	25.7%	74.3%

ALABAMA

GOVERNOR 1990

1990 Census Population	County	Total Vote	Republican	Democratic	Other	Rep.-Dem. Plurality	Percentage			
							Total Vote		Major Vote	
							Rep.	Dem.	Rep.	Dem.
74,107	TALLADEGA	19,451	10,013	9,438		575 R	51.5%	48.5%	51.5%	48.5%
38,826	TALLAPOOSA	13,668	7,440	6,227	1	1,213 R	54.4%	45.6%	54.4%	45.6%
150,522	TUSCALOOSA	39,232	19,669	19,563		106 R	50.1%	49.9%	50.1%	49.9%
67,670	WALKER	22,039	9,121	12,916	2	3,795 D	41.4%	58.6%	41.4%	58.6%
16,694	WASHINGTON	6,125	2,376	3,746	3	1,370 D	38.8%	61.2%	38.8%	61.2%
13,568	WILCOX	5,005	1,619	3,385	1	1,766 D	32.3%	67.6%	32.4%	67.6%
22,053	WINSTON	9,390	5,467	3,923		1,544 R	58.2%	41.8%	58.2%	41.8%
4,040,587	TOTAL	1,216,250	633,519	582,106	625	51,413 R	52.1%	47.9%	52.1%	47.9%

ALABAMA

SENATOR 1990

1990 Census Population	County	Total Vote	Republican	Democratic	Other	Rep.-Dem. Plurality	Percentage			
							Total Vote		Major Vote	
							Rep.	Dem.	Rep.	Dem.
34,222	AUTAUGA	11,041	5,074	5,967		893 D	46.0%	54.0%	46.0%	54.0%
98,280	BALDWIN	28,678	14,704	13,974		730 R	51.3%	48.7%	51.3%	48.7%
25,417	BARBOUR	7,454	2,245	5,209		2,964 D	30.1%	69.9%	30.1%	69.9%
16,576	BIBB	5,877	1,861	4,016		2,155 D	31.7%	68.3%	31.7%	68.3%
39,248	BLOUNT	12,376	5,232	7,144		1,912 D	42.3%	57.7%	42.3%	57.7%
11,042	BULLOCK	4,263	907	3,356		2,449 D	21.3%	78.7%	21.3%	78.7%
21,892	BUTLER	7,220	2,450	4,770		2,320 D	33.9%	66.1%	33.9%	66.1%
116,034	CALHOUN	28,020	9,052	18,968		9,916 D	32.3%	67.7%	32.3%	67.7%
36,876	CHAMBERS	9,306	3,411	5,895		2,484 D	36.7%	63.3%	36.7%	63.3%
19,543	CHEROKEE	5,206	1,349	3,857		2,508 D	25.9%	74.1%	25.9%	74.1%
32,458	CHILTON	12,301	4,771	7,528	2	2,757 D	38.8%	61.2%	38.8%	61.2%
16,018	CHOCTAW	5,773	1,387	4,384	2	2,997 D	24.0%	75.9%	24.0%	76.0%
27,240	CLARKE	8,984	3,569	5,415		1,846 D	39.7%	60.3%	39.7%	60.3%
13,252	CLAY	4,315	1,367	2,948		1,581 D	31.7%	68.3%	31.7%	68.3%
12,730	CLEBURNE	3,690	1,107	2,583		1,476 D	30.0%	70.0%	30.0%	70.0%
40,240	COFFEE	10,826	4,119	6,707		2,588 D	38.0%	62.0%	38.0%	62.0%
51,666	COLBERT	15,211	4,070	11,141		7,071 D	26.8%	73.2%	26.8%	73.2%
14,054	CONECUH	5,269	1,490	3,779		2,289 D	28.3%	71.7%	28.3%	71.7%
11,063	COOSA	3,868	1,243	2,623	2	1,380 D	32.1%	67.8%	32.2%	67.8%
36,478	COVINGTON	11,293	4,216	7,077		2,861 D	37.3%	62.7%	37.3%	62.7%
13,635	CRENSHAW	4,463	1,384	3,079		1,695 D	31.0%	69.0%	31.0%	69.0%
67,613	CULLMAN	22,404	9,336	13,067	1	3,731 D	41.7%	58.3%	41.7%	58.3%
49,633	DALE	10,321	4,519	5,801	1	1,282 D	43.8%	56.2%	43.8%	56.2%
48,130	DALLAS	15,109	5,388	9,721		4,333 D	35.7%	64.3%	35.7%	64.3%
54,651	DE KALB	16,608	6,338	10,261	9	3,923 D	38.2%	61.8%	38.2%	61.8%
49,210	ELMORE	15,342	7,708	7,634		74 R	50.2%	49.8%	50.2%	49.8%
35,518	ESCAMBIA	8,208	3,153	5,055		1,902 D	38.4%	61.6%	38.4%	61.6%
99,840	ETOWAH	31,720	9,301	22,419		13,118 D	29.3%	70.7%	29.3%	70.7%
17,962	FAYETTE	7,190	2,316	4,868	6	2,552 D	32.2%	67.7%	32.2%	67.8%
27,814	FRANKLIN	8,521	2,600	5,921		3,321 D	30.5%	69.5%	30.5%	69.5%
23,647	GENEVA	7,821	2,598	5,223		2,625 D	33.2%	66.8%	33.2%	66.8%
10,153	GREENE	3,920	608	3,312		2,704 D	15.5%	84.5%	15.5%	84.5%
15,498	HALE	5,305	1,557	3,748		2,191 D	29.3%	70.7%	29.3%	70.7%
15,374	HENRY	5,050	1,346	3,704		2,358 D	26.7%	73.3%	26.7%	73.3%
81,331	HOUSTON	21,980	9,920	12,060		2,140 D	45.1%	54.9%	45.1%	54.9%
47,796	JACKSON	9,799	2,707	7,092		4,385 D	27.6%	72.4%	27.6%	72.4%
651,525	JEFFERSON	209,938	95,005	114,524	409	19,519 D	45.3%	54.6%	45.3%	54.7%
15,715	LAMAR	4,974	1,712	3,262		1,550 D	34.4%	65.6%	34.4%	65.6%
79,661	LAUDERDALE	21,346	6,184	15,161	1	8,977 D	29.0%	71.0%	29.0%	71.0%
31,513	LAWRENCE	7,926	1,642	6,284		4,642 D	20.7%	79.3%	20.7%	79.3%
87,146	LEE	19,249	8,597	10,652		2,055 D	44.7%	55.3%	44.7%	55.3%
54,135	LIMESTONE	14,059	4,716	9,341	2	4,625 D	33.5%	66.4%	33.5%	66.5%
12,658	LOWNDES	4,156	999	3,157		2,158 D	24.0%	76.0%	24.0%	76.0%
24,928	MACON	6,801	801	6,000		5,199 D	11.8%	88.2%	11.8%	88.2%
238,912	MADISON	72,953	29,206	43,747		14,541 D	40.0%	60.0%	40.0%	60.0%
23,084	MARENGO	7,811	2,532	5,279		2,747 D	32.4%	67.6%	32.4%	67.6%
29,830	MARION	10,385	3,031	7,354		4,323 D	29.2%	70.8%	29.2%	70.8%
70,832	MARSHALL	17,652	6,394	11,257	1	4,863 D	36.2%	63.8%	36.2%	63.8%
378,643	MOBILE	94,308	40,966	53,308	34	12,342 D	43.4%	56.5%	43.5%	56.5%
23,968	MONROE	7,105	2,659	4,446		1,787 D	37.4%	62.6%	37.4%	62.6%
209,085	MONTGOMERY	67,959	30,221	37,725	13	7,504 D	44.5%	55.5%	44.5%	55.5%
100,043	MORGAN	29,354	11,941	17,408	5	5,467 D	40.7%	59.3%	40.7%	59.3%
12,759	PERRY	4,824	1,255	3,569		2,314 D	26.0%	74.0%	26.0%	74.0%
20,699	PICKENS	6,124	2,008	4,115	1	2,107 D	32.8%	67.2%	32.8%	67.2%
27,595	PIKE	9,130	2,838	6,292		3,454 D	31.1%	68.9%	31.1%	68.9%
19,881	RANDOLPH	5,726	1,933	3,793		1,860 D	33.8%	66.2%	33.8%	66.2%
46,860	RUSSELL	8,108	2,026	6,082		4,056 D	25.0%	75.0%	25.0%	75.0%
50,009	ST. CLAIR	14,094	6,695	7,399		704 D	47.5%	52.5%	47.5%	52.5%
99,358	SHELBY	30,011	17,905	12,048	58	5,857 R	59.7%	40.1%	59.8%	40.2%
16,174	SUMTER	5,332	1,066	4,261	5	3,195 D	20.0%	79.9%	20.0%	80.0%

66

ALABAMA

SENATOR 1990

1990 Census Population	County	Total Vote	Republican	Democratic	Other	Rep.-Dem. Plurality	Percentage			
							Total Vote		Major Vote	
							Rep.	Dem.	Rep.	Dem.
74,107	TALLADEGA	18,509	7,750	10,759		3,009 D	41.9%	58.1%	41.9%	58.1%
38,826	TALLAPOOSA	13,043	4,684	8,359		3,675 D	35.9%	64.1%	35.9%	64.1%
150,522	TUSCALOOSA	38,874	14,287	24,587		10,300 D	36.8%	63.2%	36.8%	63.2%
67,670	WALKER	21,053	6,567	14,484	2	7,917 D	31.2%	68.8%	31.2%	68.8%
16,694	WASHINGTON	6,061	1,748	4,308	5	2,560 D	28.8%	71.1%	28.9%	71.1%
13,568	WILCOX	4,852	1,281	3,571		2,290 D	26.4%	73.6%	26.4%	73.6%
22,053	WINSTON	9,114	4,138	4,976		838 D	45.4%	54.6%	45.4%	54.6%
4,040,587	TOTAL	1,185,563	467,190	717,814	559	250,624 D	39.4%	60.5%	39.4%	60.6%

ALABAMA

CONGRESS

CD	Year	Total Vote	Republican Vote	Candidate	Democratic Vote	Candidate	Other Vote	Rep.-Dem. Plurality	Total Vote Rep.	Total Vote Dem.	Major Vote Rep.	Major Vote Dem.
1	1990	82,530	82,185	CALLAHAN, H. L.			345	82,185 R	99.6%		100.0%	
1	1988	194,363	115,173	CALLAHAN, H. L.	77,670	TYSON, JOHN M.	1,520	37,503 R	59.3%	40.0%	59.7%	40.3%
1	1986	96,555	96,469	CALLAHAN, H. L.			86	96,469 R	99.9%		100.0%	
1	1984	200,934	102,479	CALLAHAN, H. L.	98,455	MCRIGHT, FRANK	4,024 R		51.0%	49.0%	51.0%	49.0%
1	1982	144,028	87,901	EDWARDS, JACK	54,315	GUDAC, STEVE	1,812	33,586 R	61.0%	37.7%	61.8%	38.2%
1	1980	117,221	111,089	EDWARDS, JACK			6,132	111,089 R	94.8%		100.0%	
1	1978	112,161	71,711	EDWARDS, JACK	40,450	NOONAN, L. W.		31,261 R	63.9%	36.1%	63.9%	36.1%
1	1976	157,170	98,257	EDWARDS, JACK	58,906	DAVENPORT, BILL	7	39,351 R	62.5%	37.5%	62.5%	37.5%
1	1974	102,066	60,710	EDWARDS, JACK	37,718	WILSON, AUGUSTA E.	3,638	22,992 R	59.5%	37.0%	61.7%	38.3%
1	1972	136,710	104,606	EDWARDS, JACK	24,357	MCCRORY, O. W.	7,747	80,249 R	76.5%	17.8%	81.1%	18.9%
2	1990	170,911	87,649	DICKINSON, WILLIAM	83,243	BAGGIANO, FAYE	19	4,406 R	51.3%	48.7%	51.3%	48.7%
2	1988	127,861	120,408	DICKINSON, WILLIAM			7,453	120,408 R	94.2%		100.0%	
2	1986	172,887	115,302	DICKINSON, WILLIAM	57,568	STONE, MERCER	17	57,734 R	66.7%	33.3%	66.7%	33.3%
2	1984	195,815	118,153	DICKINSON, WILLIAM	75,506	LEE, LARRY	2,156	42,647 R	60.3%	38.6%	61.0%	39.0%
2	1982	165,194	83,290	DICKINSON, WILLIAM	81,904	CAMP, BILLY JOE		1,386 R	50.4%	49.6%	50.4%	49.6%
2	1980	172,962	104,796	DICKINSON, WILLIAM	63,447	WYATT, CECIL	4,719	41,349 R	60.6%	36.7%	62.3%	37.7%
2	1978	107,265	57,924	DICKINSON, WILLIAM	49,341	MITCHELL, WENDELL		8,583 R	54.0%	46.0%	54.0%	46.0%
2	1976	156,362	90,069	DICKINSON, WILLIAM	66,288	KEAHEY, J. CAROLE	5	23,781 R	57.6%	42.4%	57.6%	42.4%
2	1974	81,818	54,089	DICKINSON, WILLIAM	27,729	CHISLER, CLAIR		26,360 R	66.1%	33.9%	66.1%	33.9%
2	1972	146,508	80,362	DICKINSON, WILLIAM	60,769	REEVES, BEN C.	5,377	19,593 R	54.9%	41.5%	56.9%	43.1%
3	1990	138,242	36,317	SLEDGE, DON	101,923	BROWDER, GLEN	2	65,606 D	26.3%	73.7%	26.3%	73.7%
3	1988	122,310			117,514	NICHOLS, BILL	4,796	117,514 D		96.1%		100.0%
3	1986	142,898	27,769	GUERIN, WHIT	115,127	NICHOLS, BILL	2	87,358 D	19.4%	80.6%	19.4%	80.6%
3	1984	125,102			120,357	NICHOLS, BILL	4,745	120,357 D		96.2%		100.0%
3	1982	104,784			100,864	NICHOLS, BILL	3,920	100,864 D		96.3%		100.0%
4	1990	130,212			129,872	BEVILL, TOM	340	129,872 D		99.7%		100.0%
4	1988	137,149			131,880	BEVILL, TOM	5,269	131,880 D		96.2%		100.0%
4	1986	171,472	38,588	DESHAZO, A. L.	132,881	BEVILL, TOM	3	94,293 D	22.5%	77.5%	22.5%	77.5%
4	1984	120,106			120,106	BEVILL, TOM		120,106 D		100.0%		100.0%
4	1982	118,607			118,595	BEVILL, TOM	12	118,595 D		100.0%		100.0%
5	1990	168,383	55,326	MCDONALD, ALBERT	113,047	CRAMER, BUD	10	57,721 D	32.9%	67.1%	32.9%	67.1%
5	1988	186,623	64,491	MCDONALD, STAN	120,142	FLIPPO, RONNIE G.	1,990	55,651 D	34.6%	64.4%	34.9%	65.1%
5	1986	158,935	33,528	MCCARLEY, H. R.	125,406	FLIPPO, RONNIE G.	1	91,878 D	21.1%	78.9%	21.1%	78.9%
5	1984	146,575			140,542	FLIPPO, RONNIE G.	6,033	140,542 D		95.9%		100.0%
5	1982	134,880	24,593	YAMBREK, LEOPOLD	108,807	FLIPPO, RONNIE G.	1,480	84,214 D	18.2%	80.7%	18.4%	81.6%
5	1980	124,967			117,626	FLIPPO, RONNIE G.	7,341	117,626 D		94.1%		100.0%
5	1978	71,236			68,985	FLIPPO, RONNIE G.	2,251	68,985 D		96.8%		100.0%
5	1976	113,560			113,553	FLIPPO, RONNIE G.	7	113,553 D		100.0%		100.0%
5	1974	56,381			56,375	JONES, ROBERT E.	6	56,375 D		100.0%		100.0%
5	1972	136,553	33,352	SCHRADER, DIETER J.	101,303	JONES, ROBERT E.	1,898	67,951 D	24.4%	74.2%	24.8%	75.2%
8	1970	90,058			76,413	JONES, ROBERT E.	13,645	76,413 D		84.8%		100.0%
8	1968	112,449			85,528	JONES, ROBERT E.	26,921	85,528 D		76.1%		100.0%
8	1966	91,386	25,404	MAYHALL, DONALD G.	65,982	JONES, ROBERT E.		40,578 D	27.8%	72.2%	27.8%	72.2%
8	1964	43,842			43,842	JONES, ROBERT E.		43,842 D		100.0%		100.0%
6	1990	145,741			134,412	ERDREICH, BEN	11,329	134,412 D		92.2%		100.0%
6	1988	209,026	68,788	CADDIS, CHARLES	138,920	ERDREICH, BEN	1,318	70,132 D	32.9%	66.5%	33.1%	66.9%
6	1986	191,997	51,924	WILLIAMS, L. MORGAN	139,608	ERDREICH, BEN	465	87,684 D	27.0%	72.7%	27.1%	72.9%
6	1984	219,710	87,550	WAGGONER, J. T.	130,973	ERDREICH, BEN	1,187	43,423 D	39.8%	59.6%	40.1%	59.9%
6	1982	165,387	76,726	SMITH, ALBERT L.	88,029	ERDREICH, BEN	632	11,303 D	46.4%	53.2%	46.6%	53.4%
7	1990	180,844	53,258	BARKER, MICHAEL D.	127,490	HARRIS, CLAUDE	96	74,232 D	29.4%	70.5%	29.5%	70.5%
7	1988	200,966	63,372	BACON, JAMES E.	136,074	HARRIS, CLAUDE	1,520	72,702 D	31.5%	67.7%	31.8%	68.2%
7	1986	180,910	72,777	MCFARLAND, BILL	108,126	HARRIS, CLAUDE	7	35,349 D	40.2%	59.8%	40.2%	59.8%
7	1984	140,332			135,834	SHELBY, RICHARD C.	4,498	135,834 D		96.8%		100.0%
7	1982	128,139			124,070	SHELBY, RICHARD C.	4,069	124,070 D		96.8%		100.0%

ALABAMA

1990 GENERAL ELECTION

Governor   Other vote was scattered write-in.

Senator   Other vote was scattered write-in.

Congress   Other vote was 8,640 Independent (Alvarez), 1,745 Independent (Ivory) and 944 scattered write-in in CD 6; scattered write-in in all other CD's.

1990 PRIMARIES

JUNE 5 REPUBLICAN

Governor   119,877 Guy Hunt; 2,927 Jim Watley; 2,313 Jack Pollard.

Senator   Bill Cabaniss, unopposed.

Congress   Unopposed in four CD's; no candidate in CD's 4 and 6. Contested as follows:

CD   5   6,097 Albert McDonald; 1,378 Jim Asquith; 1,292 Annie Wells.

JUNE 5 DEMOCRATIC

Governor   233,808 Paul R. Hubbert; 184,635 Don Siegelman; 160,121 Forrest H. James; 128,105 Ronnie G. Flippo; 31,684 Charles Bishop; 3,357 Ed Daw.

Senator   540,876 Howell Heflin; 123,508 Mrs. Frank Ross Stewart.

Congress   Unopposed in four CD's. No candidate in CD 1. Contested as follows:

CD   2   59,947 Fay Baggiano; 21,047 George Balmer.
CD   5   47,666 Bud Cramer; 20,346 Lynn Greer; 17,029 Evelyn Pratt; 12,354 Eddie Frost; 8,659 Garland D. Terry; 1,168 Bill Spears; 1,035 David A. Wood.

JUNE 26 DEMOCRATIC RUN-OFF

Governor   309,609 Paul R. Hubbert; 267,588 Don Siegelman.

Congress

CD   5   47,355 Bud Cramer; 30,978 Lynn Greer.

ALASKA

GOVERNOR
Walter J. Hickel (Alaskan Independence). Elected 1990 to a four-year term. Previously elected 1966 as a Republican.

SENATORS
Frank H. Murkowski (R). Re-elected 1986 to a six-year term. Previously elected 1980.

Ted Stevens (R). Re-elected 1990 to a six-year term. Previously elected 1984, 1978, 1972, and in 1970 to fill out term vacated by the death of Senator E. L. Bartlett; had been appointed December 1968 to fill this vacancy.

REPRESENTATIVES
At-Large. Don Young (R)

POSTWAR VOTE FOR PRESIDENT

Year	Total Vote	Republican Vote	Candidate	Democratic Vote	Candidate	Other Vote	Plurality	Total Vote Rep.	Dem.	Major Vote Rep.	Dem.
1988	200,116	119,251	Bush, George	72,584	Dukakis, Michael S.	8,281	46,667 R	59.6%	36.3%	62.2%	37.8%
1984	207,605	138,377	Reagan, Ronald	62,007	Mondale, Walter F.	7,221	76,370 R	66.7%	29.9%	69.1%	30.9%
1980	158,445	86,112	Reagan, Ronald	41,842	Carter, Jimmy	30,491	44,270 R	54.3%	26.4%	67.3%	32.7%
1976	123,574	71,555	Ford, Gerald R.	44,058	Carter, Jimmy	7,961	27,497 R	57.9%	35.7%	61.9%	38.1%
1972	95,219	55,349	Nixon, Richard M.	32,967	McGovern, George S.	6,903	22,382 R	58.1%	34.6%	62.7%	37.3%
1968	83,035	37,600	Nixon, Richard M.	35,411	Humphrey, Hubert H.	10,024	2,189 R	45.3%	42.6%	51.5%	48.5%
1964	67,259	22,930	Goldwater, Barry M.	44,329	Johnson, Lyndon B.		21,399 D	34.1%	65.9%	34.1%	65.9%
1960	60,762	30,953	Nixon, Richard M.	29,809	Kennedy, John F.		1,144 R	50.9%	49.1%	50.9%	49.1%

Alaska was formally admitted to statehood in January 1959.

POSTWAR VOTE FOR GOVERNOR

Year	Total Vote	Republican Vote	Candidate	Democratic Vote	Candidate	Other Vote	Rep-Dem. Plurality	Total Vote Rep.	Dem.	Major Vote Rep.	Dem.
1990 **	194,750	50,991	Sturgulewski, Arliss	60,201	Knowles, Tony	83,558	9,210 D	26.2%	30.9%	45.9%	54.1%
1986	179,555	76,515	Sturgulewski, Arliss	84,943	Cowper, Steve	18,097	8,428 D	42.6%	47.3%	47.4%	52.6%
1982	194,885	72,291	Fink, Tom	89,918	Sheffield, Bill	32,676	17,627 D	37.1%	46.1%	44.6%	55.4%
1978 **	126,910	49,580	Hammond, Jay S.	25,656	Croft, Chancy	51,674	23,924 R	39.1%	20.2%	65.9%	34.1%
1974	96,163	45,840	Hammond, Jay S.	45,553	Egan, William A.	4,770	287 R	47.7%	47.4%	50.2%	49.8%
1970	80,779	37,264	Miller, Keith	42,309	Egan, William A.	1,206	5,045 D	46.1%	52.4%	46.8%	53.2%
1966	66,294	33,145	Hickel, Walter J.	32,065	Egan, William A.	1,084	1,080 R	50.0%	48.4%	50.8%	49.2%
1962	56,681	27,054	Stepovich, Mike	29,627	Egan, William A.		2,573 D	47.7%	52.3%	47.7%	52.3%
1958	48,968	19,299	Butrovich, John	29,189	Egan, William A.	480	9,890 D	39.4%	59.6%	39.8%	60.2%

In 1978 other vote was 33,555 Walter J. Hickel (write-in); 15,656 Tom Kelly (Alaskans for Kelly) and 2,463 Donald R. Wright (Alaskan Independence). In 1990 Walter J. Hickel, the Alaskan Independence candidate, polled 75,721 votes (38.9% of the total vote) and won the election with a 15,520 plurality.

ALASKA

POSTWAR VOTE FOR SENATOR

Year	Total Vote	Republican Vote	Candidate	Democratic Vote	Candidate	Other Vote	Rep-Dem. Plurality	Total Vote Rep.	Total Vote Dem.	Major Vote Rep.	Major Vote Dem.
1990	189,957	125,806	Stevens, Ted	61,152	Beasley, Michael	2,999	64,654 R	66.2%	32.2%	67.3%	32.7%
1986	180,801	97,674	Murkowski, Frank H.	79,727	Olds, Glenn	3,400	17,947 R	54.0%	44.1%	55.1%	44.9%
1984	206,438	146,919	Stevens, Ted	58,804	Havelock, John E.	715	88,115 R	71.2%	28.5%	71.4%	28.6%
1980	156,762	84,159	Murkowski, Frank H.	72,007	Gruening, Clark S.	596	12,152 R	53.7%	45.9%	53.9%	46.1%
1978	122,741	92,783	Stevens, Ted	29,574	Hobbs, Donald W.	384	63,209 R	75.6%	24.1%	75.8%	24.2%
1974	93,275	38,914	Lewis, C. R.	54,361	Gravel, Mike		15,447 D	41.7%	58.3%	41.7%	58.3%
1972	96,007	74,216	Stevens, Ted	21,791	Guess, Gene		52,425 R	77.3%	22.7%	77.3%	22.7%
1970 S	80,364	47,908	Stevens, Ted	32,456	Kay, Wendell P.		15,452 R	59.6%	40.4%	59.6%	40.4%
1968	80,931	30,286	Rasmuson, Elmer	36,527	Gravel, Mike	14,118	6,241 D	37.4%	45.1%	45.3%	54.7%
1966	65,250	15,961	McKinley, Lee L.	49,289	Bartlett, E. L.		33,328 D	24.5%	75.5%	24.5%	75.5%
1962	58,181	24,354	Stevens, Ted	33,827	Gruening, Ernest		9,473 D	41.9%	58.1%	41.9%	58.1%
1960	59,978	21,937	McKinley, Lee L.	38,041	Bartlett, E. L.		16,104 D	36.6%	63.4%	36.6%	63.4%
1958 S	49,525	23,462	Stepovich, Mike	26,063	Gruening, Ernest		2,601 D	47.4%	52.6%	47.4%	52.6%
1958 S	48,837	7,299	Robertson, R. E.	40,939	Bartlett, E. L.	599	33,640 D	14.9%	83.8%	15.1%	84.9%

The two 1958 elections were held to indeterminate terms and the Senate later determined by lot that Senator Gruening would serve four years, Senator Bartlett two. The 1970 election was for a short term to fill a vacancy.

71

ALASKA

(One At Large)
Election Districts Established February 16, 1984

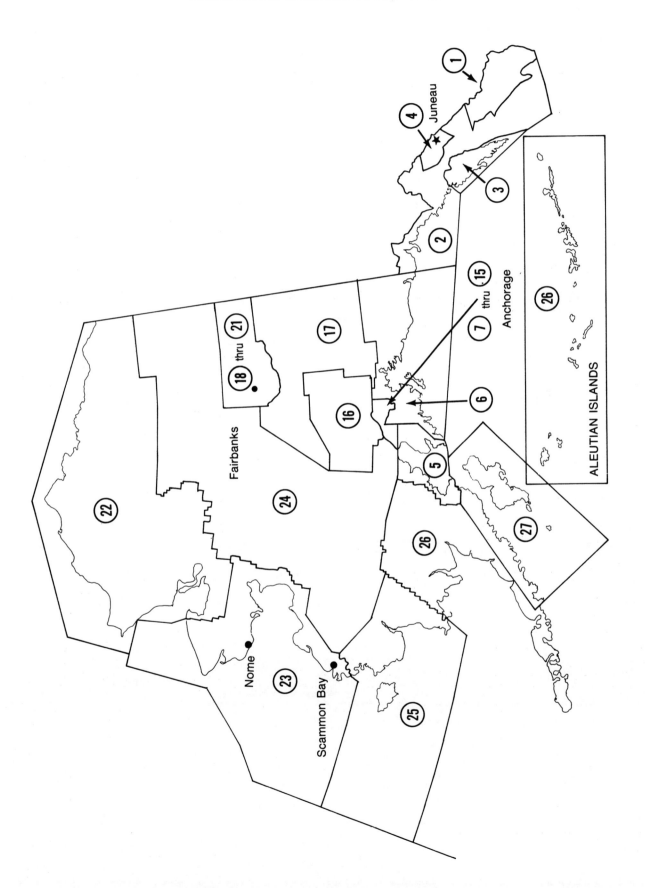

ALASKA

GOVERNOR 1990

1990 Census Population	District	Total Vote	Republican	Democratic	Alaskan	Other	Plurality	Percentage Total Vote		
								Rep.	Dem.	Alaskan
	DISTRICT 1	7,687	1,816	2,257	3,301	313	1,044 A	23.6%	29.4%	42.9%
	DISTRICT 2	4,570	923	2,068	1,333	246	735 D	20.2%	45.3%	29.2%
	DISTRICT 3	3,921	625	1,771	1,318	207	453 D	15.9%	45.2%	33.6%
	DISTRICT 4	12,512	5,031	4,535	2,546	400	496 R	40.2%	36.2%	20.3%
	DISTRICT 5	11,010	3,028	2,646	4,652	684	1,624 A	27.5%	24.0%	42.3%
	DISTRICT 6	4,148	965	1,221	1,759	203	538 A	23.3%	29.4%	42.4%
	DISTRICT 7	6,250	1,892	1,586	2,546	226	654 A	30.3%	25.4%	40.7%
	DISTRICT 8	12,043	4,010	2,771	4,885	377	875 A	33.3%	23.0%	40.6%
	DISTRICT 9	10,921	3,627	2,897	4,074	323	447 A	33.2%	26.5%	37.3%
	DISTRICT 10	10,270	3,278	2,509	4,137	346	859 A	31.9%	24.4%	40.3%
	DISTRICT 11	6,148	1,573	1,831	2,463	281	632 A	25.6%	29.8%	40.1%
	DISTRICT 12	7,182	1,971	2,650	2,274	287	376 D	27.4%	36.9%	31.7%
	DISTRICT 13	7,138	1,867	2,196	2,808	267	612 A	26.2%	30.8%	39.3%
	DISTRICT 14	9,606	3,004	2,628	3,651	323	647 A	31.3%	27.4%	38.0%
	DISTRICT 15	12,089	3,512	2,845	5,327	405	1,815 A	29.1%	23.5%	44.1%
	DISTRICT 16	14,733	3,403	2,590	7,912	828	4,509 A	23.1%	17.6%	53.7%
	DISTRICT 17	4,612	627	946	2,840	199	1,894 A	13.6%	20.5%	61.6%
	DISTRICT 18	7,132	1,526	1,348	4,064	194	2,538 A	21.4%	18.9%	57.0%
	DISTRICT 19	6,680	1,281	1,948	3,055	396	1,107 A	19.2%	29.2%	45.7%
	DISTRICT 20	8,707	1,607	2,119	4,704	277	2,585 A	18.5%	24.3%	54.0%
	DISTRICT 21	5,633	1,163	1,840	2,224	406	384 A	20.6%	32.7%	39.5%
	DISTRICT 22	3,602	393	2,610	536	63	2,074 D	10.9%	72.5%	14.9%
	DISTRICT 23	3,631	640	2,313	598	80	1,673 D	17.6%	63.7%	16.5%
	DISTRICT 24	3,450	508	2,137	715	90	1,422 D	14.7%	61.9%	20.7%
	DISTRICT 25	3,387	621	2,310	361	95	1,689 D	18.3%	68.2%	10.7%
	DISTRICT 26	3,907	1,083	1,981	697	146	898 D	27.7%	50.7%	17.8%
	DISTRICT 27	3,781	1,017	1,648	941	175	631 D	26.9%	43.6%	24.9%
550,043	TOTAL	194,750	50,991	60,201	75,721	7,837	15,520 A	26.2%	30.9%	38.9%

ALASKA

SENATOR 1990

1990 Census Population	District	Total Vote	Republican	Democratic	Other	Rep.-Dem. Plurality	Percentage Total Vote Rep.	Dem.	Major Vote Rep.	Dem.
	DISTRICT 1	7,495	5,118	2,316	61	2,802 R	68.3%	30.9%	68.8%	31.2%
	DISTRICT 2	4,463	2,813	1,618	32	1,195 R	63.0%	36.3%	63.5%	36.5%
	DISTRICT 3	3,778	2,445	1,284	49	1,161 R	64.7%	34.0%	65.6%	34.4%
	DISTRICT 4	11,998	7,014	4,807	177	2,207 R	58.5%	40.1%	59.3%	40.7%
	DISTRICT 5	10,754	6,296	4,286	172	2,010 R	58.5%	39.9%	59.5%	40.5%
	DISTRICT 6	4,065	2,607	1,381	77	1,226 R	64.1%	34.0%	65.4%	34.6%
	DISTRICT 7	6,130	3,972	2,029	129	1,943 R	64.8%	33.1%	66.2%	33.8%
	DISTRICT 8	11,755	8,235	3,232	288	5,003 R	70.1%	27.5%	71.8%	28.2%
	DISTRICT 9	10,675	7,267	3,256	152	4,011 R	68.1%	30.5%	69.1%	30.9%
	DISTRICT 10	10,010	6,640	3,103	267	3,537 R	66.3%	31.0%	68.2%	31.8%
	DISTRICT 11	5,971	3,666	2,222	83	1,444 R	61.4%	37.2%	62.3%	37.7%
	DISTRICT 12	6,913	4,246	2,561	106	1,685 R	61.4%	37.0%	62.4%	37.6%
	DISTRICT 13	7,019	4,731	2,190	98	2,541 R	67.4%	31.2%	68.4%	31.6%
	DISTRICT 14	9,378	6,340	2,865	173	3,475 R	67.6%	30.6%	68.9%	31.1%
	DISTRICT 15	11,817	7,994	3,576	247	4,418 R	67.6%	30.3%	69.1%	30.9%
	DISTRICT 16	14,497	9,293	5,017	187	4,276 R	64.1%	34.6%	64.9%	35.1%
	DISTRICT 17	4,480	3,045	1,372	63	1,673 R	68.0%	30.6%	68.9%	31.1%
	DISTRICT 18	7,041	5,138	1,757	146	3,381 R	73.0%	25.0%	74.5%	25.5%
	DISTRICT 19	6,485	4,180	2,175	130	2,005 R	64.5%	33.5%	65.8%	34.2%
	DISTRICT 20	8,327	5,528	2,651	148	2,877 R	66.4%	31.8%	67.6%	32.4%
	DISTRICT 21	5,412	3,451	1,812	149	1,639 R	63.8%	33.5%	65.6%	34.4%
	DISTRICT 22	3,579	2,748	826	5	1,922 R	76.8%	23.1%	76.9%	23.1%
	DISTRICT 23	3,583	2,727	854	2	1,873 R	76.1%	23.8%	76.2%	23.8%
	DISTRICT 24	3,432	2,571	854	7	1,717 R	74.9%	24.9%	75.1%	24.9%
	DISTRICT 25	3,335	2,395	933	7	1,462 R	71.8%	28.0%	72.0%	28.0%
	DISTRICT 26	3,850	2,867	969	14	1,898 R	74.5%	25.2%	74.7%	25.3%
	DISTRICT 27	3,715	2,479	1,206	30	1,273 R	66.7%	32.5%	67.3%	32.7%
550,043	TOTAL	189,957	125,806	61,152	2,999	64,654 R	66.2%	32.2%	67.3%	32.7%

ALASKA

CONGRESS

CD	Year	Total Vote	Republican Vote	Candidate	Democratic Vote	Candidate	Other Vote	Rep.-Dem. Plurality	Total Vote Rep.	Total Vote Dem.	Major Vote Rep.	Major Vote Dem.
AL	1990	191,647	99,003	YOUNG, DON	91,677	DEVENS, JOHN S.	967	7,326 R	51.7%	47.8%	51.9%	48.1%
AL	1988	192,955	120,595	YOUNG, DON	71,881	GRUENSTEIN, PETER	479	48,714 R	62.5%	37.3%	62.7%	37.3%
AL	1986	180,277	101,799	YOUNG, DON	74,053	BEGICH, PEGGE	4,425	27,746 R	56.5%	41.1%	57.9%	42.1%
AL	1984	206,437	113,582	YOUNG, DON	86,052	BEGICH, PEGGE	6,803	27,530 R	55.0%	41.7%	56.9%	43.1%
AL	1982	181,084	128,274	YOUNG, DON	52,011	CARLSON, DAVE	799	76,263 R	70.8%	28.7%	71.2%	28.8%
AL	1980	154,618	114,089	YOUNG, DON	39,922	PARNELL, KEVIN	607	74,167 R	73.8%	25.8%	74.1%	25.9%
AL	1978	124,187	68,811	YOUNG, DON	55,176	RODEY, PATRICK	200	13,635 R	55.4%	44.4%	55.5%	44.5%
AL	1976	118,208	83,722	YOUNG, DON	34,194	HOPSON, EBEN	292	49,528 R	70.8%	28.9%	71.0%	29.0%
AL	1974	95,921	51,641	YOUNG, DON	44,280	HENSLEY, WILLIAM L.		7,361 R	53.8%	46.2%	53.8%	46.2%
AL	1972	95,401	41,750	YOUNG, DON	53,651	BEGICH, N. J.		11,901 D	43.8%	56.2%	43.8%	56.2%
AL	1970	80,084	35,947	MURKOWSKI, FRANK H.	44,137	BEGICH, N. J.		8,190 D	44.9%	55.1%	44.9%	55.1%
AL	1968	80,362	43,577	POLLOCK, HOWARD W.	36,785	BEGICH, N. J.		6,792 R	54.2%	45.8%	54.2%	45.8%
AL	1966	65,907	34,040	POLLOCK, HOWARD W.	31,867	RIVERS, RALPH J.		2,173 R	51.6%	48.4%	51.6%	48.4%
AL	1964	67,146	32,556	THOMAS, LOWELL	34,590	RIVERS, RALPH J.		2,034 D	48.5%	51.5%	48.5%	51.5%
AL	1962	58,591	26,638	THOMAS, LOWELL	31,953	RIVERS, RALPH J.		5,315 D	45.5%	54.5%	45.5%	54.5%
AL	1960	59,063	25,517	RETTIG, R. L.	33,546	RIVERS, RALPH J.		8,029 D	43.2%	56.8%	43.2%	56.8%
AL	1958	48,647	20,699	BENSON, HENRY A.	27,948	RIVERS, RALPH J.		7,249 D	42.5%	57.5%	42.5%	57.5%
AL	1956	28,266	9,332	GILLAM, BYRON A.	18,934	BARTLETT, E. L.		9,602 D	33.0%	67.0%	33.0%	67.0%
AL	1954	26,999	7,083	DIMOCK, BARBARA D.	19,916	BARTLETT, E. L.		12,833 D	26.2%	73.8%	26.2%	73.8%
AL	1952	25,112	10,893	REEVE, ROBERT C.	14,219	BARTLETT, E. L.		3,326 D	43.4%	56.6%	43.4%	56.6%
AL	1950	18,726	5,138	PETERSON, ALMER J.	13,588	BARTLETT, E. L.		8,450 D	27.4%	72.6%	27.4%	72.6%
AL	1948	22,309	4,789	STOCK, R. H.	17,520	BARTLETT, E. L.		12,731 D	21.5%	78.5%	21.5%	78.5%
AL	1946	16,384	4,868	PETERSON, ALMER J.	11,516	BARTLETT, E. L.		6,648 D	29.7%	70.3%	29.7%	70.3%

ALASKA

1990 Population figures not available for the Alaska districts.

1990 GENERAL ELECTION

Governor   The data for Governor are presented in a four column (Republican, Democratic, Alaskan Independence and Other) tabulation and the plurality figures are calculated on a first-second party basis.
Other vote was 6,563 Green (Sykes); 942 Political (O'Callaghan) and 332 scattered write-in.

Senator   Other vote was scattered write-in.

Congress   Other vote was scattered write-in. The data for Congress on the previous page include the postwar
voting for Delegate from 1946 to 1956 and for Representative at-large since statehood.

1990 PRIMARIES

Alaska's primaries are completely open, with all candidates for an office carried on the ballot together; thus a
voter may vote for a Republican for Governor, a Democrat for Senator, and so on. Actual nominations go to the
highest vote-getter in each party, as determined in this so-called "jungle primary".

AUGUST 28 REPUBLICAN

Governor   26,906 Arliss Sturgulewski; 23,442 James O. Campbell; 22,466 Rick Halford; 1,025 Donald R. Wright.

Senator   81,968 Ted Stevens; 34,824 Robert M. Bird.

Congress   Contested as follows:

AL   78,594 Don Young; 16,567 Gary L. Sinkola.

AUGUST 28 DEMOCRATIC

Governor   36,019 Tony Knowles; 27,656 Stephen McAlpine; 586 Ryal White.

Senator   12,371 Michael Beasley; 9,329 Tom Taggart.

Congress   Unopposed at-large.

AUGUST 28 ALASKAN INDEPENDENCE

Governor   3,505 John Lindauer; 492 William DeRushe. Mr. Lindauer withdrew after the primary and Walter J.
Hickel was substituted by the party committee.

Senator   No candidate.

Congress   No candidate at-large.

ARIZONA

GOVERNOR
Fife Symington (R). Elected February 1991, in a special run-off election, to a four year term.

SENATORS
Dennis DeConcini (D). Re-elected 1988 to a six-year term. Previously elected 1982, 1976.

John McCain (R). Elected 1986 to a six-year term.

REPRESENTATIVES
1. John J. Rhodes, III (R)
2. Morris K. Udall (D) (see page 1)
3. Bob Stump (R)
4. Jon Kyl (R)
5. Jim Kolbe (R)

POSTWAR VOTE FOR PRESIDENT

Year	Total Vote	Republican Vote	Candidate	Democratic Vote	Candidate	Other Vote	Plurality	Total Vote Rep.	Dem.	Major Vote Rep.	Dem.
1988	1,171,873	702,541	Bush, George	454,029	Dukakis, Michael S.	15,303	248,512 R	60.0%	38.7%	60.7%	39.3%
1984	1,025,897	681,416	Reagan, Ronald	333,854	Mondale, Walter F.	10,627	347,562 R	66.4%	32.5%	67.1%	32.9%
1980	873,945	529,688	Reagan, Ronald	246,843	Carter, Jimmy	97,414	282,845 R	60.6%	28.2%	68.2%	31.8%
1976	742,719	418,642	Ford, Gerald R.	295,602	Carter, Jimmy	28,475	123,040 R	56.4%	39.8%	58.6%	41.4%
1972	622,926	402,812	Nixon, Richard M.	198,540	McGovern, George S.	21,574	204,272 R	64.7%	31.9%	67.0%	33.0%
1968	486,936	266,721	Nixon, Richard M.	170,514	Humphrey, Hubert H.	49,701	96,207 R	54.8%	35.0%	61.0%	39.0%
1964	480,770	242,535	Goldwater, Barry M.	237,753	Johnson, Lyndon B.	482	4,782 R	50.4%	49.5%	50.5%	49.5%
1960	398,491	221,241	Nixon, Richard M.	176,781	Kennedy, John F.	469	44,460 R	55.5%	44.4%	55.6%	44.4%
1956	290,173	176,990	Eisenhower, Dwight D.	112,880	Stevenson, Adlai E.	303	64,110 R	61.0%	38.9%	61.1%	38.9%
1952	260,570	152,042	Eisenhower, Dwight D.	108,528	Stevenson, Adlai E.		43,514 R	58.3%	41.7%	58.3%	41.7%
1948	177,065	77,597	Dewey, Thomas E.	95,251	Truman, Harry S.	4,217	17,654 D	43.8%	53.8%	44.9%	55.1%

POSTWAR VOTE FOR GOVERNOR

Year	Total Vote	Republican Vote	Candidate	Democratic Vote	Candidate	Other Vote	Rep-Dem. Plurality	Total Vote Rep.	Dem.	Major Vote Rep.	Dem.
1990 **	940,737	492,569	Symington, Fife	448,168	Goddard, Terry		44,401 R	52.4%	47.6%	52.4%	47.6%
1986 **	866,984	343,913	Mecham, Evan	298,986	Warner, Carolyn	224,085	44,927 R	39.7%	34.5%	53.5%	46.5%
1982	726,364	235,877	Corbet, Leo	453,795	Babbitt, Bruce	36,692	217,918 D	32.5%	62.5%	34.2%	65.8%
1978	538,556	241,093	Mecham, Evan	282,605	Babbitt, Bruce	14,858	41,512 D	44.8%	52.5%	46.0%	54.0%
1974	552,202	273,674	Williams, Russell	278,375	Castro, Raul H.	153	4,701 D	49.6%	50.4%	49.6%	50.4%
1970 **	411,409	209,522	Williams, John R.	201,887	Castro, Raul H.		7,635 R	50.9%	49.1%	50.9%	49.1%
1968	483,998	279,923	Williams, John R.	204,075	Goddard, Sam		75,848 R	57.8%	42.2%	57.8%	42.2%
1966	378,342	203,438	Williams, John R.	174,904	Goddard, Sam		28,534 R	53.8%	46.2%	53.8%	46.2%
1964	473,502	221,404	Kleindienst, Richard	252,098	Goddard, Sam		30,694 D	46.8%	53.2%	46.8%	53.2%
1962	365,841	200,578	Fannin, Paul	165,263	Goddard, Sam		35,315 R	54.8%	45.2%	54.8%	45.2%
1960	397,107	235,502	Fannin, Paul	161,605	Ackerman, Lee		73,897 R	59.3%	40.7%	59.3%	40.7%
1958	290,465	160,136	Fannin, Paul	130,329	Morrison, Robert		29,807 R	55.1%	44.9%	55.1%	44.9%
1956	288,592	116,744	Griffen, Horace B.	171,848	McFarland, Ernest W.		55,104 D	40.5%	59.5%	40.5%	59.5%
1954	243,970	115,866	Pyle, Howard	128,104	McFarland, Ernest W.		12,238 D	47.5%	52.5%	47.5%	52.5%
1952	260,285	156,592	Pyle, Howard	103,693	Haldiman, Joe C.		52,899 R	60.2%	39.8%	60.2%	39.8%
1950	195,227	99,109	Pyle, Howard	96,118	Frohmiller, Ana		2,991 R	50.8%	49.2%	50.8%	49.2%
1948	175,767	70,419	Brockett, Bruce	104,008	Garvey, Dan E.	1,340	33,589 D	40.1%	59.2%	40.4%	59.6%
1946	122,462	48,867	Brockett, Bruce	73,595	Osborn, Sidney P.		24,728 D	39.9%	60.1%	39.9%	60.1%

The term of office for Arizona's Governor was increased from two to four years effective with the 1970 election. In 1986 other vote was Bill Schulz (Independent). In 1990 neither major-party candidate won an absolute majority, therefore a run-off election was held February 26, 1991; the vote above is for the Feburary run-off.

ARIZONA

POSTWAR VOTE FOR SENATOR

Year	Total Vote	Republican Vote	Candidate	Democratic Vote	Candidate	Other Vote	Rep-Dem. Plurality	Percentage Total Vote Rep.	Dem.	Major Vote Rep.	Dem.
1988	1,164,539	478,060	DeGreen, Keith	660,403	DeConcini, Dennis	26,076	182,343 D	41.1%	56.7%	42.0%	58.0%
1986	862,921	521,850	McCain, John	340,965	Kimball, Richard	106	180,885 R	60.5%	39.5%	60.5%	39.5%
1982	723,885	291,749	Dunn, Pete	411,970	DeConcini, Dennis	20,166	120,221 D	40.3%	56.9%	41.5%	58.5%
1980	874,238	432,371	Goldwater, Barry M.	422,972	Schulz, Bill	18,895	9,399 R	49.5%	48.4%	50.5%	49.5%
1976	741,210	321,236	Steiger, Sam	400,334	DeConcini, Dennis	19,640	79,098 D	43.3%	54.0%	44.5%	55.5%
1974	549,919	320,396	Goldwater, Barry M.	229,523	Mar shall, Jonathan		90,873 R	58.3%	41.7%	58.3%	41.7%
1970	407,796	228,284	Fannin, Paul	179,512	Grossman, Sam		48,772 R	56.0%	44.0%	56.0%	44.0%
1968	479,945	274,607	Goldwater, Barry M.	205,338	Elson, Roy L.		69,269 R	57.2%	42.8%	57.2%	42.8%
1964	468,801	241,089	Fannin, Paul	227,712	Elson, Roy L.		13,377 R	51.4%	48.6%	51.4%	48.6%
1962	362,605	163,388	Mecham, Evan	199,217	Hayden, Carl		35,829 D	45.1%	54.9%	45.1%	54.9%
1958	293,623	164,593	Goldwater, Barry M.	129,030	McFarland, Ernest W.		35,563 R	56.1%	43.9%	56.1%	43.9%
1956	278,263	107,447	Jones, Ross F.	170,816	Hayden, Carl		63,369 D	38.6%	61.4%	38.6%	61.4%
1952	257,401	132,063	Goldwater, Barry M.	125,338	McFarland, Ernest W.		6,725 R	51.3%	48.7%	51.3%	48.7%
1950	185,092	68,846	Brockett, Bruce	116,246	Hayden, Carl		47,400 D	37.2%	62.8%	37.2%	62.8%
1946	116,239	35,022	Powers, Ward S.	80,415	McFarland, Ernest W.	802	45,393 D	30.1%	69.2%	30.3%	69.7%

ARIZONA

Districts Established April 2, 1982

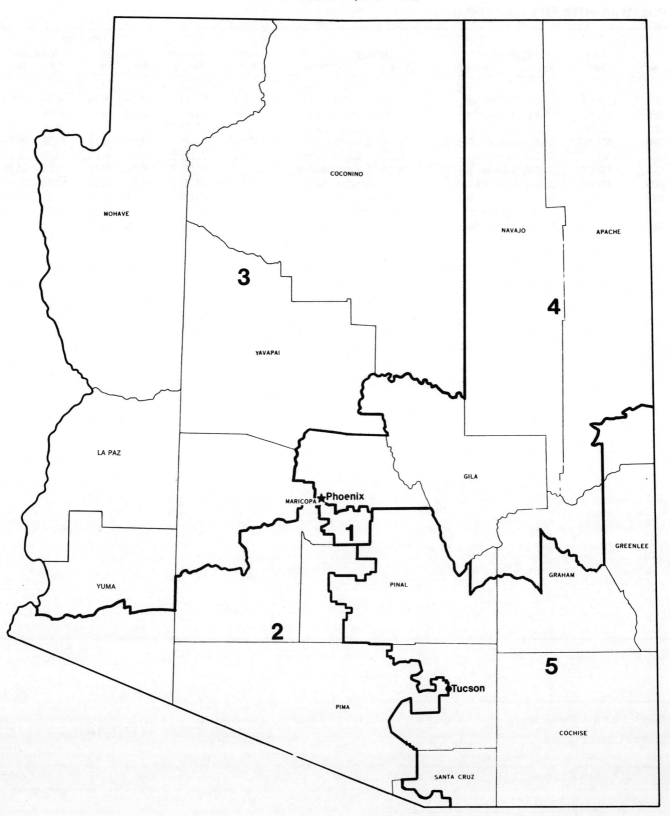

MOHAVE

COCONINO

NAVAJO

APACHE

3

YAVAPAI

4

LA PAZ

GILA

★Phoenix

MARICOPA

1

GREENLEE

YUMA

PINAL

GRAHAM

2

5

PIMA

★Tucson

COCHISE

SANTA CRUZ

© ERC

ARIZONA

GOVERNOR 1990
(NOVEMBER ELECTION)

1990 Census Population	County	Total Vote	Republican	Democratic	Other	Rep.-Dem. Plurality	Percentage			
							Total Vote		Major Vote	
							Rep.	Dem.	Rep.	Dem.
61,591	APACHE	13,234	3,638	9,485	111	5,847 D	27.5%	71.7%	27.7%	72.3%
97,624	COCHISE	24,320	11,472	12,685	163	1,213 D	47.2%	52.2%	47.5%	52.5%
96,591	COCONINO	28,522	11,330	17,050	142	5,720 D	39.7%	59.8%	39.9%	60.1%
40,216	GILA	14,317	6,283	7,893	141	1,610 D	43.9%	55.1%	44.3%	55.7%
26,554	GRAHAM	7,456	3,614	3,699	143	85 D	48.5%	49.6%	49.4%	50.6%
8,008	GREENLEE	2,918	1,071	1,836	11	765 D	36.7%	62.9%	36.8%	63.2%
13,844	LA PAZ	3,487	1,829	1,622	36	207 R	52.5%	46.5%	53.0%	47.0%
2,122,101	MARICOPA	621,199	330,261	282,409	8,529	47,852 R	53.2%	45.5%	53.9%	46.1%
93,497	MOHAVE	27,405	14,068	13,131	206	937 R	51.3%	47.9%	51.7%	48.3%
77,658	NAVAJO	17,799	7,708	9,867	224	2,159 D	43.3%	55.4%	43.9%	56.1%
666,880	PIMA	201,478	87,701	112,572	1,205	24,871 D	43.5%	55.9%	43.8%	56.2%
116,379	PINAL	28,597	11,762	16,562	273	4,800 D	41.1%	57.9%	41.5%	58.5%
29,676	SANTA CRUZ	5,956	2,140	3,801	15	1,661 D	35.9%	63.8%	36.0%	64.0%
107,714	YAVAPAI	40,731	22,682	17,567	482	5,115 R	55.7%	43.1%	56.4%	43.6%
106,895	YUMA	17,987	8,425	9,512	50	1,087 D	46.8%	52.9%	47.0%	53.0%
3,665,228	TOTAL	1,055,406	523,984	519,691	11,731	4,293 R	49.6%	49.2%	50.2%	49.8%

ARIZONA

GOVERNOR 1990
(FEBRUARY 1991 RUN-OFF ELECTION)

1990 Census Population	County	Total Vote	Republican	Democratic	Other	Rep.-Dem. Plurality	Percentage			
							Total Vote		Major Vote	
							Rep.	Dem.	Rep.	Dem.
61,591	APACHE	11,276	2,982	8,294		5,312 D	26.4%	73.6%	26.4%	73.6%
97,624	COCHISE	20,513	9,862	10,651		789 D	48.1%	51.9%	48.1%	51.9%
96,591	COCONINO	22,551	9,444	13,107		3,663 D	41.9%	58.1%	41.9%	58.1%
40,216	GILA	12,302	5,670	6,632		962 D	46.1%	53.9%	46.1%	53.9%
26,554	GRAHAM	6,264	3,512	2,752		760 R	56.1%	43.9%	56.1%	43.9%
8,008	GREENLEE	2,435	1,003	1,432		429 D	41.2%	58.8%	41.2%	58.8%
13,844	LA PAZ	2,760	1,558	1,202		356 R	56.4%	43.6%	56.4%	43.6%
2,122,101	MARICOPA	564,502	315,811	248,691		67,120 R	55.9%	44.1%	55.9%	44.1%
93,497	MOHAVE	23,828	13,106	10,722		2,384 R	55.0%	45.0%	55.0%	45.0%
77,658	NAVAJO	15,802	7,081	8,721		1,640 D	44.8%	55.2%	44.8%	55.2%
666,880	PIMA	180,367	82,594	97,773		15,179 D	45.8%	54.2%	45.8%	54.2%
116,379	PINAL	23,997	10,562	13,435		2,873 D	44.0%	56.0%	44.0%	56.0%
29,676	SANTA CRUZ	3,887	1,741	2,146		405 D	44.8%	55.2%	44.8%	55.2%
107,714	YAVAPAI	36,663	21,515	15,148		6,367 R	58.7%	41.3%	58.7%	41.3%
106,895	YUMA	13,590	6,128	7,462		1,334 D	45.1%	54.9%	45.1%	54.9%
3,665,228	TOTAL	940,737	492,569	448,168		44,401 R	52.4%	47.6%	52.4%	47.6%

80

ARIZONA

CONGRESS

CD	Year	Total Vote	Republican Vote	Republican Candidate	Democratic Vote	Democratic Candidate	Other Vote	Rep.-Dem. Plurality	Total Vote Rep.	Total Vote Dem.	Major Vote Rep.	Major Vote Dem.
1	1990	167,016	166,223	RHODES, JOHN J., III			793	166,223 R	99.5%		100.0%	
1	1988	256,027	184,639	RHODES, JOHN J., III	71,388	FILLMORE, JOHN M.		113,251 R	72.1%	27.9%	72.1%	27.9%
1	1986	178,533	127,370	RHODES, JOHN J., III	51,163	BRAUN, HARRY W.		76,207 R	71.3%	28.7%	71.3%	28.7%
1	1984	208,027	162,418	MCCAIN, JOHN	45,609	BRAUN, HARRY W.		116,809 R	78.1%	21.9%	78.1%	21.9%
1	1982	135,227	89,116	MCCAIN, JOHN	41,261	HEGARTY, WILLIAM E.	4,850	47,855 R	65.9%	30.5%	68.4%	31.6%
2	1990	116,179	39,586	SWEENEY, JOSEPH D.	76,549	UDALL, MORRIS K.	44	36,963 D	34.1%	65.9%	34.1%	65.9%
2	1988	136,204	36,309	SWEENEY, JOSEPH D.	99,895	UDALL, MORRIS K.		63,586 D	26.7%	73.3%	26.7%	73.3%
2	1986	105,407	24,522	CLARK, SHELDON	77,239	UDALL, MORRIS K.	3,646	52,717 D	23.3%	73.3%	24.1%	75.9%
2	1984	121,215			106,332	UDALL, MORRIS K.	14,883	106,332 D		87.7%		100.0%
2	1982	103,674	28,407	LAOS, ROY B.	73,468	UDALL, MORRIS K.	1,799	45,061 D	27.4%	70.9%	27.9%	72.1%
3	1990	237,297	134,279	STUMP, BOB	103,018	HARTSTONE, ROGER		31,261 R	56.6%	43.4%	56.6%	43.4%
3	1988	253,330	174,453	STUMP, BOB	72,417	MOSS, DAVE	6,460	102,036 R	68.9%	28.6%	70.7%	29.3%
3	1986	146,462	146,462	STUMP, BOB				146,462 R	100.0%		100.0%	
3	1984	218,328	156,686	STUMP, BOB	57,748	SCHUSTER, BOB	3,894	98,938 R	71.8%	26.5%	73.1%	26.9%
3	1982	159,842	101,198	STUMP, BOB	58,644	BOSCH, PAT		42,554 R	63.3%	36.7%	63.3%	36.7%
4	1990	231,238	141,843	KYL, JON	89,395	IVEY, MARK		52,448 R	61.3%	38.7%	61.3%	38.7%
4	1988	236,678	206,248	KYL, JON			30,430	206,248 R	87.1%		100.0%	
4	1986	188,833	121,939	KYL, JON	66,894	DAVIS, PHILIP R.		55,045 R	64.6%	35.4%	64.6%	35.4%
4	1984	167,615	167,558	RUDD, ELDON			57	167,558 R	100.0%		100.0%	
4	1982	145,466	95,620	RUDD, ELDON	44,182	EARLEY, WAYNE O.	5,664	51,438 R	65.7%	30.4%	68.4%	31.6%
5	1990	214,617	138,975	KOLBE, JIM	75,642	PHILLIPS, CHUCK		63,333 R	64.8%	35.2%	64.8%	35.2%
5	1988	242,577	164,462	KOLBE, JIM	78,115	BELCHER, JUDITH E.		86,347 R	67.8%	32.2%	67.8%	32.2%
5	1986	184,495	119,647	KOLBE, JIM	64,848	IRELAND, JOEL		54,799 R	64.9%	35.1%	64.9%	35.1%
5	1984	227,938	116,075	KOLBE, JIM	109,871	MCNULTY, JIM	1,992	6,204 R	50.9%	48.2%	51.4%	48.6%
5	1982	166,802	80,531	KOLBE, JIM	82,938	MCNULTY, JIM	3,333	2,407 D	48.3%	49.7%	49.3%	50.7%

ARIZONA

1990 GENERAL ELECTION

Governor   Neither major-party candidate won an absolute majority in the November election; therefore a run-off election was held February 26, 1991. Data are presented for both the November 1990 and February 1991 elections. Other vote in the November election was all for write-in candidates as follows: 10,983 Hawkins; 316 Yetman; 163 Campbell; 76 Weinstein; 75 Castronovo; 64 Winn and 54 Cojanis.

Congress   Other vote was scattered in all CD's.

1990 PRIMARIES

SEPTEMBER 11 REPUBLICAN

Governor   163,010 Fife Symington; 91,136 Evan Mecham; 61,487 Fred Koory; 49,019 Sam Steiger; 7,672 Bob Barnes.

Congress   Unopposed in three CD's. Contested as follows:

CD 1   58,763 John J. Rhodes, III; 35,458 John T. Wrzesinski.
CD 2   12,981 Joseph D. Sweeney; 7,481 Al Rodriguez.

SEPTEMBER 11 DEMOCRATIC

Governor   212,579 Terry Goddard; 40,478 Dave Moss.

Congress   Unopposed in two CD's. No candidate in CD's 1 and 3. In CD 3 Roger Hartstone received 1,470 write-in votes and became the nominee. Contested as follows:

CD 5   27,493 Chuck Phillips; 20,845 Gerald L. Coyle.

82

ARKANSAS

GOVERNOR
Bill Clinton (D). Re-elected 1990 to a four-year term. Previously elected 1986 to a four-year term and in 1984, 1982, 1978 to two-year terms.

SENATORS
Dale Bumpers (D). Re-elected 1986 to a six-year term. Previously elected 1980, 1974.

David H. Pryor (D). Re-elected 1990 to a six-year term. Previously elected 1984, 1978.

REPRESENTATIVES
1. William Alexander (D)
2. Ray Thornton (D)
3. John Hammerschmidt (R)
4. Beryl F. Anthony (D)

POSTWAR VOTE FOR PRESIDENT

Year	Total Vote	Republican Vote	Candidate	Democratic Vote	Candidate	Other Vote	Plurality	Rep.	Dem.	Rep.	Dem.
1988	827,738	466,578	Bush, George	349,237	Dukakis, Michael S.	11,923	117,341 R	56.4%	42.2%	57.2%	42.8%
1984	884,406	534,774	Reagan, Ronald	338,646	Mondale, Walter F.	10,986	196,128 R	60.5%	38.3%	61.2%	38.8%
1980	837,582	403,164	Reagan, Ronald	398,041	Carter, Jimmy	36,377	5,123 R	48.1%	47.5%	50.3%	49.7%
1976	767,535	267,903	Ford, Gerald R.	498,604	Carter, Jimmy	1,028	230,701 D	34.9%	65.0%	35.0%	65.0%
1972	651,320	448,541	Nixon, Richard M.	199,892	McGovern, George S.	2,887	248,649 R	68.9%	30.7%	69.2%	30.8%
1968 **	619,969	190,759	Nixon, Richard M.	188,228	Humphrey, Hubert H.	240,982	50,223 A	30.8%	30.4%	50.3%	49.7%
1964	560,426	243,264	Goldwater, Barry M.	314,197	Johnson, Lyndon B.	2,965	70,933 D	43.4%	56.1%	43.6%	56.4%
1960	428,509	184,508	Nixon, Richard M.	215,049	Kennedy, John F.	28,952	30,541 D	43.1%	50.2%	46.2%	53.8%
1956	406,572	186,287	Eisenhower, Dwight D.	213,277	Stevenson, Adlai E.	7,008	26,990 D	45.8%	52.5%	46.6%	53.4%
1952	404,800	177,155	Eisenhower, Dwight D.	226,300	Stevenson, Adlai E.	1,345	49,145 D	43.8%	55.9%	43.9%	56.1%
1948 **	242,475	50,959	Dewey, Thomas E.	149,659	Truman, Harry S.	41,857	98,700 D	21.0%	61.7%	25.4%	74.6%

In 1968 other vote was American (Wallace). In 1948 other vote was 40,068 States Rights; 1,037 Socialist; 751 Progressive and 1 Prohibition.

ARKANSAS

POSTWAR VOTE FOR GOVERNOR

Year	Total Vote	Republican Vote	Republican Candidate	Democratic Vote	Democratic Candidate	Other Vote	Rep-Dem. Plurality	Percentage Total Vote Rep.	Total Vote Dem.	Major Vote Rep.	Major Vote Dem.
1990	696,412	295,925	Nelson, Sheffield	400,386	Clinton, Bill	101	104,461 D	42.5%	57.5%	42.5%	57.5%
1986 **	688,551	248,427	White, Frank D.	439,882	Clinton, Bill	242	191,455 D	36.1%	63.9%	36.1%	63.9%
1984	886,548	331,987	Freeman, Woody	554,561	Clinton, Bill		222,574 D	37.4%	62.6%	37.4%	62.6%
1982	789,351	357,496	White, Frank D.	431,855	Clinton, Bill		74,359 D	45.3%	54.7%	45.3%	54.7%
1980	838,925	435,684	White, Frank D.	403,241	Clinton, Bill		32,443 R	51.9%	48.1%	51.9%	48.1%
1978	528,912	193,746	Lowe, A. Lynn	335,101	Clinton, Bill	65	141,355 D	36.6%	63.4%	36.6%	63.4%
1976	726,949	121,716	Griffith, Leon	605,083	Pryor, David H.	150	483,367 D	16.7%	83.2%	16.7%	83.3%
1974	545,974	187,872	Coon, Ken	358,018	Pryor, David H.	84	170,146 D	34.4%	65.6%	34.4%	65.6%
1972	648,069	159,177	Blaylock, Len E.	488,892	Bumpers, Dale		329,715 D	24.6%	75.4%	24.6%	75.4%
1970	609,198	197,418	Rockefeller, Winthrop	375,648	Bumpers, Dale	36,132	178,230 D	32.4%	61.7%	34.4%	65.6%
1968	615,595	322,782	Rockefeller, Winthrop	292,813	Crank, Marion		29,969 R	52.4%	47.6%	52.4%	47.6%
1966	563,527	306,324	Rockefeller, Winthrop	257,203	Johnson, James D.		49,121 R	54.4%	45.6%	54.4%	45.6%
1964	592,113	254,561	Rockefeller, Winthrop	337,489	Faubus, Orval E.	63	82,928 D	43.0%	57.0%	43.0%	57.0%
1962	308,092	82,349	Ricketts, Willis	225,743	Faubus, Orval E.		143,394 D	26.7%	73.3%	26.7%	73.3%
1960	421,985	129,921	Britt, Henry M.	292,064	Faubus, Orval E.		162,143 D	30.8%	69.2%	30.8%	69.2%
1958	286,886	50,288	Johnson, George W.	236,598	Faubus, Orval E.		186,310 D	17.5%	82.5%	17.5%	82.5%
1956	399,012	77,215	Mitchell, Roy	321,797	Faubus, Orval E.		244,582 D	19.4%	80.6%	19.4%	80.6%
1954	335,176	127,004	Remmel, Pratt C.	208,121	Faubus, Orval E.	51	81,117 D	37.9%	62.1%	37.9%	62.1%
1952	391,592	49,292	Speck, Jefferson W.	342,292	Cherry, Francis	8	293,000 D	12.6%	87.4%	12.6%	87.4%
1950	317,087	50,309	Speck, Jefferson W.	266,778	McMath, Sidney S.		216,469 D	15.9%	84.1%	15.9%	84.1%
1948	249,301	26,500	Black, Charles R.	222,801	McMath, Sidney S.		196,301 D	10.6%	89.4%	10.6%	89.4%
1946	152,162	24,133	Mills, W. T.	128,029	Laney, Ben T.		103,896 D	15.9%	84.1%	15.9%	84.1%

The term of office for Arkansas' Governor was increased from two to four years effective with the 1986 election.

POSTWAR VOTE FOR SENATOR

Year	Total Vote	Republican Vote	Republican Candidate	Democratic Vote	Democratic Candidate	Other Vote	Rep-Dem. Plurality	Percentage Total Vote Rep.	Total Vote Dem.	Major Vote Rep.	Major Vote Dem.
1990 **	494,735		—	493,910	Pryor, David H.	825	493,910 D		99.8%		100.0%
1986	695,487	262,313	Hutchinson, Asa	433,122	Bumpers, Dale	52	170,809 D	37.7%	62.3%	37.7%	62.3%
1984	875,956	373,615	Bethune, Ed	502,341	Pryor, David H.		128,726 D	42.7%	57.3%	42.7%	57.3%
1980	808,812	330,576	Clark, Bill	477,905	Bumpers, Dale	331	147,329 D	40.9%	59.1%	40.9%	59.1%
1978	522,239	84,722	Kelly, Tom	399,916	Pryor, David H.	37,601	315,194 D	16.2%	76.6%	17.5%	82.5%
1974	543,082	82,026	Jones, John H.	461,056	Bumpers, Dale		379,030 D	15.1%	84.9%	15.1%	84.9%
1972	634,636	248,238	Babbitt, Wayne H.	386,398	McClellan, John L.		138,160 D	39.1%	60.9%	39.1%	60.9%
1968	591,704	241,739	Bernard, Charles T.	349,965	Fulbright, J. W.		108,226 D	40.9%	59.1%	40.9%	59.1%
1966 **			—		McClellan, John L.						
1962	312,880	98,013	Jones, Kenneth	214,867	Fulbright, J. W.		116,854 D	31.3%	68.7%	31.3%	68.7%
1960 **			—		McClellan, John L.						
1956	399,695	68,016	Henley, Ben C.	331,679	Fulbright, J. W.		263,663 D	17.0%	83.0%	17.0%	83.0%
1954	291,058		—	291,058	McClellan, John L.		291,058 D		100.0%		100.0%
1950	302,582		—	302,582	Fulbright, J. W.		302,582 D		100.0%		100.0%
1948	216,401		—	216,401	McClellan, John L.		216,401 D		100.0%		100.0%

Senator McClellan was re-elected in 1966 and in 1960, but his vote was not canvassed in many counties. In 1990 Senator Pryor's vote was not canvassed in seven counties due to the fact that he was unopposed.

ARKANSAS

Districts Established February 25, 1981

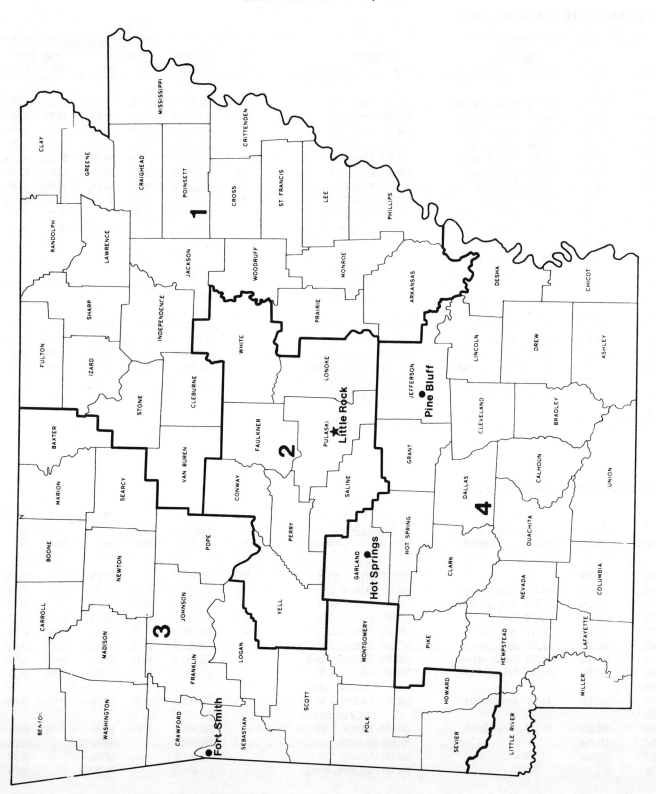

ARKANSAS

GOVERNOR 1990

1990 Census Population	County	Total Vote	Republican	Democratic	Other	Rep.-Dem. Plurality	Percentage Total Vote Rep.	Dem.	Major Vote Rep.	Dem.
21,653	ARKANSAS	6,682	2,592	4,090		1,498 D	38.8%	61.2%	38.8%	61.2%
24,319	ASHLEY	7,225	2,309	4,914	2	2,605 D	32.0%	68.0%	32.0%	68.0%
31,186	BAXTER	11,567	6,442	5,125		1,317 R	55.7%	44.3%	55.7%	44.3%
97,499	BENTON	26,709	12,699	14,010		1,311 D	47.5%	52.5%	47.5%	52.5%
28,297	BOONE	9,555	5,598	3,957		1,641 R	58.6%	41.4%	58.6%	41.4%
11,793	BRADLEY	3,658	1,495	2,163		668 D	40.9%	59.1%	40.9%	59.1%
5,826	CALHOUN	2,175	1,086	1,089		3 D	49.9%	50.1%	49.9%	50.1%
18,654	CARROLL	6,324	3,465	2,858	1	607 R	54.8%	45.2%	54.8%	45.2%
15,713	CHICOT	4,320	1,226	3,072	22	1,846 D	28.4%	71.1%	28.5%	71.5%
21,437	CLARK	6,508	2,125	4,383		2,258 D	32.7%	67.3%	32.7%	67.3%
18,107	CLAY	5,475	2,024	3,451		1,427 D	37.0%	63.0%	37.0%	63.0%
19,411	CLEBURNE	7,710	3,567	4,143		576 D	46.3%	53.7%	46.3%	53.7%
7,781	CLEVELAND	2,750	1,317	1,405	28	88 D	47.9%	51.1%	48.4%	51.6%
25,691	COLUMBIA	7,210	3,798	3,412		386 R	52.7%	47.3%	52.7%	47.3%
19,151	CONWAY	5,353	2,388	2,958	7	570 D	44.6%	55.3%	44.7%	55.3%
68,956	CRAIGHEAD	16,068	5,918	10,150		4,232 D	36.8%	63.2%	36.8%	63.2%
42,493	CRAWFORD	10,683	5,178	5,505		327 D	48.5%	51.5%	48.5%	51.5%
49,939	CRITTENDEN	11,028	3,565	7,463		3,898 D	32.3%	67.7%	32.3%	67.7%
19,225	CROSS	4,899	2,007	2,892		885 D	41.0%	59.0%	41.0%	59.0%
9,614	DALLAS	3,720	1,602	2,109	9	507 D	43.1%	56.7%	43.2%	56.8%
16,798	DESHA	4,717	1,453	3,264		1,811 D	30.8%	69.2%	30.8%	69.2%
17,369	DREW	5,029	1,859	3,170		1,311 D	37.0%	63.0%	37.0%	63.0%
60,006	FAULKNER	17,102	7,194	9,908		2,714 D	42.1%	57.9%	42.1%	57.9%
14,897	FRANKLIN	5,531	2,645	2,886		241 D	47.8%	52.2%	47.8%	52.2%
10,037	FULTON	3,130	1,420	1,710		290 D	45.4%	54.6%	45.4%	54.6%
73,397	GARLAND	25,995	10,563	15,425	7	4,862 D	40.6%	59.3%	40.6%	59.4%
13,948	GRANT	4,772	2,269	2,503		234 D	47.5%	52.5%	47.5%	52.5%
31,804	GREENE	8,550	3,208	5,342		2,134 D	37.5%	62.5%	37.5%	62.5%
21,621	HEMPSTEAD	6,134	2,655	3,479		824 D	43.3%	56.7%	43.3%	56.7%
26,115	HOT SPRING	8,328	3,468	4,860		1,392 D	41.6%	58.4%	41.6%	58.4%
13,569	HOWARD	3,681	1,629	2,052		423 D	44.3%	55.7%	44.3%	55.7%
31,192	INDEPENDENCE	10,088	4,356	5,732		1,376 D	43.2%	56.8%	43.2%	56.8%
11,364	IZARD	4,601	2,025	2,576		551 D	44.0%	56.0%	44.0%	56.0%
18,944	JACKSON	5,873	2,251	3,614	8	1,363 D	38.3%	61.5%	38.4%	61.6%
85,487	JEFFERSON	23,701	7,230	16,471		9,241 D	30.5%	69.5%	30.5%	69.5%
18,221	JOHNSON	6,010	2,700	3,310		610 D	44.9%	55.1%	44.9%	55.1%
9,643	LAFAYETTE	3,130	1,497	1,633		136 D	47.8%	52.2%	47.8%	52.2%
17,457	LAWRENCE	5,724	2,381	3,343		962 D	41.6%	58.4%	41.6%	58.4%
13,053	LEE	4,895	1,519	3,376		1,857 D	31.0%	69.0%	31.0%	69.0%
13,690	LINCOLN	4,005	1,292	2,713		1,421 D	32.3%	67.7%	32.3%	67.7%
13,966	LITTLE RIVER	3,884	1,420	2,462	2	1,042 D	36.6%	63.4%	36.6%	63.4%
20,557	LOGAN	6,976	3,417	3,557	2	140 D	49.0%	51.0%	49.0%	51.0%
39,268	LONOKE	11,166	5,082	6,084		1,002 D	45.5%	54.5%	45.5%	54.5%
11,618	MADISON	4,041	2,129	1,912		217 R	52.7%	47.3%	52.7%	47.3%
12,001	MARION	4,167	2,234	1,933		301 R	53.6%	46.4%	53.6%	46.4%
38,467	MILLER	9,567	4,354	5,208	5	854 D	45.5%	54.4%	45.5%	54.5%
57,525	MISSISSIPPI	12,280	3,967	8,313		4,346 D	32.3%	67.7%	32.3%	67.7%
11,333	MONROE	3,877	1,703	2,174		471 D	43.9%	56.1%	43.9%	56.1%
7,841	MONTGOMERY	2,790	1,362	1,428		66 D	48.8%	51.2%	48.8%	51.2%
10,101	NEVADA	3,198	1,460	1,738		278 D	45.7%	54.3%	45.7%	54.3%
7,666	NEWTON	3,770	2,258	1,512		746 R	59.9%	40.1%	59.9%	40.1%
30,574	OUACHITA	9,041	3,312	5,729		2,417 D	36.6%	63.4%	36.6%	63.4%
7,969	PERRY	2,584	1,211	1,373		162 D	46.9%	53.1%	46.9%	53.1%
28,838	PHILLIPS	9,381	2,855	6,526		3,671 D	30.4%	69.6%	30.4%	69.6%
10,086	PIKE	3,363	1,739	1,624		115 R	51.7%	48.3%	51.7%	48.3%
24,664	POINSETT	7,796	3,099	4,697		1,598 D	39.8%	60.2%	39.8%	60.2%
17,347	POLK	5,229	2,418	2,811		393 D	46.2%	53.8%	46.2%	53.8%
45,883	POPE	12,991	6,349	6,642		293 D	48.9%	51.1%	48.9%	51.1%
9,518	PRAIRIE	3,440	1,607	1,833		226 D	46.7%	53.3%	46.7%	53.3%
349,660	PULASKI	103,657	40,691	62,962	4	22,271 D	39.3%	60.7%	39.3%	60.7%

ARKANSAS

GOVERNOR 1990

1990 Census Population	County	Total Vote	Republican	Democratic	Other	Rep.-Dem. Plurality	Percentage Total Vote Rep.	Dem.	Major Vote Rep.	Dem.
16,558	RANDOLPH	3,806	1,600	2,206		606 D	42.0%	58.0%	42.0%	58.0%
28,497	ST. FRANCIS	7,109	2,683	4,426		1,743 D	37.7%	62.3%	37.7%	62.3%
64,183	SALINE	20,287	9,072	11,215		2,143 D	44.7%	55.3%	44.7%	55.3%
10,205	SCOTT	3,749	1,982	1,767		215 R	52.9%	47.1%	52.9%	47.1%
7,841	SEARCY	3,569	2,283	1,286		997 R	64.0%	36.0%	64.0%	36.0%
99,590	SEBASTIAN	27,615	12,862	14,753		1,891 D	46.6%	53.4%	46.6%	53.4%
13,637	SEVIER	3,703	1,591	2,112		521 D	43.0%	57.0%	43.0%	57.0%
14,109	SHARP	5,168	2,478	2,690		212 D	47.9%	52.1%	47.9%	52.1%
9,775	STONE	3,897	2,158	1,736	3	422 R	55.4%	44.5%	55.4%	44.6%
46,719	UNION	13,612	6,232	7,380		1,148 D	45.8%	54.2%	45.8%	54.2%
14,008	VAN BUREN	5,514	2,724	2,790		66 D	49.4%	50.6%	49.4%	50.6%
113,409	WASHINGTON	29,268	12,531	16,737		4,206 D	42.8%	57.2%	42.8%	57.2%
54,676	WHITE	17,014	7,591	9,422	1	1,831 D	44.6%	55.4%	44.6%	55.4%
9,520	WOODRUFF	2,753	816	1,937		1,121 D	29.6%	70.4%	29.6%	70.4%
17,759	YELL	5,535	2,640	2,895		255 D	47.7%	52.3%	47.7%	52.3%
2,350,725	TOTAL	696,412	295,925	400,386	101	104,461 D	42.5%	57.5%	42.5%	57.5%

ARKANSAS

SENATOR 1990

1990 Census Population	County	Total Vote	Republican	Democratic	Other	Rep.-Dem. Plurality	Percentage Total Vote Rep.	Dem.	Percentage Major Vote Rep.	Dem.
21,653	ARKANSAS	5,955		5,955		5,955 D		100.0%		100.0%
24,319	ASHLEY	5,510		5,501	9	5,501 D		99.8%		100.0%
31,186	BAXTER	8,147		8,128	19	8,128 D		99.8%		100.0%
97,499	BENTON	20,037		20,037		20,037 D		100.0%		100.0%
28,297	BOONE	5,870		5,867	3	5,867 D		99.9%		100.0%
11,793	BRADLEY	2,391		2,391		2,391 D		100.0%		100.0%
5,826	CALHOUN									
18,654	CARROLL	4,279		4,265	14	4,265 D		99.7%		100.0%
15,713	CHICOT	3,921		3,857	64	3,857 D		98.4%		100.0%
21,437	CLARK	6,103		6,100	3	6,100 D		100.0%		100.0%
18,107	CLAY	2,662		2,662		2,662 D		100.0%		100.0%
19,411	CLEBURNE	4,971		4,967	4	4,967 D		99.9%		100.0%
7,781	CLEVELAND	2,542		2,471	71	2,471 D		97.2%		100.0%
25,691	COLUMBIA	5,420		5,418	2	5,418 D		100.0%		100.0%
19,151	CONWAY	4,121		4,113	8	4,113 D		99.8%		100.0%
68,956	CRAIGHEAD	11,773		11,773		11,773 D		100.0%		100.0%
42,493	CRAWFORD	8,533		8,533		8,533 D		100.0%		100.0%
49,939	CRITTENDEN	5,938		5,900	38	5,900 D		99.4%		100.0%
19,225	CROSS	1,603		1,602	1	1,602 D		99.9%		100.0%
9,614	DALLAS	3,393		3,362	31	3,362 D		99.1%		100.0%
16,798	DESHA	3,532		3,530	2	3,530 D		99.9%		100.0%
17,369	DREW									
60,006	FAULKNER	12,829		12,812	17	12,812 D		99.9%		100.0%
14,897	FRANKLIN	2,571		2,571		2,571 D		100.0%		100.0%
10,037	FULTON	2,558		2,558		2,558 D		100.0%		100.0%
73,397	GARLAND	20,391		20,293	98	20,293 D		99.5%		100.0%
13,948	GRANT	3,139		3,134	5	3,134 D		99.8%		100.0%
31,804	GREENE	7,891		7,655	236	7,655 D		97.0%		100.0%
21,621	HEMPSTEAD	4,046		4,045	1	4,045 D		100.0%		100.0%
26,115	HOT SPRING	7,688		7,685	3	7,685 D		100.0%		100.0%
13,569	HOWARD	2,033		2,029	4	2,029 D		99.8%		100.0%
31,192	INDEPENDENCE	8,624		8,624		8,624 D		100.0%		100.0%
11,364	IZARD	3,802		3,785	17	3,785 D		99.6%		100.0%
18,944	JACKSON	4,134		4,098	36	4,098 D		99.1%		100.0%
85,487	JEFFERSON	18,345		18,345		18,345 D		100.0%		100.0%
18,221	JOHNSON	383		383		383 D		100.0%		100.0%
9,643	LAFAYETTE	1,086		1,083	3	1,083 D		99.7%		100.0%
17,457	LAWRENCE	4,742		4,742		4,742 D		100.0%		100.0%
13,053	LEE	4,094		4,094		4,094 D		100.0%		100.0%
13,690	LINCOLN	3,350		3,347	3	3,347 D		99.9%		100.0%
13,966	LITTLE RIVER	1,791		1,786	5	1,786 D		99.7%		100.0%
20,557	LOGAN	6,188		6,174	14	6,174 D		99.8%		100.0%
39,268	LONOKE	9,767		9,767		9,767 D		100.0%		100.0%
11,618	MADISON	2,723		2,723		2,723 D		100.0%		100.0%
12,001	MARION	2,577		2,569	8	2,569 D		99.7%		100.0%
38,467	MILLER	7,363		7,351	12	7,351 D		99.8%		100.0%
57,525	MISSISSIPPI	7,863		7,860	3	7,860 D		100.0%		100.0%
11,333	MONROE									
7,841	MONTGOMERY	2,100		2,098	2	2,098 D		99.9%		100.0%
10,101	NEVADA	2,185		2,185		2,185 D		100.0%		100.0%
7,666	NEWTON									
30,574	OUACHITA	7,908		7,892	16	7,892 D		99.8%		100.0%
7,969	PERRY	1,815		1,802	13	1,802 D		99.3%		100.0%
28,838	PHILLIPS	7,039		7,038	1	7,038 D		100.0%		100.0%
10,086	PIKE									
24,664	POINSETT	5,382		5,382		5,382 D		100.0%		100.0%
17,347	POLK									
45,883	POPE	11,094		11,091	3	11,091 D		100.0%		100.0%
9,518	PRAIRIE	2,261		2,254	7	2,254 D		99.7%		100.0%
349,660	PULASKI	76,598		76,581	17	76,581 D		100.0%		100.0%

ARKANSAS

SENATOR 1990

1990 Census Population	County	Total Vote	Republican	Democratic	Other	Rep.-Dem. Plurality	Percentage Total Vote Rep.	Dem.	Major Vote Rep.	Dem.
16,558	RANDOLPH	2,983		2,981	2	2,981 D		99.9%		100.0%
28,497	ST. FRANCIS	5,434		5,432	2	5,432 D		100.0%		100.0%
64,183	SALINE	16,684		16,678	6	16,678 D		100.0%		100.0%
10,205	SCOTT	815		805	10	805 D		98.8%		100.0%
7,841	SEARCY									
99,590	SEBASTIAN	21,833		21,833		21,833 D		100.0%		100.0%
13,637	SEVIER	3,093		3,090	3	3,090 D		99.9%		100.0%
14,109	SHARP	3,948		3,948		3,948 D		100.0%		100.0%
9,775	STONE	2,803		2,797	6	2,797 D		99.8%		100.0%
46,719	UNION	10,041		10,041		10,041 D		100.0%		100.0%
14,008	VAN BUREN	1,466		1,464	2	1,464 D		99.9%		100.0%
113,409	WASHINGTON	23,320		23,320		23,320 D		100.0%		100.0%
54,676	WHITE	13,540		13,540		13,540 D		100.0%		100.0%
9,520	WOODRUFF	651		651		651 D		100.0%		100.0%
17,759	YELL	5,063		5,062	1	5,062 D		100.0%		100.0%
2,350,725	TOTAL	494,735		493,910	825	493,910 D		99.8%		100.0%

ARKANSAS

CONGRESS

CD	Year	Total Vote	Republican Vote	Republican Candidate	Democratic Vote	Democratic Candidate	Other Vote	Rep.-Dem. Plurality	Total Vote Rep.	Total Vote Dem.	Major Vote Rep.	Major Vote Dem.
1	1990	157,097	56,071	HAYES, TERRY	101,026	ALEXANDER, WILLIAM		44,955 D	35.7%	64.3%	35.7%	64.3%
1	1988					ALEXANDER, WILLIAM						
1	1986	164,719	58,937	ALBIN, RICK	105,782	ALEXANDER, WILLIAM		46,845 D	35.8%	64.2%	35.8%	64.2%
1	1984	124,528			121,047	ALEXANDER, WILLIAM	3,481	121,047 D		97.2%		100.0%
1	1982	191,635	67,427	BANKS, CHUCK	124,208	ALEXANDER, WILLIAM		56,781 D	35.2%	64.8%	35.2%	64.8%
2	1990	171,271	67,800	KEET, JIM	103,471	THORNTON, RAY		35,671 D	39.6%	60.4%	39.6%	60.4%
2	1988	202,364	33,475	CARPENTER, WARREN D.	168,889	ROBINSON, TOMMY F.		135,414 D	16.5%	83.5%	16.5%	83.5%
2	1986	170,146	41,247	HAMAKER, KEITH	128,822	ROBINSON, TOMMY F.	77	87,575 D	24.2%	75.7%	24.3%	75.7%
2	1984	219,079	90,841	PETTY, JUDY	103,165	ROBINSON, TOMMY F.	25,073	12,324 D	41.5%	47.1%	46.8%	53.2%
2	1982	179,688	96,775	BETHUNE, ED	82,913	GEORGE, CHARLES L.		13,862 R	53.9%	46.1%	53.9%	46.1%
3	1990	184,208	129,876	HAMMERSCHMIDT, JOHN	54,332	IVY, DAN		75,544 R	70.5%	29.5%	70.5%	29.5%
3	1988	216,390	161,623	HAMMERSCHMIDT, JOHN	54,767	STEWART, DAVID		106,856 R	74.7%	25.3%	74.7%	25.3%
3	1986	181,856	145,127	HAMMERSCHMIDT, JOHN	36,729	SARGENT, SU		108,398 R	79.8%	20.2%	79.8%	20.2%
3	1984			HAMMERSCHMIDT, JOHN								
3	1982	202,998	133,909	HAMMERSCHMIDT, JOHN	69,089	MCDOUGAL, JIM		64,820 R	66.0%	34.0%	66.0%	34.0%
4	1990	152,495	42,130	ROOD, ROY	110,365	ANTHONY, BERYL F.		68,235 D	27.6%	72.4%	27.6%	72.4%
4	1988	187,166	57,658	BELL, ROGER N.	129,508	ANTHONY, BERYL F.		71,850 D	30.8%	69.2%	30.8%	69.2%
4	1986	148,924	22,980	KEELS, LAMAR	115,339	ANTHONY, BERYL F.	10,605	92,359 D	15.4%	77.4%	16.6%	83.4%
4	1984	119,639			117,123	ANTHONY, BERYL F.	2,516	117,123 D		97.9%		100.0%
4	1982	184,917	63,661	LESLIE, BOB	121,256	ANTHONY, BERYL F.		57,595 D	34.4%	65.6%	34.4%	65.6%

ARKANSAS

1990 GENERAL ELECTION

Governor Other vote was 79 write-in (White) and 22 write-in (Talbot). Data presented in the table are for the amended returns which include the overseas votes.

Senator As state law does not require votes to be tabulated for unopposed candidates, seven counties did not report any votes for David H. Pryor, the unopposed Democratic candidate. Data presented in the table are for the amended returns which include the overseas votes. Other vote was write-in (White).

Congress According to state law, votes are not required to be tabulated for unopposed candidates.

1990 PRIMARIES

MAY 29 REPUBLICAN

Governor 47,246 Sheffield Nelson; 39,731 Tommy F. Robinson.

Senator No candidate.

Congress Unopposed in all four CD's.

MAY 29 DEMOCRATIC

Governor 269,329 Bill Clinton; 190,887 Tom McRae; 9,659 Joe Holmes; 8,629 Jerry D. Tolliver; 8,341 O. O. Wilson; 4,301 Cyrus Young.

Senator David H. Pryor, unopposed.

Congress Unopposed in three CD's. Contested as follows:

  CD 1 72,401 William Alexander; 60,948 Mike Gibson.

CALIFORNIA

GOVERNOR
Pete Wilson (R). Elected 1990 to a four-year term.

SENATORS
Alan Cranston (D). Re-elected 1986 to a six-year term. Previously elected 1980, 1974, 1968.

John Seymour (R). Appointed December 1990 to fill the vacancy created when Senator Pete Wilson (R) was elected Governor in November 1990. Special election to be held in 1992 for the remaining two years of the term.

REPRESENTATIVES

1. Douglas H. Bosco (D)
2. Wally Herger (R)
3. Robert T. Matsui (D)
4. Vic Fazio (D)
5. Nancy Pelosi (D)
6. Barbara Boxer (D)
7. George Miller (D)
8. Ronald V. Dellums (D)
9. Fortney Stark (D)
10. Don Edwards (D)
11. Tom Lantos (D)
12. Tom Campbell (R)
13. Norman Y. Mienta (D)
14. John T. Doolittle (R)
15. Gary A. Condit (D)
16. Leon E. Panetta (D)
17. Calvin Dooley (D)
18. Richard Lehman (D)
19. Robert J. Lagomarsino (R)
20. William M. Thomas (R)
21. Elton Gallegly (R)
22. Carlos J. Moorhead (R)
23. Anthony C. Beilenson (D)
24. Henry A. Waxman (D)
25. Edward R. Roybal (D)
26. Howard L. Berman (D)
27. Mel Levine (D)
28. Julian C. Dixon (D)
29. Maxine Waters (D)
30. Matthew G. Martinez (D)
31. Mervyn M. Dymally (D)
32. Glenn M. Anderson (D)
33. David Dreier (R)
34. Esteban Torres (D)
35. Jerry Lewis (R)
36. George E. Brown (D)
37. Al McCandless (R)
38. Robert K. Dornan (R)
39. William E. Dannemeyer (R)
40. Christopher Cox (R)
41. Bill Lowery (R)
42. Dana Rohrabacher (R)
43. Ron Packard (R)
44. Randy Cunningham (R)
45. Duncan L. Hunter (R)

POSTWAR VOTE FOR PRESIDENT

Year	Total Vote	Republican Vote	Candidate	Democratic Vote	Candidate	Other Vote	Plurality	Total Vote Rep.	Total Vote Dem.	Major Vote Rep.	Major Vote Dem.
1988	9,887,065	5,054,917	Bush, George	4,702,233	Dukakis, Michael S.	129,915	352,684 R	51.1%	47.6%	51.8%	48.2%
1984	9,505,423	5,467,009	Reagan, Ronald	3,922,519	Mondale, Walter F.	115,895	1,544,490 R	57.5%	41.3%	58.2%	41.8%
1980	8,587,063	4,524,858	Reagan, Ronald	3,083,661	Carter, Jimmy	978,544	1,441,197 R	52.7%	35.9%	59.5%	40.5%
1976	7,867,117	3,882,244	Ford, Gerald R.	3,742,284	Carter, Jimmy	242,589	139,960 R	49.3%	47.6%	50.9%	49.1%
1972	8,367,862	4,602,096	Nixon, Richard M.	3,475,847	McGovern, George S.	289,919	1,126,249 R	55.0%	41.5%	57.0%	43.0%
1968	7,251,587	3,467,664	Nixon, Richard M.	3,244,318	Humphrey, Hubert H.	539,605	223,346 R	47.8%	44.7%	51.7%	48.3%
1964	7,057,586	2,879,108	Goldwater, Barry M.	4,171,877	Johnson, Lyndon B.	6,601	1,292,769 D	40.8%	59.1%	40.8%	59.2%
1960	6,506,578	3,259,722	Nixon, Richard M.	3,224,099	Kennedy, John F.	22,757	35,623 R	50.1%	49.6%	50.3%	49.7%
1956	5,466,355	3,027,668	Eisenhower, Dwight D.	2,420,135	Stevenson, Adlai E.	18,552	607,533 R	55.4%	44.3%	55.6%	44.4%
1952	5,141,849	2,897,310	Eisenhower, Dwight D.	2,197,548	Stevenson, Adlai E.	46,991	699,762 R	56.3%	42.7%	56.9%	43.1%
1948	4,021,538	1,895,269	Dewey, Thomas E.	1,913,134	Truman, Harry S.	213,135	17,865 D	47.1%	47.6%	49.8%	50.2%

CALIFORNIA

POSTWAR VOTE FOR GOVERNOR

Year	Total Vote	Republican Vote	Candidate	Democratic Vote	Candidate	Other Vote	Rep-Dem. Plurality	Percentage Total Vote Rep.	Dem.	Major Vote Rep.	Dem.
1990	7,699,467	3,791,904	Wilson, Pete	3,525,197	Feinstein, Dianne	382,366	266,707 R	49.2%	45.8%	51.8%	48.2%
1986	7,443,551	4,506,601	Deukmejian, George	2,781,714	Bradley, Tom	155,236	1,724,887 R	60.5%	37.4%	61.8%	38.2%
1982	7,876,698	3,881,014	Deukmejian, George	3,787,669	Bradley, Tom	208,015	93,345 R	49.3%	48.1%	50.6%	49.4%
1978	6,922,378	2,526,534	Younger, Evelle J.	3,878,812	Brown, Edmund G., Jr.	517,032	1,352,278 D	36.5%	56.0%	39.4%	60.6%
1974	6,248,070	2,952,954	Flournoy, Houston I.	3,131,648	Brown, Edmund G., Jr.	163,468	178,694 D	47.3%	50.1%	48.5%	51.5%
1970	6,510,072	3,439,664	Reagan, Ronald	2,938,607	Unruh, Jess	131,801	501,057 R	52.8%	45.1%	53.9%	46.1%
1966	6,503,445	3,742,913	Reagan, Ronald	2,749,174	Brown, Edmund G.	11,358	993,739 R	57.6%	42.3%	57.7%	42.3%
1962	5,853,270	2,740,351	Nixon, Richard M.	3,037,109	Brown, Edmund G.	75,810	296,758 D	46.8%	51.9%	47.4%	52.6%
1958	5,255,777	2,110,911	Knowland, William F.	3,140,076	Brown, Edmund G.	4,790	1,029,165 D	40.2%	59.7%	40.2%	59.8%
1954	4,030,368	2,290,519	Knight, Goodwin J.	1,739,368	Graves, Richard P.	481	551,151 R	56.8%	43.2%	56.8%	43.2%
1950	3,796,090	2,461,754	Warren, Earl	1,333,856	Roosevelt, James	480	1,127,898 R	64.8%	35.1%	64.9%	35.1%
1946 **	2,558,399	2,344,542	Warren, Earl	—		213,857	2,344,542 R	91.6%		100.0%	

In 1946 the Republican candidate won both major party nominations.

POSTWAR VOTE FOR SENATOR

Year	Total Vote	Republican Vote	Candidate	Democratic Vote	Candidate	Other Vote	Rep-Dem. Plurality	Percentage Total Vote Rep.	Dem.	Major Vote Rep.	Dem.
1988	9,743,598	5,143,409	Wilson, Pete	4,287,253	McCarthy, Leo	312,936	856,156 R	52.8%	44.0%	54.5%	45.5%
1986	7,398,549	3,541,804	Zschau, Ed	3,646,672	Cranston, Alan	210,073	104,868 D	47.9%	49.3%	49.3%	50.7%
1982	7,805,538	4,022,565	Wilson, Pete	3,494,968	Brown, Edmund G., Jr.	288,005	527,597 R	51.5%	44.8%	53.5%	46.5%
1980	8,327,481	3,093,426	Gann, Paul	4,705,399	Cranston, Alan	528,656	1,611,973 D	37.1%	56.5%	39.7%	60.3%
1976	7,472,268	3,748,973	Hayakawa, S. I.	3,502,862	Tunney, John V.	220,433	246,111 R	50.2%	46.9%	51.7%	48.3%
1974	6,102,432	2,210,267	Richardson, H. L.	3,693,160	Cranston, Alan	199,005	1,482,893 D	36.2%	60.5%	37.4%	62.6%
1970	6,492,157	2,877,617	Murphy, George	3,496,558	Tunney, John V.	117,982	618,941 D	44.3%	53.9%	45.1%	54.9%
1968	7,102,465	3,329,148	Rafferty, Max	3,680,352	Cranston, Alan	92,965	351,204 D	46.9%	51.8%	47.5%	52.5%
1964	7,041,821	3,628,555	Murphy, George	3,411,912	Salinger, Pierre	1,354	216,643 R	51.5%	48.5%	51.5%	48.5%
1962	5,647,952	3,180,483	Kuchel, Thomas H.	2,452,839	Richards, Richard	14,630	727,644 R	56.3%	43.4%	56.5%	43.5%
1958	5,135,221	2,204,337	Knight, Goodwin J.	2,927,693	Engle, Clair	3,191	723,356 D	42.9%	57.0%	43.0%	57.0%
1956	5,361,467	2,892,918	Kuchel, Thomas H.	2,445,816	Richards, Richard	22,733	447,102 R	54.0%	45.6%	54.2%	45.8%
1954 S	3,929,668	2,090,836	Kuchel, Thomas H.	1,788,071	Yorty, Samuel W.	50,761	302,765 R	53.2%	45.5%	53.9%	46.1%
1952 **	4,542,548	3,982,448	Knowland, William F.	—		560,100	3,982,448 R	87.7%		100.0%	
1950	3,686,315	2,183,454	Nixon, Richard M.	1,502,507	Douglas, Helen	354	680,947 R	59.2%	40.8%	59.2%	40.8%
1946	2,639,465	1,428,067	Knowland, William F.	1,167,161	Rogers, Will	44,237	260,906 R	54.1%	44.2%	55.0%	45.0%

The 1954 election was for a short term to fill a vacancy. In 1952 the Republican candidate won both major party nominations.

CALIFORNIA

Districts Established January 2, 1983

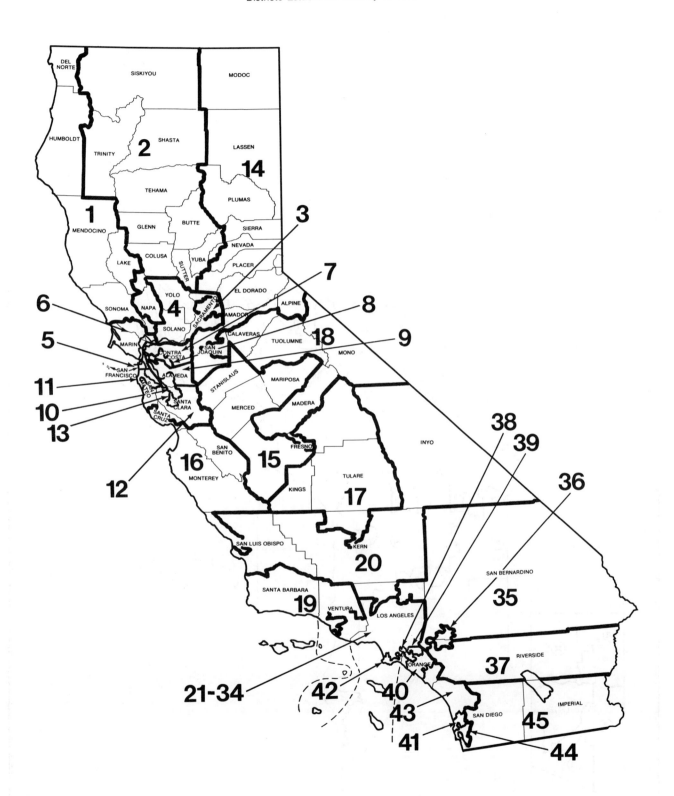

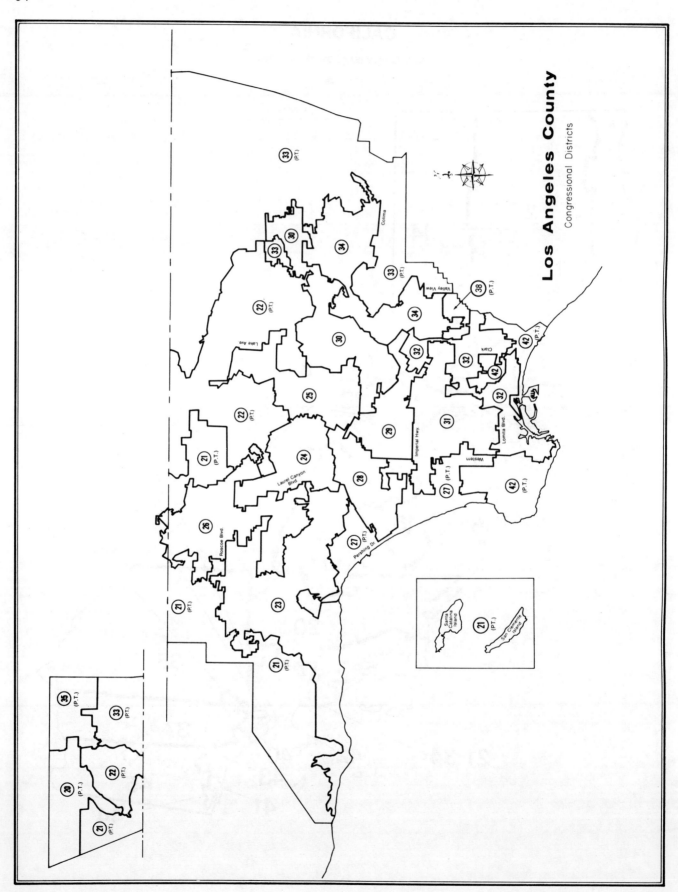

Los Angeles County
Congressional Districts

© ERC

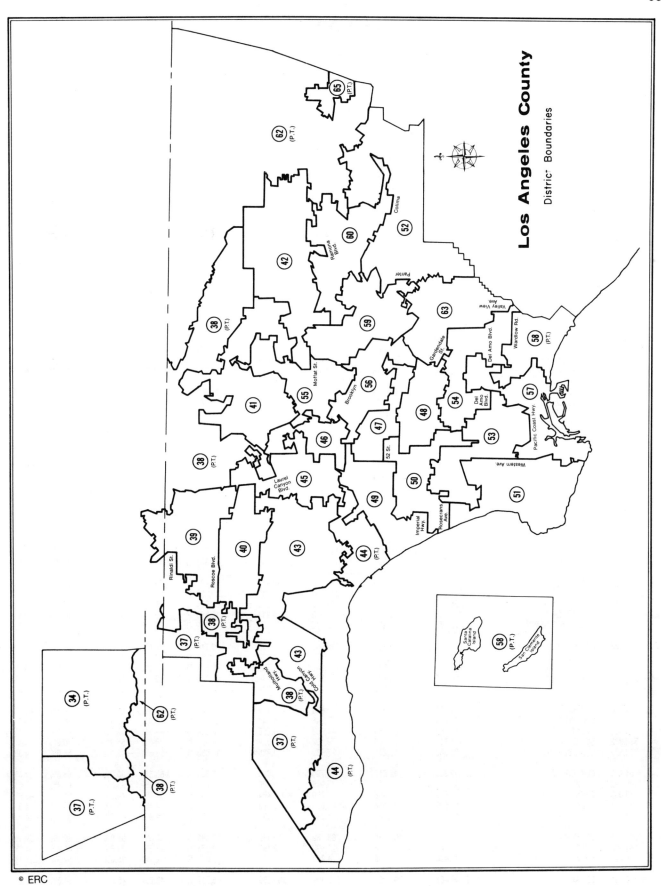

Los Angeles County

District Boundaries

© ERC

CALIFORNIA

GOVERNOR 1990

1990 Census Population	County	Total Vote	Republican	Democratic	Other	Rep.-Dem. Plurality	Percentage			
							Total Vote		Major Vote	
							Rep.	Dem.	Rep.	Dem.
1,279,182	ALAMEDA	370,178	117,107	237,345	15,726	120,238 D	31.6%	64.1%	33.0%	67.0%
1,113	ALPINE	459	242	174	43	68 R	52.7%	37.9%	58.2%	41.8%
30,039	AMADOR	11,981	6,469	4,797	715	1,672 R	54.0%	40.0%	57.4%	42.6%
182,120	BUTTE	63,801	35,048	25,422	3,331	9,626 R	54.9%	39.8%	58.0%	42.0%
31,998	CALAVERAS	13,345	7,071	5,422	852	1,649 R	53.0%	40.6%	56.6%	43.4%
16,275	COLUSA	4,486	2,798	1,455	233	1,343 R	62.4%	32.4%	65.8%	34.2%
803,732	CONTRA COSTA	272,883	119,901	144,268	8,714	24,367 D	43.9%	52.9%	45.4%	54.6%
23,460	DEL NORTE	6,794	3,615	2,717	462	898 R	53.2%	40.0%	57.1%	42.9%
125,995	EL DORADO	47,396	26,452	18,390	2,554	8,062 R	55.8%	38.8%	59.0%	41.0%
667,490	FRESNO	147,782	77,693	63,523	6,566	14,170 R	52.6%	43.0%	55.0%	45.0%
24,798	GLENN	6,862	4,190	2,182	490	2,008 R	61.1%	31.8%	65.8%	34.2%
119,118	HUMBOLDT	49,008	22,943	22,823	3,242	120 R	46.8%	46.6%	50.1%	49.9%
109,303	IMPERIAL	18,044	9,422	7,463	1,159	1,959 R	52.2%	41.4%	55.8%	44.2%
18,281	INYO	7,251	4,566	2,369	316	2,197 R	63.0%	32.7%	65.8%	34.2%
543,477	KERN	121,613	73,065	41,763	6,785	31,302 R	60.1%	34.3%	63.6%	36.4%
101,469	KINGS	17,419	9,771	6,731	917	3,040 R	56.1%	38.6%	59.2%	40.8%
50,631	LAKE	17,710	8,344	8,475	891	131 D	47.1%	47.9%	49.6%	50.4%
27,598	LASSEN	8,519	4,790	3,152	577	1,638 R	56.2%	37.0%	60.3%	39.7%
8,863,164	LOS ANGELES	1,861,893	867,781	911,413	82,699	43,632 D	46.6%	49.0%	48.8%	51.2%
88,090	MADERA	19,850	11,216	7,431	1,203	3,785 R	56.5%	37.4%	60.1%	39.9%
230,096	MARIN	96,720	35,563	57,255	3,902	21,692 D	36.8%	59.2%	38.3%	61.7%
14,302	MARIPOSA	6,430	3,336	2,634	460	702 R	51.9%	41.0%	55.9%	44.1%
80,345	MENDOCINO	28,688	11,723	14,515	2,450	2,792 D	40.9%	50.6%	44.7%	55.3%
178,403	MERCED	33,679	17,054	15,004	1,621	2,050 R	50.6%	44.6%	53.2%	46.8%
9,678	MODOC	3,688	2,115	1,320	253	795 R	57.3%	35.8%	61.6%	38.4%
9,956	MONO	3,091	1,776	1,124	191	652 R	57.5%	36.4%	61.2%	38.8%
355,660	MONTEREY	81,893	34,932	42,371	4,590	7,439 D	42.7%	51.7%	45.2%	54.8%
110,765	NAPA	40,075	18,931	19,017	2,127	86 D	47.2%	47.5%	49.9%	50.1%
78,510	NEVADA	34,058	18,458	13,588	2,012	4,870 R	54.2%	39.9%	57.6%	42.4%
2,410,556	ORANGE	667,030	425,025	208,886	33,119	216,139 R	63.7%	31.3%	67.0%	33.0%
172,796	PLACER	64,382	36,397	24,577	3,408	11,820 R	56.5%	38.2%	59.7%	40.3%
19,739	PLUMAS	8,180	4,243	3,477	460	766 R	51.9%	42.5%	55.0%	45.0%
1,170,413	RIVERSIDE	274,555	157,214	102,847	14,494	54,367 R	57.3%	37.5%	60.5%	39.5%
1,041,219	SACRAMENTO	333,848	167,982	149,215	16,651	18,767 R	50.3%	44.7%	53.0%	47.0%
36,697	SAN BENITO	9,108	4,120	4,445	543	325 D	45.2%	48.8%	48.1%	51.9%
1,418,380	SAN BERNARDINO	301,873	169,028	114,764	18,081	54,264 R	56.0%	38.0%	59.6%	40.4%
2,498,016	SAN DIEGO	672,537	383,959	244,759	43,819	139,200 R	57.1%	36.4%	61.1%	38.9%
723,959	SAN FRANCISCO	226,627	56,652	161,626	8,349	104,974 D	25.0%	71.3%	26.0%	74.0%
480,628	SAN JOAQUIN	113,213	62,249	46,653	4,311	15,596 R	55.0%	41.2%	57.2%	42.8%
217,162	SAN LUIS OBISPO	72,673	38,909	30,140	3,624	8,769 R	53.5%	41.5%	56.3%	43.7%
649,623	SAN MATEO	198,396	80,253	109,963	8,180	29,710 D	40.5%	55.4%	42.2%	57.8%
369,608	SANTA BARBARA	110,474	58,677	46,977	4,820	11,700 R	53.1%	42.5%	55.5%	44.5%
1,497,577	SANTA CLARA	418,892	178,310	218,843	21,739	40,533 D	42.6%	52.2%	44.9%	55.1%
229,734	SANTA CRUZ	80,941	26,797	48,530	5,614	21,733 D	33.1%	60.0%	35.6%	64.4%
147,036	SHASTA	48,961	28,322	17,795	2,844	10,527 R	57.8%	36.3%	61.4%	38.6%
3,318	SIERRA	1,593	813	671	109	142 R	51.0%	42.1%	54.8%	45.2%
43,531	SISKIYOU	15,813	8,320	6,346	1,147	1,974 R	52.6%	40.1%	56.7%	43.3%
340,421	SOLANO	86,482	36,755	44,969	4,758	8,214 D	42.5%	52.0%	45.0%	55.0%
388,222	SONOMA	141,723	54,706	79,093	7,924	24,387 D	38.6%	55.8%	40.9%	59.1%
370,522	STANISLAUS	88,382	47,275	37,182	3,925	10,093 R	53.5%	42.1%	56.0%	44.0%
64,415	SUTTER	19,323	12,647	5,796	880	6,851 R	65.5%	30.0%	68.6%	31.4%
49,625	TEHAMA	16,536	9,415	5,915	1,206	3,500 R	56.9%	35.8%	61.4%	38.6%
13,063	TRINITY	5,622	2,908	2,250	464	658 R	51.7%	40.0%	56.4%	43.6%
311,921	TULARE	65,629	41,186	21,670	2,773	19,516 R	62.8%	33.0%	65.5%	34.5%
48,456	TUOLUMNE	19,780	10,465	8,294	1,021	2,171 R	52.9%	41.9%	55.8%	44.2%
669,016	VENTURA	184,505	106,234	68,139	10,132	38,095 R	57.6%	36.9%	60.9%	39.1%
141,092	YOLO	44,373	19,316	22,890	2,167	3,574 D	43.5%	51.6%	45.8%	54.2%
58,228	YUBA	12,420	7,355	4,342	723	3,013 R	59.2%	35.0%	62.9%	37.1%
29,760,021	TOTAL	7,699,467	3,791,904	3,525,197	382,366	266,707 R	49.2%	45.8%	51.8%	48.2%

LOS ANGELES COUNTY

GOVERNOR 1990

1990 Census Population	Assembly District	Total Vote	Republican	Democratic	Other	Rep.-Dem. Plurality	Percentage			
							Total Vote		Major Vote	
							Rep.	Dem.	Rep.	Dem.
	DISTRICT 34 (PART)	51,327	32,880	14,969	3,478	17,911 R	64.1%	29.2%	68.7%	31.3%
	DISTRICT 37 (PART)	68,974	41,921	23,896	3,157	18,025 R	60.8%	34.6%	63.7%	36.3%
	DISTRICT 38	104,688	58,676	41,573	4,439	17,103 R	56.0%	39.7%	58.5%	41.5%
	DISTRICT 39	60,546	28,595	28,792	3,159	197 D	47.2%	47.6%	49.8%	50.2%
	DISTRICT 40	75,680	30,749	41,634	3,297	10,885 D	40.6%	55.0%	42.5%	57.5%
	DISTRICT 41	95,492	55,858	35,824	3,810	20,034 R	58.5%	37.5%	60.9%	39.1%
	DISTRICT 42	89,214	54,435	30,669	4,110	23,766 R	61.0%	34.4%	64.0%	36.0%
	DISTRICT 43	113,680	44,351	66,446	2,883	22,095 D	39.0%	58.5%	40.0%	60.0%
	DISTRICT 44	109,519	38,536	67,243	3,740	28,707 D	35.2%	61.4%	36.4%	63.6%
	DISTRICT 45	85,982	28,177	54,691	3,114	26,514 D	32.8%	63.6%	34.0%	66.0%
	DISTRICT 46	31,775	11,934	18,591	1,250	6,657 D	37.6%	58.5%	39.1%	60.9%
	DISTRICT 47	28,006	4,795	22,414	797	17,619 D	17.1%	80.0%	17.6%	82.4%
	DISTRICT 48	36,347	6,953	27,966	1,428	21,013 D	19.1%	76.9%	19.9%	80.1%
	DISTRICT 49	80,194	21,229	56,437	2,528	35,208 D	26.5%	70.4%	27.3%	72.7%
	DISTRICT 50	60,012	15,803	41,860	2,349	26,057 D	26.3%	69.8%	27.4%	72.6%
	DISTRICT 51	112,052	69,386	38,019	4,647	31,367 R	61.9%	33.9%	64.6%	35.4%
	DISTRICT 52	87,983	52,843	30,742	4,398	22,101 R	60.1%	34.9%	63.2%	36.8%
	DISTRICT 53	65,033	29,050	32,560	3,423	3,510 D	44.7%	50.1%	47.2%	52.8%
	DISTRICT 54	65,220	29,493	32,396	3,331	2,903 D	45.2%	49.7%	47.7%	52.3%
	DISTRICT 55	45,821	16,087	27,086	2,648	10,999 D	35.1%	59.1%	37.3%	62.7%
	DISTRICT 56	21,478	6,435	13,984	1,059	7,549 D	30.0%	65.1%	31.5%	68.5%
	DISTRICT 57	53,134	23,240	27,025	2,869	3,785 D	43.7%	50.9%	46.2%	53.8%
	DISTRICT 58 (PART)	58,173	30,917	24,755	2,501	6,162 R	53.1%	42.6%	55.5%	44.5%
	DISTRICT 59	61,091	26,708	30,984	3,399	4,276 D	43.7%	50.7%	46.3%	53.7%
	DISTRICT 60	44,353	20,418	20,994	2,941	576 D	46.0%	47.3%	49.3%	50.7%
	DISTRICT 62 (PART)	77,909	46,007	28,166	3,736	17,841 R	59.1%	36.2%	62.0%	38.0%
	DISTRICT 63	68,581	37,664	27,301	3,616	10,363 R	54.9%	39.8%	58.0%	42.0%
	DISTRICT 65 (PART)	9,578	4,641	4,396	541	245 R	48.5%	45.9%	51.4%	48.6%
8,863,164	TOTAL	1,861,893	867,781	911,413	82,699	43,632 D	46.6%	49.0%	48.8%	51.2%

CALIFORNIA

CONGRESS

CD	Year	Total Vote	Republican Vote	Republican Candidate	Democratic Vote	Democratic Candidate	Other Vote	Rep.-Dem. Plurality	Percentage Total Vote Rep.	Dem.	Major Vote Rep.	Dem.
1	1990	230,261	99,782	RIGGS, FRANK	96,468	BOSCO, DOUGLAS H.	34,011	3,314 R	43.3%	41.9%	50.8%	49.2%
1	1988	254,154	72,189	VANDERBILT, SAMUEL	159,815	BOSCO, DOUGLAS H.	22,150	87,626 D	28.4%	62.9%	31.1%	68.9%
1	1986	204,759	54,436	SAMPSON, FLOYD G.	138,174	BOSCO, DOUGLAS H.	12,149	83,738 D	26.6%	67.5%	28.3%	71.7%
1	1984	252,223	95,186	REDICK, DAVID	157,037	BOSCO, DOUGLAS H.		61,851 D	37.7%	62.3%	37.7%	62.3%
2	1990	209,401	133,315	HERGER, WALLY	65,333	RUSH, ERWIN E.	10,753	67,982 R	63.7%	31.2%	67.1%	32.9%
2	1988	236,351	139,010	HERGER, WALLY	91,088	MEYER, WAYNE	6,253	47,922 R	58.8%	38.5%	60.4%	39.6%
2	1986	188,414	109,758	HERGER, WALLY	74,602	SWENDIMAN, STEPHEN C.	4,054	35,156 R	58.3%	39.6%	59.5%	40.5%
2	1984	228,472	158,679	CHAPPIE, EUGENE A.	69,793	COZAD, HARRY		88,886 R	69.5%	30.5%	69.5%	30.5%
3	1990	219,088	76,148	LANDOWSKI, LOWELL	132,143	MATSUI, ROBERT T.	10,797	55,995 D	34.8%	60.3%	36.6%	63.4%
3	1988	257,766	74,296	LANDOWSKI, LOWELL	183,470	MATSUI, ROBERT T.		109,174 D	28.8%	71.2%	28.8%	71.2%
3	1986	208,974	50,265	LANDOWSKI, LOWELL	158,709	MATSUI, ROBERT T.		108,444 D	24.1%	75.9%	24.1%	75.9%
3	1984	131,565			131,369	MATSUI, ROBERT T.	196	131,369 D		99.9%		100.0%
4	1990	210,454	82,738	BAUGHMAN, MARK	115,090	FAZIO, VIC	12,626	32,352 D	39.3%	54.7%	41.8%	58.2%
4	1988	182,490			181,184	FAZIO, VIC	1,306	181,184 D		99.3%		100.0%
4	1986	182,960	54,596	HITE, JACK D.	128,364	FAZIO, VIC		73,768 D	29.8%	70.2%	29.8%	70.2%
4	1984	211,921	77,773	CANFIELD, ROGER B.	130,109	FAZIO, VIC	4,039	52,336 D	36.7%	61.4%	37.4%	62.6%
5	1990	156,304	35,671	NICHOLS, ALAN	120,633	PELOSI, NANCY		84,962 D	22.8%	77.2%	22.8%	77.2%
5	1988	174,758	33,692	O'NEILL, BRUCE M.	133,530	PELOSI, NANCY	7,536	99,838 D	19.3%	76.4%	20.1%	79.9%
5	1986	163,214	36,039	GARZA, MIKE	122,688	BURTON, SALA	4,487	86,649 D	22.1%	75.2%	22.7%	77.3%
5	1984	193,204	45,930	SPINOSA, TOM	139,692	BURTON, SALA	7,582	93,762 D	23.8%	72.3%	24.7%	75.3%
6	1990	201,708	64,402	BOERUM, BILL	137,306	BOXER, BARBARA		72,904 D	31.9%	68.1%	31.9%	68.1%
6	1988	240,819	64,174	STEINMETZ, WILLIAM	176,645	BOXER, BARBARA		112,471 D	26.6%	73.4%	26.6%	73.4%
6	1986	193,552	50,606	ERNST, FRANKLIN	142,946	BOXER, BARBARA		92,340 D	26.1%	73.9%	26.1%	73.9%
6	1984	239,096	71,011	BINDERUP, DOUGLAS	162,511	BOXER, BARBARA	5,574	91,500 D	29.7%	68.0%	30.4%	69.6%
7	1990	200,111	79,031	PAYTON, ROGER A.	121,080	MILLER, GEORGE		42,049 D	39.5%	60.5%	39.5%	60.5%
7	1988	248,484	78,478	LAST, JEAN	170,006	MILLER, GEORGE		91,528 D	31.6%	68.4%	31.6%	68.4%
7	1986	186,553	62,379	THAKAR, ROSEMARY	124,174	MILLER, GEORGE		61,795 D	33.4%	66.6%	33.4%	66.6%
7	1984	241,244	78,985	THAKAR, ROSEMARY	158,306	MILLER, GEORGE	3,953	79,321 D	32.7%	65.6%	33.3%	66.7%
8	1990	195,189	75,544	GALEWSKI, BARBARA	119,645	DELLUMS, RONALD V.		44,101 D	38.7%	61.3%	38.7%	61.3%
8	1988	245,196	76,531	CUDDIHY, JOHN J.	163,221	DELLUMS, RONALD V.	5,444	86,690 D	31.2%	66.6%	31.9%	68.1%
8	1986	202,935	76,850	EIGENBERG, STEVEN	121,790	DELLUMS, RONALD V.	4,295	44,940 D	37.9%	60.0%	38.7%	61.3%
8	1984	239,223	94,907	CONNOR, CHARLES	144,316	DELLUMS, RONALD V.		49,409 D	39.7%	60.3%	39.7%	60.3%
9	1990	162,151	67,412	ROMERO, VICTOR	94,739	STARK, FORTNEY		27,327 D	41.6%	58.4%	41.6%	58.4%
9	1988	209,522	56,656	HERTZ, HOWARD	152,866	STARK, FORTNEY		96,210 D	27.0%	73.0%	27.0%	73.0%
9	1986	162,790	49,300	WILLIAMS, DAVID M.	113,490	STARK, FORTNEY		64,190 D	30.3%	69.7%	30.3%	69.7%
9	1984	195,308	51,399	BEAVER, J. T.	136,511	STARK, FORTNEY	7,398	85,112 D	26.3%	69.9%	27.4%	72.6%
10	1990	130,637	48,747	PATROSSO, MARK	81,875	EDWARDS, DON	15	33,128 D	37.3%	62.7%	37.3%	62.7%
10	1988	165,301			142,500	EDWARDS, DON	22,801	142,500 D		86.2%		100.0%
10	1986	119,564	31,826	LA CRONE, MICHAEL R.	84,240	EDWARDS, DON	3,498	52,414 D	26.6%	70.5%	27.4%	72.6%
10	1984	164,177	56,256	HERRIOTT, BOB	102,469	EDWARDS, DON	5,452	46,213 D	34.3%	62.4%	35.4%	64.6%
11	1990	159,365	45,818	QURAISHI, G. M.	105,029	LANTOS, TOM	8,518	59,211 D	28.8%	65.9%	30.4%	69.6%
11	1988	205,471	50,505	QURAISHI, G. M.	145,484	LANTOS, TOM	9,482	94,979 D	24.6%	70.8%	25.8%	74.2%
11	1986	151,695	39,315	QURAISHI, G. M.	112,380	LANTOS, TOM		73,065 D	25.9%	74.1%	25.9%	74.1%
11	1984	211,115	59,625	HICKEY, JOHN J.	147,607	LANTOS, TOM	3,883	87,982 D	28.2%	69.9%	28.8%	71.2%
12	1990	205,698	125,157	CAMPBELL, TOM	69,270	PALMER, ROBERT	11,271	55,887 R	60.8%	33.7%	64.4%	35.6%
12	1988	263,930	136,384	CAMPBELL, TOM	121,523	ESHOO, ANNA G.	6,023	14,861 R	51.7%	46.0%	52.9%	47.1%
12	1986	187,043	111,252	KONNYU, ERNEST L.	69,564	WEIL, LANCE T.	6,227	41,688 R	59.5%	37.2%	61.5%	38.5%
12	1984	252,693	155,795	ZSCHAU, ED	91,026	CARNOY, MARTIN	5,872	64,769 R	61.7%	36.0%	63.1%	36.9%

CALIFORNIA

CONGRESS

CD	Year	Total Vote	Republican Vote	Republican Candidate	Democratic Vote	Democratic Candidate	Other Vote	Rep.-Dem. Plurality	Total Vote Rep.	Total Vote Dem.	Major Vote Rep.	Major Vote Dem.
13	1990	167,646	59,773	SMITH, DAVID E.	97,286	MINETA, NORMAN Y.	10,587	37,513 D	35.7%	58.0%	38.1%	61.9%
13	1988	214,522	63,959	SOMMER, LUKE	143,980	MINETA, NORMAN Y.	6,583	80,021 D	29.8%	67.1%	30.8%	69.2%
13	1986	154,450	46,754	NASH, BOB	107,696	MINETA, NORMAN Y.		60,942 D	30.3%	69.7%	30.3%	69.7%
13	1984	214,353	70,666	WILLIAMS, JOHN D.	139,851	MINETA, NORMAN Y.	3,836	69,185 D	33.0%	65.2%	33.6%	66.4%
14	1990	248,781	128,039	DOOLITTLE, JOHN T.	120,742	MALBERG, PATRICIA		7,297 R	51.5%	48.5%	51.5%	48.5%
14	1988	277,775	173,876	SHUMWAY, NORMAN D.	103,899	MALBERG, PATRICIA		69,977 R	62.6%	37.4%	62.6%	37.4%
14	1986	205,161	146,906	SHUMWAY, NORMAN D.	53,597	STEELE, BILL	4,658	93,309 R	71.6%	26.1%	73.3%	26.7%
14	1984	244,476	179,238	SHUMWAY, NORMAN D.	58,384	CARLSON, RUTH	6,854	120,854 R	73.3%	23.9%	75.4%	24.6%
15	1990	146,781	49,634	BURRIS, CLIFF	97,147	CONDIT, GARY A.		47,513 D	33.8%	66.2%	33.8%	66.2%
15	1988	170,193	47,957	HARNER, CAROL	118,710	COELHO, TONY	3,526	70,753 D	28.2%	69.8%	28.8%	71.2%
15	1986	131,775	35,793	HARNER, CAROL	93,600	COELHO, TONY	2,382	57,807 D	27.2%	71.0%	27.7%	72.3%
15	1984	167,406	54,730	HARNER, CAROL	109,590	COELHO, TONY	3,086	54,860 D	32.7%	65.5%	33.3%	66.7%
16	1990	181,002	39,885	REISS, JERRY M.	134,236	PANETTA, LEON E.	6,881	94,351 D	22.0%	74.2%	22.9%	77.1%
16	1988	225,827	48,375	MONTEITH, STANLEY	177,452	PANETTA, LEON E.		129,077 D	21.4%	78.6%	21.4%	78.6%
16	1986	163,498	31,386	DARRIGO, LOUIS	128,151	PANETTA, LEON E.	3,961	96,765 D	19.2%	78.4%	19.7%	80.3%
16	1984	216,687	60,065	RAMSEY, PATRICIA S.	153,377	PANETTA, LEON E.	3,245	93,312 D	27.7%	70.8%	28.1%	71.9%
17	1990	151,459	68,848	PASHAYAN, CHARLES	82,611	DOOLEY, CALVIN		13,763 D	45.5%	54.5%	45.5%	54.5%
17	1988	181,298	129,568	PASHAYAN, CHARLES	51,730	LAVERY, VINCENT		77,838 R	71.5%	28.5%	71.5%	28.5%
17	1986	147,469	88,787	PASHAYAN, CHARLES	58,682	HARTNETT, JOHN		30,105 R	60.2%	39.8%	60.2%	39.8%
17	1984	177,690	128,802	PASHAYAN, CHARLES	48,888	LAKRITZ, SIMON		79,914 R	72.5%	27.5%	72.5%	27.5%
18	1990	98,804			98,804	LEHMAN, RICHARD		98,804 D		100.0%		100.0%
18	1988	179,749	54,034	LINN, DAVID A.	125,715	LEHMAN, RICHARD		71,681 D	30.1%	69.9%	30.1%	69.9%
18	1986	142,387	40,907	CREVELT, DAVID C.	101,480	LEHMAN, RICHARD		60,573 D	28.7%	71.3%	28.7%	71.3%
18	1984	190,525	62,339	EWEN, DALE L.	128,186	LEHMAN, RICHARD		65,847 D	32.7%	67.3%	32.7%	67.3%
19	1990	173,245	94,599	LAGOMARSINO, ROBERT J.	76,991	FERGUSON, ANITA P.	1,655	17,608 R	54.6%	44.4%	55.1%	44.9%
19	1988	230,924	116,026	LAGOMARSINO, ROBERT J.	112,033	HART, GARY K.	2,865	3,993 R	50.2%	48.5%	50.9%	49.1%
19	1986	170,538	122,578	LAGOMARSINO, ROBERT J.	45,619	NORRIS, WAYNE B.	2,341	76,959 R	71.9%	26.8%	72.9%	27.1%
19	1984	227,626	153,187	LAGOMARSINO, ROBERT J.	70,278	CAREY, JAMES C.	4,161	82,909 R	67.3%	30.9%	68.6%	31.4%
20	1990	188,925	112,962	THOMAS, WILLIAM M.	65,101	THOMAS, MICHAEL A.	10,862	47,861 R	59.8%	34.5%	63.4%	36.6%
20	1988	229,006	162,779	THOMAS, WILLIAM M.	62,037	REID, LITA	4,190	100,742 R	71.1%	27.1%	72.4%	27.6%
20	1986	179,016	129,989	THOMAS, WILLIAM M.	49,027	MOQUIN, JULES H.		80,962 R	72.6%	27.4%	72.6%	27.4%
20	1984	214,039	151,732	THOMAS, WILLIAM M.	62,307	LESAGE, MIKE		89,425 R	70.9%	29.1%	70.9%	29.1%
21	1990	202,611	118,326	GALLEGLY, ELTON	68,921	FREIMAN, RICHARD D.	15,364	49,405 R	58.4%	34.0%	63.2%	36.8%
21	1988	262,671	181,413	GALLEGLY, ELTON	75,739	STEVENS, DONALD E.	5,519	105,674 R	69.1%	28.8%	70.5%	29.5%
21	1986	193,101	132,100	GALLEGLY, ELTON	54,497	SALDANA, GILBERT R.	6,504	77,603 R	68.4%	28.2%	70.8%	29.2%
21	1984	239,968	173,504	FIEDLER, BOBBI	62,085	DAVIS, CHARLES	4,379	111,419 R	72.3%	25.9%	73.6%	26.4%
22	1990	180,929	108,634	MOORHEAD, CARLOS J.	61,630	BAYER, DAVID	10,665	47,004 R	60.0%	34.1%	63.8%	36.2%
22	1988	236,811	164,699	MOORHEAD, CARLOS J.	61,555	SIMMONS, JOHN G.	10,557	103,144 R	69.5%	26.0%	72.8%	27.2%
22	1986	191,176	141,096	MOORHEAD, CARLOS J.	44,036	SIMMONS, JOHN G.	6,044	97,060 R	73.8%	23.0%	76.2%	23.8%
22	1984	217,176	184,981	MOORHEAD, CARLOS J.			32,195	184,981 R	85.2%		100.0%	
23	1990	167,093	57,118	SALOMON, JIM	103,141	BEILENSON, ANTHONY C.	6,834	46,023 D	34.2%	61.7%	35.6%	64.4%
23	1988	232,879	77,184	SALOMON, JIM	147,858	BEILENSON, ANTHONY C.	7,837	70,674 D	33.1%	63.5%	34.3%	65.7%
23	1986	184,754	58,746	WOOLVERTON, GEORGE	121,468	BEILENSON, ANTHONY C.	4,540	62,722 D	31.8%	65.7%	32.6%	67.4%
23	1984	228,134	84,093	PARRISH, CLAUDE	140,461	BEILENSON, ANTHONY C.	3,580	56,368 D	36.9%	61.6%	37.4%	62.6%
24	1990	103,875	26,607	COWLES, JOHN N.	71,562	WAXMAN, HENRY A.	5,706	44,955 D	25.6%	68.9%	27.1%	72.9%
24	1988	155,071	36,835	COWLES, JOHN N.	112,038	WAXMAN, HENRY A.	6,198	75,203 D	23.8%	72.2%	24.7%	75.3%
24	1986	118,173			103,914	WAXMAN, HENRY A.	14,259	103,914 D		87.9%		100.0%
24	1984	153,607	51,010	ZERG, JERRY	97,340	WAXMAN, HENRY A.	5,257	46,330 D	33.2%	63.4%	34.4%	65.6%

CALIFORNIA

CONGRESS

CD	Year	Total Vote	Republican Vote	Republican Candidate	Democratic Vote	Democratic Candidate	Other Vote	Rep.-Dem. Plurality	Total Vote Rep.	Total Vote Dem.	Major Vote Rep.	Major Vote Dem.
25	1990	68,717	17,021	RENSHAW, STEVEN J.	48,120	ROYBAL, EDWARD R.	3,576	31,099 D	24.8%	70.0%	26.1%	73.9%
25	1988	99,876			85,378	ROYBAL, EDWARD R.	14,498	85,378 D		85.5%		100.0%
25	1986	82,413	17,558	HARDY, GREGORY L.	62,692	ROYBAL, EDWARD R.	2,163	45,134 D	21.3%	76.1%	21.9%	78.1%
25	1984	103,602	24,968	BLOXOM, ROY D.	74,261	ROYBAL, EDWARD R.	4,373	49,293 D	24.1%	71.7%	25.2%	74.8%
26	1990	127,791	44,492	DAHLSON, ROY	78,031	BERMAN, HOWARD L.	5,268	33,539 D	34.8%	61.1%	36.3%	63.7%
26	1988	180,448	53,518	BRODERSON, G. C.	126,930	BERMAN, HOWARD L.		73,412 D	29.7%	70.3%	29.7%	70.3%
26	1986	150,753	52,662	KERNS, ROBERT M.	98,091	BERMAN, HOWARD L.		45,429 D	34.9%	65.1%	34.9%	65.1%
26	1984	186,452	69,372	OJEDA, MIRIAM	117,080	BERMAN, HOWARD L.		47,708 D	37.2%	62.8%	37.2%	62.8%
27	1990	156,098	58,140	COHEN, DAVID B.	90,857	LEVINE, MEL	7,101	32,717 D	37.2%	58.2%	39.0%	61.0%
27	1988	220,335	65,307	GALBRAITH, DENNIS	148,814	LEVINE, MEL	6,214	83,507 D	29.6%	67.5%	30.5%	69.5%
27	1986	173,320	59,410	SCRIBNER, ROBERT B.	110,403	LEVINE, MEL	3,507	50,993 D	34.3%	63.7%	35.0%	65.0%
27	1984	212,781	88,896	SCRIBNER, ROBERT B.	116,933	LEVINE, MEL	6,952	28,037 D	41.8%	55.0%	43.2%	56.8%
28	1990	95,600	21,245	ADAMS, GEORGE	69,482	DIXON, JULIAN C.	4,873	48,237 D	22.2%	72.7%	23.4%	76.6%
28	1988	144,337	28,645	ADAMS, GEORGE	109,801	DIXON, JULIAN C.	5,891	81,156 D	19.8%	76.1%	20.7%	79.3%
28	1986	121,330	25,858	ADAMS, GEORGE	92,635	DIXON, JULIAN C.	2,837	66,777 D	21.3%	76.3%	21.8%	78.2%
28	1984	149,517	33,511	JETT, BEATRICE M.	113,076	DIXON, JULIAN C.	2,930	79,565 D	22.4%	75.6%	22.9%	77.1%
29	1990	64,672	12,054	DEWITT, BILL	51,350	WATERS, MAXINE	1,268	39,296 D	18.6%	79.4%	19.0%	81.0%
29	1988	106,436	14,543	FRANCO, REUBEN D.	88,169	HAWKINS, AUGUSTUS	3,724	73,626 D	13.7%	82.8%	14.2%	85.8%
29	1986	92,415	13,432	VAN DE BROOKE, JOHN	78,132	HAWKINS, AUGUSTUS	851	64,700 D	14.5%	84.5%	14.7%	85.3%
29	1984	125,559	16,781	GOTO, ECHO Y.	108,777	HAWKINS, AUGUSTUS	1	91,996 D	13.4%	86.6%	13.4%	86.6%
30	1990	78,083	28,914	FRANCO, REUBEN D.	45,456	MARTINEZ, MATTHEW G.	3,713	16,542 D	37.0%	58.2%	38.9%	61.1%
30	1988	120,644	43,833	RAMIREZ, RALPH R.	72,253	MARTINEZ, MATTHEW G.	4,558	28,420 D	36.3%	59.9%	37.8%	62.2%
30	1986	94,985	33,705	ALMQUIST, JOHN W.	59,369	MARTINEZ, MATTHEW G.	1,911	25,664 D	35.5%	62.5%	36.2%	63.8%
30	1984	124,333	53,900	GOMEZ, RICHARD	64,378	MARTINEZ, MATTHEW G.	6,055	10,478 D	43.4%	51.8%	45.6%	54.4%
31	1990	83,987	27,593	SATO, EUNICE N.	56,394	DYMALLY, MERVYN M.		28,801 D	32.9%	67.1%	32.9%	67.1%
31	1988	141,027	36,017	MAY, ARNOLD C.	100,919	DYMALLY, MERVYN M.	4,091	64,902 D	25.5%	71.6%	26.3%	73.7%
31	1986	109,800	30,322	MCMURRAY, JACK	77,126	DYMALLY, MERVYN M.	2,352	46,804 D	27.6%	70.2%	28.2%	71.8%
31	1984	142,349	41,691	MINTURN, HENRY C.	100,658	DYMALLY, MERVYN M.		58,967 D	29.3%	70.7%	29.3%	70.7%
32	1990	110,960	42,692	KAHN, SANFORD W.	68,268	ANDERSON, GLENN M.		25,576 D	38.5%	61.5%	38.5%	61.5%
32	1988	171,349	50,710	KAHN, SANFORD W.	114,666	ANDERSON, GLENN M.	5,973	63,956 D	29.6%	66.9%	30.7%	69.3%
32	1986	132,541	39,003	ROBERTSON, JOYCE M.	90,739	ANDERSON, GLENN M.	2,799	51,736 D	29.4%	68.5%	30.1%	69.9%
32	1984	169,716	62,176	FIOLA, ROGER E.	102,961	ANDERSON, GLENN M.	4,579	40,785 D	36.6%	60.7%	37.7%	62.3%
33	1990	159,157	101,336	DREIER, DAVID	49,981	WEBB, GEORGIA H.	7,840	51,355 R	63.7%	31.4%	67.0%	33.0%
33	1988	219,383	151,704	DREIER, DAVID	57,586	GENTRY, NELSON	10,093	94,118 R	69.2%	26.2%	72.5%	27.5%
33	1986	165,353	118,541	DREIER, DAVID	44,312	HEMPEL, MONTY	2,500	74,229 R	71.7%	26.8%	72.8%	27.2%
33	1984	208,619	147,363	DREIER, DAVID	54,147	MCDONALD, CLAIRE K.	7,109	93,216 R	70.6%	26.0%	73.1%	26.9%
34	1990	91,670	36,024	EASTMAN, JOHN	55,646	TORRES, ESTEBAN		19,622 D	39.3%	60.7%	39.3%	60.7%
34	1988	145,727	50,954	HOUSE, CHARLES M.	92,087	TORRES, ESTEBAN	2,686	41,133 D	35.0%	63.2%	35.6%	64.4%
34	1986	110,063	43,659	HOUSE, CHARLES M.	66,404	TORRES, ESTEBAN		22,745 D	39.7%	60.3%	39.7%	60.3%
34	1984	145,527	58,467	JACKSON, PAUL R.	87,060	TORRES, ESTEBAN		28,593 D	40.2%	59.8%	40.2%	59.8%
35	1990	200,722	121,602	LEWIS, JERRY	66,100	NORTON, BARRY	13,020	55,502 R	60.6%	32.9%	64.8%	35.2%
35	1988	257,268	181,203	LEWIS, JERRY	71,186	SWEENEY, PAUL	4,879	110,017 R	70.4%	27.7%	71.8%	28.2%
35	1986	165,557	127,235	LEWIS, JERRY	38,322	HALL, R. SARGE		88,913 R	76.9%	23.1%	76.9%	23.1%
35	1984	206,467	176,477	LEWIS, JERRY			29,990	176,477 R	85.5%		100.0%	
36	1990	137,370	64,961	HAMMOCK, BOB	72,409	BROWN, GEORGE E.		7,448 D	47.3%	52.7%	47.3%	52.7%
36	1988	191,648	81,413	STARK, JOHN P.	103,493	BROWN, GEORGE E.	6,742	22,080 D	42.5%	54.0%	44.0%	56.0%
36	1986	136,778	58,660	HENLEY, BOB	78,118	BROWN, GEORGE E.		19,458 D	42.9%	57.1%	42.9%	57.1%
36	1984	184,661	80,212	STARK, JOHN P.	104,438	BROWN, GEORGE E.	11	24,226 D	43.4%	56.6%	43.4%	56.6%

CALIFORNIA

CONGRESS

CD	Year	Total Vote	Republican Vote	Republican Candidate	Democratic Vote	Democratic Candidate	Other Vote	Rep.-Dem. Plurality	Percentage Total Vote Rep.	Dem.	Major Vote Rep.	Dem.
37	1990	232,082	115,469	MCCANDLESS, AL	103,961	WAITE, RALPH	12,652	11,508 R	49.8%	44.8%	52.6%	47.4%
37	1988	271,242	174,284	MCCANDLESS, AL	89,666	PEARSON, JOHNNY	7,292	84,618 R	64.3%	33.1%	66.0%	34.0%
37	1986	192,224	122,416	MCCANDLESS, AL	69,808	SKINNER, DAVID E.		52,608 R	63.7%	36.3%	63.7%	36.3%
37	1984	235,863	149,955	MCCANDLESS, AL	85,908	SKINNER, DAVID E.		64,047 R	63.6%	36.4%	63.6%	36.4%
38	1990	104,254	60,561	DORNAN, ROBERT K.	43,693	JACKSON, BARBARA	16,868 R		58.1%	41.9%	58.1%	41.9%
38	1988	147,369	87,690	DORNAN, ROBERT K.	52,399	YUDELSON, JERRY	7,280	35,291 R	59.5%	35.6%	62.6%	37.4%
38	1986	119,464	66,032	DORNAN, ROBERT K.	50,625	ROBINSON, RICHARD	2,807	15,407 R	55.3%	42.4%	56.6%	43.4%
38	1984	162,797	86,545	DORNAN, ROBERT K.	73,231	PATTERSON, JERRY M.	3,021	13,314 R	53.2%	45.0%	54.2%	45.8%
39	1990	174,228	113,849	DANNEMEYER, WILLIAM E.	53,670	HOFFMAN, FRANCIS X.	6,709	60,179 R	65.3%	30.8%	68.0%	32.0%
39	1988	229,359	169,360	DANNEMEYER, WILLIAM E.	52,162	MARQUIS, DON E.	7,837	117,198 R	73.8%	22.7%	76.5%	23.5%
39	1986	176,732	131,603	DANNEMEYER, WILLIAM E.	42,377	VEST, DAVID D.	2,752	89,226 R	74.5%	24.0%	75.6%	24.4%
39	1984	230,677	175,788	DANNEMEYER, WILLIAM E.	54,889	WARD, ROBERT E.		120,899 R	76.2%	23.8%	76.2%	23.8%
40	1990	210,386	142,299	COX, CHRISTOPHER	68,087	GRATZ, EUGENE C.		74,212 R	67.6%	32.4%	67.6%	32.4%
40	1988	270,376	181,269	COX, CHRISTOPHER	80,782	LENNEY, LIDA	8,325	100,487 R	67.0%	29.9%	69.2%	30.8%
40	1986	200,518	119,829	BADHAM, ROBERT E.	75,664	SUMNER, BRUCE W.	5,025	44,165 R	59.8%	37.7%	61.3%	38.7%
40	1984	254,974	164,257	BADHAM, ROBERT E.	86,748	BRADFORD, CAROL A.	3,969	77,509 R	64.4%	34.0%	65.4%	34.6%
41	1990	214,737	105,723	LOWERY, BILL	93,586	KRIPKE, DAN	15,428	12,137 R	49.2%	43.6%	53.0%	47.0%
41	1988	285,761	187,380	LOWERY, BILL	88,192	KRIPKE, DAN	10,189	99,188 R	65.6%	30.9%	68.0%	32.0%
41	1986	196,933	133,566	LOWERY, BILL	59,816	KRIPKE, DAN	3,551	73,750 R	67.8%	30.4%	69.1%	30.9%
41	1984	253,855	161,068	LOWERY, BILL	85,475	SIMMONS, BOB	7,312	75,593 R	63.4%	33.7%	65.3%	34.7%
42	1990	184,286	109,353	ROHRABACHER, DANA	67,189	KIMBROUGH, GUY C.	7,744	42,164 R	59.3%	36.5%	61.9%	38.1%
42	1988	238,621	153,280	ROHRABACHER, DANA	78,778	KIMBROUGH, GUY C.	6,563	74,502 R	64.2%	33.0%	66.1%	33.9%
42	1986	192,711	140,364	LUNGREN, DANIEL E.	47,586	BLACKBURN, MICHAEL P.	4,761	92,778 R	72.8%	24.7%	74.7%	25.3%
42	1984	243,619	177,783	LUNGREN, DANIEL E.	60,025	BROPHY, MARY L.	5,811	117,758 R	73.0%	24.6%	74.8%	25.2%
43	1990	222,138	151,206	PACKARD, RON			70,932	151,206 R	68.1%		100.0%	
43	1988	282,529	202,478	PACKARD, RON	72,499	GREENBAUM, HOWARD	7,552	129,979 R	71.7%	25.7%	73.6%	26.4%
43	1986	187,789	137,341	PACKARD, RON	45,078	CHIRRA, JOSEPH	5,370	92,263 R	73.1%	24.0%	75.3%	24.7%
43	1984	223,517	165,643	PACKARD, RON	50,996	HUMPHREYS, LOIS E.	6,878	114,647 R	74.1%	22.8%	76.5%	23.5%
44	1990	108,711	50,377	CUNNINGHAM, RANDY	48,712	BATES, JIM	9,622	1,665 R	46.3%	44.8%	50.8%	49.2%
44	1988	152,089	55,511	BUTTERFIELD, ROB	90,796	BATES, JIM	5,782	35,285 D	36.5%	59.7%	37.9%	62.1%
44	1986	109,844	36,359	MITCHELL, BILL	70,557	BATES, JIM	2,928	34,198 D	33.1%	64.2%	34.0%	66.0%
44	1984	142,563	39,977	CAMPBELL, NEILL	99,378	BATES, JIM	3,208	59,401 D	28.0%	69.7%	28.7%	71.3%
45	1990	169,659	123,591	HUNTER, DUNCAN L.			46,068	123,591 R	72.8%		100.0%	
45	1988	224,903	166,451	HUNTER, DUNCAN L.	54,012	LEPISCOPO, PETE	4,440	112,439 R	74.0%	24.0%	75.5%	24.5%
45	1986	154,675	118,900	HUNTER, DUNCAN L.	32,800	RYAN, HEWITT F.	2,975	86,100 R	76.9%	21.2%	78.4%	21.6%
45	1984	198,307	149,011	HUNTER, DUNCAN L.	45,325	GUTHRIE, DAVID W.	3,971	103,686 R	75.1%	22.9%	76.7%	23.3%

102

CALIFORNIA

1990 GENERAL ELECTION

Governor   Other vote was 145,628 Libertarian (Thompson); 139,661 American Independent (McCready); 96,842 Peace and Freedom (Munoz); 98 write-in (Britton); 91 write-in (Mahon); 34 write-in (Geraty) and 12 write-in (Solomon). Original unamended returns gave the Mahon write-in vote as 88 and the Peace and Freedom (Munoz) vote as 96,795.

Congress   Other vote was Peace and Freedom (Comingore) in CD 1; Libertarian (Crain) in CD 2; Libertarian (McCann) in CD 3; Libertarian (Bigwood) in CD 4; write-in (James) in CD 10; Libertarian (Genis) in CD 11; Libertarian (Olson) in CD 12; Libertarian (Webster) in CD 13; Libertarian (Brian Tucker) in CD 16; write-in (Lorenz) in CD 19; 10,555 Libertarian (Dilbeck) and 307 write-in (Reid) in CD 20; Libertarian (Christensen) in CD 21; 6,702 Libertarian (Wilson) and 3,963 Peace and Freedom (Jan Tucker) in CD 22; Peace and Freedom (Honigsfeld) in CD 23; Peace and Freedom (Phair) in CD 24; Libertarian (Scott) in CD 25; Libertarian (Zimring) in CD 26; Peace and Freedom (Ferrer) in CD 27; 2,723 Peace and Freedom (Williams) and 2,150 Libertarian (Weber) in CD 28; Libertarian (Boctor) in CD 29; Libertarian (Feger) in CD 30; Libertarian (Lightfoot) in CD 33; Libertarian (Johnson) in CD 35; 6,474 American Independent (Odom) and 6,178 Libertarian (Flickinger) in CD 37; Peace and Freedom (Quirk) in CD 39; Peace and Freedom (Works) in CD 41; Libertarian (Martin) in CD 42; 40,212 Peace and Freedom (Hansen) and 30,720 Libertarian (Arnold) in CD 43; 5,237 Peace and Freedom (White) and 4,385 Libertarian (Wallner) in CD 44; Libertarian (Shea) in CD 45.

LOS ANGELES COUNTY

1990 Population by Assembly District is not available.

Governor   Other vote was 30,157 Libertarian (Thompson); 27,931 American Independent (McCready); 24,560 Peace and Freedom (Munoz) and 51 scattered write-in not available by assembly district.

1990 PRIMARIES

JUNE 5 REPUBLICAN

Governor   1,856,613 Pete Wilson; 107,397 David M. Williams; 79,083 Jeffrey T. Greene; 54,577 Donald L. Bullock; 24,058 William B. Allen (write-in).

Congress   Unopposed in twenty-five CD's. No candidate in CD 18. In CD 18 Mike Eagles received 27 write-in votes but did not qualify. Contested as follows:

CD 1   45,148 Frank Riggs; 13,244 Timothy O. Stoen.
CD 3   26,703 Lowell Landowski; 22,271 Eugene R. Borman.
CD 4   17,494 Mark Baughman; 14,449 Edward A. Anderson; 10,943 Thomas L. Koziol; 5,044 Isaac P. Yonker.
CD 7   38,527 Roger A. Payton; 5,329 Wil Watkins.
CD 8   16,846 Barbara Galewski; 13,528 John J. Cuddihy.
CD 10   11,956 Mark Patrosso; 10,043 Lowell A. King.
CD 11   20,551 G. M. Quraishi; 8,577 Barbara Rathbun-Chiodo.
CD 16   23,548 Jerry M. Reiss; 19,116 Louis Darrigo.
CD 19   47,906 Robert J. Lagomarsino; 6,054 Alan Winterbourne.
CD 20   52,669 William M. Thomas; 19,158 Rod Gregory.
CD 21   45,800 Elton Gallegly; 21,256 Sang Korman.
CD 25   5,504 Steven J. Renshaw; 4,267 Alexander S. Justice.
CD 26   16,457 Roy Dahlson; 7,865 Gary E. Forsch.
CD 27   18,908 David B. Cohen; 10,812 Hans Yeager.
CD 32   14,897 Sanford W. Kahn; 10,758 Jerry Bakke.
CD 35   53,806 Jerry Lewis; 14,361 Mark I. Blankenship.
CD 36   20,330 Bob Hammock; 11,152 Aloysius G. Casey.

CALIFORNIA

CD 37   53,298 Al McCandless; 19,128 Bud Mathewson.
CD 44   11,350 Randy Cunningham; 7,459 Joe Ghougassian; 3,968 Jim Lantry; 1,472 Kenny Harrell; 715 Eric Epifano.

JUNE 5 DEMOCRATIC

Governor   1,361,361 Dianne Feinstein; 1,067,899 John Van de Kamp; 35,900 Frank L. Thomas; 25,396 Charles Pineda; 24,251 Franklin R. Geraty; 19,697 John H. Abbott; 17,987 Charles A. Mahon; 16,280 F. Frank Wong; 16,116 Eileen Anderson; 11,975 Lydon Byrne; 7,923 Mark Calney; 68 Sue L. Digre (write-in).

Congress   Unopposed in twenty-four CD's. No candidate in CD's 43 and 45. In CD 43 Thonas R. Potocki received 374 write-in votes but did not qualify; in CD 45 Hweitt F. Ryan received 215 write-in votes but did not qualify. Contested as follows:

CD 1   62,630 Douglas H. Bosco; 32,394 Lionel Gambill.
CD 3   71,562 Robert T. Matsui; 11,857 James J. Walsh.
CD 4   60,005 Vic Fazio; 16,097 Stan Warner.
CD 12   24,818 Robert Palmer; 22,762 Gary Bond.
CD 14   62,650 Patricia Malberg; 16,645 Robert D. Ingraham.
CD 16   65,159 Leon E. Panetta; 4,848 Arthur V. Dunn.
CD 17   28,907 Calvin Dooley; 13,736 Archie Nahigian; 6,641 Paul M. Laygo.
CD 19   33,051 Anita P. Ferguson; 17,330 Mike McConnell.
CD 20   25,337 Michael A. Thomas; 24,872 Lita Reid.
CD 22   30,157 David Bayer; 6,529 Tom Vournas.
CD 26   43,676 Howard L. Berman; 6,912 Scott M. Gaulke.
CD 29   36,182 Maxine Waters; 2,666 Lionel Allen; 1,115 Twain M. Wilson; 930 Ted Andromidas.
CD 31   30,416 Mervyn M. Dymally; 6,426 Lawrence A. Grigsby; 4,965 Carl E. Robinson.
CD 33   28,495 Georgia H. Webb; 11,031 Garry M. Hamud.
CD 37   40,058 Ralph Waite; 16,203 Jeffrey E. Jacobs.
CD 38   18,048 Barbara Jackson; 9,484 Art Hoffmann.
CD 39   12,921 Francis X. Hoffman; 10,564 John W. Black; 5,642 Anthony J. Roberts; 1,687 Truman Swann.
CD 42   13,994 Guy C. Kimbrough; 13,814 James Cavuoto; 12,608 Bryan W. Stevens.
CD 44   25,419 Jim Bates; 15,209 Byron Georgiou.

JUNE 5 AMERICAN INDEPENDENT

Governor   8,921 Jerome McCready; 7,563 Chuck Morsa.

Congress   Unopposed in all CD's in which candidates were entered.

JUNE 5 LIBERTARIAN

Governor   Dennis Thompson, unopposed.

Congress   Unopposed in all CD's in which candidates were entered.

JUNE 5 PEACE AND FREEDOM

Governor   3,461 Maria E. Munoz; 2,647 Merle Woo.

Congress   Unopposed in all CD's in which candidates were entered except CD 24 as follows:

CD 24   109 Maggie Phair; 76 Vikki Murdock.

COLORADO

GOVERNOR

Roy Romer (D). Re-elected 1990 to a four-year term. Previously elected 1986.

SENATORS

Hank Brown (R). Elected 1990 to a six-year term.

Timothy E. Wirth (D). Elected 1986 to a six-year term.

REPRESENTATIVES

1. Patricia Schroeder (D)	3. Ben N. Campbell (D)	5. Joel Hefley (R)
2. David Skaggs (D)	4. Wayne Allard (R)	6. Daniel L. Schaefer (R)

POSTWAR VOTE FOR PRESIDENT

Year	Total Vote	Republican Vote	Candidate	Democratic Vote	Candidate	Other Vote	Plurality	Percentage Total Vote Rep.	Dem.	Major Vote Rep.	Dem.
1988	1,372,394	728,177	Bush, George	621,453	Dukakis, Michael S.	22,764	106,724 R	53.1%	45.3%	54.0%	46.0%
1984	1,295,380	821,817	Reagan, Ronald	454,975	Mondale, Walter F.	18,588	366,842 R	63.4%	35.1%	64.4%	35.6%
1980	1,184,415	652,264	Reagan, Ronald	367,973	Carter, Jimmy	164,178	284,291 R	55.1%	31.1%	63.9%	36.1%
1976	1,081,554	584,367	Ford, Gerald R.	460,353	Carter, Jimmy	36,834	124,014 R	54.0%	42.6%	55.9%	44.1%
1972	953,884	597,189	Nixon, Richard M.	329,980	McGovern, George S.	26,715	267,209 R	62.6%	34.6%	64.4%	35.6%
1968	811,199	409,345	Nixon, Richard M.	335,174	Humphrey, Hubert H.	66,680	74,171 R	50.5%	41.3%	55.0%	45.0%
1964	776,986	296,767	Goldwater, Barry M.	476,024	Johnson, Lyndon B.	4,195	179,257 D	38.2%	61.3%	38.4%	61.6%
1960	736,236	402,242	Nixon, Richard M.	330,629	Kennedy, John F.	3,365	71,613 R	54.6%	44.9%	54.9%	45.1%
1956	657,074	394,479	Eisenhower, Dwight D.	257,997	Stevenson, Adlai E.	4,598	136,482 R	60.0%	39.3%	60.5%	39.5%
1952	630,103	379,782	Eisenhower, Dwight D.	245,504	Stevenson, Adlai E.	4,817	134,278 R	60.3%	39.0%	60.7%	39.3%
1948	515,237	239,714	Dewey, Thomas E.	267,288	Truman, Harry S.	8,235	27,574 D	46.5%	51.9%	47.3%	52.7%

POSTWAR VOTE FOR GOVERNOR

Year	Total Vote	Republican Vote	Candidate	Democratic Vote	Candidate	Other Vote	Rep-Dem. Plurality	Percentage Total Vote Rep.	Dem.	Major Vote Rep.	Dem.
1990	1,011,272	358,403	Andrews, John	626,032	Romer, Roy	26,837	267,629 D	35.4%	61.9%	36.4%	63.3%
1986	1,058,928	434,420	Strickland, Ted	616,325	Romer, Roy	8,183	181,905 D	41.0%	58.2%	41.3%	58.7%
1982	956,021	302,740	Fuhr, John D.	627,960	Lamm, Richard D.	25,321	325,220 D	31.7%	65.7%	32.5%	67.5%
1978	823,807	317,292	Strickland, Ted	483,985	Lamm, Richard D.	22,530	166,693 D	38.5%	58.7%	39.6%	60.4%
1974	828,968	378,698	Vanderhoof, John D.	441,408	Lamm, Richard D.	8,862	62,710 D	45.7%	53.2%	46.2%	53.8%
1970	668,496	350,690	Love, John A.	302,432	Hogan, Mark	15,374	48,258 R	52.5%	45.2%	53.7%	46.3%
1966	660,063	356,730	Love, John A.	287,132	Knous, Robert L.	16,201	69,598 R	54.0%	43.5%	55.4%	44.6%
1962	616,481	349,342	Love, John A.	262,890	McNichols, Stephen	4,249	86,452 R	56.7%	42.6%	57.1%	42.9%
1958 **	549,808	228,643	Burch, Palmer L.	321,165	McNichols, Stephen		92,522 D	41.6%	58.4%	41.6%	58.4%
1956	645,233	313,950	Brotzman, Donald G.	331,283	McNichols, Stephen		17,333 D	48.7%	51.3%	48.7%	51.3%
1954	489,540	227,335	Brotzman, Donald G.	262,205	Johnson, Ed C.		34,870 D	46.4%	53.6%	46.4%	53.6%
1952	613,034	349,924	Thornton, Dan	260,044	Metzger, John W.	3,066	89,880 R	57.1%	42.4%	57.4%	42.6%
1950	450,994	236,472	Thornton, Dan	212,976	Johnson, Walter	1,546	23,496 R	52.4%	47.2%	52.6%	47.4%
1948	501,680	168,928	Hamil, David A.	332,752	Knous, William Lee		163,824 D	33.7%	66.3%	33.7%	66.3%
1946	335,087	160,483	Lavington, Leon E.	174,604	Knous, William Lee		14,121 D	47.9%	52.1%	47.9%	52.1%

The term of office of Colorado's Governor was increased from two to four years effective with the 1958 election.

COLORADO

POSTWAR VOTE FOR SENATOR

Year	Total Vote	Republican Vote	Republican Candidate	Democratic Vote	Democratic Candidate	Other Vote	Rep-Dem. Plurality	Percentage Total Vote Rep.	Percentage Total Vote Dem.	Percentage Major Vote Rep.	Percentage Major Vote Dem.
1990	1,022,027	569,048	Brown, Hank	425,746	Heath, Josie	27,233	143,302 R	55.7%	41.7%	57.2%	42.8%
1986	1,060,765	512,994	Kramer, Ken	529,449	Wirth, Timothy E.	18,322	16,455 D	48.4%	49.9%	49.2%	50.8%
1984	1,297,809	833,821	Armstrong, William L.	449,327	Dick, Nancy	14,661	384,494 R	64.2%	34.6%	65.0%	35.0%
1980	1,173,646	571,295	Buchanan, Mary E.	590,501	Hart, Gary W.	11,850	19,206 D	48.7%	50.3%	49.2%	50.8%
1978	819,150	480,596	Armstrong, William L.	330,247	Haskell, Floyd K.	8,307	150,349 R	58.7%	40.3%	59.3%	40.7%
1974	824,166	325,508	Dominick, Peter H.	471,691	Hart, Gary W.	26,967	146,183 D	39.5%	57.2%	40.8%	59.2%
1972	926,093	447,957	Allott, Gordon	457,545	Haskell, Floyd K.	20,591	9,588 D	48.4%	49.4%	49.5%	50.5%
1968	785,536	459,952	Dominick, Peter H.	325,584	McNichols, Stephen		134,368 R	58.6%	41.4%	58.6%	41.4%
1966	634,898	368,307	Allott, Gordon	266,259	Romer, Roy	332	102,048 R	58.0%	41.9%	58.0%	42.0%
1962	613,444	328,655	Dominick, Peter H.	279,586	Carroll, John A.	5,203	49,069 R	53.6%	45.6%	54.0%	46.0%
1960	727,633	389,428	Allott, Gordon	334,854	Knous, Robert L.	3,351	54,574 R	53.5%	46.0%	53.8%	46.2%
1956	636,974	317,102	Thornton, Dan	319,872	Carroll, John A.		2,770 D	49.8%	50.2%	49.8%	50.2%
1954	484,188	248,502	Allott, Gordon	235,686	Carroll, John A.		12,816 R	51.3%	48.7%	51.3%	48.7%
1950	450,176	239,734	Millikin, Eugene D.	210,442	Carroll, John A.		29,292 R	53.3%	46.7%	53.3%	46.7%
1948	510,121	165,069	Nicholson, W. F.	340,719	Johnson, Ed C.	4,333	175,650 D	32.4%	66.8%	32.6%	67.4%

COLORADO

Districts Established June 3, 1982

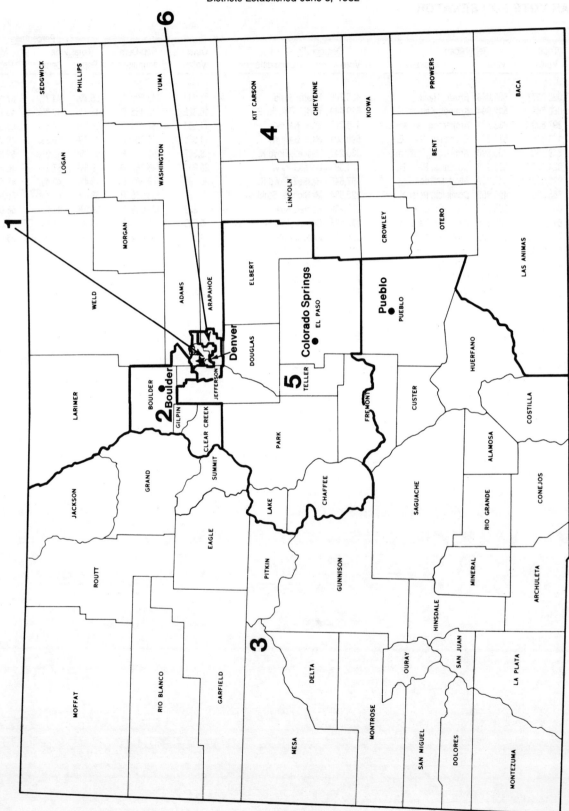

COLORADO

GOVERNOR 1990

1990 Census Population	County	Total Vote	Republican	Democratic	Other	Rep.-Dem. Plurality	Percentage			
							Total Vote		Major Vote	
							Rep.	Dem.	Rep.	Dem.
265,038	ADAMS	64,508	21,423	40,968	2,117	19,545 D	33.2%	63.5%	34.3%	65.7%
13,617	ALAMOSA	4,058	1,267	2,711	80	1,444 D	31.2%	66.8%	31.9%	68.1%
391,511	ARAPAHOE	111,649	37,396	71,709	2,544	34,313 D	33.5%	64.2%	34.3%	65.7%
5,345	ARCHULETA	1,947	802	1,092	53	290 D	41.2%	56.1%	42.3%	57.7%
4,556	BACA	2,357	807	1,509	41	702 D	34.2%	64.0%	34.8%	65.2%
5,048	BENT	1,675	498	1,143	34	645 D	29.7%	68.2%	30.3%	69.7%
225,339	BOULDER	78,317	19,986	56,126	2,205	36,140 D	25.5%	71.7%	26.3%	73.7%
12,684	CHAFFEE	4,637	1,680	2,853	104	1,173 D	36.2%	61.5%	37.1%	62.9%
2,397	CHEYENNE	998	397	580	21	183 D	39.8%	58.1%	40.6%	59.4%
7,619	CLEAR CREEK	3,020	979	1,915	126	936 D	32.4%	63.4%	33.8%	66.2%
7,453	CONEJOS	2,739	898	1,798	43	900 D	32.8%	65.6%	33.3%	66.7%
3,190	COSTILLA	1,510	328	1,148	34	820 D	21.7%	76.0%	22.2%	77.8%
3,946	CROWLEY	1,328	583	722	23	139 D	43.9%	54.4%	44.7%	55.3%
1,926	CUSTER	973	538	412	23	126 R	55.3%	42.3%	56.6%	43.4%
20,980	DELTA	7,816	3,501	4,054	261	553 D	44.8%	51.9%	46.3%	53.7%
467,610	DENVER	136,239	34,600	97,216	4,423	62,616 D	25.4%	71.4%	26.2%	73.8%
1,504	DOLORES	703	216	470	17	254 D	30.7%	66.9%	31.5%	68.5%
60,391	DOUGLAS	19,532	7,599	11,465	468	3,866 D	38.9%	58.7%	39.9%	60.1%
21,928	EAGLE	5,088	1,339	3,612	137	2,273 D	26.3%	71.0%	27.0%	73.0%
9,646	ELBERT	3,233	1,305	1,843	85	538 D	40.4%	57.0%	41.5%	58.5%
397,014	EL PASO	106,810	66,190	38,107	2,513	28,083 R	62.0%	35.7%	63.5%	36.5%
32,273	FREMONT	10,527	5,548	4,730	249	818 R	52.7%	44.9%	54.0%	46.0%
29,974	GARFIELD	8,420	2,780	5,440	200	2,660 D	33.0%	64.6%	33.8%	66.2%
3,070	GILPIN	1,370	588	684	98	96 D	42.9%	49.9%	46.2%	53.8%
7,966	GRAND	3,802	1,405	2,317	80	912 D	37.0%	60.9%	37.7%	62.3%
10,273	GUNNISON	3,361	965	2,295	101	1,330 D	28.7%	68.3%	29.6%	70.4%
467	HINSDALE	415	167	246	2	79 D	40.2%	59.3%	40.4%	59.6%
6,009	HUERFANO	2,186	774	1,373	39	599 D	35.4%	62.8%	36.1%	63.9%
1,605	JACKSON	699	327	362	10	35 D	46.8%	51.8%	47.5%	52.5%
438,430	JEFFERSON	148,013	50,778	92,770	4,465	41,992 D	34.3%	62.7%	35.4%	64.6%
1,688	KIOWA	973	425	546	2	121 D	43.7%	56.1%	43.8%	56.2%
7,140	KIT CARSON	3,147	1,012	2,093	42	1,081 D	32.2%	66.5%	32.6%	67.4%
6,007	LAKE	1,808	451	1,304	53	853 D	24.9%	72.1%	25.7%	74.3%
32,284	LA PLATA	9,947	2,919	6,752	276	3,833 D	29.3%	67.9%	30.2%	69.8%
186,136	LARIMER	60,311	18,825	39,998	1,488	21,173 D	31.2%	66.3%	32.0%	68.0%
13,765	LAS ANIMAS	4,625	1,354	3,111	160	1,757 D	29.3%	67.3%	30.3%	69.7%
4,529	LINCOLN	1,852	675	1,140	37	465 D	36.4%	61.6%	37.2%	62.8%
17,567	LOGAN	6,702	1,984	4,607	111	2,623 D	29.6%	68.7%	30.1%	69.9%
93,145	MESA	31,426	13,541	17,165	720	3,624 D	43.1%	54.6%	44.1%	55.9%
558	MINERAL	455	105	339	11	234 D	23.1%	74.5%	23.6%	76.4%
11,357	MOFFAT	3,353	1,397	1,803	153	406 D	41.7%	53.8%	43.7%	56.3%
18,672	MONTEZUMA	5,068	2,107	2,821	140	714 D	41.6%	55.7%	42.8%	57.2%
24,423	MONTROSE	8,311	3,401	4,644	266	1,243 D	40.9%	55.9%	42.3%	57.7%
21,939	MORGAN	6,828	2,243	4,457	128	2,214 D	32.9%	65.3%	33.5%	66.5%
20,185	OTERO	6,123	2,091	3,905	127	1,814 D	34.1%	63.8%	34.9%	65.1%
2,295	OURAY	1,207	534	649	24	115 D	44.2%	53.8%	45.1%	54.9%
7,174	PARK	2,621	1,071	1,431	119	360 D	40.9%	54.6%	42.8%	57.2%
4,189	PHILLIPS	2,009	598	1,382	29	784 D	29.8%	68.8%	30.2%	69.8%
12,661	PITKIN	3,896	805	2,977	114	2,172 D	20.7%	76.4%	21.3%	78.7%
13,347	PROWERS	4,367	1,236	3,010	121	1,774 D	28.3%	68.9%	29.1%	70.9%
123,051	PUEBLO	42,208	12,519	28,931	758	16,412 D	29.7%	68.5%	30.2%	69.8%
5,972	RIO BLANCO	2,071	869	1,156	46	287 D	42.0%	55.8%	42.9%	57.1%
10,770	RIO GRANDE	3,654	1,220	2,388	46	1,168 D	33.4%	65.4%	33.8%	66.2%
14,088	ROUTT	4,929	1,249	3,546	134	2,297 D	25.3%	71.9%	26.0%	74.0%
4,619	SAGUACHE	1,832	570	1,220	42	650 D	31.1%	66.6%	31.8%	68.2%
745	SAN JUAN	358	145	191	22	46 D	40.5%	53.4%	43.2%	56.8%
3,653	SAN MIGUEL	1,572	364	1,119	89	755 D	23.2%	71.2%	24.5%	75.5%
2,690	SEDGWICK	1,305	477	810	18	333 D	36.6%	62.1%	37.1%	62.9%
12,881	SUMMIT	4,124	1,017	2,996	111	1,979 D	24.7%	72.6%	25.3%	74.7%
12,468	TELLER	4,556	2,687	1,729	140	958 R	59.0%	37.9%	60.8%	39.2%

COLORADO

GOVERNOR 1990

1990 Census Population	County	Total Vote	Republican	Democratic	Other	Rep.-Dem. Plurality	Percentage Total Vote Rep.	Dem.	Major Vote Rep.	Dem.
4,812	WASHINGTON	2,141	1,025	1,083	33	58 D	47.9%	50.6%	48.6%	51.4%
131,821	WELD	35,657	12,532	22,528	597	9,996 D	35.1%	63.2%	35.7%	64.3%
8,954	YUMA	3,906	1,291	2,531	84	1,240 D	33.1%	64.8%	33.8%	66.2%
3,294,394	TOTAL	1,011,272	358,403	626,032	26,837	267,629 D	35.4%	61.9%	36.4%	63.6%

COLORADO

SENATOR 1990

1990 Census Population	County	Total Vote	Republican	Democratic	Other	Rep.-Dem. Plurality	Percentage			
							Total Vote		Major Vote	
							Rep.	Dem.	Rep.	Dem.
265,038	ADAMS	64,429	32,575	29,681	2,173	2,894 R	50.6%	46.1%	52.3%	47.7%
13,617	ALAMOSA	4,195	2,455	1,659	81	796 R	58.5%	39.5%	59.7%	40.3%
391,511	ARAPAHOE	112,781	67,696	42,733	2,352	24,963 R	60.0%	37.9%	61.3%	38.7%
5,345	ARCHULETA	1,955	1,204	694	57	510 R	61.6%	35.5%	63.4%	36.6%
4,556	BACA	2,437	1,617	783	37	834 R	66.4%	32.1%	67.4%	32.6%
5,048	BENT	1,728	963	740	25	223 R	55.7%	42.8%	56.5%	43.5%
225,339	BOULDER	80,445	36,232	42,628	1,585	6,396 D	45.0%	53.0%	45.9%	54.1%
12,684	CHAFFEE	4,657	2,701	1,833	123	868 R	58.0%	39.4%	59.6%	40.4%
2,397	CHEYENNE	1,021	652	352	17	300 R	63.9%	34.5%	64.9%	35.1%
7,619	CLEAR CREEK	3,046	1,631	1,325	90	306 R	53.5%	43.5%	55.2%	44.8%
7,453	CONEJOS	2,967	1,559	1,280	128	279 R	52.5%	43.1%	54.9%	45.1%
3,190	COSTILLA	1,507	548	916	43	368 D	36.4%	60.8%	37.4%	62.6%
3,946	CROWLEY	1,351	904	430	17	474 R	66.9%	31.8%	67.8%	32.2%
1,926	CUSTER	1,006	707	279	20	428 R	70.3%	27.7%	71.7%	28.3%
20,980	DELTA	7,900	4,598	3,103	199	1,495 R	58.2%	39.3%	59.7%	40.3%
467,610	DENVER	135,792	57,994	72,825	4,973	14,831 D	42.7%	53.6%	44.3%	55.7%
1,504	DOLORES	714	379	317	18	62 R	53.1%	44.4%	54.5%	45.5%
60,391	DOUGLAS	19,693	12,752	6,380	561	6,372 R	64.8%	32.4%	66.7%	33.3%
21,928	EAGLE	5,107	2,715	2,279	113	436 R	53.2%	44.6%	54.4%	45.6%
9,646	ELBERT	3,411	2,223	1,087	101	1,136 R	65.2%	31.9%	67.2%	32.8%
397,014	EL PASO	107,593	72,184	32,218	3,191	39,966 R	67.1%	29.9%	69.1%	30.9%
32,273	FREMONT	10,942	6,631	4,052	259	2,579 R	60.6%	37.0%	62.1%	37.9%
29,974	GARFIELD	8,633	4,534	3,930	169	604 R	52.5%	45.5%	53.6%	46.4%
3,070	GILPIN	1,397	661	682	54	21 D	47.3%	48.8%	49.2%	50.8%
7,966	GRAND	3,847	2,334	1,439	74	895 R	60.7%	37.4%	61.9%	38.1%
10,273	GUNNISON	3,374	1,576	1,717	81	141 D	46.7%	50.9%	47.9%	52.1%
467	HINSDALE	430	256	169	5	87 R	59.5%	39.3%	60.2%	39.8%
6,009	HUERFANO	2,246	1,092	1,131	23	39 D	48.6%	50.4%	49.1%	50.9%
1,605	JACKSON	737	521	206	10	315 R	70.7%	28.0%	71.7%	28.3%
438,430	JEFFERSON	148,489	83,212	60,096	5,181	23,116 R	56.0%	40.5%	58.1%	41.9%
1,688	KIOWA	1,008	662	333	13	329 R	65.7%	33.0%	66.5%	33.5%
7,140	KIT CARSON	3,233	2,337	858	38	1,479 R	72.3%	26.5%	73.1%	26.9%
6,007	LAKE	1,820	880	892	48	12 D	48.4%	49.0%	49.7%	50.3%
32,284	LA PLATA	10,051	5,899	3,954	198	1,945 R	58.7%	39.3%	59.9%	40.1%
186,136	LARIMER	61,261	37,159	23,021	1,081	14,138 R	60.7%	37.6%	61.7%	38.3%
13,765	LAS ANIMAS	4,855	2,699	2,043	113	656 R	55.6%	42.1%	56.9%	43.1%
4,529	LINCOLN	1,889	1,328	528	33	800 R	70.3%	28.0%	71.6%	28.4%
17,567	LOGAN	6,859	4,527	2,237	95	2,290 R	66.0%	32.6%	66.9%	33.1%
93,145	MESA	31,741	17,565	13,362	814	4,203 R	55.3%	42.1%	56.8%	43.2%
558	MINERAL	460	266	185	9	81 R	57.8%	40.2%	59.0%	41.0%
11,357	MOFFAT	3,379	1,942	1,316	121	626 R	57.5%	38.9%	59.6%	40.4%
18,672	MONTEZUMA	5,082	2,857	2,068	157	789 R	56.2%	40.7%	58.0%	42.0%
24,423	MONTROSE	8,401	4,767	3,410	224	1,357 R	56.7%	40.6%	58.3%	41.7%
21,939	MORGAN	6,883	4,747	2,020	116	2,727 R	69.0%	29.3%	70.1%	29.9%
20,185	OTERO	6,270	4,128	2,044	98	2,084 R	65.8%	32.6%	66.9%	33.1%
2,295	OURAY	1,215	735	460	20	275 R	60.5%	37.9%	61.5%	38.5%
7,174	PARK	2,586	1,442	1,039	105	403 R	55.8%	40.2%	58.1%	41.9%
4,189	PHILLIPS	2,075	1,371	672	32	699 R	66.1%	32.4%	67.1%	32.9%
12,661	PITKIN	3,953	1,639	2,245	69	606 R	41.5%	56.8%	42.2%	57.8%
13,347	PROWERS	4,470	2,814	1,554	102	1,260 R	63.0%	34.8%	64.4%	35.6%
123,051	PUEBLO	42,491	20,326	21,445	720	1,119 D	47.8%	50.5%	48.7%	51.3%
5,972	RIO BLANCO	2,158	1,401	714	43	687 R	64.9%	33.1%	66.2%	33.8%
10,770	RIO GRANDE	3,843	2,449	1,287	107	1,162 R	63.7%	33.5%	65.6%	34.4%
14,088	ROUTT	4,991	2,522	2,385	84	137 R	50.5%	47.8%	51.4%	48.6%
4,619	SAGUACHE	1,867	1,009	830	28	179 R	54.0%	44.5%	54.9%	45.1%
745	SAN JUAN	365	191	165	9	26 R	52.3%	45.2%	53.7%	46.3%
3,653	SAN MIGUEL	1,597	598	955	44	357 D	37.4%	59.8%	38.5%	61.5%
2,690	SEDGWICK	1,335	880	442	13	438 R	65.9%	33.1%	66.6%	33.4%
12,881	SUMMIT	4,154	2,192	1,873	89	319 R	52.8%	45.1%	53.9%	46.1%
12,468	TELLER	4,591	2,881	1,578	132	1,303 R	62.8%	34.4%	64.6%	35.4%

COLORADO

SENATOR 1990

1990 Census Population	County	Total Vote	Republican	Democratic	Other	Rep.-Dem. Plurality	Percentage Total Vote Rep.	Dem.	Major Vote Rep.	Dem.
4,812	WASHINGTON	2,220	1,524	669	27	855 R	68.6%	30.1%	69.5%	30.5%
131,821	WELD	37,129	25,429	11,084	616	14,345 R	68.5%	29.9%	69.6%	30.4%
8,954	YUMA	3,965	2,776	1,114	75	1,662 R	70.0%	28.1%	71.4%	28.6%
3,294,394	TOTAL	1,022,027	569,048	425,746	27,233	143,302 R	55.7%	41.7%	57.2%	42.8%

COLORADO

CONGRESS

CD	Year	Total Vote	Republican Vote	Republican Candidate	Democratic Vote	Democratic Candidate	Other Vote	Rep.-Dem. Plurality	Total Vote Rep.	Total Vote Dem.	Major Vote Rep.	Major Vote Dem.
1	1990	128,978	46,802	ROEMER, GLORIA G.	82,176	SCHROEDER, PATRICIA		35,374 D	36.3%	63.7%	36.3%	63.7%
1	1988	191,509	57,587	WOOD, JOY	133,922	SCHROEDER, PATRICIA		76,335 D	30.1%	69.9%	30.1%	69.9%
1	1986	155,208	49,095	WOOD, JOY	106,113	SCHROEDER, PATRICIA		57,018 D	31.6%	68.4%	31.6%	68.4%
1	1984	203,873	73,993	DOWNS, MARY	126,348	SCHROEDER, PATRICIA	3,532	52,355 D	36.3%	62.0%	36.9%	63.1%
1	1982	157,597	59,009	DECKER, ARCH	94,969	SCHROEDER, PATRICIA	3,619	35,960 D	37.4%	60.3%	38.3%	61.7%
2	1990	173,474	68,226	LEWIS, JASON	105,248	SKAGGS, DAVID		37,022 D	39.3%	60.7%	39.3%	60.7%
2	1988	235,015	87,578	BATH, DAVID	147,437	SKAGGS, DAVID		59,859 D	37.3%	62.7%	37.3%	62.7%
2	1986	177,255	86,032	NORTON, MICHAEL J.	91,223	SKAGGS, DAVID		5,191 D	48.5%	51.5%	48.5%	51.5%
2	1984	222,859	101,488	NORTON, MICHAEL J.	118,580	WIRTH, TIMOTHY E.	2,791	17,092 D	45.5%	53.2%	46.1%	53.9%
2	1982	163,654	59,590	BUECHNER, JOHN C.	101,202	WIRTH, TIMOTHY E.	2,862	41,612 D	36.4%	61.8%	37.1%	62.9%
3	1990	177,363	49,961	ELLIS, BOB	124,487	CAMPBELL, BEN N.	2,915	74,526 D	28.2%	70.2%	28.6%	71.4%
3	1988	216,909	47,625	ZARTMAN, JIM	169,284	CAMPBELL, BEN N.		121,659 D	22.0%	78.0%	22.0%	78.0%
3	1986	183,861	88,508	STRANG, MICHAEL L.	95,353	CAMPBELL, BEN N.		6,845 D	48.1%	51.9%	48.1%	51.9%
3	1984	214,970	122,669	STRANG, MICHAEL L.	90,063	MITCHELL, W	2,238	32,606 R	57.1%	41.9%	57.7%	42.3%
3	1982	172,889	77,410	WIENS, TOM	92,384	KOGOVSEK, RAY	3,095	14,974 D	44.8%	53.4%	45.6%	54.4%
4	1990	165,186	89,285	ALLARD, WAYNE	75,901	BOND, DICK		13,384 R	54.1%	45.9%	54.1%	45.9%
4	1988	213,754	156,202	BROWN, HANK	57,552	VIGIL, CHARLES S.		98,650 R	73.1%	26.9%	73.1%	26.9%
4	1986	167,761	117,089	BROWN, HANK	50,672	SPRAGUE, DAVID		66,417 R	69.8%	30.2%	69.8%	30.2%
4	1984	205,930	146,469	BROWN, HANK	56,462	BATES, MARY F.	2,999	90,007 R	71.1%	27.4%	72.2%	27.8%
4	1982	151,300	105,550	BROWN, HANK	45,750	BISHOPP, CHARLES L.		59,800 R	69.8%	30.2%	69.8%	30.2%
5	1990	192,277	127,740	HEFLEY, JOEL	57,776	JOHNSTON, CAL	6,761	69,964 R	66.4%	30.0%	68.9%	31.1%
5	1988	241,728	181,612	HEFLEY, JOEL	60,116	MITCHELL, JOHN J.		121,496 R	75.1%	24.9%	75.1%	24.9%
5	1986	173,641	121,153	HEFLEY, JOEL	52,488	STORY, BILL		68,665 R	69.8%	30.2%	69.8%	30.2%
5	1984	208,242	163,654	KRAMER, KEN	44,588	GEFFEN, WILLIAM		119,066 R	78.6%	21.4%	78.6%	21.4%
5	1982	141,871	84,479	KRAMER, KEN	57,392	CRONIN, TOM		27,087 R	59.5%	40.5%	59.5%	40.5%
6	1990	163,273	105,312	SCHAEFER, DANIEL L.	57,961	JARRETT, DON		47,351 R	64.5%	35.%	64.5%	35.5%
6	1988	216,556	136,487	SCHAEFER, DANIEL L.	77,158	EZZARD, MARTHA M.	2,911	59,329 R	63.0%	35.6%	63.9%	36.1%
6	1986	160,531	104,359	SCHAEFER, DANIEL L.	53,834	NORRIS, CHUCK	2,338	50,525 R	65.0%	33.5%	66.0%	34.0%
6	1984	191,760	171,427	SCHAEFER, DANIEL L.			20,333	171,427 R	89.4%		100.0%	
6	1982	159,112	98,909	SWIGERT, JACK	56,598	HOGAN, STEVE	3,605	42,311 R	62.2%	35.6%	63.6%	36.4%

112

COLORADO

1990 GENERAL ELECTION

Governor   Other vote was 18,930 Libertarian (Aitken) and 7,907 Prohibition (Livingston).

Senator   Other vote was 15,432 Concerns of People (Heckman) and 11,801 Prohibition (Dodge).

Congress   Other vote was Populist (Fields) in CD 3; Libertarian (Hamburger) in CD 5.

1990 PRIMARIES

AUGUST 14 REPUBLICAN

Governor   John Andrews, unopposed.

Senator   Hank Brown, unopposed.

Congress   Unopposed in five CD's. Contested as follows:

CD   4   18,592 Wayne Allard; 14,826 Jim Brandon.

AUGUST 14 DEMOCRATIC

Governor   Roy Romer, unopposed.

Senator   116,099 Josie Heath; 82,173 Carlos Lucero.

Congress   Unopposed in all six CD's.

CONNECTICUT

GOVERNOR
Lowell P. Weicker (Connecticut Party). Elected 1990 to a four-year term.

SENATORS
Christopher J. Dodd (D). Re-elected 1986 to a six-year term. Previously elected 1980.

Joseph I. Lieberman (D). Elected 1988 to a six-year term.

REPRESENTATIVES
1. Barbara B. Kennelly (D)
2. Samuel Gejdenson (D)
3. Rosa L. DeLauro (D)
4. Christopher Shays (R)
5. Gary A. Franks (R)
6. Nancy L. Johnson (R)

POSTWAR VOTE FOR PRESIDENT

		Republican		Democratic		Other		Percentage Total Vote		Major Vote	
Year	Total Vote	Vote	Candidate	Vote	Candidate	Vote	Plurality	Rep.	Dem.	Rep.	Dem.
1988	1,443,394	750,241	Bush, George	676,584	Dukakis, Michael S.	16,569	73,657 R	52.0%	46.9%	52.6%	47.4%
1984	1,466,900	890,877	Reagan, Ronald	569,597	Mondale, Walter F.	6,426	321,280 R	60.7%	38.8%	61.0%	39.0%
1980	1,406,285	677,210	Reagan, Ronald	541,732	Carter, Jimmy	187,343	135,478 R	48.2%	38.5%	55.6%	44.4%
1976	1,381,526	719,261	Ford, Gerald R.	647,895	Carter, Jimmy	14,370	71,366 R	52.1%	46.9%	52.6%	47.4%
1972	1,384,277	810,763	Nixon, Richard M.	555,498	McGovern, George S.	18,016	255,265 R	58.6%	40.1%	59.3%	40.7%
1968	1,256,232	556,721	Nixon, Richard M.	621,561	Humphrey, Hubert H.	77,950	64,840 D	44.3%	49.5%	47.2%	52.8%
1964	1,218,578	390,996	Goldwater, Barry M.	826,269	Johnson, Lyndon B.	1,313	435,273 D	32.1%	67.8%	32.1%	67.9%
1960	1,222,883	565,813	Nixon, Richard M.	657,055	Kennedy, John F.	15	91,242 D	46.3%	53.7%	46.3%	53.7%
1956	1,117,121	711,837	Eisenhower, Dwight D.	405,079	Stevenson, Adlai E.	205	306,758 R	63.7%	36.3%	63.7%	36.3%
1952	1,096,911	611,012	Eisenhower, Dwight D.	481,649	Stevenson, Adlai E.	4,250	129,363 R	55.7%	43.9%	55.9%	44.1%
1948	883,518	437,754	Dewey, Thomas E.	423,297	Truman, Harry S.	22,467	14,457 R	49.5%	47.9%	50.8%	49.2%

POSTWAR VOTE FOR GOVERNOR

		Republican		Democratic		Other	Rep-Dem.	Percentage Total Vote		Major Vote	
Year	Total Vote	Vote	Candidate	Vote	Candidate	Vote	Plurality	Rep.	Dem.	Rep.	Dem.
1990 **	1,141,122	427,840	Rowland, John G.	236,641	Morrison, Bruce A.	476,641	191,199 R	37.5%	20.7%	64.4%	35.6%
1986	993,692	408,489	Belaga, Julie D.	575,638	O'Neill, William A.	9,565	167,149 D	41.1%	57.9%	41.5%	58.5%
1982	1,084,156	497,773	Rome, Lewis B.	578,264	O'Neill, William A.	8,119	80,491 D	45.9%	53.3%	46.3%	53.7%
1978	1,036,608	422,316	Sarasin, Ronald A.	613,109	Grasso, Ella T.	1,183	190,793 D	40.7%	59.1%	40.8%	59.2%
1974	1,102,773	440,169	Steele, Robert H.	643,490	Grasso, Ella T.	19,114	203,321 D	39.9%	58.4%	40.6%	59.4%
1970	1,082,797	582,160	Meskill, Thomas J.	500,561	Daddario, Emilio	76	81,599 R	53.8%	46.2%	53.8%	46.2%
1966	1,008,557	446,536	Gengras, E. Clayton	561,599	Dempsey, John N.	422	115,063 D	44.3%	55.7%	44.3%	55.7%
1962	1,031,902	482,852	Alsop, John	549,027	Dempsey, John N.	23	66,175 D	46.8%	53.2%	46.8%	53.2%
1958	974,509	360,644	Zeller, Fred R.	607,012	Ribicoff, Abraham A.	6,853	246,368 D	37.0%	62.3%	37.3%	62.7%
1954	936,753	460,528	Lodge, John D.	463,643	Ribicoff, Abraham A.	12,582	3,115 D	49.2%	49.5%	49.8%	50.2%
1950 **	878,735	436,418	Lodge, John D.	419,404	Bowles, Chester	22,913	17,014 R	49.7%	47.7%	51.0%	49.0%
1948	875,170	429,071	Shannon, James C.	431,296	Bowles, Chester	14,803	2,225 D	49.0%	49.3%	49.9%	50.1%
1946	683,831	371,852	McConaughy, J. L.	276,335	Snow, Wilbert	35,644	95,517 R	54.4%	40.4%	57.4%	42.6%

The term of office for Connecticut's Governor was increased from two to four years effective with the 1950 election. In 1990 Lowell P. Weicker, the Connecticut Party candidate, polled 460,576 votes (40.4% of the total vote) and won the election with a 32,736 plurality.

114

CONNECTICUT

POSTWAR VOTE FOR SENATOR

Year	Total Vote	Republican Vote	Candidate	Democratic Vote	Candidate	Other Vote	Rep-Dem. Plurality	Total Vote Rep.	Dem.	Major Vote Rep.	Dem.
1988	1,383,526	678,454	Weicker, Lowell P.	688,499	Lieberman, Joseph I.	16,573	10,045 D	49.0%	49.8%	49.6%	50.4%
1986	976,933	340,438	Eddy, Roger W.	632,695	Dodd, Christopher J.	3,800	292,257 D	34.8%	64.8%	35.0%	65.0%
1982	1,083,613	545,987	Weicker, Lowell P.	499,146	Moffett, Anthony T.	38,480	46,841 R	50.4%	46.1%	52.2%	47.8%
1980	1,356,075	581,884	Buckley, James L.	763,969	Dodd, Christopher J.	10,222	182,085 D	42.9%	56.3%	43.2%	56.8%
1976	1,361,666	785,683	Weicker, Lowell P.	561,018	Schaffer, Gloria	14,965	224,665 R	57.7%	41.2%	58.3%	41.7%
1974	1,084,918	372,055	Brannen, James H.	690,820	Ribicoff, Abraham A.	22,043	318,765 D	34.3%	63.7%	35.0%	65.0%
1970	1,089,353	454,721	Weicker, Lowell P.	368,111	Duffey, Joseph D.	266,521	86,610 R	41.7%	33.8%	55.3%	44.7%
1968	1,206,537	551,455	May, Edwin H.	655,043	Ribicoff, Abraham A.	39	103,588 D	45.7%	54.3%	45.7%	54.3%
1964	1,208,163	426,939	Lodge, John D.	781,008	Dodd, Thomas J.	216	354,069 D	35.3%	64.6%	35.3%	64.7%
1962	1,029,301	501,694	Seely-Brown, Horace	527,522	Ribicoff, Abraham A.	85	25,828 D	48.7%	51.3%	48.7%	51.3%
1958	965,463	410,622	Purtell, William A.	554,841	Dodd, Thomas J.		144,219 D	42.5%	57.5%	42.5%	57.5%
1956	1,113,819	610,829	Bush, Prescott	479,460	Dodd, Thomas J.	23,530	131,369 R	54.8%	43.0%	56.0%	44.0%
1952	1,093,467	573,854	Purtell, William A.	485,066	Benton, William	34,547	88,788 R	52.5%	44.4%	54.2%	45.8%
1952 S	1,093,268	559,465	Bush, Prescott	530,505	Ribicoff, Abraham A.	3,298	28,960 R	51.2%	48.5%	51.3%	48.7%
1950	877,827	409,053	Talbot, Joseph E.	453,646	McMahon, Brien	15,128	44,593 D	46.6%	51.7%	47.4%	52.6%
1950 S	877,135	430,311	Bush, Prescott	431,413	Benton, William	15,411	1,102 D	49.1%	49.2%	49.9%	50.1%
1946	682,921	381,328	Baldwin, Raymond	276,424	Tone, Joseph M.	25,169	104,904 R	55.8%	40.5%	58.0%	42.0%

One each of the 1952 and 1950 elections was for a short term to fill a vacancy.

CONNECTICUT

Districts Established October 29, 1981

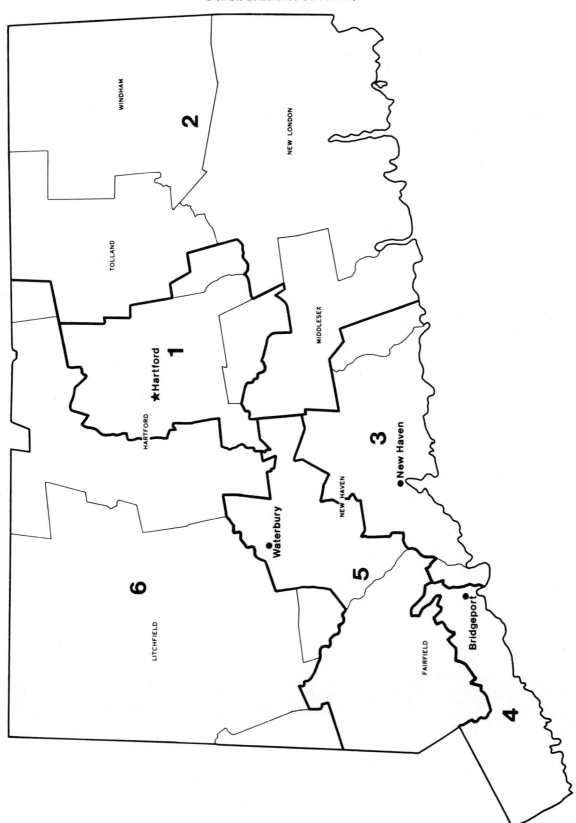

CONNECTICUT

GOVERNOR 1990

1990 Census Population	County	Total Vote	Republican	Democratic	Connecticut	Other	Plurality	Percentage Total Vote		
								Rep.	Dem.	Conn.
827,645	FAIRFIELD	271,189	139,539	42,266	86,523	2,861	53,016 R	51.5%	15.6%	31.9%
851,783	HARTFORD	302,881	82,066	63,656	152,605	4,554	70,539 C	27.1%	21.0%	50.4%
174,092	LITCHFIELD	67,288	28,495	11,817	25,801	1,175	2,694 R	42.3%	17.6%	38.3%
143,196	MIDDLESEX	57,420	16,859	11,805	28,146	610	11,287 C	29.4%	20.6%	49.0%
804,219	WEST HAVEN	282,694	112,419	74,854	90,977	4,444	21,442 R	39.8%	26.5%	32.2%
254,957	NEW LONDON	80,657	25,825	15,805	37,759	1,268	11,934 C	32.0%	19.6%	46.8%
128,699	TOLLAND	45,695	13,232	8,402	23,425	636	10,193 C	29.0%	18.4%	51.3%
102,525	WINDHAM	33,277	9,405	8,036	15,340	496	5,935 C	28.3%	24.1%	46.1%
3,287,116	TOTAL	1,141,122	427,840	236,641	460,576	16,065	32,736 C	37.5%	20.7%	40.4%

CONNECTICUT

GOVERNOR 1990

1990 Census Population	City/Town	Total Vote	Republican	Democratic	Connecticut	Other	Plurality	Percentage Total Vote		
								Rep.	Dem.	Conn.
18,403	ANSONIA	6,575	2,996	1,626	1,848	105	1,148 R	45.6%	24.7%	28.1%
19,483	BLOOMFIELD	8,394	1,427	1,875	5,020	72	3,145 C	17.0%	22.3%	59.8%
27,603	BRANFORD	11,028	3,845	3,024	4,058	101	213 C	34.9%	27.4%	36.8%
141,686	BRIDGEPORT	27,610	9,988	7,965	9,211	446	777 R	36.2%	28.8%	33.4%
60,640	BRISTOL	20,379	5,885	4,712	9,530	252	3,645 C	28.9%	23.1%	46.8%
25,684	CHESHIRE	10,888	5,146	1,553	4,052	137	1,094 R	47.3%	14.3%	37.2%
65,585	DANBURY	17,474	9,326	3,204	4,680	264	4,646 R	53.4%	18.3%	26.8%
18,196	DARIEN	7,696	5,075	531	2,050	40	3,025 R	65.9%	6.9%	26.6%
50,452	EAST HARTFORD	17,407	4,126	4,650	8,101	530	3,451 C	23.7%	26.7%	46.5%
26,144	EAST HAVEN	9,223	2,982	3,505	2,627	109	523 D	32.3%	38.0%	28.5%
45,532	ENFIELD	14,083	4,484	3,095	6,172	332	1,688 C	31.8%	22.0%	43.8%
53,418	FAIRFIELD	21,983	11,295	3,011	7,479	198	3,816 R	51.4%	13.7%	34.0%
20,608	FARMINGTON	8,921	2,652	1,238	4,919	112	2,267 C	29.7%	13.9%	55.1%
27,901	GLASTONBURY	13,166	4,484	1,791	6,785	106	2,301 C	34.1%	13.6%	51.5%
58,441	GREENWICH	21,901	10,169	1,952	9,633	147	536 R	46.4%	8.9%	44.0%
45,144	GROTON	9,672	3,288	1,935	4,284	165	996 C	34.0%	20.0%	44.3%
19,848	GUILFORD	8,333	3,115	1,788	3,363	67	248 C	37.4%	21.5%	40.4%
52,434	HAMDEN	21,430	6,450	6,656	8,088	236	1,432 C	30.1%	31.1%	37.7%
139,739	HARTFORD	23,355	2,880	9,045	11,165	265	2,120 C	12.3%	38.7%	47.8%
51,618	MANCHESTER	20,645	5,745	4,146	10,474	280	4,729 C	27.8%	20.1%	50.7%
21,103	MANSFIELD	5,019	717	1,012	3,252	38	2,240 C	14.3%	20.2%	64.8%
59,479	MERIDEN	18,653	6,880	4,461	6,923	389	43 C	36.9%	23.9%	37.1%
42,762	MIDDLETOWN	14,525	3,186	3,576	7,605	158	4,029 C	21.9%	24.6%	52.4%
49,938	MILFORD	18,854	8,719	4,464	5,449	222	3,270 R	46.2%	23.7%	28.9%
30,625	NAUGATUCK	10,074	5,226	1,946	2,650	252	2,576 R	51.9%	19.3%	26.3%
75,491	NEW BRITAIN	19,686	4,887	5,986	8,470	343	2,484 C	24.8%	30.4%	43.0%
130,474	NEW HAVEN	31,361	5,575	16,184	9,265	337	6,919 D	17.8%	51.6%	29.5%
28,540	NEW LONDON	6,487	1,557	1,781	3,016	133	1,235 C	24.0%	27.5%	46.5%
23,629	NEW MILFORD	7,035	3,717	947	2,247	124	1,470 R	52.8%	13.5%	31.9%
29,208	NEWINGTON	12,776	3,255	2,535	6,826	160	3,571 C	25.5%	19.8%	53.4%
20,779	NEWTOWN	7,972	4,502	847	2,538	85	1,964 R	56.5%	10.6%	31.8%
22,247	NORTH HAVEN	10,019	3,735	2,265	3,917	102	182 C	37.3%	22.6%	39.1%
78,331	NORWALK	22,237	10,672	3,674	7,632	259	3,040 R	48.0%	16.5%	34.3%
37,391	NORWICH	11,073	2,666	2,449	5,758	200	3,092 C	24.1%	22.1%	52.0%
20,919	RIDGEFIELD	8,940	5,419	775	2,636	110	2,783 R	60.6%	8.7%	29.5%
35,418	SHELTON	13,659	8,096	2,053	3,404	106	4,692 R	59.3%	15.0%	24.9%
22,023	SIMSBURY	10,498	3,528	1,091	5,757	122	2,229 C	33.6%	10.4%	54.8%
22,090	SOUTH WINDSOR	9,560	3,024	1,504	4,893	139	1,869 C	31.6%	15.7%	51.2%
38,518	SOUTHINGTON	14,672	5,138	2,864	6,497	173	1,359 C	35.0%	19.5%	44.3%
108,056	STAMFORD	30,324	13,736	5,330	10,909	349	2,827 R	45.3%	17.6%	36.0%
49,389	STRATFORD	19,819	9,580	4,783	5,286	170	4,294 R	48.3%	24.1%	26.7%
33,687	TORRINGTON	12,383	4,426	2,809	4,864	284	438 C	35.7%	22.7%	39.3%
32,016	TRUMBULL	14,400	8,085	1,928	4,182	205	3,903 R	56.1%	13.4%	29.0%
29,841	VERNON	10,312	3,132	2,070	4,961	149	1,829 C	30.4%	20.1%	48.1%
40,822	WALLINGFORD	15,204	5,365	4,208	5,467	164	102 C	35.3%	27.7%	36.0%
108,961	WATERBURY	34,108	17,674	6,436	8,948	1,050	8,726 R	51.8%	18.9%	26.2%
20,456	WATERTOWN	8,036	4,298	1,400	2,164	174	2,134 R	53.5%	17.4%	26.9%
60,110	WEST HARTFORD	30,077	6,673	5,445	17,421	538	10,748 C	22.2%	18.1%	57.9%
54,021	WEST HAVEN	18,991	5,792	7,011	5,899	289	1,112 D	30.5%	36.9%	31.1%
24,410	WESTPORT	10,233	5,025	1,544	3,602	62	1,423 R	49.1%	15.1%	35.2%
25,651	WETHERSFIELD	13,010	3,502	2,296	7,058	154	3,556 C	26.9%	17.6%	54.3%
22,039	WINDHAM	7,209	1,223	2,197	3,672	117	1,475 C	17.0%	30.5%	50.9%
27,817	WINDSOR	10,605	2,786	1,965	5,743	111	2,957 C	26.3%	18.5%	54.2%

CONNECTICUT

CONGRESS

CD	Year	Total Vote	Republican Vote	Republican Candidate	Democratic Vote	Democratic Candidate	Other Vote	Rep.-Dem. Plurality	Percentage Total Vote Rep.	Dem.	Major Vote Rep.	Dem.
1	1990	177,256	50,690	GARVEY, JAMES P.	126,566	KENNELLY, BARBARA B.		75,876 D	28.6%	71.4%	28.6%	71.4%
1	1988	228,448	51,985	ROBLES, MARIO	176,463	KENNELLY, BARBARA B.		124,478 D	22.8%	77.2%	22.8%	77.2%
1	1986	173,787	44,122	KLEIN, HERSCHEL A.	128,930	KENNELLY, BARBARA B.	735	84,808 D	25.4%	74.2%	25.5%	74.5%
1	1984	239,362	90,823	KLEIN, HERSCHEL A.	147,748	KENNELLY, BARBARA B.	791	56,925 D	37.9%	61.7%	38.1%	61.9%
1	1982	186,123	58,075	KLEIN, HERSCHEL A.	126,798	KENNELLY, BARBARA B.	1,250	68,723 D	31.2%	68.1%	31.4%	68.6%
2	1990	176,015	70,922	RAGSDALE, JOHN M.	105,085	GEJDENSON, SAMUEL	8	34,163 D	40.3%	59.7%	40.3%	59.7%
2	1988	225,291	81,965	CARBERRY, GLENN	143,326	GEJDENSON, SAMUEL		61,361 D	36.4%	63.6%	36.4%	63.6%
2	1986	162,098	52,869	MULLEN, FRANCIS M.	109,229	GEJDENSON, SAMUEL		56,360 D	32.6%	67.4%	32.6%	67.4%
2	1984	228,253	103,119	KOONTZ, ROBERTA F.	124,110	GEJDENSON, SAMUEL	1,024	20,991 D	45.2%	54.4%	45.4%	54.6%
2	1982	170,814	74,294	GUGLIELMO, TONY	95,254	GEJDENSON, SAMUEL	1,266	20,960 D	43.5%	55.8%	43.8%	56.2%
3	1990	174,212	83,440	SCOTT, THOMAS	90,772	DELAURO, ROSA L.		7,332 D	47.9%	52.1%	47.9%	52.1%
3	1988	221,669	74,275	PATTON, GERARD B.	147,394	MORRISON, BRUCE A.		73,119 D	33.5%	66.5%	33.5%	66.5%
3	1986	164,087	49,806	DIETTE, ERNEST J.	114,276	MORRISON, BRUCE A.	5	64,470 D	30.4%	69.6%	30.4%	69.6%
3	1984	245,795	115,939	DENARDIS, LAWRENCE J.	129,230	MORRISON, BRUCE A.	626	13,291 D	47.2%	52.6%	47.3%	52.7%
3	1982	181,458	88,951	DENARDIS, LAWRENCE J.	90,638	MORRISON, BRUCE A.	1,869	1,687 D	49.0%	49.9%	49.5%	50.5%
4	1990	138,068	105,682	SHAYS, CHRISTOPHER	32,352	SMITH, AL	34	73,330 R	76.5%	23.4%	76.6%	23.4%
4	1988	205,973	147,843	SHAYS, CHRISTOPHER	55,751	PEARSON, ROGER	2,379	92,092 R	71.8%	27.1%	72.6%	27.4%
4	1986	144,211	77,212	MCKINNEY, STEWART B.	66,999	NIEDERMEIER, CHRISTINE M.		10,213 R	53.5%	46.5%	53.5%	46.5%
4	1984	235,310	165,644	MCKINNEY, STEWART B.	69,666	ORMAN, JOHN M.		95,978 R	70.4%	29.6%	70.4%	29.6%
4	1982	165,907	93,660	MCKINNEY, STEWART B.	71,110	PHILLIPS, JOHN A.	1,137	22,550 R	56.5%	42.9%	56.8%	43.2%
5	1990	181,608	93,912	FRANKS, GARY A.	85,803	MOFFETT, ANTHONY T.	1,893	8,109 R	51.7%	47.2%	52.3%	47.7%
5	1988	222,341	163,729	ROWLAND, JOHN G.	58,612	MARINAN, JOSEPH		105,117 R	73.6%	26.4%	73.6%	26.4%
5	1986	162,035	98,664	ROWLAND, JOHN G.	63,371	COHEN, JIM		35,293 R	60.9%	39.1%	60.9%	39.1%
5	1984	240,657	130,700	ROWLAND, JOHN G.	109,425	RATCHFORD, WILLIAM	532	21,275 R	54.3%	45.5%	54.4%	45.6%
5	1982	173,376	70,808	HANLON, NEAL B.	101,362	RATCHFORD, WILLIAM	1,206	30,554 D	40.8%	58.5%	41.1%	58.9%
6	1990	189,733	141,105	JOHNSON, NANCY L.	48,628	KULAS, PAUL		92,477 R	74.4%	25.6%	74.4%	25.6%
6	1988	236,888	157,020	JOHNSON, NANCY L.	78,814	GRIFFIN, JAMES L.	1,054	78,206 R	66.3%	33.3%	66.6%	33.4%
6	1986	173,437	111,304	JOHNSON, NANCY L.	62,133	AMENTA, PAUL S.		49,171 R	64.2%	35.8%	64.2%	35.8%
6	1984	242,911	155,422	JOHNSON, NANCY L.	87,489	HOUSE, ARTHUR H.		67,933 R	64.0%	36.0%	64.0%	36.0%
6	1982	192,997	99,703	JOHNSON, NANCY L.	92,178	CURRY, WILLIAM E.	1,116	7,525 R	5.7%	47.8%	52.0%	48.0%

CONNECTICUT

1990 GENERAL ELECTION

In addition to the county-by-county figures, data are presented for selected Connecticut communities. Since not all jurisdictions of the state are listed in this special tabulation, state-wide totals are shown only with the county-by-county statistics.

Governor   The data for Governor are presented in a four column (Republican, Democratic, Connecticut and Other) tabulation and the plurality figures are calculated on a first-second party basis. Other vote was 16,044 Concerned Citizens (Zdonczyk) and 21 scattered write-in. Total for the other vote column includes these 21 write-in votes not available by county or city/town.

Congress   Other vote was 1,888 Liberty (Hare) and 5 scattered write-in in CD 5; scattered write-in in all other CD's.

1990 PRIMARIES

Party conventions nominate Connecticut candidates, subject to a system of "challenge" primaries. Any candidate who receives more than 20 percent of the convention vote is entitled to challenge the endorsed candidate in a primary.

SEPTEMBER 11 REPUBLICAN

Governor   John G. Rowland, nominated by convention.

Congress   A challenge primary was held in only one of the six CD's as follows:

   CD   3   7,500 Thomas Scott; 2,851 Gerard B. Patton.

SEPTEMBER 11 DEMOCRATIC

Governor   84,771 Bruce A. Morrison; 46,294 William J. Cibes.

Congress   Candidates in all six CD's nominated by convention.

DELAWARE

GOVERNOR
Michael N. Castle (R). Re-elected 1988 to a four-year term. Previously elected 1984.

SENATORS
Joseph R. Biden (D). Re-elected 1990 to a six-year term. Previously elected 1984, 1978, 1972.

William V. Roth (R). Re-elected 1988 to a six-year term. Previously elected 1982, 1976, 1970.

REPRESENTATIVES
At-Large. Thomas R. Carper (D)

POSTWAR VOTE FOR PRESIDENT

Year	Total Vote	Republican Vote	Candidate	Democratic Vote	Candidate	Other Vote	Plurality	Percentage Total Vote Rep.	Dem.	Major Vote Rep.	Dem.
1988	249,891	139,639	Bush, George	108,647	Dukakis, Michael S.	1,605	30,992 R	55.9%	43.5%	56.2%	43.8%
1984	254,572	152,190	Reagan, Ronald	101,656	Mondale, Walter F.	726	50,534 R	59.8%	39.9%	60.0%	40.0%
1980	235,900	111,252	Reagan, Ronald	105,754	Carter, Jimmy	18,894	5,498 R	47.2%	44.8%	51.3%	48.7%
1976	235,834	109,831	Ford, Gerald R.	122,596	Carter, Jimmy	3,407	12,765 D	46.6%	52.0%	47.3%	52.7%
1972	235,516	140,357	Nixon, Richard M.	92,283	McGovern, George S.	2,876	48,074 R	59.6%	39.2%	60.3%	39.7%
1968	214,367	96,714	Nixon, Richard M.	89,194	Humphrey, Hubert H.	28,459	7,520 R	45.1%	41.6%	52.0%	48.0%
1964	201,320	78,078	Goldwater, Barry M.	122,704	Johnson, Lyndon B.	538	44,626 D	38.8%	60.9%	38.9%	61.1%
1960	196,683	96,373	Nixon, Richard M.	99,590	Kennedy, John F.	720	3,217 D	49.0%	50.6%	49.2%	50.8%
1956	177,988	98,057	Eisenhower, Dwight D.	79,421	Stevenson, Adlai E.	510	18,636 R	55.1%	44.6%	55.3%	44.7%
1952	174,025	90,059	Eisenhower, Dwight D.	83,315	Stevenson, Adlai E.	651	6,744 R	51.8%	47.9%	51.9%	48.1%
1948	139,073	69,588	Dewey, Thomas E.	67,813	Truman, Harry S.	1,672	1,775 R	50.0%	48.8%	50.6%	49.4%

POSTWAR VOTE FOR GOVERNOR

Year	Total Vote	Republican Vote	Candidate	Democratic Vote	Candidate	Other Vote	Rep.-Dem. Plurality	Percentage Total Vote Rep.	Dem.	Major Vote Rep.	Dem.
1988	239,969	169,733	Castle, Michael N.	70,236	Kreshtoll, Jacob		99,497 R	70.7%	29.3%	70.7%	29.3%
1984	243,565	135,250	Castle, Michael N.	108,315	Quillen, William T.		26,935 R	55.5%	44.5%	55.5%	44.5%
1980	225,081	159,004	duPont, Pierre	64,217	Gordy, William J.	1,860	94,787 R	70.6%	28.5%	71.2%	28.8%
1976	229,563	130,531	duPont, Pierre	97,480	Tribbitt, Sherman W.	1,552	33,051 R	56.9%	42.5%	57.2%	42.8%
1972	228,722	109,583	Peterson, Russell W.	117,274	Tribbitt, Sherman W.	1,865	7,691 D	47.9%	51.3%	48.3%	51.7%
1968	206,834	104,474	Peterson, Russell W.	102,360	Terry, Charles L.		2,114 R	50.5%	49.5%	50.5%	49.5%
1964	200,171	97,374	Buckson, David P.	102,797	Terry, Charles L.		5,423 D	48.6%	51.4%	48.6%	51.4%
1960	194,835	94,043	Rollins, John W.	100,792	Carvel, Elbert N.		6,749 D	48.3%	51.7%	48.3%	51.7%
1956	177,012	91,965	Boggs, J. Caleb	85,047	McConnell, J. H. T.		6,918 R	52.0%	48.0%	52.0%	48.0%
1952	170,749	88,977	Boggs, J. Caleb	81,772	Carvel, Elbert N.		7,205 R	52.1%	47.9%	52.1%	47.9%
1948	140,335	64,996	George, Hyland P.	75,339	Carvel, Elbert N.		10,343 D	46.3%	53.7%	46.3%	53.7%

DELAWARE

POSTWAR VOTE FOR SENATOR

Year	Total Vote	Republican Vote	Candidate	Democratic Vote	Candidate	Other Vote	Rep.-Dem. Plurality	Total Vote Rep.	Total Vote Dem.	Major Vote Rep.	Major Vote Dem.
1990	180,152	64,554	Brady, M. Jane	112,918	Biden, Joseph R.	2,680	48,364 D	35.8%	62.7%	36.4%	63.6%
1988	243,493	151,115	Roth, William V.	92,378	Woo, S. B.		58,737 R	62.1%	37.9%	62.1%	37.9%
1984	245,932	98,101	Burris, John M.	147,831	Biden, Joseph R.		49,730 D	39.9%	60.1%	39.9%	60.1%
1982	190,960	105,357	Roth, William V.	84,413	Levinson, David N.	1,190	20,944 R	55.2%	44.2%	55.5%	44.5%
1978	162,072	66,479	Baxter, James H.	93,930	Biden, Joseph R.	1,663	27,451 D	41.0%	58.0%	41.4%	58.6%
1976	224,859	125,502	Roth, William V.	98,055	Maloney, Thomas C.	1,302	27,447 R	55.8%	43.6%	56.1%	43.9%
1972	229,828	112,844	Boggs, J. Caleb	116,006	Biden, Joseph R.	978	3,162 D	49.1%	50.5%	49.3%	50.7%
1970	161,439	94,979	Roth, William V.	64,740	Zimmerman, Jacob	1,720	30,239 R	58.8%	40.1%	59.5%	40.5%
1966	164,549	97,268	Boggs, J. Caleb	67,281	Tunnell, James M., Jr.		29,987 R	59.1%	40.9%	59.1%	40.9%
1964	200,703	103,782	Williams, John J.	96,850	Carvel, Elbert N.	71	6,932 R	51.7%	48.3%	51.7%	48.3%
1960	194,964	98,874	Boggs, J. Caleb	96,090	Frear, J. Allen		2,784 R	50.7%	49.3%	50.7%	49.3%
1958	154,432	82,280	Williams, John J.	72,152	Carvel, Elbert N.		10,128 R	53.3%	46.7%	53.3%	46.7%
1954	144,900	62,389	Warburton, H. B.	82,511	Frear, J. Allen		20,122 D	43.1%	56.9%	43.1%	56.9%
1952	170,705	93,020	Williams, John J.	77,685	Bayard, A. I. duP.		15,335 R	54.5%	45.5%	54.5%	45.5%
1948	141,362	68,246	Buck, C. Douglas	71,888	Frear, J. Allen	1,228	3,642 D	48.3%	50.9%	48.7%	51.3%
1946	113,513	62,603	Williams, John J.	50,910	Tunnell, James M.		11,693 R	55.2%	44.8%	55.2%	44.8%

DELAWARE

One At Large

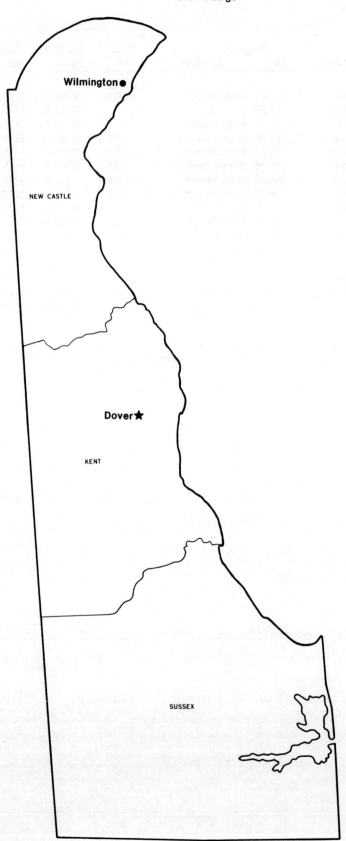

DELAWARE

SENATOR 1990

1990 Census Population	County	Total Vote	Republican	Democratic	Other	Rep.-Dem. Plurality	Percentage Total Vote Rep.	Dem.	Major Vote Rep.	Dem.
110,993	KENT	25,093	10,103	14,537	453	4,434 D	40.3%	57.9%	41.0%	59.0%
441,946	NEW CASTLE	120,121	41,149	77,105	1,867	35,956 D	34.3%	64.2%	34.8%	65.2%
113,229	SUSSEX	34,938	13,302	21,276	360	7,974 D	38.1%	60.9%	38.5%	61.5%
666,168	TOTAL	180,152	64,554	112,918	2,680	48,364 D	35.8%	62.7%	36.4%	63.6%

DELAWARE

CONGRESS

CD	Year	Total Vote	Republican Vote	Republican Candidate	Democratic Vote	Democratic Candidate	Other Vote	Rep.-Dem. Plurality	Percentage Total Vote Rep.	Dem.	Major Vote Rep.	Dem.
AL	1990	177,432	58,037	WILLIAMS, RALPH O.	116,274	CARPER, THOMAS R.	3,121	58,237 D	32.7%	65.5%	33.3%	66.7%
AL	1988	234,517	76,179	KRAPF, JAMES P.	158,338	CARPER, THOMAS R.		82,159 D	32.5%	67.5%	32.5%	67.5%
AL	1986	160,757	53,767	NEUBERGER, THOMAS S.	106,351	CARPER, THOMAS R.	639	52,584 D	33.4%	66.2%	33.6%	66.4%
AL	1984	243,014	100,650	DUPONT, ELISE	142,070	CARPER, THOMAS R.	294	41,420 D	41.4%	58.5%	41.5%	58.5%
AL	1982	188,064	87,153	EVANS, THOMAS B.	98,533	CARPER, THOMAS R.	2,378	11,380 D	46.3%	52.4%	46.9%	53.1%
AL	1980	216,629	133,842	EVANS, THOMAS B.	81,227	MAXWELL, ROBERT L.	1,560	52,615 R	61.8%	37.5%	62.2%	37.8%
AL	1978	157,566	91,689	EVANS, THOMAS B.	64,863	HINDES, GARY E.	1,014	26,826 R	58.2%	41.2%	58.6%	41.4%
AL	1976	214,799	110,677	EVANS, THOMAS B.	102,431	SHIPLEY, SAMUEL L.	1,691	8,246 R	51.5%	47.7%	51.9%	48.1%
AL	1974	160,328	93,826	DUPONT, PIERRE	63,490	SOLES, JAMES	3,012	30,336 R	58.5%	39.6%	59.6%	40.4%
AL	1972	225,851	141,237	DUPONT, PIERRE	83,230	HANDLOFF, NORMA	1,384	58,007 R	62.5%	36.9%	62.9%	37.1%
AL	1970	160,313	86,125	DUPONT, PIERRE	71,429	DANIELLO, JOHN D.	2,759	14,696 R	53.7%	44.6%	54.7%	45.3%
AL	1968	200,820	117,827	ROTH, WILLIAM V.	82,993	MCDOWELL, HARRIS B.		34,834 R	58.7%	41.3%	58.7%	41.3%
AL	1966	163,103	90,961	ROTH, WILLIAM V.	72,142	MCDOWELL, HARRIS B.		18,819 R	55.8%	44.2%	55.8%	44.2%
AL	1964	198,691	86,254	SNOWDEN, JAMES H.	112,361	MCDOWELL, HARRIS B.	76	26,107 D	43.4%	56.6%	43.4%	56.6%
AL	1962	153,356	71,934	WILLIAMS, WILMER F.	81,166	MCDOWELL, HARRIS B.	256	9,232 D	46.9%	52.9%	47.0%	53.0%
AL	1960	194,564	96,337	MCKINSTRY, JAMES T.	98,227	MCDOWELL, HARRIS B.		1,890 D	49.5%	50.5%	49.5%	50.5%
AL	1958	152,896	76,099	HASKELL, HARRY G.	76,797	MCDOWELL, HARRIS B.		698 D	49.8%	50.2%	49.8%	50.2%
AL	1956	176,182	91,538	HASKELL, HARRY G.	84,644	MCDOWELL, HARRIS B.		6,894 R	52.0%	48.0%	52.0%	48.0%
AL	1954	144,236	65,035	MARTIN, LILLIAN	79,201	MCDOWELL, HARRIS B.		14,166 D	45.1%	54.9%	45.1%	54.9%
AL	1952	170,015	88,285	WARBURTON, H. B.	81,730	SCANNELL, JOSEPH S.		6,555 R	51.9%	48.1%	51.9%	48.1%
AL	1950	129,404	73,313	BOGGS, J. CALEB	56,091	WINCHESTER, H. M.		17,222 R	56.7%	43.3%	56.7%	43.3%
AL	1948	140,535	71,127	BOGGS, J. CALEB	68,909	MCGUIGAN, J. CARL	499	2,218 R	50.6%	49.0%	50.8%	49.2%
AL	1946	112,621	63,516	BOGGS, J. CALEB	49,105	TRAYNOR, PHILIP A.		14,411 R	56.4%	43.6%	56.4%	43.6%

DELAWARE

1990 GENERAL ELECTION

Senator   Other vote was Libertarian (Rosenbaum).

Congress   Other vote was Libertarian (Cohen).

1990 PRIMARIES

SEPTEMBER 8 REPUBLICAN

Senator   M. Jane Brady, unopposed.

Congress   Unopposed at-large.

SEPTEMBER 8 DEMOCRATIC

Senator   Joseph R. Biden, unopposed.

Congress   Contested as follows:

  AL   24,561 Thomas R. Carper; 2,676 Daniel D. Rappa.

126

FLORIDA

GOVERNOR

Lawton Chiles (D). Elected 1990 to a four-year term.

SENATORS

Robert Graham (D). Elected 1986 to a six-year term.

Connie Mack (R). Elected 1988 to a six-year term.

REPRESENTATIVES

1. Earl D. Hutto (D)
2. Pete Peterson (D)
3. Charles E. Bennett (D)
4. Craig T. James (R)
5. Bill McCollum (R)
6. Clifford B. Stearns (R)
7. Sam M. Gibbons (D)

8. C. W. Young (R)
9. Michael Bilirakis (R)
10. Andrew P. Ireland (R)
11. Jim Bacchus (D)
12. Tom Lewis (R)
13. Porter J. Goss (R)

14. Harry Johnston (D)
15. Clay Shaw (R)
16. Larry Smith (D)
17. William Lehman (D)
18. Ileana Ros-Lehtinen (R)
19. Dante B. Fascell (D)

POSTWAR VOTE FOR PRESIDENT

Year	Total Vote	Republican Vote	Candidate	Democratic Vote	Candidate	Other Vote	Plurality	Total Vote Rep.	Total Vote Dem.	Major Vote Rep.	Major Vote Dem.
1988	4,302,313	2,618,885	Bush, George	1,656,701	Dukakis, Michael S.	26,727	962,184 R	60.9%	38.5%	61.3%	38.7%
1984	4,180,051	2,730,350	Reagan, Ronald	1,448,816	Mondale, Walter F.	885	1,281,534 R	65.3%	34.7%	65.3%	34.7%
1980	3,686,930	2,046,951	Reagan, Ronald	1,419,475	Carter, Jimmy	220,504	627,476 R	55.5%	38.5%	59.1%	40.9%
1976	3,150,631	1,469,531	Ford, Gerald R.	1,636,000	Carter, Jimmy	45,100	166,469 D	46.6%	51.9%	47.3%	52.7%
1972	2,583,283	1,857,759	Nixon, Richard M.	718,117	McGovern, George S.	7,407	1,139,642 R	71.9%	27.8%	72.1%	27.9%
1968 **	2,187,805	886,804	Nixon, Richard M.	676,794	Humphrey, Hubert H.	624,207	210,010 R	40.5%	30.9%	56.7%	43.3%
1964	1,854,481	905,941	Goldwater, Barry M.	948,540	Johnson, Lyndon B.		42,599 D	48.9%	51.1%	48.9%	51.1%
1960	1,544,176	795,476	Nixon, Richard M.	748,700	Kennedy, John F.		46,776 R	51.5%	48.5%	51.5%	48.5%
1956	1,125,762	643,849	Eisenhower, Dwight D.	480,371	Stevenson, Adlai E.	1,542	163,478 R	57.2%	42.7%	57.3%	42.7%
1952	989,337	544,036	Eisenhower, Dwight D.	444,950	Stevenson, Adlai E.	351	99,086 R	55.0%	45.0%	55.0%	45.0%
1948	577,643	194,280	Dewey, Thomas E.	281,988	Truman, Harry S.	101,375	87,708 D	33.6%	48.8%	40.8%	59.2%

In 1968 other vote was George Wallace party.

FLORIDA

POSTWAR VOTE FOR GOVERNOR

Year	Total Vote	Republican Vote	Candidate	Democratic Vote	Candidate	Other Vote	Rep-Dem. Plurality	Percentage Total Vote Rep.	Dem.	Major Vote Rep.	Dem.
1990	3,530,871	1,535,068	Martinez, Bob	1,995,206	Chiles, Lawton	597	460,138 D	43.5%	56.5%	43.5%	56.5%
1986	3,386,171	1,847,525	Martinez, Bob	1,538,620	Pajcic, Steve	26	308,905 R	54.6%	45.4%	54.6%	45.4%
1982	2,688,566	949,013	Bafalis, L. A.	1,739,553	Graham, Robert		790,540 D	35.3%	64.7%	35.3%	64.7%
1978	2,530,468	1,123,888	Eckerd, Jack M.	1,406,580	Graham, Robert		282,692 D	44.4%	55.6%	44.4%	55.6%
1974	1,828,392	709,438	Thomas, Jerry	1,118,954	Askew, Reubin		409,516 D	38.8%	61.2%	38.8%	61.2%
1970	1,730,813	746,243	Kirk, Claude R.	984,305	Askew, Reubin	265	238,062 D	43.1%	56.9%	43.1%	56.9%
1966	1,489,661	821,190	Kirk, Claude R.	668,233	High, Robert King	238	152,957 R	55.1%	44.9%	55.1%	44.9%
1964 S	1,663,481	686,297	Holley, Charles R.	933,554	Burns, Haydon	43,630	247,257 D	41.3%	56.1%	42.4%	57.6%
1960	1,419,343	569,936	Petersen, George C.	849,407	Bryant, Farris		279,471 D	40.2%	59.8%	40.2%	59.8%
1956	1,014,733	266,980	Washburne, W. A.	747,753	Collins, LeRoy		480,773 D	26.3%	73.7%	26.3%	73.7%
1954 S	357,783	69,852	Watson, J. Tom	287,769	Collins, LeRoy	162	217,917 D	19.5%	80.4%	19.5%	80.5%
1952	834,518	210,009	Swan, Harry S.	624,463	McCarty, Dan	46	414,454 D	25.2%	74.8%	25.2%	74.8%
1948	457,638	76,153	Acker, Bert Lee	381,459	Warren, Fuller	26	305,306 D	16.6%	83.4%	16.6%	83.4%

The 1954 election was for a short term to fill a vacancy. The 1964 election was for a two-year term to permit shifting the vote for Governor to non-Presidential years.

POSTWAR VOTE FOR SENATOR

Year	Total Vote	Republican Vote	Candidate	Democratic Vote	Candidate	Other Vote	Rep-Dem. Plurality	Percentage Total Vote Rep.	Dem.	Major Vote Rep.	Dem.
1988	4,068,209	2,051,071	Mack, Connie	2,016,553	MacKay, Buddy	585	34,518 R	50.4%	49.6%	50.4%	49.6%
1986	3,429,996	1,552,376	Hawkins, Paula	1,877,543	Graham, Robert	77	325,167 D	45.3%	54.7%	45.3%	54.7%
1982	2,653,419	1,015,330	Poole, Van B.	1,637,667	Chiles, Lawton	422	622,337 D	38.3%	61.7%	38.3%	61.7%
1980	3,528,028	1,822,460	Hawkins, Paula	1,705,409	Gunter, Bill	159	117,051 R	51.7%	48.3%	51.7%	48.3%
1976	2,857,534	1,057,886	Grady, John	1,799,518	Chiles, Lawton	130	741,632 D	37.0%	63.0%	37.0%	63.0%
1974	1,800,539	736,674	Eckerd, Jack M.	781,031	Stone, Richard	282,834	44,357 D	40.9%	43.4%	48.5%	51.5%
1970	1,675,378	772,817	Cramer, William C.	902,438	Chiles, Lawton	123	129,621 D	46.1%	53.9%	46.1%	53.9%
1968	2,024,136	1,131,499	Gurney, Edward J.	892,637	Collins, LeRoy		238,862 R	55.9%	44.1%	55.9%	44.1%
1964	1,560,337	562,212	Kirk, Claude R.	997,585	Holland, Spessard L.	540	435,373 D	36.0%	63.9%	36.0%	64.0%
1962	939,207	281,381	Rupert, Emerson H.	657,633	Smathers, George A.	193	376,252 D	30.0%	70.0%	30.0%	70.0%
1958	542,069	155,956	Hyzer, Leland	386,113	Holland, Spessard L.		230,157 D	28.8%	71.2%	28.8%	71.2%
1956	655,418		—	655,418	Smathers, George A.		655,418 D		100.0%		100.0%
1952	617,800		—	616,665	Holland, Spessard L.	1,135	616,665 D		99.8%		100.0%
1950	313,487	74,228	Booth, John P.	238,987	Smathers, George A.	272	164,759 D	23.7%	76.2%	23.7%	76.3%
1946	198,640	42,408	Schad, J. Harry	156,232	Holland, Spessard L.		113,824 D	21.3%	78.7%	21.3%	78.7%

FLORIDA

Districts Established May 21, 1982

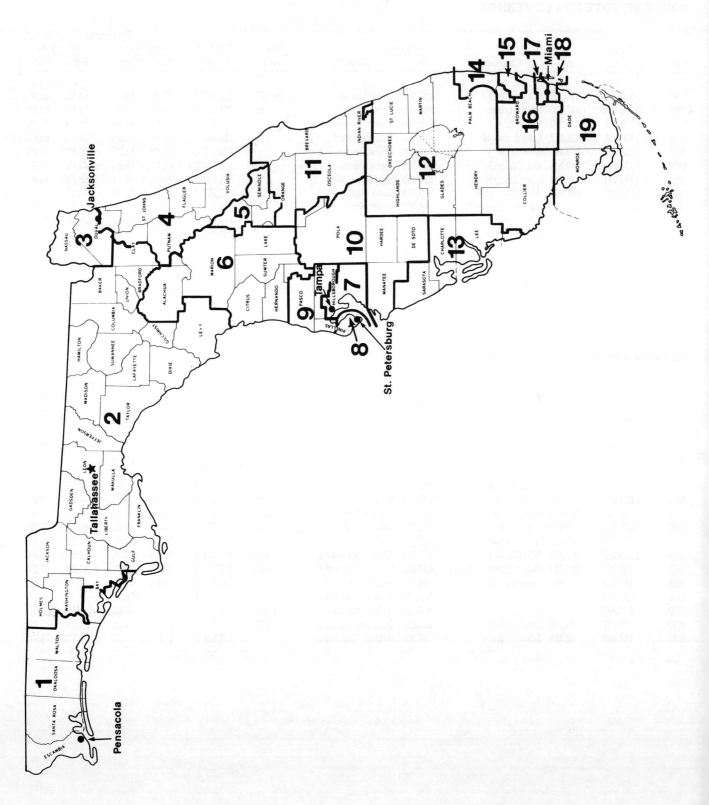

FLORIDA

GOVERNOR 1990

1990 Census Population	County	Total Vote	Republican	Democratic	Other	Rep.-Dem. Plurality	Total Vote Rep.	Total Vote Dem.	Major Vote Rep.	Major Vote Dem.
181,596	ALACHUA	49,604	15,988	33,616		17,628 D	32.2%	67.8%	32.2%	67.8%
18,486	BAKER	4,107	1,957	2,150		193 D	47.7%	52.3%	47.7%	52.3%
126,994	BAY	31,204	16,966	14,236	2	2,730 R	54.4%	45.6%	54.4%	45.6%
22,515	BRADFORD	5,709	2,468	3,241		773 D	43.2%	56.8%	43.2%	56.8%
398,978	BREVARD	127,385	65,641	61,741	3	3,900 R	51.5%	48.5%	51.5%	48.5%
1,255,488	BROWARD	331,303	113,869	217,422	12	103,553 D	34.4%	65.6%	34.4%	65.6%
11,011	CALHOUN	3,294	1,407	1,887		480 D	42.7%	57.3%	42.7%	57.3%
110,975	CHARLOTTE	41,686	21,673	20,012	1	1,661 R	52.0%	48.0%	52.0%	48.0%
93,515	CITRUS	35,434	16,152	19,282		3,130 D	45.6%	54.4%	45.6%	54.4%
105,986	CLAY	25,963	16,256	9,704	3	6,552 R	62.6%	37.4%	62.6%	37.4%
152,099	COLLIER	45,387	26,505	18,882		7,623 R	58.4%	41.6%	58.4%	41.6%
42,613	COLUMBIA	10,017	4,657	5,360		703 D	46.5%	53.5%	46.5%	53.5%
1,937,094	DADE	370,961	138,417	232,542	2	94,125 D	37.3%	62.7%	37.3%	62.7%
23,865	DESOTO	5,475	2,350	3,125		775 D	42.9%	57.1%	42.9%	57.1%
10,585	DIXIE	3,582	1,096	2,486		1,390 D	30.6%	69.4%	30.6%	69.4%
672,971	DUVAL	158,354	83,023	75,326	5	7,697 R	52.4%	47.6%	52.4%	47.6%
262,798	ESCAMBIA	69,857	39,383	30,468	6	8,915 R	56.4%	43.6%	56.4%	43.6%
28,701	FLAGLER	10,606	5,390	5,215	1	175 R	50.8%	49.2%	50.8%	49.2%
8,967	FRANKLIN	2,900	758	2,142		1,384 D	26.1%	73.9%	26.1%	73.9%
41,105	GADSDEN	10,334	3,495	6,839		3,344 D	33.8%	66.2%	33.8%	66.2%
9,667	GILCHRIST	2,873	1,229	1,644		415 D	42.8%	57.2%	42.8%	57.2%
7,591	GLADES	2,305	1,025	1,275	5	250 D	44.5%	55.3%	44.6%	55.4%
11,504	GULF	4,399	1,728	2,671		943 D	39.3%	60.7%	39.3%	60.7%
10,930	HAMILTON	2,686	992	1,694		702 D	36.9%	63.1%	36.9%	63.1%
19,499	HARDEE	4,646	2,019	2,627		608 D	43.5%	56.5%	43.5%	56.5%
25,773	HENDRY	4,461	2,107	2,354		247 D	47.2%	52.8%	47.2%	52.8%
101,115	HERNANDO	41,887	17,434	24,453		7,019 D	41.6%	58.4%	41.6%	58.4%
68,432	HIGHLANDS	23,499	11,227	12,270	2	1,043 D	47.8%	52.2%	47.8%	52.2%
834,054	HILLSBOROUGH	206,222	76,891	129,322	9	52,431 D	37.3%	62.7%	37.3%	62.7%
15,778	HOLMES	4,287	2,057	2,230		173 D	48.0%	52.0%	48.0%	52.0%
90,208	INDIAN RIVER	31,781	17,943	13,838		4,105 R	56.5%	43.5%	56.5%	43.5%
41,375	JACKSON	11,289	4,681	6,608		1,927 D	41.5%	58.5%	41.5%	58.5%
11,296	JEFFERSON	3,859	1,271	2,588		1,317 D	32.9%	67.1%	32.9%	67.1%
5,578	LAFAYETTE	1,805	767	1,038		271 D	42.5%	57.5%	42.5%	57.5%
152,104	LAKE	45,643	23,019	22,624		395 R	50.4%	49.6%	50.4%	49.6%
335,113	LEE	109,363	60,408	48,784	171	11,624 R	55.2%	44.6%	55.3%	44.7%
192,493	LEON	65,523	20,085	45,438		25,353 D	30.7%	69.3%	30.7%	69.3%
25,923	LEVY	7,249	3,153	4,090	6	937 D	43.5%	56.4%	43.5%	56.5%
5,569	LIBERTY	1,827	739	1,088		349 D	40.4%	59.6%	40.4%	59.6%
16,569	MADISON	4,342	1,832	2,510		678 D	42.2%	57.8%	42.2%	57.8%
211,707	MANATEE	69,804	31,594	37,920	290	6,326 D	45.3%	54.3%	45.4%	54.6%
194,833	MARION	57,124	30,522	26,588	14	3,934 R	53.4%	46.5%	53.4%	46.6%
100,900	MARTIN	36,574	21,229	15,344	1	5,885 R	58.0%	42.0%	58.0%	42.0%
78,024	MONROE	18,217	7,034	11,179	4	4,145 D	38.6%	61.4%	38.6%	61.4%
43,941	NASSAU	11,286	6,324	4,962		1,362 R	56.0%	44.0%	56.0%	44.0%
143,776	OKALOOSA	39,850	22,049	17,794	7	4,255 R	55.3%	44.7%	55.3%	44.7%
29,627	OKEECHOBEE	6,061	2,566	3,495		929 D	42.3%	57.7%	42.3%	57.7%
677,491	ORANGE	146,143	65,360	80,762	21	15,402 D	44.7%	55.3%	44.7%	55.3%
107,728	OSCEOLA	25,982	12,381	13,601		1,220 D	47.7%	52.3%	47.7%	52.3%
863,518	PALM BEACH	260,196	106,110	154,085	1	47,975 D	40.8%	59.2%	40.8%	59.2%
281,131	PASCO	99,956	38,783	61,172	1	22,389 D	38.8%	61.2%	38.8%	61.2%
851,659	PINELLAS	298,352	109,236	189,108	8	79,872 D	36.6%	63.4%	36.6%	63.4%
405,382	POLK	104,334	45,671	58,654	9	12,983 D	43.8%	56.2%	43.8%	56.2%
65,070	PUTNAM	17,920	8,184	9,736		1,552 D	45.7%	54.3%	45.7%	54.3%
83,829	ST. JOHNS	25,025	14,626	10,399		4,227 R	58.4%	41.6%	58.4%	41.6%
150,171	ST. LUCIE	39,527	19,487	20,040		553 D	49.3%	50.7%	49.3%	50.7%
81,608	SANTA ROSA	22,164	11,894	10,267	3	1,627 R	53.7%	46.3%	53.7%	46.3%
277,776	SARASOTA	112,095	53,153	58,941	1	5,788 D	47.4%	52.6%	47.4%	52.6%
287,529	SEMINOLE	68,134	32,107	36,027		3,920 D	47.1%	52.9%	47.1%	52.9%
31,577	SUMTER	8,516	3,409	5,107		1,698 D	40.0%	60.0%	40.0%	60.0%

FLORIDA

GOVERNOR 1990

1990 Census Population	County	Total Vote	Republican	Democratic	Other	Rep.-Dem. Plurality	Percentage Total Vote Rep.	Dem.	Major Vote Rep.	Dem.
26,780	SUWANNEE	7,098	3,566	3,532		34 R	50.2%	49.8%	50.2%	49.8%
17,111	TAYLOR	5,009	2,411	2,598		187 D	48.1%	51.9%	48.1%	51.9%
10,252	UNION	2,336	777	1,559		782 D	33.3%	66.7%	33.3%	66.7%
370,712	VOLUSIA	106,588	49,606	56,982		7,376 D	46.5%	53.5%	46.5%	53.5%
14,202	WAKULLA	5,145	2,049	3,087	9	1,038 D	39.8%	60.0%	39.9%	60.1%
27,760	WALTON	9,121	4,303	4,818		515 D	47.2%	52.8%	47.2%	52.8%
16,919	WASHINGTON	5,206	2,579	2,627		48 D	49.5%	50.5%	49.5%	50.5%
12,937,926	TOTAL	3,530,871	1,535,068	1,995,206	597	460,138 D	43.5%	56.5%	43.5%	56.5%

FLORIDA

CONGRESS

CD	Year	Total Vote	Republican Vote	Republican Candidate	Democratic Vote	Democratic Candidate	Other Vote	Rep.-Dem. Plurality	Total Vote Rep.	Total Vote Dem.	Major Vote Rep.	Major Vote Dem.
1	1990	169,267	80,851	KETCHEL, TERRY	88,416	HUTTO, EARL D.		7,565 D	47.8%	52.2%	47.8%	52.2%
1	1988	212,983	70,534	ARMBRUSTER, E. D.	142,449	HUTTO, EARL D.		71,915 D	33.1%	66.9%	33.1%	66.9%
1	1986	152,991	55,459	NEUBECK, GREG	97,532	HUTTO, EARL D.		42,073 D	36.2%	63.8%	36.2%	63.8%
1	1984					HUTTO, EARL D.		D				
1	1982	110,942	28,373	BECHTOL, J. TERRYL	82,569	HUTTO, EARL D.		54,196 D	25.6%	74.4%	25.6%	74.4%
2	1990	180,971	77,939	GRANT, BILL	103,032	PETERSON, PETE		25,093 D	43.1%	56.9%	43.1%	56.9%
2	1988	134,621			134,269	GRANT, BILL	352	134,269 D		99.7%		100.0%
2	1986	110,766			110,141	GRANT, BILL	625	110,141 D		99.4%		100.0%
2	1984					FUQUA, DON						
2	1982	128,244	49,101	MCNEIL, RON	79,143	FUQUA, DON		30,042 D	38.3%	61.7%	38.3%	61.7%
3	1990	116,007	31,727	SULLIVAN, ROD	84,280	BENNETT, CHARLES E.		52,553 D	27.3%	72.7%	27.3%	72.7%
3	1988					BENNETT, CHARLES E.						
3	1986					BENNETT, CHARLES E.						
3	1984					BENNETT, CHARLES E.						
3	1982	87,774	13,972	GRIMSLEY, GEORGE	73,802	BENNETT, CHARLES E.		59,830 D	15.9%	84.1%	15.9%	84.1%
4	1990	216,228	120,895	JAMES, CRAIG T.	95,320	HUGHES, REID	13	25,575 R	55.9%	44.1%	55.9%	44.1%
4	1988	250,425	125,608	JAMES, CRAIG T.	124,817	CHAPPELL, WILLIAM V.		791 R	50.2%	49.8%	50.2%	49.8%
4	1986					CHAPPELL, WILLIAM V.						
4	1984	207,912	73,218	STARLING, ALTON H.	134,694	CHAPPELL, WILLIAM V.		61,476 D	35.2%	64.8%	35.2%	64.8%
4	1982	125,352	41,457	GAUDET, LARRY	83,895	CHAPPELL, WILLIAM V.		42,438 D	33.1%	66.9%	33.1%	66.9%
5	1990	157,706	94,453	MCCOLLUM, BILL	63,253	FLETCHER, BOB		31,200 R	59.9%	40.1%	59.9%	40.1%
5	1988			MCCOLLUM, BILL								
5	1986			MCCOLLUM, BILL								
5	1984			MCCOLLUM, BILL								
5	1982	119,063	69,993	MCCOLLUM, BILL	49,070	BATCHELOR, DICK		20,923 R	58.8%	41.2%	58.8%	41.2%
6	1990	234,029	138,588	STEARNS, CLIFFORD B.	95,421	JOHNSON, ART	20	43,167 R	59.2%	40.8%	59.2%	40.8%
6	1988	255,171	136,415	STEARNS, CLIFFORD B.	118,756	MILLS, JON		17,659 R	53.5%	46.5%	53.5%	46.5%
6	1986	204,667	61,069	GALLAGHER, LARRY	143,598	MACKAY, BUDDY		82,529 D	29.8%	70.2%	29.8%	70.2%
6	1984	168,583			167,409	MACKAY, BUDDY	1,174	167,409 D		99.3%		100.0%
6	1982	139,897	54,059	HAVILL, ED	85,825	MACKAY, BUDDY	13	31,766 D	38.6%	61.3%	38.6%	61.4%
7	1990	147,229	47,765	PROUT, CHARLES	99,464	GIBBONS, SAM M.		51,699 D	32.4%	67.6%	32.4%	67.6%
7	1988					GIBBONS, SAM M.						
7	1986					GIBBONS, SAM M.						
7	1984	170,710	70,280	KAVOUKLIS, MICHAEL N.	100,430	GIBBONS, SAM M.		30,150 D	41.2%	58.8%	41.2%	58.8%
7	1982	114,963	29,632	AYERS, KEN	85,331	GIBBONS, SAM M.		55,699 D	25.8%	74.2%	25.8%	74.2%
8	1990			YOUNG, C. W.								
8	1988	231,704	169,165	YOUNG, C. W.	62,539	WIMBISH, C. BETTE		106,626 R	73.0%	27.0%	73.0%	27.0%
8	1986			YOUNG, C. W.								
8	1984	229,946	184,553	YOUNG, C. W.	45,393	KENT, ROBERT		139,160 R	80.3%	19.7%	80.3%	19.7%
8	1982			YOUNG, C. W.								
9	1990	244,666	142,163	BILIRAKIS, MICHAEL	102,503	KNAPP, CHERYL D.		39,660 R	58.1%	41.9%	58.1%	41.9%
9	1988	224,167	223,925	BILIRAKIS, MICHAEL			242	223,925 R	99.9%		100.0%	
9	1986	235,118	166,540	BILIRAKIS, MICHAEL	68,578	CAZARES, GABE		97,962 R	70.8%	29.2%	70.8%	29.2%
9	1984	243,493	191,343	BILIRAKIS, MICHAEL	52,150	WILSON, JACK		139,193 R	78.6%	21.4%	78.6%	21.4%
9	1982	185,742	95,009	BILIRAKIS, MICHAEL	90,697	SHELDON, GEORGE H.	36	4,312 R	51.2%	48.8%	51.2%	48.8%
10	1990			IRELAND, ANDREW P.								
10	1988	213,099	156,563	IRELAND, ANDREW P.	56,536	HIGGINBOTTOM, DAVID		100,027 R	73.5%	26.5%	73.5%	26.5%
10	1986	171,966	122,395	IRELAND, ANDREW P.	49,571	HIGGINBOTTOM, DAVID		72,824 R	71.2%	28.8%	71.2%	28.8%
10	1984	203,841	126,206	IRELAND, ANDREW P.	77,635	GLASS, PATRICIA M.		48,571 R	61.9%	38.1%	61.9%	38.1%
10	1982					IRELAND, ANDREW P.						

132

FLORIDA

CONGRESS

CD	Year	Total Vote	Republican Vote	Republican Candidate	Democratic Vote	Democratic Candidate	Other Vote	Rep.-Dem. Plurality	Total Vote Rep.	Total Vote Dem.	Major Vote Rep.	Major Vote Dem.
11	1990	232,961	111,970	TOLLEY, BILL	120,991	BACCHUS, JIM		9,021 D	48.1%	51.9%	48.1%	51.9%
11	1988	276,763	108,373	TOLLEY, BILL	168,390	NELSON, BILL		60,017 D	39.2%	60.8%	39.2%	60.8%
11	1986	205,061	55,952	ELLIS, SCOTT	149,109	NELSON, BILL		93,157 D	27.3%	72.7%	27.3%	72.7%
11	1984	240,890	95,115	QUARTEL, ROB	145,764	NELSON, BILL	11	50,649 D	39.5%	60.5%	39.5%	60.5%
11	1982	144,168	42,422	ROBINSON, JOEL	101,746	NELSON, BILL		59,324 D	29.4%	70.6%	29.4%	70.6%
12	1990			LEWIS, TOM								
12	1988			LEWIS, TOM								
12	1986	151,180	150,244	LEWIS, TOM			936	150,244 R	99.4%		100.0%	
12	1984			LEWIS, TOM								
12	1982	155,806	81,893	LEWIS, TOM	73,913	CULVERHOUSE, BRAD		7,980 R	52.6%	47.4%	52.6%	47.4%
13	1990			GOSS, PORTER J.								
13	1988	324,870	231,170	GOSS, PORTER J.	93,700	CONWAY, JACK		137,470 R	71.2%	28.8%	71.2%	28.8%
13	1986	250,555	187,846	MACK, CONNIE	62,709	GILBERT, ADDISON S.		125,137 R	75.0%	25.0%	75.0%	25.0%
13	1984			MACK, CONNIE								
13	1982	204,190	132,951	MACK, CONNIE	71,239	STEVENS, DANA N.		61,712 R	65.1%	34.9%	65.1%	34.9%
14	1990	236,304	80,249	SHORE, SCOTT	156,055	JOHNSTON, HARRY		75,806 D	34.0%	66.0%	34.0%	66.0%
14	1988	315,927	142,635	ADAMS, KEN	173,292	JOHNSTON, HARRY		30,657 D	45.1%	54.9%	45.1%	54.9%
14	1986	233,165	61,189	MARTIN, RICK	171,976	MICA, DAN		110,787 D	26.2%	73.8%	26.2%	73.8%
14	1984	277,861	123,926	ROSS, DON	153,935	MICA, DAN		30,009 D	44.6%	55.4%	44.6%	55.4%
14	1982	176,206	47,560	MITCHELL, STEVE	128,646	MICA, DAN		81,086 D	27.0%	73.0%	27.0%	73.0%
15	1990	106,669	104,295	SHAW, CLAY			2,374	104,295 R	97.8%		100.0%	
15	1988	199,836	132,090	SHAW, CLAY	67,746	KUHLE, MICHAEL A.		64,344 R	66.1%	33.9%	66.1%	33.9%
15	1986			SHAW, CLAY								
15	1984	194,930	128,097	SHAW, CLAY	66,833	HUMPHREY, BILL		61,264 R	65.7%	34.3%	65.7%	34.3%
15	1982	156,241	89,158	SHAW, CLAY	67,083	STACK, EDWARD J.		22,075 R	57.1%	42.9%	57.1%	42.9%
16	1990					SMITH, LARRY						
16	1988	220,493	67,461	SMITH, JOSEPH	153,032	SMITH, LARRY		85,571 D	30.6%	69.4%	30.6%	69.4%
16	1986	174,028	52,809	COLLINS, MARY	121,219	SMITH, LARRY		68,410 D	30.3%	69.7%	30.3%	69.7%
16	1984	192,313	83,903	BUSH, TOM	108,410	SMITH, LARRY		24,507 D	43.6%	56.4%	43.6%	56.4%
16	1982	135,346	43,458	BERKOWITZ, MAURICE	91,888	SMITH, LARRY		48,430 D	32.1%	67.9%	32.1%	67.9%
17	1990	101,599	22,029	RODNEY, EARL	79,569	LEHMAN, WILLIAM	1	57,540 D	21.7%	78.3%	21.7%	78.3%
17	1988					LEHMAN, WILLIAM						
17	1986					LEHMAN, WILLIAM						
17	1984					LEHMAN, WILLIAM						
17	1982					LEHMAN, WILLIAM						
18	1990	93,343	56,364	ROS-LEHTINEN, ILEANA	36,978	ANSCHER, BERNARD	1	19,386 R	60.4%	39.6%	60.4%	39.6%
18	1988					PEPPER, CLAUDE						
18	1986	108,876	28,814	BRODIE, TOM	80,062	PEPPER, CLAUDE		51,248 D	26.5%	735%	26.5%	73.5%
18	1984	126,222	49,818	NUNEZ, RICARDO	76,404	PEPPER, CLAUDE		26,586 D	39.5%	60.5%	39.5%	60.5%
18	1982	101,379	29,196	NUNEZ, RICARDO	72,183	PEPPER, CLAUDE		42,987 D	28.8%	71.2%	28.8%	71.2%
19	1990	141,492	53,796	ALLEN, BOB	87,696	FASCELL, DANTE B.		33,900 D	38.0%	62.0%	38.0%	62.0%
19	1988	186,983	51,628	ROCHETEAU, RALPH C.	135,355	FASCELL, DANTE B.		83,727 D	27.6%	72.4%	27.6%	72.4%
19	1986	143,678	44,463	FLANAGAN, BILL	99,215	FASCELL, DANTE B.		54,752 D	30.9%	69.1%	30.9%	69.1%
19	1984	179,951	64,317	FLANAGAN, BILL	115,631	FASCELL, DANTE B.	3	51,314 D	35.7%	64.3%	35.7%	64.3%
19	1982	126,281	51,969	RINKER, GLENN	74,312	FASCELL, DANTE B.		22,343 D	41.2%	58.8%	41.2%	58.8%

FLORIDA

1990 GENERAL ELECTION

Governor   Other vote was write-in (Floyd).

Congress   According to state law, votes are not required to be tabulated for unopposed candidates. Other vote was write-in (McCarthy) in CD 4; write-in (O'Connor) in CD 6; write-in (Goodmon) in CD 15; write-in (Evans) in CD 17; write-in (Ntweng) in CD 18. In CD 2 Bill Grant changed his party affiliation between the November 1988 and November 1990 elections. In CD 10 Andrew P. Ireland was elected as a Democrat in 1982 and as a Republican in 1984, 1986, 1988 and 1990.

1990 PRIMARIES

SEPTEMBER 4 REPUBLICAN

Governor   460,718 Bob Martinez; 132,565 Marlene Howard; 34,720 John Davis; 28,591 Anthony Martin; 11,587 Warren Folks.

Congress   Unopposed in fourteen CD's. No candidate in CD 16. Contested as follows:

CD 6   37,265 Clifford B. Stearns; 10,556 Larry Gallegher.
CD 9   36,870 Michael Bilirakis; 7,316 John Freehafer.
CD 11   21,916 Bill Tolley; 21,256 John Vogt; 6,005 Bonnie Wharton; 5,616 Frank Filiberto; 3,727 Mel Pearlman; 2,235 Lewis Oliver.
CD 12   33,826 Tom Lewis; 11,469 Kevan Boyles.

SEPTEMBER 4 DEMOCRATIC

Governor   746,325 Lawton Chiles; 327,731 Bill Nelson.

Congress   Unopposed in ten CD's. No candidate in CD's 8, 10, 12, 13, and 15. Contested as follows:

CD 1   53,648 Earl D. Hutto; 19,779 Steve Hudson.
CD 2   56,835 Pete Peterson; 37,903 Bob Boyd.
CD 4   38,924 Reid Hughes; 16,548 David Davis; 10,899 Bob Gray.
CD 6   35,349 Art Johnson; 32,754 Joan Wollin.

OCTOBER 2 REPUBLICAN RUN-OFF

Congress

CD 11   20,511 Bill Tolley; 15,674 John Vogt.

GEORGIA

GOVERNOR
Zell Miller (D). Elected 1990 to a four-year term.

SENATORS
Wyche Fowler (D). Elected 1986 to a six-year term.

Sam Nunn (D). Re-elected 1990 to a six-year term. Previously elected 1984, 1978, 1972.

REPRESENTATIVES

1. Lindsay Thomas (D)	5. John Lewis (D)	8. J. Roy Rowland (D)
2. Charles Hatcher (D)	6. Newt Gingrich (R)	9. Ed Jenkins (D)
3. Richard Ray (D)	7. George Darden (D)	10. Doug Barnard (D)
4. Ben Jones (D)		

POSTWAR VOTE FOR PRESIDENT

									Percentage			
	Total	Republican		Democratic		Other			Total Vote		Major Vote	
Year	Vote	Vote	Candidate	Vote	Candidate	Vote	Plurality		Rep.	Dem.	Rep.	Dem.
1988	1,809,672	1,081,331	Bush, George	714,792	Dukakis, Michael S.	13,549	366,539 R		59.8%	39.5%	60.2%	39.8%
1984	1,776,120	1,068,722	Reagan, Ronald	706,628	Mondale, Walter F.	770	362,094 R		60.2%	39.8%	60.2%	39.8%
1980	1,596,695	654,168	Reagan, Ronald	890,733	Carter, Jimmy	51,794	236,565 D		41.0%	55.8%	42.3%	57.7%
1976	1,467,458	483,743	Ford, Gerald R.	979,409	Carter, Jimmy	4,306	495,666 D		33.0%	66.7%	33.1%	66.9%
1972	1,174,772	881,496	Nixon, Richard M.	289,529	McGovern, George S.	3,747	591,967 R		75.0%	24.6%	75.3%	24.7%
1968 **	1,250,266	380,111	Nixon, Richard M.	334,440	Humphrey, Hubert H.	535,715	155,439 A		30.4%	26.7%	53.2%	46.8%
1964	1,139,335	616,584	Goldwater, Barry M.	522,556	Johnson, Lyndon B.	195	94,028 R		54.1%	45.9%	54.1%	45.9%
1960	733,349	274,472	Nixon, Richard M.	458,638	Kennedy, John F.	239	184,166 D		37.4%	62.5%	37.4%	62.6%
1956	669,655	222,778	Eisenhower, Dwight D.	444,688	Stevenson, Adlai E.	2,189	221,910 D		33.3%	66.4%	33.4%	66.6%
1952	655,785	198,961	Eisenhower, Dwight D.	456,823	Stevenson, Adlai E.	1	257,862 D		30.3%	69.7%	30.3%	69.7%
1948 **	418,844	76,691	Dewey, Thomas E.	254,646	Truman, Harry S.	87,507	169,511 D		18.3%	60.8%	23.1%	76.9%

In 1968 other vote was 535,550 American (Wallace) and 165 scattered. In 1948 other vote was 85,135 States Rights; 1,636 Progressive; 732 Prohibition; 3 Socialist and 1 scattered.

POSTWAR VOTE FOR GOVERNOR

									Percentage			
	Total	Republican		Democratic		Other	Rep-Dem.		Total Vote		Major Vote	
Year	Vote	Vote	Candidate	Vote	Candidate	Vote	Plurality		Rep.	Dem.	Rep.	Dem.
1990	1,449,682	645,625	Isakson, Johnny	766,662	Miller, Zell	37,395	121,037 D		44.5%	52.9%	45.7%	54.3%
1986	1,175,114	346,512	Davis, Guy	828,465	Harris, Joe Frank	137	481,953 D		29.5%	70.5%	29.5%	70.5%
1982	1,169,041	434,496	Bell, Robert H.	734,090	Harris, Joe Frank	455	299,594 D		37.2%	62.8%	37.2%	62.8%
1978	662,862	128,139	Cook, Rodney M.	534,572	Busbee, George	151	406,433 D		19.3%	80.6%	19.3%	80.7%
1974	936,438	289,113	Thompson, Ronnie	646,777	Busbee, George	548	357,664 D		30.9%	69.1%	30.9%	69.1%
1970	1,046,663	424,983	Suit, Hal	620,419	Carter, Jimmy	1,261	195,436 D		40.6%	59.3%	40.7%	59.3%
1966 **	975,019	453,665	Callaway, Howard H.	450,626	Maddox, Lester	70,728	3,039 R		46.5%	46.2%	50.2%	49.8%
1962	311,691		—	311,524	Sanders, Carl E.	167	311,524 D			99.9%		100.0%
1958	168,497		—	168,414	Vandiver, Ernest	83	168,414 D			100.0%		100.0%
1954	331,966		—	331,899	Griffin, Marvin	67	331,899 D			100.0%		100.0%
1950	234,430		—	230,771	Talmadge, Herman	3,659	230,771 D			98.4%		100.0%
1948 S	363,763		—	354,711	Talmadge, Herman	9,052	354,711 D			97.5%		100.0%
1946	145,403		—	143,279	Talmadge, Herman	2,124	143,279 D			98.5%		100.0%

The 1948 election was for a short term to fill a vacancy. In 1966, in the absence of a majority for any candidate, the State Legislature elected Lester Maddox to a four-year term.

GEORGIA

POSTWAR VOTE FOR SENATOR

Year	Total Vote	Republican Vote	Republican Candidate	Democratic Vote	Democratic Candidate	Other Vote	Rep-Dem. Plurality	Percentage Total Vote Rep.	Percentage Total Vote Dem.	Percentage Major Vote Rep.	Percentage Major Vote Dem.
1990	1,033,517	—		1,033,439	Nunn, Sam	78	1,033,439 D		100.0%		100.0%
1986	1,225,008	601,241	Mattingly, Mack	623,707	Fowler, Wyche	60	22,466 D	49.1%	50.9%	49.1%	50.9%
1984	1,681,344	337,196	Hicks, Jon Michael	1,344,104	Nunn, Sam	44	1,006,908 D	20.1%	79.9%	20.1%	79.9%
1980	1,580,340	803,686	Mattingly, Mack	776,143	Talmadge, Herman	511	27,543 R	50.9%	49.1%	50.9%	49.1%
1978	645,164	108,808	Stokes, John W.	536,320	Nunn, Sam	36	427,512 D	16.9%	83.1%	16.9%	83.1%
1974	874,555	246,866	Johnson, Jerry R.	627,376	Talmadge, Herman	313	380,510 D	28.2%	71.7%	28.2%	71.8%
1972	1,178,708	542,331	Thompson, Fletcher	635,970	Nunn, Sam	407	93,639 D	46.0%	54.0%	46.0%	54.0%
1968	1,141,889	256,796	Patton, E. Earl	885,093	Talmadge, Herman		628,297 D	22.5%	77.5%	22.5%	77.5%
1966	622,371	—		622,043	Russell, Richard B.	328	622,043 D		99.9%		100.0%
1962	306,250	—		306,250	Talmadge, Herman		306,250 D		100.0%		100.0%
1960	576,495	—		576,140	Russell, Richard B.	355	576,140 D		99.9%		100.0%
1956	541,267	—		541,094	Talmadge, Herman	173	541,094 D		100.0%		100.0%
1954	333,936	—		333,917	Russell, Richard B.	19	333,917 D		100.0%		100.0%
1950	261,293	—		261,290	George, Walter F.	3	261,290 D		100.0%		100.0%
1948	362,504	—		362,104	Russell, Richard B.	400	362,104 D		99.9%		100.0%

136

GEORGIA

Districts Established August 24, 1982

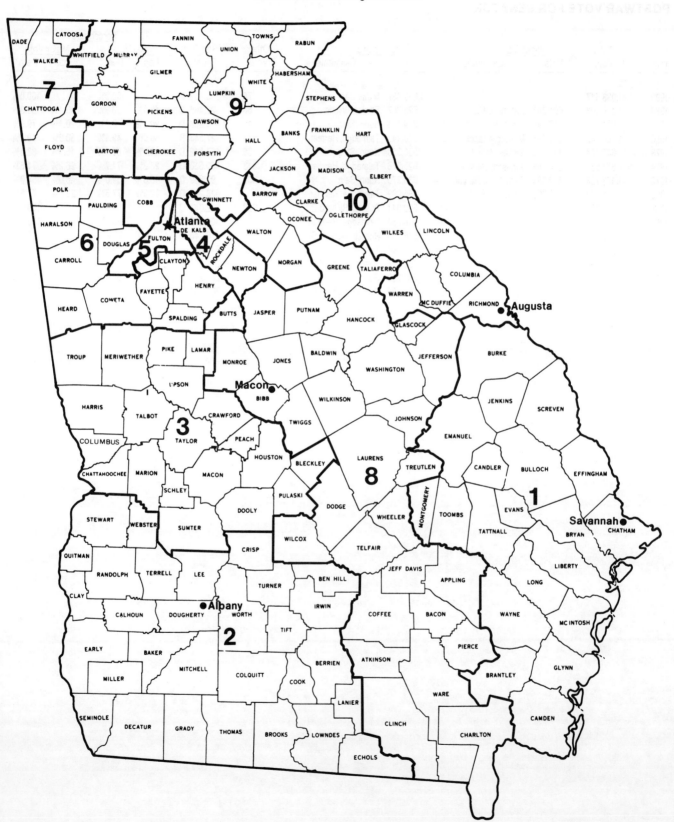

© ERC

GEORGIA

GOVERNOR 1990

1990 Census Population	County	Total Vote	Republican	Democratic	Other	Rep.-Dem. Plurality	Percentage Total Vote Rep.	Dem.	Major Vote Rep.	Dem.
15,744	APPLING	3,526	1,483	1,988	55	505 D	42.1%	56.4%	42.7%	57.3%
6,213	ATKINSON	1,463	607	844	12	237 D	41.5%	57.7%	41.8%	58.2%
9,566	BACON	1,840	745	1,072	23	327 D	40.5%	58.3%	41.0%	59.0%
3,615	BAKER	1,076	346	722	8	376 D	32.2%	67.1%	32.4%	67.6%
39,530	BALDWIN	7,844	3,241	4,473	130	1,232 D	41.3%	57.0%	42.0%	58.0%
10,308	BANKS	2,366	981	1,341	44	360 D	41.5%	56.7%	42.2%	57.8%
29,721	BARROW	6,467	2,681	3,615	171	934 D	41.5%	55.9%	42.6%	57.4%
55,911	BARTOW	9,809	3,879	5,675	255	1,796 D	39.5%	57.9%	40.6%	59.4%
16,245	BEN HILL	3,302	1,357	1,908	37	551 D	41.1%	57.8%	41.6%	58.4%
14,153	BERRIEN	2,949	1,211	1,709	29	498 D	41.1%	58.0%	41.5%	58.5%
149,967	BIBB	37,047	13,653	22,686	708	9,033 D	36.9%	61.2%	37.6%	62.4%
10,430	BLECKLEY	2,547	1,238	1,268	41	30 D	48.6%	49.8%	49.4%	50.6%
11,077	BRANTLEY	2,179	684	1,461	34	777 D	31.4%	67.0%	31.9%	68.1%
15,398	BROOKS	2,767	1,230	1,503	34	273 D	44.5%	54.3%	45.0%	55.0%
15,438	BRYAN	3,558	1,303	2,198	57	895 D	36.6%	61.8%	37.2%	62.8%
43,125	BULLOCH	7,849	3,614	4,126	109	512 D	46.0%	52.6%	46.7%	53.3%
20,579	BURKE	4,060	1,665	2,345	50	680 D	41.0%	57.8%	41.5%	58.5%
15,326	BUTTS	3,507	1,398	2,042	67	644 D	39.9%	58.2%	40.6%	59.4%
5,013	CALHOUN	1,406	452	941	13	489 D	32.1%	66.9%	32.4%	67.6%
30,167	CAMDEN	2,934	1,119	1,737	78	618 D	38.1%	59.2%	39.2%	60.8%
7,744	CANDLER	1,667	618	1,028	21	410 D	37.1%	61.7%	37.5%	62.5%
71,422	CARROLL	14,688	6,919	7,354	415	435 D	47.1%	50.1%	48.5%	51.5%
42,464	CATOOSA	9,117	3,121	5,868	128	2,747 D	34.2%	64.4%	34.7%	65.3%
8,496	CHARLTON	1,301	482	782	37	300 D	37.0%	60.1%	38.1%	61.9%
216,935	CHATHAM	46,679	16,935	28,843	901	11,908 D	36.3%	61.8%	37.0%	63.0%
16,934	CHATTAHOOCHEE	503	120	378	5	258 D	23.9%	75.1%	24.1%	75.9%
22,242	CHATTOOGA	4,573	1,624	2,836	113	1,212 D	35.5%	62.0%	36.4%	63.6%
90,204	CHEROKEE	17,931	9,409	7,926	596	1,483 R	52.5%	44.2%	54.3%	45.7%
87,594	CLARKE	19,132	8,418	9,907	807	1,489 D	44.0%	51.8%	45.9%	54.1%
3,364	CLAY	804	247	547	10	300 D	30.7%	68.0%	31.1%	68.9%
182,052	CLAYTON	36,458	15,296	20,016	1,146	4,720 D	42.0%	54.9%	43.3%	56.7%
6,160	CLINCH	1,048	353	688	7	335 D	33.7%	65.6%	33.9%	66.1%
447,745	COBB	109,600	67,709	38,250	3,641	29,459 R	61.8%	34.9%	63.9%	36.1%
29,592	COFFEE	6,220	2,869	3,246	105	377 D	46.1%	52.2%	46.9%	53.1%
36,645	COLQUITT	7,416	4,033	3,318	65	715 R	54.4%	44.7%	54.9%	45.1%
66,031	COLUMBIA	15,073	8,393	6,441	239	1,952 R	55.7%	42.7%	56.6%	43.4%
13,456	COOK	2,375	971	1,396	8	425 D	40.9%	58.8%	41.0%	59.0%
53,853	COWETA	11,953	5,813	5,815	325	2 D	48.6%	48.6%	50.0%	50.0%
8,991	CRAWFORD	2,031	704	1,277	50	573 D	34.7%	62.9%	35.5%	64.5%
20,011	CRISP	4,052	1,917	2,083	52	166 D	47.3%	51.4%	47.9%	52.1%
13,147	DADE	2,122	697	1,389	36	692 D	32.8%	65.5%	33.4%	66.6%
9,429	DAWSON	2,180	896	1,232	52	336 D	41.1%	56.5%	42.1%	57.9%
25,511	DECATUR	4,988	2,561	2,360	67	201 R	51.3%	47.3%	52.0%	48.0%
545,837	DE KALB	134,412	56,899	71,835	5,678	14,936 D	42.3%	53.4%	44.2%	55.8%
17,607	DODGE	4,063	1,718	2,280	65	562 D	42.3%	56.1%	43.0%	57.0%
9,901	DOOLY	2,547	912	1,606	29	694 D	35.8%	63.1%	36.2%	63.8%
96,311	DOUGHERTY	21,276	9,025	11,976	275	2,951 D	42.4%	56.3%	43.0%	57.0%
71,120	DOUGLAS	16,063	7,317	8,202	544	885 D	45.6%	51.1%	47.1%	52.9%
11,854	EARLY	2,621	1,139	1,455	27	316 D	43.5%	55.5%	43.9%	56.1%
2,334	ECHOLS	482	170	305	7	135 D	35.3%	63.3%	35.8%	64.2%
25,687	EFFINGHAM	5,127	1,916	3,127	84	1,211 D	37.4%	61.0%	38.0%	62.0%
18,949	ELBERT	3,701	1,339	2,345	17	1,006 D	36.2%	63.4%	36.3%	63.7%
20,546	EMANUEL	4,409	1,787	2,555	67	768 D	40.5%	57.9%	41.2%	58.8%
8,724	EVANS	2,088	732	1,327	29	595 D	35.1%	63.6%	35.6%	64.4%
15,992	FANNIN	5,642	2,310	3,282	50	972 D	40.9%	58.2%	41.3%	58.7%
62,415	FAYETTE	19,215	11,239	7,423	553	3,816 R	58.5%	38.6%	60.2%	39.8%
81,251	FLOYD	18,977	8,054	10,529	394	2,475 D	42.4%	55.5%	43.3%	56.7%
44,083	FORSYTH	10,638	4,953	5,318	367	365 D	46.6%	50.0%	48.2%	51.8%
16,650	FRANKLIN	3,393	1,222	2,158	13	936 D	36.0%	63.6%	36.2%	63.8%
648,951	FULTON	153,765	60,151	88,499	5,115	28,348 D	39.1%	57.6%	40.5%	59.5%

GEORGIA

GOVERNOR 1990

1990 Census Population	County	Total Vote	Republican	Democratic	Other	Rep.-Dem. Plurality	Percentage			
							Total Vote		Major Vote	
							Rep.	Dem.	Rep.	Dem.
13,368	GILMER	3,751	1,587	2,100	64	513 D	42.3%	56.0%	43.0%	57.0%
2,357	GLASCOCK	810	456	342	12	114 R	56.3%	42.2%	57.1%	42.9%
62,496	GLYNN	13,935	6,701	6,978	256	277 D	48.1%	50.1%	49.0%	51.0%
35,072	GORDON	6,595	2,731	3,736	128	1,005 D	41.4%	56.6%	42.2%	57.8%
20,279	GRADY	3,716	1,700	1,964	52	264 D	45.7%	52.9%	46.4%	53.6%
11,793	GREENE	2,547	829	1,694	24	865 D	32.5%	66.5%	32.9%	67.1%
352,910	GWINNETT	96,259	51,755	40,307	4,197	11,448 R	53.8%	41.9%	56.2%	43.8%
27,621	HABERSHAM	5,858	2,979	2,775	104	204 R	50.9%	47.4%	51.8%	48.2%
95,428	HALL	20,636	10,012	10,167	457	155 D	48.5%	49.3%	49.6%	50.4%
8,908	HANCOCK	1,726	433	1,272	21	839 D	25.1%	73.7%	25.4%	74.6%
21,966	HARALSON	5,167	2,385	2,647	135	262 D	46.2%	51.2%	47.4%	52.6%
17,788	HARRIS	4,327	1,762	2,488	77	726 D	40.7%	57.5%	41.5%	58.5%
19,712	HART	4,638	1,582	2,966	90	1,384 D	34.1%	63.9%	34.8%	65.2%
8,628	HEARD	1,967	656	1,271	40	615 D	33.4%	64.6%	34.0%	66.0%
58,741	HENRY	15,362	7,421	7,506	435	85 D	48.3%	48.9%	49.7%	50.3%
89,208	HOUSTON	20,718	8,844	11,299	575	2,455 D	42.7%	54.5%	43.9%	56.1%
8,649	IRWIN	1,980	923	1,034	23	111 D	46.6%	52.2%	47.2%	52.8%
30,005	JACKSON	7,010	2,952	3,952	106	1,000 D	42.1%	56.4%	42.8%	57.2%
8,453	JASPER	2,160	820	1,308	32	488 D	38.0%	60.6%	38.5%	61.5%
12,032	JEFF DAVIS	2,372	1,012	1,323	37	311 D	42.7%	55.8%	43.3%	56.7%
17,408	JEFFERSON	4,317	1,834	2,430	53	596 D	42.5%	56.3%	43.0%	57.0%
8,247	JENKINS	1,657	871	769	17	102 R	52.6%	46.4%	53.1%	46.9%
8,329	JOHNSON	2,075	903	1,143	29	240 D	43.5%	55.1%	44.1%	55.9%
20,739	JONES	5,021	1,788	3,147	86	1,359 D	35.6%	62.7%	36.2%	63.8%
13,038	LAMAR	3,061	1,203	1,792	66	589 D	39.3%	58.5%	40.2%	59.8%
5,531	LANIER	1,051	349	689	13	340 D	33.2%	65.6%	33.6%	66.4%
39,988	LAURENS	9,303	4,229	4,917	157	688 D	45.5%	52.9%	46.2%	53.8%
16,250	LEE	3,678	1,847	1,798	33	49 R	50.2%	48.9%	50.7%	49.3%
52,745	LIBERTY	4,434	1,502	2,837	95	1,335 D	33.9%	64.0%	34.6%	65.4%
7,442	LINCOLN	1,862	830	1,013	19	183 D	44.6%	54.4%	45.0%	55.0%
6,202	LONG	1,316	477	821	18	344 D	36.2%	62.4%	36.7%	63.3%
75,981	LOWNDES	12,968	6,158	6,626	184	468 D	47.5%	51.1%	48.2%	51.8%
14,573	LUMPKIN	3,229	1,298	1,820	111	522 D	40.2%	56.4%	41.6%	58.4%
20,119	MCDUFFIE	3,953	2,258	1,637	58	621 R	57.1%	41.4%	58.0%	42.0%
8,634	MCINTOSH	2,429	571	1,822	36	1,251 D	23.5%	75.0%	23.9%	76.1%
13,114	MACON	2,910	910	1,960	40	1,050 D	31.3%	67.4%	31.7%	68.3%
21,050	MADISON	4,206	1,913	2,207	86	294 D	45.5%	52.5%	46.4%	53.6%
5,590	MARION	1,587	546	1,019	22	473 D	34.4%	64.2%	34.9%	65.1%
22,411	MERIWETHER	5,371	1,733	3,589	49	1,856 D	32.3%	66.8%	32.6%	67.4%
6,280	MILLER	1,236	626	604	6	22 R	50.6%	48.9%	50.9%	49.1%
20,275	MITCHELL	4,525	1,790	2,680	55	890 D	39.6%	59.2%	40.0%	60.0%
17,113	MONROE	4,314	1,603	2,609	102	1,006 D	37.2%	60.5%	38.1%	61.9%
7,163	MONTGOMERY	1,690	720	957	13	237 D	42.6%	56.6%	42.9%	57.1%
12,883	MORGAN	3,165	1,369	1,726	70	357 D	43.3%	54.5%	44.2%	55.8%
26,147	MURRAY	3,978	1,328	2,596	54	1,268 D	33.4%	65.3%	33.8%	66.2%
179,278	MUSCOGEE	36,478	12,498	23,505	475	11,007 D	34.3%	64.4%	34.7%	65.3%
41,808	NEWTON	9,149	3,878	5,095	176	1,217 D	42.4%	55.7%	43.2%	56.8%
17,618	OCONEE	5,084	2,701	2,257	126	444 R	53.1%	44.4%	54.5%	45.5%
9,763	OGLETHORPE	2,522	1,106	1,361	55	255 D	43.9%	54.0%	44.8%	55.2%
41,611	PAULDING	8,392	3,519	4,641	232	1,122 D	41.9%	55.3%	43.1%	56.9%
21,189	PEACH	4,751	1,753	2,901	97	1,148 D	36.9%	61.1%	37.7%	62.3%
14,432	PICKENS	3,691	1,540	2,043	108	503 D	41.7%	55.4%	43.0%	57.0%
13,328	PIERCE	2,510	973	1,518	19	545 D	38.8%	60.5%	39.1%	60.9%
10,224	PIKE	2,856	1,316	1,459	81	143 D	46.1%	51.1%	47.4%	52.6%
33,815	POLK	6,871	3,034	3,710	127	676 D	44.2%	54.0%	45.0%	55.0%
8,108	PULASKI	2,245	915	1,293	37	378 D	40.8%	57.6%	41.4%	58.6%
14,137	PUTNAM	3,110	1,137	1,918	55	781 D	36.6%	61.7%	37.2%	62.8%
2,209	QUITMAN	498	125	370	3	245 D	25.1%	74.3%	25.3%	74.7%
11,648	RABUN	3,309	1,450	1,812	47	362 D	43.8%	54.8%	44.5%	55.5%
8,023	RANDOLPH	2,280	707	1,564	9	857 D	31.0%	68.6%	31.1%	68.9%

GEORGIA

GOVERNOR 1990

1990 Census Population	County	Total Vote	Republican	Democratic	Other	Rep.-Dem. Plurality	Percentage Total Vote Rep.	Dem.	Major Vote Rep.	Dem.
189,719	RICHMOND	34,494	15,593	18,382	519	2,789 D	45.2%	53.3%	45.9%	54.1%
54,091	ROCKDALE	15,083	7,931	6,686	466	1,245 R	52.6%	44.3%	54.3%	45.7%
3,588	SCHLEY	928	451	468	9	17 D	48.6%	50.4%	49.1%	50.9%
13,842	SCREVEN	2,800	1,205	1,566	29	361 D	43.0%	55.9%	43.5%	56.5%
9,010	SEMINOLE	2,151	849	1,273	29	424 D	39.5%	59.2%	40.0%	60.0%
54,457	SPALDING	11,010	4,994	5,788	228	794 D	45.4%	52.6%	46.3%	53.7%
23,257	STEPHENS	4,788	2,414	2,286	88	128 R	50.4%	47.7%	51.4%	48.6%
5,654	STEWART	1,433	393	1,019	21	626 D	27.4%	71.1%	27.8%	72.2%
30,228	SUMTER	6,062	2,976	3,014	72	38 D	49.1%	49.7%	49.7%	50.3%
6,524	TALBOT	1,616	565	1,025	26	460 D	35.0%	63.4%	35.5%	64.5%
1,915	TALIAFERRO	617	214	402	1	188 D	34.7%	65.2%	34.7%	65.3%
17,722	TATTNALL	3,974	1,427	2,512	35	1,085 D	35.9%	63.2%	36.2%	63.8%
7,642	TAYLOR	2,293	876	1,372	45	496 D	38.2%	59.8%	39.0%	61.0%
11,000	TELFAIR	2,819	1,203	1,581	35	378 D	42.7%	56.1%	43.2%	56.8%
10,653	TERRELL	2,450	916	1,524	10	608 D	37.4%	62.2%	37.5%	62.5%
38,986	THOMAS	7,587	3,879	3,639	69	240 R	51.1%	48.0%	51.6%	48.4%
34,998	TIFT	6,083	3,140	2,858	85	282 R	51.6%	47.0%	52.4%	47.6%
24,072	TOOMBS	5,066	2,413	2,565	88	152 D	47.6%	50.6%	48.5%	51.5%
6,754	TOWNS	2,447	633	1,799	15	1,166 D	25.9%	73.5%	26.0%	74.0%
5,994	TREUTLEN	1,491	530	945	16	415 D	35.5%	63.4%	35.9%	64.1%
55,536	TROUP	10,728	4,651	5,906	171	1,255 D	43.4%	55.1%	44.1%	55.9%
8,703	TURNER	1,864	722	1,126	16	404 D	38.7%	60.4%	39.1%	60.9%
9,806	TWIGGS	2,136	569	1,534	33	965 D	26.6%	71.8%	27.1%	72.9%
11,993	UNION	3,462	1,194	2,227	41	1,033 D	34.5%	64.3%	34.9%	65.1%
26,300	UPSON	5,863	2,545	3,188	130	643 D	43.4%	54.4%	44.4%	55.6%
58,340	WALKER	9,646	3,446	6,050	150	2,604 D	35.7%	62.7%	36.3%	63.7%
38,586	WALTON	8,130	3,290	4,669	171	1,379 D	40.5%	57.4%	41.3%	58.7%
35,471	WARE	6,092	2,466	3,551	75	1,085 D	40.5%	58.3%	41.0%	59.0%
6,078	WARREN	1,394	623	756	15	133 D	44.7%	54.2%	45.2%	54.8%
19,112	WASHINGTON	4,097	1,617	2,432	48	815 D	39.5%	59.4%	39.9%	60.1%
22,356	WAYNE	4,811	2,244	2,459	108	215 D	46.6%	51.1%	47.7%	52.3%
2,263	WEBSTER	606	202	398	6	196 D	33.3%	65.7%	33.7%	66.3%
4,903	WHEELER	1,021	459	550	12	91 D	45.0%	53.9%	45.5%	54.5%
13,006	WHITE	3,224	1,421	1,720	83	299 D	44.1%	53.3%	45.2%	54.8%
72,462	WHITFIELD	12,079	5,854	6,019	206	165 D	48.5%	49.8%	49.3%	50.7%
7,008	WILCOX	1,862	778	1,071	13	293 D	41.8%	57.5%	42.1%	57.9%
10,597	WILKES	2,977	1,264	1,685	28	421 D	42.5%	56.6%	42.9%	57.1%
10,228	WILKINSON	2,667	878	1,747	42	869 D	32.9%	65.5%	33.4%	66.6%
19,745	WORTH	4,359	2,077	2,230	52	153 D	47.6%	51.2%	48.2%	51.8%
6,478,216	TOTAL	1,449,682	645,625	766,662	37,395	121,037 D	44.5%	52.9%	45.7%	54.3%

GEORGIA

SENATOR 1990

1990 Census Population	County	Total Vote	Republican	Democratic	Other	Rep.-Dem. Plurality	Percentage Total Vote Rep.	Dem.	Major Vote Rep.	Dem.
15,744	APPLING	1,921		1,921		1,921 D		100.0%		100.0%
6,213	ATKINSON	833		833		833 D		100.0%		100.0%
9,566	BACON	1,122		1,122		1,122 D		100.0%		100.0%
3,615	BAKER	627		627		627 D		100.0%		100.0%
39,530	BALDWIN	5,169		5,169		5,169 D		100.0%		100.0%
10,308	BANKS	1,747		1,747		1,747 D		100.0%		100.0%
29,721	BARROW	5,105		5,105		5,105 D		100.0%		100.0%
55,911	BARTOW	6,208		6,208		6,208 D		100.0%		100.0%
16,245	BEN HILL	2,473		2,473		2,473 D		100.0%		100.0%
14,153	BERRIEN	2,357		2,357		2,357 D		100.0%		100.0%
149,967	BIBB	28,280		28,280		28,280 D		100.0%		100.0%
10,430	BLECKLEY	1,413		1,413		1,413 D		100.0%		100.0%
11,077	BRANTLEY	1,498		1,498		1,498 D		100.0%		100.0%
15,398	BROOKS	1,734		1,734		1,734 D		100.0%		100.0%
15,438	BRYAN	2,252		2,252		2,252 D		100.0%		100.0%
43,125	BULLOCH	5,587		5,587		5,587 D		100.0%		100.0%
20,579	BURKE	2,691		2,691		2,691 D		100.0%		100.0%
15,326	BUTTS	2,776		2,776		2,776 D		100.0%		100.0%
5,013	CALHOUN	1,140		1,140		1,140 D		100.0%		100.0%
30,167	CAMDEN	1,850		1,850		1,850 D		100.0%		100.0%
7,744	CANDLER	1,094		1,094		1,094 D		100.0%		100.0%
71,422	CARROLL	11,594		11,594		11,594 D		100.0%		100.0%
42,464	CATOOSA	6,081		6,081		6,081 D		100.0%		100.0%
8,496	CHARLTON	850		850		850 D		100.0%		100.0%
216,935	CHATHAM	30,658		30,658		30,658 D		100.0%		100.0%
16,934	CHATTAHOOCHEE	324		324		324 D		100.0%		100.0%
22,242	CHATTOOGA	3,732		3,732		3,732 D		100.0%		100.0%
90,204	CHEROKEE	11,315		11,315		11,315 D		100.0%		100.0%
87,594	CLARKE	14,142		14,142		14,142 D		100.0%		100.0%
3,364	CLAY	619		619		619 D		100.0%		100.0%
182,052	CLAYTON	25,908		25,908		25,908 D		100.0%		100.0%
6,160	CLINCH	741		741		741 D		100.0%		100.0%
447,745	COBB	76,341		76,341		76,341 D		100.0%		100.0%
29,592	COFFEE	3,583		3,583		3,583 D		100.0%		100.0%
36,645	COLQUITT	4,508		4,508		4,508 D		100.0%		100.0%
66,031	COLUMBIA	10,486		10,486		10,486 D		100.0%		100.0%
13,456	COOK	1,908		1,908		1,908 D		100.0%		100.0%
53,853	COWETA	8,406		8,406		8,406 D		100.0%		100.0%
8,991	CRAWFORD	1,237		1,237		1,237 D		100.0%		100.0%
20,011	CRISP	2,765		2,765		2,765 D		100.0%		100.0%
13,147	DADE	1,161		1,161		1,161 D		100.0%		100.0%
9,429	DAWSON	1,385		1,385		1,385 D		100.0%		100.0%
25,511	DECATUR	2,885		2,885		2,885 D		100.0%		100.0%
545,837	DE KALB	102,965		102,965		102,965 D		100.0%		100.0%
17,607	DODGE	2,332		2,332		2,332 D		100.0%		100.0%
9,901	DOOLY	1,581		1,581		1,581 D		100.0%		100.0%
96,311	DOUGHERTY	16,323		16,323		16,323 D		100.0%		100.0%
71,120	DOUGLAS	10,783		10,783		10,783 D		100.0%		100.0%
11,854	EARLY	2,031		2,031		2,031 D		100.0%		100.0%
2,334	ECHOLS	327		327		327 D		100.0%		100.0%
25,687	EFFINGHAM	3,284		3,284		3,284 D		100.0%		100.0%
18,949	ELBERT	2,515		2,515		2,515 D		100.0%		100.0%
20,546	EMANUEL	2,681		2,681		2,681 D		100.0%		100.0%
8,724	EVANS	1,347		1,347		1,347 D		100.0%		100.0%
15,992	FANNIN	3,471		3,471		3,471 D		100.0%		100.0%
62,415	FAYETTE	13,823		13,823		13,823 D		100.0%		100.0%
81,251	FLOYD	13,682		13,682		13,682 D		100.0%		100.0%
44,083	FORSYTH	6,946		6,946		6,946 D		100.0%		100.0%
16,650	FRANKLIN	2,694		2,694		2,694 D		100.0%		100.0%
648,951	FULTON	119,559		119,559		119,559 D		100.0%		100.0%

GEORGIA

SENATOR 1990

1990 Census Population	County	Total Vote	Republican	Democratic	Other	Rep.-Dem. Plurality	Percentage Total Vote Rep.	Dem.	Major Vote Rep.	Dem.
13,368	GILMER	2,248		2,248		2,248 D		100.0%		100.0%
2,357	GLASCOCK	471		471		471 D		100.0%		100.0%
62,496	GLYNN	10,240		10,240		10,240 D		100.0%		100.0%
35,072	GORDON	4,168		4,168		4,168 D		100.0%		100.0%
20,279	GRADY	2,550		2,550		2,550 D		100.0%		100.0%
11,793	GREENE	2,049		2,049		2,049 D		100.0%		100.0%
352,910	GWINNETT	70,648		70,648		70,648 D		100.0%		100.0%
27,621	HABERSHAM	3,711		3,711		3,711 D		100.0%		100.0%
95,428	HALL	15,931		15,931		15,931 D		100.0%		100.0%
8,908	HANCOCK	1,112		1,112		1,112 D		100.0%		100.0%
21,966	HARALSON	3,956		3,956		3,956 D		100.0%		100.0%
17,788	HARRIS	2,784		2,784		2,784 D		100.0%		100.0%
19,712	HART	3,283		3,283		3,283 D		100.0%		100.0%
8,628	HEARD	1,538		1,538		1,538 D		100.0%		100.0%
58,741	HENRY	11,330		11,330		11,330 D		100.0%		100.0%
89,208	HOUSTON	11,043		11,043		11,043 D		100.0%		100.0%
8,649	IRWIN	1,328		1,328		1,328 D		100.0%		100.0%
30,005	JACKSON	5,222		5,222		5,222 D		100.0%		100.0%
8,453	JASPER	1,457		1,457		1,457 D		100.0%		100.0%
12,032	JEFF DAVIS	1,370		1,370		1,370 D		100.0%		100.0%
17,408	JEFFERSON	2,495		2,495		2,495 D		100.0%		100.0%
8,247	JENKINS	999		999		999 D		100.0%		100.0%
8,329	JOHNSON	1,251		1,251		1,251 D		100.0%		100.0%
20,739	JONES	3,169		3,169		3,169 D		100.0%		100.0%
13,038	LAMAR	2,050		2,050		2,050 D		100.0%		100.0%
5,531	LANIER	714		714		714 D		100.0%		100.0%
39,988	LAURENS	5,710		5,710		5,710 D		100.0%		100.0%
16,250	LEE	2,563		2,563		2,563 D		100.0%		100.0%
52,745	LIBERTY	2,908		2,908		2,908 D		100.0%		100.0%
7,442	LINCOLN	1,385		1,385		1,385 D		100.0%		100.0%
6,202	LONG	770		770		770 D		100.0%		100.0%
75,981	LOWNDES	10,298		10,298		10,298 D		100.0%		100.0%
14,573	LUMPKIN	2,346		2,346		2,346 D		100.0%		100.0%
20,119	MCDUFFIE	2,593		2,593		2,593 D		100.0%		100.0%
8,634	MCINTOSH	1,636		1,636		1,636 D		100.0%		100.0%
13,114	MACON	1,912		1,912		1,912 D		100.0%		100.0%
21,050	MADISON	2,808		2,808		2,808 D		100.0%		100.0%
5,590	MARION	1,126		1,126		1,126 D		100.0%		100.0%
22,411	MERIWETHER	3,538		3,538		3,538 D		100.0%		100.0%
6,280	MILLER	776		776		776 D		100.0%		100.0%
20,275	MITCHELL	3,460		3,460		3,460 D		100.0%		100.0%
17,113	MONROE	3,206		3,206		3,206 D		100.0%		100.0%
7,163	MONTGOMERY	1,060		1,060		1,060 D		100.0%		100.0%
12,883	MORGAN	2,530		2,530		2,530 D		100.0%		100.0%
26,147	MURRAY	2,500		2,500		2,500 D		100.0%		100.0%
179,278	MUSCOGEE	28,815		28,815		28,815 D		100.0%		100.0%
41,808	NEWTON	6,184		6,184		6,184 D		100.0%		100.0%
17,618	OCONEE	3,982		3,982		3,982 D		100.0%		100.0%
9,763	OGLETHORPE	1,928		1,928		1,928 D		100.0%		100.0%
41,611	PAULDING	5,622		5,622		5,622 D		100.0%		100.0%
21,189	PEACH	3,125		3,125		3,125 D		100.0%		100.0%
14,432	PICKENS	2,307		2,307		2,307 D		100.0%		100.0%
13,328	PIERCE	1,738		1,738		1,738 D		100.0%		100.0%
10,224	PIKE	1,726		1,726		1,726 D		100.0%		100.0%
33,815	POLK	4,639		4,639		4,639 D		100.0%		100.0%
8,108	PULASKI	1,521		1,521		1,521 D		100.0%		100.0%
14,137	PUTNAM	2,034		2,034		2,034 D		100.0%		100.0%
2,209	QUITMAN	349		349		349 D		100.0%		100.0%
11,648	RABUN	2,203		2,203		2,203 D		100.0%		100.0%
8,023	RANDOLPH	1,582		1,582		1,582 D		100.0%		100.0%

142

GEORGIA

SENATOR 1990

1990 Census Population	County	Total Vote	Republican	Democratic	Other	Rep.-Dem. Plurality	Percentage Total Vote Rep.	Dem.	Major Vote Rep.	Dem.
189,719	RICHMOND	25,980		25,980		25,980 D		100.0%		100.0%
54,091	ROCKDALE	9,882		9,882		9,882 D		100.0%		100.0%
3,588	SCHLEY	597		597		597 D		100.0%		100.0%
13,842	SCREVEN	1,730		1,730		1,730 D		100.0%		100.0%
9,010	SEMINOLE	1,540		1,540		1,540 D		100.0%		100.0%
54,457	SPALDING	7,073		7,073		7,073 D		100.0%		100.0%
23,257	STEPHENS	3,225		3,225		3,225 D		100.0%		100.0%
5,654	STEWART	898		898		898 D		100.0%		100.0%
30,228	SUMTER	4,152		4,152		4,152 D		100.0%		100.0%
6,524	TALBOT	1,087		1,087		1,087 D		100.0%		100.0%
1,915	TALIAFERRO	481		481		481 D		100.0%		100.0%
17,722	TATTNALL	2,534		2,534		2,534 D		100.0%		100.0%
7,642	TAYLOR	1,746		1,746		1,746 D		100.0%		100.0%
11,000	TELFAIR	1,588		1,588		1,588 D		100.0%		100.0%
10,653	TERRELL	1,612		1,612		1,612 D		100.0%		100.0%
38,986	THOMAS	5,737		5,737		5,737 D		100.0%		100.0%
34,998	TIFT	4,056		4,056		4,056 D		100.0%		100.0%
24,072	TOOMBS	2,938		2,938		2,938 D		100.0%		100.0%
6,754	TOWNS	1,554		1,554		1,554 D		100.0%		100.0%
5,994	TREUTLEN	1,125		1,125		1,125 D		100.0%		100.0%
55,536	TROUP	8,319		8,319		8,319 D		100.0%		100.0%
8,703	TURNER	1,467		1,467		1,467 D		100.0%		100.0%
9,806	TWIGGS	1,584		1,584		1,584 D		100.0%		100.0%
11,993	UNION	2,201		2,201		2,201 D		100.0%		100.0%
26,300	UPSON	4,653		4,653		4,653 D		100.0%		100.0%
58,340	WALKER	6,612		6,612		6,612 D		100.0%		100.0%
38,586	WALTON	5,530		5,530		5,530 D		100.0%		100.0%
35,471	WARE	4,200		4,200		4,200 D		100.0%		100.0%
6,078	WARREN	919		919		919 D		100.0%		100.0%
19,112	WASHINGTON	2,634		2,634		2,634 D		100.0%		100.0%
22,356	WAYNE	3,256		3,256		3,256 D		100.0%		100.0%
2,263	WEBSTER	290		290		290 D		100.0%		100.0%
4,903	WHEELER	611		611		611 D		100.0%		100.0%
13,006	WHITE	2,229		2,229		2,229 D		100.0%		100.0%
72,462	WHITFIELD	8,200		8,200		8,200 D		100.0%		100.0%
7,008	WILCOX	1,418		1,418		1,418 D		100.0%		100.0%
10,597	WILKES	2,185		2,185		2,185 D		100.0%		100.0%
10,228	WILKINSON	1,571		1,571		1,571 D		100.0%		100.0%
19,745	WORTH	3,178		3,178		3,178 D		100.0%		100.0%
6,478,216	TOTAL	1,033,517		1,033,439	78	1,033,439 D		100.0%		100.0%

GEORGIA

CONGRESS

CD	Year	Total Vote	Republican Vote	Candidate	Democratic Vote	Candidate	Other Vote	Rep.-Dem. Plurality	Percentage Total Vote Rep.	Dem.	Major Vote Rep.	Dem.
1	1990	113,047	32,532	MEREDITH, JOHN C.	80,515	THOMAS, LINDSAY		47,983 D	28.8%	71.2%	28.8%	71.2%
1	1988	141,083	46,552	MEREDITH, JOHN C.	94,531	THOMAS, LINDSAY		47,979 D	33.0%	67.0%	33.0%	67.0%
1	1986	69,442			69,440	THOMAS, LINDSAY	2	69,440 D		100.0%		100.0%
1	1984	154,545	28,460	DOWNING, ERIE L.	126,082	THOMAS, LINDSAY	3	97,622 D	18.4%	81.6%	18.4%	81.6%
1	1982	102,425	36,799	JONES, HERB	65,625	THOMAS, LINDSAY	1	28,826 D	35.9%	64.1%	35.9%	64.1%
2	1990	106,691	28,781	WATERS, JONATHAN P.	77,910	HATCHER, CHARLES		49,129 D	27.0%	73.0%	27.0%	73.0%
2	1988	137,836	52,807	HUDGENS, RALPH T.	85,029	HATCHER, CHARLES		32,222 D	38.3%	61.7%	38.3%	61.7%
2	1986	72,490			72,482	HATCHER, CHARLES	8	72,482 D		100.0%		100.0%
2	1984	110,566			110,561	HATCHER, CHARLES	5	110,561 D		100.0%		100.0%
2	1982	73,905			73,897	HATCHER, CHARLES	8	73,897 D		100.0%		100.0%
3	1990	115,522	42,561	BROUN, PAUL	72,961	RAY, RICHARD		30,400 D	36.8%	63.2%	36.8%	63.2%
3	1988	97,663			97,663	RAY, RICHARD		97,663 D		100.0%		100.0%
3	1986	76,062			75,850	RAY, RICHARD	212	75,850 D		99.7%		100.0%
3	1984	136,473	25,410	CANTU, MITCHELL	111,061	RAY, RICHARD	2	85,651 D	18.6%	81.4%	18.6%	81.4%
3	1982	105,171	30,537	ELLIOTT, TYRON	74,626	RAY, RICHARD	8	44,089 D	29.0%	71.0%	29.0%	71.0%
4	1990	184,098	87,569	LINDER, JOHN	96,526	JONES, BEN	3	8,957 D	47.6%	52.4%	47.6%	52.4%
4	1988	246,139	97,745	SWINDALL, PATRICK L.	148,394	JONES, BEN		50,649 D	39.7%	60.3%	39.7%	60.3%
4	1986	162,266	86,366	SWINDALL, PATRICK L.	75,892	JONES, BEN	8	10,474 R	53.2%	46.8%	53.2%	46.8%
4	1984	226,835	120,456	SWINDALL, PATRICK L.	106,376	LEVITAS, ELLIOTT H.	3	14,080 R	53.1%	46.9%	53.1%	46.9%
4	1982	59,185	20,418	WINDER, DICK	38,758	LEVITAS, ELLIOTT H.	9	18,340 D	34.5%	65.5%	34.5%	65.5%
5	1990	113,820	27,781	TIBBS, J. W.	86,037	LEWIS, JOHN	2	58,256 D	24.4%	75.6%	24.4%	75.6%
5	1988	172,887	37,693	TIBBS, J. W.	135,194	LEWIS, JOHN		97,501 D	21.8%	78.2%	21.8%	78.2%
5	1986	123,800	30,562	SCOTT, PORTIA A.	93,229	LEWIS, JOHN	9	62,667 D	24.7%	75.3%	24.7%	75.3%
5	1984	151,250			151,233	FOWLER, WYCHE	17	151,233 D		100.0%		100.0%
5	1982	65,955	3,633	JONES, PAUL	53,264	FOWLER, WYCHE	9,058	49,631 D	5.5%	80.8%	6.4%	93.6%
6	1990	156,566	78,768	GINGRICH, NEWT	77,794	WORLEY, DAVE	4	974 R	50.3%	49.7%	50.3%	49.7%
6	1988	187,011	110,169	GINGRICH, NEWT	76,824	WORLEY, DAVE	18	33,345 R	58.9%	41.1%	58.9%	41.1%
6	1986	126,941	75,583	GINGRICH, NEWT	51,352	BRAY, CRANDLE	6	24,231 R	59.5%	40.5%	59.5%	40.5%
6	1984	168,717	116,655	GINGRICH, NEWT	52,061	JOHNSON, GERALD L.	1	64,594 R	69.1%	30.9%	69.1%	30.9%
6	1982	112,812	62,352	GINGRICH, NEWT	50,459	WOOD, JIM	1	11,893 R	55.3%	44.7%	55.3%	44.7%
7	1990	159,405	63,588	BEVERLY, AL	95,817	DARDEN, GEORGE		32,229 D	39.9%	60.1%	39.9%	60.1%
7	1988	208,481	73,425	LAMUTT, ROBERT	135,056	DARDEN, GEORGE		61,631 D	35.2%	64.8%	35.2%	64.8%
7	1986	133,534	44,891	MORECRAFT, JOE	88,636	DARDEN, GEORGE	7	43,745 D	33.6%	66.4%	33.6%	66.4%
7	1984	193,020	86,431	BRONSON, BILL	106,586	DARDEN, GEORGE	3	20,155 D	44.8%	55.2%	44.8%	55.2%
7	1982	117,224	45,569	SELLERS, DAVE	71,647	MCDONALD, LARRY	8	26,078 D	38.9%	61.1%	38.9%	61.1%
8	1990	118,326	36,980	CUNNINGHAM, ROBERT F.	81,344	ROWLAND, J. ROY	2	44,364 D	31.3%	68.7%	31.3%	68.7%
8	1988	102,696			102,696	ROWLAND, J. ROY		102,696 D		100.0%		100.0%
8	1986	95,206	12,952	MCDOWELL, EDDIE	82,254	ROWLAND, J. ROY		69,302 D	13.6%	86.4%	13.6%	86.4%
8	1984	100,940			100,936	ROWLAND, J. ROY	4	100,936 D		100.0%		100.0%
8	1982	75,035			75,009	ROWLAND, J. ROY	26	75,009 D		100.0%		100.0%
9	1990	172,318	76,121	HOFFMAN, JOE	96,197	JENKINS, ED		20,076 D	44.2%	55.8%	44.2%	55.8%
9	1988	193,705	71,905	HOFFMAN, JOE	121,800	JENKINS, ED		49,895 D	37.1%	62.9%	37.1%	62.9%
9	1986	84,320			84,303	JENKINS, ED	17	84,303 D		100.0%		100.0%
9	1984	162,156	52,731	COFER, FRANK	109,422	JENKINS, ED	3	56,691 D	32.5%	67.5%	32.5%	67.5%
9	1982	112,422	25,907	SHERWOOD, CHARLES	86,514	JENKINS, ED	1	60,607 D	23.0%	77.0%	23.0%	77.0%
10	1990	153,867	64,184	JONES, SAM	89,683	BARNARD, DOUG		25,499 D	41.7%	58.3%	41.7%	58.3%
10	1988	184,677	66,521	MYERS, MARK	118,156	BARNARD, DOUG		51,635 D	36.0%	64.0%	36.0%	64.0%
10	1986	118,267	38,714	HILL, JIM	79,548	BARNARD, DOUG	5	40,834 D	32.7%	67.3%	32.7%	67.3%
10	1984	116,374			116,364	BARNARD, DOUG	10	116,364 D		100.0%		100.0%
10	1982	80,323			80,311	BARNARD, DOUG	12	80,311 D		100.0%		100.0%

144

GEORGIA

1990 GENERAL ELECTION

Governor Other vote was 37,365 Libertarian (Rand); 16 write-in (Dixon) and 14 write-in (Williams). Total for other vote column includes these write-in votes not available by county.

Senator Other vote was write-in (Kolis). The total line for the other vote column represents these write-in votes not available by county.

Congress Other vote was scattered write-in in all CD's.

1990 PRIMARIES

JULY 17 REPUBLICAN

Governor 87,795 Johnny Isakson; 14,496 Bob Wood; 13,062 Greeley Ellis; 2,765 Eli Veazey.

Senator No candidate.

Congress Unopposed in eight CD's. Contested as follows:

  CD 7 9,585 Al Beverly; 9,130 Robert Rivard.
  CD 10 9,543 Sam Jones; 5,757 Mark Myers.

JULY 17 DEMOCRATIC

Governor 434,405 Zell Miller; 303,159 Andrew Young; 219,136 Roy E. Barnes; 64,212 Lauren McDonald; 31,403 Lester Maddox.

Senator Sam Nunn, unopposed.

Congress Unopposed in eight CD's. Contested as follows:

  CD 6 49,952 Dave Worley; 18,583 Joe Forrest; 18,058 Roger B. Marietta.
  CD 10 61,976 Doug Barnard; 25,276 Scott A. Starling.

AUGUST 7 DEMOCRATIC RUN-OFF

Governor 591,166 Zell Miller; 364,861 Andrew Young.

HAWAII

GOVERNOR
John Waihee (D). Re-elected 1990 to a four-year term. Previously elected 1986.

SENATORS
Daniel K. Akaka (D). Elected 1990 to fill out the remaining four years of the term vacated by the death of Senator Spark M. Matsunaga (D); had previously been appointed May 1990 to fill this vacancy.

Daniel K. Inouye (D). Re-elected 1986 to a six-year term. Previously elected 1980, 1974, 1968, 1962.

REPRESENTATIVES
1. Neil Abercrombie (D)   2. Patsy T. Mink (D)

POSTWAR VOTE FOR PRESIDENT

Year	Total Vote	Republican Vote	Candidate	Democratic Vote	Candidate	Other Vote	Plurality	Total Vote Rep.	Total Vote Dem.	Major Vote Rep.	Major Vote Dem.
1988	354,461	158,625	Bush, George	192,364	Dukakis, Michael S.	3,472	33,739 D	44.8%	54.3%	45.2%	54.8%
1984	335,846	185,050	Reagan, Ronald	147,154	Mondale, Walter F.	3,642	37,896 R	55.1%	43.8%	55.7%	44.3%
1980	303,287	130,112	Reagan, Ronald	135,879	Carter, Jimmy	37,296	5,767 D	42.9%	44.8%	48.9%	51.1%
1976	291,301	140,003	Ford, Gerald R.	147,375	Carter, Jimmy	3,923	7,372 D	48.1%	50.6%	48.7%	51.3%
1972	270,274	168,865	Nixon, Richard M.	101,409	McGovern, George S.		67,456 R	62.5%	37.5%	62.5%	37.5%
1968	236,218	91,425	Nixon, Richard M.	141,324	Humphrey, Hubert H.	3,469	49,899 D	38.7%	59.8%	39.3%	60.7%
1964	207,271	44,022	Goldwater, Barry M.	163,249	Johnson, Lyndon B.		119,227 D	21.2%	78.8%	21.2%	78.8%
1960	184,705	92,295	Nixon, Richard M.	92,410	Kennedy, John F.		115 D	50.0%	50.0%	50.0%	50.0%

Hawaii was formally admitted to statehood in August 1959.

POSTWAR VOTE FOR GOVERNOR

Year	Total Vote	Republican Vote	Candidate	Democratic Vote	Candidate	Other Vote	Rep.-Dem. Plurality	Total Vote Rep.	Total Vote Dem.	Major Vote Rep.	Major Vote Dem.
1990	340,132	131,310	Hemmings, Fred	203,491	Waihee, John	5,331	72,181 D	38.6%	59.8%	39.2%	60.8%
1986	334,115	160,460	Anderson, D. G.	173,655	Waihee, John		13,195 D	48.0%	52.0%	48.0%	52.0%
1982 **	311,853	81,507	Anderson, D. G.	141,043	Ariyoshi, George R.	89,303	59,536 D	26.1%	45.2%	36.6%	63.4%
1978	281,587	124,610	Leopold, John	153,394	Ariyoshi, George R.	3,583	28,784 D	44.3%	54.5%	44.8%	55.2%
1974	249,650	113,388	Crossley, Randolph	136,262	Ariyoshi, George R.		22,874 D	45.4%	54.6%	45.4%	54.6%
1970	239,061	101,249	King, Samuel P.	137,812	Burns, John A.		36,563 D	42.4%	57.6%	42.4%	57.6%
1966	213,164	104,324	Crossley, Randolph	108,840	Burns, John A.		4,516 D	48.9%	51.1%	48.9%	51.1%
1962	196,015	81,707	Quinn, William F.	114,308	Burns, John A.		32,601 D	41.7%	58.3%	41.7%	58.3%
1959 S	168,662	86,213	Quinn, William F.	82,074	Burns, John A.	375	4,139 R	51.1%	48.7%	51.2%	48.8%

The 1959 election was for a short term pending the regular vote in 1962. In 1982 other vote was Independent Democrat (Frank F. Fasi) who ran second.

HAWAII

POSTWAR VOTE FOR SENATOR

Year	Total Vote	Republican Vote	Candidate	Democratic Vote	Candidate	Other Vote	Rep-Dem. Plurality	Total Vote Rep.	Total Vote Dem.	Major Vote Rep.	Major Vote Dem.
1990 S	349,666	155,978	Saiki, Patricia	188,901	Akaka, Daniel K.	4,787	32,923 D	44.6%	54.0%	45.2%	54.8%
1988	323,876	66,987	Hustace, Maria M.	247,941	Matsunaga, Spark M.	8,948	180,954 D	20.7%	76.6%	21.3%	78.7%
1986	328,797	86,910	Hutchinson, Frank	241,887	Inouye, Daniel K.		154,977 D	26.4%	73.6%	26.4%	73.6%
1982	306,410	52,071	Brown, Clarence J.	245,386	Matsunaga, Spark M.	8,953	193,315 D	17.0%	80.1%	17.5%	82.5%
1980	288,006	53,068	Brown, Cooper	224,485	Inouye, Daniel K.	10,453	171,417 D	18.4%	77.9%	19.1%	80.9%
1976	302,092	122,724	Quinn, William F.	162,305	Matsunaga, Spark M.	17,063	39,581 D	40.6%	53.7%	43.1%	56.9%
1974	250,221		—	207,454	Inouye, Daniel K.	42,767	207,454 D		82.9%		100.0%
1970	240,760	124,163	Fong, Hiram L.	116,597	Heftel, Cecil		7,566 R	51.6%	48.4%	51.6%	48.4%
1968	226,927	34,008	Thiessen, Wayne C.	189,248	Inouye, Daniel K.	3,671	155,240 D	15.0%	83.4%	15.2%	84.8%
1964	208,814	110,747	Fong, Hiram L.	96,789	Gill, Thomas P.	1,278	13,958 R	53.0%	46.4%	53.4%	46.6%
1962	196,361	60,067	Dillingham, Ben F.	136,294	Inouye, Daniel K.		76,227 D	30.6%	69.4%	30.6%	69.4%
1959 **	164,808	87,161	Fong, Hiram L.	77,647	Fasi, Frank F.		9,514 R	52.9%	47.1%	52.9%	47.1%
1959 S	163,875	79,123	Tsukiyama, W. C.	83,700	Long, Oren E.	1,052	4,577 D	48.3%	51.1%	48.6%	51.4%

The two 1959 elections were held to indeterminate terms and the Senate later determined by lot that Senator Long would serve a short term, Senator Fong a long term. The 1990 election was for a short term to fill a vacancy.

HAWAII

Districts Established April 9, 1984

PRINCIPAL ISLANDS

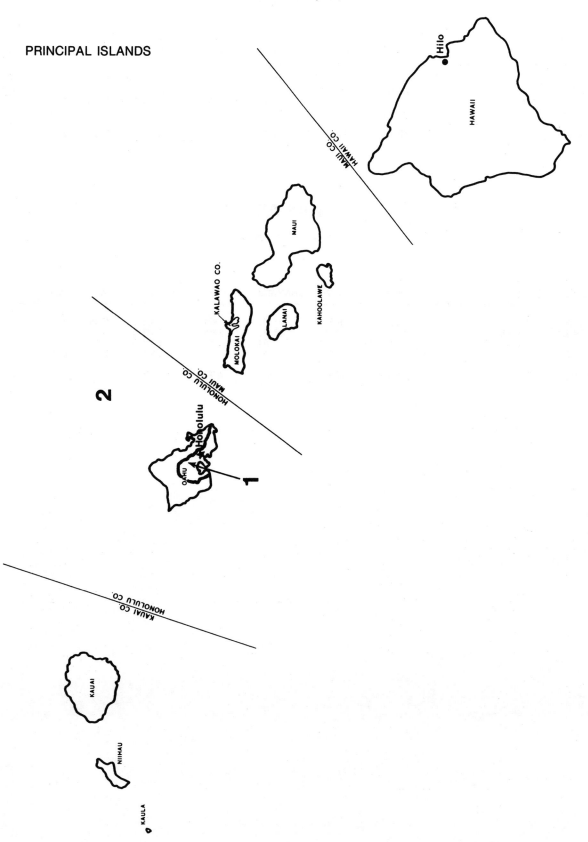

© ERC

HAWAII

GOVERNOR 1990

1990 Census Population	County	Total Vote	Republican	Democratic	Other	Rep.-Dem. Plurality	Percentage Total Vote Rep.	Dem.	Major Vote Rep.	Dem.
120,317	HAWAII	42,828	15,024	26,832	972	11,808 D	35.1%	62.7%	35.9%	64.1%
836,231	HONOLULU	243,501	100,111	140,232	3,158	40,121 D	41.1%	57.6%	41.7%	58.3%
51,177	KAUAI	20,466	4,984	15,088	394	10,104 D	24.4%	73.7%	24.8%	75.2%
100,504	MAUI	33,337	11,191	21,339	807	10,148 D	33.6%	64.0%	34.4%	65.6%
1,108,229	TOTAL	340,132	131,310	203,491	5,331	72,181 D	38.6%	59.8%	39.2%	60.8%

HAWAII

SENATOR 1990

1990 Census Population	County	Total Vote	Republican	Democratic	Other	Rep.-Dem. Plurality	Percentage Total Vote Rep.	Dem.	Major Vote Rep.	Dem.
120,317	HAWAII	43,983	17,574	25,508	901	7,934 D	40.0%	58.0%	40.8%	59.2%
836,231	HONOLULU	249,988	118,336	128,783	2,869	10,447 D	47.3%	51.5%	47.9%	52.1%
51,177	KAUAI	21,159	7,020	13,874	265	6,854 D	33.2%	65.6%	33.6%	66.4%
100,504	MAUI	34,536	13,048	20,736	752	7,688 D	37.8%	60.0%	38.6%	61.4%
1,108,229	TOTAL	349,666	155,978	188,901	4,787	32,923 D	44.6%	54.0%	45.2%	54.8%

HAWAII

CONGRESS

CD	Year	Total Vote	Republican Vote	Candidate	Democratic Vote	Candidate	Other Vote	Rep.-Dem. Plurality	Percentage Total Vote Rep.	Dem.	Major Vote Rep.	Dem.
1	1990	162,711	62,982	LIU, MIKE	97,622	ABERCROMBIE, NEIL	2,107	34,640 D	38.7%	60.0%	39.2%	60.8%
1	1988	177,020	96,848	SAIKI, PATRICIA	76,394	BITTERMAN, MARY	3,778	20,454 R	54.7%	43.2%	55.9%	44.1%
1	1986	168,377	99,683	SAIKI, PATRICIA	63,061	HANNEMANN, MUFI	5,633	36,622 R	59.2%	37.5%	61.3%	38.7%
1	1984	138,865	20,608	BEARD, WILLARD F.	114,884	HEFTEL, CECIL	3,373	94,276 D	14.8%	82.7%	15.2%	84.8%
2	1990	178,288	54,625	POEPOE, ANDY	118,155	MINK, PATSY T.	5,508	63,530 D	30.6%	66.3%	31.6%	68.4%
2	1988	162,808			144,802	AKAKA, DANIEL K.	18,006	144,802 D		88.9%		100.0%
2	1986	162,819	35,371	HUSTACE, MARIA M.	123,830	AKAKA, DANIEL K.	3,618	88,459 D	21.7%	76.1%	22.2%	77.8%
2	1984	136,741	20,000	SHIPLEY, ARBIS D.	112,377	AKAKA, DANIEL K.	4,364	92,377 D	14.6%	82.2%	15.1%	84.9%

150

HAWAII

Kalawao county, an area of 14 square miles on Molokai Island with a population of 130, consists entirely of the Kalaupapa Hansen's desease settlement. The population and voting data for this settlement are included in the Maui county statistics.

1990 GENERAL ELECTION

Governor   Other vote was 2,885 Libertarian (Smith) and 2,446 Nonpartisan (Ross).

Senator   Other vote was Libertarian (Schoolland).

Congress   Other vote was Libertarian (Taylor) in CD 1; Libertarian (Mallan) in CD 2.

1990 PRIMARIES

SEPTEMBER 22 REPUBLICAN

Governor   38,827 Fred Hemmings; 1,343 Leonard Mednick; 1,049 Charles Y. Hirayasu; 844 Ichiro Izuka; 593 Herman P. U'o; 448 Robert Measel.

Senator   39,847 Patricia Saiki; 2,443 Richard I. C. Sutton; 2,096 Robert Zimmerman; 2,049 Maria M. Hustace.

Congress   Contested as follows:

CD 1   11,154 Mike Liu; 9,150 Frank Hutchinson; 885 John L. Sabey.
CD 2   13,363 Andy Poepoe; 4,354 Stanley Monsef; 892 Jose S. Pillos.

SEPTEMBER 22 DEMOCRATIC

Governor   179,383 John Waihee; 9,735 Benjamin Hopkins; 9,112 Robert H. Garner; 4,517 Elbert Marshall.

Senator   180,235 Daniel K. Akaka; 18,427 Paul Snider.

Congress   Contested as follows:

CD 1   43,480 Neil Abercrombie; 30,942 Norman Mizuguchi; 21,128 Matt Matsunaga.
CD 2   47,998 Patsy T. Mink; 44,536 Mufi Hannemann; 20,845 Ron Menor; 6,522 Mike Crozier.

SEPTEMBER 22 LIBERTARIAN

Governor   Triaka-Don Smith, unopposed.

Senator   Ken Schoolland, unopposed

Congress   Unopposed in both CD's.

IDAHO

GOVERNOR
Cecil D. Andrus (D). Re-elected 1990 to a four-year term. Previously elected 1986,1974, 1970.

SENATORS
Larry Craig (R). Elected 1990 to a six-year term.

Steven D. Symms (R). Re-elected 1986 to a six-year term. Previously elected 1980.

REPRESENTATIVES
1. Larry LaRocco (D)   2. Richard Stallings (D)

POSTWAR VOTE FOR PRESIDENT

Year	Total Vote	Republican Vote	Candidate	Democratic Vote	Candidate	Other Vote	Plurality	Percentage Total Vote Rep.	Dem.	Major Vote Rep.	Dem.
1988	408,968	253,881	Bush, George	147,272	Dukakis, Michael S.	7,815	106,609 R	62.1%	36.0%	63.3%	36.7%
1984	411,144	297,523	Reagan, Ronald	108,510	Mondale, Walter F.	5,111	189,013 R	72.4%	26.4%	73.3%	26.7%
1980	437,431	290,699	Reagan, Ronald	110,192	Carter, Jimmy	36,540	180,507 R	66.5%	25.2%	72.5%	27.5%
1976	344,071	204,151	Ford, Gerald R.	126,549	Carter, Jimmy	13,371	77,602 R	59.3%	36.8%	61.7%	38.3%
1972	310,379	199,384	Nixon, Richard M.	80,826	McGovern, George S.	30,169	118,558 R	64.2%	26.0%	71.2%	28.8%
1968	291,183	165,369	Nixon, Richard M.	89,273	Humphrey, Hubert H.	36,541	76,096 R	56.8%	30.7%	64.9%	35.1%
1964	292,477	143,557	Goldwater, Barry M.	148,920	Johnson, Lyndon B.		5,363 D	49.1%	50.9%	49.1%	50.9%
1960	300,450	161,597	Nixon, Richard M.	138,853	Kennedy, John F.		22,744 R	53.8%	46.2%	53.8%	46.2%
1956	272,989	166,979	Eisenhower, Dwight D.	105,868	Stevenson, Adlai E.	142	61,111 R	61.2%	38.8%	61.2%	38.8%
1952	276,254	180,707	Eisenhower, Dwight D.	95,081	Stevenson, Adlai E.	466	85,626 R	65.4%	34.4%	65.5%	34.5%
1948	214,816	101,514	Dewey, Thomas E.	107,370	Truman, Harry S.	5,932	5,856 D	47.3%	50.0%	48.6%	51.4%

POSTWAR VOTE FOR GOVERNOR

Year	Total Vote	Republican Vote	Candidate	Democratic Vote	Candidate	Other Vote	Rep-Dem. Plurality	Percentage Total Vote Rep.	Dem.	Major Vote Rep.	Dem.
1990	320,610	101,937	Fairchild, Roger	218,673	Andrus, Cecil D.		116,736 D	31,8%	68.2%	31.8%	68.2%
1986	387,426	189,794	Leroy, David H.	193,429	Andrus, Cecil D.	4,203	3,635 D	49.0%	49.9%	49.5%	50.5%
1982	326,522	161,157	Batt, Philip	165,365	Evans, John V.		4,208 D	49.4%	50.6%	49.4%	50.6%
1978	288,566	114,149	Larsen, Allan	169,540	Evans, John V.	4,877	55,391 D	39.6%	58.8%	40.2%	59.8%
1974	259,632	68,731	Murphy, Jack M.	184,142	Andrus, Cecil D.	6,759	115,411 D	26.5%	70.9%	27.2%	72.8%
1970	245,112	117,108	Samuelson, Don	128,004	Andrus, Cecil D.		10,896 D	47.8%	52.2%	47.8%	52.2%
1966	252,593	104,586	Samuelson, Don	93,744	Andrus, Cecil D.	54,263	10,842 R	41.4%	37.1%	52.7%	47.3%
1962	255,454	139,578	Smylie, Robert E.	115,876	Smith, Vernon K.		23,702 R	54.6%	45.4%	54.6%	45.4%
1958	239,046	121,810	Smylie, Robert E.	117,236	Derr, A. M.		4,574 R	51.0%	49.0%	51.0%	49.0%
1954	228,685	124,038	Smylie, Robert E.	104,647	Hamilton, Clark		19,391 R	54.2%	45.8%	54.2%	45.8%
1950	204,792	107,642	Jordan, Len B.	97,150	Wright, Calvin E.		10,492 R	52.6%	47.4%	52.6%	47.4%
1946	181,364	102,233	Robins, C. A.	79,131	Williams, Arnold		23,102 R	56.4%	43.6%	56.4%	43.6%

IDAHO

POSTWAR VOTE FOR SENATOR

Year	Total Vote	Republican Vote	Candidate	Democratic Vote	Candidate	Other Vote	Rep-Dem. Plurality	Percentage Total Vote Rep.	Dem.	Major Vote Rep.	Dem.
1990	315,936	193,641	Craig, Larry	122,295	Twilegar, Ron J.		71,346 R	61.3%	38.7%	61.3%	38.7%
1986	382,024	196,958	Symms, Steven D.	185,066	Evans, John V.		11,892 R	51.6%	48.4%	51.6%	48.4%
1984	406,168	293,193	McClure, James A.	105,591	Busch, Peter M.	7,384	187,602 R	72.2%	26.0%	73.5%	26.5%
1980	439,647	218,701	Symms, Steven D.	214,439	Church, Frank	6,507	4,262 R	49.7%	48.8%	50.5%	49.5%
1978	284,047	194,412	McClure, James A.	89,635	Jensen, Dwight		104,777 R	68.4%	31.6%	68.4%	31.6%
1974	258,847	109,072	Smith, Robert L.	145,140	Church, Frank	4,635	36,068 D	42.1%	56.1%	42.9%	57.1%
1972	309,602	161,804	McClure, James A.	140,913	Davis, William E.	6,885	20,891 R	52.3%	45.5%	53.5%	46.5%
1968	287,876	114,394	Hansen, George V.	173,482	Church, Frank		59,088 D	39.7%	60.3%	39.7%	60.3%
1966	252,456	139,819	Jordan, Len B.	112,637	Harding, Ralph R.		27,182 R	55.4%	44.6%	55.4%	44.6%
1962	258,786	117,129	Hawley, Jack	141,657	Church, Frank		24,528 D	45.3%	54.7%	45.3%	54.7%
1962 S	257,677	131,279	Jordan, Len B.	126,398	Pfost, Gracie		4,881 R	50.9%	49.1%	50.9%	49.1%
1960	292,096	152,648	Dworshak, Henry C.	139,448	McLaughlin, Bob		13,200 R	52.3%	47.7%	52.3%	47.7%
1956	265,292	102,781	Welker, Herman	149,096	Church, Frank	13,415	46,315 D	38.7%	56.2%	40.8%	59.2%
1954	226,408	142,269	Dworshak, Henry C.	84,139	Taylor, Glen H.		58,130 R	62.8%	37.2%	62.8%	37.2%
1950	201,417	124,237	Welker, Herman	77,180	Clark, D. Worth		47,057 R	61.7%	38.3%	61.7%	38.3%
1950 S	201,970	104,068	Dworshak, Henry C.	97,902	Burtenshaw, Claude		6,166 R	51.5%	48.5%	51.5%	48.5%
1948	214,188	103,868	Dworshak, Henry C.	107,000	Miller, Bert H.	3,320	3,132 D	48.5%	50.0%	49.3%	50.7%
1946 S	180,152	105,523	Dworshak, Henry C.	74,629	Donart, George E.		30,894 R	58.6%	41.4%	58.6%	41.4%

The 1946 election and one each of the 1962 and 1950 elections were for short terms to fill vacancies.

IDAHO

Districts Established July 30, 1981

IDAHO

GOVERNOR 1990

1990 Census Population	County	Total Vote	Republican	Democratic	Other	Rep.-Dem. Plurality	Percentage Total Vote Rep.	Dem.	Major Vote Rep.	Dem.
205,775	ADA	73,189	18,012	55,177		37,165 D	24.6%	75.4%	24.6%	75.4%
3,254	ADAMS	1,411	617	794		177 D	43.7%	56.3%	43.7%	56.3%
66,026	BANNOCK	21,187	4,631	16,556		11,925 D	21.9%	78.1%	21.9%	78.1%
6,084	BEAR LAKE	2,183	1,031	1,152		121 D	47.2%	52.8%	47.2%	52.8%
7,937	BENEWAH	2,351	767	1,584		817 D	32.6%	67.4%	32.6%	67.4%
37,583	BINGHAM	11,561	4,054	7,507		3,453 D	35.1%	64.9%	35.1%	64.9%
13,552	BLAINE	4,760	824	3,936		3,112 D	17.3%	82.7%	17.3%	82.7%
3,509	BOISE	1,419	513	906		393 D	36.2%	63.8%	36.2%	63.8%
26,622	BONNER	8,697	2,755	5,942		3,187 D	31.7%	68.3%	31.7%	68.3%
72,207	BONNEVILLE	23,606	9,276	14,330		5,054 D	39.3%	60.7%	39.3%	60.7%
8,332	BOUNDARY	2,785	1,169	1,616		447 D	42.0%	58.0%	42.0%	58.0%
2,918	BUTTE	1,113	448	665		217 D	40.3%	59.7%	40.3%	59.7%
727	CAMAS	429	145	284		139 D	33.8%	66.2%	33.8%	66.2%
90,076	CANYON	25,165	8,919	16,246		7,327 D	35.4%	64.6%	35.4%	64.6%
6,963	CARIBOU	2,405	977	1,428		451 D	40.6%	59.4%	40.6%	59.4%
19,532	CASSIA	5,484	2,537	2,947		410 D	46.3%	53.7%	46.3%	53.7%
762	CLARK	385	190	195		5 D	49.4%	50.6%	49.4%	50.6%
8,505	CLEARWATER	2,901	726	2,175		1,449 D	25.0%	75.0%	25.0%	75.0%
4,133	CUSTER	1,288	635	653		18 D	49.3%	50.7%	49.3%	50.7%
21,205	ELMORE	4,349	1,365	2,984		1,619 D	31.4%	68.6%	31.4%	68.6%
9,232	FRANKLIN	2,749	1,348	1,401		53 D	49.0%	51.0%	49.0%	51.0%
10,937	FREMONT	3,695	1,668	2,027		359 D	45.1%	54.9%	45.1%	54.9%
11,844	GEM	4,273	1,328	2,945		1,617 D	31.1%	68.9%	31.1%	68.9%
11,633	GOODING	3,944	1,276	2,668		1,392 D	32.4%	67.6%	32.4%	67.6%
13,783	IDAHO	4,877	2,166	2,711		545 D	44.4%	55.6%	44.4%	55.6%
16,543	JEFFERSON	4,960	2,636	2,324		312 R	53.1%	46.9%	53.1%	46.9%
15,138	JEROME	4,474	1,622	2,852		1,230 D	36.3%	63.7%	36.3%	63.7%
69,795	KOOTENAI	21,001	6,637	14,364		7,727 D	31.6%	68.4%	31.6%	68.4%
30,617	LATAH	9,910	2,351	7,559		5,208 D	23.7%	76.3%	23.7%	76.3%
6,899	LEMHI	2,429	1,322	1,107		215 R	54.4%	45.6%	54.4%	45.6%
3,516	LEWIS	1,254	352	902		550 D	28.1%	71.9%	28.1%	71.9%
3,308	LINCOLN	1,214	385	829		444 D	31.7%	68.3%	31.7%	68.3%
23,674	MADISON	5,233	2,467	2,766		299 D	47.1%	52.9%	47.1%	52.9%
19,361	MINIDOKA	5,244	1,882	3,362		1,480 D	35.9%	64.1%	35.9%	64.1%
33,754	NEZ PERCE	11,002	2,747	8,255		5,508 D	25.0%	75.0%	25.0%	75.0%
3,492	ONEIDA	1,473	587	886		299 D	39.9%	60.1%	39.9%	60.1%
8,392	OWYHEE	2,059	924	1,135		211 D	44.9%	55.1%	44.9%	55.1%
16,434	PAYETTE	4,572	1,391	3,181		1,790 D	30.4%	69.6%	30.4%	69.6%
7,086	POWER	2,113	539	1,574		1,035 D	25.5%	74.5%	25.5%	74.5%
13,931	SHOSHONE	4,718	946	3,772		2,826 D	20.1%	79.9%	20.1%	79.9%
3,439	TETON	1,242	583	659		76 D	46.9%	53.1%	46.9%	53.1%
53,580	TWIN FALLS	15,674	5,264	10,410		5,146 D	33.6%	66.4%	33.6%	66.4%
6,109	VALLEY	2,648	813	1,835		1,022 D	30.7%	69.3%	30.7%	69.3%
8,550	WASHINGTON	3,184	1,112	2,072		960 D	34.9%	65.1%	34.9%	65.1%
1,006,749	TOTAL	320,610	101,937	218,673		116,736 D	31.8%	68.2%	31.8%	68.2%

IDAHO

SENATOR 1990

1990 Census Population	County	Total Vote	Republican	Democratic	Other	Rep.-Dem. Plurality	Percentage Total Vote Rep.	Dem.	Major Vote Rep.	Dem.
205,775	ADA	72,836	44,954	27,882		17,072 R	61.7%	38.3%	61.7%	38.3%
3,254	ADAMS	1,445	1,056	389		667 R	73.1%	26.9%	73.1%	26.9%
66,026	BANNOCK	20,766	10,465	10,301		164 R	50.4%	49.6%	50.4%	49.6%
6,084	BEAR LAKE	2,011	1,398	613		785 R	69.5%	30.5%	69.5%	30.5%
7,937	BENEWAH	2,276	1,204	1,072		132 R	52.9%	47.1%	52.9%	47.1%
37,583	BINGHAM	11,387	7,392	3,995		3,397 R	64.9%	35.1%	64.9%	35.1%
13,552	BLAINE	4,670	1,912	2,758		846 D	40.9%	59.1%	40.9%	59.1%
3,509	BOISE	1,403	986	417		569 R	70.3%	29.7%	70.3%	29.7%
26,622	BONNER	8,398	4,307	4,091		216 R	51.3%	48.7%	51.3%	48.7%
72,207	BONNEVILLE	23,263	14,748	8,515		6,233 R	63.4%	36.6%	63.4%	36.6%
8,332	BOUNDARY	2,720	1,749	971		778 R	64.3%	35.7%	64.3%	35.7%
2,918	BUTTE	1,088	678	410		268 R	62.3%	37.7%	62.3%	37.7%
727	CAMAS	420	298	122		176 R	71.0%	29.0%	71.0%	29.0%
90,076	CANYON	25,250	17,582	7,668		9,914 R	69.6%	30.4%	69.6%	30.4%
6,963	CARIBOU	2,309	1,578	731		847 R	68.3%	31.7%	68.3%	31.7%
19,532	CASSIA	5,383	3,956	1,427		2,529 R	73.5%	26.5%	73.5%	26.5%
762	CLARK	367	267	100		167 R	72.8%	27.2%	72.8%	27.2%
8,505	CLEARWATER	2,829	1,456	1,373		83 R	51.5%	48.5%	51.5%	48.5%
4,133	CUSTER	1,269	826	443		383 R	65.1%	34.9%	65.1%	34.9%
21,205	ELMORE	4,183	2,548	1,635		913 R	60.9%	39.1%	60.9%	39.1%
9,232	FRANKLIN	2,664	1,951	713		1,238 R	73.2%	26.8%	73.2%	26.8%
10,937	FREMONT	3,554	2,560	994		1,566 R	72.0%	28.0%	72.0%	28.0%
11,844	GEM	4,274	2,718	1,556		1,162 R	63.6%	36.4%	63.6%	36.4%
11,633	GOODING	3,718	2,335	1,383		952 R	62.8%	37.2%	62.8%	37.2%
13,783	IDAHO	4,786	3,000	1,786		1,214 R	62.7%	37.3%	62.7%	37.3%
16,543	JEFFERSON	4,895	3,599	1,296		2,303 R	73.5%	26.5%	73.5%	26.5%
15,138	JEROME	4,231	2,771	1,460		1,311 R	65.5%	34.5%	65.5%	34.5%
69,795	KOOTENAI	20,773	11,607	9,166		2,441 R	55.9%	44.1%	55.9%	44.1%
30,617	LATAH	9,812	4,786	5,026		240 D	48.8%	51.2%	48.8%	51.2%
6,899	LEMHI	2,404	1,584	820		764 R	65.9%	34.1%	65.9%	34.1%
3,516	LEWIS	1,216	666	550		116 R	54.8%	45.2%	54.8%	45.2%
3,308	LINCOLN	1,132	694	438		256 R	61.3%	38.7%	61.3%	38.7%
23,674	MADISON	5,185	4,113	1,072		3,041 R	79.3%	20.7%	79.3%	20.7%
19,361	MINIDOKA	5,136	3,345	1,791		1,554 R	65.1%	34.9%	65.1%	34.9%
33,754	NEZ PERCE	10,849	5,211	5,638		427 D	48.0%	52.0%	48.0%	52.0%
3,492	ONEIDA	1,355	911	444		467 R	67.2%	32.8%	67.2%	32.8%
8,392	OWYHEE	2,031	1,547	484		1,063 R	76.2%	23.8%	76.2%	23.8%
16,434	PAYETTE	4,614	3,249	1,365		1,884 R	70.4%	29.6%	70.4%	29.6%
7,086	POWER	1,984	1,240	744		496 R	62.5%	37.5%	62.5%	37.5%
13,931	SHOSHONE	4,661	2,121	2,540		419 D	45.5%	54.5%	45.5%	54.5%
3,439	TETON	1,184	768	416		352 R	64.9%	35.1%	64.9%	35.1%
53,580	TWIN FALLS	15,419	9,529	5,890		3,639 R	61.8%	38.2%	61.8%	38.2%
6,109	VALLEY	2,623	1,700	923		777 R	64.8%	35.2%	64.8%	35.2%
8,550	WASHINGTON	3,163	2,276	887		1,389 R	72.0%	28.0%	72.0%	28.0%
1,006,749	TOTAL	315,936	193,641	122,295		71,346 R	61.3%	38.7%	61.3%	38.7%

IDAHO

CONGRESS

CD	Year	Total Vote	Republican Vote	Candidate	Democratic Vote	Candidate	Other Vote	Rep.-Dem. Plurality	Percentage Total Vote Rep.	Dem.	Major Vote Rep.	Dem.
1	1990	160,460	75,406	SMYSER, C. A.	85,054	LAROCCO, LARRY		9,648 D	47.0%	53.0%	47.0%	53.0%
1	1988	205,549	135,221	CRAIG, LARRY	70,328	GIVENS, JEANNE		64,893 R	65.8%	34.2%	65.8%	34.2%
1	1986	186,196	121,625	CRAIG, LARRY	59,723	CURRIE, BILL	4,848	61,902 R	65.3%	32.1%	67.1%	32.9%
1	1984	202,676	139,085	CRAIG, LARRY	63,591	HELLAR, BILL		75,494 R	68.6%	31.4%	68.6%	31.4%
1	1982	160,665	86,277	CRAIG, LARRY	74,388	LAROCCO, LARRY		11,889 R	53.7%	46.3%	53.7%	46.3%
2	1990	154,052	56,044	MCDEVITT, SEAN	98,008	STALLINGS, RICHARD		41,964 D	36.4%	63.6%	36.4%	63.6%
2	1988	201,885	68,226	WATKINS, DANE H.	127,956	STALLINGS, RICHARD	5,703	59,730 D	33.8%	63.4%	34.8%	65.2%
2	1986	189,563	86,528	RICHARDSON, MEL	103,035	STALLINGS, RICHARD		16,507 D	45.6%	54.4%	45.6%	54.4%
2	1984	202,404	101,117	HANSEN, GEORGE V.	101,287	STALLINGS, RICHARD		170 D	50.0%	50.0%	50.0%	50.0%
2	1982	160,481	83,873	HANSEN, GEORGE V.	76,608	STALLINGS, RICHARD		7,265 R	52.3%	47.7%	52.3%	47.7%

IDAHO

1990 GENERAL ELECTION

Governor

Senator

Congress

1990 PRIMARIES

MAY 22 REPUBLICAN

Governor   37,728 Roger Fairchild; 33,483 Rachel S. Gilbert; 30,514 Milton E. Erhart.

Senator   65,830 Larry Craig; 45,733 Jim Jones.

Congress   Unopposed in CD 1. Contested as follows:

  CD 2   21,608 Sean McDevitt; 19,217 Ann Rydalch; 6,410 Dan Hawkley; 5,645 Janet L. Reid.

MAY 22 DEMOCRATIC

Governor   Cecil D. Andrus, unopposed.

Senator   30,154 Ron J. Twilegar; 16,587 David C. Steed.

Congress   Unopposed in CD 2. Contested as follows:

  CD 1   14,001 Larry LaRocco; 10,725 Jeanne Givens; 7,472 Dick Rush.

ILLINOIS

GOVERNOR
Jim Edgar (R). Elected 1990 to a four-year term.

SENATORS
Alan J. Dixon (D). Re-elected 1986 to a six-year term. Previously elected 1980.

Paul Simon (D). Re-elected 1990 to a six-year term. Previously elected 1984.

REPRESENTATIVES
1. Charles A. Hayes (D)
2. Gus Savage (D)
3. Martin A. Russo (D)
4. George E. Sangmeister (D)
5. William O. Lipinski (D)
6. Henry J. Hyde (R)
7. Cardiss Collins (D)
8. Daniel Rostenkowski (D)
9. Sindey R. Yates (D)
10. John E. Porter (R)
11. Frank Annunzio (D)
12. Philip M. Crane (R)
13. Harris W. Fawell (R)
14. J. Dennis Hastert (R)
15. Edward R. Madigan (R) (see page 1)
16. John W. Cox (D)
17. Lane Evans (D)
18. Robert H. Michel (R)
19. Terry L. Bruce (D)
20. Richard J. Durbin (D)
21. Jerry F. Costello (D)
22. Glenn Poshard (D)

POSTWAR VOTE FOR PRESIDENT

Year	Total Vote	Republican Vote	Republican Candidate	Democratic Vote	Democratic Candidate	Other Vote	Plurality	Total Vote Rep.	Total Vote Dem.	Major Vote Rep.	Major Vote Dem.
1988	4,559,120	2,310,939	Bush, George	2,215,940	Dukakis, Michael S.	32,241	94,999 R	50.7%	48.6%	51.0%	49.0%
1984	4,819,088	2,707,103	Reagan, Ronald	2,086,499	Mondale, Walter F.	25,486	620,604 R	56.2%	43.3%	56.5%	43.5%
1980	4,749,721	2,358,049	Reagan, Ronald	1,981,413	Carter, Jimmy	410,259	376,636 R	49.6%	41.7%	54.3%	45.7%
1976	4,718,914	2,364,269	Ford, Gerald R.	2,271,295	Carter, Jimmy	83,350	92,974 R	50.1%	48.1%	51.0%	49.0%
1972	4,723,236	2,788,179	Nixon, Richard M.	1,913,472	McGovern, George S.	21,585	874,707 R	59.0%	40.5%	59.3%	40.7%
1968	4,619,749	2,174,774	Nixon, Richard M.	2,039,814	Humphrey, Hubert H.	405,161	134,960 R	47.1%	44.2%	51.6%	48.4%
1964	4,702,841	1,905,946	Goldwater, Barry M.	2,796,833	Johnson, Lyndon B.	62	890,887 D	40.5%	59.5%	40.5%	59.5%
1960	4,757,409	2,368,988	Nixon, Richard M.	2,377,846	Kennedy, John F.	10,575	8,858 D	49.8%	50.0%	49.9%	50.1%
1956	4,407,407	2,623,327	Eisenhower, Dwight D.	1,775,682	Stevenson, Adlai E.	8,398	847,645 R	59.5%	40.3%	59.6%	40.4%
1952	4,481,058	2,457,327	Eisenhower, Dwight D.	2,013,920	Stevenson, Adlai E.	9,811	443,407 R	54.8%	44.9%	55.0%	45.0%
1948	3,984,046	1,961,103	Dewey, Thomas E.	1,994,715	Truman, Harry S.	28,228	33,612 D	49.2%	50.1%	49.6%	50.4%

ILLINOIS

POSTWAR VOTE FOR GOVERNOR

Year	Total Vote	Republican Vote	Republican Candidate	Democratic Vote	Democratic Candidate	Other Vote	Rep-Dem. Plurality	Total Vote Rep.	Total Vote Dem.	Major Vote Rep.	Major Vote Dem.
1990	3,257,410	1,653,126	Edgar, Jim	1,569,217	Hartigan, Neil F.	35,067	83,909 R	50.7%	48.2%	51.3%	48.7%
1986 **	3,143,978	1,655,849	Thompson, James R.	208,830	[See note below]	1,279,299	1,447,019 R	52.7%	6.6%	88.8%	11.2%
1982	3,673,681	1,816,101	Thompson, James R.	1,811,027	Stevenson, Adlai E., III	46,553	5,074 R	49.4%	49.3%	50.1%	49.9%
1978	3,150,095	1,859,684	Thompson, James R.	1,263,134	Bakalis, Michael	27,277	596,550 R	59.0%	40.1%	59.6%	40.4%
1976 S	4,638,997	3,000,395	Thompson, James R.	1,610,258	Howlett, Michael J.	28,344	1,390,137 R	64.7%	34.7%	65.1%	34.9%
1972	4,678,804	2,293,809	Ogilvie, Richard B.	2,371,303	Walker, Daniel	13,692	77,494 D	49.0%	50.7%	49.2%	50.8%
1968	4,506,000	2,307,295	Ogilvie, Richard B.	2,179,501	Shapiro, Samuel H.	19,204	127,794 R	51.2%	48.4%	51.4%	48.6%
1964	4,657,500	2,239,095	Percy, Charles H.	2,418,394	Kerner, Otto	11	179,299 D	48.1%	51.9%	48.1%	51.9%
1960	4,674,187	2,070,479	Stratton, William G.	2,594,731	Kerner, Otto	8,977	524,252 D	44.3%	55.5%	44.4%	55.6%
1956	4,314,611	2,171,786	Stratton, William G.	2,134,909	Austin, Richard B.	7,916	36,877 R	50.3%	49.5%	50.4%	49.6%
1952	4,415,864	2,317,363	Stratton, William G.	2,089,721	Dixon, Sherwood	8,780	227,642 R	52.5%	47.3%	52.6%	47.4%
1948	3,940,257	1,678,007	Green, Dwight H.	2,250,074	Stevenson, Adlai E.	12,176	572,067 D	42.6%	57.1%	42.7%	57.3%

The 1976 vote was for a two-year term to permit shifting the vote for Governor to non-Presidential years. In 1986 there was no Democratic candidate for Governor on the ballot, Mark Fairchild being the "paired" Democrat for Lt. Governor and the Democratic vote above was cast for this ticket of "no name" and Fairchild. Other vote in this election was 1,256,626 Adlai E. Stevenson III (Solidarity) who received 40.0% of the total vote and came in second; 15,646 Gary L. Shilts (Libertarian); 6,843 Diane Roling (Socialist Workers) and 184 scattered.

POSTWAR VOTE FOR SENATOR

Year	Total Vote	Republican Vote	Republican Candidate	Democratic Vote	Democratic Candidate	Other Vote	Rep-Dem. Plurality	Total Vote Rep.	Total Vote Dem.	Major Vote Rep.	Major Vote Dem.
1990	3,251,005	1,135,628	Martin, Lynn	2,115,377	Simon, Paul		979,749 D	34.9%	65.1%	34.9%	65.1%
1986	3,122,883	1,053,734	Koehler, Judy	2,033,783	Dixon, Alan J.	35,366	980,049 D	33.7%	65.1%	34.1%	65.9%
1984	4,787,473	2,308,039	Percy, Charles H.	2,397,303	Simon, Paul	82,131	89,264 D	48.2%	50.1%	49.1%	50.9%
1980	4,580,029	1,946,296	O'Neal, David C.	2,565,302	Dixon, Alan J.	68,431	619,006 D	42.5%	56.0%	43.1%	56.9%
1978	3,184,764	1,698,711	Percy, Charles H.	1,448,187	Seith, Alex	37,866	250,524 R	53.3%	45.5%	54.0%	46.0%
1974	2,914,666	1,084,884	Burditt, George M.	1,811,496	Stevenson, Adlai E., III	18,286	726,612 D	37.2%	62.2%	37.5%	62.5%
1972	4,608,380	2,867,078	Percy, Charles H.	1,721,031	Pucinski, Roman C.	20,271	1,146,047 R	62.2%	37.3%	62.5%	37.5%
1970 S	3,599,272	1,519,718	Smith, Ralph T.	2,065,054	Stevenson, Adlai E., III	14,500	545,336 D	42.2%	57.4%	42.4%	57.6%
1968	4,449,757	2,358,947	Dirksen, Everett M.	2,073,242	Clark, William G.	17,568	285,705 R	53.0%	46.6%	53.2%	46.8%
1966	3,822,725	2,100,449	Percy, Charles H.	1,678,147	Douglas, Paul H.	44,129	422,302 R	54.9%	43.9%	55.6%	44.4%
1962	3,709,216	1,961,202	Dirksen, Everett M.	1,748,007	Yates, Sidney R.	7	213,195 R	52.9%	47.1%	52.9%	47.1%
1960	4,632,796	2,093,846	Witwer, Samuel W.	2,530,943	Douglas, Paul H.	8,007	437,097 D	45.2%	54.6%	45.3%	54.7%
1956	4,264,830	2,307,352	Dirksen, Everett M.	1,949,883	Stengel, Richard	7,595	357,469 R	54.1%	45.7%	54.2%	45.8%
1954	3,368,025	1,563,683	Meek, Joseph T.	1,804,338	Douglas, Paul H.	4	240,655 D	46.4%	53.6%	46.4%	53.6%
1950	3,622,673	1,951,984	Dirksen, Everett M.	1,657,630	Lucas, Scott W.	13,059	294,354 R	53.9%	45.8%	54.1%	45.9%
1948	3,900,285	1,740,026	Brooks, C. Wayland	2,147,754	Douglas, Paul H.	12,505	407,728 D	44.6%	55.1%	44.8%	55.2%

The 1970 election was for a short term to fill a vacancy.

ILLINOIS

Districts Established November 23, 1981

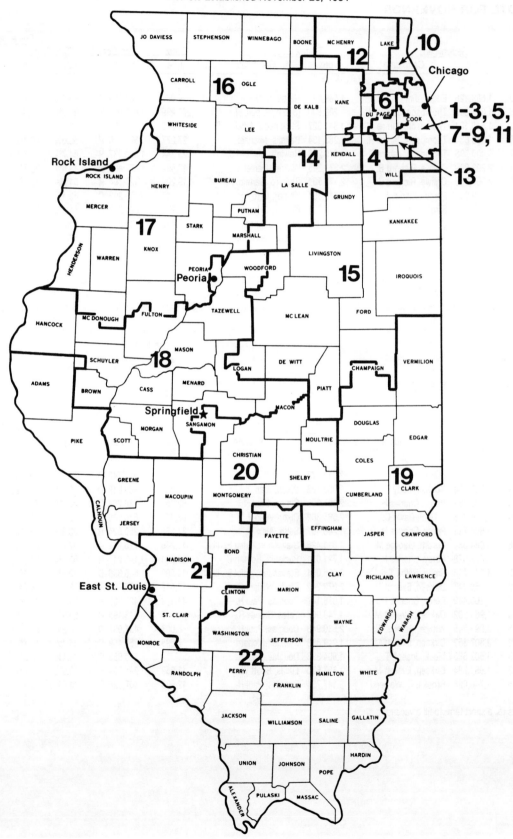

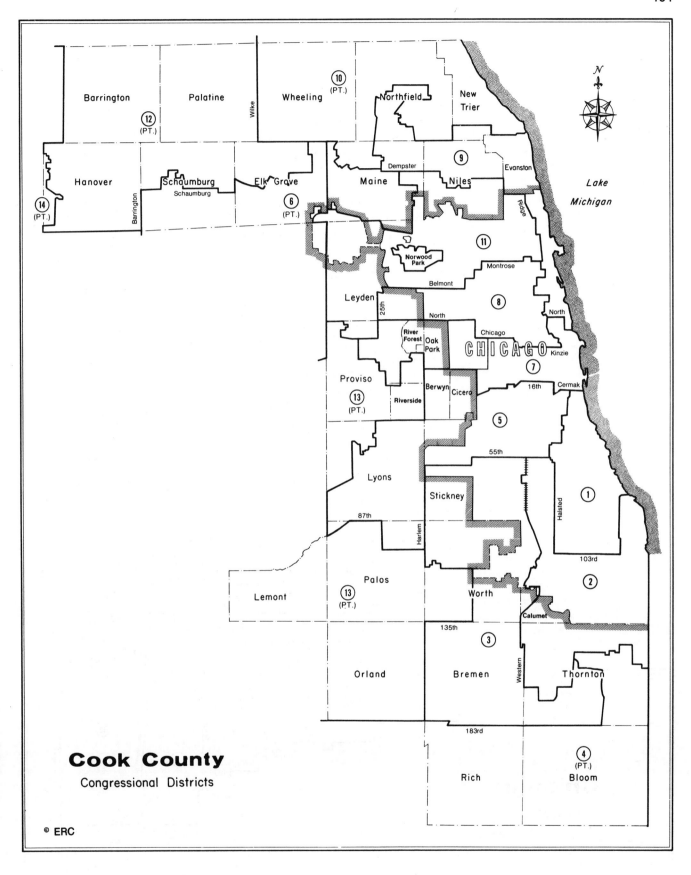

Cook County

Congressional Districts

© ERC

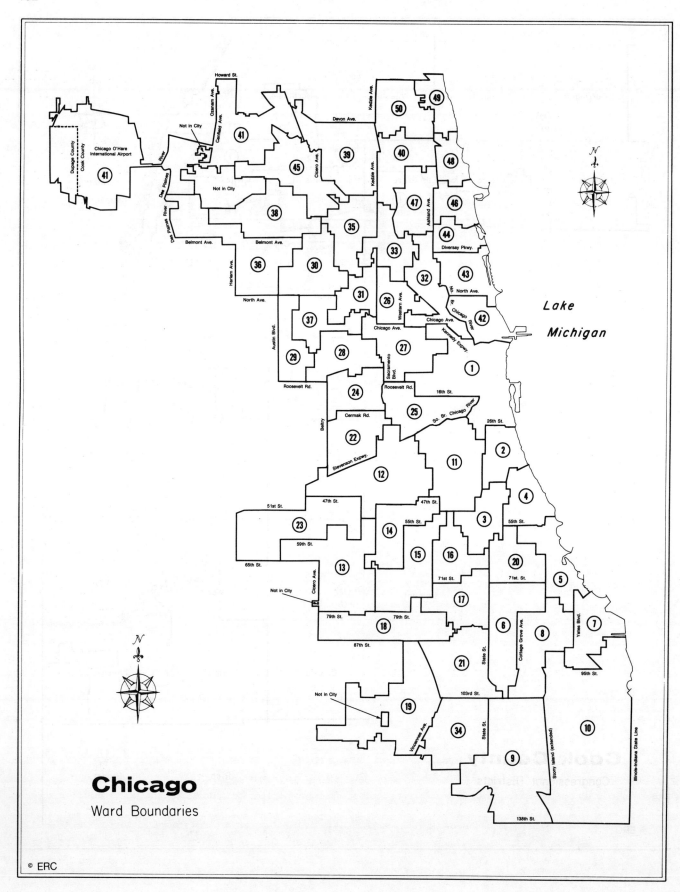

Chicago

Ward Boundaries

© ERC

ILLINOIS

GOVERNOR 1990

1990 Census Population	County	Total Vote	Republican	Democratic	Other	Rep.-Dem. Plurality	Percentage Total Vote Rep.	Dem.	Major Vote Rep.	Dem.
66,090	ADAMS	24,638	14,167	10,288	183	3,879 R	57.5%	41.8%	57.9%	42.1%
10,626	ALEXANDER	4,011	1,442	2,550	19	1,108 D	36.0%	63.6%	36.1%	63.9%
14,991	BOND	6,385	3,101	3,247	37	146 D	48.6%	50.9%	48.9%	51.1%
30,806	BOONE	8,118	4,856	3,166	96	1,690 R	59.8%	39.0%	60.5%	39.5%
5,836	BROWN	2,555	1,403	1,130	22	273 R	54.9%	44.2%	55.4%	44.6%
35,688	BUREAU	14,448	7,009	7,279	160	270 D	48.5%	50.4%	49.1%	50.9%
5,322	CALHOUN	2,803	1,128	1,653	22	525 D	40.2%	59.0%	40.6%	59.4%
16,805	CARROLL	6,655	4,015	2,566	74	1,449 R	60.3%	38.6%	61.0%	39.0%
13,437	CASS	5,327	2,372	2,913	42	541 D	44.5%	54.7%	44.9%	55.1%
173,025	CHAMPAIGN	46,266	29,197	16,279	790	12,918 R	63.1%	35.2%	64.2%	35.8%
34,418	CHRISTIAN	14,589	5,890	8,586	113	2,696 D	40.4%	58.9%	40.7%	59.3%
15,921	CLARK	6,865	3,721	3,090	54	631 R	54.2%	45.0%	54.6%	45.4%
14,460	CLAY	5,425	2,292	3,079	54	787 D	42.2%	56.8%	42.7%	57.3%
33,944	CLINTON	12,017	4,894	7,027	96	2,133 D	40.7%	58.5%	41.1%	58.9%
51,644	COLES	16,525	10,057	6,336	132	3,721 R	60.9%	38.3%	61.3%	38.7%
5,105,067	COOK	1,320,958	596,642	707,523	16,793	110,881 D	45.2%	53.6%	45.7%	54.3%
19,464	CRAWFORD	7,466	4,296	3,130	40	1,166 R	57.5%	41.9%	57.9%	42.1%
10,670	CUMBERLAND	4,572	2,265	2,256	51	9 R	49.5%	49.3%	50.1%	49.9%
77,932	DE KALB	20,667	12,279	8,120	268	4,159 R	59.4%	39.3%	60.2%	39.8%
16,516	DE WITT	5,814	3,109	2,641	64	468 R	53.5%	45.4%	54.1%	45.9%
19,464	DOUGLAS	6,815	3,905	2,869	41	1,036 R	57.3%	42.1%	57.6%	42.4%
781,666	DU PAGE	219,280	149,436	67,927	1,917	81,509 R	68.1%	31.0%	68.7%	31.3%
19,595	EDGAR	8,095	4,695	3,352	48	1,343 R	58.0%	41.4%	58.3%	41.7%
7,440	EDWARDS	2,901	1,788	1,098	15	690 R	61.6%	37.8%	62.0%	38.0%
31,704	EFFINGHAM	11,930	4,925	6,917	88	1,992 D	41.3%	58.0%	41.6%	58.4%
20,893	FAYETTE	8,818	3,879	4,902	37	1,023 D	44.0%	55.6%	44.2%	55.8%
14,275	FORD	4,874	3,122	1,703	49	1,419 R	64.1%	34.9%	64.7%	35.3%
40,319	FRANKLIN	16,370	5,545	10,653	172	5,108 D	33.9%	65.1%	34.2%	65.8%
38,080	FULTON	13,960	6,773	7,056	131	283 D	48.5%	50.5%	49.0%	51.0%
6,909	GALLATIN	3,538	893	2,623	22	1,730 D	25.2%	74.1%	25.4%	74.6%
15,317	GREENE	6,345	2,988	3,310	47	322 D	47.1%	52.2%	47.4%	52.6%
32,337	GRUNDY	12,431	6,844	5,452	135	1,392 R	55.1%	43.9%	55.7%	44.3%
8,499	HAMILTON	4,418	1,500	2,906	12	1,406 D	34.0%	65.8%	34.0%	66.0%
21,373	HANCOCK	7,937	4,637	3,221	79	1,416 R	58.4%	40.6%	59.0%	41.0%
5,189	HARDIN	2,675	1,066	1,592	17	526 D	39.9%	59.5%	40.1%	59.9%
8,096	HENDERSON	3,321	1,589	1,706	26	117 D	47.8%	51.4%	48.2%	51.8%
51,159	HENRY	17,125	9,197	7,750	178	1,447 R	53.7%	45.3%	54.3%	45.7%
30,787	IROQUOIS	11,669	7,392	4,150	127	3,242 R	63.3%	35.6%	64.0%	36.0%
61,067	JACKSON	16,162	7,612	8,349	201	737 D	47.1%	51.7%	47.7%	52.3%
10,609	JASPER	4,759	2,180	2,535	44	355 D	45.8%	53.3%	46.2%	53.8%
37,020	JEFFERSON	12,368	4,925	7,370	73	2,445 D	39.8%	59.6%	40.1%	59.9%
20,539	JERSEY	7,835	3,017	4,747	71	1,730 D	38.5%	60.6%	38.9%	61.1%
21,821	JO DAVIESS	7,971	4,611	3,293	67	1,318 R	57.8%	41.3%	58.3%	41.7%
11,347	JOHNSON	4,307	2,170	2,112	25	58 R	50.4%	49.0%	50.7%	49.3%
317,471	KANE	73,707	44,531	28,298	878	16,233 R	60.4%	38.4%	61.1%	38.9%
96,255	KANKAKEE	26,980	14,210	12,580	190	1,630 R	52.7%	46.6%	53.0%	47.0%
39,413	KENDALL	12,199	7,566	4,503	130	3,063 R	62.0%	36.9%	62.7%	37.3%
56,393	KNOX	19,037	10,535	8,315	187	2,220 R	55.3%	43.7%	55.9%	44.1%
516,418	LAKE	126,059	77,512	47,337	1,210	30,175 R	61.5%	37.6%	62.1%	37.9%
106,913	LA SALLE	38,774	17,624	20,780	370	3,156 D	45.5%	53.6%	45.9%	54.1%
15,972	LAWRENCE	5,565	2,509	3,027	29	518 D	45.1%	54.4%	45.3%	54.7%
34,392	LEE	11,162	6,326	4,729	107	1,597 R	56.7%	42.4%	57.2%	42.8%
39,301	LIVINGSTON	12,816	7,838	4,878	100	2,960 R	61.2%	38.1%	61.6%	38.4%
30,798	LOGAN	11,135	6,545	4,528	62	2,017 R	58.8%	40.7%	59.1%	40.9%
35,244	MCDONOUGH	10,067	6,402	3,575	90	2,827 R	63.6%	35.5%	64.2%	35.8%
183,241	MCHENRY	48,879	30,655	17,468	756	13,187 R	62.7%	35.7%	63.7%	36.3%
129,180	MCLEAN	34,042	22,355	11,302	385	11,053 R	65.7%	33.2%	66.4%	33.6%
117,206	MACON	38,378	19,005	19,073	300	68 D	49.5%	49.7%	49.9%	50.1%
47,679	MACOUPIN	18,373	7,106	11,128	139	4,022 D	38.7%	60.6%	39.0%	61.0%
249,238	MADISON	70,581	29,260	40,561	760	11,301 D	41.5%	57.5%	41.9%	58.1%

ILLINOIS

GOVERNOR 1990

1990 Census Population	County	Total Vote	Republican	Democratic	Other	Rep.-Dem. Plurality	Percentage Total Vote Rep.	Dem.	Major Vote Rep.	Dem.
41,561	MARION	14,277	5,816	8,363	98	2,547 D	40.7%	58.6%	41.0%	59.0%
12,846	MARSHALL	5,048	2,575	2,411	62	164 R	51.0%	47.8%	51.6%	48.4%
16,269	MASON	5,959	3,039	2,865	55	174 R	51.0%	48.1%	51.5%	48.5%
14,752	MASSAC	5,013	2,458	2,516	39	58 D	49.0%	50.2%	49.4%	50.6%
11,164	MENARD	5,428	3,074	2,316	38	758 R	56.6%	42.7%	57.0%	43.0%
17,290	MERCER	6,949	3,689	3,159	101	530 R	53.1%	45.5%	53.9%	46.1%
22,422	MONROE	7,797	3,874	3,865	58	9 R	49.7%	49.6%	50.1%	49.9%
30,728	MONTGOMERY	12,158	5,369	6,682	107	1,313 D	44.2%	55.0%	44.6%	55.4%
36,397	MORGAN	13,093	7,162	5,831	100	1,331 R	54.7%	44.5%	55.1%	44.9%
13,930	MOULTRIE	4,855	2,441	2,384	30	57 R	50.3%	49.1%	50.6%	49.4%
45,957	OGLE	13,410	8,477	4,785	148	3,692 R	63.2%	35.7%	63.9%	36.1%
182,827	PEORIA	49,776	28,540	20,752	484	7,788 R	57.3%	41.7%	57.9%	42.1%
21,412	PERRY	9,130	3,514	5,567	49	2,053 D	38.5%	61.0%	38.7%	61.3%
15,548	PIATT	6,143	3,374	2,710	59	664 R	54.9%	44.1%	55.5%	44.5%
17,577	PIKE	7,771	3,866	3,845	60	21 R	49.7%	49.5%	50.1%	49.9%
4,373	POPE	2,069	1,007	1,052	10	45 D	48.7%	50.8%	48.9%	51.1%
7,523	PULASKI	3,182	1,507	1,660	15	153 D	47.4%	52.2%	47.6%	52.4%
5,730	PUTNAM	2,816	1,146	1,630	40	484 D	40.7%	57.9%	41.3%	58.7%
34,583	RANDOLPH	14,543	5,093	9,374	76	4,281 D	35.0%	64.5%	35.2%	64.8%
16,545	RICHLAND	5,976	3,071	2,854	51	217 R	51.4%	47.8%	51.8%	48.2%
148,723	ROCK ISLAND	44,461	20,413	23,572	476	3,159 D	45.9%	53.0%	46.4%	53.6%
262,852	ST. CLAIR	64,225	27,079	36,453	693	9,374 D	42.2%	56.8%	42.6%	57.4%
26,551	SALINE	10,447	4,278	6,120	49	1,842 D	40.9%	58.6%	41.1%	58.9%
178,386	SANGAMON	81,668	45,490	35,697	481	9,793 R	55.7%	43.7%	56.0%	44.0%
7,498	SCHUYLER	3,328	1,793	1,509	26	284 R	53.9%	45.3%	54.3%	45.7%
5,644	SCOTT	2,671	1,318	1,333	20	15 D	49.3%	49.9%	49.7%	50.3%
22,261	SHELBY	9,119	4,153	4,904	62	751 D	45.5%	53.8%	45.9%	54.1%
6,534	STARK	2,871	1,613	1,234	24	379 R	56.2%	43.0%	56.7%	43.3%
48,052	STEPHENSON	14,392	8,654	5,616	122	3,038 R	60.1%	39.0%	60.6%	39.4%
123,692	TAZEWELL	39,159	22,393	16,260	506	6,133 R	57.2%	41.5%	57.9%	42.1%
17,619	UNION	7,836	3,530	4,262	44	732 D	45.0%	54.4%	45.3%	54.7%
88,257	VERMILION	27,769	13,750	13,662	357	88 R	49.5%	49.2%	50.2%	49.8%
13,111	WABASH	4,329	2,377	1,917	35	460 R	54.9%	44.3%	55.4%	44.6%
19,181	WARREN	6,225	3,860	2,329	36	1,531 R	62.0%	37.4%	62.4%	37.6%
14,965	WASHINGTON	6,053	3,021	2,988	44	33 R	49.9%	49.4%	50.3%	49.7%
17,241	WAYNE	7,262	3,738	3,450	74	288 R	51.5%	47.5%	52.0%	48.0%
16,522	WHITE	8,026	3,171	4,806	49	1,635 D	39.5%	59.9%	39.8%	60.2%
60,186	WHITESIDE	19,461	9,857	9,435	169	422 R	50.7%	48.5%	51.1%	48.9%
357,313	WILL	88,608	47,386	40,540	682	6,846 R	53.5%	45.8%	53.9%	46.1%
57,733	WILLIAMSON	21,437	9,304	11,937	196	2,633 D	43.4%	55.7%	43.8%	56.2%
252,913	WINNEBAGO	71,592	40,910	29,990	692	10,920 R	57.1%	41.9%	57.7%	42.3%
32,653	WOODFORD	11,316	7,143	4,048	125	3,095 R	63.1%	35.8%	63.8%	36.2%
11,430,602	TOTAL	3,257,410	1,653,126	1,569,217	35,067	83,909 R	50.7%	48.2%	51.3%	48.7%

ILLINOIS

SENATOR 1990

1990 Census Population	County	Total Vote	Republican	Democratic	Other	Rep.-Dem. Plurality	Percentage Total Vote Rep.	Dem.	Major Vote Rep.	Dem.
66,090	ADAMS	24,516	8,383	16,133		7,750 D	34.2%	65.8%	34.2%	65.8%
10,626	ALEXANDER	4,006	907	3,099		2,192 D	22.6%	77.4%	22.6%	77.4%
14,991	BOND	6,344	2,332	4,012		1,680 D	36.8%	63.2%	36.8%	63.2%
30,806	BOONE	8,139	3,770	4,369		599 D	46.3%	53.7%	46.3%	53.7%
5,836	BROWN	2,494	898	1,596		698 D	36.0%	64.0%	36.0%	64.0%
35,688	BUREAU	14,315	5,326	8,989		3,663 D	37.2%	62.8%	37.2%	62.8%
5,322	CALHOUN	2,791	869	1,922		1,053 D	31.1%	68.9%	31.1%	68.9%
16,805	CARROLL	6,675	2,873	3,802		929 D	43.0%	57.0%	43.0%	57.0%
13,437	CASS	5,304	1,713	3,591		1,878 D	32.3%	67.7%	32.3%	67.7%
173,025	CHAMPAIGN	45,960	17,298	28,662		11,364 D	37.6%	62.4%	37.6%	62.4%
34,418	CHRISTIAN	14,468	4,459	10,009		5,550 D	30.8%	69.2%	30.8%	69.2%
15,921	CLARK	6,664	3,098	3,566		468 D	46.5%	53.5%	46.5%	53.5%
14,460	CLAY	5,310	1,955	3,355		1,400 D	36.8%	63.2%	36.8%	63.2%
33,944	CLINTON	11,867	4,507	7,360		2,853 D	38.0%	62.0%	38.0%	62.0%
51,644	COLES	16,337	5,983	10,354		4,371 D	36.6%	63.4%	36.6%	63.4%
5,105,067	COOK	1,323,533	381,604	941,929		560,325 D	28.8%	71.2%	28.8%	71.2%
19,464	CRAWFORD	7,416	3,290	4,126		836 D	44.4%	55.6%	44.4%	55.6%
10,670	CUMBERLAND	4,529	1,951	2,578		627 D	43.1%	56.9%	43.1%	56.9%
77,932	DE KALB	20,666	8,763	11,903		3,140 D	42.4%	57.6%	42.4%	57.6%
16,516	DE WITT	5,756	2,199	3,557		1,358 D	38.2%	61.8%	38.2%	61.8%
19,464	DOUGLAS	6,755	2,650	4,105		1,455 D	39.2%	60.8%	39.2%	60.8%
781,666	DU PAGE	218,898	108,923	109,975		1,052 D	49.8%	50.2%	49.8%	50.2%
19,595	EDGAR	8,017	3,832	4,185		353 D	47.8%	52.2%	47.8%	52.2%
7,440	EDWARDS	2,836	1,466	1,370		96 R	51.7%	48.3%	51.7%	48.3%
31,704	EFFINGHAM	11,927	4,511	7,416		2,905 D	37.8%	62.2%	37.8%	62.2%
20,893	FAYETTE	8,787	3,277	5,510		2,233 D	37.3%	62.7%	37.3%	62.7%
14,275	FORD	4,876	2,394	2,482		88 D	49.1%	50.9%	49.1%	50.9%
40,319	FRANKLIN	16,307	3,550	12,757		9,207 D	21.8%	78.2%	21.8%	78.2%
38,080	FULTON	13,907	4,162	9,745		5,583 D	29.9%	70.1%	29.9%	70.1%
6,909	GALLATIN	3,530	706	2,824		2,118 D	20.0%	80.0%	20.0%	80.0%
15,317	GREENE	6,266	2,245	4,021		1,776 D	35.8%	64.2%	35.8%	64.2%
32,337	GRUNDY	12,354	5,147	7,207		2,060 D	41.7%	58.3%	41.7%	58.3%
8,499	HAMILTON	4,230	1,093	3,137		2,044 D	25.8%	74.2%	25.8%	74.2%
21,373	HANCOCK	7,884	2,822	5,062		2,240 D	35.8%	64.2%	35.8%	64.2%
5,189	HARDIN	2,644	641	2,003		1,362 D	24.2%	75.8%	24.2%	75.8%
8,096	HENDERSON	3,292	1,134	2,158		1,024 D	34.4%	65.6%	34.4%	65.6%
51,159	HENRY	17,065	6,176	10,889		4,713 D	36.2%	63.8%	36.2%	63.8%
30,787	IROQUOIS	11,709	5,311	6,398		1,087 D	45.4%	54.6%	45.4%	54.6%
61,067	JACKSON	16,216	4,094	12,122		8,028 D	25.2%	74.8%	25.2%	74.8%
10,609	JASPER	4,657	1,901	2,756		855 D	40.8%	59.2%	40.8%	59.2%
37,020	JEFFERSON	12,292	3,743	8,549		4,806 D	30.5%	69.5%	30.5%	69.5%
20,539	JERSEY	7,762	2,668	5,094		2,426 D	34.4%	65.6%	34.4%	65.6%
21,821	JO DAVIESS	8,052	3,430	4,622		1,192 D	42.6%	57.4%	42.6%	57.4%
11,347	JOHNSON	4,247	1,380	2,867		1,487 D	32.5%	67.5%	32.5%	67.5%
317,471	KANE	73,413	32,812	40,601		7,789 D	44.7%	55.3%	44.7%	55.3%
96,255	KANKAKEE	26,939	9,545	17,394		7,849 D	35.4%	64.6%	35.4%	64.6%
39,413	KENDALL	12,179	5,992	6,187		195 D	49.2%	50.8%	49.2%	50.8%
56,393	KNOX	18,871	5,984	12,887		6,903 D	31.7%	68.3%	31.7%	68.3%
516,418	LAKE	126,987	56,036	70,951		14,915 D	44.1%	55.9%	44.1%	55.9%
106,913	LA SALLE	38,307	13,367	24,940		11,573 D	34.9%	65.1%	34.9%	65.1%
15,972	LAWRENCE	5,492	2,265	3,227		962 D	41.2%	58.8%	41.2%	58.8%
34,392	LEE	11,142	5,189	5,953		764 D	46.6%	53.4%	46.6%	53.4%
39,301	LIVINGSTON	12,676	5,829	6,847		1,018 D	46.0%	54.0%	46.0%	54.0%
30,798	LOGAN	11,107	4,700	6,407		1,707 D	42.3%	57.7%	42.3%	57.7%
35,244	MCDONOUGH	9,949	3,490	6,459		2,969 D	35.1%	64.9%	35.1%	64.9%
183,241	MCHENRY	48,748	25,209	23,539		1,670 R	51.7%	48.3%	51.7%	48.3%
129,180	MCLEAN	33,877	14,280	19,597		5,317 D	42.2%	57.8%	42.2%	57.8%
117,206	MACON	38,305	12,352	25,953		13,601 D	32.2%	67.8%	32.2%	67.8%
47,679	MACOUPIN	18,311	5,901	12,410		6,509 D	32.2%	67.8%	32.2%	67.8%
249,238	MADISON	70,341	22,722	47,619		24,897 D	32.3%	67.7%	32.3%	67.7%

ILLINOIS

SENATOR 1990

1990 Census Population	County	Total Vote	Republican	Democratic	Other	Rep.-Dem. Plurality	Percentage			
							Total Vote		Major Vote	
							Rep.	Dem.	Rep.	Dem.
41,561	MARION	14,144	4,996	9,148		4,152 D	35.3%	64.7%	35.3%	64.7%
12,846	MARSHALL	5,021	1,808	3,213		1,405 D	36.0%	64.0%	36.0%	64.0%
16,269	MASON	5,927	1,831	4,096		2,265 D	30.9%	69.1%	30.9%	69.1%
14,752	MASSAC	4,987	1,327	3,660		2,333 D	26.6%	73.4%	26.6%	73.4%
11,164	MENARD	5,334	2,342	2,992		650 D	43.9%	56.1%	43.9%	56.1%
17,290	MERCER	6,890	2,323	4,567		2,244 D	33.7%	66.3%	33.7%	66.3%
22,422	MONROE	7,716	3,045	4,671		1,626 D	39.5%	60.5%	39.5%	60.5%
30,728	MONTGOMERY	12,133	4,373	7,760		3,387 D	36.0%	64.0%	36.0%	64.0%
36,397	MORGAN	13,187	5,519	7,668		2,149 D	41.9%	58.1%	41.9%	58.1%
13,930	MOULTRIE	4,796	1,575	3,221		1,646 D	32.8%	67.2%	32.8%	67.2%
45,957	OGLE	13,397	6,386	7,011		625 D	47.7%	52.3%	47.7%	52.3%
182,827	PEORIA	49,038	17,044	31,994		14,950 D	34.8%	65.2%	34.8%	65.2%
21,412	PERRY	9,113	2,257	6,856		4,599 D	24.8%	75.2%	24.8%	75.2%
15,548	PIATT	6,080	2,273	3,807		1,534 D	37.4%	62.6%	37.4%	62.6%
17,577	PIKE	7,711	2,492	5,219		2,727 D	32.3%	67.7%	32.3%	67.7%
4,373	POPE	2,076	633	1,443		810 D	30.5%	69.5%	30.5%	69.5%
7,523	PULASKI	3,127	874	2,253		1,379 D	28.0%	72.0%	28.0%	72.0%
5,730	PUTNAM	2,801	952	1,849		897 D	34.0%	66.0%	34.0%	66.0%
34,583	RANDOLPH	14,337	3,974	10,363		6,389 D	27.7%	72.3%	27.7%	72.3%
16,545	RICHLAND	5,917	2,742	3,175		433 D	46.3%	53.7%	46.3%	53.7%
148,723	ROCK ISLAND	44,403	13,824	30,579		16,755 D	31.1%	68.9%	31.1%	68.9%
262,852	ST. CLAIR	62,647	19,949	42,698		22,749 D	31.8%	68.2%	31.8%	68.2%
26,551	SALINE	10,264	2,459	7,805		5,346 D	24.0%	76.0%	24.0%	76.0%
178,386	SANGAMON	80,060	31,465	48,595		17,130 D	39.3%	60.7%	39.3%	60.7%
7,498	SCHUYLER	3,354	1,281	2,073		792 D	38.2%	61.8%	38.2%	61.8%
5,644	SCOTT	2,629	992	1,637		645 D	37.7%	62.3%	37.7%	62.3%
22,261	SHELBY	9,115	2,968	6,147		3,179 D	32.6%	67.4%	32.6%	67.4%
6,534	STARK	2,862	1,091	1,771		680 D	38.1%	61.9%	38.1%	61.9%
48,052	STEPHENSON	14,540	5,954	8,586		2,632 D	40.9%	59.1%	40.9%	59.1%
123,692	TAZEWELL	39,118	14,232	24,886		10,654 D	36.4%	63.6%	36.4%	63.6%
17,619	UNION	7,759	1,887	5,872		3,985 D	24.3%	75.7%	24.3%	75.7%
88,257	VERMILION	27,709	9,949	17,760		7,811 D	35.9%	64.1%	35.9%	64.1%
13,111	WABASH	4,308	1,834	2,474		640 D	42.6%	57.4%	42.6%	57.4%
19,181	WARREN	6,238	2,494	3,744		1,250 D	40.0%	60.0%	40.0%	60.0%
14,965	WASHINGTON	5,966	2,729	3,237		508 D	45.7%	54.3%	45.7%	54.3%
17,241	WAYNE	7,209	3,352	3,857		505 D	46.5%	53.5%	46.5%	53.5%
16,522	WHITE	8,001	2,997	5,004		2,007 D	37.5%	62.5%	37.5%	62.5%
60,186	WHITESIDE	19,261	7,055	12,206		5,151 D	36.6%	63.4%	36.6%	63.4%
357,313	WILL	88,801	34,829	53,972		19,143 D	39.2%	60.8%	39.2%	60.8%
57,733	WILLIAMSON	21,394	5,394	16,000		10,606 D	25.2%	74.8%	25.2%	74.8%
252,913	WINNEBAGO	72,104	29,961	42,143		12,182 D	41.6%	58.4%	41.6%	58.4%
32,653	WOODFORD	11,287	5,059	6,228		1,169 D	44.8%	55.2%	44.8%	55.2%
11,430,602	TOTAL	3,251,005	1,135,628	2,115,377		979,749 D	34.9%	65.1%	34.9%	65.1%

CHICAGO

GOVERNOR 1990

1990 Census Population	Ward	Total Vote	Republican	Democratic	Other	Rep.-Dem. Plurality	Total Vote Rep.	Total Vote Dem.	Major Vote Rep.	Major Vote Dem.
	WARD 1	12,919	4,590	8,095	234	3,505 D	35.5%	62.7%	36.2%	63.8%
	WARD 2	10,118	1,966	7,856	296	5,890 D	19.4%	77.6%	20.0%	80.0%
	WARD 3	7,840	1,002	6,642	196	5,640 D	12.8%	84.7%	13.1%	86.9%
	WARD 4	11,412	2,769	8,306	337	5,537 D	24.3%	72.8%	25.0%	75.0%
	WARD 5	13,674	3,577	9,672	425	6,095 D	26.2%	70.7%	27.0%	73.0%
	WARD 6	18,143	4,137	13,474	532	9,337 D	22.8%	74.3%	23.5%	76.5%
	WARD 7	9,482	1,928	7,270	284	5,342 D	20.3%	76.7%	21.0%	79.0%
	WARD 8	16,518	3,240	12,758	520	9,518 D	19.6%	77.2%	20.3%	79.7%
	WARD 9	11,102	3,512	7,254	336	3,742 D	31.6%	65.3%	32.6%	67.4%
	WARD 10	15,902	6,997	8,694	211	1,697 D	44.0%	54.7%	44.6%	55.4%
	WARD 11	15,648	3,311	12,214	123	8,903 D	21.2%	78.1%	21.3%	78.7%
	WARD 12	12,170	4,223	7,834	113	3,611 D	34.7%	64.4%	35.0%	65.0%
	WARD 13	25,614	8,314	17,150	150	8,836 D	32.5%	67.0%	32.7%	67.3%
	WARD 14	11,779	3,368	8,279	132	4,911 D	28.6%	70.3%	28.9%	71.1%
	WARD 15	10,016	2,331	7,370	315	5,039 D	23.3%	73.6%	24.0%	76.0%
	WARD 16	9,772	1,130	8,327	315	7,197 D	11.6%	85.2%	11.9%	88.1%
	WARD 17	11,969	1,888	9,673	408	7,785 D	15.8%	80.8%	16.3%	83.7%
	WARD 18	19,434	6,801	12,319	314	5,518 D	35.0%	63.4%	35.6%	64.4%
	WARD 19	24,873	10,619	14,035	219	3,416 D	42.7%	56.4%	43.1%	56.9%
	WARD 20	9,609	1,558	7,728	323	6,170 D	16.2%	80.4%	16.8%	83.2%
	WARD 21	16,230	3,318	12,346	566	9,028 D	20.4%	76.1%	21.2%	78.8%
	WARD 22	4,041	1,045	2,937	59	1,892 D	25.9%	72.7%	26.2%	73.8%
	WARD 23	22,725	9,615	12,977	133	3,362 D	42.3%	57.1%	42.6%	57.4%
	WARD 24	9,915	1,147	8,437	331	7,290 D	11.6%	85.1%	12.0%	88.0%
	WARD 25	5,312	1,370	3,837	105	2,467 D	25.8%	72.2%	26.3%	73.7%
	WARD 26	7,116	1,714	5,256	146	3,542 D	24.1%	73.9%	24.6%	75.4%
	WARD 27	7,431	1,376	5,851	204	4,475 D	18.5%	78.7%	19.0%	81.0%
	WARD 28	8,399	1,072	7,088	239	6,016 D	12.8%	84.4%	13.1%	86.9%
	WARD 29	9,816	1,538	7,999	279	6,461 D	15.7%	81.5%	16.1%	83.9%
	WARD 30	11,645	4,005	7,486	154	3,481 D	34.4%	64.3%	34.9%	65.1%
	WARD 31	6,703	1,586	4,981	136	3,395 D	23.7%	74.3%	24.2%	75.8%
	WARD 32	10,329	2,910	7,253	166	4,343 D	28.2%	70.2%	28.6%	71.4%
	WARD 33	11,892	3,358	8,338	196	4,980 D	28.2%	70.1%	28.7%	71.3%
	WARD 34	14,564	2,626	11,518	420	8,892 D	18.0%	79.1%	18.6%	81.4%
	WARD 35	12,147	5,206	6,809	132	1,603 D	42.9%	56.1%	43.3%	56.7%
	WARD 36	19,513	8,597	10,775	141	2,178 D	44.1%	55.2%	44.4%	55.6%
	WARD 37	9,024	1,249	7,536	239	6,287 D	13.8%	83.5%	14.2%	85.8%
	WARD 38	19,744	10,010	9,603	131	407 R	50.7%	48.6%	51.0%	49.0%
	WARD 39	15,444	7,035	8,292	117	1,257 D	45.6%	53.7%	45.9%	54.1%
	WARD 40	11,861	4,923	6,802	136	1,879 D	41.5%	57.3%	42.0%	58.0%
	WARD 41	23,788	13,038	10,601	149	2,437 R	54.8%	44.6%	55.2%	44.8%
	WARD 42	17,375	7,950	9,251	174	1,301 D	45.8%	53.2%	46.2%	53.8%
	WARD 43	19,047	9,751	9,164	132	587 R	51.2%	48.1%	51.6%	48.4%
	WARD 44	16,118	6,662	9,277	179	2,615 D	41.3%	57.6%	41.8%	58.2%
	WARD 45	20,860	10,112	10,588	160	476 D	48.5%	50.8%	48.9%	51.1%
	WARD 46	12,454	4,663	7,571	220	2,908 D	37.4%	60.8%	38.1%	61.9%
	WARD 47	14,739	5,478	9,103	158	3,625 D	37.2%	61.8%	37.6%	62.4%
	WARD 48	12,531	4,682	7,630	219	2,948 D	37.4%	60.9%	38.0%	62.0%
	WARD 49	11,498	3,584	7,713	201	4,129 D	31.2%	67.1%	31.7%	68.3%
	WARD 50	16,938	5,579	11,243	116	5,664 D	32.9%	66.4%	33.2%	66.8%
	ABSENTEE	8,664	2,798	5,830	36	3,032 D	32.3%	67.3%	32.4%	67.6%
2,783,726	TOTAL	685,857	225,258	449,042	11,557	223,784 D	32.8%	65.5%	33.4%	66.6%

CHICAGO

SENATOR 1990

1990 Census Population	Ward	Total Vote	Republican	Democratic	Other	Rep.-Dem. Plurality	Percentage Total Vote Rep.	Dem.	Major Vote Rep.	Dem.
	WARD 1	12,960	2,718	10,242		7,524 D	21.0%	79.0%	21.0%	79.0%
	WARD 2	10,170	715	9,455		8,740 D	7.0%	93.0%	7.0%	93.0%
	WARD 3	7,927	431	7,496		7,065 D	5.4%	94.6%	5.4%	94.6%
	WARD 4	11,634	901	10,733		9,832 D	7.7%	92.3%	7.7%	92.3%
	WARD 5	13,898	1,224	12,674		11,450 D	8.8%	91.2%	8.8%	91.2%
	WARD 6	18,467	1,078	17,389		16,311 D	5.8%	94.2%	5.8%	94.2%
	WARD 7	9,548	801	8,747		7,946 D	8.4%	91.6%	8.4%	91.6%
	WARD 8	16,708	997	15,711		14,714 D	6.0%	94.0%	6.0%	94.0%
	WARD 9	11,257	779	10,478		9,699 D	6.9%	93.1%	6.9%	93.1%
	WARD 10	15,877	4,429	11,448		7,019 D	27.9%	72.1%	27.9%	72.1%
	WARD 11	15,626	2,072	13,554		11,482 D	13.3%	86.7%	13.3%	86.7%
	WARD 12	12,176	2,703	9,473		6,770 D	22.2%	77.8%	22.2%	77.8%
	WARD 13	25,572	5,859	19,713		13,854 D	22.9%	77.1%	22.9%	77.1%
	WARD 14	11,815	2,226	9,589		7,363 D	18.8%	81.2%	18.8%	81.2%
	WARD 15	10,027	1,186	8,841		7,655 D	11.8%	88.2%	11.8%	88.2%
	WARD 16	9,840	441	9,399		8,958 D	4.5%	95.5%	4.5%	95.5%
	WARD 17	12,118	627	11,491		10,864 D	5.2%	94.8%	5.2%	94.8%
	WARD 18	19,560	4,027	15,533		11,506 D	20.6%	79.4%	20.6%	79.4%
	WARD 19	24,870	7,259	17,611		10,352 D	29.2%	70.8%	29.2%	70.8%
	WARD 20	9,785	581	9,204		8,623 D	5.9%	94.1%	5.9%	94.1%
	WARD 21	16,429	981	15,448		14,467 D	6.0%	94.0%	6.0%	94.0%
	WARD 22	4,021	532	3,489		2,957 D	13.2%	86.8%	13.2%	86.8%
	WARD 23	22,546	6,287	16,259		9,972 D	27.9%	72.1%	27.9%	72.1%
	WARD 24	9,955	453	9,502		9,049 D	4.6%	95.4%	4.6%	95.4%
	WARD 25	5,278	737	4,541		3,804 D	14.0%	86.0%	14.0%	86.0%
	WARD 26	7,034	960	6,074		5,114 D	13.6%	86.4%	13.6%	86.4%
	WARD 27	7,393	685	6,708		6,023 D	9.3%	90.7%	9.3%	90.7%
	WARD 28	8,433	408	8,025		7,617 D	4.8%	95.2%	4.8%	95.2%
	WARD 29	9,891	663	9,228		8,565 D	6.7%	93.3%	6.7%	93.3%
	WARD 30	11,634	2,445	9,189		6,744 D	21.0%	79.0%	21.0%	79.0%
	WARD 31	6,659	863	5,796		4,933 D	13.0%	87.0%	13.0%	87.0%
	WARD 32	10,381	1,718	8,663		6,945 D	16.5%	83.5%	16.5%	83.5%
	WARD 33	11,841	2,059	9,782		7,723 D	17.4%	82.6%	17.4%	82.6%
	WARD 34	14,759	790	13,969		13,179 D	5.4%	94.6%	5.4%	94.6%
	WARD 35	12,150	3,180	8,970		5,790 D	26.2%	73.8%	26.2%	73.8%
	WARD 36	19,449	5,402	14,047		8,645 D	27.8%	72.2%	27.8%	72.2%
	WARD 37	9,076	489	8,587		8,098 D	5.4%	94.6%	5.4%	94.6%
	WARD 38	19,618	6,178	13,440		7,262 D	31.5%	68.5%	31.5%	68.5%
	WARD 39	15,382	4,515	10,867		6,352 D	29.4%	70.6%	29.4%	70.6%
	WARD 40	11,821	3,054	8,767		5,713 D	25.8%	74.2%	25.8%	74.2%
	WARD 41	23,727	9,084	14,643		5,559 D	38.3%	61.7%	38.3%	61.7%
	WARD 42	17,479	5,196	12,283		7,087 D	29.7%	70.3%	29.7%	70.3%
	WARD 43	19,129	5,986	13,143		7,157 D	31.3%	68.7%	31.3%	68.7%
	WARD 44	16,209	3,576	12,633		9,057 D	22.1%	77.9%	22.1%	77.9%
	WARD 45	20,765	6,589	14,176		7,587 D	31.7%	68.3%	31.7%	68.3%
	WARD 46	12,487	2,535	9,952		7,417 D	20.3%	79.7%	20.3%	79.7%
	WARD 47	14,762	3,302	11,460		8,158 D	22.4%	77.6%	22.4%	77.6%
	WARD 48	12,608	2,748	9,860		7,112 D	21.8%	78.2%	21.8%	78.2%
	WARD 49	11,565	2,107	9,458		7,351 D	18.2%	81.8%	18.2%	81.8%
	WARD 50	17,018	2,840	14,178		11,338 D	16.7%	83.3%	16.7%	83.3%
	ABSENTEE	8,666	1,705	6,961		5,256 D	19.7%	80.3%	19.7%	80.3%
2,783,726	TOTAL	688,000	129,121	558,879		429,758 D	18.8%	81.2%	18.8%	81.2%

ILLINOIS

CONGRESS

CD	Year	Total Vote	Republican Vote	Republican Candidate	Democratic Vote	Democratic Candidate	Other Vote	Rep.-Dem. Plurality	Total Vote Rep.	Total Vote Dem.	Major Vote Rep.	Major Vote Dem.
1	1990	107,598	6,708	PEYTON, BABETTE	100,890	HAYES, CHARLES A.		94,182 D	6.2%	93.8%	6.2%	93.8%
1	1988	170,878	6,753	EVANS, STEPHEN J.	164,125	HAYES, CHARLES A.		157,372 D	4.0%	96.0%	4.0%	96.0%
1	1986	126,948	4,572	FAULKNER, JOSEPH C.	122,376	HAYES, CHARLES A.		117,804 D	3.6%	96.4%	3.6%	96.4%
1	1984	185,534			177,438	HAYES, CHARLES A.	8,096	177,438 D		95.6%		100.0%
1	1982	177,462	4,820	TALIAFERRO, CHARLES A.	172,641	WASHINGTON, HAROLD	1	167,821 D	2.7%	97.3%	2.7%	97.3%
2	1990	102,595	22,350	HESPEL, WILLIAM T.	80,245	SAVAGE, GUS		57,895 D	21.8%	78.2%	21.8%	78.2%
2	1988	167,087	28,831	HESPEL, WILLIAM T.	138,256	SAVAGE, GUS		109,425 D	17.3%	82.7%	17.3%	82.7%
2	1986	118,417	19,149	TAYLOR, RON	99,268	SAVAGE, GUS		80,119 D	16.2%	83.8%	16.2%	83.8%
2	1984	187,215	31,865	HARMAN, DALE F.	155,349	SAVAGE, GUS	1	123,484 D	17.0%	83.0%	17.0%	83.0%
2	1982	161,794	20,670	SPARKS, KEVIN W.	140,827	SAVAGE, GUS	297	120,157 D	12.8%	87.0%	12.8%	87.2%
3	1990	155,811	45,299	KLEIN, CARL L.	110,512	RUSSO, MARTIN A.		65,213 D	29.1%	70.9%	29.1%	70.9%
3	1988	212,292	80,181	MCCARTHY, JOSEPH J.	132,111	RUSSO, MARTIN A.		51,930 D	37.8%	62.2%	37.8%	62.2%
3	1986	155,567	52,618	TIERNEY, JAMES J.	102,949	RUSSO, MARTIN A.		50,331 D	33.8%	66.2%	33.8%	66.2%
3	1984	222,582	79,218	MURPHY, RICHARD D.	143,363	RUSSO, MARTIN A.	1	64,145 D	35.6%	64.4%	35.6%	64.4%
3	1982	185,659	48,268	MURPHY, RICHARD D.	137,391	RUSSO, MARTIN A.		89,123 D	26.0%	74.0%	26.0%	74.0%
4	1990	130,548	53,258	HOFFMAN, MANNY	77,290	SANGMEISTER, GEORGE E.		24,032 D	40.8%	59.2%	40.8%	59.2%
4	1988	181,525	90,243	DAVIS, JACK	91,282	SANGMEISTER, GEORGE E.		1,039 D	49.7%	50.3%	49.7%	50.3%
4	1986	119,356	61,583	DAVIS, JACK	57,773	COLLINS, SHAWN		3,810 R	51.6%	48.4%	51.6%	48.4%
4	1984	190,291	121,744	O'BRIEN, GEORGE M.	68,547	MARLOW, DENNIS E.		53,197 R	64.0%	36.0%	64.0%	36.0%
4	1982	146,172	79,842	O'BRIEN, GEORGE M.	66,323	MURER, MICHAEL A.	7	13,519 R	54.6%	45.4%	54.6%	45.4%
5	1990	111,246	34,440	SHESTOKAS, DAVID J.	73,805	LIPINSKI, WILLIAM O.	3,001	39,365 D	31.0%	66.3%	31.8%	68.2%
5	1988	152,695	59,128	HOLOWINSKI, JOHN J.	93,567	LIPINSKI, WILLIAM O.		34,439 D	38.7%	61.3%	38.7%	61.3%
5	1986	117,204	34,738	SOBIESKI, DANIEL J.	82,466	LIPINSKI, WILLIAM O.		47,728 D	29.6%	70.4%	29.6%	70.4%
5	1984	167,708	61,109	PACZKOWSKI, JOHN M.	106,597	LIPINSKI, WILLIAM O.	2	45,488 D	36.4%	63.6%	36.4%	63.6%
5	1982	146,322	35,970	PARTYKA, DANIEL J.	110,351	LIPINSKI, WILLIAM O.	1	74,381 D	24.6%	75.4%	24.6%	75.4%
6	1990	144,565	96,410	HYDE, HENRY J.	48,155	CASSIDY, ROBERT J.		48,255 R	66.7%	33.3%	66.7%	33.3%
6	1988	208,229	153,425	HYDE, HENRY J.	54,804	ANDREL, WILLIAM J.		98,621 R	73.7%	26.3%	73.7%	26.3%
6	1986	130,260	98,196	HYDE, HENRY J.	32,064	RENSHAW, ROBERT H.		66,132 R	75.4%	24.6%	75.4%	24.6%
6	1984	209,562	157,370	HYDE, HENRY J.	52,189	RENSHAW, ROBERT H.	3	105,181 R	75.1%	24.9%	75.1%	24.9%
6	1982	143,168	97,918	HYDE, HENRY J.	45,237	KENNEL, LEROY E.	13	52,681 R	68.4%	31.6%	68.4%	31.6%
7	1990	100,120	20,099	DOOLEY, MICHAEL	80,021	COLLINS, CARDISS		59,922 D	20.1%	79.9%	20.1%	79.9%
7	1988	135,331			135,331	COLLINS, CARDISS		135,331 D		100.0%		100.0%
7	1986	113,164	21,055	KALLAS, CAROLINE K.	90,761	COLLINS, CARDISS	1,348	69,706 D	18.6%	80.2%	18.8%	81.2%
7	1984	172,908	37,411	BEVEL, JAMES L.	135,493	COLLINS, CARDISS	4	98,082 D	21.6%	78.4%	21.6%	78.4%
7	1982	154,974	20,994	CHEEKS, DANSBY	133,978	COLLINS, CARDISS	2	112,984 D	13.5%	86.5%	13.5%	86.5%
8	1990	88,680			70,151	ROSTENKOWSKI, DANIEL	18,529	70,151 D		79.1%		100.0%
8	1988	144,324	34,659	VETTER, V. STEPHEN	107,728	ROSTENKOWSKI, DANIEL	1,937	73,069 D	24.0%	74.6%	24.3%	75.7%
8	1986	105,256	22,383	DE FAZIO, THOMAS J.	82,873	ROSTENKOWSKI, DANIEL		60,490 D	21.3%	78.7%	21.3%	78.7%
8	1984	160,417	46,030	GEORGESON, SPIRO F.	114,385	ROSTENKOWSKI, DANIEL	2	68,355 D	28.7%	71.3%	28.7%	71.3%
8	1982	148,985	24,666	HICKEY, BONNIE	124,318	ROSTENKOWSKI, DANIEL	1	99,652 D	16.6%	83.4%	16.6%	83.4%
9	1990	135,588	39,031	SOHN, HERBERT	96,557	YATES, SIDNEY R.		57,526 D	28.8%	71.2%	28.8%	71.2%
9	1988	205,187	67,604	SOHN, HERBERT	135,583	YATES, SIDNEY R.	2,000	67,979 D	32.9%	66.1%	33.3%	66.7%
9	1986	129,453	36,715	SOHN, HERBERT	92,738	YATES, SIDNEY R.		56,023 D	28.4%	71.6%	28.4%	71.6%
9	1984	214,495	69,613	SOHN, HERBERT	144,879	YATES, SIDNEY R.	3	75,266 D	32.5%	67.5%	32.5%	67.5%
9	1982	171,529	54,851	BERTINI, CATHERINE	114,083	YATES, SIDNEY R.	2,595	59,232 D	32.0%	66.5%	32.5%	67.5%
10	1990	153,599	104,070	PORTER, JOHN E.	47,286	MCNAMARA, PEG	2,243	56,784 R	67.8%	30.8%	68.8%	31.2%
10	1988	218,706	158,519	PORTER, JOHN E.	60,187	FRIEDMAN, EUGENE F.		98,332 R	72.5%	27.5%	72.5%	27.5%
10	1986	116,520	87,530	PORTER, JOHN E.	28,990	CLELAND, ROBERT A.		58,540 R	75.1%	24.9%	75.1%	24.9%
10	1984	211,140	153,330	PORTER, JOHN E.	57,809	BRAVER, RUTH C.	1	95,521 R	72.6%	27.4%	72.6%	27.4%
10	1982	153,868	90,750	PORTER, JOHN E.	63,115	CHAPMAN, EUGENIA S.	3	27,635 R	59.0%	41.0%	59.0%	41.0%

ILLINOIS

CONGRESS

CD	Year	Total Vote	Republican Vote	Candidate	Democratic Vote	Candidate	Other Vote	Rep.-Dem. Plurality	Total Vote Rep.	Dem.	Major Vote Rep.	Dem.
11	1990	154,245	68,850	DUDYCZ, WALTER W.	82,703	ANNUNZIO, FRANK	2,692	13,853 D	44.6%	53.6%	45.4%	54.6%
11	1988	204,242	72,489	GOTTLIEB, GEORGE S.	131,753	ANNUNZIO, FRANK		59,264 D	35.5%	64.5%	35.5%	64.5%
11	1986	151,311	44,341	GOTTLIEB, GEORGE S.	106,970	ANNUNZIO, FRANK		62,629 D	29.3%	70.7%	29.3%	70.7%
11	1984	220,690	82,518	THEUSCH, CHARLES J.	138,171	ANNUNZIO, FRANK	1	55,653 D	37.4%	62.6%	37.4%	62.6%
11	1982	185,722	50,967	MOYNIHAN, JAMES F.	134,755	ANNUNZIO, FRANK		83,788 D	27.4%	72.6%	27.4%	72.6%
12	1990	137,531	113,081	CRANE, PHILIP M.			24,450	113,081 R	82.2%		100.0%	
12	1988	220,682	165,913	CRANE, PHILIP M.	54,769	LEONARDI, JOHN A.		111,144 R	75.2%	24.8%	75.2%	24.8%
12	1986	114,580	89,044	CRANE, PHILIP M.	25,536	LEONARDI, JOHN A.		63,508 R	77.7%	22.3%	77.7%	22.3%
12	1984	205,119	159,582	CRANE, PHILIP M.	45,537	LA FLAMME, EDWARD J.		114,045 R	77.8%	22.2%	77.8%	22.2%
12	1982	130,701	86,487	CRANE, PHILIP M.	40,108	DEFOSSE, DANIEL G.	4,106	46,379 R	66.2%	30.7%	68.3%	31.7%
13	1990	176,353	116,048	FAWELL, HARRIS W.	60,305	THOMAS, STEVEN		55,743 R	65.8%	34.2%	65.8%	34.2%
13	1988	249,416	174,992	FAWELL, HARRIS W.	74,424	CRAIG, EVELYN E.		100,568 R	70.2%	29.8%	70.2%	29.8%
13	1986	146,101	107,227	FAWELL, HARRIS W.	38,874	JEFFREY, DOMINICK J.		68,353 R	73.4%	26.6%	73.4%	26.6%
13	1984	235,234	157,603	FAWELL, HARRIS W.	77,623	DONOHUE, MICHAEL J.	8	79,980 R	67.0%	33.0%	67.0%	33.0%
13	1982	162,530	113,423	ERLENBORN, JOHN N.	49,105	BILY, ROBERT	2	64,318 R	69.8%	30.2%	69.8%	30.2%
14	1990	167,975	112,383	HASTERT, J. DENNIS	55,592	WESTPHAL, DONALD J.		56,791 R	66.9%	33.1%	66.9%	33.1%
14	1988	218,628	161,146	HASTERT, J. DENNIS	57,482	YOUHANAIE, STEPHEN		103,664 R	73.7%	26.3%	73.7%	26.3%
14	1986	147,581	77,288	HASTERT, J. DENNIS	70,293	KEARNS, MARY LOU		6,995 R	52.4%	47.6%	52.4%	47.6%
14	1984	218,738	135,967	GROTBERG, JOHN E.	82,756	MCGRATH, DAN	15	53,211 R	62.2%	37.8%	62.2%	37.8%
14	1982	152,180	98,262	CORCORAN, TOM	53,914	MCGRATH, DAN	4	44,348 R	64.6%	35.4%	64.6%	35.4%
15	1990	119,822	119,812	MADIGAN, EDWARD R.			10	119,812 R	100.0%		100.0%	
15	1988	195,431	140,171	MADIGAN, EDWARD R.	55,260	CURL, THOMAS J.		84,911 R	71.7%	28.3%	71.7%	28.3%
15	1986	115,284	115,284	MADIGAN, EDWARD R.				115,284 R	100.0%		100.0%	
15	1984	203,613	149,096	MADIGAN, EDWARD R.	54,516	HOFFMANN, JOHN M.	1	94,580 R	73.2%	26.8%	73.2%	26.8%
15	1982	158,344	105,038	MADIGAN, EDWARD R.	53,303	HALL, TIM L.	3	51,735 R	66.3%	33.7%	66.3%	33.7%
16	1990	152,166	69,105	HALLOCK, JOHN W.	83,061	COX, JOHN W.		13,956 D	45.4%	54.6%	45.4%	54.6%
16	1988	200,796	128,365	MARTIN, LYNN	72,431	MAHAN, STEVEN E.		55,934 R	63.9%	36.1%	63.9%	36.1%
16	1986	139,069	92,982	MARTIN, LYNN	46,087	BOHNSACK, KENNETH F.		46,895 R	66.9%	33.1%	66.9%	33.1%
16	1984	218,538	127,684	MARTIN, LYNN	90,850	SCHWERDTFEGER, CARL R.	4	36,834 R	58.4%	41.6%	58.4%	41.6%
16	1982	156,287	89,405	MARTIN, LYNN	66,877	SCHWERDTFEGER, CARL R.	5	22,528 R	57.2%	42.8%	57.2%	42.8%
17	1990	153,442	51,380	LEE, DAN	102,062	EVANS, LANE		50,682 D	33.5%	66.5%	33.5%	66.5%
17	1988	203,690	71,560	STEWART, WILLIAM E.	132,130	EVANS, LANE		60,570 D	35.1%	64.9%	35.1%	64.9%
17	1986	153,543	68,101	MCHARD, SAM	85,442	EVANS, LANE		17,341 D	44.4%	55.6%	44.4%	55.6%
17	1984	226,345	98,069	MCMILLAN, KENNETH G.	128,273	EVANS, LANE	3	30,204 D	43.3%	56.7%	43.3%	56.7%
17	1982	178,887	84,347	MCMILLAN, KENNETH G.	94,483	EVANS, LANE	57	10,136 D	47.2%	52.8%	47.2%	52.8%
18	1990	107,370	105,693	MICHEL, ROBERT H.			1,677	105,693 R	98.4%		100.0%	
18	1988	209,221	114,458	MICHEL, ROBERT H.	94,763	STEPHENS, G. DOUGLAS		19,695 R	54.7%	45.3%	54.7%	45.3%
18	1986	150,639	94,308	MICHEL, ROBERT H.	56,331	DAWSON, JIM		37,977 R	62.6%	37.4%	62.6%	37.4%
18	1984	223,106	136,183	MICHEL, ROBERT H.	86,884	BRADLEY, GERALD A.	39	49,299 R	61.0%	38.9%	61.1%	38.9%
18	1982	188,694	97,406	MICHEL, ROBERT H.	91,281	STEPHENS, G. DOUGLAS	7	6,125 R	51.6%	48.4%	51.6%	48.4%
19	1990	171,888	55,680	KERANS, ROBERT F.	113,958	BRUCE, TERRY L.	2,250	58,278 D	32.4%	66.3%	32.8%	67.2%
19	1988	206,870	73,981	KERANS, ROBERT F.	132,889	BRUCE, TERRY L.		58,908 D	35.8%	64.2%	35.8%	64.2%
19	1986	167,291	56,186	SALVI, AL	111,105	BRUCE, TERRY L.		54,919 D	33.6%	66.4%	33.6%	66.4%
19	1984	225,103	107,463	CRANE, DANIEL B.	117,634	BRUCE, TERRY L.	6	10,171 D	47.7%	52.3%	47.7%	52.3%
19	1982	182,064	94,833	CRANE, DANIEL B.	87,231	GWINN, JOHN		7,602 R	52.1%	47.9%	52.1%	47.9%
20	1990	196,547	66,433	JURGENS, PAUL E.	130,114	DURBIN, RICHARD J.		63,681 D	33.8%	66.2%	33.8%	66.2%
20	1988	222,644	69,303	JURGENS, PAUL E.	153,341	DURBIN, RICHARD J.		84,038 D	31.1%	68.9%	31.1%	68.9%
20	1986	185,847	59,291	MCCARTHY, KEVIN B.	126,556	DURBIN, RICHARD J.		67,265 D	31.9%	68.1%	31.9%	68.1%
20	1984	236,821	91,728	AUSTIN, RICHARD G.	145,092	DURBIN, RICHARD J.	1	53,364 D	38.7%	61.3%	38.7%	61.3%
20	1982	200,109	99,348	FINDLEY, PAUL	100,758	DURBIN, RICHARD J.	3	1,410 D	49.6%	50.4%	49.6%	50.4%

ILLINOIS

CONGRESS

CD	Year	Total Vote	Republican Vote	Candidate	Democratic Vote	Candidate	Other Vote	Rep.-Dem. Plurality	Percentage Total Vote Rep.	Dem.	Major Vote Rep.	Dem.
21	1990	144,157	48,949	GAFFNER, ROBERT H.	95,208	COSTELLO, JERRY F.		46,259 D	34.0%	66.0%	34.0%	66.0%
21	1988	201,221	95,385	GAFFNER, ROBERT H.	105,836	COSTELLO, JERRY F.		10,451 D	47.4%	52.6%	47.4%	52.6%
21	1986	130,501	64,779	GAFFNER, ROBERT H.	65,722	PRICE, MELVIN		943 D	49.6%	50.4%	49.6%	50.4%
21	1984	211,194	84,148	GAFFNER, ROBERT H.	127,046	PRICE, MELVIN		42,898 D	39.8%	60.2%	39.8%	60.2%
21	1982	140,608	46,764	GAFFNER, ROBERT H.	89,500	PRICE, MELVIN	4,344	42,736 D	33.3%	63.7%	34.3%	65.7%
22	1990	165,321			138,425	POSHARD, GLENN	26,896	138,425 D		83.7%		100.0%
22	1988	214,854	75,462	KELLEY, PATRICK J.	139,392	POSHARD, GLENN		63,930 D	35.1%	64.9%	35.1%	64.9%
22	1986	183,318	85,733	PATCHETT, RANDY	97,585	GRAY, KENNETH J.		11,852 D	46.8%	53.2%	46.8%	53.2%
22	1984	232,728	115,775	PATCHETT, RANDY	116,952	GRAY, KENNETH J.	1	1,177 D	49.7%	50.3%	49.7%	50.3%
22	1982	186,972	63,279	PRINEAS, PETER G.	123,693	SIMON, PAUL		60,414 D	33.8%	66.2%	33.8%	66.2%

ILLINOIS

1990 GENERAL ELECTION

Governor   Other vote was Solidarity (Fields).

Senator

Congress   Other vote was Solidarity (Bartos) in CD 5; Libertarian (Marshall) in CD 8; Solidarity (Gorrell) in CD 10; Solidarity (Saska) in CD 11; Solidarity (Pedersen) in CD 12; write-in (Decker) in CD 15; 1,524 write-in (Gillin) and 153 write-in (Port) in CD 18; Solidarity (O'Neill) in CD 19; Wham Party (Wham) in CD 22.

CHICAGO

1990 Population figures not available by ward for Chicago.

Governor   Other vote was Solidarity (Fields).

Senator

1990 PRIMARIES

MARCH 20 REPUBLICAN

Governor   482,441 Jim Edgar; 256,889 Steven Baer; 28,365 Robert Marshall.

Senator   Lynn Martin, unopposed.

Congress   Unopposed in sixteen CD's. No candidate in CD's 3, 8, and 22. In CD 3 Carl L. Klein was nominated by the local party committee; in CD 8 William A. Radatz received 4 write-in votes but did not qualify. Contested as follows:

CD 2   2,187 William T. Hespel; 1,642 Ron Taylor; 1,154 Sidney Welch.
CD 16   33,623 John W. Hallock; 28,681 Donald Manzullo.
CD 19   23,764 Robert F. Kerans; 21,797 Lane Harvey.

MARCH 20 DEMOCRATIC

Governor   Neil F. Hartigan, unopposed.

Senator   Paul Simon, unopposed.

Congress   Unopposed in fourteen CD's. No candidate in CD's 12, 15, and 18. John L. Grandin, the unopposed candidate in CD 13, withdrew after the primary and Steven Thomas was substituted by the local party committee. Contested as follows:

CD 1   83,098 Charles A. Hayes; 6,676 Gilbert S. Marchman.
CD 2   41,837 Gus Savage; 35,012 Melvin J. Reynolds; 4,412 Ernest Washington.
CD 7   52,763 Cardiss Collins; 7,005 Sharon E. Butler; 2,084 James Hammonds; 1,529 Rosalind Collins; 1,273 Earnest L. Thomas.
CD 9   53,758 Sidney R. Yates; 20,821 Edwin W. Eisendrath; 2,289 James Chiakulas.
CD 16   6,778 John W. Cox; 6,205 Stephen J. Eytalis; 4,990 James E. Dixon; 2,299 Robert E. Brinkmeier.

MARCH 20 SOLIDARITY

Governor   Jeff W. Smith received 13 write-in votes but did not qualify. Jessie Fields was nominated by the state party committee.

Senator   No candidate.

ILLINOIS

Congress   Unopposed in all CD's in which candidates were entered except CD 12 below. Larry Saska, the unopposed candidate in CD 11, withdrew after the primary and no substitution was made.

CD 12   10 Steve Pedersen; 4 Steve Lasko.

INDIANA

GOVERNOR
Evan Bayh (D). Elected 1988 to a four-year term.

SENATORS
Daniel R. Coats (R). Elected 1990 to fill out the remaining two years of the term vacated when Senator J. Danforth Quayle (R) resigned to become Vice-President; had previously been appointed January 1989 to fill this vacancy.

Richard G. Lugar (R). Re-elected 1988 to a six-year term. Previously elected 1982, 1976.

REPRESENTATIVES

1. Peter J. Visclosky (D)
2. Philip R. Sharp (D)
3. Timothy J. Roemer (D)
4. Jill L. Long (D)
5. Jim Jontz (D)
6. Dan Burton (R)
7. John T. Myers (R)
8. Francis McCloskey (D)
9. Lee H. Hamilton (D)
10. Andrew Jacobs, Jr. (D)

POSTWAR VOTE FOR PRESIDENT

Year	Total Vote	Republican Vote	Candidate	Democratic Vote	Candidate	Other Vote	Plurality	Rep.	Dem.	Rep.	Dem.
								Total Vote		Major Vote	
1988	2,168,621	1,297,763	Bush, George	860,643	Dukakis, Michael S.	10,215	437,120 R	59.8%	39.7%	60.1%	39.9%
1984	2,233,069	1,377,230	Reagan, Ronald	841,481	Mondale, Walter F.	14,358	535,749 R	61.7%	37.7%	62.1%	37.9%
1980	2,242,033	1,255,656	Reagan, Ronald	844,197	Carter, Jimmy	142,180	411,459 R	56.0%	37.7%	59.8%	40.2%
1976	2,220,362	1,183,958	Ford, Gerald R.	1,014,714	Carter, Jimmy	21,690	169,244 R	53.3%	45.7%	53.8%	46.2%
1972	2,125,529	1,405,154	Nixon, Richard M.	708,568	McGovern, George S.	11,807	696,586 R	66.1%	33.3%	66.5%	33.5%
1968	2,123,597	1,067,885	Nixon, Richard M.	806,659	Humphrey, Hubert H.	249,053	261,226 R	50.3%	38.0%	57.0%	43.0%
1964	2,091,606	911,118	Goldwater, Barry M.	1,170,848	Johnson, Lyndon B.	9,640	259,730 D	43.6%	56.0%	43.8%	56.2%
1960	2,135,360	1,175,120	Nixon, Richard M.	952,358	Kennedy, John F.	7,882	222,762 R	55.0%	44.6%	55.2%	44.8%
1956	1,974,607	1,182,811	Eisenhower, Dwight D.	783,908	Stevenson, Adlai E.	7,888	398,903 R	59.9%	39.7%	60.1%	39.9%
1952	1,955,049	1,136,259	Eisenhower, Dwight D.	801,530	Stevenson, Adlai E.	17,260	334,729 R	58.1%	41.0%	58.6%	41.4%
1948	1,656,212	821,079	Dewey, Thomas E.	807,831	Truman, Harry S.	27,302	13,248 R	49.6%	48.8%	50.4%	49.6%

POSTWAR VOTE FOR GOVERNOR

Year	Total Vote	Republican Vote	Candidate	Democratic Vote	Candidate	Other Vote	Rep.-Dem. Plurality	Rep.	Dem.	Rep.	Dem.
								Total Vote		Major Vote	
1988	2,140,781	1,002,207	Mutz, John M.	1,138,574	Bayh, Evan		136,367 D	46.8%	53.2%	46.8%	53.2%
1984	2,197,988	1,146,497	Orr, Robert D.	1,036,922	Townsend, W. Wayne	14,569	109,575 R	52.2%	47.2%	52.5%	47.5%
1980	2,178,403	1,257,383	Orr, Robert D.	913,116	Hillenbrand, John A.	7,904	344,267 R	57.7%	41.9%	57.9%	42.1%
1976	2,175,324	1,236,555	Bowen, Otis R.	927,243	Conrad, Larry A.	11,526	309,312 R	56.8%	42.6%	57.1%	42.9%
1972	2,120,847	1,203,903	Bowen, Otis R.	900,489	Welsh, Matthew E.	16,455	303,414 R	56.8%	42.5%	57.2%	42.8%
1968	2,049,072	1,080,271	Whitcomb, Edgar D.	965,816	Rock, Robert L.	2,985	114,455 R	52.7%	47.1%	52.8%	47.2%
1964	2,072,915	901,342	Ristine, Richard O.	1,164,620	Branigin, Roger D.	6,953	263,278 D	43.5%	56.2%	43.6%	56.4%
1960	2,128,965	1,049,540	Parker, Crawford F.	1,072,717	Welsh, Matthew E.	6,708	23,177 D	49.3%	50.4%	49.5%	50.5%
1956	1,954,290	1,086,868	Handley, Harold W.	859,393	Tucker, Ralph	8,029	227,475 R	55.6%	44.0%	55.8%	44.2%
1952	1,931,869	1,075,685	Craig, George N.	841,984	Watkins, John A.	14,200	233,701 R	55.7%	43.6%	56.1%	43.9%
1948	1,652,321	745,892	Creighton, Hobart	884,995	Schricker, Henry F.	21,434	139,103 D	45.1%	53.6%	45.7%	54.3%

INDIANA

POSTWAR VOTE FOR SENATOR

Year	Total Vote	Republican Vote	Candidate	Democratic Vote	Candidate	Other Vote	Rep-Dem. Plurality	Total Vote Rep.	Total Vote Dem.	Major Vote Rep.	Major Vote Dem.
1990 S	1,504,302	806,048	Coats, Daniel R.	696,639	Hill, Baron P.	1,615	109,409 R	53.6%	46.3%	53.6%	46.4%
1988	2,099,303	1,430,525	Lugar, Richard G.	668,778	Wickes, Jack		761,747 R	68.1%	31.9%	68.1%	31.9%
1986	1,545,563	936,143	Quayle, J. Danforth	595,192	Long, Jill L.	14,228	340,951 R	60.6%	38.5%	61.1%	38.9%
1982	1,817,287	978,301	Lugar, Richard G.	828,400	Fithian, Floyd	10,586	149,901 R	53.8%	45.6%	54.1%	45.9%
1980	2,198,376	1,182,414	Quayle, J. Danforth	1,015,962	Bayh, Birch		166,452 R	53.8%	46.2%	53.8%	46.2%
1976	2,171,187	1,275,833	Lugar, Richard G.	878,522	Hartke, R. Vance	16,832	397,311 R	58.8%	40.5%	59.2%	40.8%
1974	1,752,978	814,117	Lugar, Richard G.	889,269	Bayh, Birch	49,592	75,152 D	46.4%	50.7%	47.8%	52.2%
1970	1,737,697	866,707	Roudebush, Richard	870,990	Hartke, R. Vance		4,283 D	49.9%	50.1%	49.9%	50.1%
1968	2,053,118	988,571	Ruckelshaus, William	1,060,456	Bayh, Birch	4,091	71,885 D	48.1%	51.7%	48.2%	51.8%
1964	2,076,963	941,519	Bontrager, D. Russell	1,128,505	Hartke, R. Vance	6,939	186,986 D	45.3%	54.3%	45.5%	54.5%
1962	1,800,038	894,547	Capehart, Homer E.	905,491	Bayh, Birch		10,944 D	49.7%	50.3%	49.7%	50.3%
1958	1,724,598	731,635	Handley, Harold W.	973,636	Hartke, R. Vance	19,327	242,001 D	42.4%	56.5%	42.9%	57.1%
1956	1,963,986	1,084,262	Capehart, Homer E.	871,781	Wickard, Claude	7,943	212,481 R	55.2%	44.4%	55.4%	44.6%
1952	1,946,118	1,020,605	Jenner, William E.	911,169	Schricker, Henry F.	14,344	109,436 R	52.4%	46.8%	52.8%	47.2%
1950	1,598,724	844,303	Capehart, Homer E.	741,025	Campbell, Alex M.	13,396	103,278 R	52.8%	46.4%	53.3%	46.7%
1946	1,347,434	739,809	Jenner, William E.	584,288	Townsend, M. Clifford	23,337	155,521 R	54.9%	43.4%	55.9%	44.1%

The 1990 election was for a short term to fill a vacancy.

INDIANA

Districts Established September 1, 1981

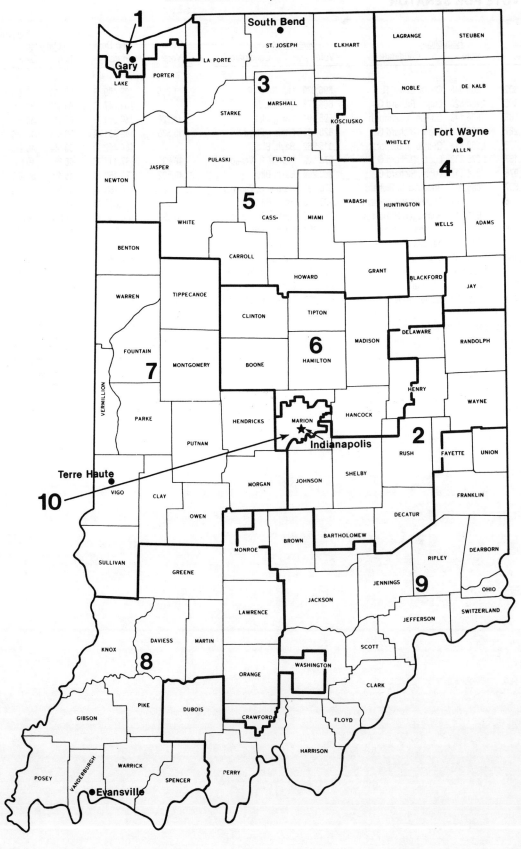

INDIANA

SENATOR 1990

1990 Census Population	County	Total Vote	Republican	Democratic	Other	Rep.-Dem. Plurality	Percentage Total Vote Rep.	Dem.	Major Vote Rep.	Dem.
31,095	ADAMS	10,383	6,589	3,790	4	2,799 R	63.5%	36.5%	63.5%	36.5%
300,836	ALLEN	80,191	47,183	32,904	104	14,279 R	58.8%	41.0%	58.9%	41.1%
63,657	BARTHOLOMEW	19,820	10,820	8,985	15	1,835 R	54.6%	45.3%	54.6%	45.4%
9,441	BENTON	3,608	2,253	1,336	19	917 R	62.4%	37.0%	62.8%	37.2%
14,067	BLACKFORD	4,427	2,307	2,120		187 R	52.1%	47.9%	52.1%	47.9%
38,147	BOONE	11,463	7,525	3,929	9	3,596 R	65.6%	34.3%	65.7%	34.3%
14,080	BROWN	4,508	2,484	2,020	4	464 R	55.1%	44.8%	55.2%	44.8%
18,809	CARROLL	6,749	3,817	2,915	17	902 R	56.6%	43.2%	56.7%	43.3%
38,413	CASS	12,041	6,491	5,550		941 R	53.9%	46.1%	53.9%	46.1%
87,777	CLARK	18,314	7,876	10,436	2	2,560 D	43.0%	57.0%	43.0%	57.0%
24,705	CLAY	7,899	4,178	3,707	14	471 R	52.9%	46.9%	53.0%	47.0%
30,974	CLINTON	8,369	4,879	3,489	1	1,390 R	58.3%	41.7%	58.3%	41.7%
9,914	CRAWFORD	3,957	1,830	2,127		297 D	46.2%	53.8%	46.2%	53.8%
27,533	DAVIESS	8,346	4,785	3,561		1,224 R	57.3%	42.7%	57.3%	42.7%
38,835	DEARBORN	9,041	4,967	4,072	2	895 R	54.9%	45.0%	55.0%	45.0%
23,645	DECATUR	7,714	4,371	3,342	1	1,029 R	56.7%	43.3%	56.7%	43.3%
35,324	DE KALB	10,918	6,621	4,296	1	2,325 R	60.6%	39.3%	60.6%	39.4%
119,659	DELAWARE	35,270	19,510	15,727	33	3,783 R	55.3%	44.6%	55.4%	44.6%
36,616	DUBOIS	9,475	3,882	5,593		1,711 D	41.0%	59.0%	41.0%	59.0%
156,198	ELKHART	35,062	23,559	11,496	7	12,063 R	67.2%	32.8%	67.2%	32.8%
26,015	FAYETTE	8,376	4,285	4,090	1	195 R	51.2%	48.8%	51.2%	48.8%
64,404	FLOYD	16,771	7,733	9,038		1,305 D	46.1%	53.9%	46.1%	53.9%
17,808	FOUNTAIN	6,742	3,954	2,786	2	1,168 R	58.6%	41.3%	58.7%	41.3%
19,580	FRANKLIN	4,981	2,600	2,375	6	225 R	52.2%	47.7%	52.3%	47.7%
18,840	FULTON	6,806	3,689	3,115	2	574 R	54.2%	45.8%	54.2%	45.8%
31,913	GIBSON	12,236	4 947	7,289		2,342 D	40.4%	59.6%	40.4%	59.6%
74,169	GRANT	19,489	11,494	7,984	11	3,510 R	59.0%	41.0%	59.0%	41.0%
30,410	GREENE	11,077	5,483	5,594		111 D	49.5%	50.5%	49.5%	50.5%
108,936	HAMILTON	27,135	19,461	7,644	30	11,817 R	71.7%	28.2%	71.8%	28.2%
45,527	HANCOCK	13,668	8,460	5,208		3,252 R	61.9%	38.1%	61.9%	38.1%
29,890	HARRISON	9,455	5,031	4,420	4	611 R	53.2%	46.7%	53.2%	46.8%
75,717	HENDRICKS	16,589	10,846	5,714	29	5,132 R	65.4%	34.4%	65.5%	34.5%
48,139	HENRY	13,845	7,619	6,225	1	1,394 R	55.0%	45.0%	55.0%	45.0%
80,827	HOWARD	23,845	13,653	10,144	48	3,509 R	57.3%	42.5%	57.4%	42.6%
35,427	HUNTINGTON	11,798	7,395	4,402	1	2,993 R	62.7%	37.3%	62.7%	37.3%
37,730	JACKSON	12,545	4,815	7,730		2,915 D	38.4%	61.6%	38.4%	61.6%
24,960	JASPER	5,913	3,756	2,155	2	1,601 R	63.5%	36.4%	63.5%	36.5%
21,512	JAY	7,262	4,496	2,765	1	1,731 R	61.9%	38.1%	61.9%	38.1%
29,797	JEFFERSON	9,336	4,467	4,869		402 D	47.8%	52.2%	47.8%	52.2%
23,661	JENNINGS	7,891	4,098	3,793		305 R	51.9%	48.1%	51.9%	48.1%
88,109	JOHNSON	22,546	14,473	8,008	65	6,465 R	64.2%	35.5%	64.4%	35.6%
39,884	KNOX	13,413	6,780	6,633		147 R	50.5%	49.5%	50.5%	49.5%
65,294	KOSCIUSKO	16,734	11,537	5,195	2	6,342 R	68.9%	31.0%	69.0%	31.0%
29,477	LAGRANGE	5,244	3,428	1,787	29	1,641 R	65.4%	34.1%	65.7%	34.3%
475,594	LAKE	95,946	36,107	59,822	17	23,715 D	37.6%	62.3%	37.6%	62.4%
107,066	LA PORTE	27,991	14,618	13,351	22	1,267 R	52.2%	47.7%	52.3%	47.7%
42,836	LAWRENCE	11,756	6,308	5,440	8	868 R	53.7%	46.3%	53.7%	46.3%
130,669	MADISON	42,090	21,180	20,904	6	276 R	50.3%	49.7%	50.3%	49.7%
797,159	MARION	191,205	100,222	90,603	380	9,619 R	52.4%	47.4%	52.5%	47.5%
42,182	MARSHALL	12,756	7,982	4,773	1	3,209 R	62.6%	37.4%	62.6%	37.4%
10,369	MARTIN	4,493	2,054	2,434	5	380 D	45.7%	54.2%	45.8%	54.2%
36,897	MIAMI	10,777	6,209	4,565	3	1,644 R	57.6%	42.4%	57.6%	42.4%
108,978	MONROE	22,429	10,943	11,357	129	414 D	48.8%	50.6%	49.1%	50.9%
34,436	MONTGOMERY	9,632	6,250	3,361	21	2,889 R	64.9%	34.9%	65.0%	35.0%
55,920	MORGAN	13,434	8,299	5,135		3,164 R	61.8%	38.2%	61.8%	38.2%
13,551	NEWTON	4,038	2,427	1,608	3	819 R	60.1%	39.8%	60.1%	39.9%
37,877	NOBLE	10,133	6,235	3,896	2	2,339 R	61.5%	38.4%	61.5%	38.5%
5,315	OHIO	1,965	968	996	1	28 D	49.3%	50.7%	49.3%	50.7%
18,409	ORANGE	6,533	3,727	2,804	2	923 R	57.0%	42.9%	57.1%	42.9%
17,281	OWEN	5,355	3,063	2,283	9	780 R	57.2%	42.6%	57.3%	42.7%

INDIANA

SENATOR 1990

1990 Census Population	County	Total Vote	Republican	Democratic	Other	Rep.-Dem. Plurality	Percentage Total Vote Rep.	Dem.	Major Vote Rep.	Dem.
15,410	PARKE	6,181	3,426	2,755		671 R	55.4%	44.6%	55.4%	44.6%
19,107	PERRY	7,985	3,051	4,928	6	1,877 D	38.2%	61.7%	38.2%	61.8%
12,509	PIKE	5,412	2,296	3,116		820 D	42.4%	57.6%	42.4%	57.6%
128,932	PORTER	34,284	19,034	15,165	85	3,869 R	55.5%	44.2%	55.7%	44.3%
25,968	POSEY	8,875	3,846	4,989	40	1,143 D	43.3%	56.2%	43.5%	56.5%
12,643	PULASKI	4,328	2,545	1,783		762 R	58.8%	41.2%	58.8%	41.2%
30,315	PUTNAM	9,025	5,257	3,712	56	1,545 R	58.2%	41.1%	58.6%	41.4%
27,148	RANDOLPH	8,503	5,374	3,106	23	2,268 R	63.2%	36.5%	63.4%	36.6%
24,616	RIPLEY	7,275	4,182	3,089	4	1,093 R	57.5%	42.5%	57.5%	42.5%
18,129	RUSH	6,054	3,649	2,399	6	1,250 R	60.3%	39.6%	60.3%	39.7%
247,052	ST. JOSEPH	67,978	32,406	35,560	12	3,154 D	47.7%	52.3%	47.7%	52.3%
20,991	SCOTT	5,468	2,031	3,437		1,406 D	37.1%	62.9%	37.1%	62.9%
40,307	SHELBY	11,023	6,251	4,767	5	1,484 R	56.7%	43.2%	56.7%	43.3%
19,490	SPENCER	8,165	3,826	4,339		513 D	46.9%	53.1%	46.9%	53.1%
22,747	STARKE	6,663	3,264	3,399		135 D	49.0%	51.0%	49.0%	51.0%
27,446	STEUBEN	7,969	4,881	3,082	6	1,799 R	61.2%	38.7%	61.3%	38.7%
18,993	SULLIVAN	7,254	3,367	3,879	8	512 D	46.4%	53.5%	46.5%	53.5%
7,738	SWITZERLAND	2,327	1,146	1,176	5	30 D	49.2%	50.5%	49.4%	50.6%
130,598	TIPPECANOE	32,642	18,845	13,619	178	5,226 R	57.7%	41.7%	58.0%	42.0%
16,119	TIPTON	6,497	3,952	2,541	4	1,411 R	60.8%	39.1%	60.9%	39.1%
6,976	UNION	2,271	1,363	905	3	458 R	60.0%	39.9%	60.1%	39.9%
165,058	VANDERBURGH	52,242	23,584	28,658		5,074 D	45.1%	54.9%	45.1%	54.9%
16,773	VERMILLION	5,954	2,525	3,426	3	901 D	42.4%	57.5%	42.4%	57.6%
106,107	VIGO	27,674	13,075	14,558	41	1,483 D	47.2%	52.6%	47.3%	52.7%
35,069	WABASH	10,099	6,395	3,703	1	2,692 R	63.3%	36.7%	63.3%	36.7%
8,176	WARREN	3,363	1,864	1,497	2	367 R	55.4%	44.5%	55.5%	44.5%
44,920	WARRICK	13,309	5,338	7,971		2,633 D	40.1%	59.9%	40.1%	59.9%
23,717	WASHINGTON	6,604	3,724	2,876	4	848 R	56.4%	43.5%	56.4%	43.6%
71,951	WAYNE	19,483	11,674	7,787	22	3,887 R	59.9%	40.0%	60.0%	40.0%
25,948	WELLS	9,879	6,309	3,570		2,739 R	63.9%	36.1%	63.9%	36.1%
23,265	WHITE	7,972	4,675	3,286	11	1,389 R	58.6%	41.2%	58.7%	41.3%
27,651	WHITLEY	9,759	5,874	3,871	14	2,003 R	60.2%	39.7%	60.3%	39.7%
5,544,159	TOTAL	1,504,302	806,048	696,639	1,615	109,409 R	53.6%	46.3%	53.6%	46.4%

INDIANA

CONGRESS

CD	Year	Total Vote	Republican Vote	Republican Candidate	Democratic Vote	Democratic Candidate	Other Vote	Rep.-Dem. Plurality	Total Vote Rep.	Total Vote Dem.	Major Vote Rep.	Major Vote Dem.
1	1990	104,370	35,450	COSTAS, WILLIAM	68,920	VISCLOSKY, PETER J.		33,470 D	34.0%	66.0%	34.0%	66.0%
1	1988	179,327	41,076	CRUMPACKER, OWEN W.	138,251	VISCLOSKY, PETER J.		97,175 D	22.9%	77.1%	22.9%	77.1%
1	1986	118,441	30,395	COSTAS, WILLIAM	86,983	VISCLOSKY, PETER J.	1,063	56,588 D	25.7%	73.4%	25.9%	74.1%
1	1984	207,964	59,986	GRENCHIK, JOSEPH B.	147,035	VISCLOSKY, PETER J.	943	87,049 D	28.8%	70.7%	29.0%	71.0%
1	1982	155,096	66,921	KRIEGER, THOMAS	87,369	HALL, KATIE	806	20,448 D	43.1%	56.3%	43.4%	56.6%
2	1990	157,475	63,980	PENCE, MIKE	93,495	SHARP, PHILIP R.		29,515 D	40.6%	59.4%	40.6%	59.4%
2	1988	219,761	102,846	PENCE, MIKE	116,915	SHARP, PHILIP R.		14,069 D	46.8%	53.2%	46.8%	53.2%
2	1986	165,625	62,013	LYNCH, DONALD J.	102,456	SHARP, PHILIP R.	1,156	40,443 D	37.4%	61.9%	37.7%	62.3%
2	1984	222,663	103,061	MACKENZIE, KEN	118,965	SHARP, PHILIP R.	637	15,904 D	46.3%	53.4%	46.4%	53.6%
2	1982	190,891	83,593	VAN NATTA, RALPH	107,298	SHARP, PHILIP R.		23,705 D	43.8%	56.2%	43.8%	56.2%
3	1990	158,651	77,911	HILER, JOHN P.	80,740	ROEMER, TIMOTHY J.		2,829 D	49.1%	50.9%	49.1%	50.9%
3	1988	214,243	116,309	HILER, JOHN P.	97,934	WARD, THOMAS W.		18,375 R	54.3%	45.7%	54.3%	45.7%
3	1986	152,509	75,979	HILER, JOHN P.	75,932	WARD, THOMAS W.	598	47 R	49.8%	49.8%	50.0%	50.0%
3	1984	219,752	115,139	HILER, JOHN P.	103,961	BARNES, MICHAEL P.	652	11,178 R	52.4%	47.3%	52.6%	47.4%
3	1982	170,004	86,958	HILER, JOHN P.	83,046	BODINE, RICHARD C.		3,912 R	51.2%	48.8%	51.2%	48.8%
4	1990	163,971	64,415	HAWKS, RICHARD W.	99,347	LONG, JILL L.	209	34,932 D	39.3%	60.6%	39.3%	60.7%
4	1988	213,758	132,843	COATS, DANIEL R.	80,915	LONG, JILL L.		51,928 R	62.1%	37.9%	62.1%	37.9%
4	1986	143,572	99,865	COATS, DANIEL R.	43,105	SCHER, GREGORY A.	602	56,760 R	69.6%	30.0%	69.9%	30.1%
4	1984	213,119	129,674	COATS, DANIEL R.	82,053	BARNARD, MICHAEL H.	1,392	47,621 R	60.8%	38.5%	61.2%	38.8%
4	1982	171,238	110,155	COATS, DANIEL R.	60,054	MILLER, ROGER M.	1,029	50,101 R	64.3%	35.1%	64.7%	35.3%
5	1990	153,123	71,750	JOHNSON, JOHN A.	81,373	JONTZ, JIM		9,623 D	46.9%	53.1%	46.9%	53.1%
5	1988	206,403	90,163	WILLIAMS, PATRICIA L.	116,240	JONTZ, JIM		26,077 D	43.7%	56.3%	43.7%	56.3%
5	1986	157,006	75,507	BUTCHER, JAMES R.	80,772	JONTZ, JIM	727	5,265 D	48.1%	51.4%	48.3%	51.7%
5	1984	211,355	143,560	HILLIS, ELWOOD H.	66,631	MAXWELL, ALLEN	1,164	76,929 R	67.9%	31.5%	68.3%	31.7%
5	1982	172,707	105,469	HILLIS, ELWOOD H.	67,238	MAXWELL, ALLEN		38,231 R	61.1%	38.9%	61.1%	38.9%
6	1990	183,494	116,470	BURTON, DAN	67,024	FADELY, JAMES P.		49,446 R	63.5%	36.5%	63.5%	36.5%
6	1988	263,511	192,064	BURTON, DAN	71,447	HOLLAND, GEORGE T.		120,617 R	72.9%	27.1%	72.9%	27.1%
6	1986	173,165	118,363	BURTON, DAN	53,431	MCKENNA, THOMAS F.	1,371	64,932 R	68.4%	30.9%	68.9%	31.1%
6	1984	245,864	178,814	BURTON, DAN	65,772	CAMPBELL, HOWARD O.	1,278	113,042 R	72.7%	26.8%	73.1%	26.9%
6	1982	201,864	131,100	BURTON, DAN	70,764	GRABIANOWSKI, GEORGE E.		60,336 R	64.9%	35.1%	64.9%	35.1%
7	1990	154,550	88,598	MYERS, JOHN T.	65,248	RILEY, JOHN W.	704	23,350 R	57.3%	42.2%	57.6%	42.4%
7	1988	211,316	130,578	MYERS, JOHN T.	80,738	WATERFILL, MARK R.		49,840 R	61.8%	38.2%	61.8%	38.2%
7	1986	157,163	104,965	MYERS, JOHN T.	49,675	SMITH, EUGENE	2,523	55,290 R	66.8%	31.6%	67.9%	32.1%
7	1984	219,694	147,787	MYERS, JOHN T.	69,097	SMITH, ARTHUR E.	2,810	78,690 R	67.3%	31.5%	68.1%	31.9%
7	1982	186,133	115,884	MYERS, JOHN T.	70,249	BONNEY, STEPHEN S.		45,635 R	62.3%	37.7%	62.3%	37.7%
8	1990	178,110	80,645	MOURDOCK, RICHARD	97,465	MCCLOSKEY, FRANCIS		16,820 D	45.3%	54.7%	45.3%	54.7%
8	1988	228,676	87,321	MYERS, JOHN L.	141,355	MCCLOSKEY, FRANCIS		54,034 D	38.2%	61.8%	38.2%	61.8%
8	1986	201,157	93,586	MCINTYRE, RICHARD D.	106,662	MCCLOSKEY, FRANCIS	909	13,076 D	46.5%	53.0%	46.7%	53.3%
8	1984	234,092	116,641	MCINTYRE, RICHARD D.	116,645	MCCLOSKEY, FRANCIS	806	4 D	49.8%	49.8%	50.0%	50.0%
8	1982	195,725	94,127	DECKARD, H. JOEL	100,592	MCCLOSKEY, FRANCIS	1,006	6,465 D	48.1%	51.4%	48.3%	51.7%
9	1990	155,851	48,325	COATES, FLOYD E.	107,526	HAMILTON, LEE H.		59,201 D	31.0%	69.0%	31.0%	69.0%
9	1988	208,139	60,946	COATES, FLOYD E.	147,193	HAMILTON, LEE H.		86,247 D	29.3%	70.7%	29.3%	70.7%
9	1986	167,703	46,398	KILROY, ROBERT W.	120,586	HAMILTON, LEE H.	719	74,188 D	27.7%	71.9%	27.8%	72.2%
9	1984	210,340	72,652	COATES, FLOYD E.	137,018	HAMILTON, LEE H.	670	64,366 D	34.5%	65.1%	34.7%	65.3%
9	1982	180,539	58,532	COATES, FLOYD E.	121,094	HAMILTON, LEE H.	913	62,562 D	32.4%	67.1%	32.6%	67.4%
10	1990	104,411	35,049	HORVATH, JANOS	69,362	JACOBS, ANDREW, JR.		34,313 D	33.6%	66.4%	33.6%	66.4%
10	1988	174,824	68,978	CUMMINGS, JAMES C.	105,846	JACOBS, ANDREW, JR.		36,868 D	39.5%	60.5%	39.5%	60.5%
10	1986	119,166	49,064	EYNON, JIM	68,817	JACOBS, ANDREW, JR.	1,285	19,753 D	41.2%	57.7%	41.6%	58.4%
10	1984	195,493	79,342	WATKINS, JOSEPH P.	115,274	JACOBS, ANDREW, JR.	877	35,932 D	40.6%	59.0%	40.8%	59.2%
10	1982	171,863	56,992	CARROLL, MICHAEL	114,674	JACOBS, ANDREW, JR.	197	57,682 D	33.2%	66.7%	33.2%	66.8%

INDIANA

1990 GENERAL ELECTION

Senator   Other vote was 1,144 write-in (Dillon); 305 write-in (Eisenhour) and 166 write-in (Plemons).

Congress   Other vote was write-in (Bisson) in CD 4; write-in (Bourland) in CD 7.

1990 PRIMARIES

MAY 8 REPUBLICAN

Senator   Daniel R. Coats, unopposed.

Congress   Unopposed in six CD's. Contested as follows:

CD 1   6,352 William Costas; 1,525 Donald Ewen; 1,430 Owen W. Crumpacker; 762 David W. Shaw; 356 Lawrence C. Sarsoun.
CD 4   36,494 Richard W. Hawks; 6,522 Douglas G. Brown; 6,240 Phillip J. Troyer.
CD 5   36,082 John A. Johnson; 7,950 Daniel C. Langmesser.
CD 10   8,385 Janos Horvath; 6,633 Keith Allen Beaven; 1,206 Fred Ray; 1,015 F. Perry Ray.

MAY 8 DEMOCRATIC

Senator   Baron P. Hill, unopposed.

Congress   Unopposed in two CD's. Contested as follows:

CD 1   37,286 Peter J. Visclosky; 21,749 Katie Hall; 9,712 Gregory S. Reising; 3,754 Sandra K. Smith.
CD 3   22,898 Timothy J. Roemer; 8,101 Daniel T. Durham; 2,357 Sally Lou Croff; 1,362 Samuel E. Lehman; 1,107 Christopher A. Mikulak.
CD 4   30,505 Jill L. Long; 1,914 J. Carolyn Williams.
CD 6   18,457 James P. Fadely; 11,802 George T. Holland.
CD 7   24,650 John W. Riley; 13,178 Ellen E. Wedum.
CD 8   44,906 Francis McCloskey; 5,814 John W. Taylor.
CD 9   67,056 Lee H. Hamilton; 5,930 Lendall B. Terry.
CD 10   21,554 Andrew Jacobs, Jr.; 2,482 Jocelyn E. Tandy.

IOWA

GOVERNOR
Terry E. Branstad (R). Re-elected 1990 to a four-year term. Previously elected 1986, 1982.

SENATORS
Charles E. Grassley (R). Re-elected 1986 to a six-year term. Previously elected 1980.

Tom Harkin (D). Re-elected 1990 to a six-year term. Previously elected 1984.

REPRESENTATIVES
1. James A. Leach (R)
2. Jim Nussle (R)
3. David R. Nagle (D)
4. Neal Smith (D)
5. Jim R. Lightfoot (R)
6. Fred Grandy (R)

POSTWAR VOTE FOR PRESIDENT

Year	Total Vote	Republican Vote	Candidate	Democratic Vote	Candidate	Other Vote	Plurality	Total Vote Rep.	Dem.	Major Vote Rep.	Dem.
1988	1,225,614	545,355	Bush, George	670,557	Dukakis, Michael S.	9,702	125,202 D	44.5%	54.7%	44.9%	55.1%
1984	1,319,805	703,088	Reagan, Ronald	605,620	Mondale, Walter F.	11,097	97,468 R	53.3%	45.9%	53.7%	46.3%
1980	1,317,661	676,026	Reagan, Ronald	508,672	Carter, Jimmy	132,963	167,354 R	51.3%	38.6%	57.1%	42.9%
1976	1,279,306	632,863	Ford, Gerald R.	619,931	Carter, Jimmy	26,512	12,932 R	49.5%	48.5%	50.5%	49.5%
1972	1,225,944	706,207	Nixon, Richard M.	496,206	McGovern, George S.	23,531	210,001 R	57.6%	40.5%	58.7%	41.3%
1968	1,167,931	619,106	Nixon, Richard M.	476,699	Humphrey, Hubert H.	72,126	142,407 R	53.0%	40.8%	56.5%	43.5%
1964	1,184,539	449,148	Goldwater, Barry M.	733,030	Johnson, Lyndon B.	2,361	283,882 D	37.9%	61.9%	38.0%	62.0%
1960	1,273,810	722,381	Nixon, Richard M.	550,565	Kennedy, John F.	864	171,816 R	56.7%	43.2%	56.7%	43.3%
1956	1,234,564	729,187	Eisenhower, Dwight D.	501,858	Stevenson, Adlai E.	3,519	227,329 R	59.1%	40.7%	59.2%	40.8%
1952	1,268,773	808,906	Eisenhower, Dwight D.	451,513	Stevenson, Adlai E.	8,354	357,393 R	63.8%	35.6%	64.2%	35.8%
1948	1,038,264	494,018	Dewey, Thomas E.	522,380	Truman, Harry S.	21,866	28,362 D	47.6%	50.3%	48.6%	51.4%

IOWA

POSTWAR VOTE FOR GOVERNOR

Year	Total Vote	Republican Vote	Candidate	Democratic Vote	Candidate	Other Vote	Rep-Dem. Plurality	Total Vote Rep.	Dem.	Major Vote Rep.	Dem.
1990	976,483	591,852	Branstad, Terry E.	379,372	Avenson, Donald D.	5,259	212,480 R	60.6%	38.9%	60.9%	39.1%
1986	910,623	472,712	Branstad, Terry E.	436,987	Junkins, Lowell L.	924	35,725 R	51.9%	48.0%	52.0%	48.0%
1982	1,038,229	548,313	Branstad, Terry E.	483,291	Conlin, Roxanne	6,625	65,022 R	52.8%	46.5%	53.2%	46.8%
1978	843,190	491,713	Ray, Robert	345,519	Fitzgerald, Jerome D.	5,958	146,194 R	58.3%	41.0%	58.7%	41.3%
1974 **	920,458	534,518	Ray, Robert	377,553	Schaben, James, F.	8,387	156,965 R	58.1%	41.0%	58.6%	41.4%
1972	1,210,222	707,177	Ray, Robert	487,282	Franzenburg, Paul	15,763	219,895 R	58.4%	40.3%	59.2%	40.8%
1970	791,241	403,394	Ray, Robert	368,911	Fulton, Robert	18,936	34,483 R	51.0%	46.6%	52.2%	47.8%
1968	1,136,489	614,328	Ray, Robert	521,216	Franzenburg, Paul	945	93,112 R	54.1%	45.9%	54.1%	45.9%
1966	893,175	394,518	Murray, William G.	494,259	Hughes, Harold E.	4,398	99,741 D	44.2%	55.3%	44.4%	55.6%
1964	1,167,734	365,131	Hultman, Evan	794,610	Hughes, Harold E.	7,993	429,479 D	31.3%	68.0%	31.5%	68.5%
1962	819,854	388,955	Erbe, Norman A.	430,899	Hughes, Harold E.		41,944 D	47.4%	52.6%	47.4%	52.6%
1960	1,237,089	645,026	Erbe, Norman A.	592,063	McManus, E. J.		52,963 R	52.1%	47.9%	52.1%	47.9%
1958	859,095	394,071	Murray, William G.	465,024	Loveless, Herschel C.		70,953 D	45.9%	54.1%	45.9%	54.1%
1956	1,204,235	587,383	Hoegh, Leo A.	616,852	Loveless, Herschel C.		29,469 D	48.8%	51.2%	48.8%	51.2%
1954	848,592	435,944	Hoegh, Leo A.	410,255	Herring, Clyde E.	2,393	25,689 R	51.4%	48.3%	51.5%	48.5%
1952	1,230,045	638,388	Beardsley, William	587,671	Loveless, Herschel C.	3,986	50,717 R	51.9%	47.8%	52.1%	47.9%
1950	857,213	506,642	Beardsley, William	347,176	Gillette, Lester S.	3,395	159,466 R	59.1%	40.5%	59.3%	40.7%
1948	994,833	553,900	Beardsley, William	434,432	Switzer, Carroll O.	6,501	119,468 R	55.7%	43.7%	56.0%	44.0%
1946	631,681	362,592	Blue, Robert D.	266,190	Miles, Frank	2,899	96,402 R	57.4%	42.1%	57.7%	42.3%

The term of office of Iowa's Governor was increased from two to four years effective with the 1974 election.

POSTWAR VOTE FOR SENATOR

Year	Total Vote	Republican Vote	Candidate	Democratic Vote	Candidate	Other Vote	Rep-Dem. Plurality	Total Vote Rep.	Dem.	Major Vote Rep.	Dem.
1990	983,933	446,869	Tauke, Tom	535,975	Harkin, Tom	1,089	89,106 D	45.4%	54.5%	45.5%	54.5%
1986	891,762	588,880	Grassley, Charles E.	299,406	Roehrick, John P.	3,476	289,474 R	66.0%	33.6%	66.3%	33.7%
1984	1,292,700	564,381	Jepsen, Roger W.	716,883	Harkin, Tom	11,436	152,502 D	43.7%	55.5%	44.0%	56.0%
1980	1,277,034	683,014	Grassley, Charles E.	581,545	Culver, John C.	12,475	101,469 R	53.5%	45.5%	54.0%	46.0%
1978	824,654	421,598	Jepsen, Roger W.	395,066	Clark, Richard	7,990	26,532 R	51.1%	47.9%	51.6%	48.4%
1974	889,561	420,546	Stanley, David M.	462,947	Culver, John C.	6,068	42,401 D	47.3%	52.0%	47.6%	52.4%
1972	1,203,333	530,525	Miller, Jack	662,637	Clark, Richard	10,171	132,112 D	44.1%	55.1%	44.5%	55.5%
1968	1,144,086	568,469	Stanley, David M.	574,884	Hughes, Harold E.	733	6,415 D	49.7%	50.2%	49.7%	50.3%
1966	857,496	522,339	Miller, Jack	324,114	Smith, E. B.	11,043	198,225 R	60.9%	37.8%	61.7%	38.3%
1962	807,972	431,364	Hickenlooper, Bourke B.	376,602	Smith, E. B.	6	54,762 R	53.4%	46.6%	53.4%	46.6%
1960	1,237,582	642,463	Miller, Jack	595,119	Loveless, Herschel C.		47,344 R	51.9%	48.1%	51.9%	48.1%
1956	1,178,655	635,499	Hickenlooper, Bourke B.	543,156	Evans, R. M.		92,343 R	53.9%	46.1%	53.9%	46.1%
1954	847,355	442,409	Martin, Thomas E.	402,712	Gillette, Guy	2,234	39,697 R	52.2%	47.5%	52.3%	47.7%
1950	858,523	470,613	Hickenlooper, Bourke B.	383,766	Loveland, A. J.	4,144	86,847 R	54.8%	44.7%	55.1%	44.9%
1948	1,000,412	415,778	Wilson, George A.	578,226	Gillette, Guy	6,408	162,448 D	41.6%	57.8%	41.8%	58.2%

IOWA

Districts Established August 20, 1981

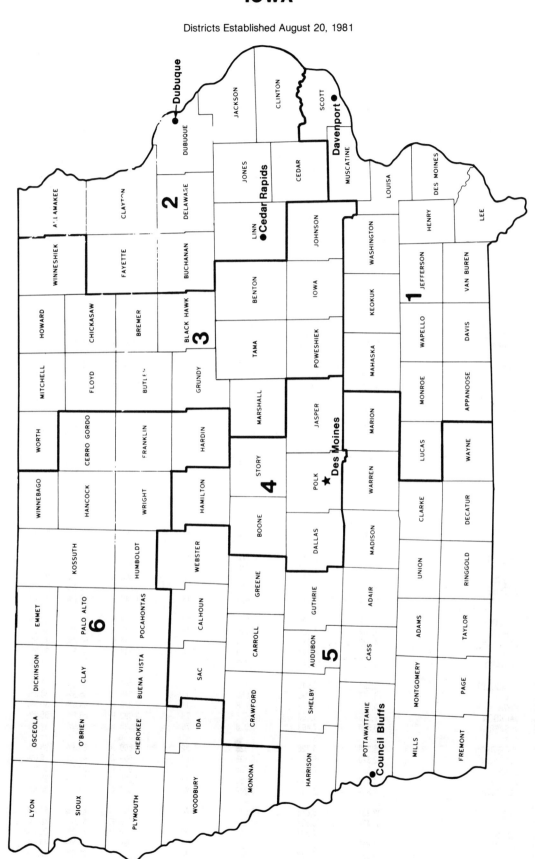

IOWA

GOVERNOR 1990

1990 Census Population	County	Total Vote	Republican	Democratic	Other	Rep.-Dem. Plurality	Total Vote Rep.	Total Vote Dem.	Major Vote Rep.	Major Vote Dem.
8,409	ADAIR	3,727	2,463	1,256	8	1,207 R	66.1%	33.7%	66.2%	33.8%
4,866	ADAMS	1,945	1,312	632	1	680 R	67.5%	32.5%	67.5%	32.5%
13,855	ALLAMAKEE	5,218	3,567	1,631	20	1,936 R	68.4%	31.3%	68.6%	31.4%
13,743	APPANOOSE	4,644	2,753	1,880	11	873 R	59.3%	40.5%	59.4%	40.6%
7,334	AUDUBON	3,326	2,157	1,150	19	1,007 R	64.9%	34.6%	65.2%	34.8%
22,429	BENTON	8,158	5,061	3,053	44	2,008 R	62.0%	37.4%	62.4%	37.6%
123,798	BLACK HAWK	42,821	25,640	17,018	163	8,622 R	59.9%	39.7%	60.1%	39.9%
25,186	BOONE	9,489	5,270	4,187	32	1,083 R	55.5%	44.1%	55.7%	44.3%
22,813	BREMER	8,309	5,593	2,690	26	2,903 R	67.3%	32.4%	67.5%	32.5%
20,844	BUCHANAN	6,565	3,929	2,575	61	1,354 R	59.8%	39.2%	60.4%	39.6%
19,965	BUENA VISTA	7,244	4,835	2,385	24	2,450 R	66.7%	32.9%	67.0%	33.0%
15,731	BUTLER	5,119	3,712	1,397	10	2,315 R	72.5%	27.3%	72.7%	27.3%
11,508	CALHOUN	4,261	2,775	1,473	13	1,302 R	65.1%	34.6%	65.3%	34.7%
21,423	CARROLL	7,259	4,584	2,651	24	1,933 R	63.1%	36.5%	63.4%	36.6%
15,128	CASS	5,944	4,265	1,648	31	2,617 R	71.8%	27.7%	72.1%	27.9%
17,381	CEDAR	6,090	3,917	2,103	70	1,814 R	64.3%	34.5%	65.1%	34.9%
46,733	CERRO GORDO	17,701	10,434	7,224	43	3,210 R	58.9%	40.8%	59.1%	40.9%
14,098	CHEROKEE	5,731	3,628	2,076	27	1,552 R	63.3%	36.2%	63.6%	36.4%
13,295	CHICKASAW	5,204	3,227	1,933	44	1,294 R	62.0%	37.1%	62.5%	37.5%
8,287	CLARKE	3,461	1,966	1,465	30	501 R	56.8%	42.3%	57.3%	42.7%
17,585	CLAY	6,078	3,807	2,249	22	1,558 R	62.6%	37.0%	62.9%	37.1%
19,054	CLAYTON	7,152	4,815	2,312	25	2,503 R	67.3%	32.3%	67.6%	32.4%
51,040	CLINTON	18,140	10,960	7,100	80	3,860 R	60.4%	39.1%	60.7%	39.3%
16,775	CRAWFORD	5,463	3,250	2,193	20	1,057 R	59.5%	40.1%	59.7%	40.3%
29,755	DALLAS	9,780	5,423	4,281	76	1,142 R	55.4%	43.8%	55.9%	44.1%
8,312	DAVIS	3,126	1,608	1,509	9	99 R	51.4%	48.3%	51.6%	48.4%
8,338	DECATUR	2,913	1,783	1,109	21	674 R	61.2%	38.1%	61.7%	38.3%
18,035	DELAWARE	6,546	4,684	1,840	22	2,844 R	71.6%	28.1%	71.8%	28.2%
42,614	DES MOINES	15,339	8,595	6,699	45	1,896 R	56.0%	43.7%	56.2%	43.8%
14,909	DICKINSON	5,793	3,758	2,011	24	1,747 R	64.9%	34.7%	65.1%	34.9%
86,403	DUBUQUE	31,732	18,541	12,972	219	5,569 R	58.4%	40.9%	58.8%	41.2%
11,569	EMMET	3,917	2,446	1,460	11	986 R	62.4%	37.3%	62.6%	37.4%
21,843	FAYETTE	9,120	5,331	3,762	27	1,569 R	58.5%	41.3%	58.6%	41.4%
17,058	FLOYD	6,039	3,670	2,339	30	1,331 R	60.8%	38.7%	61.1%	38.9%
11,364	FRANKLIN	4,260	2,884	1,359	17	1,525 R	67.7%	31.9%	68.0%	32.0%
8,226	FREMONT	3,203	2,215	972	16	1,243 R	69.2%	30.3%	69.5%	30.5%
10,045	GREENE	4,431	2,797	1,615	19	1,182 R	63.1%	36.4%	63.4%	36.6%
12,029	GRUNDY	4,793	3,573	1,205	15	2,368 R	74.5%	25.1%	74.8%	25.2%
10,935	GUTHRIE	4,095	2,451	1,631	13	820 R	59.9%	39.8%	60.0%	40.0%
16,071	HAMILTON	6,174	3,684	2,474	16	1,210 R	59.7%	40.1%	59.8%	40.2%
12,638	HANCOCK	4,602	3,199	1,371	32	1,828 R	69.5%	29.8%	70.0%	30.0%
19,094	HARDIN	7,702	4,809	2,819	74	1,990 R	62.4%	36.6%	63.0%	37.0%
14,730	HARRISON	4,506	3,075	1,424	7	1,651 R	68.2%	31.6%	68.3%	31.7%
19,226	HENRY	6,399	4,243	2,110	46	2,133 R	66.3%	33.0%	66.8%	33.2%
9,809	HOWARD	3,881	2,547	1,302	32	1,245 R	65.6%	33.5%	66.2%	33.8%
10,756	HUMBOLDT	4,391	2,912	1,472	7	1,440 R	66.3%	33.5%	66.4%	33.6%
8,365	IDA	3,158	2,095	1,050	13	1,045 R	66.3%	33.2%	66.6%	33.4%
14,630	IOWA	5,869	4,078	1,778	13	2,300 R	69.5%	30.3%	69.6%	30.4%
19,950	JACKSON	7,323	4,669	2,576	78	2,093 R	63.8%	35.2%	64.4%	35.6%
34,795	JASPER	13,560	7,403	6,078	79	1,325 R	54.6%	44.8%	54.9%	45.1%
16,310	JEFFERSON	5,708	3,728	1,928	52	1,800 R	65.3%	33.8%	65.9%	34.1%
96,119	JOHNSON	32,370	15,687	16,196	487	509 D	48.5%	50.0%	49.2%	50.8%
19,444	JONES	6,865	4,331	2,505	29	1,826 R	63.1%	36.5%	63.4%	36.6%
11,624	KEOKUK	4,424	2,816	1,590	18	1,226 R	63.7%	35.9%	63.9%	36.1%
18,591	KOSSUTH	7,383	5,110	2,249	24	2,861 R	69.2%	30.5%	69.4%	30.6%
38,687	LEE	13,137	6,066	7,011	60	945 D	46.2%	53.4%	46.4%	53.6%
168,767	LINN	60,434	35,597	24,278	559	11,319 R	58.9%	40.2%	59.5%	40.5%
11,592	LOUISA	3,743	2,367	1,337	39	1,030 R	63.2%	35.7%	63.9%	36.1%
9,070	LUCAS	3,610	2,149	1,453	8	696 R	59.5%	40.2%	59.7%	40.3%
11,952	LYON	4,031	3,130	891	10	2,239 R	77.6%	22.1%	77.8%	22.2%

IOWA

GOVERNOR 1990

1990 Census Population	County	Total Vote	Republican	Democratic	Other	Rep.-Dem. Plurality	Percentage Total Vote Rep.	Dem.	Major Vote Rep.	Dem.
12,483	MADISON	5,205	3,101	2,085	19	1,016 R	59.6%	40.1%	59.8%	40.2%
21,522	MAHASKA	7,712	5,404	2,280	28	3,124 R	70.1%	29.6%	70.3%	29.7%
30,001	MARION	10,830	6,617	4,187	26	2,430 R	61.1%	38.7%	61.2%	38.8%
38,276	MARSHALL	14,824	8,154	6,560	110	1,594 R	55.0%	44.3%	55.4%	44.6%
13,202	MILLS	3,930	2,760	1,153	17	1,607 R	70.2%	29.3%	70.5%	29.5%
10,928	MITCHELL	4,472	2,969	1,478	25	1,491 R	66.4%	33.1%	66.8%	33.2%
10,034	MONONA	3,388	2,086	1,287	15	799 R	61.6%	38.0%	61.8%	38.2%
8,114	MONROE	3,265	1,861	1,401	3	460 R	57.0%	42.9%	57.1%	42.9%
12,076	MONTGOMERY	3,988	2,970	1,009	9	1,961 R	74.5%	25.3%	74.6%	25.4%
39,907	MUSCATINE	11,278	7,323	3,919	36	3,404 R	64.9%	34.7%	65.1%	34.9%
15,444	O'BRIEN	5,532	4,090	1,421	21	2,669 R	73.9%	25.7%	74.2%	25.8%
7,267	OSCEOLA	2,553	1,835	713	5	1,122 R	71.9%	27.9%	72.0%	28.0%
16,870	PAGE	5,290	4,142	1,115	33	3,027 R	78.3%	21.1%	78.8%	21.2%
10,669	PALO ALTO	4,132	2,560	1,558	14	1,002 R	62.0%	37.7%	62.2%	37.8%
23,388	PLYMOUTH	7,271	5,087	2,160	24	2,927 R	70.0%	29.7%	70.2%	29.8%
9,525	POCAHONTAS	3,737	2,522	1,195	20	1,327 R	67.5%	32.0%	67.9%	32.1%
327,140	POLK	114,361	61,780	52,004	577	9,776 R	54.0%	45.5%	54.3%	45.7%
82,628	POTTAWATTAMIE	23,224	14,886	8,254	84	6,632 R	64.1%	35.5%	64.3%	35.7%
19,033	POWESHIEK	6,947	3,980	2,926	41	1,054 R	57.3%	42.1%	57.6%	42.4%
5,420	RINGGOLD	2,476	1,617	858	1	759 R	65.3%	34.7%	65.3%	34.7%
12,324	SAC	4,091	2,725	1,356	10	1,369 R	66.6%	33.1%	66.8%	33.2%
150,979	SCOTT	46,980	29,834	16,905	241	12,929 R	63.5%	36.0%	63.8%	36.2%
13,230	SHELBY	4,808	3,543	1,245	20	2,298 R	73.7%	25.9%	74.0%	26.0%
29,903	SIOUX	10,725	9,316	1,381	28	7,935 R	86.9%	12.9%	87.1%	12.9%
74,252	STORY	25,286	14,167	10,945	174	3,222 R	56.0%	43.3%	56.4%	43.6%
17,419	TAMA	6,667	4,095	2,548	24	1,547 R	61.4%	38.2%	61.6%	38.4%
7,114	TAYLOR	2,954	1,915	1,027	12	888 R	64.8%	34.8%	65.1%	34.9%
12,750	UNION	4,855	2,891	1,950	14	941 R	59.5%	40.2%	59.7%	40.3%
7,676	VAN BUREN	2,961	1,688	1,264	9	424 R	57.0%	42.7%	57.2%	42.8%
35,687	WAPELLO	12,161	5,446	6,668	47	1,222 D	44.8%	54.8%	45.0%	55.0%
36,033	WARREN	13,648	7,581	6,018	49	1,563 R	55.5%	44.1%	55.7%	44.3%
19,612	WASHINGTON	6,228	4,177	2,023	28	2,154 R	67.1%	32.5%	67.4%	32.6%
7,067	WAYNE	2,958	1,821	1,135	2	686 R	61.6%	38.4%	61.6%	38.4%
40,342	WEBSTER	13,892	7,845	6,011	36	1,834 R	56.5%	43.3%	56.6%	43.4%
12,122	WINNEBAGO	5,064	3,497	1,549	18	1,948 R	69.1%	30.6%	69.3%	30.7%
20,847	WINNESHIEK	7,342	4,965	2,334	43	2,631 R	67.6%	31.8%	68.0%	32.0%
98,276	WOODBURY	29,639	18,104	11,274	261	6,830 R	61.1%	38.0%	61.6%	38.4%
7,991	WORTH	3,476	1,990	1,454	32	536 R	57.2%	41.8%	57.8%	42.2%
14,269	WRIGHT	4,927	3,134	1,785	8	1,349 R	63.6%	36.2%	63.7%	36.3%
2,776,755	TOTAL	976,483	591,852	379,372	5,259	212,480 R	60.6%	38.9%	60.9%	39.1%

IOWA

SENATOR 1990

1990 Census Population	County	Total Vote	Republican	Democratic	Other	Rep.-Dem. Plurality	Percentage Total Vote Rep.	Dem.	Major Vote Rep.	Dem.
8,409	ADAIR	3,704	1,562	2,139	3	577 D	42.2%	57.7%	42.2%	57.8%
4,866	ADAMS	1,952	921	1,031		110 D	47.2%	52.8%	47.2%	52.8%
13,855	ALLAMAKEE	5,255	3,207	2,048		1,159 R	61.0%	39.0%	61.0%	39.0%
13,743	APPANOOSE	4,559	1,943	2,616		673 D	42.6%	57.4%	42.6%	57.4%
7,334	AUDUBON	3,327	1,513	1,814		301 D	45.5%	54.5%	45.5%	54.5%
22,429	BENTON	8,057	3,675	4,381	1	706 D	45.6%	54.4%	45.6%	54.4%
123,798	BLACK HAWK	42,800	19,577	23,205	18	3,628 D	45.7%	54.2%	45.8%	54.2%
25,186	BOONE	9,501	3,392	6,109		2,717 D	35.7%	64.3%	35.7%	64.3%
22,813	BREMER	8,123	4,051	4,071	1	20 D	49.9%	50.1%	49.9%	50.1%
20,844	BUCHANAN	7,290	3,694	3,591	5	103 R	50.7%	49.3%	50.7%	49.3%
19,965	BUENA VISTA	7,145	3,622	3,523		99 R	50.7%	49.3%	50.7%	49.3%
15,731	BUTLER	5,071	3,045	2,026		1,019 R	60.0%	40.0%	60.0%	40.0%
11,508	CALHOUN	4,217	2,034	2,183		149 D	48.2%	51.8%	48.2%	51.8%
21,423	CARROLL	7,236	3,831	3,401	4	430 R	52.9%	47.0%	53.0%	47.0%
15,128	CASS	6,045	3,303	2,737	5	566 R	54.6%	45.3%	54.7%	45.3%
17,381	CEDAR	6,081	3,100	2,977	4	123 R	51.0%	49.0%	51.0%	49.0%
46,733	CERRO GORDO	17,559	8,717	8,841	1	124 D	49.6%	50.4%	49.6%	50.4%
14,098	CHEROKEE	5,656	2,697	2,958	1	261 D	47.7%	52.3%	47.7%	52.3%
13,295	CHICKASAW	5,197	2,464	2,725	8	261 D	47.4%	52.4%	47.5%	52.5%
8,287	CLARKE	3,477	1,212	2,262	3	1,050 D	34.9%	65.1%	34.9%	65.1%
17,585	CLAY	5,939	2,778	3,160	1	382 D	46.8%	53.2%	46.8%	53.2%
19,054	CLAYTON	7,133	3,914	3,218	1	696 R	54.9%	45.1%	54.9%	45.1%
51,040	CLINTON	17,986	9,398	8,586	2	812 R	52.3%	47.7%	52.3%	47.7%
16,775	CRAWFORD	5,541	2,733	2,807	1	74 D	49.3%	50.7%	49.3%	50.7%
29,755	DALLAS	10,736	3,967	6,754	15	2,787 D	37.0%	62.9%	37.0%	63.0%
8,312	DAVIS	3,063	1,118	1,942	3	824 D	36.5%	63.4%	36.5%	63.5%
8,338	DECATUR	2,934	1,024	1,909	1	885 D	34.9%	65.1%	34.9%	65.1%
18,035	DELAWARE	6,440	3,966	2,474		1,492 R	61.6%	38.4%	61.6%	38.4%
42,614	DES MOINES	15,277	6,149	9,125	3	2,976 D	40.3%	59.7%	40.3%	59.7%
14,909	DICKINSON	5,748	2,969	2,779		190 R	51.7%	48.3%	51.7%	48.3%
86,403	DUBUQUE	31,932	17,964	13,939	29	4,025 R	56.3%	43.7%	56.3%	43.7%
11,569	EMMET	3,892	1,977	1,914	1	63 R	50.8%	49.2%	50.8%	49.2%
21,843	FAYETTE	8,975	4,861	4,112	2	749 R	54.2%	45.8%	54.2%	45.8%
17,058	FLOYD	6,041	2,928	3,108	5	180 D	48.5%	51.4%	48.5%	51.5%
11,364	FRANKLIN	4,259	2,094	2,165		71 D	49.2%	50.8%	49.2%	50.8%
8,226	FREMONT	3,245	1,859	1,386		473 R	57.3%	42.7%	57.3%	42.7%
10,045	GREENE	4,451	1,706	2,744	1	1,038 D	38.3%	61.6%	38.3%	61.7%
12,029	GRUNDY	4,719	2,803	1,916		887 R	59.4%	40.6%	59.4%	40.6%
10,935	GUTHRIE	4,101	1,605	2,496		891 D	39.1%	60.9%	39.1%	60.9%
16,071	HAMILTON	6,068	2,648	3,420		772 D	43.6%	56.4%	43.6%	56.4%
12,638	HANCOCK	4,632	1,918	2,706	8	788 D	41.4%	58.4%	41.5%	58.5%
19,094	HARDIN	7,700	3,364	4,328	8	964 D	43.7%	56.2%	43.7%	56.3%
14,730	HARRISON	4,538	2,437	2,100	1	337 R	53.7%	46.3%	53.7%	46.3%
19,226	HENRY	6,400	3,040	3,360		320 D	47.5%	52.5%	47.5%	52.5%
9,809	HOWARD	3,970	2,117	1,850	3	267 R	53.3%	46.6%	53.4%	46.6%
10,756	HUMBOLDT	4,352	2,142	2,210		68 D	49.2%	50.8%	49.2%	50.8%
8,365	IDA	3,112	1,524	1,587	1	63 D	49.0%	51.0%	49.0%	51.0%
14,630	IOWA	5,677	2,758	2,918	1	160 D	48.6%	51.4%	48.6%	51.4%
19,950	JACKSON	7,296	3,982	3,309	5	673 R	54.6%	45.4%	54.6%	45.4%
34,795	JASPER	13,688	5,288	8,386	14	3,098 D	38.6%	61.3%	38.7%	61.3%
16,310	JEFFERSON	5,647	2,682	2,962	3	280 D	47.5%	52.5%	47.5%	52.5%
96,119	JOHNSON	32,536	10,420	22,027	89	11,607 D	32.0%	67.7%	32.1%	67.9%
19,444	JONES	6,951	3,647	3,300	4	347 R	52.5%	47.5%	52.5%	47.5%
11,624	KEOKUK	4,378	1,942	2,436		494 D	44.4%	55.6%	44.4%	55.6%
18,591	KOSSUTH	7,318	4,067	3,251		816 R	55.6%	44.4%	55.6%	44.4%
38,687	LEE	13,000	5,301	7,697	2	2,396 D	40.8%	59.2%	40.8%	59.2%
168,767	LINN	63,547	30,193	33,212	142	3,019 D	47.5%	52.3%	47.6%	52.4%
11,592	LOUISA	3,764	1,733	2,027	4	294 D	46.0%	53.9%	46.1%	53.9%
9,070	LUCAS	3,569	1,336	2,231	2	895 D	37.4%	62.5%	37.5%	62.5%
11,952	LYON	4,050	2,846	1,204		1,642 R	70.3%	29.7%	70.3%	29.7%

IOWA

SENATOR 1990

1990 Census Population	County	Total Vote	Republican	Democratic	Other	Rep.-Dem. Plurality	Percentage Total Vote Rep.	Dem.	Major Vote Rep.	Dem.
12,483	MADISON	5,157	3,259	1,893	5	1,366 R	63.2%	36.7%	63.3%	36.7%
21,522	MAHASKA	7,585	4,086	3,499		587 R	53.9%	46.1%	53.9%	46.1%
30,001	MARION	10,789	4,773	6,015	1	1,242 D	44.2%	55.8%	44.2%	55.8%
38,276	MARSHALL	14,813	6,174	8,628	11	2,454 D	41.7%	58.2%	41.7%	58.3%
13,202	MILLS	3,842	2,282	1,560		722 R	59.4%	40.6%	59.4%	40.6%
10,928	MITCHELL	4,405	2,460	1,945		515 R	55.8%	44.2%	55.8%	44.2%
10,034	MONONA	3,378	1,544	1,832	2	288 D	45.7%	54.2%	45.7%	54.3%
8,114	MONROE	3,232	1,243	1,988	1	745 D	38.5%	61.5%	38.5%	61.5%
12,076	MONTGOMERY	3,956	2,424	1,528	4	896 R	61.3%	38.6%	61.3%	38.7%
39,907	MUSCATINE	11,212	5,565	5,646	1	81 D	49.6%	50.4%	49.6%	50.4%
15,444	O'BRIEN	5,564	3,424	2,140		1,284 R	61.5%	38.5%	61.5%	38.5%
7,267	OSCEOLA	2,528	1,539	989		550 R	60.9%	39.1%	60.9%	39.1%
16,870	PAGE	5,208	3,409	1,799		1,610 R	65.5%	34.5%	65.5%	34.5%
10,669	PALO ALTO	4,110	1,982	2,128		146 D	48.2%	51.8%	48.2%	51.8%
23,388	PLYMOUTH	7,212	4,100	3,106	6	994 R	56.8%	43.1%	56.9%	43.1%
9,525	POCAHONTAS	3,648	1,782	1,866		84 D	48.8%	51.2%	48.8%	51.2%
327,140	POLK	119,469	43,289	75,892	288	32,603 D	36.2%	63.5%	36.3%	63.7%
82,628	POTTAWATTAMIE	22,959	11,472	11,486	1	14 D	50.0%	50.0%	50.0%	50.0%
19,033	POWESHIEK	6,784	2,707	4,077		1,370 D	39.9%	60.1%	39.9%	60.1%
5,420	RINGGOLD	2,523	942	1,581		639 D	37.3%	62.7%	37.3%	62.7%
12,324	SAC	4,056	2,088	1,968		120 R	51.5%	48.5%	51.5%	48.5%
150,979	SCOTT	46,737	22,023	24,704	10	2,681 D	47.1%	52.9%	47.1%	52.9%
13,230	SHELBY	4,816	2,877	1,939		938 R	59.7%	40.3%	59.7%	40.3%
29,903	SIOUX	10,732	2,164	8,568		6,404 D	20.2%	79.8%	20.2%	79.8%
74,252	STORY	25,277	9,198	16,068	11	6,870 D	36.4%	63.6%	36.4%	63.6%
17,419	TAMA	6,551	2,909	3,642		733 D	44.4%	55.6%	44.4%	55.6%
7,114	TAYLOR	3,046	1,338	1,708		370 D	43.9%	56.1%	43.9%	56.1%
12,750	UNION	4,803	1,895	2,908		1,013 D	39.5%	60.5%	39.5%	60.5%
7,676	VAN BUREN	2,908	1,440	1,465	3	25 D	49.5%	50.4%	49.6%	50.4%
35,687	WAPELLO	12,161	4,013	8,147	1	4,134 D	33.0%	67.0%	33.0%	67.0%
36,033	WARREN	13,691	4,822	8,865	4	4,043 D	35.2%	64.8%	35.2%	64.8%
19,612	WASHINGTON	6,145	3,037	3,107	1	70 D	49.4%	50.6%	49.4%	50.6%
7,067	WAYNE	2,864	961	1,901	2	940 D	33.6%	66.4%	33.6%	66.4%
40,342	WEBSTER	13,896	5,731	8,165		2,434 D	41.2%	58.8%	41.2%	58.8%
12,122	WINNEBAGO	4,970	2,809	2,160	1	649 R	56.5%	43.5%	56.5%	43.5%
20,847	WINNESHIEK	7,274	3,710	3,564		146 R	51.0%	49.0%	51.0%	49.0%
98,276	WOODBURY	30,405	14,486	15,595	324	1,109 D	47.6%	51.3%	48.2%	51.8%
7,991	WORTH	3,489	1,826	1,660	3	166 R	52.3%	47.6%	52.4%	47.6%
14,269	WRIGHT	4,881	2,328	2,550	3	222 D	47.7%	52.2%	47.7%	52.3%
2,776,755	TOTAL	983,933	446,869	535,975	1,089	89,106 D	45.4%	54.5%	45.5%	54.5%

IOWA

CONGRESS

CD	Year	Total Vote	Republican Vote	Candidate	Democratic Vote	Candidate	Other Vote	Rep.-Dem. Plurality	Total Vote Rep.	Total Vote Dem.	Major Vote Rep.	Major Vote Dem.
1	1990	90,193	90,042	LEACH, JAMES A.			151	90,042 R	99.8%		100.0%	
1	1988	185,716	112,746	LEACH, JAMES A.	71,280	GLUBA, WILLIAM E.	1,690	41,466 R	60.7%	38.4%	61.3%	38.7%
1	1986	130,825	86,834	LEACH, JAMES A.	43,985	WHITAKER, JOHN R.	6	42,849 R	66.4%	33.6%	66.4%	33.6%
1	1984	196,489	131,182	LEACH, JAMES A.	65,293	READY, KEVIN	14	65,889 R	66.8%	33.2%	66.8%	33.2%
1	1982	151,332	89,585	LEACH, JAMES A.	61,734	GLUBA, WILLIAM E.	13	27,851 R	59.2%	40.8%	59.2%	40.8%
2	1990	166,106	82,650	NUSSLE, JIM	81,008	TABOR, ERIC	2,448	1,642 R	49.8%	48.8%	50.5%	49.5%
2	1988	200,041	113,543	TAUKE, TOM	86,438	TABOR, ERIC	60	27,105 R	56.8%	43.2%	56.8%	43.2%
2	1986	144,630	88,708	TAUKE, TOM	55,903	TABOR, ERIC	19	32,805 R	61.3%	38.7%	61.3%	38.7%
2	1984	214,255	136,893	TAUKE, TOM	77,335	WELSH, JOE	27	59,558 R	63.9%	36.1%	63.9%	36.1%
2	1982	169,037	99,478	TAUKE, TOM	69,539	APPEL, BRENT	20	29,939 R	58.8%	41.1%	58.9%	41.1%
3	1990	101,780			100,947	NAGLE, DAVID R.	833	100,947 D		99.2%		100.0%
3	1988	203,932	74,682	REDFERN, DONALD	129,204	NAGLE, DAVID R.	46	54,522 D	36.6%	63.4%	36.6%	63.4%
3	1986	152,920	69,386	MCINTEE, JOHN	83,504	NAGLE, DAVID R.	30	14,118 D	45.4%	54.6%	45.4%	54.6%
3	1984	220,375	133,737	EVANS, COOPER	86,574	JOHNSTON, JOE	64	47,163 R	60.7%	39.3%	60.7%	39.3%
3	1982	187,675	104,072	EVANS, COOPER	83,581	CUTLER, LYNN G.	22	20,491 R	55.5%	44.5%	55.5%	44.5%
4	1990	130,590			127,812	SMITH, NEAL	2,778	127,812 D		97.9%		100.0%
4	1988	219,223	62,056	LUNDE, PAUL	157,065	SMITH, NEAL	102	95,009 D	28.3%	71.6%	28.3%	71.7%
4	1986	156,952	49,641	LOCKARD, ROBERT R.	107,271	SMITH, NEAL	40	57,630 D	31.6%	68.3%	31.6%	68.4%
4	1984	225,674	88,717	LOCKARD, ROBERT R.	136,922	SMITH, NEAL	35	48,205 D	39.3%	60.7%	39.3%	60.7%
4	1982	179,972	60,534	READINGER, DAVE	118,849	SMITH, NEAL	589	58,315 D	33.6%	66.0%	33.7%	66.3%
5	1990	147,012	99,978	LIGHTFOOT, JIM R.	47,022	POWELL, ROD	12	52,956 R	68.0%	32.0%	68.0%	32.0%
5	1988	184,368	117,761	LIGHTFOOT, JIM R.	66,599	FREUND, GENE	8	51,162 R	63.9%	36.1%	63.9%	36.1%
5	1986	143,589	85,025	LIGHTFOOT, JIM R.	58,552	HUGHES, SCOTT	12	26,473 R	59.2%	40.8%	59.2%	40.8%
5	1984	206,072	104,632	LIGHTFOOT, JIM R.	101,435	FITZGERALD, JERRY	5	3,197 R	50.8%	49.2%	50.8%	49.2%
5	1982	158,563	65,200	DANKER, ARLYN E.	93,333	HARKIN, TOM	30	28,133 D	41.1%	58.9%	41.1%	58.9%
6	1990	156,459	112,333	GRANDY, FRED	44,063	EARLL, MIKE D.	63	68,270 R	71.8%	28.2%	71.8%	28.2%
6	1988	195,478	125,859	GRANDY, FRED	69,614	O'BRIEN, DAVE	5	56,245 R	64.4%	35.6%	64.4%	35.6%
6	1986	160,679	81,861	GRANDY, FRED	78,807	HODGSON, CLAYTON	11	3,054 R	50.9%	49.0%	51.0%	49.0%
6	1984	205,894	78,182	RENSINK, DARREL	127,706	BEDELL, BERKLEY	6	49,524 D	38.0%	62.0%	38.0%	62.0%
6	1982	158,184	56,487	BREMER, AL	101,690	BEDELL, BERKLEY	7	45,203 D	35.7%	64.3%	35.7%	64.3%

IOWA

1990 GENERAL ELECTION

Governor   Other vote was 4,263 Socialist Workers (Bailey) and 996 scattered write-in.

Senator   Other vote was scattered write-in.

Congress   Other vote was 2,325 Independent (Zonneveld) and 123 scattered write-in in CD 2; scattered write-in in all other CD's.

1990 PRIMARIES

JUNE 5 REPUBLICAN

Governor   Terry E. Branstad, unopposed.

Senator   Tom Tauke, unopposed.

Congress   Unopposed in four CD's. No candidate in CD 4. Jeff Abbas, the unopposed candidate in CD 3, withdrew after the primary and no substitution was made. Contested as follows:

CD 2   8,209 Jim Nussle; 7,455 Joe Ertl; 4,845 Wayne A. Moldenhauer; 17 scattered write-in.

JUNE 5 DEMOCRATIC

Governor   79,022 Donald D. Avenson; 63,364 Tom Miller; 52,170 John Chrystal; 4,475 Jo Ann Zimmerman; 1,167 Darold Powers; 107 scattered write-in.

Senator   Tom Harkin, unopposed.

Congress   Unopposed in four CD's. No candidate in CD 1. Contested as follows:

CD 2   19,806 Eric Tabor; 15,248 Steve Sovern; 31 scattered write-in.

KANSAS

GOVERNOR
Joan Finney (D). Elected 1990 to a four-year term.

SENATORS
Robert Dole (R). Re-elected 1986 to a six-year term. Previously elected 1980, 1974, 1968.

Nancy Landon Kassebaum (R). Re-elected 1990 to a six-year term. Previously elected 1984, 1978.

REPRESENTATIVES
1. Pat Roberts (R)
2. Jim Slattery (D)
3. Jan Meyers (R)
4. Dan Glickman (D)
5. Dick Nichols (R)

POSTWAR VOTE FOR PRESIDENT

		Republican		Democratic		Other		Percentage Total Vote		Major Vote	
Year	Total Vote	Vote	Candidate	Vote	Candidate	Vote	Plurality	Rep.	Dem.	Rep.	Dem.
1988	993,044	554,049	Bush, George	422,636	Dukakis, Michael S.	16,359	131,413 R	55.8%	42.6%	56.7%	43.3%
1984	1,021,991	677,296	Reagan, Ronald	333,149	Mondale, Walter F.	11,546	344,147 R	66.3%	32.6%	67.0%	33.0%
1980	979,795	566,812	Reagan, Ronald	326,150	Carter, Jimmy	86,833	240,662 R	57.9%	33.3%	63.5%	36.5%
1976	957,845	502,752	Ford, Gerald R.	430,421	Carter, Jimmy	24,672	72,331 R	52.5%	44.9%	53.9%	46.1%
1972	916,095	619,812	Nixon, Richard M.	270,287	McGovern, George S.	25,996	349,525 R	67.7%	29.5%	69.6%	30.4%
1968	872,783	478,674	Nixon, Richard M.	302,996	Humphrey, Hubert H.	91,113	175,678 R	54.8%	34.7%	61.2%	38.8%
1964	857,901	386,579	Goldwater, Barry M.	464,028	Johnson, Lyndon B.	7,294	77,449 D	45.1%	54.1%	45.4%	54.6%
1960	928,825	561,474	Nixon, Richard M.	363,213	Kennedy, John F.	4,138	198,261 R	60.4%	39.1%	60.7%	39.3%
1956	866,243	566,878	Eisenhower, Dwight D.	296,317	Stevenson, Adlai E.	3,048	270,561 R	65.4%	34.2%	65.7%	34.3%
1952	896,166	616,302	Eisenhower, Dwight D.	273,296	Stevenson, Adlai E.	6,568	343,006 R	68.8%	30.5%	69.3%	30.7%
1948	788,819	423,039	Dewey, Thomas E.	351,902	Truman, Harry S.	13,878	71,137 R	53.6%	44.6%	54.6%	45.4%

POSTWAR VOTE FOR GOVERNOR

		Republican		Democratic		Other	Rep.-Dem.	Percentage Total Vote		Major Vote	
Year	Total Vote	Vote	Candidate	Vote	Candidate	Vote	Plurality	Rep.	Dem.	Rep.	Dem.
1990	783,325	333,589	Hayden, Mike	380,609	Finney, Joan	69,127	47,020 D	42.6%	48.6%	46.7%	53.3%
1986	840,605	436,267	Hayden, Mike	404,338	Docking, Thomas R.		31,929 R	51.9%	48.1%	51.9%	48.1%
1982	763,263	339,356	Hardage, Sam	405,772	Carlin, John	18,135	66,416 D	44.5%	53.2%	45.5%	54.5%
1978	736,246	348,015	Bennett, Robert F.	363,835	Carlin, John	24,396	15,820 D	47.3%	49.4%	48.9%	51.1%
1974 **	783,875	387,792	Bennett, Robert F.	384,115	Miller, Vern	11,968	3,677 R	49.5%	49.0%	50.2%	49.8%
1972	921,552	341,440	Kay, Morris	571,256	Docking, Robert	8,856	229,816 D	37.1%	62.0%	37.4%	62.6%
1970	745,196	333,227	Frizzell, Kent	404,611	Docking, Robert	7,358	71,384 D	44.7%	54.3%	45.2%	54.8%
1968	862,473	410,673	Harman, Rick	447,269	Docking, Robert	4,531	36,596 D	47.6%	51.9%	47.9%	52.1%
1966	692,955	304,325	Avery, William H.	380,030	Docking, Robert	8,600	75,705 D	43.9%	54.8%	44.5%	55.5%
1964	850,414	432,667	Avery, William H.	400,264	Wiles, Harry G.	17,483	32,403 R	50.9%	47.1%	51.9%	48.1%
1962	638,798	341,257	Anderson, John	291,285	Saffels, Dale E.	6,256	49,972 R	53.4%	45.6%	54.0%	46.0%
1960	922,522	511,534	Anderson, John	402,261	Docking, George	8,727	109,273 R	55.4%	43.6%	56.0%	44.0%
1958	735,939	313,036	Reed, Clyde M.	415,506	Docking, George	7,397	102,470 D	42.5%	56.5%	43.0%	57.0%
1956	864,935	364,340	Shaw, Warren W.	479,701	Docking, George	20,894	115,361 D	42.1%	55.5%	43.2%	56.8%
1954	622,633	329,868	Hall, Fred	286,218	Docking, George	6,547	43,650 R	53.0%	46.0%	53.5%	46.5%
1952	872,139	491,338	Arn, Edward F.	363,482	Rooney, Charles	17,319	127,856 R	56.3%	41.7%	57.5%	42.5%
1950	619,310	333,001	Arn, Edward F.	275,494	Anderson, Kenneth	10,815	57,507 R	53.8%	44.5%	54.7%	45.3%
1948	760,407	433,396	Carlson, Frank	307,485	Carpenter, Randolph	19,526	125,911 R	57.0%	40.4%	58.5%	41.5%
1946	577,694	309,064	Carlson, Frank	254,283	Woodring, Harry H.	14,347	54,781 R	53.5%	44.0%	54.9%	45.1%

The term of office of Kansas' Governor was increased from two to four years effective with the 1974 election.

KANSAS

POSTWAR VOTE FOR SENATOR

Year	Total Vote	Republican Vote	Candidate	Democratic Vote	Candidate	Other Vote	Rep-Dem. Plurality	Percentage Total Vote Rep.	Dem.	Major Vote Rep.	Dem.
1990	786,235	578,605	Kassebaum, Nancy Landon	207,491	Williams, Dick	139	371,114 R	73.6%	26.4%	73.6%	26.4%
1986	823,566	576,902	Dole, Robert	246,664	MacDonald, Guy		330,238 R	70.0%	30.0%	70.0%	30.0%
1984	996,729	757,402	Kassebaum, Nancy Landon	211,664	Maher, James	27,663	545,738 R	76.0%	21.2%	78.2%	21.8%
1980	938,957	598,686	Dole, Robert	340,271	Simpson, John		258,415 R	63.8%	36.2%	63.8%	36.2%
1978	748,839	403,354	Kassebaum, Nancy Landon	317,602	Roy, William R.	27,883	85,752 R	53.9%	42.4%	55.9%	44.1%
1974	794,437	403,983	Dole, Robert	390,451	Roy, William R.	3	13,532 R	50.9%	49.1%	50.9%	49.1%
1972	871,722	622,591	Pearson, James B.	200,764	Tetzlaff, Arch O.	48,367	421,827 R	71.4%	23.0%	75.6%	24.4%
1968	817,096	490,911	Dole, Robert	315,911	Robinson, William I.	10,274	175,000 R	60.1%	38.7%	60.8%	39.2%
1966	671,345	350,077	Pearson, James B.	303,223	Breeding, J. Floyd	18,045	46,854 R	52.1%	45.2%	53.6%	46.4%
1962	622,232	388,500	Carlson, Frank	223,630	Smith, K. L.	10,102	164,870 R	62.4%	35.9%	63.5%	36.5%
1962 S	613,250	344,689	Pearson, James B.	260,756	Aylward, Paul L.	7,805	83,933 R	56.2%	42.5%	56.9%	43.1%
1960	888,592	485,499	Schoeppel, Andrew F.	388,895	Theis, Frank	14,198	96,604 R	54.6%	43.8%	55.5%	44.5%
1956	825,280	477,822	Carlson, Frank	333,939	Hart, George	13,519	143,883 R	57.9%	40.5%	58.9%	41.1%
1954	618,063	348,144	Schoeppel, Andrew F.	258,575	McGill, George	11,344	89,569 R	56.3%	41.8%	57.4%	42.6%
1950	619,104	335,880	Carlson, Frank	271,365	Aiken, Paul	11,859	64,515 R	54.3%	43.8%	55.3%	44.7%
1948	716,342	393,412	Schoeppel, Andrew F.	305,987	McGill, George	16,943	87,425 R	54.9%	42.7%	56.3%	43.7%

One of the 1962 elections was for a short term to fill a vacancy.

KANSAS

Districts Established June 2, 1982

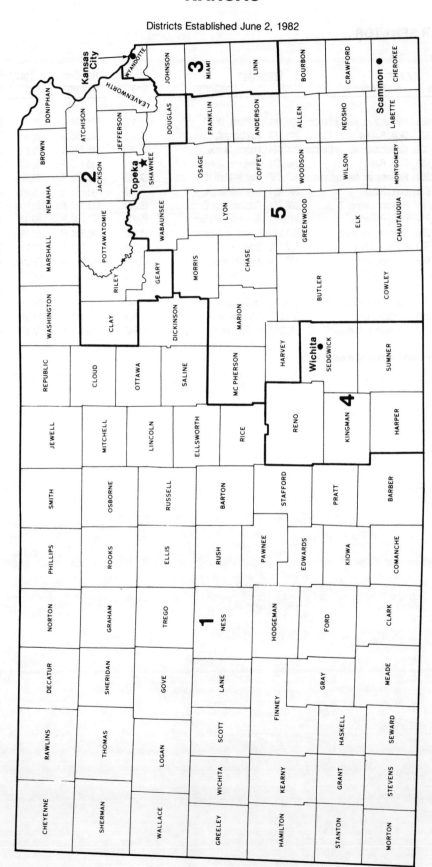

KANSAS

GOVERNOR 1990

1990 Census Population	County	Total Vote	Republican	Democratic	Other	Rep.-Dem. Plurality	Percentage Total Vote Rep.	Dem.	Major Vote Rep.	Dem.
14,638	ALLEN	4,873	2,240	2,164	469	76 R	46.0%	44.4%	50.9%	49.1%
7,803	ANDERSON	3,009	1,134	1,347	528	213 D	37.7%	44.8%	45.7%	54.3%
16,932	ATCHISON	4,932	1,529	2,966	437	1,437 D	31.0%	60.1%	34.0%	66.0%
5,874	BARBER	2,224	905	1,152	167	247 D	40.7%	51.8%	44.0%	56.0%
29,382	BARTON	10,105	4,907	4,413	785	494 R	48.6%	43.7%	52.7%	47.3%
14,966	BOURBON	5,005	1,938	2,676	391	738 D	38.7%	53.5%	42.0%	58.0%
11,128	BROWN	4,076	2,126	1,575	375	551 R	52.2%	38.6%	57.4%	42.6%
50,580	BUTLER	16,721	7,005	8,230	1,486	1,225 D	41.9%	49.2%	46.0%	54.0%
3,021	CHASE	1,205	534	525	146	9 R	44.3%	43.6%	50.4%	49.6%
4,407	CHAUTAUQUA	1,400	675	613	112	62 R	48.2%	43.8%	52.4%	47.6%
21,374	CHEROKEE	6,462	2,738	3,296	428	558 D	42.4%	51.0%	45.4%	54.6%
3,243	CHEYENNE	1,257	862	332	63	530 R	68.6%	26.4%	72.2%	27.8%
2,418	CLARK	1,121	610	410	101	200 R	54.4%	36.6%	59.8%	40.2%
9,158	CLAY	3,704	1,765	1,595	344	170 R	47.7%	43.1%	52.5%	47.5%
11,023	CLOUD	4,052	1,504	2,254	294	750 D	37.1%	55.6%	40.0%	60.0%
8,404	COFFEY	3,577	1,825	1,325	427	500 R	51.0%	37.0%	57.9%	42.1%
2,313	COMANCHE	954	584	325	45	259 R	61.2%	34.1%	64.2%	35.8%
36,915	COWLEY	11,266	4,570	5,675	1,021	1,105 D	40.6%	50.4%	44.6%	55.4%
35,568	CRAWFORD	11,675	4,383	6,346	946	1,963 D	37.5%	54.4%	40.9%	59.1%
4,021	DECATUR	1,737	1,218	448	71	770 R	70.1%	25.8%	73.1%	26.9%
18,958	DICKINSON	6,617	3,121	2,816	680	305 R	47.2%	42.6%	52.6%	47.4%
8,134	DONIPHAN	2,926	1,135	1,536	255	401 D	38.8%	52.5%	42.5%	57.5%
81,798	DOUGLAS	24,635	12,579	8,993	3,063	3,586 R	51.1%	36.5%	58.3%	41.7%
3,787	EDWARDS	1,531	663	743	125	80 D	43.3%	48.5%	47.2%	52.8%
3,327	ELK	1,407	673	628	106	45 R	47.8%	44.6%	51.7%	48.3%
26,004	ELLIS	9,056	3,652	4,845	559	1,193 D	40.3%	53.5%	43.0%	57.0%
6,586	ELLSWORTH	2,613	1,283	1,149	181	134 R	49.1%	44.0%	52.8%	47.2%
33,070	FINNEY	7,070	3,905	2,791	374	1,114 R	55.2%	39.5%	58.3%	41.7%
27,463	FORD	7,939	3,979	3,466	494	513 R	50.1%	43.7%	53.4%	46.6%
21,994	FRANKLIN	6,733	2,664	3,013	1,056	349 D	39.6%	44.7%	46.9%	53.1%
30,453	GEARY	4,915	2,419	2,142	354	277 R	49.2%	43.6%	53.0%	47.0%
3,231	GOVE	1,465	676	669	120	7 R	46.1%	45.7%	50.3%	49.7%
3,543	GRAHAM	1,423	750	568	105	182 R	52.7%	39.9%	56.9%	43.1%
7,159	GRANT	1,967	1,138	689	140	449 R	57.9%	35.0%	62.3%	37.7%
5,396	GRAY	1,741	998	603	140	395 R	57.3%	34.6%	62.3%	37.7%
1,774	GREELEY	679	394	219	66	175 R	58.0%	32.3%	64.3%	35.7%
7,847	GREENWOOD	3,362	1,433	1,588	341	155 D	42.6%	47.2%	47.4%	52.6%
2,388	HAMILTON	1,066	656	372	38	284 R	61.5%	34.9%	63.8%	36.2%
7,124	HARPER	2,742	1,123	1,424	195	301 D	41.0%	51.9%	44.1%	55.9%
31,028	HARVEY	10,586	4,304	5,329	953	1,025 D	40.7%	50.3%	44.7%	55.3%
3,886	HASKELL	1,202	695	430	77	265 R	57.8%	35.8%	61.8%	38.2%
2,177	HODGEMAN	997	591	353	53	238 R	59.3%	35.4%	62.6%	37.4%
11,525	JACKSON	4,379	1,927	2,139	313	212 D	44.0%	48.8%	47.4%	52.6%
15,905	JEFFERSON	5,735	2,028	3,143	564	1,115 D	35.4%	54.8%	39.2%	60.8%
4,251	JEWELL	1,751	1,045	605	101	440 R	59.7%	34.6%	63.3%	36.7%
355,054	JOHNSON	102,861	46,116	45,046	11,699	1,070 R	44.8%	43.8%	50.6%	49.4%
4,027	KEARNY	1,314	786	435	93	351 R	59.8%	33.1%	64.4%	35.6%
8,292	KINGMAN	3,416	1,310	1,851	255	541 D	38.3%	54.2%	41.4%	58.6%
3,660	KIOWA	1,421	823	480	118	343 R	57.9%	33.8%	63.2%	36.8%
23,693	LABETTE	7,633	3,389	3,825	419	436 D	44.4%	50.1%	47.0%	53.0%
2,375	LANE	1,064	686	315	63	371 R	64.5%	29.6%	68.5%	31.5%
64,371	LEAVENWORTH	13,891	3,748	8,649	1,494	4,901 D	27.0%	62.3%	30.2%	69.8%
3,653	LINCOLN	2,059	1,155	720	184	435 R	56.1%	35.0%	61.6%	38.4%
8,254	LINN	2,738	1,181	1,355	202	174 D	43.1%	49.5%	46.6%	53.4%
3,081	LOGAN	1,231	695	441	95	254 R	56.5%	35.8%	61.2%	38.8%
34,732	LYON	10,371	3,795	5,410	1,166	1,615 D	36.6%	52.2%	41.2%	58.8%
27,268	MCPHERSON	9,811	4,288	4,556	967	268 D	43.7%	46.4%	48.5%	51.5%
12,888	MARION	4,916	2,617	1,912	387	705 R	53.2%	38.9%	57.8%	42.2%
11,705	MARSHALL	4,801	1,931	2,482	388	551 D	40.2%	51.7%	43.8%	56.2%
4,247	MEADE	1,648	942	628	78	314 R	57.2%	38.1%	60.0%	40.0%

KANSAS

GOVERNOR 1990

1990 Census Population	County	Total Vote	Republican	Democratic	Other	Rep.-Dem. Plurality		Percentage Total Vote Rep.	Dem.	Major Vote Rep.	Dem.
23,466	MIAMI	6,793	2,225	3,853	715	1,628	D	32.8%	56.7%	36.6%	63.4%
7,203	MITCHELL	3,059	1,570	1,237	252	333	R	51.3%	40.4%	55.9%	44.1%
38,816	MONTGOMERY	11,545	4,780	5,905	860	1,125	D	41.4%	51.1%	44.7%	55.3%
6,198	MORRIS	2,476	1,061	1,126	289	65	D	42.9%	45.5%	48.5%	51.5%
3,480	MORTON	1,314	692	504	118	188	R	52.7%	38.4%	57.9%	42.1%
10,446	NEMAHA	4,651	1,827	2,577	247	750	D	39.3%	55.4%	41.5%	58.5%
17,035	NEOSHO	5,941	2,396	3,037	508	641	D	40.3%	51.1%	44.1%	55.9%
4,033	NESS	1,885	920	807	158	113	R	48.8%	42.8%	53.3%	46.7%
5,947	NORTON	2,573	1,520	891	162	629	R	59.1%	34.6%	63.0%	37.0%
15,248	OSAGE	5,772	2,055	3,080	637	1,025	D	35.6%	53.4%	40.0%	60.0%
4,867	OSBORNE	2,186	1,156	882	148	274	R	52.9%	40.3%	56.7%	43.3%
5,634	OTTAWA	2,242	1,155	898	189	257	R	51.5%	40.1%	56.3%	43.7%
7,555	PAWNEE	2,796	1,534	1,075	187	459	R	54.9%	38.4%	58.8%	41.2%
6,590	PHILLIPS	2,649	1,674	810	165	864	R	63.2%	30.6%	67.4%	32.6%
16,128	POTTAWATOMIE	5,702	2,243	2,866	593	623	D	39.3%	50.3%	43.9%	56.1%
9,702	PRATT	3,654	1,704	1,627	323	77	R	46.6%	44.5%	51.2%	48.8%
3,404	RAWLINS	1,830	1,395	371	64	1,024	R	76.2%	20.3%	79.0%	21.0%
62,389	RENO	20,573	8,467	10,224	1,882	1,757	D	41.2%	49.7%	45.3%	54.7%
6,482	REPUBLIC	2,942	1,569	1,122	251	447	R	53.3%	38.1%	58.3%	41.7%
10,610	RICE	4,122	1,714	2,029	379	315	D	41.6%	49.2%	45.8%	54.2%
67,139	RILEY	12,533	6,331	4,859	1,343	1,472	R	50.5%	38.8%	56.6%	43.4%
6,039	ROOKS	2,535	1,242	1,069	224	173	R	49.0%	42.2%	53.7%	46.3%
3,842	RUSH	1,849	829	879	141	50	D	44.8%	47.5%	48.5%	51.5%
7,835	RUSSELL	3,445	1,561	1,646	238	85	D	45.3%	47.8%	48.7%	51.3%
49,301	SALINE	16,836	7,786	7,530	1,520	256	R	46.2%	44.7%	50.8%	49.2%
5,289	SCOTT	1,985	1,249	593	143	656	R	62.9%	29.9%	67.8%	32.2%
403,662	SEDGWICK	123,324	50,664	62,299	10,361	11,635	D	41.1%	50.5%	44.9%	55.1%
18,743	SEWARD	4,338	2,415	1,592	331	823	R	55.7%	36.7%	60.3%	39.7%
160,976	SHAWNEE	64,685	24,156	36,130	4,399	11,974	D	37.3%	55.9%	40.1%	59.9%
3,043	SHERIDAN	1,397	728	568	101	160	R	52.1%	40.7%	56.2%	43.8%
6,926	SHERMAN	2,520	1,478	837	205	641	R	58.7%	33.2%	63.8%	36.2%
5,078	SMITH	2,253	1,302	754	197	548	R	57.8%	33.5%	63.3%	36.7%
5,365	STAFFORD	2,213	1,082	964	167	118	R	48.9%	43.6%	52.9%	47.1%
2,333	STANTON	873	550	255	68	295	R	63.0%	29.2%	68.3%	31.7%
5,048	STEVENS	1,744	903	690	151	213	R	51.8%	39.6%	56.7%	43.3%
25,841	SUMNER	8,287	2,982	4,564	741	1,582	D	36.0%	55.1%	39.5%	60.5%
8,258	THOMAS	3,126	1,734	1,090	302	644	R	55.5%	34.9%	61.4%	38.6%
3,694	TREGO	1,582	819	643	120	176	R	51.8%	40.6%	56.0%	44.0%
6,603	WABAUNSEE	2,875	1,285	1,320	270	35	D	44.7%	45.9%	49.3%	50.7%
1,821	WALLACE	792	499	224	69	275	R	63.0%	28.3%	69.0%	31.0%
7,073	WASHINGTON	2,966	1,500	1,203	263	297	R	50.6%	40.6%	55.5%	44.5%
2,758	WICHITA	851	444	356	51	88	R	52.2%	41.8%	55.5%	44.5%
10,289	WILSON	3,526	1,864	1,391	271	473	R	52.9%	39.4%	57.3%	42.7%
4,116	WOODSON	1,565	789	669	107	120	R	50.4%	42.7%	54.1%	45.9%
161,993	WYANDOTTE	37,453	7,395	27,538	2,520	20,143	D	19.7%	73.5%	21.2%	78.8%
2,477,574	TOTAL	783,325	333,589	380,609	69,127	47,020	D	42.6%	48.6%	46.7%	53.3%

KANSAS

SENATOR 1990

1990 Census Population	County	Total Vote	Republican	Democratic	Other	Rep.-Dem. Plurality	Total Vote Rep.	Total Vote Dem.	Major Vote Rep.	Major Vote Dem.
14,638	ALLEN	4,886	3,670	1,216		2,454 R	75.1%	24.9%	75.1%	24.9%
7,803	ANDERSON	3,065	2,154	911		1,243 R	70.3%	29.7%	70.3%	29.7%
16,932	ATCHISON	5,099	3,466	1,633		1,833 R	68.0%	32.0%	68.0%	32.0%
5,874	BARBER	2,225	1,641	584		1,057 R	73.8%	26.2%	73.8%	26.2%
29,382	BARTON	10,339	7,988	2,351		5,637 R	77.3%	22.7%	77.3%	22.7%
14,966	BOURBON	5,040	3,599	1,441		2,158 R	71.4%	28.6%	71.4%	28.6%
11,128	BROWN	4,114	3,224	890		2,334 R	78.4%	21.6%	78.4%	21.6%
50,580	BUTLER	16,814	12,425	4,389		8,036 R	73.9%	26.1%	73.9%	26.1%
3,021	CHASE	1,205	986	219		767 R	81.8%	18.2%	81.8%	18.2%
4,407	CHAUTAUQUA	1,417	1,009	408		601 R	71.2%	28.8%	71.2%	28.8%
21,374	CHEROKEE	6,582	4,181	2,401		1,780 R	63.5%	36.5%	63.5%	36.5%
3,243	CHEYENNE	1,241	953	288		665 R	76.8%	23.2%	76.8%	23.2%
2,418	CLARK	1,123	892	231		661 R	79.4%	20.6%	79.4%	20.6%
9,158	CLAY	3,782	3,268	514		2,754 R	86.4%	13.6%	86.4%	13.6%
11,023	CLOUD	4,078	2,980	1,098		1,882 R	73.1%	26.9%	73.1%	26.9%
8,404	COFFEY	3,600	2,899	701		2,198 R	80.5%	19.5%	80.5%	19.5%
2,313	COMANCHE	970	788	182		606 R	81.2%	18.8%	81.2%	18.8%
36,915	COWLEY	11,344	8,311	3,033		5,278 R	73.3%	26.7%	73.3%	26.7%
35,568	CRAWFORD	11,908	8,013	3,895		4,118 R	67.3%	32.7%	67.3%	32.7%
4,021	DECATUR	1,720	1,367	353		1,014 R	79.5%	20.5%	79.5%	20.5%
18,958	DICKINSON	6,849	5,567	1,282		4,285 R	81.3%	18.7%	81.3%	18.7%
8,134	DONIPHAN	2,957	1,922	1,035		887 R	65.0%	35.0%	65.0%	35.0%
81,798	DOUGLAS	25,188	18,609	6,579		12,030 R	73.9%	26.1%	73.9%	26.1%
3,787	EDWARDS	1,538	1,108	430		678 R	72.0%	28.0%	72.0%	28.0%
3,327	ELK	1,423	1,071	352		719 R	75.3%	24.7%	75.3%	24.7%
26,004	ELLIS	9,124	6,712	2,412		4,300 R	73.6%	26.4%	73.6%	26.4%
6,586	ELLSWORTH	2,634	2,037	597		1,440 R	77.3%	22.7%	77.3%	22.7%
33,070	FINNEY	7,223	5,810	1,413		4,397 R	80.4%	19.6%	80.4%	19.6%
27,463	FORD	7,971	6,226	1,745		4,481 R	78.1%	21.9%	78.1%	21.9%
21,994	FRANKLIN	6,815	4,769	2,046		2,723 R	70.0%	30.0%	70.0%	30.0%
30,453	GEARY	4,980	3,490	1,490		2,000 R	70.1%	29.9%	70.1%	29.9%
3,231	GOVE	1,458	1,139	319		820 R	78.1%	21.9%	78.1%	21.9%
3,543	GRAHAM	1,423	1,102	321		781 R	77.4%	22.6%	77.4%	22.6%
7,159	GRANT	2,148	1,507	641		866 R	70.2%	29.8%	70.2%	29.8%
5,396	GRAY	1,745	1,453	292		1,161 R	83.3%	16.7%	83.3%	16.7%
1,774	GREELEY	680	524	156		368 R	77.1%	22.9%	77.1%	22.9%
7,847	GREENWOOD	3,193	2,360	833		1,527 R	73.9%	26.1%	73.9%	26.1%
2,388	HAMILTON	1,038	804	234		570 R	77.5%	22.5%	77.5%	22.5%
7,124	HARPER	2,754	2,077	677		1,400 R	75.4%	24.6%	75.4%	24.6%
31,028	HARVEY	10,724	8,286	2,438		5,848 R	77.3%	22.7%	77.3%	22.7%
3,886	HASKELL	1,210	970	240		730 R	80.2%	19.8%	80.2%	19.8%
2,177	HODGEMAN	1,002	791	211		580 R	78.9%	21.1%	78.9%	21.1%
11,525	JACKSON	4,476	3,555	921		2,634 R	79.4%	20.6%	79.4%	20.6%
15,905	JEFFERSON	5,815	4,223	1,592		2,631 R	72.6%	27.4%	72.6%	27.4%
4,251	JEWELL	1,761	1,394	367		1,027 R	79.2%	20.8%	79.2%	20.8%
355,054	JOHNSON	104,282	77,449	26,833		50,616 R	74.3%	25.7%	74.3%	25.7%
4,027	KEARNY	1,321	1,074	247		827 R	81.3%	18.7%	81.3%	18.7%
8,292	KINGMAN	3,429	2,577	852		1,725 R	75.2%	24.8%	75.2%	24.8%
3,660	KIOWA	1,417	1,126	291		835 R	79.5%	20.5%	79.5%	20.5%
23,693	LABETTE	7,711	5,546	2,165		3,381 R	71.9%	28.1%	71.9%	28.1%
2,375	LANE	1,062	917	145		772 R	86.3%	13.7%	86.3%	13.7%
64,371	LEAVENWORTH	14,005	8,606	5,399		3,207 R	61.4%	38.6%	61.4%	38.6%
3,653	LINCOLN	2,075	1,765	310		1,455 R	85.1%	14.9%	85.1%	14.9%
8,254	LINN	2,823	1,872	951		921 R	66.3%	33.7%	66.3%	33.7%
3,081	LOGAN	1,223	919	304		615 R	75.1%	24.9%	75.1%	24.9%
34,732	LYON	10,442	7,818	2,624		5,194 R	74.9%	25.1%	74.9%	25.1%
27,268	MCPHERSON	9,895	8,041	1,854		6,187 R	81.3%	18.7%	81.3%	18.7%
12,888	MARION	4,973	4,177	796		3,381 R	84.0%	16.0%	84.0%	16.0%
11,705	MARSHALL	4,812	3,435	1,377		2,058 R	71.4%	28.6%	71.4%	28.6%
4,247	MEADE	1,649	1,329	320		1,009 R	80.6%	19.4%	80.6%	19.4%

KANSAS

SENATOR 1990

1990 Census Population	County	Total Vote	Republican	Democratic	Other	Rep.-Dem. Plurality	Total Vote Rep.	Total Vote Dem.	Major Vote Rep.	Major Vote Dem.
23,466	MIAMI	6,903	4,279	2,624		1,655 R	62.0%	38.0%	62.0%	38.0%
7,203	MITCHELL	3,078	2,568	510		2,058 R	83.4%	16.6%	83.4%	16.6%
38,816	MONTGOMERY	11,896	8,321	3,575		4,746 R	69.9%	30.1%	69.9%	30.1%
6,198	MORRIS	2,496	2,043	453		1,590 R	81.9%	18.1%	81.9%	18.1%
3,480	MORTON	1,303	917	386		531 R	70.4%	29.6%	70.4%	29.6%
10,446	NEMAHA	4,659	3,693	966		2,727 R	79.3%	20.7%	79.3%	20.7%
17,035	NEOSHO	6,012	4,413	1,599		2,814 R	73.4%	26.6%	73.4%	26.6%
4,033	NESS	1,892	1,418	474		944 R	74.9%	25.1%	74.9%	25.1%
5,947	NORTON	2,572	1,961	611		1,350 R	76.2%	23.8%	76.2%	23.8%
15,248	OSAGE	5,779	4,157	1,622		2,535 R	71.9%	28.1%	71.9%	28.1%
4,867	OSBORNE	2,195	1,783	412		1,371 R	81.2%	18.8%	81.2%	18.8%
5,634	OTTAWA	2,263	1,879	384		1,495 R	83.0%	17.0%	83.0%	17.0%
7,555	PAWNEE	2,780	2,153	627		1,526 R	77.4%	22.6%	77.4%	22.6%
6,590	PHILLIPS	2,653	2,139	514		1,625 R	80.6%	19.4%	80.6%	19.4%
16,128	POTTAWATOMIE	5,674	4,476	1,198		3,278 R	78.9%	21.1%	78.9%	21.1%
9,702	PRATT	3,701	2,759	942		1,817 R	74.5%	25.5%	74.5%	25.5%
3,404	RAWLINS	1,821	1,426	395		1,031 R	78.3%	21.7%	78.3%	21.7%
62,389	RENO	20,785	14,812	5,973		8,839 R	71.3%	28.7%	71.3%	28.7%
6,482	REPUBLIC	2,964	2,235	729		1,506 R	75.4%	24.6%	75.4%	24.6%
10,610	RICE	4,132	3,133	999		2,134 R	75.8%	24.2%	75.8%	24.2%
67,139	RILEY	12,719	10,317	2,402		7,915 R	81.1%	18.9%	81.1%	18.9%
6,039	ROOKS	2,555	1,939	616		1,323 R	75.9%	24.1%	75.9%	24.1%
3,842	RUSH	1,837	1,367	470		897 R	74.4%	25.6%	74.4%	25.6%
7,835	RUSSELL	3,453	2,629	824		1,805 R	76.1%	23.9%	76.1%	23.9%
49,301	SALINE	16,957	13,580	3,377		10,203 R	80.1%	19.9%	80.1%	19.9%
5,289	SCOTT	1,990	1,652	338		1,314 R	83.0%	17.0%	83.0%	17.0%
403,662	SEDGWICK	123,262	91,084	32,178		58,906 R	73.9%	26.1%	73.9%	26.1%
18,743	SEWARD	4,372	3,343	1,029		2,314 R	76.5%	23.5%	76.5%	23.5%
160,976	SHAWNEE	64,500	48,809	15,691		33,118 R	75.7%	24.3%	75.7%	24.3%
3,043	SHERIDAN	1,397	1,063	334		729 R	76.1%	23.9%	76.1%	23.9%
6,926	SHERMAN	2,504	1,936	568		1,368 R	77.3%	22.7%	77.3%	22.7%
5,078	SMITH	2,272	1,735	537		1,198 R	76.4%	23.6%	76.4%	23.6%
5,365	STAFFORD	2,217	1,674	543		1,131 R	75.5%	24.5%	75.5%	24.5%
2,333	STANTON	884	706	178		528 R	79.9%	20.1%	79.9%	20.1%
5,048	STEVENS	1,737	1,293	444		849 R	74.4%	25.6%	74.4%	25.6%
25,841	SUMNER	8,329	5,923	2,406		3,517 R	71.1%	28.9%	71.1%	28.9%
8,258	THOMAS	3,064	2,170	894		1,276 R	70.8%	29.2%	70.8%	29.2%
3,694	TREGO	1,592	1,224	368		856 R	76.9%	23.1%	76.9%	23.1%
6,603	WABAUNSEE	2,885	2,271	614		1,657 R	78.7%	21.3%	78.7%	21.3%
1,821	WALLACE	775	591	184		407 R	76.3%	23.7%	76.3%	23.7%
7,073	WASHINGTON	2,959	2,221	738		1,483 R	75.1%	24.9%	75.1%	24.9%
2,758	WICHITA	849	668	181		487 R	78.7%	21.3%	78.7%	21.3%
10,289	WILSON	3,537	2,615	922		1,693 R	73.9%	26.1%	73.9%	26.1%
4,116	WOODSON	1,564	1,166	398		768 R	74.6%	25.4%	74.6%	25.4%
161,993	WYANDOTTE	34,528	18,093	16,435		1,658 R	52.4%	47.6%	52.4%	47.6%
2,477,574	TOTAL	786,235	578,605	207,491	139	371,114 R	73.6%	26.4%	73.6%	26.4%

KANSAS

CONGRESS

CD	Year	Total Vote	Republican Vote	Republican Candidate	Democratic Vote	Democratic Candidate	Other Vote	Rep.-Dem. Plurality	Total Vote Rep.	Total Vote Dem.	Major Vote Rep.	Major Vote Dem.
1	1990	164,388	102,974	ROBERTS, PAT	61,396	WEST, DUANE	18	41,578 R	62.6%	37.3%	62.6%	37.4%
1	1988	168,754	168,700	ROBERTS, PAT			54	168,700 R	100.0%		100.0%	
1	1986	184,656	141,297	ROBERTS, PAT	43,359	LYON, DALE		97,938 R	76.5%	23.5%	76.5%	23.5%
1	1984	210,763	159,931	ROBERTS, PAT	49,015	RINGER, DARRELL T.	1,817	110,916 R	75.9%	23.3%	76.5%	23.5%
1	1982	169,133	115,749	ROBERTS, PAT	51,079	ROTH, KENT	2,305	64,670 R	68.4%	30.2%	69.4%	30.6%
2	1990	157,745	58,643	MORGAN, SCOTT	99,093	SLATTERY, JIM	9	40,450 D	37.2%	62.8%	37.2%	62.8%
2	1988	185,296	49,498	MEINHARDT, PHIL	135,694	SLATTERY, JIM	104	86,196 D	26.7%	73.2%	26.7%	73.3%
2	1986	156,766	46,029	KLINE, PHILL	110,737	SLATTERY, JIM		64,708 D	29.4%	70.6%	29.4%	70.6%
2	1984	187,052	73,045	VAN SLYKE, JIM	112,263	SLATTERY, JIM	1,744	39,218 D	39.1%	60.0%	39.4%	60.6%
2	1982	150,228	63,942	KAY, MORRIS	86,286	SLATTERY, JIM		22,344 D	42.6%	57.4%	42.6%	57.4%
3	1990	147,726	88,725	MEYERS, JAN	58,923	JONES, LEROY	78	29,802 R	60.1%	39.9%	60.1%	39.9%
3	1988	204,221	150,223	MEYERS, JAN	53,959	KUNST, LIONEL	39	96,264 R	73.6%	26.4%	73.6%	26.4%
3	1986	109,266	109,266	MEYERS, JAN				109,266 R	100.0%		100.0%	
3	1984	213,902	117,159	MEYERS, JAN	85,441	REARDON, JOHN E.	11,302	31,718 R	54.8%	39.9%	57.8%	42.2%
3	1982	138,696	82,117	WINN, LARRY	53,140	KOSTAR, WILLIAM L.	3,439	28,977 R	59.2%	38.3%	60.7%	39.3%
4	1990	158,316	46,283	GRUND, ROGER M.	112,015	GLICKMAN, DAN	18	65,732 D	29.2%	70.8%	29.2%	70.8%
4	1988	191,957	69,165	THOMPSON, LEE	122,777	GLICKMAN, DAN	15	53,612 D	36.0%	64.0%	36.0%	64.0%
4	1986	172,342	61,178	KNIGHT, BOB	111,164	GLICKMAN, DAN		49,986 D	35.5%	64.5%	35.5%	64.5%
4	1984	186,693	47,776	KRAUSE, WILLIAM V.	138,917	GLICKMAN, DAN		91,141 D	25.6%	74.4%	25.6%	74.4%
4	1982	145,167	35,478	CAYWOOD, GERALD	107,326	GLICKMAN, DAN	2,363	71,848 D	24.4%	73.9%	24.8%	75.2%
5	1990	152,823	90,555	NICHOLS, DICK	62,244	WINGERT, GEORGE D.	24	28,311 R	59.3%	40.7%	59.3%	40.7%
5	1988	182,079	127,722	WHITTAKER, ROBERT	54,327	BARNES, JOHN A.	30	73,395 R	70.1%	29.8%	70.2%	29.8%
5	1986	164,340	116,800	WHITTAKER, ROBERT	47,540	MYERS, KYM E.		69,260 R	71.1%	28.9%	71.1%	28.9%
5	1984	195,915	144,075	WHITTAKER, ROBERT	49,435	BARNES, JOHN A.	2,405	94,640 R	73.5%	25.2%	74.5%	25.5%
5	1982	153,121	103,551	WHITTAKER, ROBERT	47,676	ROWE, LEE	1,894	55,875 R	67.6%	31.1%	68.5%	31.5%

KANSAS

1990 GENERAL ELECTION

Governor   Other vote was Independent (Campbell-Cline).

Senator   Other vote was scattered write-in. The total line for the other vote column represents these write-in votes not available by county.

Congress   Other vote was scattered write-in in all CD's.

1990 PRIMARIES

AUGUST 7 REPUBLICAN

Governor   138,467 Mike Hayden; 130,816 Nestor Weigand; 29,033 Richard Peckham; 4,225 Louis A. Klemp; 3,823 Jack J. H. Beemont; 3,196 Harold Knight.

Senator   267,946 Nancy Landon Kassebaum; 39,379 R. Gregory Walstrom.

Congress   Unopposed in four CD's. Contested as follows:

CD 5   18,599 Dick Nichols; 17,839 Shelia C. Bair; 11,686 Doyle Talkington; 7,614 Ed Roitz; 6,133 Kent Hodges; 2,290 Bill Otto.

AUGUST 7 DEMOCRATIC

Governor   81,250 Joan Finney; 79,406 John Carlin; 11,572 Fred Phelps.

Senator   86,174 William R. Roy; 65,395 Dick Williams. Mr. Roy withdrew after the primary and Mr. Williams was substituted by the state party committee.

Congress   Unopposed in two CD's. James W. Parrish, the unopposed candidate in CD 1, withdrew after the primary and Duane West was substituted by the local party committee. Contested as follows:

CD 2   30,287 Jim Slattery; 5,020 Mark Creamer.
CD 3   11,088 Leroy Jones; 8,665 Charles B. Masterson; 7,378 Lionel Kunst.
CD 5   11,355 George D. Wingert; 9,757 Charles M. Benjamin; 7,108 John A. Barnes; 6,561 Kym Myers.

KENTUCKY

GOVERNOR
Wallace G. Wilkinson (D). Elected 1987 to a four-year term.

SENATORS
Wendell H. Ford (D). Re-elected 1986 to a six-year term. Previously elected 1980, 1974.

Mitch McConnell (R). Re-elected 1990 to a six-year term. Previously elected 1984.

REPRESENTATIVES
1. Carroll Hubbard (D)
2. William H. Natcher (D)
3. Romano L. Mazzoli (D)
4. Jim Bunning (R)
5. Harold Rogers (R)
6. Larry J. Hopkins (R)
7. Carl C. Perkins (D)

POSTWAR VOTE FOR PRESIDENT

		Republican		Democratic		Other		Percentage Total Vote		Major Vote	
Year	Total Vote	Vote	Candidate	Vote	Candidate	Vote	Plurality	Rep.	Dem.	Rep.	Dem.
1988	1,322,517	734,281	Bush, George	580,368	Dukakis, Michael S.	7,868	153,913 R	55.5%	43.9%	55.9%	44.1%
1984	1,369,345	821,702	Reagan, Ronald	539,539	Mondale, Walter F.	8,104	282,163 R	60.0%	39.4%	60.4%	39.6%
1980	1,294,627	635,274	Reagan, Ronald	616,417	Carter, Jimmy	42,936	18,857 R	49.1%	47.6%	50.8%	49.2%
1976	1,167,142	531,852	Ford, Gerald R.	615,717	Carter, Jimmy	19,573	83,865 D	45.6%	52.8%	46.3%	53.7%
1972	1,067,499	676,446	Nixon, Richard M.	371,159	McGovern, George S.	19,894	305,287 R	63.4%	34.8%	64.6%	35.4%
1968	1,055,893	462,411	Nixon, Richard M.	397,541	Humphrey, Hubert H.	195,941	64,870 R	43.8%	37.6%	53.8%	46.2%
1964	1,046,105	372,977	Goldwater, Barry M.	669,659	Johnson, Lyndon B.	3,469	296,682 D	35.7%	64.0%	35.8%	64.2%
1960	1,124,462	602,607	Nixon, Richard M.	521,855	Kennedy, John F.		80,752 R	53.6%	46.4%	53.6%	46.4%
1956	1,053,805	572,192	Eisenhower, Dwight D.	476,453	Stevenson, Adlai E.	5,160	95,739 R	54.3%	45.2%	54.6%	45.4%
1952	993,148	495,029	Eisenhower, Dwight D.	495,729	Stevenson, Adlai E.	2,390	700 D	49.8%	49.9%	50.0%	50.0%
1948	822,658	341,210	Dewey, Thomas E.	466,756	Truman, Harry S.	14,692	125,546 D	41.5%	56.7%	42.2%	57.8%

POSTWAR VOTE FOR GOVERNOR

		Republican		Democratic		Other	Rep-Dem.	Percentage Total Vote		Major Vote	
Year	Total Vote	Vote	Candidate	Vote	Candidate	Vote	Plurality	Rep.	Dem.	Rep.	Dem.
1987	777,815	273,141	Harper, John	504,674	Wilkinson, Wallace G.		231,533 D	35.1%	64.9%	35.1%	64.9%
1983	1,030,671	454,650	Bunning, Jim	561,674	Collins, Martha Layne	14,347	107,024 D	44.1%	54.5%	44.7%	55.3%
1979	939,366	381,278	Nunn, Louie B.	558,088	Brown, J. Y., Jr.		176,810 D	40.6%	59.4%	40.6%	59.4%
1975	748,157	277,998	Gable, Robert E.	470,159	Carroll, Julian		192,161 D	37.2%	62.8%	37.2%	62.8%
1971	930,790	412,653	Emberton, Thomas	470,720	Ford, Wendell H.	47,417	58,067 D	44.3%	50.6%	46.7%	53.3%
1967	886,946	454,123	Nunn, Louie B.	425,674	Ward, Henry	7,149	28,449 R	51.2%	48.0%	51.6%	48.4%
1963	886,047	436,496	Nunn, Louie B.	449,551	Breathitt, Edward T.		13,055 D	49.3%	50.7%	49.3%	50.7%
1959	853,005	336,456	Robsion, John M.	516,549	Combs, Bert T.		180,093 D	39.4%	60.6%	39.4%	60.6%
1955	778,488	322,671	Denney, Edwin R.	451,647	Chandler, Albert B.	4,170	128,976 D	41.4%	58.0%	41.7%	58.3%
1951	634,359	288,014	Siler, Eugene	346,345	Wetherby, Lawrence		58,331 D	45.4%	54.6%	45.4%	54.6%
1947	672,372	287,130	Dummit, Eldon S.	385,242	Clements, Earle C.		98,112 D	42.7%	57.3%	42.7%	57.3%

KENTUCKY

POSTWAR VOTE FOR SENATOR

Year	Total Vote	Republican Vote	Candidate	Democratic Vote	Candidate	Other Vote	Rep-Dem. Plurality	Total Vote Rep.	Dem.	Major Vote Rep.	Dem.
1990	916,010	478,034	McConnell, Mitch	437,976	Sloane, Harvey		40,058 R	52.2%	47.8%	52.2%	47.8%
1986	677,280	173,330	Andrews, Jackson M.	503,775	Ford, Wendell H.	175	330,445 D	25.6%	74.4%	25.6%	74.4%
1984	1,292,407	644,990	McConnell, Mitch	639,721	Huddleston, Walter	7,696	5,269 R	49.9%	49.5%	50.2%	49.8%
1980	1,106,890	386,029	Foust, Mary Louise	720,861	Ford, Wendell H.		334,832 D	34.9%	65.1%	34.9%	65.1%
1978	476,783	175,766	Guenthner, Louie	290,730	Huddleston, Walter	10,287	114,964 D	36.9%	61.0%	37.7%	62.3%
1974	745,994	328,982	Cook, Marlow W.	399,406	Ford, Wendell H.	17,606	70,424 D	44.1%	53.5%	45.2%	54.8%
1972	1,037,861	494,337	Nunn, Louie B.	528,550	Huddleston, Walter	14,974	34,213 D	47.6%	50.9%	48.3%	51.7%
1968	942,865	484,260	Cook, Marlow W.	448,960	Peden, Katherine	9,645	35,300 R	51.4%	47.6%	51.9%	48.1%
1966	749,884	483,805	Cooper, John Sherman	266,079	Brown, J. Y.		217,726 R	64.5%	35.5%	64.5%	35.5%
1962	820,088	432,648	Morton, Thruston B.	387,440	Wyatt, Wilson W.		45,208 R	52.8%	47.2%	52.8%	47.2%
1960	1,088,377	644,087	Cooper, John Sherman	444,290	Johnson, Keen		199,797 R	59.2%	40.8%	59.2%	40.8%
1956	1,006,825	506,903	Morton, Thruston B.	499,922	Clements, Earle C.	6,981	R	50.3%	49.7%	50.3%	49.7%
1956 S	1,011,645	538,505	Cooper, John Sherman	473,140	Wetherby, Lawrence		65,365 R	53.2%	46.8%	53.2%	46.8%
1954	797,057	362,948	Cooper, John Sherman	434,109	Barkley, Alben W.		71,161 D	45.5%	54.5%	45.5%	54.5%
1952 S	960,228	494,576	Cooper, John Sherman	465,652	Underwood, Thomas R.		28,924 R	51.5%	48.5%	51.5%	48.5%
1950	612,617	278,368	Dawson, Charles L.	334,249	Clements, Earle C.		55,881 D	45.4%	54.6%	45.4%	54.6%
1948	794,469	383,776	Cooper, John Sherman	408,256	Chapman, Virgil	2,437	24,480 D	48.3%	51.4%	48.5%	51.5%
1946 S	615,119	327,652	Cooper, John Sherman	285,829	Brown, J. Y.	1,638	41,823 R	53.3%	46.5%	53.4%	46.6%

One of the 1956 elections and those in 1952 and 1946 were for short terms to fill vacancies.

KENTUCKY

Districts Established March 10, 1982

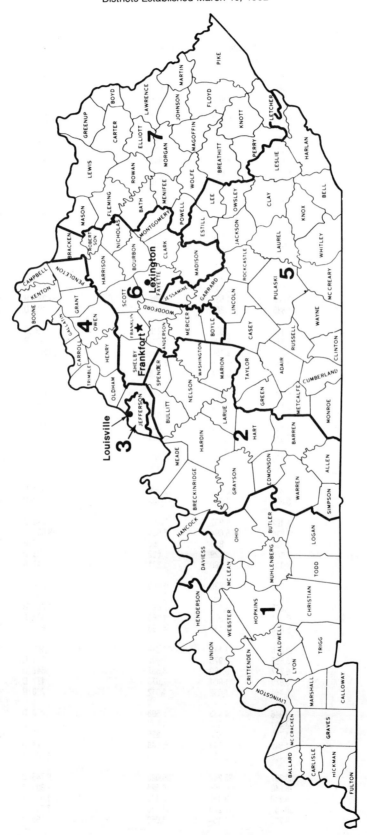

KENTUCKY

SENATOR 1990

1990 Census Population	County	Total Vote	Republican	Democratic	Other	Rep.-Dem. Plurality	Percentage Total Vote Rep.	Dem.	Major Vote Rep.	Dem.
15,360	ADAIR	4,568	2,979	1,589		1,390 R	65.2%	34.8%	65.2%	34.8%
14,628	ALLEN	2,580	1,707	873		834 R	66.2%	33.8%	66.2%	33.8%
14,571	ANDERSON	3,975	2,025	1,950		75 R	50.9%	49.1%	50.9%	49.1%
7,902	BALLARD	2,920	1,450	1,470		20 D	49.7%	50.3%	49.7%	50.3%
34,001	BARREN	8,655	5,080	3,575		1,505 R	58.7%	41.3%	58.7%	41.3%
9,692	BATH	2,680	1,159	1,521		362 D	43.2%	56.8%	43.2%	56.8%
31,506	BELL	7,424	4,610	2,814		1,796 R	62.1%	37.9%	62.1%	37.9%
57,589	BOONE	12,672	8,129	4,543		3,586 R	64.1%	35.9%	64.1%	35.9%
19,236	BOURBON	4,207	1,991	2,216		225 D	47.3%	52.7%	47.3%	52.7%
51,150	BOYD	13,339	6,829	6,510		319 R	51.2%	48.8%	51.2%	48.8%
25,641	BOYLE	5,729	2,846	2,883		37 D	49.7%	50.3%	49.7%	50.3%
7,766	BRACKEN	1,981	1,208	773		435 R	61.0%	39.0%	61.0%	39.0%
15,703	BREATHITT	3,187	1,143	2,044		901 D	35.9%	64.1%	35.9%	64.1%
16,312	BRECKINRIDGE	4,717	2,546	2,171		375 R	54.0%	46.0%	54.0%	46.0%
47,567	BULLITT	11,089	5,744	5,345		399 R	51.8%	48.2%	51.8%	48.2%
11,245	BUTLER	3,006	2,036	970		1,066 R	67.7%	32.3%	67.7%	32.3%
13,232	CALDWELL	3,782	1,988	1,794		194 R	52.6%	47.4%	52.6%	47.4%
30,735	CALLOWAY	7,088	3,611	3,477		134 R	50.9%	49.1%	50.9%	49.1%
83,866	CAMPBELL	19,039	11,536	7,503		4,033 R	60.6%	39.4%	60.6%	39.4%
5,238	CARLISLE	1,835	866	969		103 D	47.2%	52.8%	47.2%	52.8%
9,292	CARROLL	2,110	892	1,218		326 D	42.3%	57.7%	42.3%	57.7%
24,340	CARTER	6,214	3,590	2,624		966 R	57.8%	42.2%	57.8%	42.2%
14,211	CASEY	3,059	2,150	909		1,241 R	70.3%	29.7%	70.3%	29.7%
68,941	CHRISTIAN	9,342	5,385	3,957		1,428 R	57.6%	42.4%	57.6%	42.4%
29,496	CLARK	6,650	3,234	3,416		182 D	48.6%	51.4%	48.6%	51.4%
21,746	CLAY	5,855	3,607	2,248		1,359 R	61.6%	38.4%	61.6%	38.4%
9,135	CLINTON	2,860	2,150	710		1,440 R	75.2%	24.8%	75.2%	24.8%
9,196	CRITTENDEN	2,464	1,415	1,049		366 R	57.4%	42.6%	57.4%	42.6%
6,784	CUMBERLAND	1,407	1,048	359		689 R	74.5%	25.5%	74.5%	25.5%
87,189	DAVIESS	27,123	13,234	13,889		655 D	48.8%	51.2%	48.8%	51.2%
10,357	EDMONSON	2,500	1,636	864		772 R	65.4%	34.6%	65.4%	34.6%
6,455	ELLIOTT	1,750	674	1,076		402 D	38.5%	61.5%	38.5%	61.5%
14,614	ESTILL	3,135	1,693	1,442		251 R	54.0%	46.0%	54.0%	46.0%
225,366	FAYETTE	48,949	26,440	22,509		3,931 R	54.0%	46.0%	54.0%	46.0%
12,292	FLEMING	3,081	1,547	1,534		13 R	50.2%	49.8%	50.2%	49.8%
43,586	FLOYD	11,192	3,957	7,235		3,278 D	35.4%	64.6%	35.4%	64.6%
43,781	FRANKLIN	14,818	5,894	8,924		3,030 D	39.8%	60.2%	39.8%	60.2%
8,271	FULTON	1,933	973	960		13 R	50.3%	49.7%	50.3%	49.7%
5,393	GALLATIN	1,151	529	622		93 D	46.0%	54.0%	46.0%	54.0%
11,579	GARRARD	3,311	1,980	1,331		649 R	59.8%	40.2%	59.8%	40.2%
15,737	GRANT	3,296	1,836	1,460		376 R	55.7%	44.3%	55.7%	44.3%
33,550	GRAVES	9,930	4,467	5,463		996 D	45.0%	55.0%	45.0%	55.0%
21,050	GRAYSON	5,275	3,181	2,094		1,087 R	60.3%	39.7%	60.3%	39.7%
10,371	GREEN	3,131	1,971	1,160		811 R	63.0%	37.0%	63.0%	37.0%
36,742	GREENUP	9,608	5,110	4,498		612 R	53.2%	46.8%	53.2%	46.8%
7,864	HANCOCK	2,356	1,117	1,239		122 D	47.4%	52.6%	47.4%	52.6%
89,240	HARDIN	15,585	7,978	7,607		371 R	51.2%	48.8%	51.2%	48.8%
36,574	HARLAN	6,707	3,180	3,527		347 D	47.4%	52.6%	47.4%	52.6%
16,248	HARRISON	3,979	1,901	2,078		177 D	47.8%	52.2%	47.8%	52.2%
14,890	HART	3,444	1,832	1,612		220 R	53.2%	46.8%	53.2%	46.8%
43,044	HENDERSON	9,946	4,438	5,508		1,070 D	44.6%	55.4%	44.6%	55.4%
12,823	HENRY	3,401	1,560	1,841		281 D	45.9%	54.1%	45.9%	54.1%
5,566	HICKMAN	1,719	864	855		9 R	50.3%	49.7%	50.3%	49.7%
46,126	HOPKINS	11,546	5,501	6,045		544 D	47.6%	52.4%	47.6%	52.4%
11,955	JACKSON	3,408	2,688	720		1,968 R	78.9%	21.1%	78.9%	21.1%
664,937	JEFFERSON	200,307	95,282	105,025		9,743 D	47.6%	52.4%	47.6%	52.4%
30,508	JESSAMINE	6,849	4,325	2,524		1,801 R	63.1%	36.9%	63.1%	36.9%
23,248	JOHNSON	5,248	3,132	2,116		1,016 R	59.7%	40.3%	59.7%	40.3%
142,031	KENTON	30,751	19,233	11,518		7,715 R	62.5%	37.5%	62.5%	37.5%
17,906	KNOTT	4,223	1,164	3,059		1,895 D	27.6%	72.4%	27.6%	72.4%

KENTUCKY

SENATOR 1990

1990 Census Population	County	Total Vote	Republican	Democratic	Other	Rep.-Dem. Plurality	Percentage Total Vote Rep.	Dem.	Major Vote Rep.	Dem.
29,676	KNOX	5,820	3,726	2,094		1,632 R	64.0%	36.0%	64.0%	36.0%
11,679	LARUE	3,061	1,485	1,576		91 D	48.5%	51.5%	48.5%	51.5%
43,438	LAUREL	8,283	5,589	2,694		2,895 R	67.5%	32.5%	67.5%	32.5%
13,998	LAWRENCE	4,107	2,324	1,783		541 R	56.6%	43.4%	56.6%	43.4%
7,422	LEE	1,792	1,012	780		232 R	56.5%	43.5%	56.5%	43.5%
13,642	LESLIE	3,628	2,523	1,105		1,418 R	69.5%	30.5%	69.5%	30.5%
27,000	LETCHER	5,121	2,040	3,081		1,041 D	39.8%	60.2%	39.8%	60.2%
13,029	LEWIS	3,293	2,356	937		1,419 R	71.5%	28.5%	71.5%	28.5%
20,045	LINCOLN	3,721	2,112	1,609		503 R	56.8%	43.2%	56.8%	43.2%
9,062	LIVINGSTON	2,651	1,261	1,390		129 D	47.6%	52.4%	47.6%	52.4%
24,416	LOGAN	5,058	2,940	2,118		822 R	58.1%	41.9%	58.1%	41.9%
6,624	LYON	1,834	877	957		80 D	47.8%	52.2%	47.8%	52.2%
62,879	MCCRACKEN	17,562	9,535	8,027		1,508 R	54.3%	45.7%	54.3%	45.7%
15,603	MCCREARY	3,069	2,205	864		1,341 R	71.8%	28.2%	71.8%	28.2%
9,628	MCLEAN	2,768	1,220	1,548		328 D	44.1%	55.9%	44.1%	55.9%
57,508	MADISON	10,893	5,815	5,078		737 R	53.4%	46.6%	53.4%	46.6%
13,077	MAGOFFIN	2,972	1,335	1,637		302 D	44.9%	55.1%	44.9%	55.1%
16,499	MARION	4,029	1,608	2,421		813 D	39.9%	60.1%	39.9%	60.1%
27,205	MARSHALL	8,128	3,533	4,595		1,062 D	43.5%	56.5%	43.5%	56.5%
12,526	MARTIN	2,475	1,578	897		681 R	63.8%	36.2%	63.8%	36.2%
16,666	MASON	3,671	2,016	1,655		361 R	54.9%	45.1%	54.9%	45.1%
24,170	MEADE	4,461	2,093	2,368		275 D	46.9%	53.1%	46.9%	53.1%
5,092	MENIFEE	1,042	404	638		234 D	38.8%	61.2%	38.8%	61.2%
19,148	MERCER	4,601	2,283	2,318		35 D	49.6%	50.4%	49.6%	50.4%
8,963	METCALFE	2,406	1,465	941		524 R	60.9%	39.1%	60.9%	39.1%
11,401	MONROE	2,876	2,314	562		1,752 R	80.5%	19.5%	80.5%	19.5%
19,561	MONTGOMERY	4,579	2,099	2,480		381 D	45.8%	54.2%	45.8%	54.2%
11,648	MORGAN	2,797	1,100	1,697		597 D	39.3%	60.7%	39.3%	60.7%
31,318	MUHLENBERG	7,236	3,027	4,209		1,182 D	41.8%	58.2%	41.8%	58.2%
29,710	NELSON	7,395	3,003	4,392		1,389 D	40.6%	59.4%	40.6%	59.4%
6,725	NICHOLAS	1,682	817	865		48 D	48.6%	51.4%	48.6%	51.4%
21,105	OHIO	5,861	3,196	2,665		531 R	54.5%	45.5%	54.5%	45.5%
33,263	OLDHAM	9,673	6,028	3,645		2,383 R	62.3%	37.7%	62.3%	37.7%
9,035	OWEN	2,295	1,100	1,195		95 D	47.9%	52.1%	47.9%	52.1%
5,036	OWSLEY	1,105	781	324		457 R	70.7%	29.3%	70.7%	29.3%
12,036	PENDLETON	2,887	1,581	1,306		275 R	54.8%	45.2%	54.8%	45.2%
30,283	PERRY	7,469	3,488	3,981		493 D	46.7%	53.3%	46.7%	53.3%
72,583	PIKE	16,948	7,172	9,776		2,604 D	42.3%	57.7%	42.3%	57.7%
11,686	POWELL	2,386	1,051	1,335		284 D	44.0%	56.0%	44.0%	56.0%
49,489	PULASKI	10,247	6,749	3,498		3,251 R	65.9%	34.1%	65.9%	34.1%
2,124	ROBERTSON	648	326	322		4 R	50.3%	49.7%	50.3%	49.7%
14,803	ROCKCASTLE	2,903	1,979	924		1,055 R	68.2%	31.8%	68.2%	31.8%
20,353	ROWAN	4,203	2,155	2,048		107 R	51.3%	48.7%	51.3%	48.7%
14,716	RUSSELL	3,573	2,473	1,100		1,373 R	69.2%	30.8%	69.2%	30.8%
23,867	SCOTT	5,351	2,696	2,655		41 R	50.4%	49.6%	50.4%	49.6%
24,824	SHELBY	6,662	3,524	3,138		386 R	52.9%	47.1%	52.9%	47.1%
15,145	SIMPSON	2,336	1,329	1,007		322 R	56.9%	43.1%	56.9%	43.1%
6,801	SPENCER	1,808	877	931		54 D	48.5%	51.5%	48.5%	51.5%
21,146	TAYLOR	5,481	3,020	2,461		559 R	55.1%	44.9%	55.1%	44.9%
10,940	TODD	2,320	1,412	908		504 R	60.9%	39.1%	60.9%	39.1%
10,361	TRIGG	2,851	1,420	1,431		11 D	49.8%	50.2%	49.8%	50.2%
6,090	TRIMBLE	1,968	832	1,136		304 D	42.3%	57.7%	42.3%	57.7%
16,557	UNION	3,971	1,578	2,393		815 D	39.7%	60.3%	39.7%	60.3%
76,673	WARREN	20,204	11,136	9,068		2,068 R	55.1%	44.9%	55.1%	44.9%
10,441	WASHINGTON	3,617	1,921	1,696		225 R	53.1%	46.9%	53.1%	46.9%
17,468	WAYNE	3,852	2,300	1,552		748 R	59.7%	40.3%	59.7%	40.3%
13,955	WEBSTER	3,881	1,468	2,413		945 D	37.8%	62.2%	37.8%	62.2%
33,326	WHITLEY	7,408	4,927	2,481		2,446 R	66.5%	33.5%	66.5%	33.5%
6,503	WOLFE	1,368	499	869		370 D	36.5%	63.5%	36.5%	63.5%
19,955	WOODFORD	5,637	3,050	2,587		463 R	54.1%	45.9%	54.1%	45.9%
3,685,296	TOTAL	916,010	478,034	437,976		40,058 R	52.2%	47.8%	52.2%	47.8%

KENTUCKY

CONGRESS

CD	Year	Total Vote	Republican Vote	Republican Candidate	Democratic Vote	Democratic Candidate	Other Vote	Rep.-Dem. Plurality	Total Vote Rep.	Total Vote Dem.	Major Vote Rep.	Major Vote Dem.
1	1990	98,202			85,323	HUBBARD, CARROLL	12,879	85,323 D		86.9%		100.0%
1	1988	123,410			117,288	HUBBARD, CARROLL	6,122	117,288 D		95.0%		100.0%
1	1986	64,332			64,315	HUBBARD, CARROLL	17	64,315 D		100.0%		100.0%
1	1984	112,180			112,180	HUBBARD, CARROLL		112,180 D		100.0%		100.0%
1	1982	48,356			48,342	HUBBARD, CARROLL	14	48,342 D		100.0%		100.0%
2	1990	116,681	39,624	TORI, MARTIN A.	77,057	NATCHER, WILLIAM H.		37,433 D	34.0%	66.0%	34.0%	66.0%
2	1988	152,099	59,907	TORI, MARTIN A.	92,184	NATCHER, WILLIAM H.	8	32,277 D	39.4%	60.6%	39.4%	60.6%
2	1986	57,652			57,644	NATCHER, WILLIAM H.	8	57,644 D		100.0%		100.0%
2	1984	149,742	56,700	MORRISON, TIMOTHY A.	93,042	NATCHER, WILLIAM H.		36,342 D	37.9%	62.1%	37.9%	62.1%
2	1982	67,143	17,561	WATSON, MARK T.	49,571	NATCHER, WILLIAM H.	11	32,010 D	26.2%	73.8%	26.2%	73.8%
3	1990	139,938	55,188	BROWN, AL	84,750	MAZZOLI, ROMANO L.		29,562 D	39.4%	60.6%	39.4%	60.6%
3	1988	189,368	57,387	DUNNAGAN, PHILIP	131,981	MAZZOLI, ROMANO L.		74,594 D	30.3%	69.7%	30.3%	69.7%
3	1986	112,233	29,348	HOLMES, LEE	81,943	MAZZOLI, ROMANO L.	942	52,595 D	26.1%	73.0%	26.4%	73.6%
3	1984	215,138	68,185	WARNER, SUZANNE M.	145,680	MAZZOLI, ROMANO L.	1,273	77,495 D	31.7%	67.7%	31.9%	68.1%
3	1982	142,597	45,900	BROWN, CARL	92,849	MAZZOLI, ROMANO L.	3,848	46,949 D	32.2%	65.1%	33.1%	66.9%
4	1990	146,659	101,680	BUNNING, JIM	44,979	MARTIN, GALEN		56,701 R	69.3%	30.7%	69.3%	30.7%
4	1988	196,184	145,609	BUNNING, JIM	50,575	BELILES, RICHARD V.		95,034 R	74.2%	25.8%	74.2%	25.8%
4	1986	122,763	67,626	BUNNING, JIM	53,906	MANN, TERRY L.	1,231	13,720 R	55.1%	43.9%	55.6%	44.4%
4	1984	202,038	108,398	SNYDER, M. G.	93,640	MULLOY, WILLIAM P.		14,758 R	53.7%	46.3%	53.7%	46.3%
4	1982	136,750	74,109	SNYDER, M. G.	61,937	MANN, TERRY L.	704	12,172 R	54.2%	45.3%	54.5%	45.5%
5	1990	64,660	64,660	ROGERS, HAROLD				64,660 R	100.0%		100.0%	
5	1988	104,501	104,467	ROGERS, HAROLD			34	104,467 R	100.0%		100.0%	
5	1986	56,764	56,760	ROGERS, HAROLD			4	56,760 R	100.0%		100.0%	
5	1984	164,947	125,164	ROGERS, HAROLD	39,783	MCINTOSH, SHERMAN W.		85,381 R	75.9%	24.1%	75.9%	24.1%
5	1982	81,217	52,928	ROGERS, HAROLD	28,285	DAVENPORT, DOYE	4	24,643 R	65.2%	34.8%	65.2%	34.8%
6	1990	76,859	76,859	HOPKINS, LARRY J.				76,859 R	100.0%		100.0%	
6	1988	174,277	128,898	HOPKINS, LARRY J.	45,339	PATTON, MILTON	40	83,559 R	74.0%	26.0%	74.0%	26.0%
6	1986	102,224	75,906	HOPKINS, LARRY J.	26,315	HAMMOND, JERRY	3	49,591 R	74.3%	25.7%	74.3%	25.7%
6	1984	177,108	126,525	HOPKINS, LARRY J.	49,657	HAMMOND, JERRY	926	76,868 R	71.4%	28.0%	71.8%	28.2%
6	1982	120,360	68,418	HOPKINS, LARRY J.	49,839	MILLS, DON	2,103	18,579 R	56.8%	41.4%	57.9%	42.1%
7	1990	120,707	59,377	SCOTT, WILLIAM T.	61,330	PERKINS, CARL C.		1,953 D	49.2%	50.8%	49.2%	50.8%
7	1988	165,112	68,165	SCOTT, WILLIAM T.	96,946	PERKINS, CARL C.	1	28,781 D	41.3%	58.7%	41.3%	58.7%
7	1986	113,828	23,209	POLLEY, JAMES T.	90,619	PERKINS, CARL C.		67,410 D	20.4%	79.6%	20.4%	79.6%
7	1984	166,569	43,890	RUSSELL, AUBREY	122,679	PERKINS, CARL C.		78,789 D	26.3%	73.7%	26.3%	73.7%
7	1982	103,899	21,436	HAMBY, TOM	82,463	PERKINS, CARL D.		61,027 D	20.6%	79.4%	20.6%	79.4%

KENTUCKY

1990 GENERAL ELECTION

Senator

Congress   Other vote was Populist (Seat) in CD 1.

1990 PRIMARIES

MAY 29 REPUBLICAN

Senator   64,063 Mitch McConnell; 8,310 Tommy Klein.

Congress   Unopposed in three CD's. No candidate in CD 1. Contested as follows:

CD 2   4,711 Martin A. Tori; 3,171 Linda S. Pepper.
CD 3   5,747 Al Brown; 5,354 Tim Hardy.
CD 7   8,216 William T. Scott; 2,123 Larry M. Leslie.

MAY 29 DEMOCRATIC

Senator   183,789 Harvey Sloane; 126,318 John Brock.

Congress   Unopposed in three CD's. No candidate in CD's 5 and 6. Contested as follows:

CD 3   28,103 Romano L. Mazzoli; 20,152 Jeff Hutter; 13,768 Paul C. Bather.
CD 7   30,748 Carl C. Perkins; 14,195 Jerry Cecil.

LOUISIANA

GOVERNOR
Charles Roemer (D). Elected October 1987 to a four-year term. In March 1991 Governor Roemer announced his change of party affiliation to Republican.

SENATORS
John B. Breaux (D). Elected 1986 to a six-year term.

J. Bennett Johnston (D). Re-elected 1990 to a six-year term. Previously elected 1984, 1978, 1972.

REPRESENTATIVES
1. Bob Livingston (R)
2. William J. Jefferson (D)
3. W. J. Tauzin (D)
4. Jim McCrery (R)
5. Jerry Huckaby (D)
6. Richard H. Baker (R)
7. James A. Hayes (D)
8. Clyde C. Holloway (R)

POSTWAR VOTE FOR PRESIDENT

Year	Total Vote	Republican Vote	Candidate	Democratic Vote	Candidate	Other Vote	Plurality	Percentage Total Vote Rep.	Dem.	Major Vote Rep.	Dem.
1988	1,628,202	883,702	Bush, George	717,460	Dukakis, Michael S.	27,040	166,242 R	54.3%	44.1%	55.2%	44.8%
1984	1,706,822	1,037,299	Reagan, Ronald	651,586	Mondale, Walter F.	17,937	385,713 R	60.8%	38.2%	61.4%	38.6%
1980	1,548,591	792,853	Reagan, Ronald	708,453	Carter, Jimmy	47,285	84,400 R	51.2%	45.7%	52.8%	47.2%
1976	1,278,439	587,446	Ford, Gerald R.	661,365	Carter, Jimmy	29,628	73,919 D	46.0%	51.7%	47.0%	53.0%
1972	1,051,491	686,852	Nixon, Richard M.	298,142	McGovern, George S.	66,497	388,710 R	65.3%	28.4%	69.7%	30.3%
1968 **	1,097,450	257,535	Nixon, Richard M.	309,615	Humphrey, Hubert H.	530,300	220,685 A	23.5%	28.2%	45.4%	54.6%
1964	896,293	509,225	Goldwater, Barry M.	387,068	Johnson, Lyndon B.		122,157 R	56.8%	43.2%	56.8%	43.2%
1960	807,891	230,980	Nixon, Richard M.	407,339	Kennedy, John F.	169,572	176,359 D	28.6%	50.4%	36.2%	63.8%
1956	617,544	329,047	Eisenhower, Dwight D.	243,977	Stevenson, Adlai E.	44,520	85,070 R	53.3%	39.5%	57.4%	42.6%
1952	651,952	306,925	Eisenhower, Dwight D.	345,027	Stevenson, Adlai E.		38,102 D	47.1%	52.9%	47.1%	52.9%
1948 **	416,336	72,657	Dewey, Thomas E.	136,344	Truman, Harry S.	207,335	67,946 SR	17.5%	32.7%	34.8%	65.2%

In 1968 other vote was American (Wallace). In 1948 other vote was 204,290 States Rights; 3,035 Progressive and 10 scattered.

LOUISIANA

POSTWAR VOTE FOR GOVERNOR

Year	Total Vote	Republican Vote	Candidate	Democratic Vote	Candidate	Other Vote	Rep-Dem. Plurality	Percentage Total Vote Rep.	Dem.	Major Vote Rep.	Dem.
1987 **		—			Roemer, Charles						
1983 **		—			Edwards, Edwin W.						
1979	1,371,825	690,691	Treen, David C.	681,134	Lambert, Louis		9,557 R	50.3%	49.7%	50.3%	49.7%
1975	430,095		—	430,095	Edwards, Edwin W.		430,095 D		100.0%		100.0%
1972	1,121,570	480,424	Treen, David C.	641,146	Edwards, Edwin W.		160,722 D	42.8%	57.2%	42.8%	57.2%
1968	372,762		—	372,762	McKeithen, John J.		372,762 D		100.0%		100.0%
1964	773,390	297,753	Lyons, C. H.	469,589	McKeithen, John J.	6,048	171,836 D	38.5%	60.7%	38.8%	61.2%
1960	506,562	86,135	Grevemberg, F. C.	407,907	Davis, Jimmie H.	12,520	321,772 D	17.0%	80.5%	17.4%	82.6%
1956	172,291		—	172,291	Long, Earl K.		172,291 D		100.0%		100.0%
1952	123,681	4,958	Bagwell, Harrison G.	118,723	Kennon, Robert F.		113,765 D	4.0%	96.0%	4.0%	96.0%
1948	76,566		—	76,566	Long, Earl K.		76,566 D		100.0%		100.0%

For the 1987 and 1983 elections, no run-off general elections were required (see note section).

POSTWAR VOTE FOR SENATOR

Year	Total Vote	Republican Vote	Candidate	Democratic Vote	Candidate	Other Vote	Rep-Dem. Plurality	Percentage Total Vote Rep.	Dem.	Major Vote Rep.	Dem.
1990 **		—			Johnston, J. Bennett						
1986	1,369,897	646,311	Moore, W. Henson	723,586	Breaux, John B.		77,275 D	47.2%	52.8%	47.2%	52.8%
1984 **		—			Johnston, J. Bennett						
1980 **		—			Long, Russell B.						
1978 **		—			Johnston, J. Bennett						
1974	434,643		—	434,643	Long, Russell B.		434,643 D		100.0%		100.0%
1972	1,084,904	206,846	Toledano, Ben C.	598,987	Johnston, J. Bennett	279,071	392,141 D	19.1%	55.2%	25.7%	74.3%
1968	518,586		—	518,586	Long, Russell B.		518,586 D		100.0%		100.0%
1966	437,695		—	437,695	Ellender, Allen J.		437,695 D		100.0%		100.0%
1962	421,904	103,066	O'Hearn, Taylor W.	318,838	Long, Russell B.		215,772 D	24.4%	75.6%	24.4%	75.6%
1960	541,928	109,698	Reese, George W.	432,228	Ellender, Allen J.	2	322,530 D	20.2%	79.8%	20.2%	79.8%
1956	335,564		—	335,564	Long, Russell B.		335,564 D		100.0%		100.0%
1954	207,115		—	207,115	Ellender, Allen J.		207,115 D		100.0%		100.0%
1950	251,838	30,931	Gerth, Charles S.	220,907	Long, Russell B.		189,976 D	12.3%	87.7%	12.3%	87.7%
1948	330,124		—	330,115	Ellender, Allen J.	9	330,115 D		100.0%		100.0%
1948 S	408,667	102,331	Clarke, Clem S.	306,336	Long, Russell B.		204,005 D	25.0%	75.0%	25.0%	75.0%

One of the 1948 elections was for a short term to fill a vacancy. For the 1978, 1980, 1984 and 1990 elections, no run-off general elections were required (see note section).

LOUISIANA

Districts Established December 19, 1983

LOUISIANA

SENATOR 1990
(PRIMARY ELECTION)

1990 Census Population	Parish	Total Vote	Duke	Johnston	Other	Plurality	Percentage Total Vote Duke	Johnston	Major Vote Duke	Johnston
55,882	ACADIA	21,900	10,511	10,763	626	252 JBJ	48.0%	49.1%	49.4%	50.6%
21,226	ALLEN	9,249	3,551	5,560	138	2,009 JBJ	38.4%	60.1%	39.0%	61.0%
58,214	ASCENSION	22,418	10,855	11,046	517	191 JBJ	48.4%	49.3%	49.6%	50.4%
22,753	ASSUMPTION	9,777	4,236	5,119	422	883 JBJ	43.3%	52.4%	45.3%	54.7%
39,159	AVOYELLES	15,470	8,021	6,780	669	1,241 DED	51.8%	43.8%	54.2%	45.8%
30,083	BEAUREGARD	10,521	5,037	5,166	318	129 JBJ	47.9%	49.1%	49.4%	50.6%
15,979	BIENVILLE	6,962	3,075	3,684	203	609 JBJ	44.2%	52.9%	45.5%	54.5%
86,088	BOSSIER	24,499	12,300	11,811	388	489 DED	50.2%	48.2%	51.0%	49.0%
248,253	CADDO	79,040	28,410	49,712	918	21,302 JBJ	35.9%	62.9%	36.4%	63.6%
168,134	CALCASIEU	49,422	18,012	30,299	1,111	12,287 JBJ	36.4%	61.3%	37.3%	62.7%
9,810	CALDWELL	4,714	2,786	1,808	120	978 DED	59.1%	38.4%	60.6%	39.4%
9,260	CAMERON	3,319	1,315	1,945	59	630 JBJ	39.6%	58.6%	40.3%	59.7%
11,065	CATAHOULA	5,364	2,843	2,342	179	501 DED	53.0%	43.7%	54.8%	45.2%
17,405	CLAIBORNE	5,955	2,749	3,086	120	337 JBJ	46.2%	51.8%	47.1%	52.9%
20,828	CONCORDIA	7,238	3,912	3,054	272	858 DED	54.0%	42.2%	56.2%	43.8%
25,346	DE SOTO	9,332	4,204	4,925	203	721 JBJ	45.0%	52.8%	46.1%	53.9%
380,105	EAST BATON ROUGE	120,312	45,928	72,352	2,032	26,424 JBJ	38.2%	60.1%	38.8%	61.2%
9,709	EAST CARROLL	3,224	1,101	1,865	258	764 JBJ	34.2%	57.8%	37.1%	62.9%
19,211	EAST FELICIANA	6,621	2,970	3,516	135	546 JBJ	44.9%	53.1%	45.8%	54.2%
33,274	EVANGELINE	14,243	7,147	6,647	449	500 DED	50.2%	46.7%	51.8%	48.2%
22,387	FRANKLIN	8,334	4,851	3,272	211	1,579 DED	58.2%	39.3%	59.7%	40.3%
17,526	GRANT	6,923	3,787	2,861	275	926 DED	54.7%	41.3%	57.0%	43.0%
68,297	IBERIA	22,806	10,012	11,983	811	1,971 JBJ	43.9%	52.5%	45.5%	54.5%
31,049	IBERVILLE	15,001	5,645	9,028	328	3,383 JBJ	37.6%	60.2%	38.5%	61.5%
15,705	JACKSON	6,710	3,317	3,143	250	174 DED	49.4%	46.8%	51.3%	48.7%
448,306	JEFFERSON	135,993	70,339	63,136	2,518	7,203 DED	51.7%	46.4%	52.7%	47.3%
30,722	JEFFERSON DAVIS	11,409	4,212	6,924	273	2,712 JBJ	36.9%	60.7%	37.8%	62.2%
164,762	LAFAYETTE	50,850	19,769	29,089	1,992	9,320 JBJ	38.9%	57.2%	40.5%	59.5%
85,860	LAFOURCHE	27,911	12,908	14,035	968	1,127 JBJ	46.2%	50.3%	47.9%	52.1%
13,662	LA SALLE	5,982	3,749	1,980	253	1,769 DED	62.7%	33.1%	65.4%	34.6%
41,745	LINCOLN	12,411	4,414	7,536	461	3,122 JBJ	35.6%	60.7%	36.9%	63.1%
70,526	LIVINGSTON	24,968	15,972	8,551	445	7,421 DED	64.0%	34.2%	65.1%	34.9%
12,463	MADISON	4,407	1,649	2,467	291	818 JBJ	37.4%	56.0%	40.1%	59.9%
31,938	MOREHOUSE	10,339	5,321	4,638	380	683 DED	51.5%	44.9%	53.4%	46.6%
36,689	NATCHITOCHES	11,895	5,437	5,947	511	510 JBJ	45.7%	50.0%	47.8%	52.2%
496,938	ORLEANS	143,606	30,423	110,395	2,788	79,972 JBJ	21.2%	76.9%	21.6%	78.4%
142,191	OUACHITA	42,722	21,582	19,799	1,341	1,783 DED	50.5%	46.3%	52.2%	47.8%
25,575	PLAQUEMINES	10,407	5,029	5,242	136	213 JBJ	48.3%	50.4%	49.0%	51.0%
22,540	POINTE COUPEE	10,818	4,648	5,893	277	1,245 JBJ	43.0%	54.5%	44.1%	55.9%
131,556	RAPIDES	40,875	18,714	20,701	1,460	1,987 JBJ	45.8%	50.6%	47.5%	52.5%
9,387	RED RIVER	3,888	2,011	1,780	97	231 DED	51.7%	45.8%	53.0%	47.0%
20,629	RICHLAND	7,405	4,206	2,984	215	1,222 DED	56.8%	40.3%	58.5%	41.5%
22,646	SABINE	8,483	4,342	3,853	288	489 DED	51.2%	45.4%	53.0%	47.0%
66,631	ST. BERNARD	27,634	18,545	8,571	518	9,974 DED	67.1%	31.0%	68.4%	31.6%
42,437	ST. CHARLES	16,039	7,208	8,527	304	1,319 JBJ	44.9%	53.2%	45.8%	54.2%
9,874	ST. HELENA	5,329	2,382	2,827	120	445 JBJ	44.7%	53.0%	45.7%	54.3%
20,879	ST. JAMES	10,479	3,883	6,169	427	2,286 JBJ	37.1%	58.9%	38.6%	61.4%
39,996	ST. JOHN THE BAPTIST	13,529	5,665	7,361	503	1,696 JBJ	41.9%	54.4%	43.5%	56.5%
80,331	ST. LANDRY	32,818	14,134	17,948	736	3,814 JBJ	43.1%	54.7%	44.1%	55.9%
43,978	ST. MARTIN	17,220	6,867	9,618	735	2,751 JBJ	39.9%	55.9%	41.7%	58.3%
58,086	ST. MARY	20,039	8,042	10,518	1,479	2,476 JBJ	40.1%	52.5%	43.3%	56.7%
144,508	ST. TAMMANY	45,625	24,239	20,430	956	3,809 DED	53.1%	44.8%	54.3%	45.7%
85,709	TANGIPAHOA	28,395	15,261	12,525	609	2,736 DED	53.7%	44.1%	54.9%	45.1%
7,103	TENSAS	2,847	1,175	1,560	112	385 JBJ	41.3%	54.8%	43.0%	57.0%
96,982	TERREBONNE	27,830	12,575	14,487	768	1,912 JBJ	45.2%	52.1%	46.5%	53.5%
20,690	UNION	8,928	4,894	3,792	242	1,102 DED	54.8%	42.5%	56.3%	43.7%
50,055	VERMILION	20,271	8,177	11,276	818	3,099 JBJ	40.3%	55.6%	42.0%	58.0%
61,961	VERNON	11,711	5,217	6,089	405	872 JBJ	44.5%	52.0%	46.1%	53.9%
43,185	WASHINGTON	15,871	8,833	6,763	275	2,070 DED	55.7%	42.6%	56.6%	43.4%
41,989	WEBSTER	15,240	7,726	7,168	346	558 DED	50.7%	47.0%	51.9%	48.1%

210

LOUISIANA

SENATOR 1990
(PRIMARY ELECTION)

1990 Census Population	Parish	Total Vote	Duke	Johnston	Other	Plurality		Total Vote Duke	Johnston	Major Vote Duke	Johnston
19,419	WEST BATON ROUGE	8,105	3,576	4,360	169	784	JBJ	44.1%	53.8%	45.1%	54.9%
12,093	WEST CARROLL	4,159	2,712	1,234	213	1,478	DED	65.2%	29.7%	68.7%	31.3%
12,915	WEST FELICIANA	3,661	1,458	2,109	94	651	JBJ	39.8%	57.6%	40.9%	59.1%
16,269	WINN	6,660	3,522	2,853	285	669	DED	52.9%	42.8%	55.2%	44.8%
4,219,973	TOTAL	1,396,113	607,391	752,902	35,820	145,511	JBJ	43.5%	53.9%	44.7%	55.3%

LOUISIANA

CONGRESS

CD	Year	Total Vote	Republican Vote	Candidate	Democratic Vote	Candidate	Other Vote	Rep.-Dem. Plurality	Percentage Total Vote Rep.	Dem.	Major Vote Rep.	Dem.
1	1990			LIVINGSTON, BOB								
1	1988			LIVINGSTON, BOB								
1	1986			LIVINGSTON, BOB								
1	1984			LIVINGSTON, BOB								
2	1990	105,853			105,853	JEFFERSON/MORIAL		105,853 D	100.0%		100.0%	
2	1988					BOGGS, LINDY						
2	1986					BOGGS, LINDY						
2	1984					BOGGS, LINDY						
3	1990					TAUZIN, W. J.						
3	1988					TAUZIN, W. J.						
3	1986					TAUZIN, W. J.						
3	1984					TAUZIN, W. J.						
4	1990			MCCRERY, JIM								
4	1988			MCCRERY, JIM								
4	1986					ROEMER, CHARLES						
4	1984					ROEMER, CHARLES						
4	1982					ROEMER, CHARLES						
5	1990					HUCKABY, JERRY						
5	1988					HUCKABY, JERRY						
5	1986					HUCKABY, JERRY						
5	1984					HUCKABY, JERRY						
5	1982					HUCKABY, JERRY						
6	1990			BAKER, RICHARD H.								
6	1988			BAKER, RICHARD H.								
6	1986			BAKER, RICHARD H.								
6	1984			MOORE, W. HENSON								
6	1982			MOORE, W. HENSON								
7	1990					HAYES, JAMES A.						
7	1988					HAYES, JAMES A.						
7	1986	191,498			191,498	HAYES AND LOWENTHAL		191,498 D	100.0%		100.0%	
7	1984					BREAUX, JOHN B.						
7	1982					BREAUX, JOHN B.						
8	1990			HOLLOWAY, CLYDE C.								
8	1988	204,805	116,241	HOLLOWAY, CLYDE C.	88,564	WILLIAMS, FAYE		27,677 R	56.8%	43.2%	56.8%	43.2%
8	1986	199,140	102,276	HOLLOWAY, CLYDE C.	96,864	WILLIAMS, FAYE		5,412 R	51.4%	48.6%	51.4%	48.6%
8	1984					LONG, GILLIS W.						
8	1982					LONG, GILLIS W.						

LOUISIANA

1990 GENERAL ELECTION

Senator   The data carried in the table for Senator 1990 are for the primary contest between the candidates listed below. The vote by parish is presented in three columns (Duke (R), Johnston (D) and Other). The other vote column represents votes for Accardo (D) and Crowe (D). In the plurality column JBJ and DED are used to designate pluralities for Johnston and Duke.

Congress   See primary note section below. Since candidates who are unopposed in the primary or who receive a majority in the primary are elected unopposed, CD 2 was the only district to have a run-off election in November. In that CD, the the run-off was between two Democratic candidates; William J. Jefferson received 55,621 votes and Marc H. Morial received 50,232 votes giving Mr. Jefferson the election with 52.5% of the vote and a plurality of 5,389.

1990 PRIMARIES

Louisiana holds an open primary election with candidates from all parties running on the same ballot. Any candidate who receives a majority is elected. If no candidate receives 50 percent, there is a run-off election between the top two finishers, without regard to party affiliation, in November.

OCTOBER 6 OPEN PRIMARY

Senator   752,902 J. Bennett Johnston (D); 607,391 David E. Duke (R); 21,485 Nick J. Accardo (D); 14,335 Larry Crowe (D).

Congress   Unopposed in CD 6. Contested as follows:

CD 1   132,855 Bob Livingston (R); 25,494 Vincent J. Bruno (R).

CD 2   32,237 William J. Jefferson (D); 29,366 Marc H. Morial (D); 25,468 Jon D. Johnson (D); 24,175 Harwood Koppel (D); 9,017 Edgar Chase (D); 4,742 Michael G. Bagneris (D); 3,048 Jeffrey A. Barach (R); 1,742 Jane E. Booth (I); 1,143 Roger C. Johnson (R); 411 Michael G. Roccaforte (D); 393 Jeffrey H. Diket (I); 304 Leon A. Waters (D).

CD 3   155,351 W. J. Tauzin (D); 14,909 Ronald P. Duplantis (I); 6,562 Millard F. Clement (I).

CD 4   89,859 Jim McCrery (R); 74,388 Foster L. Campbell (D).

CD 5   128,137 Jerry Huckaby (D); 24,050 Carl Batey (D); 16,331 Bradley T. Roark (R); 5,776 L. D. Knox (I).

CD 7   103,308 James A. Hayes (D); 68,530 David Thibodaux (R); 7,369 Johnny Myers (D).

CD 8   113,607 Clyde C. Holloway (R); 59,511 Cleo Fields (D); 28,170 Joe McPherson (D).

MAINE

GOVERNOR

John R. McKernan (R). Re-elected 1990 to a four-year term. Previously elected 1986.

SENATORS

William S. Cohen (R). Re-elected 1990 to a six-year term. Previously elected 1984, 1978.

George J. Mitchell (D). Re-elected 1988 to a six-year term. Previously elected 1982. Appointed May 1980 to fill our the term vacated by the resignation of Senator Edmund S. Muskie to become Secretary of State.

REPRESENTATIVES

1. Thomas H. Andrews (D)   2. Olympia J. Snowe (R)

POSTWAR VOTE FOR PRESIDENT

| | Total | Republican | | Democratic | | Other | | Percentage Total Vote | | Major Vote | |
Year	Vote	Vote	Candidate	Vote	Candidate	Vote	Plurality	Rep.	Dem.	Rep.	Dem.
1988	555,035	307,131	Bush, George	243,569	Dukakis, Michael S.	4,335	63,562 R	55.3%	43.9%	55.8%	44.2%
1984	553,144	336,500	Reagan, Ronald	214,515	Mondale, Walter F.	2,129	121,985 R	60.8%	38.8%	61.1%	38.9%
1980	523,011	238,522	Reagan, Ronald	220,974	Carter, Jimmy	63,515	17,548 R	45.6%	42.3%	51.9%	48.1%
1976	483,216	236,320	Ford, Gerald R.	232,279	Carter, Jimmy	14,617	4,041 R	48.9%	48.1%	50.4%	49.6%
1972	417,042	256,458	Nixon, Richard M.	160,584	McGovern, George S.		95,874 R	61.5%	38.5%	61.5%	38.5%
1968	392,936	169,254	Nixon, Richard M.	217,312	Humphrey, Hubert H.	6,370	48,058 D	43.1%	55.3%	43.8%	56.2%
1964	380,965	118,701	Goldwater, Barry M.	262,264	Johnson, Lyndon B.		143,563 D	31.2%	68.8%	31.2%	68.8%
1960	421,767	240,608	Nixon, Richard M.	181,159	Kennedy, John F.		59,449 R	57.0%	43.0%	57.0%	43.0%
1956	351,706	249,238	Eisenhower, Dwight D.	102,468	Stevenson, Adlai E.		146,770 R	70.9%	29.1%	70.9%	29.1%
1952	351,786	232,353	Eisenhower, Dwight D.	118,806	Stevenson, Adlai E.	627	113,547 R	66.0%	33.8%	66.2%	33.8%
1948	264,787	150,234	Dewey, Thomas E.	111,916	Truman, Harry S.	2,637	38,318 R	56.7%	42.3%	57.3%	42.7%

POSTWAR VOTE FOR GOVERNOR

| | Total | Republican | | Democratic | | Other | Rep-Dem. | Percentage Total Vote | | Major Vote | |
Year	Vote	Vote	Candidate	Vote	Candidate	Vote	Plurality	Rep.	Dem.	Rep.	Dem.
1990	522,492	243,766	McKernan, John R.	230,038	Brennan, Joseph E.	48,688	13,728 R	46.7%	44.0%	51.4%	48.6%
1986 **	426,861	170,312	McKernan, John R.	128,744	Tierney, James	127,805	41,568 R	39.9%	30.2%	56.9%	43.1%
1982	460,295	172,949	Cragin, Charles L.	281,066	Brennan, Joseph E.	6,280	108,117 D	37.6%	61.1%	38.1%	61.9%
1978	370,258	126,862	Palmer, Linwood E.	176,493	Brennan, Joseph E.	66,903	49,631 D	34.3%	47.7%	41.8%	58.2%
1974 **	363,945	84,176	Erwin, James S.	132,219	Mitchell, George J.	147,550	48,043 D	23.1%	36.3%	38.9%	61.1%
1970	325,386	162,248	Erwin, James S.	163,138	Curtis, Kenneth M.		890 D	49.9%	50.1%	49.9%	50.1%
1966	323,838	151,802	Reed, John H.	172,036	Curtis, Kenneth M.		20,234 D	46.9%	53.1%	46.9%	53.1%
1962	292,725	146,604	Reed, John H.	146,121	Dolloff, Maynard C.		483 R	50.1%	49.9%	50.1%	49.9%
1960 S	417,315	219,768	Reed, John H.	197,547	Coffin, Frank M.		22,221 R	52.7%	47.3%	52.7%	47.3%
1958 **	280,295	134,572	Hildreth, Horace A.	145,723	Clauson, Clinton A.		11,151 D	48.0%	52.0%	48.0%	52.0%
1956	304,649	124,395	Trafton, Willis A.	180,254	Muskie, Edmund S.		55,859 D	40.8%	59.2%	40.8%	59.2%
1954	248,971	113,298	Cross, Burton M.	135,673	Muskie, Edmund S.		22,375 D	45.5%	54.5%	45.5%	54.5%
1952	248,441	128,532	Cross, Burton M.	82,538	Oliver, James C.	37,371	45,994 R	51.7%	33.2%	60.9%	39.1%
1950	241,177	145,823	Payne, Frederick G.	94,304	Grant, Earl S.	1,050	51,519 R	60.5%	39.1%	60.7%	39.3%
1948	222,500	145,956	Payne, Frederick G.	76,544	Lausier, Louis B.		69,412 R	65.6%	34.4%	65.6%	34.4%
1946	179,951	110,327	Hildreth, Horace A.	69,624	Clark, F. Davis		40,703 R	61.3%	38.7%	61.3%	38.7%

The term of office of Maine's Governor was increased from two to four years effective with the 1958 election. The 1960 election was for a short term to fill a vacancy. In 1974 James B. Longley, an Independent candidate, polled 142,464 votes (39.1% of the total vote) and won the election with a 10,245 plurality. In 1986 other vote was 64,317 Sherry F. Huber (Independent); 63,474 John E. Menario (Independent) and 14 scattered.

MAINE

POSTWAR VOTE FOR SENATOR

Year	Total Vote	Republican Vote	Candidate	Democratic Vote	Candidate	Other Vote	Rep.-Dem. Plurality		Percentage Total Vote Rep.	Dem.	Major Vote Rep.	Dem.
1990	520,320	319,167	Cohen, William S.	201,053	Rolde, Neil	100	118,114	R	61.3%	38.6%	61.4%	38.6%
1988	557,375	104,758	Wyman, Jasper S.	452,590	Mitchell, George J.	27	347,832	D	18.8%	81.2%	18.8%	81.2%
1984	551,406	404,414	Cohen, William S.	142,626	Mitchell, Elizabeth H.	4,366	261,788	R	73.3%	25.9%	73.9%	26.1%
1982	459,715	179,882	Emery, David F.	279,819	Mitchell, George J.	14	99,937	D	39.1%	60.9%	39.1%	60.9%
1978	375,172	212,294	Cohen, William S.	127,327	Hathaway, William D.	35,551	84,967	R	56.6%	33.9%	62.5%	37.5%
1976	486,254	193,489	Monks, Robert A. G.	292,704	Muskie, Edmund S.	61	99,215	D	39.8%	60.2%	39.8%	60.2%
1972	421,310	197,040	Smith, Margaret Chase	224,270	Hathaway, William D.		27,230	D	46.8%	53.2%	46.8%	53.2%
1970	323,860	123,906	Bishop, Neil S.	199,954	Muskie, Edmund S.		76,048	D	38.3%	61.7%	38.3%	61.7%
1966	319,535	188,291	Smith, Margaret Chase	131,136	Violette, Elmer H.	108	57,155	R	58.9%	41.0%	58.9%	41.1%
1964	380,551	127,040	McIntire, Clifford	253,511	Muskie, Edmund S.		126,471	D	33.4%	66.6%	33.4%	66.6%
1960	416,699	256,890	Smith, Margaret Chase	159,809	Cormier, Lucia M.		97,081	R	61.6%	38.4%	61.6%	38.4%
1958	284,226	111,522	Payne, Frederick G.	172,704	Muskie, Edmund S.		61,182	D	39.2%	60.8%	39.2%	60.8%
1954	246,605	144,530	Smith, Margaret Chase	102,075	Fullam, Paul A.		42,455	R	58.6%	41.4%	58.6%	41.4%
1952	237,164	139,205	Payne, Frederick G.	82,665	Dube, Roger P.	15,294	56,540	R	58.7%	34.9%	62.7%	37.3%
1948	223,256	159,182	Smith, Margaret Chase	64,074	Scolten, Adrian H.		95,108	R	71.3%	28.7%	71.3%	28.7%
1946	175,014	111,215	Brewster, Owen	63,799	MacDonald, Peter		47,416	R	63.5%	36.5%	63.5%	36.5%

MAINE

Districts Established March 28, 1983

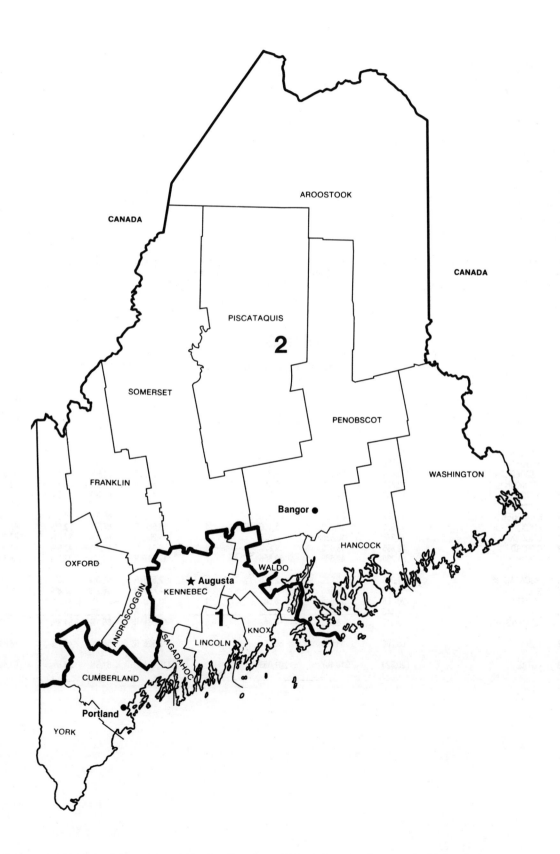

216

MAINE

GOVERNOR 1990

1990 Census Population	County	Total Vote	Republican	Democratic	Other	Rep.-Dem. Plurality	Total Vote Rep.	Total Vote Dem.	Major Vote Rep.	Major Vote Dem.
105,259	ANDROSCOGGIN	43,806	16,098	21,880	5,828	5,782 D	36.7%	49.9%	42.4%	57.6%
86,936	AROOSTOOK	27,352	13,922	10,964	2,466	2,958 R	50.9%	40.1%	55.9%	44.1%
243,135	CUMBERLAND	111,186	50,752	52,163	8,271	1,411 D	45.6%	46.9%	49.3%	50.7%
29,008	FRANKLIN	12,909	6,050	5,723	1,136	327 R	46.9%	44.3%	51.4%	48.6%
46,948	HANCOCK	21,529	11,877	7,426	2,226	4,451 R	55.2%	34.5%	61.5%	38.5%
115,904	KENNEBEC	51,073	22,535	24,025	4,513	1,490 D	44.1%	47.0%	48.4%	51.6%
36,310	KNOX	15,903	8,499	5,810	1,594	2,689 R	53.4%	36.5%	59.4%	40.6%
30,357	LINCOLN	15,550	8,368	5,571	1,611	2,797 R	53.8%	35.8%	60.0%	40.0%
52,602	OXFORD	22,882	9,783	10,474	2,625	691 D	42.8%	45.8%	48.3%	51.7%
146,601	PENOBSCOT	61,121	30,507	24,816	5,798	5,691 R	49.9%	40.6%	55.1%	44.9%
18,653	PISCATAQUIS	8,177	4,177	3,213	787	964 R	51.1%	39.3%	56.5%	43.5%
33,535	SAGADAHOC	14,544	6,634	6,399	1,511	235 R	45.6%	44.0%	50.9%	49.1%
49,767	SOMERSET	20,356	8,784	9,610	1,962	826 D	43.2%	47.2%	47.8%	52.2%
33,018	WALDO	14,262	7,373	5,300	1,589	2,073 R	51.7%	37.2%	58.2%	41.8%
35,308	WASHINGTON	12,910	6,378	5,258	1,274	1,120 R	49.4%	40.7%	54.8%	45.2%
164,587	YORK	68,932	32,029	31,406	5,497	623 R	46.5%	45.6%	50.5%	49.5%
1,227,928	TOTAL	522,492	243,766	230,038	48,688	13,728 R	46.7%	44.0%	51.4%	48.6%

MAINE

SENATOR 1990

1990 Census Population	County	Total Vote	Republican	Democratic	Other	Rep.-Dem. Plurality	Total Vote Rep.	Total Vote Dem.	Major Vote Rep.	Major Vote Dem.
105,259	ANDROSCOGGIN	43,849	24,239	19,599	11	4,640 R	55.3%	44.7%	55.3%	44.7%
86,936	AROOSTOOK	26,986	16,829	10,154	3	6,675 R	62.4%	37.6%	62.4%	37.6%
243,135	CUMBERLAND	110,891	68,614	42,242	35	26,372 R	61.9%	38.1%	61.9%	38.1%
29,008	FRANKLIN	12,821	7,678	5,143		2,535 R	59.9%	40.1%	59.9%	40.1%
46,948	HANCOCK	21,463	14,449	7,005	9	7,444 R	67.3%	32.6%	67.3%	32.7%
115,904	KENNEBEC	50,669	30,425	20,235	9	10,190 R	60.0%	39.9%	60.1%	39.9%
36,310	KNOX	15,879	10,722	5,156	1	5,566 R	67.5%	32.5%	67.5%	32.5%
30,357	LINCOLN	15,375	10,336	5,038	1	5,298 R	67.2%	32.8%	67.2%	32.8%
52,602	OXFORD	22,895	13,070	9,822	3	3,248 R	57.1%	42.9%	57.1%	42.9%
146,601	PENOBSCOT	61,230	40,565	20,658	7	19,907 R	66.3%	33.7%	66.3%	33.7%
18,653	PISCATAQUIS	7,908	5,222	2,686		2,536 R	66.0%	34.0%	66.0%	34.0%
33,535	SAGADAHOC	14,475	9,586	4,888	1	4,698 R	66.2%	33.8%	66.2%	33.8%
49,767	SOMERSET	20,155	11,646	8,508	1	3,138 R	57.8%	42.2%	57.8%	42.2%
33,018	WALDO	14,148	8,753	5,392	3	3,361 R	61.9%	38.1%	61.9%	38.1%
35,308	WASHINGTON	12,810	8,343	4,462	5	3,881 R	65.1%	34.8%	65.2%	34.8%
164,587	YORK	68,766	38,690	30,065	11	8,625 R	56.3%	43.7%	56.3%	43.7%
1,227,928	TOTAL	520,320	319,167	201,053	100	118,114 R	61.3%	38.6%	61.4%	38.6%

MAINE

GOVERNOR 1990

1990 Census Population	City/Town	Total Vote	Republican	Democratic	Other	Rep.-Dem. Plurality	Total Vote Rep.	Total Vote Dem.	Major Vote Rep.	Major Vote Dem.
24,309	AUBURN	10,638	4,524	4,821	1,293	297 D	42.5%	45.3%	48.4%	51.6%
21,325	AUGUSTA	8,646	3,706	4,263	677	557 D	42.9%	49.3%	46.5%	53.5%
33,181	BANGOR	12,828	6,854	5,057	917	1,797 R	53.4%	39.4%	57.5%	42.5%
9,799	BATH	4,066	1,861	1,842	363	19 R	45.8%	45.3%	50.3%	49.7%
6,355	BELFAST	2,656	1,447	929	280	518 R	54.5%	35.0%	60.9%	39.1%
5,995	BERWICK	1,648	857	673	118	184 R	52.0%	40.8%	56.0%	44.0%
20,710	BIDDEFORD	8,259	2,435	5,077	747	2,642 D	29.5%	61.5%	32.4%	67.6%
9,021	BREWER	4,432	2,559	1,476	397	1,083 R	57.7%	33.3%	63.4%	36.6%
20,906	BRUNSWICK	8,002	3,517	3,880	605	363 D	44.0%	48.5%	47.5%	52.5%
6,494	BUXTON	3,018	1,369	1,323	326	46 R	45.4%	43.8%	50.9%	49.1%
5,060	CAMDEN	2,643	1,477	977	189	500 R	55.9%	37.0%	60.2%	39.8%
8,854	CAPE ELIZABETH	4,949	2,925	1,809	215	1,116 R	59.1%	36.6%	61.8%	38.2%
9,415	CARIBOU	2,684	1,608	869	207	739 R	59.9%	32.4%	64.9%	35.1%
5,836	CUMBERLAND TOWN	3,403	2,185	1,041	177	1,144 R	64.2%	30.6%	67.7%	32.3%
5,329	ELIOT	2,117	1,229	784	104	445 R	58.1%	37.0%	61.1%	38.9%
5,975	ELLSWORTH	2,706	1,718	748	240	970 R	63.5%	27.6%	69.7%	30.3%
6,718	FAIRFIELD	2,602	961	1,385	256	424 D	36.9%	53.2%	41.0%	59.0%
7,610	FALMOUTH	4,480	2,629	1,594	257	1,035 R	58.7%	35.6%	62.3%	37.7%
7,436	FARMINGTON	2,883	1,605	1,069	209	536 R	55.7%	37.1%	60.0%	40.0%
6,905	FREEPORT	3,380	1,606	1,493	281	113 R	47.5%	44.2%	51.8%	48.2%
6,746	GARDINER	3,016	1,223	1,471	322	248 D	40.6%	48.8%	45.4%	54.6%
11,856	GORHAM	5,170	2,616	2,121	433	495 R	50.6%	41.0%	55.2%	44.8%
5,904	GRAY	2,783	1,425	1,083	275	342 R	51.2%	38.9%	56.8%	43.2%
5,974	HAMPDEN	2,703	1,626	859	218	767 R	60.2%	31.8%	65.4%	34.6%
5,012	HARPSWELL	2,782	1,418	1,112	252	306 R	51.0%	40.0%	56.0%	44.0%
6,613	HOULTON	2,386	1,443	756	187	687 R	60.5%	31.7%	65.6%	34.4%
5,080	JAY	2,443	666	1,645	132	979 D	27.3%	67.3%	28.8%	71.2%
8,004	KENNEBUNK	4,085	2,486	1,375	224	1,111 R	60.9%	33.7%	64.4%	35.6%
9,372	KITTERY	3,287	1,634	1,493	160	141 R	49.7%	45.4%	52.3%	47.7%
39,757	LEWISTON	16,059	4,658	9,321	2,080	4,663 D	29.0%	58.0%	33.3%	66.7%
7,587	LIMESTONE	710	395	235	80	160 R	55.6%	33.1%	62.7%	37.3%
5,587	LINCOLN TOWN	2,177	1,078	875	224	203 R	49.5%	40.2%	55.2%	44.8%
9,457	LISBON	3,324	1,308	1,483	533	175 D	39.4%	44.6%	46.9%	53.1%
6,956	MILLINOCKET	3,221	1,190	1,638	393	448 D	36.9%	50.9%	42.1%	57.9%
5,595	OAKLAND	2,119	981	951	187	30 R	46.3%	44.9%	50.8%	49.2%
7,789	OLD ORCHARD BEACH	3,884	1,606	1,954	324	348 D	41.3%	50.3%	45.1%	54.9%
8,317	OLD TOWN	3,840	1,559	2,029	252	470 D	40.6%	52.8%	43.5%	56.5%
10,573	ORONO	3,837	1,938	1,690	209	248 R	50.5%	44.0%	53.4%	46.6%
64,358	PORTLAND	27,456	9,539	16,421	1,496	6,882 D	34.7%	59.8%	36.7%	63.3%
10,550	PRESQUE ISLE	3,394	2,100	1,047	247	1,053 R	61.9%	30.8%	66.7%	33.3%
7,972	ROCKLAND	2,378	1,168	986	224	182 R	49.1%	41.5%	54.2%	45.8%
7,078	RUMFORD	3,260	949	1,975	336	1,026 D	29.1%	60.6%	32.5%	67.5%
15,181	SACO	6,811	2,803	3,462	546	659 D	41.2%	50.8%	44.7%	55.3%
20,463	SANFORD	7,253	2,821	3,799	633	978 D	38.9%	52.4%	42.6%	57.4%
12,518	SCARBOROUGH	6,032	3,189	2,387	456	802 R	52.9%	39.6%	57.2%	42.8%
8,725	SKOWHEGAN	3,513	1,479	1,811	223	332 D	42.1%	51.6%	45.0%	55.0%
5,877	SOUTH BERWICK	2,234	1,246	840	148	406 R	55.8%	37.6%	59.7%	40.3%
23,163	SOUTH PORTLAND	10,508	4,272	5,429	807	1,157 D	40.7%	51.7%	44.0%	56.0%
7,678	STANDISH	3,188	1,577	1,330	281	247 R	49.5%	41.7%	54.2%	45.8%
8,746	TOPSHAM	3,637	1,635	1,633	369	2 R	45.0%	44.9%	50.0%	50.0%
17,173	WATERVILLE	6,415	2,404	3,646	365	1,242 D	37.5%	56.8%	39.7%	60.3%
7,778	WELLS	3,370	1,879	1,280	211	599 R	55.8%	38.0%	59.5%	40.5%
16,121	WESTBROOK	7,150	2,689	3,857	604	1,168 D	37.6%	53.9%	41.1%	58.9%
13,020	WINDHAM	5,646	2,695	2,369	582	326 R	47.7%	42.0%	53.2%	46.8%
7,997	WINSLOW	3,447	1,310	1,873	264	563 D	38.0%	54.3%	41.2%	58.8%
5,968	WINTHROP	3,059	1,598	1,201	260	397 R	52.2%	39.3%	57.1%	42.9%
7,862	YARMOUTH	4,294	2,525	1,540	229	985 R	58.8%	35.9%	62.1%	37.9%
9,818	YORK TOWN	4,802	2,789	1,764	249	1,025 R	58.1%	36.7%	61.3%	38.7%

MAINE

SENATOR 1990

1990 Census Population	City/Town	Total Vote	Republican	Democratic	Other	Rep.-Dem. Plurality	Percentage Total Vote Rep.	Total Vote Dem.	Major Vote Rep.	Major Vote Dem.
24,309	AUBURN	10,625	6,434	4,191		2,243 R	60.6%	39.4%	60.6%	39.4%
21,325	AUGUSTA	8,259	4,928	3,331		1,597 R	59.7%	40.3%	59.7%	40.3%
33,181	BANGOR	12,845	8,899	3,946		4,953 R	69.3%	30.7%	69.3%	30.7%
9,799	BATH	4,037	2,755	1,282		1,473 R	68.2%	31.8%	68.2%	31.8%
6,355	BELFAST	2,649	1,715	934		781 R	64.7%	35.3%	64.7%	35.3%
5,995	BERWICK	1,642	1,026	616		410 R	62.5%	37.5%	62.5%	37.5%
20,710	BIDDEFORD	8,270	3,700	4,570		870 D	44.7%	55.3%	44.7%	55.3%
9,021	BREWER	4,412	3,254	1,158		2,096 R	73.8%	26.2%	73.8%	26.2%
20,906	BRUNSWICK	8,009	5,042	2,965	2	2,077 R	63.0%	37.0%	63.0%	37.0%
6,494	BUXTON	2,992	1,728	1,263	1	465 R	57.8%	42.2%	57.8%	42.2%
5,060	CAMDEN	2,681	1,849	832		1,017 R	69.0%	31.0%	69.0%	31.0%
8,854	CAPE ELIZABETH	4,942	3,602	1,340		2,262 R	72.9%	27.1%	72.9%	27.1%
9,415	CARIBOU	2,569	1,824	745		1,079 R	71.0%	29.0%	71.0%	29.0%
5,836	CUMBERLAND TOWN	3,388	2,568	820		1,748 R	75.8%	24.2%	75.8%	24.2%
5,329	ELIOT	2,161	1,415	746		669 R	65.5%	34.5%	65.5%	34.5%
5,975	ELLSWORTH	2,706	2,004	702		1,302 R	74.1%	25.9%	74.1%	25.9%
6,718	FAIRFIELD	2,578	1,384	1,194		190 R	53.7%	46.3%	53.7%	46.3%
7,610	FALMOUTH	4,486	3,255	1,231		2,024 R	72.6%	27.4%	72.6%	27.4%
7,436	FARMINGTON	2,855	1,946	909		1,037 R	68.2%	31.8%	68.2%	31.8%
6,905	FREEPORT	3,383	2,181	1,202		979 R	64.5%	35.5%	64.5%	35.5%
6,746	GARDINER	3,006	1,810	1,196		614 R	60.2%	39.8%	60.2%	39.8%
11,856	GORHAM	5,158	3,477	1,679	2	1,798 R	67.4%	32.6%	67.4%	32.6%
5,904	GRAY	2,805	1,788	1,017		771 R	63.7%	36.3%	63.7%	36.3%
5,974	HAMPDEN	2,701	2,018	683		1,335 R	74.7%	25.3%	74.7%	25.3%
5,012	HARPSWELL	2,758	1,878	880		998 R	68.1%	31.9%	68.1%	31.9%
6,613	HOULTON	2,361	1,769	592		1,177 R	74.9%	25.1%	74.9%	25.1%
5,080	JAY	2,431	995	1,436		441 D	40.9%	59.1%	40.9%	59.1%
8,004	KENNEBUNK	4,058	2,779	1,276	3	1,503 R	68.5%	31.4%	68.5%	31.5%
9,372	KITTERY	3,268	1,745	1,518	5	227 R	53.4%	46.5%	53.5%	46.5%
39,757	LEWISTON	15,961	7,764	8,188	9	424 D	48.6%	51.3%	48.7%	51.3%
7,587	LIMESTONE	707	501	206		295 R	70.9%	29.1%	70.9%	29.1%
5,587	LINCOLN TOWN	2,163	1,402	761		641 R	64.8%	35.2%	64.8%	35.2%
9,457	LISBON	3,489	2,041	1,448		593 R	58.5%	41.5%	58.5%	41.5%
6,956	MILLINOCKET	3,212	1,814	1,398		416 R	56.5%	43.5%	56.5%	43.5%
5,595	OAKLAND	2,118	1,254	863	1	391 R	59.2%	40.7%	59.2%	40.8%
7,789	OLD ORCHARD BEACH	3,842	2,119	1,722	1	397 R	55.2%	44.8%	55.2%	44.8%
8,317	OLD TOWN	3,846	2,290	1,556		734 R	59.5%	40.5%	59.5%	40.5%
10,573	ORONO	3,843	2,563	1,280		1,283 R	66.7%	33.3%	66.7%	33.3%
64,358	PORTLAND	27,367	14,414	12,936	17	1,478 R	52.7%	47.3%	52.7%	47.3%
10,550	PRESQUE ISLE	3,371	2,372	999		1,373 R	70.4%	29.6%	70.4%	29.6%
7,972	ROCKLAND	2,330	1,494	836		658 R	64.1%	35.9%	64.1%	35.9%
7,078	RUMFORD	3,429	1,588	1,841		253 D	46.3%	53.7%	46.3%	53.7%
15,181	SACO	6,859	3,768	3,091		677 R	54.9%	45.1%	54.9%	45.1%
20,463	SANFORD	7,204	3,782	3,422		360 R	52.5%	47.5%	52.5%	47.5%
12,518	SCARBOROUGH	6,019	4,101	1,908	10	2,193 R	68.1%	31.7%	68.2%	31.8%
8,725	SKOWHEGAN	3,501	2,027	1,474		553 R	57.9%	42.1%	57.9%	42.1%
5,877	SOUTH BERWICK	2,228	1,436	792		644 R	64.5%	35.5%	64.5%	35.5%
23,163	SOUTH PORTLAND	10,497	6,087	4,410		1,677 R	58.0%	42.0%	58.0%	42.0%
7,678	STANDISH	3,179	1,944	1,235		709 R	61.2%	38.8%	61.2%	38.8%
8,746	TOPSHAM	3,628	2,384	1,244		1,140 R	65.7%	34.3%	65.7%	34.3%
17,173	WATERVILLE	6,391	3,417	2,973	1	444 R	53.5%	46.5%	53.5%	46.5%
7,778	WELLS	3,366	2,151	1,215		936 R	63.9%	36.1%	63.9%	36.1%
16,121	WESTBROOK	7,183	3,996	3,184	3	812 R	55.6%	44.3%	55.7%	44.3%
13,020	WINDHAM	5,654	3,610	2,044		1,566 R	63.8%	36.2%	63.8%	36.2%
7,997	WINSLOW	3,494	1,847	1,646	1	201 R	52.9%	47.1%	52.9%	47.1%
5,968	WINTHROP	3,209	2,208	1,001		1,207 R	68.8%	31.2%	68.8%	31.2%
7,862	YARMOUTH	4,284	3,109	1,174	1	1,935 R	72.6%	27.4%	72.6%	27.4%
9,818	YORK TOWN	4,814	2,260	2,554		294 D	46.9%	53.1%	46.9%	53.1%

MAINE

CONGRESS

CD	Year	Total Vote	Republican Vote	Republican Candidate	Democratic Vote	Democratic Candidate	Other Vote	Rep.-Dem. Plurality	Total Vote Rep.	Total Vote Dem.	Major Vote Rep.	Major Vote Dem.
1	1990	278,872	110,836	EMERY, DAVID F.	167,623	ANDREWS, THOMAS H.	413	56,787 D	39.7%	60.1%	39.8%	60.2%
1	1988	302,163	111,125	O'MEARA, EDWARD S.	190,989	BRENNAN, JOSEPH E.	49	79,864 D	36.8%	63.2%	36.8%	63.2%
1	1986	229,233	100,260	IVES, H. ROLLIN	121,848	BRENNAN, JOSEPH E.	7,125	21,588 D	43.7%	53.2%	45.1%	54.9%
1	1984	287,765	182,785	MCKERNAN, JOHN R.	104,972	HOBBINS, BARRY J.	8	77,813 R	63.5%	36.5%	63.5%	36.5%
2	1990	238,522	121,704	SNOWE, OLYMPIA J.	116,798	MCGOWAN, PATRICK K.	20	4,906 R	51.0%	49.0%	51.0%	49.0%
2	1988	252,721	167,226	SNOWE, OLYMPIA J.	85,346	HAYES, KENNETH P.	149	81,880 R	66.2%	33.8%	66.2%	33.8%
2	1986	192,397	148,770	SNOWE, OLYMPIA J.	43,614	CHARETTE, RICHARD R.	13	105,156 R	77.3%	22.7%	77.3%	22.7%
2	1984	253,773	192,166	SNOWE, OLYMPIA J.	57,347	BULL, CHIPMAN C.	4,260	134,819 R	75.7%	22.6%	77.0%	23.0%

220

MAINE

1990 GENERAL ELECTION

In addition to the county-by-county figures, data are presented for selected Maine communities. Since not all jurisdictions of the state are listed in this special tabulation, state-wide totals are shown only with the county-by-county statistics.

Governor   Other vote was 48,377 Independent (Adam) and 311 scattered write-in.

Senator   Other vote was scattered write-in.

Congress   Other vote was scattered write-in in both CD's.

1990 PRIMARIES

JUNE 12 REPUBLICAN

Governor   John R. McKernan, unopposed.

Senator   William S. Cohen, unopposed.

Congress   Unopposed in CD 2. Contested as follows:

CD   1   20,638 David F. Emery; 12,748 John S. McCormick; 7 scattered write-in.

JUNE 12 DEMOCRATIC

Governor   Joseph E. Brennan, unopposed.

Senator   Neil Rolde, unopposed.

Congress   Unopposed in CD 2. Contested as follows:

CD   1   16,158 Thomas H. Andrews: 14,995 James E. Tierney; 7,634 Elizabeth H. Mitchell; 4,957 Linda E. Abromson; 762 Ralph W. Conant.

MARYLAND

GOVERNOR
William D. Schaefer (D). Re-elected 1990 to a four-year term. Previously elected 1986.

SENATORS
Barbara A. Mikulski (D). Elected 1986 to a six-year term.

Paul S. Sarbanes (D). Re-elected 1988 to a six-year term. Previously elected 1982, 1976.

REPRESENTATIVES
1. Wayne T. Gilchrest (R)
2. Helen D. Bentley (R)
3. Benjamin L. Cardin (D)
4. Thomas McMillen (D)
5. Steny H. Hoyer (D)
6. Beverly B. Byron (D)
7. Kweisi Mfume (D)
8. Constance A. Morella (R)

POSTWAR VOTE FOR PRESIDENT

Year	Total Vote	Republican Vote	Candidate	Democratic Vote	Candidate	Other Vote	Plurality	Total Vote Rep.	Dem.	Major Vote Rep.	Dem.
1988	1,714,358	876,167	Bush, George	826,304	Dukakis, Michael S.	11,887	49,863 R	51.1%	48.2%	51.5%	48.5%
1984	1,675,873	879,918	Reagan, Ronald	787,935	Mondale, Walter F.	8,020	91,983 R	52.5%	47.0%	52.8%	47.2%
1980	1,540,496	680,606	Reagan, Ronald	726,161	Carter, Jimmy	133,729	45,555 D	44.2%	47.1%	48.4%	51.6%
1976	1,439,897	672,661	Ford, Gerald R.	759,612	Carter, Jimmy	7,624	86,951 D	46.7%	52.8%	47.0%	53.0%
1972	1,353,812	829,305	Nixon, Richard M.	505,781	McGovern, George S.	18,726	323,524 R	61.3%	37.4%	62.1%	37.9%
1968	1,235,039	517,995	Nixon, Richard M.	538,310	Humphrey, Hubert H.	178,734	20,315 D	41.9%	43.6%	49.0%	51.0%
1964	1,116,457	385,495	Goldwater, Barry M.	730,912	Johnson, Lyndon B.	50	345,417 D	34.5%	65.5%	34.5%	65.5%
1960	1,055,349	489,538	Nixon, Richard M.	565,808	Kennedy, John F.	3	76,270 D	46.4%	53.6%	46.4%	53.6%
1956	932,827	559,738	Eisenhower, Dwight D.	372,613	Stevenson, Adlai E.	476	187,125 R	60.0%	39.9%	60.0%	40.0%
1952	902,074	499,424	Eisenhower, Dwight D.	395,337	Stevenson, Adlai E.	7,313	104,087 R	55.4%	43.8%	55.8%	44.2%
1948	596,748	294,814	Dewey, Thomas E.	286,521	Truman, Harry S.	15,413	8,293 R	49.4%	48.0%	50.7%	49.3%

POSTWAR VOTE FOR GOVERNOR

Year	Total Vote	Republican Vote	Candidate	Democratic Vote	Candidate	Other Vote	Rep.-Dem. Plurality	Total Vote Rep.	Dem.	Major Vote Rep.	Dem.
1990	1,111,088	446,980	Shepard, William S.	664,015	Schaefer, William D.	93	217,035 D	40.2%	59.8%	40.2%	59.8%
1986	1,101,476	194,185	Mooney, Thomas J.	907,291	Schaefer, William D.		713,106 D	17.6%	82.4%	17.6%	82.4%
1982	1,139,149	432,826	Pascal, Robert A.	705,910	Hughes, Harry	413	273,084 D	38.0%	62.0%	38.0%	62.0%
1978	1,011,963	293,635	Beall, J. Glenn, Jr.	718,328	Hughes, Harry		424,693 D	29.0%	71.0%	29.0%	71.0%
1974	949,097	346,449	Gore, Louise	602,648	Mandel, Marvin		256,199 D	36.5%	63.5%	36.5%	63.5%
1970	973,099	314,336	Blain, C. Stanley	639,579	Mandel, Marvin	19,184	325,243 D	32.3%	65.7%	33.0%	67.0%
1966	918,761	455,318	Agnew, Spiro T.	373,543	Mahoney, George P.	89,900	81,775 R	49.6%	40.7%	54.9%	45.1%
1962	775,101	343,051	Small, Frank	432,045	Tawes, J. Millard	5	88,994 D	44.3%	55.7%	44.3%	55.7%
1958	763,234	278,173	Devereux, James	485,061	Tawes, J. Millard		206,888 D	36.4%	63.6%	36.4%	63.6%
1954	700,484	381,451	McKeldin, Theodore	319,033	Byrd, Harry C.		62,418 R	54.5%	45.5%	54.5%	45.5%
1950	645,631	369,807	McKeldin, Theodore	275,824	Lane, William P.		93,983 R	57.3%	42.7%	57.3%	42.7%
1946	489,836	221,752	McKeldin, Theodore	268,084	Lane, William P.		46,332 D	45.3%	54.7%	45.3%	54.7%

MARYLAND

POSTWAR VOTE FOR SENATOR

Year	Total Vote	Republican Vote	Candidate	Democratic Vote	Candidate	Other Vote	Rep.-Dem. Plurality	Total Vote Rep.	Dem.	Major Vote Rep.	Dem.
1988	1,617,065	617,537	Keyes, Alan L.	999,166	Sarbanes, Paul S.	362	381,629 D	38.2%	61.8%	38.2%	61.8%
1986	1,112,637	437,411	Chavez, Linda	675,225	Mikulski, Barbara A.	1	237,814 D	39.3%	60.7%	39.3%	60.7%
1982	1,114,690	407,334	Hogan, Lawrence J.	707,356	Sarbanes, Paul S.		300,022 D	36.5%	63.5%	36.5%	63.5%
1980	1,286,088	850,970	Mathias, Charles	435,118	Conroy, Edward T.		415,852 R	66.2%	33.8%	66.2%	33.8%
1976	1,365,568	530,439	Beall, J. Glenn, Jr.	772,101	Sarbanes, Paul S.	63,028	241,662 D	38.8%	56.5%	40.7%	59.3%
1974	877,786	503,223	Mathias, Charles	374,563	Mikulski, Barbara A.		128,660 R	57.3%	42.7%	57.3%	42.7%
1970	956,370	484,960	Beall, J. Glenn, Jr.	460,422	Tydings, Joseph D.	10,988	24,538 R	50.7%	48.1%	51.3%	48.7%
1968	1,133,727	541,893	Mathias, Charles	443,367	Brewster, Daniel B.	148,467	98,526 R	47.8%	39.1%	55.0%	45.0%
1964	1,081,049	402,393	Beall, J. Glenn	678,649	Tydings, Joseph D.	7	276,256 D	37.2%	62.8%	37.2%	62.8%
1962	714,248	270,312	Miller, Edward T.	443,935	Brewster, Daniel B.	1	173,623 D	37.8%	62.2%	37.8%	62.2%
1958	749,291	382,021	Beall, J. Glenn	367,270	D'Alesandro, Thomas		14,751 R	51.0%	49.0%	51.0%	49.0%
1956	892,167	473,059	Butler, John Marshall	419,108	Mahoney, George P.		53,951 R	53.0%	47.0%	53.0%	47.0%
1952	856,193	449,823	Beall, J. Glenn	406,370	Mahoney, George P.		43,453 R	52.5%	47.5%	52.5%	47.5%
1950	615,614	326,291	Butler, John Marshall	283,180	Tydings, Millard E.	6,143	43,111 R	53.0%	46.0%	53.5%	46.5%
1946	472,232	235,000	Markey, David John	237,232	O'Conor, Herbert R.		2,232 D	49.8%	50.2%	49.8%	50.2%

MARYLAND

Districts Established April 13, 1982

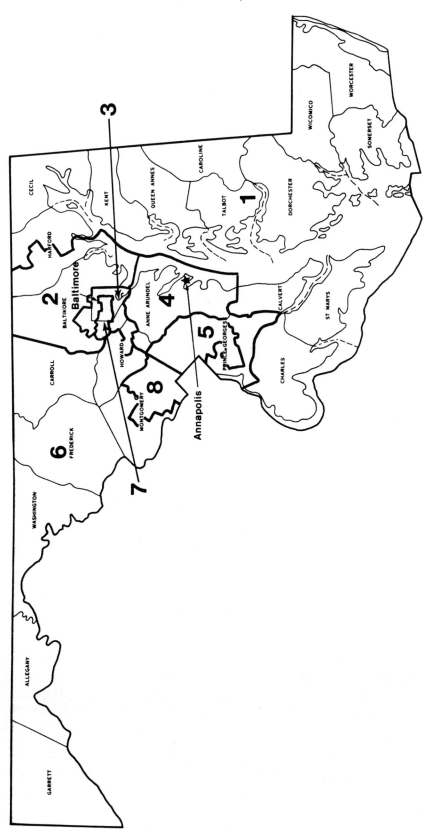

MARYLAND

GOVERNOR 1990

1990 Census Population	County	Total Vote	Republican	Democratic	Other	Rep.-Dem. Plurality	Percentage Total Vote Rep.	Dem.	Major Vote Rep.	Dem.
74,946	ALLEGANY	21,969	7,345	14,624		7,279 D	33.4%	66.6%	33.4%	66.6%
427,239	ANNE ARUNDEL	114,773	58,507	56,253	13	2,254 R	51.0%	49.0%	51.0%	49.0%
736,014	BALTIMORE CITY	113,809	32,260	81,542	7	49,282 D	28.3%	71.6%	28.3%	71.7%
692,134	BALTIMORE COUNTY	197,302	92,602	104,689	11	12,087 D	46.9%	53.1%	46.9%	53.1%
51,372	CALVERT	13,299	5,295	8,003	1	2,708 D	39.8%	60.2%	39.8%	60.2%
27,035	CAROLINE	5,661	3,910	1,751		2,159 R	69.1%	30.9%	69.1%	30.9%
123,372	CARROLL	31,318	18,281	13,037		5,244 R	58.4%	41.6%	58.4%	41.6%
71,347	CECIL	15,147	7,473	7,671	3	198 D	49.3%	50.6%	49.3%	50.7%
101,154	CHARLES	19,832	6,969	12,861	2	5,892 D	35.1%	64.8%	35.1%	64.9%
30,236	DORCHESTER	7,923	5,324	2,599		2,725 R	67.2%	32.8%	67.2%	32.8%
150,208	FREDERICK	33,120	17,718	15,398	4	2,320 R	53.5%	46.5%	53.5%	46.5%
28,138	GARRETT	6,632	4,010	2,621	1	1,389 R	60.5%	39.5%	60.5%	39.5%
182,132	HARFORD	42,924	20,832	22,090	2	1,258 D	48.5%	51.5%	48.5%	51.5%
187,328	HOWARD	51,981	19,809	32,158	14	12,349 D	38.1%	61.9%	38.1%	61.9%
17,842	KENT	5,388	3,095	2,293		802 R	57.4%	42.6%	57.4%	42.6%
757,027	MONTGOMERY	205,392	61,444	143,948		82,504 D	29.9%	70.1%	29.9%	70.1%
729,268	PRINCE GEORGES	130,194	27,520	102,642	32	75,122 D	21.1%	78.8%	21.1%	78.9%
33,953	QUEEN ANNES	9,203	6,382	2,821		3,561 R	69.3%	30.7%	69.3%	30.7%
75,974	ST. MARYS	13,997	5,159	8,838		3,679 D	36.9%	63.1%	36.9%	63.1%
23,440	SOMERSET	6,133	3,221	2,912		309 R	52.5%	47.5%	52.5%	47.5%
30,549	TALBOT	8,988	5,612	3,375	1	2,237 R	62.4%	37.6%	62.4%	37.6%
121,393	WASHINGTON	26,562	16,941	9,619	2	7,322 R	63.8%	36.2%	63.8%	36.2%
74,339	WICOMICO	18,704	12,057	6,647		5,410 R	64.5%	35.5%	64.5%	35.5%
35,028	WORCESTER	10,837	5,214	5,623		409 D	48.1%	51.9%	48.1%	51.9%
4,781,468	TOTAL	1,111,088	446,980	664,015	93	217,035 D	40.2%	59.8%	40.2%	59.8%

MARYLAND

CONGRESS

CD	Year	Total Vote	Republican Vote	Republican Candidate	Democratic Vote	Democratic Candidate	Other Vote	Rep.-Dem. Plurality	Percentage Total Vote Rep.	Total Vote Dem.	Major Vote Rep.	Major Vote Dem.
1	1990	156,438	88,920	GILCHREST, WAYNE T.	67,518	DYSON, ROY		21,402 R	56.8%	43.2%	56.8%	43.2%
1	1988	190,716	94,588	GILCHREST, WAYNE T.	96,128	DYSON, ROY		1,540 D	49.6%	50.4%	49.6%	50.4%
1	1986	131,877	43,764	WILLIAMS, HARLAN C.	88,113	DYSON, ROY		44,349 D	33.2%	66.8%	33.2%	66.8%
1	1984	165,538	68,865	WILLIAMS, HARLAN C.	96,673	DYSON, ROY		27,808 D	41.6%	58.4%	41.6%	58.4%
1	1982	129,159	39,656	HOPKINS, C. A. PORTER	89,503	DYSON, ROY		49,847 D	30.7%	69.3%	30.7%	69.3%
2	1990	155,183	115,398	BENTLEY, HELEN D.	39,785	BOWERS, RONALD P.		75,613 R	74.4%	25.6%	74.4%	25.6%
2	1988	221,070	157,956	BENTLEY, HELEN D.	63,114	BARTENFELDER, JOSEPH		94,842 R	71.5%	28.5%	71.5%	28.5%
2	1986	164,946	96,745	BENTLEY, HELEN D.	68,200	TOWNSEND, KATHLEEN K.	1	28,545 R	58.7%	41.3%	58.7%	41.3%
2	1984	217,089	111,517	BENTLEY, HELEN D.	105,571	LONG, CLARENCE D.	1	5,946 R	51.4%	48.6%	51.4%	48.6%
2	1982	158,380	75,062	BENTLEY, HELEN D.	83,318	LONG, CLARENCE D.		8,256 D	47.4%	52.6%	47.4%	52.6%
3	1990	118,386	35,841	NICHOLS, HARWOOD	82,545	CARDIN, BENJAMIN L.		46,704 D	30.3%	69.7%	30.3%	69.7%
3	1988	183,512	49,733	PIERPONT, ROSS Z.	133,779	CARDIN, BENJAMIN L.		84,046 D	27.1%	72.9%	27.1%	72.9%
3	1986	126,613	26,452	PIERPONT, ROSS Z.	100,161	CARDIN, BENJAMIN L.		73,709 D	20.9%	79.1%	20.9%	79.1%
3	1984	195,261	59,493	PIERPONT, ROSS Z.	133,189	MIKULSKI, BARBARA A.	2,579	73,696 D	30.5%	68.2%	30.9%	69.1%
3	1982	148,301	38,259	SCHERR, H. ROBERT	110,042	MIKULSKI, BARBARA A.		71,783 D	25.8%	74.2%	25.8%	74.2%
4	1990	145,447	59,846	DUCKWORTH, ROBERT P.	85,601	MCMILLEN, THOMAS		25,755 D	41.1%	58.9%	41.1%	58.9%
4	1988	188,312	59,688	MCCLANAHAN, BRADLYN	128,624	MCMILLEN, THOMAS		68,936 D	31.7%	68.3%	31.7%	68.3%
4	1986	129,714	64,643	NEALL, ROBERT R.	65,071	MCMILLEN, THOMAS		428 D	49.8%	50.2%	49.8%	50.2%
4	1984	172,743	114,430	HOLT, MARJORIE S.	58,312	GREENEBAUM, HOWARD	1	56,118 R	66.2%	33.8%	66.2%	33.8%
4	1982	123,564	75,617	HOLT, MARJORIE S.	47,947	AIKEN, PATRICIA O'B.		27,670 R	61.2%	38.8%	61.2%	38.8%
5	1990	105,061	20,314	BREUER, LEE F.	84,747	HOYER, STENY H.		64,433 D	19.3%	80.7%	19.3%	80.7%
5	1988	163,346	34,909	SELLNER, JOHN E.	128,437	HOYER, STENY H.		93,528 D	21.4%	78.6%	21.4%	78.6%
5	1986	100,200	18,102	SELLNER, JOHN E.	82,098	HOYER, STENY H.		63,996 D	18.1%	81.9%	18.1%	81.9%
5	1984	161,149	44,839	RITCHIE, JOHN E.	116,310	HOYER, STENY H.		71,471 D	27.8%	72.2%	27.8%	72.2%
5	1982	105,470	21,533	GUTHRIE, WILLIAM P.	83,937	HOYER, STENY H.		62,404 D	20.4%	79.6%	20.4%	79.6%
6	1990	162,981	56,479	FIOTES, CHRISTOPHER P.	106,502	BYRON, BEVERLY B.		50,023 D	34.7%	65.3%	34.7%	65.3%
6	1988	221,281	54,528	HALSEY, KENNETH W.	166,753	BYRON, BEVERLY B.		112,225 D	24.6%	75.4%	24.6%	75.4%
6	1986	142,575	39,600	VANDENBERGE, JOHN	102,975	BYRON, BEVERLY B.		63,375 D	27.8%	72.2%	27.8%	72.2%
6	1984	189,442	66,056	FICKER, ROBIN	123,383	BYRON, BEVERLY B.	3	57,327 D	34.9%	65.1%	34.9%	65.1%
6	1982	137,917	35,321	BARTLETT, ROSCOE	102,596	BYRON, BEVERLY B.		67,275 D	25.6%	74.4%	25.6%	74.4%
7	1990	70,160	10,529	KONDNER, KENNETH	59,628	MFUME, KWEISI	3	49,099 D	15.0%	85.0%	15.0%	85.0%
7	1988	117,650			117,650	MFUME, KWEISI		117,650 D		100.0%		100.0%
7	1986	91,398	12,170	CROSSE, ST. GEORGE I.	79,226	MFUME, KWEISI	2	67,056 D	13.3%	86.7%	13.3%	86.7%
7	1984	139,489			139,488	MITCHELL, PARREN J.	1	139,488 D		100.0%		100.0%
7	1982	117,699	14,203	JONES, M. LEONORA	103,496	MITCHELL, PARREN J.		89,293 D	12.1%	87.9%	12.1%	87.9%
8	1990	176,887	130,059	MORELLA, CONSTANCE A.	39,343	WALKER, JAMES W.	7,485	90,716 R	73.5%	22.2%	76.8%	23.2%
8	1988	275,097	172,619	MORELLA, CONSTANCE A.	102,478	FRANCHOT, PETER		70,141 R	62.7%	37.3%	62.7%	37.3%
8	1986	175,742	92,917	MORELLA, CONSTANCE A.	82,825	BAINUM, STEWART		10,092 R	52.9%	47.1%	52.9%	47.1%
8	1984	254,569	70,715	CECCONE, ALBERT	181,947	BARNES, MICHAEL D.	1,907	111,232 D	27.8%	71.5%	28.0%	72.0%
8	1982	170,671	48,910	SPENCER, ELIZABETH W.	121,761	BARNES, MICHAEL D.		72,851 D	28.7%	71.3%	28.7%	71.3%

MARYLAND

1990 GENERAL ELECTION

Governor   Other vote was write-in (Thies).

Congress   Other vote was write-in (Scott) in CD 7; Independent (Altman) in CD 8.

1990 PRIMARIES

SEPTEMBER 11 REPUBLICAN

Governor   66,966 William S. Shepard; 60,065 Ross Z. Pierpont.

Congress   Unopposed in two CD's. Contested as follows:

CD	1	9,095 Wayne T. Gilchrest; 4,330 Barry J. Sullivan; 3,996 Mark R. Frazer; 3,894 Richard F. Colburn; 3,700 Raymond J. Briscuso; 3,623 Luis A. Luna; 2,114 Perry Weed; 1,104 Charles G. Grace.
CD	3	3,153 Harwood Nichols; 3,050 Fredric M. Parker.
CD	4	11,736 Robert P. Duckworth; 4,744 Bradlyn McClanahan; 2,504 Michael D. Hathaway.
CD	5	5,355 Lee F. Breuer; 2,161 Gregory K. Washington.
CD	6	9,393 Christopher P. Fiotes; 8,859 Kenneth W. Halsey; 8,822 Frank K. Nethken.
CD	8	20,010 Constance A. Morella; 2,990 Asa Beck.

SEPTEMBER 11 DEMOCRATIC

Governor   358,534 William D. Schaefer; 100,816 Frederick M. Griisser.

Congress   Contested as follows:

CD	1	37,683 Roy Dyson; 21,828 Barbara O. Kreamer; 5,706 Morris C. Durham; 3,977 Michael C. Hickey.
CD	2	22,136 Ronald P. Bowers; 13,488 Cornelius U. Morgan.
CD	3	43,496 Benjamin L. Cardin; 8,788 Martin Glaser.
CD	4	47,863 Thomas McMillen; 6,636 Jack A. Blum; 2,956 John W. Dotterweich.
CD	5	49,473 Steny H. Hoyer; 13,141 Abdul Alim Muhammad.
CD	6	31,384 Beverly B. Byron; 17,512 Anthony P. Puca.
CD	7	41,238 Kweisi Mfume; 5,270 Michael V. Dobson.
CD	8	19,019 James W. Walker; 15,791 Joseph S. Incarnato; 8,556 George W. Benns.

MASSACHUSETTS

GOVERNOR
William F. Weld (R). Elected 1990 to a four year term.

SENATORS
Edward M. Kennedy (D). Re-elected 1988 to a six-year term. Previously elected 1982, 1976, 1970, 1964 and in 1962 to fill out term vacated by the resignation of Senator John F. Kennedy.

John F. Kerry (D). Re-elected 1990 to a six-year term. Previously elected 1984.

REPRESENTATIVES
1. Silvio O. Conte (R) (see page 1)
2. Richard E. Neal (D)
3. Joseph D. Early (D)
4. Barney Frank (D)
5. Chester G. Atkins (D)
6. Nicholas Mavroules (D)
7. Edwward J. Markey (D)
8. Joseph P. Kennedy (D)
9. John J. Moakley (D)
10. Gerry E. Studds (D)
11. Brian J. Donnelly (D)

POSTWAR VOTE FOR PRESIDENT

Year	Total Vote	Republican Vote	Candidate	Democratic Vote	Candidate	Other Vote	Plurality	Percentage Total Vote Rep.	Dem.	Major Vote Rep.	Dem.
1988	2,632,805	1,194,635	Bush, George	1,401,415	Dukakis, Michael S.	36,755	206,780 D	45.4%	53.2%	46.0%	54.0%
1984	2,559,453	1,310,936	Reagan, Ronald	1,239,606	Mondale, Walter F.	8,911	71,330 R	51.2%	48.4%	51.4%	48.6%
1980	2,524,298	1,057,631	Reagan, Ronald	1,053,802	Carter, Jimmy	412,865	3,829 R	41.9%	41.7%	50.1%	49.9%
1976	2,547,558	1,030,276	Ford, Gerald R.	1,429,475	Carter, Jimmy	87,807	399,199 D	40.4%	56.1%	41.9%	58.1%
1972	2,458,756	1,112,078	Nixon, Richard M.	1,332,540	McGovern, George S.	14,138	220,462 D	45.2%	54.2%	45.5%	54.5%
1968	2,331,752	766,844	Nixon, Richard M.	1,469,218	Humphrey, Hubert H.	95,690	702,374 D	32.9%	63.0%	34.3%	65.7%
1964	2,344,798	549,727	Goldwater, Barry M.	1,786,422	Johnson, Lyndon B.	8,649	1,236,695 D	23.4%	76.2%	23.5%	76.5%
1960	2,469,480	976,750	Nixon, Richard M.	1,487,174	Kennedy, John F.	5,556	510,424 D	39.6%	60.2%	39.6%	60.4%
1956	2,348,506	1,393,197	Eisenhower, Dwight D.	948,190	Stevenson, Adlai E.	7,119	445,007 R	59.3%	40.4%	59.5%	40.5%
1952	2,383,398	1,292,325	Eisenhower, Dwight D.	1,083,525	Stevenson, Adlai E.	7,548	208,800 R	54.2%	45.5%	54.4%	45.6%
1948	2,107,146	909,370	Dewey, Thomas E.	1,151,788	Truman, Harry S.	45,988	242,418 D	43.2%	54.7%	44.1%	55.9%

MASSACHUSETTS

POSTWAR VOTE FOR GOVERNOR

Year	Total Vote	Republican Vote	Candidate	Democratic Vote	Candidate	Other Vote	Rep-Dem. Plurality	Percentage Total Vote Rep.	Dem.	Major Vote Rep.	Dem.
1990	2,342,927	1,175,817	Weld, William F.	1,099,878	Silber, John	67,232	75,939 R	50.2%	46.9%	51.7%	48.3%
1986	1,684,079	525,364	Kariotis, George	1,157,786	Dukakis, Michael S.	929	632,422 D	31.2%	68.7%	31.2%	68.8%
1982	2,050,254	749,679	Sears, John W.	1,219,109	Dukakis, Michael S.	81,466	469,430 D	36.6%	59.5%	38.1%	61.9%
1978	1,962,251	926,072	Hatch, Francis W.	1,030,294	King, Edward J.	5,885	104,222 D	47.2%	52.5%	47.3%	52.7%
1974	1,854,798	784,353	Sargent, Francis W.	992,284	Dukakis, Michael S.	78,161	207,931 D	42.3%	53.5%	44.1%	55.9%
1970	1,867,906	1,058,623	Sargent, Francis W.	799,269	White, Kevin H.	10,014	259,354 R	56.7%	42.8%	57.0%	43.0%
1966 **	2,041,177	1,277,358	Volpe, John A.	752,720	McCormack, Edward J.	11,099	524,638 R	62.6%	36.9%	62.9%	37.1%
1964	2,340,130	1,176,462	Volpe, John A.	1,153,416	Bellotti, Francis X.	10,252	23,046 R	50.3%	49.3%	50.5%	49.5%
1962	2,109,089	1,047,891	Volpe, John A.	1,053,322	Peabody, Endicott	7,876	5,431 D	49.7%	49.9%	49.9%	50.1%
1960	2,417,133	1,269,295	Volpe, John A.	1,130,810	Ward, Joseph D.	17,028	138,485 R	52.5%	46.8%	52.9%	47.1%
1958	1,899,117	818,463	Gibbons, Charles	1,067,020	Furcolo, Foster	13,634	248,557 D	43.1%	56.2%	43.4%	56.6%
1956	2,339,884	1,096,759	Whittier, Sumner G.	1,234,618	Furcolo, Foster	8,507	137,859 D	46.9%	52.8%	47.0%	53.0%
1954	1,903,774	985,339	Herter, Christian A.	910,087	Murphy, Robert F.	8,348	75,252 R	51.8%	47.8%	52.0%	48.0%
1952	2,356,298	1,175,955	Herter, Christian A.	1,161,499	Dever, Paul A.	18,844	14,456 R	49.9%	49.3%	50.3%	49.7%
1950	1,910,180	824,069	Coolidge, Arthur W.	1,074,570	Dever, Paul A.	11,541	250,501 D	43.1%	56.3%	43.4%	56.6%
1948	2,099,250	849,895	Bradford, Robert F.	1,239,247	Dever, Paul A.	10,108	389,352 D	40.5%	59.0%	40.7%	59.3%
1946	1,683,452	911,152	Bradford, Robert F.	762,743	Tobin, Maurice	9,557	148,409 R	54.1%	45.3%	54.4%	45.6%

The term of office of Massachusetts' Governor was increased from two to four years effective with the 1966 election.

POSTWAR VOTE FOR SENATOR

Year	Total Vote	Republican Vote	Candidate	Democratic Vote	Candidate	Other Vote	Rep-Dem. Plurality	Percentage Total Vote Rep.	Dem.	Major Vote Rep.	Dem.
1990	2,316,212	992,917	Rappaport, Jim	1,321,712	Kerry, John F.	1,583	328,795 D	42.9%	57.1%	42.9%	57.1%
1988	2,606,225	884,267	Malone, Joseph	1,693,344	Kennedy, Edward M.	28,614	809,077 D	33.9%	65.0%	34.3%	65.7%
1984	2,530,195	1,136,806	Shamie, Raymond	1,392,981	Kerry, John F.	408	256,175 D	44.9%	55.1%	44.9%	55.1%
1982	2,050,769	784,602	Shamie, Raymond	1,247,084	Kennedy, Edward M.	19,083	462,482 D	38.3%	60.8%	38.6%	61.4%
1978	1,985,700	890,584	Brooke, Edward W.	1,093,283	Tsongas, Paul E.	1,833	202,699 D	44.8%	55.1%	44.9%	55.1%
1976	2,491,255	722,641	Robertson, Michael	1,726,657	Kennedy, Edward M.	41,957	1,004,016 D	29.0%	69.3%	29.5%	70.5%
1972	2,370,676	1,505,932	Brooke, Edward W.	823,278	Droney, John J.	41,466	682,654 R	63.5%	34.7%	64.7%	35.3%
1970	1,935,607	715,978	Spaulding, Josiah A.	1,202,856	Kennedy, Edward M.	16,773	486,878 D	37.0%	62.1%	37.3%	62.7%
1966	1,999,949	1,213,473	Brooke, Edward W.	774,761	Peabody, Endicott	11,715	438,712 R	60.7%	38.7%	61.0%	39.0%
1964	2,312,028	587,663	Whitmore, Howard	1,716,907	Kennedy, Edward M.	7,458	1,129,244 D	25.4%	74.3%	25.5%	74.5%
1962 S	2,097,085	877,669	Lodge, George C.	1,162,611	Kennedy, Edward M.	56,805	284,942 D	41.9%	55.4%	43.0%	57.0%
1960	2,417,813	1,358,556	Saltonstall, Leverett	1,050,725	O'Connor, Thomas J.	8,532	307,831 R	56.2%	43.5%	56.4%	43.6%
1958	1,862,041	488,318	Celeste, Vincent J.	1,362,926	Kennedy, John F.	10,797	874,608 D	26.2%	73.2%	26.4%	73.6%
1954	1,892,710	956,605	Saltonstall, Leverett	927,899	Furcolo, Foster	8,206	28,706 R	50.5%	49.0%	50.8%	49.2%
1952	2,360,425	1,141,247	Lodge, Henry Cabot	1,211,984	Kennedy, John F.	7,194	70,737 D	48.3%	51.3%	48.5%	51.5%
1948	2,055,798	1,088,475	Saltonstall, Leverett	954,398	Fitzgerald, John I.	12,925	134,077 R	52.9%	46.4%	53.3%	46.7%
1946	1,662,063	989,736	Lodge, Henry Cabot	660,200	Walsh, David I.	12,127	329,536 R	59.5%	39.7%	60.0%	40.0%

The 1962 election was for a short term to fill a vacancy.

MASSACHUSETTS

Districts Established December 3, 1981

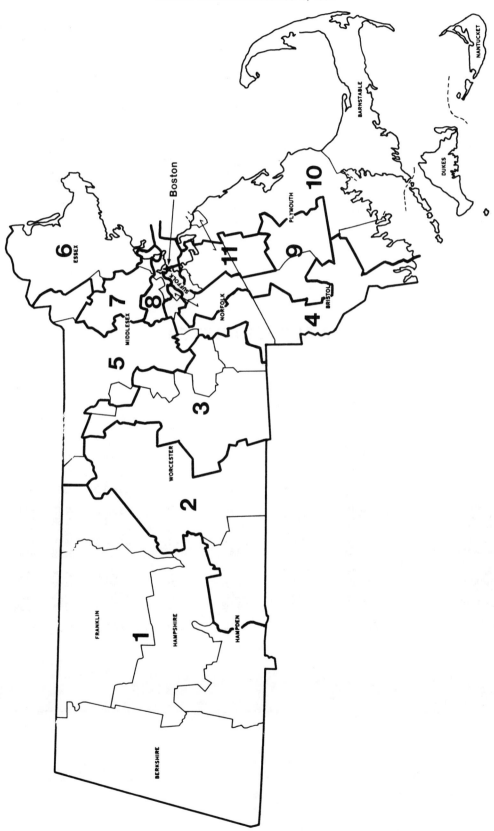

© ERC

MASSACHUSETTS

GOVERNOR 1990

1990 Census Population	County	Total Vote	Republican	Democratic	Other	Rep.-Dem. Plurality	Percentage Total Vote Rep.	Dem.	Major Vote Rep.	Dem.
186,605	BARNSTABLE	90,876	50,911	37,474	2,491	13,437 R	56.0%	41.2%	57.6%	42.4%
139,352	BERKSHIRE	50,930	23,562	24,953	2,415	1,391 D	46.3%	49.0%	48.6%	51.4%
506,325	BRISTOL	174,516	71,420	97,046	6,050	25,626 D	40.9%	55.6%	42.4%	57.6%
11,639	DUKES	5,526	2,559	2,720	247	161 D	46.3%	49.2%	48.5%	51.5%
670,080	ESSEX	276,893	144,583	125,734	6,576	18,849 R	52.2%	45.4%	53.5%	46.5%
70,092	FRANKLIN	28,372	15,101	11,822	1,449	3,279 R	53.2%	41.7%	56.1%	43.9%
456,310	HAMPDEN	146,125	67,360	73,356	5,409	5,996 D	46.1%	50.2%	47.9%	52.1%
146,568	HAMPSHIRE	52,358	26,626	23,495	2,237	3,131 R	50.9%	44.9%	53.1%	46.9%
1,398,468	MIDDLESEX	596,682	320,188	259,059	17,435	61,129 R	53.7%	43.4%	55.3%	44.7%
6,012	NANTUCKET	2,717	1,466	1,166	85	300 R	54.0%	42.9%	55.7%	44.3%
616,087	NORFOLK	288,674	149,521	132,141	7,012	17,380 R	51.8%	45.8%	53.1%	46.9%
435,276	PLYMOUTH	178,838	95,137	79,039	4,662	16,098 R	53.2%	44.2%	54.6%	45.4%
663,906	SUFFOLK	184,415	77,119	102,392	4,904	25,273 D	41.8%	55.5%	43.0%	57.0%
709,705	WORCESTER	266,005	130,264	129,481	6,260	783 R	49.0%	48.7%	50.2%	49.8%
6,016,425	TOTAL	2,342,927	1,175,817	1,099,878	67,232	75,939 R	50.2%	46.9%	51.7%	48.3%

MASSACHUSETTS

SENATOR 1990

1990 Census Population	County	Total Vote	Republican	Democratic	Other	Rep.-Dem. Plurality	Percentage Total Vote Rep.	Dem.	Major Vote Rep.	Dem.
186,605	BARNSTABLE	89,854	42,952	46,884	18	3,932 D	47.8%	52.2%	47.8%	52.2%
139,352	BERKSHIRE	51,191	22,839	28,308	44	5,469 D	44.6%	55.3%	44.7%	55.3%
506,325	BRISTOL	173,508	76,140	97,274	94	21,134 D	43.9%	56.1%	43.9%	56.1%
11,639	DUKES	5,658	2,054	3,597	7	1,543 D	36.3%	63.6%	36.3%	63.7%
670,080	ESSEX	272,488	123,300	148,915	273	25,615 D	45.2%	54.7%	45.3%	54.7%
70,092	FRANKLIN	28,972	12,671	16,223	78	3,552 D	43.7%	56.0%	43.9%	56.1%
456,310	HAMPDEN	145,475	70,493	74,905	77	4,412 D	48.5%	51.5%	48.5%	51.5%
146,568	HAMPSHIRE	54,646	22,951	31,650	45	8,699 D	42.0%	57.9%	42.0%	58.0%
1,398,468	MIDDLESEX	589,815	232,438	356,898	479	124,460 D	39.4%	60.5%	39.4%	60.6%
6,012	NANTUCKET	2,729	1,053	1,676		623 D	38.6%	61.4%	38.6%	61.4%
616,087	NORFOLK	283,266	117,525	165,486	255	47,961 D	41.5%	58.4%	41.5%	58.5%
435,276	PLYMOUTH	175,827	87,737	88,019	71	282 D	49.9%	50.1%	49.9%	50.1%
663,906	SUFFOLK	180,427	54,959	125,458	10	70,499 D	30.5%	69.5%	30.5%	69.5%
709,705	WORCESTER	262,356	125,805	136,419	132	10,614 D	48.0%	52.0%	48.0%	52.0%
6,016,425	TOTAL	2,316,212	992,917	1,321,712	1,583	328,795 D	42.9%	57.1%	42.9%	57.1%

MASSACHUSETTS

GOVERNOR 1990

1990 Census Population	City/Town	Total Vote	Republican	Democratic	Other	Rep.-Dem. Plurality	Percentage Total Vote Rep.	Dem.	Percentage Major Vote Rep.	Dem.
27,323	AGAWAM	9,998	5,003	4,598	397	405 R	50.0%	46.0%	52.1%	47.9%
35,228	AMHERST	8,127	4,201	3,572	354	629 R	51.7%	44.0%	54.0%	46.0%
29,151	ANDOVER	14,354	8,608	5,500	246	3,108 R	60.0%	38.3%	61.0%	39.0%
44,630	ARLINGTON	23,181	11,881	10,556	744	1,325 R	51.3%	45.5%	53.0%	47.0%
38,383	ATTLEBORO	12,269	6,321	5,486	462	835 R	51.5%	44.7%	53.5%	46.5%
40,949	BARNSTABLE TOWN	18,397	10,041	7,920	436	2,121 R	54.6%	43.1%	55.9%	44.1%
24,720	BELMONT	13,310	7,512	5,507	291	2,005 R	56.4%	41.4%	57.7%	42.3%
38,195	BEVERLY	17,064	9,527	7,068	469	2,459 R	55.8%	41.4%	57.4%	42.6%
37,609	BILLERICA	14,719	8,100	6,146	473	1,954 R	55.0%	41.8%	56.9%	43.1%
574,283	BOSTON	151,441	63,109	84,235	4,097	21,126 D	41.7%	55.6%	42.8%	57.2%
33,836	BRAINTREE	16,880	8,376	8,137	367	239 R	49.6%	48.2%	50.7%	49.3%
21,249	BRIDGEWATER	7,153	3,790	3,169	194	621 R	53.0%	44.3%	54.5%	45.5%
92,788	BROCKTON	27,497	13,256	13,486	755	230 D	48.2%	49.0%	49.6%	50.4%
54,718	BROOKLINE	23,179	12,483	10,190	506	2,293 R	53.9%	44.0%	55.1%	44.9%
23,302	BURLINGTON	11,058	5,906	4,824	328	1,082 R	53.4%	43.6%	55.0%	45.0%
95,802	CAMBRIDGE	32,486	17,581	13,573	1,332	4,008 R	54.1%	41.8%	56.4%	43.6%
32,383	CHELMSFORD	15,641	9,012	6,202	427	2,810 R	57.6%	39.7%	59.2%	40.8%
28,710	CHELSEA	7,434	2,775	4,470	189	1,695 D	37.3%	60.1%	38.3%	61.7%
56,632	CHICOPEE	19,340	7,777	10,766	797	2,989 D	40.2%	55.7%	41.9%	58.1%
24,174	DANVERS	11,559	6,257	5,011	291	1,246 R	54.1%	43.4%	55.5%	44.5%
27,244	DARTMOUTH	10,207	4,283	5,562	362	1,279 D	42.0%	54.5%	43.5%	56.5%
23,782	DEDHAM	12,011	5,911	5,841	259	70 R	49.2%	48.6%	50.3%	49.7%
25,594	DRACUT	10,890	5,298	5,219	373	79 R	48.7%	47.9%	50.4%	49.6%
35,701	EVERETT	14,300	6,204	7,711	385	1,507 D	43.4%	53.9%	44.6%	55.4%
92,703	FALL RIVER	25,642	6,614	18,283	745	11,669 D	25.8%	71.3%	26.6%	73.4%
27,960	FALMOUTH	13,266	6,761	6,156	349	605 R	51.0%	46.4%	52.3%	47.7%
41,194	FITCHBURG	12,707	5,413	6,930	364	1,517 D	42.6%	54.5%	43.9%	56.1%
64,989	FRAMINGHAM	26,163	13,708	11,732	723	1,976 R	52.4%	44.8%	53.9%	46.1%
22,095	FRANKLIN	9,054	4,793	3,998	263	795 R	52.9%	44.2%	54.5%	45.5%
20,125	GARDNER	7,272	3,164	3,911	197	747 D	43.5%	53.8%	44.7%	55.3%
28,716	GLOUCESTER	11,799	6,214	5,316	269	898 R	52.7%	45.1%	53.9%	46.1%
51,418	HAVERHILL	19,191	9,658	9,027	506	631 R	50.3%	47.0%	51.7%	48.3%
43,704	HOLYOKE	12,512	4,595	7,487	430	2,892 D	36.7%	59.8%	38.0%	62.0%
70,207	LAWRENCE	14,937	6,227	8,334	376	2,107 D	41.7%	55.8%	42.8%	57.2%
38,145	LEOMINSTER	14,375	6,936	7,039	400	103 D	48.3%	49.0%	49.6%	50.4%
28,974	LEXINGTON	15,065	8,920	5,778	367	3,142 R	59.2%	38.4%	60.7%	39.3%
103,439	LOWELL	28,232	12,142	15,100	990	2,958 D	43.0%	53.5%	44.6%	55.4%
81,245	LYNN	27,403	11,367	15,277	759	3,910 D	41.5%	55.7%	42.7%	57.3%
53,884	MALDEN	20,633	9,247	10,782	604	1,535 D	44.8%	52.3%	46.2%	53.8%
31,813	MARLBOROUGH	13,040	7,515	5,100	425	2,415 R	57.6%	39.1%	59.6%	40.4%
21,531	MARSHFIELD	10,356	5,307	4,826	223	481 R	51.2%	46.6%	52.4%	47.6%
57,407	MEDFORD	25,024	11,763	12,595	666	832 D	47.0%	50.3%	48.3%	51.7%
28,150	MELROSE	14,439	7,518	6,557	364	961 R	52.1%	45.4%	53.4%	46.6%
39,990	METHUEN	16,669	8,117	8,149	403	32 D	48.7%	48.9%	49.9%	50.1%
25,355	MILFORD	9,911	4,895	4,766	250	129 R	49.4%	48.1%	50.7%	49.3%
25,725	MILTON	14,104	6,353	7,477	274	1,124 D	45.0%	53.0%	45.9%	54.1%
30,510	NATICK	14,789	8,034	6,368	387	1,666 R	54.3%	43.1%	55.8%	44.2%
27,557	NEEDHAM	15,492	8,866	6,290	336	2,576 R	57.2%	40.6%	58.5%	41.5%
99,922	NEW BEDFORD	29,318	9,452	18,486	1,380	9,034 D	32.2%	63.1%	33.8%	66.2%
82,585	NEWTON	38,645	21,764	16,104	777	5,660 R	56.3%	41.7%	57.5%	42.5%
29,289	NORTHAMPTON	10,794	5,637	4,748	409	889 R	52.2%	44.0%	54.3%	45.7%
22,792	NORTH ANDOVER	10,693	5,914	4,561	218	1,353 R	55.3%	42.7%	56.5%	43.5%
25,038	NORTH ATTLEBOROUGH	8,326	4,647	3,366	313	1,281 R	55.8%	40.4%	58.0%	42.0%
28,700	NORWOOD	13,245	6,278	6,639	328	361 D	47.4%	50.1%	48.6%	51.4%
47,039	PEABODY	21,383	10,031	10,863	489	832 D	46.9%	50.8%	48.0%	52.0%
48,622	PITTSFIELD	17,275	7,444	8,989	842	1,545 D	43.1%	52.0%	45.3%	54.7%
45,608	PLYMOUTH TOWN	17,284	9,178	7,621	485	1,557 R	53.1%	44.1%	54.6%	45.4%
84,985	QUINCY	36,263	16,606	18,629	1,028	2,023 D	45.8%	51.4%	47.1%	52.9%
30,093	RANDOLPH	13,061	6,449	6,280	332	169 R	49.4%	48.1%	50.7%	49.3%
22,539	READING	12,208	6,961	4,960	287	2,001 R	57.0%	40.6%	58.4%	41.6%

MASSACHUSETTS

GOVERNOR 1990

1990 Census Population	City/Town	Total Vote	Republican	Democratic	Other	Rep.-Dem. Plurality	Percentage			
							Total Vote		Major Vote	
							Rep.	Dem.	Rep.	Dem.
42,786	REVERE	17,019	7,265	9,348	406	2,083 D	42.7%	54.9%	43.7%	56.3%
38,091	SALEM	15,634	7,130	8,068	436	938 D	45.6%	51.6%	46.9%	53.1%
25,549	SAUGUS	10,726	5,413	5,040	273	373 R	50.5%	47.0%	51.8%	48.2%
24,146	SHREWSBURY	11,165	5,829	5,131	205	698 R	52.2%	46.0%	53.2%	46.8%
76,210	SOMERVILLE	26,263	12,016	12,801	1,446	785 D	45.8%	48.7%	48.4%	51.6%
156,983	SPRINGFIELD	37,882	15,869	20,491	1,522	4,622 D	41.9%	54.1%	43.6%	56.4%
22,203	STONEHAM	10,143	5,255	4,615	273	640 R	51.8%	45.5%	53.2%	46.8%
26,777	STOUGHTON	11,335	5,809	5,231	295	578 R	51.2%	46.1%	52.6%	47.4%
49,832	TAUNTON	16,138	6,888	8,759	491	1,871 D	42.7%	54.3%	44.0%	56.0%
27,266	TEWKSBURY	11,908	6,263	5,271	374	992 R	52.6%	44.3%	54.3%	45.7%
24,825	WAKEFIELD	12,674	6,775	5,612	287	1,163 R	53.5%	44.3%	54.7%	45.3%
20,212	WALPOLE	9,892	5,250	4,415	227	835 R	53.1%	44.6%	54.3%	45.7%
57,878	WALTHAM	20,751	10,519	9,447	785	1,072 R	50.7%	45.5%	52.7%	47.3%
33,284	WATERTOWN	14,842	7,535	6,925	382	610 R	50.8%	46.7%	52.1%	47.9%
26,615	WELLESLEY	12,815	7,876	4,742	197	3,134 R	61.5%	37.0%	62.4%	37.6%
27,537	WEST SPRINGFIELD	9,930	4,822	4,764	344	58 R	48.6%	48.0%	50.3%	49.7%
38,372	WESTFIELD	13,566	6,876	6,148	542	728 R	50.7%	45.3%	52.8%	47.2%
54,063	WEYMOUTH	24,733	11,983	12,038	712	55 D	48.4%	48.7%	49.9%	50.1%
20,267	WINCHESTER	10,914	6,211	4,513	190	1,698 R	56.9%	41.4%	57.9%	42.1%
35,943	WOBURN	16,116	7,800	7,819	497	19 D	48.4%	48.5%	49.9%	50.1%
169,759	WORCESTER CITY	51,795	21,124	29,659	1,012	8,535 D	40.8%	57.3%	41.6%	58.4%
21,174	YARMOUTH	10,685	6,100	4,322	263	1,778 R	57.1%	40.4%	58.5%	41.5%

MASSACHUSETTS

SENATOR 1990

1990 Census Population	City/Town	Total Vote	Republican	Democratic	Other	Rep.-Dem. Plurality	Total Vote Rep.	Dem.	Major Vote Rep.	Dem.
27,323	AGAWAM	9,968	5,231	4,736	1	495 R	52.5%	47.5%	52.5%	47.5%
35,228	AMHERST	9,083	2,216	6,859	8	4,643 D	24.4%	75.5%	24.4%	75.6%
29,151	ANDOVER	14,188	7,217	6,971		246 R	50.9%	49.1%	50.9%	49.1%
44,630	ARLINGTON	22,922	7,539	15,377	6	7,838 D	32.9%	67.1%	32.9%	67.1%
38,383	ATTLEBORO	12,157	6,502	5,655		847 R	53.5%	46.5%	53.5%	46.5%
40,949	BARNSTABLE TOWN	18,029	8,577	9,452		875 D	47.6%	52.4%	47.6%	52.4%
24,720	BELMONT	13,091	4,908	8,183		3,275 D	37.5%	62.5%	37.5%	62.5%
38,195	BEVERLY	16,838	7,663	9,175		1,512 D	45.5%	54.5%	45.5%	54.5%
37,609	BILLERICA	14,479	7,177	7,302		125 D	49.6%	50.4%	49.6%	50.4%
574,283	BOSTON	148,196	42,808	105,381	7	62,573 D	28.9%	71.1%	28.9%	71.1%
33,836	BRAINTREE	16,521	7,505	9,012	4	1,507 D	45.4%	54.5%	45.4%	54.6%
21,249	BRIDGEWATER	7,065	3,826	3,234	5	592 R	54.2%	45.8%	54.2%	45.8%
92,788	BROCKTON	26,851	12,908	13,940	3	1,032 D	48.1%	51.9%	48.1%	51.9%
54,718	BROOKLINE	23,401	5,305	18,092	4	12,787 D	22.7%	77.3%	22.7%	77.3%
23,302	BURLINGTON	10,836	4,912	5,919	5	1,007 D	45.3%	54.6%	45.4%	54.6%
95,802	CAMBRIDGE	33,238	6,394	26,833	11	20,439 D	19.2%	80.7%	19.2%	80.8%
32,383	CHELMSFORD	15,418	7,891	7,448	79	443 R	51.2%	48.3%	51.4%	48.6%
28,710	CHELSEA	7,326	2,457	4,869		2,412 D	33.5%	66.5%	33.5%	66.5%
56,632	CHICOPEE	19,369	8,987	10,335	47	1,348 D	46.4%	53.4%	46.5%	53.5%
24,174	DANVERS	11,350	5,416	5,932	2	516 D	47.7%	52.3%	47.7%	52.3%
27,244	DARTMOUTH	10,274	4,407	5,866	1	1,459 D	42.9%	57.1%	42.9%	57.1%
23,782	DEDHAM	11,620	4,905	6,715		1,810 D	42.2%	57.8%	42.2%	57.8%
25,594	DRACUT	10,667	5,503	5,142	22	361 R	51.6%	48.2%	51.7%	48.3%
35,701	EVERETT	14,038	5,469	8,569		3,100 D	39.0%	61.0%	39.0%	61.0%
92,703	FALL RIVER	25,416	8,861	16,552	3	7,691 D	34.9%	65.1%	34.9%	65.1%
27,960	FALMOUTH	13,155	5,448	7,703	4	2,255 D	41.4%	58.6%	41.4%	58.6%
41,194	FITCHBURG	12,525	5,602	6,923		1,321 D	44.7%	55.3%	44.7%	55.3%
64,989	FRAMINGHAM	25,847	9,879	15,961	7	6,082 D	38.2%	61.8%	38.2%	61.8%
22,095	FRANKLIN	8,952	3,958	4,992	2	1,034 D	44.2%	55.8%	44.2%	55.8%
20,125	GARDNER	7,253	3,169	4,084		915 D	43.7%	56.3%	43.7%	56.3%
28,716	GLOUCESTER	11,729	4,832	6,897		2,065 D	41.2%	58.8%	41.2%	58.8%
51,418	HAVERHILL	18,941	8,449	10,459	33	2,010 D	44.6%	55.2%	44.7%	55.3%
43,704	HOLYOKE	12,406	5,560	6,845	1	1,285 D	44.8%	55.2%	44.8%	55.2%
70,207	LAWRENCE	14,756	6,705	8,047	4	1,342 D	45.4%	54.5%	45.5%	54.5%
38,145	LEOMINSTER	14,218	7,047	7,168	3	121 D	49.6%	50.4%	49.6%	50.4%
28,974	LEXINGTON	14,920	5,300	9,616	4	4,316 D	35.5%	64.5%	35.5%	64.5%
103,439	LOWELL	27,797	12,188	15,608	1	3,420 D	43.8%	56.1%	43.8%	56.2%
81,245	LYNN	26,416	10,740	15,674	2	4,934 D	40.7%	59.3%	40.7%	59.3%
53,884	MALDEN	20,302	7,315	12,984	3	5,669 D	36.0%	64.0%	36.0%	64.0%
31,813	MARLBOROUGH	12,806	5,910	6,883	13	973 D	46.2%	53.7%	46.2%	53.8%
21,531	MARSHFIELD	10,204	4,697	5,507		810 D	46.0%	54.0%	46.0%	54.0%
57,407	MEDFORD	24,682	9,041	15,641		6,600 D	36.6%	63.4%	36.6%	63.4%
28,150	MELROSE	14,153	5,815	8,338		2,523 D	41.1%	58.9%	41.1%	58.9%
39,990	METHUEN	16,500	8,606	7,894		712 R	52.2%	47.8%	52.2%	47.8%
25,355	MILFORD	9,781	4,417	5,364		947 D	45.2%	54.8%	45.2%	54.8%
25,725	MILTON	13,731	5,360	8,370	1	3,010 D	39.0%	61.0%	39.0%	61.0%
30,510	NATICK	14,683	5,687	8,996		3,309 D	38.7%	61.3%	38.7%	61.3%
27,557	NEEDHAM	15,218	6,072	9,142	4	3,070 D	39.9%	60.1%	39.9%	60.1%
99,922	NEW BEDFORD	29,346	9,635	19,702	9	10,067 D	32.8%	67.1%	32.8%	67.2%
82,585	NEWTON	38,622	10,581	28,041		17,460 D	27.4%	72.6%	27.4%	72.6%
29,289	NORTHAMPTON	11,795	4,147	7,641	7	3,494 D	35.2%	64.8%	35.2%	64.8%
22,792	NORTH ANDOVER	10,462	5,340	5,122		218 R	51.0%	49.0%	51.0%	49.0%
25,038	NORTH ATTLEBOROUGH	8,154	4,513	3,641		872 R	55.3%	44.7%	55.3%	44.7%
28,700	NORWOOD	12,941	5,243	7,695	3	2,452 D	40.5%	59.5%	40.5%	59.5%
47,039	PEABODY	21,132	8,496	12,500	136	4,004 D	40.2%	59.2%	40.5%	59.5%
48,622	PITTSFIELD	17,329	7,348	9,981		2,633 D	42.4%	57.6%	42.4%	57.6%
45,608	PLYMOUTH TOWN	17,007	8,046	8,959	2	913 D	47.3%	52.7%	47.3%	52.7%
84,985	QUINCY	35,425	14,426	20,999		6,573 D	40.7%	59.3%	40.7%	59.3%
30,093	RANDOLPH	12,922	4,877	7,991	54	3,114 D	37.7%	61.8%	37.9%	62.1%
22,539	READING	11,950	5,486	6,459	5	973 D	45.9%	54.1%	45.9%	54.1%

MASSACHUSETTS

SENATOR 1990

1990 Census Population	City/Town	Total Vote	Republican	Democratic	Other	Rep.-Dem. Plurality	Percentage			
							Total Vote		Major Vote	
							Rep.	Dem.	Rep.	Dem.
42,786	REVERE	16,574	6,459	10,112	3	3,653 D	39.0%	61.0%	39.0%	61.0%
38,091	SALEM	15,396	5,518	9,875	3	4,357 D	35.8%	64.1%	35.8%	64.2%
25,549	SAUGUS	10,553	4,603	5,949	1	1,346 D	43.6%	56.4%	43.6%	56.4%
24,146	SHREWSBURY	10,932	5,280	5,651	1	371 D	48.3%	51.7%	48.3%	51.7%
76,210	SOMERVILLE	26,153	7,169	18,805	179	11,636 D	27.4%	71.9%	27.6%	72.4%
156,983	SPRINGFIELD	37,751	15,804	21,944	3	6,140 D	41.9%	58.1%	41.9%	58.1%
22,203	STONEHAM	9,852	4,188	5,663	1	1,475 D	42.5%	57.5%	42.5%	57.5%
26,777	STOUGHTON	11,107	4,644	6,448	15	1,804 D	41.8%	58.1%	41.9%	58.1%
49,832	TAUNTON	15,854	7,170	8,684		1,514 D	45.2%	54.8%	45.2%	54.8%
27,266	TEWKSBURY	11,772	5,699	6,040	33	341 D	48.4%	51.3%	48.5%	51.5%
24,825	WAKEFIELD	12,407	5,339	7,063	5	1,724 D	43.0%	56.9%	43.0%	57.0%
20,212	WALPOLE	9,635	4,576	5,056	3	480 D	47.5%	52.5%	47.5%	52.5%
57,878	WALTHAM	20,313	8,133	12,179	1	4,046 D	40.0%	60.0%	40.0%	60.0%
33,284	WATERTOWN	14,864	4,652	10,212		5,560 D	31.3%	68.7%	31.3%	68.7%
26,615	WELLESLEY	12,569	5,201	7,365	3	2,164 D	41.4%	58.6%	41.4%	58.6%
27,537	WEST SPRINGFIELD	9,879	5,175	4,704		471 R	52.4%	47.6%	52.4%	47.6%
38,372	WESTFIELD	13,523	7,116	6,400	7	716 R	52.6%	47.3%	52.6%	47.4%
54,063	WEYMOUTH	23,939	10,542	13,395	2	2,853 D	44.0%	56.0%	44.0%	56.0%
20,267	WINCHESTER	10,722	4,506	6,215	1	1,709 D	42.0%	58.0%	42.0%	58.0%
35,943	WOBURN	15,814	6,662	9,152		2,490 D	42.1%	57.9%	42.1%	57.9%
169,759	WORCESTER CITY	51,166	19,871	31,294	1	11,423 D	38.8%	61.2%	38.8%	61.2%
21,174	YARMOUTH	10,481	5,330	5,151		179 R	50.9%	49.1%	50.9%	49.1%

MASSACHUSETTS

CONGRESS

CD	Year	Total Vote	Republican Vote	Republican Candidate	Democratic Vote	Democratic Candidate	Other Vote	Rep.-Dem. Plurality	Total Vote Rep.	Total Vote Dem.	Major Vote Rep.	Major Vote Dem.
1	1990	194,504	150,748	CONTE, SILVIO O.	43,611	ARDEN, JOHN R.	145	107,137 R	77.5%	22.4%	77.6%	22.4%
1	1988	225,291	186,356	CONTE, SILVIO O.	38,907	ARDEN, JOHN R.	28	147,449 R	82.7%	17.3%	82.7%	17.3%
1	1986	146,090	113,653	CONTE, SILVIO O.	32,396	WEINER, ROBERT S.	41	81,257 R	77.8%	22.2%	77.8%	22.2%
1	1984	223,037	162,646	CONTE, SILVIO O.	60,372	WENTWORTH, MARY L.	19	102,274 R	72.9%	27.1%	72.9%	27.1%
1	1982	146,197	145,417	* CONTE, SILVIO O.			780	145,417 R	99.5%		100.0%	
2	1990	134,429			134,152	NEAL, RICHARD E.	277	134,152 D		99.8%		100.0%
2	1988	194,760			156,262	NEAL, RICHARD E.	38,498	156,262 D		80.2%		100.0%
2	1986	138,062	47,022	LEES, BRIAN P.	91,033	BOLAND, EDWARD P.	7	44,011 D	34.1%	65.9%	34.1%	65.9%
2	1984	193,254	60,463	SWANK, THOMAS P.	132,693	BOLAND, EDWARD P.	98	72,230 D	31.3%	68.7%	31.3%	68.7%
2	1982	162,773	44,544	SWANK, THOMAS P.	118,215	BOLAND, EDWARD P.	14	73,671 D	27.4%	72.6%	27.4%	72.6%
3	1990	151,910			150,992	EARLY, JOSEPH D.	918	150,992 D		99.4%		100.0%
3	1988	191,387			191,009	EARLY, JOSEPH D.	378	191,009 D		99.8%		100.0%
3	1986	120,279			120,222	EARLY, JOSEPH D.	57	120,222 D		100.0%		100.0%
3	1984	220,254	71,765	REDDING, KENNETH J.	148,461	EARLY, JOSEPH D.	28	76,696 D	32.6%	67.4%	32.6%	67.4%
3	1982	142,740			142,611	EARLY, JOSEPH D.	129	142,611 D		99.9%		100.0%
4	1990	218,969	75,454	SOTO, JOHN R.	143,473	FRANK, BARNEY	42	68,019 D	34.5%	65.5%	34.5%	65.5%
4	1988	241,414	71,661	TUCKER, DEBRA R.	169,729	FRANK, BARNEY	24	98,068 D	29.7%	70.3%	29.7%	70.3%
4	1986	151,265			134,387	FRANK, BARNEY	16,878	134,387 D		88.8%		100.0%
4	1984	233,032	60,121	FORTE, JIM	172,903	FRANK, BARNEY	8	112,782 D	25.8%	74.2%	25.8%	74.2%
4	1982	204,615	82,804	HECKLER, MARGARET M.	121,802	FRANK, BARNEY	9	38,998 D	40.5%	59.5%	40.5%	59.5%
5	1990	211,334	101,017	MACGOVERN, JOHN F.	110,232	ATKINS, CHESTER G.	85	9,215 D	47.8%	52.2%	47.8%	52.2%
5	1988	216,290			181,877	ATKINS, CHESTER G.	34,413	181,877 D		84.1%		100.0%
5	1986	113,747			113,690	ATKINS, CHESTER G.	57	113,690 D		99.9%		100.0%
5	1984	224,927	104,912	HYATT, GREGORY S.	120,008	ATKINS, CHESTER G.	7	15,096 D	46.6%	53.4%	46.6%	53.4%
5	1982	165,598			140,177	SHANNON, JAMES M.	25,421	140,177 D		84.6%		100.0%
6	1990	229,546	80,177	KELLEY, EDGAR L.	149,284	MAVROULES, NICHOLAS	85	69,107 D	34.9%	65.0%	34.9%	65.1%
6	1988	255,067	77,186	MCCARTHY, PAUL	177,643	MAVROULES, NICHOLAS	238	100,457 D	30.3%	69.6%	30.3%	69.7%
6	1986	131,137			131,051	MAVROULES, NICHOLAS	86	131,051 D		99.9%		100.0%
6	1984	239,649	63,363	LEBER, FREDERICK S.	168,662	MAVROULES, NICHOLAS	7,624	105,299 D	26.4%	70.4%	27.3%	72.7%
6	1982	203,584	85,849	TRIMARCO, THOMAS H.	117,723	MAVROULES, NICHOLAS	12	31,874 D	42.2%	57.8%	42.2%	57.8%
7	1990	155,509			155,380	MARKEY, EDWARD J.	129	155,380 D		99.9%		100.0%
7	1988	188,710			188,647	MARKEY, EDWARD J.	63	188,647 D		100.0%		100.0%
7	1986	124,245			124,183	MARKEY, EDWARD J.	62	124,183 D		100.0%		100.0%
7	1984	234,190	66,930	RALPH, S. LESTER	167,211	MARKEY, EDWARD J.	49	100,281 D	28.6%	71.4%	28.6%	71.4%
7	1982	194,369	43,063	BASILE, DAVID M.	151,305	MARKEY, EDWARD J.	1	108,242 D	22.2%	77.8%	22.2%	77.8%
8	1990	173,689	39,310	FISCUS, GLENN W.	125,479	KENNEDY, JOSEPH P.	8,900	86,169 D	22.6%	72.2%	23.9%	76.1%
8	1988	206,189	40,316	FISCUS, GLENN W.	165,745	KENNEDY, JOSEPH P.	128	125,429 D	19.6%	80.4%	19.6%	80.4%
8	1986	145,358	40,259	ABT, CLARK C.	104,651	KENNEDY, JOSEPH P.	448	64,392 D	27.7%	72.0%	27.8%	72.2%
8	1984	195,603			179,617	O'NEILL, THOMAS P.	15,986	179,617 D		91.8%		100.0%
8	1982	164,672	41,370	MCNAMARA, FRANK L.	123,296	O'NEILL, THOMAS P.	6	81,926 D	25.1%	74.9%	25.1%	74.9%
9	1990	177,248			124,534	MOAKLEY, JOHN J.	52,714	124,534 D		70.3%		100.0%
9	1988	161,042			160,799	MOAKLEY, JOHN J.	243	160,799 D		99.8%		100.0%
9	1986	131,330			110,026	MOAKLEY, JOHN J.	21,304	110,026 D		83.8%		100.0%
9	1984	153,252			153,132	MOAKLEY, JOHN J.	120	153,132 D		99.9%		100.0%
9	1982	160,225	55,030	COCHRAN, DEBORAH R.	102,665	MOAKLEY, JOHN J.	2,530	47,635 D	34.3%	64.1%	34.9%	65.1%
10	1990	258,061	120,217	BRYAN, JON L.	137,805	STUDDS, GERRY E.	39	17,588 D	46.6%	53.4%	46.6%	53.4%
10	1988	280,767	93,564	BRYAN, JON L.	187,178	STUDDS, GERRY E.	25	93,614 D	33.3%	66.7%	33.3%	66.7%
10	1986	186,726	49,451	BARROS, RICARDO M.	121,578	STUDDS, GERRY E.	15,697	72,127 D	26.5%	65.1%	28.9%	71.1%
10	1984	256,824	113,745	CRAMPTON, LEWIS	143,062	STUDDS, GERRY E.	17	29,317 D	44.3%	55.7%	44.3%	55.7%
10	1982	201,436	63,014	CONWAY, JOHN E.	138,418	STUDDS, GERRY E.	4	75,404 D	31.3%	68.7%	31.3%	68.7%

MASSACHUSETTS

CONGRESS

CD	Year	Total Vote	Republican Vote	Republican Candidate	Democratic Vote	Democratic Candidate	Other Vote	Rep.-Dem. Plurality	Percentage Total Vote Rep.	Percentage Total Vote Dem.	Percentage Major Vote Rep.	Percentage Major Vote Dem.
11	1990	145,972			145,480	DONNELLY, BRIAN J.	492	145,480 D		99.7%		100.0%
11	1988	209,988	40,277	GILLERAN, MICHAEL C.	169,692	DONNELLY, BRIAN J.	19	129,415 D	19.2%	80.8%	19.2%	80.8%
11	1986	114,929			114,926	DONNELLY, BRIAN J.	3	114,926 D		100.0%		100.0%
11	1984	172,025			172,010	DONNELLY, BRIAN J.	15	172,010 D		100.0%		100.0%
11	1982	144,157			144,132	DONNELLY, BRIAN J.	25	144,132 D		100.0%		100.0%

MASSACHUSETTS

1990 GENERAL ELECTION

In addition to the county-by-county figures, data are presented for selected Massachusetts communities. Since not all jurisdictions of the state are listed in this special tabulation, state-wide totals are shown only with the county-by-county statistics.

Governor   Other vote was 62,703 Independent High Tech (Umina); 872 write-in Stevens and 3,657 scattered write-in.

Senator   Other vote was scattered write-in.

Congress   An asterisk in the Congressional vote table indicates a candidate received votes from another party endorsing his/her candidacy. Other vote was 8,806 New Alliance (Davies) and 94 scattered write-in in CD 8; 52,660 Independent (Horan) and 54 scattered write-in in CD 9; scattered write-in in all other CD's.

1990 PRIMARIES

SEPTEMBER 18 REPUBLICAN

Governor   270,455 William F. Weld; 176,184 Steven D. Pierce; 283 scattered write-in.

Senator   265,093 Jim Rappaport; 135,647 Daniel W. Daly; 202 scattered write-in.

Congress   Unopposed in four CD's. No candidate in CD's 2, 3, 7, 9, and 11. Contested as follows:

CD 4   17,481 John R. Soto; 13,663 James L. Nuzzo; 51 scattered write-in.
CD 5   26,940 John F. MacGovern; 14,548 Donal T. Coleman; 37 scattered write-in.

SEPTEMBER 18 DEMOCRATIC

Governor   562,222 John Silber; 459,128 Francis X. Bellotti; 30,054 Evelyn F. Murphy; 1,028 scattered write-in.

Senator   John F. Kerry, unopposed.

Congress   Unopposed in ten CD's. Contested as follows:

CD 2   51,615 Richard E. Neal; 29,520 Theodore E. Dimauro; 5 scattered write-in.

MICHIGAN

GOVERNOR
John Engler (R). Elected 1990 to a four-year term.

SENATORS
Carl Levin (D). Re-elected 1990 to a six-year term. Previously elected 1984, 1978.

Donald W. Riegle (D). Re-elected 1988 to a six-year term. Previously elected 1982, 1976.

REPRESENTATIVES

1. John Conyers (D)	7. Dale E. Kildee (D)	13. Barbara-Rose Collins (D)
2. Carl D. Pursell (R)	8. J. Robert Traxler (D)	14. Dennis M. Hertel (D)
3. Howard Wolpe (D)	9. Guy Vander Jagt (R)	15. William D. Ford (D)
4. Frederick Upton (R)	10. Dave Camp (R)	16. John D. Dingell, Jr.(D)
5. Paul Henry (R)	11. Robert W. Davis (R)	17. Sander Levin (D)
6. M. Robert Carr (D)	12. David E. Bonior (D)	18. William S. Broomfield (R)

POSTWAR VOTE FOR PRESIDENT

Year	Total Vote	Republican Vote	Candidate	Democratic Vote	Candidate	Other Vote	Plurality	Total Vote Rep.	Total Vote Dem.	Major Vote Rep.	Major Vote Dem.
1988	3,669,163	1,965,486	Bush, George	1,675,783	Dukakis, Michael S.	27,894	289,703 R	53.6%	45.7%	54.0%	46.0%
1984	3,801,658	2,251,571	Reagan, Ronald	1,529,638	Mondale, Walter F.	20,449	721,933 R	59.2%	40.2%	59.5%	40.5%
1980	3,909,725	1,915,225	Reagan, Ronald	1,661,532	Carter, Jimmy	332,968	253,693 R	49.0%	42.5%	53.5%	46.5%
1976	3,653,749	1,893,742	Ford, Gerald R.	1,696,714	Carter, Jimmy	63,293	197,028 R	51.8%	46.4%	52.7%	47.3%
1972	3,489,727	1,961,721	Nixon, Richard M.	1,459,435	McGovern, George S.	68,571	502,286 R	56.2%	41.8%	57.3%	42.7%
1968	3,306,250	1,370,665	Nixon, Richard M.	1,593,082	Humphrey, Hubert H.	342,503	222,417 D	41.5%	48.2%	46.2%	53.8%
1964	3,203,102	1,060,152	Goldwater, Barry M.	2,136,615	Johnson, Lyndon B.	6,335	1,076,463 D	33.1%	66.7%	33.2%	66.8%
1960	3,318,097	1,620,428	Nixon, Richard M.	1,687,269	Kennedy, John F.	10,400	66,841 D	48.8%	50.9%	49.0%	51.0%
1956	3,080,468	1,713,647	Eisenhower, Dwight D.	1,359,898	Stevenson, Adlai E.	6,923	353,749 R	55.6%	44.1%	55.8%	44.2%
1952	2,798,592	1,551,529	Eisenhower, Dwight D.	1,230,657	Stevenson, Adlai E.	16,406	320,872 R	55.4%	44.0%	55.8%	44.2%
1948	2,109,609	1,038,595	Dewey, Thomas E.	1,003,448	Truman, Harry S.	67,566	35,147 R	49.2%	47.6%	50.9%	49.1%

MICHIGAN

POSTWAR VOTE FOR GOVERNOR

Year	Total Vote	Republican Vote	Candidate	Democratic Vote	Candidate	Other Vote	Rep-Dem. Plurality	Percentage Total Vote Rep.	Dem.	Major Vote Rep.	Dem.
1990	2,564,563	1,276,134	Engler, John	1,258,539	Blanchard, James J.	29,890	17,595 R	49.8%	49.1%	50.3%	49.7%
1986	2,396,564	753,647	Lucas, William	1,632,138	Blanchard, James J.	10,779	878,491 D	31.4%	68.1%	31.6%	68.4%
1982	3,040,008	1,369,582	Headlee, Richard H.	1,561,291	Blanchard, James J.	109,135	191,709 D	45.1%	51.4%	46.7%	53.3%
1978	2,867,212	1,628,485	Milliken, William G.	1,237,256	Fitzgerald, William	1,471	391,229 R	56.8%	43.2%	56.8%	43.2%
1974	2,657,017	1,356,865	Milliken, William G.	1,242,247	Levin, Sander	57,905	114,618 R	51.1%	46.8%	52.2%	47.8%
1970	2,656,162	1,339,047	Milliken, William G.	1,294,638	Levin, Sander	22,477	44,409 R	50.4%	48.7%	50.8%	49.2%
1966 **	2,461,909	1,490,430	Romney, George W.	963,383	Ferency, Zolton A.	8,096	527,047 R	60.5%	39.1%	60.7%	39.3%
1964	3,158,102	1,764,355	Romney, George W.	1,381,442	Staebler, Neil	12,305	382,913 R	55.9%	43.7%	56.1%	43.9%
1962	2,764,839	1,420,086	Romney, George W.	1,339,513	Swainson, John B.	5,240	80,573 R	51.4%	48.4%	51.5%	48.5%
1960	3,255,991	1,602,022	Bagwell, Paul D.	1,643,634	Swainson, John B.	10,335	41,612 D	49.2%	50.5%	49.4%	50.6%
1958	2,312,184	1,078,089	Bagwell, Paul D.	1,225,533	Williams, G. Mennen	8,562	147,444 D	46.6%	53.0%	46.8%	53.2%
1956	3,049,651	1,376,376	Cobo, Albert E.	1,666,689	Williams, G. Mennen	6,586	290,313 D	45.1%	54.7%	45.2%	54.8%
1954	2,187,027	963,300	Leonard, Donald S.	1,216,308	Williams, G. Mennen	7,419	253,008 D	44.0%	55.6%	44.2%	55.8%
1952	2,865,980	1,423,275	Alger, Fred M.	1,431,893	Williams, G. Mennen	10,812	8,618 D	49.7%	50.0%	49.8%	50.2%
1950	1,879,382	933,998	Kelly, Harry F.	935,152	Williams, G. Mennen	10,232	1,154 D	49.7%	49.8%	50.0%	50.0%
1948	2,113,122	964,810	Sigler, Kim	1,128,664	Williams, G. Mennen	19,648	163,854 D	45.7%	53.4%	46.1%	53.9%
1946	1,665,475	1,003,878	Sigler, Kim	644,540	Van Wagoner, Murray	17,057	359,338 R	60.3%	38.7%	60.9%	39.1%

The term of office of Michigan's Governor was increased from two to four years effective with the 1966 election.

POSTWAR VOTE FOR SENATOR

Year	Total Vote	Republican Vote	Candidate	Democratic Vote	Candidate	Other Vote	Rep-Dem. Plurality	Percentage Total Vote Rep.	Dem.	Major Vote Rep.	Dem.
1990	2,560,494	1,055,695	Schuette, Bill	1,471,753	Levin, Carl	33,046	416,058 D	41.2%	57.5%	41.8%	58.2%
1988	3,505,985	1,348,219	Dunn, Jim	2,116,865	Riegle, Donald W.	40,901	768,646 D	38.5%	60.4%	38.9%	61.1%
1984	3,700,938	1,745,302	Lousma, Jack	1,915,831	Levin, Carl	39,805	170,529 D	47.2%	51.8%	47.7%	52.3%
1982	2,994,334	1,223,288	Ruppe, Philip E.	1,728,793	Riegle, Donald W.	42,253	505,505 D	40.9%	57.7%	41.4%	58.6%
1978	2,846,630	1,362,165	Griffin, Robert P.	1,484,193	Levin, Carl	272	122,028 D	47.9%	52.1%	47.9%	52.1%
1976	3,490,664	1,635,087	Esch, Marvin L.	1,831,031	Riegle, Donald W.	24,546	195,944 D	46.8%	52.5%	47.2%	52.8%
1972	3,406,906	1,781,065	Griffin, Robert P.	1,577,178	Kelley, Frank J.	48,663	203,887 R	52.3%	46.3%	53.0%	47.0%
1970	2,610,839	858,470	Romney, Lenore	1,744,716	Hart, Philip A.	7,653	886,246 D	32.9%	66.8%	33.0%	67.0%
1966	2,439,365	1,363,530	Griffin, Robert P.	1,069,484	Williams, G. Mennen	6,351	294,046 R	55.9%	43.8%	56.0%	44.0%
1964	3,101,667	1,096,272	Peterson, Elly M.	1,996,912	Hart, Philip A.	8,483	900,640 D	35.3%	64.4%	35.4%	64.6%
1960	3,226,647	1,548,873	Bentley, Alvin M.	1,669,179	McNamara, Patrick V.	8,595	120,306 D	48.0%	51.7%	48.1%	51.9%
1958	2,271,644	1,046,963	Potter, Charles E.	1,216,966	Hart, Philip A.	7,715	170,003 D	46.1%	53.6%	46.2%	53.8%
1954	2,144,840	1,049,420	Ferguson, Homer	1,088,550	McNamara, Patrick V.	6,870	39,130 D	48.9%	50.8%	49.1%	50.9%
1952	2,821,133	1,428,352	Potter, Charles E.	1,383,416	Moody, Blair	9,365	44,936 R	50.6%	49.0%	50.8%	49.2%
1948	2,062,097	1,045,156	Ferguson, Homer	1,000,329	Hook, Frank E.	16,612	44,827 R	50.7%	48.5%	51.1%	48.9%
1946	1,618,720	1,085,570	Vandenberg, Arthur	517,923	Lee, James H.	15,227	567,647 R	67.1%	32.0%	67.7%	32.3%

MICHIGAN

Districts Established May 24, 1982

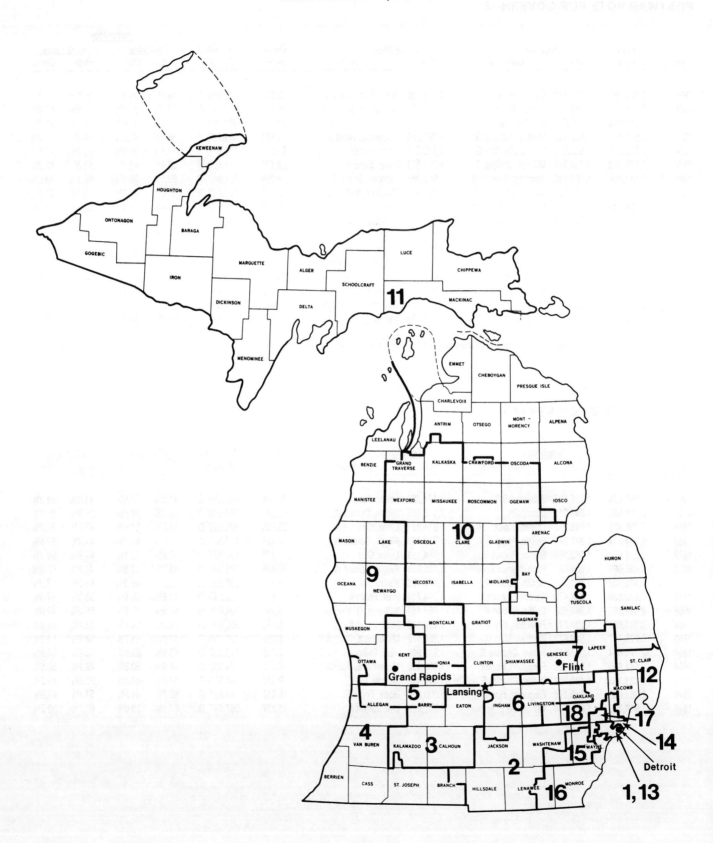

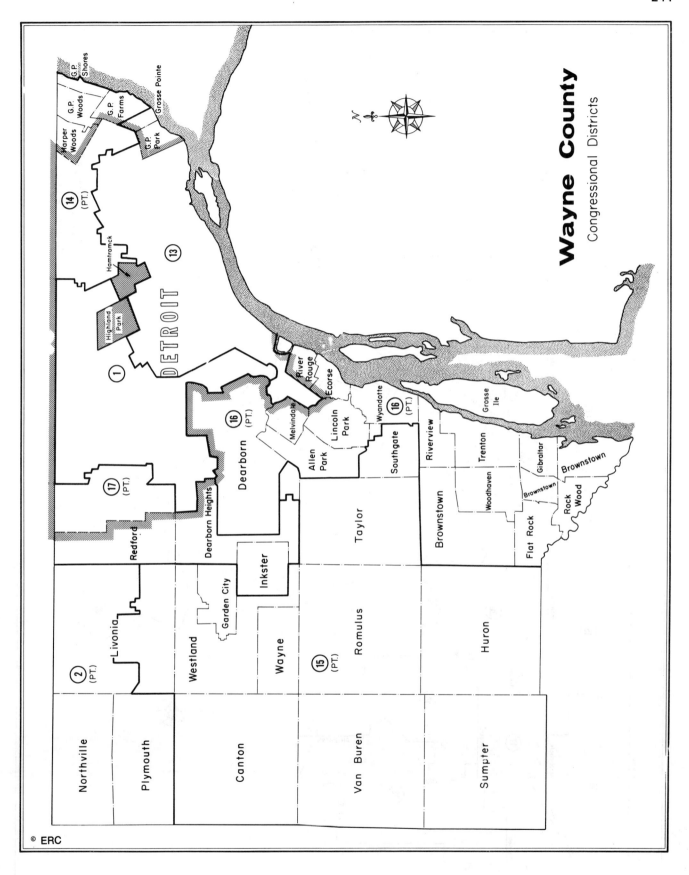

Wayne County

Congressional Districts

N

①

② (PT.)

⑬

⑭ (PT.)

⑮ (PT.)

⑯ (PT.)

⑰ (PT.)

DETROIT

Hamtramck

Highland Park

G.P. Shores

G.P.
Woods

G.P.
Farms

Harper
Woods

G.P. Park

Grosse Pointe

River
Rouge

Ecorse

Melvindale

Lincoln
Park

Wyandotte

Allen
Park

Southgate

Riverview

Grosse
Ile

Trenton

Gibraltar

Brownstown

Woodhaven

Brownstown

Rock
Wood

Flat Rock

Dearborn

Taylor

Brownstown

Dearborn Heights

Redford

Inkster

Garden City

Wayne

Romulus

Huron

Livonia

Westland

Northville

Plymouth

Canton

Van Buren

Sumpter

© ERC

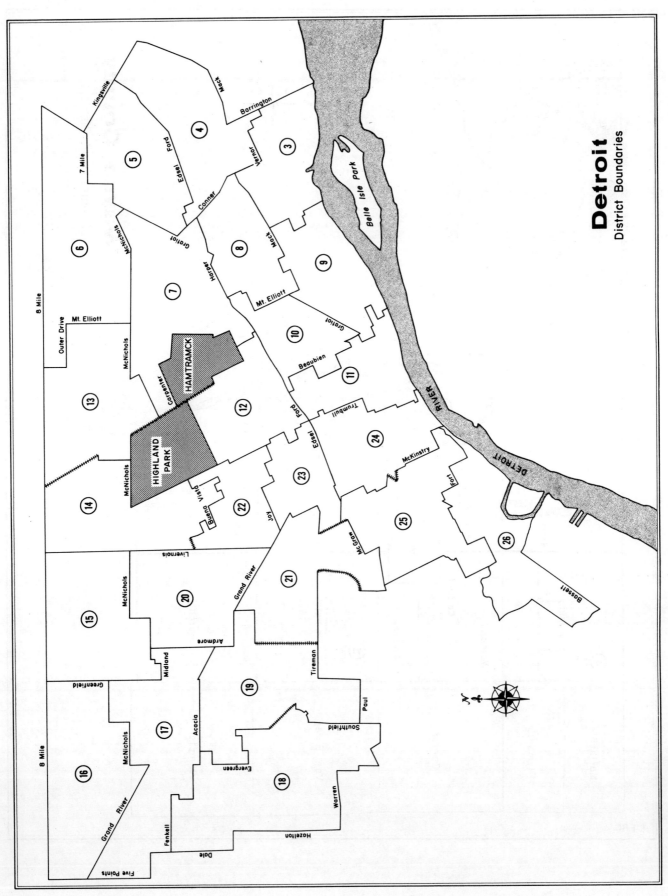

Detroit
District Boundaries

MICHIGAN

GOVERNOR 1990

1990 Census Population	County	Total Vote	Republican	Democratic	Other	Rep.-Dem. Plurality	Percentage Total Vote Rep.	Dem.	Major Vote Rep.	Dem.
10,145	ALCONA	3,358	2,031	1,313	14	718 R	60.5%	39.1%	60.7%	39.3%
8,972	ALGER	3,531	1,700	1,821	10	121 D	48.1%	51.6%	48.3%	51.7%
90,509	ALLEGAN	24,520	16,342	7,934	244	8,408 R	66.6%	32.4%	67.3%	32.7%
30,605	ALPENA	8,710	4,333	4,319	58	14 R	49.7%	49.6%	50.1%	49.9%
18,185	ANTRIM	6,331	3,572	2,711	48	861 R	56.4%	42.8%	56.9%	43.1%
14,931	ARENAC	4,269	1,937	2,305	27	368 D	45.4%	54.0%	45.7%	54.3%
7,954	BARAGA	2,491	1,298	1,181	12	117 R	52.1%	47.4%	52.4%	47.6%
50,057	BARRY	14,543	8,785	5,567	191	3,218 R	60.4%	38.3%	61.2%	38.8%
111,723	BAY	34,766	14,886	19,646	234	4,760 D	42.8%	56.5%	43.1%	56.9%
12,200	BENZIE	4,251	2,305	1,917	29	388 R	54.2%	45.1%	54.6%	45.4%
161,378	BERRIEN	37,845	24,019	13,480	346	10,539 R	63.5%	35.6%	64.1%	35.9%
41,502	BRANCH	9,789	5,946	3,778	65	2,168 R	60.7%	38.6%	61.1%	38.9%
135,982	CALHOUN	36,196	18,819	16,823	554	1,996 R	52.0%	46.5%	52.8%	47.2%
49,477	CASS	10,505	6,149	4,308	48	1,841 R	58.5%	41.0%	58.8%	41.2%
21,468	CHARLEVOIX	7,113	3,863	3,109	141	754 R	54.3%	43.7%	55.4%	44.6%
21,398	CHEBOYGAN	6,392	3,461	2,895	36	566 R	54.1%	45.3%	54.5%	45.5%
34,604	CHIPPEWA	8,974	4,442	4,493	39	51 D	49.5%	50.1%	49.7%	50.3%
24,952	CLARE	7,642	3,741	3,765	136	24 D	49.0%	49.3%	49.8%	50.2%
57,883	CLINTON	19,669	11,023	8,412	234	2,611 R	56.0%	42.8%	56.7%	43.3%
12,260	CRAWFORD	3,220	1,961	1,197	62	764 R	60.9%	37.2%	62.1%	37.9%
37,780	DELTA	11,872	5,155	6,675	42	1,520 D	43.4%	56.2%	43.6%	56.4%
26,831	DICKINSON	9,007	4,190	4,803	14	613 D	46.5%	53.3%	46.6%	53.4%
92,879	EATON	30,598	16,264	13,818	516	2,446 R	53.2%	45.2%	54.1%	45.9%
25,040	EMMET	7,814	4,338	3,343	133	995 R	55.5%	42.8%	56.5%	43.5%
430,459	GENESEE	114,223	45,456	67,057	1,710	21,601 D	39.8%	58.7%	40.4%	59.6%
21,896	GLADWIN	6,378	3,097	3,170	111	73 D	48.6%	49.7%	49.4%	50.6%
18,052	GOGEBIC	6,098	2,089	3,989	20	1,900 D	34.3%	65.4%	34.4%	65.6%
64,273	GRAND TRAVERSE	21,005	12,344	8,519	142	3,825 R	58.8%	40.6%	59.2%	40.8%
38,982	GRATIOT	10,171	5,283	4,799	89	484 R	51.9%	47.2%	52.4%	47.6%
43,431	HILLSDALE	10,683	6,779	3,823	81	2,956 R	63.5%	35.8%	63.9%	36.1%
35,446	HOUGHTON	10,440	5,696	4,686	58	1,010 R	54.6%	44.9%	54.9%	45.1%
34,951	HURON	11,174	6,365	4,769	40	1,596 R	57.0%	42.7%	57.2%	42.8%
281,912	INGHAM	83,234	34,878	46,143	2,213	11,265 D	41.9%	55.4%	43.0%	57.0%
57,024	IONIA	15,524	8,721	6,658	145	2,063 R	56.2%	42.9%	56.7%	43.3%
30,209	IOSCO	8,293	4,258	3,904	131	354 R	51.3%	47.1%	52.2%	47.8%
13,175	IRON	4,930	2,397	2,512	21	115 D	48.6%	51.0%	48.8%	51.2%
54,624	ISABELLA	13,663	6,913	6,541	209	372 R	50.6%	47.9%	51.4%	48.6%
149,756	JACKSON	39,183	22,051	16,702	430	5,349 R	56.3%	42.6%	56.9%	43.1%
223,411	KALAMAZOO	60,329	30,431	29,086	812	1,345 R	50.4%	48.2%	51.1%	48.9%
13,497	KALKASKA	3,765	2,289	1,450	26	839 R	60.8%	38.5%	61.2%	38.8%
500,631	KENT	147,747	95,254	50,060	2,433	45,194 R	64.5%	33.9%	65.6%	34.4%
1,701	KEWEENAW	892	449	442	1	7 R	50.3%	49.6%	50.4%	49.6%
8,583	LAKE	2,875	1,385	1,423	67	38 D	48.2%	49.5%	49.3%	50.7%
74,768	LAPEER	19,878	11,792	7,639	447	4,153 R	59.3%	38.4%	60.7%	39.3%
16,527	LEELANAU	6,419	3,757	2,620	42	1,137 R	58.5%	40.8%	58.9%	41.1%
91,476	LENAWEE	25,102	13,753	11,239	110	2,514 R	54.8%	44.8%	55.0%	45.0%
115,645	LIVINGSTON	33,820	21,102	12,162	556	8,940 R	62.4%	36.0%	63.4%	36.6%
5,763	LUCE	2,053	1,053	994	6	59 R	51.3%	48.4%	51.4%	48.6%
10,674	MACKINAC	4,132	2,206	1,901	25	305 R	53.4%	46.0%	53.7%	46.3%
717,400	MACOMB	209,284	110,387	96,088	2,809	14,299 R	52.7%	45.9%	53.5%	46.5%
21,265	MANISTEE	7,721	4,289	3,386	46	903 R	55.5%	43.9%	55.9%	44.1%
70,887	MARQUETTE	18,103	7,305	10,676	122	3,371 D	40.4%	59.0%	40.6%	59.4%
25,537	MASON	9,204	5,138	3,964	102	1,174 R	55.8%	43.1%	56.4%	43.6%
37,308	MECOSTA	9,255	5,170	4,019	66	1,151 R	55.9%	43.4%	56.3%	43.7%
24,920	MENOMINEE	6,556	2,979	3,559	18	580 D	45.4%	54.3%	45.6%	54.4%
75,651	MIDLAND	26,206	13,087	12,783	336	304 R	49.9%	48.8%	50.6%	49.4%
12,147	MISSAUKEE	3,960	2,585	1,306	69	1,279 R	65.3%	33.0%	66.4%	33.6%
133,600	MONROE	31,875	16,865	14,811	199	2,054 R	52.9%	46.5%	53.2%	46.8%
53,059	MONTCALM	14,028	8,036	5,863	129	2,173 R	57.3%	41.8%	57.8%	42.2%
8,936	MONTMORENCY	2,564	1,556	997	11	559 R	60.7%	38.9%	60.9%	39.1%

MICHIGAN

GOVERNOR 1990

1990 Census Population	County	Total Vote	Republican	Democratic	Other	Rep.-Dem. Plurality	Total Vote Rep.	Total Vote Dem.	Major Vote Rep.	Major Vote Dem.
158,983	MUSKEGON	43,770	21,519	21,948	303	429 D	49.2%	50.1%	49.5%	50.5%
38,202	NEWAYGO	11,111	6,902	4,120	89	2,782 R	62.1%	37.1%	62.6%	37.4%
1,083,592	OAKLAND	329,112	172,462	153,429	3,221	19,033 R	52.4%	46.6%	52.9%	47.1%
22,454	OCEANA	6,788	3,933	2,794	61	1,139 R	57.9%	41.2%	58.5%	41.5%
18,681	OGEMAW	5,893	2,824	2,981	88	157 D	47.9%	50.6%	48.6%	51.4%
8,854	ONTONAGON	3,405	1,699	1,687	19	12 R	49.9%	49.5%	50.2%	49.8%
20,146	OSCEOLA	5,774	3,436	2,299	39	1,137 R	59.5%	39.8%	59.9%	40.1%
7,842	OSCODA	2,237	1,361	839	37	522 R	60.8%	37.5%	61.9%	38.1%
17,957	OTSEGO	5,703	3,241	2,400	62	841 R	56.8%	42.1%	57.5%	42.5%
187,768	OTTAWA	60,344	43,993	15,888	463	28,105 R	72.9%	26.3%	73.5%	26.5%
13,743	PRESQUE ISLE	4,547	2,328	2,168	51	160 R	51.2%	47.7%	51.8%	48.2%
19,776	ROSCOMMON	7,422	3,891	3,478	53	413 R	52.4%	46.9%	52.8%	47.2%
211,946	SAGINAW	65,878	29,130	36,036	712	6,906 D	44.2%	54.7%	44.7%	55.3%
145,607	ST. CLAIR	39,186	22,858	15,757	571	7,101 R	58.3%	40.2%	59.2%	40.8%
58,913	ST. JOSEPH	14,155	8,661	5,404	90	3,257 R	61.2%	38.2%	61.6%	38.4%
39,928	SANILAC	12,566	7,778	4,732	56	3,046 R	61.9%	37.7%	62.2%	37.8%
8,302	SCHOOLCRAFT	3,128	1,332	1,786	10	454 D	42.6%	57.1%	42.7%	57.3%
69,770	SHIAWASSEE	21,428	10,473	10,751	204	278 D	48.9%	50.2%	49.3%	50.7%
55,498	TUSCOLA	15,268	8,118	7,046	104	1,072 R	53.2%	46.1%	53.5%	46.5%
70,060	VAN BUREN	17,210	9,827	7,230	153	2,597 R	57.1%	42.0%	57.6%	42.4%
282,937	WASHTENAW	77,893	32,942	43,934	1,017	10,992 D	42.3%	56.4%	42.9%	57.1%
2,111,687	WAYNE	489,617	175,344	308,902	5,371	133,558 D	35.8%	63.1%	36.2%	63.8%
26,360	WEXFORD	7,955	4,327	3,577	51	750 R	54.4%	45.0%	54.7%	45.3%
9,295,297	TOTAL	2,564,563	1,276,134	1,258,539	29,890	17,595 R	49.8%	49.1%	50.3%	49.7%

MICHIGAN

SENATOR 1990

1990 Census Population	County	Total Vote	Republican	Democratic	Other	Rep.-Dem. Plurality	Percentage Total Vote Rep.	Dem.	Major Vote Rep.	Dem.
10,145	ALCONA	3,292	1,656	1,624	12	32 R	50.3%	49.3%	50.5%	49.5%
8,972	ALGER	3,374	1,020	2,340	14	1,320 D	30.2%	69.4%	30.4%	69.6%
90,509	ALLEGAN	24,169	14,389	9,600	180	4,789 R	59.5%	39.7%	60.0%	40.0%
30,605	ALPENA	8,693	3,167	5,437	89	2,270 D	36.4%	62.5%	36.8%	63.2%
18,185	ANTRIM	6,274	2,885	3,343	46	458 D	46.0%	53.3%	46.3%	53.7%
14,931	ARENAC	4,011	1,712	2,279	20	567 D	42.7%	56.8%	42.9%	57.1%
7,954	BARAGA	2,456	750	1,702	4	952 D	30.5%	69.3%	30.6%	69.4%
50,057	BARRY	14,403	7,273	7,000	130	273 R	50.5%	48.6%	51.0%	49.0%
111,723	BAY	34,544	12,154	22,246	144	10,092 D	35.2%	64.4%	35.3%	64.7%
12,200	BENZIE	4,224	1,834	2,371	19	537 D	43.4%	56.1%	43.6%	56.4%
161,378	BERRIEN	37,511	22,679	13,840	992	8,839 R	60.5%	36.9%	62.1%	37.9%
41,502	BRANCH	9,625	4,931	4,643	51	288 R	51.2%	48.2%	51.5%	48.5%
135,982	CALHOUN	36,209	15,409	20,105	695	4,696 D	42.6%	55.5%	43.4%	56.6%
49,477	CASS	10,052	5,446	4,503	103	943 R	54.2%	44.8%	54.7%	45.3%
21,468	CHARLEVOIX	7,132	2,997	3,929	206	932 D	42.0%	55.1%	43.3%	56.7%
21,398	CHEBOYGAN	6,313	2,573	3,715	25	1,142 D	40.8%	58.8%	40.9%	59.1%
34,604	CHIPPEWA	8,894	3,383	5,478	33	2,095 D	38.0%	61.6%	38.2%	61.8%
24,952	CLARE	7,737	3,405	4,171	161	766 D	44.0%	53.9%	44.9%	55.1%
57,883	CLINTON	19,575	10,369	9,033	173	1,336 R	53.0%	46.1%	53.4%	46.6%
12,260	CRAWFORD	3,272	1,625	1,544	103	81 R	49.7%	47.2%	51.3%	48.7%
37,780	DELTA	11,732	3,774	7,919	39	4,145 D	32.2%	67.5%	32.3%	67.7%
26,831	DICKINSON	8,806	3,134	5,652	20	2,518 D	35.6%	64.2%	35.7%	64.3%
92,879	EATON	30,543	14,461	15,544	538	1,083 D	47.3%	50.9%	48.2%	51.8%
25,040	EMMET	7,839	3,428	4,236	175	808 D	43.7%	54.0%	44.7%	55.3%
430,459	GENESEE	115,126	37,016	76,148	1,962	39,132 D	32.2%	66.1%	32.7%	67.3%
21,896	GLADWIN	6,456	2,943	3,387	126	444 D	45.6%	52.5%	46.5%	53.5%
18,052	GOGEBIC	5,980	1,771	4,170	39	2,399 D	29.6%	69.7%	29.8%	70.2%
64,273	GRAND TRAVERSE	20,858	9,609	11,141	108	1,532 D	46.1%	53.4%	46.3%	53.7%
38,982	GRATIOT	10,248	5,606	4,565	77	1,041 R	54.7%	44.5%	55.1%	44.9%
43,431	HILLSDALE	10,509	5,840	4,603	66	1,237 R	55.6%	43.8%	55.9%	44.1%
35,446	HOUGHTON	10,281	3,432	6,816	33	3,384 D	33.4%	66.3%	33.5%	66.5%
34,951	HURON	11,025	5,398	5,597	30	199 D	49.0%	50.8%	49.1%	50.9%
281,912	INGHAM	83,841	31,157	50,518	2,166	19,361 D	37.2%	60.3%	38.1%	61.9%
57,024	IONIA	15,128	7,091	7,933	104	842 D	46.9%	52.4%	47.2%	52.8%
30,209	IOSCO	8,369	3,804	4,352	213	548 D	45.5%	52.0%	46.6%	53.4%
13,175	IRON	4,866	1,493	3,328	45	1,835 D	30.7%	68.4%	31.0%	69.0%
54,624	ISABELLA	13,753	6,369	7,198	186	829 D	46.3%	52.3%	46.9%	53.1%
149,756	JACKSON	39,194	18,142	20,546	506	2,404 D	46.3%	52.4%	46.9%	53.1%
223,411	KALAMAZOO	60,354	27,265	32,006	1,083	4,741 D	45.2%	53.0%	46.0%	54.0%
13,497	KALKASKA	3,749	1,800	1,929	20	129 D	48.0%	51.5%	48.3%	51.7%
500,631	KENT	147,880	76,954	68,554	2,372	8,400 R	52.0%	46.4%	52.9%	47.1%
1,701	KEWEENAW	865	257	607	1	350 D	29.7%	70.2%	29.7%	70.3%
8,583	LAKE	2,903	963	1,823	117	860 D	33.2%	62.8%	34.6%	65.4%
74,768	LAPEER	20,088	9,319	10,243	526	924 D	46.4%	51.0%	47.6%	52.4%
16,527	LEELANAU	6,398	2,918	3,444	36	526 D	45.6%	53.8%	45.9%	54.1%
91,476	LENAWEE	24,607	11,832	12,653	122	821 D	48.1%	51.4%	48.3%	51.7%
115,645	LIVINGSTON	33,918	17,467	15,700	751	1,767 R	51.5%	46.3%	52.7%	47.3%
5,763	LUCE	2,003	804	1,195	4	391 D	40.1%	59.7%	40.2%	59.8%
10,674	MACKINAC	4,096	1,718	2,330	48	612 D	41.9%	56.9%	42.4%	57.6%
717,400	MACOMB	209,195	84,750	121,136	3,309	36,386 D	40.5%	57.9%	41.2%	58.8%
21,265	MANISTEE	7,637	3,301	4,296	40	995 D	43.2%	56.3%	43.5%	56.5%
70,887	MARQUETTE	18,034	4,516	13,327	191	8,811 D	25.0%	73.9%	25.3%	74.7%
25,537	MASON	9,232	3,831	5,151	250	1,320 D	41.5%	55.8%	42.7%	57.3%
37,308	MECOSTA	9,280	4,714	4,511	55	203 R	50.8%	48.6%	51.1%	48.9%
24,920	MENOMINEE	6,311	2,576	3,718	17	1,142 D	40.8%	58.9%	40.9%	59.1%
75,651	MIDLAND	26,377	14,058	12,003	316	2,055 R	53.3%	45.5%	53.9%	46.1%
12,147	MISSAUKEE	3,979	2,287	1,594	98	693 R	57.5%	40.1%	58.9%	41.1%
133,600	MONROE	31,623	13,684	17,619	320	3,935 D	43.3%	55.7%	43.7%	56.3%
53,059	MONTCALM	13,772	6,685	7,005	82	320 D	48.5%	50.9%	48.8%	51.2%
8,936	MONTMORENCY	2,521	1,139	1,370	12	231 D	45.2%	54.3%	45.4%	54.6%

MICHIGAN

SENATOR 1990

1990 Census Population	County	Total Vote	Republican	Democratic	Other	Rep.-Dem. Plurality	Percentage			
							Total Vote		Major Vote	
							Rep.	Dem.	Rep.	Dem.
158,983	MUSKEGON	43,327	17,929	25,193	205	7,264 D	41.4%	58.1%	41.6%	58.4%
38,202	NEWAYGO	11,014	5,806	5,142	66	664 R	52.7%	46.7%	53.0%	47.0%
1,083,592	OAKLAND	329,373	141,264	184,675	3,434	43,411 D	42.9%	56.1%	43.3%	56.7%
22,454	OCEANA	6,738	3,237	3,459	42	222 D	48.0%	51.3%	48.3%	51.7%
18,681	OGEMAW	5,963	2,608	3,242	113	634 D	43.7%	54.4%	44.6%	55.4%
8,854	ONTONAGON	3,303	1,037	2,228	38	1,191 D	31.4%	67.5%	31.8%	68.2%
20,146	OSCEOLA	5,773	3,034	2,715	24	319 R	52.6%	47.0%	52.8%	47.2%
7,842	OSCODA	2,255	1,078	1,103	74	25 D	47.8%	48.9%	49.4%	50.6%
17,957	OTSEGO	5,640	2,377	3,190	73	813 D	42.1%	56.6%	42.7%	57.3%
187,768	OTTAWA	59,731	39,506	20,011	214	19,495 R	66.1%	33.5%	66.4%	33.6%
13,743	PRESQUE ISLE	4,581	1,652	2,824	105	1,172 D	36.1%	61.6%	36.9%	63.1%
19,776	ROSCOMMON	7,436	3,408	3,981	47	573 D	45.8%	53.5%	46.1%	53.9%
211,946	SAGINAW	66,267	25,630	39,695	942	14,065 D	38.7%	59.9%	39.2%	60.8%
145,607	ST. CLAIR	39,217	17,407	20,999	811	3,592 D	44.4%	53.5%	45.3%	54.7%
58,913	ST. JOSEPH	13,684	7,777	5,834	73	1,943 R	56.8%	42.6%	57.1%	42.9%
39,928	SANILAC	12,470	6,397	5,995	78	402 R	51.3%	48.1%	51.6%	48.4%
8,302	SCHOOLCRAFT	3,045	925	2,110	10	1,185 D	30.4%	69.3%	30.5%	69.5%
69,770	SHIAWASSEE	21,495	9,878	11,489	128	1,611 D	46.0%	53.4%	46.2%	53.8%
55,498	TUSCOLA	15,093	6,903	8,087	103	1,184 D	45.7%	53.6%	46.1%	53.9%
70,060	VAN BUREN	16,815	8,489	8,183	143	306 R	50.5%	48.7%	50.9%	49.1%
282,937	WASHTENAW	77,986	27,181	49,791	1,014	22,610 D	34.9%	63.8%	35.3%	64.7%
2,111,687	WAYNE	490,197	141,440	342,893	5,864	201,453 D	28.9%	70.0%	29.2%	70.8%
26,360	WEXFORD	7,955	3,769	4,144	42	375 D	47.4%	52.1%	47.6%	52.4%
9,295,297	TOTAL	2,560,494	1,055,695	1,471,753	33,046	416,058 D	41.2%	57.5%	41.8%	58.2%

DETROIT

GOVERNOR 1990

1990 Census Population	District	Total Vote	Republican	Democratic	Other	Rep.-Dem. Plurality	Percentage			
							Total Vote		Major Vote	
							Rep.	Dem.	Rep.	Dem.
	DISTRICT 3	2,828	216	2,580	32	2,364 D	7.6%	91.2%	7.7%	92.3%
	DISTRICT 4	7,041	1,777	5,162	102	3,385 D	25.2%	73.3%	25.6%	74.4%
	DISTRICT 5	6,485	1,465	4,950	70	3,485 D	22.6%	76.3%	22.8%	77.2%
	DISTRICT 6	7,454	2,129	5,237	88	3,108 D	28.6%	70.3%	28.9%	71.1%
	DISTRICT 7	4,250	522	3,678	50	3,156 D	12.3%	86.5%	12.4%	87.6%
	DISTRICT 8	4,394	152	4,219	23	4,067 D	3.5%	96.0%	3.5%	96.5%
	DISTRICT 9	5,491	567	4,859	65	4,292 D	10.3%	88.5%	10.4%	89.6%
	DISTRICT 10	1,802	96	1,685	21	1,589 D	5.3%	93.5%	5.4%	94.6%
	DISTRICT 11	2,863	357	2,447	59	2,090 D	12.5%	85.5%	12.7%	87.3%
	DISTRICT 12	3,583	198	3,348	37	3,150 D	5.5%	93.4%	5.6%	94.4%
	DISTRICT 13	7,602	567	6,962	73	6,395 D	7.5%	91.6%	7.5%	92.5%
	DISTRICT 14	7,555	570	6,894	91	6,324 D	7.5%	91.3%	7.6%	92.4%
	DISTRICT 15	13,459	593	12,767	99	12,174 D	4.4%	94.9%	4.4%	95.6%
	DISTRICT 16	9,967	1,038	8,825	104	7,787 D	10.4%	88.5%	10.5%	89.5%
	DISTRICT 17	10,085	1,539	8,414	132	6,875 D	15.3%	83.4%	15.5%	84.5%
	DISTRICT 18	7,815	2,405	5,291	119	2,886 D	30.8%	67.7%	31.3%	68.8%
	DISTRICT 19	7,140	790	6,269	81	5,479 D	11.1%	87.8%	11.2%	88.8%
	DISTRICT 20	7,816	303	7,434	79	7,131 D	3.9%	95.1%	3.9%	96.1%
	DISTRICT 21	7,193	556	6,563	74	6,007 D	7.7%	91.2%	7.8%	92.2%
	DISTRICT 22	5,322	199	5,077	46	4,878 D	3.7%	95.4%	3.8%	96.2%
	DISTRICT 23	4,192	121	4,033	38	3,912 D	2.9%	96.2%	2.9%	97.1%
	DISTRICT 24	2,192	274	1,881	37	1,607 D	12.5%	85.8%	12.7%	87.3%
	DISTRICT 25	3,745	1,156	2,527	62	1,371 D	30.9%	67.5%	31.4%	68.6%
	DISTRICT 26	2,969	318	2,616	35	2,298 D	10.7%	88.1%	10.8%	89.2%
	ABSENTEE	42,484	6,348	35,878	258	29,530 D	14.9%	84.5%	15.0%	85.0%
1,027,974	TOTAL	185,727	24,256	159,596	1,875	105,810 D	12.5%	86.4%	12.6%	87.4%

DETROIT

SENATOR 1990

1990 Census Population	District	Total Vote	Republican	Democratic	Other	Rep.-Dem. Plurality	Total Vote Rep.	Total Vote Dem.	Major Vote Rep.	Major Vote Dem.
	DISTRICT 3	2,827	156	2,645	26	2,489 D	5.5%	93.6%	5.6%	94.4%
	DISTRICT 4	7,058	1,384	5,563	111	4,179 D	19.6%	78.8%	19.9%	80.1%
	DISTRICT 5	6,504	1,154	5,251	99	4,097 D	17.7%	80.7%	18.0%	82.0%
	DISTRICT 6	7,492	1,667	5,704	121	4,037 D	22.3%	76.1%	22.6%	77.4%
	DISTRICT 7	4,282	413	3,806	63	3,393 D	9.6%	88.9%	9.8%	90.2%
	DISTRICT 8	4,390	89	4,267	34	4,178 D	2.0%	97.2%	2.0%	98.0%
	DISTRICT 9	5,508	421	5,026	61	4,605 D	7.6%	91.2%	7.7%	92.3%
	DISTRICT 10	1,799	75	1,709	15	1,634 D	4.2%	95.0%	4.2%	95.8%
	DISTRICT 11	2,876	280	2,532	64	2,252 D	9.7%	88.0%	10.0%	90.0%
	DISTRICT 12	3,583	144	3,390	49	3,246 D	4.0%	94.6%	4.1%	95.9%
	DISTRICT 13	7,651	413	7,166	72	6,753 D	5.4%	93.7%	5.4%	94.6%
	DISTRICT 14	7,590	389	7,113	88	6,724 D	5.1%	93.7%	5.2%	94.8%
	DISTRICT 15	13,494	368	13,024	102	12,656 D	2.7%	96.5%	2.7%	97.3%
	DISTRICT 16	10,001	779	9,107	115	8,328 D	7.8%	91.1%	7.9%	92.1%
	DISTRICT 17	10,107	1,128	8,855	124	7,727 D	11.2%	87.6%	11.3%	88.7%
	DISTRICT 18	7,848	1,863	5,854	131	3,991 D	23.7%	74.6%	24.1%	75.9%
	DISTRICT 19	7,175	571	6,521	83	5,950 D	8.0%	90.9%	8.1%	91.9%
	DISTRICT 20	7,860	203	7,579	78	7,376 D	2.6%	96.4%	2.6%	97.4%
	DISTRICT 21	7,268	408	6,782	78	6,374 D	5.6%	93.3%	5.7%	94.3%
	DISTRICT 22	5,340	124	5,166	50	5,042 D	2.3%	96.7%	2.3%	97.7%
	DISTRICT 23	4,172	73	4,050	49	3,977 D	1.7%	97.1%	1.8%	98.2%
	DISTRICT 24	2,198	195	1,972	31	1,777 D	8.9%	89.7%	9.0%	91.0%
	DISTRICT 25	3,638	870	2,684	84	1,814 D	23.9%	73.8%	24.5%	75.5%
	DISTRICT 26	2,985	222	2,707	56	2,485 D	7.4%	90.7%	7.6%	92.4%
	ABSENTEE	42,724	5,461	37,015	248	31,554 D	12.8%	86.6%	12.9%	87.1%
1,027,974	TOTAL	186,370	18,850	165,488	2,032	146,638 D	10.1%	88.8%	10.2%	89.8%

MICHIGAN

CONGRESS

CD	Year	Total Vote	Republican Vote	Candidate	Democratic Vote	Candidate	Other Vote	Rep.-Dem. Plurality	Total Vote Rep.	Total Vote Dem.	Major Vote Rep.	Major Vote Dem.
1	1990	85,756	7,298	SHOULDERS, RAY	76,556	CONYERS, JOHN	1,902	69,258 D	8.5%	89.3%	8.7%	91.3%
1	1988	140,138	10,979	ASHE, BILL	127,800	CONYERS, JOHN	1,359	116,821 D	7.8%	91.2%	7.9%	92.1%
1	1986	105,784	10,407	ASHE, BILL	94,307	CONYERS, JOHN	1,070	83,900 D	9.8%	89.2%	9.9%	90.1%
1	1984	170,510	17,393	MACK, EDWARD	152,432	CONYERS, JOHN	685	135,039 D	10.2%	89.4%	10.2%	89.8%
1	1982	129,850			125,517	CONYERS, JOHN	4,333	125,517 D		96.7%		100.0%
2	1990	149,766	95,962	PURSELL, CARL D.	49,678	WHITE, ELMER	4,126	46,284 R	64.1%	33.2%	65.9%	34.1%
2	1988	219,692	120,070	PURSELL, CARL D.	98,290	POLLACK, LANA	1,332	21,780 R	54.7%	44.7%	55.0%	45.0%
2	1986	134,778	79,567	PURSELL, CARL D.	55,204	BAKER, DEAN	7	24,363 R	59.0%	41.0%	59.0%	41.0%
2	1984	205,132	140,688	PURSELL, CARL D.	62,374	MCCAULEY, MIKE	2,070	78,314 R	68.6%	30.4%	69.3%	30.7%
2	1982	163,414	106,960	PURSELL, CARL D.	53,040	SALLADE, GEORGE W.	3,414	53,920 R	65.5%	32.5%	66.9%	33.2%
3	1990	142,390	60,007	HASKINS, BRAD	82,376	WOLPE, HOWARD	7	22,369 D	42.1%	57.9%	42.1%	57.9%
3	1988	196,375	83,769	ALLGAIER, CAL	112,605	WOLPE, HOWARD	1	28,836 D	42.7%	57.3%	42.7%	57.3%
3	1986	130,400	51,678	MCGREGOR, JACKIE	78,720	WOLPE, HOWARD	2	27,042 D	39.6%	60.4%	39.6%	60.4%
3	1984	201,224	94,714	MCGREGOR, JACKIE	106,505	WOLPE, HOWARD	5	11,791 D	47.1%	52.9%	47.1%	52.9%
3	1982	171,961	73,315	MILLIMAN, RICHARD L.	96,842	WOLPE, HOWARD	1,804	23,527 D	42.6%	56.3%	43.1%	56.9%
4	1990	131,302	75,850	UPTON, FREDERICK	55,449	MCFARLAND, JOANNE	3	20,401 R	57.8%	42.2%	57.8%	42.2%
4	1988	186,703	132,270	UPTON, FREDERICK	54,428	RIVERS, NORMAN	5	77,842 R	70.8%	29.2%	70.8%	29.2%
4	1986	113,633	70,331	UPTON, FREDERICK	41,624	ROCHE, DANIEL	1,678	28,707 R	61.9%	36.6%	62.8%	37.2%
4	1984	191,087	127,907	SILJANDER, MARK D.	63,159	RODEBAUGH, CHARLES	21	64,748 R	66.9%	33.1%	66.9%	33.1%
4	1982	146,605	87,489	SILJANDER, MARK D.	56,877	MASIOKAS, DAVID A.	2,239	30,612 R	59.7%	38.8%	60.6%	39.4%
5	1990	167,498	126,308	HENRY, PAUL	41,170	TRZYBINSKI, THOMAS	20	85,138 R	75.4%	24.6%	75.4%	24.6%
5	1988	229,440	166,569	HENRY, PAUL	62,868	CATCHICK, JAMES	3	103,701 R	72.6%	27.4%	72.6%	27.4%
5	1986	141,186	100,577	HENRY, PAUL	40,608	DECKER, TERESA	1	59,969 R	71.2%	28.8%	71.2%	28.8%
5	1984	226,678	140,131	HENRY, PAUL	85,232	MCINERNEY, GARY	1,315	54,899 R	61.8%	37.6%	62.2%	37.8%
5	1982	185,881	98,650	SAWYER, HAROLD S.	87,229	MONSMA, STEPHEN V.	2	11,421 R	53.1%	46.9%	53.1%	46.9%
6	1990	97,791			97,547	CARR, M. ROBERT	244	97,547 D		99.8%		100.0%
6	1988	204,625	81,079	SCHULTZ, SCOTT	120,581	CARR, M. ROBERT	2,965	39,502 D	39.6%	58.9%	40.2%	59.8%
6	1986	132,217	57,283	DUNN, JIM	74,927	CARR, M. ROBERT	7	17,644 D	43.3%	56.7%	43.3%	56.7%
6	1984	203,530	95,113	RITTER, TOM	106,705	CARR, M. ROBERT	1,712	11,592 D	46.7%	52.4%	47.1%	52.9%
6	1982	164,987	78,388	DUNN, JIM	84,778	CARR, M. ROBERT	1,821	6,390 D	47.5%	51.4%	48.0%	52.0%
7	1990	132,068	41,759	MORRILL, DAVID	90,307	KILDEE, DALE E.	2	48,548 D	31.6%	68.4%	31.6%	68.4%
7	1988	199,080	47,071	COAD, JEFF	150,832	KILDEE, DALE E.	1,177	103,761 D	23.6%	75.8%	23.8%	76.2%
7	1986	127,172	24,848	CALLIHAN, TRUDIE	101,225	KILDEE, DALE E.	1,099	76,377 D	19.5%	79.6%	19.7%	80.3%
7	1984	155,748			145,070	KILDEE, DALE E.	10,678	145,070 D		93.1%		100.0%
7	1982	157,254	36,303	DARRAH, GEORGE R.	118,538	KILDEE, DALE E.	2,413	82,235 D	23.1%	75.4%	23.4%	76.6%
8	1990	144,165	45,259	WHITE, JAMES	98,903	TRAXLER, J. ROBERT	3	53,644 D	31.4%	68.6%	31.4%	68.6%
8	1988	194,104	54,195	BUHL, LLOYD F.	139,904	TRAXLER, J. ROBERT	5	85,709 D	27.9%	72.1%	27.9%	72.1%
8	1986	134,101	36,695	LEVI, JOHN	97,406	TRAXLER, J. ROBERT		60,711 D	27.4%	72.6%	27.4%	72.6%
8	1984	195,845	69,683	HEUSSNER, JOHN	126,161	TRAXLER, J. ROBERT	1	56,478 D	35.6%	64.4%	35.6%	64.4%
8	1982	124,737			113,515	TRAXLER, J. ROBERT	11,222	113,515 D		91.0%		100.0%
9	1990	162,694	89,078	VANDER JAGT, GUY	73,604	GREENE, GERALDINE	12	15,474 R	54.8%	45.2%	54.8%	45.2%
9	1988	214,594	149,748	VANDER JAGT, GUY	64,843	GAWRON, DAVID	3	84,905 R	69.8%	30.2%	69.8%	30.2%
9	1986	139,693	89,991	VANDER JAGT, GUY	49,702	ANDERSON, RICHARD		40,289 R	64.4%	35.6%	64.4%	35.6%
9	1984	212,805	150,885	VANDER JAGT, GUY	61,233	SENGER, JOHN	687	89,652 R	70.9%	28.8%	71.1%	28.9%
9	1982	173,439	112,504	VANDER JAGT, GUY	60,932	WARNER, GERALD D.	3	51,572 R	64.9%	35.1%	64.9%	35.1%
10	1990	153,716	99,952	CAMP, DAVE	50,923	DENNISON, JOAN	2,841	49,029 R	65.0%	33.1%	66.2%	33.8%
10	1988	209,863	152,646	SCHUETTE, BILL	55,398	FORBES, MATHIAS	1,819	97,248 R	72.7%	26.4%	73.4%	26.6%
10	1986	153,424	78,475	SCHUETTE, BILL	74,941	ALBOSTA, DONALD J.	8	3,534 R	51.1%	48.8%	51.2%	48.8%
10	1984	209,645	104,950	SCHUETTE, BILL	103,636	ALBOSTA, DONALD J.	1,059	1,314 R	50.1%	49.4%	50.3%	49.7%
10	1982	169,687	66,080	REED, LAWRENCE W.	102,048	ALBOSTA, DONALD J.	1,559	35,968 D	38.9%	60.1%	39.3%	60.7%

MICHIGAN

CONGRESS

CD	Year	Total Vote	Republican Vote	Republican Candidate	Democratic Vote	Democratic Candidate	Other Vote	Rep.-Dem. Plurality	Total Vote Rep.	Total Vote Dem.	Major Vote Rep.	Major Vote Dem.
11	1990	154,316	94,555	DAVIS, ROBERT W.	59,759	GOULD, MARCIA	2	34,796 R	61.3%	38.7%	61.3%	38.7%
11	1988	216,417	129,085	DAVIS, ROBERT W.	86,526	IRWIN, MITCH	806	42,559 R	59.6%	40.0%	59.9%	40.1%
11	1986	145,404	91,575	DAVIS, ROBERT W.	53,180	ANDERSON, ROBERT	649	38,395 R	63.0%	36.6%	63.3%	36.7%
11	1984	216,634	126,992	DAVIS, ROBERT W.	89,640	STEWART, TOM	2	37,352 R	58.6%	41.4%	58.6%	41.4%
11	1982	175,222	106,039	DAVIS, ROBERT W.	69,181	BOURLAND, KENT	2	36,858 R	60.5%	39.5%	60.5%	39.5%
12	1990	151,825	51,119	DINGEMAN, JIM	98,232	BONIOR, DAVID E.	2,474	47,113 D	33.7%	64.7%	34.2%	65.8%
12	1988	201,798	91,780	CARL, DOUGLAS	108,158	BONIOR, DAVID E.	1,860	16,378 D	45.5%	53.6%	45.9%	54.1%
12	1986	132,089	44,442	MILLER, CANDICE	87,643	BONIOR, DAVID E.	4	43,201 D	33.6%	66.4%	33.6%	66.4%
12	1984	194,984	79,824	TYZA, EUGENE J.	113,772	BONIOR, DAVID E.	1,388	33,948 D	40.9%	58.3%	41.2%	58.8%
12	1982	157,664	52,312	CONTESTI, RAY	103,851	BONIOR, DAVID E.	1,501	51,539 D	33.2%	65.9%	33.5%	66.5%
13	1990	67,824	11,203	EDWARDS, CARL	54,345	COLLINS, BARBARA-ROSE	2,276	43,142 D	16.5%	80.1%	17.1%	82.9%
13	1988	114,700	13,196	SAVAGE, JOHN	99,751	CROCKETT, GEORGE W.	1,753	86,555 D	11.5%	87.0%	11.7%	88.3%
13	1986	89,746	12,395	GRIFFIN, MARY	76,435	CROCKETT, GEORGE W.	916	64,040 D	13.8%	85.2%	14.0%	86.0%
13	1984	152,638	20,416	MURPHY, ROBERT	132,222	CROCKETT, GEORGE W.		111,806 D	13.4%	86.6%	13.4%	86.6%
13	1982	123,195	13,732	GUPTA, LETTY	108,351	CROCKETT, GEORGE W.	1,112	94,619 D	11.1%	88.0%	11.2%	88.8%
14	1990	123,421	40,499	MCNEALY, KENNETH	78,506	HERTEL, DENNIS M.	4,416	38,007 D	32.8%	63.6%	34.0%	66.0%
14	1988	178,410	64,750	MCNEALY, KENNETH	111,612	HERTEL, DENNIS M.	2,048	46,862 D	36.3%	62.6%	36.7%	63.3%
14	1986	126,667	33,831	GROT, STANLEY	92,328	HERTEL, DENNIS M.	508	58,497 D	26.7%	72.9%	26.8%	73.2%
14	1984	192,142	77,427	LAUVE, JOHN	113,610	HERTEL, DENNIS M.	1,105	36,183 D	40.3%	59.1%	40.5%	59.5%
14	1982	122,613			116,421	HERTEL, DENNIS M.	6,192	116,421 D		94.9%		100.0%
15	1990	112,335	41,092	ADKINS, BURL C.	68,742	FORD, WILLIAM D.	2,501	27,650 D	36.6%	61.2%	37.4%	62.6%
15	1988	163,842	56,963	ADKINS, BURL C.	104,596	FORD, WILLIAM D.	2,283	47,633 D	34.8%	63.8%	35.3%	64.7%
15	1986	103,612	25,078	KASSEL, GLEN	77,950	FORD, WILLIAM D.	584	52,872 D	24.2%	75.2%	24.3%	75.7%
15	1984	165,152	66,172	CARLSON, GERALD	98,973	FORD, WILLIAM D.	7	32,801 D	40.1%	59.9%	40.1%	59.9%
15	1982	130,409	33,904	MORAN, MITCHELL	94,950	FORD, WILLIAM D.	1,555	61,046 D	26.0%	72.8%	26.3%	73.7%
16	1990	133,614	42,629	BEAUMONT, FRANK	88,962	DINGELL, JOHN D., JR.	2,023	46,333 D	31.9%	66.6%	32.4%	67.6%
16	1988	136,357			132,775	DINGELL, JOHN D., JR.	3,582	132,775 D		97.4%		100.0%
16	1986	130,636	28,971	GRZYWACKI, FRANK	101,659	DINGELL, JOHN D., JR.	6	72,688 D	22.2%	77.8%	22.2%	77.8%
16	1984	190,622	68,116	GRZYWACKI, FRANK	121,463	DINGELL, JOHN D., JR.	1,043	53,347 D	35.7%	63.7%	35.9%	64.1%
16	1982	154,756	39,227	HASKINS, DAVID K.	114,006	DINGELL, JOHN D., JR.	1,523	74,779 D	25.3%	73.7%	25.6%	74.4%
17	1990	132,314	40,100	LANKFORD, BLAINE	92,205	LEVIN, SANDER	9	52,105 D	30.3%	69.7%	30.3%	69.7%
17	1988	193,027	55,197	FLESSLAND, DENNIS	135,493	LEVIN, SANDER	2,337	80,296 D	28.6%	70.2%	28.9%	71.1%
17	1986	137,390	30,879	WILLIAMS, CALVIN	105,031	LEVIN, SANDER	1,480	74,152 D	22.5%	76.4%	22.7%	77.3%
17	1984	133,105			133,064	LEVIN, SANDER	41	133,064 D		100.0%		100.0%
17	1982	175,480	55,620	ROSEN, GERALD E.	116,901	LEVIN, SANDER	2,959	61,281 D	31.7%	66.6%	32.2%	67.8%
18	1990	190,834	126,629	BROOMFIELD, WILLIAM S.	64,185	BRIGGS, WALTER	20	62,444 R	66.4%	33.6%	66.4%	33.6%
18	1988	257,228	195,579	BROOMFIELD, WILLIAM S.	57,643	KOHUT, GARY	4,006	137,936 R	76.0%	22.4%	77.2%	22.8%
18	1986	149,244	110,099	BROOMFIELD, WILLIAM S.	39,144	KOHUT, GARY	1	70,955 R	73.8%	26.2%	73.8%	26.2%
18	1984	234,884	186,505	BROOMFIELD, WILLIAM S.	46,191	SMARGON, VIVIAN	2,188	140,314 R	79.4%	19.7%	80.1%	19.9%
18	1982	181,262	132,902	BROOMFIELD, WILLIAM S.	46,545	SIPHER, ALLEN J.	1,815	86,357 R	73.3%	25.7%	74.1%	25.9%

MICHIGAN

1990 GENERAL ELECTION

Governor   Other vote was 28,091 Workers World (Roundtree) and 1,799 scattered write-in.

Senator   Other vote was 32,796 Workers World (Farquhar) and 250 scattered write-in.

Congress   Other vote was 1,134 Independent (Mays), 764 Libertarian (Flint) and 4 scattered write-in in CD 1; 4,119 Tisch Independent Citizens (Jensen) and 7 scattered write-in in CD 2; 2,496 Libertarian (Congdon) and 345 scattered write-in in CD 10; 2,472 Libertarian (Roddis) and 2 scattered write-in in CD 12; 1,090 Workers World (Griffin), 649 Libertarian (Hampton), 530 Independent (Pulley) and 7 scattered write-in in CD 13; 2,692 Tisch Independent Citizens (Gale), 1,721 Libertarian (Morris) and 3 scattered write-in in CD 14; 2,497 Libertarian (Hunt) and 4 scattered write-in in CD 15; 2,019 Libertarian (Pope) and 4 scattered write-in in CD 16; scattered write-in in all other CD's.

DETROIT

1990 Population data are not available for the Detroit districts.

Governor   Other vote was Workers World (Roundtree). There were 273 scattered write-in votes in Wayne county not reported by districts in Detroit.

Senator   Other vote was Workers World (Farquhar). There were 46 scattered write-in votes in Wayne county not reported by districts in Detroit.

1990 PRIMARIES

AUGUST 7 REPUBLICAN

Governor   409,747 John Engler; 63,457 John Lauve; 19 scattered write-in.

Senator   270,434 Bill Schuette; 182,592 Clark Durant; 9 scattered write-in.

Congress   Unopposed in twelve CD's. No candidate in CD 6. In CD 6 write-in votes were 1,210 Joseph Cox and 15 scattered; Mr. Cox did not quality. Contested as follows:

CD 4   29,480 Frederick Upton; 17,140 Ed Fredricks.
CD 10   17,794 Dave Camp; 16,127 Al Cropsey; 10,197 Richard Allen; 9,898 Jim Dunn; 524 Joseph Simcox; 1 scattered write-in.
CD 12   14,330 Jim Dingeman; 5,624 Rene Napiorkowski.
CD 13   1,224 Carl Edwards; 813 John Savage; 382 Philip Lenud.
CD 15   6,848 Burl C. Adkins; 4,390 Glen Kassel.

AUGUST 7 DEMOCRATIC

Governor   James J. Blanchard, unopposed.

Senator   Carl Levin, unopposed.

Congress   Unopposed in fourteen CD's. Contested as follows:

CD 10   8,572 Joan Dennison; 5,905 Leon Keys; 12 scattered write-in.
CD 11   17,997 Marcia Gould; 14,534 Sven Johnson; 8 scattered write-in.
CD 12   23,121 David E. Bonior; 3,890 Leah Peltier.
CD 13   11,994 Barbara-Rose Collins; 6,742 Tom Barrow; 6,430 Charles Vincent; 5,162 Alberta Tinsley-Williams; 2,333 Mike Patterson; 1,666 Juanita Watkins; 472 Michael J. Hartt; 429 Henry Stallings.

MINNESOTA

GOVERNOR
Arne Carlson (R). Elected 1990 to a four-year term.

SENATORS
David Durenberger (R). Re-elected 1988 to a six-year term. Previously elected 1982 and in 1978 to fill out the remaining four years of the term vacated by the death of Senator Hubert H. Humphrey.

Paul D. Wellstone (D). Elected 1990 to a six-year term.

REPRESENTATIVES
1. Timothy J. Penny (D)
2. Vin Weber (R)
3. Jim Ramstad (R)
4. Bruce F. Vento (D)
5. Martin O. Sabo (D)
6. Gerry Sikorski (D)
7. Collin C. Peterson (D)
8. James L. Oberstar (D)

POSTWAR VOTE FOR PRESIDENT

Year	Total Vote	Republican Vote	Candidate	Democratic Vote	Candidate	Other Vote	Plurality	Total Vote Rep.	Total Vote Dem.	Major Vote Rep.	Major Vote Dem.
1988	2,096,790	962,337	Bush, George	1,109,471	Dukakis, Michael S.	24,982	147,134 D	45.9%	52.9%	46.4%	53.6%
1984	2,084,449	1,032,603	Reagan, Ronald	1,036,364	Mondale, Walter F.	15,482	3,761 D	49.5%	49.7%	49.9%	50.1%
1980	2,051,980	873,268	Reagan, Ronald	954,174	Carter, Jimmy	224,538	80,906 D	42.6%	46.5%	47.8%	52.2%
1976	1,949,931	819,395	Ford, Gerald R.	1,070,440	Carter, Jimmy	60,096	251,045 D	42.0%	54.9%	43.4%	56.6%
1972	1,741,652	898,269	Nixon, Richard M.	802,346	McGovern, George S.	41,037	95,923 R	51.6%	46.1%	52.8%	47.2%
1968	1,588,506	658,643	Nixon, Richard M.	857,738	Humphrey, Hubert H.	72,125	199,095 D	41.5%	54.0%	43.4%	56.6%
1964	1,554,462	559,624	Goldwater, Barry M.	991,117	Johnson, Lyndon B.	3,721	431,493 D	36.0%	63.8%	36.1%	63.9%
1960	1,541,887	757,915	Nixon, Richard M.	779,933	Kennedy, John F.	4,039	22,018 D	49.2%	50.6%	49.3%	50.7%
1956	1,340,005	719,302	Eisenhower, Dwight D.	617,525	Stevenson, Adlai E.	3,178	101,777 R	53.7%	46.1%	53.8%	46.2%
1952	1,379,483	763,211	Eisenhower, Dwight D.	608,458	Stevenson, Adlai E.	7,814	154,753 R	55.3%	44.1%	55.6%	44.4%
1948	1,212,226	483,617	Dewey, Thomas E.	692,966	Truman, Harry S.	35,643	209,349 D	39.9%	57.2%	41.1%	58.9%

MINNESOTA

POSTWAR VOTE FOR GOVERNOR

Year	Total Vote	Republican Vote	Candidate	Democratic Vote	Candidate	Other Vote	Rep-Dem. Plurality	Percentage Total Vote Rep.	Dem.	Major Vote Rep.	Dem.
1990	1,806,777	895,988	Carlson, Arne	836,218	Perpich, Rudy	74,571	59,770 R	49.6%	46.3%	51.7%	48.3%
1986	1,415,989	606,755	Ludeman, Cal R.	790,138	Perpich, Rudy	19,096	183,383 D	42.9%	55.8%	43.4%	56.6%
1982	1,789,539	715,796	Whitney, Wheelock	1,049,104	Perpich, Rudy	24,639	333,308 D	40.0%	58.6%	40.6%	59.4%
1978	1,585,702	830,019	Quie, Albert H.	718,244	Perpich, Rudy	37,439	111,775 R	52.3%	45.3%	53.6%	46.4%
1974	1,252,898	367,722	Johnson, John W.	786,787	Anderson, Wendell R.	98,389	419,065 D	29.3%	62.8%	31.9%	68.1%
1970	1,365,443	621,780	Head, Douglas M.	737,921	Anderson, Wendell R.	5,742	116,141 D	45.5%	54.0%	45.7%	54.3%
1966	1,295,058	680,593	LeVander, Harold	607,943	Rolvaag, Karl F.	6,522	72,650 R	52.6%	46.9%	52.8%	47.2%
1962 **	1,246,904	619,751	Andersen, Elmer L.	619,842	Rolvaag, Karl F.	7,311	91 D	49.7%	49.7%	50.0%	50.0%
1960	1,550,265	783,813	Andersen, Elmer L.	760,934	Freeman, Orville L.	5,518	22,879 R	50.6%	49.1%	50.7%	49.3%
1958	1,159,915	490,731	MacKinnon, George	658,326	Freeman, Orville L.	10,858	167,595 D	42.3%	56.8%	42.7%	57.3%
1956	1,422,161	685,196	Nelsen, Ancher	731,180	Freeman, Orville L.	5,785	45,984 D	48.2%	51.4%	48.4%	51.6%
1954	1,151,417	538,865	Anderson, C. Elmer	607,099	Freeman, Orville L.	5,453	68,234 D	46.8%	52.7%	47.0%	53.0%
1952	1,418,869	785,125	Anderson, C. Elmer	624,480	Freeman, Orville L.	9,264	160,645 R	55.3%	44.0%	55.7%	44.3%
1950	1,046,632	635,800	Youngdahl, Luther	400,637	Peterson, Harry H.	10,195	235,163 R	60.7%	38.3%	61.3%	38.7%
1948	1,210,894	643,572	Youngdahl, Luther	545,766	Halsted, Charles L.	21,556	97,806 R	53.1%	45.1%	54.1%	45.9%
1946	880,348	519,067	Youngdahl, Luther	349,565	Barker, Harold H.	11,716	169,502 R	59.0%	39.7%	59.8%	40.2%

The term of office of Minnesota's Governor was increased from two to four years effective with the 1962 election.

POSTWAR VOTE FOR SENATOR

Year	Total Vote	Republican Vote	Candidate	Democratic Vote	Candidate	Other Vote	Rep-Dem. Plurality	Percentage Total Vote Rep.	Dem.	Major Vote Rep.	Dem.
1990	1,808,045	864,375	Boschwitz, Rudy	911,999	Wellstone, Paul D.	31,671	47,624 D	47.8%	50.4%	48.7%	51.3%
1988	2,093,953	1,176,210	Durenberger, David	856,694	Humphrey, Hubert H.,III	61,049	319,516 R	56.2%	40.9%	57.9%	42.1%
1984	2,066,143	1,199,926	Boschwitz, Rudy	852,844	Growe, Joan Anderson	13,373	347,082 R	58.1%	41.3%	58.5%	41.5%
1982	1,804,675	949,207	Durenberger, David	840,401	Dayton, Mark	15,067	108,806 R	52.6%	46.6%	53.0%	47.0%
1978	1,580,778	894,092	Boschwitz, Rudy	638,375	Anderson, Wendell R.	48,311	255,717 R	56.6%	40.4%	58.3%	41.7%
1978 S	1,560,724	957,908	Durenberger, David	538,675	Short, Robert E.	64,141	419,233 R	61.4%	34.5%	64.0%	36.0%
1976	1,912,068	478,611	Brekke, Gerald W.	1,290,736	Humphrey, Hubert H.	142,721	812,125 D	25.0%	67.5%	27.1%	72.9%
1972	1,731,653	742,121	Hansen, Philip	981,340	Mondale, Walter F.	8,192	239,219 D	42.9%	56.7%	43.1%	56.9%
1970	1,364,887	568,025	MacGregor, Clark	788,256	Humphrey, Hubert H.	8,606	220,231 D	41.6%	57.8%	41.9%	58.1%
1966	1,271,426	574,868	Forsythe, Robert A.	685,840	Mondale, Walter F.	10,718	110,972 D	45.2%	53.9%	45.6%	54.4%
1964	1,543,590	605,933	Whitney, Wheelock	931,353	McCarthy, Eugene J.	6,304	325,420 D	39.3%	60.3%	39.4%	60.6%
1960	1,536,839	648,586	Peterson, P. K.	884,168	Humphrey, Hubert H.	4,085	235,582 D	42.2%	57.5%	42.3%	57.7%
1958	1,150,883	536,629	Thye, Edward J.	608,847	McCarthy, Eugene J.	5,407	72,218 D	46.6%	52.9%	46.8%	53.2%
1954	1,138,952	479,619	Bjornson, Val	642,193	Humphrey, Hubert H.	17,140	162,574 D	42.1%	56.4%	42.8%	57.2%
1952	1,387,419	785,649	Thye, Edward J.	590,011	Carlson, William E.	11,759	195,638 R	56.6%	42.5%	57.1%	42.9%
1948	1,220,250	485,801	Ball, Joseph H.	729,494	Humphrey, Hubert H.	4,955	243,693 D	39.8%	59.8%	40.0%	60.0%
1946	878,731	517,775	Thye, Edward J.	349,520	Jorgenson, Theodore	11,436	168,255 R	58.9%	39.8%	59.7%	40.3%

One of the 1978 elections was for a short term to fill a vacancy.

254

MINNESOTA

Districts Established March 11, 1982

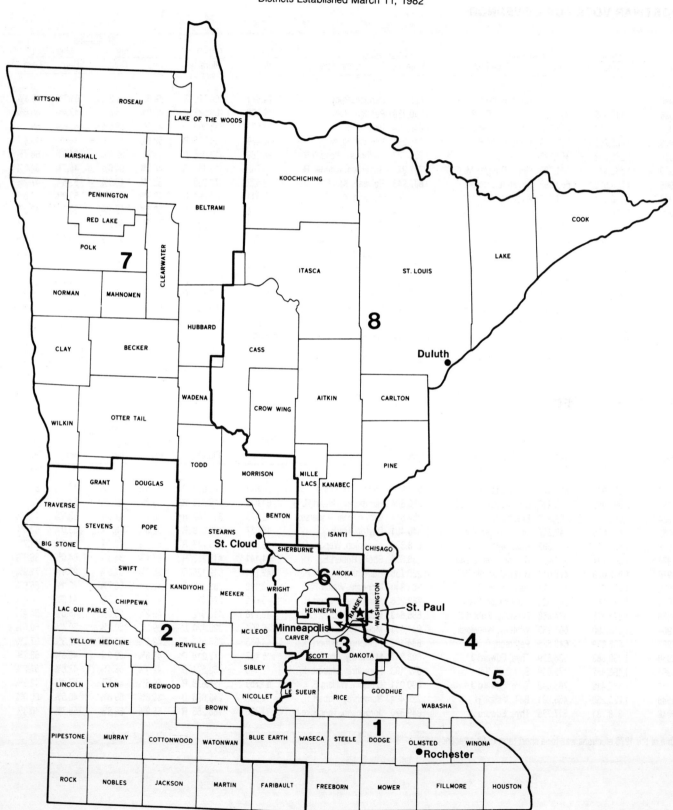

© ERC

MINNESOTA

GOVERNOR 1990

1990 Census Population	County	Total Vote	Republican	Democratic	Other	Rep.-Dem. Plurality	Percentage Total Vote Rep.	Dem.	Major Vote Rep.	Dem.
12,425	AITKIN	6,386	2,735	3,313	338	578 D	42.8%	51.9%	45.2%	54.8%
243,641	ANOKA	91,260	42,993	45,029	3,238	2,036 D	47.1%	49.3%	48.8%	51.2%
27,881	BECKER	11,020	5,043	5,503	474	460 D	45.8%	49.9%	47.8%	52.2%
34,384	BELTRAMI	11,759	5,306	5,896	557	590 D	45.1%	50.1%	47.4%	52.6%
30,185	BENTON	10,972	4,826	5,517	629	691 D	44.0%	50.3%	46.7%	53.3%
6,285	BIG STONE	3,214	1,337	1,759	118	422 D	41.6%	54.7%	43.2%	56.8%
54,044	BLUE EARTH	21,186	11,372	8,949	865	2,423 R	53.7%	42.2%	56.0%	44.0%
26,984	BROWN	10,153	5,562	4,251	340	1,311 R	54.8%	41.9%	56.7%	43.3%
29,259	CARLTON	12,003	2,860	8,806	337	5,946 D	23.8%	73.4%	24.5%	75.5%
47,915	CARVER	19,386	11,065	7,614	707	3,451 R	57.1%	39.3%	59.2%	40.8%
21,791	CASS	9,845	4,821	4,510	514	311 R	49.0%	45.8%	51.7%	48.3%
13,228	CHIPPEWA	5,660	2,800	2,655	205	145 R	49.5%	46.9%	51.3%	48.7%
30,521	CHISAGO	13,023	6,260	6,197	566	63 R	48.1%	47.6%	50.3%	49.7%
50,422	CLAY	17,452	7,544	9,471	437	1,927 D	43.2%	54.3%	44.3%	55.7%
8,309	CLEARWATER	3,300	1,294	1,892	114	598 D	39.2%	57.3%	40.6%	59.4%
3,868	COOK	1,876	771	962	143	191 D	41.1%	51.3%	44.5%	55.5%
12,694	COTTONWOOD	5,579	3,037	2,352	190	685 R	54.4%	42.2%	56.4%	43.6%
44,249	CROW WING	20,180	9,920	9,305	955	615 R	49.2%	46.1%	51.6%	48.4%
275,227	DAKOTA	111,807	63,354	44,230	4,223	19,124 R	56.7%	39.6%	58.9%	41.1%
15,731	DODGE	6,055	3,249	2,574	232	675 R	53.7%	42.5%	55.8%	44.2%
28,674	DOUGLAS	12,831	6,196	6,093	542	103 R	48.3%	47.5%	50.4%	49.6%
16,937	FARIBAULT	7,864	4,391	3,209	264	1,182 R	55.8%	40.8%	57.8%	42.2%
20,777	FILLMORE	7,830	4,461	3,168	201	1,293 R	57.0%	40.5%	58.5%	41.5%
33,060	FREEBORN	13,118	6,542	6,199	377	343 R	49.9%	47.3%	51.3%	48.7%
40,690	GOODHUE	16,581	10,167	6,008	406	4,159 R	61.3%	36.2%	62.9%	37.1%
6,246	GRANT	3,323	1,480	1,741	102	261 D	44.5%	52.4%	45.9%	54.1%
1,032,431	HENNEPIN	457,748	246,340	189,861	21,547	56,479 R	53.8%	41.5%	56.5%	43.5%
18,497	HOUSTON	7,799	3,563	4,002	234	439 D	45.7%	51.3%	47.1%	52.9%
14,939	HUBBARD	6,884	3,575	3,009	300	566 R	51.9%	43.7%	54.3%	45.7%
25,921	ISANTI	10,437	4,139	5,855	443	1,716 D	39.7%	56.1%	41.4%	58.6%
40,863	ITASCA	17,691	5,011	11,874	806	6,863 D	28.3%	67.1%	29.7%	70.3%
11,677	JACKSON	5,501	2,536	2,678	287	142 D	46.1%	48.7%	48.6%	51.4%
12,802	KANABEC	5,052	2,161	2,704	187	543 D	42.8%	53.5%	44.4%	55.6%
38,761	KANDIYOHI	15,420	6,878	7,955	587	1,077 D	44.6%	51.6%	46.4%	53.6%
5,767	KITTSON	2,449	1,011	1,366	72	355 D	41.3%	55.8%	42.5%	57.5%
16,299	KOOCHICHING	6,009	2,171	3,560	278	1,389 D	36.1%	59.2%	37.9%	62.1%
8,924	LAC QUI PARLE	4,540	2,058	2,360	122	302 D	45.3%	52.0%	46.6%	53.4%
10,415	LAKE	5,727	1,226	4,209	292	2,983 D	21.4%	73.5%	22.6%	77.4%
4,076	LAKE OF THE WOODS	1,692	609	983	100	374 D	36.0%	58.1%	38.3%	61.7%
23,239	LE SUEUR	9,927	4,595	5,007	325	412 D	46.3%	50.4%	47.9%	52.1%
6,890	LINCOLN	2,979	1,513	1,406	60	107 R	50.8%	47.2%	51.8%	48.2%
24,789	LYON	9,998	5,591	4,016	391	1,575 R	55.9%	40.2%	58.2%	41.8%
32,030	MCLEOD	11,922	6,504	4,818	600	1,686 R	54.6%	40.4%	57.4%	42.6%
5,044	MAHNOMEN	2,375	707	1,538	130	831 D	29.8%	64.8%	31.5%	68.5%
10,993	MARSHALL	4,781	1,681	3,004	96	1,323 D	35.2%	62.8%	35.9%	64.1%
22,914	MARTIN	8,980	5,314	3,395	271	1,919 R	59.2%	37.8%	61.0%	39.0%
20,846	MEEKER	9,005	4,453	4,171	381	282 R	49.5%	46.3%	51.6%	48.4%
18,670	MILLE LACS	7,942	3,330	4,219	393	889 D	41.9%	53.1%	44.1%	55.9%
29,604	MORRISON	11,429	4,438	6,438	553	2,000 D	38.8%	56.3%	40.8%	59.2%
37,385	MOWER	14,942	6,555	7,935	452	1,380 D	43.9%	53.1%	45.2%	54.8%
9,660	MURRAY	4,640	2,034	2,419	187	385 D	43.8%	52.1%	45.7%	54.3%
28,076	NICOLLET	11,825	6,763	4,704	358	2,059 R	57.2%	39.8%	59.0%	41.0%
20,098	NOBLES	7,638	3,059	4,340	239	1,281 D	40.0%	56.8%	41.3%	58.7%
7,975	NORMAN	3,633	1,392	2,123	118	731 D	38.3%	58.4%	39.6%	60.4%
106,470	OLMSTED	40,243	23,294	15,605	1,344	7,689 R	57.9%	38.8%	59.9%	40.1%
50,714	OTTER TAIL	21,229	10,398	10,169	662	229 R	49.0%	47.9%	50.6%	49.4%
13,306	PENNINGTON	4,943	1,801	3,030	112	1,229 D	36.4%	61.3%	37.3%	62.7%
21,264	PINE	8,747	3,125	5,176	446	2,051 D	35.7%	59.2%	37.6%	62.4%
10,491	PIPESTONE	3,848	1,746	1,984	118	238 D	45.4%	51.6%	46.8%	53.2%
32,498	POLK	11,284	4,387	6,617	280	2,230 D	38.9%	58.6%	39.9%	60.1%

MINNESOTA

GOVERNOR 1990

1990 Census Population	County	Total Vote	Republican	Democratic	Other	Rep.-Dem. Plurality	Percentage			
							Total Vote		Major Vote	
							Rep.	Dem.	Rep.	Dem.
10,745	POPE	4,946	2,345	2,444	157	99 D	47.4%	49.4%	49.0%	51.0%
485,765	RAMSEY	199,984	107,125	83,672	9,187	23,453 R	53.6%	41.8%	56.1%	43.9%
4,525	RED LAKE	2,349	590	1,664	95	1,074 D	25.1%	70.8%	26.2%	73.8%
17,254	REDWOOD	7,132	4,125	2,709	298	1,416 R	57.8%	38.0%	60.4%	39.6%
17,673	RENVILLE	7,857	4,189	3,365	303	824 R	53.3%	42.8%	55.5%	44.5%
49,183	RICE	18,349	9,095	8,503	751	592 R	49.6%	46.3%	51.7%	48.3%
9,806	ROCK	4,358	2,177	2,097	84	80 R	50.0%	48.1%	50.9%	49.1%
15,026	ROSEAU	5,685	2,130	3,355	200	1,225 D	37.5%	59.0%	38.8%	61.2%
198,213	ST. LOUIS	84,724	19,996	62,149	2,579	42,153 D	23.6%	73.4%	24.3%	75.7%
57,846	SCOTT	22,592	11,332	10,377	883	955 R	50.2%	45.9%	52.2%	47.8%
41,945	SHERBURNE	15,073	6,880	7,448	745	568 D	45.6%	49.4%	48.0%	52.0%
14,366	SIBLEY	5,811	3,303	2,288	220	1,015 R	56.8%	39.4%	59.1%	40.9%
118,791	STEARNS	44,427	19,694	22,046	2,687	2,352 R	44.3%	49.6%	47.2%	52.8%
30,729	STEELE	11,779	6,529	4,934	316	1,595 R	55.4%	41.9%	57.0%	43.0%
10,634	STEVENS	4,771	2,233	2,360	178	127 D	46.8%	49.5%	48.6%	51.4%
10,724	SWIFT	5,203	2,035	2,999	169	964 D	39.1%	57.6%	40.4%	59.6%
23,363	TODD	9,237	3,656	5,145	436	1,489 D	39.6%	55.7%	41.5%	58.5%
4,463	TRAVERSE	2,163	1,036	1,052	75	16 D	47.9%	48.6%	49.6%	50.4%
19,744	WABASHA	8,286	4,393	3,575	318	818 R	53.0%	43.1%	55.1%	44.9%
13,154	WADENA	5,763	2,945	2,528	290	417 R	51.1%	43.9%	53.8%	46.2%
18,079	WASECA	7,566	4,141	3,180	245	961 R	54.7%	42.0%	56.6%	43.4%
145,896	WASHINGTON	60,844	36,506	22,049	2,289	14,457 R	60.0%	36.2%	62.3%	37.7%
11,682	WATONWAN	4,929	2,718	2,075	136	643 R	55.1%	42.1%	56.7%	43.3%
7,516	WILKIN	2,805	1,221	1,497	87	276 D	43.5%	53.4%	44.9%	55.1%
47,828	WINONA	15,423	7,626	7,229	568	397 R	49.4%	46.9%	51.3%	48.7%
68,710	WRIGHT	26,265	11,715	13,293	1,257	1,578 D	44.6%	50.6%	46.8%	53.2%
11,684	YELLOW MEDICINE	5,534	2,909	2,452	173	457 R	52.6%	44.3%	54.3%	45.7%
4,375,099	TOTAL	1,806,777	895,988	836,218	74,571	59,770 R	49.6%	46.3%	51.7%	48.3%

MINNESOTA

SENATOR 1990

1990 Census Population	County	Total Vote	Republican	Democratic	Other	Rep.-Dem. Plurality	Percentage Total Vote Rep.	Dem.	Major Vote Rep.	Dem.
12,425	AITKIN	6,506	2,974	3,393	139	419 D	45.7%	52.2%	46.7%	53.3%
243,641	ANOKA	91,430	41,617	48,002	1,811	6,385 D	45.5%	52.5%	46.4%	53.6%
27,881	BECKER	11,183	5,732	5,246	205	486 R	51.3%	46.9%	52.2%	47.8%
34,384	BELTRAMI	11,817	5,355	6,270	192	915 D	45.3%	53.1%	46.1%	53.9%
30,185	BENTON	11,017	5,750	4,985	282	765 R	52.2%	45.2%	53.6%	46.4%
6,285	BIG STONE	3,250	1,551	1,647	52	96 D	47.7%	50.7%	48.5%	51.5%
54,044	BLUE EARTH	21,303	11,353	9,542	408	1,811 R	53.3%	44.8%	54.3%	45.7%
26,984	BROWN	10,167	6,217	3,779	171	2,438 R	61.1%	37.2%	62.2%	37.8%
29,259	CARLTON	11,504	4,123	7,153	228	3,030 D	35.8%	62.2%	36.6%	63.4%
47,915	CARVER	19,208	10,889	7,955	364	2,934 R	56.7%	41.4%	57.8%	42.2%
21,791	CASS	10,032	5,134	4,674	224	460 R	51.2%	46.6%	52.3%	47.7%
13,228	CHIPPEWA	5,585	2,797	2,705	83	92 R	50.1%	48.4%	50.8%	49.2%
30,521	CHISAGO	13,128	5,917	6,957	254	1,040 D	45.1%	53.0%	46.0%	54.0%
50,422	CLAY	17,275	9,510	7,568	197	1,942 R	55.1%	43.8%	55.7%	44.3%
8,309	CLEARWATER	3,369	1,647	1,652	70	5 D	48.9%	49.0%	49.9%	50.1%
3,868	COOK	1,899	846	1,019	34	173 D	44.5%	53.7%	45.4%	54.6%
12,694	COTTONWOOD	5,700	3,103	2,491	106	612 R	54.4%	43.7%	55.5%	44.5%
44,249	CROW WING	20,105	10,736	8,947	422	1,789 R	53.4%	44.5%	54.5%	45.5%
275,227	DAKOTA	112,033	54,964	55,272	1,797	308 D	49.1%	49.3%	49.9%	50.1%
15,731	DODGE	5,953	3,539	2,246	168	1,293 R	59.4%	37.7%	61.2%	38.8%
28,674	DOUGLAS	13,189	7,596	5,398	195	2,198 R	57.6%	40.9%	58.5%	41.5%
16,937	FARIBAULT	7,989	4,928	2,903	158	2,025 R	61.7%	36.3%	62.9%	37.1%
20,777	FILLMORE	7,856	4,625	3,093	138	1,532 R	58.9%	39.4%	59.9%	40.1%
33,060	FREEBORN	12,963	6,892	5,822	249	1,070 R	53.2%	44.9%	54.2%	45.8%
40,690	GOODHUE	16,358	8,893	7,174	291	1,719 R	54.4%	43.9%	55.3%	44.7%
6,246	GRANT	3,385	1,630	1,703	52	73 D	48.2%	50.3%	48.9%	51.1%
1,032,431	HENNEPIN	455,296	206,917	240,818	7,561	33,901 D	45.4%	52.9%	46.2%	53.8%
18,497	HOUSTON	7,786	4,648	2,946	192	1,702 R	59.7%	37.8%	61.2%	38.8%
14,939	HUBBARD	6,934	3,553	3,239	142	314 R	51.2%	46.7%	52.3%	47.7%
25,921	ISANTI	10,594	5,053	5,351	190	298 D	47.7%	50.5%	48.6%	51.4%
40,863	ITASCA	17,300	7,357	9,583	360	2,226 D	42.5%	55.4%	43.4%	56.6%
11,677	JACKSON	5,447	3,133	2,232	82	901 R	57.5%	41.0%	58.4%	41.6%
12,802	KANABEC	5,136	2,566	2,458	112	108 R	50.0%	47.9%	51.1%	48.9%
38,761	KANDIYOHI	15,487	8,142	7,105	240	1,037 R	52.6%	45.9%	53.4%	46.6%
5,767	KITTSON	2,507	1,229	1,253	25	24 D	49.0%	50.0%	49.5%	50.5%
16,299	KOOCHICHING	6,087	2,637	3,344	106	707 D	43.3%	54.9%	44.1%	55.9%
8,924	LAC QUI PARLE	4,532	2,126	2,320	86	194 D	46.9%	51.2%	47.8%	52.2%
10,415	LAKE	5,653	1,910	3,648	95	1,738 D	33.8%	64.5%	34.4%	65.6%
4,076	LAKE OF THE WOODS	1,724	885	806	33	79 R	51.3%	46.8%	52.3%	47.7%
23,239	LE SUEUR	9,952	5,478	4,327	147	1,151 R	55.0%	43.5%	55.9%	44.1%
6,890	LINCOLN	3,015	1,422	1,501	92	79 D	47.2%	49.8%	48.6%	51.4%
24,789	LYON	10,118	5,484	4,466	168	1,018 R	54.2%	44.1%	55.1%	44.9%
32,030	MCLEOD	11,853	7,009	4,648	196	2,361 R	59.1%	39.2%	60.1%	39.9%
5,044	MAHNOMEN	2,428	1,191	1,180	57	11 R	49.1%	48.6%	50.2%	49.8%
10,993	MARSHALL	4,867	2,491	2,297	79	194 R	51.2%	47.2%	52.0%	48.0%
22,914	MARTIN	9,121	5,523	3,466	132	2,057 R	60.6%	38.0%	61.4%	38.6%
20,846	MEEKER	9,148	4,936	4,030	182	906 R	54.0%	44.1%	55.1%	44.9%
18,670	MILLE LACS	7,583	3,687	3,756	140	69 D	48.6%	49.5%	49.5%	50.5%
29,604	MORRISON	11,537	6,231	5,038	268	1,193 R	54.0%	43.7%	55.3%	44.7%
37,385	MOWER	14,888	6,701	7,906	281	1,205 D	45.0%	53.1%	45.9%	54.1%
9,660	MURRAY	4,745	2,388	2,239	118	149 R	50.3%	47.2%	51.6%	48.4%
28,076	NICOLLET	12,203	6,563	5,433	207	1,130 R	53.8%	44.5%	54.7%	45.3%
20,098	NOBLES	7,732	4,311	3,255	166	1,056 R	55.8%	42.1%	57.0%	43.0%
7,975	NORMAN	3,681	1,863	1,748	70	115 R	50.6%	47.5%	51.6%	48.4%
106,470	OLMSTED	40,575	24,627	15,243	705	9,384 R	60.7%	37.6%	61.8%	38.2%
50,714	OTTER TAIL	21,568	12,336	8,924	308	3,412 R	57.2%	41.4%	58.0%	42.0%
13,306	PENNINGTON	4,916	2,563	2,295	58	268 R	52.1%	46.7%	52.8%	47.2%
21,264	PINE	8,843	4,085	4,540	218	455 D	46.2%	51.3%	47.4%	52.6%
10,491	PIPESTONE	3,924	2,169	1,687	68	482 R	55.3%	43.0%	56.3%	43.8%
32,498	POLK	10,877	5,887	4,839	151	1,048 R	54.1%	44.5%	54.9%	45.1%

MINNESOTA

SENATOR 1990

1990 Census Population	County	Total Vote	Republican	Democratic	Other	Rep.-Dem. Plurality	Percentage			
							Total Vote		Major Vote	
							Rep.	Dem.	Rep.	Dem.
10,745	POPE	4,999	2,702	2,210	87	492 R	54.1%	44.2%	55.0%	45.0%
485,765	RAMSEY	200,778	79,525	117,972	3,281	38,447 D	39.6%	58.8%	40.3%	59.7%
4,525	RED LAKE	2,401	1,287	1,073	41	214 R	53.6%	44.7%	54.5%	45.5%
17,254	REDWOOD	7,331	4,491	2,691	149	1,800 R	61.3%	36.7%	62.5%	37.5%
17,673	RENVILLE	7,869	3,990	3,725	154	265 R	50.7%	47.3%	51.7%	48.3%
49,183	RICE	18,077	8,243	9,624	210	1,381 D	45.6%	53.2%	46.1%	53.9%
9,806	ROCK	4,443	2,733	1,659	51	1,074 R	61.5%	37.3%	62.2%	37.8%
15,026	ROSEAU	5,761	3,032	2,605	124	427 R	52.6%	45.2%	53.8%	46.2%
198,213	ST. LOUIS	83,971	26,043	56,638	1,290	30,595 D	31.0%	67.4%	31.5%	68.5%
57,846	SCOTT	22,667	11,831	10,413	423	1,418 R	52.2%	45.9%	53.2%	46.8%
41,945	SHERBURNE	15,096	7,723	7,092	281	631 R	51.2%	47.0%	52.1%	47.9%
14,366	SIBLEY	5,919	3,454	2,377	88	1,077 R	58.4%	40.2%	59.2%	40.8%
118,791	STEARNS	45,339	25,276	19,073	990	6,203 R	55.7%	42.1%	57.0%	43.0%
30,729	STEELE	11,697	7,434	4,094	169	3,340 R	63.6%	35.0%	64.5%	35.5%
10,634	STEVENS	4,845	2,665	2,118	62	547 R	55.0%	43.7%	55.7%	44.3%
10,724	SWIFT	5,231	2,438	2,698	95	260 D	46.6%	51.6%	47.5%	52.5%
23,363	TODD	9,412	5,132	4,038	242	1,094 R	54.5%	42.9%	56.0%	44.0%
4,463	TRAVERSE	2,188	1,114	1,046	28	68 R	50.9%	47.8%	51.6%	48.4%
19,744	WABASHA	8,344	4,763	3,360	221	1,403 R	57.1%	40.3%	58.6%	41.4%
13,154	WADENA	5,925	3,336	2,455	134	881 R	56.3%	41.4%	57.6%	42.4%
18,079	WASECA	7,430	4,328	2,954	148	1,374 R	58.3%	39.8%	59.4%	40.6%
145,896	WASHINGTON	60,394	28,007	31,391	996	3,384 D	46.4%	52.0%	47.2%	52.8%
11,682	WATONWAN	4,979	2,783	2,124	72	659 R	55.9%	42.7%	56.7%	43.3%
7,516	WILKIN	2,836	1,770	1,025	41	745 R	62.4%	36.1%	63.3%	36.7%
47,828	WINONA	15,539	8,290	6,931	318	1,359 R	53.3%	44.6%	54.5%	45.5%
68,710	WRIGHT	26,691	13,870	12,262	559	1,608 R	52.0%	45.9%	53.1%	46.9%
11,684	YELLOW MEDICINE	5,622	2,696	2,834	92	138 D	48.0%	50.4%	48.8%	51.2%
4,375,099	TOTAL	1,808,045	864,375	911,999	31,671	47,624 D	47.8%	50.4%	48.7%	51.3%

MINNESOTA

CONGRESS

CD	Year	Total Vote	Republican Vote	Republican Candidate	Democratic Vote	Democratic Candidate	Other Vote	Rep.-Dem. Plurality	Total Vote Rep.	Total Vote Dem.	Major Vote Rep.	Major Vote Dem.
1	1990	200,663	43,856	ANDERSEN, DOUG	156,749	PENNY, TIMOTHY J.	58	112,893 D	21.9%	78.1%	21.9%	78.1%
1	1988	229,813	67,709	SCHRIMPF, CURT	161,118	PENNY, TIMOTHY J.	986	93,409 D	29.5%	70.1%	29.6%	70.4%
1	1986	172,877	47,750	GRAWE, PAUL H.	125,115	PENNY, TIMOTHY J.	12	77,365 D	27.6%	72.4%	27.6%	72.4%
1	1984	245,837	105,723	SPICER, KEITH	140,095	PENNY, TIMOTHY J.	19	34,372 D	43.0%	57.0%	43.0%	57.0%
1	1982	213,520	102,298	HAGEDORN, TOM	109,257	PENNY, TIMOTHY J.	1,965	6,959 D	47.9%	51.2%	48.4%	51.6%
2	1990	204,404	126,367	WEBER, VIN	77,935	STONE, JIM	102	48,432 R	61.8%	38.1%	61.9%	38.1%
2	1988	227,701	131,639	WEBER, VIN	96,016	PETERSON, DOUG	46	35,623 R	57.8%	42.2%	57.8%	42.2%
2	1986	194,315	100,249	WEBER, VIN	94,048	JOHNSON, DAVE	18	6,201 R	51.6%	48.4%	51.6%	48.4%
2	1984	243,097	153,308	WEBER, VIN	89,770	LUNDQUIST, TODD	19	63,538 R	63.1%	36.9%	63.1%	36.9%
2	1982	226,751	123,508	WEBER, VIN	103,243	NICHOLS, JAMES W.		20,265 R	54.5%	45.5%	54.5%	45.5%
3	1990	292,852	195,833	RAMSTAD, JIM	96,395	DEMARS, LOU	624	99,438 R	66.9%	32.9%	67.0%	33.0%
3	1988	315,609	215,322	FRENZEL, BILL	99,770	CARLSON, DAVE	517	115,552 R	68.2%	31.6%	68.3%	31.7%
3	1986	181,729	127,434	FRENZEL, BILL	54,261	STOCK, RAY	34	73,173 R	70.1%	29.9%	70.1%	29.9%
3	1984	283,978	207,819	FRENZEL, BILL	76,132	PETERSON, DAVE	27	131,687 R	73.2%	26.8%	73.2%	26.8%
3	1982	231,311	166,891	FRENZEL, BILL	60,993	SALITERMAN, JOEL A.	3,427	105,898 R	72.2%	26.4%	73.2%	26.8%
4	1990	221,396	77,639	MAITLAND, IAN	143,353	VENTO, BRUCE F.	404	65,714 D	35.1%	64.7%	35.1%	64.9%
4	1988	250,327	67,073	MAITLAND, IAN	181,227	VENTO, BRUCE F.	2,027	114,154 D	26.8%	72.4%	27.0%	73.0%
4	1986	154,635	41,926	STASSEN, HAROLD E.	112,662	VENTO, BRUCE F.	47	70,736 D	27.1%	72.9%	27.1%	72.9%
4	1984	228,071	57,450	RACHNER, MARY JANE	167,678	VENTO, BRUCE F.	2,943	110,228 D	25.2%	73.5%	25.5%	74.5%
4	1982	209,742	56,248	JAMES, BILL	153,494	VENTO, BRUCE F.		97,246 D	26.8%	73.2%	26.8%	73.2%
5	1990	198,886	53,720	GILBERTSON, RAYMOND	144,682	SABO, MARTIN O.	484	90,962 D	27.0%	72.7%	27.1%	72.9%
5	1988	241,798	60,646	GILBERTSON, RAYMOND	174,416	SABO, MARTIN O.	6,736	113,770 D	25.1%	72.1%	25.8%	74.2%
5	1986	145,031	37,583	SERRA, RICK	105,410	SABO, MARTIN O.	2,038	67,827 D	25.9%	72.7%	26.3%	73.7%
5	1984	235,470	62,642	WEIBLEN, RICHARD	165,075	SABO, MARTIN O.	7,753	102,433 D	26.6%	70.1%	27.5%	72.5%
5	1982	208,452	61,184	JOHNSON, KEITH W.	136,634	SABO, MARTIN O.	10,634	75,450 D	29.4%	65.5%	30.9%	69.1%
6	1990	255,219	90,138	ANDERSON, BRUCE D.	164,816	SIKORSKI, GERRY	265	74,678 D	35.3%	64.6%	35.4%	64.6%
6	1988	259,035	89,209	PLOETZ, RAY	169,486	SIKORSKI, GERRY	340	80,277 D	34.4%	65.4%	34.5%	65.5%
6	1986	168,077	57,460	SYKORA, BARBARA Z.	110,598	SIKORSKI, GERRY	19	53,138 D	34.2%	65.8%	34.2%	65.8%
6	1984	255,692	101,058	TRUEMAN, PATRICK	154,603	SIKORSKI, GERRY	31	53,545 D	39.5%	60.5%	39.5%	60.5%
6	1982	214,980	105,734	ERDAHL, ARLEN	109,246	SIKORSKI, GERRY		3,512 D	49.2%	50.8%	49.2%	50.8%
7	1990	200,186	92,876	STANGELAND, ARLAN	107,126	PETERSON, COLLIN C.	184	14,250 D	46.4%	53.5%	46.4%	53.6%
7	1988	222,496	121,396	STANGELAND, ARLAN	101,011	HANSON, MARV	89	20,385 R	54.6%	45.4%	54.6%	45.4%
7	1986	189,264	94,024	STANGELAND, ARLAN	93,903	PETERSON, COLLIN C.	1,337	121 R	49.7%	49.6%	50.0%	50.0%
7	1984	236,839	135,087	STANGELAND, ARLAN	101,720	PETERSON, COLLIN C.	32	33,367 R	57.0%	42.9%	57.0%	43.0%
7	1982	215,316	108,254	STANGELAND, ARLAN	107,062	WENSTROM, GENE		1,192 R	50.3%	49.7%	50.3%	49.7%
8	1990	207,312	56,068	SHUSTER, JERRY	151,145	OBERSTAR, JAMES L.	99	95,077 D	27.0%	72.9%	27.1%	72.9%
8	1988	222,311	56,630	SHUSTER, JERRY	165,656	OBERSTAR, JAMES L.	25	109,026 D	25.5%	74.5%	25.5%	74.5%
8	1986	187,045	51,315	RUED, DAVE	135,718	OBERSTAR, JAMES L.	12	84,403 D	27.4%	72.6%	27.4%	72.6%
8	1984	246,483	79,181	RUED, DAVE	165,727	OBERSTAR, JAMES L.	1,575	86,546 D	32.1%	67.2%	32.3%	67.7%
8	1982	229,859	53,467	LUCE, MARJORY L.	176,392	OBERSTAR, JAMES L.		122,925 D	23.3%	76.7%	23.3%	76.7%

MINNESOTA

1990 GENERAL ELECTION

In Minnesota the Democratic party is known as the Democratic-Farmer-Labor party and the Republican party as the Independent-Republican party; candidates appear on the ballot with these designations.

Governor   Other vote was 21,139 Earth Rights (Chosa); 17,176 Grassroots (Culerhouse); 10,941 Jon Grunseth, the original Republican nominee; 6,701 Socialist Workers (Lyons); 18,614 scattered write-in. Jon Grunseth, the original Republican nominee withdrew (October 29) too late to remove his name from the November 6 ballot. Voters were given a supplemental ballot with Arne Carlson as the Republican candidate, but some voters chose to vote for Mr. Grunseth.

Senator   Other vote was 29,820 Grassroots (Bentley) and 1,851 scattered write-in.

Congress   Other vote was scattered write-in in all CD's.

1990 PRIMARIES

SEPTEMBER 11 REPUBLICAN

Governor   169,451 Jon Grunseth; 108,446 Arne Carlson; 57,872 Doug Kelley; 2,944 Mary Jane Rachner; 2,557 Samuel A. Faulk; 1,609 Beatrice Mooney. Mr. Grunseth withdrew after the primary and Arne Carlson was substituted by the state party committee.

Senator   293,619 Rudy Boschwitz; 44,202 John J. Zeleniak.

Congress   Unopposed in six CD's. Contested as follows:

CD 1   28,970 Doug Andersen; 8,102 Germain A. Davison.
CD 3   43,252 Jim Ramstad; 11,387 Dave Drummond.

SEPTEMBER 11 DEMOCRATIC

Governor   218,410 Rudy Perpich; 166,183 Mike Hatch; 8,978 Kent S. Herschbach.

Senator   226,306 Paul D. Wellstone; 129,302 James W. Nichols; 19,379 Gene Schenk.

Congress   Unopposed in seven CD's. Contested as follows:

CD 2   24,189 Jim Stone; 8,293 Gary LeGare.

MISSISSIPPI

GOVERNOR
Ray Mabus (D). Elected 1987 to a four-year term.

SENATORS
Thad Cochran (R). Re-elected 1990 to a six-year term. Previously elected 1984, 1978.

Trent Lott (R). Elected 1988 to a six-year term.

REPRESENTATIVES
1. Jamie L. Whitten (D)
2. Mike Espy (D)
3. G. V. Montgomery (D)
4. Mike Parker (D)
5. Gene Taylor (D)

POSTWAR VOTE FOR PRESIDENT

Year	Total Vote	Republican Vote	Candidate	Democratic Vote	Candidate	Other Vote	Plurality	Rep.	Dem.	Rep.	Dem.
1988	931,527	557,890	Bush, George	363,921	Dukakis, Michael S.	9,716	193,969 R	59.9%	39.1%	60.5%	39.5%
1984	941,104	582,377	Reagan, Ronald	352,192	Mondale, Walter F.	6,535	230,185 R	61.9%	37.4%	62.3%	37.7%
1980	892,620	441,089	Reagan, Ronald	429,281	Carter, Jimmy	22,250	11,808 R	49.4%	48.1%	50.7%	49.3%
1976	769,361	366,846	Ford, Gerald R.	381,309	Carter, Jimmy	21,206	14,463 D	47.7%	49.6%	49.0%	51.0%
1972	645,963	505,125	Nixon, Richard M.	126,782	McGovern, George S.	14,056	378,343 R	78.2%	19.6%	79.9%	20.1%
1968 **	654,509	88,516	Nixon, Richard M.	150,644	Humphrey, Hubert H.	415,349	264,705 A	13.5%	23.0%	37.0%	63.0%
1964	409,146	356,528	Goldwater, Barry M.	52,618	Johnson, Lyndon B.		303,910 R	87.1%	12.9%	87.1%	12.9%
1960 **	298,171	73,561	Nixon, Richard M.	108,362	Kennedy, John F.	116,248	7,886 U	24.7%	36.3%	40.4%	59.6%
1956	248,104	60,685	Eisenhower, Dwight D.	144,453	Stevenson, Adlai E.	42,966	83,768 D	24.5%	58.2%	29.6%	70.4%
1952	285,532	112,966	Eisenhower, Dwight D.	172,566	Stevenson, Adlai E.		59,600 D	39.6%	60.4%	39.6%	60.4%
1948 **	192,190	5,043	Dewey, Thomas E.	19,384	Truman, Harry S.	167,763	148,154 SR	2.6%	10.1%	20.6%	79.4%

In 1968 other vote was Independent (Wallace). In 1960 other vote was Unpledged Independent Democratic. In 1948 other vote was 167,538 States Rights and 225 Progressive.

POSTWAR VOTE FOR GOVERNOR

Year	Total Vote	Republican Vote	Candidate	Democratic Vote	Candidate	Other Vote	Rep-Dem. Plurality	Rep.	Dem.	Rep.	Dem.
1987	721,695	336,006	Reed, Jack	385,689	Mabus, Ray		49,683 D	46.6%	53.4%	46.6%	53.4%
1983	742,737	288,764	Bramlett, Leon	409,209	Allain, William A.	44,764	120,445 D	38.9%	55.1%	41.4%	58.6%
1979	677,322	263,702	Carmichael, Gil	413,620	Winter, William F.		149,918 D	38.9%	61.1%	38.9%	61.1%
1975	708,033	319,632	Carmichael, Gil	369,568	Finch, Cliff	18,833	49,936 D	45.1%	52.2%	46.4%	53.6%
1971	780,537		—	601,122	Waller, William L.	179,415	601,122 D		77.0%		100.0%
1967	448,697	133,379	Phillips, Rubel L.	315,318	Williams, John Bell		181,939 D	29.7%	70.3%	29.7%	70.3%
1963	363,971	138,515	Phillips, Rubel L.	225,456	Johnson, Paul B.		86,941 D	38.1%	61.9%	38.1%	61.9%
1959	57,671		—	57,671	Barnett, Ross R.		57,671 D		100.0%		100.0%
1955	40,707		—	40,707	Coleman, James P.		40,707 D		100.0%		100.0%
1951	43,422		—	43,422	White, Hugh		43,422 D		100.0%		100.0%
1947	166,095		—	161,993	Wright, Fielding L.	4,102	161,993 D		97.5%		100.0%

MISSISSIPPI

POSTWAR VOTE FOR SENATOR

Year	Total Vote	Republican Vote	Republican Candidate	Democratic Vote	Democratic Candidate	Other Vote	Rep-Dem. Plurality	Total Vote Rep.	Total Vote Dem.	Major Vote Rep.	Major Vote Dem.
1990	274,244	274,244	Cochran, Thad		—		274,244 R	100.0%		100.0%	
1988	946,719	510,380	Lott, Trent	436,339	Dowdy, Wayne		74,041 R	53.9%	46.1%	53.9%	46.1%
1984	952,240	580,314	Cochran, Thad	371,926	Winter, William F.		208,388 R	60.9%	39.1%	60.9%	39.1%
1982	645,026	230,927	Barbour, Haley	414,099	Stennis, John		183,172 D	35.8%	64.2%	35.8%	64.2%
1978	583,936	263,089	Cochran, Thad	185,454	Dantin, Maurice	135,393	77,635 R	45.1%	31.8%	58.7%	41.3%
1976	554,433		—	554,433	Stennis, John		554,433 D		100.0%		100.0%
1972	645,746	249,779	Carmichael, Gil	375,102	Eastland, James O.	20,865	125,323 D	38.7%	58.1%	40.0%	60.0%
1970	324,215		—	286,622	Stennis, John	37,593	286,622 D		88.4%		100.0%
1966	393,900	105,150	Walker, Prentiss	258,248	Eastland, James O.	30,502	153,098 D	26.7%	65.6%	28.9%	71.1%
1964	343,364		—	343,364	Stennis, John		343,364 D		100.0%		100.0%
1960	266,148	21,807	Moore, Joe A.	244,341	Eastland, James O.		222,534 D	8.2%	91.8%	8.2%	91.8%
1958	61,039		—	61,039	Stennis, John		61,039 D		100.0%		100.0%
1954	105,526	4,678	White, James A.	100,848	Eastland, James O.		96,170 D	4.4%	95.6%	4.4%	95.6%
1952	233,919		—	233,919	Stennis, John		233,919 D		100.0%		100.0%
1948	151,478		—	151,478	Eastland, James O.		151,478 D		100.0%		100.0%
1947 S	193,709		[See note below]								
1946	46,747		—	46,747	Bilbo, Theodore		46,747 D		100.0%		100.0%

The 1947 election was for a short term to fill a vacancy and was held without party designation or nomination; John Stennis polled 52,068 votes (26.9% of the total vote) and won the election with a 6,343 plurality. Other candidate votes in this election were 45,725 W. M. Colmer; 43,642 Forrest B. Jackson; 27,159 Paul B. Johnson; 24,492 John E. Rankin and 623 R. L. Collins.

MISSISSIPPI

Districts Established January 6, 1984

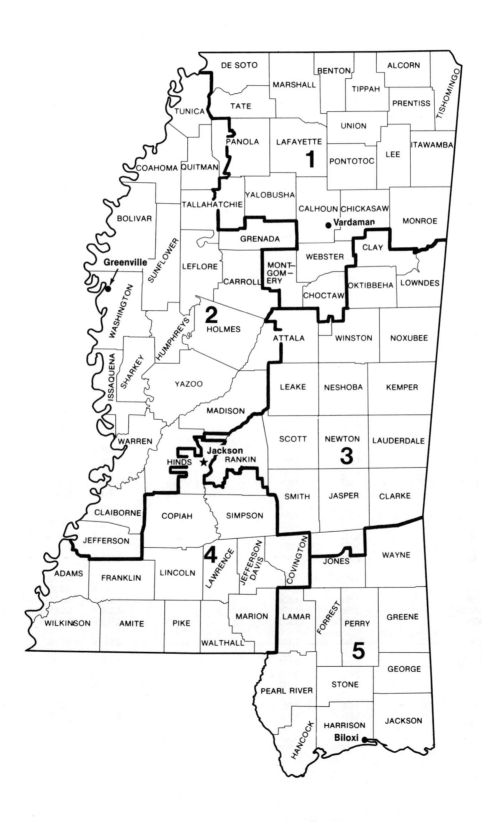

MISSISSIPPI

SENATOR 1990

1990 Census Population	County	Total Vote	Republican	Democratic	Other	Rep.-Dem. Plurality	Percentage Total Vote Rep.	Dem.	Major Vote Rep.	Dem.
35,356	ADAMS	6,170	6,170			6,170 R	100.0%		100.0%	
31,722	ALCORN	1,495	1,495			1,495 R	100.0%		100.0%	
13,328	AMITE	2,354	2,354			2,354 R	100.0%		100.0%	
18,481	ATTALA	1,412	1,412			1,412 R	100.0%		100.0%	
8,046	BENTON	1,020	1,020			1,020 R	100.0%		100.0%	
41,875	BOLIVAR	2,243	2,243			2,243 R	100.0%		100.0%	
14,908	CALHOUN	2,663	2,663			2,663 R	100.0%		100.0%	
9,237	CARROLL	986	986			986 R	100.0%		100.0%	
18,085	CHICKASAW	1,016	1,016			1,016 R	100.0%		100.0%	
9,071	CHOCTAW	922	922			922 R	100.0%		100.0%	
11,370	CLAIBORNE	1,748	1,748			1,748 R	100.0%		100.0%	
17,313	CLARKE	1,885	1,885			1,885 R	100.0%		100.0%	
21,120	CLAY	1,440	1,440			1,440 R	100.0%		100.0%	
31,665	COAHOMA	1,221	1,221			1,221 R	100.0%		100.0%	
27,592	COPIAH	2,067	2,067			2,067 R	100.0%		100.0%	
16,527	COVINGTON	2,039	2,039			2,039 R	100.0%		100.0%	
67,910	DE SOTO	5,937	5,937			5,937 R	100.0%		100.0%	
68,314	FORREST	8,411	8,411			8,411 R	100.0%		100.0%	
8,377	FRANKLIN	1,389	1,389			1,389 R	100.0%		100.0%	
16,673	GEORGE	2,893	2,893			2,893 R	100.0%		100.0%	
10,220	GREENE	1,161	1,161			1,161 R	100.0%		100.0%	
21,555	GRENADA	1,308	1,308			1,308 R	100.0%		100.0%	
31,760	HANCOCK	5,357	5,357			5,357 R	100.0%		100.0%	
165,365	HARRISON	24,963	24,963			24,963 R	100.0%		100.0%	
254,441	HINDS	16,840	16,840			16,840 R	100.0%		100.0%	
21,604	HOLMES	1,759	1,759			1,759 R	100.0%		100.0%	
12,134	HUMPHREYS	1,529	1,529			1,529 R	100.0%		100.0%	
1,909	ISSAQUENA	490	490			490 R	100.0%		100.0%	
20,017	ITAWAMBA	1,720	1,720			1,720 R	100.0%		100.0%	
115,243	JACKSON	21,274	21,274			21,274 R	100.0%		100.0%	
17,114	JASPER	1,884	1,884			1,884 R	100.0%		100.0%	
8,653	JEFFERSON	1,356	1,356			1,356 R	100.0%		100.0%	
14,051	JEFFERSON DAVIS	1,857	1,857			1,857 R	100.0%		100.0%	
62,031	JONES	6,413	6,413			6,413 R	100.0%		100.0%	
10,356	KEMPER	2,425	2,425			2,425 R	100.0%		100.0%	
31,826	LAFAYETTE	2,231	2,231			2,231 R	100.0%		100.0%	
30,424	LAMAR	5,955	5,955			5,955 R	100.0%		100.0%	
75,555	LAUDERDALE	5,768	5,768			5,768 R	100.0%		100.0%	
12,458	LAWRENCE	1,527	1,527			1,527 R	100.0%		100.0%	
18,436	LEAKE	1,934	1,934			1,934 R	100.0%		100.0%	
65,581	LEE	4,206	4,206			4,206 R	100.0%		100.0%	
37,341	LEFLORE	4,034	4,034			4,034 R	100.0%		100.0%	
30,278	LINCOLN	4,142	4,142			4,142 R	100.0%		100.0%	
59,308	LOWNDES	2,377	2,377			2,377 R	100.0%		100.0%	
53,794	MADISON	2,604	2,604			2,604 R	100.0%		100.0%	
25,544	MARION	1,462	1,462			1,462 R	100.0%		100.0%	
30,361	MARSHALL	2,142	2,142			2,142 R	100.0%		100.0%	
36,582	MONROE	1,824	1,824			1,824 R	100.0%		100.0%	
12,388	MONTGOMERY	1,256	1,256			1,256 R	100.0%		100.0%	
24,800	NESHOBA	1,908	1,908			1,908 R	100.0%		100.0%	
20,291	NEWTON	3,140	3,140			3,140 R	100.0%		100.0%	
12,604	NOXUBEE	839	839			839 R	100.0%		100.0%	
38,375	OKTIBBEHA	2,168	2,168			2,168 R	100.0%		100.0%	
29,996	PANOLA	2,473	2,473			2,473 R	100.0%		100.0%	
38,714	PEARL RIVER	4,617	4,617			4,617 R	100.0%		100.0%	
10,865	PERRY	1,699	1,699			1,699 R	100.0%		100.0%	
36,882	PIKE	8,575	8,575			8,575 R	100.0%		100.0%	
22,237	PONTOTOC	1,925	1,925			1,925 R	100.0%		100.0%	
23,278	PRENTISS	4,238	4,238			4,238 R	100.0%		100.0%	
10,490	QUITMAN	1,760	1,760			1,760 R	100.0%		100.0%	

MISSISSIPPI

SENATOR 1990

1990 Census Population	County	Total Vote	Republican	Democratic	Other	Rep.-Dem. Plurality	Percentage Total Vote Rep.	Dem.	Major Vote Rep.	Dem.
87,161	RANKIN	9,901	9,901			9,901 R	100.0%		100.0%	
24,137	SCOTT	1,645	1,645			1,645 R	100.0%		100.0%	
7,066	SHARKEY	959	959			959 R	100.0%		100.0%	
23,953	SIMPSON	2,602	2,602			2,602 R	100.0%		100.0%	
14,798	SMITH	1,617	1,617			1,617 R	100.0%		100.0%	
10,750	STONE	1,859	1,859			1,859 R	100.0%		100.0%	
32,867	SUNFLOWER	2,019	2,019			2,019 R	100.0%		100.0%	
15,210	TALLAHATCHIE	3,208	3,208			3,208 R	100.0%		100.0%	
21,432	TATE	2,151	2,151			2,151 R	100.0%		100.0%	
19,523	TIPPAH	2,326	2,326			2,326 R	100.0%		100.0%	
17,683	TISHOMINGO	2,443	2,443			2,443 R	100.0%		100.0%	
8,164	TUNICA	1,099	1,099			1,099 R	100.0%		100.0%	
22,085	UNION	2,165	2,165			2,165 R	100.0%		100.0%	
14,352	WALTHALL	1,877	1,877			1,877 R	100.0%		100.0%	
47,880	WARREN	8,842	8,842			8,842 R	100.0%		100.0%	
67,935	WASHINGTON	6,106	6,106			6,106 R	100.0%		100.0%	
19,517	WAYNE									
10,222	WEBSTER	2,144	2,144			2,144 R	100.0%		100.0%	
9,678	WILKINSON	2,047	2,047			2,047 R	100.0%		100.0%	
19,433	WINSTON	1,665	1,665			1,665 R	100.0%		100.0%	
12,033	YALOBUSHA	1,014	1,014			1,014 R	100.0%		100.0%	
25,506	YAZOO	2,104	2,104			2,104 R	100.0%		100.0%	
2,573,216	TOTAL	274,244	274,244			274,244 R	100.0%		100.0%	

MISSISSIPPI

CONGRESS

CD	Year	Total Vote	Republican Vote	Candidate	Democratic Vote	Candidate	Other Vote	Rep.-Dem. Plurality	Total Vote Rep.	Total Vote Dem.	Major Vote Rep.	Major Vote Dem.
1	1990	67,318	23,650	BOWLIN, BILL	43,668	WHITTEN, JAMIE L.		20,018 D	35.1%	64.9%	35.1%	64.9%
1	1988	175,826	38,381	BUSH, JIM	137,445	WHITTEN, JAMIE L.		99,064 D	21.8%	78.2%	21.8%	78.2%
1	1986	90,137	30,267	COBB, LARRY	59,870	WHITTEN, JAMIE L.		29,603 D	33.6%	66.4%	33.6%	66.4%
1	1984	154,521			136,530	WHITTEN, JAMIE L.	17,991	136,530 D		88.4%		100.0%
2	1990	70,617	11,224	BENFORD, DOROTHY	59,393	ESPY, MIKE		48,169 D	15.9%	84.1%	15.9%	84.1%
2	1988	173,631	59,827	COLEMAN, JACK	112,401	ESPY, MIKE	1,403	52,574 D	34.5%	64.7%	34.7%	65.3%
2	1986	141,411	68,292	FRANKLIN, WEBB	73,119	ESPY, MIKE		4,827 D	48.3%	51.7%	48.3%	51.7%
2	1984	182,420	92,392	FRANKLIN, WEBB	89,154	CLARK, ROBERT G.	874	3,238 R	50.6%	48.9%	50.9%	49.1%
3	1990	49,162			49,162	MONTGOMERY, G. V.		49,162 D		100.0%		100.0%
3	1988	185,380	20,729	BOURLAND, JIMMIE RAY	164,651	MONTGOMERY, G. V.		143,922 D	11.2%	88.8%	11.2%	88.8%
3	1986	80,575			80,575	MONTGOMERY, G. V.		80,575 D		100.0%		100.0%
3	1984	158,002			158,002	MONTGOMERY, G. V.		158,002 D		100.0%		100.0%
4	1990	70,891	13,754	PARKS, JERRY	57,137	PARKER, MIKE		43,383 D	19.4%	80.6%	19.4%	80.6%
4	1988	201,063	88,433	COLLINS, THOMAS	110,184	PARKER, MIKE	2,446	21,751 D	44.0%	54.8%	44.5%	55.5%
4	1986	120,009	34,190	HEALY, GAIL	85,819	DOWDY, WAYNE		51,629 D	28.5%	71.5%	28.5%	71.5%
4	1984	205,432	91,797	ARMSTRONG, DAVID	113,635	DOWDY, WAYNE		21,838 D	44.7%	55.3%	44.7%	55.3%
5	1990	110,514	20,588	SMITH, SHEILA	89,926	TAYLOR, GENE		69,338 D	18.6%	81.4%	18.6%	81.4%
5	1988	182,219	100,185	SMITH, LARKIN	82,034	TAYLOR, GENE		18,151 R	55.0%	45.0%	55.0%	45.0%
5	1986	91,431	75,288	LOTT, TRENT	16,143	ALBRITTON, LARRY L.		59,145 R	82.3%	17.7%	82.3%	17.7%
5	1984	168,477	142,637	LOTT, TRENT	25,840	COATE, ARLON		116,797 R	84.7%	15.3%	84.7%	15.3%

MISSISSIPPI

1990 GENERAL ELECTION

Senator   Wayne county did not report votes for the unopposed candidate Thad Cochran; therefore the certified results do not include any returns for Wayne county.

Congress

1990 PRIMARIES

JUNE 5 REPUBLICAN

Senator   Thad Cochran, unopposed.

Congress   Unopposed in four CD's. No candidate in CD 3.

JUNE 5 DEMOCRATIC

Senator   No candidate.

Congress   Unopposed in all five CD's.

MISSOURI

GOVERNOR
John Ashcroft (R). Re-elected 1988 to a four-year term. Previously elected 1984.

SENATORS
Christopher Bond (R). Elected 1986 to a six-year term.

John C. Danforth (R). Re-elected 1988 to a six-year term. Previously elected 1982, 1976.

REPRESENTATIVES
1. William Clay (D)
2. Joan Kelly Horn (D)
3. Richard A. Gephardt (D)
4. Ike Skelton (D)
5. Alan Wheat (D)
6. E. Thomas Coleman (R)
7. Melton D. Hancock (R)
8. Bill Emerson (R)
9. Harold Volkmer (D)

POSTWAR VOTE FOR PRESIDENT

| | | Republican | | Democratic | | Other | | Percentage Total Vote | | Major Vote | |
| | Total | | | | | | | | | | |
Year	Vote	Vote	Candidate	Vote	Candidate	Vote	Plurality	Rep.	Dem.	Rep.	Dem.
1988	2,093,713	1,084,953	Bush, George	1,001,619	Dukakis, Michael S.	7,141	83,334 R	51.8%	47.8%	52.0%	48.0%
1984	2,122,783	1,274,188	Reagan, Ronald	848,583	Mondale, Walter F.	12	425,605 R	60.0%	40.0%	60.0%	40.0%
1980	2,099,824	1,074,181	Reagan, Ronald	931,182	Carter, Jimmy	94,461	142,999 R	51.2%	44.3%	53.6%	46.4%
1976	1,953,600	927,443	Ford, Gerald R.	998,387	Carter, Jimmy	27,770	70,944 D	47.5%	51.1%	48.2%	51.8%
1972	1,855,803	1,153,852	Nixon, Richard M.	697,147	McGovern, George S.	4,804	456,705 R	62.2%	37.6%	62.3%	37.7%
1968	1,809,502	811,932	Nixon, Richard M.	791,444	Humphrey, Hubert H.	206,126	20,488 R	44.9%	43.7%	50.6%	49.4%
1964	1,817,879	653,535	Goldwater, Barry M.	1,164,344	Johnson, Lyndon B.		510,809 D	36.0%	64.0%	36.0%	64.0%
1960	1,934,422	962,221	Nixon, Richard M.	972,201	Kennedy, John F.		9,980 D	49.7%	50.3%	49.7%	50.3%
1956	1,832,562	914,289	Eisenhower, Dwight D.	918,273	Stevenson, Adlai E.		3,984 D	49.9%	50.1%	49.9%	50.1%
1952	1,892,062	959,429	Eisenhower, Dwight D.	929,830	Stevenson, Adlai E.	2,803	29,599 R	50.7%	49.1%	50.8%	49.2%
1948	1,578,628	655,039	Dewey, Thomas E.	917,315	Truman, Harry S.	6,274	262,276 D	41.5%	58.1%	41.7%	58.3%

POSTWAR VOTE FOR GOVERNOR

| | | Republican | | Democratic | | Other | Rep-Dem. | Percentage Total Vote | | Major Vote | |
| | Total | | | | | | | | | | |
Year	Vote	Vote	Candidate	Vote	Candidate	Vote	Plurality	Rep.	Dem.	Rep.	Dem.
1988	2,085,928	1,339,531	Ashcroft, John	724,919	Hearnes, Betty C.	21,478	614,612 R	64.2%	34.8%	64.9%	35.1%
1984	2,108,210	1,194,506	Ashcroft, John	913,700	Rothman, Kenneth J.	4	280,806 R	56.7%	43.3%	56.7%	43.3%
1980	2,088,028	1,098,950	Bond, Christopher	981,884	Teasdale, Joseph P.	7,194	117,066 R	52.6%	47.0%	52.8%	47.2%
1976	1,933,575	958,110	Bond, Christopher	971,184	Teasdale, Joseph P.	4,281	13,074 D	49.6%	50.2%	49.7%	50.3%
1972	1,865,683	1,029,451	Bond, Christopher	832,751	Dowd, Edward L.	3,481	196,700 R	55.2%	44.6%	55.3%	44.7%
1968	1,764,602	691,797	Roos, Lawrence K.	1,072,805	Hearnes, Warren E.		381,008 D	39.2%	60.8%	39.2%	60.8%
1964	1,789,600	678,949	Shepley, Ethan	1,110,651	Hearnes, Warren E.		431,702 D	37.9%	62.1%	37.9%	62.1%
1960	1,887,331	792,131	Farmer, Edward G.	1,095,200	Dalton, John M.		303,069 D	42.0%	58.0%	42.0%	58.0%
1956	1,808,338	866,810	Hocker, Lon	941,528	Blair, James T.		74,718 D	47.9%	52.1%	47.9%	52.1%
1952	1,871,095	886,370	Elliott, Howard	983,166	Donnelly, Phil M.	1,559	96,796 D	47.4%	52.5%	47.4%	52.6%
1948	1,567,338	670,064	Thompson, Murray	893,092	Smith, Forrest	4,182	223,028 D	42.8%	57.0%	42.9%	57.1%

MISSOURI

POSTWAR VOTE FOR SENATOR

Year	Total Vote	Republican Vote	Candidate	Democratic Vote	Candidate	Other Vote	Rep-Dem. Plurality	Total Vote Rep.	Dem.	Major Vote Rep.	Dem.
1988	2,078,875	1,407,416	Danforth, John C.	660,045	Nixon, Jeremiah W.	11,414	747,371 R	67.7%	31.8%	68.1%	31.9%
1986	1,477,327	777,612	Bond, Christopher	699,624	Woods, Harriett	91	77,988 R	52.6%	47.4%	52.6%	47.4%
1982	1,543,521	784,876	Danforth, John C.	758,629	Woods, Harriett	16	26,247 R	50.8%	49.1%	50.9%	49.1%
1980	2,066,965	985,399	McNary, Gene	1,074,859	Eagleton, Thomas F.	6,707	89,460 D	47.7%	52.0%	47.8%	52.2%
1976	1,914,777	1,090,067	Danforth, John C.	813,571	Hearnes, Warren E.	11,139	276,496 R	56.9%	42.5%	57.3%	42.7%
1974	1,224,303	480,900	Curtis, Thomas B.	735,433	Eagleton, Thomas F.	7,970	254,533 D	39.3%	60.1%	39.5%	60.5%
1970	1,283,912	617,903	Danforth, John C.	655,431	Symington, Stuart	10,578	37,528 D	48.1%	51.0%	48.5%	51.5%
1968	1,737,958	850,544	Curtis, Thomas B.	887,414	Eagleton, Thomas F.		36,870 D	48.9%	51.1%	48.9%	51.1%
1964	1,783,043	596,377	Bradshaw, Jean P.	1,186,666	Symington, Stuart		590,289 D	33.4%	66.6%	33.4%	66.6%
1962	1,222,259	555,330	Kemper, Crosby	666,929	Long, Edward V.		111,599 D	45.4%	54.6%	45.4%	54.6%
1960 S	1,880,232	880,576	Hocker, Lon	999,656	Long, Edward V.		119,080 D	46.8%	53.2%	46.8%	53.2%
1958	1,173,903	393,847	Palmer, Hazel	780,056	Symington, Stuart		386,209 D	33.6%	66.4%	33.6%	66.4%
1956	1,800,984	785,048	Douglas, Herbert	1,015,936	Hennings, Thomas C.		230,888 D	43.6%	56.4%	43.6%	56.4%
1952	1,868,083	858,170	Kem, James P.	1,008,523	Symington, Stuart	1,390	150,353 D	45.9%	54.0%	46.0%	54.0%
1950	1,279,414	592,922	Donnell, Forrest C.	685,732	Hennings, Thomas C.	760	92,810 D	46.3%	53.6%	46.4%	53.6%
1946	1,084,100	572,556	Kem, James P.	511,544	Briggs, Frank P.		61,012 R	52.8%	47.2%	52.8%	47.2%

The 1960 election was for a short term to fill a vacancy.

MISSOURI

Districts Established January 7, 1982

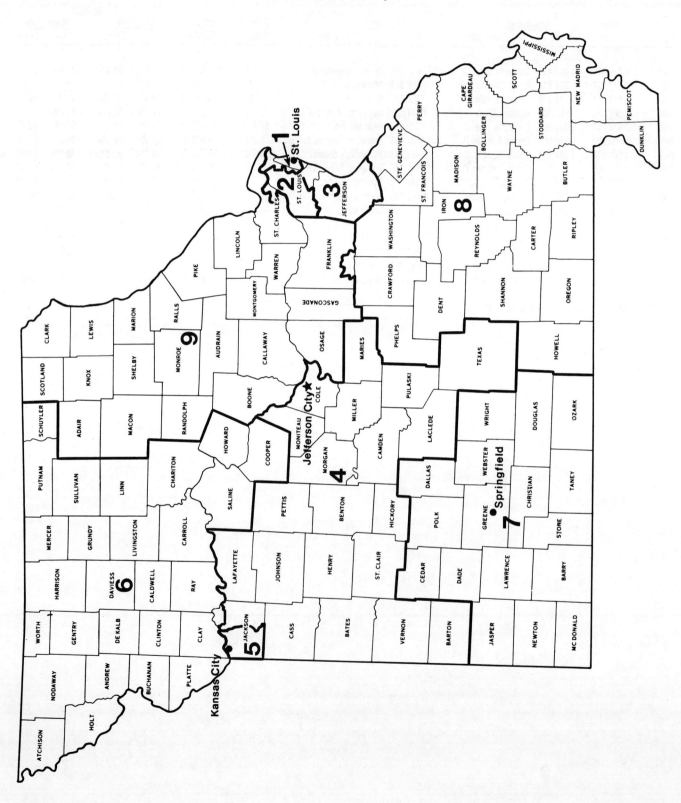

MISSOURI

CONGRESS

CD	Year	Total Vote	Republican Vote	Republican Candidate	Democratic Vote	Democratic Candidate	Other Vote	Rep.-Dem. Plurality	Percentage Total Vote Rep.	Percentage Total Vote Dem.	Major Vote Rep.	Major Vote Dem.
1	1990	102,710	40,160	PIOTROWSKI, WAYNE G.	62,550	CLAY, WILLIAM		22,390 D	39.1%	60.9%	39.1%	60.9%
1	1988	196,658	53,109	SCHWAN, JOSEPH A.	140,751	CLAY, WILLIAM	2,798	87,642 D	27.0%	71.6%	27.4%	72.6%
1	1986	137,643	46,599	WITTMANN, ROBERT J.	91,044	CLAY, WILLIAM		44,445 D	33.9%	66.1%	33.9%	66.1%
1	1984	215,974	68,538	RATHBONE, ERIC	147,436	CLAY, WILLIAM		78,898 D	31.7%	68.3%	31.7%	68.3%
1	1982	155,255	52,599	WHITE, WILLIAM E.	102,656	CLAY, WILLIAM		50,057 D	33.9%	66.1%	33.9%	66.1%
2	1990	188,702	94,324	BUECHNER, JOHN	94,378	HORN, JOAN KELLY		54 D	50.0%	50.0%	50.0%	50.0%
2	1988	281,109	186,450	BUECHNER, JOHN	91,645	FEIGENBAUM, ROBERT H.	3,014	94,805 R	66.3%	32.6%	67.0%	33.0%
2	1986	194,548	101,010	BUECHNER, JOHN	93,538	YOUNG, ROBERT A.		7,472 R	51.9%	48.1%	51.9%	48.1%
2	1984	268,616	127,710	BUECHNER, JOHN	139,123	YOUNG, ROBERT A.	1,783	11,413 D	47.5%	51.8%	47.9%	52.1%
2	1982	178,203	77,433	DIELMANN, HAROLD L.	100,770	YOUNG, ROBERT A.		23,337 D	43.5%	56.5%	43.5%	56.5%
3	1990	156,609	67,659	HOLEKAMP, MALCOLM L.	88,950	GEPHARDT, RICHARD A.		21,291 D	43.2%	56.8%	43.2%	56.8%
3	1988	239,203	86,763	HEARNE, MARK F.	150,205	GEPHARDT, RICHARD A.	2,235	63,442 D	36.3%	62.8%	36.6%	63.4%
3	1986	168,785	52,382	AMELUNG, ROY C.	116,403	GEPHARDT, RICHARD A.		64,021 D	31.0%	69.0%	31.0%	69.0%
3	1984	193,537			193,537	GEPHARDT, RICHARD A.		193,537 D		100.0%		100.0%
3	1982	168,954	37,388	FORISTEL, RICHARD	131,566	GEPHARDT, RICHARD A.		94,178 D	22.1%	77.9%	22.1%	77.9%
4	1990	170,622	65,095	EYERLY, DAVID	105,527	SKELTON, IKE		40,432 D	38.2%	61.8%	38.2%	61.8%
4	1988	231,873	65,393	EYERLY, DAVID	166,480	SKELTON, IKE		101,087 D	28.2%	71.8%	28.2%	71.8%
4	1986	129,471			129,471	SKELTON, IKE		129,471 D		100.0%		100.0%
4	1984	225,058	74,434	RUSSELL, CARL D.	150,624	SKELTON, IKE		76,190 D	33.1%	66.9%	33.1%	66.9%
4	1982	175,953	79,565	BAILEY, WENDELL	96,388	SKELTON, IKE		16,823 D	45.2%	54.8%	45.2%	54.8%
5	1990	115,787	43,897	GARDNER, ROBERT H.	71,890	WHEAT, ALAN		27,993 D	37.9%	62.1%	37.9%	62.1%
5	1988	212,139	60,453	LOBB, MARY ELLEN	149,166	WHEAT, ALAN	2,520	88,713 D	28.5%	70.3%	28.8%	71.2%
5	1986	142,574	39,340	FISHER, GREG	101,030	WHEAT, ALAN	2,204	61,690 D	27.6%	70.9%	28.0%	72.0%
5	1984	228,230	72,477	KENWORTHY, JIM	150,675	WHEAT, ALAN	5,078	78,198 D	31.8%	66.0%	32.5%	67.5%
5	1982	165,989	66,664	SHARP, JOHN A.	96,059	WHEAT, ALAN	3,266	29,395 D	40.2%	57.9%	41.0%	59.0%
6	1990	152,049	78,956	COLEMAN, E. THOMAS	73,093	MCCLURE, BOB		5,863 R	51.9%	48.1%	51.9%	48.1%
6	1988	229,011	135,883	COLEMAN, E. THOMAS	93,128	HUGHES, DOUG R.		42,755 R	59.3%	40.7%	59.3%	40.7%
6	1986	169,020	95,865	COLEMAN, E. THOMAS	73,155	HUGHES, DOUG R.		22,710 R	56.7%	43.3%	56.7%	43.3%
6	1984	232,913	150,996	COLEMAN, E. THOMAS	81,917	HENSLEY, KENNETH C.		69,079 R	64.8%	35.2%	64.8%	35.2%
6	1982	177,046	97,993	COLEMAN, E. THOMAS	79,053	RUSSELL, JIM		18,940 R	55.3%	44.7%	55.3%	44.7%
7	1990	160,334	83,609	HANCOCK, MELTON D.	76,725	DEATON, THOMAS P.		6,884 R	52.1%	47.9%	52.1%	47.9%
7	1988	240,911	127,939	HANCOCK, MELTON D.	111,244	BACON, MAX	1,728	16,695 R	53.1%	46.2%	53.5%	46.5%
7	1986	170,501	114,210	TAYLOR, GENE	56,291	YOUNG, KEN		57,919 R	67.0%	33.0%	67.0%	33.0%
7	1984	236,453	164,586	TAYLOR, GENE	71,867	YOUNG, KEN		92,719 R	69.6%	30.4%	69.6%	30.4%
7	1982	180,940	91,391	TAYLOR, GENE	89,549	GEISLER, DAVID A.		1,842 R	50.5%	49.5%	50.5%	49.5%
8	1990	142,203	81,452	EMERSON, BILL	60,751	CARNAHAN, RUSS		20,701 R	57.3%	42.7%	57.3%	42.7%
8	1988	202,402	117,601	EMERSON, BILL	84,801	CRYTS, WAYNE		32,800 R	58.1%	41.9%	58.1%	41.9%
8	1986	150,674	79,142	EMERSON, BILL	71,532	CRYTS, WAYNE		7,610 R	52.5%	47.5%	52.5%	47.5%
8	1984	205,108	134,186	EMERSON, BILL	70,922	BLUE, BILL		63,264 R	65.4%	34.6%	65.4%	34.6%
8	1982	162,906	86,493	EMERSON, BILL	76,413	FORD, JERRY		10,080 R	53.1%	46.9%	53.1%	46.9%
9	1990	163,670	69,514	CURTIS, DON	94,156	VOLKMER, HAROLD		24,642 D	42.5%	57.5%	42.5%	57.5%
9	1988	236,880	76,008	DUDLEY, KEN A.	160,872	VOLKMER, HAROLD		84,864 D	32.1%	67.9%	32.1%	67.9%
9	1986	166,911	70,972	UTHLAUT, RALPH	95,939	VOLKMER, HAROLD		24,967 D	42.5%	57.5%	42.5%	57.5%
9	1984	233,688	110,100	FRANCKE, CARRIE	123,588	VOLKMER, HAROLD		13,488 D	47.1%	52.9%	47.1%	52.9%
9	1982	163,170	63,942	MEAD, LARRY E.	99,228	VOLKMER, HAROLD		35,286 D	39.2%	60.8%	39.2%	60.8%

272

MISSOURI

1990 GENERAL ELECTION

Congress   The vote carried in CD 2 is for the recount.

1990 PRIMARIES

AUGUST 7 REPUBLICAN

Congress   Unopposed in three CD's. Contested as follows:

CD 1   3,293 Wayne G. Piotrowski; 3,050 Kyle Z. Knight; 1,821 Joseph A. Schwan.
CD 3   9,512 Malcolm L. Holekamp; 4,748 Wallace Anderson; 1,679 Paul G. Stein; 1,214 Bernard L. Mazurkiewicz.
CD 5   8,403 Robert H. Gardner; 5,998 Joyce Lea; 3,332 Joseph A. Privitera.
CD 6   27,382 E. Thomas Coleman; 5,197 Don R. Sartain.
CD 7   75,860 Melton D. Hancock; 8,032 Jim Mundy; 4,605 Ray Eaton.
CD 9   14,725 Don Curtis; 12,379 Ken A. Dudley.

AUGUST 7 DEMOCRATIC

Congress   Unopposed in three CD's. Contested as follows:

CD 2   17,165 Joan Kelly Horn; 7,440 John M. Baine; 1,485 Leif O. Johnson.
CD 3   34,919 Richard A. Gephardt; 8,523 Nicholas F. Clement.
CD 5   54,664 Alan Wheat; 13,620 Gus Dubbert.
CD 6   38,917 Bob McClure; 24,943 John Gallagher.
CD 7   9,727 Thomas P. Deaton; 6,544 William Jacobs.
CD 8   38,795 Russ Carnahan; 11,896 Thad Bullock; 7,666 Francis L. Brokaw.

MONTANA

GOVERNOR
Stan Stephens (R). Elected 1988 to a four-year term.

SENATORS
Max S. Baucus (D). Re-elected 1990 to a six-year term. Previously elected 1984, 1978.

Conrad Burns (R). Elected 1988 to a six-year term.

REPRESENTATIVES
1. Pat Williams (D)   2. Ron Marlenee (R)

POSTWAR VOTE FOR PRESIDENT

Year	Total Vote	Republican Vote	Candidate	Democratic Vote	Candidate	Other Vote	Plurality	Total Vote Rep.	Dem.	Major Vote Rep.	Dem.
1988	365,674	190,412	Bush, George	168,936	Dukakis, Michael S.	6,326	21,476 R	52.1%	46.2%	53.0%	47.0%
1984	384,377	232,450	Reagan, Ronald	146,742	Mondale, Walter F.	5,185	85,708 R	60.5%	38.2%	61.3%	38.7%
1980	363,952	206,814	Reagan, Ronald	118,032	Carter, Jimmy	39,106	88,782 R	56.8%	32.4%	63.7%	36.3%
1976	328,734	173,703	Ford, Gerald R.	149,259	Carter, Jimmy	5,772	24,444 R	52.8%	45.4%	53.8%	46.2%
1972	317,603	183,976	Nixon, Richard M.	120,197	McGovern, George S.	13,430	63,779 R	57.9%	37.8%	60.5%	39.5%
1968	274,404	138,835	Nixon, Richard M.	114,117	Humphrey, Hubert H.	21,452	24,718 R	50.6%	41.6%	54.9%	45.1%
1964	278,628	113,032	Goldwater, Barry M.	164,246	Johnson, Lyndon B.	1,350	51,214 D	40.6%	58.9%	40.8%	59.2%
1960	277,579	141,841	Nixon, Richard M.	134,891	Kennedy, John F.	847	6,950 R	51.1%	48.6%	51.3%	48.7%
1956	271,171	154,933	Eisenhower, Dwight D.	116,238	Stevenson, Adlai E.		38,695 R	57.1%	42.9%	57.1%	42.9%
1952	265,037	157,394	Eisenhower, Dwight D.	106,213	Stevenson, Adlai E.	1,430	51,181 R	59.4%	40.1%	59.7%	40.3%
1948	224,278	96,770	Dewey, Thomas E.	119,071	Truman, Harry S.	8,437	22,301 D	43.1%	53.1%	44.8%	55.2%

POSTWAR VOTE FOR GOVERNOR

Year	Total Vote	Republican Vote	Candidate	Democratic Vote	Candidate	Other Vote	Rep-Dem. Plurality	Total Vote Rep.	Dem.	Major Vote Rep.	Dem.
1988	367,021	190,604	Stephens, Stan	169,313	Judge, Thomas L.	7,104	21,291 R	51.9%	46.1%	53.0%	47.0%
1984	378,970	100,070	Goodover, Pat M.	266,578	Schwinden, Ted	12,322	166,508 D	26.4%	70.3%	27.3%	72.7%
1980	360,466	160,892	Ramirez, Jack	199,574	Schwinden, Ted		38,682 D	44.6%	55.4%	44.6%	55.4%
1976	316,720	115,848	Woodahl, Robert	195,420	Judge, Thomas L.	5,452	79,572 D	36.6%	61.7%	37.2%	62.8%
1972	318,754	146,231	Smith, Ed	172,523	Judge, Thomas L.		26,292 D	45.9%	54.1%	45.9%	54.1%
1968	278,112	116,432	Babcock, Tim M.	150,481	Anderson, Forrest H.	11,199	34,049 D	41.9%	54.1%	43.6%	56.4%
1964	280,975	144,113	Babcock, Tim M.	136,862	Renne, Roland		7,251 R	51.3%	48.7%	51.3%	48.7%
1960	279,881	154,230	Nutter, Donald G.	125,651	Cannon, Paul		28,579 R	55.1%	44.9%	55.1%	44.9%
1956	270,366	138,878	Aronson, J. Hugo	131,488	Olsen, Arnold H.		7,390 R	51.4%	48.6%	51.4%	48.6%
1952	263,792	134,423	Aronson, J. Hugo	129,369	Bonner, John W.		5,054 R	51.0%	49.0%	51.0%	49.0%
1948	222,964	97,792	Ford, Sam C.	124,267	Bonner, John W.	905	26,475 D	43.9%	55.7%	44.0%	56.0%

MONTANA

POSTWAR VOTE FOR SENATOR

Year	Total Vote	Republican		Democratic		Other Vote	Rep-Dem. Plurality	Percentage			
		Vote	Candidate	Vote	Candidate			Total Vote		Major Vote	
								Rep.	Dem.	Rep.	Dem.
1990	319,336	93,836	Kolstad, Allen C.	217,563	Baucus, Max S.	7,937	123,727 D	29.4%	68.1%	30.1%	69.9%
1988	365,254	189,445	Burns, Conrad	175,809	Melcher, John		13,636 R	51.9%	48.1%	51.9%	48.1%
1984	379,155	154,308	Cozzens, Chuck	215,704	Baucus, Max S.	9,143	61,396 D	40.7%	56.9%	41.7%	58.3%
1982	321,062	133,789	Williams, Larry	174,861	Melcher, John	12,412	41,072 D	41.7%	54.5%	43.3%	56.7%
1978	287,942	127,589	Williams, Larry	160,353	Baucus, Max S.		32,764 D	44.3%	55.7%	44.3%	55.7%
1976	321,445	115,213	Burger, Stanley C.	206,232	Melcher, John		91,019 D	35.8%	64.2%	35.8%	64.2%
1972	314,925	151,316	Hibbard, Henry S.	163,609	Metcalf, Lee		12,293 D	48.0%	52.0%	48.0%	52.0%
1970	247,869	97,809	Wallace, Harold E.	150,060	Mansfield, Mike		52,251 D	39.5%	60.5%	39.5%	60.5%
1966	259,863	121,697	Babcock, Tim M.	138,166	Metcalf, Lee		16,469 D	46.8%	53.2%	46.8%	53.2%
1964	280,010	99,367	Blewett, Alex	180,643	Mansfield, Mike		81,276 D	35.5%	64.5%	35.5%	64.5%
1960	276,612	136,281	Fjare, Orvin B.	140,331	Metcalf, Lee		4,050 D	49.3%	50.7%	49.3%	50.7%
1958	229,483	54,573	Welch. Lou W.	174,910	Mansfield, Mike		120,337 D	23.8%	76.2%	23.8%	76.2%
1954	227,454	112,863	D'Ewart, Wesley A.	114,591	Murray, James E.		1,728 D	49.6%	50.4%	49.6%	50.4%
1952	262,297	127,360	Ecton, Zales N.	133,109	Mansfield, Mike	1,828	5,749 D	48.6%	50.7%	48.9%	51.1%
1948	221,003	94,458	David, Tom J.	125,193	Murray, James E.	1,352	30,735 D	42.7%	56.6%	43.0%	57.0%
1946	190,566	101,901	Ecton, Zales N.	86,476	Erickson, Leif	2,189	15,425 R	53.5%	45.4%	54.1%	45.9%

275

MONTANA

Districts Established March 4, 1983

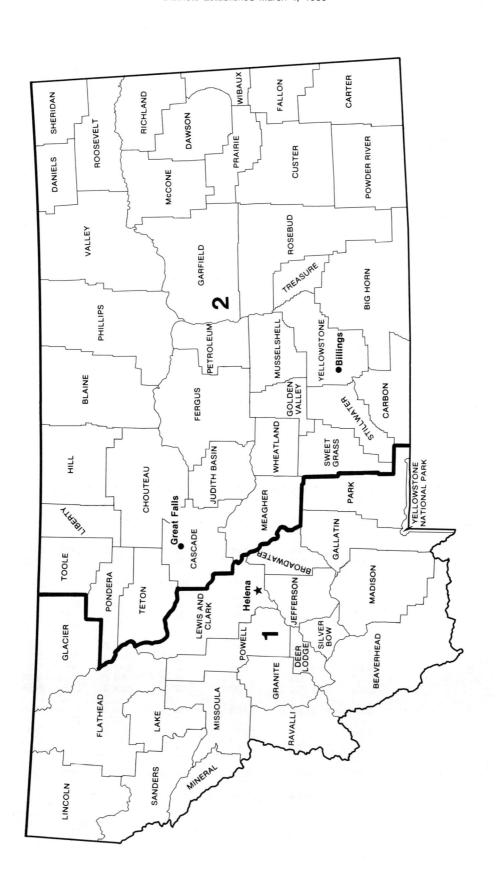

© ERC

MONTANA

SENATOR 1990

1990 Census Population	County	Total Vote	Republican	Democratic	Other	Rep.-Dem. Plurality	Percentage Total Vote Rep.	Dem.	Major Vote Rep.	Dem.
8,424	BEAVERHEAD	3,318	1,620	1,607	91	13 R	48.8%	48.4%	50.2%	49.8%
11,337	BIG HORN	3,705	746	2,886	73	2,140 D	20.1%	77.9%	20.5%	79.5%
6,728	BLAINE	2,535	596	1,894	45	1,298 D	23.5%	74.7%	23.9%	76.1%
3,318	BROADWATER	1,607	678	877	52	199 D	42.2%	54.6%	43.6%	56.4%
8,080	CARBON	3,984	1,002	2,900	82	1,898 D	25.2%	72.8%	25.7%	74.3%
1,503	CARTER	852	408	430	14	22 D	47.9%	50.5%	48.7%	51.3%
77,691	CASCADE	28,236	6,507	21,113	616	14,606 D	23.0%	74.8%	23.6%	76.4%
5,452	CHOUTEAU	3,002	1,029	1,905	68	876 D	34.3%	63.5%	35.1%	64.9%
11,697	CUSTER	4,698	1,148	3,459	91	2,311 D	24.4%	73.6%	24.9%	75.1%
2,266	DANIELS	1,283	394	875	14	481 D	30.7%	68.2%	31.0%	69.0%
9,505	DAWSON	4,332	1,235	3,038	59	1,803 D	28.5%	70.1%	28.9%	71.1%
10,278	DEER LODGE	4,301	582	3,658	61	3,076 D	13.5%	85.0%	13.7%	86.3%
3,103	FALLON	1,555	596	938	21	342 D	38.3%	60.3%	38.9%	61.1%
12,083	FERGUS	5,695	1,938	3,642	115	1,704 D	34.0%	64.0%	34.7%	65.3%
59,218	FLATHEAD	22,183	7,845	13,505	833	5,660 D	35.4%	60.9%	36.7%	63.3%
50,463	GALLATIN	19,327	7,282	11,574	471	4,292 D	37.7%	59.9%	38.6%	61.4%
1,589	GARFIELD	833	318	491	24	173 D	38.2%	58.9%	39.3%	60.7%
12,121	GLACIER	3,114	963	2,000	151	1,037 D	30.9%	64.2%	32.5%	67.5%
912	GOLDEN VALLEY	531	207	316	8	109 D	39.0%	59.5%	39.6%	60.4%
2,548	GRANITE	1,247	549	653	45	104 D	44.0%	52.4%	45.7%	54.3%
17,654	HILL	6,603	1,857	4,624	122	2,767 D	28.1%	70.0%	28.7%	71.3%
7,939	JEFFERSON	3,407	1,097	2,204	106	1,107 D	32.2%	64.7%	33.2%	66.8%
2,282	JUDITH BASIN	1,269	346	896	27	550 D	27.3%	70.6%	27.9%	72.1%
21,041	LAKE	7,800	2,937	4,648	215	1,711 D	37.7%	59.6%	38.7%	61.3%
47,495	LEWIS AND CLARK	20,124	4,999	14,605	520	9,606 D	24.8%	72.6%	25.5%	74.5%
2,295	LIBERTY	1,145	565	554	26	11 R	49.3%	48.4%	50.5%	49.5%
17,481	LINCOLN	6,666	2,717	3,716	233	999 D	40.8%	55.7%	42.2%	57.8%
2,276	MCCONE	1,353	441	895	17	454 D	32.6%	66.1%	33.0%	67.0%
5,989	MADISON	2,635	1,223	1,342	70	119 D	46.4%	50.9%	47.7%	52.3%
1,819	MEAGHER	877	301	553	23	252 D	34.3%	63.1%	35.2%	64.8%
3,315	MINERAL	1,417	364	1,017	36	653 D	25.7%	71.8%	26.4%	73.6%
78,687	MISSOULA	28,532	7,393	20,310	829	12,917 D	25.9%	71.2%	26.7%	73.3%
4,106	MUSSELSHELL	1,999	554	1,399	46	845 D	27.7%	70.0%	28.4%	71.6%
14,562	PARK	6,165	2,292	3,761	112	1,469 D	37.2%	61.0%	37.9%	62.1%
519	PETROLEUM	261	84	164	13	80 D	32.2%	62.8%	33.9%	66.1%
5,163	PHILLIPS	2,433	731	1,662	40	931 D	30.0%	68.3%	30.5%	69.5%
6,433	PONDERA	2,849	1,066	1,732	51	666 D	37.4%	60.8%	38.1%	61.9%
2,090	POWDER RIVER	970	377	571	22	194 D	38.9%	58.9%	39.8%	60.2%
6,620	POWELL	2,533	891	1,591	51	700 D	35.2%	62.8%	35.9%	64.1%
1,383	PRAIRIE	737	225	497	15	272 D	30.5%	67.4%	31.2%	68.8%
25,010	RAVALLI	10,961	4,602	5,979	380	1,377 D	42.0%	54.5%	43.5%	56.5%
10,716	RICHLAND	4,279	1,345	2,865	69	1,520 D	31.4%	67.0%	31.9%	68.1%
10,999	ROOSEVELT	3,516	878	2,508	130	1,630 D	25.0%	71.3%	25.9%	74.1%
10,505	ROSEBUD	3,178	684	2,362	132	1,678 D	21.5%	74.3%	22.5%	77.5%
8,669	SANDERS	3,905	1,318	2,454	133	1,136 D	33.8%	62.8%	34.9%	65.1%
4,732	SHERIDAN	2,526	598	1,902	26	1,304 D	23.7%	75.3%	23.9%	76.1%
33,941	SILVER BOW	15,473	2,472	12,695	306	10,223 D	16.0%	82.0%	16.3%	83.7%
6,536	STILLWATER	3,039	751	2,215	73	1,464 D	24.7%	72.9%	25.3%	74.7%
3,154	SWEET GRASS	1,597	622	939	36	317 D	38.9%	58.8%	39.8%	60.2%
6,271	TETON	2,953	937	1,963	53	1,026 D	31.7%	66.5%	32.3%	67.7%
5,046	TOOLE	2,576	905	1,603	68	698 D	35.1%	62.2%	36.1%	63.9%
874	TREASURE	506	116	383	7	267 D	22.9%	75.7%	23.2%	76.8%
8,239	VALLEY	3,883	1,093	2,696	94	1,603 D	28.1%	69.4%	28.8%	71.2%
2,246	WHEATLAND	1,054	329	712	13	383 D	31.2%	67.6%	31.6%	68.4%
1,191	WIBAUX	679	209	454	16	245 D	30.8%	66.9%	31.5%	68.5%
113,419	YELLOWSTONE	43,098	10,874	31,331	893	20,457 D	25.2%	72.7%	25.8%	74.2%
799,065	TOTAL	319,336	93,836	217,563	7,937	123,727 D	29.4%	68.1%	30.1%	69.9%

MONTANA

CONGRESS

CD	Year	Total Vote	Republican Vote	Candidate	Democratic Vote	Candidate	Other Vote	Rep.-Dem. Plurality	Total Vote Rep.	Dem.	Major Vote Rep.	Dem.
1	1990	164,246	63,837	JOHNSON, BRAD	100,409	WILLIAMS, PAT		36,572 D	38.9%	61.1%	38.9%	61.1%
1	1988	189,683	74,405	FENLASON, JIM	115,278	WILLIAMS, PAT		40,873 D	39.2%	60.8%	39.2%	60.8%
1	1986	159,731	61,230	ALLEN, DON	98,501	WILLIAMS, PAT		37,271 D	38.3%	61.7%	38.3%	61.7%
1	1984	193,452	61,794	CARLSON, GARY K.	126,998	WILLIAMS, PAT	4,660	65,204 D	31.9%	65.6%	32.7%	67.3%
2	1990	153,188	96,449	MARLENEE, RON	56,739	BURRIS, DON		39,710 R	63.0%	37.0%	63.0%	37.0%
2	1988	175,534	97,465	MARLENEE, RON	78,069	O'BRIEN, BUCK		19,396 R	55.5%	44.5%	55.5%	44.5%
2	1986	158,131	84,548	MARLENEE, RON	73,583	O'BRIEN, BUCK		10,965 R	53.5%	46.5%	53.5%	46.5%
2	1984	177,377	116,932	MARLENEE, RON	60,445	BLAYLOCK, CHET		56,487 R	65.9%	34.1%	65.9%	34.1%

MONTANA

Population total includes 52 persons living in Yellowstone National Park and not under any county jurisidction.

1990 GENERAL ELECTION

Senator   Other vote was Libertarian (Deitchler).

Congress

1990 PRIMARIES

JUNE 5 REPUBLICAN

Senator   38,097 Allen C. Kolstad; 30,837 Bruce Vorhauer; 11,833 Bill Farrell; 6,654 John Domenech.

Congress   Unopposed in both CD's.

JUNE 5 DEMOCRATIC

Senator   81,687 Max S. Baucus; 12,622 John Driscoll; 4,367 Curly Thornton.

Congress   Unopposed in both CD's.

NEBRASKA

GOVERNOR
Ben Nelson (D). Elected 1990 to a four-year term.

SENATORS
J. J. Exon (D). Re-elected 1990 to a six-year term. Previously elected 1984, 1978.

Bob Kerrey (D). Elected 1988 to a six-year term.

REPRESENTATIVES
1. Douglas K. Bereuter (R)   2. Peter Hoagland (D)   3. Bill Barrett (R)

POSTWAR VOTE FOR PRESIDENT

| | | | | | | | | Percentage | | | |
| | | Republican | | Democratic | | | | Total Vote | | Major Vote | |
Year	Total Vote	Vote	Candidate	Vote	Candidate	Other Vote	Plurality	Rep.	Dem.	Rep.	Dem.
1988	661,465	397,956	Bush, George	259,235	Dukakis, Michael S.	4,274	138,721 R	60.2%	39.2%	60.6%	39.4%
1984	652,090	460,054	Reagan, Ronald	187,866	Mondale, Walter F.	4,170	272,188 R	70.6%	28.8%	71.0%	29.0%
1980	640,854	419,937	Reagan, Ronald	166,851	Carter, Jimmy	54,066	253,086 R	65.5%	26.0%	71.6%	28.4%
1976	607,668	359,705	Ford, Gerald R.	233,692	Carter, Jimmy	14,271	126,013 R	59.2%	38.5%	60.6%	39.4%
1972	576,289	406,298	Nixon, Richard M.	169,991	McGovern, George S.		236,307 R	70.5%	29.5%	70.5%	29.5%
1968	536,851	321,163	Nixon, Richard M.	170,784	Humphrey, Hubert H.	44,904	150,379 R	59.8%	31.8%	65.3%	34.7%
1964	584,154	276,847	Goldwater, Barry M.	307,307	Johnson, Lyndon B.		30,460 D	47.4%	52.6%	47.4%	52.6%
1960	613,095	380,553	Nixon, Richard M.	232,542	Kennedy, John F.		148,011 R	62.1%	37.9%	62.1%	37.9%
1956	577,137	378,108	Eisenhower, Dwight D.	199,029	Stevenson, Adlai E.		179,079 R	65.5%	34.5%	65.5%	34.5%
1952	609,660	421,603	Eisenhower, Dwight D.	188,057	Stevenson, Adlai E.		233,546 R	69.2%	30.8%	69.2%	30.8%
1948	488,940	264,774	Dewey, Thomas E.	224,165	Truman, Harry S.	1	40,609 R	54.2%	45.8%	54.2%	45.8%

POSTWAR VOTE FOR GOVERNOR

| | | | | | | | | Percentage | | | |
| | | Republican | | Democratic | | | | Total Vote | | Major Vote | |
Year	Total Vote	Vote	Candidate	Vote	Candidate	Other Vote	Rep-Dem. Plurality	Rep.	Dem.	Rep.	Dem.
1990	586,542	288,741	Orr, Kay	292,771	Nelson, Ben	5,030	4,030 D	49.2%	49.9%	49.7%	50.3%
1986	564,422	298,325	Orr, Kay	265,156	Boosalis, Helen	941	33,169 R	52.9%	47.0%	52.9%	47.1%
1982	547,902	270,203	Thone, Charles	277,436	Kerrey, Bob	263	7,233 D	49.3%	50.6%	49.3%	50.7%
1978	492,423	275,473	Thone, Charles	216,754	Whelan, Gerald T.	196	58,719 R	55.9%	44.0%	56.0%	44.0%
1974	451,306	159,780	Marvel, Richard D.	267,012	Exon, J. J.	24,514	107,232 D	35.4%	59.2%	37.4%	62.6%
1970	461,619	201,994	Tiemann, Norbert T.	248,552	Exon, J. J.	11,073	46,558 D	43.8%	53.8%	44.8%	55.2%
1966 **	486,396	299,245	Tiemann, Norbert T.	186,985	Sorensen, Philip C.	166	112,260 R	61.5%	38.4%	61.5%	38.5%
1964	578,090	231,029	Burney, Dwight W.	347,026	Morrison, Frank B.	35	115,997 D	40.0%	60.0%	40.0%	60.0%
1962	464,585	221,885	Seaton, Fred A.	242,669	Morrison, Frank B.	31	20,784 D	47.8%	52.2%	47.8%	52.2%
1960	598,971	287,302	Cooper, John R.	311,344	Morrison, Frank B.	325	24,042 D	48.0%	52.0%	48.0%	52.0%
1958	421,067	209,705	Anderson, Victor E.	211,345	Brooks, Ralph G.	17	1,640 D	49.8%	50.2%	49.8%	50.2%
1956	567,933	308,293	Anderson, Victor E.	228,048	Sorrell, Frank	31,592	80,245 R	54.3%	40.2%	57.5%	42.5%
1954	414,841	250,080	Anderson, Victor E.	164,753	Ritchie, William	8	85,327 R	60.3%	39.7%	60.3%	39.7%
1952	595,714	366,009	Crosby, Robert B.	229,700	Raecke, Walter R.	5	136,309 R	61.4%	38.6%	61.4%	38.6%
1950	449,720	247,081	Peterson, Val	202,638	Raecke, Walter R.	1	44,443 R	54.9%	45.1%	54.9%	45.1%
1948	476,352	286,119	Peterson, Val	190,214	Sorrell, Frank	19	95,905 R	60.1%	39.9%	60.1%	39.9%
1946	380,835	249,468	Peterson, Val	131,367	Sorrell, Frank		118,101 R	65.5%	34.5%	65.5%	34.5%

The term of office of Nebraska's Governor was increased from two to four years effective with the 1966 election.

NEBRASKA

POSTWAR VOTE FOR SENATOR

Year	Total Vote	Republican Vote	Candidate	Democratic Vote	Candidate	Other Vote	Rep-Dem. Plurality	Total Vote Rep.	Dem.	Major Vote Rep.	Dem.
1990	593,828	243,013	Daub, Harold J.	349,779	Exon, J. J.	1,036	106,766 D	40.9%	58.9%	41.0%	59.0%
1988	667,860	278,250	Karnes, David	378,717	Kerrey, Bob	10,893	100,467 D	41.7%	56.7%	42.4%	57.6%
1984	639,668	307,147	Hoch, Nancy	332,217	Exon, J. J.	304	25,070 D	48.0%	51.9%	48.0%	52.0%
1982	545,647	155,760	Keck, Jim	363,350	Zorinsky, Edward	26,537	207,590 D	28.5%	66.6%	30.0%	70.0%
1978	494,368	159,806	Shasteen, Donald	334,276	Exon, J. J.	286	174,470 D	32.3%	67.6%	32.3%	67.7%
1976	598,314	284,284	McCollister, John Y.	313,809	Zorinsky, Edward	221	29,525 D	47.5%	52.4%	47.5%	52.5%
1972	568,580	301,841	Curtis, Carl T.	265,922	Carpenter, Terry	817	35,919 R	53.1%	46.8%	53.2%	46.8%
1970	458,966	240,894	Hruska, Roman L.	217,681	Morrison, Frank B.	391	23,213 R	52.5%	47.4%	52.5%	47.5%
1966	485,101	296,116	Curtis, Carl T.	187,950	Morrison, Frank B.	1,035	108,166 R	61.0%	38.7%	61.2%	38.8%
1964	563,401	345,772	Hruska, Roman L.	217,605	Arndt, Raymond W.	24	128,167 R	61.4%	38.6%	61.4%	38.6%
1960	598,743	352,748	Curtis, Carl T.	245,837	Conrad, Robert	158	106,911 R	58.9%	41.1%	58.9%	41.1%
1958	417,385	232,227	Hruska, Roman L.	185,152	Morrison, Frank B.	6	47,075 R	55.6%	44.4%	55.6%	44.4%
1954	418,691	255,695	Curtis, Carl T.	162,990	Neville, Keith	6	92,705 R	61.1%	38.9%	61.1%	38.9%
1954 S	411,225	250,341	Hruska, Roman L.	160,881	Green, James F.	3	89,460 R	60.9%	39.1%	60.9%	39.1%
1952	591,749	408,971	Butler, Hugh	164,660	Long, Stanley D.	18,118	244,311 R	69.1%	27.8%	71.3%	28.7%
1952 S	581,750	369,841	Griswold, Dwight	211,898	Ritchie, William	11	157,943 R	63.6%	36.4%	63.6%	36.4%
1948	471,895	267,575	Wherry, Kenneth S.	204,320	Carpenter, Terry		63,255 R	56.7%	43.3%	56.7%	43.3%
1946	382,958	271,208	Butler, Hugh	111,750	Mekota, John E.		159,458 R	70.8%	29.2%	70.8%	29.2%

One each of the 1954 and 1952 elections was for a short term to fill a vacancy.

NEBRASKA

Districts Established May 28, 1981

NEBRASKA

GOVERNOR 1990

1990 Census Population	County	Total Vote	Republican	Democratic	Other	Rep.-Dem. Plurality	Percentage Total Vote Rep.	Dem.	Major Vote Rep.	Dem.
29,625	ADAMS	10,732	5,344	5,227	161	117 R	49.8%	48.7%	50.6%	49.4%
7,965	ANTELOPE	3,293	1,920	1,373		547 R	58.3%	41.7%	58.3%	41.7%
462	ARTHUR	192	146	46		100 R	76.0%	24.0%	76.0%	24.0%
852	BANNER	447	302	140	5	162 R	67.6%	31.3%	68.3%	31.7%
675	BLAINE	420	277	141	2	136 R	66.0%	33.6%	66.3%	33.7%
6,667	BOONE	2,736	1,487	1,221	28	266 R	54.3%	44.6%	54.9%	45.1%
13,130	BOX BUTTE	4,886	2,305	2,568	13	263 D	47.2%	52.6%	47.3%	52.7%
2,835	BOYD	1,714	702	1,012		310 D	41.0%	59.0%	41.0%	59.0%
3,657	BROWN	1,684	1,029	628	27	401 R	61.1%	37.3%	62.1%	37.9%
37,447	BUFFALO	14,097	7,234	6,803	60	431 R	51.3%	48.3%	51.5%	48.5%
7,868	BURT	3,437	1,497	1,933	7	436 D	43.6%	56.2%	43.6%	56.4%
8,601	BUTLER	3,403	1,364	2,039		675 D	40.1%	59.9%	40.1%	59.9%
21,318	CASS	7,607	3,059	4,446	102	1,387 D	40.2%	58.4%	40.8%	59.2%
10,131	CEDAR	4,043	1,818	2,225		407 D	45.0%	55.0%	45.0%	55.0%
4,381	CHASE	1,950	1,076	857	17	219 R	55.2%	43.9%	55.7%	44.3%
6,307	CHERRY	2,503	1,622	868	13	754 R	64.8%	34.7%	65.1%	34.9%
9,494	CHEYENNE	3,543	2,144	1,358	41	786 R	60.5%	38.3%	61.2%	38.8%
7,123	CLAY	3,249	1,673	1,554	22	119 R	51.5%	47.8%	51.8%	48.2%
9,139	COLFAX	3,616	1,664	1,931	21	267 D	46.0%	53.4%	46.3%	53.7%
10,117	CUMING	3,765	2,291	1,468	6	823 R	60.8%	39.0%	60.9%	39.1%
12,270	CUSTER	4,665	2,732	1,909	24	823 R	58.6%	40.9%	58.9%	41.1%
16,742	DAKOTA	4,570	1,784	2,771	15	987 D	39.0%	60.6%	39.2%	60.8%
9,021	DAWES	3,410	1,747	1,662	1	85 R	51.2%	48.7%	51.2%	48.8%
19,940	DAWSON	6,933	4,131	2,800	2	1,331 R	59.6%	40.4%	59.6%	40.4%
2,237	DEUEL	924	529	381	14	148 R	57.3%	41.2%	58.1%	41.9%
6,143	DIXON	2,655	1,366	1,281	8	85 R	51.5%	48.2%	51.6%	48.4%
34,500	DODGE	13,249	6,046	7,098	105	1,052 D	45.6%	53.6%	46.0%	54.0%
416,444	DOUGLAS	151,882	75,722	75,114	1,046	608 R	49.9%	49.5%	50.2%	49.8%
2,582	DUNDY	1,167	593	574		19 R	50.8%	49.2%	50.8%	49.2%
7,103	FILLMORE	3,017	1,476	1,541		65 D	48.9%	51.1%	48.9%	51.1%
3,938	FRANKLIN	1,880	811	1,043	26	232 D	43.1%	55.5%	43.7%	56.3%
3,101	FRONTIER	1,356	816	539	1	277 R	60.2%	39.7%	60.2%	39.8%
5,553	FURNAS	2,401	1,204	1,179	18	25 R	50.1%	49.1%	50.5%	49.5%
22,794	GAGE	8,737	3,877	4,799	61	922 D	44.4%	54.9%	44.7%	55.3%
2,460	GARDEN	1,310	751	556	3	195 R	57.3%	42.4%	57.5%	42.5%
2,141	GARFIELD	861	500	345	16	155 R	58.1%	40.1%	59.2%	40.8%
1,928	GOSPER	856	457	399		58 R	53.4%	46.6%	53.4%	46.6%
769	GRANT	370	239	130	1	109 R	64.6%	35.1%	64.8%	35.2%
3,006	GREELEY	1,101	495	600	6	105 D	45.0%	54.5%	45.2%	54.8%
48,925	HALL	16,667	8,193	8,306	168	113 D	49.2%	49.8%	49.7%	50.3%
8,862	HAMILTON	3,809	2,201	1,598	10	603 R	57.8%	42.0%	57.9%	42.1%
3,810	HARLAN	2,183	1,034	1,123	26	89 D	47.4%	51.4%	47.9%	52.1%
1,222	HAYES	528	299	227	2	72 R	56.6%	43.0%	56.8%	43.2%
3,750	HITCHCOCK	1,480	661	808	11	147 D	44.7%	54.6%	45.0%	55.0%
12,599	HOLT	4,710	2,443	2,216	51	227 R	51.9%	47.0%	52.4%	47.6%
793	HOOKER	440	285	155		130 R	64.8%	35.2%	64.8%	35.2%
6,055	HOWARD	2,378	1,059	1,302	17	243 D	44.5%	54.8%	44.9%	55.1%
8,759	JEFFERSON	4,101	1,793	2,244	64	451 D	43.7%	54.7%	44.4%	55.6%
4,673	JOHNSON	2,231	852	1,345	34	493 D	38.2%	60.3%	38.8%	61.2%
6,629	KEARNEY	2,851	1,449	1,363	39	86 R	50.8%	47.8%	51.5%	48.5%
8,584	KEITH	3,347	2,024	1,306	17	718 R	60.5%	39.0%	60.8%	39.2%
1,029	KEYA PAHA	601	399	192	10	207 R	66.4%	31.9%	67.5%	32.5%
4,108	KIMBALL	1,554	958	581	15	377 R	61.6%	37.4%	62.2%	37.8%
9,534	KNOX	3,796	1,875	1,920	1	45 D	49.4%	50.6%	49.4%	50.6%
213,641	LANCASTER	81,502	34,692	45,074	1,736	10,382 D	42.6%	55.3%	43.5%	56.5%
32,508	LINCOLN	12,661	6,533	6,103	25	430 R	51.6%	48.2%	51.7%	48.3%
878	LOGAN	452	280	172		108 R	61.9%	38.1%	61.9%	38.1%
683	LOUP	312	171	135	6	36 R	54.8%	43.3%	55.9%	44.1%
546	MCPHERSON	269	199	69	1	130 R	74.0%	25.7%	74.3%	25.7%
32,655	MADISON	10,072	6,203	3,842	27	2,361 R	61.6%	38.1%	61.8%	38.2%

NEBRASKA

GOVERNOR 1990

1990 Census Population	County	Total Vote	Republican	Democratic	Other	Rep.-Dem. Plurality	Percentage Total Vote Rep.	Percentage Total Vote Dem.	Percentage Major Vote Rep.	Percentage Major Vote Dem.
8,042	MERRICK	3,035	1,727	1,301	7	426 R	56.9%	42.9%	57.0%	43.0%
5,423	MORRILL	2,306	1,250	1,013	43	237 R	54.2%	43.9%	55.2%	44.8%
4,275	NANCE	1,735	778	953	4	175 D	44.8%	54.9%	44.9%	55.1%
7,980	NEMAHA	3,743	1,662	2,028	53	366 D	44.4%	54.2%	45.0%	55.0%
5,786	NUCKOLLS	2,653	1,064	1,542	47	478 D	40.1%	58.1%	40.8%	59.2%
14,252	OTOE	5,870	2,686	3,142	42	456 D	45.8%	53.5%	46.1%	53.9%
3,317	PAWNEE	1,724	682	1,025	17	343 D	39.6%	59.5%	40.0%	60.0%
3,367	PERKINS	1,451	779	666	6	113 R	53.7%	45.9%	53.9%	46.1%
9,715	PHELPS	4,130	2,392	1,702	36	690 R	57.9%	41.2%	58.4%	41.6%
7,827	PIERCE	3,043	1,689	1,347	7	342 R	55.5%	44.3%	55.6%	44.4%
29,820	PLATTE	10,453	6,020	4,398	35	1,622 R	57.6%	42.1%	57.8%	42.2%
5,675	POLK	2,563	1,355	1,166	42	189 R	52.9%	45.5%	53.7%	46.3%
11,705	RED WILLOW	4,523	1,895	2,608	20	713 D	41.9%	57.7%	42.1%	57.9%
9,937	RICHARDSON	4,345	1,879	2,429	37	550 D	43.2%	55.9%	43.6%	56.4%
2,019	ROCK	837	498	301	38	197 R	59.5%	36.0%	62.3%	37.7%
12,715	SALINE	4,997	1,559	3,372	66	1,813 D	31.2%	67.5%	31.6%	68.4%
102,583	SARPY	27,063	13,695	13,351	17	344 R	50.6%	49.3%	50.6%	49.4%
18,285	SAUNDERS	7,699	3,195	4,480	24	1,285 D	41.5%	58.2%	41.6%	58.4%
36,025	SCOTTS BLUFF	11,626	6,743	4,876	7	1,867 R	58.0%	41.9%	58.0%	42.0%
15,450	SEWARD	5,798	2,531	3,211	56	680 D	43.7%	55.4%	44.1%	55.9%
6,750	SHERIDAN	2,581	1,694	846	41	848 R	65.6%	32.8%	66.7%	33.3%
3,718	SHERMAN	1,624	639	973	12	334 D	39.3%	59.9%	39.6%	60.4%
1,549	SIOUX	668	395	271	2	124 R	59.1%	40.6%	59.3%	40.7%
6,244	STANTON	2,058	1,023	1,028	7	5 D	49.7%	50.0%	49.9%	50.1%
6,635	THAYER	3,097	1,365	1,652	80	287 D	44.1%	53.3%	45.2%	54.8%
851	THOMAS	402	263	139		124 R	65.4%	34.6%	65.4%	34.6%
6,936	THURSTON	2,028	764	1,228	36	464 D	37.7%	60.6%	38.4%	61.6%
5,169	VALLEY	2,066	1,090	963	13	127 R	52.8%	46.6%	53.1%	46.9%
16,607	WASHINGTON	6,468	3,276	3,158	34	118 R	50.6%	48.8%	50.9%	49.1%
9,364	WAYNE	3,273	1,974	1,298	1	676 R	60.3%	39.7%	60.3%	39.7%
4,279	WEBSTER	2,071	812	1,228	31	416 D	39.2%	59.3%	39.8%	60.2%
948	WHEELER	429	239	185	5	54 R	55.7%	43.1%	56.4%	43.6%
14,428	YORK	5,578	3,295	2,251	32	1,044 R	59.1%	40.4%	59.4%	40.6%
1,578,385	TOTAL	586,542	288,741	292,771	5,030	4,030 D	49.2%	49.9%	49.7%	50.3%

NEBRASKA

SENATOR 1990

1990 Census Population	County	Total Vote	Republican	Democratic	Other	Rep.-Dem. Plurality	Percentage Total Vote Rep.	Dem.	Major Vote Rep.	Dem.
29,625	ADAMS	10,869	4,793	6,054	22	1,261 D	44.1%	55.7%	44.2%	55.8%
7,965	ANTELOPE	3,334	1,744	1,590		154 R	52.3%	47.7%	52.3%	47.7%
462	ARTHUR	203	149	54		95 R	73.4%	26.6%	73.4%	26.6%
852	BANNER	454	218	236		18 D	48.0%	52.0%	48.0%	52.0%
675	BLAINE	425	292	133		159 R	68.7%	31.3%	68.7%	31.3%
6,667	BOONE	2,801	1,176	1,625		449 D	42.0%	58.0%	42.0%	58.0%
13,130	BOX BUTTE	4,918	1,916	3,002		1,086 D	39.0%	61.0%	39.0%	61.0%
2,835	BOYD	1,682	1,052	630		422 R	62.5%	37.5%	62.5%	37.5%
3,657	BROWN	1,715	1,389	326		1,063 R	81.0%	19.0%	81.0%	19.0%
37,447	BUFFALO	14,418	6,082	8,336		2,254 D	42.2%	57.8%	42.2%	57.8%
7,868	BURT	3,502	1,356	2,146		790 D	38.7%	61.3%	38.7%	61.3%
8,601	BUTLER	3,540	1,101	2,439		1,338 D	31.1%	68.9%	31.1%	68.9%
21,318	CASS	7,659	2,868	4,773	18	1,905 D	37.4%	62.3%	37.5%	62.5%
10,131	CEDAR	4,043	1,613	2,430		817 D	39.9%	60.1%	39.9%	60.1%
4,381	CHASE	1,940	913	1,027		114 D	47.1%	52.9%	47.1%	52.9%
6,307	CHERRY	2,524	1,891	633		1,258 R	74.9%	25.1%	74.9%	25.1%
9,494	CHEYENNE	3,578	1,878	1,693	7	185 R	52.5%	47.3%	52.6%	47.4%
7,123	CLAY	3,352	1,388	1,945	19	557 D	41.4%	58.0%	41.6%	58.4%
9,139	COLFAX	3,650	1,185	2,464	1	1,279 D	32.5%	67.5%	32.5%	67.5%
10,117	CUMING	3,849	1,692	2,155	2	463 D	44.0%	56.0%	44.0%	56.0%
12,270	CUSTER	4,741	2,315	2,426		111 D	48.8%	51.2%	48.8%	51.2%
16,742	DAKOTA	4,570	1,866	2,703	1	837 D	40.8%	59.1%	40.8%	59.2%
9,021	DAWES	3,433	1,814	1,618	1	196 R	52.8%	47.1%	52.9%	47.1%
19,940	DAWSON	7,052	3,538	3,514		24 R	50.2%	49.8%	50.2%	49.8%
2,237	DEUEL	917	569	348		221 R	62.1%	37.9%	62.1%	37.9%
6,143	DIXON	2,723	1,268	1,453	2	185 D	46.6%	53.4%	46.6%	53.4%
34,500	DODGE	13,344	4,677	8,653	14	3,976 D	35.0%	64.8%	35.1%	64.9%
416,444	DOUGLAS	152,257	61,981	89,724	552	27,743 D	40.7%	58.9%	40.9%	59.1%
2,582	DUNDY	1,172	554	618		64 D	47.3%	52.7%	47.3%	52.7%
7,103	FILLMORE	3,184	1,097	2,085	2	988 D	34.5%	65.5%	34.5%	65.5%
3,938	FRANKLIN	1,914	773	1,141		368 D	40.4%	59.6%	40.4%	59.6%
3,101	FRONTIER	1,368	630	738		108 D	46.1%	53.9%	46.1%	53.9%
5,553	FURNAS	2,418	1,021	1,397		376 D	42.2%	57.8%	42.2%	57.8%
22,794	GAGE	9,076	2,875	6,201		3,326 D	31.7%	68.3%	31.7%	68.3%
2,460	GARDEN	1,324	786	538		248 R	59.4%	40.6%	59.4%	40.6%
2,141	GARFIELD	883	522	361		161 R	59.1%	40.9%	59.1%	40.9%
1,928	GOSPER	869	381	488		107 D	43.8%	56.2%	43.8%	56.2%
769	GRANT	376	241	135		106 R	64.1%	35.9%	64.1%	35.9%
3,006	GREELEY	1,114	348	766		418 D	31.2%	68.8%	31.2%	68.8%
48,925	HALL	16,828	7,256	9,532	40	2,276 D	43.1%	56.6%	43.2%	56.8%
8,862	HAMILTON	3,945	1,684	2,261		577 D	42.7%	57.3%	42.7%	57.3%
3,810	HARLAN	2,168	921	1,247		326 D	42.5%	57.5%	42.5%	57.5%
1,222	HAYES	534	264	270		6 D	49.4%	50.6%	49.4%	50.6%
3,750	HITCHCOCK	1,485	625	860		235 D	42.1%	57.9%	42.1%	57.9%
12,599	HOLT	4,830	3,231	1,599		1,632 R	66.9%	33.1%	66.9%	33.1%
793	HOOKER	453	282	171		111 R	62.3%	37.7%	62.3%	37.7%
6,055	HOWARD	2,436	924	1,512		588 D	37.9%	62.1%	37.9%	62.1%
8,759	JEFFERSON	4,256	1,512	2,743	1	1,231 D	35.5%	64.5%	35.5%	64.5%
4,673	JOHNSON	2,260	712	1,545	3	833 D	31.5%	68.4%	31.5%	68.5%
6,629	KEARNEY	2,911	1,271	1,638	2	367 D	43.7%	56.3%	43.7%	56.3%
8,584	KEITH	3,422	2,169	1,252	1	917 R	63.4%	36.6%	63.4%	36.6%
1,029	KEYA PAHA	614	531	83		448 R	86.5%	13.5%	86.5%	13.5%
4,108	KIMBALL	1,579	832	747		85 R	52.7%	47.3%	52.7%	47.3%
9,534	KNOX	3,815	1,866	1,949		83 D	48.9%	51.1%	48.9%	51.1%
213,641	LANCASTER	82,707	24,573	57,849	285	33,276 D	29.7%	69.9%	29.8%	70.2%
32,508	LINCOLN	12,894	5,222	7,662	10	2,440 D	40.5%	59.4%	40.5%	59.5%
878	LOGAN	465	265	200		65 R	57.0%	43.0%	57.0%	43.0%
683	LOUP	315	174	141		33 R	55.2%	44.8%	55.2%	44.8%
546	MCPHERSON	271	176	95		81 R	64.9%	35.1%	64.9%	35.1%
32,655	MADISON	10,212	5,615	4,591	6	1,024 R	55.0%	45.0%	55.0%	45.0%

NEBRASKA

SENATOR 1990

1990 Census Population	County	Total Vote	Republican	Democratic	Other	Rep.-Dem. Plurality	Percentage Total Vote Rep.	Dem.	Major Vote Rep.	Dem.
8,042	MERRICK	3,094	1,374	1,720		346 D	44.4%	55.6%	44.4%	55.6%
5,423	MORRILL	2,323	1,203	1,117	3	86 R	51.8%	48.1%	51.9%	48.1%
4,275	NANCE	1,768	581	1,187		606 D	32.9%	67.1%	32.9%	67.1%
7,980	NEMAHA	3,766	1,379	2,385	2	1,006 D	36.6%	63.3%	36.6%	63.4%
5,786	NUCKOLLS	2,726	1,020	1,704	2	684 D	37.4%	62.5%	37.4%	62.6%
14,252	OTOE	5,931	2,115	3,815	1	1,700 D	35.7%	64.3%	35.7%	64.3%
3,317	PAWNEE	1,751	623	1,128		505 D	35.6%	64.4%	35.6%	64.4%
3,367	PERKINS	1,454	776	678		98 R	53.4%	46.6%	53.4%	46.6%
9,715	PHELPS	4,243	2,236	2,007		229 R	52.7%	47.3%	52.7%	47.3%
7,827	PIERCE	3,063	1,534	1,527	2	7 R	50.1%	49.9%	50.1%	49.9%
29,820	PLATTE	10,695	4,459	6,230	6	1,771 D	41.7%	58.3%	41.7%	58.3%
5,675	POLK	2,599	963	1,632	4	669 D	37.1%	62.8%	37.1%	62.9%
11,705	RED WILLOW	4,575	1,999	2,575	1	576 D	43.7%	56.3%	43.7%	56.3%
9,937	RICHARDSON	4,372	1,795	2,577		782 D	41.1%	58.9%	41.1%	58.9%
2,019	ROCK	856	584	272		312 R	68.2%	31.8%	68.2%	31.8%
12,715	SALINE	5,088	1,114	3,968	6	2,854 D	21.9%	78.0%	21.9%	78.1%
102,583	SARPY	27,297	12,403	14,894		2,491 D	45.4%	54.6%	45.4%	54.6%
18,285	SAUNDERS	7,775	2,503	5,262	10	2,759 D	32.2%	67.7%	32.2%	67.8%
36,025	SCOTTS BLUFF	11,946	5,728	6,218		490 D	47.9%	52.1%	47.9%	52.1%
15,450	SEWARD	5,948	1,877	4,070	1	2,193 D	31.6%	68.4%	31.6%	68.4%
6,750	SHERIDAN	2,606	1,697	909		788 R	65.1%	34.9%	65.1%	34.9%
3,718	SHERMAN	1,648	571	1,077		506 D	34.6%	65.4%	34.6%	65.4%
1,549	SIOUX	683	333	350		17 D	48.8%	51.2%	48.8%	51.2%
6,244	STANTON	2,104	899	1,202	3	303 D	42.7%	57.1%	42.8%	57.2%
6,635	THAYER	3,175	1,156	2,019		863 D	36.4%	63.6%	36.4%	63.6%
851	THOMAS	408	253	155		98 R	62.0%	38.0%	62.0%	38.0%
6,936	THURSTON	2,040	693	1,347		654 D	34.0%	66.0%	34.0%	66.0%
5,169	VALLEY	2,118	958	1,160		202 D	45.2%	54.8%	45.2%	54.8%
16,607	WASHINGTON	6,526	3,035	3,486	5	451 D	46.5%	53.4%	46.5%	53.5%
9,364	WAYNE	3,325	1,691	1,634		57 R	50.9%	49.1%	50.9%	49.1%
4,279	WEBSTER	2,112	771	1,341		570 D	36.5%	63.5%	36.5%	63.5%
948	WHEELER	440	210	230		20 D	47.7%	52.3%	47.7%	52.3%
14,428	YORK	5,782	2,423	3,358	1	935 D	41.9%	58.1%	41.9%	58.1%
1,578,385	TOTAL	593,828	243,013	349,779	1,036	106,766 D	40.9%	58.9%	41.0%	59.0%

NEBRASKA

CONGRESS

CD	Year	Total Vote	Republican Vote	Candidate	Democratic Vote	Candidate	Other Vote	Rep.-Dem. Plurality	Percentage Total Vote Rep.	Dem.	Major Vote Rep.	Dem.
1	1990	200,381	129,654	BEREUTER, DOUGLAS K.	70,587	HALL, LARRY	140	59,067 R	64.7%	35.2%	64.7%	35.3%
1	1988	218,502	146,231	BEREUTER, DOUGLAS K.	72,167	JONES, CORKY	104	74,064 R	66.9%	33.0%	67.0%	33.0%
1	1986	188,986	121,772	BEREUTER, DOUGLAS K.	67,137	BURNS, STEVE	77	54,635 R	64.4%	35.5%	64.5%	35.5%
1	1984	214,364	158,836	BEREUTER, DOUGLAS K.	55,508	BAUER, MONICA	20	103,328 R	74.1%	25.9%	74.1%	25.9%
1	1982	183,368	137,675	BEREUTER, DOUGLAS K.	45,676	DONALDSON, CURT	17	91,999 R	75.1%	24.9%	75.1%	24.9%
2	1990	193,421	80,845	MILDER, ALLY	111,903	HOAGLAND, PETER	673	31,058 D	41.8%	57.9%	41.9%	58.1%
2	1988	222,275	109,193	SCHENKEN, JERRY	112,174	HOAGLAND, PETER	908	2,981 D	49.1%	50.5%	49.3%	50.7%
2	1986	170,267	99,569	DAUB, HAROLD J.	70,372	CALINGER, WALTER M.	326	29,197 R	58.5%	41.3%	58.6%	41.4%
2	1984	214,883	139,384	DAUB, HAROLD J.	75,210	CAVANAUGH, THOMAS F.	289	64,174 R	64.9%	35.0%	65.0%	35.0%
2	1982	163,349	92,639	DAUB, HAROLD J.	70,431	FELLMAN, RICHARD M.	279	22,208 R	56.7%	43.1%	56.8%	43.2%
3	1990	192,944	98,607	BARRETT, BILL	94,234	SCOFIELD, SANDRA K.	103	4,373 R	51.1%	48.8%	51.1%	48.9%
3	1988	215,501	170,302	SMITH, VIRGINIA	45,183	RACEK, JOHN D.	16	125,119 R	79.0%	21.0%	79.0%	21.0%
3	1986	196,184	136,985	SMITH, VIRGINIA	59,182	SIDWELL, SCOTT E.	17	77,803 R	69.8%	30.2%	69.8%	30.2%
3	1984	220,814	183,901	SMITH, VIRGINIA	36,899	VICKERS, TOM	14	147,002 R	83.3%	16.7%	83.3%	16.7%
3	1982	172,364	171,853	SMITH, VIRGINIA			511	171,853 R	99.7%		100.0%	

NEBRASKA

1990 GENERAL ELECTION

Governor   Other vote was 1,887 write-in (Sullivan) and 3,143 scattered write-in.

Senator   Other vote was scattered write-in.

Congress   Other vote was scattered write-in in all CD's.

1990 PRIMARIES

MAY 15 REPUBLICAN

Governor   130,045 Kay Orr; 59,048 Mort Sullivan; 1,848 scattered write-in.

Senator   178,232 Harold J. Daub; 16,367 Otis Glebe; 711 scattered write-in.

Congress   Unopposed in CD 1. Contested as follows:

CD 2   29,678 Ally Milder; 22,808 Ronald L. Staskiewicz; 185 scattered write-in.
CD 3   25,199 Bill Barrett; 23,097 Merlyn Carlson; 20,390 Fred Lockwood; 12,961 Rod Johnson; 3,021 Dan A. Govier; 39 scattered write-in.

MAY 15 DEMOCRATIC

Governor   44,721 Ben Nelson; 44,679 Bill Hoppner; 41,227 Mike Boyle; 31,527 Bill Harris; 2,759 Robert J. Prokop; 1,320 Don Eret; 726 Robb Nimic; 150 scattered write-in. The figures for Nelson and Hoppner are for the re-count.

Senator   J. J. Exon, unopposed.

Congress   Contested as follows:

CD 1   39,126 Larry Hall; 8,725 Marlin R. Pals; 132 scattered write-in.
CD 2   49,693 Peter Hoagland; 7,439 Jess M. Pritchett; 251 scattered write-in.
CD 3   27,734 Sandra K. Scofield; 17,329 Scott E. Sidwell; 3,168 Bill Haivala; 48 scattered write-in.

NEVADA

GOVERNOR

Robert J. Miller (D). Elected 1990 to a four-year term. Had been elected Lieutenant-Governor 1986 and became Governor January 1989 on the resignation of Governor Richard H. Bryan (D) following his election November 1988 to the U. S. Senate.

SENATORS

Richard H. Bryan (D). Elected 1988 to a six-year term.

Harry Reid (D). Elected 1986 to a six-year term.

REPRESENTATIVES

1. James Bilbray (D)   2. Barbara Vucanovich (R)

POSTWAR VOTE FOR PRESIDENT

| | | Republican | | Democratic | | Other | | Percentage Total Vote | | Percentage Major Vote | |
| | Total | | | | | | | | | | |
Year	Vote	Vote	Candidate	Vote	Candidate	Vote	Plurality	Rep.	Dem.	Rep.	Dem.
1988	350,067	206,040	Bush, George	132,738	Dukakis, Michael S.	11,289	73,302 R	58.9%	37.9%	60.8%	39.2%
1984	286,667	188,770	Reagan, Ronald	91,655	Mondale, Walter F.	6,242	97,115 R	65.8%	32.0%	67.3%	32.7%
1980	247,885	155,017	Reagan, Ronald	66,666	Carter, Jimmy	26,202	88,351 R	62.5%	26.9%	69.9%	30.1%
1976	201,876	101,273	Ford, Gerald R.	92,479	Carter, Jimmy	8,124	8,794 R	50.2%	45.8%	52.3%	47.7%
1972	181,766	115,750	Nixon, Richard M.	66,016	McGovern, George S.		49,734 R	63.7%	36.3%	63.7%	36.3%
1968	154,218	73,188	Nixon, Richard M.	60,598	Humphrey, Hubert H.	20,432	12,590 R	47.5%	39.3%	54.7%	45.3%
1964	135,433	56,094	Goldwater, Barry M.	79,339	Johnson, Lyndon B.		23,245 D	41.4%	58.6%	41.4%	58.6%
1960	107,267	52,387	Nixon, Richard M.	54,880	Kennedy, John F.		2,493 D	48.8%	51.2%	48.8%	51.2%
1956	96,689	56,049	Eisenhower, Dwight D.	40,640	Stevenson, Adlai E.		15,409 R	58.0%	42.0%	58.0%	42.0%
1952	82,190	50,502	Eisenhower, Dwight D.	31,688	Stevenson, Adlai E.		18,814 R	61.4%	38.6%	61.4%	38.6%
1948	62,117	29,357	Dewey, Thomas E.	31,291	Truman, Harry S.	1,469	1,934 D	47.3%	50.4%	48.4%	51.6%

POSTWAR VOTE FOR GOVERNOR

| | | Republican | | Democratic | | Other | Rep-Dem. | Percentage Total Vote | | Percentage Major Vote | |
| | Total | | | | | | | | | | |
Year	Vote	Vote	Candidate	Vote	Candidate	Vote	Plurality	Rep.	Dem.	Rep.	Dem.
1990	320,743	95,789	Gallaway, Jim	207,878	Miller, Robert J.	17,076	112,089 D	29.9%	64.8%	31.5%	68.5%
1986	260,375	65,081	Cafferata, Patty	187,268	Bryan, Richard H.	8,026	122,187 D	25.0%	71.9%	25.8%	74.2%
1982	239,751	100,104	List, Robert F.	128,132	Bryan, Richard H.	11,515	28,028 D	41.8%	53.4%	43.9%	56.1%
1978	192,445	108,097	List, Robert F.	76,361	Rose, Robert E.	7,987	31,736 R	56.2%	39.7%	58.6%	41.4%
1974	169,358	28,959	Crumpler, Shirley	114,114	O'Callaghan, Mike	26,285	85,155 D	17.1%	67.4%	20.2%	79.8%
1970	146,991	64,400	Fike, Ed	70,697	O'Callaghan, Mike	11,894	6,297 D	43.8%	48.1%	47.7%	52.3%
1966	137,677	71,807	Laxalt, Paul	65,870	Sawyer, Grant		5,937 R	52.2%	47.8%	52.2%	47.8%
1962	96,929	32,145	Gragson, Oran K.	64,784	Sawyer, Grant		32,639 D	33.2%	66.8%	33.2%	66.8%
1958	84,889	34,025	Russell, Charles H.	50,864	Sawyer, Grant		16,839 D	40.1%	59.9%	40.1%	59.9%
1954	78,462	41,665	Russell, Charles H.	36,797	Pittman, Vail		4,868 R	53.1%	46.9%	53.1%	46.9%
1950	61,773	35,609	Russell, Charles H.	26,164	Pittman, Vail		9,445 R	57.6%	42.4%	57.6%	42.4%
1946	49,902	21,247	Jepson, Melvin E.	28,655	Pittman, Vail		7,408 D	42.6%	57.4%	42.6%	57.4%

NEVADA

POSTWAR VOTE FOR SENATOR

Year	Total Vote	Republican Vote	Republican Candidate	Democratic Vote	Democratic Candidate	Other Vote	Rep-Dem. Plurality	Percentage Total Vote Rep.	Dem.	Major Vote Rep.	Dem.
1988	349,649	161,336	Hecht, Chic	175,548	Bryan, Richard H.	12,765	14,212 D	46.1%	50.2%	47.9%	52.1%
1986	261,932	116,606	Santini, James	130,955	Reid, Harry	14,371	14,349 D	44.5%	50.0%	47.1%	52.9%
1982	240,394	120,377	Hecht, Chic	114,720	Cannon, Howard W.	5,297	5,657 R	50.1%	47.7%	51.2%	48.8%
1980	246,436	144,224	Laxalt, Paul	92,129	Gojack, Mary	10,083	52,095 R	58.5%	37.4%	61.0%	39.0%
1976	201,980	63,471	Towell, David	127,295	Cannon, Howard W.	11,214	63,824 D	31.4%	63.0%	33.3%	66.7%
1974	169,473	79,605	Laxalt, Paul	78,981	Reid, Harry	10,887	624 R	47.0%	46.6%	50.2%	49.8%
1970	147,768	60,838	Raggio, William J.	85,187	Cannon, Howard W.	1,743	24,349 D	41.2%	57.6%	41.7%	58.3%
1968	152,690	69,068	Fike, Ed	83,622	Bible, Alan		14,554 D	45.2%	54.8%	45.2%	54.8%
1964	134,624	67,288	Laxalt, Paul	67,336	Cannon, Howard W.		48 D	50.0%	50.0%	50.0%	50.0%
1962	97,192	33,749	Wright, William B.	63,443	Bible, Alan		29,694 D	34.7%	65.3%	34.7%	65.3%
1958	84,492	35,760	Malone, George W.	48,732	Cannon, Howard W.		12,972 D	42.3%	57.7%	42.3%	57.7%
1956	96,389	45,712	Young, Clifton	50,677	Bible, Alan		4,965 D	47.4%	52.6%	47.4%	52.6%
1954 S	77,513	32,470	Brown, Ernest S.	45,043	Bible, Alan		12,573 D	41.9%	58.1%	41.9%	58.1%
1952	81,090	41,906	Malone, George W.	39,184	Mechling, Thomas B.		2,722 R	51.7%	48.3%	51.7%	48.3%
1950	61,762	25,933	Marshall, George E.	35,829	McCarran, Pat		9,896 D	42.0%	58.0%	42.0%	58.0%
1946	50,354	27,801	Malone, George W.	22,553	Bunker, Berkeley		5,248 R	55.2%	44.8%	55.2%	44.8%

The 1954 election was for a short term to fill a vacancy.

NEVADA

Districts Established June 4, 1981

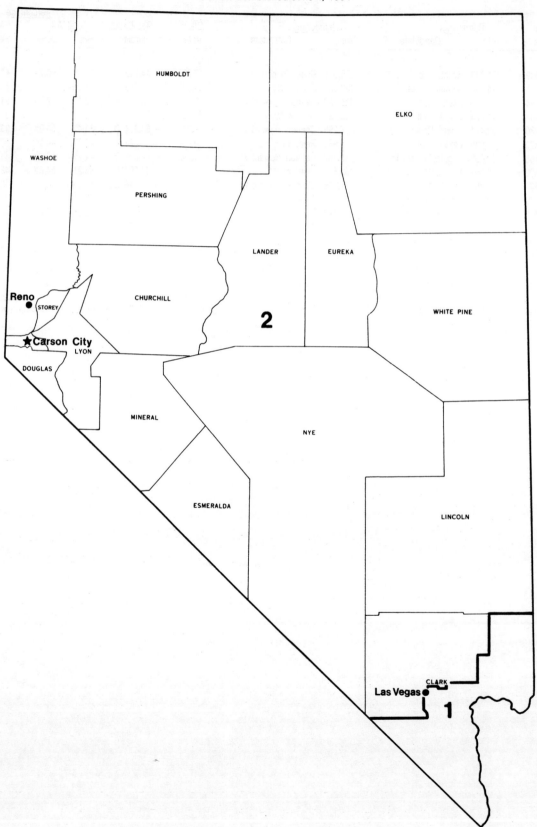

NEVADA

GOVERNOR 1990

1990 Census Population	County	Total Vote	Republican	Democratic	Other	Rep.-Dem. Plurality	Total Vote Rep.	Total Vote Dem.	Major Vote Rep.	Major Vote Dem.
40,443	CARSON CITY	14,966	4,675	9,517	774	4,842 D	31.2%	63.6%	32.9%	67.1%
17,938	CHURCHILL	5,825	2,173	3,315	337	1,142 D	37.3%	56.9%	39.6%	60.4%
741,459	CLARK	173,403	49,938	114,687	8,778	64,749 D	28.8%	66.1%	30.3%	69.7%
27,637	DOUGLAS	10,678	3,500	6,611	567	3,111 D	32.8%	61.9%	34.6%	65.4%
33,530	ELKO	8,363	3,832	3,908	623	76 D	45.8%	46.7%	49.5%	50.5%
1,344	ESMERALDA	523	221	256	46	35 D	42.3%	48.9%	46.3%	53.7%
1,547	EUREKA	681	279	347	55	68 D	41.0%	51.0%	44.6%	55.4%
12,844	HUMBOLDT	3,704	1,406	2,071	227	665 D	38.0%	55.9%	40.4%	59.6%
6,266	LANDER	1,654	765	792	97	27 D	46.3%	47.9%	49.1%	50.9%
3,775	LINCOLN	1,517	378	1,052	87	674 D	24.9%	69.3%	26.4%	73.6%
20,001	LYON	7,148	2,004	4,815	329	2,811 D	28.0%	67.4%	29.4%	70.6%
6,475	MINERAL	2,543	691	1,719	133	1,028 D	27.2%	67.6%	28.7%	71.3%
17,781	NYE	5,806	2,120	3,172	514	1,052 D	36.5%	54.6%	40.1%	59.9%
4,336	PERSHING	1,342	426	814	102	388 D	31.7%	60.7%	34.4%	65.6%
2,526	STOREY	1,283	327	874	82	547 D	25.5%	68.1%	27.2%	72.8%
254,667	WASHOE	78,023	22,235	51,746	4,042	29,511 D	28.5%	66.3%	30.1%	69.9%
9,264	WHITE PINE	3,284	819	2,182	283	1,363 D	24.9%	66.4%	27.3%	72.7%
1,201,833	TOTAL	320,743	95,789	207,878	17,076	112,089 D	29.9%	64.8%	31.5%	68.5%

NEVADA

CONGRESS

CD	Year	Total Vote	Republican Vote	Candidate	Democratic Vote	Candidate	Other Vote	Rep.-Dem. Plurality	Percentage Total Vote Rep.	Dem.	Major Vote Rep.	Dem.
1	1990	137,852	47,377	DICKINSON, BOB	84,650	BILBRAY, JAMES	5,825	37,273 D	34.4%	61.4%	35.9%	64.1%
1	1988	159,076	53,588	LUSK, LUCILLE	101,764	BILBRAY, JAMES	3,724	48,176 D	33.7%	64.0%	34.5%	65.5%
1	1986	114,317	50,342	RYAN, BOB	61,830	BILBRAY, JAMES	2,145	11,488 D	44.0%	54.1%	44.9%	55.1%
1	1984	130,518	55,391	CAVNAR, PEGGY	73,242	REID, HARRY	1,885	17,851 D	42.4%	56.1%	43.1%	56.9%
1	1982	107,576	45,675	CAVNAR, PEGGY	61,901	REID, HARRY		16,226 D	42.5%	57.5%	42.5%	57.5%
2	1990	175,209	103,508	VUCANOVICH, BARBARA	59,581	WISDOM, JANE	12,120	43,927 R	59.1%	34.0%	63.5%	36.5%
2	1988	185,097	105,981	VUCANOVICH, BARBARA	75,163	SPOO, JAMES	3,953	30,818 R	57.3%	40.6%	58.5%	41.5%
2	1986	142,912	83,479	VUCANOVICH, BARBARA	59,433	SFERRAZZA, PETE		24,046 R	58.4%	41.6%	58.4%	41.6%
2	1984	140,106	99,775	VUCANOVICH, BARBARA	36,130	BARBANO, ANDREW	4,201	63,645 R	71.2%	25.8%	73.4%	26.6%
2	1982	126,496	70,188	VUCANOVICH, BARBARA	52,265	GOJACK, MARY	4,043	17,923 R	55.5%	41.3%	57.3%	42.7%

NEVADA

1990 GENERAL ELECTION

Governor   Other vote was 8,059 Libertarian (Frye) and 9,017 "None of these Candidates".

Congress   Other vote was Libertarian (Moore) in CD 1; Libertarian (Becan) in CD 2.

1990 PRIMARIES

SEPTEMBER 4 REPUBLICAN

Governor   37,467 Jim Gallaway; 16,067 Charlie Brown; 1,490 John Glab; 1,095 M. L. Stover; 1,054 Vince L. Thompson; 914 Loyd Ellis; 799 Ronald L. Spilsbury; 577 Denis A. Sholty; 16,565 "None of these Candidates".

Congress   Contested as follows:

CD   1   13,699 Bob Dickinson; 4,773 Bob Roland; 4,049 Gregory Nyberg.
CD   2   42,166 Barbara Vucanovich; 5,144 Dick Baker; 2,816 Brooklyn Harris.

SEPTEMBER 4 DEMOCRATIC

Governor   71,537 Robert J. Miller; 2,451 Rhinestone Cowboy; 2,201 Knight Allen; 2,002 William H. Morrison; 1,707 Robert J. Edwards; 1,005 Frederick G. Wilson; 7,394 "None of these Candidates".

Congress   Unopposed in CD 2. Contested as follows:

CD   1   30,747 James Bilbray; 4,883 Josh Elliott.

NEW HAMPSHIRE

GOVERNOR
Judd Gregg (R). Re-elected 1990 to a two-year term. Previously elected 1988.

SENATORS
Warren Rudman (R). Re-elected 1986 to a six-year term. Previously elected 1980.

Robert C. Smith (R). Elected 1990 to a six-year term; appointed December 1990 to fill the last few weeks of the term vacated when Senator Gordon J. Humphrey resigned to be sworn in as a state senator in New Hampshire.

REPRESENTATIVES
1. Bill Zeliff (R)   2. Dick Swett (D)

POSTWAR VOTE FOR PRESIDENT

Year	Total Vote	Republican Vote	Candidate	Democratic Vote	Candidate	Other Vote	Plurality	Rep.	Dem.	Rep.	Dem.
1988	451,074	281,537	Bush, George	163,696	Dukakis, Michael S.	5,841	117,841 R	62.4%	36.3%	63.2%	36.8%
1984	389,066	267,051	Reagan, Ronald	120,395	Mondale, Walter F.	1,620	146,656 R	68.6%	30.9%	68.9%	31.1%
1980	383,990	221,705	Reagan, Ronald	108,864	Carter, Jimmy	53,421	112,841 R	57.7%	28.4%	67.1%	32.9%
1976	339,618	185,935	Ford, Gerald R.	147,635	Carter, Jimmy	6,048	38,300 R	54.7%	43.5%	55.7%	44.3%
1972	334,055	213,724	Nixon, Richard M.	116,435	McGovern, George S.	3,896	97,289 R	64.0%	34.9%	64.7%	35.3%
1968	297,298	154,903	Nixon, Richard M.	130,589	Humphrey, Hubert H.	11,806	24,314 R	52.1%	43.9%	54.3%	45.7%
1964	288,093	104,029	Goldwater, Barry M.	184,064	Johnson, Lyndon B.		80,035 D	36.1%	63.9%	36.1%	63.9%
1960	295,761	157,989	Nixon, Richard M.	137,772	Kennedy, John F.		20,217 R	53.4%	46.6%	53.4%	46.6%
1956	266,994	176,519	Eisenhower, Dwight D.	90,364	Stevenson, Adlai E.	111	86,155 R	66.1%	33.8%	66.1%	33.9%
1952	272,950	166,287	Eisenhower, Dwight D.	106,663	Stevenson, Adlai E.		59,624 R	60.9%	39.1%	60.9%	39.1%
1948	231,440	121,299	Dewey, Thomas E.	107,995	Truman, Harry S.	2,146	13,304 R	52.4%	46.7%	52.9%	47.1%

NEW HAMPSHIRE

POSTWAR VOTE FOR GOVERNOR

Year	Total Vote	Republican Vote	Candidate	Democratic Vote	Candidate	Other Vote	Rep-Dem. Plurality	Total Vote Rep.	Total Vote Dem.	Major Vote Rep.	Major Vote Dem.
1990	295,018	177,773	Gregg, Judd	101,923	Grandmaison, J. Joseph	15,322	75,850 R	60.3%	34.5%	63.6%	36.4%
1988	441,923	267,064	Gregg, Judd	172,543	McEachern, Paul	2,316	94,521 R	60.4%	39.0%	60.8%	39.2%
1986	251,107	134,824	Sununu, John H.	116,142	McEachern, Paul	141	18,682 R	53.7%	46.3%	53.7%	46.3%
1984	383,910	256,574	Sununu, John H.	127,156	Spirou, Chris	180	129,418 R	66.8%	33.1%	66.9%	33.1%
1982	282,588	145,389	Sununu, John H.	132,317	Gallen, Hugh J.	4,882	13,072 R	51.4%	46.8%	52.4%	47.6%
1980	384,031	156,178	Thomson, Meldrim	226,436	Gallen, Hugh J.	1,417	70,258 D	40.7%	59.0%	40.8%	59.2%
1978	269,587	122,464	Thomson, Meldrim	133,133	Gallen, Hugh J.	13,990	10,669 D	45.4%	49.4%	47.9%	52.1%
1976	342,669	197,589	Thomson, Meldrim	145,015	Spanos, Harry V.	65	52,574 R	57.7%	42.3%	57.7%	42.3%
1974	226,665	115,933	Thomson, Meldrim	110,591	Leonard, Richard W.	141	5,342 R	51.1%	48.8%	51.2%	48.8%
1972	323,102	133,702	Thomson, Meldrim	126,107	Crowley, Roger J.	63,293	7,595 R	41.4%	39.0%	51.5%	48.5%
1970	222,441	102,298	Peterson, Walter R.	98,098	Crowley, Roger J.	22,045	4,200 R	46.0%	44.1%	51.0%	49.0%
1968	285,342	149,902	Peterson, Walter R.	135,378	Bussiere, Emile R.	62	14,524 R	52.5%	47.4%	52.5%	47.5%
1966	233,642	107,259	Gregg, Hugh	125,882	King, John W.	501	18,623 D	45.9%	53.9%	46.0%	54.0%
1964	285,863	94,824	Pillsbury, John	190,863	King, John W.	176	96,039 D	33.2%	66.8%	33.2%	66.8%
1962	230,048	94,567	Pillsbury, John	135,481	King, John W.		40,914 D	41.1%	58.9%	41.1%	58.9%
1960	290,527	161,123	Powell, Wesley	129,404	Boutin, Bernard L.		31,719 R	55.5%	44.5%	55.5%	44.5%
1958	206,745	106,790	Powell, Wesley	99,955	Boutin, Bernard L.		6,835 R	51.7%	48.3%	51.7%	48.3%
1956	258,695	141,578	Dwinell, Lane	117,117	Shaw, John		24,461 R	54.7%	45.3%	54.7%	45.3%
1954	194,631	107,287	Dwinell, Lane	87,344	Shaw, John		19,943 R	55.1%	44.9%	55.1%	44.9%
1952	265,715	167,791	Gregg, Hugh	97,924	Craig, William H.		69,867 R	63.1%	36.9%	63.1%	36.9%
1950	191,239	108,907	Adams, Sherman	82,258	Bingham, Robert P.	74	26,649 R	56.9%	43.0%	57.0%	43.0%
1948	222,571	116,212	Adams, Sherman	105,207	Hill, Herbert W.	1,152	11,005 R	52.2%	47.3%	52.5%	47.5%
1946	163,451	103,204	Dale, Charles M.	60,247	Keefe, F. Clyde		42,957 R	63.1%	36.9%	63.1%	36.9%

POSTWAR VOTE FOR SENATOR

Year	Total Vote	Republican Vote	Candidate	Democratic Vote	Candidate	Other Vote	Rep-Dem. Plurality	Total Vote Rep.	Total Vote Dem.	Major Vote Rep.	Major Vote Dem.
1990	291,393	189,792	Smith, Robert C.	91,299	Durkin, John A.	10,302	98,493 R	65.1%	31.3%	67.5%	32.5%
1986	244,797	154,090	Rudman, Warren	79,225	Peabody, Endicott	11,482	74,865 R	62.9%	32.4%	66.0%	34.0%
1984	384,406	225,828	Humphrey, Gordon J.	157,447	D'Amours, Norman E.	1,131	68,381 R	58.7%	41.0%	58.9%	41.1%
1980	375,064	195,563	Rudman, Warren	179,455	Durkin, John A.	46	16,108 R	52.1%	47.8%	52.1%	47.9%
1978	263,779	133,745	Humphrey, Gordon J.	127,945	McIntyre, Thomas J.	2,089	5,800 R	50.7%	48.5%	51.1%	48.9%
1975 S	262,682	113,007	Wyman, Louis C.	140,778	Durkin, John A.	8,897	27,771 D	43.0%	53.6%	44.5%	55.5%
1974 **	223,363	110,926	Wyman, Louis C.	110,924	Durkin, John A.	1,513	2 R	49.7%	49.7%	50.0%	50.0%
1972	324,354	139,852	Powell, Wesley	184,495	McIntyre, Thomas J.	7	44,643 D	43.1%	56.9%	43.1%	56.9%
1968	286,989	170,163	Cotton, Norris	116,816	King, John W.	10	53,347 R	59.3%	40.7%	59.3%	40.7%
1966	229,305	105,241	Thyng, Harrison R.	123,888	McIntyre, Thomas J.	176	18,647 D	45.9%	54.0%	45.9%	54.1%
1962	224,479	134,035	Cotton, Norris	90,444	Catalfo, Alfred		43,591 R	59.7%	40.3%	59.7%	40.3%
1962 S	224,811	107,199	Bass, Perkins	117,612	McIntyre, Thomas J.		10,413 D	47.7%	52.3%	47.7%	52.3%
1960	287,545	173,521	Bridges, Styles	114,024	Hill, Herbert W.		59,497 R	60.3%	39.7%	60.3%	39.7%
1956	251,943	161,424	Cotton, Norris	90,519	Pickett, Laurence M.		70,905 R	64.1%	35.9%	64.1%	35.9%
1954	194,536	117,150	Bridges, Styles	77,386	Morin, Gerard L.		39,764 R	60.2%	39.8%	60.2%	39.8%
1954 S	189,558	114,068	Cotton, Norris	75,490	Bentley, Stanley J.		38,578 R	60.2%	39.8%	60.2%	39.8%
1950	190,573	106,142	Tobey, Charles W.	72,473	Kelley, Emmet J.	11,958	33,669 R	55.7%	38.0%	59.4%	40.6%
1948	222,898	129,600	Bridges, Styles	91,760	Fortin, Alfred E.	1,538	37,840 R	58.1%	41.2%	58.5%	41.5%

One each of the 1962 and 1954 elections were for short terms to fill vacancies. Following the 1974 election, neither candidate was seated and the 1975 special election was held for the remaining years of this term.

NEW HAMPSHIRE

Districts Established March 4, 1982

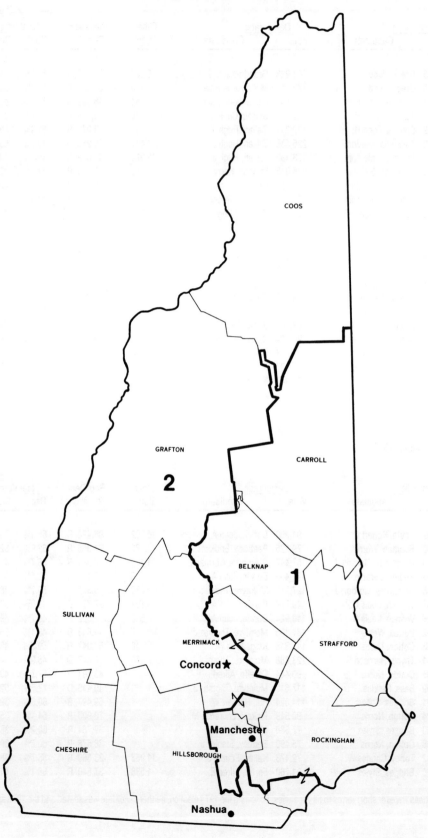

COOS

GRAFTON

2

CARROLL

BELKNAP

1

SULLIVAN

STRAFFORD

MERRIMACK

Concord ★

Manchester ●

ROCKINGHAM

CHESHIRE

HILLSBOROUGH

Nashua ●

NEW HAMPSHIRE

GOVERNOR 1990

1990 Census Population	County	Total Vote	Republican	Democratic	Other	Rep.-Dem. Plurality	Percentage Total Vote Rep.	Dem.	Major Vote Rep.	Dem.
49,216	BELKNAP	15,332	9,298	5,269	765	4,029 R	60.6%	34.4%	63.8%	36.2%
35,410	CARROLL	12,534	8,779	3,158	597	5,621 R	70.0%	25.2%	73.5%	26.5%
70,121	CHESHIRE	17,474	8,158	8,327	989	169 D	46.7%	47.7%	49.5%	50.5%
34,828	COOS	8,695	5,253	3,205	237	2,048 R	60.4%	36.9%	62.1%	37.9%
74,929	GRAFTON	19,900	11,572	7,661	667	3,911 R	58.2%	38.5%	60.2%	39.8%
336,073	HILLSBOROUGH	87,824	57,345	26,064	4,415	31,281 R	65.3%	29.7%	68.8%	31.2%
120,005	MERRIMACK	34,737	18,537	14,159	2,041	4,378 R	53.4%	40.8%	56.7%	43.3%
245,845	ROCKINGHAM	63,652	39,957	19,767	3,928	20,190 R	62.8%	31.1%	66.9%	33.1%
104,233	STRAFFORD	24,169	13,218	9,693	1,258	3,525 R	54.7%	40.1%	57.7%	42.3%
38,592	SULLIVAN	10,701	5,656	4,620	425	1,036 R	52.9%	43.2%	55.0%	45.0%
1,109,252	TOTAL	295,018	177,773	101,923	15,322	75,850 R	60.3%	34.5%	63.6%	36.4%

NEW HAMPSHIRE

SENATOR 1990

1990 Census Population	County	Total Vote	Republican	Democratic	Other	Rep.-Dem. Plurality	Percentage Total Vote Rep.	Dem.	Major Vote Rep.	Dem.
49,216	BELKNAP	15,252	10,648	4,119	485	6,529 R	69.8%	27.0%	72.1%	27.9%
35,410	CARROLL	12,653	9,128	3,188	337	5,940 R	72.1%	25.2%	74.1%	25.9%
70,121	CHESHIRE	16,877	9,569	6,707	601	2,862 R	56.7%	39.7%	58.8%	41.2%
34,828	COOS	8,706	5,416	3,168	122	2,248 R	62.2%	36.4%	63.1%	36.9%
74,929	GRAFTON	19,481	12,377	6,554	550	5,823 R	63.5%	33.6%	65.4%	34.6%
336,073	HILLSBOROUGH	86,368	58,129	25,023	3,216	33,106 R	67.3%	29.0%	69.9%	30.1%
120,005	MERRIMACK	34,157	21,116	11,602	1,439	9,514 R	61.8%	34.0%	64.5%	35.5%
245,845	ROCKINGHAM	63,009	41,818	18,691	2,500	23,127 R	66.4%	29.7%	69.1%	30.9%
104,233	STRAFFORD	24,196	15,157	8,257	782	6,900 R	62.6%	34.1%	64.7%	35.3%
38,592	SULLIVAN	10,694	6,434	3,990	270	2,444 R	60.2%	37.3%	61.7%	38.3%
1,109,252	TOTAL	291,393	189,792	91,299	10,302	98,493 R	65.1%	31.3%	67.5%	32.5%

NEW HAMPSHIRE

GOVERNOR 1990

1990 Census Population	City/Town	Total Vote	Republican	Democratic	Other	Rep.-Dem. Plurality	Percentage Total Vote Rep.	Dem.	Major Vote Rep.	Dem.
9,068	AMHERST	2,895	2,057	680	158	1,377 R	71.1%	23.5%	75.2%	24.8%
5,188	ATKINSON	1,485	1,068	331	86	737 R	71.9%	22.3%	76.3%	23.7%
6,164	BARRINGTON	1,429	749	565	115	184 R	52.4%	39.5%	57.0%	43.0%
12,563	BEDFORD	4,541	3,380	941	220	2,439 R	74.4%	20.7%	78.2%	21.8%
5,796	BELMONT	1,257	732	439	86	293 R	58.2%	34.9%	62.5%	37.5%
11,824	BERLIN	3,027	1,593	1,359	75	234 R	52.6%	44.9%	54.0%	46.0%
5,500	BOW	2,051	1,269	656	126	613 R	61.9%	32.0%	65.9%	34.1%
13,902	CLAREMONT	3,468	1,651	1,692	125	41 D	47.6%	48.8%	49.4%	50.6%
36,006	CONCORD	10,100	4,439	5,054	607	615 D	44.0%	50.0%	46.8%	53.2%
7,940	CONWAY	2,133	1,569	562	2	1,007 R	73.6%	26.3%	73.6%	26.4%
29,603	DERRY	5,390	3,587	1,409	394	2,178 R	66.5%	26.1%	71.8%	28.2%
25,042	DOVER	6,417	3,614	2,482	321	1,132 R	56.3%	38.7%	59.3%	40.7%
11,818	DURHAM	2,205	960	1,140	105	180 D	43.5%	51.7%	45.7%	54.3%
5,162	EPPING	1,146	697	367	82	330 R	60.8%	32.0%	65.5%	34.5%
12,481	EXETER	3,707	2,157	1,295	255	862 R	58.2%	34.9%	62.5%	37.5%
5,739	FARMINGTON	1,049	657	350	42	307 R	62.6%	33.4%	65.2%	34.8%
8,304	FRANKLIN	1,812	1,089	651	72	438 R	60.1%	35.9%	62.6%	37.4%
5,867	GILFORD	2,234	1,399	729	106	670 R	62.6%	32.6%	65.7%	34.3%
14,621	GOFFSTOWN	3,901	2,699	1,027	175	1,672 R	69.2%	26.3%	72.4%	27.6%
6,732	HAMPSTEAD	1,774	1,272	410	92	862 R	71.7%	23.1%	75.6%	24.4%
12,278	HAMPTON	4,047	2,295	1,446	306	849 R	56.7%	35.7%	61.3%	38.7%
9,212	HANOVER	2,353	978	1,335	40	357 D	41.6%	56.7%	42.3%	57.7%
5,705	HOLLIS	2,020	1,361	555	104	806 R	67.4%	27.5%	71.0%	29.0%
8,767	HOOKSETT	2,506	1,818	594	94	1,224 R	72.5%	23.7%	75.4%	24.6%
19,530	HUDSON	4,481	2,809	1,349	323	1,460 R	62.7%	30.1%	67.6%	32.4%
5,361	JAFFREY	1,254	744	456	54	288 R	59.3%	36.4%	62.0%	38.0%
22,430	KEENE	5,728	2,307	3,055	366	748 D	40.3%	53.3%	43.0%	57.0%
5,591	KINGSTON	1,343	896	357	90	539 R	66.7%	26.6%	71.5%	28.5%
15,743	LACONIA	4,711	2,795	1,765	151	1,030 R	59.3%	37.5%	61.3%	38.7%
12,183	LEBANON	2,618	1,278	1,271	69	7 R	48.8%	48.5%	50.1%	49.9%
5,516	LITCHFIELD	1,240	830	325	85	505 R	66.9%	26.2%	71.9%	28.1%
5,827	LITTLETON	1,385	966	377	42	589 R	69.7%	27.2%	71.9%	28.1%
19,781	LONDONDERRY	4,673	3,312	1,076	285	2,236 R	70.9%	23.0%	75.5%	24.5%
99,567	MANCHESTER	25,311	16,619	7,864	828	8,755 R	65.7%	31.1%	67.9%	32.1%
22,156	MERRIMACK TOWN	5,328	3,597	1,385	346	2,212 R	67.5%	26.0%	72.2%	27.8%
11,795	MILFORD	2,755	1,921	692	142	1,229 R	69.7%	25.1%	73.5%	26.5%
79,662	NASHUA	19,991	12,177	6,704	1,110	5,473 R	60.9%	33.5%	64.5%	35.5%
7,157	NEWMARKET	1,753	871	780	102	91 R	49.7%	44.5%	52.8%	47.2%
6,110	NEWPORT	1,463	812	593	58	219 R	55.5%	40.5%	57.8%	42.2%
9,408	PELHAM	2,258	1,587	543	128	1,044 R	70.3%	24.0%	74.5%	25.5%
6,561	PEMBROKE	1,750	928	729	93	199 R	53.0%	41.7%	56.0%	44.0%
5,239	PETERBOROUGH	1,773	1,051	655	67	396 R	59.3%	36.9%	61.6%	38.4%
7,316	PLAISTOW	1,431	965	401	65	564 R	67.4%	28.0%	70.6%	29.4%
5,811	PLYMOUTH	1,206	673	479	54	194 R	55.8%	39.7%	58.4%	41.6%
25,925	PORTSMOUTH	6,200	2,952	2,935	313	17 R	47.6%	47.3%	50.1%	49.9%
8,713	RAYMOND	1,743	1,186	448	109	738 R	68.0%	25.7%	72.6%	27.4%
26,630	ROCHESTER	5,828	3,454	2,113	261	1,341 R	59.3%	36.3%	62.0%	38.0%
25,746	SALEM	6,798	4,403	2,056	339	2,347 R	64.8%	30.2%	68.2%	31.8%
6,503	SEABROOK	1,763	1,196	480	87	716 R	67.8%	27.2%	71.4%	28.6%
11,249	SOMERSWORTH	2,639	1,347	1,190	102	157 R	51.0%	45.1%	53.1%	46.9%
6,236	SWANZEY	1,436	670	664	102	6 R	46.7%	46.2%	50.2%	49.8%
6,193	WEARE	1,544	985	425	134	560 R	63.8%	27.5%	69.9%	30.1%
9,000	WINDHAM	2,222	1,571	486	165	1,085 R	70.7%	21.9%	76.4%	23.6%

NEW HAMPSHIRE

SENATOR 1990

1990 Census Population	City/Town	Total Vote	Republican	Democratic	Other	Rep.-Dem. Plurality	Percentage Total Vote Rep.	Dem.	Major Vote Rep.	Dem.
9,068	AMHERST	2,842	2,051	674	117	1,377 R	72.2%	23.7%	75.3%	24.7%
5,188	ATKINSON	1,488	1,146	293	49	853 R	77.0%	19.7%	79.6%	20.4%
6,164	BARRINGTON	1,450	938	440	72	498 R	64.7%	30.3%	68.1%	31.9%
12,563	BEDFORD	4,541	3,486	914	141	2,572 R	76.8%	20.1%	79.2%	20.8%
5,796	BELMONT	1,271	908	303	60	605 R	71.4%	23.8%	75.0%	25.0%
11,824	BERLIN	3,047	1,540	1,472	35	68 R	50.5%	48.3%	51.1%	48.9%
5,500	BOW	2,041	1,402	552	87	850 R	68.7%	27.0%	71.8%	28.2%
13,902	CLAREMONT	3,531	2,021	1,458	52	563 R	57.2%	41.3%	58.1%	41.9%
36,006	CONCORD	9,922	5,268	4,136	518	1,132 R	53.1%	41.7%	56.0%	44.0%
7,940	CONWAY	2,208	1,606	601	1	1,005 R	72.7%	27.2%	72.8%	27.2%
29,603	DERRY	5,352	3,545	1,513	294	2,032 R	66.2%	28.3%	70.1%	29.9%
25,042	DOVER	6,371	3,964	2,212	195	1,752 R	62.2%	34.7%	64.2%	35.8%
11,818	DURHAM	2,131	1,033	1,026	72	7 R	48.5%	48.1%	50.2%	49.8%
5,162	EPPING	1,158	797	296	65	501 R	68.8%	25.6%	72.9%	27.1%
12,481	EXETER	3,561	2,212	1,217	132	995 R	62.1%	34.2%	64.5%	35.5%
5,739	FARMINGTON	1,072	756	285	31	471 R	70.5%	26.6%	72.6%	27.4%
8,304	FRANKLIN	1,787	1,235	529	23	706 R	69.1%	29.6%	70.0%	30.0%
5,867	GILFORD	2,215	1,563	581	71	982 R	70.6%	26.2%	72.9%	27.1%
14,621	GOFFSTOWN	3,898	2,793	977	128	1,816 R	71.7%	25.1%	74.1%	25.9%
6,732	HAMPSTEAD	1,769	1,309	387	73	922 R	74.0%	21.9%	77.2%	22.8%
12,278	HAMPTON	3,985	2,461	1,390	134	1,071 R	61.8%	34.9%	63.9%	36.1%
9,212	HANOVER	2,259	1,003	1,189	67	186 D	44.4%	52.6%	45.8%	54.2%
5,705	HOLLIS	2,019	1,407	536	76	871 R	69.7%	26.5%	72.4%	27.6%
8,767	HOOKSETT	2,498	1,951	500	47	1,451 R	78.1%	20.0%	79.6%	20.4%
19,530	HUDSON	4,445	2,922	1,263	260	1,659 R	65.7%	28.4%	69.8%	30.2%
5,361	JAFFREY	1,235	822	371	42	451 R	66.6%	30.0%	68.9%	31.1%
22,430	KEENE	5,355	2,820	2,341	194	479 R	52.7%	43.7%	54.6%	45.4%
5,591	KINGSTON	1,358	980	332	46	648 R	72.2%	24.4%	74.7%	25.3%
15,743	LACONIA	4,672	3,225	1,330	117	1,895 R	69.0%	28.5%	70.8%	29.2%
12,183	LEBANON	2,500	1,381	1,019	100	362 R	55.2%	40.8%	57.5%	42.5%
5,516	LITCHFIELD	1,225	849	304	72	545 R	69.3%	24.8%	73.6%	26.4%
5,827	LITTLETON	1,375	999	356	20	643 R	72.7%	25.9%	73.7%	26.3%
19,781	LONDONDERRY	4,658	3,242	1,202	214	2,040 R	69.6%	25.8%	73.0%	27.0%
99,567	MANCHESTER	25,156	16,857	7,671	628	9,186 R	67.0%	30.5%	68.7%	31.3%
22,156	MERRIMACK TOWN	5,288	3,670	1,392	226	2,278 R	69.4%	26.3%	72.5%	27.5%
11,795	MILFORD	2,704	1,996	625	83	1,371 R	73.8%	23.1%	76.2%	23.8%
79,662	NASHUA	19,081	11,798	6,438	845	5,360 R	61.8%	33.7%	64.7%	35.3%
7,157	NEWMARKET	1,735	1,021	641	73	380 R	58.8%	36.9%	61.4%	38.6%
6,110	NEWPORT	1,469	925	504	40	421 R	63.0%	34.3%	64.7%	35.3%
9,408	PELHAM	2,228	1,555	584	89	971 R	69.8%	26.2%	72.7%	27.3%
6,561	PEMBROKE	1,716	1,092	572	52	520 R	63.6%	33.3%	65.6%	34.4%
5,239	PETERBOROUGH	1,744	1,067	618	59	449 R	61.2%	35.4%	63.3%	36.7%
7,316	PLAISTOW	1,438	1,024	369	45	655 R	71.2%	25.7%	73.5%	26.5%
5,811	PLYMOUTH	1,174	761	377	36	384 R	64.8%	32.1%	66.9%	33.1%
25,925	PORTSMOUTH	6,050	3,050	2,769	231	281 R	50.4%	45.8%	52.4%	47.6%
8,713	RAYMOND	1,764	1,251	433	80	818 R	70.9%	24.5%	74.3%	25.7%
26,630	ROCHESTER	5,912	3,942	1,820	150	2,122 R	66.7%	30.8%	68.4%	31.6%
25,746	SALEM	6,753	4,466	2,031	256	2,435 R	66.1%	30.1%	68.7%	31.3%
6,503	SEABROOK	1,763	1,241	477	45	764 R	70.4%	27.1%	72.2%	27.8%
11,249	SOMERSWORTH	2,635	1,616	963	56	653 R	61.3%	36.5%	62.7%	37.3%
6,236	SWANZEY	1,434	877	492	65	385 R	61.2%	34.3%	64.1%	35.9%
6,193	WEARE	1,525	1,068	379	78	689 R	70.0%	24.9%	73.8%	26.2%
9,000	WINDHAM	2,198	1,574	520	104	1,054 R	71.6%	23.7%	75.2%	24.8%

NEW HAMPSHIRE

CONGRESS

CD	Year	Total Vote	Republican Vote	Candidate	Democratic Vote	Candidate	Other Vote	Rep.-Dem. Plurality	Percentage Total Vote Rep.	Dem.	Major Vote Rep.	Dem.
1	1990	148,368	81,684	ZELIFF, BILL	66,176	KEEFE, JOSEPH F.	508	15,508 R	55.1%	44.6%	55.2%	44.8%
1	1988	218,505	131,824	SMITH, ROBERT C.	86,623	KEEFE, JOSEPH F.	58	45,201 R	60.3%	39.6%	60.3%	39.7%
1	1986	125,547	70,739	SMITH, ROBERT C.	54,787	DEMERS, JAMES M.	21	15,952 R	56.3%	43.6%	56.4%	43.6%
1	1984	190,516	111,627	SMITH, ROBERT C.	76,854	DUDLEY, DUDLEY	2,035	34,773 R	58.6%	40.3%	59.2%	40.8%
1	1982	138,911	61,876	SMITH, ROBERT C.	76,281	D'AMOURS, NORMAN E.	754	14,405 D	44.5%	54.9%	44.8%	55.2%
2	1990	142,263	67,225	DOUGLAS, CHUCK	74,866	SWETT, DICK	172	7,641 D	47.3%	52.6%	47.3%	52.7%
2	1988	210,994	119,742	DOUGLAS, CHUCK	89,677	DONCHESS, JAMES W.	1,575	30,065 R	56.8%	42.5%	57.2%	42.8%
2	1986	115,200	85,479	GREGG, JUDD	29,688	CRAIG-GREEN, LAURENCE	33	55,791 R	74.2%	25.8%	74.2%	25.8%
2	1984	182,444	138,975	GREGG, JUDD	42,257	CONVERSE, LARRY	1,212	96,718 R	76.2%	23.2%	76.7%	23.3%
2	1982	130,007	92,098	GREGG, JUDD	37,906	DUPAY, ROBERT L.	3	54,192 R	70.8%	29.2%	70.8%	29.2%

NEW HAMPSHIRE

1990 GENERAL ELECTION

In addition to the county-by-county figures, data are presented for selected New Hampshire communities. Since not all jurisdictions of the state are listed in this special tabulation, state-wide totals are shown only with the county-by-county statistics.

Governor   Other vote was 14,348 Libertarian (Luce); 385 write-in (Preston); 252 write-in (Chichester) and 337 scattered write-in.

Senator   Other vote was 9,717 Libertarian (Elsnau) and 585 scattered write-in.

Congress   Other vote was scattered write-in in both CD's.

1990 PRIMARIES

SEPTEMBER 11 REPUBLICAN

Governor   67,934 Judd Gregg; 15,207 Robert A. Bonser; 894 scattered write-in.

Senator   56,215 Robert C. Smith; 25,286 Tom Christo; 2,768 Theo de Winter; 2,009 Ewing E. J. Smith; 208 scattered write-in.

Congress   Unopposed in CD 2. Contested as follows:

CD 1   13,266 Bill Zeliff; 12,952 Larry Brady; 12,678 Doug Scamman; 3,637 Dean Dexter; 3,069 Bill Johnson; 1,633 Chris Tremblay; 697 Dennis C. Hogan; 582 Michael R. Weddle; 59 scattered write-in.

SEPTEMBER 11 DEMOCRATIC

Governor   22,246 J. Joseph Grandmaison; 21,653 Robert F. Preston; 3,923 Paul Blacketor; 847 scattered write-in.

Senator   20,222 John A. Durkin; 15,205 James W. Donchess; 12,935 John Rauh; 523 scattered write-in.

Congress   Unopposed in CD 2. Contested as follows:

CD 1   17,610 Joseph F. Keefe; 9,472 Robert A. Stephen; 278 scattered write-in.

NEW JERSEY

GOVERNOR
James J. Florio (D). Elected 1989 to a four-year term.

SENATORS
Bill Bradley (D). Re-elected 1990 to a six-year term. Previously elected 1984, 1978.

Frank R. Lautenberg (D). Re-elected 1988 to a six-year term. Previously elected 1982.

REPRESENTATIVES
1. Robert E. Andrews (D)
2. William J. Hughes (D)
3. Frank Pallone (D)
4. Christopher H. Smith (R)
5. Margaret S. Roukema (R)
6. Bernard J. Dwyer (D)
7. Matthew J. Rinaldo (R)
8. Robert A. Roe (D)
9. Robert G. Torricelli (D)
10. Donald M. Payne (D)
11. Dean A. Gallo (R)
12. Dick Zimmer (R)
13. H. James Saxton (R)
14. Frank J. Guarini (D)

POSTWAR VOTE FOR PRESIDENT

Year	Total Vote	Republican Vote	Candidate	Democratic Vote	Candidate	Other Vote	Plurality	Total Vote Rep.	Dem.	Major Vote Rep.	Dem.
1988	3,099,553	1,743,192	Bush, George	1,320,352	Dukakis, Michael S.	36,009	422,840 R	56.2%	42.6%	56.9%	43.1%
1984	3,217,862	1,933,630	Reagan, Ronald	1,261,323	Mondale, Walter F.	22,909	672,307 R	60.1%	39.2%	60.5%	39.5%
1980	2,975,684	1,546,557	Reagan, Ronald	1,147,364	Carter, Jimmy	281,763	399,193 R	52.0%	38.6%	57.4%	42.6%
1976	3,014,472	1,509,688	Ford, Gerald R.	1,444,653	Carter, Jimmy	60,131	65,035 R	50.1%	47.9%	51.1%	48.9%
1972	2,997,229	1,845,502	Nixon, Richard M.	1,102,211	McGovern, George S.	49,516	743,291 R	61.6%	36.8%	62.6%	37.4%
1968	2,875,395	1,325,467	Nixon, Richard M.	1,264,206	Humphrey, Hubert H.	285,722	61,261 R	46.1%	44.0%	51.2%	48.8%
1964	2,847,663	964,174	Goldwater, Barry M.	1,868,231	Johnson, Lyndon B.	15,258	904,057 D	33.9%	65.6%	34.0%	66.0%
1960	2,773,111	1,363,324	Nixon, Richard M.	1,385,415	Kennedy, John F.	24,372	22,091 D	49.2%	50.0%	49.6%	50.4%
1956	2,484,312	1,606,942	Eisenhower, Dwight D.	850,337	Stevenson, Adlai E.	27,033	756,605 R	64.7%	34.2%	65.4%	34.6%
1952	2,418,554	1,373,613	Eisenhower, Dwight D.	1,015,902	Stevenson, Adlai E.	29,039	357,711 R	56.8%	42.0%	57.5%	42.5%
1948	1,949,555	981,124	Dewey, Thomas E.	895,455	Truman, Harry S.	72,976	85,669 R	50.3%	45.9%	52.3%	47.7%

POSTWAR VOTE FOR GOVERNOR

Year	Total Vote	Republican Vote	Candidate	Democratic Vote	Candidate	Other Vote	Rep.-Dem. Plurality	Total Vote Rep.	Dem.	Major Vote Rep.	Dem.
1989	2,253,764	838,553	Courter, James A.	1,379,937	Florio, James J.	35,274	541,384 D	37.2%	61.2%	37.8%	62.2%
1985	1,972,624	1,372,631	Kean, Thomas H.	578,402	Shapiro, Peter	21,591	794,229 R	69.6%	29.3%	70.4%	29.6%
1981	2,317,239	1,145,999	Kean, Thomas H.	1,144,202	Florio, James J.	27,038	1,797 R	49.5%	49.4%	50.0%	50.0%
1977	2,126,264	888,880	Bateman, Raymond H.	1,184,564	Byrne, Brendan T.	52,820	295,684 D	41.8%	55.7%	42.9%	57.1%
1973	2,122,009	676,235	Sandman, Charles W.	1,414,613	Byrne, Brendan T.	31,161	738,378 D	31.9%	66.7%	32.3%	67.7%
1969	2,366,606	1,411,905	Cahill, William T.	911,003	Meyner, Robert B.	43,698	500,902 R	59.7%	38.5%	60.8%	39.2%
1965	2,229,583	915,996	Dumont, Wayne	1,279,568	Hughes, Richard J.	34,019	363,572 D	41.1%	57.4%	41.7%	58.3%
1961	2,152,662	1,049,274	Mitchell, James P.	1,084,194	Hughes, Richard J.	19,194	34,920 D	48.7%	50.4%	49.2%	50.8%
1957	2,018,488	897,321	Forbes, Malcolm S.	1,101,130	Meyner, Robert B.	20,037	203,809 D	44.5%	54.6%	44.9%	55.1%
1953	1,810,812	809,068	Troast, Paul L.	962,710	Meyner, Robert B.	39,034	153,642 D	44.7%	53.2%	45.7%	54.3%
1949 **	1,718,788	885,882	Driscoll, Alfred	810,022	Wene, Elmer H.	22,884	75,860 R	51.5%	47.1%	52.2%	47.8%
1946	1,414,527	807,378	Driscoll, Alfred	585,960	Hansen, Lewis G.	21,189	221,418 R	57.1%	41.4%	57.9%	42.1%

The term of office of New Jersey's Governor was increased from three to four years effective with the 1949 election.

NEW JERSEY

POSTWAR VOTE FOR SENATOR

Year	Total Vote	Republican Vote	Candidate	Democratic Vote	Candidate	Other Vote	Rep-Dem. Plurality	Percentage Total Vote Rep.	Dem.	Major Vote Rep.	Dem.
1990	1,938,454	918,874	Whitman, Christine T.	977,810	Bradley, Bill	41,770	58,936 D	47.4%	50.4%	48.4%	51.6%
1988	2,987,634	1,349,937	Dawkins, Peter M.	1,599,905	Lautenberg, Frank R.	37,792	249,968 D	45.2%	53.6%	45.8%	54.2%
1984	3,096,456	1,080,100	Mochary, Mary V.	1,986,644	Bradley, Bill	29,712	906,544 D	34.9%	64.2%	35.2%	64.8%
1982	2,193,945	1,047,626	Fenwick, Millicent	1,117,549	Lautenberg, Frank R.	28,770	69,923 D	47.8%	50.9%	48.4%	51.6%
1978	1,957,515	844,200	Bell, Jeffrey	1,082,960	Bradley, Bill	30,355	238,760 D	43.1%	55.3%	43.8%	56.2%
1976	2,771,390	1,054,508	Norcross, David F.	1,681,140	Williams, Harrison	35,742	626,632 D	38.0%	60.7%	38.5%	61.5%
1972	2,791,907	1,743,854	Case, Clifford P.	963,573	Krebs, Paul J.	84,480	780,281 R	62.5%	34.5%	64.4%	35.6%
1970	2,142,105	903,026	Gross, Nelson G.	1,157,074	Williams, Harrison	82,005	254,048 D	42.2%	54.0%	43.8%	56.2%
1966	2,131,188	1,279,343	Case, Clifford P.	788,021	Wilentz, Warren W.	63,824	491,322 R	60.0%	37.0%	61.9%	38.1%
1964	2,710,441	1,011,610	Shanley, Bernard M.	1,678,051	Williams, Harrison	20,780	666,441 D	37.3%	61.9%	37.6%	62.4%
1960	2,664,556	1,483,832	Case, Clifford P.	1,151,385	Lord, Thorn	29,339	332,447 R	55.7%	43.2%	56.3%	43.7%
1958	1,881,329	882,287	Kean, Robert W.	966,832	Williams, Harrison	32,210	84,545 D	46.9%	51.4%	47.7%	52.3%
1954	1,770,557	861,528	Case, Clifford P.	858,158	Howell, Charles R.	50,871	3,370 R	48.7%	48.5%	50.1%	49.9%
1952	2,318,232	1,286,782	Smith, H. Alexander	1,011,187	Alexander, Archibald	20,263	275,595 R	55.5%	43.6%	56.0%	44.0%
1948	1,869,882	934,720	Hendrickson, Robert	884,414	Alexander, Archibald	50,748	50,306 R	50.0%	47.3%	51.4%	48.6%
1946	1,367,155	799,808	Smith, H. Alexander	548,458	Brunner, George E.	18,889	251,350 R	58.5%	40.1%	59.3%	40.7%

NEW JERSEY

Districts Established February 17, 1984

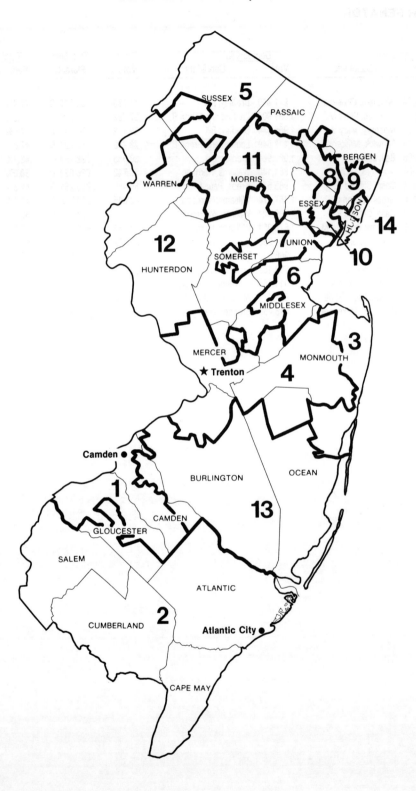

NEW JERSEY

GOVERNOR 1989

1990 Census Population	County	Total Vote	Republican	Democratic	Other	Rep.-Dem. Plurality	Percentage Total Vote Rep.	Dem.	Major Vote Rep.	Dem.
224,327	ATLANTIC	61,602	21,087	39,917	598	18,830 D	34.2%	64.8%	34.6%	65.4%
825,380	BERGEN	278,812	109,184	165,104	4,524	55,920 D	39.2%	59.2%	39.8%	60.2%
395,066	BURLINGTON	107,719	38,774	67,600	1,345	28,826 D	36.0%	62.8%	36.5%	63.5%
502,824	CAMDEN	149,291	41,007	106,836	1,448	65,829 D	27.5%	71.6%	27.7%	72.3%
95,089	CAPE MAY	35,495	15,408	19,642	445	4,234 D	43.4%	55.3%	44.0%	56.0%
138,053	CUMBERLAND	37,649	13,304	23,906	439	10,602 D	35.3%	63.5%	35.8%	64.2%
778,206	ESSEX	191,247	57,206	131,835	2,206	74,629 D	29.9%	68.9%	30.3%	69.7%
230,082	GLOUCESTER	69,408	20,871	47,760	777	26,889 D	30.1%	68.8%	30.4%	69.6%
553,099	HUDSON	129,091	32,215	95,122	1,754	62,907 D	25.0%	73.7%	25.3%	74.7%
107,776	HUNTERDON	33,048	18,046	14,164	838	3,882 R	54.6%	42.9%	56.0%	44.0%
325,824	MERCER	99,208	29,887	67,962	1,359	38,075 D	30.1%	68.5%	30.5%	69.5%
671,780	MIDDLESEX	190,960	67,054	120,157	3,749	53,103 D	35.1%	62.9%	35.8%	64.2%
553,124	MONMOUTH	176,896	72,403	101,995	2,498	29,592 D	40.9%	57.7%	41.5%	58.5%
421,353	MORRIS	130,837	67,592	61,678	1,567	5,914 R	51.7%	47.1%	52.3%	47.7%
433,203	OCEAN	148,956	62,700	83,587	2,669	20,887 D	42.1%	56.1%	42.9%	57.1%
453,060	PASSAIC	112,311	42,106	67,934	2,271	25,828 D	37.5%	60.5%	38.3%	61.7%
65,294	SALEM	20,219	7,938	11,644	637	3,706 D	39.3%	57.6%	40.5%	59.5%
240,279	SOMERSET	73,653	34,815	37,159	1,679	2,344 D	47.3%	50.5%	48.4%	51.6%
130,943	SUSSEX	35,887	20,096	14,901	890	5,195 R	56.0%	41.5%	57.4%	42.6%
493,819	UNION	146,094	53,636	89,419	3,039	35,783 D	36.7%	61.2%	37.5%	62.5%
91,607	WARREN	25,381	13,224	11,615	542	1,609 R	52.1%	45.8%	53.2%	46.8%
7,730,188	TOTAL	2,253,764	838,553	1,379,937	35,274	541,384 D	37.2%	61.2%	37.8%	62.2%

NEW JERSEY

SENATOR 1990

1990 Census Population	County	Total Vote	Republican	Democratic	Other	Rep.-Dem. Plurality	Percentage Total Vote Rep.	Dem.	Major Vote Rep.	Dem.
224,327	ATLANTIC	48,048	19,481	27,905	662	8,424 D	40.5%	58.1%	41.1%	58.9%
825,380	BERGEN	245,800	121,600	121,020	3,180	580 R	49.5%	49.2%	50.1%	49.9%
395,066	BURLINGTON	95,100	46,287	46,912	1,901	625 D	48.7%	49.3%	49.7%	50.3%
502,824	CAMDEN	127,381	52,790	72,328	2,263	19,538 D	41.4%	56.8%	42.2%	57.8%
95,089	CAPE MAY	30,728	13,528	16,627	573	3,099 D	44.0%	54.1%	44.9%	55.1%
138,053	CUMBERLAND	32,004	12,765	18,186	1,053	5,421 D	39.9%	56.8%	41.2%	58.8%
778,206	ESSEX	152,313	56,722	93,052	2,539	36,330 D	37.2%	61.1%	37.9%	62.1%
230,082	GLOUCESTER	62,060	25,374	35,379	1,307	10,005 D	40.9%	57.0%	41.8%	58.2%
553,099	HUDSON	99,430	32,311	65,242	1,877	32,931 D	32.5%	65.6%	33.1%	66.9%
107,776	HUNTERDON	30,044	18,309	10,849	886	7,460 R	60.9%	36.1%	62.8%	37.2%
325,824	MERCER	86,141	39,570	45,036	1,535	5,466 D	45.9%	52.3%	46.8%	53.2%
671,780	MIDDLESEX	161,798	77,165	80,080	4,553	2,915 D	47.7%	49.5%	49.1%	50.9%
553,124	MONMOUTH	157,358	80,126	74,934	2,298	5,192 R	50.9%	47.6%	51.7%	48.3%
421,353	MORRIS	115,280	66,369	46,928	1,983	19,441 R	57.6%	40.7%	58.6%	41.4%
433,203	OCEAN	137,119	76,948	54,714	5,457	22,234 R	56.1%	39.9%	58.4%	41.6%
453,060	PASSAIC	86,536	43,867	40,312	2,357	3,555 R	50.7%	46.6%	52.1%	47.9%
65,294	SALEM	18,681	7,999	10,086	596	2,087 D	42.8%	54.0%	44.2%	55.8%
240,279	SOMERSET	68,254	38,426	27,508	2,320	10,918 R	56.3%	40.3%	58.3%	41.7%
130,943	SUSSEX	33,329	19,789	12,814	726	6,975 R	59.4%	38.4%	60.7%	39.3%
493,819	UNION	126,988	57,628	66,176	3,184	8,548 D	45.4%	52.1%	46.5%	53.5%
91,607	WARREN	24,062	11,820	11,722	520	98 R	49.1%	48.7%	50.2%	49.8%
7,730,188	TOTAL	1,938,454	918,874	977,810	41,770	58,936 D	47.4%	50.4%	48.4%	51.6%

NEW JERSEY

CONGRESS

CD	Year	Total Vote	Republican Vote	Candidate	Democratic Vote	Candidate	Other Vote	Rep.-Dem. Plurality	Total Vote Rep.	Total Vote Dem.	Major Vote Rep.	Major Vote Dem.
1	1990	133,794	57,299	MANGINI, DANIEL J.	72,415	ANDREWS, ROBERT E.	4,080	15,116 D	42.8%	54.1%	44.2%	55.8%
1	1988	203,153	60,037	CRISTAUDO, FRANK A.	141,988	FLORIO, JAMES J.	1,128	81,951 D	29.6%	69.9%	29.7%	70.3%
1	1986	123,603	29,175	BUSCH, FREDERICK A.	93,497	FLORIO, JAMES J.	931	64,322 D	23.6%	75.6%	23.8%	76.2%
1	1984	211,711	58,800	BUSCH, FREDERICK A.	152,125	FLORIO, JAMES J.	786	93,325 D	27.8%	71.9%	27.9%	72.1%
2	1990	110,818			97,698	HUGHES, WILLIAM J.	13,120	97,698 D		88.2%		100.0%
2	1988	204,636	67,759	CONOVER, KIRK W.	134,505	HUGHES, WILLIAM J.	2,372	66,746 D	33.1%	65.7%	33.5%	66.5%
2	1986	122,800	35,167	BENNINGTON, ALFRED J.	83,821	HUGHES, WILLIAM J.	3,812	48,654 D	28.6%	68.3%	29.6%	70.4%
2	1984	210,072	77,231	MASSIE, RAYMOND G.	132,841	HUGHES, WILLIAM J.		55,610 D	36.8%	63.2%	36.8%	63.2%
3	1990	158,643	73,696	KAPALKO, PAUL A.	77,866	PALLONE, FRANK	7,081	4,170 D	46.5%	49.1%	48.6%	51.4%
3	1988	226,610	107,479	AZZOLINA, JOSEPH	117,024	PALLONE, FRANK	2,107	9,545 D	47.4%	51.6%	47.9%	52.1%
3	1986	125,625	51,882	KENNEDY, BRIAN T.	73,743	HOWARD, JAMES J.		21,861 D	41.3%	58.7%	41.3%	58.7%
3	1984	229,422	105,028	KENNEDY, BRIAN T.	122,291	HOWARD, JAMES J.	2,103	17,263 D	45.8%	53.3%	46.2%	53.8%
4	1990	159,299	99,920	SMITH, CHRISTOPHER H.	54,961	SETARO, MARK	4,418	44,959 R	62.7%	34.5%	64.5%	35.5%
4	1988	236,194	155,283	SMITH, CHRISTOPHER H.	79,006	HOLLAND, BETTY	1,905	76,277 R	65.7%	33.4%	66.3%	33.7%
4	1986	128,778	78,699	SMITH, CHRISTOPHER H.	49,290	LAURENTI, JEFFREY	789	29,409 R	61.1%	38.3%	61.5%	38.5%
4	1984	227,203	139,295	SMITH, CHRISTOPHER H.	87,908	HEDDEN, JAMES C.		51,387 R	61.3%	38.7%	61.3%	38.7%
5	1990	156,109	118,101	ROUKEMA, MARGARET S.	35,010	OLSEN, LAWRENCE W.	2,998	83,091 R	75.7%	22.4%	77.1%	22.9%
5	1988	231,936	175,562	ROUKEMA, MARGARET S.	54,828	MONACO, LEE	1,546	120,734 R	75.7%	23.6%	76.2%	23.8%
5	1986	126,398	94,253	ROUKEMA, MARGARET S.	32,145	JOLLEY, H. VERNON		62,108 R	74.6%	25.4%	74.6%	25.4%
5	1984	241,645	171,979	ROUKEMA, MARGARET S.	69,666	BRUNETTO, ROSE		102,313 R	71.2%	28.8%	71.2%	28.8%
6	1990	126,022	58,147	DANIELCZYK, PAUL	63,745	DWYER, BERNARD J.	4,130	5,598 D	46.1%	50.6%	47.7%	52.3%
6	1988	196,598	74,824	SICA, PETER J.	120,125	DWYER, BERNARD J.	1,649	45,301 D	38.1%	61.1%	38.4%	61.6%
6	1986	97,769	28,286	SCALAMONTI, JOHN D.	67,460	DWYER, BERNARD J.	2,023	39,174 D	28.9%	69.0%	29.5%	70.5%
6	1984	212,080	90,862	ADAMS, DENNIS	118,532	DWYER, BERNARD J.	2,686	27,670 D	42.8%	55.9%	43.4%	56.6%
7	1990	134,072	100,066	RINALDO, MATTHEW J.	31,099	BERGEN, BRUCE H.	2,907	68,967 R	74.6%	23.2%	76.3%	23.7%
7	1988	205,539	153,350	RINALDO, MATTHEW J.	52,189	HELY, JAMES		101,161 R	74.6%	25.4%	74.6%	25.4%
7	1986	116,716	92,254	RINALDO, MATTHEW J.	24,462	FISCHER, JUNE S.		67,792 R	79.0%	21.0%	79.0%	21.0%
7	1984	223,282	165,685	RINALDO, MATTHEW J.	56,798	FEELEY, JOHN F.	799	108,887 R	74.2%	25.4%	74.5%	25.5%
8	1990	72,540			55,797	ROE, ROBERT A.	16,743	55,797 D		76.9%		100.0%
8	1988	96,036			96,036	ROE, ROBERT A.		96,036 D		100.0%		100.0%
8	1986	92,088	34,268	ZAMPINO, THOMAS P.	57,820	ROE, ROBERT A.		23,552 D	37.2%	62.8%	37.2%	62.8%
8	1984	189,395	69,973	PAGE, MARGUERITE A.	118,793	ROE, ROBERT A.	629	48,820 D	36.9%	62.7%	37.1%	62.9%
9	1990	154,766	69,658	RUSSO, PETER J.	82,535	TORRICELLI, ROBERT G.	2,573	12,877 D	45.0%	53.3%	45.8%	54.2%
9	1988	211,494	68,363	LANE, ROGER J.	142,012	TORRICELLI, ROBERT G.	1,119	73,649 D	32.3%	67.1%	32.5%	67.5%
9	1986	129,860	40,226	JONES, ARTHUR F.	89,634	TORRICELLI, ROBERT G.		49,408 D	31.0%	69.0%	31.0%	69.0%
9	1984	238,659	89,166	ROMANO, NEIL	149,493	TORRICELLI, ROBERT G.		60,327 D	37.4%	62.6%	37.4%	62.6%
10	1990	51,703	8,954	BERKELEY, HOWARD E.	42,106	PAYNE, DONALD M.	643	33,152 D	17.3%	81.4%	17.5%	82.5%
10	1988	109,473	13,848	WEBB, MICHAEL	84,681	PAYNE, DONALD M.	10,944	70,833 D	12.6%	77.4%	14.1%	85.9%
10	1986	48,643			46,666	RODINO, PETER W.	1,977	46,666 D		95.9%		100.0%
10	1984	132,956	21,712	BERKELEY, HOWARD E.	111,244	RODINO, PETER W.		89,532 D	16.3%	83.7%	16.3%	83.7%
11	1990	143,686	92,681	GALLO, DEAN A.	47,414	GORDON, MICHAEL	3,591	45,267 R	64.5%	33.0%	66.2%	33.8%
11	1988	219,427	154,654	GALLO, DEAN A.	64,773	SHAW, JOHN C.		89,881 R	70.5%	29.5%	70.5%	29.5%
11	1986	110,317	75,037	GALLO, DEAN A.	35,280	ASKIN, FRANK		39,757 R	68.0%	32.0%	68.0%	32.0%
11	1984	239,700	133,662	GALLO, DEAN A.	106,038	MINISH, JOSEPH G.		27,624 R	55.8%	44.2%	55.8%	44.2%
12	1990	168,390	107,851	ZIMMER, DICK	52,256	CHANDLER, MARGUERITE	8,283	55,595 R	64.0%	31.0%	67.4%	32.6%
12	1988	239,537	165,918	COURTER, JAMES A.	71,596	WEINSTEIN, NORMAN J.	2,023	94,322 R	69.3%	29.9%	69.9%	30.1%
12	1986	114,933	72,966	COURTER, JAMES A.	41,967	CRABIEL, DAVID B.		30,999 R	63.5%	36.5%	63.5%	36.5%
12	1984	227,833	148,042	COURTER, JAMES A.	78,167	BEARSE, PETER	1,624	69,875 R	65.0%	34.3%	65.4%	34.6%

NEW JERSEY

CONGRESS

CD	Year	Total Vote	Republican Vote	Republican Candidate	Democratic Vote	Democratic Candidate	Other Vote	Rep.-Dem. Plurality	Total Vote Rep.	Total Vote Dem.	Major Vote Rep.	Major Vote Dem.
13	1990	171,406	99,688	SAXTON, H. JAMES	67,587	ADLER, JOHN H.	4,131	32,101 R	58.2%	39.4%	59.6%	40.4%
13	1988	241,031	167,470	SAXTON, H. JAMES	73,561	SMITH, JAMES B.		93,909 R	69.5%	30.5%	69.5%	30.5%
13	1986	126,786	82,866	SAXTON, H. JAMES	43,920	WYDRA, JOHN		38,946 R	65.4%	34.6%	65.4%	34.6%
13	1984	232,483	141,136	SAXTON, H. JAMES	89,307	SMITH, JAMES B.	2,040	51,829 R	60.7%	38.4%	61.2%	38.8%
14	1990	85,276	24,870	THEEMLING, FRED J.	56,455	GUARINI, FRANK J.	3,951	31,585 D	29.2%	66.2%	30.6%	69.4%
14	1988	154,440	47,293	THEEMLING, FRED J.	104,001	GUARINI, FRANK J.	3,146	56,708 D	30.6%	67.3%	31.3%	68.7%
14	1986	89,229	23,822	SIRES, ALBIO	63,057	GUARINI, FRANK J.	2,350	39,235 D	26.7%	70.7%	27.4%	72.6%
14	1984	175,217	58,265	MAGEE, EDWARD T.	115,117	GUARINI, FRANK J.	1,835	56,852 D	33.3%	65.7%	33.6%	66.4%

NEW JERSEY

1989 GENERAL ELECTION

Governor   Other vote was 11,878 Libertarian (Karlan); 10,210 Better Affordable Government (Ziruolo); 6,989 One Eye On (Fuscaldo) and 6,197 Socialist Workers (Sedwick).

1990 GENERAL ELECTION

Senator   Other vote was 19,978 Populist (Kucek); 13,988 Libertarian (Stefanelli) and 7,804 Socialist Workers (Mackle).

Congress   There was some confusion in the releasing of the canvass for New Jersey Congress. The returns marked "Unofficial" were actually the final corrected canvass and these returns are the ones reported here. Other vote was 1,592 Libertarian (Zeldin), 1,422 Pride and Honesty (Konstanty) and 1,066 Populist (Harris) in CD 1; Populist (Kanengiser) in CD 2; 4,377 Independent (McKean), 1,833 Libertarian (Stewart) and 871 Populist (Plonski)in CD 3; 2,178 Libertarian (Peters), 1,206 Populist (Notarangelo) and 1,034 God We Trust (Carter) in CD 4; Populist (Richards) in CD 5; 2,348 Populist (Waller) and 1,782 Libertarian (Schoen) in CD 6; Populist (Sarnowski) in CD 7; 13,180 Independent (Sibilia) and 3,563 Populiat (Eden) in CD 8; Populist (Grabowski) in CD 9; Socialist Workers (Mehrabian) in CD 10; Populist (Gould) in CD 11; 4,441 Back To Basics (Bottcher), 2,431 Independent Reform (Kortepeter) and 1,411 Populist (Notarangelo) in CD 12; World Without War (Pearlman) in CD 13; 1,822 Better Affordable Goernment (Ziruolo), 1,318 Socialist Workers (Harris), 502 Populist (Stoveken) and 309 Right to Vote (Vernotico) in CD 14.

1989 PRIMARIES

JUNE 6 REPUBLICAN

Governor   112,326 James A. Courter; 85,313 Cary Edwards; 82,392 Chuck Hardwick; 66,430 Bill Gormley; 32,250 Gerald Cardinale; 3,791 Tom Blomquist; 2,553 Lois G. Rand; 1,963 James A. Kolyer.

JUNE 6 DEMOCRATIC

Governor   251,979 James J. Florio; 61,033 Barbara Boggs Sigmund; 56,311 Alan J. Karcher.

1990 PRIMARIES

JUNE 5 REPUBLICAN

Senator   Christine T. Whitman, unopposed.

Congress   Unopposed in eight CD's. No candidate in CD's 2 and 8. Contested as follows:

CD 6   3,893 Paul Danielczyk; 920 Rodger Zepka.
CD 12   15,834 Dick Zimmer; 12,925 Phil McConkey; 12,257 Rodney P. Frelinghuysen; 989 Joseph F. Shanahan.
CD 13   16,719 H. James Saxton; 1,186 William Monk.
CD 14   2,928 Fred J. Theemling; 2,661 Jorge T. Gallo.

JUNE 5 DEMOCRATIC

Senator   197,454 Bill Bradley; 16,287 Daniel Z. Seyler.

Congress   Unopposed in four CD's. Contested as follows:

CD 1   14,589 Robert E. Andrews; 8,290 Linda Bowker; 3,922 John A. Dramesi; 908 Joel S. Farley.
CD 3   12,544 Frank Pallone; 2,555 Pat Daly; 551 Irwin Zucker.
CD 5   6,317 Lawrence W. Olsen; 409 Elliot Greenspan.

NEW JERSEY

CD	6	22,440 Bernard J. Dwyer; 2,994 Sebastian Del Duca.
CD	8	11,559 Robert A. Roe; 2,955 Edward S. Hochman.
CD	9	12,734 Robert G. Torricelli; 486 Robert Wesser.
CD	11	7,587 Michael Gordon; 1,161 Mary J. Frueholz.
CD	12	12,058 Marguerite Chandler; 1,021 James J. Cleary.
CD	13	10,126 John H. Adler; 2,724 Michael DiMarco; 2,055 Eugene Creech.
CD	14	32,637 Frank J. Guarini; 3,337 Gil Corby.

NEW MEXICO

GOVERNOR

Bruce King (D). Elected 1990 to a four-year term. Previously elected 1978, 1970.

SENATORS

Jeff Bingaman (D). Re-elected 1988 to a six-year term. Previously elected 1982.

Peter V. Domenici (R). Re-elected 1990 to a six-year term. Previously elected 1984, 1978, 1972.

REPRESENTATIVES

1. Steven H. Schiff (R)   2. Joseph R. Skeen (R)   3. Bill Richardson (D)

POSTWAR VOTE FOR PRESIDENT

Year	Total Vote	Republican Vote	Candidate	Democratic Vote	Candidate	Other Vote	Plurality	Total Vote Rep.	Dem.	Major Vote Rep.	Dem.
1988	521,287	270,341	Bush, George	244,497	Dukakis, Michael S.	6,449	25,844 R	51.9%	46.9%	52.5%	47.5%
1984	514,370	307,101	Reagan, Ronald	201,769	Mondale, Walter F.	5,500	105,332 R	59.7%	39.2%	60.3%	39.7%
1980	456,971	250,779	Reagan, Ronald	167,826	Carter, Jimmy	38,366	82,953 R	54.9%	36.7%	59.9%	40.1%
1976	418,409	211,419	Ford, Gerald R.	201,148	Carter, Jimmy	5,842	10,271 R	50.5%	48.1%	51.2%	48.8%
1972	386,241	235,606	Nixon, Richard M.	141,084	McGovern, George S.	9,551	94,522 R	61.0%	36.5%	62.5%	37.5%
1968	327,350	169,692	Nixon, Richard M.	130,081	Humphrey, Hubert H.	27,577	39,611 R	51.8%	39.7%	56.6%	43.4%
1964	328,645	132,838	Goldwater, Barry M.	194,015	Johnson, Lyndon B.	1,792	61,177 D	40.4%	59.0%	40.6%	59.4%
1960	311,107	153,733	Nixon, Richard M.	156,027	Kennedy, John F.	1,347	2,294 D	49.4%	50.2%	49.6%	50.4%
1956	253,926	146,788	Eisenhower, Dwight D.	106,098	Stevenson, Adlai E.	1,040	40,690 R	57.8%	41.8%	58.0%	42.0%
1952	238,608	132,170	Eisenhower, Dwight D.	105,661	Stevenson, Adlai E.	777	26,509 R	55.4%	44.3%	55.6%	44.4%
1948	187,063	80,303	Dewey, Thomas E.	105,464	Truman, Harry S.	1,296	25,161 D	42.9%	56.4%	43.2%	56.8%

POSTWAR VOTE FOR GOVERNOR

Year	Total Vote	Republican Vote	Candidate	Democratic Vote	Candidate	Other Vote	Rep-Dem. Plurality	Total Vote Rep.	Dem.	Major Vote Rep.	Dem.
1990	411,236	185,692	Bond, Frank M.	224,564	King, Bruce	980	38,872 D	45.2%	54.6%	45.3%	54.7%
1986	394,833	209,455	Carruthers, Garrey E.	185,378	Powell. Ray B.		24,077 R	53.0%	47.0%	53.0%	47.0%
1982	407,466	191,626	Irick, John B.	215,840	Anaya, Toney		24,214 D	47.0%	53.0%	47.0%	53.0%
1978	345,577	170,848	Skeen, Joseph R.	174,631	King, Bruce	98	3,783 D	49.4%	50.5%	49.5%	50.5%
1974	328,742	160,430	Skeen, Joseph R.	164,172	Apodaca, Jerry	4,140	3,742 D	48.8%	49.9%	49.4%	50.6%
1970 **	290,375	134,640	Domenici, Peter V.	148,835	King, Bruce	6,900	14,195 D	46.4%	51.3%	47.5%	52.5%
1968	318,975	160,140	Cargo, David F.	157,230	Chavez, Fabian	1,605	2,910 R	50.2%	49.3%	50.5%	49.5%
1966	260,232	134,625	Cargo, David F.	125,587	Lusk, Thomas E.	20	9,038 R	51.7%	48.3%	51.7%	48.3%
1964	318,042	126,540	Tucker, Merle H.	191,497	Campbell, Jack M.	5	64,957 D	39.8%	60.2%	39.8%	60.2%
1962	247,135	116,184	Mechem, Edwin L.	130,933	Campbell, Jack M.	18	14,749 D	47.0%	53.0%	47.0%	53.0%
1960	305,542	153,765	Mechem, Edwin L.	151,777	Burroughs, John		1,988 R	50.3%	49.7%	50.3%	49.7%
1958	205,048	101,567	Mechem, Edwin L.	103,481	Burroughs, John		1,914 D	49.5%	50.5%	49.5%	50.5%
1956	251,751	131,488	Mechem, Edwin L.	120,263	Simms, John F.		11,225 R	52.2%	47.8%	52.2%	47.8%
1954	193,956	83,373	Stockton, Alvin	110,583	Simms, John F.		27,210 D	43.0%	57.0%	43.0%	57.0%
1952	240,150	129,116	Mechem, Edwin L.	111,034	Grantham, Everett		18,082 R	53.8%	46.2%	53.8%	46.2%
1950	180,205	96,846	Mechem, Edwin L.	83,359	Miles, John E.		13,487 R	53.7%	46.3%	53.7%	46.3%
1948	189,992	86,023	Lujan, Manuel	103,969	Mabry, Thomas J.		17,946 D	45.3%	54.7%	45.3%	54.7%
1946	132,930	62,875	Safford, Edward L.	70,055	Mabry, Thomas J.		7,180 D	47.3%	52.7%	47.3%	52.7%

The term of New Mexico's Governor was increased from two to four years effective with the 1970 election.

NEW MEXICO

POSTWAR VOTE FOR SENATOR

Year	Total Vote	Republican Vote	Republican Candidate	Democratic Vote	Democratic Candidate	Other Vote	Rep-Dem. Plurality	Percentage Total Vote Rep.	Percentage Total Vote Dem.	Percentage Major Vote Rep.	Percentage Major Vote Dem.
1990	406,938	296,712	Domenici, Peter V.	110,033	Benavides, Tom R.	193	186,679 R	72.9%	27.0%	72.9%	27.1%
1988	508,598	186,579	Valentine, William	321,983	Bingaman, Jeff	36	135,404 D	36.7%	63.3%	36.7%	63.3%
1984	502,634	361,371	Domenici, Peter V.	141,253	Pratt, Judith A.	10	220,118 R	71.9%	28.1%	71.9%	28.1%
1982	404,810	187,128	Schmitt, Harrison	217,682	Bingaman, Jeff		30,554 D	46.2%	53.8%	46.2%	53.8%
1978	343,554	183,442	Domenici, Peter V.	160,045	Anaya, Toney	67	23,397 R	53.4%	46.6%	53.4%	46.6%
1976	413,141	234,681	Schmitt, Harrison	176,382	Montoya, Joseph M.	2,078	58,299 R	56.8%	42.7%	57.1%	42.9%
1972	378,330	204,253	Domenici, Peter V.	173,815	Daniels, Jack	262	30,438 R	54.0%	45.9%	54.0%	46.0%
1970	289,906	135,004	Carter, Anderson	151,486	Montoya, Joseph M.	3,416	16,482 D	46.6%	52.3%	47.1%	52.9%
1966	258,203	120,988	Carter, Anderson	137,205	Anderson, Clinton P.	10	16,217 D	46.9%	53.1%	46.9%	53.1%
1964	325,774	147,562	Mechem, Edwin L.	178,209	Montoya, Joseph M.	3	30,647 D	45.3%	54.7%	45.3%	54.7%
1960	300,551	109,897	Colwes, William F.	190,654	Anderson, Clinton P.		80,757 D	36.6%	63.4%	36.6%	63.4%
1958	203,323	75,827	Atchley, Forrest S.	127,496	Chavez, Dennis		51,669 D	37.3%	62.7%	37.3%	62.7%
1954	194,422	83,071	Mechem, Edwin L.	111,351	Anderson, Clinton P.		28,280 D	42.7%	57.3%	42.7%	57.3%
1952	239,711	117,168	Hurley, Patrick J.	122,543	Chavez, Dennis		5,375 D	48.9%	51.1%	48.9%	51.1%
1948	188,495	80,226	Hurley, Patrick J.	108,269	Anderson, Clinton P.		28,043 D	42.6%	57.4%	42.6%	57.4%
1946	133,282	64,632	Hurley, Patrick J.	68,650	Chavez, Dennis		4,018 D	48.5%	51.5%	48.5%	51.5%

312

NEW MEXICO

Districts Established January 19, 1982

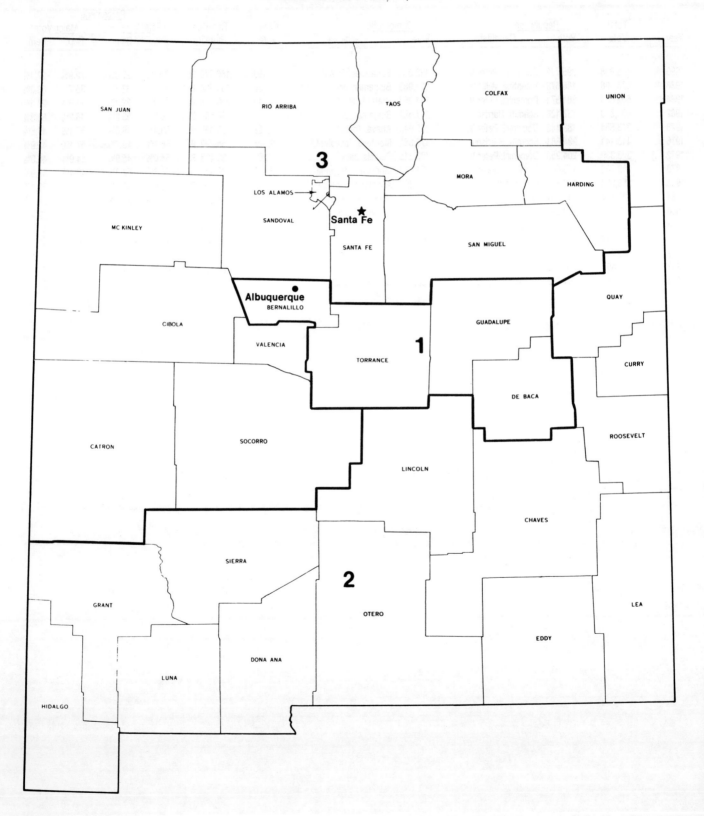

© ERC

NEW MEXICO

GOVERNOR 1990

1990 Census Population	County	Total Vote	Republican	Democratic	Other	Rep.-Dem. Plurality	Percentage Total Vote Rep.	Dem.	Major Vote Rep.	Dem.
480,577	BERNALILLO	132,975	64,601	67,965	409	3,364 D	48.6%	51.1%	48.7%	51.3%
2,563	CATRON	1,358	630	719	9	89 D	46.4%	52.9%	46.7%	53.3%
57,849	CHAVES	15,175	9,156	5,997	22	3,159 R	60.3%	39.5%	60.4%	39.6%
23,794	CIBOLA	5,441	1,779	3,658	4	1,879 D	32.7%	67.2%	32.7%	67.3%
12,925	COLFAX	4,169	1,598	2,571		973 D	38.3%	61.7%	38.3%	61.7%
42,207	CURRY	9,045	4,399	4,637	9	238 D	48.6%	51.3%	48.7%	51.3%
2,252	DE BACA	1,151	570	579	2	9 D	49.5%	50.3%	49.6%	50.4%
135,510	DONA ANA	30,855	15,365	15,443	47	78 D	49.8%	50.1%	49.9%	50.1%
48,605	EDDY	13,968	6,583	7,368	17	785 D	47.1%	52.7%	47.2%	52.8%
27,676	GRANT	8,134	3,107	5,011	16	1,904 D	38.2%	61.6%	38.3%	61.7%
4,156	GUADALUPE	2,200	624	1,576		952 D	28.4%	71.6%	28.4%	71.6%
987	HARDING	619	269	350		81 D	43.5%	56.5%	43.5%	56.5%
5,958	HIDALGO	1,910	825	1,085		260 D	43.2%	56.8%	43.2%	56.8%
55,765	LEA	12,971	7,568	5,392	11	2,176 R	58.3%	41.6%	58.4%	41.6%
12,219	LINCOLN	4,577	2,656	1,908	13	748 R	58.0%	41.7%	58.2%	41.8%
18,115	LOS ALAMOS	8,146	4,959	3,146	41	1,813 R	60.9%	38.6%	61.2%	38.8%
18,110	LUNA	5,171	2,526	2,625	20	99 D	48.8%	50.8%	49.0%	51.0%
60,686	MCKINLEY	12,018	3,937	8,081		4,144 D	32.8%	67.2%	32.8%	67.2%
4,264	MORA	2,478	822	1,656		834 D	33.2%	66.8%	33.2%	66.8%
51,928	OTERO	12,315	6,450	5,833	32	617 R	52.4%	47.4%	52.5%	47.5%
10,823	QUAY	3,469	1,458	2,010	1	552 D	42.0%	57.9%	42.0%	58.0%
34,365	RIO ARRIBA	10,225	2,599	7,626		5,027 D	25.4%	74.6%	25.4%	74.6%
16,702	ROOSEVELT	4,617	2,296	2,318	3	22 D	49.7%	50.2%	49.8%	50.2%
63,319	SANDOVAL	15,384	6,481	8,841	62	2,360 D	42.1%	57.5%	42.3%	57.7%
91,605	SAN JUAN	21,159	10,610	10,471	78	139 R	50.1%	49.5%	50.3%	49.7%
25,743	SAN MIGUEL	7,682	1,760	5,919	3	4,159 D	22.9%	77.1%	22.9%	77.1%
98,928	SANTA FE	29,106	8,942	20,025	139	11,083 D	30.7%	68.8%	30.9%	69.1%
9,912	SIERRA	3,633	1,846	1,774	13	72 R	50.8%	48.8%	51.0%	49.0%
14,764	SOCORRO	5,449	2,123	3,317	9	1,194 D	39.0%	60.9%	39.0%	61.0%
23,118	TAOS	6,742	2,108	4,625	9	2,517 D	31.3%	68.6%	31.3%	68.7%
10,285	TORRANCE	3,822	1,080	2,738	4	1,658 D	28.3%	71.6%	28.3%	71.7%
4,124	UNION	1,708	800	906	2	106 D	46.8%	53.0%	46.9%	53.1%
45,235	VALENCIA	13,564	5,165	8,394	5	3,229 D	38.1%	61.9%	38.1%	61.9%
1,515,069	TOTAL	411,236	185,692	224,564	980	38,872 D	45.2%	54.6%	45.3%	54.7%

NEW MEXICO

SENATOR 1990

1990 Census Population	County	Total Vote	Republican	Democratic	Other	Rep.-Dem. Plurality	Percentage Total Vote Rep.	Dem.	Major Vote Rep.	Dem.
480,577	BERNALILLO	132,352	103,209	29,061	82	74,148 R	78.0%	22.0%	78.0%	22.0%
2,563	CATRON	1,325	959	366		593 R	72.4%	27.6%	72.4%	27.6%
57,849	CHAVES	14,843	11,585	3,258		8,327 R	78.1%	21.9%	78.1%	21.9%
23,794	CIBOLA	5,441	3,600	1,840	1	1,760 R	66.2%	33.8%	66.2%	33.8%
12,925	COLFAX	4,069	2,882	1,186	1	1,696 R	70.8%	29.1%	70.8%	29.2%
42,207	CURRY	8,939	6,881	2,041	17	4,840 R	77.0%	22.8%	77.1%	22.9%
2,252	DE BACA	1,139	939	200		739 R	82.4%	17.6%	82.4%	17.6%
135,510	DONA ANA	30,664	21,863	8,792	9	13,071 R	71.3%	28.7%	71.3%	28.7%
48,605	EDDY	13,576	9,208	4,364	4	4,844 R	67.8%	32.1%	67.8%	32.2%
27,676	GRANT	8,063	5,027	3,036		1,991 R	62.3%	37.7%	62.3%	37.7%
4,156	GUADALUPE	2,116	1,327	789		538 R	62.7%	37.3%	62.7%	37.3%
987	HARDING	601	481	120		361 R	80.0%	20.0%	80.0%	20.0%
5,958	HIDALGO	1,841	1,278	563		715 R	69.4%	30.6%	69.4%	30.6%
55,765	LEA	12,718	9,419	3,297	2	6,122 R	74.1%	25.9%	74.1%	25.9%
12,219	LINCOLN	4,499	3,825	674		3,151 R	85.0%	15.0%	85.0%	15.0%
18,115	LOS ALAMOS	8,110	6,823	1,286	1	5,537 R	84.1%	15.9%	84.1%	15.9%
18,110	LUNA	5,022	3,426	1,594	2	1,832 R	68.2%	31.7%	68.2%	31.8%
60,686	MCKINLEY	11,592	7,416	4,176		3,240 R	64.0%	36.0%	64.0%	36.0%
4,264	MORA	2,403	1,407	996		411 R	58.6%	41.4%	58.6%	41.4%
51,928	OTERO	12,077	9,318	2,758	1	6,560 R	77.2%	22.8%	77.2%	22.8%
10,823	QUAY	3,322	2,340	982		1,358 R	70.4%	29.6%	70.4%	29.6%
34,365	RIO ARRIBA	9,926	5,292	4,634		658 R	53.3%	46.7%	53.3%	46.7%
16,702	ROOSEVELT	4,546	3,712	834		2,878 R	81.7%	18.3%	81.7%	18.3%
63,319	SANDOVAL	15,331	10,805	4,499	27	6,306 R	70.5%	29.3%	70.6%	29.4%
91,605	SAN JUAN	21,141	15,128	5,976	37	9,152 R	71.6%	28.3%	71.7%	28.3%
25,743	SAN MIGUEL	7,424	4,395	3,028	1	1,367 R	59.2%	40.8%	59.2%	40.8%
98,928	SANTA FE	29,114	19,991	9,118	5	10,873 R	68.7%	31.3%	68.7%	31.3%
9,912	SIERRA	3,529	2,594	935		1,659 R	73.5%	26.5%	73.5%	26.5%
14,764	SOCORRO	5,280	3,723	1,557		2,166 R	70.5%	29.5%	70.5%	29.5%
23,118	TAOS	7,356	4,737	2,619		2,118 R	64.4%	35.6%	64.4%	35.6%
10,285	TORRANCE	3,654	2,601	1,053		1,548 R	71.2%	28.8%	71.2%	28.8%
4,124	UNION	1,625	1,253	369	3	884 R	77.1%	22.7%	77.3%	22.7%
45,235	VALENCIA	13,300	9,268	4,032		5,236 R	69.7%	30.3%	69.7%	30.3%
1,515,069	TOTAL	406,938	296,712	110,033	193	186,679 R	72.9%	27.0%	72.9%	27.1%

NEW MEXICO

CONGRESS

CD	Year	Total Vote	Republican Vote	Republican Candidate	Democratic Vote	Democratic Candidate	Other Vote	Rep.-Dem. Plurality	Total Vote Rep.	Total Vote Dem.	Major Vote Rep.	Major Vote Dem.
1	1990	138,681	97,375	SCHIFF, STEVEN H.	41,306	VIGIL-GIRON, REBECCA		56,069 R	70.2%	29.8%	70.2%	29.8%
1	1988	177,962	89,985	SCHIFF, STEVEN H.	84,138	UDALL, TOM	3,839	5,847 R	50.6%	47.3%	51.7%	48.3%
1	1986	127,632	90,476	LUJAN, MANUEL, JR.	37,138	GARCIA, MANNY	18	53,338 R	70.9%	29.1%	70.9%	29.1%
1	1984	178,342	115,808	LUJAN, MANUEL, JR.	60,598	ASBURY, CHARLES T.	1,936	55,210 R	64.9%	34.0%	65.6%	34.4%
1	1982	141,993	74,459	LUJAN, MANUEL, JR.	67,534	HARTKE, JAN A.		6,925 R	52.4%	47.6%	52.4%	47.6%
2	1990	80,677	80,677	SKEEN, JOSEPH R.				80,677 R	100.0%		100.0%	
2	1988	100,324	100,324	SKEEN, JOSEPH R.				100,324 R	100.0%		100.0%	
2	1986	123,711	77,787	SKEEN, JOSEPH R.	45,924	RUNNELS, MIKE		31,863 R	62.9%	37.1%	62.9%	37.1%
2	1984	156,069	116,006	SKEEN, JOSEPH R.	40,063	YORK, PETER R.		75,943 R	74.3%	25.7%	74.3%	25.7%
2	1982	121,620	71,021	SKEEN, JOSEPH R.	50,599	CHANDLER, CALEB J.		20,422 R	58.4%	41.6%	58.4%	41.6%
3	1990	139,976	35,751	ARCHULETTA, PHIL T.	104,225	RICHARDSON, BILL		68,474 D	25.5%	74.5%	25.5%	74.5%
3	1988	170,892	45,954	SALAZAR, CECILIA M.	124,938	RICHARDSON, BILL		78,984 D	26.9%	73.1%	26.9%	73.1%
3	1986	134,312	38,552	CARGO, DAVID F.	95,760	RICHARDSON, BILL		57,208 D	28.7%	71.3%	28.7%	71.3%
3	1984	165,209	62,351	GALLEGOS, LOUIS H.	100,470	RICHARDSON, BILL	2,388	38,119 D	37.7%	60.8%	38.3%	61.7%
3	1982	131,293	46,466	CHAMBERS, MARJORIE B.	84,669	RICHARDSON, BILL	158	38,203 D	35.4%	64.5%	35.4%	64.6%

NEW MEXICO

1990 GENERAL ELECTION

Governor   Other vote was 788 write-in (Knight) and 192 write-in (Macaione).

Senator   Other vote was 129 write-in (Cole) and 64 write-in (Chapman).

Congress

1990 PRIMARIES

JUNE 5 REPUBLICAN

Governor   44,928 Frank M. Bond; 27,073 Les Houston; 4,681 James A. Caudell; 4,289 Harry F. Kinney.

Senator   Pete V. Domenici, unopposed.

Congress   Unopposed in all three CD's.

JUNE 5 DEMOCRATIC

Governor   95,884 Bruce King; 70,169 Paul Bardacke; 8,931 Tony Scarborough; 6,256 Bob Gold.

Senator   Tom R. Benavides, unopposed.

Congress   Unopposed in CD 3. No candidate in CD 2. Contested as follows:

   CD   1   19,104 Rebecca Vigil-Giron; 18,839 James B. Lewis; 8,118 Richard J. Chapman.

NEW YORK

GOVERNOR
Mario M. Cuomo (D). Re-elected 1990 to a four-year term. Previously elected 1986, 1982.

SENATORS
Alfonse M. D'Amato (R). Re-elected 1986 to a six-year term. Previously elected 1980.

Daniel P. Moynihan (D). Re-elected 1988 to a six-year term. Previously elected 1982, 1976.

REPRESENTATIVES

1. George J. Hochbrueckner (D)
2. Thomas J. Downey (D)
3. Robert J. Mrazek (D)
4. Norman F. Lent (R)
5. Raymond J. McGrath (R)
6. Floyd H. Flake (D)
7. Gary L. Ackerman (D)
8. James H. Scheuer (D)
9. Thomas J. Manton (D)
10. Charles E. Schumer (D)
11. Edolphus Towns (D)
12. Major R. Owens (D)
13. Stephen J. Solarz (D)
14. Susan Molinari (R)
15. S. William Green (R)
16. Charles B. Rangel (D)
17. Theodore S. Weiss (D)
18. Jose E. Serrano (D)
19. Eliot L. Engel (D)
20. Nita M. Lowey (D)
21. Hamilton Fish (R)
22. Benjamin A. Gilman (R)
23. Michael R. McNulty (D)
24. Gerald B. Solomon (R)
25. Sherwood L. Boehlert (R)
26. David O'B. Martin (R)
27. James T. Walsh (R)
28. Matthew F. McHugh (D)
29. Frank J. Horton (R)
30. Louise M. Slaughter (D)
31. L. William Paxon (R)
32. John J. LaFalce (D)
33. Henry J. Nowak (D)
34. Amory Houghton (R)

POSTWAR VOTE FOR PRESIDENT

Year	Total Vote	Republican Vote	Candidate	Democratic Vote	Candidate	Other Vote	Plurality	Percentage Total Vote Rep.	Dem.	Major Vote Rep.	Dem.
1988	6,485,683	3,081,871	Bush, George	3,347,882	Dukakis, Michael S.	55,930	266,011 D	47.5%	51.6%	47.9%	52.1%
1984	6,806,810	3,664,763	Reagan, Ronald	3,119,609	Mondale, Walter F.	22,438	545,154 R	53.8%	45.8%	54.0%	46.0%
1980	6,201,959	2,893,831	Reagan, Ronald	2,728,372	Carter, Jimmy	579,756	165,459 R	46.7%	44.0%	51.5%	48.5%
1976	6,534,170	3,100,791	Ford, Gerald R.	3,389,558	Carter, Jimmy	43,821	288,767 D	47.5%	51.9%	47.8%	52.2%
1972	7,165,919	4,192,778	Nixon, Richard M.	2,951,084	McGovern, George S.	22,057	1,241,694 R	58.5%	41.2%	58.7%	41.3%
1968	6,791,688	3,007,932	Nixon, Richard M.	3,378,470	Humphrey, Hubert H.	405,286	370,538 D	44.3%	49.7%	47.1%	52.9%
1964	7,166,275	2,243,559	Goldwater, Barry M.	4,913,102	Johnson, Lyndon B.	9,614	2,669,543 D	31.3%	68.6%	31.3%	68.7%
1960	7,291,079	3,446,419	Nixon, Richard M.	3,830,085	Kennedy, John F.	14,575	383,666 D	47.3%	52.5%	47.4%	52.6%
1956	7,095,971	4,345,506	Eisenhower, Dwight D.	2,747,944	Stevenson, Adlai E.	2,521	1,597,562 R	61.2%	38.7%	61.3%	38.7%
1952	7,128,239	3,952,813	Eisenhower, Dwight D.	3,104,601	Stevenson, Adlai E.	70,825	848,212 R	55.5%	43.6%	56.0%	44.0%
1948	6,177,337	2,841,163	Dewey, Thomas E.	2,780,204	Truman, Harry S.	555,970	60,959 R	46.0%	45.0%	50.5%	49.5%

318

NEW YORK

POSTWAR VOTE FOR GOVERNOR

Year	Total Vote	Republican Vote	Candidate	Democratic Vote	Candidate	Other Vote	Rep-Dem. Plurality	Percentage Total Vote Rep.	Dem.	Major Vote Rep.	Dem.
1990 * *	4,056,896	865,948	Rinfret, Pierre A.	2,157,087	Cuomo, Mario M.	1,033,861	1,291,139 D	21.3%	53.2%	28.6%	71.4%
1986	4,294,124	1,363,810	O'Rourke, Andrew P.	2,775,229	Cuomo, Mario M.	155,085	1,411,419 D	31.8%	64.6%	32.9%	67.1%
1982	5,254,891	2,494,827	Lehrman, Lew	2,675,213	Cuomo, Mario M.	84,851	180,386 D	47.5%	50.9%	48.3%	51.7%
1978	4,768,820	2,156,404	Duryea, Perry B.	2,429,272	Carey, Hugh L.	183,144	272,868 D	45.2%	50.9%	47.0%	53.0%
1974	5,293,176	2,219,667	Wilson, Malcolm	3,028,503	Carey, Hugh L.	45,006	808,836 D	41.9%	57.2%	42.3%	57.7%
1970	6,013,064	3,151,432	Rockefeller, Nelson A.	2,421,426	Goldberg, Arthur	440,206	730,006 R	52.4%	40.3%	56.5%	43.5%
1966 * *	6,031,585	2,690,626	Rockefeller, Nelson A.	2,298,363	O'Connor, Frank D.	1,042,596	392,263 R	44.6%	38.1%	53.9%	46.1%
1962	5,805,631	3,081,587	Rockefeller, Nelson A.	2,552,418	Morgenthau, Robert M.	171,626	529,169 R	53.1%	44.0%	54.7%	45.3%
1958	5,712,665	3,126,929	Rockefeller, Nelson A.	2,553,895	Harriman, Averell	31,841	573,034 R	54.7%	44.7%	55.0%	45.0%
1954	5,161,942	2,549,613	Ives, Irving M.	2,560,738	Harriman, Averell	51,591	11,125 D	49.4%	49.6%	49.9%	50.1%
1950	5,308,889	2,819,523	Dewey, Thomas E.	2,246,855	Lynch, Walter A.	242,511	572,668 R	53.1%	42.3%	55.7%	44.3%
1946	4,964,552	2,825,633	Dewey, Thomas E.	2,138,482	Mead, James M.	437	687,151 R	56.9%	43.1%	56.9%	43.1%

In 1966 other vote was 510,023 Conservative (Adams); 507,234 Liberal (F. D. Roosevelt, Jr.); 12,730 Socialist Labor (Herder); 12,506 Socialist Workers (White) and 103 scattered. In 1990 other vote was 827,614 Conservative (London); 137,804 Right to Life (Wein); 31,089 New Alliance (Fulani); 24,611 Libertarian (Johnson) and 12,743 Socialist Workers (Gannon).

POSTWAR VOTE FOR SENATOR

Year	Total Vote	Republican Vote	Candidate	Democratic Vote	Candidate	Other Vote	Rep-Dem. Plurality	Percentage Total Vote Rep.	Dem.	Major Vote Rep.	Dem.
1988	6,040,980	1,875,784	McMillan, Robert	4,048,649	Moynihan, Daniel P.	116,547	2,172,865 D	31.1%	67.0%	31.7%	68.3%
1986	4,179,447	2,378,197	D'Amato, Alfonse M.	1,723,216	Green, Mark	78,034	654,981 R	56.9%	41.2%	58.0%	42.0%
1982	4,967,729	1,696,766	Sullivan, Florence M.	3,232,146	Moynihan, Daniel P.	38,817	1,535,380 D	34.2%	65.1%	34.4%	65.6%
1980	6,014,914	2,699,652	D'Amato, Alfonse M.	2,618,661	Holtzman, Elizabeth	696,601	80,991 R	44.9%	43.5%	50.8%	49.2%
1976	6,319,755	2,836,633	Buckley, James L.	3,422,594	Moynihan, Daniel P.	60,528	585,961 D	44.9%	54.2%	45.3%	54.7%
1974	5,163,600	2,340,188	Javits, Jacob K.	1,973,781	Clark, Ramsey	849,631	366,407 R	45.3%	38.2%	54.2%	45.8%
1970 * *	5,904,782	1,434,472	Goodell, Charles	2,171,232	Ottinger, Richard L.	2,299,078	736,760 D	24.3%	36.8%	39.8%	60.2%
1968 * *	6,581,587	3,269,772	Javits, Jacob K.	2,150,695	O'Dwyer, Paul	1,161,120	1,119,077 R	49.7%	32.7%	60.3%	39.7%
1964	7,151,686	3,104,056	Keating, Kenneth B.	3,823,749	Kennedy, Robert F.	223,881	719,693 D	43.4%	53.5%	44.8%	55.2%
1962	5,700,186	3,269,417	Javits, Jacob K.	2,289,341	Donovan, James B.	141,428	980,076 R	57.4%	40.2%	58.8%	41.2%
1958	5,602,088	2,842,942	Keating, Kenneth B.	2,709,950	Hogan, Frank S.	49,196	132,992 R	50.7%	48.4%	51.2%	48.8%
1956	6,991,136	3,723,933	Javits, Jacob K.	3,265,159	Wagner, Robert F.	2,044	458,774 R	53.3%	46.7%	53.3%	46.7%
1952	6,980,259	3,853,934	Ives, Irving M.	2,521,736	Cashmore, John	604,589	1,332,198 R	55.2%	36.1%	60.4%	39.6%
1950	5,228,403	2,367,353	Hanley, Joe R.	2,632,313	Lehman, Herbert H.	228,737	264,960 D	45.3%	50.3%	47.4%	52.6%
1949 S	4,966,878	2,384,381	Dulles, John Foster	2,582,438	Lehman, Herbert H.	59	198,057 D	48.0%	52.0%	48.0%	52.0%
1946	4,867,564	2,559,365	Ives, Irving M.	2,308,112	Lehman, Herbert H.	87	251,253 R	52.6%	47.4%	52.6%	47.4%

The 1949 election was for a short term to fill a vacancy. In 1968 other vote was 1,139,402 Conservative (Buckley); 8,775 Freedom and Peace (Ferguson); 7,964 Socialist Labor (Emanuel); 4,979 Socialist Workers (Garza). In 1970 James L. Buckley, the Conservative candidate, polled 2,288,190 votes (38.8% of the total vote) and won the election with a 116,958 plurality.

319

NEW YORK

Districts Established September 27, 1983

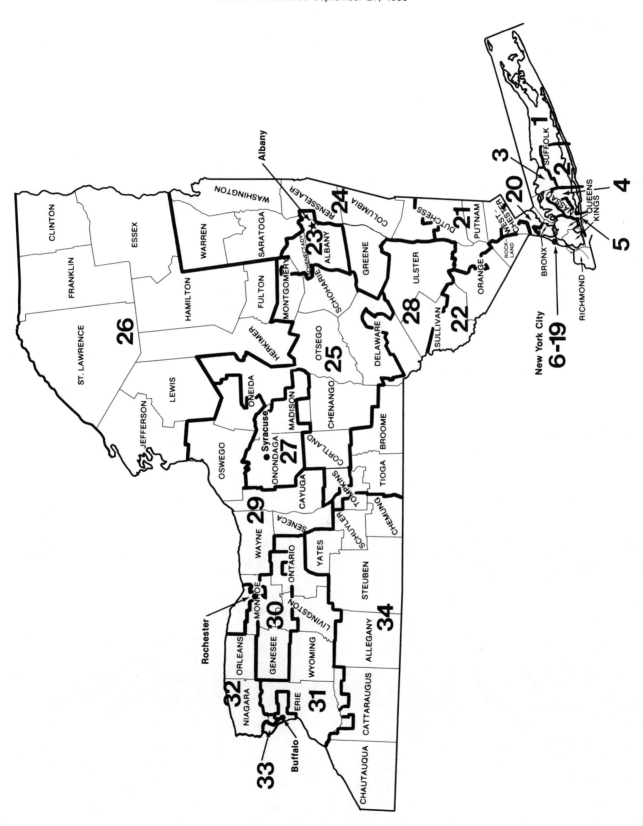

© ERC

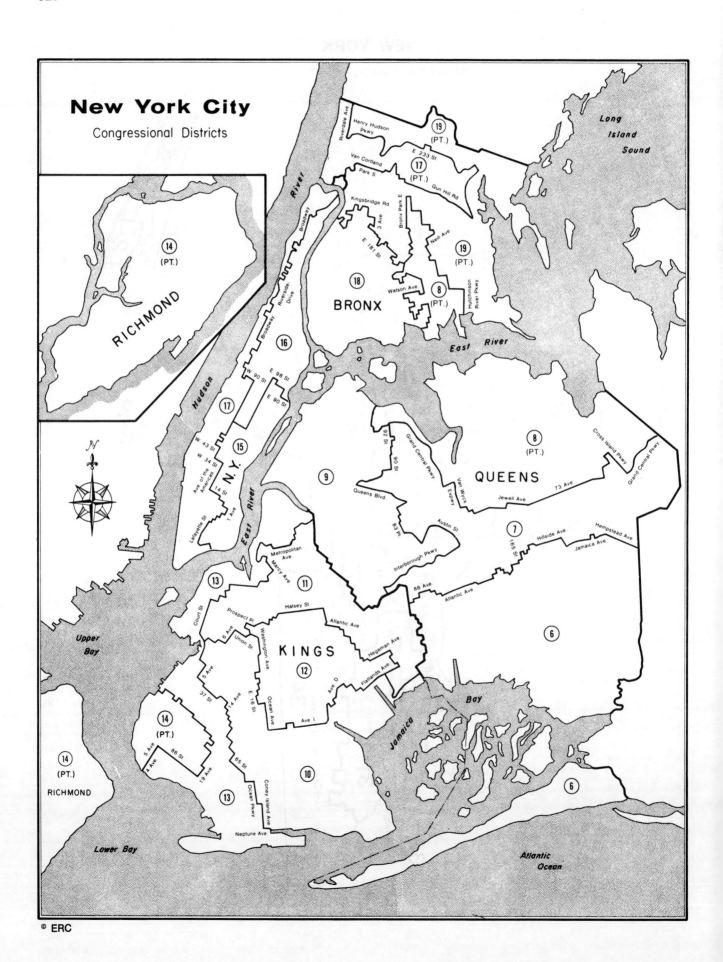

New York City

Congressional Districts

RICHMOND

⑭ (PT.)

Long Island Sound

Riverdale Ave
Henry Hudson Pkwy

⑲ (PT.)

E 233 St

Van Cortland Park S

⑰ (PT.)

Gun Hill Rd

Kingsbridge Rd

3 Ave

Bronx Park E

Neill Ave

⑲ (PT.)

E 181 St

⑱

BRONX

Watson Ave

⑧ (PT.)

Hutchinson River Pkwy

Broadway

Riverside Drive

⑯

Broadway

East River

Hudson

W 90 St

E 98 St

E 90 St

⑰

N.Y.

W 43 St

W 34 St

⑮

Ave of the Americas

14 St

Lafayette St

1 Ave

East River

⑨

Queens Blvd.

St 26

90 St

Grand Central Pkwy

Van Wyck Expwy

⑧ (PT.)

Cross Island Pkwy

QUEENS

Grand Central Pkwy

73 Ave

Jewell Ave

Austin St

83 Pl

Interborough Pkwy

⑦

165 St

Hillside Ave

Hempstead Ave

Jamaica Ave

88 Ave

Atlantic Ave

Metropolitan Ave

Marcy Ave

⑬

⑪

Court St

Prospect Pl

Halsey St

Atlantic Ave

6 Ave

Union St

Washington Ave

KINGS

Hegeman Ave

⑥

5 Ave

⑫

Ave D

Flatlands Ave

37 St

14 Ave

E 16 St

Ocean Ave

Ave I

Jamaica Bay

Upper Bay

⑭ (PT.)

5 Ave

86 St

4 Ave

65 St

19 Ave

⑩

⑭ (PT.)

RICHMOND

⑬

Ocean Pkwy

Coney Island Ave

⑥

Neptune Ave

Lower Bay

Atlantic Ocean

© ERC

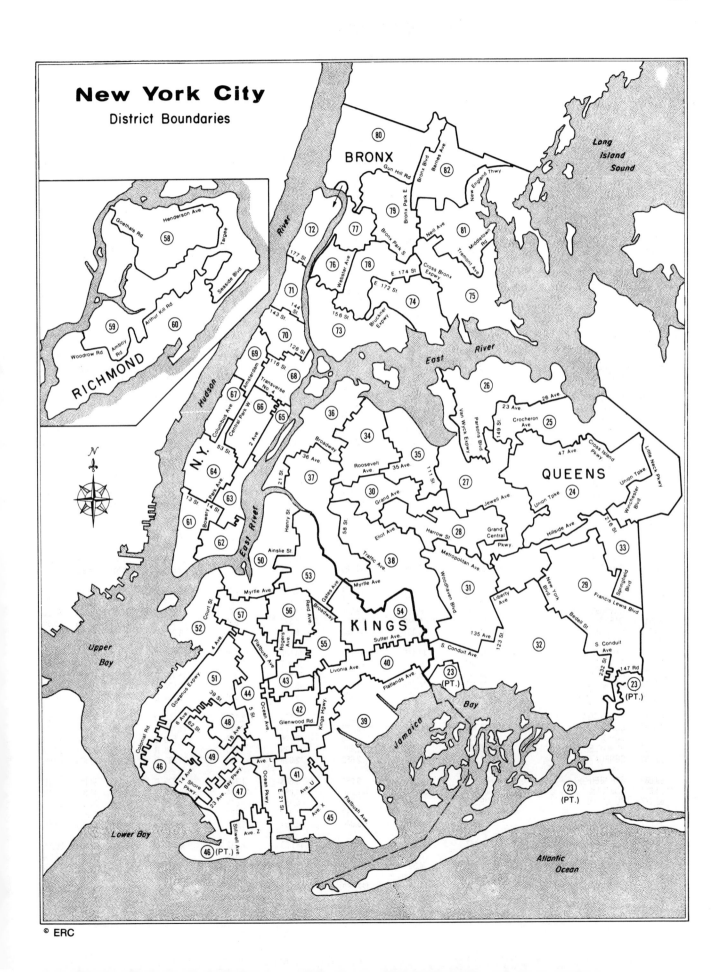

New York City
District Boundaries

© ERC

NEW YORK

GOVERNOR 1990

1990 Census Population	County	Total Vote	Republican	Democratic	Conservative	Other	Plurality	Rep.	Dem.	Con.
292,594	ALBANY	111,027	14,413	62,922	28,740	4,952	34,182 D	13.0%	56.7%	25.9%
50,470	ALLEGANY	11,535	4,392	3,457	2,852	834	935 R	38.1%	30.0%	24.7%
1,203,789	BRONX	152,831	12,962	117,054	15,071	7,744	101,983 D	8.5%	76.6%	9.9%
212,160	BROOME	69,660	19,470	39,603	7,710	2,877	20,133 D	28.0%	56.9%	11.1%
84,234	CATTARAUGUS	21,873	6,701	8,480	5,342	1,350	1,779 D	30.6%	38.8%	24.4%
82,313	CAYUGA	22,618	5,531	7,139	9,105	843	1,966 C	24.5%	31.6%	40.3%
141,895	CHAUTAUQUA	40,217	10,221	15,866	12,329	1,801	3,537 D	25.4%	39.5%	30.7%
95,195	CHEMUNG	25,992	7,359	12,729	4,520	1,384	5,370 D	28.3%	49.0%	17.4%
51,768	CHENANGO	13,859	5,590	4,935	2,702	632	655 R	40.3%	35.6%	19.5%
85,969	CLINTON	18,627	6,826	8,278	2,282	1,241	1,452 D	36.6%	44.4%	12.3%
62,982	COLUMBIA	19,942	4,075	7,597	7,297	973	300 D	20.4%	38.1%	36.6%
48,963	CORTLAND	12,350	4,249	4,177	3,182	742	72 R	34.4%	33.8%	25.8%
47,225	DELAWARE	14,079	5,355	4,006	3,973	745	1,349 R	38.0%	28.5%	28.2%
259,462	DUTCHESS	67,518	19,985	24,878	18,910	3,745	4,893 D	29.6%	36.8%	28.0%
968,532	ERIE	272,681	46,689	152,975	59,814	13,203	93,161 D	17.1%	56.1%	21.9%
37,152	ESSEX	12,317	5,715	3,956	1,803	843	1,759 R	46.4%	32.1%	14.6%
46,540	FRANKLIN	13,120	4,824	5,939	1,646	711	1,115 D	36.8%	45.3%	12.5%
54,191	FULTON	15,624	3,994	5,578	5,312	740	266 D	25.6%	35.7%	34.0%
60,060	GENESEE	16,084	4,935	5,427	4,647	1,075	492 D	30.7%	33.7%	28.9%
44,739	GREENE	14,952	3,762	5,111	5,310	769	199 C	25.2%	34.2%	35.5%
5,279	HAMILTON	2,946	1,078	605	1,101	162	23 C	36.6%	20.5%	37.4%
65,797	HERKIMER	20,914	8,186	7,192	4,603	933	994 R	39.1%	34.4%	22.0%
110,943	JEFFERSON	24,283	7,864	10,545	4,727	1,147	2,681 D	32.4%	43.4%	19.5%
2,300,664	KINGS	295,398	28,302	217,163	35,209	14,724	181,954 D	9.6%	73.5%	11.9%
26,796	LEWIS	7,735	3,625	2,233	1,474	403	1,392 R	46.9%	28.9%	19.1%
62,372	LIVINGSTON	16,991	5,503	5,891	4,618	979	388 D	32.4%	34.7%	27.2%
69,120	MADISON	19,498	5,562	7,183	5,867	886	1,316 D	28.5%	36.8%	30.1%
713,968	MONROE	219,188	43,512	111,164	55,482	9,030	55,682 D	19.9%	50.7%	25.3%
51,981	MONTGOMERY	16,925	3,843	7,035	5,318	729	1,717 D	22.7%	41.6%	31.4%
1,287,348	NASSAU	355,070	92,486	175,153	66,485	20,946	82,667 D	26.0%	49.3%	18.7%
1,487,536	NEW YORK	257,490	22,779	202,306	21,261	11,144	179,527 D	8.8%	78.6%	8.3%
220,756	NIAGRA	53,993	12,104	22,914	16,152	2,823	6,762 D	22.4%	42.4%	29.9%
250,836	ONEIDA	80,751	26,991	32,519	17,369	3,872	5,528 D	33.4%	40.3%	21.5%
468,973	ONONDAGA	139,691	29,861	65,850	37,885	6,095	27,965 D	21.4%	47.1%	27.1%
95,101	ONTARIO	29,457	8,480	11,463	8,324	1,190	2,983 D	28.8%	38.9%	28.3%
307,647	ORANGE	71,043	20,558	27,044	19,716	3,725	6,486 D	28.9%	38.1%	27.8%
41,846	ORLEANS	10,200	3,479	3,325	2,926	470	154 R	34.1%	32.6%	28.7%
121,771	OSWEGO	32,945	9,353	9,989	11,913	1,690	1,924 C	28.4%	30.3%	36.2%
60,517	OTSEGO	17,306	5,942	6,001	4,373	990	59 D	34.3%	34.7%	25.3%
83,941	PUTNAM	24,846	6,301	10,447	6,463	1,635	3,984 D	25.4%	42.0%	26.0%
1,951,598	QUEENS	291,478	40,175	191,721	46,686	12,896	145,035 D	13.8%	65.8%	16.0%
154,429	RENSSELAER	52,588	9,361	22,001	18,217	3,009	3,784 D	17.8%	41.8%	34.6%
378,977	RICHMOND	83,113	13,829	47,700	16,523	5,061	31,177 D	16.6%	57.4%	19.9%
265,475	ROCKLAND	73,939	14,552	38,889	16,361	4,137	22,528 D	19.7%	52.6%	22.1%
111,974	ST. LAWRENCE	27,465	8,872	12,326	4,643	1,624	3,454 D	32.3%	44.9%	16.9%
181,276	SARATOGA	54,130	11,772	22,246	17,554	2,558	4,692 D	21.7%	41.1%	32.4%
149,285	SCHENECTADY	52,760	9,543	26,933	13,773	2,511	13,160 D	18.1%	51.0%	26.1%
31,859	SCHOHARIE	9,852	2,312	3,786	3,226	528	560 D	23.5%	38.4%	32.7%
18,662	SCHUYLER	5,084	1,860	1,832	1,129	263	28 R	36.6%	36.0%	22.2%
33,683	SENECA	9,503	3,327	2,652	2,938	586	389 R	35.0%	27.9%	30.9%
99,088	STEUBEN	24,276	9,076	8,251	5,603	1,346	825 R	37.4%	34.0%	23.1%
1,321,864	SUFFOLK	307,410	93,863	142,250	51,893	19,404	48,387 D	30.5%	46.3%	16.9%
69,277	SULLIVAN	19,585	6,586	6,770	5,350	879	184 D	33.6%	34.6%	27.3%
52,337	TIOGA	14,295	5,029	6,382	1,961	923	1,353 D	35.2%	44.6%	13.7%
94,097	TOMPKINS	23,794	5,756	13,844	3,194	1,000	8,088 D	24.2%	58.2%	13.4%
165,304	ULSTER	53,157	13,273	20,892	16,060	2,932	4,832 D	25.0%	39.3%	30.2%
59,209	WARREN	17,841	5,290	6,933	5,004	614	1,643 D	29.7%	38.9%	28.0%
59,330	WASHINGTON	16,545	4,391	5,852	5,487	815	365 D	26.5%	35.4%	33.2%
89,123	WAYNE	24,029	9,831	6,727	6,417	1,054	3,104 R	40.9%	28.0%	26.7%
874,866	WESTCHESTER	235,523	48,849	127,862	46,589	12,223	79,013 D	20.7%	54.3%	19.8%

NEW YORK

GOVERNOR 1990

1990 Census Population	County	Total Vote	Republican	Democratic	Conservative	Other	Plurality	Percentage Total Vote		
								Rep.	Dem.	Con.
42,507	WYOMING	10,451	3,206	3,060	3,385	800	179 C	30.7%	29.3%	32.4%
22,810	YATES	6,502	2,338	2,049	1,808	307	289 R	36.0%	31.5%	27.8%
17,990,455	TOTAL	4,056,896	865,948	2,157,087	827,614	206,247	1,291,139 D	21.3%	53.2%	20.4%

NEW YORK CITY

BRONX COUNTY
GOVERNOR 1990

1990 Census Population	District	Total Vote	Republican	Democratic	Conservative	Other	Plurality	Percentage Total Vote		
								Rep.	Dem.	Con.
	DISTRICT 73	13,614	500	12,274	183	657	11,774 D	3.7%	90.2%	1.3%
	DISTRICT 74	13,446	763	11,383	411	889	10,620 D	5.7%	84.7%	3.1%
	DISTRICT 75	18,325	2,682	11,146	3,542	955	7,604 D	14.6%	60.8%	19.3%
	DISTRICT 76	10,018	324	8,969	131	594	8,645 D	3.2%	89.5%	1.3%
	DISTRICT 77	9,369	493	8,041	340	495	7,548 D	5.3%	85.8%	3.6%
	DISTRICT 78	12,546	495	11,199	290	562	10,704 D	3.9%	89.3%	2.3%
	DISTRICT 79	14,764	1,502	10,469	2,074	719	8,395 D	10.2%	70.9%	14.0%
	DISTRICT 80	22,082	2,241	15,131	3,707	1,003	11,424 D	10.1%	68.5%	16.8%
	DISTRICT 81	23,466	3,091	15,788	3,634	953	12,154 D	13.2%	67.3%	15.5%
	DISTRICT 82	15,201	871	12,654	759	917	11,783 D	5.7%	83.2%	5.0%
1,203,789	TOTAL	152,831	12,962	117,054	15,071	7,744	101,983 D	8.5%	76.6%	9.9%

NEW YORK CITY

KINGS COUNTY
GOVERNOR 1990

1990 Census Population	District	Total Vote	Republican	Democratic	Conservative	Other	Plurality	Percentage Total Vote		
								Rep.	Dem.	Con.
	DISTRICT 39	18,440	2,380	12,470	3,132	458	9,338 D	12.9%	67.6%	17.0%
	DISTRICT 40	12,947	265	11,632	125	925	11,367 D	2.0%	89.8%	1.0%
	DISTRICT 41	21,450	2,330	14,130	4,013	977	10,117 D	10.9%	65.9%	18.7%
	DISTRICT 42	10,996	669	8,690	805	832	7,885 D	6.1%	79.0%	7.3%
	DISTRICT 43	11,270	226	9,887	342	815	9,545 D	2.0%	87.7%	3.0%
	DISTRICT 44	18,612	1,746	13,688	2,333	845	11,355 D	9.4%	73.5%	12.5%
	DISTRICT 45	20,297	2,409	13,548	3,773	567	9,775 D	11.9%	66.7%	18.6%
	DISTRICT 46	20,084	2,624	13,309	3,481	670	9,828 D	13.1%	66.3%	17.3%
	DISTRICT 47	15,765	2,349	10,438	2,564	414	7,874 D	14.9%	66.2%	16.3%
	DISTRICT 48	15,256	2,140	9,500	3,139	477	6,361 D	14.0%	62.3%	20.6%
	DISTRICT 49	14,595	2,666	8,838	2,720	371	6,118 D	18.3%	60.6%	18.6%
	DISTRICT 50	15,102	1,523	11,409	1,439	731	9,886 D	10.1%	75.5%	9.5%
	DISTRICT 51	14,781	1,756	10,221	2,012	792	8,209 D	11.9%	69.1%	13.6%
	DISTRICT 52	22,465	2,699	14,912	3,885	969	11,027 D	12.0%	66.4%	17.3%
	DISTRICT 53	11,006	863	9,349	390	404	8,486 D	7.8%	84.9%	3.5%
	DISTRICT 54	9,484	651	7,991	382	460	7,340 D	6.9%	84.3%	4.0%
	DISTRICT 55	13,238	246	12,066	108	818	11,820 D	1.9%	91.1%	0.8%
	DISTRICT 56	13,925	265	11,870	110	1,680	11,605 D	1.9%	85.2%	0.8%
	DISTRICT 57	15,685	495	13,215	456	1,519	12,720 D	3.2%	84.3%	2.9%
2,300,664	TOTAL	295,398	28,302	217,163	35,209	14,724	181,954 D	9.6%	73.5%	11.9%

NEW YORK CITY

NEW YORK COUNTY
GOVERNOR 1990

1990 Census Population	District	Total Vote	Republican	Democratic	Conservative	Other	Plurality	Percentage Total Vote Rep.	Dem.	Con.
	DISTRICT 61	27,445	2,184	21,719	2,277	1,265	19,442 D	8.0%	79.1%	8.3%
	DISTRICT 62	15,050	1,398	12,157	981	514	10,759 D	9.3%	80.8%	6.5%
	DISTRICT 63	27,101	2,986	19,553	3,505	1,057	16,048 D	11.0%	72.1%	12.9%
	DISTRICT 64	23,229	2,057	18,176	2,065	931	16,111 D	8.9%	78.2%	8.9%
	DISTRICT 65	25,798	3,317	18,484	3,226	771	15,167 D	12.9%	71.6%	12.5%
	DISTRICT 66	26,015	4,296	17,468	3,683	568	13,172 D	16.5%	67.1%	14.2%
	DISTRICT 67	27,285	2,170	22,059	2,131	925	19,889 D	8.0%	80.8%	7.8%
	DISTRICT 68	16,420	684	14,555	348	833	13,871 D	4.2%	88.6%	2.1%
	DISTRICT 69	23,829	1,350	20,000	1,206	1,273	18,650 D	5.7%	83.9%	5.1%
	DISTRICT 70	16,137	367	14,303	150	1,317	13,936 D	2.3%	88.6%	0.9%
	DISTRICT 71	14,965	597	13,012	289	1,067	12,415 D	4.0%	86.9%	1.9%
	DISTRICT 72	14,626	1,410	11,157	1,419	640	9,738 D	9.6%	76.3%	9.7%
1,487,536	TOTAL	257,490	22,779	202,306	21,261	11,144	179,527 D	8.8%	78.6%	8.3%

NEW YORK CITY

QUEENS COUNTY
GOVERNOR 1990

1990 Census Population	District	Total Vote	Republican	Democratic	Conservative	Other	Plurality	Percentage Total Vote Rep.	Dem.	Con.
	DISTRICT 23	18,320	2,106	12,081	3,168	965	8,913 D	11.5%	65.9%	17.3%
	DISTRICT 24	27,234	3,509	18,107	4,763	855	13,344 D	12.9%	66.5%	17.5%
	DISTRICT 25	26,133	4,796	14,138	5,988	1,211	8,150 D	18.4%	54.1%	22.9%
	DISTRICT 26	21,254	2,989	13,749	3,849	667	9,900 D	14.1%	64.7%	18.1%
	DISTRICT 27	18,828	2,613	12,480	3,063	672	9,417 D	13.9%	66.3%	16.3%
	DISTRICT 28	22,889	2,828	15,772	3,659	630	12,113 D	12.4%	68.9%	16.0%
	DISTRICT 29	19,610	628	17,141	570	1,271	16,513 D	3.2%	87.4%	2.9%
	DISTRICT 30	14,050	2,311	8,842	2,410	487	6,432 D	16.4%	62.9%	17.2%
	DISTRICT 31	16,698	3,135	8,840	3,973	750	4,867 D	18.8%	52.9%	23.8%
	DISTRICT 32	19,408	1,153	15,545	1,423	1,287	14,122 D	5.9%	80.1%	7.3%
	DISTRICT 33	13,682	913	11,099	794	876	10,186 D	6.7%	81.1%	5.8%
	DISTRICT 34	15,614	2,745	9,211	2,972	686	6,239 D	17.6%	59.0%	19.0%
	DISTRICT 35	10,332	984	8,188	697	463	7,204 D	9.5%	79.2%	6.7%
	DISTRICT 36	14,070	2,332	9,202	1,951	585	6,870 D	16.6%	65.4%	13.9%
	DISTRICT 37	13,693	2,639	8,063	2,357	634	5,424 D	19.3%	58.9%	17.2%
	DISTRICT 38	19,663	4,494	9,263	5,049	857	4,214 D	22.9%	47.1%	25.7%
1,951,598	TOTAL	291,478	40,175	191,721	46,686	12,896	145,035 D	13.8%	65.8%	16.0%

NEW YORK CITY

RICHMOND COUNTY
GOVERNOR 1990

1990 Census Population	District	Total Vote	Republican	Democratic	Conservative	Other	Plurality	Percentage Total Vote		
								Rep.	Dem.	Con.
	DISTRICT 58	26,905	4,234	16,296	4,690	1,685	11,606 D	15.7%	60.6%	17.4%
	DISTRICT 59	25,142	3,961	15,339	4,465	1,377	10,874 D	15.8%	61.0%	17.8%
	DISTRICT 60	31,066	5,634	16,065	7,368	1,999	8,697 D	18.1%	51.7%	23.7%
378,977	TOTAL	83,113	13,829	47,700	16,523	5,061	31,177 D	16.6%	57.4%	19.9%

NEW YORK CITY

GOVERNOR 1990

1990 Census Population	County	Total Vote	Republican	Democratic	Conservative	Other	Plurality	Percentage Total Vote		
								Rep.	Dem.	Con.
1,203,789	BRONX	152,831	12,962	117,054	15,071	7,744	101,983 D	8.5%	76.6%	9.9%
2,300,664	KINGS	295,398	28,302	217,163	35,209	14,724	181,954 D	9.6%	73.5%	11.9%
1,487,536	NEW YORK	257,490	22,779	202,306	21,261	11,144	179,527 D	8.8%	78.6%	8.3%
1,951,598	QUEENS	291,478	40,175	191,721	46,686	12,896	145,035 D	13.8%	65.8%	16.0%
378,977	RICHMOND	83,113	13,829	47,700	16,523	5,061	31,177 D	16.6%	57.4%	19.9%
7,322,564	TOTAL	1,080,310	118,047	775,944	134,750	51,569	641,194 D	10.9%	71.8%	12.5%

NEW YORK

CONGRESS

CD	Year	Total Vote	Republican Vote	Republican Candidate	Democratic Vote	Democratic Candidate	Other Vote	Rep.-Dem. Plurality	Total Vote Rep.	Total Vote Dem.	Major Vote Rep.	Major Vote Dem.
1	1990	133,585	46,380	CREIGHTON, FRANCIS W.	75,211	* HOCHBRUECKNER, GEORGE J.	11,994	28,831 D	34.7%	56.3%	38.1%	61.9%
1	1988	207,951	102,327	* ROMAINE, EDWARD P.	105,624	* HOCHBRUECKNER, GEORGE J.		3,297 D	49.2%	50.8%	49.2%	50.8%
1	1986	131,031	55,413	* BLASS, GREGORY J.	67,139	* HOCHBRUECKNER, GEORGE J.	8,479	11,726 D	42.3%	51.2%	45.2%	54.8%
1	1984	201,580	107,029	* CARNEY, WILLIAM	94,551	* HOCHBRUECKNER, GEORGE J.		12,478 R	53.1%	46.9%	53.1%	46.9%
1	1982	138,021	88,234	* CARNEY, WILLIAM	49,787	ELDON, ETHAN C.		38,447 R	63.9%	36.1%	63.9%	36.1%
2	1990	101,731	36,859	* BUGLER, JOHN W.	56,722	DOWNEY, THOMAS J.	8,150	19,863 D	36.2%	55.8%	39.4%	60.6%
2	1988	174,618	66,972	* CARDINO, JOSEPH	107,646	* DOWNEY, THOMAS J.		40,674 D	38.4%	61.6%	38.4%	61.6%
2	1986	108,554	35,132	* BUTZKE, JEFFREY A.	69,771	* DOWNEY, THOMAS J.	3,651	34,639 D	32.4%	64.3%	33.5%	66.5%
2	1984	178,503	80,855	* ANIBOLI, PAUL	97,648	* DOWNEY, THOMAS J.		16,793 D	45.3%	54.7%	45.3%	54.7%
2	1982	126,712	42,790	* COSTELLO, PAUL G.	80,951	* DOWNEY, THOMAS J.	2,971	38,161 D	33.8%	63.9%	34.6%	65.4%
3	1990	137,033	59,089	* PREVIDI, ROBERT	73,029	* MRAZEK, ROBERT J.	4,915	13,940 D	43.1%	53.3%	44.7%	55.3%
3	1988	224,306	91,122	* PREVIDI, ROBERT	128,336	MRAZEK, ROBERT J.	4,848	37,214 D	40.6%	57.2%	41.5%	58.5%
3	1986	148,792	60,367	* GUARINO, JOSEPH A.	83,985	MRAZEK, ROBERT J.	4,440	23,618 D	40.6%	56.4%	41.8%	58.2%
3	1984	235,751	112,909	* QUINN, ROBERT P.	120,191	MRAZEK, ROBERT J.	2,651	7,282 D	47.9%	51.0%	48.4%	51.6%
4	1990	129,661	79,304	* LENT, NORMAN F.	41,308	GOBAN, FRANCIS T.	9,049	37,996 R	61.2%	31.9%	65.8%	34.2%
4	1988	215,386	151,038	* LENT, NORMAN F.	59,479	* GOBAN, FRANCIS T.	4,869	91,559 R	70.1%	27.6%	71.7%	28.3%
4	1986	142,288	92,214	* LENT, NORMAN F.	43,581	* SULLIVAN, PATRICIA	6,493	48,633 R	64.8%	30.6%	67.9%	32.1%
4	1984	224,679	154,875	* LENT, NORMAN F.	65,678	* ENGELHARD, SHELDON	4,126	89,197 R	68.9%	29.2%	70.2%	29.8%
5	1990	131,868	71,948	* MCGRATH, RAYMOND J.	53,920	* EPSTEIN, MARK S.	6,000	18,028 R	54.6%	40.9%	57.2%	42.8%
5	1988	207,313	134,881	* MCGRATH, RAYMOND J.	68,930	KELLY, WILLIAM G.	3,502	65,951 R	65.1%	33.2%	66.2%	33.8%
5	1986	143,201	93,473	* MCGRATH, RAYMOND J.	49,728	* SULLIVAN, MICHAEL T.		43,745 R	65.3%	34.7%	65.3%	34.7%
5	1984	222,191	138,560	* MCGRATH, RAYMOND J.	78,429	* D'INNOCENZO, MICHAEL	5,202	60,131 R	62.4%	35.3%	63.9%	36.1%
6	1990	60,641	13,224	SAMPOL, WILLIAM	44,306	* FLAKE, FLOYD H.	3,111	31,082 D	21.8%	73.1%	23.0%	77.0%
6	1988	110,053			94,506	* FLAKE, FLOYD H.	15,547	94,506 D		85.9%		100.0%
6	1986	86,090	27,773	* DIETL, RICHARD	58,317	FLAKE, FLOYD H.		30,544 D	32.3%	67.7%	32.3%	67.7%
6	1984	145,138	25,040	* VELTRE, PHILIP J.	120,098	* ADDABBO, JOSEPH P.		95,058 D	17.3%	82.7%	17.3%	82.7%
7	1990	51,091			51,091	* ACKERMAN, GARY L.		51,091 D		100.0%		100.0%
7	1988	93,120			93,120	* ACKERMAN, GARY L.		93,120 D		100.0%		100.0%
7	1986	81,220	18,384	* RODRIGUEZ, EDWARD N.	62,836	ACKERMAN, GARY L.		44,452 D	22.6%	77.4%	22.6%	77.4%
7	1984	141,044	43,370	* REIFENKUGEL, GUSTAVE A.	97,674	* ACKERMAN, GARY L.		54,304 D	30.7%	69.3%	30.7%	69.3%
8	1990	78,042	21,646	* REIFENKUGEL, GUSTAVE A.	56,396	* SCHEUER, JAMES H.		34,750 D	27.7%	72.3%	27.7%	72.3%
8	1988	100,240			100,240	* SCHEUER, JAMES H.		100,240 D		100.0%		100.0%
8	1986	78,284			70,605	* SCHEUER, JAMES H.	7,679	70,605 D		90.2%		100.0%
8	1984	166,573	62,015	* BRANDOFINO, ROBERT L.	104,558	* SCHEUER, JAMES H.		42,543 D	37.2%	62.8%	37.2%	62.8%
9	1990	54,644	13,330	DARBY, ANN P.	35,177	MANTON, THOMAS J.	6,137	21,847 D	24.4%	64.4%	27.5%	72.5%
9	1988	72,851			72,851	MANTON, THOMAS J.		72,851 D		100.0%		100.0%
9	1986	73,126	18,040	CALISE, SALVATORE J.	50,738	MANTON, THOMAS J.	4,348	32,698 D	24.7%	69.4%	26.2%	73.8%
9	1984	135,330	63,910	* MALTESE, SERPHIN R.	71,420	MANTON, THOMAS J.		7,510 D	47.2%	52.8%	47.2%	52.8%
9	1982	102,820	20,352	WEIGANDT, JOHN L.	75,286	FERRARO, GERALDINE A.	7,182	54,934 D	19.8%	73.2%	21.3%	78.7%
10	1990	76,431	14,963	* KINSELLA, PATRICK J.	61,468	* SCHUMER, CHARLES E.		46,505 D	19.6%	80.4%	19.6%	80.4%
10	1988	136,488	24,313	POPIELARSKI, GEORGE S.	107,056	* SCHUMER, CHARLES E.	5,119	82,743 D	17.8%	78.4%	18.5%	81.5%
10	1986	81,790			76,318	* SCHUMER, CHARLES E.	5,472	76,318 D		93.3%		100.0%
10	1984	159,992	42,009	* FOX, JOHN H.	115,867	* SCHUMER, CHARLES E.	2,116	73,858 D	26.3%	72.4%	26.6%	73.4%
11	1990	39,056			36,286	* TOWNS, EDOLPHUS	2,770	36,286 D		92.9%		100.0%
11	1988	83,158	7,418	HUSSAIN, RIAZ B.	73,755	* TOWNS, EDOLPHUS	1,985	66,337 D	8.9%	88.7%	9.1%	90.9%
11	1986	46,616	4,053	HENDRICKS, NATHANIEL	41,689	* TOWNS, EDOLPHUS	874	37,636 D	8.7%	89.4%	8.9%	91.1%
11	1984	95,064	12,494	HENDRICKS, NATHANIEL	81,002	* TOWNS, EDOLPHUS	1,568	68,508 D	13.1%	85.2%	13.4%	86.6%

NEW YORK

CONGRESS

CD	Year	Total Vote	Republican Vote	Republican Candidate	Democratic Vote	Democratic Candidate	Other Vote	Rep.-Dem. Plurality	Total Vote Rep.	Total Vote Dem.	Major Vote Rep.	Major Vote Dem.
12	1990	42,750			40,570	* OWENS, MAJOR R.	2,180	40,570 D		94.9%		100.0%
12	1988	79,886	5,582	* AUGUSTINE, OWEN	74,304	* OWENS, MAJOR R.		68,722 D	7.0%	93.0%	7.0%	93.0%
12	1986	46,058	2,752	AUGUSTINE, OWEN	42,138	* OWENS, MAJOR R.	1,168	39,386 D	6.0%	91.5%	6.1%	93.9%
12	1984	90,656	8,609	* CAESAR, JOSEPH N.	82,047	* OWENS, MAJOR R.		73,438 D	9.5%	90.5%	9.5%	90.5%
12	1982	49,259	3,215	KATAN, DAVID	44,586	* OWENS, MAJOR R.	1,458	41,371 D	6.5%	90.5%	6.7%	93.3%
13	1990	59,003	11,557	* RAMOS, EDWIN	47,446	* SOLARZ, STEPHEN J.		35,889 D	19.6%	80.4%	19.6%	80.4%
13	1988	108,841	27,536	* CURCI, ANTHONY M.	81,305	* SOLARZ, STEPHEN J.		53,769 D	25.3%	74.7%	25.3%	74.7%
13	1986	74,136	10,941	NADROWSKI, LEON	61,089	* SOLARZ, STEPHEN J.	2,106	50,148 D	14.8%	82.4%	15.2%	84.8%
13	1984	125,347	42,737	* LEVIN, LEW Y.	82,610	* SOLARZ, STEPHEN J.		39,873 D	34.1%	65.9%	34.1%	65.9%
14	1990	97,611	58,616	* MOLINARI, SUSAN	34,625	* POCCHIA, ANTHONY J.	4,370	23,991 R	60.1%	35.5%	62.9%	37.1%
14	1988	156,682	99,179	* MOLINARI, GUY V.	57,503	* O'DONOVAN, JEROME X.		41,676 R	63.3%	36.7%	63.3%	36.7%
14	1986	93,972	64,647	* MOLINARI, GUY V.	27,950	WALLA, BARBARA	1,375	36,697 R	68.8%	29.7%	69.8%	30.2%
14	1984	166,817	117,041	* MOLINARI, GUY V.	49,776	SHEEHY, KEVIN		67,265 R	70.2%	29.8%	70.2%	29.8%
15	1990	90,037	52,919	* GREEN, S. WILLIAM	33,464	* REITER, FRANCES L.	3,654	19,455 R	58.8%	37.2%	61.3%	38.7%
15	1988	175,483	107,599	* GREEN, S. WILLIAM	64,425	DOUKAS, PETER G.	3,459	43,174 R	61.3%	36.7%	62.5%	37.5%
15	1986	100,361	58,214	* GREEN, S. WILLIAM	42,147	* HIRSCH, GEORGE A.		16,067 R	58.0%	42.0%	58.0%	42.0%
15	1984	192,048	107,644	* GREEN, S. WILLIAM	84,404	* STEIN, ANDREW J.		23,240 R	56.1%	43.9%	56.1%	43.9%
15	1982	123,698	66,262	* GREEN, S. WILLIAM	55,483	* LALL, BETTY G.	1,953	10,779 R	53.6%	44.9%	54.4%	45.6%
16	1990	57,474			55,882	* RANGEL, CHARLES B.	1,592	55,882 D		97.2%		100.0%
16	1988	110,850			107,620	* RANGEL, CHARLES B.	3,230	107,620 D		97.1%		100.0%
16	1986	63,545			61,262	* RANGEL, CHARLES B.	2,283	61,262 D		96.4%		100.0%
16	1984	121,398			117,759	* RANGEL, CHARLES B.	3,639	117,759 D		97.0%		100.0%
16	1982	78,605			76,626	* RANGEL, CHARLES B.	1,979	76,626 D		97.5%		100.0%
17	1990	98,395	15,219	KOEPPEL, WILLIAM W.	79,161	* WEISS, THEODORE S.	4,015	63,942 D	15.5%	80.5%	16.1%	83.9%
17	1988	186,495	29,156	* ALBERT, MYRNA C.	157,339	* WEISS, THEODORE S.		128,183 D	15.6%	84.4%	15.6%	84.4%
17	1986	111,262	15,587	* CHORBA, THOMAS A.	95,094	* WEISS, THEODORE S.	581	79,507 D	14.0%	85.5%	14.1%	85.9%
17	1984	199,479	33,316	KATZMAN, KENNETH	162,489	* WEISS, THEODORE S.	3,674	129,173 D	16.7%	81.5%	17.0%	83.0%
17	1982	133,100	19,928	* ANTONELLI, LOUIS S.	113,172	* WEISS, THEODORE S.		93,244 D	15.0%	85.0%	15.0%	85.0%
18	1990	40,796	1,189	CHIAVARO, JOSEPH	38,024	* SERRANO, JOSE E.	1,583	36,835 D	2.9%	93.2%	3.0%	97.0%
18	1988	82,866	5,764	BROWN, FRED	75,459	* GARCIA, ROBERT	1,643	69,695 D	7.0%	91.1%	7.1%	92.9%
18	1986	46,353	2,479	CHASE, MELANIE	43,343	* GARCIA, ROBERT	531	40,864 D	5.3%	93.5%	5.4%	94.6%
18	1984	96,328	8,970	JOHNSON, CURTIS	85,960	* GARCIA, ROBERT	1,398	76,990 D	9.3%	89.2%	9.4%	90.6%
19	1990	74,761	17,135	GOULDMAN, WILLIAM J.	45,758	* ENGEL, ELIOT L.	11,868	28,623 D	22.9%	61.2%	27.2%	72.8%
19	1988	137,743	37,454	BIAGGI, MARIO	77,158	* ENGEL, ELIOT L.	23,131	39,704 D	27.2%	56.0%	32.7%	67.3%
19	1986	97,349			87,774	* BIAGGI, MARIO	9,575	87,774 D		90.2%		100.0%
19	1984	163,539			155,067	* BIAGGI, MARIO	8,472	155,067 D		94.8%		100.0%
20	1990	130,808	35,575	BELLITTO, GLENN D.	82,203	LOWEY, NITA M.	13,030	46,628 D	27.2%	62.8%	30.2%	69.8%
20	1988	203,263	96,465	* DIOGUARDI, JOSEPH J.	102,235	LOWEY, NITA M.	4,563	5,770 D	47.5%	50.3%	48.5%	51.5%
20	1986	148,920	80,220	* DIOGUARDI, JOSEPH J.	66,359	ABZUG, BELLA S.	2,341	13,861 R	53.9%	44.6%	54.7%	45.3%
20	1984	213,349	106,958	* DIOGUARDI, JOSEPH J.	102,842	TEICHER, OREN J.	3,549	4,116 R	50.1%	48.2%	51.0%	49.0%
21	1990	139,919	99,866	* FISH, HAMILTON	34,128	BARBUTO, RICHARD L.	5,925	65,738 R	71.4%	24.4%	74.5%	25.5%
21	1988	201,607	150,443	* FISH, HAMILTON	47,294	GRUNBERGER, LAWRENCE W.	3,870	103,149 R	74.6%	23.5%	76.1%	23.9%
21	1986	133,397	102,070	* FISH, HAMILTON	28,339	GRUNBERGER, LAWRENCE W.	2,988	73,731 R	76.5%	21.2%	78.3%	21.7%
21	1984	204,327	160,053	* FISH, HAMILTON	44,274	GRUNBERGER, LAWRENCE W.		115,779 R	78.3%	21.7%	78.3%	21.7%
21	1982	156,124	117,460	* FISH, HAMILTON	38,664	STRONG, J. MORGAN		78,796 R	75.2%	24.8%	75.2%	24.8%
22	1990	139,185	95,495	GILMAN, BENJAMIN A.	37,034	DOW, JOHN G.	6,656	58,461 R	68.6%	26.6%	72.1%	27.9%
22	1988	203,635	144,227	GILMAN, BENJAMIN A.	54,312	BURLINGHAM, ELEANOR F.	5,096	89,915 R	70.8%	26.7%	72.6%	27.4%
22	1986	135,656	94,244	GILMAN, BENJAMIN A.	36,852	BURLINGHAM, ELEANOR F.	4,560	57,392 R	69.5%	27.2%	71.9%	28.1%
22	1984	210,486	144,278	GILMAN, BENJAMIN A.	57,934	* LEVINE, BRUCE M.	8,274	86,344 R	68.5%	27.5%	71.3%	28.7%
22	1982	174,286	92,266	GILMAN, BENJAMIN A.	73,124	* PEYSER, PETER A.	8,896	19,142 R	52.9%	42.0%	55.8%	44.2%

NEW YORK

CONGRESS

CD	Year	Total Vote	Republican Vote	Republican Candidate	Democratic Vote	Democratic Candidate	Other Vote	Rep.-Dem. Plurality	Total Vote Rep.	Total Vote Dem.	Major Vote Rep.	Major Vote Dem.
23	1990	182,999	65,760	BUHRMASTER, MARGARET B.	117,239	* MCNULTY, MICHAEL R.		51,479 D	35.9%	64.1%	35.9%	64.1%
23	1988	234,898	89,858	* BAKAL, PETER M.	145,040	MCNULTY, MICHAEL R.		55,182 D	38.3%	61.7%	38.3%	61.7%
23	1986	146,038			140,759	STRATTON, SAMUEL S.	5,279	140,759 D		96.4%		100.0%
23	1984	241,846	53,060	* WICKS, FRANK	188,144	STRATTON, SAMUEL S.	642	135,084 D	21.9%	77.8%	22.0%	78.0%
23	1982	216,083	41,386	* WICKS, FRANK	164,427	STRATTON, SAMUEL S.	10,270	123,041 D	19.2%	76.1%	20.1%	79.9%
24	1990	177,877	121,206	* SOLOMON, GERALD B.	56,671	LAWRENCE, BOB		64,535 R	68.1%	31.9%	68.1%	31.9%
24	1988	225,139	162,962	* SOLOMON, GERALD B.	62,177	BAYE, FRED		100,785 R	72.4%	27.6%	72.4%	27.6%
24	1986	166,510	117,285	* SOLOMON, GERALD B.	49,225	BLOCH, EDWARD J.		68,060 R	70.4%	29.6%	70.4%	29.6%
24	1984	224,207	164,019	* SOLOMON, GERALD B.	60,188	BLOCH, EDWARD J.		103,831 R	73.2%	26.8%	73.2%	26.8%
24	1982	189,737	140,296	* SOLOMON, GERALD B.	49,441	ESIASON, ROY		90,855 R	73.9%	26.1%	73.9%	26.1%
25	1990	108,829	91,348	BOEHLERT, SHERWOOD L.			17,481	91,348 R	83.9%		100.0%	
25	1988	130,122	130,122	BOEHLERT, SHERWOOD L.				130,122 R	100.0%		100.0%	
25	1986	151,079	104,216	BOEHLERT, SHERWOOD L.	33,864	CONWAY, KEVIN J.	12,999	70,352 R	69.0%	22.4%	75.5%	24.5%
25	1984	192,690	140,256	BOEHLERT, SHERWOOD L.	52,434	BALL, JAMES J.		87,822 R	72.8%	27.2%	72.8%	27.2%
26	1990	97,340	97,340	* MARTIN, DAVID O'B.				97,340 R	100.0%		100.0%	
26	1988	174,628	131,043	* MARTIN, DAVID O'B.	43,585	RAVENSCROFT, DONALD R.		87,458 R	75.0%	25.0%	75.0%	25.0%
26	1986	94,840	94,840	* MARTIN, DAVID O'B.				94,840 R	100.0%		100.0%	
26	1984	185,920	131,257	* MARTIN, DAVID O'B.	54,663	LAMMERS, BERNARD J.		76,594 R	70.6%	29.4%	70.6%	29.4%
26	1982	152,170	108,962	* MARTIN, DAVID O'B.	43,208	LANDY, DAVID P.		65,754 R	71.6%	28.4%	71.6%	28.4%
27	1990	150,755	95,220	* WALSH, JAMES T.	52,438	* MURRAY, PEGGY L.	3,097	42,782 R	63.2%	34.8%	64.5%	35.5%
27	1988	217,426	124,928	* WALSH, JAMES T.	90,854	* POOLER, ROSEMARY S.	1,644	34,074 R	57.5%	41.8%	57.9%	42.1%
27	1986	168,026	83,430	* WORTLEY, GEORGE C.	82,491	* POOLER, ROSEMARY S.	2,105	939 R	49.7%	49.1%	50.3%	49.7%
27	1984	215,816	122,215	* WORTLEY, GEORGE C.	93,601	* BUCKEL, THOMAS C.		28,614 R	56.6%	43.4%	56.6%	43.4%
28	1990	150,892	53,077	KRIEGER, SEYMOUR	97,815	MCHUGH, MATTHEW F.		44,738 D	35.2%	64.8%	35.2%	64.8%
28	1988	152,371			141,976	MCHUGH, MATTHEW F.	10,395	141,976 D		93.2%		100.0%
28	1986	152,121	48,213	* MASTERSON, MARK R.	103,908	MCHUGH, MATTHEW F.		55,695 D	31.7%	68.3%	31.7%	68.3%
28	1984	218,061	90,324	COOK, CONSTANCE E.	123,334	MCHUGH, MATTHEW F.	4,403	33,010 D	41.4%	56.6%	42.3%	57.7%
29	1990	141,417	89,105	HORTON, FRANK J.	34,835	EBER, ALTON F.	17,477	54,270 R	63.0%	24.6%	71.9%	28.1%
29	1988	192,661	132,608	HORTON, FRANK J.	51,243	VOGEL, JAMES R.	8,810	81,365 R	68.8%	26.6%	72.1%	27.9%
29	1986	141,008	99,704	HORTON, FRANK J.	34,194	VOGEL, JAMES R.	7,110	65,510 R	70.7%	24.2%	74.5%	25.5%
29	1984	198,662	138,362	HORTON, FRANK J.	48,301	TOOLE, JAMES R.	11,999	90,061 R	69.6%	24.3%	74.1%	25.9%
30	1990	164,814	67,534	* REGAN, JOHN M.	97,280	SLAUGHTER, LOUISE M.		29,746 D	41.0%	59.0%	41.0%	59.0%
30	1988	225,712	89,126	BOUCHARD, JOHN D.	128,364	SLAUGHTER, LOUISE M.	8,222	39,238 D	39.5%	56.9%	41.0%	59.0%
30	1986	170,179	83,402	* ECKERT, FRED J.	86,777	SLAUGHTER, LOUISE M.		3,375 D	49.0%	51.0%	49.0%	51.0%
30	1984	220,273	119,844	* ECKERT, FRED J.	100,066	CALL, W. DOUGLAS	363	19,778 R	54.4%	45.4%	54.5%	45.5%
30	1982	174,620	119,105	CONABLE, BARBER B.	48,764	BENET, BILL	6,751	70,341 R	68.2%	27.9%	71.0%	29.0%
31	1990	159,565	90,237	* PAXON, L. WILLIAM	69,328	* GAUGHAN, KEVIN P.		20,909 R	56.6%	43.4%	56.6%	43.4%
31	1988	220,487	117,710	* PAXON, L. WILLIAM	102,777	* SWARTS, DAVID J.		14,933 R	53.4%	46.6%	53.4%	46.6%
31	1986	160,995	92,508	* KEMP, JACK F.	67,574	* KEANE, JAMES P.	913	24,934 R	57.5%	42.0%	57.8%	42.2%
31	1984	224,488	168,332	* KEMP, JACK F.	56,156	* MARTINELLI, PETER J.		112,176 R	75.0%	25.0%	75.0%	25.0%
32	1990	124,273	39,053	WARING, MICHAEL T.	68,367	* LAFALCE, JOHN J.	16,853	29,314 D	31.4%	55.0%	36.4%	63.6%
32	1988	184,146	50,229	* EVERETT, EMIL K.	133,917	* LAFALCE, JOHN J.		83,688 D	27.3%	72.7%	27.3%	72.7%
32	1986	109,657			99,745	* LAFALCE, JOHN J.	9,912	99,745 D		91.0%		100.0%
32	1984	201,776	61,797	* MURTY, ANTHONY J.	139,979	* LAFALCE, JOHN J.		78,182 D	30.6%	69.4%	30.6%	69.4%
32	1982	127,383			116,386	* LAFALCE, JOHN J.	10,997	116,386 D		91.4%		100.0%
33	1990	109,546	18,181	KEPFER, THOMAS K.	84,905	* NOWAK, HENRY J.	6,460	66,724 D	16.6%	77.5%	17.6%	82.4%
33	1988	139,604			139,604	* NOWAK, HENRY J.		139,604 D		100.0%		100.0%
33	1986	128,403	19,147	* WALKER, CHARLES A.	109,256	* NOWAK, HENRY J.		90,109 D	14.9%	85.1%	14.9%	85.1%
33	1984	200,078	44,880	* LEWANDOWSKI, DAVID S.	155,198	* NOWAK, HENRY J.		110,318 D	22.4%	77.6%	22.4%	77.6%
33	1982	149,977	19,791	* PILLICH, WALTER J.	126,091	* NOWAK, HENRY J.	4,095	106,300 D	13.2%	84.1%	13.6%	86.4%

NEW YORK

CONGRESS

CD	Year	Total Vote	Republican Vote	Candidate	Democratic Vote	Candidate	Other Vote	Rep.-Dem. Plurality	Percentage Total Vote Rep.	Dem.	Major Vote Rep.	Dem.
34	1990	129,059	89,831	* HOUGHTON, AMORY	37,421	LEAHEY, JOSEPH P.	1,807	52,410 R	69.6%	29.0%	70.6%	29.4%
34	1988	135,875	131,078	* HOUGHTON, AMORY			4,797	131,078 R	96.5%		100.0%	
34	1986	142,754	85,856	* HOUGHTON, AMORY	56,898	HIMELEIN, LARRY M.		28,958 R	60.1%	39.9%	60.1%	39.9%
34	1984	204,478	91,016	* EMERY, JILL H.	110,902	LUNDINE, STANLEY N.	2,560	19,886 D	44.5%	54.2%	45.1%	54.9%

NEW YORK

1990 GENERAL ELECTION

Governor The data for Governor are presented in a four column (Republican, Democratic, Conservative and Other) tabulation and the plurality figures are calculated on a first-second party basis. The Democratic candidate was also the Liberal nominee and 71,017 of his votes were received as the Liberal candidate. Other vote was 137,804 Right to Life (Wein); 31,089 New Alliance (Fulani); 24,611 Libertarian (Johnson), 12,743 Socialist Workers (Gannon).

Congress An asterisk in the Congressional vote table indicates a candidate received votes as the nominee of an additional party/parties. Other vote was 6,883 Conservative (Baldwin) and 5,111 Right to Life (O'Hara) in CD 1; Conservative (Curcio) in CD 2; Right to Life (Dreger) in CD 3; 6,706 Right to Life (Dunkle) and 2,343 Liberal (Heyman) in CD 4; Right to Life (Kitt) in CD 5; Right to Life (Cronin) in CD 6; Conservative (Ognibene) in CD 9; 1,676 Conservative (Johnson) and 1,094 New Alliance (Stevens) in CD 11; 1,159 Conservative (Caesar) and 1,021 New Alliance (Moore) in CD 12; Right to Life (Sacchi) in CD 14; Conservative (Berns) in CD 15; New Alliance (Frazier) in CD 16; 2,928 Conservative (Goret) and 1,087 New Alliance (Patterson) in CD 17; 866 New Alliance (Rivera) and 717 Conservative (Johnson) in CD 18; 8,451 Conservative plus 3,417 Right to Life (Brawley) in CD 19; 8,610 Conservative plus 4,420 Right to Life (Schafer) in CD 20; Right to Life (Curtin) in CD 21; Right to Life (Beirne) in CD 22; Liberal (Griffen) in CD 25; Right to Life (Hoff) in CD 27; 12,599 Conservative (DeMauro) and 4,878 Right to Life (Peters) in CD 29; 11,792 Conservative plus 5,061 Right to Life (Kowalski) in CD 32; Conservative (Corrigan) in CD 33; Liberal (Eklund) in CD 34.

NEW YORK CITY

The City is composed of five counties, each of which for municipal government purposes is known as a borough. Names of the counties and boroughs are the same save in the case of New York county (Manhattan borough), Kings county (Brooklyn borough) and Richmond county (Staten Island borough). 1990 Population by Assembly District is not available.

Governor The data for New York City Governor are presented in the same four column format as the state tabulation and the plurality figures are calculated on a first-second party basis. The Democratic vote includes 29,501 votes cast for Mario M. Cuomo as the Liberal candidate. Other vote was 21,403 Right to Life (Wein); 22,125 New Alliance (Fulani); 3,944 Libertarian (Johnson) and 4,097 Socialist Workers (Gannon). In the New York county detail by assembly district, there are small differences between the state certified totals for the candidates and the addition of the vote by assembly district. The state certified totals are used in the total line and the breakdown by assembly district is from the New York City Board of Elections.

1990 PRIMARIES

SEPTEMBER 11 REPUBLICAN

Governor Pierre A. Rinfret, unopposed.

Congress Unopposed in thirty CD's. No candidate in CD's 7, 11, 12, and 16.

SEPTEMBER 11 DEMOCRATIC

Governor Mario M. Cuomo, unopposed.

Congress Unopposed in twenty-seven CD's. No candidate in CD's 25 and 26. Contested as follows:

CD 18 17,983 Jose E. Serrano; 2,329 Ismael Betancourt.
CD 19 12,521 Eliot L. Engel; 4,928 Dominick A. Fusco.
CD 22 6,975 John G. Dow; 5,607 Sean O'B. Strub.
CD 29 3,630 Alton F. Eber; 1,870 Keith R. T. Perez.
CD 33 28,117 Henry J. Nowak; 2,934 Louis P. Corrigan; 1,336 John A. Basar.

NEW YORK

SEPTEMBER 11 CONSERVATIVE

Governor   Herbert I. London, unopposed.

Congress   Other party candidates endorsed or nominees unopposed in all CD's in which a candidate was named.

SEPTEMBER 11 LIBERAL

Governor   Mario M. Cuomo, unopposed.

Congress   Other party candidates endorsed or nominees unopposed in all CD's in which a candidate was named.

SEPTEMBER 11 RIGHT TO LIFE

Governor   Louis P. Wein, unopposed.

Congress   Other party candidates endorsed or nominees unopposed in all CD's in which a candidate was named.

NORTH CAROLINA

GOVERNOR
James G. Martin (R). Re-elected 1988 to a four-year term. Previously elected 1984.

SENATORS
Jesse Helms (R). Re-elected 1990 to a six-year term. Previously elected 1984, 1978, 1972.

Terry Sanford (D). Elected 1986 to a six-year term.

REPRESENTATIVES
1. Walter B. Jones (D)
2. I. T. Valentine (D)
3. Martin Lancaster (D)
4. David E. Price (D)
5. Stephen L. Neal (D)
6. Howard Coble (R)
7. Charles G. Rose (D)
8. W. G. Hefner (D)
9. J. Alex McMillan (R)
10. Cass Ballenger (R)
11. Charles H. Taylor (R)

POSTWAR VOTE FOR PRESIDENT

Year	Total Vote	Republican Vote	Republican Candidate	Democratic Vote	Democratic Candidate	Other Vote	Plurality	Total Vote Rep.	Total Vote Dem.	Major Vote Rep.	Major Vote Dem.
1988	2,134,370	1,237,258	Bush, George	890,167	Dukakis, Michael S.	6,945	347,091 R	58.0%	41.7%	58.2%	41.8%
1984	2,175,361	1,346,481	Reagan, Ronald	824,287	Mondale, Walter F.	4,593	522,194 R	61.9%	37.9%	62.0%	38.0%
1980	1,855,833	915,018	Reagan, Ronald	875,635	Carter, Jimmy	65,180	39,383 R	49.3%	47.2%	51.1%	48.9%
1976	1,678,914	741,960	Ford, Gerald R.	927,365	Carter, Jimmy	9,589	185,405 D	44.2%	55.2%	44.4%	55.6%
1972	1,518,612	1,054,889	Nixon, Richard M.	438,705	McGovern, George S.	25,018	616,184 R	69.5%	28.9%	70.6%	29.4%
1968 **	1,587,493	627,192	Nixon, Richard M.	464,113	Humphrey, Hubert H.	496,188	131,004 R	39.5%	29.2%	57.5%	42.5%
1964	1,424,983	624,844	Goldwater, Barry M.	800,139	Johnson, Lyndon B.		175,295 D	43.8%	56.2%	43.8%	56.2%
1960	1,368,556	655,420	Nixon, Richard M.	713,136	Kennedy, John F.		57,716 D	47.9%	52.1%	47.9%	52.1%
1956	1,165,592	575,062	Eisenhower, Dwight D.	590,530	Stevenson, Adlai E.		15,468 D	49.3%	50.7%	49.3%	50.7%
1952	1,210,910	558,107	Eisenhower, Dwight D.	652,803	Stevenson, Adlai E.		94,696 D	46.1%	53.9%	46.1%	53.9%
1948	791,209	258,572	Dewey, Thomas E.	459,070	Truman, Harry S.	73,567	200,498 D	32.7%	58.0%	36.0%	64.0%

In 1968 other vote was American (Wallace).

POSTWAR VOTE FOR GOVERNOR

Year	Total Vote	Republican Vote	Republican Candidate	Democratic Vote	Democratic Candidate	Other Vote	Rep-Dem. Plurality	Total Vote Rep.	Total Vote Dem.	Major Vote Rep.	Major Vote Dem.
1988	2,180,025	1,222,338	Martin, James G.	957,687	Jordan, Robert B.		264,651 R	56.1%	43.9%	56.1%	43.9%
1984	2,226,727	1,208,167	Martin, James G.	1,011,209	Edmisten, Rufus	7,351	196,958 R	54.3%	45.4%	54.4%	45.6%
1980	1,847,432	691,449	Lake, Beverly	1,143,145	Hunt, James B.	12,838	451,696 D	37.4%	61.9%	37.7%	62.3%
1976	1,663,824	564,102	Flaherty, David T.	1,081,293	Hunt, James B.	18,429	517,191 D	33.9%	65.0%	34.3%	65.7%
1972	1,504,785	767,470	Holshouser, James E.	729,104	Bowles, Hargrove	8,211	38,366 R	51.0%	48.5%	51.3%	48.7%
1968	1,558,308	737,075	Gardner, James C.	821,233	Scott, Robert W.		84,158 D	47.3%	52.7%	47.3%	52.7%
1964	1,396,508	606,165	Gavin, Robert L.	790,343	Moore, Dan K.		184,178 D	43.4%	56.6%	43.4%	56.6%
1960	1,350,360	613,975	Gavin, Robert L.	735,248	Sanford, Terry	1,137	121,273 D	45.5%	54.4%	45.5%	54.5%
1956	1,135,859	375,379	Hayes, Kyle	760,480	Hodges, Luther H.		385,101 D	33.0%	67.0%	33.0%	67.0%
1952	1,179,635	383,329	Seawell, H. F.	796,306	Umstead, William B.		412,977 D	32.5%	67.5%	32.5%	67.5%
1948	780,525	206,166	Pritchard, George	570,995	Scott, William Kerr	3,364	364,829 D	26.4%	73.2%	26.5%	73.5%

NORTH CAROLINA

POSTWAR VOTE FOR SENATOR

Year	Total Vote	Republican Vote	Candidate	Democratic Vote	Candidate	Other Vote	Rep-Dem. Plurality	Percentage Total Vote Rep.	Dem.	Major Vote Rep.	Dem.
1990	2,069,585	1,087,331	Helms, Jesse	981,573	Gantt, Harvy B.	681	105,758 R	52.5%	47.4%	52.6%	47.4%
1986	1,591,330	767,668	Broyhill, James T.	823,662	Sanford, Terry		55,994 D	48.2%	51.8%	48.2%	51.8%
1984	2,239,051	1,156,768	Helms, Jesse	1,070,488	Hunt, James B.	11,795	86,280 R	51.7%	47.8%	51.9%	48.1%
1980	1,797,665	898,064	East, John P.	887,653	Morgan, Robert	11,948	10,411 R	50.0%	49.4%	50.3%	49.7%
1978	1,135,814	619,151	Helms, Jesse	516,663	Ingram, John		102,488 R	54.5%	45.5%	54.5%	45.5%
1974	1,020,367	377,618	Stevens, William E.	633,775	Morgan, Robert	8,974	256,157 D	37.0%	62.1%	37.3%	62.7%
1972	1,472,541	795,248	Helms, Jesse	677,293	Galifianakis, Nick		117,955 R	54.0%	46.0%	54.0%	46.0%
1968	1,437,340	566,934	Somers, Robert V.	870,406	Ervin, Sam J.		303,472 D	39.4%	60.6%	39.4%	60.6%
1966	901,978	400,502	Shallcross, John S.	501,440	Jordan, B. Everett	36	100,938 D	44.4%	55.6%	44.4%	55.6%
1962	813,155	321,635	Greene, Claude L.	491,520	Ervin, Sam J.		169,885 D	39.6%	60.4%	39.6%	60.4%
1960	1,291,485	497,964	Hayes, Kyle	793,521	Jordan, B. Everett		295,557 D	38.6%	61.4%	38.6%	61.4%
1958 S	616,469	184,977	Clarke, Richard C.	431,492	Jordan, B. Everett		246,515 D	30.0%	70.0%	30.0%	70.0%
1956	1,098,828	367,475	Johnson, Joel A.	731,353	Ervin, Sam J.		363,878 D	33.4%	66.6%	33.4%	66.6%
1954	619,634	211,322	West, Paul C.	408,312	Scott, William Kerr		196,990 D	34.1%	65.9%	34.1%	65.9%
1954 S	410,574	—		410,574	Ervin, Sam J.		410,574 D		100.0%		100.0%
1950	548,276	171,804	Leavitt, Halsey B.	376,472	Hoey, Clyde R.		204,668 D	31.3%	68.7%	31.3%	68.7%
1950 S	544,924	177,753	Gavin, E. L.	364,912	Smith, Willis	2,259	187,159 D	32.6%	67.0%	32.8%	67.2%
1948	764,559	220,307	Wilkinson, John A.	540,762	Broughton, J. M.	3,490	320,455 D	28.8%	70.7%	28.9%	71.1%

The 1958 election and one each of the 1954 and 1950 elections were for short terms to fill vacancies.

NORTH CAROLINA

Districts Established February 11, 1982

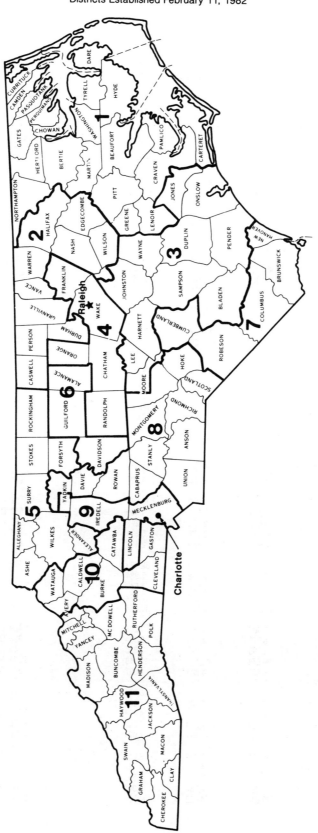

© ERC

NORTH CAROLINA

SENATOR 1990

1990 Census Population	County	Total Vote	Republican	Democratic	Other	Rep.-Dem. Plurality	Percentage Total Vote Rep.	Dem.	Major Vote Rep.	Dem.
108,213	ALAMANCE	36,252	22,546	13,706		8,840 R	62.2%	37.8%	62.2%	37.8%
27,544	ALEXANDER	12,599	8,075	4,524		3,551 R	64.1%	35.9%	64.1%	35.9%
9,590	ALLEGHANY	4,072	2,298	1,774		524 R	56.4%	43.6%	56.4%	43.6%
23,474	ANSON	7,241	3,093	4,148		1,055 D	42.7%	57.3%	42.7%	57.3%
22,209	ASHE	9,566	5,853	3,697	16	2,156 R	61.2%	38.6%	61.3%	38.7%
14,867	AVERY	5,611	4,139	1,469	3	2,670 R	73.8%	26.2%	73.8%	26.2%
42,283	BEAUFORT	12,451	7,608	4,842	1	2,766 R	61.1%	38.9%	61.1%	38.9%
20,388	BERTIE	5,814	2,442	3,372		930 D	42.0%	58.0%	42.0%	58.0%
28,663	BLADEN	8,168	4,058	4,110		52 D	49.7%	50.3%	49.7%	50.3%
50,985	BRUNSWICK	16,850	9,147	7,703		1,444 R	54.3%	45.7%	54.3%	45.7%
174,821	BUNCOMBE	59,011	29,371	29,640		269 D	49.8%	50.2%	49.8%	50.2%
75,744	BURKE	24,506	14,092	10,414		3,678 R	57.5%	42.5%	57.5%	42.5%
98,935	CABARRUS	32,344	19,627	12,641	76	6,986 R	60.7%	39.1%	60.8%	39.2%
70,709	CALDWELL	20,756	12,955	7,790	11	5,165 R	62.4%	37.5%	62.4%	37.6%
5,904	CAMDEN	2,027	1,035	992		43 R	51.1%	48.9%	51.1%	48.9%
52,556	CARTERET	16,461	9,455	7,005	1	2,450 R	57.4%	42.6%	57.4%	42.6%
20,693	CASWELL	6,842	3,311	3,531		220 D	48.4%	51.6%	48.4%	51.6%
118,412	CATAWBA	38,796	23,743	14,904	149	8,839 R	61.2%	38.4%	61.4%	38.6%
38,759	CHATHAM	14,988	7,043	7,945		902 D	47.0%	53.0%	47.0%	53.0%
20,170	CHEROKEE	6,675	3,818	2,857		961 R	57.2%	42.8%	57.2%	42.8%
13,506	CHOWAN	3,851	1,875	1,976		101 D	48.7%	51.3%	48.7%	51.3%
7,155	CLAY	3,787	2,099	1,688		411 R	55.4%	44.6%	55.4%	44.6%
84,714	CLEVELAND	24,181	13,028	11,153		1,875 R	53.9%	46.1%	53.9%	46.1%
49,587	COLUMBUS	16,330	8,389	7,941		448 R	51.4%	48.6%	51.4%	48.6%
81,613	CRAVEN	20,071	10,680	9,391		1,289 R	53.2%	46.8%	53.2%	46.8%
274,566	CUMBERLAND	50,399	23,905	26,334	160	2,429 D	47.4%	52.3%	47.6%	52.4%
13,736	CURRITUCK	3,709	2,022	1,686	1	336 R	54.5%	45.5%	54.5%	45.5%
22,746	DARE	7,888	3,907	3,980	1	73 D	49.5%	50.5%	49.5%	50.5%
126,677	DAVIDSON	37,946	24,992	12,953	1	12,039 R	65.9%	34.1%	65.9%	34.1%
27,859	DAVIE	10,263	7,202	3,061		4,141 R	70.2%	29.8%	70.2%	29.8%
39,995	DUPLIN	11,898	6,768	5,130		1,638 R	56.9%	43.1%	56.9%	43.1%
181,835	DURHAM	64,984	23,670	41,313	1	17,643 D	36.4%	63.6%	36.4%	63.6%
56,558	EDGECOMBE	18,619	8,089	10,527	3	2,438 D	43.4%	56.5%	43.5%	56.5%
265,878	FORSYTH	89,580	46,477	43,077	26	3,400 R	51.9%	48.1%	51.9%	48.1%
36,414	FRANKLIN	11,811	6,384	5,427		957 R	54.1%	45.9%	54.1%	45.9%
175,093	GASTON	46,797	29,962	16,835		13,127 R	64.0%	36.0%	64.0%	36.0%
9,305	GATES	2,790	1,089	1,699	2	610 D	39.0%	60.9%	39.1%	60.9%
7,196	GRAHAM	3,610	2,331	1,279		1,052 R	64.6%	35.4%	64.6%	35.4%
38,345	GRANVILLE	10,709	5,372	5,331	6	41 R	50.2%	49.8%	50.2%	49.8%
15,384	GREENE	4,965	2,859	2,106		753 R	57.6%	42.4%	57.6%	42.4%
347,420	GUILFORD	118,169	56,030	62,139		6,109 D	47.4%	52.6%	47.4%	52.6%
55,516	HALIFAX	15,152	7,218	7,934		716 D	47.6%	52.4%	47.6%	52.4%
67,822	HARNETT	16,616	10,065	6,548	3	3,517 R	60.6%	39.4%	60.6%	39.4%
46,942	HAYWOOD	15,555	7,830	7,722	3	108 R	50.3%	49.6%	50.3%	49.7%
69,285	HENDERSON	24,016	13,993	10,023		3,970 R	58.3%	41.7%	58.3%	41.7%
22,523	HERTFORD	7,007	2,769	4,238		1,469 D	39.5%	60.5%	39.5%	60.5%
22,856	HOKE	5,329	2,154	3,174	1	1,020 D	40.4%	59.6%	40.4%	59.6%
5,411	HYDE	1,795	870	925		55 D	48.5%	51.5%	48.5%	51.5%
92,931	IREDELL	29,671	17,450	12,149	72	5,301 R	58.8%	40.9%	59.0%	41.0%
26,846	JACKSON	8,822	4,225	4,597		372 D	47.9%	52.1%	47.9%	52.1%
81,306	JOHNSTON	24,040	16,029	8,011		8,018 R	66.7%	33.3%	66.7%	33.3%
9,414	JONES	3,377	1,746	1,631		115 R	51.7%	48.3%	51.7%	48.3%
41,374	LEE	10,908	6,480	4,428		2,052 R	59.4%	40.6%	59.4%	40.6%
57,274	LENOIR	16,167	9,820	6,342	5	3,478 R	60.7%	39.2%	60.8%	39.2%
50,319	LINCOLN	18,222	11,151	7,071		4,080 R	61.2%	38.8%	61.2%	38.8%
35,681	MCDOWELL	10,255	6,308	3,947		2,361 R	61.5%	38.5%	61.5%	38.5%
23,499	MACON	8,712	4,563	4,149		414 R	52.4%	47.6%	52.4%	47.6%
16,953	MADISON	7,464	3,901	3,563		338 R	52.3%	47.7%	52.3%	47.7%
25,078	MARTIN	7,095	4,054	3,041		1,013 R	57.1%	42.9%	57.1%	42.9%
511,433	MECKLENBURG	179,086	74,822	104,264		29,442 D	41.8%	58.2%	41.8%	58.2%

NORTH CAROLINA

SENATOR 1990

1990 Census Population	County	Total Vote	Republican	Democratic	Other	Rep.-Dem. Plurality	Percentage			
							Total Vote		Major Vote	
							Rep.	Dem.	Rep.	Dem.
14,433	MITCHELL	5,482	4,101	1,381		2,720 R	74.8%	25.2%	74.8%	25.2%
23,346	MONTGOMERY	7,543	4,068	3,475		593 R	53.9%	46.1%	53.9%	46.1%
59,013	MOORE	22,151	12,847	9,304		3,543 R	58.0%	42.0%	58.0%	42.0%
76,677	NASH	23,192	14,647	8,545		6,102 R	63.2%	36.8%	63.2%	36.8%
120,284	NEW HANOVER	35,814	18,105	17,705	4	400 R	50.6%	49.4%	50.6%	49.4%
20,798	NORTHAMPTON	7,547	3,013	4,534		1,521 D	39.9%	60.1%	39.9%	60.1%
149,838	ONSLOW	19,256	11,648	7,515	93	4,133 R	60.5%	39.0%	60.8%	39.2%
93,851	ORANGE	37,772	10,752	26,997	23	16,245 D	28.5%	71.5%	28.5%	71.5%
11,372	PAMLICO	4,468	2,336	2,132		204 R	52.3%	47.7%	52.3%	47.7%
31,298	PASQUOTANK	7,602	3,310	4,292		982 D	43.5%	56.5%	43.5%	56.5%
28,855	PENDER	9,355	4,856	4,499		357 R	51.9%	48.1%	51.9%	48.1%
10,447	PERQUIMANS	3,066	1,514	1,552		38 D	49.4%	50.6%	49.4%	50.6%
30,180	PERSON	8,571	5,352	3,219		2,133 R	62.4%	37.6%	62.4%	37.6%
107,924	PITT	31,592	15,614	15,978		364 D	49.4%	50.6%	49.4%	50.6%
14,416	POLK	5,466	3,001	2,465		536 R	54.9%	45.1%	54.9%	45.1%
106,546	RANDOLPH	30,576	21,351	9,224	1	12,127 R	69.8%	30.2%	69.8%	30.2%
44,518	RICHMOND	12,726	5,751	6,974	1	1,223 D	45.2%	54.8%	45.2%	54.8%
105,179	ROBESON	26,543	10,299	16,244		5,945 D	38.8%	61.2%	38.8%	61.2%
86,064	ROCKINGHAM	23,652	14,556	9,092	4	5,464 R	61.5%	38.4%	61.6%	38.4%
110,605	ROWAN	32,470	19,658	12,812		6,846 R	60.5%	39.5%	60.5%	39.5%
56,918	RUTHERFORD	16,603	9,954	6,649		3,305 R	60.0%	40.0%	60.0%	40.0%
47,297	SAMPSON	17,493	9,577	7,916		1,661 R	54.7%	45.3%	54.7%	45.3%
33,754	SCOTLAND	6,654	2,866	3,786	2	920 D	43.1%	56.9%	43.1%	56.9%
51,765	STANLY	18,199	11,881	6,318		5,563 R	65.3%	34.7%	65.3%	34.7%
37,223	STOKES	14,044	9,217	4,827		4,390 R	65.6%	34.4%	65.6%	34.4%
61,704	SURRY	17,662	11,103	6,559		4,544 R	62.9%	37.1%	62.9%	37.1%
11,268	SWAIN	3,722	2,001	1,721		280 R	53.8%	46.2%	53.8%	46.2%
25,520	TRANSYLVANIA	10,476	5,659	4,813	4	846 R	54.0%	45.9%	54.0%	46.0%
3,856	TYRRELL	1,321	695	626		69 R	52.6%	47.4%	52.6%	47.4%
84,211	UNION	24,925	15,827	9,098		6,729 R	63.5%	36.5%	63.5%	36.5%
38,892	VANCE	11,322	5,740	5,581	1	159 R	50.7%	49.3%	50.7%	49.3%
423,380	WAKE	152,018	66,379	85,635	4	19,256 D	43.7%	56.3%	43.7%	56.3%
17,265	WARREN	6,642	2,513	4,129		1,616 D	37.8%	62.2%	37.8%	62.2%
13,997	WASHINGTON	4,242	2,223	2,019		204 R	52.4%	47.6%	52.4%	47.6%
36,952	WATAUGA	14,871	6,976	7,893	2	917 D	46.9%	53.1%	46.9%	53.1%
104,666	WAYNE	24,757	15,172	9,585		5,587 R	61.3%	38.7%	61.3%	38.7%
59,393	WILKES	20,201	13,822	6,379		7,443 R	68.4%	31.6%	68.4%	31.6%
66,061	WILSON	18,895	10,519	8,376		2,143 R	55.7%	44.3%	55.7%	44.3%
30,488	YADKIN	9,855	7,370	2,485		4,885 R	74.8%	25.2%	74.8%	25.2%
15,419	YANCEY	8,163	4,771	3,392		1,379 R	58.4%	41.6%	58.4%	41.6%
6,628,637	TOTAL	2,069,585	1,087,331	981,573	681	105,758 R	52.5%	47.4%	52.6%	47.4%

NORTH CAROLINA

CONGRESS

CD	Year	Total Vote	Republican Vote	Republican Candidate	Democratic Vote	Democratic Candidate	Other Vote	Rep.-Dem. Plurality	Total Vote Rep.	Total Vote Dem.	Major Vote Rep.	Major Vote Dem.
1	1990	163,358	57,526	MOYE, HOWARD	105,832	JONES, WALTER B.		48,306 D	35.2%	64.8%	35.2%	64.8%
1	1988	181,040	63,013	MOYE, HOWARD	118,027	JONES, WALTER B.		55,014 D	34.8%	65.2%	34.8%	65.2%
1	1986	131,034	39,912	MOYE, HOWARD	91,122	JONES, WALTER B.		51,210 D	30.5%	69.5%	30.5%	69.5%
1	1984	182,968	60,153	LEE, HERBERT W.	122,815	JONES, WALTER B.		62,662 D	32.9%	67.1%	32.9%	67.1%
1	1982	98,342	17,478	MCINTYRE, JAMES F.	79,954	JONES, WALTER B.	910	62,476 D	17.8%	81.3%	17.9%	82.1%
2	1990	175,242	44,263	SHARPE, HAL C.	130,979	VALENTINE, I. T.		86,716 D	25.3%	74.7%	25.3%	74.7%
2	1988	128,832			128,832	VALENTINE, I. T.		128,832 D		100.0%		100.0%
2	1986	127,835	32,515	MCELHANEY, BUD	95,320	VALENTINE, I. T.		62,805 D	25.4%	74.6%	25.4%	74.6%
2	1984	180,604	58,312	HILL, FRANK H.	122,292	VALENTINE, I. T.		63,980 D	32.3%	67.7%	32.3%	67.7%
2	1982	111,326	34,293	MARIN, JOHN W.	59,617	VALENTINE, I. T.	17,416	25,324 D	30.8%	53.6%	36.5%	63.5%
3	1990	141,535	57,605	DAVIS, DON	83,930	LANCASTER, MARTIN		26,325 D	40.7%	59.3%	40.7%	59.3%
3	1988	95,323			95,323	LANCASTER, MARTIN		95,323 D		100.0%		100.0%
3	1986	110,868	39,408	HURST, GERALD B.	71,460	LANCASTER, MARTIN		32,052 D	35.5%	64.5%	35.5%	64.5%
3	1984	156,281	56,096	MOODY, DANNY G.	100,185	WHITLEY, CHARLES		44,089 D	35.9%	64.1%	35.9%	64.1%
3	1982	108,473	39,046	MCDANIEL, EUGENE	68,936	WHITLEY, CHARLES	491	29,890 D	36.0%	63.6%	36.2%	63.8%
4	1990	240,057	100,661	CARRINGTON, JOHN	139,396	PRICE, DAVID E.		38,735 D	41.9%	58.1%	41.9%	58.1%
4	1988	227,378	95,482	FETZER, TOM	131,896	PRICE, DAVID E.		36,414 D	42.0%	58.0%	42.0%	58.0%
4	1986	165,685	73,469	COBEY, WILLIAM	92,216	PRICE, DAVID E.		18,747 D	44.3%	55.7%	44.3%	55.7%
4	1984	231,898	117,436	COBEY, WILLIAM	114,462	ANDREWS, IKE F.		2,974 R	50.6%	49.4%	50.6%	49.4%
4	1982	137,044	64,955	COBEY, WILLIAM	70,369	ANDREWS, IKE F.	1,720	5,414 D	47.4%	51.3%	48.0%	52.0%
5	1990	192,561	78,747	BELL, KEN	113,814	NEAL, STEPHEN L.		35,067 D	40.9%	59.1%	40.9%	59.1%
5	1988	210,056	99,540	GRAY, LYONS	110,516	NEAL, STEPHEN L.		10,976 D	47.4%	52.6%	47.4%	52.6%
5	1986	159,671	73,261	EPPERSON, STUART	86,410	NEAL, STEPHEN L.		13,149 D	45.9%	54.1%	45.9%	54.1%
5	1984	216,430	106,599	EPPERSON, STUART	109,831	NEAL, STEPHEN L.		3,232 D	49.3%	50.7%	49.3%	50.7%
5	1982	145,707	57,083	BAGNAL, ANNE	87,819	NEAL, STEPHEN L.	805	30,736 D	39.2%	60.3%	39.4%	60.6%
6	1990	188,305	125,392	COBLE, HOWARD	62,913	ALLEGRONE, HELEN R.		62,479 R	66.6%	33.4%	66.6%	33.4%
6	1988	186,542	116,534	COBLE, HOWARD	70,008	GILMORE, TOM		46,526 R	62.5%	37.5%	62.5%	37.5%
6	1986	144,579	72,329	COBLE, HOWARD	72,250	BRITT, C. ROBIN		79 R	50.0%	50.0%	50.0%	50.0%
6	1984	203,473	102,925	COBLE, HOWARD	100,263	BRITT, C. ROBIN	285	2,662 R	50.6%	49.3%	50.7%	49.3%
6	1982	127,619	58,244	JOHNSTON, EUGENE	68,696	BRITT, C. ROBIN	679	10,452 D	45.6%	53.8%	45.9%	54.1%
7	1990	144,627	49,681	ANDERSON, ROBERT C.	94,946	ROSE, CHARLES G.		45,265 D	34.4%	65.6%	34.4%	65.6%
7	1988	152,247	49,855	THOMPSON, GEORGE G.	102,392	ROSE, CHARLES G.		52,537 D	32.7%	67.3%	32.7%	67.3%
7	1986	109,760	39,289	HARRELSON, THOMAS J.	70,471	ROSE, CHARLES G.		31,182 D	35.8%	64.2%	35.8%	64.2%
7	1984	155,782	63,625	RHODES, S. THOMAS	92,157	ROSE, CHARLES G.		28,532 D	40.8%	59.2%	40.8%	59.2%
7	1982	96,534	27,015	JOHNSON, EDWARD	68,529	ROSE, CHARLES G.	990	41,514 D	28.0%	71.0%	28.3%	71.7%
8	1990	179,552	80,852	BLANTON, TED	98,700	HEFNER, W. G.		17,848 D	45.0%	55.0%	45.0%	55.0%
8	1988	192,677	93,463	BLANTON, TED	99,214	HEFNER, W. G.		5,751 D	48.5%	51.5%	48.5%	51.5%
8	1986	139,900	58,941	HAMBY, WILLIAM G.	80,959	HEFNER, W. G.		22,018 D	42.1%	57.9%	42.1%	57.9%
8	1984	196,085	96,354	BLAKE, HARRIS D.	99,731	HEFNER, W. G.		3,377 D	49.1%	50.9%	49.1%	50.9%
8	1982	124,938	52,417	BLAKE, HARRIS D.	71,691	HEFNER, W. G.	830	19,274 D	42.0%	57.4%	42.2%	57.8%
9	1990	212,738	131,936	MCMILLAN, J. ALEX	80,802	MCKNIGHT, DAVID P.		51,134 R	62.0%	38.0%	62.0%	38.0%
9	1988	210,816	139,014	MCMILLAN, J. ALEX	71,802	SHOLANDER, MARK		67,212 R	65.9%	34.1%	65.9%	34.1%
9	1986	156,592	80,352	MCMILLAN, J. ALEX	76,240	MARTIN, D. G.		4,112 R	51.3%	48.7%	51.3%	48.7%
9	1984	218,519	109,420	MCMILLAN, J. ALEX	109,099	MARTIN, D. G.		321 R	50.1%	49.9%	50.1%	49.9%
9	1982	112,786	64,297	MARTIN, JAMES G.	47,258	CORNELIUS, PRESTON	1,231	17,039 R	57.0%	41.9%	57.6%	42.4%
10	1990	172,110	106,400	BALLENGER, CASS	65,710	GREEN, DANIEL R.		40,690 R	61.8%	38.2%	61.8%	38.2%
10	1988	184,419	112,554	BALLENGER, CASS	71,865	RHYNE, JACK L.		40,689 R	61.0%	39.0%	61.0%	39.0%
10	1986	145,937	83,902	BALLENGER, CASS	62,035	ROARK, LESTER D.		21,867 R	57.5%	42.5%	57.5%	42.5%
10	1984	194,733	142,873	BROYHILL, JAMES T.	51,860	POOVEY, TED A.		91,013 R	73.4%	26.6%	73.4%	26.6%
10	1982	87,264	80,904	BROYHILL, JAMES T.			6,360	80,904 R	92.7%		100.0%	

NORTH CAROLINA

CONGRESS

CD	Year	Total Vote	Republican Vote	Republican Candidate	Democratic Vote	Democratic Candidate	Other Vote	Rep.-Dem. Plurality	Total Vote Rep.	Total Vote Dem.	Major Vote Rep.	Major Vote Dem.
11	1990	201,309	101,991	TAYLOR, CHARLES H.	99,318	CLARKE, JAMES MCC.		2,673 R	50.7%	49.3%	50.7%	49.3%
11	1988	215,343	106,907	TAYLOR, CHARLES H.	108,436	CLARKE, JAMES MCC.		1,529 D	49.6%	50.4%	49.6%	50.4%
11	1986	180,644	89,069	HENDON, WILLIAM M.	91,575	CLARKE, JAMES MCC.		2,506 D	49.3%	50.7%	49.3%	50.7%
11	1984	220,882	112,598	HENDON, WILLIAM M.	108,284	CLARKE, JAMES MCC.		4,314 R	51.0%	49.0%	51.0%	49.0%
11	1982	171,047	84,085	HENDON, WILLIAM M.	85,410	CLARKE, JAMES MCC.	1,552	1,325 D	49.2%	49.9%	49.6%	50.4%

NORTH CAROLINA

1990 GENERAL ELECTION

Senator   Other vote was write-in (Stuart).

Congress

1990 PRIMARIES

MAY 8 REPUBLICAN

Senator   157,345 Jesse Helms; 15,355 L. C. Nixon; 13,895 George Wimbish.

Congress   Unopposed in five CD's. Contested as follows:

CD 1   6,072 Howard Moye; 3,175 Marvin R. Jones.
CD 3   5,518 Don Davis; 2,389 William K. Brosman; 1,543 Henry M. Stenhouse.
CD 5   11,209 Ken Bell; 10,565 Steve Royal.
CD 7   6,730 Robert C. Anderson; 4,589 Fries Shaffner.
CD 10   17,052 Cass Ballenger; 2,508 Cherie K. Berry.
CD 11   16,381 Charles H. Taylor; 6,089 Herschel Morgan; 4,158 Lanier M. Cansler; 1,630 Richard Bridges; 945 James T. Harper.

MAY 8 DEMOCRATIC

Senator   260,179 Harvey B. Gantt; 209,934 Mike Easley; 120,990 John Ingram; 82,883 R. P. Thomas; 11,528 Lloyd Garner; 7,982 Robert L. Hannon.

Congress   Unopposed in eight CD's. Contested as follows:

CD 4   51,122 David E. Price; 2,482 Robert B. Coats; 2,377 Paul E. Moore.
CD 8   50,832 W. G. Hefner; 12,111 Helen Ann Garrels.
CD 10   20,782 Daniel R. Green; 11,370 Rita W. McElwaine.

JUNE 5 DEMOCRATIC RUN-OFF

Senator   273,567 Harvey B. Gantt; 207,283 Mike Easley.

NORTH DAKOTA

GOVERNOR
George Sinner (D). Re-elected 1988 to a four-year term. Previously elected 1984.

SENATORS
Quentin N. Burdick (D). Re-elected 1988 to a six-year term. Previously elected 1982, 1976, 1970, 1964 and in June 1960 to fill our term vacated by the death of Senator William Langer.

Kent Conrad (D). Elected 1986 to a six-year term.

REPRESENTATIVES
At-large. Byron L. Dorgan (D)

POSTWAR VOTE FOR PRESIDENT

Year	Total Vote	Republican Vote	Candidate	Democratic Vote	Candidate	Other Vote	Plurality	Total Vote Rep.	Dem.	Major Vote Rep.	Dem.
1988	297,261	166,559	Bush, George	127,739	Dukakis, Michael S.	2,963	38,820 R	56.0%	43.0%	56.6%	43.4%
1984	308,971	200,336	Reagan, Ronald	104,429	Mondale, Walter F.	4,206	95,907 R	64.8%	33.8%	65.7%	34.3%
1980	301,545	193,695	Reagan, Ronald	79,189	Carter, Jimmy	28,661	114,506 R	64.2%	26.3%	71.0%	29.0%
1976	297,188	153,470	Ford, Gerald R.	136,078	Carter, Jimmy	7,640	17,392 R	51.6%	45.8%	53.0%	47.0%
1972	280,514	174,109	Nixon, Richard M.	100,384	McGovern, George S.	6,021	73,725 R	62.1%	35.8%	63.4%	36.6%
1968	247,882	138,669	Nixon, Richard M.	94,769	Humphrey, Hubert H.	14,444	43,900 R	55.9%	38.2%	59.4%	40.6%
1964	258,389	108,207	Goldwater, Barry M.	149,784	Johnson, Lyndon B.	398	41,577 D	41.9%	58.0%	41.9%	58.1%
1960	278,431	154,310	Nixon, Richard M.	123,963	Kennedy, John F.	158	30,347 R	55.4%	44.5%	55.5%	44.5%
1956	253,991	156,766	Eisenhower, Dwight D.	96,742	Stevenson, Adlai E.	483	60,024 R	61.7%	38.1%	61.8%	38.2%
1952	270,127	191,712	Eisenhower, Dwight D.	76,694	Stevenson, Adlai E.	1,721	115,018 R	71.0%	28.4%	71.4%	28.6%
1948	220,716	115,139	Dewey, Thomas E.	95,812	Truman, Harry S.	9,765	19,327 R	52.2%	43.4%	54.6%	45.4%

POSTWAR VOTE FOR GOVERNOR

Year	Total Vote	Republican Vote	Candidate	Democratic Vote	Candidate	Other Vote	Rep-Dem. Plurality	Total Vote Rep.	Dem.	Major Vote Rep.	Dem.
1988	299,080	119,986	Mallberg, Leon L.	179,094	Sinner, George		59,108 D	40.1%	59.9%	40.1%	59.9%
1984	314,382	140,460	Olson, Allen I.	173,922	Sinner, George		33,462 D	44.7%	55.3%	44.7%	55.3%
1980	302,621	162,230	Olson, Allen I.	140,391	Link, Arthur A.		21,839 R	53.6%	46.4%	53.6%	46.4%
1976	297,249	138,321	Elkin, Richard	153,309	Link, Arthur A.	5,619	14,988 D	46.5%	51.6%	47.4%	52.6%
1972	281,931	138,032	Larsen, Richard	143,899	Link, Arthur A.		5,867 D	49.0%	51.0%	49.0%	51.0%
1968	248,000	108,382	McCarney, Robert P.	135,955	Guy, William L.	3,663	27,573 D	43.7%	54.8%	44.4%	55.6%
1964 **	262,661	116,247	Halcrow, Donald M.	146,414	Guy, William L.		30,167 D	44.3%	55.7%	44.3%	55.7%
1962	228,509	113,251	Andrews, Mark	115,258	Guy, William L.		2,007 D	49.6%	50.4%	49.6%	50.4%
1960	275,375	122,486	Dahl, C. P.	136,148	Guy, William L.	16,741	13,662 D	44.5%	49.4%	47.4%	52.6%
1958	210,599	111,836	Davis, John E.	98,763	Lord, John F.		13,073 R	53.1%	46.9%	53.1%	46.9%
1956	252,435	147,566	Davis, John E.	104,869	Warner, Wallace E.		42,697 R	58.5%	41.5%	58.5%	41.5%
1954	193,501	124,253	Brunsdale, C. Norman	69,248	Bymers, Cornelius		55,005 R	64.2%	35.8%	64.2%	35.8%
1952	253,934	199,944	Brunsdale, C. Norman	53,990	Johnson, Ole C.		145,954 R	78.7%	21.3%	78.7%	21.3%
1950	183,772	121,822	Brunsdale, C. Norman	61,950	Byerly, Clyde G.		59,872 R	66.3%	33.7%	66.3%	33.7%
1948	214,858	131,764	Aandahl, Fred G.	80,555	Henry, Howard	2,539	51,209 R	61.3%	37.5%	62.1%	37.9%
1946	169,391	116,672	Aandahl, Fred G.	52,719	Burdick, Quentin N.		63,953 R	68.9%	31.1%	68.9%	31.1%

The term of office of North Dakota's Governor was increased from two to four years effective with the 1964 election.

NORTH DAKOTA

POSTWAR VOTE FOR SENATOR

Year	Total Vote	Republican Vote	Republican Candidate	Democratic Vote	Democratic Candidate	Other Vote	Rep-Dem. Plurality	Total Vote Rep.	Total Vote Dem.	Major Vote Rep.	Major Vote Dem.
1988	289,170	112,937	Striden, Earl	171,899	Burdick, Quentin N.	4,334	58,962 D	39.1%	59.4%	39.6%	60.4%
1986	288,998	141,797	Andrews, Mark	143,932	Conrad, Kent	3,269	2,135 D	49.1%	49.8%	49.6%	50.4%
1982	262,465	89,304	Knorr, Gene	164,873	Burdick, Quentin N.	8,288	75,569 D	34.0%	62.8%	35.1%	64.9%
1980	299,272	210,347	Andrews, Mark	86,658	Johanneson, Kent	2,267	123,689 R	70.3%	29.0%	70.8%	29.2%
1976	283,062	103,466	Stroup, Richard	175,772	Burdick, Quentin N.	3,824	72,306 D	36.6%	62.1%	37.1%	62.9%
1974	235,661	114,117	Young, Milton R.	113,931	Guy, William L.	7,613	186 R	48.4%	48.3%	50.0%	50.0%
1970	219,560	82,996	Kleppe, Tom	134,519	Burdick, Quentin N.	2,045	51,523 D	37.8%	61.3%	38.2%	61.8%
1968	239,776	154,968	Young, Milton R.	80,815	Lashkowitz, Herschel	3,993	74,153 R	64.6%	33.7%	65.7%	34.3%
1964	258,945	109,681	Kleppe, Tom	149,264	Burdick, Quentin N.		39,583 D	42.4%	57.6%	42.4%	57.6%
1962	223,737	135,705	Young, Milton R.	88,032	Lanier, William		47,673 R	60.7%	39.3%	60.7%	39.3%
1960 S	210,349	103,475	Davis, John E.	104,593	Burdick, Quentin N.	2,281	1,118 D	49.2%	49.7%	49.7%	50.3%
1958	204,635	117,070	Langer, William	84,892	Vendsel, Raymond	2,673	32,178 R	57.2%	41.5%	58.0%	42.0%
1956	244,161	155,305	Young, Milton R.	87,919	Burdick, Quentin N.	937	67,386 R	63.6%	36.0%	63.9%	36.1%
1952	237,995	157,907	Langer, William	55,347	Morrison, Harold A.	24,741	102,560 R	66.3%	23.3%	74.0%	26.0%
1950	186,716	126,209	Young, Milton R.	60,507	O'Brien, Harry		65,702 R	67.6%	32.4%	67.6%	32.4%
1946 **	165,382	88,210	Langer, William	38,368	Larson, Abner B.	38,804	49,842 R	53.3%	23.2%	69.7%	30.3%
1946 S	136,852	75,998	Young, Milton R.	37,507	Lanier, William	23,347	38,491 R	55.5%	27.4%	67.0%	33.0%

The 1960 and 1946 special elections were held in June for short terms to fill vacancies. In 1946 other vote was Arthur Thompson (Independent) who received 23.5% of the total vote and ran second.

343

NORTH DAKOTA

One At Large

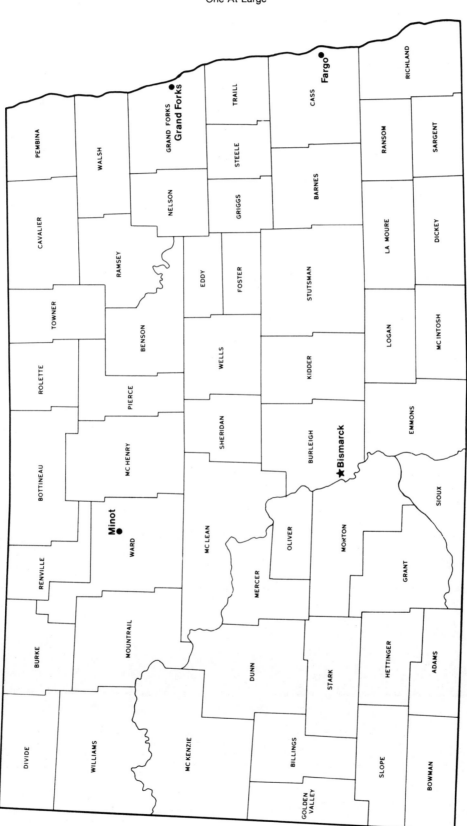

© ERC

NORTH DAKOTA

CONGRESS

CD	Year	Total Vote	Republican Vote	Republican Candidate	Democratic Vote	Democratic Candidate	Other Vote	Rep.-Dem. Plurality	Percentage Total Vote Rep.	Percentage Total Vote Dem.	Percentage Major Vote Rep.	Percentage Major Vote Dem.
AL	1990	233,979	81,443	SCHAFER, EDWARD T.	152,530	DORGAN, BYRON L.	6	71,087 D	34.8%	65.2%	34.8%	65.2%
AL	1988	299,982	84,475	SYDNESS, STEVE	212,583	DORGAN, BYRON L.	2,924	128,108 D	28.2%	70.9%	28.4%	71.6%
AL	1986	286,361	66,989	VINJE, SYVER	216,258	DORGAN, BYRON L.	3,114	149,269 D	23.4%	75.5%	23.7%	76.3%
AL	1984	308,729	65,761	ALTENBURG, LOIS I.	242,968	DORGAN, BYRON L.		177,207 D	21.3%	78.7%	21.3%	78.7%
AL	1982	260,499	72,241	JONES, KENT	186,534	DORGAN, BYRON L.	1,724	114,293 D	27.7%	71.6%	27.9%	72.1%
AL	1980	293,076	124,707	SMYKOWSKI, JIM	166,437	DORGAN, BYRON L.	1,932	41,730 D	42.6%	56.8%	42.8%	57.2%
AL	1978	220,348	147,746	ANDREWS, MARK	68,016	HAGEN, BRUCE	4,586	79,730 R	67.1%	30.9%	68.5%	31.5%
AL	1976	289,881	181,018	ANDREWS, MARK	104,263	OMDAHL, LLOYD B.	4,600	76,755 R	62.4%	36.0%	63.5%	36.5%
AL	1974	233,688	130,184	ANDREWS, MARK	103,504	DORGAN, BYRON L.		26,680 R	55.7%	44.3%	55.7%	44.3%
AL	1972	268,721	195,360	ANDREWS, MARK	72,850	ISTA, RICHARD	511	122,510 R	72.7%	27.1%	72.8%	27.2%

NORTH DAKOTA

1990 GENERAL ELECTION

Congress   Other vote at-large was scattered write-in.

1990 PRIMARIES

JUNE 12 REPUBLICAN

Congress   Contested as follows:

AL   35,749 Edward T. Schafer; 5,912 Avone Kukla.

JUNE 12 DEMOCRATIC

Congress   Contested as follows:

AL   60,359 Byron L. Dorgan; 4,244 Gerald W. Kopp.

346

OHIO

GOVERNOR
George Voinovich (R). Elected 1990 to a four-year term.

SENATORS
John H. Glenn (D). Re-elected 1986 to a six-year term. Previously elected 1980, 1974.

Howard Metzenbaum (D). Re-elected 1988 to a six-year term. Previously elected 1982, 1976.

REPRESENTATIVES

1. Charles Luken (D)
2. Willis D. Gradison (R)
3. Tony P. Hall (D)
4. Michael G. Oxley (R)
5. Paul E. Gillmor (R)
6. Bob McEwen (R)
7. David L. Hobson (R)
8. John A. Boehner (R)
9. Marcy Kaptur (D)
10. Clarence E. Miller (R)
11. Dennis E. Eckart (D)
12. John R. Kasich (R)
13. Donald J. Pease (D)
14. Thomas C. Sawyer (D)
15. Chalmers P. Wylie (R)
16. Ralph S. Regula (R)
17. James A. Traficant (D)
18. Douglas Applegate (D)
19. Edward F. Feighan (D)
20. Mary Rose Oakar (D)
21. Louis Stokes (D)

POSTWAR VOTE FOR PRESIDENT

Year	Total Vote	Republican Vote	Candidate	Democratic Vote	Candidate	Other Vote	Plurality	Rep.	Dem.	Rep.	Dem.
1988	4,393,699	2,416,549	Bush, George	1,939,629	Dukakis, Michael S.	37,521	476,920 R	55.0%	44.1%	55.5%	44.5%
1984	4,547,619	2,678,560	Reagan, Ronald	1,825,440	Mondale, Walter F.	43,619	853,120 R	58.9%	40.1%	59.5%	40.5%
1980	4,283,603	2,206,545	Reagan, Ronald	1,752,414	Carter, Jimmy	324,644	454,131 R	51.5%	40.9%	55.7%	44.3%
1976	4,111,873	2,000,505	Ford, Gerald R.	2,011,621	Carter, Jimmy	99,747	11,116 D	48.7%	48.9%	49.9%	50.1%
1972	4,094,787	2,441,827	Nixon, Richard M.	1,558,889	McGovern, George S.	94,071	882,938 R	59.6%	38.1%	61.0%	39.0%
1968	3,959,698	1,791,014	Nixon, Richard M.	1,700,586	Humphrey, Hubert H.	468,098	90,428 R	45.2%	42.9%	51.3%	48.7%
1964	3,969,196	1,470,865	Goldwater, Barry M.	2,498,331	Johnson, Lyndon B.		1,027,466 D	37.1%	62.9%	37.1%	62.9%
1960	4,161,859	2,217,611	Nixon, Richard M.	1,944,248	Kennedy, John F.		273,363 R	53.3%	46.7%	53.3%	46.7%
1956	3,702,265	2,262,610	Eisenhower, Dwight D.	1,439,655	Stevenson, Adlai E.		822,955 R	61.1%	38.9%	61.1%	38.9%
1952	3,700,758	2,100,391	Eisenhower, Dwight D.	1,600,367	Stevenson, Adlai E.		500,024 R	56.8%	43.2%	56.8%	43.2%
1948	2,936,071	1,445,684	Dewey, Thomas E.	1,452,791	Truman, Harry S.	37,596	7,107 D	49.2%	49.5%	49.9%	50.1%

OHIO

POSTWAR VOTE FOR GOVERNOR

Year	Total Vote	Republican Vote	Candidate	Democratic Vote	Candidate	Other Vote	Rep-Dem. Plurality	Percentage Total Vote Rep.	Dem.	Major Vote Rep.	Dem.
1990	3,477,650	1,938,103	Voinovich, George	1,539,416	Celebrezze, Anthony J.	131	398,687 R	55.7%	44.3%	55.7%	44.3%
1986	3,066,611	1,207,264	Rhodes, James A.	1,858,372	Celeste, Richard F.	975	651,108 D	39.4%	60.6%	39.4%	60.6%
1982	3,356,721	1,303,962	Brown, Clarence, Jr.	1,981,882	Celeste, Richard F.	70,877	677,920 D	38.8%	59.0%	39.7%	60.3%
1978	2,843,351	1,402,167	Rhodes, James A.	1,354,631	Celeste, Richard F.	86,553	47,536 R	49.3%	47.6%	50.9%	49.1%
1974	3,072,010	1,493,679	Rhodes, James A.	1,482,191	Gilligan, John J.	96,140	11,488 R	48.6%	48.2%	50.2%	49.8%
1970	3,184,133	1,382,659	Cloud, Roger	1,725,560	Gilligan, John J.	75,914	342,901 D	43.4%	54.2%	44.5%	55.5%
1966	2,887,331	1,795,277	Rhodes, James A.	1,092,054	Reams, Frazier, Jr.		703,223 R	62.2%	37.8%	62.2%	37.8%
1962	3,116,711	1,836,190	Rhodes, James A.	1,280,521	DiSalle, Michael V.		555,669 R	58.9%	41.1%	58.9%	41.1%
1958 **	3,284,134	1,414,874	O'Neill, C. William	1,869,260	DiSalle, Michael V.		454,386 D	43.1%	56.9%	43.1%	56.9%
1956	3,542,091	1,984,988	O'Neill, C. William	1,557,103	DiSalle, Michael V.		427,885 R	56.0%	44.0%	56.0%	44.0%
1954	2,597,790	1,192,528	Rhodes, James A.	1,405,262	Lausche, Frank J.		212,734 D	45.9%	54.1%	45.9%	54.1%
1952	3,605,168	1,590,058	Taft, Charles P.	2,015,110	Lausche, Frank J.		425,052 D	44.1%	55.9%	44.1%	55.9%
1950	2,892,819	1,370,570	Ebright, Don H.	1,522,249	Lausche, Frank J.		151,679 D	47.4%	52.6%	47.4%	52.6%
1948	3,018,289	1,398,514	Herbert, Thomas J.	1,619,775	Lausche, Frank J.		221,261 D	46.3%	53.7%	46.3%	53.7%
1946	2,303,750	1,166,550	Herbert, Thomas J.	1,125,997	Lausche, Frank J.	11,203	40,553 R	50.6%	48.9%	50.9%	49.1%

The term of office of Ohio's Governor was increased from two to four years effective with the 1958 election.

POSTWAR VOTE FOR SENATOR

Year	Total Vote	Republican Vote	Candidate	Democratic Vote	Candidate	Other Vote	Rep-Dem. Plurality	Percentage Total Vote Rep.	Dem.	Major Vote Rep.	Dem.
1988	4,352,905	1,872,716	Voinovich, George	2,480,038	Metzenbaum, Howard	151	607,322 D	43.0%	57.0%	43.0%	57.0%
1986	3,121,189	1,171,893	Kindness, Thomas N.	1,949,208	Glenn, John H.	88	777,315 D	37.5%	62.5%	37.5%	62.5%
1982	3,395,463	1,396,790	Pfeifer, Paul E.	1,923,767	Metzenbaum, Howard	74,906	526,977 D	41.1%	56.7%	42.1%	57.9%
1980	4,027,303	1,137,695	Betts, James E.	2,770,786	Glenn, John H.	118,822	1,633,091 D	28.2%	68.8%	29.1%	70.9%
1976	3,920,613	1,823,774	Taft, Robert A.,Jr.	1,941,113	Metzenbaum, Howard	155,726	117,339 D	46.5%	49.5%	48.4%	51.6%
1974	2,987,951	918,133	Perk, Ralph J.	1,930,670	Glenn, John H.	139,148	1,012,537 D	30.7%	64.6%	32.2%	67.8%
1970	3,151,274	1,565,682	Taft, Robert A.,Jr.	1,495,262	Metzenbaum, Howard	90,330	70,420 R	49.7%	47.4%	51.2%	48.8%
1968	3,743,121	1,928,964	Saxbe, William B.	1,814,152	Gilligan, John J.	5	114,812 R	51.5%	48.5%	51.5%	48.5%
1964	3,830,389	1,906,781	Taft, Robert A.,Jr.	1,923,608	Young, Stephen M.		16,827 D	49.8%	50.2%	49.8%	50.2%
1962	2,994,986	1,151,173	Briley, John M.	1,843,813	Lausche, Frank J.		692,640 D	38.4%	61.6%	38.4%	61.6%
1958	3,149,410	1,497,199	Bricker, John W.	1,652,211	Young, Stephen M.		155,012 D	47.5%	52.5%	47.5%	52.5%
1956	3,525,499	1,660,910	Bender, George H.	1,864,589	Lausche, Frank J.		203,679 D	47.1%	52.9%	47.1%	52.9%
1954 S	2,512,778	1,257,874	Bender, George H.	1,254,904	Burke, Thomas A.		2,970 R	50.1%	49.9%	50.1%	49.9%
1952	3,442,291	1,878,961	Bricker, John W.	1,563,330	DiSalle, Michael V.		315,631 R	54.6%	45.4%	54.6%	45.4%
1950	2,860,102	1,645,643	Taft, Robert A.	1,214,459	Ferguson, Joseph T.		431,184 R	57.5%	42.5%	57.5%	42.5%
1946	2,237,269	1,275,774	Bricker, John W.	947,610	Huffman, James W.	13,885	328,164 R	57.0%	42.4%	57.4%	42.6%

The 1954 election was for a short term to fill a vacancy.

OHIO

Districts Established July 12, 1985

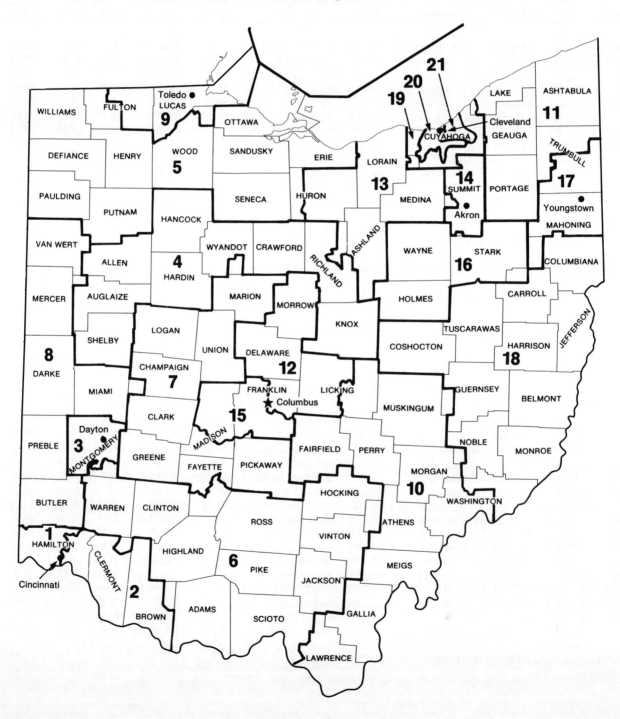

OHIO

GOVERNOR 1990

1990 Census Population	County	Total Vote	Republican	Democratic	Other	Rep.-Dem. Plurality	Percentage			
							Total Vote		Major Vote	
							Rep.	Dem.	Rep.	Dem.
25,371	ADAMS	8,375	4,754	3,621		1,133 R	56.8%	43.2%	56.8%	43.2%
109,755	ALLEN	35,559	23,095	12,464		10,631 R	64.9%	35.1%	64.9%	35.1%
47,507	ASHLAND	15,701	10,369	5,332		5,037 R	66.0%	34.0%	66.0%	34.0%
99,821	ASHTABULA	32,388	16,761	15,627		1,134 R	51.8%	48.2%	51.8%	48.2%
59,549	ATHENS	15,893	7,250	8,642	1	1,392 D	45.6%	54.4%	45.6%	54.4%
44,585	AUGLAIZE	14,718	9,800	4,918		4,882 R	66.6%	33.4%	66.6%	33.4%
71,074	BELMONT	24,820	9,611	15,209		5,598 D	38.7%	61.3%	38.7%	61.3%
34,966	BROWN	10,606	5,624	4,981	1	643 R	53.0%	47.0%	53.0%	47.0%
291,479	BUTLER	79,556	50,951	28,605		22,346 R	64.0%	36.0%	64.0%	36.0%
26,521	CARROLL	8,985	4,883	4,102		781 R	54.3%	45.7%	54.3%	45.7%
36,019	CHAMPAIGN	11,072	7,359	3,712	1	3,647 R	66.5%	33.5%	66.5%	33.5%
147,548	CLARK	43,812	25,819	17,990	3	7,829 R	58.9%	41.1%	58.9%	41.1%
150,187	CLERMONT	36,696	23,414	13,280	2	10,134 R	63.8%	36.2%	63.8%	36.2%
35,415	CLINTON	10,118	6,802	3,316		3,486 R	67.2%	32.8%	67.2%	32.8%
108,276	COLUMBIANA	35,272	18,283	16,989		1,294 R	51.8%	48.2%	51.8%	48.2%
35,427	COSHOCTON	11,529	6,055	5,474		581 R	52.5%	47.5%	52.5%	47.5%
47,870	CRAWFORD	15,527	9,645	5,881	1	3,764 R	62.1%	37.9%	62.1%	37.9%
1,412,140	CUYAHOGA	480,712	244,192	236,511	9	7,681 R	50.8%	49.2%	50.8%	49.2%
53,619	DARKE	17,535	11,074	6,461		4,613 R	63.2%	36.8%	63.2%	36.8%
39,350	DEFIANCE	12,974	7,826	5,148		2,678 R	60.3%	39.7%	60.3%	39.7%
66,929	DELAWARE	25,397	16,591	8,803	3	7,788 R	65.3%	34.7%	65.3%	34.7%
76,779	ERIE	24,483	13,711	10,772		2,939 R	56.0%	44.0%	56.0%	44.0%
103,461	FAIRFIELD	34,910	20,290	14,618	2	5,672 R	58.1%	41.9%	58.1%	41.9%
27,466	FAYETTE	6,613	4,286	2,327		1,959 R	64.8%	35.2%	64.8%	35.2%
961,437	FRANKLIN	293,860	158,907	134,941	12	23,966 R	54.1%	45.9%	54.1%	45.9%
38,498	FULTON	12,016	7,713	4,302	1	3,411 R	64.2%	35.8%	64.2%	35.8%
30,954	GALLIA	10,842	6,040	4,802		1,238 R	55.7%	44.3%	55.7%	44.3%
81,129	GEAUGA	28,181	19,686	8,495		11,191 R	69.9%	30.1%	69.9%	30.1%
136,731	GREENE	44,025	29,420	14,601	4	14,819 R	66.8%	33.2%	66.8%	33.2%
39,024	GUERNSEY	12,152	6,758	5,393	1	1,365 R	55.6%	44.4%	55.6%	44.4%
866,228	HAMILTON	279,862	167,288	112,569	5	54,719 R	59.8%	40.2%	59.8%	40.2%
65,536	HANCOCK	22,014	14,928	7,086		7,842 R	67.8%	32.2%	67.8%	32.2%
31,111	HARDIN	9,857	5,668	4,189		1,479 R	57.5%	42.5%	57.5%	42.5%
16,085	HARRISON	6,245	2,739	3,506		767 D	43.9%	56.1%	43.9%	56.1%
29,108	HENRY	9,825	6,383	3,442		2,941 R	65.0%	35.0%	65.0%	35.0%
35,728	HIGHLAND	11,285	6,796	4,489		2,307 R	60.2%	39.8%	60.2%	39.8%
25,533	HOCKING	7,704	3,788	3,916		128 D	49.2%	50.8%	49.2%	50.8%
32,849	HOLMES	6,170	4,122	2,048		2,074 R	66.8%	33.2%	66.8%	33.2%
56,240	HURON	17,609	11,156	6,453		4,703 R	63.4%	36.6%	63.4%	36.6%
30,230	JACKSON	9,457	5,029	4,428		601 R	53.2%	46.8%	53.2%	46.8%
80,298	JEFFERSON	29,423	12,388	17,035		4,647 D	42.1%	57.9%	42.1%	57.9%
47,473	KNOX	16,073	8,689	7,384		1,305 R	54.1%	45.9%	54.1%	45.9%
215,499	LAKE	73,110	45,847	27,263		18,584 R	62.7%	37.3%	62.7%	37.3%
61,834	LAWRENCE	18,334	9,323	9,011		312 R	50.9%	49.1%	50.9%	49.1%
128,300	LICKING	43,105	22,575	20,530		2,045 R	52.4%	47.6%	52.4%	47.6%
42,310	LOGAN	12,844	8,830	4,014		4,816 R	68.7%	31.3%	68.7%	31.3%
271,126	LORAIN	87,003	46,514	40,488	1	6,026 R	53.5%	46.5%	53.5%	46.5%
462,361	LUCAS	139,247	68,228	71,015	4	2,787 D	49.0%	51.0%	49.0%	51.0%
37,068	MADISON	9,876	6,227	3,649		2,578 R	63.1%	36.9%	63.1%	36.9%
264,806	MAHONING	96,689	41,162	55,495	32	14,333 D	42.6%	57.4%	42.6%	57.4%
64,274	MARION	20,277	11,894	8,383		3,511 R	58.7%	41.3%	58.7%	41.3%
122,354	MEDINA	40,768	26,195	14,573		11,622 R	64.3%	35.7%	64.3%	35.7%
22,987	MEIGS	7,776	4,377	3,399		978 R	56.3%	43.7%	56.3%	43.7%
39,443	MERCER	13,826	9,122	4,704		4,418 R	66.0%	34.0%	66.0%	34.0%
93,182	MIAMI	29,731	19,054	10,677		8,377 R	64.1%	35.9%	64.1%	35.9%
15,497	MONROE	6,018	2,313	3,704	1	1,391 D	38.4%	61.5%	38.4%	61.6%
573,809	MONTGOMERY	165,375	90,638	74,722	15	15,916 R	54.8%	45.2%	54.8%	45.2%
14,194	MORGAN	5,308	3,034	2,274		760 R	57.2%	42.8%	57.2%	42.8%
27,749	MORROW	8,976	5,196	3,780		1,416 R	57.9%	42.1%	57.9%	42.1%
82,068	MUSKINGUM	25,684	13,279	12,404	1	875 R	51.7%	48.3%	51.7%	48.3%

OHIO

GOVERNOR 1990

1990 Census Population	County	Total Vote	Republican	Democratic	Other	Rep.-Dem. Plurality	Percentage Total Vote Rep.	Dem.	Major Vote Rep.	Dem.
11,336	NOBLE	4,895	2,630	2,265		365 R	53.7%	46.3%	53.7%	46.3%
40,029	OTTAWA	13,785	7,516	6,269		1,247 R	54.5%	45.5%	54.5%	45.5%
20,488	PAULDING	6,966	4,068	2,898		1,170 R	58.4%	41.6%	58.4%	41.6%
31,557	PERRY	10,097	4,805	5,292		487 D	47.6%	52.4%	47.6%	52.4%
48,255	PICKAWAY	13,122	7,698	5,423	1	2,275 R	58.7%	41.3%	58.7%	41.3%
24,249	PIKE	8,084	3,592	4,492		900 D	44.4%	55.6%	44.4%	55.6%
142,585	PORTAGE	43,225	23,631	19,586	8	4,045 R	54.7%	45.3%	54.7%	45.3%
40,113	PREBLE	12,773	7,740	5,031	2	2,709 R	60.6%	39.4%	60.6%	39.4%
33,819	PUTNAM	12,776	8,763	4,013		4,750 R	68.6%	31.4%	68.6%	31.4%
126,137	RICHLAND	42,704	26,152	16,550	2	9,602 R	61.2%	38.8%	61.2%	38.8%
69,330	ROSS	19,631	10,454	9,177		1,277 R	53.3%	46.7%	53.3%	46.7%
61,963	SANDUSKY	19,969	11,572	8,397		3,175 R	57.9%	42.1%	57.9%	42.1%
80,327	SCIOTO	24,033	11,612	12,420	1	808 D	48.3%	51.7%	48.3%	51.7%
59,733	SENECA	18,817	11,280	7,537		3,743 R	59.9%	40.1%	59.9%	40.1%
44,915	SHELBY	14,463	9,338	5,125		4,213 R	64.6%	35.4%	64.6%	35.4%
367,585	STARK	132,071	76,921	55,150		21,771 R	58.2%	41.8%	58.2%	41.8%
514,990	SUMMIT	171,458	93,480	77,972	6	15,508 R	54.5%	45.5%	54.5%	45.5%
227,813	TRUMBULL	78,429	33,135	45,294		12,159 D	42.2%	57.8%	42.2%	57.8%
84,090	TUSCARAWAS	27,031	13,993	13,036	2	957 R	51.8%	48.2%	51.8%	48.2%
31,969	UNION	10,084	6,636	3,448		3,188 R	65.8%	34.2%	65.8%	34.2%
30,464	VAN WERT	10,009	6,682	3,327		3,355 R	66.8%	33.2%	66.8%	33.2%
11,098	VINTON	3,914	1,863	2,051		188 D	47.6%	52.4%	47.6%	52.4%
113,909	WARREN	31,161	21,299	9,861	1	11,438 R	68.4%	31.6%	68.4%	31.6%
62,254	WASHINGTON	18,448	10,400	8,048		2,352 R	56.4%	43.6%	56.4%	43.6%
101,461	WAYNE	30,235	19,665	10,564	6	9,101 R	65.0%	34.9%	65.1%	34.9%
36,956	WILLIAMS	11,349	7,398	3,951		3,447 R	65.2%	34.8%	65.2%	34.8%
113,269	WOOD	36,261	20,971	15,288	2	5,683 R	57.8%	42.2%	57.8%	42.2%
22,254	WYANDOT	8,062	5,058	3,004		2,054 R	62.7%	37.3%	62.7%	37.3%
10,847,115	TOTAL	3,477,650	1,938,103	1,539,416	131	398,687 R	55.7%	44.3%	55.7%	44.3%

OHIO

CONGRESS

CD	Year	Total Vote	Republican Vote	Candidate	Democratic Vote	Candidate	Other Vote	Rep.-Dem. Plurality	Total Vote Rep.	Total Vote Dem.	Major Vote Rep.	Major Vote Dem.
1	1990	164,294	80,362	BLACKWELL, J. KENNETH	83,932	LUKEN, CHARLES		3,570 D	48.9%	51.1%	48.9%	51.1%
1	1988	208,420	90,738	CHABOT, STEVE	117,682	LUKEN, THOMAS A.		26,944 D	43.5%	56.5%	43.5%	56.5%
1	1986	146,577	56,100	MORR, FRED E.	90,477	LUKEN, THOMAS A.		34,377 D	38.3%	61.7%	38.3%	61.7%
2	1990	161,162	103,817	GRADISON, WILLIS D.	57,345	YATES, TYRONE K.		46,472 R	64.4%	35.6%	64.4%	35.6%
2	1988	211,799	153,162	GRADISON, WILLIS D.	58,637	STIDHAM, CHUCK R.		94,525 R	72.3%	27.7%	72.3%	27.7%
2	1986	148,509	105,061	GRADISON, WILLIS D.	43,448	STINEMAN, WILLIAM F.		61,613 R	70.7%	29.3%	70.7%	29.3%
3	1990	116,797			116,797	HALL, TONY P.		116,797 D		100.0%		100.0%
3	1988	184,617	42,664	CRUTCHER, RON	141,953	HALL, TONY P.		99,289 D	23.1%	76.9%	23.1%	76.9%
3	1986	133,478	35,167	CRUTCHER, RON	98,311	HALL, TONY P.		63,144 D	26.3%	73.7%	26.3%	73.7%
4	1990	168,364	103,897	OXLEY, MICHAEL G.	64,467	BURKHART, THOMAS E.		39,430 R	61.7%	38.3%	61.7%	38.3%
4	1988	160,637	160,099	OXLEY, MICHAEL G.			538	160,099 R	99.7%		100.0%	
4	1986	154,068	115,751	OXLEY, MICHAEL G.	26,320	CRATTY, CLEM	11,997	89,431 R	75.1%	17.1%	81.5%	18.5%
5	1990	165,920	113,615	GILLMOR, PAUL E.	41,693	MANGE, P. SCOTT	10,612	71,922 R	68.5%	25.1%	73.2%	26.8%
5	1988	204,130	123,838	GILLMOR, PAUL E.	80,292	MURRAY, TOM		43,546 R	60.7%	39.3%	60.7%	39.3%
5	1986	156,880	102,016	LATTA, DELBERT L.	54,864	MURRAY, TOM		47,152 R	65.0%	35.0%	65.0%	35.0%
6	1990	164,635	117,220	MCEWEN, BOB	47,415	MITCHELL, RAYMOND J.		69,805 R	71.2%	28.8%	71.2%	28.8%
6	1988	204,870	152,235	MCEWEN, BOB	52,635	ROBERTS, GORDON		99,600 R	74.3%	25.7%	74.3%	25.7%
6	1986	151,338	106,354	MCEWEN, BOB	42,155	ROBERTS, GORDON	2,829	64,199 R	70.3%	27.9%	71.6%	28.4%
7	1990	156,472	97,123	HOBSON, DAVID L.	59,349	SCHIRA, JACK		37,774 R	62.1%	37.9%	62.1%	37.9%
7	1988	193,020	142,597	DEWINE, MICHAEL	50,423	SCHIRA, JACK		92,174 R	73.9%	26.1%	73.9%	26.1%
7	1986	119,238	119,238	DEWINE, MICHAEL				119,238 R	100.0%		100.0%	
8	1990	163,539	99,955	BOEHNER, JOHN A.	63,584	JOLIVETTE, GREGORY V.		36,371 R	61.1%	38.9%	61.1%	38.9%
8	1988	203,248	154,164	LUKENS, DONALD E.	49,084	GRIFFIN, JOHN W.		105,080 R	75.9%	24.1%	75.9%	24.1%
8	1986	144,670	98,475	LUKENS, DONALD E.	46,195	GRIFFIN, JOHN W.		52,280 R	68.1%	31.9%	68.1%	31.9%
9	1990	151,472	33,791	LAMMERS, JERRY D.	117,681	KAPTUR, MARCY		83,890 D	22.3%	77.7%	22.3%	77.7%
9	1988	193,812	36,183	HAWKINS, AL	157,557	KAPTUR, MARCY	72	121,374 D	18.7%	81.3%	18.7%	81.3%
9	1986	136,289	30,643	SHUFELDT, MIKE	105,646	KAPTUR, MARCY		75,003 D	22.5%	77.5%	22.5%	77.5%
10	1990	167,665	106,009	MILLER, CLARENCE E.	61,656	BUCHANAN, JOHN M.		44,353 R	63.2%	36.8%	63.2%	36.8%
10	1988	200,566	143,673	MILLER, CLARENCE E.	56,893	BUCHANAN, JOHN M.		86,780 R	71.6%	28.4%	71.6%	28.4%
10	1986	151,717	106,870	MILLER, CLARENCE E.	44,847	BUCHANAN, JOHN M.		62,023 R	70.4%	29.6%	70.4%	29.6%
11	1990	170,305	58,372	MUELLER, MARGARET R.	111,923	ECKART, DENNIS E.	10	53,551 D	34.3%	65.7%	34.3%	65.7%
11	1988	202,628	78,028	MUELLER, MARGARET R.	124,600	ECKART, DENNIS E.		46,572 D	38.5%	61.5%	38.5%	61.5%
11	1986	144,568	35,944	MUELLER, MARGARET R.	104,740	ECKART, DENNIS E.	3,884	68,796 D	24.9%	72.5%	25.5%	74.5%
12	1990	181,279	130,495	KASICH, JOHN R.	50,784	GELPI, MIKE		79,711 R	72.0%	28.0%	72.0%	28.0%
12	1988	195,905	154,727	KASICH, JOHN R.	41,178	BROWN, MARK P.		113,549 R	79.0%	21.0%	79.0%	21.0%
12	1986	160,632	117,905	KASICH, JOHN R.	42,727	JOCHIM, TIMOTHY C.		75,178 R	73.4%	26.6%	73.4%	26.6%
13	1990	164,862	60,925	NIELSEN, WILLIAM D.	93,431	PEASE, DONALD J.	10,506	32,506 D	37.0%	56.7%	39.5%	60.5%
13	1988	196,361	59,287	BROWN, DWIGHT	137,074	PEASE, DONALD J.		77,787 D	30.2%	69.8%	30.2%	69.8%
13	1986	141,064	52,452	NIELSEN, WILLIAM D.	88,612	PEASE, DONALD J.		36,160 D	37.2%	62.8%	37.2%	62.8%
14	1990	164,335	66,460	BENDER, JEAN E.	97,875	SAWYER, THOMAS C.		31,415 D	40.4%	59.6%	40.4%	59.6%
14	1988	199,307	50,356	LANG, LORETTA A.	148,951	SAWYER, THOMAS C.		98,595 D	25.3%	74.7%	25.3%	74.7%
14	1986	154,970	71,713	SLABY, LYNN	83,257	SAWYER, THOMAS C.		11,544 D	46.3%	53.7%	46.3%	53.7%
15	1990	167,919	99,251	WYLIE, CHALMERS P.	68,510	ERNEY, THOMAS V.	158	30,741 R	59.1%	40.8%	59.2%	40.8%
15	1988	196,295	146,854	WYLIE, CHALMERS P.	49,441	FROEHLICH, MARK S.		97,413 R	74.8%	25.2%	74.8%	25.2%
15	1986	153,495	97,745	WYLIE, CHALMERS P.	55,750	JACKSON, DAVID L.		41,995 R	63.7%	36.3%	63.7%	36.3%

OHIO

CONGRESS

CD	Year	Total Vote	Republican Vote	Candidate	Democratic Vote	Candidate	Other Vote	Rep.-Dem. Plurality	Total Vote Rep.	Dem.	Major Vote Rep.	Dem.
16	1990	171,613	101,097	REGULA, RALPH S.	70,516	MENDENHALL, WARNER D.		30,581 R	58.9%	41.1%	58.9%	41.1%
16	1988	202,180	158,824	REGULA, RALPH S.	43,356	GRAVELY, MELVIN J.		115,468 R	78.6%	21.4%	78.6%	21.4%
16	1986	154,845	118,206	REGULA, RALPH S.	36,639	KENNICK, WILLIAM J.		81,567 R	76.3%	23.7%	76.3%	23.7%
17	1990	171,406	38,199	DEJULIO, ROBERT R.	133,207	TRAFICANT, JAMES A.		95,008 D	22.3%	77.7%	22.3%	77.7%
17	1988	210,455	47,929	LENZ, FREDERICK W.	162,526	TRAFICANT, JAMES A.		114,597 D	22.8%	77.2%	22.8%	77.2%
17	1986	156,189	43,334	FULKS, JAMES H.	112,855	TRAFICANT, JAMES A.		69,521 D	27.7%	72.3%	27.7%	72.3%
18	1990	162,605	41,823	HALES, JOHN A.	120,782	APPLEGATE, DOUGLAS		78,959 D	25.7%	74.3%	25.7%	74.3%
18	1988	197,436	46,130	ABRAHAM, WILLIAM C.	151,306	APPLEGATE, DOUGLAS		105,176 D	23.4%	76.6%	23.4%	76.6%
18	1986	126,526			126,526	APPLEGATE, DOUGLAS		126,526 D		100.0%		100.0%
19	1990	205,266	72,315	LAWKO, SUSAN M.	132,951	FEIGHAN, EDWARD F.		60,636 D	35.2%	64.8%	35.2%	64.8%
19	1988	238,424	70,359	ROBERTS, NOEL F.	168,065	FEIGHAN, EDWARD F.		97,706 D	29.5%	70.5%	29.5%	70.5%
19	1986	178,557	80,743	SUHADOLNIK, GARY C.	97,814	FEIGHAN, EDWARD F.		17,071 D	45.2%	54.8%	45.2%	54.8%
20	1990	149,139	39,749	SMITH, BILL	109,390	OAKAR, MARY ROSE		69,641 D	26.7%	73.3%	26.7%	73.3%
20	1988	177,659	30,944	SAJNA, MICHAEL	146,715	OAKAR, MARY ROSE		115,771 D	17.4%	82.6%	17.4%	82.6%
20	1986	130,770	19,794	SMITH, BILL	110,976	OAKAR, MARY ROSE		91,182 D	15.1%	84.9%	15.1%	84.9%
21	1990	129,249	25,906	ROSKI, FRANKLIN H.	103,338	STOKES, LOUIS	5	77,432 D	20.0%	80.0%	20.0%	80.0%
21	1988	173,192	24,804	ROSKI, FRANKLIN H.	148,388	STOKES, LOUIS		123,584 D	14.3%	85.7%	14.3%	85.7%
21	1986	122,472	22,594	ROSKI, FRANKLIN H.	99,878	STOKES, LOUIS		77,284 D	18.4%	81.6%	18.4%	81.6%

OHIO

1990 GENERAL ELECTION

Governor   Other vote was 82 write-in (Marshall); 49 write-in (Attia).

Congress   Other vote was Independent (Jackson) in CD 5; write-in (Mononen) in CD 11; Independent (Ryan) in CD 13; write-in (Buckel) in CD 15; write-in (Ware) in CD 21.

1990 PRIMARIES

MAY 8 REPUBLICAN

Governor   George Voinovich, unopposed.

Congress   Unopposed in fourteen CD's. No candidate in CD 3. In CD 3, Mr. Wright received 100 write-in votes but did not qualify. Contested as follows:

CD 7   28,530 David L. Hobson; 7,516 Todd Gordon.
CD 8   25,071 John A. Boehner; 16,360 Thomas N. Kindness; 8,686 Donald E. Lukens; 719 Mort W. Meier.
CD 9   6,500 Jerry D. Lammers; 4,273 George L. Carpenter; 2,026 Ellsworth R. Fraley.
CD 14   10,624 Jean E. Bender; 9,549 William A. Fink.
CD 15   31,798 Chalmers P. Wylie; 8,863 Clifford Arnebeck.
CD 18   7,348 John A. Hales; 7,225 D. Randall Sells; 7,084 Charles L. Graber.

MAY 8 DEMOCRATIC

Governor   683,932 Anthony J. Celebrezze; 131,564 Michael H. Lord.

Congress   Unopposed in ten CD's. Contested as follows:

CD 4   14,956 Thomas E. Burkhart; 12,247 Tom Watkins.
CD 6   12,889 Raymond J. Mitchell; 9,374 Leon Bailey.
CD 7   17,570 Jack Schira; 5,786 Donald Scott; 2,788 Steve Tatone.
CD 8   13,174 Gregory V. Jolivette; 9,056 Harrt T. Wilks; 3,183 Ricky L. Mattox.
CD 12   14,107 Mike Gelpi; 9,041 Ralph A. Applegate; 2,603 Dennis Slaggy.
CD 14   34,343 Thomas C. Sawyer; 12,454 Lillian Ryan.
CD 16   18,201 Warner D. Mendenhall; 12,161 William J. Kennick; 8,291 Ernie Murphy.
CD 17   78,470 James A. Traficant; 3,466 Leonard A. Viselli; 3,436 Michael J. Metaxas.
CD 18   64,104 Douglas Applegate; 8,973 Donald K. Dickey.
CD 19   65,771 Edward F. Feighan; 11,813 Bruce L. Edwards.
CD 20   65,890 Mary Rose Oakar; 16,892 David Perry.

OKLAHOMA

GOVERNOR
David Walters (D). Elected 1990 to a four-year term.

SENATORS
David L. Boren (D). Re-elected 1990 to a six-year term. Previously elected 1984, 1978.

Don Nickles (R). Re-elected 1986 to a six-year term. Previously elected 1980.

REPRESENTATIVES
1. James M. Inhofe (R)
2. Mike Synar (D)
3. Bill Brewster (D)
4. Dave McCurdy (D)
5. M. H. Edwards (R)
6. Glenn English (D)

POSTWAR VOTE FOR PRESIDENT

Year	Total Vote	Republican Vote	Candidate	Democratic Vote	Candidate	Other Vote	Plurality	Total Vote Rep.	Dem.	Major Vote Rep.	Dem.
1988	1,171,036	678,367	Bush, George	483,423	Dukakis, Michael S.	9,246	194,944 R	57.9%	41.3%	58.4%	41.6%
1984	1,255,676	861,530	Reagan, Ronald	385,080	Mondale, Walter F.	9,066	476,450 R	68.6%	30.7%	69.1%	30.9%
1980	1,149,708	695,570	Reagan, Ronald	402,026	Carter, Jimmy	52,112	293,544 R	60.5%	35.0%	63.4%	36.6%
1976	1,092,251	545,708	Ford, Gerald R.	532,442	Carter, Jimmy	14,101	13,266 R	50.0%	48.7%	50.6%	49.4%
1972	1,029,900	759,025	Nixon, Richard M.	247,147	McGovern, George S.	23,728	511,878 R	73.7%	24.0%	75.4%	24.6%
1968	943,086	449,697	Nixon, Richard M.	301,658	Humphrey, Hubert H.	191,731	148,039 R	47.7%	32.0%	59.9%	40.1%
1964	932,499	412,665	Goldwater, Barry M.	519,834	Johnson, Lyndon B.		107,169 D	44.3%	55.7%	44.3%	55.7%
1960	903,150	533,039	Nixon, Richard M.	370,111	Kennedy, John F.		162,928 R	59.0%	41.0%	59.0%	41.0%
1956	859,350	473,769	Eisenhower, Dwight D.	385,581	Stevenson, Adlai E.		88,188 R	55.1%	44.9%	55.1%	44.9%
1952	948,984	518,045	Eisenhower, Dwight D.	430,939	Stevenson, Adlai E.		87,106 R	54.6%	45.4%	54.6%	45.4%
1948	721,599	268,817	Dewey, Thomas E.	452,782	Truman, Harry S.		183,965 D	37.3%	62.7%	37.3%	62.7%

POSTWAR VOTE FOR GOVERNOR

Year	Total Vote	Republican Vote	Candidate	Democratic Vote	Candidate	Other Vote	Rep-Dem. Plurality	Total Vote Rep.	Dem.	Major Vote Rep.	Dem.
1990	911,314	297,584	Price, Bill	523,196	Walters, David	90,534	225,612 D	32.7%	57.4%	36.3%	63.7%
1986	909,925	431,762	Bellmon, Henry	405,295	Walters, David	72,868	26,467 R	47.5%	44.5%	51.6%	48.4%
1982	883,130	332,207	Daxon, Tom	548,159	Nigh, George	2,764	215,952 D	37.6%	62.1%	37.7%	62.3%
1978	777,414	367,055	Shotts, Ron	402,240	Nigh, George	8,119	35,185 D	47.2%	51.7%	47.7%	52.3%
1974	804,848	290,459	Inhofe, James M.	514,389	Boren, David L.		223,930 D	36.1%	63.9%	36.1%	63.9%
1970	698,790	336,157	Bartlett, Dewey F.	338,338	Hall, David	24,295	2,181 D	48.1%	48.4%	49.8%	50.2%
1966	677,258	377,078	Bartlett, Dewey F.	296,328	Moore, Preston J.	3,852	80,750 R	55.7%	43.8%	56.0%	44.0%
1962	709,763	392,316	Bellmon, Henry	315,357	Atkinson, W. P.	2,090	76,959 R	55.3%	44.4%	55.4%	44.6%
1958	538,839	107,495	Ferguson, Phil	399,504	Edmondson, J. Howard	31,840	292,009 D	19.9%	74.1%	21.2%	78.8%
1954	609,194	251,808	Sparks, Reuben K.	357,386	Gary, Raymond		105,578 D	41.3%	58.7%	41.3%	58.7%
1950	644,276	313,205	Ferguson, Jo O.	329,308	Murray, Johnston	1,763	16,103 D	48.6%	51.1%	48.7%	51.3%
1946	494,599	227,426	Flynn, Olney F.	259,491	Turner, Roy J.	7,682	32,065 D	46.0%	52.5%	46.7%	53.3%

OKLAHOMA

POSTWAR VOTE FOR SENATOR

Year	Total Vote	Republican Vote	Candidate	Democratic Vote	Candidate	Other Vote	Rep-Dem. Plurality	Rep.	Dem.	Rep.	Dem.
1990	884,498	148,814	Jones, Stephen	735,684	Boren, David L.		586,870 D	16.8%	83.2%	16.8%	83.2%
1986	893,666	493,436	Nickles, Don	400,230	Jones, James R.		93,206 R	55.2%	44.8%	55.2%	44.8%
1984	1,197,937	280,638	Crozier, Will E.	906,131	Boren, David L.	11,168	625,493 D	23.4%	75.6%	23.6%	76.4%
1980	1,098,294	587,252	Nickles, Don	478,283	Coats, Andrew	32,759	108,969 R	53.5%	43.5%	55.1%	44.9%
1978	754,264	247,857	Kamm, Robert B.	493,953	Boren, David L.	12,454	246,096 D	32.9%	65.5%	33.4%	66.6%
1974	791,809	390,997	Bellmon, Henry	387,162	Edmondson, Ed	13,650	3,835 R	49.4%	48.9%	50.2%	49.8%
1972	1,005,148	516,934	Bartlett, Dewey F.	478,212	Edmondson, Ed	10,002	38,722 R	51.4%	47.6%	51.9%	48.1%
1968	909,119	470,120	Bellmon, Henry	419,658	Monroney, A. S. Mike	19,341	50,462 R	51.7%	46.2%	52.8%	47.2%
1966	638,742	295,585	Patterson, Pat J.	343,157	Harris, Fred R.		47,572 D	46.3%	53.7%	46.3%	53.7%
1964 S	912,174	445,392	Wilkinson, Bud	466,782	Harris, Fred R.		21,390 D	48.8%	51.2%	48.8%	51.2%
1962	664,712	307,966	Crawford, B. Hayden	353,890	Monroney, A. S. Mike	2,856	45,924 D	46.3%	53.2%	46.5%	53.5%
1960	864,475	385,646	Crawford, B. Hayden	474,116	Kerr, Robert S.	4,713	88,470 D	44.6%	54.8%	44.9%	55.1%
1956	831,142	371,146	McKeever, Douglas	459,996	Monroney, A. S. Mike		88,850 D	44.7%	55.3%	44.7%	55.3%
1954	600,120	262,013	Mock, Fred M.	335,127	Kerr, Robert S.	2,980	73,114 D	43.7%	55.8%	43.9%	56.1%
1950	631,177	285,224	Alexander, W. H.	345,953	Monroney, A. S. Mike		60,729 D	45.2%	54.8%	45.2%	54.8%
1948	708,931	265,169	Rizley, Ross	441,654	Kerr, Robert S.	2,108	176,485 D	37.4%	62.3%	37.5%	62.5%

The 1964 election was for a short term to fill a vacancy.

356

OKLAHOMA

Districts Established July 22, 1981

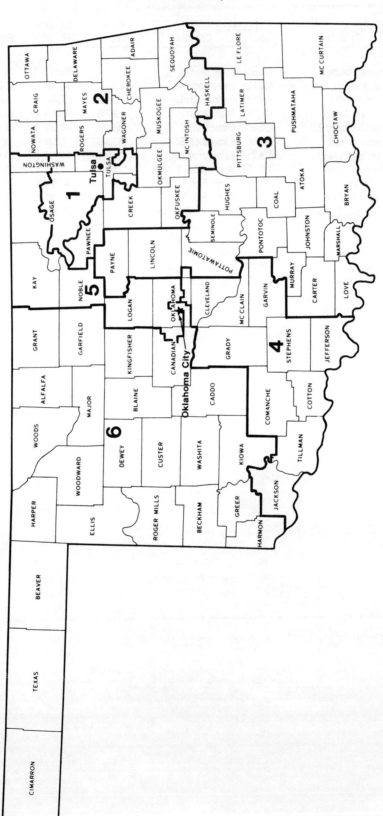

© ERC

OKLAHOMA

GOVERNOR 1990

1990 Census Population	County	Total Vote	Republican	Democratic	Other	Rep.-Dem. Plurality	Rep.	Dem.	Rep.	Dem.
18,421	ADAIR	3,994	1,168	2,512	314	1,344 D	29.2%	62.9%	31.7%	68.3%
6,416	ALFALFA	2,659	874	1,313	472	439 D	32.9%	49.4%	40.0%	60.0%
12,778	ATOKA	3,793	818	2,826	149	2,008 D	21.6%	74.5%	22.4%	77.6%
6,023	BEAVER	2,319	1,082	1,025	212	57 R	46.7%	44.2%	51.4%	48.6%
18,812	BECKHAM	5,661	1,321	4,041	299	2,720 D	23.3%	71.4%	24.6%	75.4%
11,470	BLAINE	4,509	1,262	2,517	730	1,255 D	28.0%	55.8%	33.4%	66.6%
32,089	BRYAN	8,058	1,969	5,805	284	3,836 D	24.4%	72.0%	25.3%	74.7%
29,550	CADDO	8,402	1,846	5,833	723	3,987 D	22.0%	69.4%	24.0%	76.0%
74,409	CANADIAN	21,584	8,721	10,200	2,663	1,479 D	40.4%	47.3%	46.1%	53.9%
42,919	CARTER	12,712	3,557	8,249	906	4,692 D	28.0%	64.9%	30.1%	69.9%
34,049	CHEROKEE	9,877	2,180	6,750	947	4,570 D	22.1%	68.3%	24.4%	75.6%
15,302	CHOCTAW	5,084	1,086	3,878	120	2,792 D	21.4%	76.3%	21.9%	78.1%
3,301	CIMARRON	1,406	635	683	88	48 D	45.2%	48.6%	48.2%	51.8%
174,253	CLEVELAND	46,786	16,802	24,222	5,762	7,420 D	35.9%	51.8%	41.0%	59.0%
5,780	COAL	2,181	429	1,621	131	1,192 D	19.7%	74.3%	20.9%	79.1%
111,486	COMANCHE	22,006	7,890	13,159	957	5,269 D	35.9%	59.8%	37.5%	62.5%
6,651	COTTON	2,355	524	1,777	54	1,253 D	22.3%	75.5%	22.8%	77.2%
14,104	CRAIG	4,380	1,161	2,862	357	1,701 D	26.5%	65.3%	28.9%	71.1%
60,915	CREEK	14,851	4,176	8,904	1,771	4,728 D	28.1%	60.0%	31.9%	68.1%
26,897	CUSTER	8,739	2,475	5,516	748	3,041 D	28.3%	63.1%	31.0%	69.0%
28,070	DELAWARE	7,388	2,132	4,581	675	2,449 D	28.9%	62.0%	31.8%	68.2%
5,551	DEWEY	2,411	637	1,459	315	822 D	26.4%	60.5%	30.4%	69.6%
4,497	ELLIS	1,981	623	1,078	280	455 D	31.4%	54.4%	36.6%	63.4%
56,735	GARFIELD	18,192	5,806	9,543	2,843	3,737 D	31.9%	52.5%	37.8%	62.2%
26,605	GARVIN	8,578	2,312	5,335	931	3,023 D	27.0%	62.2%	30.2%	69.8%
41,747	GRADY	12,418	3,817	7,387	1,214	3,570 D	30.7%	59.5%	34.1%	65.9%
5,689	GRANT	2,635	786	1,317	532	531 D	29.8%	50.0%	37.4%	62.6%
6,559	GREER	2,524	608	1,745	171	1,137 D	24.1%	69.1%	25.8%	74.2%
3,793	HARMON	1,471	300	1,116	55	816 D	20.4%	75.9%	21.2%	78.8%
4,063	HARPER	1,806	597	901	308	304 D	33.1%	49.9%	39.9%	60.1%
10,940	HASKELL	4,141	750	3,137	254	2,387 D	18.1%	75.8%	19.3%	80.7%
13,023	HUGHES	4,391	900	3,008	483	2,108 D	20.5%	68.5%	23.0%	77.0%
28,764	JACKSON	6,520	1,796	4,310	414	2,514 D	27.5%	66.1%	29.4%	70.6%
7,010	JEFFERSON	2,387	470	1,831	86	1,361 D	19.7%	76.7%	20.4%	79.6%
10,032	JOHNSTON	2,780	599	2,015	166	1,416 D	21.5%	72.5%	22.9%	77.1%
48,056	KAY	15,054	5,439	7,737	1,878	2,298 D	36.1%	51.4%	41.3%	58.7%
13,212	KINGFISHER	5,076	2,087	2,306	683	219 D	41.1%	45.4%	47.5%	52.5%
11,347	KIOWA	3,948	923	2,805	220	1,882 D	23.4%	71.0%	24.8%	75.2%
10,333	LATIMER	3,087	608	2,245	234	1,637 D	19.7%	72.7%	21.3%	78.7%
43,270	LE FLORE	11,517	2,622	8,602	293	5,980 D	22.8%	74.7%	23.4%	76.6%
29,216	LINCOLN	9,035	2,860	4,995	1,180	2,135 D	31.7%	55.3%	36.4%	63.6%
29,011	LOGAN	9,761	3,446	5,247	1,068	1,801 D	35.3%	53.8%	39.6%	60.4%
8,157	LOVE	2,418	471	1,804	143	1,333 D	19.5%	74.6%	20.7%	79.3%
22,795	MCCLAIN	7,397	2,177	4,389	831	2,212 D	29.4%	59.3%	33.2%	66.8%
33,433	MCCURTAIN	7,236	1,434	5,584	218	4,150 D	19.8%	77.2%	20.4%	79.6%
16,779	MCINTOSH	6,168	1,229	4,466	473	3,237 D	19.9%	72.4%	21.6%	78.4%
8,055	MAJOR	3,264	1,120	1,581	563	461 D	34.3%	48.4%	41.5%	58.5%
10,829	MARSHALL	4,026	930	2,880	216	1,950 D	23.1%	71.5%	24.4%	75.6%
33,366	MAYES	10,278	2,702	6,539	1,037	3,837 D	26.3%	63.6%	29.2%	70.8%
12,042	MURRAY	4,272	987	2,824	461	1,837 D	23.1%	66.1%	25.9%	74.1%
68,078	MUSKOGEE	17,742	4,526	11,525	1,691	6,999 D	25.5%	65.0%	28.2%	71.8%
11,045	NOBLE	4,250	1,417	2,144	689	727 D	33.3%	50.4%	39.8%	60.2%
9,992	NOWATA	3,252	920	1,996	336	1,076 D	28.3%	61.4%	31.6%	68.4%
11,551	OKFUSKEE	3,524	794	2,390	340	1,596 D	22.5%	67.8%	24.9%	75.1%
599,611	OKLAHOMA	170,772	69,514	85,019	16,239	15,505 D	40.7%	49.8%	45.0%	55.0%
36,490	OKMULGEE	10,435	2,432	6,811	1,192	4,379 D	23.3%	65.3%	26.3%	73.7%
41,645	OSAGE	11,377	2,829	7,249	1,299	4,420 D	24.9%	63.7%	28.1%	71.9%
30,561	OTTAWA	8,285	2,014	5,854	417	3,840 D	24.3%	70.7%	25.6%	74.4%
15,575	PAWNEE	4,695	1,372	2,703	620	1,331 D	29.2%	57.6%	33.7%	66.3%
61,507	PAYNE	17,944	5,803	9,921	2,220	4,118 D	32.3%	55.3%	36.9%	63.1%

OKLAHOMA

GOVERNOR 1990

1990 Census Population	County	Total Vote	Republican	Democratic	Other	Rep.-Dem. Plurality	Total Vote Rep.	Dem.	Major Vote Rep.	Dem.
40,581	PITTSBURG	12,718	3,010	8,797	911	5,787 D	23.7%	69.2%	25.5%	74.5%
34,119	PONTOTOC	10,885	3,605	5,785	1,495	2,180 D	33.1%	53.1%	38.4%	61.6%
58,760	POTTAWATOMIE	17,877	5,823	10,141	1,913	4,318 D	32.6%	56.7%	36.5%	63.5%
10,997	PUSHMATAHA	3,982	749	3,121	112	2,372 D	18.8%	78.4%	19.4%	80.6%
4,147	ROGER MILLS	1,970	459	1,304	207	845 D	23.3%	66.2%	26.0%	74.0%
55,170	ROGERS	16,653	5,075	9,517	2,061	4,442 D	30.5%	57.1%	34.8%	65.2%
25,412	SEMINOLE	8,019	2,135	5,157	727	3,022 D	26.6%	64.3%	29.3%	70.7%
33,828	SEQUOYAH	9,615	1,970	7,250	395	5,280 D	20.5%	75.4%	21.4%	78.6%
42,299	STEPHENS	14,247	4,784	8,556	907	3,772 D	33.6%	60.1%	35.9%	64.1%
16,419	TEXAS	4,942	2,585	2,063	294	522 R	52.3%	41.7%	55.6%	44.4%
10,384	TILLMAN	3,016	743	2,166	107	1,423 D	24.6%	71.8%	25.5%	74.5%
503,341	TULSA	137,843	49,403	72,730	15,710	23,327 D	35.8%	52.8%	40.5%	59.5%
47,883	WAGONER	12,617	3,911	7,334	1,372	3,423 D	31.0%	58.1%	34.8%	65.2%
48,066	WASHINGTON	16,198	6,419	8,072	1,707	1,653 D	39.6%	49.8%	44.3%	55.7%
11,441	WASHITA	4,332	800	3,175	357	2,375 D	18.5%	73.3%	20.1%	79.9%
9,103	WOODS	3,968	1,259	2,215	494	956 D	31.7%	55.8%	36.2%	63.8%
18,976	WOODWARD	6,640	2,089	3,741	810	1,652 D	31.5%	56.3%	35.8%	64.2%
3,145,585	TOTAL	911,314	297,584	523,196	90,534	225,612 D	32.7%	57.4%	36.3%	63.7%

OKLAHOMA

SENATOR 1990

1990 Census Population	County	Total Vote	Republican	Democratic	Other	Rep.-Dem. Plurality	Percentage Total Vote Rep.	Dem.	Major Vote Rep.	Dem.
18,421	ADAIR	3,833	735	3,098		2,363 D	19.2%	80.8%	19.2%	80.8%
6,416	ALFALFA	2,633	405	2,228		1,823 D	15.4%	84.6%	15.4%	84.6%
12,778	ATOKA	3,549	347	3,202		2,855 D	9.8%	90.2%	9.8%	90.2%
6,023	BEAVER	2,270	769	1,501		732 D	33.9%	66.1%	33.9%	66.1%
18,812	BECKHAM	5,545	685	4,860		4,175 D	12.4%	87.6%	12.4%	87.6%
11,470	BLAINE	4,457	828	3,629		2,801 D	18.6%	81.4%	18.6%	81.4%
32,089	BRYAN	7,654	913	6,741		5,828 D	11.9%	88.1%	11.9%	88.1%
29,550	CADDO	8,182	1,001	7,181		6,180 D	12.2%	87.8%	12.2%	87.8%
74,409	CANADIAN	21,126	4,383	16,743		12,360 D	20.7%	79.3%	20.7%	79.3%
42,919	CARTER	11,971	1,658	10,313		8,655 D	13.9%	86.1%	13.9%	86.1%
34,049	CHEROKEE	9,514	1,505	8,009		6,504 D	15.8%	84.2%	15.8%	84.2%
15,302	CHOCTAW	4,690	463	4,227		3,764 D	9.9%	90.1%	9.9%	90.1%
3,301	CIMARRON	1,334	386	948		562 D	28.9%	71.1%	28.9%	71.1%
174,253	CLEVELAND	45,619	8,964	36,655		27,691 D	19.6%	80.4%	19.6%	80.4%
5,780	COAL	2,034	186	1,848		1,662 D	9.1%	90.9%	9.1%	90.9%
111,486	COMANCHE	21,083	4,647	16,436		11,789 D	22.0%	78.0%	22.0%	78.0%
6,651	COTTON	2,212	275	1,937		1,662 D	12.4%	87.6%	12.4%	87.6%
14,104	CRAIG	4,232	561	3,671		3,110 D	13.3%	86.7%	13.3%	86.7%
60,915	CREEK	14,214	2,312	11,902		9,590 D	16.3%	83.7%	16.3%	83.7%
26,897	CUSTER	8,449	1,107	7,342		6,235 D	13.1%	86.9%	13.1%	86.9%
28,070	DELAWARE	7,129	1,521	5,608		4,087 D	21.3%	78.7%	21.3%	78.7%
5,551	DEWEY	2,352	299	2,053		1,754 D	12.7%	87.3%	12.7%	87.3%
4,497	ELLIS	1,916	366	1,550		1,184 D	19.1%	80.9%	19.1%	80.9%
56,735	GARFIELD	18,062	3,879	14,183		10,304 D	21.5%	78.5%	21.5%	78.5%
26,605	GARVIN	8,333	939	7,394		6,455 D	11.3%	88.7%	11.3%	88.7%
41,747	GRADY	12,048	1,893	10,155		8,262 D	15.7%	84.3%	15.7%	84.3%
5,689	GRANT	2,583	471	2,112		1,641 D	18.2%	81.8%	18.2%	81.8%
6,559	GREER	2,431	279	2,152		1,873 D	11.5%	88.5%	11.5%	88.5%
3,793	HARMON	1,437	90	1,347		1,257 D	6.3%	93.7%	6.3%	93.7%
4,063	HARPER	1,750	418	1,332		914 D	23.9%	76.1%	23.9%	76.1%
10,940	HASKELL	3,976	438	3,538		3,100 D	11.0%	89.0%	11.0%	89.0%
13,023	HUGHES	4,250	366	3,884		3,518 D	8.6%	91.4%	8.6%	91.4%
28,764	JACKSON	6,384	873	5,511		4,638 D	13.7%	86.3%	13.7%	86.3%
7,010	JEFFERSON	2,250	271	1,979		1,708 D	12.0%	88.0%	12.0%	88.0%
10,032	JOHNSTON	2,632	258	2,374		2,116 D	9.8%	90.2%	9.8%	90.2%
48,056	KAY	14,671	3,263	11,408		8,145 D	22.2%	77.8%	22.2%	77.8%
13,212	KINGFISHER	4,907	799	4,108		3,309 D	16.3%	83.7%	16.3%	83.7%
11,347	KIOWA	3,885	402	3,483		3,081 D	10.3%	89.7%	10.3%	89.7%
10,333	LATIMER	2,914	312	2,602		2,290 D	10.7%	89.3%	10.7%	89.3%
43,270	LE FLORE	10,845	1,361	9,484		8,123 D	12.5%	87.5%	12.5%	87.5%
29,216	LINCOLN	8,803	1,418	7,385		5,967 D	16.1%	83.9%	16.1%	83.9%
29,011	LOGAN	9,414	1,692	7,722		6,030 D	18.0%	82.0%	18.0%	82.0%
8,157	LOVE	2,273	240	2,033		1,793 D	10.6%	89.4%	10.6%	89.4%
22,795	MCCLAIN	7,107	1,096	6,011		4,915 D	15.4%	84.6%	15.4%	84.6%
33,433	MCCURTAIN	6,582	868	5,714		4,846 D	13.2%	86.8%	13.2%	86.8%
16,779	MCINTOSH	5,879	682	5,197		4,515 D	11.6%	88.4%	11.6%	88.4%
8,055	MAJOR	3,190	686	2,504		1,818 D	21.5%	78.5%	21.5%	78.5%
10,829	MARSHALL	3,783	382	3,401		3,019 D	10.1%	89.9%	10.1%	89.9%
33,366	MAYES	9,997	1,586	8,411		6,825 D	15.9%	84.1%	15.9%	84.1%
12,042	MURRAY	4,112	388	3,724		3,336 D	9.4%	90.6%	9.4%	90.6%
68,078	MUSKOGEE	17,038	2,414	14,624		12,210 D	14.2%	85.8%	14.2%	85.8%
11,045	NOBLE	4,118	673	3,445		2,772 D	16.3%	83.7%	16.3%	83.7%
9,992	NOWATA	3,119	568	2,551		1,983 D	18.2%	81.8%	18.2%	81.8%
11,551	OKFUSKEE	3,240	386	2,854		2,468 D	11.9%	88.1%	11.9%	88.1%
599,611	OKLAHOMA	167,219	31,076	136,143		105,067 D	18.6%	81.4%	18.6%	81.4%
36,490	OKMULGEE	10,002	1,194	8,808		7,614 D	11.9%	88.1%	11.9%	88.1%
41,645	OSAGE	10,963	1,511	9,452		7,941 D	13.8%	86.2%	13.8%	86.2%
30,561	OTTAWA	7,880	1,688	6,192		4,504 D	21.4%	78.6%	21.4%	78.6%
15,575	PAWNEE	4,533	769	3,764		2,995 D	17.0%	83.0%	17.0%	83.0%
61,507	PAYNE	17,698	3,011	14,687		11,676 D	17.0%	83.0%	17.0%	83.0%

OKLAHOMA

SENATOR 1990

1990 Census Population	County	Total Vote	Republican	Democratic	Other	Rep.-Dem. Plurality	Percentage Total Vote Rep.	Dem.	Major Vote Rep.	Dem.
40,581	PITTSBURG	12,296	1,546	10,750		9,204 D	12.6%	87.4%	12.6%	87.4%
34,119	PONTOTOC	10,529	997	9,532		8,535 D	9.5%	90.5%	9.5%	90.5%
58,760	POTTAWATOMIE	17,414	2,546	14,868		12,322 D	14.6%	85.4%	14.6%	85.4%
10,997	PUSHMATAHA	3,680	343	3,337		2,994 D	9.3%	90.7%	9.3%	90.7%
4,147	ROGER MILLS	1,903	261	1,642		1,381 D	13.7%	86.3%	13.7%	86.3%
55,170	ROGERS	16,033	2,700	13,333		10,633 D	16.8%	83.2%	16.8%	83.2%
25,412	SEMINOLE	7,916	863	7,053		6,190 D	10.9%	89.1%	10.9%	89.1%
33,828	SEQUOYAH	9,039	1,252	7,787		6,535 D	13.9%	86.1%	13.9%	86.1%
42,299	STEPHENS	13,796	1,972	11,824		9,852 D	14.3%	85.7%	14.3%	85.7%
16,419	TEXAS	4,766	1,571	3,195		1,624 D	33.0%	67.0%	33.0%	67.0%
10,384	TILLMAN	2,887	335	2,552		2,217 D	11.6%	88.4%	11.6%	88.4%
503,341	TULSA	135,232	23,426	111,806		88,380 D	17.3%	82.7%	17.3%	82.7%
47,883	WAGONER	12,186	2,147	10,039		7,892 D	17.6%	82.4%	17.6%	82.4%
48,066	WASHINGTON	16,043	3,702	12,341		8,639 D	23.1%	76.9%	23.1%	76.9%
11,441	WASHITA	4,143	513	3,630		3,117 D	12.4%	87.6%	12.4%	87.6%
9,103	WOODS	3,893	599	3,294		2,695 D	15.4%	84.6%	15.4%	84.6%
18,976	WOODWARD	6,436	1,085	5,351		4,266 D	16.9%	83.1%	16.9%	83.1%
3,145,585	TOTAL	884,498	148,814	735,684		586,870 D	16.8%	83.2%	16.8%	83.2%

OKLAHOMA

CONGRESS

CD	Year	Total Vote	Republican Vote	Candidate	Democratic Vote	Candidate	Other Vote	Rep.-Dem. Plurality	Total Vote Rep.	Total Vote Dem.	Major Vote Rep.	Major Vote Dem.
1	1990	135,139	75,618	INHOFE, JAMES M.	59,521	GLASSCO, KURT		16,097 R	56.0%	44.0%	56.0%	44.0%
1	1988	196,559	103,458	INHOFE, JAMES M.	93,101	GLASSCO, KURT		10,357 R	52.6%	47.4%	52.6%	47.4%
1	1986	144,037	78,919	INHOFE, JAMES M.	61,663	ALLISON, GARY D.	3,455	17,256 R	54.8%	42.8%	56.1%	43.9%
1	1984	218,093	103,098	KEATING, FRANK	113,919	JONES, JAMES R.	1,076	10,821 D	47.3%	52.2%	47.5%	52.5%
1	1982	141,083	64,704	FREEMAN, RICHARD C.	76,379	JONES, JAMES R.		11,675 D	45.9%	54.1%	45.9%	54.1%
2	1990	148,151	57,331	GORHAM, TERRY M.	90,820	SYNAR, MIKE		33,489 D	38.7%	61.3%	38.7%	61.3%
2	1988	209,668	73,659	PHILLIPS, IRA	136,009	SYNAR, MIKE		62,350 D	35.1%	64.9%	35.1%	64.9%
2	1986	156,338	41,795	RICE, GARY K.	114,543	SYNAR, MIKE		72,748 D	26.7%	73.3%	26.7%	73.3%
2	1984	200,013	51,889	RICE, GARY K.	148,124	SYNAR, MIKE		96,235 D	25.9%	74.1%	25.9%	74.1%
2	1982	154,193	42,298	STRIEGEL, LOU	111,895	SYNAR, MIKE		69,597 D	27.4%	72.6%	27.4%	72.6%
3	1990	133,902	26,261	MILLER, PATRICK K.	107,641	BREWSTER, BILL		81,380 D	19.6%	80.4%	19.6%	80.4%
3	1988					WATKINS, WES						
3	1986	145,921	31,913	MILLER, PATRICK K.	114,008	WATKINS, WES		82,095 D	21.9%	78.1%	21.9%	78.1%
3	1984	177,418	39,454	MILLER, PATRICK K.	137,964	WATKINS, WES		98,510 D	22.2%	77.8%	22.2%	77.8%
3	1982	148,005	26,335	MILLER, PATRICK K.	121,670	WATKINS, WES		95,335 D	17.8%	82.2%	17.8%	82.2%
4	1990	137,111	36,232	BELL, HOWARD	100,879	MCCURDY, DAVE		64,647 D	26.4%	73.6%	26.4%	73.6%
4	1988					MCCURDY, DAVE						
4	1986	124,681	29,697	HUMPHREYS, LARRY	94,984	MCCURDY, DAVE		65,287 D	23.8%	76.2%	23.8%	76.2%
4	1984	172,039	60,844	SMITH, JERRY	109,447	MCCURDY, DAVE	1,748	48,603 D	35.4%	63.6%	35.7%	64.3%
4	1982	129,504	44,351	RUTLEDGE, HOWARD	84,205	MCCURDY, DAVE	948	39,854 D	34.2%	65.0%	34.5%	65.5%
5	1990	164,694	114,608	EDWARDS, M. H.	50,086	BAGGETT, BRYCE		64,522 R	69.6%	30.4%	69.6%	30.4%
5	1988	192,850	139,182	EDWARDS, M. H.	53,668	MONTGOMERY, TERRY J.		85,514 R	72.2%	27.8%	72.2%	27.8%
5	1986	154,030	108,774	EDWARDS, M. H.	45,256	COMPTON, DONNA		63,518 R	70.6%	29.4%	70.6%	29.4%
5	1984	178,726	135,167	EDWARDS, M. H.	39,089	GREESON, ALLEN	4,470	96,078 R	75.6%	21.9%	77.6%	22.4%
5	1982	147,209	98,979	EDWARDS, M. H.	42,453	LANE, DAN	5,777	56,526 R	67.2%	28.8%	70.0%	30.0%
6	1990	137,640	27,540	BURNS, ROBERT	110,100	ENGLISH, GLENN		82,560 D	20.0%	80.0%	20.0%	80.0%
6	1988	168,126	45,239	BROWN, MIKE	122,887	ENGLISH, GLENN		77,648 D	26.9%	73.1%	26.9%	73.1%
6	1986					ENGLISH, GLENN						
6	1984	164,595	67,601	DODD, CRAIG	96,994	ENGLISH, GLENN		29,393 D	41.1%	58.9%	41.1%	58.9%
6	1982	136,330	33,519	MOORE, ED	102,811	ENGLISH, GLENN		69,292 D	24.6%	75.4%	24.6%	75.4%

362

OKLAHOMA

1990 GENERAL ELECTION

Governor   Other vote was Independent (Ledgerwood).

Senator

Congress   According to state law, votes are not required to be tabulated for unopposed candidates.

1990 PRIMARIES

AUGUST 28 REPUBLICAN

Governor   75,992 Vince Orza; 51,355 Bill Price; 33,641 Burns Hargis; 25,670 Jerry Brown; 2,792 Jerry Hoyt.

Senator   Stephen Jones, unopposed.

Congress   Unopposed in four CD's. Contested as follows:

CD 2   12,349 Terry M. Gorham; 6,084 Marshall Farrier; 4,515 William S. Vardeman.
CD 3   6,806 Patrick K. Miller; 5,859 Barbara Hudkins.

AUGUST 28 DEMOCRATIC

Governor   175,568 Wes Watkins; 171,730 David Walters; 160,455 Steve Lewis; 23,648 John Barnett; 11,605 Anne H. Langston.

Senator   445,969 David L. Boren; 57,909 Virginia Jenner; 25,169 Manuel Ybarra.

Congress   Unopposed in three CD's. Contested as follows:

CD 1   32,199 Kurt Glassco; 9,540 Emily Warner; 4,798 Helen M. Guthrie; 3,707 Robert P. Jackman.
CD 2   63,584 Mike Synar; 50,255 Jack Ross.
CD 3   67,069 Bill Brewster; 54,471 Robert S. Kerr, III; 8,141 Will Robison; 2,173 Eugene V. Poling.

SEPTEMBER 18 REPUBLICAN RUN-OFF

Governor   94,682 Bill Price; 91,599 Vince Orza.

SEPTEMBER 18 DEMOCRATIC RUN-OFF

Governor   243,252 David Walters; 236,597 Wes Watkins.

OREGON

GOVERNOR
Barbara Roberts (D). Elected 1990 to a four-year term.

SENATORS
Mark Hatfield (R). Re-elected 1990 to a six-year term. Previously elected 1984, 1978, 1972, 1966.

Robert W. Packwood (R). Re-elected 1986 to a six-year term. Previously elected 1980, 1974, 1968.

REPRESENTATIVES
1. Les AuCoin (D)
2. Robert F. Smith (R)
3. Ron Wyden (D)
4. Peter A. DeFazio (D)
5. Mike Kopetski (D)

POSTWAR VOTE FOR PRESIDENT

Year	Total Vote	Republican Vote	Republican Candidate	Democratic Vote	Democratic Candidate	Other Vote	Plurality	Total Vote Rep.	Total Vote Dem.	Major Vote Rep.	Major Vote Dem.
1988	1,201,694	560,126	Bush, George	616,206	Dukakis, Michael S.	25,362	56,080 D	46.6%	51.3%	47.6%	52.4%
1984	1,226,527	685,700	Reagan, Ronald	536,479	Mondale, Walter F.	4,348	149,221 R	55.9%	43.7%	56.1%	43.9%
1980	1,181,516	571,044	Reagan, Ronald	456,890	Carter, Jimmy	153,582	114,154 R	48.3%	38.7%	55.6%	44.4%
1976	1,029,876	492,120	Ford, Gerald R.	490,407	Carter, Jimmy	47,349	1,713 R	47.8%	47.6%	50.1%	49.9%
1972	927,946	486,686	Nixon, Richard M.	392,760	McGovern, George S.	48,500	93,926 R	52.4%	42.3%	55.3%	44.7%
1968	819,622	408,433	Nixon, Richard M.	358,866	Humphrey, Hubert H.	52,323	49,567 R	49.8%	43.8%	53.2%	46.8%
1964	786,305	282,779	Goldwater, Barry M.	501,017	Johnson, Lyndon B.	2,509	218,238 D	36.0%	63.7%	36.1%	63.9%
1960	776,421	408,060	Nixon, Richard M.	367,402	Kennedy, John F.	959	40,658 R	52.6%	47.3%	52.6%	47.4%
1956	736,132	406,393	Eisenhower, Dwight D.	329,204	Stevenson, Adlai E.	535	77,189 R	55.2%	44.7%	55.2%	44.8%
1952	695,059	420,815	Eisenhower, Dwight D.	270,579	Stevenson, Adlai E.	3,665	150,236 R	60.5%	38.9%	60.9%	39.1%
1948	524,080	260,904	Dewey, Thomas E.	243,147	Truman, Harry S.	20,029	17,757 R	49.8%	46.4%	51.8%	48.2%

POSTWAR VOTE FOR GOVERNOR

Year	Total Vote	Republican Vote	Republican Candidate	Democratic Vote	Democratic Candidate	Other Vote	Rep-Dem. Plurality	Total Vote Rep.	Total Vote Dem.	Major Vote Rep.	Major Vote Dem.
1990	1,112,847	444,646	Frohnmayer, Dave	508,749	Roberts, Barbara	159,452	64,103 D	40.0%	45.7%	46.6%	53.4%
1986	1,059,630	506,986	Paulus, Norma	549,456	Goldschmidt, Neil	3,188	42,470 D	47.8%	51.9%	48.0%	52.0%
1982	1,042,009	639,841	Atiyeh, Victor	374,316	Kulongoski, Ted	27,852	265,525 R	61.4%	35.9%	63.1%	36.9%
1978	911,143	498,452	Atiyeh, Victor	409,411	Straub, Robert W.	3,280	89,041 R	54.7%	44.9%	54.9%	45.1%
1974	770,574	324,751	Atiyeh, Victor	444,812	Straub, Robert W.	1,011	120,061 D	42.1%	57.7%	42.2%	57.8%
1970	666,394	369,964	McCall, Tom	293,892	Straub, Robert W.	2,538	76,072 R	55.5%	44.1%	55.7%	44.3%
1966	682,862	377,346	McCall, Tom	305,008	Straub, Robert W.	508	72,338 R	55.3%	44.7%	55.3%	44.7%
1962	637,407	345,497	Hatfield, Mark	265,359	Thornton, Robert Y.	26,551	80,138 R	54.2%	41.6%	56.6%	43.4%
1958	599,994	331,900	Hatfield, Mark	267,934	Holmes, Robert D.	160	63,966 R	55.3%	44.7%	55.3%	44.7%
1956 S	731,279	361,840	Smith, Elmo E.	369,439	Holmes, Robert D.		7,599 D	49.5%	50.5%	49.5%	50.5%
1954	566,701	322,522	Patterson, Paul	244,179	Carson, Joseph K.		78,343 R	56.9%	43.1%	56.9%	43.1%
1950	505,910	334,160	McKay, Douglas	171,750	Flegel, Austin F.		162,410 R	66.1%	33.9%	66.1%	33.9%
1948 S	509,633	271,295	McKay, Douglas	226,958	Wallace, Lew	11,380	44,337 R	53.2%	44.5%	54.4%	45.6%
1946	344,155	237,681	Snell, Earl	106,474	Donaugh, Carl C.		131,207 R	69.1%	30.9%	69.1%	30.9%

The 1956 and 1948 elections were for short terms to fill vacancies.

OREGON

POSTWAR VOTE FOR SENATOR

Year	Total Vote	Republican Vote	Candidate	Democratic Vote	Candidate	Other Vote	Rep-Dem. Plurality	Percentage Total Vote Rep.	Dem.	Major Vote Rep.	Dem.
1990	1,099,255	590,095	Hatfield, Mark	507,743	Lonsdale, Harry	1,417	82,352 R	53.7%	46.2%	53.8%	46.2%
1986	1,042,555	656,317	Packwood, Robert W.	375,735	Bauman, Rick	10,503	280,582 R	63.0%	36.0%	63.6%	36.4%
1984	1,214,735	808,152	Hatfield, Mark	406,122	Hendriksen, Margie	461	402.030 R	66.5%	33.4%	66.6%	33.4%
1980	1,140,494	594,290	Packwood, Robert W.	501,963	Kulongoski, Ted	44,241	92,327 R	52.1%	44.0%	54.2%	45.8%
1978	892,518	550,165	Hatfield, Mark	341,616	Cook, Vernon	737	208,549 R	61.6%	38.3%	61.7%	38.3%
1974	766,414	420,984	Packwood, Robert W.	338,591	Roberts, Betty	6,839	82,393 R	54.9%	44.2%	55.4%	44.6%
1972	920,833	494,671	Hatfield, Mark	425,036	Morse, Wayne L.	1,126	69,635 R	53.7%	46.2%	53.8%	46.2%
1968	814,176	408,646	Packwood, Robert W.	405,353	Morse, Wayne L.	177	3,293 R	50.2%	49.8%	50.2%	49.8%
1966	685,067	354,391	Hatfield, Mark	330,374	Duncan, Robert B.	302	24,017 R	51.7%	48.2%	51.8%	48.2%
1962	636,558	291,587	Unander, Sig	344,716	Morse, Wayne L.	255	53,129 D	45.8%	54.2%	45.8%	54.2%
1960	755,875	343,009	Smith, Elmo E.	412,757	Neuberger, Maurine	109	69,748 D	45.4%	54.6%	45.4%	54.6%
1956	732,254	335,405	McKay, Douglas	396,849	Morse, Wayne L.		61,444 D	45.8%	54.2%	45.8%	54.2%
1954	569,088	283,313	Cordon, Guy	285,775	Neuberger, Richard L.		2,462 D	49.8%	50.2%	49.8%	50.2%
1950	503,455	376,510	Morse, Wayne L.	116,780	Latourette, Howard	10,165	259,730 R	74.8%	23.2%	76.3%	23.7%
1948	498,570	299,295	Cordon, Guy	199,275	Wilson, Manley J.		100,020 R	60.0%	40.0%	60.0%	40.0%

OREGON

Districts Established July 28, 1981

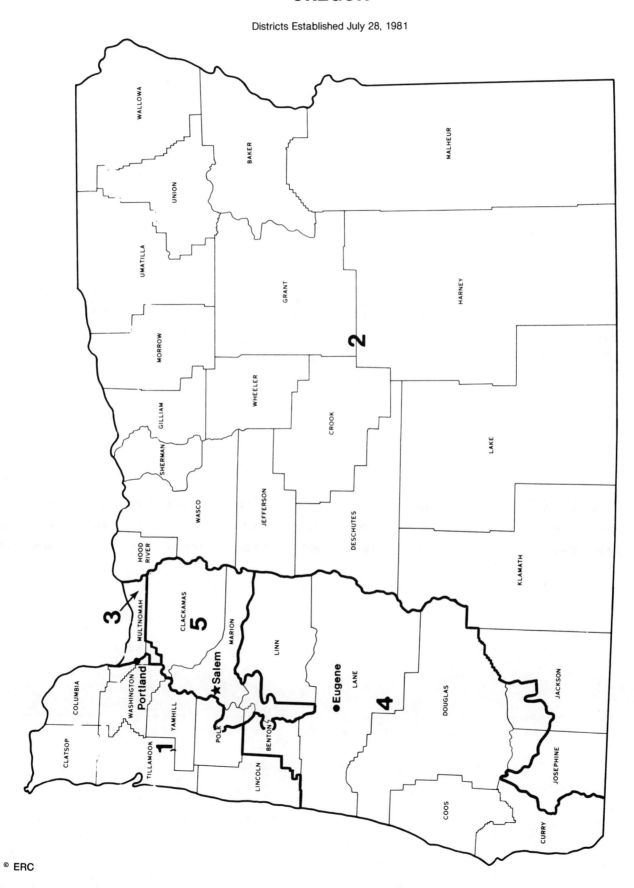

OREGON

GOVERNOR 1990

1990 Census Population	County	Total Vote	Republican	Democratic	Other	Rep.-Dem. Plurality	Percentage Total Vote Rep.	Dem.	Major Vote Rep.	Dem.
15,317	BAKER	6,089	2,947	2,080	1,062	867 R	48.4%	34.2%	58.6%	41.4%
70,811	BENTON	29,413	12,084	12,961	4,368	877 D	41.1%	44.1%	48.2%	51.8%
278,850	CLACKAMAS	118,231	47,470	56,674	14,087	9,204 D	40.2%	47.9%	45.6%	54.4%
33,301	CLATSOP	12,895	4,551	6,442	1,902	1,891 D	35.3%	50.0%	41.4%	58.6%
37,557	COLUMBIA	15,489	6,249	6,142	3,098	107 R	40.3%	39.7%	50.4%	49.6%
60,273	COOS	22,583	8,795	10,023	3,765	1,228 D	38.9%	44.4%	46.7%	53.3%
14,111	CROOK	5,358	2,924	1,859	575	1,065 R	54.6%	34.7%	61.1%	38.9%
19,327	CURRY	8,169	3,940	3,168	1,061	772 R	48.2%	38.8%	55.4%	44.6%
74,958	DESCHUTES	29,314	14,082	11,236	3,996	2,846 R	48.0%	38.3%	55.6%	44.4%
94,649	DOUGLAS	34,462	15,928	10,578	7,956	5,350 R	46.2%	30.7%	60.1%	39.9%
1,717	GILLIAM	857	366	339	152	27 R	42.7%	39.6%	51.9%	48.1%
7,853	GRANT	3,185	1,286	894	1,005	392 R	40.4%	28.1%	59.0%	41.0%
7,060	HARNEY	2,940	1,516	863	561	653 R	51.6%	29.4%	63.7%	36.3%
16,903	HOOD RIVER	6,061	2,627	2,542	892	85 R	43.3%	41.9%	50.8%	49.2%
146,389	JACKSON	56,012	26,347	20,383	9,282	5,964 R	47.0%	36.4%	56.4%	43.6%
13,676	JEFFERSON	4,373	2,238	1,716	419	522 R	51.2%	39.2%	56.6%	43.4%
62,649	JOSEPHINE	23,939	11,974	8,244	3,721	3,730 R	50.0%	34.4%	59.2%	40.8%
57,702	KLAMATH	20,189	11,183	6,118	2,888	5,065 R	55.4%	30.3%	64.6%	35.4%
7,186	LAKE	3,102	1,633	836	633	797 R	52.6%	27.0%	66.1%	33.9%
282,912	LANE	110,263	45,107	49,814	15,342	4,707 D	40.9%	45.2%	47.5%	52.5%
38,889	LINCOLN	16,264	5,264	8,503	2,497	3,239 D	32.4%	52.3%	38.2%	61.8%
91,227	LINN	34,314	14,314	11,626	8,374	2,688 R	41.7%	33.9%	55.2%	44.8%
26,038	MALHEUR	8,154	3,925	2,200	2,029	1,725 R	48.1%	27.0%	64.1%	35.9%
228,483	MARION	85,291	35,498	33,765	16,028	1,733 R	41.6%	39.6%	51.3%	48.7%
7,625	MORROW	2,556	1,062	1,013	481	49 R	41.5%	39.6%	51.2%	48.8%
583,887	MULTNOMAH	240,509	75,738	142,804	21,967	67,066 D	31.5%	59.4%	34.7%	65.3%
49,541	POLK	20,457	8,121	7,824	4,512	297 R	39.7%	38.2%	50.9%	49.1%
1,918	SHERMAN	1,034	492	391	151	101 R	47.6%	37.8%	55.7%	44.3%
21,570	TILLAMOOK	9,543	3,506	4,683	1,354	1,177 D	36.7%	49.1%	42.8%	57.2%
59,249	UMATILLA	15,926	6,615	6,436	2,875	179 R	41.5%	40.4%	50.7%	49.3%
23,598	UNION	8,925	3,714	3,399	1,812	315 R	41.6%	38.1%	52.2%	47.8%
6,911	WALLOWA	3,310	1,199	983	1,128	216 R	36.2%	29.7%	54.9%	45.1%
21,683	WASCO	8,898	3,488	3,948	1,462	460 D	39.2%	44.4%	46.9%	53.1%
311,554	WASHINGTON	120,237	49,340	57,815	13,082	8,475 D	41.0%	48.1%	46.0%	54.0%
1,396	WHEELER	655	332	189	134	143 R	50.7%	28.9%	63.7%	36.3%
65,551	YAMHILL	23,850	8,791	10,258	4,801	1,467 D	36.9%	43.0%	46.1%	53.9%
2,842,321	TOTAL	1,112,847	444,646	508,749	159,452	64,103 D	40.0%	45.7%	46.6%	53.4%

OREGON

SENATOR 1990

1990 Census Population	County	Total Vote	Republican	Democratic	Other	Rep.-Dem. Plurality	Percentage Total Vote Rep.	Dem.	Major Vote Rep.	Dem.
15,317	BAKER	5,997	2,975	3,005	17	30 D	49.6%	50.1%	49.7%	50.3%
70,811	BENTON	29,122	16,382	12,733	7	3,649 R	56.3%	43.7%	56.3%	43.7%
278,850	CLACKAMAS	117,099	65,299	51,775	25	13,524 R	55.8%	44.2%	55.8%	44.2%
33,301	CLATSOP	12,893	7,007	5,886		1,121 R	54.3%	45.7%	54.3%	45.7%
37,557	COLUMBIA	15,352	7,620	7,658	74	38 D	49.6%	49.9%	49.9%	50.1%
60,273	COOS	22,423	11,184	11,130	109	54 R	49.9%	49.6%	50.1%	49.9%
14,111	CROOK	5,269	2,930	2,334	5	596 R	55.6%	44.3%	55.7%	44.3%
19,327	CURRY	8,139	4,109	3,988	42	121 R	50.5%	49.0%	50.7%	49.3%
74,958	DESCHUTES	28,961	14,592	14,354	15	238 R	50.4%	49.6%	50.4%	49.6%
94,649	DOUGLAS	33,975	19,177	14,787	11	4,390 R	56.4%	43.5%	56.5%	43.5%
1,717	GILLIAM	846	461	383	2	78 R	54.5%	45.3%	54.6%	45.4%
7,853	GRANT	3,148	1,669	1,475	4	194 R	53.0%	46.9%	53.1%	46.9%
7,060	HARNEY	2,894	1,663	1,229	2	434 R	57.5%	42.5%	57.5%	42.5%
16,903	HOOD RIVER	5,981	3,395	2,586		809 R	56.8%	43.2%	56.8%	43.2%
146,389	JACKSON	55,331	26,868	28,447	16	1,579 D	48.6%	51.4%	48.6%	51.4%
13,676	JEFFERSON	4,345	2,313	2,029	3	284 R	53.2%	46.7%	53.3%	46.7%
62,649	JOSEPHINE	23,642	12,016	11,618	8	398 R	50.8%	49.1%	50.8%	49.2%
57,702	KLAMATH	19,813	10,010	9,801	2	209 R	50.5%	49.5%	50.5%	49.5%
7,186	LAKE	3,071	1,677	1,394		283 R	54.6%	45.4%	54.6%	45.4%
282,912	LANE	107,429	56,497	50,903	29	5,594 R	52.6%	47.4%	52.6%	47.4%
38,889	LINCOLN	16,071	7,108	8,957	6	1,849 D	44.2%	55.7%	44.2%	55.8%
91,227	LINN	33,534	20,287	13,241	6	7,046 R	60.5%	39.5%	60.5%	39.5%
26,038	MALHEUR	8,054	4,943	3,100	11	1,843 R	61.4%	38.5%	61.5%	38.5%
228,483	MARION	84,697	51,242	33,172	283	18,070 R	60.5%	39.2%	60.7%	39.3%
7,625	MORROW	2,529	1,439	1,084	6	355 R	56.9%	42.9%	57.0%	43.0%
583,887	MULTNOMAH	238,226	117,366	120,408	452	3,042 D	49.3%	50.5%	49.4%	50.6%
49,541	POLK	19,824	12,170	7,653	1	4,517 R	61.4%	38.6%	61.4%	38.6%
1,918	SHERMAN	1,016	594	420	2	174 R	58.5%	41.3%	58.6%	41.4%
21,570	TILLAMOOK	9,493	4,892	4,596	5	296 R	51.5%	48.4%	51.6%	48.4%
59,249	UMATILLA	15,632	8,926	6,704	2	2,222 R	57.1%	42.9%	57.1%	42.9%
23,598	UNION	8,837	4,834	3,982	21	852 R	54.7%	45.1%	54.8%	45.2%
6,911	WALLOWA	3,276	1,812	1,461	3	351 R	55.3%	44.6%	55.4%	44.6%
21,683	WASCO	8,795	4,978	3,816	1	1,162 R	56.6%	43.4%	56.6%	43.4%
311,554	WASHINGTON	119,435	68,134	51,268	33	16,866 R	57.0%	42.9%	57.1%	42.9%
1,396	WHEELER	795	340	309	146	31 R	42.8%	38.9%	52.4%	47.6%
65,551	YAMHILL	23,311	13,186	10,057	68	3,129 R	56.6%	43.1%	56.7%	43.3%
2,842,321	TOTAL	1,099,255	590,095	507,743	1,417	82,352 R	53.7%	46.2%	53.8%	46.2%

OREGON

CONGRESS

CD	Year	Total Vote	Republican Vote	Candidate	Democratic Vote	Candidate	Other Vote	Rep.-Dem. Plurality	Percentage Total Vote Rep.	Total Vote Dem.	Major Vote Rep.	Major Vote Dem.
1	1990	238,421	72,382	MOLANDER, EARL	150,292	AUCOIN, LES	15,747	77,910 D	30.4%	63.0%	32.5%	67.5%
1	1988	258,603	78,626	MOLANDER, EARL	179,915	AUCOIN, LES	62	101,289 D	30.4%	69.6%	30.4%	69.6%
1	1986	229,495	87,874	MEEKER, ANTHONY	141,585	AUCOIN, LES	36	53,711 D	38.3%	61.7%	38.3%	61.7%
1	1984	260,667	122,247	MOSHOFSKY, BILL	138,393	AUCOIN, LES	27	16,146 D	46.9%	53.1%	46.9%	53.1%
1	1982	220,378	101,720	MOSHOFSKY, BILL	118,638	AUCOIN, LES	20	16,918 D	46.2%	53.8%	46.2%	53.8%
2	1990	188,185	127,998	SMITH, ROBERT F.	60,131	SMILEY, JIM	56	67,867 R	68.0%	32.0%	68.0%	32.0%
2	1988	200,079	125,366	SMITH, ROBERT F.	74,700	TUTTLE, LARRY	13	50,666 R	62.7%	37.3%	62.7%	37.3%
2	1986	188,716	113,566	SMITH, ROBERT F.	75,124	TUTTLE, LARRY	26	38,442 R	60.2%	39.8%	60.2%	39.8%
2	1984	232,826	132,649	SMITH, ROBERT F.	100,152	WILLIS, LARRYANN	25	32,497 R	57.0%	43.0%	57.0%	43.0%
2	1982	192,427	106,912	SMITH, ROBERT F.	85,495	WILLIS, LARRYANN	20	21,417 R	55.6%	44.4%	55.6%	44.4%
3	1990	210,193	40,216	MOONEY, PHILIP E.	169,731	WYDEN, RON	246	129,515 D	19.1%	80.8%	19.2%	80.8%
3	1988	191,825			190,684	WYDEN, RON	1,141	190,684 D		99.4%		100.0%
3	1986	209,581	29,321	PHELAN, THOMAS H.	180,067	WYDEN, RON	193	150,746 D	14.0%	85.9%	14.0%	86.0%
3	1984	239,897	66,394	DAVIS, DREW	173,438	WYDEN, RON	65	107,044 D	27.7%	72.3%	27.7%	72.3%
3	1982	203,662	44,162	PHELAN, THOMAS H.	159,416	WYDEN, RON	84	115,254 D	21.7%	78.3%	21.7%	78.3%
4	1990	189,352			162,494	DEFAZIO, PETER A.	26,858	162,494 D		85.8%		100.0%
4	1988	150,735	42,220	HOWARD, JIM	108,483	DEFAZIO, PETER A.	32	66,263 D	28.0%	72.0%	28.0%	72.0%
4	1986	195,548	89,795	LONG, BRUCE	105,697	DEFAZIO, PETER A.	56	15,902 D	45.9%	54.1%	45.9%	54.1%
4	1984	230,687	96,487	LONG, BRUCE	134,190	WEAVER, JAMES	10	37,703 D	41.8%	58.2%	41.8%	58.2%
4	1982	195,524	80,054	ANTHONY, ROSS	115,448	WEAVER, JAMES	22	35,394 D	40.9%	59.0%	40.9%	59.1%
5	1990	226,550	101,650	SMITH, DENNY	124,610	KOPETSKI, MIKE	290	22,960 D	44.9%	55.0%	44.9%	55.1%
5	1990	222,354	111,489	SMITH, DENNY	110,782	KOPETSKI, MIKE	83	707 R	50.1%	49.8%	50.2%	49.8%
5	1986	208,204	125,906	SMITH, DENNY	82,290	ROSS, BARBARA	8	43,616 R	60.5%	39.5%	60.5%	39.5%
5	1984	239,414	130,424	SMITH, DENNY	108,919	MCFARLAND, RUTH	71	21,505 R	54.5%	45.5%	54.5%	45.5%
5	1982	202,901	103,906	SMITH, DENNY	98,952	MCFARLAND, RUTH	43	4,954 R	51.2%	48.8%	51.2%	48.8%

OREGON

1990 GENERAL ELECTION

Governor   Other vote was 144,062 Independent (Mobley); 14,583 Libertarian (Oerther) and 807 scattered write-in.

Senator   Other vote was scattered write-in.

Congress   Other vote was 15,585 Independent (Livingston) and 162 scatttered write-in in CD 1; 26,432 Libertarian (Nathan) and 426 scattered write-in in CD 4; scattered write-in in all other CD's.

1990 PRIMARIES

MAY 15 REPUBLICAN

Governor   227,867 Dave Frohnmayer; 32,397 John K. Lim; 8,285 Ed Christie; 7,412 Terry Hutchison; 4,847 Edward T. Steubs; 2,466 William Sparks; 2,006 Sanford Blau; 2,760 scattered write-in.

Senator   220,449 Mark Hatfield; 59,970 Randy Prince; 1,167 scattered write-in.

Congress   Unopposed in CD 5. No candidate in CD 4. Contested as follows:

    CD 1   25,292 Earl Molander; 14,177 Carolyn Browne; 7,768 Griff Thomas; 143 scattered write-in.
    CD 2   51,951 Robert F. Smith; 7,250 Dane Coefer; 36 scattered write-in.
    CD 3   11,736 Philip E. Mooney; 10,208 Berna Plummer; 8,278 Don Bowie; 356 scattered write-in.

MAY 15 DEMOCRATIC

Governor   Barbara Roberts, unopposed.

Senator   162,529 Harry Lonsdale; 34,305 Steve Anderson; 20,684 Neale S. Hyatt; 13,766 Brooks Washburne; 12,383 Bob Reuschlein; 8,235 Frank A. Clough; 1,535 scattered write-in.

Congress   Unopposed in three CD's. Contested as follows:

    CD 2   20,371 Jim Smiley; 15,796 Treva R. Tumbleson; 475 scattered write-in.
    CD 3   63,178 Ron Wyden; 4,908 Sam Kahl; 42 scattered write-in.

370

PENNSYLVANIA

GOVERNOR
Robert Casey (D). Re-elected 1990 to a four-year term. Previously elected 1986.

SENATORS
Harris Wofford (D). Appointed May 1991 upon the death in April 1991 of Senator H. John Heinz (R). As of publication the date for a special election to fill the remaining years of the term had not been set.

Arlen Specter (R). Re-elected 1986 to a six-year term. Previously elected 1980.

REPRESENTATIVES
1. Thomas M. Foglietta (D)
2. William H. Gray (D)
3. Robert A. Borski (D)
4. Joseph P. Kolter (D)
5. Richard T. Schulze (R)
6. Gus Yatron (D)
7. Curt Weldon (R)
8. Peter H. Kostmayer (D)
9. E. G. Shuster (R)
10. Joseph M. McDade (R)
11. Paul E. Kanjorski (D)
12. John P. Murtha (D)
13. R. Lawrence Coughlin (R)
14. William J. Coyne (D)
15. Donald L. Ritter (R)
16. Robert S. Walker (R)
17. George W. Gekas (R)
18. Rick Santorum (R)
19. William F. Goodling (R)
20. Joseph M. Gaydos (D)
21. Thomas J. Ridge (R)
22. Austin J. Murphy (D)
23. William F. Clinger (R)

POSTWAR VOTE FOR PRESIDENT

Year	Total Vote	Republican Vote	Candidate	Democratic Vote	Candidate	Other Vote	Plurality	Total Vote Rep.	Total Vote Dem.	Major Vote Rep.	Major Vote Dem.
1988	4,536,251	2,300,087	Bush, George	2,194,944	Dukakis, Michael S.	41,220	105,143 R	50.7%	48.4%	51.2%	48.8%
1984	4,844,903	2,584,323	Reagan, Ronald	2,228,131	Mondale, Walter F.	32,449	356,192 R	53.3%	46.0%	53.7%	46.3%
1980	4,561,501	2,261,872	Reagan, Ronald	1,937,540	Carter, Jimmy	362,089	324,332 R	49.6%	42.5%	53.9%	46.1%
1976	4,620,787	2,205,604	Ford, Gerald R.	2,328,677	Carter, Jimmy	86,506	123,073 D	47.7%	50.4%	48.6%	51.4%
1972	4,592,106	2,714,521	Nixon, Richard M.	1,796,951	McGovern, George S.	80,634	917,570 R	59.1%	39.1%	60.2%	39.8%
1968	4,747,928	2,090,017	Nixon, Richard M.	2,259,405	Humphrey, Hubert H.	398,506	169,388 D	44.0%	47.6%	48.1%	51.9%
1964	4,822,690	1,673,657	Goldwater, Barry M.	3,130,954	Johnson, Lyndon B.	18,079	1,457,297 D	34.7%	64.9%	34.8%	65.2%
1960	5,006,541	2,439,956	Nixon, Richard M.	2,556,282	Kennedy, John F.	10,303	116,326 D	48.7%	51.1%	48.8%	51.2%
1956	4,576,503	2,585,252	Eisenhower, Dwight D.	1,981,769	Stevenson, Adlai E.	9,482	603,483 R	56.5%	43.3%	56.6%	43.4%
1952	4,580,969	2,415,789	Eisenhower, Dwight D.	2,146,269	Stevenson, Adlai E.	18,911	269,520 R	52.7%	46.9%	53.0%	47.0%
1948	3,735,348	1,902,197	Dewey, Thomas E.	1,752,426	Truman, Harry S.	80,725	149,771 R	50.9%	46.9%	52.0%	48.0%

PENNSYLVANIA

POSTWAR VOTE FOR GOVERNOR

Year	Total Vote	Republican Vote	Republican Candidate	Democratic Vote	Democratic Candidate	Other Vote	Rep-Dem. Plurality	Total Vote Rep.	Total Vote Dem.	Major Vote Rep.	Major Vote Dem.
1990	3,052,760	987,516	Hafer, Barbara	2,065,244	Casey, Robert		1,077,728 D	32.3%	67.7%	32.3%	67.7%
1986	3,388,275	1,638,268	Scranton, William W.,III	1,717,484	Casey, Robert	32,523	79,216 D	48.4%	50.7%	48.8%	51.2%
1982	3,683,985	1,872,784	Thornburgh, Richard L.	1,772,353	Ertel, Allen E.	38,848	100,431 R	50.8%	48.1%	51.4%	48.6%
1978	3,741,969	1,966,042	Thornburgh, Richard L.	1,737,888	Flaherty, Peter	38,039	228,154 R	52.5%	46.4%	53.1%	46.9%
1974	3,491,234	1,578,917	Lewis, Andrew L.	1,878,252	Shapp, Milton	34,065	299,335 D	45.2%	53.8%	45.7%	54.3%
1970	3,700,060	1,542,854	Broderick, Raymond	2,043,029	Shapp, Milton	114,177	500,175 D	41.7%	55.2%	43.0%	57.0%
1966	4,050,668	2,110,349	Shafer, Raymond P.	1,868,719	Shapp, Milton	71,600	241,630 R	52.1%	46.1%	53.0%	47.0%
1962	4,378,042	2,424,918	Scranton, William W.	1,938,627	Dilworth, Richardson	14,497	486,291 R	55.4%	44.3%	55.6%	44.4%
1958	3,986,918	1,948,769	McGonigle, A. T.	2,024,852	Lawrence, David	13,297	76,083 D	48.9%	50.8%	49.0%	51.0%
1954	3,720,457	1,717,070	Wood, Lloyd H.	1,996,266	Leader, George M.	7,121	279,196 D	46.2%	53.7%	46.2%	53.8%
1950	3,540,059	1,796,119	Fine, John S.	1,710,355	Dilworth, Richardson	33,585	85,764 R	50.7%	48.3%	51.2%	48.8%
1946	3,123,994	1,828,462	Duff, James H.	1,270,947	Rice, John S.	24,585	557,515 R	58.5%	40.7%	59.0%	41.0%

POSTWAR VOTE FOR SENATOR

Year	Total Vote	Republican Vote	Republican Candidate	Democratic Vote	Democratic Candidate	Other Vote	Rep-Dem. Plurality	Total Vote Rep.	Total Vote Dem.	Major Vote Rep.	Major Vote Dem.
1988	4,366,598	2,901,715	Heinz, H. John	1,416,764	Vignola, Joseph C.	48,119	1,484,951 R	66.5%	32.4%	67.2%	32.8%
1986	3,378,226	1,906,537	Specter, Arlen	1,448,219	Edgar, Robert W.	23,470	458,318 R	56.4%	42.9%	56.8%	43.2%
1982	3,604,108	2,136,418	Heinz, H. John	1,412,965	Wecht, Cyril H.	54,725	723,453 R	59.3%	39.2%	60.2%	39.8%
1980	4,418,042	2,230,404	Specter, Arlen	2,122,391	Flaherty, Peter	65,247	108,013 R	50.5%	48.0%	51.2%	48.8%
1976	4,546,353	2,381,891	Heinz, H. John	2,126,977	Green, William J., III	37,485	254,914 R	52.4%	46.8%	52.8%	47.2%
1974	3,477,812	1,843,317	Schweiker, Richard S.	1,596,121	Flaherty, Peter	38,374	247,196 R	53.0%	45.9%	53.6%	46.4%
1970	3,644,305	1,874,106	Scott, Hugh	1,653,774	Sesler, William G.	116,425	220,332 R	51.4%	45.4%	53.1%	46.9%
1968	4,624,218	2,399,762	Schweiker, Richard S.	2,117,662	Clark, Joseph S.	106,794	282,100 R	51.9%	45.8%	53.1%	46.9%
1964	4,803,835	2,429,858	Scott, Hugh	2,359,223	Blatt, Genevieve	14,754	70,635 R	50.6%	49.1%	50.7%	49.3%
1962	4,383,475	2,134,649	Van Zandt, James E.	2,238,383	Clark, Joseph S.	10,443	103,734 D	48.7%	51.1%	48.8%	51.2%
1958	3,988,622	2,042,586	Scott, Hugh	1,929,821	Leader, George M.	16,215	112,765 R	51.2%	48.4%	51.4%	48.6%
1956	4,529,874	2,250,671	Duff, James H.	2,268,641	Clark, Joseph S.	10,562	17,970 D	49.7%	50.1%	49.8%	50.2%
1952	4,519,761	2,331,034	Martin, Edward	2,168,546	Bard, Guy Kurtz	20,181	162,488 R	51.6%	48.0%	51.8%	48.2%
1950	3,548,703	1,820,400	Duff, James H.	1,694,076	Myers, Francis J.	34,227	126,324 R	51.3%	47.7%	51.8%	48.2%
1946	3,127,860	1,853,458	Martin, Edward	1,245,338	Guffey, Joseph F.	29,064	608,120 R	59.3%	39.8%	59.8%	40.2%

PENNSYLVANIA

Districts Established March 3, 1982

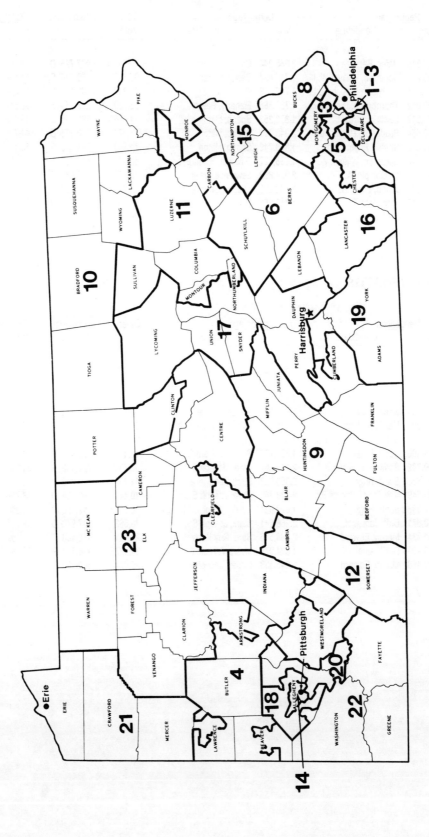

373

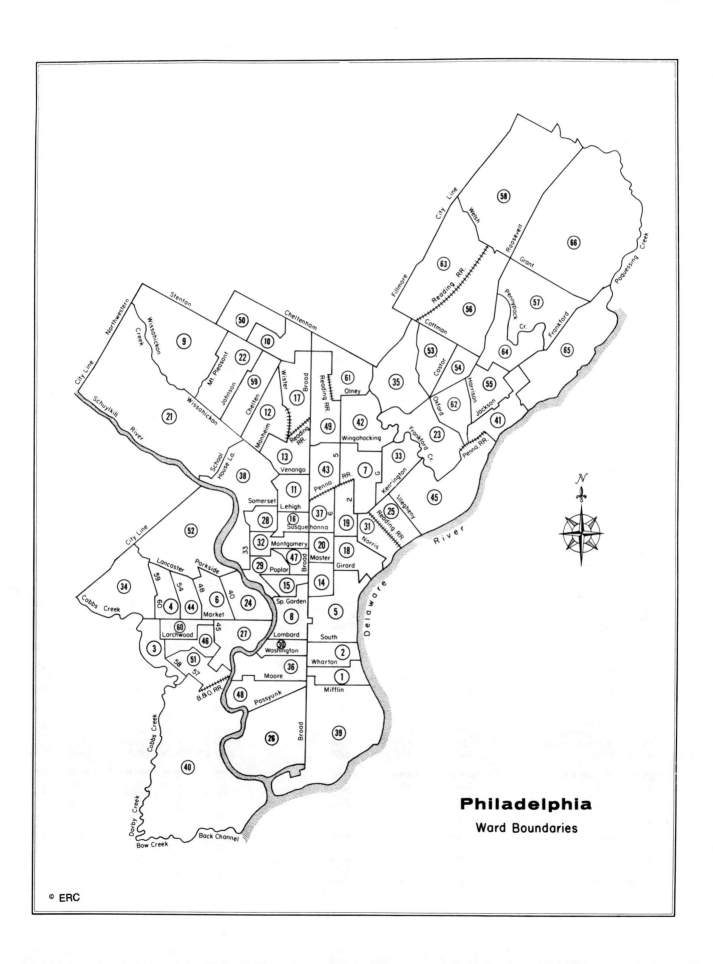

Philadelphia

Ward Boundaries

© ERC

PENNSYLVANIA

GOVERNOR 1990

1990 Census Population	County	Total Vote	Republican	Democratic	Other	Rep.-Dem. Plurality	Percentage			
							Total Vote		Major Vote	
							Rep.	Dem.	Rep.	Dem.
78,274	ADAMS	19,577	5,687	13,890		8,203 D	29.0%	71.0%	29.0%	71.0%
1,336,449	ALLEGHENY	391,778	109,895	281,883		171,988 D	28.1%	71.9%	28.1%	71.9%
73,478	ARMSTRONG	20,269	6,192	14,077		7,885 D	30.5%	69.5%	30.5%	69.5%
186,093	BEAVER	56,927	13,577	43,350		29,773 D	23.8%	76.2%	23.8%	76.2%
47,919	BEDFORD	12,585	4,876	7,709		2,833 D	38.7%	61.3%	38.7%	61.3%
336,523	BERKS	77,487	29,600	47,887		18,287 D	38.2%	61.8%	38.2%	61.8%
130,542	BLAIR	30,321	9,608	20,713		11,105 D	31.7%	68.3%	31.7%	68.3%
60,967	BRADFORD	12,726	5,663	7,063		1,400 D	44.5%	55.5%	44.5%	55.5%
541,174	BUCKS	139,498	57,783	81,715		23,932 D	41.4%	58.6%	41.4%	58.6%
152,013	BUTLER	38,044	12,715	25,329		12,614 D	33.4%	66.6%	33.4%	66.6%
163,029	CAMBRIA	50,435	10,104	40,331		30,227 D	20.0%	80.0%	20.0%	80.0%
5,913	CAMERON	2,035	721	1,314		593 D	35.4%	64.6%	35.4%	64.6%
56,846	CARBON	13,942	4,169	9,773		5,604 D	29.9%	70.1%	29.9%	70.1%
123,786	CENTRE	29,367	11,925	17,442		5,517 D	40.6%	59.4%	40.6%	59.4%
376,396	CHESTER	93,197	44,262	48,935		4,673 D	47.5%	52.5%	47.5%	52.5%
41,699	CLARION	11,046	3,811	7,235		3,424 D	34.5%	65.5%	34.5%	65.5%
78,097	CLEARFIELD	22,257	5,793	16,464		10,671 D	26.0%	74.0%	26.0%	74.0%
37,182	CLINTON	9,628	2,832	6,796		3,964 D	29.4%	70.6%	29.4%	70.6%
63,202	COLUMBIA	13,885	4,436	9,449		5,013 D	31.9%	68.1%	31.9%	68.1%
86,169	CRAWFORD	24,210	8,056	16,154		8,098 D	33.3%	66.7%	33.3%	66.7%
195,257	CUMBERLAND	49,179	16,692	32,487		15,795 D	33.9%	66.1%	33.9%	66.1%
237,813	DAUPHIN	59,896	16,833	43,063		26,230 D	28.1%	71.9%	28.1%	71.9%
547,651	DELAWARE	169,396	76,531	92,865		16,334 D	45.2%	54.8%	45.2%	54.8%
34,878	ELK	11,332	2,575	8,757		6,182 D	22.7%	77.3%	22.7%	77.3%
275,572	ERIE	72,689	20,424	52,265		31,841 D	28.1%	71.9%	28.1%	71.9%
145,351	FAYETTE	34,601	5,882	28,719		22,837 D	17.0%	83.0%	17.0%	83.0%
4,802	FOREST	1,699	595	1,104		509 D	35.0%	65.0%	35.0%	65.0%
121,082	FRANKLIN	23,587	8,461	15,126		6,665 D	35.9%	64.1%	35.9%	64.1%
13,837	FULTON	3,112	1,173	1,939		766 D	37.7%	62.3%	37.7%	62.3%
39,550	GREENE	10,155	2,157	7,998		5,841 D	21.2%	78.8%	21.2%	78.8%
44,164	HUNTINGDON	10,146	3,490	6,656		3,166 D	34.4%	65.6%	34.4%	65.6%
89,994	INDIANA	22,314	6,622	15,692		9,070 D	29.7%	70.3%	29.7%	70.3%
46,083	JEFFERSON	12,035	3,918	8,117		4,199 D	32.6%	67.4%	32.6%	67.4%
20,625	JUNIATA	6,254	1,637	4,617		2,980 D	26.2%	73.8%	26.2%	73.8%
219,039	LACKAWANNA	60,223	10,941	49,282		38,341 D	18.2%	81.8%	18.2%	81.8%
422,822	LANCASTER	90,634	24,565	66,069		41,504 D	27.1%	72.9%	27.1%	72.9%
96,246	LAWRENCE	26,845	7,282	19,563		12,281 D	27.1%	72.9%	27.1%	72.9%
113,744	LEBANON	26,831	8,055	18,776		10,721 D	30.0%	70.0%	30.0%	70.0%
291,130	LEHIGH	67,111	24,519	42,592		18,073 D	36.5%	63.5%	36.5%	63.5%
328,149	LUZERNE	74,530	14,487	60,043		45,556 D	19.4%	80.6%	19.4%	80.6%
118,710	LYCOMING	25,866	8,628	17,238		8,610 D	33.4%	66.6%	33.4%	66.6%
47,131	MCKEAN	9,044	3,893	5,151		1,258 D	43.0%	57.0%	43.0%	57.0%
121,003	MERCER	34,557	10,479	24,078		13,599 D	30.3%	69.7%	30.3%	69.7%
46,197	MIFFLIN	9,253	2,781	6,472		3,691 D	30.1%	69.9%	30.1%	69.9%
95,709	MONROE	19,004	6,761	12,243		5,482 D	35.6%	64.4%	35.6%	64.4%
678,111	MONTGOMERY	179,516	90,051	89,465		586 R	50.2%	49.8%	50.2%	49.8%
17,735	MONTOUR	3,867	1,201	2,666		1,465 D	31.1%	68.9%	31.1%	68.9%
247,105	NORTHAMPTON	57,025	18,153	38,872		20,719 D	31.8%	68.2%	31.8%	68.2%
96,771	NORTHUMBERLAND	24,336	6,388	17,948		11,560 D	26.2%	73.8%	26.2%	73.8%
41,172	PERRY	9,447	3,242	6,205		2,963 D	34.3%	65.7%	34.3%	65.7%
1,585,577	PHILADELPHIA	390,780	114,390	276,390		162,000 D	29.3%	70.7%	29.3%	70.7%
27,966	PIKE	5,651	2,529	3,122		593 D	44.8%	55.2%	44.8%	55.2%
16,717	POTTER	4,164	1,766	2,398		632 D	42.4%	57.6%	42.4%	57.6%
152,585	SCHUYLKILL	42,422	12,590	29,832		17,242 D	29.7%	70.3%	29.7%	70.3%
36,680	SNYDER	7,474	2,697	4,777		2,080 D	36.1%	63.9%	36.1%	63.9%
78,218	SOMERSET	24,547	6,937	17,610		10,673 D	28.3%	71.7%	28.3%	71.7%
6,104	SULLIVAN	2,042	835	1,207		372 D	40.9%	59.1%	40.9%	59.1%
40,380	SUSQUEHANNA	9,859	3,204	6,655		3,451 D	32.5%	67.5%	32.5%	67.5%
41,126	TIOGA	10,007	4,270	5,737		1,467 D	42.7%	57.3%	42.7%	57.3%
36,176	UNION	7,134	2,440	4,694		2,254 D	34.2%	65.8%	34.2%	65.8%

PENNSYLVANIA

GOVERNOR 1990

1990 Census Population	County	Total Vote	Republican	Democratic	Other	Rep.-Dem. Plurality	Percentage			
							Total Vote		Major Vote	
							Rep.	Dem.	Rep.	Dem.
59,381	VENANGO	14,898	4,899	9,999		5,100 D	32.9%	67.1%	32.9%	67.1%
45,050	WARREN	13,413	4,153	9,260		5,107 D	31.0%	69.0%	31.0%	69.0%
204,584	WASHINGTON	54,088	13,734	40,354		26,620 D	25.4%	74.6%	25.4%	74.6%
39,944	WAYNE	9,385	3,503	5,882		2,379 D	37.3%	62.7%	37.3%	62.7%
370,321	WESTMORELAND	95,961	24,039	71,922		47,883 D	25.1%	74.9%	25.1%	74.9%
28,076	WYOMING	6,403	1,969	4,434		2,465 D	30.8%	69.2%	30.8%	69.2%
339,574	YORK	80,834	23,440	57,394		33,954 D	29.0%	71.0%	29.0%	71.0%
11,881,643	TOTAL	3,052,760	987,516	2,065,244		1,077,728 D	32.3%	67.7%	32.3%	67.7%

PHILIDELPHIA

GOVERNOR 1990

1990 Census Population	Ward	Total Vote	Republican	Democratic	Other	Rep.-Dem. Plurality	Percentage			
							Total Vote		Major Vote	
							Rep.	Dem.	Rep.	Dem.
	WARD 1	5,334	1,719	3,615		1,896 D	32.2%	67.8%	32.2%	67.8%
	WARD 2	5,558	2,313	3,245		932 D	41.6%	58.4%	41.6%	58.4%
	WARD 3	5,389	498	4,891		4,393 D	9.2%	90.8%	9.2%	90.8%
	WARD 4	4,639	432	4,207		3,775 D	9.3%	90.7%	9.3%	90.7%
	WARD 5	5,620	3,200	2,420		780 R	56.9%	43.1%	56.9%	43.1%
	WARD 6	2,702	273	2,429		2,156 D	10.1%	89.9%	10.1%	89.9%
	WARD 7	2,986	950	2,036		1,086 D	31.8%	68.2%	31.8%	68.2%
	WARD 8	7,904	4,889	3,015		1,874 R	61.9%	38.1%	61.9%	38.1%
	WARD 9	5,978	2,819	3,159		340 D	47.2%	52.8%	47.2%	52.8%
	WARD 10	7,472	645	6,827		6,182 D	8.6%	91.4%	8.6%	91.4%
	WARD 11	3,286	295	2,991		2,696 D	9.0%	91.0%	9.0%	91.0%
	WARD 12	4,208	791	3,417		2,626 D	18.8%	81.2%	18.8%	81.2%
	WARD 13	4,055	591	3,464		2,873 D	14.6%	85.4%	14.6%	85.4%
	WARD 14	1,651	185	1,466		1,281 D	11.2%	88.8%	11.2%	88.8%
	WARD 15	4,455	1,923	2,532		609 D	43.2%	56.8%	43.2%	56.8%
	WARD 16	3,225	191	3,034		2,843 D	5.9%	94.1%	5.9%	94.1%
	WARD 17	5,864	551	5,313		4,762 D	9.4%	90.6%	9.4%	90.6%
	WARD 18	2,973	923	2,050		1,127 D	31.0%	69.0%	31.0%	69.0%
	WARD 19	2,003	264	1,739		1,475 D	13.2%	86.8%	13.2%	86.8%
	WARD 20	1,592	119	1,473		1,354 D	7.5%	92.5%	7.5%	92.5%
	WARD 21	14,352	5,261	9,091		3,830 D	36.7%	63.3%	36.7%	63.3%
	WARD 22	7,675	1,805	5,870		4,065 D	23.5%	76.5%	23.5%	76.5%
	WARD 23	5,983	2,278	3,705		1,427 D	38.1%	61.9%	38.1%	61.9%
	WARD 24	2,652	474	2,178		1,704 D	17.9%	82.1%	17.9%	82.1%
	WARD 25	5,462	1,862	3,600		1,738 D	34.1%	65.9%	34.1%	65.9%
	WARD 26	5,698	1,544	4,154		2,610 D	27.1%	72.9%	27.1%	72.9%
	WARD 27	1,871	747	1,124		377 D	39.9%	60.1%	39.9%	60.1%
	WARD 28	3,053	225	2,828		2,603 D	7.4%	92.6%	7.4%	92.6%
	WARD 29	3,109	284	2,825		2,541 D	9.1%	90.9%	9.1%	90.9%
	WARD 30	2,854	856	1,998		1,142 D	30.0%	70.0%	30.0%	70.0%
	WARD 31	4,146	1,450	2,696		1,246 D	35.0%	65.0%	35.0%	65.0%
	WARD 32	4,284	357	3,927		3,570 D	8.3%	91.7%	8.3%	91.7%
	WARD 33	6,298	1,935	4,363		2,428 D	30.7%	69.3%	30.7%	69.3%
	WARD 34	9,949	2,352	7,597		5,245 D	23.6%	76.4%	23.6%	76.4%
	WARD 35	10,399	3,595	6,804		3,209 D	34.6%	65.4%	34.6%	65.4%
	WARD 36	7,448	881	6,567		5,686 D	11.8%	88.2%	11.8%	88.2%
	WARD 37	2,904	185	2,719		2,534 D	6.4%	93.6%	6.4%	93.6%
	WARD 38	4,280	1,019	3,261		2,242 D	23.8%	76.2%	23.8%	76.2%
	WARD 39	12,939	3,710	9,229		5,519 D	28.7%	71.3%	28.7%	71.3%
	WARD 40	9,477	2,302	7,175		4,873 D	24.3%	75.7%	24.3%	75.7%
	WARD 41	8,025	2,669	5,356		2,687 D	33.3%	66.7%	33.3%	66.7%
	WARD 42	5,109	1,384	3,725		2,341 D	27.1%	72.9%	27.1%	72.9%
	WARD 43	3,223	405	2,818		2,413 D	12.6%	87.4%	12.6%	87.4%
	WARD 44	3,240	337	2,903		2,566 D	10.4%	89.6%	10.4%	89.6%
	WARD 45	7,706	2,764	4,942		2,178 D	35.9%	64.1%	35.9%	64.1%
	WARD 46	4,437	1,145	3,292		2,147 D	25.8%	74.2%	25.8%	74.2%
	WARD 47	1,677	151	1,526		1,375 D	9.0%	91.0%	9.0%	91.0%
	WARD 48	4,821	1,255	3,566		2,311 D	26.0%	74.0%	26.0%	74.0%
	WARD 49	4,222	740	3,482		2,742 D	17.5%	82.5%	17.5%	82.5%
	WARD 50	7,938	876	7,062		6,186 D	11.0%	89.0%	11.0%	89.0%
	WARD 51	4,036	384	3,652		3,268 D	9.5%	90.5%	9.5%	90.5%
	WARD 52	6,996	1,744	5,252		3,508 D	24.9%	75.1%	24.9%	75.1%
	WARD 53	8,197	3,166	5,031		1,865 D	38.6%	61.4%	38.6%	61.4%
	WARD 54	6,923	2,775	4,148		1,373 D	40.1%	59.9%	40.1%	59.9%
	WARD 55	9,149	3,028	6,121		3,093 D	33.1%	66.9%	33.1%	66.9%
	WARD 56	12,054	4,873	7,181		2,308 D	40.4%	59.6%	40.4%	59.6%
	WARD 57	8,245	3,255	4,990		1,735 D	39.5%	60.5%	39.5%	60.5%
	WARD 58	13,621	6,625	6,996		371 D	48.6%	51.4%	48.6%	51.4%
	WARD 59	4,421	967	3,454		2,487 D	21.9%	78.1%	21.9%	78.1%
	WARD 60	4,345	451	3,894		3,443 D	10.4%	89.6%	10.4%	89.6%

PHILIDELPHIA

GOVERNOR 1990

1990 Census Population	County	Total Vote	Republican	Democratic	Other	Rep.-Dem. Plurality	Percentage			
							Total Vote		Major Vote	
							Rep.	Dem.	Rep.	Dem.
	WARD 61	6,487	2,118	4,369		2,251 D	32.6%	67.4%	32.6%	67.4%
	WARD 62	9,167	3,137	6,030		2,893 D	34.2%	65.8%	34.2%	65.8%
	WARD 63	7,951	3,633	4,318		685 D	45.7%	54.3%	45.7%	54.3%
	WARD 64	5,850	2,251	3,599		1,348 D	38.5%	61.5%	38.5%	61.5%
	WARD 65	7,958	2,768	5,190		2,422 D	34.8%	65.2%	34.8%	65.2%
	WARD 66	13,247	4,802	8,445		3,643 D	36.2%	63.8%	36.2%	63.8%
1,585,577	TOTAL	390,780	114,390	276,390		162,000 D	29.3%	70.7%	29.3%	70.7%

PENNSYLVANIA

CONGRESS

CD	Year	Total Vote	Republican Vote	Republican Candidate	Democratic Vote	Democratic Candidate	Other Vote	Rep.-Dem. Plurality	Total Vote Rep.	Total Vote Dem.	Major Vote Rep.	Major Vote Dem.
1	1990	92,441	19,018	JACKSON, JAMES L.	73,423	FOGLIETTA, THOMAS M.		54,405 D	20.6%	79.4%	20.6%	79.4%
1	1988	167,825	39,749	O'BRIEN, WILLIAM J.	128,076	FOGLIETTA, THOMAS M.		88,327 D	23.7%	76.3%	23.7%	76.3%
1	1986	118,035	29,811	MUCCIOLO, ANTHONY J.	88,224	FOGLIETTA, THOMAS M.		58,413 D	25.3%	74.7%	25.3%	74.7%
1	1984	197,682	49,559	DI BIASE, CARMINE	148,123	FOGLIETTA, THOMAS M.		98,564 D	25.1%	74.9%	25.1%	74.9%
1	1982	143,416	38,155	MARINO, MICHAEL	103,626	FOGLIETTA, THOMAS M.	1,635	65,471 D	26.6%	72.3%	26.9%	73.1%
2	1990	102,702	8,118	BAKOVE, DONALD	94,584	GRAY, WILLIAM H.		86,466 D	7.9%	92.1%	7.9%	92.1%
2	1988	196,687	12,365	HARSCH, RICHARD L.	184,322	GRAY, WILLIAM H.		171,957 D	6.3%	93.7%	6.3%	93.7%
2	1986	130,495			128,399	GRAY, WILLIAM H.	2,096	128,399 D		98.4%		100.0%
2	1984	220,295	18,224	SHARPER, RONALD J.	200,484	GRAY, WILLIAM H.	1,587	182,260 D	8.3%	91.0%	8.3%	91.7%
2	1982	158,675			120,744	GRAY, WILLIAM H.	37,931	120,744 D		76.1%		100.0%
3	1990	149,809	59,901	MCCOLGAN, JOSEPH M.	89,908	BORSKI, ROBERT A.		30,007 D	40.0%	60.0%	40.0%	60.0%
3	1988	214,499	78,909	MATTHEWS, MARK	135,590	BORSKI, ROBERT A.		56,681 D	36.8%	63.2%	36.8%	63.2%
3	1986	174,497	66,693	ROVNER, ROBERT A.	107,804	BORSKI, ROBERT A.		41,111 D	38.2%	61.8%	38.2%	61.8%
3	1984	238,786	85,358	BECKER, FLORA L.	152,598	BORSKI, ROBERT A.	830	67,240 D	35.7%	63.9%	35.9%	64.1%
3	1982	193,954	94,497	DOUGHERTY, CHARLES F.	97,161	BORSKI, ROBERT A.	2,296	2,664 D	48.7%	50.1%	49.3%	50.7%
4	1990	132,583	58,469	JOHNSTON, GORDON R.	74,114	KOLTER, JOSEPH P.		15,645 D	44.1%	55.9%	44.1%	55.9%
4	1988	177,699	52,402	JOHNSTON, GORDON R.	124,041	KOLTER, JOSEPH P.	1,256	71,639 D	29.5%	69.8%	29.7%	70.3%
4	1986	142,594	55,165	LINDSAY, AL	86,133	KOLTER, JOSEPH P.	1,296	30,968 D	38.7%	60.4%	39.0%	61.0%
4	1984	200,809	86,769	KUNDER, JAMES	114,040	KOLTER, JOSEPH P.		27,271 D	43.2%	56.8%	43.2%	56.8%
4	1982	167,102	64,539	ATKINSON, EUGENE V.	100,481	KOLTER, JOSEPH P.	2,082	35,942 D	38.6%	60.1%	39.1%	60.9%
5	1990	131,489	75,097	SCHULZE, RICHARD T.	50,597	STRETTON, SAMUEL C.	5,795	24,500 R	57.1%	38.5%	59.7%	40.3%
5	1988	196,211	153,453	SCHULZE, RICHARD T.	42,758	HADLEY, DONALD		110,695 R	78.2%	21.8%	78.2%	21.8%
5	1986	133,241	87,593	SCHULZE, RICHARD T.	45,648	RINGGOLD, TIM		41,945 R	65.7%	34.3%	65.7%	34.3%
5	1984	195,551	141,965	SCHULZE, RICHARD T.	53,586	FANTI, LOUIS J.		88,379 R	72.6%	27.4%	72.6%	27.4%
5	1982	134,818	90,648	SCHULZE, RICHARD T.	44,170	BURGER, BOB		46,478 R	67.2%	32.8%	67.2%	32.8%
6	1990	130,487	56,093	HICKS, JOHN F.	74,394	YATRON, GUS		18,301 D	43.0%	57.0%	43.0%	57.0%
6	1988	180,745	65,278	ERWIN, JAMES R.	114,119	YATRON, GUS	1,348	48,841 D	36.1%	63.1%	36.4%	63.6%
6	1986	142,000	43,858	BERTASAVAGE, NORMAN W.	98,142	YATRON, GUS		54,284 D	30.9%	69.1%	30.9%	69.1%
6	1984	181,165			181,165	* YATRON, GUS		181,165 D		100.0%		100.0%
6	1982	150,385	42,155	MARTIN, HARRY B.	108,230	YATRON, GUS		66,075 D	28.0%	72.0%	28.0%	72.0%
7	1990	162,160	105,868	WELDON, CURT	56,292	INNELLI, JOHN		49,576 R	65.3%	34.7%	65.3%	34.7%
7	1988	229,132	155,387	WELDON, CURT	73,745	LANDAU, DAVID		81,642 R	67.8%	32.2%	67.8%	32.2%
7	1986	179,675	110,118	WELDON, CURT	69,557	SPINGLER, BILL		40,561 R	61.3%	38.7%	61.3%	38.7%
7	1984	248,504	124,046	WELDON, CURT	124,458	EDGAR, ROBERT W.		412 D	49.9%	50.1%	49.9%	50.1%
7	1982	190,798	85,023	JOACHIM, STEVE	105,775	EDGAR, ROBERT W.		20,752 D	44.6%	55.4%	44.6%	55.4%
8	1990	150,115	65,100	SCHALLER, AUDRIE Z.	85,015	KOSTMAYER, PETER H.		19,915 D	43.4%	56.6%	43.4%	56.6%
8	1988	225,566	93,648	HOWARD, ED	128,153	KOSTMAYER, PETER H.	3,765	34,505 D	41.5%	56.8%	42.2%	57.8%
8	1986	155,778	70,047	CHRISTIAN, DAVID A.	85,731	KOSTMAYER, PETER H.		15,684 D	45.0%	55.0%	45.0%	55.0%
8	1984	221,344	108,696	CHRISTIAN, DAVID A.	112,648	KOSTMAYER, PETER H.		3,952 D	49.1%	50.9%	49.1%	50.9%
8	1982	165,535	80,928	COYNE, JAMES K.	83,242	KOSTMAYER, PETER H.	1,365	2,314 D	48.9%	50.3%	49.3%	50.7%
9	1990	106,632	106,632	* SHUSTER, E. G.				106,632 R	100.0%		100.0%	
9	1988	158,702	158,702	* SHUSTER, E. G.				158,702 R	100.0%		100.0%	
9	1986	120,890	120,890	* SHUSTER, E. G.				120,890 R	100.0%		100.0%	
9	1984	177,986	118,437	SHUSTER, E. G.	59,549	KULP, NANCY		58,888 R	66.5%	33.5%	66.5%	33.5%
9	1982	141,905	92,322	SHUSTER, E. G.	49,583	DUNCAN, EUGENE J.		42,739 R	65.1%	34.9%	65.1%	34.9%
10	1990	113,490	113,490	* MCDADE, JOSEPH M.				113,490 R	100.0%		100.0%	
10	1988	191,275	140,096	MCDADE, JOSEPH M.	51,179	CORDARO, ROBERT C.		88,917 R	73.2%	26.8%	73.2%	26.8%
10	1986	158,851	118,603	MCDADE, JOSEPH M.	40,248	BOLUS, ROBERT C.		78,355 R	74.7%	25.3%	74.7%	25.3%
10	1984	194,737	150,166	MCDADE, JOSEPH M.	44,571	BASALYGA, GENE		105,595 R	77.1%	22.9%	77.1%	22.9%
10	1982	153,485	103,617	MCDADE, JOSEPH M.	49,868	RAFALKO, ROBERT J.		53,749 R	67.5%	32.5%	67.5%	32.5%

PENNSYLVANIA

CONGRESS

CD	Year	Total Vote	Republican Vote	Republican Candidate	Democratic Vote	Democratic Candidate	Other Vote	Rep.-Dem. Plurality	Total Vote Rep.	Total Vote Dem.	Major Vote Rep.	Major Vote Dem.
11	1990	88,219			88,219	KANJORSKI, PAUL E.		88,219 D		100.0%		100.0%
11	1988	120,706			120,706	KANJORSKI, PAUL E.		120,706 D		100.0%		100.0%
11	1986	159,190	46,785	HOLTZMAN, MARC	112,405	KANJORSKI, PAUL E.		65,620 D	29.4%	70.6%	29.4%	70.6%
11	1984	185,122	76,692	HUDOCK, ROBERT P.	108,430	KANJORSKI, PAUL E.		31,738 D	41.4%	58.6%	41.4%	58.6%
11	1982	168,856	78,485	NELLIGAN, JAMES L.	90,371	HARRISON, FRANK		11,886 D	46.5%	53.5%	46.5%	53.5%
12	1990	130,693	50,007	CHOBY, WILLEAM A.	80,686	MURTHA, JOHN P.		30,679 D	38.3%	61.7%	38.3%	61.7%
12	1988	133,081			133,081	MURTHA, JOHN P.		133,081 D		100.0%		100.0%
12	1986	144,072	46,937	HOLTZMAN, KATHY	97,135	MURTHA, JOHN P.		50,198 D	32.6%	67.4%	32.6%	67.4%
12	1984	194,494	57,446	FULLARD, THOMAS J.	134,384	MURTHA, JOHN P.	2,664	76,938 D	29.5%	69.1%	29.9%	70.1%
12	1982	157,640	54,212	TUSCANO, WILLIAM N.	96,369	MURTHA, JOHN P.	7,059	42,157 D	34.4%	61.1%	36.0%	64.0%
13	1990	148,544	89,577	COUGHLIN, R. LAWRENCE	58,967	TOMKIN, BERNARD		30,610 R	60.3%	39.7%	60.3%	39.7%
13	1988	228,615	152,191	COUGHLIN, R. LAWRENCE	76,424	TOMKIN, BERNARD		75,767 R	66.6%	33.4%	66.6%	33.4%
13	1986	172,082	100,701	COUGHLIN, R. LAWRENCE	71,381	HOEFFEL, JOSEPH M.		29,320 R	58.5%	41.5%	58.5%	41.5%
13	1984	238,704	133,948	COUGHLIN, R. LAWRENCE	104,756	HOEFFEL, JOSEPH M.		29,192 R	56.1%	43.9%	56.1%	43.9%
13	1982	169,824	109,198	COUGHLIN, R. LAWRENCE	59,709	CUNNINGHAM, MARTIN J.	917	49,489 R	64.3%	35.2%	64.6%	35.4%
14	1990	108,133	30,497	CALIGIURI, RICHARD E.	77,636	COYNE, WILLIAM J.		47,139 D	28.2%	71.8%	28.2%	71.8%
14	1988	171,900	36,719	CALIGIURI, RICHARD E.	135,181	COYNE, WILLIAM J.		98,462 D	21.4%	78.6%	21.4%	78.6%
14	1986	116,859			104,726	COYNE, WILLIAM J.	12,133	104,726 D		89.6%		100.0%
14	1984	213,797	42,616	CLARK, JOHN R.	163,818	COYNE, WILLIAM J.	7,363	121,202 D	19.9%	76.6%	20.6%	79.4%
14	1982	161,577	32,780	CLARK, JOHN R.	120,980	COYNE, WILLIAM J.	7,817	88,200 D	20.3%	74.9%	21.3%	78.7%
15	1990	127,411	77,178	RITTER, DONALD L.	50,233	ORLOSKI, RICHARD J.		26,945 R	60.6%	39.4%	60.6%	39.4%
15	1988	186,078	106,951	RITTER, DONALD L.	79,127	REIBMAN, ED		27,824 R	57.5%	42.5%	57.5%	42.5%
15	1986	131,801	74,829	RITTER, DONALD L.	56,972	SIMONETTA, JOE		17,857 R	56.8%	43.2%	56.8%	43.2%
15	1984	189,828	110,338	RITTER, DONALD L.	79,490	WELLS-SCHOOLEY, JANE		30,848 R	58.1%	41.9%	58.1%	41.9%
15	1982	137,457	79,455	RITTER, DONALD L.	58,002	ORLOSKI, RICHARD J.		21,453 R	57.8%	42.2%	57.8%	42.2%
16	1990	129,445	85,596	WALKER, ROBERT S.	43,849	GUYLL, ERNEST E.		41,747 R	66.1%	33.9%	66.1%	33.9%
16	1988	185,113	136,944	WALKER, ROBERT S.	48,169	GUYLL, ERNEST E.		88,775 R	74.0%	26.0%	74.0%	26.0%
16	1986	135,183	100,784	WALKER, ROBERT S.	34,399	HAGELGANS, JAMES D.		66,385 R	74.6%	25.4%	74.6%	25.4%
16	1984	177,992	138,477	WALKER, ROBERT S.	39,515	BARD, MARTIN L.		98,962 R	77.8%	22.2%	77.8%	22.2%
16	1982	130,398	93,034	WALKER, ROBERT S.	37,364	MOWERY, JEAN D.		55,670 R	71.3%	28.7%	71.3%	28.7%
17	1990	110,317	110,317	* GEKAS, GEORGE W.				110,317 R	100.0%		100.0%	
17	1988	166,289	166,289	* GEKAS, GEORGE W.				166,289 R	100.0%		100.0%	
17	1986	137,184	101,027	GEKAS, GEORGE W.	36,157	OGDEN, MICHAEL S.		64,870 R	73.6%	26.4%	73.6%	26.4%
17	1984	178,651	129,716	GEKAS, GEORGE W.	48,935	ANDERSON, STEPHEN A.		80,781 R	72.6%	27.4%	72.6%	27.4%
17	1982	146,265	84,291	GEKAS, GEORGE W.	61,974	HOCHENDONER, LARRY J.		22,317 R	57.6%	42.4%	57.6%	42.4%
18	1990	166,577	85,697	SANTORUM, RICK	80,880	WALGREN, DOUGLAS		4,817 R	51.4%	48.6%	51.4%	48.6%
18	1988	218,488	80,975	NEWMAN, JOHN A.	136,924	WALGREN, DOUGLAS	589	55,949 D	37.1%	62.7%	37.2%	62.8%
18	1986	165,328	61,164	BUCKMAN, ERNIE	104,164	WALGREN, DOUGLAS		43,000 D	37.0%	63.0%	37.0%	63.0%
18	1984	238,489	87,521	MAXWELL, JOHN G.	149,628	WALGREN, DOUGLAS	1,340	62,107 D	36.7%	62.7%	36.9%	63.1%
18	1982	187,683	84,428	JACOB, TED	101,807	WALGREN, DOUGLAS	1,448	17,379 D	45.0%	54.2%	45.3%	54.7%
19	1990	96,336	96,336	GOODLING, WILLIAM F.				96,336 R	100.0%		100.0%	
19	1988	188,200	145,381	GOODLING, WILLIAM F.	42,819	RITCHEY, PAUL E.		102,562 R	77.2%	22.8%	77.2%	22.8%
19	1986	137,278	100,055	GOODLING, WILLIAM F.	37,223	THORNTON, RICHARD F.		62,832 R	72.9%	27.1%	72.9%	27.1%
19	1984	186,742	141,196	GOODLING, WILLIAM F.	44,117	RARIG, JOHN	1,429	97,079 R	75.6%	23.6%	76.2%	23.8%
19	1982	142,950	101,163	GOODLING, WILLIAM F.	41,787	BECKER, LARRY		59,376 R	70.8%	29.2%	70.8%	29.2%
20	1990	125,134	43,054	LEE, ROBERT C.	82,080	GAYDOS, JOSEPH M.		39,026 D	34.4%	65.6%	34.4%	65.6%
20	1988	139,616			137,472	GAYDOS, JOSEPH M.	2,144	137,472 D		98.5%		100.0%
20	1986	138,752			136,638	* GAYDOS, JOSEPH M.	2,114	136,638 D		98.5%		100.0%
20	1984	208,998	50,247	LLOYD, DANIEL	158,751	GAYDOS, JOSEPH M.		108,504 D	24.0%	76.0%	24.0%	76.0%
20	1982	167,428	38,212	RAY, TERRY T.	127,281	GAYDOS, JOSEPH M.	1,935	89,069 D	22.8%	76.0%	23.1%	76.9%

PENNSYLVANIA

CONGRESS

CD	Year	Total Vote	Republican Vote	Candidate	Democratic Vote	Candidate	Other Vote	Rep.-Dem. Plurality	Total Vote Rep.	Total Vote Dem.	Major Vote Rep.	Major Vote Dem.
21	1990	92,732	92,732	RIDGE, THOMAS J.				92,732 R	100.0%		100.0%	
21	1988	180,120	141,832	RIDGE, THOMAS J.	38,288	ELDER, GEORGE R.		103,544 R	78.7%	21.3%	78.7%	21.3%
21	1986	137,472	111,148	RIDGE, THOMAS J.	26,324	BLACKWELL, JOYLYN		84,824 R	80.9%	19.1%	80.9%	19.1%
21	1984	192,109	125,730	RIDGE, THOMAS J.	65,594	YOUNG, JAMES A.	785	60,136 R	65.4%	34.1%	65.7%	34.3%
21	1982	159,631	80,180	RIDGE, THOMAS J.	79,451	ANDREZESKI, ANTHONY		729 R	50.2%	49.8%	50.2%	49.8%
22	1990	123,884	45,509	HAYDEN, SUZANNE	78,375	MURPHY, AUSTIN J.		32,866 D	36.7%	63.3%	36.7%	63.3%
22	1988	170,467	47,039	HODGKISS, WILLIAM	123,428	MURPHY, AUSTIN J.		76,389 D	27.6%	72.4%	27.6%	72.4%
22	1986	131,650			131,650	* MURPHY, AUSTIN J.		131,650 D		100.0%		100.0%
22	1984	194,428	39,752	PRYOR, NANCY S.	153,514	MURPHY, AUSTIN J.	1,162	113,762 D	20.4%	79.0%	20.6%	79.4%
22	1982	157,215	32,176	PATERRA, FRANK J.	123,716	MURPHY, AUSTIN J.	1,323	91,540 D	20.5%	78.7%	20.6%	79.4%
23	1990	131,654	78,189	CLINGER, WILLIAM F.	53,465	SHANNON, DANIEL J.		24,724 R	59.4%	40.6%	59.4%	40.6%
23	1988	170,160	105,575	CLINGER, WILLIAM F.	63,476	SHAKESPEARE, HOWARD	1,109	42,099 R	62.0%	37.3%	62.5%	37.5%
23	1986	143,470	79,595	CLINGER, WILLIAM F.	63,875	WACHOB, BILL		15,720 R	55.5%	44.5%	55.5%	44.5%
23	1984	183,909	94,952	CLINGER, WILLIAM F.	88,957	WACHOB, BILL		5,995 R	51.6%	48.4%	51.6%	48.4%
23	1982	141,721	92,424	CLINGER, WILLIAM F.	49,297	CALLA, JOSEPH J.		43,127 R	65.2%	34.8%	65.2%	34.8%

PENNSYLVANIA

1990 GENERAL ELECTION

Governor

Congress   An asterisk in the Congressional vote table indicates a candidate received votes as the nominee of an additional party. Other vote was American Systems (Smith) in CD 5.

PHILADELPHIA

Philadelphia city and county are coterminous. 1990 Population by wards is not available.

Governor   In the table of the vote by wards, there are small differences between the state certified totals for the candidates and the addition of the vote by wards. The state certified totals are used in the total line and the breakdown by wards is from the Philadelphia Registration Commission.

1990 PRIMARIES

MAY 15 REPUBLICAN

Governor   321,026 Barbara Hafer; 268,773 Marguerite A. Luksik.

Congress   Unopposed in nineteen CD's. No candidate in CD 11. Contested as follows:

   CD 4   16,549 Gordon R. Johnston; 8,703 John Loth.
   CD 12   12,229 Willeam A. Choby; 11,040 Tony Joseph.
   CD 19   33,139 William F. Goodling; 4,689 Francis Worley.

MAY 15 DEMOCRATIC

Governor   636,594 Robert Casey; 184,365 Philip J. Berg.

Congress   Unopposed in eleven CD's. No candidate in CD's 9, 10, 17, 19, and 21. In CD 9 E. G. Shuster, the Republican nominee, received write-in votes in the Democratic parimay and became the nominee of both parties. In CD 10 Joseph M. McDade, the Republican nominee, received write-in votes in the Democratic primary and became the nominee of both parties. In CD 17 George W. Gekas, the Repbulican nominee, received write-in votes in the Democratic primary and became the nominee of both parties. Contested as follows:

   CD 1   28,394 Thomas M. Foglietta; 5,977 Willis W. Berry.
   CD 4   31,955 Joseph P. Kolter; 6,613 Frank M. Clark.
   CD 5   8,254 Samuel C. Stretton; 2,337 Donald Hadley.
   CD 12   29,369 John P. Murtha; 24,594 Kenneth B. Burkley; 3,679 John K. Shrader.
   CD 15   11,734 Richard J. Orloski; 8,560 John B. Drescher; 3,624 Charles Buss.
   CD 20   42,910 Joseph M. Gaydos; 21,831 Emil Mrkonic.
   CD 22   48,455 Austin J. Murphy; 20,713 William A. Nicolella.

RHODE ISLAND

GOVERNOR
Bruce G. Sundlun (D). Elected 1990 to a two-year term.

SENATORS
John H. Chafee (R). Re-elected 1988 to a six-year term. Previously elected 1982, 1976.

Claiborne Pell (D). Re-elected 1990 to a six-year term. Previously elected 1984, 1978, 1972, 1966, 1960.

REPRESENTATIVES
1. Ronald K. Machtley (R)   2. John F. Reed (D)

POSTWAR VOTE FOR PRESIDENT

Year	Total Vote	Republican Vote	Republican Candidate	Democratic Vote	Democratic Candidate	Other Vote	Plurality	Percentage Total Vote Rep.	Dem.	Major Vote Rep.	Dem.
1988	404,620	177,761	Bush, George	225,123	Dukakis, Michael S.	1,736	47,362 D	43.9%	55.6%	44.1%	55.9%
1984	410,492	212,080	Reagan, Ronald	197,106	Mondale, Walter F.	1,306	14,974 R	51.7%	48.0%	51.8%	48.2%
1980	416,072	154,793	Reagan, Ronald	198,342	Carter, Jimmy	62,937	43,549 D	37.2%	47.7%	43.8%	56.2%
1976	411,170	181,249	Ford, Gerald R.	227,636	Carter, Jimmy	2,285	46,387 D	44.1%	55.4%	44.3%	55.7%
1972	415,808	220,383	Nixon, Richard M.	194,645	McGovern, George S.	780	25,738 R	53.0%	46.8%	53.1%	46.9%
1968	385,000	122,359	Nixon, Richard M.	246,518	Humphrey, Hubert H.	16,123	124,159 D	31.8%	64.0%	33.2%	66.8%
1964	390,091	74,615	Goldwater, Barry M.	315,463	Johnson, Lyndon B.	13	240,848 D	19.1%	80.9%	19.1%	80.9%
1960	405,535	147,502	Nixon, Richard M.	258,032	Kennedy, John F.	1	110,530 D	36.4%	63.6%	36.4%	63.6%
1956	387,609	225,819	Eisenhower, Dwight D.	161,790	Stevenson, Adlai E.		64,029 R	58.3%	41.7%	58.3%	41.7%
1952	414,498	210,935	Eisenhower, Dwight D.	203,293	Stevenson, Adlai E.	270	7,642 R	50.9%	49.0%	50.9%	49.1%
1948	327,702	135,787	Dewey, Thomas E.	188,736	Truman, Harry S.	3,179	52,949 D	41.4%	57.6%	41.8%	58.2%

RHODE ISLAND

POSTWAR VOTE FOR GOVERNOR

Year	Total Vote	Republican Vote	Candidate	Democratic Vote	Candidate	Other Vote	Rep-Dem. Plurality	Percentage Total Vote Rep.	Dem.	Major Vote Rep.	Dem.
1990	356,672	92,177	DiPrete, Edward	264,411	Sundlun, Bruce G.	84	172,234 D	25.8%	74.1%	25.8%	74.2%
1988	400,516	203,550	DiPrete, Edward	196,936	Sundlun, Bruce G.	30	6,614 R	50.8%	49.2%	50.8%	49.2%
1986	322,724	208,822	DiPrete, Edward	104,508	Sundlun, Bruce G.	9,394	104,314 R	64.7%	32.4%	66.6%	33.4%
1984	408,375	245,059	DiPrete, Edward	163,311	Solomon, Anthony J.	5	81,748 R	60.0%	40.0%	60.0%	40.0%
1982	337,259	79,602	Marzullo, Vincent	247,208	Garrahy, J. Joseph	10,449	167,606 D	23.6%	73.3%	24.4%	75.6%
1980	405,916	106,729	Cianci, Vincent A.	299,174	Garrahy, J. Joseph	13	192,445 D	26.3%	73.7%	26.3%	73.7%
1978	314,363	96,596	Almond, Lincoln	197,386	Garrahy, J. Joseph	20,381	100,790 D	30.7%	62.8%	32.9%	67.1%
1976	398,683	178,254	Taft, James L.	218,561	Garrahy, J. Joseph	1,868	40,307 D	44.7%	54.8%	44.9%	55.1%
1974	321,660	69,224	Nugent, James W.	252,436	Noel, Philip W.		183,212 D	21.5%	78.5%	21.5%	78.5%
1972	412,866	194,315	DeSimone, Herbert F.	216,953	Noel, Philip W.	1,598	22,638 D	47.1%	52.5%	47.2%	52.8%
1970	346,342	171,549	DeSimone, Herbert F.	173,420	Licht, Frank	1,373	1,871 D	49.5%	50.1%	49.7%	50.3%
1968	383,725	187,958	Chafee, John H.	195,766	Licht, Frank	1	7,808 D	49.0%	51.0%	49.0%	51.0%
1966	332,064	210,202	Chafee, John H.	121,862	Hobbs, Horace E.		88,340 R	63.3%	36.7%	63.3%	36.7%
1964	391,668	239,501	Chafee, John H.	152,165	Gallogly, Edward P.	2	87,336 R	61.1%	38.9%	61.1%	38.9%
1962	327,506	163,952	Chafee, John H.	163,554	Notte, John A.		398 R	50.1%	49.9%	50.1%	49.9%
1960	401,362	174,044	Del Sesto, Christopher	227,318	Notte, John A.		53,274 D	43.4%	56.6%	43.4%	56.6%
1958	346,780	176,505	Del Sesto, Christopher	170,275	Roberts, Dennis J.		6,230 R	50.9%	49.1%	50.9%	49.1%
1956	383,919	191,604	Del Sesto, Christopher	192,315	Roberts, Dennis J.		711 D	49.9%	50.1%	49.9%	50.1%
1954	328,670	137,131	Lewis, Dean J.	189,595	Roberts, Dennis J.	1,944	52,464 D	41.7%	57.7%	42.0%	58.0%
1952	409,689	194,102	Archambault, Raoul	215,587	Roberts, Dennis J.		21,485 D	47.4%	52.6%	47.4%	52.6%
1950	296,809	120,684	Lachapelle, E. T.	176,125	Roberts, Dennis J.		55,441 D	40.7%	59.3%	40.7%	59.3%
1948	323,863	124,441	Ruerat, Albert P.	198,056	Pastore, John O.	1,366	73,615 D	38.4%	61.2%	38.6%	61.4%
1946	275,341	126,456	Murphy, John G.	148,885	Pastore, John O.		22,429 D	45.9%	54.1%	45.9%	54.1%

POSTWAR VOTE FOR SENATOR

Year	Total Vote	Republican Vote	Candidate	Democratic Vote	Candidate	Other Vote	Rep-Dem. Plurality	Percentage Total Vote Rep.	Dem.	Major Vote Rep.	Dem.
1990	364,062	138,947	Schneider, Claudine	225,105	Pell, Claiborne	10	86,158 D	38.2%	61.8%	38.2%	61.8%
1988	397,996	217,273	Chafee, John H.	180,717	Licht, Richard A.	6	36,556 R	54.6%	45.4%	54.6%	45.4%
1984	395,285	108,492	Leonard, Barbara	286,780	Pell, Claiborne	13	178,288 D	27.4%	72.6%	27.4%	72.6%
1982	342,779	175,495	Chafee, John H.	167,283	Michaelson, Julius C.	1	8,212 R	51.2%	48.8%	51.2%	48.8%
1978	305,618	76,061	Reynolds, James G.	229,557	Pell, Claiborne		153,496 D	24.9%	75.1%	24.9%	75.1%
1976	398,906	230,329	Chafee, John H.	167,665	Lorber, Richard P.	912	62,664 R	57.7%	42.0%	57.9%	42.1%
1972	413,432	188,990	Chafee, John H.	221,942	Pell, Claiborne	2,500	32,952 D	45.7%	53.7%	46.0%	54.0%
1970	341,222	107,351	McLaughlin, John	230,469	Pastore, John O.	3,402	123,118 D	31.5%	67.5%	31.8%	68.2%
1966	324,173	104,838	Briggs, Ruth M.	219,331	Pell, Claiborne	4	114,493 D	32.3%	67.7%	32.3%	67.7%
1964	386,322	66,715	Lagueux, Ronald R.	319,607	Pastore, John O.		252,892 D	17.3%	82.7%	17.3%	82.7%
1960	399,983	124,408	Archambault, Raoul	275,575	Pell, Claiborne		151,167 D	31.1%	68.9%	31.1%	68.9%
1958	344,519	122,353	Ewing, Bayard	222,166	Pastore, John O.		99,813 D	35.5%	64.5%	35.5%	64.5%
1954	326,624	132,970	Sundlun, Walter I.	193,654	Green, Theodore F.		60,684 D	40.7%	59.3%	40.7%	59.3%
1952	410,978	185,850	Ewing, Bayard	225,128	Pastore, John O.		39,278 D	45.2%	54.8%	45.2%	54.8%
1950 S	297,909	114,184	Levy, Austin T.	183,725	Pastore, John O.		69,541 D	38.3%	61.7%	38.3%	61.7%
1948	320,420	130,262	Hazard, Thomas P.	190,158	Green, Theodore F.		59,896 D	40.7%	59.3%	40.7%	59.3%
1946	273,528	122,780	Dyer, W. Gurnee	150,748	McGrath, J. Howard		27,968 D	44.9%	55.1%	44.9%	55.1%

The 1950 election was for a short term to fill a vacancy.

RHODE ISLAND

Districts Established April 9, 1982

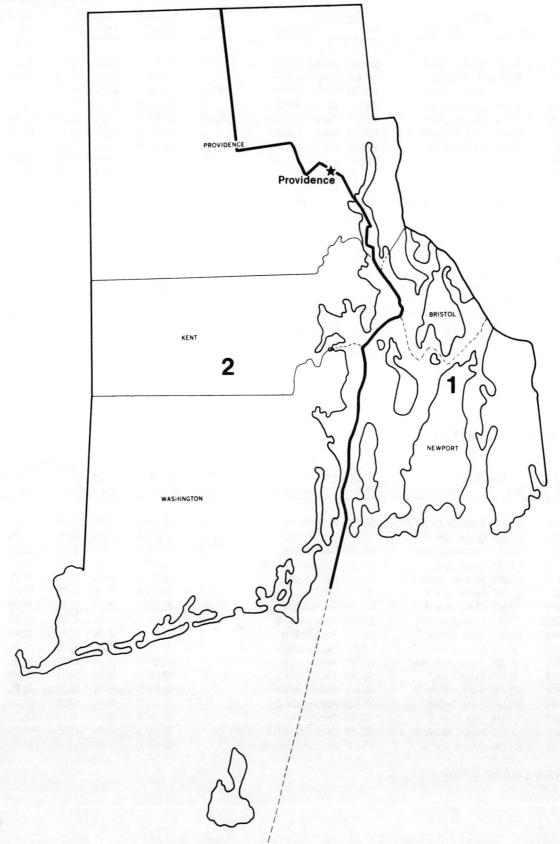

RHODE ISLAND

GOVERNOR 1990

1990 Census Population	County	Total Vote	Republican	Democratic	Other	Rep.-Dem. Plurality	Percentage			
							Total Vote		Major Vote	
							Rep.	Dem.	Rep.	Dem.
48,859	BRISTOL	19,160	5,745	13,415		7,670 D	30.0%	70.0%	30.0%	70.0%
161,135	KENT	65,257	16,555	48,702		32,147 D	25.4%	74.6%	25.4%	74.6%
87,194	NEWPORT	28,896	7,915	20,981		13,066 D	27.4%	72.6%	27.4%	72.6%
596,270	PROVIDENCE	204,412	50,629	153,783		103,154 D	24.8%	75.2%	24.8%	75.2%
110,006	WASHINGTON	38,863	11,333	27,530		16,197 D	29.2%	70.8%	29.2%	70.8%
1,003,464	TOTAL	356,672	92,177	264,411	84	172,234 D	25.8%	74.1%	25.8%	74.2%

RHODE ISLAND

SENATOR 1990

1990 Census Population	County	Total Vote	Republican	Democratic	Other	Rep.-Dem. Plurality	Percentage			
							Total Vote		Major Vote	
							Rep.	Dem.	Rep.	Dem.
48,859	BRISTOL	19,718	8,122	11,596		3,474 D	41.2%	58.8%	41.2%	58.8%
161,135	KENT	66,588	29,475	37,113		7,638 D	44.3%	55.7%	44.3%	55.7%
87,194	NEWPORT	29,689	11,143	18,546		7,403 D	37.5%	62.5%	37.5%	62.5%
596,270	PROVIDENCE	207,907	71,526	136,381		64,855 D	34.4%	65.6%	34.4%	65.6%
110,006	WASHINGTON	40,150	18,681	21,469		2,788 D	46.5%	53.5%	46.5%	53.5%
1,003,464	TOTAL	364,062	138,947	225,105	10	86,158 D	38.2%	61.8%	38.2%	61.8%

RHODE ISLAND

GOVERNOR 1990

1990 Census Population	City/Town	Total Vote	Republican	Democratic	Other	Rep.-Dem. Plurality	Percentage Total Vote Rep.	Dem.	Major Vote Rep.	Dem.
15,849	BARRINGTON	7,526	2,366	5,160		2,794 D	31.4%	68.6%	31.4%	68.6%
21,625	BRISTOL TOWN	7,703	2,285	5,418		3,133 D	29.7%	70.3%	29.7%	70.3%
16,230	BURRILLVILLE	4,943	1,217	3,726		2,509 D	24.6%	75.4%	24.6%	75.4%
17,637	CENTRAL FALLS	3,443	583	2,860		2,277 D	16.9%	83.1%	16.9%	83.1%
6,478	CHARLESTOWN	2,297	785	1,512		727 D	34.2%	65.8%	34.2%	65.8%
31,083	COVENTRY	11,362	2,971	8,391		5,420 D	26.1%	73.9%	26.1%	73.9%
76,060	CRANSTON	33,445	11,890	21,555		9,665 D	35.6%	64.4%	35.6%	64.4%
29,038	CUMBERLAND	12,421	2,995	9,426		6,431 D	24.1%	75.9%	24.1%	75.9%
11,865	EAST GREENWICH	5,151	1,626	3,525		1,899 D	31.6%	68.4%	31.6%	68.4%
50,380	EAST PROVIDENCE	16,876	3,756	13,120		9,364 D	22.3%	77.7%	22.3%	77.7%
5,461	EXETER	1,928	558	1,370		812 D	28.9%	71.1%	28.9%	71.1%
4,316	FOSTER	1,696	468	1,228		760 D	27.6%	72.4%	27.6%	72.4%
9,227	GLOCESTER	3,308	912	2,396		1,484 D	27.6%	72.4%	27.6%	72.4%
6,873	HOPKINTON	2,305	736	1,569		833 D	31.9%	68.1%	31.9%	68.1%
4,999	JAMESTOWN	2,499	601	1,898		1,297 D	24.0%	76.0%	24.0%	76.0%
26,542	JOHNSTON	11,466	2,701	8,765		6,064 D	23.6%	76.4%	23.6%	76.4%
18,045	LINCOLN	8,026	2,007	6,019		4,012 D	25.0%	75.0%	25.0%	75.0%
3,339	LITTLE COMPTON	1,647	564	1,083		519 D	34.2%	65.8%	34.2%	65.8%
19,460	MIDDLETOWN	5,282	1,408	3,874		2,466 D	26.7%	73.3%	26.7%	73.3%
14,985	NARRAGANSETT	5,582	1,571	4,011		2,440 D	28.1%	71.9%	28.1%	71.9%
28,227	NEWPORT CITY	7,885	1,880	6,005		4,125 D	23.8%	76.2%	23.8%	76.2%
836	NEW SHOREHAM	701	262	439		177 D	37.4%	62.6%	37.4%	62.6%
23,786	NORTH KINGSTOWN	9,477	2,463	7,014		4,551 D	26.0%	74.0%	26.0%	74.0%
32,090	NORTH PROVIDENCE	14,268	3,177	11,091		7,914 D	22.3%	77.7%	22.3%	77.7%
10,497	NORTH SMITHFIELD	4,532	1,262	3,270		2,008 D	27.8%	72.2%	27.8%	72.2%
72,644	PAWTUCKET	21,790	4,132	17,658		13,526 D	19.0%	81.0%	19.0%	81.0%
16,857	PORTSMOUTH	6,276	1,817	4,459		2,642 D	29.0%	71.0%	29.0%	71.0%
160,728	PROVIDENCE CITY	44,946	9,906	35,040		25,134 D	22.0%	78.0%	22.0%	78.0%
5,351	RICHMOND	1,950	530	1,420		890 D	27.2%	72.8%	27.2%	72.8%
9,796	SCITUATE	4,046	1,292	2,754		1,462 D	31.9%	68.1%	31.9%	68.1%
19,163	SMITHFIELD	7,370	1,715	5,655		3,940 D	23.3%	76.7%	23.3%	76.7%
24,631	SOUTH KINGSTOWN	7,458	2,098	5,360		3,262 D	28.1%	71.9%	28.1%	71.9%
14,312	TIVERTON	5,307	1,645	3,662		2,017 D	31.0%	69.0%	31.0%	69.0%
11,385	WARREN	3,931	1,094	2,837		1,743 D	27.8%	72.2%	27.8%	72.2%
85,427	WARWICK	36,519	8,805	27,714		18,909 D	24.1%	75.9%	24.1%	75.9%
21,605	WESTERLY	7,165	2,330	4,835		2,505 D	32.5%	67.5%	32.5%	67.5%
3,492	WEST GREENWICH	1,603	467	1,136		669 D	29.1%	70.9%	29.1%	70.9%
29,268	WEST WARWICK	10,622	2,686	7,936		5,250 D	25.3%	74.7%	25.3%	74.7%
43,877	WOONSOCKET	11,836	2,616	9,220		6,604 D	22.1%	77.9%	22.1%	77.9%
1,003,464	TOTAL	356,672	92,177	264,411	84	172,234 D	25.8%	74.1%	25.8%	74.2%

RHODE ISLAND

SENATOR 1990

1990 Census Population	City/Town	Total Vote	Republican	Democratic	Other	Rep.-Dem. Plurality	Percentage			
							Total Vote		Major Vote	
							Rep.	Dem.	Rep.	Dem.
15,849	BARRINGTON	7,717	3,631	4,086		455 D	47.1%	52.9%	47.1%	52.9%
21,625	BRISTOL TOWN	7,956	2,884	5,072		2,188 D	36.2%	63.8%	36.2%	63.8%
16,230	BURRILLVILLE	5,054	2,209	2,845		636 D	43.7%	56.3%	43.7%	56.3%
17,637	CENTRAL FALLS	3,477	994	2,483		1,489 D	28.6%	71.4%	28.6%	71.4%
6,478	CHARLESTOWN	2,371	1,270	1,101		169 R	53.6%	46.4%	53.6%	46.4%
31,083	COVENTRY	11,572	5,517	6,055		538 D	47.7%	52.3%	47.7%	52.3%
76,060	CRANSTON	33,953	13,155	20,798		7,643 D	38.7%	61.3%	38.7%	61.3%
29,038	CUMBERLAND	12,699	4,750	7,949		3,199 D	37.4%	62.6%	37.4%	62.6%
11,865	EAST GREENWICH	5,396	2,955	2,441		514 R	54.8%	45.2%	54.8%	45.2%
50,380	EAST PROVIDENCE	17,215	5,807	11,408		5,601 D	33.7%	66.3%	33.7%	66.3%
5,461	EXETER	1,971	1,033	938		95 R	52.4%	47.6%	52.4%	47.6%
4,316	FOSTER	1,748	867	881		14 D	49.6%	50.4%	49.6%	50.4%
9,227	GLOCESTER	3,375	1,650	1,725		75 D	48.9%	51.1%	48.9%	51.1%
6,873	HOPKINTON	2,369	1,237	1,132		105 R	52.2%	47.8%	52.2%	47.8%
4,999	JAMESTOWN	2,542	1,030	1,512		482 D	40.5%	59.5%	40.5%	59.5%
26,542	JOHNSTON	11,690	4,099	7,591		3,492 D	35.1%	64.9%	35.1%	64.9%
18,045	LINCOLN	8,162	3,426	4,736		1,310 D	42.0%	58.0%	42.0%	58.0%
3,339	LITTLE COMPTON	1,690	750	940		190 D	44.4%	55.6%	44.4%	55.6%
19,460	MIDDLETOWN	5,452	2,042	3,410		1,368 D	37.5%	62.5%	37.5%	62.5%
14,985	NARRAGANSETT	5,781	2,407	3,374		967 D	41.6%	58.4%	41.6%	58.4%
28,227	NEWPORT CITY	8,109	2,407	5,702		3,295 D	29.7%	70.3%	29.7%	70.3%
836	NEW SHOREHAM	751	345	406		61 D	45.9%	54.1%	45.9%	54.1%
23,786	NORTH KINGSTOWN	9,837	4,782	5,055		273 D	48.6%	51.4%	48.6%	51.4%
32,090	NORTH PROVIDENCE	14,375	4,408	9,967		5,559 D	30.7%	69.3%	30.7%	69.3%
10,497	NORTH SMITHFIELD	4,641	1,852	2,789		937 D	39.9%	60.1%	39.9%	60.1%
72,644	PAWTUCKET	21,886	6,877	15,009		8,132 D	31.4%	68.6%	31.4%	68.6%
16,857	PORTSMOUTH	6,460	2,664	3,796		1,132 D	41.2%	58.8%	41.2%	58.8%
160,728	PROVIDENCE CITY	45,796	12,255	33,541		21,286 D	26.8%	73.2%	26.8%	73.2%
5,351	RICHMOND	2,005	1,017	988		29 R	50.7%	49.3%	50.7%	49.3%
9,796	SCITUATE	4,157	2,316	1,841		475 R	55.7%	44.3%	55.7%	44.3%
19,163	SMITHFIELD	7,556	2,958	4,598		1,640 D	39.1%	60.9%	39.1%	60.9%
24,631	SOUTH KINGSTOWN	7,684	3,439	4,245		806 D	44.8%	55.2%	44.8%	55.2%
14,312	TIVERTON	5,436	2,250	3,186		936 D	41.4%	58.6%	41.4%	58.6%
11,385	WARREN	4,045	1,607	2,438		831 D	39.7%	60.3%	39.7%	60.3%
85,427	WARWICK	37,086	15,462	21,624		6,162 D	41.7%	58.3%	41.7%	58.3%
21,605	WESTERLY	7,381	3,151	4,230		1,079 D	42.7%	57.3%	42.7%	57.3%
3,492	WEST GREENWICH	1,630	842	788		54 R	51.7%	48.3%	51.7%	48.3%
29,268	WEST WARWICK	10,904	4,699	6,205		1,506 D	43.1%	56.9%	43.1%	56.9%
43,877	WOONSOCKET	12,123	3,903	8,220		4,317 D	32.2%	67.8%	32.2%	67.8%
1,003,464	TOTAL	364,062	138,947	225,105	10	86,158 D	38.2%	61.8%	38.2%	61.8%

RHODE ISLAND

CONGRESS

CD	Year	Total Vote	Republican Vote	Republican Candidate	Democratic Vote	Democratic Candidate	Other Vote	Rep.-Dem. Plurality	Percentage Total Vote Rep.	Dem.	Major Vote Rep.	Dem.
1	1990	163,094	89,963	MACHTLEY, RONALD K.	73,131	WOLF, SCOTT		16,832 R	55.2%	44.8%	55.2%	44.8%
1	1988	189,647	105,506	MACHTLEY, RONALD K.	84,141	ST. GERMAIN, FERNAND		21,365 R	55.6%	44.4%	55.6%	44.4%
1	1986	147,474	62,397	HOLMES, JOHN A.	85,077	ST. GERMAIN, FERNAND		22,680 D	42.3%	57.7%	42.3%	57.7%
1	1984	190,511	59,926	REGO, ALFRED	130,585	ST. GERMAIN, FERNAND		70,659 D	31.5%	68.5%	31.5%	68.5%
1	1982	160,131	61,253	STALLWOOD, BURTON	97,254	ST. GERMAIN, FERNAND	1,624	36,001 D	38.3%	60.7%	38.6%	61.4%
2	1990	183,771	74,953	COXE, GERTRUDE M.	108,818	REED, JOHN F.		33,865 D	40.8%	59.2%	40.8%	59.2%
2	1988	201,347	145,218	SCHNEIDER, CLAUDINE	56,129	MORGENTHAU, RUTH S.		89,089 R	72.1%	27.9%	72.1%	27.9%
2	1986	158,189	113,603	SCHNEIDER, CLAUDINE	44,586	FERRY, DONALD J.		69,017 R	71.8%	28.2%	71.8%	28.2%
2	1984	199,508	135,151	SCHNEIDER, CLAUDINE	64,357	SINAPI, RICHARD		70,794 R	67.7%	32.3%	67.7%	32.3%
2	1982	173,051	96,282	SCHNEIDER, CLAUDINE	76,769	AUKERMAN, JAMES V.		19,513 R	55.6%	44.4%	55.6%	44.4%

RHODE ISLAND

1990 GENERAL ELECTION

In addition to the county-by-county figures, data are presented by cities and towns.

Governor The total in the other vote column represents scattered write-in votes not available by county or city/town.

Senator The total in the other vote column represents scattered write-in votes not available by county or city/town.

Congress There were 14 scattered write-in votes not available by CD's.

1990 PRIMARIES

SEPTEMBER 11 REPUBLICAN

Governor 7,644 Edward DiPrete; 3,157 Steve White.

Senator Claudine Schneider, unopposed.

Congress Unopposed in CD 1. Contested as follows:

  CD 2 4,729 Gertrude M. Coxe; 2,057 David A. Gingerella.

SEPTEMBER 11 DEMOCRATIC

Governor 68,021 Bruce G. Sundlun; 53,821 Francis X. Flaherty; 46,074 Joseph R. Paolino.

Senator Claiborne Pell, unopposed.

Congress Unopposed in CD 1. Contested as follows:

  CD 2 36,315 John F. Reed; 20,308 Edward P. Beard; 10,861 Charles H. Gifford; 6,613 Rodney D. Driver.

SOUTH CAROLINA

GOVERNOR
Carroll Campbell (R). Re-elected 1990 to a four-year term. Previously elected 1986.

SENATORS
Ernest F. Hollings (D). Re-elected 1986 to a six-year term. Previously elected 1980, 1974, 1968 and in 1966 to fill out term vacated by the death of Senator Olin D. Johnston.

Strom Thurmond (R). Re-elected 1990 to a six-year term. Previously elected 1984, 1978, 1972, 1966, 1960 and in 1956 to fill out term vacated by his own resignation in April 1956; had been elected to this term in 1954 as an Independent Democrat. Changed party affiliation from Democrat to Republican in September 1964.

REPRESENTATIVES
1. Arthur Ravenel (R)
2. Floyd Spence (R)
3. Butler Derrick (D)
4. Elizabeth J. Patterson (D)
5. John Spratt (D)
6. Robert M. Tallon (D)

POSTWAR VOTE FOR PRESIDENT

Year	Total Vote	Republican Vote	Candidate	Democratic Vote	Candidate	Other Vote	Plurality	Total Vote Rep.	Dem.	Major Vote Rep.	Dem.
1988	986,009	606,443	Bush, George	370,554	Dukakis, Michael S.	9,012	235,889 R	61.5%	37.6%	62.1%	37.9%
1984	968,529	615,539	Reagan, Ronald	344,459	Mondale, Walter F.	8,531	271,080 R	63.6%	35.6%	64.1%	35.9%
1980	894,071	441,841	Reagan, Ronald	430,385	Carter, Jimmy	21,845	11,456 R	49.4%	48.1%	50.7%	49.3%
1976	802,583	346,149	Ford, Gerald R.	450,807	Carter, Jimmy	5,627	104,658 D	43.1%	56.2%	43.4%	56.6%
1972	673,960	477,044	Nixon, Richard M.	186,824	McGovern, George S.	10,092	290,220 R	70.8%	27.7%	71.9%	28.1%
1968 **	666,978	254,062	Nixon, Richard M.	197,486	Humphrey, Hubert H.	215,430	38,632 R	38.1%	29.6%	56.3%	43.7%
1964	524,779	309,048	Goldwater, Barry M.	215,723	Johnson, Lyndon B.	8	93,325 R	58.9%	41.1%	58.9%	41.1%
1960	386,688	188,558	Nixon, Richard M.	198,129	Kennedy, John F.	1	9,571 D	48.8%	51.2%	48.8%	51.2%
1956 **	300,583	75,700	Eisenhower, Dwight D.	136,372	Stevenson, Adlai E.	88,511	47,863 D	25.2%	45.4%	35.7%	64.3%
1952	341,087	168,082	Eisenhower, Dwight D.	173,004	Stevenson, Adlai E.	1	4,922 D	49.3%	50.7%	49.3%	50.7%
1948 **	142,571	5,386	Dewey, Thomas E.	34,423	Truman, Harry S.	102,762	68,184 SR	3.8%	24.1%	13.5%	86.5%

In 1968 other vote was Independent (Wallace). In 1956 other vote was 88,509 Independent (Uncommitted States Rights) and 2 scattered. In 1948 other vote was 102,607 States Rights; 154 Progressive and 1 Socialist.

POSTWAR VOTE FOR GOVERNOR

Year	Total Vote	Republican Vote	Candidate	Democratic Vote	Candidate	Other Vote	Rep-Dem. Plurality	Total Vote Rep.	Dem.	Major Vote Rep.	Dem.
1990	760,965	528,831	Campbell, Carroll	212,034	Mitchell, Theo	20,100	316,797 R	69.5%	27.9%	71.4%	28.6%
1986	753,751	384,565	Campbell, Carroll	361,325	Daniel, Mike	7,861	23,240 R	51.0%	47.9%	51.6%	48.4%
1982	671,625	202,806	Workman, W. D.	468,819	Riley, Richard W.		266,013 D	30.2%	69.8%	30.2%	69.8%
1978	627,182	236,946	Young, Edward L.	384,898	Riley, Richard W.	5,338	147,952 D	37.8%	61.4%	38.1%	61.9%
1974	523,199	266,109	Edwards, James B.	248,938	Dorn, W. J. Bryan	8,152	17,171 R	50.9%	47.6%	51.7%	48.3%
1970	484,857	221,233	Watson, Albert W.	250,551	West, John C.	13,073	29,318 D	45.6%	51.7%	46.9%	53.1%
1966	439,942	184,088	Rogers, Joseph O.	255,854	McNair, Robert E.		71,766 D	41.8%	58.2%	41.8%	58.2%
1962	253,721	—		253,704	Russell, Donald S.	17	253,704 D		100.0%		100.0%
1958	77,740	—		77,714	Hollings, Ernest F.	26	77,714 D		100.0%		100.0%
1954	214,212	—		214,204	Timmerman, George B.	8	214,204 D		100.0%		100.0%
1950	50,642	—		50,633	Byrnes, James F.	9	50,633 D		100.0%		100.0%
1946	26,520	—		26,520	Thurmond, Strom		26,520 D		100.0%		100.0%

SOUTH CAROLINA

POSTWAR VOTE FOR SENATOR

Year	Total Vote	Republican Vote	Candidate	Democratic Vote	Candidate	Other Vote	Rep-Dem. Plurality	Percentage Total Vote Rep.	Dem.	Major Vote Rep.	Dem.
1990	750,716	482,032	Thurmond, Strom	244,112	Cunningham, Bob	24,572	237,920 R	64.2%	32.5%	66.4%	33.6%
1986	737,962	262,886	McMaster, Henry D.	465,500	Hollings, Ernest F.	9,576	202,614 D	35.6%	63.1%	36.1%	63.9%
1984	965,130	644,815	Thurmond, Strom	306,982	Purvis, Melvin	13,333	337,833 R	66.8%	31.8%	67.7%	32.3%
1980	870,594	257,946	Mays, Marshall T.	612,554	Hollings, Ernest F.	94	354,608 D	29.6%	70.4%	29.6%	70.4%
1978	632,852	351,733	Thurmond, Strom	281,119	Ravenel, Charles D.		70,614 R	55.6%	44.4%	55.6%	44.4%
1974	512,397	146,645	Bush, Gwenyfred	356,126	Hollings, Ernest F.	9,626	209,481 D	28.6%	69.5%	29.2%	70.8%
1972	672,246	426,601	Thurmond, Strom	245,457	Zeigler, Eugene N.	188	181,144 R	63.5%	36.5%	63.5%	36.5%
1968	652,855	248,780	Parker, Marshall	404,060	Hollings, Ernest F.	15	155,280 D	38.1%	61.9%	38.1%	61.9%
1966	436,252	271,297	Thurmond, Strom	164,955	Morrah, Bradley		106,342 R	62.2%	37.8%	62.2%	37.8%
1966 S	435,822	212,032	Parker, Marshall	223,790	Hollings, Ernest F.		11,758 D	48.7%	51.3%	48.7%	51.3%
1962	312,647	133,930	Workman, W. D.	178,712	Johnston, Olin D.	5	44,782 D	42.8%	57.2%	42.8%	57.2%
1960	330,266		—	330,164	Thurmond, Strom	102	330,164 D		100.0%		100.0%
1956	279,845	49,695	Crawford, Leon P.	230,150	Johnston, Olin D.		180,455 D	17.8%	82.2%	17.8%	82.2%
1956 S	251,907		—	251,907	Thurmond, Strom		251,907 D		100.0%		100.0%
1954 **	227,232		—	83,525	Brown, Edgar A.	143,707	83,525 D		36.8%		100.0%
1950	50,277		—	50,240	Johnston, Olin D.	37	50,240 D		99.9%		100.0%
1948	141,006	5,008	Gerald, J. Bates	135,998	Maybank, Burnet R.		130,990 D	3.6%	96.4%	3.6%	96.4%

One each of the 1966 and 1956 elections was for a short term to fill a vacancy. In 1954, Strom Thurmond polled 143,444 votes as an Independent Democratic write-in candidate (63.1% of the total vote) and won the election with a 59,919 pluarlity.

392

SOUTH CAROLINA

Districts Established April 30, 1982

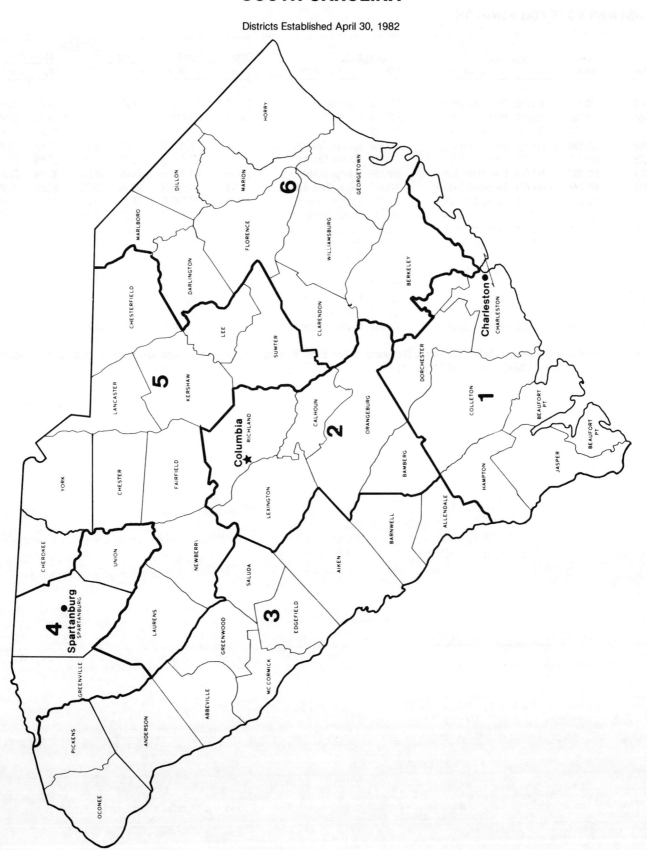

SOUTH CAROLINA

GOVERNOR 1990

1990 Census Population	County	Total Vote	Republican	Democratic	Other	Rep.-Dem. Plurality	Total Vote Rep.	Total Vote Dem.	Major Vote Rep.	Major Vote Dem.
23,862	ABBEVILLE	5,593	3,663	1,805	125	1,858 R	65.5%	32.3%	67.0%	33.0%
120,940	AIKEN	27,485	20,853	5,868	764	14,985 R	75.9%	21.3%	78.0%	22.0%
11,722	ALLENDALE	2,520	1,179	1,311	30	132 D	46.8%	52.0%	47.3%	52.7%
145,196	ANDERSON	31,231	23,386	6,607	1,238	16,779 R	74.9%	21.2%	78.0%	22.0%
16,902	BAMBERG	4,118	2,235	1,844	39	391 R	54.3%	44.8%	54.8%	45.2%
20,293	BARNWELL	4,727	3,157	1,497	73	1,660 R	66.8%	31.7%	67.8%	32.2%
86,425	BEAUFORT	19,297	13,561	5,295	441	8,266 R	70.3%	27.4%	71.9%	28.1%
128,776	BERKELEY	22,868	15,687	6,629	552	9,058 R	68.6%	29.0%	70.3%	29.7%
12,753	CALHOUN	3,640	2,343	1,241	56	1,102 R	64.4%	34.1%	65.4%	34.6%
295,039	CHARLESTON	61,130	40,394	19,208	1,528	21,186 R	66.1%	31.4%	67.8%	32.2%
44,506	CHEROKEE	9,590	6,658	2,387	545	4,271 R	69.4%	24.9%	73.6%	26.4%
32,170	CHESTER	6,897	4,452	2,286	159	2,166 R	64.5%	33.1%	66.1%	33.9%
38,577	CHESTERFIELD	7,390	5,049	2,204	137	2,845 R	68.3%	29.8%	69.6%	30.4%
28,450	CLARENDON	6,871	3,628	3,197	46	431 R	52.8%	46.5%	53.2%	46.8%
34,377	COLLETON	7,904	4,672	3,118	114	1,554 R	59.1%	39.4%	60.0%	40.0%
61,851	DARLINGTON	11,571	7,558	3,824	189	3,734 R	65.3%	33.0%	66.4%	33.6%
29,114	DILLON	5,869	3,610	2,201	58	1,409 R	61.5%	37.5%	62.1%	37.9%
83,060	DORCHESTER	16,494	11,624	4,459	411	7,165 R	70.5%	27.0%	72.3%	27.7%
18,375	EDGEFIELD	4,888	2,987	1,828	73	1,159 R	61.1%	37.4%	62.0%	38.0%
22,295	FAIRFIELD	5,191	2,583	2,521	87	62 R	49.8%	48.6%	50.6%	49.4%
114,344	FLORENCE	23,608	15,846	7,350	412	8,496 R	67.1%	31.1%	68.3%	31.7%
46,302	GEORGETOWN	9,859	5,912	3,779	168	2,133 R	60.0%	38.3%	61.0%	39.0%
320,167	GREENVILLE	80,241	61,884	15,492	2,865	46,392 R	77.1%	19.3%	80.0%	20.0%
59,567	GREENWOOD	11,730	8,216	3,225	289	4,991 R	70.0%	27.5%	71.8%	28.2%
18,191	HAMPTON	6,214	3,001	3,121	92	120 D	48.3%	50.2%	49.0%	51.0%
144,053	HORRY	30,927	24,016	6,366	545	17,650 R	77.7%	20.6%	79.0%	21.0%
15,487	JASPER	4,381	1,847	2,498	36	651 D	42.2%	57.0%	42.5%	57.5%
43,599	KERSHAW	12,576	9,478	2,718	380	6,760 R	75.4%	21.6%	77.7%	22.3%
54,516	LANCASTER	11,315	8,506	2,624	185	5,882 R	75.2%	23.2%	76.4%	23.6%
58,092	LAURENS	10,528	7,470	2,769	289	4,701 R	71.0%	26.3%	73.0%	27.0%
18,437	LEE	5,687	3,059	2,568	60	491 R	53.8%	45.2%	54.4%	45.6%
167,611	LEXINGTON	41,310	34,789	5,027	1,494	29,762 R	84.2%	12.2%	87.4%	12.6%
8,868	MCCORMICK	2,071	1,064	967	40	97 R	51.4%	46.7%	52.4%	47.6%
33,899	MARION	6,139	3,664	2,396	79	1,268 R	59.7%	39.0%	60.5%	39.5%
29,361	MARLBORO	4,428	2,683	1,696	49	987 R	60.6%	38.3%	61.3%	38.7%
33,172	NEWBERRY	8,132	5,977	1,930	225	4,047 R	73.5%	23.7%	75.6%	24.4%
57,494	OCONEE	12,024	9,041	2,397	586	6,644 R	75.2%	19.9%	79.0%	21.0%
84,803	ORANGEBURG	23,605	12,545	10,753	307	1,792 R	53.1%	45.6%	53.8%	46.2%
93,894	PICKENS	17,942	14,196	3,059	687	11,137 R	79.1%	17.0%	82.3%	17.7%
285,720	RICHLAND	65,392	41,847	22,216	1,329	19,631 R	64.0%	34.0%	65.3%	34.7%
16,357	SALUDA	4,668	3,334	1,175	159	2,159 R	71.4%	25.2%	73.9%	26.1%
226,800	SPARTANBURG	44,202	31,739	10,562	1,901	21,177 R	71.8%	23.9%	75.0%	25.0%
102,637	SUMTER	16,824	10,892	5,622	310	5,270 R	64.7%	33.4%	66.0%	34.0%
30,337	UNION	7,988	5,544	2,192	252	3,352 R	69.4%	27.4%	71.7%	28.3%
36,815	WILLIAMSBURG	10,127	5,040	5,012	75	28 R	49.8%	49.5%	50.1%	49.9%
131,497	YORK	23,773	17,962	5,190	621	12,772 R	75.6%	21.8%	77.6%	22.4%
3,486,703	TOTAL	760,965	528,831	212,034	20,100	316,797 R	69.5%	27.9%	71.4%	28.6%

393

SOUTH CAROLINA

SENATOR 1990

1990 Census Population	County	Total Vote	Republican	Democratic	Other	Rep.-Dem. Plurality	Total Vote Rep.	Total Vote Dem.	Major Vote Rep.	Major Vote Dem.
23,862	ABBEVILLE	5,503	3,247	2,160	96	1,087 R	59.0%	39.3%	60.1%	39.9%
120,940	AIKEN	27,494	17,885	8,038	1,571	9,847 R	65.1%	29.2%	69.0%	31.0%
11,722	ALLENDALE	2,405	1,118	1,232	55	114 D	46.5%	51.2%	47.6%	52.4%
145,196	ANDERSON	31,362	20,903	9,358	1,101	11,545 R	66.7%	29.8%	69.1%	30.9%
16,902	BAMBERG	4,005	2,193	1,724	88	469 R	54.8%	43.0%	56.0%	44.0%
20,293	BARNWELL	4,599	3,041	1,456	102	1,585 R	66.1%	31.7%	67.6%	32.4%
86,425	BEAUFORT	19,225	11,467	6,971	787	4,496 R	59.6%	36.3%	62.2%	37.8%
128,776	BERKELEY	22,307	14,840	6,635	832	8,205 R	66.5%	29.7%	69.1%	30.9%
12,753	CALHOUN	3,403	2,087	1,242	74	845 R	61.3%	36.5%	62.7%	37.3%
295,039	CHARLESTON	59,572	38,227	19,661	1,684	18,566 R	64.2%	33.0%	66.0%	34.0%
44,506	CHEROKEE	9,693	6,537	2,871	285	3,666 R	67.4%	29.6%	69.5%	30.5%
32,170	CHESTER	6,871	3,999	2,636	236	1,363 R	58.2%	38.4%	60.3%	39.7%
38,577	CHESTERFIELD	7,368	4,615	2,636	117	1,979 R	62.6%	35.8%	63.6%	36.4%
28,450	CLARENDON	6,947	3,445	3,179	323	266 R	49.6%	45.8%	52.0%	48.0%
34,377	COLLETON	7,733	4,593	2,957	183	1,636 R	59.4%	38.2%	60.8%	39.2%
61,851	DARLINGTON	11,305	6,844	4,090	371	2,754 R	60.5%	36.2%	62.6%	37.4%
29,114	DILLON	5,744	3,321	2,332	91	989 R	57.8%	40.6%	58.7%	41.3%
83,060	DORCHESTER	16,287	10,869	4,847	571	6,022 R	66.7%	29.8%	69.2%	30.8%
18,375	EDGEFIELD	4,737	2,694	1,896	147	798 R	56.9%	40.0%	58.7%	41.3%
22,295	FAIRFIELD	4,921	2,387	2,386	148	1 R	48.5%	48.5%	50.0%	50.0%
114,344	FLORENCE	23,588	14,778	8,230	580	6,548 R	62.7%	34.9%	64.2%	35.8%
46,302	GEORGETOWN	9,686	5,326	4,136	224	1,190 R	55.0%	42.7%	56.3%	43.7%
320,167	GREENVILLE	80,000	56,021	21,405	2,574	34,616 R	70.0%	26.8%	72.4%	27.6%
59,567	GREENWOOD	11,164	7,121	3,582	461	3,539 R	63.8%	32.1%	66.5%	33.5%
18,191	HAMPTON	6,068	3,016	2,937	115	79 R	49.7%	48.4%	50.7%	49.3%
144,053	HORRY	29,841	19,851	8,907	1,083	10,944 R	66.5%	29.8%	69.0%	31.0%
15,487	JASPER	4,356	1,786	2,496	74	710 D	41.0%	57.3%	41.7%	58.3%
43,599	KERSHAW	12,527	8,868	3,228	431	5,640 R	70.8%	25.8%	73.3%	26.7%
54,516	LANCASTER	11,167	7,555	3,406	206	4,149 R	67.7%	30.5%	68.9%	31.1%
58,092	LAURENS	10,333	6,853	3,273	207	3,580 R	66.3%	31.7%	67.7%	32.3%
18,437	LEE	5,475	2,895	2,488	92	407 R	52.9%	45.4%	53.8%	46.2%
167,611	LEXINGTON	41,877	31,765	8,179	1,933	23,586 R	75.9%	19.5%	79.5%	20.5%
8,868	MCCORMICK	1,912	832	1,024	56	192 D	43.5%	53.6%	44.8%	55.2%
33,899	MARION	5,890	3,304	2,422	164	882 R	56.1%	41.1%	57.7%	42.3%
29,361	MARLBORO	4,275	2,438	1,770	67	668 R	57.0%	41.4%	57.9%	42.1%
33,172	NEWBERRY	7,948	5,233	2,073	642	3,160 R	65.8%	26.1%	71.6%	28.4%
57,494	OCONEE	12,004	7,846	3,636	522	4,210 R	65.4%	30.3%	68.3%	31.7%
84,803	ORANGEBURG	23,598	12,216	10,960	422	1,256 R	51.8%	46.4%	52.7%	47.3%
93,894	PICKENS	18,030	13,017	4,283	730	8,734 R	72.2%	23.8%	75.2%	24.8%
285,720	RICHLAND	63,333	37,890	23,236	2,207	14,654 R	59.8%	36.7%	62.0%	38.0%
16,357	SALUDA	4,620	3,068	1,391	161	1,677 R	66.4%	30.1%	68.8%	31.2%
226,800	SPARTANBURG	43,234	30,223	11,502	1,509	18,721 R	69.9%	26.6%	72.4%	27.6%
102,637	SUMTER	16,791	10,205	6,194	392	4,011 R	60.8%	36.9%	62.2%	37.8%
30,337	UNION	7,762	5,230	2,425	107	2,805 R	67.4%	31.2%	68.3%	31.7%
36,815	WILLIAMSBURG	9,996	4,916	4,995	85	79 D	49.2%	50.0%	49.6%	50.4%
131,497	YORK	23,760	15,467	7,627	666	7,840 R	65.1%	32.1%	67.0%	33.0%
3,486,703	TOTAL	750,716	482,032	244,112	24,572	237,920 R	64.2%	32.5%	66.4%	33.6%

SOUTH CAROLINA

CONGRESS

CD	Year	Total Vote	Republican Vote	Republican Candidate	Democratic Vote	Democratic Candidate	Other Vote	Rep.-Dem. Plurality	Total Vote Rep.	Total Vote Dem.	Major Vote Rep.	Major Vote Dem.
1	1990	123,503	80,839	RAVENEL, ARTHUR	42,555	PLATT, EUGENE	109	38,284 R	65.5%	34.5%	65.5%	34.5%
1	1988	159,263	101,572	RAVENEL, ARTHUR	57,691	TILLMAN, WHEELER		43,881 R	63.8%	36.2%	63.8%	36.2%
1	1986	115,232	59,969	RAVENEL, ARTHUR	55,262	STUCKEY, JIMMY	1	4,707 R	52.0%	48.0%	52.0%	48.0%
1	1984	167,310	103,288	HARTNETT, THOMAS F.	64,022	PENDARVIS, ED		39,266 R	61.7%	38.3%	61.7%	38.3%
1	1982	117,832	63,945	HARTNETT, THOMAS F.	52,916	MCLEOD, W. MULLINS	971	11,029 R	54.3%	44.9%	54.7%	45.3%
2	1990	101,529	90,054	SPENCE, FLOYD			11,475	90,054 R	88.7%		100.0%	
2	1988	179,999	94,960	SPENCE, FLOYD	83,978	LEVENTIS, JIM	1,061	10,982 R	52.8%	46.7%	53.1%	46.9%
2	1986	137,052	73,455	SPENCE, FLOYD	63,592	ZEIGLER, FRED	5	9,863 R	53.6%	46.4%	53.6%	46.4%
2	1984	174,027	108,085	SPENCE, FLOYD	63,932	MOSELY, KEN	2,010	44,153 R	62.1%	36.7%	62.8%	37.2%
2	1982	122,318	71,569	SPENCE, FLOYD	50,749	MOSELY, KEN		20,820 R	58.5%	41.5%	58.5%	41.5%
3	1990	125,050	52,419	HASKETT, RAY	72,561	DERRICK, BUTLER	70	20,142 D	41.9%	58.0%	41.9%	58.1%
3	1988	165,825	75,571	JORDAN, HENRY S.	89,071	DERRICK, BUTLER	1,183	13,500 D	45.6%	53.7%	45.9%	54.1%
3	1986	115,683	36,495	DICKISON, RICHARD	79,109	DERRICK, BUTLER	79	42,614 D	31.5%	68.4%	31.6%	68.4%
3	1984	152,166	61,739	TAYLOR, CLARENCE E.	88,917	DERRICK, BUTLER	1,510	27,178 D	40.6%	58.4%	41.0%	59.0%
3	1982	85,339			77,125	DERRICK, BUTLER	8,214	77,125 D		90.4%		100.0%
4	1990	133,535	51,338	HASKINS, TERRY	81,927	PATTERSON, ELIZABETH J.	270	30,589 D	38.4%	61.4%	38.5%	61.5%
4	1988	173,027	82,793	WHITE, KNOX	90,234	PATTERSON, ELIZABETH J.		7,441 D	47.8%	52.2%	47.8%	52.2%
4	1986	130,407	61,648	WORKMAN, W. D.,III	67,012	PATTERSON, ELIZABETH J.	1,747	5,364 D	47.3%	51.4%	47.9%	52.1%
4	1984	164,424	105,139	CAMPBELL, CARROLL	57,854	SMITH, JEFF	1,431	47,285 R	63.9%	35.2%	64.5%	35.5%
4	1982	110,196	69,802	CAMPBELL, CARROLL	40,394	TYUS, MARION E.		29,408 R	63.3%	36.7%	63.3%	36.7%
5	1990	91,898			91,775	SPRATT, JOHN	123	91,775 D		99.9%		100.0%
5	1988	154,581	46,622	CARLEY, ROBERT K.	107,959	SPRATT, JOHN		61,337 D	30.2%	69.8%	30.2%	69.8%
5	1986	96,149			95,859	SPRATT, JOHN	290	95,859 D		99.7%		100.0%
5	1984	107,291			98,513	SPRATT, JOHN	8,778	98,513 D		91.8%		100.0%
5	1982	102,536	33,191	WILKERSON, JOHN S.	69,345	SPRATT, JOHN		36,154 D	32.4%	67.6%	32.4%	67.6%
6	1990	94,524			94,121	TALLON, ROBERT M.	403	94,121 D		99.6%		100.0%
6	1988	158,677	37,958	CUNNINGHAM, ROBBIE	120,719	TALLON, ROBERT M.		82,761 D	23.9%	76.1%	23.9%	76.1%
6	1986	122,343	29,922	CUNNINGHAM, ROBBIE	92,398	TALLON, ROBERT M.	23	62,476 D	24.5%	75.5%	24.5%	75.5%
6	1984	162,384	63,005	EARGLE, LOIS	97,329	TALLON, ROBERT M.	2,050	34,324 D	38.8%	59.9%	39.3%	60.7%
6	1982	119,235	56,653	NAPIER, JOHN L.	62,582	TALLON, ROBERT M.		5,929 D	47.5%	52.5%	47.5%	52.5%

SOUTH CAROLINA

1990 GENERAL ELECTION

Governor   Other vote was 17,302 American (Peeples) and 2,798 scattered write-in.

Senator   Other vote was 13,805 Libertarian (Griffin); 10,317 American (Metts) and 450 scattered write-in.

Congress   Other vote was 11,101 Libertarian (Sommer) and 374 scattered write-in in CD 2; scattered write-in in all other CD's.

1990 PRIMARIES

JUNE 12 REPUBLICAN

Governor   Carroll Campbell, unopposed.

Senator   Strom Thurmond, unopposed.

Congress   Unopposed in three CD's. No candidate in CD's 5 and 6. Contested as follows:

CD 1   20,032 Arthur Ravenel; 2,302 Benjamin Hunt.

JUNE 12 DEMOCRATIC

Governor   116,471 Theo Mitchell; 77,429 Ernie Passailaigue.

Senator   Bob Cunningham, unopposed.

Congress   Unopposed in five CD's. No candidate in CD 2.

SOUTH DAKOTA

GOVERNOR
George S. Mickelson (R). Re-elected 1990 to a four-year term. Previously elected 1986.

SENATORS
Thomas A. Daschle (D). Elected 1986 to a six-year term.

Larry Pressler (R). Re-elected 1990 to a six-year term. Previously elected 1984, 1978.

REPRESENTATIVES
At-Large. Tim Johnson (D)

POSTWAR VOTE FOR PRESIDENT

Year	Total Vote	Republican Vote	Candidate	Democratic Vote	Candidate	Other Vote	Plurality	Total Vote Rep.	Dem.	Major Vote Rep.	Dem.
1988	312,991	165,415	Bush, George	145,560	Dukakis, Michael S.	2,016	19,855 R	52.8%	46.5%	53.2%	46.8%
1984	317,867	200,267	Reagan, Ronald	116,113	Mondale, Walter F.	1,487	84,154 R	63.0%	36.5%	63.3%	36.7%
1980	327,703	198,343	Reagan, Ronald	103,855	Carter, Jimmy	25,505	94,488 R	60.5%	31.7%	65.6%	34.4%
1976	300,678	151,505	Ford, Gerald R.	147,068	Carter, Jimmy	2,105	4,437 R	50.4%	48.9%	50.7%	49.3%
1972	307,415	166,476	Nixon, Richard M.	139,945	McGovern, George S.	994	26,531 R	54.2%	45.5%	54.3%	45.7%
1968	281,264	149,841	Nixon, Richard M.	118,023	Humphrey, Hubert H.	13,400	31,818 R	53.3%	42.0%	55.9%	44.1%
1964	293,118	130,108	Goldwater, Barry M.	163,010	Johnson, Lyndon B.		32,902 D	44.4%	55.6%	44.4%	55.6%
1960	306,487	178,417	Nixon, Richard M.	128,070	Kennedy, John F.		50,347 R	58.2%	41.8%	58.2%	41.8%
1956	293,857	171,569	Eisenhower, Dwight D.	122,288	Stevenson, Adlai E.		49,281 R	58.4%	41.6%	58.4%	41.6%
1952	294,283	203,857	Eisenhower, Dwight D.	90,426	Stevenson, Adlai E.		113,431 R	69.3%	30.7%	69.3%	30.7%
1948	250,105	129,651	Dewey, Thomas E.	117,653	Truman, Harry S.	2,801	11,998 R	51.8%	47.0%	52.4%	47.6%

POSTWAR VOTE FOR GOVERNOR

Year	Total Vote	Republican Vote	Candidate	Democratic Vote	Candidate	Other Vote	Rep.-Dem. Plurality	Total Vote Rep.	Dem.	Major Vote Rep.	Dem.
1990	256,723	151,198	Mickelson, George S.	105,525	Samuelson, Bob L.		45,673 R	58.9%	41.1%	58.9%	41.1%
1986	294,441	152,543	Mickelson, George S.	141,898	Herseth, R. Lars		10,645 R	51.8%	48.2%	51.8%	48.2%
1982	278,562	197,426	Janklow, William J.	81,136	O'Connor, Michael J.		116,290 R	70.9%	29.1%	70.9%	29.1%
1978	259,795	147,116	Janklow, William J.	112,679	McKellips, Roger		34,437 R	56.6%	43.4%	56.6%	43.4%
1974 **	278,228	129,077	Olson, John E.	149,151	Kneip, Richard F.		20,074 D	46.4%	53.6%	46.4%	53.6%
1972	308,177	123,165	Thompson, Carveth	185,012	Kneip, Richard F.		61,847 D	40.0%	60.0%	40.0%	60.0%
1970	239,963	108,347	Farrar, Frank	131,616	Kneip, Richard F.		23,269 D	45.2%	54.8%	45.2%	54.8%
1968	276,906	159,646	Farrar, Frank	117,260	Chamberlin, Robert		42,386 R	57.7%	42.3%	57.7%	42.3%
1966	228,214	131,710	Boe, Nils A.	96,504	Chamberlin, Robert		35,206 R	57.7%	42.3%	57.7%	42.3%
1964	290,570	150,151	Boe, Nils A.	140,419	Lindley, John F.		9,732 R	51.7%	48.3%	51.7%	48.3%
1962	256,120	143,682	Gubbrud, Archie M.	112,438	Herseth, Ralph		31,244 R	56.1%	43.9%	56.1%	43.9%
1960	304,625	154,530	Gubbrud, Archie M.	150,095	Herseth, Ralph		4,435 R	50.7%	49.3%	50.7%	49.3%
1958	258,281	125,520	Saunders, Phil	132,761	Herseth, Ralph		7,241 D	48.6%	51.4%	48.6%	51.4%
1956	292,017	158,819	Foss, Joe J.	133,198	Herseth, Ralph		25,621 R	54.4%	45.6%	54.4%	45.6%
1954	236,255	133,878	Foss, Joe J.	102,377	Martin, Ed C.		31,501 R	56.7%	43.3%	56.7%	43.3%
1952	289,515	203,102	Anderson, Sigurd	86,413	Iverson, Sherman A.		116,689 R	70.2%	29.8%	70.2%	29.8%
1950	253,316	154,254	Anderson, Sigurd	99,062	Robbie, Joseph		55,192 R	60.9%	39.1%	60.9%	39.1%
1948	245,372	149,883	Mickelson, George	95,489	Volz, Harold J.		54,394 R	61.1%	38.9%	61.1%	38.9%
1946	162,292	108,998	Mickelson, George	53,294	Haeder, Richard		55,704 R	67.2%	32.8%	67.2%	32.8%

The term of office of South Dakota's Governor was increased from two to four years effective with the 1974 election.

SOUTH DAKOTA

POSTWAR VOTE FOR SENATOR

Year	Total Vote	Republican Vote	Candidate	Democratic Vote	Candidate	Other Vote	Rep-Dem. Plurality	Percentage Total Vote Rep.	Dem.	Major Vote Rep.	Dem.
1990	258,976	135,682	Pressler, Larry	116,727	Muenster, Ted	6,567	18,955 R	52.4%	45.1%	53.8%	46.2%
1986	295,830	143,173	Abdnor, James	152,657	Daschle, Thomas A.		9,484 D	48.4%	51.6%	48.4%	51.6%
1984	315,713	235,176	Pressler, Larry	80,537	Cunningham, George V.		154,639 R	74.5%	25.5%	74.5%	25.5%
1980	327,478	190,594	Abdnor, James	129,018	McGovern, George S.	7,866	61,576 R	58.2%	39.4%	59.6%	40.4%
1978	255,599	170,832	Pressler, Larry	84,767	Barnett, Don		86,065 R	66.8%	33.2%	66.8%	33.2%
1974	278,884	130,955	Thorsness, Leo K.	147,929	McGovern, George S.		16,974 D	47.0%	53.0%	47.0%	53.0%
1972	306,386	131,613	Hirsch, Robert W.	174,773	Abourezk, James		43,160 D	43.0%	57.0%	43.0%	57.0%
1968	279,912	120,951	Gubbrud, Archie M.	158,961	McGovern, George S.		38,010 D	43.2%	56.8%	43.2%	56.8%
1966	227,080	150,517	Mundt, Karl E.	76,563	Wright, Donn H.		73,954 R	66.3%	33.7%	66.3%	33.7%
1962	254,319	126,861	Bottum, Joe H.	127,458	McGovern, George S.		597 D	49.9%	50.1%	49.9%	50.1%
1960	305,442	160,181	Mundt, Karl E.	145,261	McGovern, George S.		14,920 R	52.4%	47.6%	52.4%	47.6%
1956	290,622	147,621	Case, Francis	143,001	Holum, Kenneth		4,620 R	50.8%	49.2%	50.8%	49.2%
1954	235,745	135,071	Mundt, Karl E.	100,674	Holum, Kenneth		34,397 R	57.3%	42.7%	57.3%	42.7%
1950	251,362	160,670	Case, Francis	90,692	Engel, John A.		69,978 R	63.9%	36.1%	63.9%	36.1%
1948	242,833	144,084	Mundt, Karl E.	98,749	Engel, John A.		45,335 R	59.3%	40.7%	59.3%	40.7%

SOUTH DAKOTA

One At Large

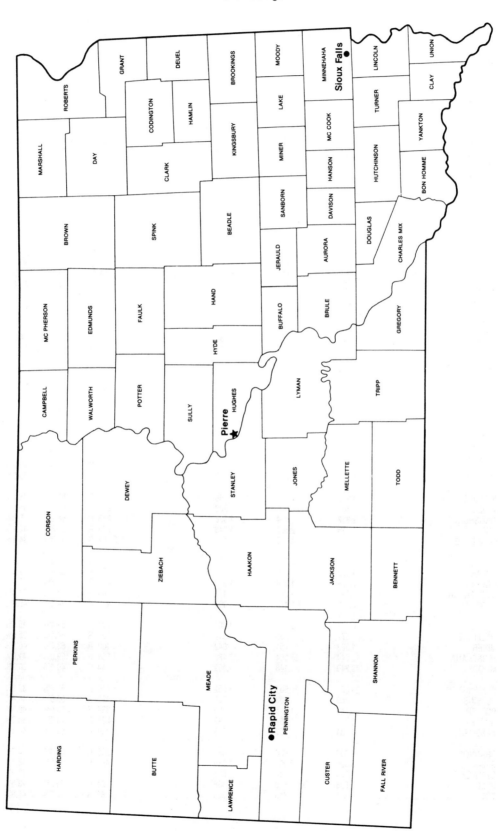

SOUTH DAKOTA

GOVERNOR 1990

1990 Census Population	County	Total Vote	Republican	Democratic	Other	Rep.-Dem. Plurality	Total Vote Rep.	Total Vote Dem.	Major Vote Rep.	Major Vote Dem.
3,135	AURORA	1,574	753	821		68 D	47.8%	52.2%	47.8%	52.2%
18,253	BEADLE	7,579	4,420	3,159		1,261 R	58.3%	41.7%	58.3%	41.7%
3,206	BENNETT	1,137	747	390		357 R	65.7%	34.3%	65.7%	34.3%
7,089	BONHOMME	2,945	1,604	1,341		263 R	54.5%	45.5%	54.5%	45.5%
25,207	BROOKINGS	8,459	5,171	3,288		1,883 R	61.1%	38.9%	61.1%	38.9%
35,580	BROWN	14,288	8,906	5,382		3,524 R	62.3%	37.7%	62.3%	37.7%
5,485	BRULE	2,197	1,136	1,061		75 R	51.7%	48.3%	51.7%	48.3%
1,759	BUFFALO	767	395	372		23 R	51.5%	48.5%	51.5%	48.5%
7,914	BUTTE	2,868	1,859	1,009		850 R	64.8%	35.2%	64.8%	35.2%
1,965	CAMPBELL	1,073	684	389		295 R	63.7%	36.3%	63.7%	36.3%
9,131	CHARLES MIX	3,408	1,727	1,681		46 R	50.7%	49.3%	50.7%	49.3%
4,403	CLARK	2,157	990	1,167		177 D	45.9%	54.1%	45.9%	54.1%
13,186	CLAY	3,676	2,031	1,645		386 R	55.3%	44.7%	55.3%	44.7%
22,698	CODINGTON	8,307	4,081	4,226		145 D	49.1%	50.9%	49.1%	50.9%
4,195	CORSON	1,136	623	513		110 R	54.8%	45.2%	54.8%	45.2%
6,179	CUSTER	2,657	1,708	949		759 R	64.3%	35.7%	64.3%	35.7%
17,503	DAVISON	6,672	4,088	2,584		1,504 R	61.3%	38.7%	61.3%	38.7%
6,978	DAY	3,057	1,441	1,616		175 D	47.1%	52.9%	47.1%	52.9%
4,522	DEUEL	2,235	1,101	1,134		33 D	49.3%	50.7%	49.3%	50.7%
5,523	DEWEY	1,563	809	754		55 R	51.8%	48.2%	51.8%	48.2%
3,746	DOUGLAS	1,804	1,185	619		566 R	65.7%	34.3%	65.7%	34.3%
4,356	EDMUNDS	2,167	1,172	995		177 R	54.1%	45.9%	54.1%	45.9%
7,353	FALL RIVER	2,871	1,771	1,100		671 R	61.7%	38.3%	61.7%	38.3%
2,744	FAULK	1,519	851	668		183 R	56.0%	44.0%	56.0%	44.0%
8,372	GRANT	3,754	2,444	1,310		1,134 R	65.1%	34.9%	65.1%	34.9%
5,359	GREGORY	2,261	1,296	965		331 R	57.3%	42.7%	57.3%	42.7%
2,624	HAAKON	1,169	712	457		255 R	60.9%	39.1%	60.9%	39.1%
4,974	HAMLIN	2,212	1,038	1,174		136 D	46.9%	53.1%	46.9%	53.1%
4,272	HAND	2,407	1,375	1,032		343 R	57.1%	42.9%	57.1%	42.9%
2,994	HANSON	1,320	715	605		110 R	54.2%	45.8%	54.2%	45.8%
1,669	HARDING	806	541	265		276 R	67.1%	32.9%	67.1%	32.9%
14,817	HUGHES	6,385	4,038	2,347		1,691 R	63.2%	36.8%	63.2%	36.8%
8,262	HUTCHINSON	3,676	2,348	1,328		1,020 R	63.9%	36.1%	63.9%	36.1%
1,696	HYDE	867	440	427		13 R	50.7%	49.3%	50.7%	49.3%
2,811	JACKSON	1,090	703	387		316 R	64.5%	35.5%	64.5%	35.5%
2,425	JERAULD	1,206	640	566		74 R	53.1%	46.9%	53.1%	46.9%
1,324	JONES	807	519	288		231 R	64.3%	35.7%	64.3%	35.7%
5,925	KINGSBURY	2,832	1,534	1,298		236 R	54.2%	45.8%	54.2%	45.8%
10,550	LAKE	4,615	2,667	1,948		719 R	57.8%	42.2%	57.8%	42.2%
20,655	LAWRENCE	7,209	4,745	2,464		2,281 R	65.8%	34.2%	65.8%	34.2%
15,427	LINCOLN	5,543	3,357	2,186		1,171 R	60.6%	39.4%	60.6%	39.4%
3,638	LYMAN	1,160	666	494		172 R	57.4%	42.6%	57.4%	42.6%
5,688	MCCOOK	2,369	1,294	1,075		219 R	54.6%	45.4%	54.6%	45.4%
3,228	MCPHERSON	1,509	1,036	473		563 R	68.7%	31.3%	68.7%	31.3%
4,844	MARSHALL	2,173	1,173	1,000		173 R	54.0%	46.0%	54.0%	46.0%
21,878	MEADE	6,771	3,684	3,087		597 R	54.4%	45.6%	54.4%	45.6%
2,137	MELLETTE	877	565	312		253 R	64.4%	35.6%	64.4%	35.6%
3,272	MINER	1,393	751	642		109 R	53.9%	46.1%	53.9%	46.1%
123,809	MINNEHAHA	42,644	25,164	17,480		7,684 R	59.0%	41.0%	59.0%	41.0%
6,507	MOODY	2,340	1,148	1,192		44 D	49.1%	50.9%	49.1%	50.9%
81,343	PENNINGTON	24,553	16,501	8,052		8,449 R	67.2%	32.8%	67.2%	32.8%
3,932	PERKINS	1,769	983	786		197 R	55.6%	44.4%	55.6%	44.4%
3,190	POTTER	1,740	1,035	705		330 R	59.5%	40.5%	59.5%	40.5%
9,914	ROBERTS	3,746	1,754	1,992		238 D	46.8%	53.2%	46.8%	53.2%
2,833	SANBORN	1,531	856	675		181 R	55.9%	44.1%	55.9%	44.1%
9,902	SHANNON	1,060	630	430		200 R	59.4%	40.6%	59.4%	40.6%
7,981	SPINK	3,525	2,006	1,519		487 R	56.9%	43.1%	56.9%	43.1%
2,453	STANLEY	1,084	510	574		64 D	47.0%	53.0%	47.0%	53.0%
1,589	SULLY	996	560	436		124 R	56.2%	43.8%	56.2%	43.8%
8,352	TODD	1,341	713	628		85 R	53.2%	46.8%	53.2%	46.8%

SOUTH DAKOTA

GOVERNOR 1990

1990 Census Population	County	Total Vote	Republican	Democratic	Other	Rep.-Dem. Plurality	Percentage Total Vote Rep.	Dem.	Major Vote Rep.	Dem.
6,924	TRIPP	3,108	2,019	1,089		930 R	65.0%	35.0%	65.0%	35.0%
8,576	TURNER	3,574	2,198	1,376		822 R	61.5%	38.5%	61.5%	38.5%
10,189	UNION	3,485	1,932	1,553		379 R	55.4%	44.6%	55.4%	44.6%
6,087	WALWORTH	2,625	1,510	1,115		395 R	57.5%	42.5%	57.5%	42.5%
19,252	YANKTON	6,359	3,917	2,442		1,475 R	61.6%	38.4%	61.6%	38.4%
2,220	ZIEBACH	716	228	488		260 D	31.8%	68.2%	31.8%	68.2%
696,004	TOTAL	256,723	151,198	105,525		45,673 R	58.9%	41.1%	58.9%	41.1%

SOUTH DAKOTA

SENATOR 1990

1990 Census Population	County	Total Vote	Republican	Democratic	Other	Rep.-Dem. Plurality	Percentage Total Vote Rep.	Dem.	Major Vote Rep.	Dem.
3,135	AURORA	1,565	839	697	29	142 R	53.6%	44.5%	54.6%	45.4%
18,253	BEADLE	7,581	3,901	3,511	169	390 R	51.5%	46.3%	52.6%	47.4%
3,206	BENNETT	1,127	703	382	42	321 R	62.4%	33.9%	64.8%	35.2%
7,089	BONHOMME	2,987	1,771	1,166	50	605 R	59.3%	39.0%	60.3%	39.7%
25,207	BROOKINGS	8,535	4,497	3,774	264	723 R	52.7%	44.2%	54.4%	45.6%
35,580	BROWN	14,301	5,951	7,934	416	1,983 D	41.6%	55.5%	42.9%	57.1%
5,485	BRULE	2,400	1,236	1,098	66	138 R	51.5%	45.8%	53.0%	47.0%
1,759	BUFFALO	777	431	320	26	111 R	55.5%	41.2%	57.4%	42.6%
7,914	BUTTE	2,846	1,790	986	70	804 R	62.9%	34.6%	64.5%	35.5%
1,965	CAMPBELL	1,074	621	427	26	194 R	57.8%	39.8%	59.3%	40.7%
9,131	CHARLES MIX	3,421	1,810	1,548	63	262 R	52.9%	45.2%	53.9%	46.1%
4,403	CLARK	2,161	1,013	1,093	55	80 D	46.9%	50.6%	48.1%	51.9%
13,186	CLAY	3,699	1,774	1,775	150	1 D	48.0%	48.0%	50.0%	50.0%
22,698	CODINGTON	8,357	3,604	4,509	244	905 D	43.1%	54.0%	44.4%	55.6%
4,195	CORSON	1,134	663	423	48	240 R	58.5%	37.3%	61.0%	39.0%
6,179	CUSTER	2,691	1,564	1,034	93	530 R	58.1%	38.4%	60.2%	39.8%
17,503	DAVISON	6,704	3,628	2,904	172	724 R	54.1%	43.3%	55.5%	44.5%
6,978	DAY	3,050	1,234	1,747	69	513 D	40.5%	57.3%	41.4%	58.6%
4,522	DEUEL	2,183	1,091	1,020	72	71 R	50.0%	46.7%	51.7%	48.3%
5,523	DEWEY	1,549	905	600	44	305 R	58.4%	38.7%	60.1%	39.9%
3,746	DOUGLAS	1,805	1,256	527	22	729 R	69.6%	29.2%	70.4%	29.6%
4,356	EDMUNDS	2,151	976	1,131	44	155 D	45.4%	52.6%	46.3%	53.7%
7,353	FALL RIVER	2,897	1,677	1,132	88	545 R	57.9%	39.1%	59.7%	40.3%
2,744	FAULK	1,514	703	773	38	70 D	46.4%	51.1%	47.6%	52.4%
8,372	GRANT	3,741	1,974	1,681	86	293 R	52.8%	44.9%	54.0%	46.0%
5,359	GREGORY	2,422	1,298	1,079	45	219 R	53.6%	44.5%	54.6%	45.4%
2,624	HAAKON	1,172	898	246	28	652 R	76.6%	21.0%	78.5%	21.5%
4,974	HAMLIN	2,199	1,073	1,068	58	5 R	48.8%	48.6%	50.1%	49.9%
4,272	HAND	2,391	1,335	1,003	53	332 R	55.8%	41.9%	57.1%	42.9%
2,994	HANSON	1,328	785	520	23	265 R	59.1%	39.2%	60.2%	39.8%
1,669	HARDING	811	548	247	16	301 R	67.6%	30.5%	68.9%	31.1%
14,817	HUGHES	6,799	3,379	3,254	166	125 R	49.7%	47.9%	50.9%	49.1%
8,262	HUTCHINSON	3,695	2,258	1,380	57	878 R	61.1%	37.3%	62.1%	37.9%
1,696	HYDE	863	424	406	33	18 R	49.1%	47.0%	51.1%	48.9%
2,811	JACKSON	1,078	717	333	28	384 R	66.5%	30.9%	68.3%	31.7%
2,425	JERAULD	1,204	694	489	21	205 R	57.6%	40.6%	58.7%	41.3%
1,324	JONES	811	496	267	48	229 R	61.2%	32.9%	65.0%	35.0%
5,925	KINGSBURY	2,833	1,429	1,322	82	107 R	50.4%	46.7%	51.9%	48.1%
10,550	LAKE	4,626	2,462	2,048	116	414 R	53.2%	44.3%	54.6%	45.4%
20,655	LAWRENCE	7,299	4,059	2,963	277	1,096 R	55.6%	40.6%	57.8%	42.2%
15,427	LINCOLN	5,546	3,022	2,420	104	602 R	54.5%	43.6%	55.5%	44.5%
3,638	LYMAN	1,233	664	529	40	135 R	53.9%	42.9%	55.7%	44.3%
5,688	MCCOOK	2,558	1,480	1,028	50	452 R	57.9%	40.2%	59.0%	41.0%
3,228	MCPHERSON	1,507	893	561	53	332 R	59.3%	37.2%	61.4%	38.6%
4,844	MARSHALL	2,167	980	1,155	32	175 D	45.2%	53.3%	45.9%	54.1%
21,878	MEADE	6,788	3,848	2,770	170	1,078 R	56.7%	40.8%	58.1%	41.9%
2,137	MELLETTE	875	532	321	22	211 R	60.8%	36.7%	62.4%	37.6%
3,272	MINER	1,508	785	678	45	107 R	52.1%	45.0%	53.7%	46.3%
123,809	MINNEHAHA	43,111	21,710	20,420	981	1,290 R	50.4%	47.4%	51.5%	48.5%
6,507	MOODY	2,346	1,145	1,146	55	1 D	48.8%	48.8%	50.0%	50.0%
81,343	PENNINGTON	24,565	13,679	10,351	535	3,328 R	55.7%	42.1%	56.9%	43.1%
3,932	PERKINS	1,767	1,022	689	56	333 R	57.8%	39.0%	59.7%	40.3%
3,190	POTTER	1,729	829	865	35	36 D	47.9%	50.0%	48.9%	51.1%
9,914	ROBERTS	3,746	1,742	1,924	80	182 D	46.5%	51.4%	47.5%	52.5%
2,833	SANBORN	1,549	890	614	45	276 R	57.5%	39.6%	59.2%	40.8%
9,902	SHANNON	1,081	433	579	69	146 D	40.1%	53.6%	42.8%	57.2%
7,981	SPINK	3,512	1,632	1,802	78	170 D	46.5%	51.3%	47.5%	52.5%
2,453	STANLEY	1,154	562	555	37	7 R	48.7%	48.1%	50.3%	49.7%
1,589	SULLY	989	509	448	32	61 R	51.5%	45.3%	53.2%	46.8%
8,352	TODD	1,355	646	649	60	3 D	47.7%	47.9%	49.9%	50.1%

SOUTH DAKOTA

SENATOR 1990

1990 Census Population	County	Total Vote	Republican	Democratic	Other	Rep.-Dem. Plurality	Percentage Total Vote Rep.	Dem.	Major Vote Rep.	Dem.
6,924	TRIPP	3,143	1,859	1,217	67	642 R	59.1%	38.7%	60.4%	39.6%
8,576	TURNER	3,592	2,110	1,409	73	701 R	58.7%	39.2%	60.0%	40.0%
10,189	UNION	3,523	1,861	1,566	96	295 R	52.8%	44.5%	54.3%	45.7%
6,087	WALWORTH	2,608	1,274	1,247	87	27 R	48.8%	47.8%	50.5%	49.5%
19,252	YANKTON	6,543	3,747	2,647	149	1,100 R	57.3%	40.5%	58.6%	41.4%
2,220	ZIEBACH	700	361	320	19	41 R	51.6%	45.7%	53.0%	47.0%
696,004	TOTAL	258,976	135,682	116,727	6,567	18,955 R	52.4%	45.1%	53.8%	46.2%

SOUTH DAKOTA

CONGRESS

CD	Year	Total Vote	Republican Vote	Republican Candidate	Democratic Vote	Democratic Candidate	Other Vote	Rep.-Dem. Plurality	Total Vote Rep.	Total Vote Dem.	Major Vote Rep.	Major Vote Dem.
AL	1990	257,298	83,484	FRANKENFELD, DON	173,814	JOHNSON, TIM		90,330 D	32.4%	67.6%	32.4%	67.6%
AL	1988	311,916	88,157	VOLK, DAVID	223,759	JOHNSON, TIM		135,602 D	28.3%	71.7%	28.3%	71.7%
AL	1986	289,723	118,261	BELL, DALE	171,462	JOHNSON, TIM		53,201 D	40.8%	59.2%	40.8%	59.2%
AL	1984	316,222	134,821	BELL, DALE	181,401	DASCHLE, THOMAS A.		46,580 D	42.6%	57.4%	42.6%	57.4%
AL	1982	275,652	133,530	ROBERTS, CLINT	142,122	DASCHLE, THOMAS A.		8,592 D	48.4%	51.6%	48.4%	51.6%

SOUTH DAKOTA

1990 GENERAL ELECTION

Governor

Senator   Other vote was Independent (Sinclair).

Congress

1990 PRIMARIES

JUNE 5 REPUBLICAN

Governor   George S. Mickelson, unopposed.

Senator   Larry Pressler, unopposed.

Congress   Unopposed at-large.

JUNE 5 DEMOCRATIC

Governor   Bob L. Samuelson, unopposed.

Senator   Ted Muenster, unopposed.

Congress   Unopposed at-large.

TENNESSEE

GOVERNOR
Ned McWherter (D). Re-elected 1990 to a four-year term. Previously elected 1986.

SENATORS
Albert Gore, Jr. (D). Re-elected 1990 to a six-year term. Previously elected 1984.

James R. Sasser (D). Re-elected 1988 to a six-year term. Previously elected 1982, 1976.

REPRESENTATIVES
1. James H. Quillen (R)
2. John J. Duncan, Jr. (R)
3. Marilyn Lloyd (D)
4. Jim Cooper (D)
5. Bob Clement (D)
6. Bart Gordon (D)
7. Don Sundquist (R)
8. John Tanner (D)
9. Harold E. Ford (D)

POSTWAR VOTE FOR PRESIDENT

Year	Total Vote	Republican Vote	Candidate	Democratic Vote	Candidate	Other Vote	Plurality	Total Vote Rep.	Dem.	Major Vote Rep.	Dem.
1988	1,636,250	947,233	Bush, George	679,794	Dukakis, Michael S.	9,223	267,439 R	57.9%	41.5%	58.2%	41.8%
1984	1,711,994	990,212	Reagan, Ronald	711,714	Mondale, Walter F.	10,068	278,498 R	57.8%	41.6%	58.2%	41.8%
1980	1,617,616	787,761	Reagan, Ronald	783,051	Carter, Jimmy	46,804	4,710 R	48.7%	48.4%	50.1%	49.9%
1976	1,476,345	633,969	Ford, Gerald R.	825,879	Carter, Jimmy	16,497	191,910 D	42.9%	55.9%	43.4%	56.6%
1972	1,201,182	813,147	Nixon, Richard M.	357,293	McGovern, George S.	30,742	455,854 R	67.7%	29.7%	69.5%	30.5%
1968 **	1,248,617	472,592	Nixon, Richard M.	351,233	Humphrey, Hubert H.	424,792	47,800 R	37.8%	28.1%	57.4%	42.6%
1964	1,143,946	508,965	Goldwater, Barry M.	634,947	Johnson, Lyndon B.	34	125,982 D	44.5%	55.5%	44.5%	55.5%
1960	1,051,792	556,577	Nixon, Richard M.	481,453	Kennedy, John F.	13,762	75,124 R	52.9%	45.8%	53.6%	46.4%
1956	939,404	462,288	Eisenhower, Dwight D.	456,507	Stevenson, Adlai E.	20,609	5,781 R	49.2%	48.6%	50.3%	49.7%
1952	892,553	446,147	Eisenhower, Dwight D.	443,710	Stevenson, Adlai E.	2,696	2,437 R	50.0%	49.7%	50.1%	49.9%
1948	550,283	202,914	Dewey, Thomas E.	270,402	Truman, Harry S.	76,967	67,488 D	36.9%	49.1%	42.9%	57.1%

In 1968 other vote was American (Wallace).

TENNESSEE

POSTWAR VOTE FOR GOVERNOR

Year	Total Vote	Republican Vote	Candidate	Democratic Vote	Candidate	Other Vote	Rep-Dem. Plurality	Total Vote Rep.	Dem.	Major Vote Rep.	Dem.
1990	790,441	289,348	Henry, Dwight	480,885	McWherter, Ned	20,208	191,537 D	36.6%	60.8%	37.6%	62.4%
1986	1,210,339	553,449	Dunn, Winfield	656,602	McWherter, Ned	288	103,153 D	45.7%	54.2%	45.7%	54.3%
1982	1,238,927	737,963	Alexander, Lamar	500,937	Tyree, Randy	27	237,026 R	59.6%	40.4%	59.6%	40.4%
1978	1,189,695	661,959	Alexander, Lamar	523,495	Butcher, Jake	4,241	138,464 R	55.6%	44.0%	55.8%	44.2%
1974	1,040,714	455,467	Alexander, Lamar	576,833	Blanton, Ray	8,414	121,366 D	43.8%	55.4%	44.1%	55.9%
1970	1,108,247	575,777	Dunn, Winfield	509,521	Hooker, John J.	22,949	66,256 R	52.0%	46.0%	53.1%	46.9%
1966 **	656,566		—	532,998	Ellington, Buford	123,568	532,998 D		81.2%		100.0%
1962 **	621,064	100,190	Patty, Hubert D.	315,648	Clement, Frank G.	205,226	215,458 D	16.1%	50.8%	24.1%	75.9%
1958 **	432,545	35,938	Wall, Thomas P.	248,874	Ellington, Buford	147,733	212,936 D	8.3%	57.5%	12.6%	87.4%
1954 **	322,586		—	281,291	Clement, Frank G.	41,295	281,291 D		87.2%		100.0%
1952	806,771	166,377	Witt, R. Beecher	640,290	Clement, Frank G.	104	473,913 D	20.6%	79.4%	20.6%	79.4%
1950	236,194		—	184,437	Browning, Gordon	51,757	184,437 D		78.1%		100.0%
1948	543,881	179,957	Acuff, Roy	363,903	Browning, Gordon	21	183,946 D	33.1%	66.9%	33.1%	66.9%
1946	229,456	73,222	Lowe, W. O.	149,937	McCord, Jim Nance	6,297	76,715 D	31.9%	65.3%	32.8%	67.2%

The term of office of Tennessee's Governor was increased from two to four years effective with the 1954 election. In 1958 Jim Nance McCord (Independent) received 136,399 votes (31.5% of the total vote) and ran second. In 1962 other vote was 203,765 William R. Anderson (Independent) who ran second; 1,441 E. B. Bowles (Independent) and 20 scattered. In 1966 other vote was 64,602 H. L. Crawford (Independent); 50,221 Charles Moffett (Independent); 8,407 Charles G. Vick (Independent) and 338 scattered.

POSTWAR VOTE FOR SENATOR

Year	Total Vote	Republican Vote	Candidate	Democratic Vote	Candidate	Other Vote	Rep-Dem. Plurality	Total Vote Rep.	Dem.	Major Vote Rep.	Dem.
1990	783,922	233,703	Hawkins, William R.	530,898	Gore, Albert, Jr.	19,321	297,195 D	29.8%	67.7%	30.6%	69.4%
1988	1,567,181	541,033	Anderson, Bill	1,020,061	Sasser, James R.	6,087	479,028 D	34.5%	65.1%	34.7%	65.3%
1984	1,648,064	557,016	Ashe, Victor	1,000,607	Gore, Albert, Jr.	90,441	443,591 D	33.8%	60.7%	35.8%	64.2%
1982	1,259,785	479,642	Beard, Robin L.	780,113	Sasser, James R.	30	300,471 D	38.1%	61.9%	38.1%	61.9%
1978	1,157,094	642,644	Baker, Howard H., Jr.	466,228	Eskind, Jane	48,222	176,416 R	55.5%	40.3%	58.0%	42.0%
1976	1,432,046	673,231	Brock, William E.	751,180	Sasser, James R.	7,635	77,949 D	47.0%	52.5%	47.3%	52.7%
1972	1,164,195	716,539	Baker, Howard H., Jr.	440,599	Blanton, Ray	7,057	275,940 R	61.5%	37.8%	61.9%	38.1%
1970	1,097,041	562,645	Brock, William E.	519,858	Gore, Albert	14,538	42,787 R	51.3%	47.4%	52.0%	48.0%
1966	866,961	483,063	Baker, Howard H., Jr.	383,843	Clement, Frank G.	55	99,220 R	55.7%	44.3%	55.7%	44.3%
1964	1,064,018	493,475	Kuykendall, Daniel H.	570,542	Gore, Albert	1	77,067 D	46.4%	53.6%	46.4%	53.6%
1964 S	1,091,093	517,330	Baker, Howard H., Jr.	568,905	Bass, Ross	4,858	51,575 D	47.4%	52.1%	47.6%	52.4%
1960	828,519	234,053	Frazier, A. Bradley	594,460	Kefauver, Estes	6	360,407 D	28.2%	71.7%	28.2%	71.8%
1958	401,666	76,371	Atkins, Hobart F.	317,324	Gore, Albert	7,971	240,953 D	19.0%	79.0%	19.4%	80.6%
1954	356,094	106,971	Wall, Thomas P.	249,121	Kefauver, Estes	2	142,150 D	30.0%	70.0%	30.0%	70.0%
1952	735,219	153,479	Atkins, Hobart F.	545,432	Gore, Albert	36,308	391,953 D	20.9%	74.2%	22.0%	78.0%
1948	499,218	166,947	Reece, B. Carroll	326,142	Kefauver, Estes	6,129	159,195 D	33.4%	65.3%	33.9%	66.1%
1946	218,714	57,238	Ladd, William B.	145,654	McKellar, Kenneth	15,822	88,416 D	26.2%	66.6%	28.2%	71.8%

One of the 1964 elections was for a short term to fill a vacancy.

TENNESSEE

Districts Established June 18, 1981

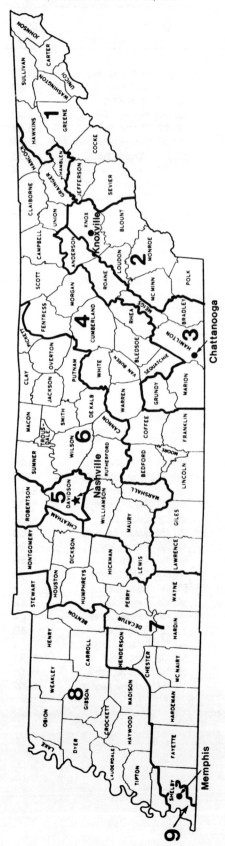

TENNESSEE

GOVERNOR 1990

1990 Census Population	County	Total Vote	Republican	Democratic	Other	Rep.-Dem. Plurality	Percentage Total Vote Rep.	Dem.	Major Vote Rep.	Dem.
68,250	ANDERSON	13,628	5,232	8,088	308	2,856 D	38.4%	59.3%	39.3%	60.7%
30,411	BEDFORD	2,898	769	2,066	63	1,297 D	26.5%	71.3%	27.1%	72.9%
14,524	BENTON	2,223	761	1,354	108	593 D	34.2%	60.9%	36.0%	64.0%
9,669	BLEDSOE	1,967	853	1,063	51	210 D	43.4%	54.0%	44.5%	55.5%
85,969	BLOUNT	12,706	6,022	6,397	287	375 D	47.4%	50.3%	48.5%	51.5%
73,712	BRADLEY	8,692	4,195	4,196	301	1 D	48.3%	48.3%	50.0%	50.0%
35,079	CAMPBELL	4,897	1,662	3,139	96	1,477 D	33.9%	64.1%	34.6%	65.4%
10,467	CANNON	1,332	385	899	48	514 D	28.9%	67.5%	30.0%	70.0%
27,514	CARROLL	4,351	1,304	2,965	82	1,661 D	30.0%	68.1%	30.5%	69.5%
51,505	CARTER	5,786	2,352	3,282	152	930 D	40.6%	56.7%	41.7%	58.3%
27,140	CHEATHAM	2,578	839	1,653	86	814 D	32.5%	64.1%	33.7%	66.3%
12,819	CHESTER	2,264	971	1,258	35	287 D	42.9%	55.6%	43.6%	56.4%
26,137	CLAIBORNE	3,465	1,210	2,189	66	979 D	34.9%	63.2%	35.6%	64.4%
7,238	CLAY	949	290	636	23	346 D	30.6%	67.0%	31.3%	68.7%
29,141	COCKE	3,148	1,282	1,784	82	502 D	40.7%	56.7%	41.8%	58.2%
40,339	COFFEE	6,086	2,323	3,594	169	1,271 D	38.2%	59.1%	39.3%	60.7%
13,378	CROCKETT	1,960	693	1,188	79	495 D	35.4%	60.6%	36.8%	63.2%
34,736	CUMBERLAND	6,470	3,055	3,224	191	169 D	47.2%	49.8%	48.7%	51.3%
510,784	DAVIDSON	75,553	23,389	49,744	2,420	26,355 D	31.0%	65.8%	32.0%	68.0%
10,472	DECATUR	1,723	674	1,016	33	342 D	39.1%	59.0%	39.9%	60.1%
14,360	DE KALB	1,765	559	1,147	59	588 D	31.7%	65.0%	32.8%	67.2%
35,061	DICKSON	5,038	1,465	3,456	117	1,991 D	29.1%	68.6%	29.8%	70.2%
34,854	DYER	5,116	1,855	3,027	234	1,172 D	36.3%	59.2%	38.0%	62.0%
25,559	FAYETTE	3,713	1,374	2,249	90	875 D	37.0%	60.6%	37.9%	62.1%
14,669	FENTRESS	2,051	850	1,159	42	309 D	41.4%	56.5%	42.3%	57.7%
34,725	FRANKLIN	5,196	1,451	3,616	129	2,165 D	27.9%	69.6%	28.6%	71.4%
46,315	GIBSON	8,954	2,234	6,514	206	4,280 D	24.9%	72.7%	25.5%	74.5%
25,741	GILES	3,211	712	2,453	46	1,741 D	22.2%	76.4%	22.5%	77.5%
17,095	GRAINGER	1,588	775	768	45	7 R	48.8%	48.4%	50.2%	49.8%
55,853	GREENE	5,984	2,643	3,199	142	556 D	44.2%	53.5%	45.2%	54.8%
13,362	GRUNDY	1,587	466	1,090	31	624 D	29.4%	68.7%	29.9%	70.1%
50,480	HAMBLEN	7,808	3,425	4,216	167	791 D	43.9%	54.0%	44.8%	55.2%
285,536	HAMILTON	51,670	19,874	30,056	1,740	10,182 D	38.5%	58.2%	39.8%	60.2%
6,739	HANCOCK	969	349	608	12	259 D	36.0%	62.7%	36.5%	63.5%
23,377	HARDEMAN	5,186	1,517	3,573	96	2,056 D	29.3%	68.9%	29.8%	70.2%
22,633	HARDIN	4,765	1,839	2,848	78	1,009 D	38.6%	59.8%	39.2%	60.8%
44,565	HAWKINS	7,423	2,727	4,583	113	1,856 D	36.7%	61.7%	37.3%	62.7%
19,437	HAYWOOD	2,311	643	1,615	53	972 D	27.8%	69.9%	28.5%	71.5%
21,844	HENDERSON	3,081	1,646	1,374	61	272 R	53.4%	44.6%	54.5%	45.5%
27,888	HENRY	3,765	965	2,707	93	1,742 D	25.6%	71.9%	26.3%	73.7%
16,754	HICKMAN	2,170	537	1,593	40	1,056 D	24.7%	73.4%	25.2%	74.8%
7,018	HOUSTON	1,241	279	928	34	649 D	22.5%	74.8%	23.1%	76.9%
15,795	HUMPHREYS	2,027	480	1,493	54	1,013 D	23.7%	73.7%	24.3%	75.7%
9,297	JACKSON	1,527	506	976	45	470 D	33.1%	63.9%	34.1%	65.9%
33,016	JEFFERSON	4,046	1,923	2,009	114	86 D	47.5%	49.7%	48.9%	51.1%
13,766	JOHNSON	1,697	667	1,006	24	339 D	39.3%	59.3%	39.9%	60.1%
335,749	KNOX	57,442	24,363	31,848	1,231	7,485 D	42.4%	55.4%	43.3%	56.7%
7,129	LAKE	634	162	453	19	291 D	25.6%	71.5%	26.3%	73.7%
23,491	LAUDERDALE	2,387	859	1,448	80	589 D	36.0%	60.7%	37.2%	62.8%
35,303	LAWRENCE	7,187	2,179	4,916	92	2,737 D	30.3%	68.4%	30.7%	69.3%
9,247	LEWIS	2,104	579	1,493	32	914 D	27.5%	71.0%	27.9%	72.1%
28,157	LINCOLN	3,634	839	2,732	63	1,893 D	23.1%	75.2%	23.5%	76.5%
31,255	LOUDON	4,480	2,171	2,171	138		48.5%	48.5%	50.0%	50.0%
42,383	MCMINN	8,716	4,578	3,963	175	615 R	52.5%	45.5%	53.6%	46.4%
22,422	MCNAIRY	5,454	2,111	3,286	57	1,175 D	38.7%	60.2%	39.1%	60.9%
15,906	MACON	1,432	514	894	24	380 D	35.9%	62.4%	36.5%	63.5%
77,982	MADISON	18,537	6,217	11,895	425	5,678 D	33.5%	64.2%	34.3%	65.7%
24,860	MARION	5,231	2,020	2,958	253	938 D	38.6%	56.5%	40.6%	59.4%
21,539	MARSHALL	2,324	746	1,521	57	775 D	32.1%	65.4%	32.9%	67.1%
54,812	MAURY	7,744	2,612	4,977	155	2,365 D	33.7%	64.3%	34.4%	65.6%

TENNESSEE

GOVERNOR 1990

1990 Census Population	County	Total Vote	Republican	Democratic	Other	Rep.-Dem. Plurality	Percentage Total Vote Rep.	Dem.	Major Vote Rep.	Dem.
8,033	MEIGS	1,479	735	719	25	16 R	49.7%	48.6%	50.6%	49.4%
30,541	MONROE	4,748	2,330	2,331	87	1 D	49.1%	49.1%	50.0%	50.0%
100,498	MONTGOMERY	14,984	3,164	11,584	236	8,420 D	21.1%	77.3%	21.5%	78.5%
4.721	MOORE	636	192	425	19	233 D	30.2%	66.8%	31.1%	68.9%
17,300	MORGAN	1,930	712	1,186	32	474 D	36.9%	61.5%	37.5%	62.5%
31,717	OBION	4,376	1,387	2,856	133	1,469 D	31.7%	65.3%	32.7%	67.3%
17,636	OVERTON	2,126	651	1,426	49	775 D	30.6%	67.1%	31.3%	68.7%
6,612	PERRY	965	283	666	16	383 D	29.3%	69.0%	29.8%	70.2%
4,548	PICKETT	764	351	403	10	52 D	45.9%	52.7%	46.6%	53.4%
13,643	POLK	2,100	754	1,298	48	544 D	35.9%	61.8%	36.7%	63.3%
51,373	PUTNAM	8,865	3,719	4,844	302	1,125 D	42.0%	54.6%	43.4%	56.6%
24,344	RHEA	5,224	2,153	2,978	93	825 D	41.2%	57.0%	42.0%	58.0%
47,227	ROANE	10,870	4,231	6,327	312	2,096 D	38.9%	58.2%	40.1%	59.9%
41,494	ROBERTSON	4,602	1,213	3,237	152	2,024 D	26.4%	70.3%	27.3%	72.7%
118,570	RUTHERFORD	14,412	4,840	9,121	451	4,281 D	33.6%	63.3%	34.7%	65.3%
18,358	SCOTT	1,534	577	923	34	346 D	37.6%	60.2%	38.5%	61.5%
8,863	SEQUATCHIE	1,571	622	920	29	298 D	39.6%	58.6%	40.3%	59.7%
51,043	SEVIER	5,695	2,909	2,608	178	301 R	51.1%	45.8%	52.7%	47.3%
826,330	SHELBY	156,943	60,427	92,455	4,061	32,028 D	38.5%	58.9%	39.5%	60.5%
14,143	SMITH	2,310	562	1,712	36	1,150 D	24.3%	74.1%	24.7%	75.3%
9,479	STEWART	1,643	368	1,224	51	856 D	22.4%	74.5%	23.1%	76.9%
143,596	SULLIVAN	23,058	8,294	14,240	524	5,946 D	36.0%	61.8%	36.8%	63.2%
103,281	SUMNER	14,024	4,490	9,222	312	4,732 D	32.0%	65.8%	32.7%	67.3%
37,568	TIPTON	4,036	1,837	2,047	152	210 D	45.5%	50.7%	47.3%	52.7%
5,920	TROUSDALE	2,018	328	1,650	40	1,322 D	16.3%	81.8%	16.6%	83.4%
16,549	UNICOI	2,022	652	1,334	36	682 D	32.2%	66.0%	32.8%	67.2%
13,694	UNION	1,728	825	871	32	46 D	47.7%	50.4%	48.6%	51.4%
4,846	VAN BUREN	856	224	611	21	387 D	26.2%	71.4%	26.8%	73.2%
32,992	WARREN	7,017	1,897	4,936	184	3,039 D	27.0%	70.3%	27.8%	72.2%
92,315	WASHINGTON	15,675	5,290	10,124	261	4,834 D	33.7%	64.6%	34.3%	65.7%
13,935	WAYNE	1,591	758	813	20	55 D	47.6%	51.1%	48.2%	51.8%
31,972	WEAKLEY	5,537	1,359	4,015	163	2,656 D	24.5%	72.5%	25.3%	74.7%
20,090	WHITE	2,304	756	1,461	87	705 D	32.8%	63.4%	34.1%	65.9%
81,021	WILLIAMSON	14,176	6,016	7,846	314	1,830 D	42.4%	55.3%	43.4%	56.6%
67,675	WILSON	14,751	4,470	9,919	362	5,449 D	30.3%	67.2%	31.1%	68.9%
4,877,185	TOTAL	790,441	289,348	480,885	20,208	191,537 D	36.6%	60.8%	37.6%	62.4%

TENNESSEE

SENATOR 1990

1990 Census Population	County	Total Vote	Republican	Democratic	Other	Rep.-Dem. Plurality	Percentage			
							Total Vote		Major Vote	
							Rep.	Dem.	Rep.	Dem.
68,250	ANDERSON	13,801	4,018	9,542	241	5,524 D	29.1%	69.1%	29.6%	70.4%
30,411	BEDFORD	2,930	621	2,259	50	1,638 D	21.2%	77.1%	21.6%	78.4%
14,524	BENTON	2,264	441	1,735	88	1,294 D	19.5%	76.6%	20.3%	79.7%
9,669	BLEDSOE	1,997	734	1,229	34	495 D	36.8%	61.5%	37.4%	62.6%
85,969	BLOUNT	12,644	4,803	7,563	278	2,760 D	38.0%	59.8%	38.8%	61.2%
73,712	BRADLEY	8,700	3,533	4,942	225	1,409 D	40.6%	56.8%	41.7%	58.3%
35,079	CAMPBELL	4,845	1,253	3,527	65	2,274 D	25.9%	72.8%	26.2%	73.8%
10,467	CANNON	1,349	316	992	41	676 D	23.4%	73.5%	24.2%	75.8%
27,514	CARROLL	4,389	998	3,306	85	2,308 D	22.7%	75.3%	23.2%	76.8%
51,505	CARTER	5,621	2,042	3,431	148	1,389 D	36.3%	61.0%	37.3%	62.7%
27,140	CHEATHAM	2,557	672	1,818	67	1,146 D	26.3%	71.1%	27.0%	73.0%
12,819	CHESTER	2,251	758	1,468	25	710 D	33.7%	65.2%	34.1%	65.9%
26,137	CLAIBORNE	3,473	938	2,486	49	1,548 D	27.0%	71.6%	27.4%	72.6%
7,238	CLAY	945	219	711	15	492 D	23.2%	75.2%	23.5%	76.5%
29,141	COCKE	3,009	914	1,996	99	1,082 D	30.4%	66.3%	31.4%	68.6%
40,339	COFFEE	6,156	2,013	3,994	149	1,981 D	32.7%	64.9%	33.5%	66.5%
13,378	CROCKETT	1,952	535	1,361	56	826 D	27.4%	69.7%	28.2%	71.8%
34,736	CUMBERLAND	6,390	2,513	3,680	197	1,167 D	39.3%	57.6%	40.6%	59.4%
510,784	DAVIDSON	75,329	19,008	54,267	2,054	35,259 D	25.2%	72.0%	25.9%	74.1%
10,472	DECATUR	1,738	509	1,200	29	691 D	29.3%	69.0%	29.8%	70.2%
14,360	DE KALB	1,812	421	1,342	49	921 D	23.2%	74.1%	23.9%	76.1%
35,061	DICKSON	4,953	1,127	3,740	86	2,613 D	22.8%	75.5%	23.2%	76.8%
34,854	DYER	5,099	1,374	3,536	189	2,162 D	26.9%	69.3%	28.0%	72.0%
25,559	FAYETTE	3,645	1,137	2,378	130	1,241 D	31.2%	65.2%	32.3%	67.7%
14,669	FENTRESS	1,999	519	1,446	34	927 D	26.0%	72.3%	26.4%	73.6%
34,725	FRANKLIN	5,269	1,210	3,971	88	2,761 D	23.0%	75.4%	23.4%	76.6%
46,315	GIBSON	8,810	1,671	6,972	167	5,301 D	19.0%	79.1%	19.3%	80.7%
25,741	GILES	3,212	608	2,558	46	1,950 D	18.9%	79.6%	19.2%	80.8%
17,095	GRAINGER	1,595	625	936	34	311 D	39.2%	58.7%	40.0%	60.0%
55,853	GREENE	5,910	2,283	3,511	116	1,228 D	38.6%	59.4%	39.4%	60.6%
13,362	GRUNDY	1,616	344	1,251	21	907 D	21.3%	77.4%	21.6%	78.4%
50,480	HAMBLEN	7,771	2,842	4,792	137	1,950 D	36.6%	61.7%	37.2%	62.8%
285,536	HAMILTON	51,313	20,671	28,928	1,714	8,257 D	40.3%	56.4%	41.7%	58.3%
6,739	HANCOCK	920	260	651	9	391 D	28.3%	70.8%	28.5%	71.5%
23,377	HARDEMAN	5,027	1,034	3,873	120	2,839 D	20.6%	77.0%	21.1%	78.9%
22,633	HARDIN	4,788	1,374	3,343	71	1,969 D	28.7%	69.8%	29.1%	70.9%
44,565	HAWKINS	7,263	2,239	4,943	81	2,704 D	30.8%	68.1%	31.2%	68.8%
19,437	HAYWOOD	2,313	568	1,685	60	1,117 D	24.6%	72.8%	25.2%	74.8%
21,844	HENDERSON	3,040	1,141	1,857	42	716 D	37.5%	61.1%	38.1%	61.9%
27,888	HENRY	3,710	868	2,756	86	1,888 D	23.4%	74.3%	24.0%	76.0%
16,754	HICKMAN	2,195	421	1,741	33	1,320 D	19.2%	79.3%	19.5%	80.5%
7,018	HOUSTON	1,237	185	1,017	35	832 D	15.0%	82.2%	15.4%	84.6%
15,795	HUMPHREYS	2,053	393	1,605	55	1,212 D	19.1%	78.2%	19.7%	80.3%
9,297	JACKSON	1,494	231	1,243	20	1,012 D	15.5%	83.2%	15.7%	84.3%
33,016	JEFFERSON	4,067	1,504	2,454	109	950 D	37.0%	60.3%	38.0%	62.0%
13,766	JOHNSON	1,622	561	1,027	34	466 D	34.6%	63.3%	35.3%	64.7%
335,749	KNOX	56,947	18,675	37,254	1,018	18,579 D	32.8%	65.4%	33.4%	66.6%
7,129	LAKE	619	113	486	20	373 D	18.3%	78.5%	18.9%	81.1%
23,491	LAUDERDALE	2,405	593	1,748	64	1,155 D	24.7%	72.7%	25.3%	74.7%
35,303	LAWRENCE	7,118	1,862	5,198	58	3,336 D	26.2%	73.0%	26.4%	73.6%
9,247	LEWIS	2,132	404	1,704	24	1,300 D	18.9%	79.9%	19.2%	80.8%
28,157	LINCOLN	3,612	807	2,743	62	1,936 D	22.3%	75.9%	22.7%	77.3%
31,255	LOUDON	4,259	1,655	2,479	125	824 D	38.9%	58.2%	40.0%	60.0%
42,383	MCMINN	8,663	3,065	5,442	156	2,377 D	35.4%	62.8%	36.0%	64.0%
22,422	MCNAIRY	5,322	1,654	3,622	46	1,968 D	31.1%	68.1%	31.3%	68.7%
15,906	MACON	1,446	392	1,030	24	638 D	27.1%	71.2%	27.6%	72.4%
77,982	MADISON	18,457	4,499	13,500	458	9,001 D	24.4%	73.1%	25.0%	75.0%
24,860	MARION	5,273	1,399	3,743	131	2,344 D	26.5%	71.0%	27.2%	72.8%
21,539	MARSHALL	2,313	623	1,629	61	1,006 D	26.9%	70.4%	27.7%	72.3%
54,812	MAURY	7,754	2,332	5,289	133	2,957 D	30.1%	68.2%	30.6%	69.4%

TENNESSEE

SENATOR 1990

1990 Census Population	County	Total Vote	Republican	Democratic	Other	Rep.-Dem. Plurality	Percentage Total Vote Rep.	Dem.	Major Vote Rep.	Dem.
8,033	MEIGS	1,476	556	900	20	344 D	37.7%	61.0%	38.2%	61.8%
30,541	MONROE	4,697	1,922	2,715	60	793 D	40.9%	57.8%	41.4%	58.6%
100,498	MONTGOMERY	14,686	2,864	11,567	255	8,703 D	19.5%	78.8%	19.8%	80.2%
4,721	MOORE	631	156	465	10	309 D	24.7%	73.7%	25.1%	74.9%
17,300	MORGAN	1,959	457	1,457	45	1,000 D	23.3%	74.4%	23.9%	76.1%
31,717	OBION	4,176	858	3,210	108	2,352 D	20.5%	76.9%	21.1%	78.9%
17,636	OVERTON	2,117	317	1,761	39	1,444 D	15.0%	83.2%	15.3%	84.7%
6,612	PERRY	965	194	762	9	568 D	20.1%	79.0%	20.3%	79.7%
4,548	PICKETT	777	262	506	9	244 D	33.7%	65.1%	34.1%	65.9%
13,643	POLK	2,130	615	1,485	30	870 D	28.9%	69.7%	29.3%	70.7%
51,373	PUTNAM	8,875	2,032	6,663	180	4,631 D	22.9%	75.1%	23.4%	76.6%
24,344	RHEA	5,138	1,954	3,124	60	1,170 D	38.0%	60.8%	38.5%	61.5%
47,227	ROANE	10,882	3,069	7,583	230	4,514 D	28.2%	69.7%	28.8%	71.2%
41,494	ROBERTSON	4,619	883	3,602	134	2,719 D	19.1%	78.0%	19.7%	80.3%
118,570	RUTHERFORD	14,415	3,860	10,184	371	6,324 D	26.8%	70.6%	27.5%	72.5%
18,358	SCOTT	1,523	465	1,021	37	556 D	30.5%	67.0%	31.3%	68.7%
8,863	SEQUATCHIE	1,556	538	996	22	458 D	34.6%	64.0%	35.1%	64.9%
51,043	SEVIER	5,594	2,158	3,278	158	1,120 D	38.6%	58.6%	39.7%	60.3%
826,330	SHELBY	153,823	49,860	98,841	5,122	48,981 D	32.4%	64.3%	33.5%	66.5%
14,143	SMITH	2,376	341	1,996	39	1,655 D	14.4%	84.0%	14.6%	85.4%
9,479	STEWART	1,637	337	1,247	53	910 D	20.6%	76.2%	21.3%	78.7%
143,596	SULLIVAN	22,790	7,398	14,871	521	7,473 D	32.5%	65.3%	33.2%	66.8%
103,281	SUMNER	14,179	3,539	10,376	264	6,837 D	25.0%	73.2%	25.4%	74.6%
37,568	TIPTON	4,021	1,465	2,375	181	910 D	36.4%	59.1%	38.2%	61.8%
5,920	TROUSDALE	2,104	216	1,867	21	1,651 D	10.3%	88.7%	10.4%	89.6%
16,549	UNICOI	1,992	567	1,395	30	828 D	28.5%	70.0%	28.9%	71.1%
13,694	UNION	1,713	629	1,054	30	425 D	36.7%	61.5%	37.4%	62.6%
4,846	VAN BUREN	860	124	728	8	604 D	14.4%	84.7%	14.6%	85.4%
32,992	WARREN	7,140	1,117	5,837	186	4,720 D	15.6%	81.8%	16.1%	83.9%
92,315	WASHINGTON	15,037	3,973	10,730	334	6,757 D	26.4%	71.4%	27.0%	73.0%
13,935	WAYNE	1,552	632	896	24	264 D	40.7%	57.7%	41.4%	58.6%
31,972	WEAKLEY	5,498	1,072	4,290	136	3,218 D	19.5%	78.0%	20.0%	80.0%
20,090	WHITE	2,349	459	1,818	72	1,359 D	19.5%	77.4%	20.2%	79.8%
81,021	WILLIAMSON	14,167	5,189	8,664	314	3,475 D	36.6%	61.2%	37.5%	62.5%
67,675	WILSON	15,075	3,103	11,704	268	8,601 D	20.6%	77.6%	21.0%	79.0%
4,877,185	TOTAL	783,922	233,703	530,898	19,321	297,195 D	29.8%	67.7%	30.6%	69.4%

TENNESSEE

CONGRESS

CD	Year	Total Vote	Republican Vote	Republican Candidate	Democratic Vote	Democratic Candidate	Other Vote	Rep.-Dem. Plurality	Total Vote Rep.	Total Vote Dem.	Major Vote Rep.	Major Vote Dem.
1	1990	47,860	47,796	QUILLEN, JAMES H.			64	47,796 R	99.9%		100.0%	
1	1988	148,998	119,526	QUILLEN, JAMES H.	29,469	SMITH, SIDNEY S.	3	90,057 R	80.2%	19.8%	80.2%	19.8%
1	1986	116,570	80,289	QUILLEN, JAMES H.	36,278	RUSSELL, JOHN B.	3	44,011 R	68.9%	31.1%	68.9%	31.1%
1	1984	113,442	113,407	QUILLEN, JAMES H.			35	113,407 R	100.0%		100.0%	
1	1982	120,858	89,497	QUILLEN, JAMES H.	27,580	CABLE, JESSIE J.	3,781	61,917 R	74.1%	22.8%	76.4%	23.6%
2	1990	77,944	62,797	DUNCAN, JOHN J., JR.			15,147	62,797 R	80.6%		100.0%	
2	1988	177,174	99,631	DUNCAN, JOHN J., JR.	77,540	TAYLOR, DUDLEY W.	3	22,091 R	56.2%	43.8%	56.2%	43.8%
2	1986	126,486	96,396	DUNCAN, JOHN J.	30,088	BOWEN, JOHN F.	2	66,308 R	76.2%	23.8%	76.2%	23.8%
2	1984	171,453	132,604	DUNCAN, JOHN J.	38,846	BOWEN, JOHN F.	3	93,758 R	77.3%	22.7%	77.3%	22.7%
2	1982	109,057	109,045	DUNCAN, JOHN J.			12	109,045 R	100.0%		100.0%	
3	1990	93,665	36,855	RHODEN, GRADY L.	49,662	LLOYD, MARILYN	7,148	12,807 D	39.3%	53.0%	42.6%	57.4%
3	1988	188,638	80,372	COKER, HAROLD L.	108,264	LLOYD, MARILYN	2	27,892 D	42.6%	57.4%	42.6%	57.4%
3	1986	139,120	64,084	GOLDEN, JIM	75,034	LLOYD, MARILYN	2	10,950 D	46.1%	53.9%	46.1%	53.9%
3	1984	189,683	90,216	DAVIS, JOHN	99,465	LLOYD, MARILYN	2	9,249 D	47.6%	52.4%	47.6%	52.4%
3	1982	137,493	49,885	BYERS, GLEN	84,967	BOUQUARD, MARILYN LLOYD	2,641	35,082 D	36.3%	61.8%	37.0%	63.0%
4	1990	77,276	22,890	SANDERS, CLAIBORNE	52,101	COOPER, JIM	2,285	29,211 D	29.6%	67.4%	30.5%	69.5%
4	1988	94,151			94,129	COOPER, JIM	22	94,129 D		100.0%		100.0%
4	1986	87,005			86,997	COOPER, JIM	8	86,997 D		100.0%		100.0%
4	1984	124,863	31,011	SEIGNEUR, JAMES B.	93,848	COOPER, JIM	4	62,837 D	24.8%	75.2%	24.8%	75.2%
4	1982	141,322	47,865	BAKER, CISSY	93,453	COOPER, JIM	4	45,588 D	33.9%	66.1%	33.9%	66.1%
5	1990	76,760			55,607	CLEMENT, BOB	21,153	55,607 D		72.4%		100.0%
5	1988	155,140			155,068	CLEMENT, BOB	72	155,068 D		100.0%		100.0%
5	1986	147,147	58,701	HOLCOMB, TERRY	85,126	BONER, BILL	3,320	26,425 D	39.9%	57.9%	40.8%	59.2%
5	1984	138,286			138,233	BONER, BILL	53	138,233 D		100.0%		100.0%
5	1982	136,349	27,061	STEINHICE, LAUREL	109,282	BONER, BILL	6	82,221 D	19.8%	80.1%	19.8%	80.2%
6	1990	90,768	26,424	COCHRAN, GREGORY	60,538	GORDON, BART	3,806	34,114 D	29.1%	66.7%	30.4%	69.6%
6	1988	161,687	38,033	EMBRY, WALLACE	123,652	GORDON, BART	2	85,619 D	23.5%	76.5%	23.5%	76.5%
6	1986	133,004	30,823	VAIL, FRED	102,180	GORDON, BART	1	71,357 D	23.2%	76.8%	23.2%	76.8%
6	1984	165,565	61,559	SIMPKINS, JOE	103,989	GORDON, BART	17	42,430 D	37.2%	62.8%	37.2%	62.8%
6	1982	104,105			104,094	GORE, ALBERT, JR.	11	104,094 D		100.0%		100.0%
7	1990	106,676	66,141	SUNDQUIST, DON	40,516	BLOODWORTH, KEN	19	25,625 R	62.0%	38.0%	62.0%	38.0%
7	1988	177,266	142,025	SUNDQUIST, DON	35,237	BLOODWORTH, KEN	4	106,788 R	80.1%	19.9%	80.1%	19.9%
7	1986	129,878	93,902	SUNDQUIST, DON	35,966	HILER, M. LLOYD	10	57,936 R	72.3%	27.7%	72.3%	27.7%
7	1984	107,278	107,257	SUNDQUIST, DON			21	107,257 R	100.0%		100.0%	
7	1982	146,197	73,835	SUNDQUIST, DON	72,359	CLEMENT, BOB	3	1,476 R	50.5%	49.5%	50.5%	49.5%
8	1990	62,266			62,241	TANNER, JOHN	25	62,241 D		100.0%		100.0%
8	1988	151,465	56,893	BRYANT, ED	94,571	TANNER, JOHN	1	37,678 D	37.6%	62.4%	37.6%	62.4%
8	1986	126,503	24,792	CAMPBELL, DAN H.	101,699	JONES, ED	12	76,907 D	19.6%	80.4%	19.6%	80.4%
8	1984	118,668			118,653	JONES, ED	15	118,653 D		100.0%		100.0%
8	1982	125,472	31,527	BENSON, BRUCE	93,945	JONES, ED		62,418 D	25.1%	74.9%	25.1%	74.9%
9	1990	83,657	25,730	DAVIS, AARON C.	48,629	FORD, HAROLD E.	9,298	22,899 D	30.8%	58.1%	34.6%	65.4%
9	1988	154,802			126,280	FORD, HAROLD E.	28,522	126,280 D		81.6%		100.0%
9	1986	99,516			83,006	FORD, HAROLD E.	16,510	83,006 D		83.4%		100.0%
9	1984	186,497	53,064	THOMPSON, WILLIAM B.	133,428	FORD, HAROLD E.	5	80,364 D	28.5%	71.5%	28.5%	71.5%
9	1982	154,830	40,812	CRAWFORD, JOE	112,143	FORD, HAROLD E.	1,875	71,331 D	26.4%	72.4%	26.7%	73.3%

TENNESSEE

1990 GENERAL ELECTION

Governor   Other vote was 10,993 Independent (W. Curtis Jacox); 9,109 Independent (Shepard) and 106 scattered write-in.

Senator   Other vote was 11,191 Independent (Bill Jacox); 8,021 Independent (Vick) and 109 scattered write-in.

Congress   Other vote was 15,127 Independent (Hebert) and 20 scattered write-in in CD 2; 5,598 Independent (Melcher), 1,546 Independent (Googe) and 4 scattered write-in in CD 3; 2,281 Independent (Bullington) and 4 scattered write-in in CD 4; 13,577 Independent (Stone), 5,383 Independent (Borgman), 2,192 Independent (Kuttab) and 1 scattered write-in in CD 5; 3,793 Independent (Brown) and 13 scattered in CD 6; 7,249 Independent (Davidson), 2,032 Independent (Richmond) and 17 scattered write-in in CD 9; scattered write-in in all other CD's.

1990 PRIMARIES

AUGUST 2 REPUBLICAN

Governor   92,100 Dwight Henry; 26,363 Charles R. Moffett; 18,153 Terry A. Williams; 16,293 Carroll Turner; 10,097 Hubert D. Patty; 8,893 Robert O. Watson; 102 scattered write-in.

Senator   54,317 William R. Hawkins; 53,873 Ralph Brown; 31,515 Patrick K. Hales; 70 scattered write-in.

Congress   Unopposed in six CD's. No candidate in CD's 5 and 8. Contested as follows:

CD   6   5,310 Gregory Cochran; 4,572 Wallace Embry; 3,789 Jack Nugent; 2 scattered write-in.

AUGUST 2 DEMOCRATIC

Governor   Ned McWherter, unopposed.

Senator   Albert Gore, Jr., unopposed.

Congress   Unopposed in five CD's. No candidate in CD's 1 and 2. Contested as follows:

CD   3   36,607 Marilyn Lloyd; 5,973 David R. Stacy; 2 scattered write-in.
CD   9   55,247 Harold E. Ford; 21,689 Pam Gaia; 2,862 Mark F. Flanagan.

TEXAS

GOVERNOR
Ann Richards (D). Elected 1990 to a four-year term.

SENATORS
Lloyd Bentsen (D). Re-elected 1988 to a six-year term. Previously elected 1982, 1976, 1970.

Phil Gramm (R). Re-elected 1990 to a six-year term. Previously elected 1984.

REPRESENTATIVES

1. James L. Chapman (D)
2. Charles Wilson (D)
3. Steve Bartlett (R) (see page 1)
4. Ralph M. Hall (D)
5. John Bryant (D)
6. Joe L. Barton (R)
7. W. R. Archer (R)
8. Jack Fields (R)
9. Jack B. Brooks (D)
10. Jake Pickle (D)
11. Chet Edwards (D)
12. Pete Geren (D)
13. Bill Sarpalius (D)
14. Greg Laughlin (D)
15. Eligio de la Garza (D)
16. Ronald Coleman (D)
17. Charles W. Stenholm (D)
18. Craig A. Washington (D)
19. Larry Combest (R)
20. Henry B. Gonzalez (D)
21. Lamar Smith (R)
22. Thomas D. DeLay (R)
23. Albert G. Bustamante (D)
24. Martin Frost (D)
25. Mike Andrews (D)
26. Dick Armey (R)
27. Solomon P. Ortiz (D)

POSTWAR VOTE FOR PRESIDENT

Year	Total Vote	Republican Vote	Candidate	Democratic Vote	Candidate	Other Vote	Plurality	Rep.	Dem.	Rep.	Dem.
1988	5,427,410	3,036,829	Bush, George	2,352,748	Dukakis, Michael S.	37,833	684,081 R	56.0%	43.3%	56.3%	43.7%
1984	5,397,571	3,433,428	Reagan, Ronald	1,949,276	Mondale, Walter F.	14,867	1,484,152 R	63.6%	36.1%	63.8%	36.2%
1980	4,541,636	2,510,705	Reagan, Ronald	1,881,147	Carter, Jimmy	149,784	629,558 R	55.3%	41.4%	57.2%	42.8%
1976	4,071,884	1,953,300	Ford, Gerald R.	2,082,319	Carter, Jimmy	36,265	129,019 D	48.0%	51.1%	48.4%	51.6%
1972	3,471,281	2,298,896	Nixon, Richard M.	1,154,289	McGovern, George S.	18,096	1,144,607 R	66.2%	33.3%	66.6%	33.4%
1968 **	3,079,216	1,227,844	Nixon, Richard M.	1,266,804	Humphrey, Hubert H.	584,568	38,960 D	39.9%	41.1%	49.2%	50.8%
1964	2,626,811	958,566	Goldwater, Barry M.	1,663,185	Johnson, Lyndon B.	5,060	704,619 D	36.5%	63.3%	36.6%	63.4%
1960	2,311,084	1,121,310	Nixon, Richard M.	1,167,567	Kennedy, John F.	22,207	46,257 D	48.5%	50.5%	49.0%	51.0%
1956	1,955,168	1,080,619	Eisenhower, Dwight D.	859,958	Stevenson, Adlai E.	14,591	220,661 R	55.3%	44.0%	55.7%	44.3%
1952	2,075,946	1,102,878	Eisenhower, Dwight D.	969,228	Stevenson, Adlai E.	3,840	133,650 R	53.1%	46.7%	53.2%	46.8%
1948	1,249,577	303,467	Dewey, Thomas E.	824,235	Truman, Harry S.	121,875	520,768 D	24.3%	66.0%	26.9%	73.1%

In 1968 other vote was 584,269 American (Wallace) and 299 scattered.

TEXAS

POSTWAR VOTE FOR GOVERNOR

| | | Republican | | Democratic | | | | Percentage | | | |
Year	Total Vote	Vote	Candidate	Vote	Candidate	Other Vote	Rep-Dem. Plurality	Total Vote Rep.	Dem.	Major Vote Rep.	Dem.
1990	3,892,746	1,826,431	Williams, Clayton	1,925,670	Richards, Ann	140,645	99,239 D	46.9%	49.5%	48.7%	51.3%
1986	3,441,460	1,813,779	Clements, William P.	1,584,515	White, Mark	43,166	229,264 R	52.7%	46.0%	53.4%	46.6%
1982	3,191,091	1,465,937	Clements, William P.	1,697,870	White, Mark	27,284	231,933 D	45.9%	53.2%	46.3%	53.7%
1978	2,369,764	1,183,839	Clements, William P.	1,166,979	Hill, John	18,946	16,860 R	50.0%	49.2%	50.4%	49.6%
1974 **	1,654,984	514,725	Granberry, Jim	1,016,334	Briscoe, Dolph	123,925	501,609 D	31.1%	61.4%	33.6%	66.4%
1972	3,410,128	1,534,060	Grover, Henry C.	1,633,970	Briscoe, Dolph	242,098	99,910 D	45.0%	47.9%	48.4%	51.6%
1970	2,235,847	1,037,723	Eggers, Paul W.	1,197,726	Smith, Preston	398	160,003 D	46.4%	53.6%	46.4%	53.6%
1968	2,916,509	1,254,333	Eggers, Paul W.	1,662,019	Smith, Preston	157	407,686 D	43.0%	57.0%	43.0%	57.0%
1966	1,425,861	368,025	Kennerly, T. E.	1,037,517	Connally, John B.	20,319	669,492 D	25.8%	72.8%	26.2%	73.8%
1964	2,544,753	661,675	Crichton, Jack	1,877,793	Connally, John B.	5,285	1,216,118 D	26.0%	73.8%	26.1%	73.9%
1962	1,569,181	715,025	Cox, Jack	847,036	Connally, John B.	7,120	132,011 D	45.6%	54.0%	45.8%	54.2%
1960	2,250,718	612,963	Steger, William M.	1,637,755	Daniel, Price		1,024,792 D	27.2%	72.8%	27.2%	72.8%
1958	789,133	94,098	Mayer, Edwin S.	695,035	Daniel, Price		600,937 D	11.9%	88.1%	11.9%	88.1%
1956	1,828,161	271,088	Bryant, William R.	1,433,051	Daniel, Price	124,022	1,161,963 D	14.8%	78.4%	15.9%	84.1%
1954	636,892	66,154	Adams, Tod R.	569,533	Shivers, Allan	1,205	503,379 D	10.4%	89.4%	10.4%	89.6%
1952	1,881,202		—	1,844,530	Shivers, Allan	36,672	1,844,530 D		98.1%		100.0%
1950	394,747	39,737	Currie, Ralph W.	355,010	Shivers, Allan		315,273 D	10.1%	89.9%	10.1%	89.9%
1948	1,208,860	177,399	Lane, Alvin H.	1,024,160	Jester, Beauford	7,301	846,761 D	14.7%	84.7%	14.8%	85.2%
1946	378,744	33,231	Nolte, Eugene	345,513	Jester, Beauford		312,282 D	8.8%	91.2%	8.8%	91.2%

The term of office of Texas' Governor was increased from two to four years effective with the 1974 election.

POSTWAR VOTE FOR SENATOR

| | | Republican | | Democratic | | | | Percentage | | | |
Year	Total Vote	Vote	Candidate	Vote	Candidate	Other Vote	Rep-Dem. Plurality	Total Vote Rep.	Dem.	Major Vote Rep.	Dem.
1990	3,822,157	2,302,357	Gramm, Phil	1,429,986	Parmer, Hugh	89,814	872,371 R	60.2%	37.4%	61.7%	38.3%
1988	5,323,606	2,129,228	Boulter, Beau	3,149,806	Bentsen, Lloyd	44,572	1,020,578 D	40.0%	59.2%	40.3%	59.7%
1984	5,319,178	3,116,348	Gramm, Phil	2,202,557	Doggett, Lloyd	273	913,791 R	58.6%	41.4%	58.6%	41.4%
1982	3,103,167	1,256,759	Collins, James M.	1,818,223	Bentsen, Lloyd	28,185	561,464 D	40.5%	58.6%	40.9%	59.1%
1978	2,312,540	1,151,376	Tower, John G.	1,139,149	Krueger, Robert	22,015	12,227 R	49.8%	49.3%	50.3%	49.7%
1976	3,874,516	1,636,370	Steelman, Alan	2,199,956	Bentsen, Lloyd	38,190	563,586 D	42.2%	56.8%	42.7%	57.3%
1972	3,413,903	1,822,877	Tower, John G.	1,511,985	Sanders, Barefoot	79,041	310,892 R	53.4%	44.3%	54.7%	45.3%
1970	2,231,671	1,035,794	Bush, George	1,194,069	Bentsen, Lloyd	1,808	158,275 D	46.4%	53.5%	46.5%	53.5%
1966	1,493,182	842,501	Tower, John G.	643,855	Carr, Waggoner	6,826	198,646 R	56.4%	43.1%	56.7%	43.3%
1964	2,603,856	1,134,337	Bush, George	1,463,958	Yarborough, Ralph	5,561	329,621 D	43.6%	56.2%	43.7%	56.3%
1961 S	886,091	448,217	Tower, John G.	437,874	Blakley, William A.		10,343 R	50.6%	49.4%	50.6%	49.4%
1960	2,253,784	926,653	Tower, John G.	1,306,625	Johnson, Lyndon B.	20,506	379,972 D	41.1%	58.0%	41.5%	58.5%
1958	787,128	185,926	Whittenburg, Roy	587,030	Yarborough, Ralph	14,172	401,104 D	23.6%	74.6%	24.1%	75.9%
1957 S	957,298		[See note below]								
1954	636,475	94,131	Watson, Carlos G.	539,319	Johnson, Lyndon B.	3,025	445,188 D	14.8%	84.7%	14.9%	85.1%
1952	1,895,192		—	1,895,192	Daniel, Price		1,895,192 D		100.0%		100.0%
1948	1,061,563	349,665	Porter, Jack	702,985	Johnson, Lyndon B.	8,913	353,320 D	32.9%	66.2%	33.2%	66.8%
1946	380,681	43,750	Sells, Murray C.	336,931	Connally, Tom		293,181 D	11.5%	88.5%	11.5%	88.5%

The May 1961 and April 1957 elections were for short terms to fill vacancies. Though neither vote was held with official party designations, the 1961 vote above was a run-off contest between unofficial party candidates. In 1957 there was a single ballot without run-off and Ralph Yarborough polled 364,605 votes (38.1% of the total vote) and won the election with a 73,802 plurality.

TEXAS

Districts Established June 19, 1983

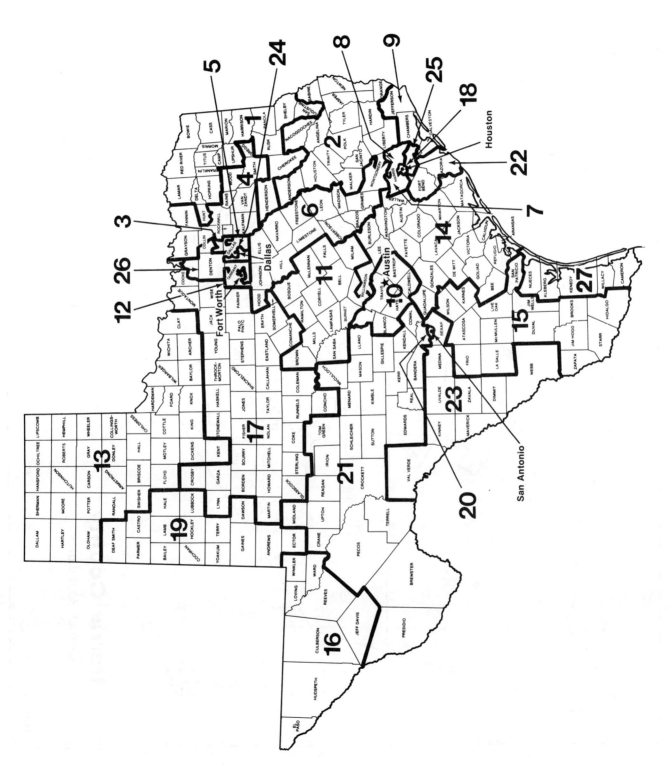

418

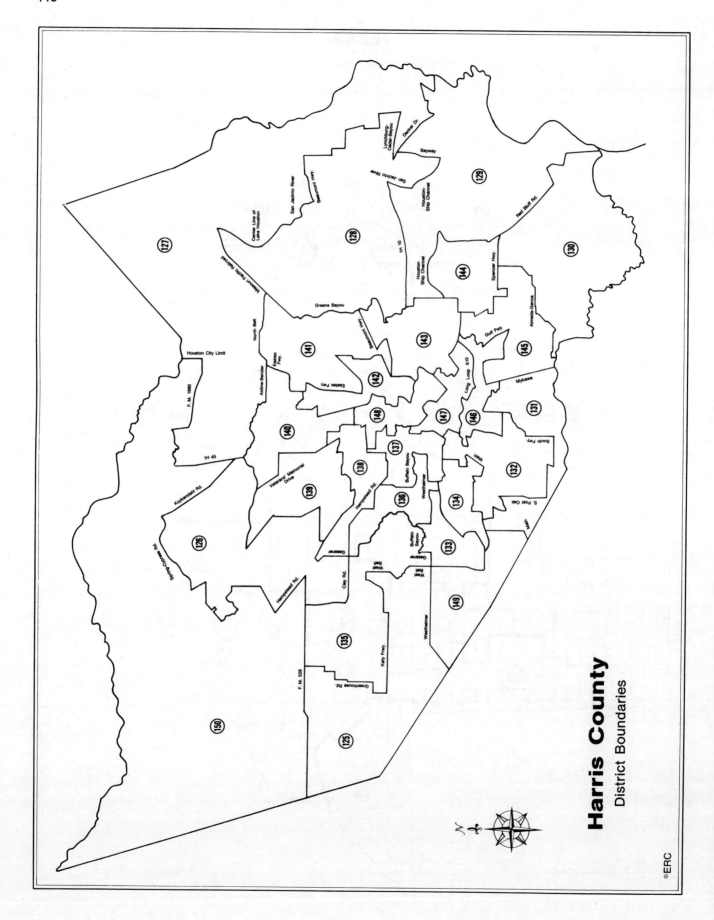

Harris County

District Boundaries

©ERC

TEXAS

GOVERNOR 1990

1990 Census Population	County	Total Vote	Republican	Democratic	Other	Rep.-Dem. Plurality	Percentage Total Vote Rep.	Dem.	Major Vote Rep.	Dem.
48,024	ANDERSON	10,081	5,133	4,796	152	337 R	50.9%	47.6%	51.7%	48.3%
14,338	ANDREWS	3,123	2,272	787	64	1,485 R	72.8%	25.2%	74.3%	25.7%
69,884	ANGELINA	16,568	7,385	8,665	518	1,280 D	44.6%	52.3%	46.0%	54.0%
17,892	ARANSAS	4,765	2,405	2,079	281	326 R	50.5%	43.6%	53.6%	46.4%
7,973	ARCHER	3,052	1,419	1,509	124	90 D	46.5%	49.4%	48.5%	51.5%
2,021	ARMSTRONG	759	433	271	55	162 R	57.0%	35.7%	61.5%	38.5%
30,533	ATASCOSA	6,877	3,420	3,185	272	235 R	49.7%	46.3%	51.8%	48.2%
19,832	AUSTIN	5,717	3,465	2,093	159	1,372 R	60.6%	36.6%	62.3%	37.7%
7,064	BAILEY	1,750	996	696	58	300 R	56.9%	39.8%	58.9%	41.1%
10,562	BANDERA	3,624	2,266	1,152	206	1,114 R	62.5%	31.8%	66.3%	33.7%
38,263	BASTROP	10,489	4,135	6,101	253	1,966 D	39.4%	58.2%	40.4%	59.6%
4,385	BAYLOR	1,460	538	895	27	357 D	36.8%	61.3%	37.5%	62.5%
25,135	BEE	6,777	3,026	3,556	195	530 D	44.7%	52.5%	46.0%	54.0%
191,088	BELL	32,374	15,903	15,621	850	282 R	49.1%	48.3%	50.4%	49.6%
1,185,394	BEXAR	229,288	99,478	120,468	9,342	20,990 D	43.4%	52.5%	45.2%	54.8%
5,972	BLANCO	2,377	1,392	895	90	497 R	58.6%	37.7%	60.9%	39.1%
799	BORDEN	397	250	140	7	110 R	63.0%	35.3%	64.1%	35.9%
15,125	BOSQUE	5,154	2,592	2,409	153	183 R	50.3%	46.7%	51.8%	48.2%
81,665	BOWIE	18,514	8,180	9,640	694	1,460 D	44.2%	52.1%	45.9%	54.1%
191,707	BRAZORIA	45,685	23,579	19,850	2,256	3,729 R	51.6%	43.4%	54.3%	45.7%
121,862	BRAZOS	32,936	17,225	14,357	1,354	2,868 R	52.3%	43.6%	54.5%	45.5%
8,681	BREWSTER	2,311	1,321	940	50	381 R	57.2%	40.7%	58.4%	41.6%
1,971	BRISCOE	833	319	484	30	165 D	38.3%	58.1%	39.7%	60.3%
8,204	BROOKS	2,134	420	1,685	29	1,265 D	19.7%	79.0%	20.0%	80.0%
34,371	BROWN	9,045	4,762	4,017	266	745 R	52.6%	44.4%	54.2%	45.8%
13,625	BURLESON	4,251	2,012	2,174	65	162 D	47.3%	51.1%	48.1%	51.9%
22,677	BURNET	7,840	4,088	3,561	191	527 R	52.1%	45.4%	53.4%	46.6%
26,392	CALDWELL	5,697	1,906	3,659	132	1,753 D	33.5%	64.2%	34.2%	65.8%
19,053	CALHOUN	5,618	2,634	2,771	213	137 D	46.9%	49.3%	48.7%	51.3%
11,859	CALLAHAN	4,043	2,333	1,607	103	726 R	57.7%	39.7%	59.2%	40.8%
260,120	CAMERON	36,533	14,989	20,704	840	5,715 D	41.0%	56.7%	42.0%	58.0%
9,904	CAMP	2,968	1,245	1,646	77	401 D	41.9%	55.5%	43.1%	56.9%
6,576	CARSON	2,577	1,296	1,136	145	160 R	50.3%	44.1%	53.3%	46.7%
29,982	CASS	7,509	3,141	4,244	124	1,103 D	41.8%	56.5%	42.5%	57.5%
9,070	CASTRO	2,147	1,046	1,008	93	38 R	48.7%	46.9%	50.9%	49.1%
20,088	CHAMBERS	5,049	2,554	2,284	211	270 R	50.6%	45.2%	52.8%	47.2%
41,049	CHEROKEE	9,220	4,808	4,141	271	667 R	52.1%	44.9%	53.7%	46.3%
5,953	CHILDRESS	1,647	751	881	15	130 D	45.6%	53.5%	46.0%	54.0%
10,024	CLAY	3,300	1,331	1,836	133	505 D	40.3%	55.6%	42.0%	58.0%
4,377	COCHRAN	1,042	529	468	45	61 R	50.8%	44.9%	53.1%	46.9%
3,424	COKE	1,229	678	522	29	156 R	55.2%	42.5%	56.5%	43.5%
9,710	COLEMAN	3,033	1,676	1,307	50	369 R	55.3%	43.1%	56.2%	43.8%
264,036	COLLIN	71,844	40,427	27,435	3,982	12,992 R	56.3%	38.2%	59.6%	40.4%
3,573	COLLINGSWORTH	1,167	476	638	53	162 D	40.8%	54.7%	42.7%	57.3%
18,383	COLORADO	5,280	2,934	2,222	124	712 R	55.6%	42.1%	56.9%	43.1%
51,832	COMAL	14,923	8,763	5,369	791	3,394 R	58.7%	36.0%	62.0%	38.0%
13,381	COMANCHE	3,620	1,542	1,978	100	436 D	42.6%	54.6%	43.8%	56.2%
3,044	CONCHO	990	521	450	19	71 R	52.6%	45.5%	53.7%	46.3%
30,777	COOKE	8,305	4,770	3,097	438	1,673 R	57.4%	37.3%	60.6%	39.4%
64,213	CORYELL	8,123	4,055	3,753	315	302 R	49.9%	46.2%	51.9%	48.1%
2,247	COTTLE	774	224	528	22	304 D	28.9%	68.2%	29.8%	70.2%
4,652	CRANE	1,729	1,208	464	57	744 R	69.9%	26.8%	72.2%	27.8%
4,078	CROCKETT	1,034	679	340	15	339 R	65.7%	32.9%	66.6%	33.4%
7,304	CROSBY	1,761	844	869	48	25 D	47.9%	49.3%	49.3%	50.7%
3,407	CULBERSON	712	373	322	17	51 R	52.4%	45.2%	53.7%	46.3%
5,461	DALLAM	1,405	762	535	108	227 R	54.2%	38.1%	58.8%	41.2%
1,852,810	DALLAS	421,984	192,105	211,728	18,151	19,623 D	45.5%	50.2%	47.6%	52.4%
14,349	DAWSON	3,800	2,534	1,168	98	1,366 R	66.7%	30.7%	68.4%	31.6%
19,153	DEAF SMITH	4,116	2,491	1,435	190	1,056 R	60.5%	34.9%	63.4%	36.6%
4,857	DELTA	1,470	550	901	19	351 D	37.4%	61.3%	37.9%	62.1%

TEXAS

GOVERNOR 1990

1990 Census Population	County	Total Vote	Republican	Democratic	Other	Rep.-Dem. Plurality	Percentage Total Vote Rep.	Dem.	Major Vote Rep.	Dem.
273,525	DENTON	61,088	30,971	26,560	3,557	4,411 R	50.7%	43.5%	53.8%	46.2%
18,840	DE WITT	4,521	2,728	1,689	104	1,039 R	60.3%	37.4%	61.8%	38.2%
2,571	DICKENS	875	402	448	25	46 D	45.9%	51.2%	47.3%	52.7%
10,433	DIMMIT	3,425	1,194	2,205	26	1,011 D	34.9%	64.4%	35.1%	64.9%
3,696	DONLEY	1,339	692	574	73	118 R	51.7%	42.9%	54.7%	45.3%
12,918	DUVAL	4,203	881	3,174	148	2,293 D	21.0%	75.5%	21.7%	78.3%
18,488	EASTLAND	5,668	3,008	2,493	167	515 R	53.1%	44.0%	54.7%	45.3%
118,934	ECTOR	25,513	16,458	8,347	708	8,111 R	64.5%	32.7%	66.3%	33.7%
2,266	EDWARDS	811	527	272	12	255 R	65.0%	33.5%	66.0%	34.0%
85,167	ELLIS	21,949	11,210	9,746	993	1,464 R	51.1%	44.4%	53.5%	46.5%
591,610	EL PASO	76,863	32,740	41,624	2,499	8,884 D	42.6%	54.2%	44.0%	56.0%
27,991	ERATH	7,005	3,515	3,286	204	229 R	50.2%	46.9%	51.7%	48.3%
17,712	FALLS	4,436	1,792	2,576	68	784 D	40.4%	58.1%	41.0%	59.0%
24,804	FANNIN	6,312	2,272	3,822	218	1,550 D	36.0%	60.6%	37.3%	62.7%
20,095	FAYETTE	7,206	4,224	2,811	171	1,413 R	58.6%	39.0%	60.0%	40.0%
4,842	FISHER	1,750	582	1,123	45	541 D	33.3%	64.2%	34.1%	65.9%
8,497	FLOYD	2,412	1,405	958	49	447 R	58.3%	39.7%	59.5%	40.5%
1,794	FOARD	643	182	454	7	272 D	28.3%	70.6%	28.6%	71.4%
225,421	FORT BEND	47,930	25,040	21,333	1,557	3,707 R	52.2%	44.5%	54.0%	46.0%
7,802	FRANKLIN	2,211	1,088	1,061	62	27 R	49.2%	48.0%	50.6%	49.4%
15,818	FREESTONE	4,628	2,364	2,153	111	211 R	51.1%	46.5%	52.3%	47.7%
13,472	FRIO	2,622	1,130	1,458	34	328 D	43.1%	55.6%	43.7%	56.3%
14,123	GAINES	2,825	1,820	905	100	915 R	64.4%	32.0%	66.8%	33.2%
217,399	GALVESTON	52,013	21,006	29,303	1,704	8,297 D	40.4%	56.3%	41.8%	58.2%
5,143	GARZA	1,323	788	494	41	294 R	59.6%	37.3%	61.5%	38.5%
17,204	GILLESPIE	5,772	3,895	1,619	258	2,276 R	67.5%	28.0%	70.6%	29.4%
1,447	GLASSCOCK	535	421	101	13	320 R	78.7%	18.9%	80.7%	19.3%
5,980	GOLIAD	2,000	1,079	872	49	207 R	54.0%	43.6%	55.3%	44.7%
17,205	GONZALES	4,100	2,234	1,783	83	451 R	54.5%	43.5%	55.6%	44.4%
23,967	GRAY	8,128	4,845	2,679	604	2,166 R	59.6%	33.0%	64.4%	35.6%
95,021	GRAYSON	23,048	10,410	11,597	1,041	1,187 D	45.2%	50.3%	47.3%	52.7%
104,948	GREGG	28,329	15,344	12,053	932	3,291 R	54.2%	42.5%	56.0%	44.0%
18,828	GRIMES	4,008	2,020	1,873	115	147 R	50.4%	46.7%	51.9%	48.1%
64,873	GUADALUPE	15,179	8,586	5,756	837	2,830 R	56.6%	37.9%	59.9%	40.1%
34,671	HALE	6,492	3,971	2,363	158	1,608 R	61.2%	36.4%	62.7%	37.3%
3,905	HALL	1,294	514	753	27	239 D	39.7%	58.2%	40.6%	59.4%
7,733	HAMILTON	2,966	1,535	1,363	68	172 R	51.8%	46.0%	53.0%	47.0%
5,848	HANSFORD	2,079	1,495	476	108	1,019 R	71.9%	22.9%	75.8%	24.2%
5,283	HARDEMAN	1,390	518	827	45	309 D	37.3%	59.5%	38.5%	61.5%
41,320	HARDIN	9,491	3,931	5,151	409	1,220 D	41.4%	54.3%	43.3%	56.7%
2,818,199	HARRIS	556,735	259,821	280,159	16,755	20,338 D	46.7%	50.3%	48.1%	51.9%
57,483	HARRISON	14,697	7,104	7,186	407	82 D	48.3%	48.9%	49.7%	50.3%
3,634	HARTLEY	1,560	891	569	100	322 R	57.1%	36.5%	61.0%	39.0%
6,820	HASKELL	2,330	922	1,366	42	444 D	39.6%	58.6%	40.3%	59.7%
65,614	HAYS	17,736	7,157	10,044	535	2,887 D	40.4%	56.6%	41.6%	58.4%
3,720	HEMPHILL	1,548	862	595	91	267 R	55.7%	38.4%	59.2%	40.8%
58,543	HENDERSON	17,257	8,032	8,472	753	440 D	46.5%	49.1%	48.7%	51.3%
383,545	HIDALGO	53,063	18,942	33,167	954	14,225 D	35.7%	62.5%	36.4%	63.6%
27,146	HILL	7,601	3,519	3,816	266	297 D	46.3%	50.2%	48.0%	52.0%
24,199	HOCKLEY	4,957	2,761	1,994	202	767 R	55.7%	40.2%	58.1%	41.9%
28,981	HOOD	9,827	5,053	4,257	517	796 R	51.4%	43.3%	54.3%	45.7%
28,833	HOPKINS	8,184	3,714	4,219	251	505 D	45.4%	51.6%	46.8%	53.2%
21,375	HOUSTON	5,923	2,728	3,037	158	309 D	46.1%	51.3%	47.3%	52.7%
32,343	HOWARD	8,027	4,512	3,270	245	1,242 R	56.2%	40.7%	58.0%	42.0%
2,915	HUDSPETH	585	335	234	16	101 R	57.3%	40.0%	58.9%	41.1%
64,343	HUNT	15,672	7,978	7,030	664	948 R	50.9%	44.9%	53.2%	46.8%
25,689	HUTCHINSON	8,390	4,645	3,118	627	1,527 R	55.4%	37.2%	59.8%	40.2%
1,629	IRION	616	352	245	19	107 R	57.1%	39.8%	59.0%	41.0%
6,981	JACK	2,128	1,053	999	76	54 R	49.5%	46.9%	51.3%	48.7%
13,039	JACKSON	3,785	2,080	1,591	114	489 R	55.0%	42.0%	56.7%	43.3%

TEXAS

GOVERNOR 1990

1990 Census Population	County	Total Vote	Republican	Democratic	Other	Rep.-Dem. Plurality	Percentage Total Vote Rep.	Dem.	Major Vote Rep.	Dem.
31,102	JASPER	7,411	2,881	4,176	354	1,295 D	38.9%	56.3%	40.8%	59.2%
1,946	JEFF DAVIS	693	416	257	20	159 R	60.0%	37.1%	61.8%	38.2%
239,397	JEFFERSON	63,978	21,718	40,288	1,972	18,570 D	33.9%	63.0%	35.0%	65.0%
5,109	JIM HOGG	1,704	381	1,318	5	937 D	22.4%	77.3%	22.4%	77.6%
37,679	JIM WELLS	8,211	2,624	5,464	123	2,840 D	32.0%	66.5%	32.4%	67.6%
97,165	JOHNSON	23,663	11,491	10,945	1,227	546 R	48.6%	46.3%	51.2%	48.8%
16,490	JONES	4,231	2,080	2,057	94	23 R	49.2%	48.6%	50.3%	49.7%
12,455	KARNES	3,252	1,902	1,267	83	635 R	58.5%	39.0%	60.0%	40.0%
52,220	KAUFMAN	12,366	5,885	5,987	494	102 D	47.6%	48.4%	49.6%	50.4%
14,589	KENDALL	4,793	3,177	1,359	257	1,818 R	66.3%	28.4%	70.0%	30.0%
460	KENEDY	151	65	82	4	17 D	43.0%	54.3%	44.2%	55.8%
1,010	KENT	214	99	98	17	1 R	46.3%	45.8%	50.3%	49.7%
36,304	KERR	10,617	6,761	3,301	555	3,460 R	63.7%	31.1%	67.2%	32.8%
4,122	KIMBLE	1,559	976	529	54	447 R	62.6%	33.9%	64.9%	35.1%
354	KING	190	109	76	5	33 R	57.4%	40.0%	58.9%	41.1%
3,119	KINNEY	1,110	590	487	33	103 R	53.2%	43.9%	54.8%	45.2%
30,274	KLEBERG	6,399	2,500	3,743	156	1,243 D	39.1%	58.5%	40.0%	60.0%
4,837	KNOX	1,427	519	876	32	357 D	36.4%	61.4%	37.2%	62.8%
43,949	LAMAR	10,623	4,517	5,826	280	1,309 D	42.5%	54.8%	43.7%	56.3%
15,072	LAMB	3,481	2,017	1,364	100	653 R	57.9%	39.2%	59.7%	40.3%
13,521	LAMPASAS	3,734	2,023	1,622	89	401 R	54.2%	43.4%	55.5%	44.5%
5,254	LA SALLE	1,558	481	1,059	18	578 D	30.9%	68.0%	31.2%	68.8%
18,690	LAVACA	5,348	2,675	2,510	163	165 R	50.0%	46.9%	51.6%	48.4%
12,854	LEE	4,255	2,537	1,642	76	895 R	59.6%	38.6%	60.7%	39.3%
12,665	LEON	3,967	2,040	1,821	106	219 R	51.4%	45.9%	52.8%	47.2%
52,726	LIBERTY	11,690	5,961	5,389	340	572 R	51.0%	46.1%	52.5%	47.5%
20,946	LIMESTONE	5,050	2,141	2,788	121	647 D	42.4%	55.2%	43.4%	56.6%
3,143	LIPSCOMB	1,225	676	428	121	248 R	55.2%	34.9%	61.2%	38.8%
9,556	LIVE OAK	2,627	1,465	1,060	102	405 R	55.8%	40.4%	58.0%	42.0%
11,631	LLANO	5,535	3,205	2,223	107	982 R	57.9%	40.2%	59.0%	41.0%
107	LOVING	96	65	31		34 R	67.7%	32.3%	67.7%	32.3%
222,636	LUBBOCK	51,445	29,100	20,643	1,702	8,457 R	56.6%	40.1%	58.5%	41.5%
6,758	LYNN	1,700	998	663	39	335 R	58.7%	39.0%	60.1%	39.9%
8,778	MCCULLOCH	2,573	1,323	1,204	46	119 R	51.4%	46.8%	52.4%	47.6%
189,123	MCLENNAN	50,377	21,671	27,414	1,292	5,743 D	43.0%	54.4%	44.1%	55.9%
817	MCMULLEN	324	217	89	18	128 R	67.0%	27.5%	70.9%	29.1%
10,931	MADISON	2,825	1,392	1,417	16	25 D	49.3%	50.2%	49.6%	50.4%
9,984	MARION	3,528	1,385	2,015	128	630 D	39.3%	57.1%	40.7%	59.3%
4,956	MARTIN	1,226	876	330	20	546 R	71.5%	26.9%	72.6%	27.4%
3,423	MASON	1,303	787	485	31	302 R	60.4%	37.2%	61.9%	38.1%
36,928	MATAGORDA	9,018	4,574	4,146	298	428 R	50.7%	46.0%	52.5%	47.5%
36,378	MAVERICK	5,061	1,439	3,553	69	2,114 D	28.4%	70.2%	28.8%	71.2%
27,312	MEDINA	6,952	3,953	2,727	272	1,226 R	56.9%	39.2%	59.2%	40.8%
2,252	MENARD	954	465	458	31	7 R	48.7%	48.0%	50.4%	49.6%
106,611	MIDLAND	30,641	23,184	6,672	785	16,512 R	75.7%	21.8%	77.7%	22.3%
22,946	MILAM	6,945	2,758	4,069	118	1,311 D	39.7%	58.6%	40.4%	59.6%
4,531	MILLS	1,572	832	709	31	123 R	52.9%	45.1%	54.0%	46.0%
8,016	MITCHELL	2,515	1,216	1,259	40	43 D	48.3%	50.1%	49.1%	50.9%
17,274	MONTAGUE	5,083	2,280	2,510	293	230 D	44.9%	49.4%	47.6%	52.4%
182,201	MONTGOMERY	45,575	27,499	16,454	1,622	11,045 R	60.3%	36.1%	62.6%	37.4%
17,865	MOORE	4,415	2,513	1,542	360	971 R	56.9%	34.9%	62.0%	38.0%
13,200	MORRIS	3,956	1,353	2,528	75	1,175 D	34.2%	63.9%	34.9%	65.1%
1,532	MOTLEY	618	362	223	33	139 R	58.6%	36.1%	61.9%	38.1%
54,753	NACOGDOCHES	12,634	6,298	5,958	378	340 R	49.8%	47.2%	51.4%	48.6%
39,926	NAVARRO	10,478	4,763	5,343	372	580 D	45.5%	51.0%	47.1%	52.9%
13,569	NEWTON	3,269	909	2,274	86	1,365 D	27.8%	69.6%	28.6%	71.4%
16,594	NOLAN	4,283	2,058	2,080	145	22 D	48.1%	48.6%	49.7%	50.3%
291,145	NUECES	63,299	24,317	37,019	1,963	12,702 D	38.4%	58.5%	39.6%	60.4%
9,128	OCHILTREE	2,824	2,042	636	146	1,406 R	72.3%	22.5%	76.3%	23.7%
2,278	OLDHAM	764	422	274	68	148 R	55.2%	35.9%	60.6%	39.4%

422

TEXAS

GOVERNOR 1990

1990 Census Population	County	Total Vote	Republican	Democratic	Other	Rep.-Dem. Plurality	Percentage Total Vote Rep.	Dem.	Major Vote Rep.	Dem.
80,509	ORANGE	19,860	6,727	12,366	767	5,639 D	33.9%	62.3%	35.2%	64.8%
25,055	PALO PINTO	6,618	3,128	3,197	293	69 D	47.3%	48.3%	49.5%	50.5%
22,035	PANOLA	6,194	2,908	3,166	120	258 D	46.9%	51.1%	47.9%	52.1%
64,785	PARKER	17,803	9,380	7,344	1,079	2,036 R	52.7%	41.3%	56.1%	43.9%
9,863	PARMER	2,061	1,288	685	88	603 R	62.5%	33.2%	65.3%	34.7%
14,675	PECOS	4,761	3,256	1,441	64	1,815 R	68.4%	30.3%	69.3%	30.7%
30,687	POLK	8,938	4,265	4,321	352	56 D	47.7%	48.3%	49.7%	50.3%
97,874	POTTER	20,102	9,855	9,233	1,014	622 R	49.0%	45.9%	51.6%	48.4%
6,637	PRESIDIO	1,720	635	1,062	23	427 D	36.9%	61.7%	37.4%	62.6%
6,715	RAINS	2,120	1,016	1,041	63	25 D	47.9%	49.1%	49.4%	50.6%
89,673	RANDALL	30,239	17,924	10,842	1,473	7,082 R	59.3%	35.9%	62.3%	37.7%
4,514	REAGAN	1,065	807	242	16	565 R	75.8%	22.7%	76.9%	23.1%
2,412	REAL	1,132	671	418	43	253 R	59.3%	36.9%	61.6%	38.4%
14,317	RED RIVER	4,014	1,711	2,179	124	468 D	42.6%	54.3%	44.0%	56.0%
15,852	REEVES	3,336	1,686	1,600	50	86 R	50.5%	48.0%	51.3%	48.7%
7,976	REFUGIO	2,865	1,246	1,553	66	307 D	43.5%	54.2%	44.5%	55.5%
1,025	ROBERTS	528	331	165	32	166 R	62.7%	31.3%	66.7%	33.3%
15,511	ROBERTSON	4,638	1,676	2,883	79	1,207 D	36.1%	62.2%	36.8%	63.2%
25,604	ROCKWALL	7,828	4,625	2,752	451	1,873 R	59.1%	35.2%	62.7%	37.3%
11,294	RUNNELS	3,192	1,894	1,200	98	694 R	59.3%	37.6%	61.2%	38.8%
43,735	RUSK	11,286	6,197	4,699	390	1,498 R	54.9%	41.6%	56.9%	43.1%
9,586	SABINE	3,147	1,336	1,728	83	392 D	42.5%	54.9%	43.6%	56.4%
7,999	SAN AUGUSTINE	3,136	1,290	1,753	93	463 D	41.1%	55.9%	42.4%	57.6%
16,372	SAN JACINTO	4,154	2,023	2,009	122	14 R	48.7%	48.4%	50.2%	49.8%
58,749	SAN PATRICIO	11,769	5,088	6,202	479	1,114 D	43.2%	52.7%	45.1%	54.9%
5,401	SAN SABA	1,560	847	692	21	155 R	54.3%	44.4%	55.0%	45.0%
2,990	SCHLEICHER	882	535	321	26	214 R	60.7%	36.4%	62.5%	37.5%
18,634	SCURRY	4,896	3,107	1,614	175	1,493 R	63.5%	33.0%	65.8%	34.2%
3,316	SHACKELFORD	1,152	719	406	27	313 R	62.4%	35.2%	63.9%	36.1%
22,034	SHELBY	5,640	2,264	3,247	129	983 D	40.1%	57.6%	41.1%	58.9%
2,858	SHERMAN	1,039	627	311	101	316 R	60.3%	29.9%	66.8%	33.2%
151,309	SMITH	40,855	23,493	15,874	1,488	7,619 R	57.5%	38.9%	59.7%	40.3%
5,360	SOMERVELL	1,883	951	819	113	132 R	50.5%	43.5%	53.7%	46.3%
40,518	STARR	4,260	653	3,582	25	2,929 D	15.3%	84.1%	15.4%	84.6%
9,010	STEPHENS	2,865	1,707	1,033	125	674 R	59.6%	36.1%	62.3%	37.7%
1,438	STERLING	510	357	146	7	211 R	70.0%	28.6%	71.0%	29.0%
2,013	STONEWALL	840	308	519	13	211 D	36.7%	61.8%	37.2%	62.8%
4,135	SUTTON	1,042	639	383	20	256 R	61.3%	36.8%	62.5%	37.5%
8,133	SWISHER	2,318	799	1,440	79	641 D	34.5%	62.1%	35.7%	64.3%
1,170,103	TARRANT	285,772	131,234	139,788	14,750	8,554 D	45.9%	48.9%	48.4%	51.6%
119,655	TAYLOR	29,469	16,705	11,976	788	4,729 R	56.7%	40.6%	58.2%	41.8%
1,410	TERRELL	499	242	250	7	8 D	48.5%	50.1%	49.2%	50.8%
13,218	TERRY	3,369	1,897	1,354	118	543 R	56.3%	40.2%	58.4%	41.6%
1,880	THROCKMORTON	775	367	374	34	7 D	47.4%	48.3%	49.5%	50.5%
24,009	TITUS	5,776	2,503	3,138	135	635 D	43.3%	54.3%	44.4%	55.6%
98,458	TOM GREEN	23,542	13,040	9,607	895	3,433 R	55.4%	40.8%	57.6%	42.4%
576,407	TRAVIS	195,829	63,376	128,120	4,333	64,744 D	32.4%	65.4%	33.1%	66.9%
11,445	TRINITY	3,740	1,712	1,919	109	207 D	45.8%	51.3%	47.1%	52.9%
16,646	TYLER	4,775	1,840	2,763	172	923 D	38.5%	57.9%	40.0%	60.0%
31,370	UPSHUR	8,300	3,851	4,159	290	308 D	46.4%	50.1%	48.1%	51.9%
4,447	UPTON	1,356	1,005	313	38	692 R	74.1%	23.1%	76.3%	23.7%
23,340	UVALDE	5,519	2,891	2,472	156	419 R	52.4%	44.8%	53.9%	46.1%
38,721	VAL VERDE	6,675	2,682	3,856	137	1,174 D	40.2%	57.8%	41.0%	59.0%
37,944	VAN ZANDT	10,579	5,406	4,750	423	656 R	51.1%	44.9%	53.2%	46.8%
74,361	VICTORIA	18,567	10,373	7,600	594	2,773 R	55.9%	40.9%	57.7%	42.3%
50,917	WALKER	10,346	4,924	5,160	262	236 D	47.6%	49.9%	48.8%	51.2%
23,390	WALLER	6,475	2,790	3,541	144	751 D	43.1%	54.7%	44.1%	55.9%
13,115	WARD	3,860	2,527	1,229	104	1,298 R	65.5%	31.8%	67.3%	32.7%
26,154	WASHINGTON	8,660	5,324	3,128	208	2,196 R	61.5%	36.1%	63.0%	37.0%
133,239	WEBB	14,643	3,521	10,947	175	7,426 D	24.0%	74.8%	24.3%	75.7%

TEXAS

GOVERNOR 1990

1990 Census Population	County	Total Vote	Republican	Democratic	Other	Rep.-Dem. Plurality	Percentage Total Vote Rep.	Dem.	Major Vote Rep.	Dem.
39,955	WHARTON	8,962	4,794	3,939	229	855 R	53.5%	44.0%	54.9%	45.1%
5,879	WHEELER	2,212	1,191	884	137	307 R	53.8%	40.0%	57.4%	42.6%
122,378	WICHITA	30,699	12,926	16,397	1,376	3,471 D	42.1%	53.4%	44.1%	55.9%
15,121	WILBARGER	3,477	1,586	1,769	122	183 D	45.6%	50.9%	47.3%	52.7%
17,705	WILLACY	3,867	1,385	2,410	72	1,025 D	35.8%	62.3%	36.5%	63.5%
139,551	WILLIAMSON	38,930	18,148	19,737	1,045	1,589 D	46.6%	50.7%	47.9%	52.1%
22,650	WILSON	6,928	3,624	3,109	195	515 R	52.3%	44.9%	53.8%	46.2%
8,626	WINKLER	2,091	1,419	644	28	775 R	67.9%	30.8%	68.8%	31.2%
34,679	WISE	9,139	4,255	4,458	426	203 D	46.6%	48.8%	48.8%	51.2%
29,380	WOOD	8,488	4,678	3,479	331	1,199 R	55.1%	41.0%	57.3%	42.7%
8,786	YOAKUM	1,976	1,204	676	96	528 R	60.9%	34.2%	64.0%	36.0%
18,126	YOUNG	5,845	3,142	2,414	289	728 R	53.8%	41.3%	56.6%	43.4%
9,279	ZAPATA	1,711	587	1,111	13	524 D	34.3%	64.9%	34.6%	65.4%
12,162	ZAVALA	2,499	483	1,989	27	1,506 D	19.3%	79.6%	19.5%	80.5%
16,986,510	TOTAL	3,892,746	1,826,431	1,925,670	140,645	99,239 D	46.9%	49.5%	48.7%	51.3%

TEXAS

SENATOR 1990

1990 Census Population	County	Total Vote	Republican	Democratic	Other	Rep.-Dem. Plurality	Percentage Total Vote Rep.	Dem.	Percentage Major Vote Rep.	Dem.
48,024	ANDERSON	10,261	6,263	3,826	172	2,437 R	61.0%	37.3%	62.1%	37.9%
14,338	ANDREWS	2,730	2,152	530	48	1,622 R	78.8%	19.4%	80.2%	19.8%
69,884	ANGELINA	16,609	9,522	6,828	259	2,694 R	57.3%	41.1%	58.2%	41.8%
17,892	ARANSAS	4,759	3,229	1,416	114	1,813 R	67.9%	29.8%	69.5%	30.5%
7,973	ARCHER	3,049	1,813	1,194	42	619 R	59.5%	39.2%	60.3%	39.7%
2,021	ARMSTRONG	757	523	209	25	314 R	69.1%	27.6%	71.4%	28.6%
30,533	ATASCOSA	6,755	3,920	2,622	213	1,298 R	58.0%	38.8%	59.9%	40.1%
19,832	AUSTIN	5,677	3,890	1,706	81	2,184 R	68.5%	30.1%	69.5%	30.5%
7,064	BAILEY	1,718	1,163	530	25	633 R	67.7%	30.8%	68.7%	31.3%
10,562	BANDERA	3,637	2,474	985	178	1,489 R	68.0%	27.1%	71.5%	28.5%
38,263	BASTROP	10,385	4,842	5,206	337	364 D	46.6%	50.1%	48.2%	51.8%
4,385	BAYLOR	1,417	669	733	15	64 D	47.2%	51.7%	47.7%	52.3%
25,135	BEE	6,757	3,814	2,838	105	976 R	56.4%	42.0%	57.3%	42.7%
191,088	BELL	31,817	18,596	12,590	631	6,006 R	58.4%	39.6%	59.6%	40.4%
1,185,394	BEXAR	218,369	124,138	87,040	7,191	37,098 R	56.8%	39.9%	58.8%	41.2%
5,972	BLANCO	2,319	1,441	790	88	651 R	62.1%	34.1%	64.6%	35.4%
799	BORDEN	373	258	109	6	149 R	69.2%	29.2%	70.3%	29.7%
15,125	BOSQUE	5,118	2,891	2,167	60	724 R	56.5%	42.3%	57.2%	42.8%
81,665	BOWIE	17,620	10,211	6,935	474	3,276 R	58.0%	39.4%	59.6%	40.4%
191,707	BRAZORIA	43,334	27,430	14,763	1,141	12,667 R	63.3%	34.1%	65.0%	35.0%
121,862	BRAZOS	32,026	22,233	9,120	673	13,113 R	69.4%	28.5%	70.9%	29.1%
8,681	BREWSTER	2,224	1,328	819	77	509 R	59.7%	36.8%	61.9%	38.1%
1,971	BRISCOE	812	403	401	8	2 R	49.6%	49.4%	50.1%	49.9%
8,204	BROOKS	2,089	592	1,463	34	871 D	28.3%	70.0%	28.8%	71.2%
34,371	BROWN	9,104	5,651	3,333	120	2,318 R	62.1%	36.6%	62.9%	37.1%
13,625	BURLESON	4,217	2,219	1,956	42	263 R	52.6%	46.4%	53.1%	46.9%
22,677	BURNET	7,768	4,254	3,359	155	895 R	54.8%	43.2%	55.9%	44.1%
26,392	CALDWELL	6,221	2,903	3,140	178	237 D	46.7%	50.5%	48.0%	52.0%
19,053	CALHOUN	5,599	3,392	2,118	89	1,274 R	60.6%	37.8%	61.6%	38.4%
11,859	CALLAHAN	4,007	2,636	1,319	52	1,317 R	65.8%	32.9%	66.6%	33.4%
260,120	CAMERON	33,493	18,211	14,367	915	3,844 R	54.4%	42.9%	55.9%	44.1%
9,904	CAMP	2,865	1,496	1,345	24	151 R	52.2%	46.9%	52.7%	47.3%
6,576	CARSON	2,641	1,661	921	59	740 R	62.9%	34.9%	64.3%	35.7%
29,982	CASS	7,303	3,885	3,355	63	530 R	53.2%	45.9%	53.7%	46.3%
9,070	CASTRO	2,131	1,362	742	27	620 R	63.9%	34.8%	64.7%	35.3%
20,088	CHAMBERS	4,902	2,986	1,809	107	1,177 R	60.9%	36.9%	62.3%	37.7%
41,049	CHEROKEE	9,160	5,774	3,262	124	2,512 R	63.0%	35.6%	63.9%	36.1%
5,953	CHILDRESS	1,645	965	668	12	297 R	58.7%	40.6%	59.1%	40.9%
10,024	CLAY	3,247	1,709	1,506	32	203 R	52.6%	46.4%	53.2%	46.8%
4,377	COCHRAN	1,034	643	361	30	282 R	62.2%	34.9%	64.0%	36.0%
3,424	COKE	1,202	787	395	20	392 R	65.5%	32.9%	66.6%	33.4%
9,710	COLEMAN	2,963	1,921	1,018	24	903 R	64.8%	34.4%	65.4%	34.6%
264,036	COLLIN	71,806	54,151	15,516	2,139	38,635 R	75.4%	21.6%	77.7%	22.3%
3,573	COLLINGSWORTH	1,134	630	495	9	135 R	55.6%	43.7%	56.0%	44.0%
18,383	COLORADO	5,304	3,380	1,850	74	1,530 R	63.7%	34.9%	64.6%	35.4%
51,832	COMAL	14,912	10,193	4,093	626	6,100 R	68.4%	27.4%	71.3%	28.7%
13,381	COMANCHE	3,596	1,773	1,773	50		49.3%	49.3%	50.0%	50.0%
3,044	CONCHO	949	577	357	15	220 R	60.8%	37.6%	61.8%	38.2%
30,777	COOKE	8,183	5,359	2,651	173	2,708 R	65.5%	32.4%	66.9%	33.1%
64,213	CORYELL	8,188	4,666	3,340	182	1,326 R	57.0%	40.8%	58.3%	41.7%
2,247	COTTLE	748	260	474	14	214 D	34.8%	63.4%	35.4%	64.6%
4,652	CRANE	1,658	1,218	419	21	799 R	73.5%	25.3%	74.4%	25.6%
4,078	CROCKETT	1,015	752	245	18	507 R	74.1%	24.1%	75.4%	24.6%
7,304	CROSBY	1,757	1,008	725	24	283 R	57.4%	41.3%	58.2%	41.8%
3,407	CULBERSON	609	369	225	15	144 R	60.6%	36.9%	62.1%	37.9%
5,461	DALLAM	1,397	910	453	34	457 R	65.1%	32.4%	66.8%	33.2%
1,852,810	DALLAS	419,995	254,951	153,363	11,681	101,588 R	60.7%	36.5%	62.4%	37.6%
14,349	DAWSON	3,648	2,611	994	43	1,617 R	71.6%	27.2%	72.4%	27.6%
19,153	DEAF SMITH	4,148	2,896	1,158	94	1,738 R	69.8%	27.9%	71.4%	28.6%
4,857	DELTA	1,441	753	678	10	75 R	52.3%	47.1%	52.6%	47.4%

TEXAS

SENATOR 1990

1990 Census Population	County	Total Vote	Republican	Democratic	Other	Rep.-Dem. Plurality	Percentage Total Vote Rep.	Dem.	Major Vote Rep.	Dem.
273,525	DENTON	60,898	41,751	17,132	2,015	24,619 R	68.6%	28.1%	70.9%	29.1%
18,840	DE WITT	4,444	3,056	1,327	61	1,729 R	68.8%	29.9%	69.7%	30.3%
2,571	DICKENS	887	406	474	7	68 D	45.8%	53.4%	46.1%	53.9%
10,433	DIMMIT	3,322	1,266	2,012	44	746 D	38.1%	60.6%	38.6%	61.4%
3,696	DONLEY	1,316	814	484	18	330 R	61.9%	36.8%	62.7%	37.3%
12,918	DUVAL	3,729	797	2,895	37	2,098 D	21.4%	77.6%	21.6%	78.4%
18,488	EASTLAND	5,623	3,429	2,096	98	1,333 R	61.0%	37.3%	62.1%	37.9%
118,934	ECTOR	23,225	17,238	5,521	466	11,717 R	74.2%	23.8%	75.7%	24.3%
2,266	EDWARDS	780	581	184	15	397 R	74.5%	23.6%	75.9%	24.1%
85,167	ELLIS	22,510	14,227	7,751	532	6,476 R	63.2%	34.4%	64.7%	35.3%
591,610	EL PASO	76,290	45,185	29,033	2,072	16,152 R	59.2%	38.1%	60.9%	39.1%
27,991	ERATH	7,067	4,279	2,645	143	1,634 R	60.5%	37.4%	61.8%	38.2%
17,712	FALLS	4,400	1,963	2,399	38	436 D	44.6%	54.5%	45.0%	55.0%
24,804	FANNIN	6,209	2,859	3,239	111	380 D	46.0%	52.2%	46.9%	53.1%
20,095	FAYETTE	7,205	4,630	2,456	119	2,174 R	64.3%	34.1%	65.3%	34.7%
4,842	FISHER	1,723	742	965	16	223 D	43.1%	56.0%	43.5%	56.5%
8,497	FLOYD	2,364	1,608	745	11	863 R	68.0%	31.5%	68.3%	31.7%
1,794	FOARD	613	232	379	2	147 D	37.8%	61.8%	38.0%	62.0%
225,421	FORT BEND	48,250	32,115	15,310	825	16,805 R	66.6%	31.7%	67.7%	32.3%
7,802	FRANKLIN	2,180	1,255	896	29	359 R	57.6%	41.1%	58.3%	41.7%
15,818	FREESTONE	4,621	2,729	1,838	54	891 R	59.1%	39.8%	59.8%	40.2%
13,472	FRIO	2,575	1,252	1,279	44	27 D	48.6%	49.7%	49.5%	50.5%
14,123	GAINES	2,355	1,666	647	42	1,019 R	70.7%	27.5%	72.0%	28.0%
217,399	GALVESTON	51,971	26,576	24,138	1,257	2,438 R	51.1%	46.4%	52.4%	47.6%
5,143	GARZA	1,275	829	429	17	400 R	65.0%	33.6%	65.9%	34.1%
17,204	GILLESPIE	5,791	4,284	1,297	210	2,987 R	74.0%	22.4%	76.8%	23.2%
1,447	GLASSCOCK	510	407	95	8	312 R	79.8%	18.6%	81.1%	18.9%
5,980	GOLIAD	1,931	1,306	601	24	705 R	67.6%	31.1%	68.5%	31.5%
17,205	GONZALES	3,973	2,546	1,379	48	1,167 R	64.1%	34.7%	64.9%	35.1%
23,967	GRAY	8,191	6,043	1,942	206	4,101 R	73.8%	23.7%	75.7%	24.3%
95,021	GRAYSON	23,005	13,551	8,910	544	4,641 R	58.9%	38.7%	60.3%	39.7%
104,948	GREGG	20,868	18,485	1,850	533	16,635 R	88.6%	8.9%	90.9%	9.1%
18,828	GRIMES	3,987	2,361	1,565	61	796 R	59.2%	39.3%	60.1%	39.9%
64,873	GUADALUPE	15,301	10,111	4,587	603	5,524 R	66.1%	30.0%	68.8%	31.2%
34,671	HALE	6,608	4,632	1,905	71	2,727 R	70.1%	28.8%	70.9%	29.1%
3,905	HALL	1,246	596	636	14	40 D	47.8%	51.0%	48.4%	51.6%
7,733	HAMILTON	2,899	1,636	1,211	52	425 R	56.4%	41.8%	57.5%	42.5%
5,848	HANSFORD	2,056	1,677	347	32	1,330 R	81.6%	16.9%	82.9%	17.1%
5,283	HARDEMAN	1,369	641	714	14	73 D	46.8%	52.2%	47.3%	52.7%
41,320	HARDIN	9,545	5,497	3,868	180	1,629 R	57.6%	40.5%	58.7%	41.3%
2,818,199	HARRIS	542,266	327,411	203,551	11,304	123,860 R	60.4%	37.5%	61.7%	38.3%
57,483	HARRISON	14,565	8,688	5,611	266	3,077 R	59.6%	38.5%	60.8%	39.2%
3,634	HARTLEY	1,564	1,115	430	19	685 R	71.3%	27.5%	72.2%	27.8%
6,820	HASKELL	2,361	1,216	1,123	22	93 R	51.5%	47.6%	52.0%	48.0%
65,614	HAYS	17,493	9,081	7,823	589	1,258 R	51.9%	44.7%	53.7%	46.3%
3,720	HEMPHILL	1,525	1,120	376	29	744 R	73.4%	24.7%	74.9%	25.1%
58,543	HENDERSON	17,199	9,711	7,163	325	2,548 R	56.5%	41.6%	57.6%	42.4%
383,545	HIDALGO	48,625	23,882	23,369	1,374	513 R	49.1%	48.1%	50.5%	49.5%
27,146	HILL	7,641	4,158	3,330	153	828 R	54.4%	43.6%	55.5%	44.5%
24,199	HOCKLEY	4,915	3,412	1,389	114	2,023 R	69.4%	28.3%	71.1%	28.9%
28,981	HOOD	9,975	6,169	3,558	248	2,611 R	61.8%	35.7%	63.4%	36.6%
28,833	HOPKINS	7,977	4,515	3,381	81	1,134 R	56.6%	42.4%	57.2%	42.8%
21,375	HOUSTON	5,896	3,536	2,305	55	1,231 R	60.0%	39.1%	60.5%	39.5%
32,343	HOWARD	7,059	4,332	2,583	144	1,749 R	61.4%	36.6%	62.6%	37.4%
2,915	HUDSPETH	539	350	183	6	167 R	64.9%	34.0%	65.7%	34.3%
64,343	HUNT	15,754	9,814	5,584	356	4,230 R	62.3%	35.4%	63.7%	36.3%
25,689	HUTCHINSON	8,588	6,014	2,377	197	3,637 R	70.0%	27.7%	71.7%	28.3%
1,629	IRION	602	436	152	14	284 R	72.4%	25.2%	74.1%	25.9%
6,981	JACK	2,073	1,188	847	38	341 R	57.3%	40.9%	58.4%	41.6%
13,039	JACKSON	3,736	2,496	1,203	37	1,293 R	66.8%	32.2%	67.5%	32.5%

TEXAS

SENATOR 1990

1990 Census Population	County	Total Vote	Republican	Democratic	Other	Rep.-Dem. Plurality	Percentage Total Vote Rep.	Dem.	Major Vote Rep.	Dem.
31,102	JASPER	7,397	3,915	3,362	120	553 R	52.9%	45.5%	53.8%	46.2%
1,946	JEFF DAVIS	646	449	179	18	270 R	69.5%	27.7%	71.5%	28.5%
239,397	JEFFERSON	63,346	32,018	30,431	897	1,587 R	50.5%	48.0%	51.3%	48.7%
5,109	JIM HOGG	1,664	567	1,081	16	514 D	34.1%	65.0%	34.4%	65.6%
37,679	JIM WELLS	7,893	3,455	4,372	66	917 D	43.8%	55.4%	44.1%	55.9%
97,165	JOHNSON	23,972	14,388	8,909	675	5,479 R	60.0%	37.2%	61.8%	38.2%
16,490	JONES	4,174	2,546	1,583	45	963 R	61.0%	37.9%	61.7%	38.3%
12,455	KARNES	3,158	1,958	1,136	64	822 R	62.0%	36.0%	63.3%	36.7%
52,220	KAUFMAN	12,214	6,992	4,861	361	2,131 R	57.2%	39.8%	59.0%	41.0%
14,589	KENDALL	4,844	3,617	1,043	184	2,574 R	74.7%	21.5%	77.6%	22.4%
460	KENEDY	148	84	59	5	25 R	56.8%	39.9%	58.7%	41.3%
1,010	KENT	575	319	243	13	76 R	55.5%	42.3%	56.8%	43.2%
36,304	KERR	10,717	7,477	2,791	449	4,686 R	69.8%	26.0%	72.8%	27.2%
4,122	KIMBLE	1,519	1,115	370	34	745 R	73.4%	24.4%	75.1%	24.9%
354	KING	185	121	59	5	62 R	65.4%	31.9%	67.2%	32.8%
3,119	KINNEY	1,048	631	392	25	239 R	60.2%	37.4%	61.7%	38.3%
30,274	KLEBERG	6,150	3,257	2,800	93	457 R	53.0%	45.5%	53.8%	46.2%
4,837	KNOX	1,427	680	733	14	53 D	47.7%	51.4%	48.1%	51.9%
43,949	LAMAR	10,672	6,110	4,490	72	1,620 R	57.3%	42.1%	57.6%	42.4%
15,072	LAMB	3,496	2,313	1,136	47	1,177 R	66.2%	32.5%	67.1%	32.9%
13,521	LAMPASAS	3,718	2,129	1,535	54	594 R	57.3%	41.3%	58.1%	41.9%
5,254	LA SALLE	1,498	513	969	16	456 D	34.2%	64.7%	34.6%	65.4%
18,690	LAVACA	5,225	3,128	2,017	80	1,111 R	59.9%	38.6%	60.8%	39.2%
12,854	LEE	4,139	2,446	1,648	45	798 R	59.1%	39.8%	59.7%	40.3%
12,665	LEON	3,954	2,411	1,503	40	908 R	61.0%	38.0%	61.6%	38.4%
52,726	LIBERTY	11,680	6,873	4,613	194	2,260 R	58.8%	39.5%	59.8%	40.2%
20,946	LIMESTONE	5,062	2,505	2,502	55	3 R	49.5%	49.4%	50.0%	50.0%
3,143	LIPSCOMB	1,219	885	307	27	578 R	72.6%	25.2%	74.2%	25.8%
9,556	LIVE OAK	2,613	1,724	830	59	894 R	66.0%	31.8%	67.5%	32.5%
11,631	LLANO	5,577	3,271	2,215	91	1,056 R	58.7%	39.7%	59.6%	40.4%
107	LOVING	82	62	19	1	43 R	75.6%	23.2%	76.5%	23.5%
222,636	LUBBOCK	51,559	38,147	12,526	886	25,621 R	74.0%	24.3%	75.3%	24.7%
6,758	LYNN	1,682	1,049	612	21	437 R	62.4%	36.4%	63.2%	36.8%
8,778	MCCULLOCH	2,543	1,610	912	21	698 R	63.3%	35.9%	63.8%	36.2%
189,123	MCLENNAN	50,846	28,094	22,121	631	5,973 R	55.3%	43.5%	55.9%	44.1%
817	MCMULLEN	326	249	74	3	175 R	76.4%	22.7%	77.1%	22.9%
10,931	MADISON	587	293	290	4	3 R	49.9%	49.4%	50.3%	49.7%
9,984	MARION	3,135	1,730	1,348	57	382 R	55.2%	43.0%	56.2%	43.8%
4,956	MARTIN	1,182	838	333	11	505 R	70.9%	28.2%	71.6%	28.4%
3,423	MASON	1,284	840	422	22	418 R	65.4%	32.9%	66.6%	33.4%
36,928	MATAGORDA	9,011	5,310	3,547	154	1,763 R	58.9%	39.4%	60.0%	40.0%
36,378	MAVERICK	4,746	2,147	2,486	113	339 D	45.2%	52.4%	46.3%	53.7%
27,312	MEDINA	6,884	4,358	2,317	209	2,041 R	63.3%	33.7%	65.3%	34.7%
2,252	MENARD	922	593	319	10	274 R	64.3%	34.6%	65.0%	35.0%
106,611	MIDLAND	30,654	24,496	5,379	779	19,117 R	79.9%	17.5%	82.0%	18.0%
22,946	MILAM	6,778	2,907	3,787	84	880 D	42.9%	55.9%	43.4%	56.6%
4,531	MILLS	1,579	858	686	35	172 R	54.3%	43.4%	55.6%	44.4%
8,016	MITCHELL	2,405	1,490	896	19	594 R	62.0%	37.3%	62.4%	37.6%
17,274	MONTAGUE	4,965	2,799	2,032	134	767 R	56.4%	40.9%	57.9%	42.1%
182,201	MONTGOMERY	45,043	31,806	12,266	971	19,540 R	70.6%	27.2%	72.2%	27.8%
17,865	MOORE	4,450	3,167	1,191	92	1,976 R	71.2%	26.8%	72.7%	27.3%
13,200	MORRIS	3,849	1,704	2,107	38	403 D	44.3%	54.7%	44.7%	55.3%
1,532	MOTLEY	603	403	192	8	211 R	66.8%	31.8%	67.7%	32.3%
54,753	NACOGDOCHES	12,691	8,365	4,056	270	4,309 R	65.9%	32.0%	67.3%	32.7%
39,926	NAVARRO	10,533	5,826	4,508	199	1,318 R	55.3%	42.8%	56.4%	43.6%
13,569	NEWTON	3,147	1,246	1,862	39	616 D	39.6%	59.2%	40.1%	59.9%
16,594	NOLAN	4,231	2,561	1,583	87	978 R	60.5%	37.4%	61.8%	38.2%
291,145	NUECES	61,012	36,102	23,711	1,199	12,391 R	59.2%	38.9%	60.4%	39.6%
9,128	OCHILTREE	2,841	2,386	399	56	1,987 R	84.0%	14.0%	85.7%	14.3%
2,278	OLDHAM	751	512	224	15	288 R	68.2%	29.8%	69.6%	30.4%

TEXAS

SENATOR 1990

1990 Census Population	County	Total Vote	Republican	Democratic	Other	Rep.-Dem. Plurality	Percentage Total Vote Rep.	Dem.	Major Vote Rep.	Dem.
80,509	ORANGE	19,975	9,954	9,628	393	326 R	49.8%	48.2%	50.8%	49.2%
25,055	PALO PINTO	6,569	3,705	2,715	149	990 R	56.4%	41.3%	57.7%	42.3%
22,035	PANOLA	6,064	3,417	2,566	81	851 R	56.3%	42.3%	57.1%	42.9%
64,785	PARKER	18,032	11,245	6,224	563	5,021 R	62.4%	34.5%	64.4%	35.6%
9,863	PARMER	2,137	1,417	678	42	739 R	66.3%	31.7%	67.6%	32.4%
14,675	PECOS	3,969	2,471	1,416	82	1,055 R	62.3%	35.7%	63.6%	36.4%
30,687	POLK	8,893	4,869	3,839	185	1,030 R	54.8%	43.2%	55.9%	44.1%
97,874	POTTER	20,034	12,991	6,493	550	6,498 R	64.8%	32.4%	66.7%	33.3%
6,637	PRESIDIO	1,604	649	933	22	284 D	40.5%	58.2%	41.0%	59.0%
6,715	RAINS	2,054	1,097	926	31	171 R	53.4%	45.1%	54.2%	45.8%
89,673	RANDALL	29,137	22,460	6,156	521	16,304 R	77.1%	21.1%	78.5%	21.5%
4,514	REAGAN	1,041	864	173	4	691 R	83.0%	16.6%	83.3%	16.7%
2,412	REAL	1,111	785	299	27	486 R	70.7%	26.9%	72.4%	27.6%
14,317	RED RIVER	3,880	1,948	1,888	44	60 R	50.2%	48.7%	50.8%	49.2%
15,852	REEVES	2,942	1,536	1,360	46	176 R	52.2%	46.2%	53.0%	47.0%
7,976	REFUGIO	2,783	1,670	1,073	40	597 R	60.0%	38.6%	60.9%	39.1%
1,025	ROBERTS	524	393	123	8	270 R	75.0%	23.5%	76.2%	23.8%
15,511	ROBERTSON	4,645	2,001	2,601	43	600 D	43.1%	56.0%	43.5%	56.5%
25,604	ROCKWALL	7,737	5,660	1,851	226	3,809 R	73.2%	23.9%	75.4%	24.6%
11,294	RUNNELS	3,126	2,132	946	48	1,186 R	68.2%	30.3%	69.3%	30.7%
43,735	RUSK	10,957	7,413	3,361	183	4,052 R	67.7%	30.7%	68.8%	31.2%
9,586	SABINE	3,017	1,555	1,414	48	141 R	51.5%	46.9%	52.4%	47.6%
7,999	SAN AUGUSTINE	2,846	1,500	1,291	55	209 R	52.7%	45.4%	53.7%	46.3%
16,372	SAN JACINTO	4,023	2,239	1,708	76	531 R	55.7%	42.5%	56.7%	43.3%
58,749	SAN PATRICIO	11,246	6,492	4,525	229	1,967 R	57.7%	40.2%	58.9%	41.1%
5,401	SAN SABA	1,546	801	729	16	72 R	51.8%	47.2%	52.4%	47.6%
2,990	SCHLEICHER	868	620	240	8	380 R	71.4%	27.6%	72.1%	27.9%
18,634	SCURRY	4,122	3,000	1,059	63	1,941 R	72.8%	25.7%	73.9%	26.1%
3,316	SHACKELFORD	1,125	776	334	15	442 R	69.0%	29.7%	69.9%	30.1%
22,034	SHELBY	5,578	3,090	2,334	154	756 R	55.4%	41.8%	57.0%	43.0%
2,858	SHERMAN	1,090	749	281	60	468 R	68.7%	25.8%	72.7%	27.3%
151,309	SMITH	40,796	27,984	12,025	787	15,959 R	68.6%	29.5%	69.9%	30.1%
5,360	SOMERVELL	1,833	1,107	666	60	441 R	60.4%	36.3%	62.4%	37.6%
40,518	STARR	4,186	988	3,144	54	2,156 D	23.6%	75.1%	23.9%	76.1%
9,010	STEPHENS	2,829	1,967	826	36	1,141 R	69.5%	29.2%	70.4%	29.6%
1,438	STERLING	482	396	80	6	316 R	82.2%	16.6%	83.2%	16.8%
2,013	STONEWALL	834	386	437	11	51 D	46.3%	52.4%	46.9%	53.1%
4,135	SUTTON	1,029	764	259	6	505 R	74.2%	25.2%	74.7%	25.3%
8,133	SWISHER	2,300	1,027	1,244	29	217 D	44.7%	54.1%	45.2%	54.8%
1,170,103	TARRANT	288,850	175,629	104,985	8,236	70,644 R	60.8%	36.3%	62.6%	37.4%
119,655	TAYLOR	29,310	21,220	7,603	487	13,617 R	72.4%	25.9%	73.6%	26.4%
1,410	TERRELL	460	242	213	5	29 R	52.6%	46.3%	53.2%	46.8%
13,218	TERRY	3,409	2,268	1,087	54	1,181 R	66.5%	31.9%	67.6%	32.4%
1,880	THROCKMORTON	764	424	327	13	97 R	55.5%	42.8%	56.5%	43.5%
24,009	TITUS	5,733	3,215	2,460	58	755 R	56.1%	42.9%	56.7%	43.3%
98,458	TOM GREEN	23,497	16,730	6,321	446	10,409 R	71.2%	26.9%	72.6%	27.4%
576,407	TRAVIS	191,970	87,145	98,983	5,842	11,838 D	45.4%	51.6%	46.8%	53.2%
11,445	TRINITY	3,616	2,008	1,567	41	441 R	55.5%	43.3%	56.2%	43.8%
16,646	TYLER	4,679	2,480	2,139	60	341 R	53.0%	45.7%	53.7%	46.3%
31,370	UPSHUR	8,301	4,755	3,391	155	1,364 R	57.3%	40.9%	58.4%	41.6%
4,447	UPTON	1,299	1,010	261	28	749 R	77.8%	20.1%	79.5%	20.5%
23,340	UVALDE	5,410	3,384	1,923	103	1,461 R	62.6%	35.5%	63.8%	36.2%
38,721	VAL VERDE	6,645	3,394	3,125	126	269 R	51.1%	47.0%	52.1%	47.9%
37,944	VAN ZANDT	10,405	6,221	4,014	170	2,207 R	59.8%	38.6%	60.8%	39.2%
74,361	VICTORIA	18,007	12,750	5,001	256	7,749 R	70.8%	27.8%	71.8%	28.2%
50,917	WALKER	10,440	6,810	3,452	178	3,358 R	65.2%	33.1%	66.4%	33.6%
23,390	WALLER	6,360	3,271	3,012	77	259 R	51.4%	47.4%	52.1%	47.9%
13,115	WARD	3,246	2,185	996	65	1,189 R	67.3%	30.7%	68.7%	31.3%
26,154	WASHINGTON	8,668	6,069	2,490	109	3,579 R	70.0%	28.7%	70.9%	29.1%
133,239	WEBB	14,294	6,982	7,026	286	44 D	48.8%	49.2%	49.8%	50.2%

TEXAS

SENATOR 1990

1990 Census Population	County	Total Vote	Republican	Democratic	Other	Rep.-Dem. Plurality	Percentage Total Vote Rep.	Dem.	Major Vote Rep.	Dem.
39,955	WHARTON	8,993	5,629	3,250	114	2,379 R	62.6%	36.1%	63.4%	36.6%
5,879	WHEELER	2,178	1,458	689	31	769 R	66.9%	31.6%	67.9%	32.1%
122,378	WICHITA	30,628	18,038	12,002	588	6,036 R	58.9%	39.2%	60.0%	40.0%
15,121	WILBARGER	3,445	1,974	1,441	30	533 R	57.3%	41.8%	57.8%	42.2%
17,705	WILLACY	3,589	1,719	1,814	56	95 D	47.9%	50.5%	48.7%	51.3%
139,551	WILLIAMSON	39,134	23,068	15,033	1,033	8,035 R	58.9%	38.4%	60.5%	39.5%
22,650	WILSON	6,573	3,746	2,664	163	1,082 R	57.0%	40.5%	58.4%	41.6%
8,626	WINKLER	1,769	1,247	494	28	753 R	70.5%	27.9%	71.6%	28.4%
34,679	WISE	9,226	4,957	3,993	276	964 R	53.7%	43.3%	55.4%	44.6%
29,380	WOOD	8,479	5,425	2,869	185	2,556 R	64.0%	33.8%	65.4%	34.6%
8,786	YOAKUM	1,642	1,172	436	34	736 R	71.4%	26.6%	72.9%	27.1%
18,126	YOUNG	5,860	3,862	1,918	80	1,944 R	65.9%	32.7%	66.8%	33.2%
9,279	ZAPATA	1,668	767	889	12	122 D	46.0%	53.3%	46.3%	53.7%
12,162	ZAVALA	2,328	531	1,777	20	1,246 D	22.8%	76.3%	23.0%	77.0%
16,986,510	TOTAL	3,822,157	2,302,357	1,429,986	89,814	872,371 R	60.2%	37.4%	61.7%	38.3%

HARRIS COUNTY

GOVERNOR 1990

1990 Census Population	District	Total Vote	Republican	Democratic	Other	Rep.-Dem. Plurality	Percentage Total Vote Rep.	Dem.	Major Vote Rep.	Dem.
	DISTRICT 125	32,758	20,367	11,339	1,052	9,028 R	62.2%	34.6%	64.2%	35.8%
	DISTRICT 126	36,221	21,895	13,123	1,203	8,772 R	60.4%	36.2%	62.5%	37.5%
	DISTRICT 127	27,931	16,867	10,136	928	6,731 R	60.4%	36.3%	62.5%	37.5%
	DISTRICT 128	15,072	6,120	8,506	446	2,386 D	40.6%	56.4%	41.8%	58.2%
	DISTRICT 129	16,248	7,892	7,803	553	89 R	48.6%	48.0%	50.3%	49.7%
	DISTRICT 130	28,409	14,825	12,383	1,201	2,442 R	52.2%	43.6%	54.5%	45.5%
	DISTRICT 131	16,832	3,779	12,785	268	9,006 D	22.5%	76.0%	22.8%	77.2%
	DISTRICT 132	24,539	7,867	16,097	575	8,230 D	32.1%	65.6%	32.8%	67.2%
	DISTRICT 133	14,654	7,483	6,713	458	770 R	51.1%	45.8%	52.7%	47.3%
	DISTRICT 134	20,683	9,778	10,270	635	492 D	47.3%	49.7%	48.8%	51.2%
	DISTRICT 135	29,742	18,690	10,226	826	8,464 R	62.8%	34.4%	64.6%	35.4%
	DISTRICT 136	22,746	14,214	7,968	564	6,246 R	62.5%	35.0%	64.1%	35.9%
	DISTRICT 137	18,382	5,535	12,373	474	6,838 D	30.1%	67.3%	30.9%	69.1%
	DISTRICT 138	15,996	6,861	8,715	420	1,854 D	42.9%	54.5%	44.0%	56.0%
	DISTRICT 139	18,615	6,914	11,225	476	4,311 D	37.1%	60.3%	38.1%	61.9%
	DISTRICT 140	10,854	5,233	5,336	285	103 D	48.2%	49.2%	49.5%	50.5%
	DISTRICT 141	12,444	1,119	11,182	143	10,063 D	9.0%	89.9%	9.1%	90.9%
	DISTRICT 142	11,366	975	10,294	97	9,319 D	8.6%	90.6%	8.7%	91.3%
	DISTRICT 143	10,606	2,436	7,977	193	5,541 D	23.0%	75.2%	23.4%	76.6%
	DISTRICT 144	12,108	5,868	5,815	425	53 R	48.5%	48.0%	50.2%	49.8%
	DISTRICT 145	15,164	6,782	7,916	466	1,134 D	44.7%	52.2%	46.1%	53.9%
	DISTRICT 146	13,468	2,418	10,862	188	8,444 D	18.0%	80.7%	18.2%	81.8%
	DISTRICT 147	9,800	1,462	8,193	145	6,731 D	14.9%	83.6%	15.1%	84.9%
	DISTRICT 148	9,543	2,365	6,969	209	4,604 D	24.8%	73.0%	25.3%	74.7%
	DISTRICT 149	25,010	11,708	12,449	853	741 D	46.8%	49.8%	48.5%	51.5%
	DISTRICT 150	34,981	21,440	12,302	1,239	9,138 R	61.3%	35.2%	63.5%	36.5%
	ABSENTEE	51,353	28,928	21,202	1,223	7,726 R	56.3%	41.3%	57.7%	42.3%
2,818,199	TOTAL	556,735	259,821	280,159	16,755	20,338 D	46.7%	50.3%	48.1%	51.9%

HARRIS COUNTY

SENATOR 1990

1990 Census Population	District	Total Vote	Republican	Democratic	Other	Rep.-Dem. Plurality	Percentage			
							Total Vote		Major Vote	
							Rep.	Dem.	Rep.	Dem.
	DISTRICT 125	32,569	25,721	6,219	629	19,502 R	79.0%	19.1%	80.5%	19.5%
	DISTRICT 126	35,897	27,387	7,788	722	19,599 R	76.3%	21.7%	77.9%	22.1%
	DISTRICT 127	27,413	20,564	6,316	533	14,248 R	75.0%	23.0%	76.5%	23.5%
	DISTRICT 128	14,498	7,431	6,749	318	682 R	51.3%	46.6%	52.4%	47.6%
	DISTRICT 129	15,780	9,677	5,693	410	3,984 R	61.3%	36.1%	63.0%	37.0%
	DISTRICT 130	28,186	19,582	7,897	707	11,685 R	69.5%	28.0%	71.3%	28.7%
	DISTRICT 131	16,042	5,158	10,596	288	5,438 D	32.2%	66.1%	32.7%	67.3%
	DISTRICT 132	23,741	11,510	11,771	460	261 D	48.5%	49.6%	49.4%	50.6%
	DISTRICT 133	14,585	10,034	4,190	361	5,844 R	68.8%	28.7%	70.5%	29.5%
	DISTRICT 134	20,492	13,454	6,577	461	6,877 R	65.7%	32.1%	67.2%	32.8%
	DISTRICT 135	29,579	23,318	5,687	574	17,631 R	78.8%	19.2%	80.4%	19.6%
	DISTRICT 136	22,566	17,355	4,770	441	12,585 R	76.9%	21.1%	78.4%	21.6%
	DISTRICT 137	17,618	8,546	8,505	567	41 R	48.5%	48.3%	50.1%	49.9%
	DISTRICT 138	15,474	8,337	6,823	314	1,514 R	53.9%	44.1%	55.0%	45.0%
	DISTRICT 139	17,985	8,602	9,041	342	439 D	47.8%	50.3%	48.8%	51.2%
	DISTRICT 140	10,307	5,871	4,257	179	1,614 R	57.0%	41.3%	58.0%	42.0%
	DISTRICT 141	11,769	1,557	10,089	123	8,532 D	13.2%	85.7%	13.4%	86.6%
	DISTRICT 142	10,683	1,245	9,330	108	8,085 D	11.7%	87.3%	11.8%	88.2%
	DISTRICT 143	9,946	3,029	6,760	157	3,731 D	30.5%	68.0%	30.9%	69.1%
	DISTRICT 144	11,736	6,729	4,692	315	2,037 R	57.3%	40.0%	58.9%	41.1%
	DISTRICT 145	14,608	8,171	6,086	351	2,085 R	55.9%	41.7%	57.3%	42.7%
	DISTRICT 146	12,749	3,008	9,571	170	6,563 D	23.6%	75.1%	23.9%	76.1%
	DISTRICT 147	9,167	2,040	6,962	165	4,922 D	22.3%	75.9%	22.7%	77.3%
	DISTRICT 148	8,916	3,272	5,423	221	2,151 D	36.7%	60.8%	37.6%	62.4%
	DISTRICT 149	24,665	16,329	7,737	599	8,592 R	66.2%	31.4%	67.9%	32.1%
	DISTRICT 150	34,552	26,380	7,392	780	18,988 R	76.3%	21.4%	78.1%	21.9%
	ABSENTEE	50,716	33,104	16,630	982	16,474 R	65.3%	32.8%	66.6%	33.4%
2,818,199	TOTAL	542,266	327,411	203,551	11,304	123,860 R	60.4%	37.5%	61.7%	38.3%

TEXAS

CONGRESS

CD	Year	Total Vote	Republican Vote	Republican Candidate	Democratic Vote	Democratic Candidate	Other Vote	Rep.-Dem. Plurality	Total Vote Rep.	Total Vote Dem.	Major Vote Rep.	Major Vote Dem.
1	1990	146,195	56,954	HODGES, HAMP	89,241	CHAPMAN, JAMES L.		32,287 D	39.0%	61.0%	39.0%	61.0%
1	1988	196,923	74,357	MCQUEEN, HORACE	122,566	CHAPMAN, JAMES L.		48,209 D	37.8%	62.2%	37.8%	62.2%
1	1986	84,445			84,445	CHAPMAN, JAMES L.		84,445 D		100.0%		100.0%
1	1984	139,829			139,829	HALL, SAM B.		139,829 D		100.0%		100.0%
1	1982	103,283			100,685	HALL, SAM B.	2,598	100,685 D		97.5%		100.0%
2	1990	138,529	61,555	PETERSON, DONNA	76,974	WILSON, CHARLES		15,419 D	44.4%	55.6%	44.4%	55.6%
2	1988	166,089			145,614	WILSON, CHARLES	20,475	145,614 D		87.7%		100.0%
2	1986	138,353	55,986	GORDON, JULIAN	78,529	WILSON, CHARLES	3,838	22,543 D	40.5%	56.8%	41.6%	58.4%
2	1984	191,067	77,842	DUGAS, LOUIS	113,225	WILSON, CHARLES		35,383 D	40.7%	59.3%	40.7%	59.3%
2	1982	97,346			91,762	WILSON, CHARLES	5,584	91,762 D		94.3%		100.0%
3	1990	154,474	153,857	BARTLETT, STEVE			617	153,857 R	99.6%		100.0%	
3	1988	278,509	227,882	BARTLETT, STEVE	50,627	COWDEN, BLAKE		177,255 R	81.8%	18.2%	81.8%	18.2%
3	1986	152,385	143,381	BARTLETT, STEVE			9,004	143,381 R	94.1%		100.0%	
3	1984	275,709	228,819	BARTLETT, STEVE	46,890	WESTBROOK, JIM		181,929 R	83.0%	17.0%	83.0%	17.0%
4	1990	108,694			108,300	HALL, RALPH M.	394	108,300 D		99.6%		100.0%
4	1988	209,868	67,337	SUTTON, RANDY	139,379	HALL, RALPH M.	3,152	72,042 D	32.1%	66.4%	32.6%	67.4%
4	1986	136,118	38,578	BLOW, THOMAS	97,540	HALL, RALPH M.		58,962 D	28.3%	71.7%	28.3%	71.7%
4	1984	208,341	87,553	BLOW, THOMAS	120,749	HALL, RALPH M.	39	33,196 D	42.0%	58.0%	42.0%	58.0%
4	1982	127,496	32,221	COLLUMB, PETER J.	94,134	HALL, RALPH M.	1,141	61,913 D	25.3%	73.8%	25.5%	74.5%
5	1990	109,474	41,307	RUCKER, JERRY	65,228	BRYANT, JOHN	2,939	23,921 D	37.7%	59.6%	38.8%	61.2%
5	1988	157,039	59,877	WILLIAMS, LON	95,376	BRYANT, JOHN	1,786	35,499 D	38.1%	60.7%	38.6%	61.4%
5	1986	98,104	39,945	CARTER, TOM	57,410	BRYANT, JOHN	749	17,465 D	40.7%	58.5%	41.0%	59.0%
5	1984	94,391			94,391	BRYANT, JOHN		94,391 D		100.0%		100.0%
5	1982	80,530	27,121	DEVANY, JOE	52,214	BRYANT, JOHN	1,195	25,093 D	33.7%	64.8%	34.2%	65.8%
6	1990	188,130	125,049	BARTON, JOE L.	62,344	WELCH, JOHN E.	737	62,705 R	66.5%	33.1%	66.7%	33.3%
6	1988	243,478	164,692	BARTON, JOE L.	78,786	KENDRICK, N. P.		85,906 R	67.6%	32.4%	67.6%	32.4%
6	1986	154,460	86,190	BARTON, JOE L.	68,270	GEREN, PETE		17,920 R	55.8%	44.2%	55.8%	44.2%
6	1984	232,281	131,482	BARTON, JOE L.	100,799	KUBIAK, DAN		30,683 R	56.6%	43.4%	56.6%	43.4%
7	1990	114,254	114,254	ARCHER, W. R.				114,254 R	100.0%		100.0%	
7	1988	234,027	185,203	ARCHER, W. R.	48,824	RICHARDS, DIANNE		136,379 R	79.1%	20.9%	79.1%	20.9%
7	1986	148,395	129,673	ARCHER, W. R.	17,635	KNIFFEN, HARRY	1,087	112,038 R	87.4%	11.9%	88.0%	12.0%
7	1984	246,315	213,480	ARCHER, W. R.	32,835	WILLIBEY, BILLY		180,645 R	86.7%	13.3%	86.7%	13.3%
7	1982	127,922	108,718	ARCHER, W. R.	17,866	SCOGGINS, DENNIS G.	1,338	90,852 R	85.0%	14.0%	85.9%	14.1%
8	1990	60,603	60,603	FIELDS, JACK				60,603 R	100.0%		100.0%	
8	1988	90,503	90,503	FIELDS, JACK				90,503 R	100.0%		100.0%	
8	1986	96,903	66,280	FIELDS, JACK	30,617	MANN, BLAINE	6	35,663 R	68.4%	31.6%	68.4%	31.6%
8	1984	175,103	113,031	FIELDS, JACK	62,072	BUFORD, DON		50,959 R	64.6%	35.4%	64.6%	35.4%
8	1982	89,218	50,630	FIELDS, JACK	38,041	ALLEE, HENRY E.	547	12,589 R	56.7%	42.6%	57.1%	42.9%
9	1990	138,185	58,399	MEYERS, MAURY	79,786	BROOKS, JACK B.		21,387 D	42.3%	57.7%	42.3%	57.7%
9	1988	137,270			137,270	BROOKS, JACK B.		137,270 D		100.0%		100.0%
9	1986	119,119	45,834	DUPERIER, LISA	73,285	BROOKS, JACK B.		27,451 D	38.5%	61.5%	38.5%	61.5%
9	1984	204,865	84,306	MAHAN, JIM	120,559	BROOKS, JACK B.		36,253 D	41.2%	58.8%	41.2%	58.8%
9	1982	116,897	35,422	LEWIS, JOHN W.	78,965	BROOKS, JACK B.	2,510	43,543 D	30.3%	67.6%	31.0%	69.0%
10	1990	235,496	73,766	BEILHARZ, DAVID	152,784	PICKLE, JAKE	8,946	79,018 D	31.3%	64.9%	32.6%	67.4%
10	1988	248,494			232,213	PICKLE, JAKE	16,281	232,213 D		93.4%		100.0%
10	1986	187,863	52,000	RYLANDER, CAROLE K.	135,863	PICKLE, JAKE		83,863 D	27.7%	72.3%	27.7%	72.3%
10	1984	186,785			186,447	PICKLE, JAKE	338	186,447 D		99.8%		100.0%
10	1982	134,276			121,030	PICKLE, JAKE	13,246	121,030 D		90.1%		100.0%

432

TEXAS

CONGRESS

CD	Year	Total Vote	Republican Vote	Republican Candidate	Democratic Vote	Democratic Candidate	Other Vote	Rep.-Dem. Plurality	Total Vote Rep.	Total Vote Dem.	Major Vote Rep.	Major Vote Dem.
11	1990	138,079	64,269	SHINE, HUGH D.	73,810	EDWARDS, CHET		9,541 D	46.5%	53.5%	46.5%	53.5%
11	1988	140,740			134,207	LEATH, J. MARVIN	6,533	134,207 D		95.4%		100.0%
11	1986	84,201			84,201	LEATH, J. MARVIN		84,201 D		100.0%		100.0%
11	1984	112,940			112,940	LEATH, J. MARVIN		112,940 D		100.0%		100.0%
11	1982	86,395			83,236	LEATH, J. MARVIN	3,159	83,236 D		96.3%		100.0%
12	1990	137,464	39,438	MCGINN, MIKE	98,026	GEREN, PETE		58,588 D	28.7%	71.3%	28.7%	71.3%
12	1988	136,456			135,459	WRIGHT, JAMES C.	997	135,459 D		99.3%		100.0%
12	1986	123,451	38,620	MCNEIL, DON	84,831	WRIGHT, JAMES C.		46,211 D	31.3%	68.7%	31.3%	68.7%
12	1984	106,302			106,299	WRIGHT, JAMES C.	3	106,299 D		100.0%		100.0%
13	1990	144,860	63,045	WATERFIELD, DICK	81,815	SARPALIUS, BILL		18,770 D	43.5%	56.5%	43.5%	56.5%
13	1988	187,450	89,105	MILNER, LARRY S.	98,345	SARPALIUS, BILL		9,240 D	47.5%	52.5%	47.5%	52.5%
13	1986	130,887	84,980	BOULTER, BEAU	45,907	SEAL, DOUG		39,073 R	64.9%	35.1%	64.9%	35.1%
13	1984	202,967	107,600	BOULTER, BEAU	95,367	HIGHTOWER, JOHN		12,233 R	53.0%	47.0%	53.0%	47.0%
13	1982	135,820	47,877	SLOVER, RON	86,376	HIGHTOWER, JOHN	1,567	38,499 D	35.3%	63.6%	35.7%	64.3%
14	1990	164,349	75,098	DIAL, JOE	89,251	LAUGHLIN, GREG		14,153 D	45.7%	54.3%	45.7%	54.3%
14	1988	209,216	96,042	SWEENEY, MAC	111,395	LAUGHLIN, GREG	1,779	15,353 D	45.9%	53.2%	46.3%	53.7%
14	1986	142,323	74,471	SWEENEY, MAC	67,852	LAUGHLIN, GREG		6,619 R	52.3%	47.7%	52.3%	47.7%
14	1984	203,066	104,181	SWEENEY, MAC	98,885	PATMAN, WILLIAM N.		5,296 R	51.3%	48.7%	51.3%	48.7%
14	1982	126,712	48,942	WYATT, JOE	76,851	PATMAN, WILLIAM N.	919	27,909 D	38.6%	60.7%	38.9%	61.1%
15	1990	72,461			72,461	DE LA GARZA, ELIGIO		72,461 D		100.0%		100.0%
15	1988	99,805			93,672	DE LA GARZA, ELIGIO	6,133	93,672 D		93.9%		100.0%
15	1986	70,777			70,777	DE LA GARZA, ELIGIO		70,777 D		100.0%		100.0%
15	1984	104,863			104,863	DE LA GARZA, ELIGIO		104,863 D		100.0%		100.0%
15	1982	80,002			76,544	DE LA GARZA, ELIGIO	3,458	76,544 D		95.7%		100.0%
16	1990	65,309			62,455	COLEMAN, RONALD	2,854	62,455 D		95.6%		100.0%
16	1988	104,514			104,514	COLEMAN, RONALD		104,514 D		100.0%		100.0%
16	1986	77,011	26,421	GILLIA, ROY	50,590	COLEMAN, RONALD		24,169 D	34.3%	65.7%	34.3%	65.7%
16	1984	132,964	56,589	HAMMOND, JACK	76,375	COLEMAN, RONALD		19,786 D	42.6%	57.4%	42.6%	57.4%
16	1982	81,671	36,064	HAGGERTY, PAT	44,024	COLEMAN, RONALD	1,583	7,960 D	44.2%	53.9%	45.0%	55.0%
17	1990	104,100			104,100	STENHOLM, CHARLES W.		104,100 D		100.0%		100.0%
17	1988	149,064			149,064	STENHOLM, CHARLES W.		149,064 D		100.0%		100.0%
17	1986	97,791			97,791	STENHOLM, CHARLES W.		97,791 D		100.0%		100.0%
17	1984	143,012			143,012	STENHOLM, CHARLES W.		143,012 D		100.0%		100.0%
17	1982	112,630			109,359	STENHOLM, CHARLES W.	3,271	109,359 D		97.1%		100.0%
18	1990	54,720			54,477	WASHINGTON, CRAIG A.	243	54,477 D		99.6%		100.0%
18	1988	101,643			94,408	LELAND, MICKEY	7,235	94,408 D		92.9%		100.0%
18	1986	70,219			63,335	LELAND, MICKEY	6,884	63,335 D		90.2%		100.0%
18	1984	139,110	26,400	BEAMAN, GLEN E.	109,626	LELAND, MICKEY	3,084	83,226 D	19.0%	78.8%	19.4%	80.6%
18	1982	82,335	12,104	PICKETT, C. LEON	68,014	LELAND, MICKEY	2,217	55,910 D	14.7%	82.6%	15.1%	84.9%
19	1990	83,795	83,795	COMBEST, LARRY				83,795 R	100.0%		100.0%	
19	1988	167,000	113,068	COMBEST, LARRY	53,932	MCCATHERN, GERALD		59,136 R	67.7%	32.3%	67.7%	32.3%
19	1986	110,824	68,695	COMBEST, LARRY	42,129	MCCATHERN, GERALD		26,566 R	62.0%	38.0%	62.0%	38.0%
19	1984	176,849	102,805	COMBEST, LARRY	74,044	RICHARDS, DON R.		28,761 R	58.1%	41.9%	58.1%	41.9%
19	1982	109,970	19,062	HICKS, E. L.	89,702	HANCE, KENT	1,206	70,640 D	17.3%	81.6%	17.5%	82.5%
20	1990	56,318			56,318	GONZALEZ, HENRY B.		56,318 D		100.0%		100.0%
20	1988	133,696	36,801	TREVINO, LEE	94,527	GONZALEZ, HENRY B.	2,368	57,726 D	27.5%	70.7%	28.0%	72.0%
20	1986	55,363			55,363	GONZALEZ, HENRY B.		55,363 D		100.0%		100.0%
20	1984	100,443			100,443	GONZALEZ, HENRY B.		100,443 D		100.0%		100.0%

TEXAS

CONGRESS

CD	Year	Total Vote	Republican Vote	Republican Candidate	Democratic Vote	Democratic Candidate	Other Vote	Rep.-Dem. Plurality	Total Vote Rep.	Total Vote Dem.	Major Vote Rep.	Major Vote Dem.
21	1990	193,155	144,570	SMITH, LAMAR	48,585	ROBERTS, KIRBY J.		95,985 R	74.8%	25.2%	74.8%	25.2%
21	1988	218,790	203,989	SMITH, LAMAR			14,801	203,989 R	93.2%		100.0%	
21	1986	165,567	100,346	SMITH, LAMAR	63,779	SNELSON, PETE	1,442	36,567 R	60.6%	38.5%	61.1%	38.9%
21	1984	247,980	199,909	LOEFFLER, TOM	48,039	SULLIVAN, JOE	32	151,870 R	80.6%	19.4%	80.6%	19.4%
22	1990	131,146	93,425	DELAY, THOMAS D.	37,721	DIRECTOR, BRUCE		55,704 R	71.2%	28.8%	71.2%	28.8%
22	1988	186,484	125,733	DELAY, THOMAS D.	58,471	WALKER, WAYNE	2,280	67,262 R	67.4%	31.4%	68.3%	31.7%
22	1986	106,538	76,459	DELAY, THOMAS D.	30,079	DIRECTOR, SUSAN		46,380 R	71.8%	28.2%	71.8%	28.2%
22	1984	191,751	125,225	DELAY, THOMAS D.	66,495	WILLIAMS, DOUG	31	58,730 R	65.3%	34.7%	65.3%	34.7%
22	1982	67,479	66,536	PAUL, RON			943	66,536 R	98.6%		100.0%	
23	1990	111,908	40,856	GONZALES, JEROME L.	71,052	BUSTAMANTE, ALBERT G.		30,196 D	36.5%	63.5%	36.5%	63.5%
23	1988	180,430	60,559	GONZALES, JEROME L.	116,423	BUSTAMANTE, ALBERT G.	3,448	55,864 D	33.6%	64.5%	34.2%	65.8%
23	1986	75,132			68,131	BUSTAMANTE, ALBERT G.	7,001	68,131 D		90.7%		100.0%
23	1984	95,721			95,721	BUSTAMANTE, ALBERT G.		95,721 D		100.0%		100.0%
24	1990	86,297			86,297	FROST, MARTIN		86,297 D		100.0%		100.0%
24	1988	146,635			135,794	FROST, MARTIN	10,841	135,794 D		92.6%		100.0%
24	1986	103,191	33,819	BURK, BOB	69,368	FROST, MARTIN	4	35,549 D	32.8%	67.2%	32.8%	67.2%
24	1984	176,918	71,703	BURK, BOB	105,210	FROST, MARTIN	5	33,507 D	40.5%	59.5%	40.5%	59.5%
25	1990	67,427			67,427	ANDREWS, MIKE		67,427 D		100.0%		100.0%
25	1988	159,036	44,043	LOEFFLER, GEORGE H.	113,499	ANDREWS, MIKE	1,494	69,456 D	27.7%	71.4%	28.0%	72.0%
25	1986	67,435			67,435	ANDREWS, MIKE		67,435 D		100.0%		100.0%
25	1984	177,920	63,974	PATTERSON, JERRY	113,946	ANDREWS, MIKE		49,972 D	36.0%	64.0%	36.0%	64.0%
25	1982	105,914	40,112	FAUBION, MIKE	63,974	ANDREWS, MIKE	1,828	23,862 D	37.9%	60.4%	38.5%	61.5%
26	1990	210,014	147,856	ARMEY, DICK	62,158	CATON, JOHN W.		85,698 R	70.4%	29.6%	70.4%	29.6%
26	1988	281,446	194,944	ARMEY, DICK	86,490	REYES, JO ANN	12	108,454 R	69.3%	30.7%	69.3%	30.7%
26	1986	149,386	101,735	ARMEY, DICK	47,651	RICHARDSON, GEORGE		54,084 R	68.1%	31.9%	68.1%	31.9%
26	1984	247,094	126,641	ARMEY, DICK	120,451	VANDERGRIFF, TOM	2	6,190 R	51.3%	48.7%	51.3%	48.7%
27	1990	62,822			62,822	ORTIZ, SOLOMON P.		62,822 D		100.0%		100.0%
27	1988	105,085			105,085	ORTIZ, SOLOMON P.		105,085 D		100.0%		100.0%
27	1986	64,165			64,165	ORTIZ, SOLOMON P.		64,165 D		100.0%		100.0%
27	1984	165,799	60,283	MOORE, RICHARD	105,516	ORTIZ, SOLOMON P.		45,233 D	36.4%	63.6%	36.4%	63.6%
27	1982	104,044	35,209	LUBY, JASON	66,604	ORTIZ, SOLOMON P.	2,231	31,395 D	33.8%	64.0%	34.6%	65.4%

434

TEXAS

1990 GENERAL ELECTION

Governor   Other vote was 129,128 Libertarian (Daiell) and write-in votes for the following nineteen candidates: 3,275 Cash; 1,566 Wright; 1,395 Pierson; 1,027 Bridges; 783 Calkins; 608 Landry; 543 Hickerson-Bull; 381 Hearn-Haynes; 355 Fain; 258 Mabrito; 226 Yancy; 196 Wolfe; 188 Summers; 186 Christopher; 155 Mitchell; 137 Garrett; 127 Scott; 86 Larson; 25 Southmayd. When the returns for Governor were canvassed by the State Legislature the Daiell total was amended to 129,157 and the Christopher total to 186. The state did not amend any county figures, therefore the original data are presented in the table for Governor.

Senator   Other vote was 89,089 Libertarian (Johnson) and 725 write-in (Calkins). There appears to be an undercount in the Democratic vote in Gregg county. The state certified returns give the vote as 1,850; however when queried, the Gregg county clerk's office gave the vote as 8,350.

Congress   Other vote was Libertarian (Ashby) in CD 5; 8,905 Libertarian (Davis) and 41 scattered write-in in CD 10; scattered write-in in all other CD's.

HARRIS COUNTY

1990 Population data not available by districts.

Governor   Other vote was 15,545 Libertarian (Daiell) and 1,210 write-in votes not available by district. The total in the other vote column includes these write-in votes.

Senator   Other vote was 11,277 Libertarian (Johnson) and 27 write-in votes not available by district. The total in the other vote column includes these write-in votes.

1990 PRIMARIES

MARCH 13 REPUBLICAN

Governor   520,014 Clayton Williams; 132,142 Kent Hance; 115,835 Tom Luce; 82,461 Jack Rains; 2,310 W. N. Otwell; 1,392 Royce X. Owens; 1,077 Ed Cude.

Senator   Phil Gramm, unopposed.

Congress   Unopposed in fourteen CD's. No candidate in CD's 4, 15, 16, 17, 18, 20, 24, 25 and 27. Contested as follows:

  CD 9   7,383 Maury Meyers; 6,755 Steve Stockman; 2,435 Steve Clifford.
  CD 10   15,870 David Beilharz; 14,130 Matt Harnest.
  CD 11   11,852 Hugh D. Shine; 8,239 Jim Mathis; 8,017 David Sibley.
  CD 13   21,117 Dick Waterfield; 9,324 Robert Price.

MARCH 13 DEMOCRATIC

Governor   580,191 Ann Richards; 546,103 Jim Mattox; 286,161 Mark White; 31,395 Theresa Hearn-Haynes; 17,904 Earl Holmes; 16,118 Stanley Adams; 9,388 Ray Rachal.

Senator   766,284 Hugh Parmer; 249,445 Harley Schlanger.

Congress   Unopposed in twenty CD's. No candidate in CD's 3, 7, 8, and 19. Contested as follows:

  CD 9   44,781 Jack B. Brooks; 17,268 Jack Brookshire.
  CD 10   83,989 Jake Pickle; 6,116 Robin Mills; 4,589 John Longsworth.
  CD 26   17,051 John W. Caton; 9,208 Craig Holtzclaw.

TEXAS

APRIL 10 DEMOCRATIC RUN-OFF

Governor   640,995 Ann Richards; 481,739 Jim Mattox.

UTAH

GOVERNOR
Norman H. Bangerter (R). Re-elected 1988 to a four-year term. Previously elected 1984.

SENATORS
E. J. Garn (R). Re-elected 1986 to a six-year term. Previously elected 1980, 1974.

Orrin G. Hatch (R). Re-elected 1988 to a six-year term. Previously elected 1982, 1976.

REPRESENTATIVES
1. James V. Hansen (R) 2. Wayne Owens (D) 3. Bill Orton (D)

POSTWAR VOTE FOR PRESIDENT

		Republican		Democratic		Other		Percentage Total Vote		Major Vote	
Year	Total Vote	Vote	Candidate	Vote	Candidate	Vote	Plurality	Rep.	Dem.	Rep.	Dem.
1988	647,008	428,442	Bush, George	207,343	Dukakis, Michael S.	11,223	221,099 R	66.2%	32.0%	67.4%	32.6%
1984	629,656	469,105	Reagan, Ronald	155,369	Mondale, Walter F.	5,182	313,736 R	74.5%	24.7%	75.1%	24.9%
1980	604,222	439,687	Reagan, Ronald	124,266	Carter, Jimmy	40,269	315,421 R	72.8%	20.6%	78.0%	22.0%
1976	541,198	337,908	Ford, Gerald R.	182,110	Carter, Jimmy	21,180	155,798 R	62.4%	33.6%	65.0%	35.0%
1972	478,476	323,643	Nixon, Richard M.	126,284	McGovern, George S.	28,549	197,359 R	67.6%	26.4%	71.9%	28.1%
1968	422,568	238,728	Nixon, Richard M.	156,665	Humphrey, Hubert H.	27,175	82,063 R	56.5%	37.1%	60.4%	39.6%
1964	401,413	181,785	Goldwater, Barry M.	219,628	Johnson, Lyndon B.		37,843 D	45.3%	54.7%	45.3%	54.7%
1960	374,709	205,361	Nixon, Richard M.	169,248	Kennedy, John F.	100	36,113 R	54.8%	45.2%	54.8%	45.2%
1956	333,995	215,631	Eisenhower, Dwight D.	118,364	Stevenson, Adlai E.		97,267 R	64.6%	35.4%	64.6%	35.4%
1952	329,554	194,190	Eisenhower, Dwight D.	135,364	Stevenson, Adlai E.		58,826 R	58.9%	41.1%	58.9%	41.1%
1948	276,306	124,402	Dewey, Thomas E.	149,151	Truman, Harry S.	2,753	24,749 D	45.0%	54.0%	45.5%	54.5%

POSTWAR VOTE FOR GOVERNOR

		Republican		Democratic		Other	Rep.-Dem.	Percentage Total Vote		Major Vote	
Year	Total Vote	Vote	Candidate	Vote	Candidate	Vote	Plurality	Rep.	Dem.	Rep.	Dem.
1988 **	649,114	260,462	Bangerter, Norman H.	249,321	Wilson, Ted	139,331	11,141 R	40.1%	38.4%	51.1%	48.9%
1984	629,619	351,792	Bangerter, Norman H.	275,669	Owens, Wayne	2,158	76,123 R	55.9%	43.8%	56.1%	43.9%
1980	600,019	266,578	Wright, Bob	330,974	Matheson, Scott M.	2,467	64,396 D	44.4%	55.2%	44.6%	55.4%
1976	539,649	248,027	Romney, Vernon B.	280,706	Matheson, Scott M.	10,916	32,679 D	46.0%	52.0%	46.9%	53.1%
1972	476,447	144,449	Strike, Nicholas L.	331,998	Rampton, Calvin L.		187,549 D	30.3%	69.7%	30.3%	69.7%
1968	421,012	131,729	Buehner, Carl W.	289,283	Rampton, Calvin L.		157,554 D	31.3%	68.7%	31.3%	68.7%
1964	398,256	171,300	Melich, Mitchell	226,956	Rampton, Calvin L.		55,656 D	43.0%	57.0%	43.0%	57.0%
1960	371,489	195,634	Clyde, George D.	175,855	Barlocker, W. A.		19,779 R	52.7%	47.3%	52.7%	47.3%
1956 **	332,889	127,164	Clyde, George D.	111,297	Romney, L. C.	94,428	15,867 R	38.2%	33.4%	53.3%	46.7%
1952	327,704	180,516	Lee, J. Bracken	147,188	Glade, Earl J.		33,328 R	55.1%	44.9%	55.1%	44.9%
1948	275,067	151,253	Lee, J. Bracken	123,814	Maw, Herbert B.		27,439 R	55.0%	45.0%	55.0%	45.0%

In 1956 other vote was Independent (Lee). In 1988 other vote was 136,651 Independent (Cook); 1,661 Libertarian (Burton) and 1,019 American (Pedersen).

UTAH

POSTWAR VOTE FOR SENATOR

Year	Total Vote	Republican Vote	Candidate	Democratic Vote	Candidate	Other Vote	Rep-Dem. Plurality	Total Vote Rep.	Dem.	Major Vote Rep.	Dem.
1988	640,702	430,089	Hatch, Orrin G.	203,364	Moss, Brian H.	7,249	226,725 R	67.1%	31.7%	67.9%	32.1%
1986	435,111	314,608	Garn, E. J.	115,523	Oliver, Craig	4,980	199,085 R	72.3%	26.6%	73.1%	26.9%
1982	530,802	309,332	Hatch, Orrin G.	219,482	Wilson, Ted	1,988	89,850 R	58.3%	41.3%	58.5%	41.5%
1980	594,298	437,675	Garn, E. J.	151,454	Berman, Dan	5,169	286,221 R	73.6%	25.5%	74.3%	25.7%
1976	540,108	290,221	Hatch, Orrin G.	241,948	Moss, Frank E.	7,939	48,273 R	53.7%	44.8%	54.5%	45.5%
1974	420,642	210,299	Garn, E. J.	185,377	Owens, Wayne	24,966	24,922 R	50.0%	44.1%	53.1%	46.9%
1970	374,303	159,004	Burton, Laurence J.	210,207	Moss, Frank E.	5,092	51,203 D	42.5%	56.2%	43.1%	56.9%
1968	419,262	225,075	Bennett, Wallace F.	192,168	Weilenmann, Milton	2,019	32,907 R	53.7%	45.8%	53.9%	46.1%
1964	397,384	169,562	Wilkinson, Ernest L.	227,822	Moss, Frank E.		58,260 D	42.7%	57.3%	42.7%	57.3%
1962	318,411	166,755	Bennett, Wallace F.	151,656	King, David S.		15,099 R	52.4%	47.6%	52.4%	47.6%
1958 **	291,311	101,471	Watkins, Arthur V.	112,827	Moss, Frank E.	77,013	11,356 D	34.8%	38.7%	47.4%	52.6%
1956	330,381	178,261	Bennett, Wallace F.	152,120	Hopkin, Alonzo F.		26,141 R	54.0%	46.0%	54.0%	46.0%
1952	327,033	177,435	Watkins, Arthur V.	149,598	Granger, Walter K.		27,837 R	54.3%	45.7%	54.3%	45.7%
1950	264,440	142,427	Bennett, Wallace F.	121,198	Thomas, Elbert D.	815	21,229 R	53.9%	45.8%	54.0%	46.0%
1946	197,399	101,142	Watkins, Arthur V.	96,257	Murdock, Abe		4,885 R	51.2%	48.8%	51.2%	48.8%

In 1958 other vote was Independent (Lee).

438

UTAH

Districts Established January 1, 1982

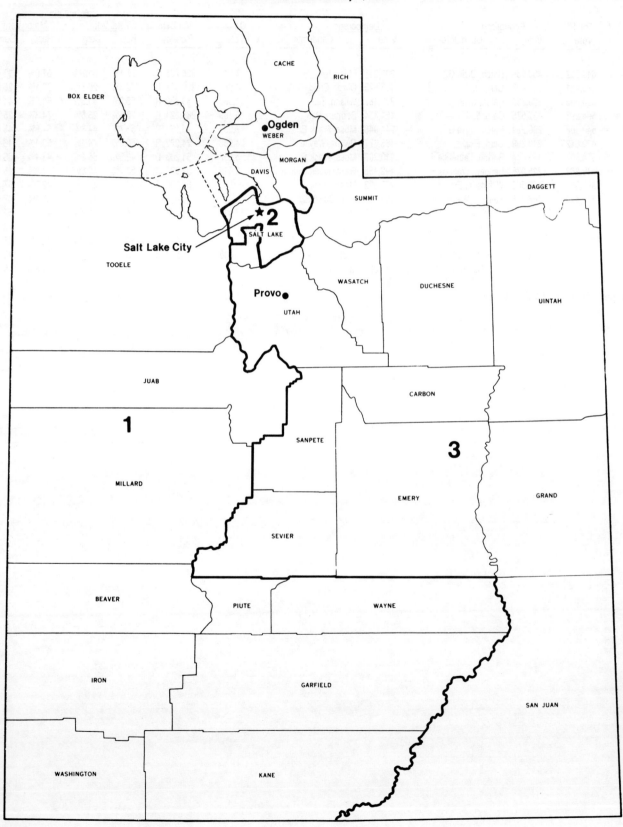

© ERC

UTAH

CONGRESS

CD	Year	Total Vote	Republican Vote	Republican Candidate	Democratic Vote	Democratic Candidate	Other Vote	Rep.-Dem. Plurality	Total Vote Rep.	Total Vote Dem.	Major Vote Rep.	Major Vote Dem.
1	1990	158,666	82,746	HANSEN, JAMES V.	69,491	BRUNSDALE, KENLEY	6,429	13,255 R	52.2%	43.8%	54.4%	45.6%
1	1988	218,869	130,893	HANSEN, JAMES V.	87,976	MCKAY, GUNN		42,917 R	59.8%	40.2%	59.8%	40.2%
1	1986	159,331	82,151	HANSEN, JAMES V.	77,180	MCKAY, GUNN		4,971 R	51.6%	48.4%	51.6%	48.4%
1	1984	200,717	142,952	HANSEN, JAMES V.	56,619	ABRAMS, MILTON C.	1,146	86,333 R	71.2%	28.2%	71.6%	28.4%
1	1982	177,422	111,416	HANSEN, JAMES V.	66,006	DIRKS, A. STEPHEN		45,410 R	62.8%	37.2%	62.8%	37.2%
2	1990	147,871	58,869	ATWOOD, GENEVIEVE	85,167	OWENS, WAYNE	3,835	26,298 D	39.8%	57.6%	40.9%	59.1%
2	1988	195,338	80,212	SNELGROVE, RICHARD	112,129	OWENS, WAYNE	2,997	31,917 D	41.1%	57.4%	41.7%	58.3%
2	1986	139,390	60,967	SHIMIZU, TOM	76,921	OWENS, WAYNE	1,502	15,954 D	43.7%	55.2%	44.2%	55.8%
2	1984	213,793	105,540	MONSON, DAVID S.	105,044	FARLEY, FRANCES	3,209	496 R	49.4%	49.1%	50.1%	49.9%
2	1982	171,090	92,109	MARRIOTT, DAN	78,981	FARLEY, FRANCES		13,128 R	53.8%	46.2%	53.8%	46.2%
3	1990	135,676	49,452	SNOW, KARL	79,163	ORTON, BILL	7,061	29,711 D	36.4%	58.3%	38.4%	61.6%
3	1988	194,461	129,951	NIELSON, HOWARD C.	60,018	STRINGHAM, ROBERT W.	4,492	69,933 R	66.8%	30.9%	68.4%	31.6%
3	1986	130,074	86,599	NIELSON, HOWARD C.	42,582	GARDINER, DALE F.	893	44,017 R	66.6%	32.7%	67.0%	33.0%
3	1984	186,572	138,918	NIELSON, HOWARD C.	46,560	BAIRD, BRUCE R.	1,094	92,358 R	74.5%	25.0%	74.9%	25.1%
3	1982	141,139	108,478	NIELSON, HOWARD C.			32,661	108,478 R	76.9%		100.0%	

UTAH

1990 GENERAL ELECTION

Congress   Other vote was American (Wadsworth) in CD 1; 3,424 Independent (Topham) and 411 Socialist Workers (Garcia) in CD 2; 6,542 American (Smith) and 519 Socialist Workers (Dutrow) in CD 3.

1990 PRIMARIES

SEPTEMBER 11 REPUBLICAN

Congress   Nominated by convention in CD 1. Contested as follows:

CD   2   22,089 Genevieve Atwood; 15,716 Dan Marriott.
CD   3   29,367 Karl Snow; 14,988 John Harmer.

SEPTEMBER 11 DEMOCRATIC

Congress   Nominated by convention in all three CD's.

VERMONT

GOVERNOR
Richard A. Snelling (R). Elected 1990 to a two year term. Previously elected 1982, 1980, 1978, 1976.

SENATORS
James M. Jeffords (R). Elected 1988 to a six-year term.

Patrick J. Leahy (D). Re-elected 1986 to a six-year term. Previously elected 1980, 1974.

REPRESENTATIVES
At-Large. Bernard Sanders (I)

POSTWAR VOTE FOR PRESIDENT

Year	Total Vote	Republican Vote	Candidate	Democratic Vote	Candidate	Other Vote	Plurality	Total Vote Rep.	Dem.	Major Vote Rep.	Dem.
1988	243,328	124,331	Bush, George	115,775	Dukakis, Michael S.	3,222	8,556 R	51.1%	47.6%	51.8%	48.2%
1984	234,561	135,865	Reagan, Ronald	95,730	Mondale, Walter F.	2,966	40,135 R	57.9%	40.8%	58.7%	41.3%
1980	213,299	94,628	Reagan, Ronald	81,952	Carter, Jimmy	36,719	12,676 R	44.4%	38.4%	53.6%	46.4%
1976	187,765	102,085	Ford, Gerald R.	80,954	Carter, Jimmy	4,726	21,131 R	54.4%	43.1%	55.8%	44.2%
1972	186,947	117,149	Nixon, Richard M.	68,174	McGovern, George S.	1,624	48,975 R	62.7%	36.5%	63.2%	36.8%
1968	161,404	85,142	Nixon, Richard M.	70,255	Humphrey, Hubert H.	6,007	14,887 R	52.8%	43.5%	54.8%	45.2%
1964	163,089	54,942	Goldwater, Barry M.	108,127	Johnson, Lyndon B.	20	53,185 D	33.7%	66.3%	33.7%	66.3%
1960	167,324	98,131	Nixon, Richard M.	69,186	Kennedy, John F.	7	28,945 R	58.6%	41.3%	58.6%	41.4%
1956	152,978	110,390	Eisenhower, Dwight D.	42,549	Stevenson, Adlai E.	39	67,841 R	72.2%	27.8%	72.2%	27.8%
1952	153,557	109,717	Eisenhower, Dwight D.	43,355	Stevenson, Adlai E.	485	66,362 R	71.5%	28.2%	71.7%	28.3%
1948	123,382	75,926	Dewey, Thomas E.	45,557	Truman, Harry S.	1,899	30,369 R	61.5%	36.9%	62.5%	37.5%

442

VERMONT

POSTWAR VOTE FOR GOVERNOR

Year	Total Vote	Republican Vote	Candidate	Democratic Vote	Candidate	Other Vote	Rep-Dem. Plurality	Total Vote Rep.	Dem.	Major Vote Rep.	Dem.
1990	211,422	109,540	Snelling, Richard A.	97,321	Welch, Peter	4,561	12,219 R	51.8%	46.0%	53.0%	47.0%
1988	243,130	105,319	Bernhardt, Michael	134,594	Kunin, Madeleine M.	3,253	29,275 D	43.3%	55.4%	43.9%	56.1%
1986 **	196,716	75,162	Smith, Peter	92,379	Kunin, Madeleine M.	29,175	17,217 D	38.2%	47.0%	44.9%	55.1%
1984	233,753	113,264	Easton, John J.	116,938	Kunin, Madeleine M.	3,551	3,674 D	48.5%	50.0%	49.2%	50.8%
1982	169,251	93,111	Snelling, Richard A.	74,394	Kunin, Madeleine M.	1,746	18,717 R	55.0%	44.0%	55.6%	44.4%
1980	210,381	123,229	Snelling, Richard A.	77,363	Diamond, J. Jerome	9,789	45,866 R	58.6%	36.8%	61.4%	38.6%
1978	124,482	78,181	Snelling, Richard A.	42,482	Granai, Edwin C.	3,819	35,699 R	62.8%	34.1%	64.8%	35.2%
1976	185,929	99,268	Snelling, Richard A.	75,262	Hackel, Stella B.	11,399	24,006 R	53.4%	40.5%	56.9%	43.1%
1974	141,156	53,672	Kennedy, Walter L.	79,842	Salmon, Thomas P.	7,642	26,170 D	38.0%	56.6%	40.2%	59.8%
1972	189,237	82,491	Hackett, Luther F.	104,533	Salmon, Thomas P.	2,213	22,042 D	43.6%	55.2%	44.1%	55.9%
1970	153,528	87,458	Davis, Deane C.	66,028	O'Brien, Leo	42	21,430 R	57.0%	43.0%	57.0%	43.0%
1968	161,089	89,387	Davis, Deane C.	71,656	Daley, John J.	46	17,731 R	55.5%	44.5%	55.5%	44.5%
1966	136,262	57,577	Snelling, Richard A.	78,669	Hoff, Philip H.	16	21,092 D	42.3%	57.7%	42.3%	57.7%
1964	164,199	57,576	Foote, Ralph A.	106,611	Hoff, Philip H.	12	49,035 D	35.1%	64.9%	35.1%	64.9%
1962	121,422	60,035	Keyser, F. Ray	61,383	Hoff, Philip H.	4	1,348 D	49.4%	50.6%	49.4%	50.6%
1960	164,632	92,861	Keyser, F. Ray	71,755	Niquette, Russell F.	16	21,106 R	56.4%	43.6%	56.4%	43.6%
1958	123,728	62,222	Stafford, Robert T.	61,503	Leddy, Bernard J.	3	719 R	50.3%	49.7%	50.3%	49.7%
1956	153,809	88,379	Johnson, Joseph B.	65,420	Branon, E. Frank	10	22,959 R	57.5%	42.5%	57.5%	42.5%
1954	114,360	59,778	Johnson, Joseph B.	54,554	Branon, E. Frank	28	5,224 R	52.3%	47.7%	52.3%	47.7%
1952	150,862	78,338	Emerson, Lee E.	60,051	Larrow, Robert W.	12,473	18,287 R	51.9%	39.8%	56.6%	43.4%
1950	87,155	64,915	Emerson, Lee E.	22,227	Moran, J. Edward	13	42,688 R	74.5%	25.5%	74.5%	25.5%
1948	120,183	86,394	Gibson, Ernest W., Jr.	33,588	Ryan, Charles F.	201	52,806 R	71.9%	27.9%	72.0%	28.0%
1946	72,044	57,849	Gibson, Ernest W., Jr.	14,096	Coburn, Berthold	99	43,753 R	80.3%	19.6%	80.4%	19.6%

In 1986, in the absence of a majority for any candidate, the State Legislature elected Madeleine M. Kunin to a two-year term.

POSTWAR VOTE FOR SENATOR

Year	Total Vote	Republican Vote	Candidate	Democratic Vote	Candidate	Other Vote	Rep-Dem. Plurality	Total Vote Rep.	Dem.	Major Vote Rep.	Dem.
1988	240,111	163,203	Jeffords, James M.	71,469	Gray, William	5,439	91,736 R	68.0%	29.8%	69.5%	30.5%
1986	196,532	67,798	Snelling, Richard A.	124,123	Leahy, Patrick J.	4,611	56,325 D	34.5%	63.2%	35.3%	64.7%
1982	168,003	84,450	Stafford, Robert T.	79,340	Guest, James A.	4,213	5,110 R	50.3%	47.2%	51.6%	48.4%
1980	209,124	101,421	Ledbetter, Stewart M.	104,176	Leahy, Patrick J.	3,527	2,755 D	48.5%	49.8%	49.3%	50.7%
1976	189,060	94,481	Stafford, Robert T.	85,682	Salmon, Thomas P.	8,897	8,799 R	50.0%	45.3%	52.4%	47.6%
1974	142,772	66,223	Mallary, Richard W.	70,629	Leahy, Patrick J.	5,920	4,406 D	46.4%	49.5%	48.4%	51.6%
1972 S	71,348	45,888	Stafford, Robert T.	23,842	Major, Randolph T.	1,618	22,046 R	64.3%	33.4%	65.8%	34.2%
1970	154,899	91,198	Prouty, Winston L.	62,271	Hoff, Philip H.	1,430	28,927 R	58.9%	40.2%	59.4%	40.6%
1968 **	157,375	157,154	Aiken, George D.	—		221	157,154 R	99.9%	0.0	100.0%	
1964	164,350	87,879	Prouty, Winston L.	76,457	Fayette, Frederick J.	14	11,422 R	53.5%	46.5%	53.5%	46.5%
1962	121,571	81,241	Aiken, George D.	40,134	Johnson, W. Robert	196	41,107 R	66.8%	33.0%	66.9%	33.1%
1958	124,442	64,900	Prouty, Winston L.	59,536	Fayette, Frederick J.	6	5,364 R	52.2%	47.8%	52.2%	47.8%
1956	155,289	103,101	Aiken, George D.	52,184	O'Shea, Bernard G.	4	50,917 R	66.4%	33.6%	66.4%	33.6%
1952	154,052	111,406	Flanders, Ralph E.	42,630	Johnston, Allan R.	16	68,776 R	72.3%	27.7%	72.3%	27.7%
1950	89,171	69,543	Aiken, George D.	19,608	Bigelow, James E.	20	49,935 R	78.0%	22.0%	78.0%	22.0%
1946	73,340	54,729	Flanders, Ralph E.	18,594	McDevitt, Charles P.	17	36,135 R	74.6%	25.4%	74.6%	25.4%

In 1968 the Republican candidate won both major party nominations. The January 1972 election was for a short term to fill a vacancy.

VERMONT

One At Large

VERMONT

GOVERNOR 1990

1990 Census Population	County	Total Vote	Republican	Democratic	Other	Rep.-Dem. Plurality	Percentage			
							Total Vote		Major Vote	
							Rep.	Dem.	Rep.	Dem.
32,953	ADDISON	13,246	6,676	6,282	288	394 R	50.4%	47.4%	51.5%	48.5%
35,845	BENNINGTON	11,924	6,016	5,641	267	375 R	50.5%	47.3%	51.6%	48.4%
27,846	CALEDONIA	9,552	6,242	3,072	238	3,170 R	65.3%	32.2%	67.0%	33.0%
131,761	CHITTENDEN	50,857	24,285	25,700	872	1,415 D	47.8%	50.5%	48.6%	51.4%
6,405	ESSEX	2,033	1,320	654	59	666 R	64.9%	32.2%	66.9%	33.1%
39,980	FRANKLIN	14,066	7,235	6,577	254	658 R	51.4%	46.8%	52.4%	47.6%
5,318	GRAND ISLE	2,686	1,425	1,210	51	215 R	53.1%	45.0%	54.1%	45.9%
19,735	LAMOILLE	7,065	3,899	3,014	152	885 R	55.2%	42.7%	56.4%	43.6%
26,149	ORANGE	10,222	5,570	4,275	377	1,295 R	54.5%	41.8%	56.6%	43.4%
24,053	ORLEANS	8,488	4,505	3,799	184	706 R	53.1%	44.8%	54.3%	45.7%
62,142	RUTLAND	22,226	12,544	9,258	424	3,286 R	56.4%	41.7%	57.5%	42.5%
54,928	WASHINGTON	23,691	12,732	10,524	435	2,208 R	53.7%	44.4%	54.7%	45.3%
41,588	WINDHAM	14,616	6,934	7,239	443	305 D	47.4%	49.5%	48.9%	51.1%
54,055	WINDSOR	20,750	10,157	10,076	517	81 R	48.9%	48.6%	50.2%	49.8%
562,758	TOTAL	211,422	109,540	97,321	4,561	12,219 R	51.8%	46.0%	53.0%	47.0%

VERMONT

GOVERNOR 1990

1990 Census Population	City/Town	Total Vote	Republican	Democratic	Other	Rep.-Dem. Plurality	Percentage			
							Total Vote		Major Vote	
							Rep.	Dem.	Rep.	Dem.
9,482	BARRE CITY	3,751	2,012	1,686	53	326 R	53.6%	44.9%	54.4%	45.6%
7,411	BARRE TOWN	3,094	1,853	1,206	35	647 R	59.9%	39.0%	60.6%	39.4%
16,451	BENNINGTON TOWN	4,872	2,084	2,699	89	615 D	42.8%	55.4%	43.6%	56.4%
12,241	BRATTLEBORO	3,933	1,665	2,161	107	496 D	42.3%	54.9%	43.5%	56.5%
39,127	BURLINGTON	14,475	5,407	8,765	303	3,358 D	37.4%	60.6%	38.2%	61.8%
14,731	COLCHESTER	4,570	2,309	2,190	71	119 R	50.5%	47.9%	51.3%	48.7%
16,498	ESSEX TOWN	6,371	3,647	2,643	81	1,004 R	57.2%	41.5%	58.0%	42.0%
9,404	HARTFORD	2,799	1,249	1,499	51	250 D	44.6%	53.6%	45.5%	54.5%
5,371	LYNDON	1,451	977	437	37	540 R	67.3%	30.1%	69.1%	30.9%
8,034	MIDDLEBURY	2,903	1,323	1,530	50	207 D	45.6%	52.7%	46.4%	53.6%
8,404	MILTON	2,697	1,420	1,211	66	209 R	52.7%	44.9%	54.0%	46.0%
8,247	MONTPELIER	3,931	1,972	1,888	71	84 R	50.2%	48.0%	51.1%	48.9%
5,610	NORTHFIELD	1,919	1,118	747	54	371 R	58.3%	38.9%	59.9%	40.1%
5,484	ROCKINGHAM	1,780	782	951	47	169 D	43.9%	53.4%	45.1%	54.9%
18,230	RUTLAND CITY	6,351	3,350	2,898	103	452 R	52.7%	45.6%	53.6%	46.4%
7,339	ST. ALBANS CITY	2,493	1,268	1,198	27	70 R	50.9%	48.1%	51.4%	48.6%
7,608	ST. JOHNSBURY	2,490	1,790	655	45	1,135 R	71.9%	26.3%	73.2%	26.8%
5,871	SHELBURNE	2,996	1,756	1,206	34	550 R	58.6%	40.3%	59.3%	40.7%
12,809	SOUTH BURLINGTON	5,614	2,834	2,705	75	129 R	50.5%	48.2%	51.2%	48.8%
9,579	SPRINGFIELD	3,191	1,585	1,555	51	30 R	49.7%	48.7%	50.5%	49.5%
5,636	SWANTON	1,868	987	842	39	145 R	52.8%	45.1%	54.0%	46.0%
6,649	WINOOSKI	1,920	677	1,209	34	532 D	35.3%	63.0%	35.9%	64.1%

VERMONT

CONGRESS

CD	Year	Total Vote	Republican Vote	Candidate	Democratic Vote	Candidate	Other Vote	Rep.-Dem. Plurality	Total Vote Rep.	Dem.	Major Vote Rep.	Dem.
AL	1990	209,856	82,938	SMITH, PETER	6,315	SANDOVAL, DOLORES	120,603	76,623 R	39.5%	3.0%	92.9%	7.1%
AL	1988	240,131	98,937	SMITH, PETER	45,330	POIRIER, PAUL N	95,864	53,607 R	41.2%	18.9%	68.6%	31.4%
AL	1986	188,954	168,403	* JEFFORDS, JAMES M.			20,551	168,403 R	89.1%		100.0%	
AL	1984	226,297	148,025	JEFFORDS, JAMES M.	60,360	POLLINA, ANTHONY	17,912	87,665 R	65.4%	26.7%	71.0%	29.0%
AL	1982	164,951	114,191	JEFFORDS, JAMES M.	38,296	KAPLAN, MARK A.	12,464	75,895 R	69.2%	23.2%	74.9%	25.1%
AL	1980	194,697	154,274	JEFFORDS, JAMES M.			40,423	154,274 R	79.2%		100.0%	
AL	1978	120,502	90,688	JEFFORDS, JAMES M.	23,228	DIETZ, S. MARIE	6,586	67,460 R	75.3%	19.3%	79.6%	20.4%
AL	1976	184,783	124,458	JEFFORDS, JAMES M.	60,202	* BURGESS, JOHN A.	123	64,256 R	67.4%	32.6%	67.4%	32.6%
AL	1974	140,899	74,561	JEFFORDS, JAMES M.	56,342	* CAIN, FRANCIS J.	9,996	18,219 R	52.9%	40.0%	57.0%	43.0%
AL	1972	186,028	120,924	MALLARY, RICHARD W.	65,062	MEYER, WILLIAM H.	42	55,862 R	65.0%	35.0%	65.0%	35.0%
AL	1970	152,557	103,806	STAFFORD, ROBERT T.	44,415	O'SHEA, BERNARD G.	4,336	59,391 R	68.0%	29.1%	70.0%	30.0%
AL	1968	157,133	156,956	* STAFFORD, ROBERT T.			177	156,956 R	99.9%		100.0%	
AL	1966	135,748	89,097	STAFFORD, ROBERT T.	46,643	RYAN, WILLIAM J.	8	42,454 R	65.6%	34.4%	65.6%	34.4%
AL	1964	163,452	92,252	STAFFORD, ROBERT T.	71,193	O'SHEA, BERNARD G.	7	21,059 R	56.4%	43.6%	56.4%	43.6%
AL	1962	121,381	68,822	STAFFORD, ROBERT T.	52,535	RAYNOLDS, HAROLD	24	16,287 R	56.7%	43.3%	56.7%	43.3%
AL	1960	166,035	94,905	STAFFORD, ROBERT T.	71,111	MEYER, WILLIAM H.	19	23,794 R	57.2%	42.8%	57.2%	42.8%
AL	1958	122,702	59,536	ARTHUR, HAROLD J.	63,131	MEYER, WILLIAM H.	35	3,595 D	48.5%	51.5%	48.5%	51.5%
AL	1956	154,536	103,736	PROUTY, WINSTON L.	50,797	ST. AMOUR, CAMILLE	3	52,939 R	67.1%	32.9%	67.1%	32.9%
AL	1954	114,289	70,143	PROUTY, WINSTON L.	44,141	BOYLAN, JOHN J.	5	26,002 R	61.4%	38.6%	61.4%	38.6%
AL	1952	153,060	109,871	PROUTY, WINSTON L.	43,187	COMINGS, HERBERT B.	2	66,684 R	71.8%	28.2%	71.8%	28.2%
AL	1950	38,851	65,248	PROUTY, WINSTON L.	22,709	COMINGS, HERBERT B.	894	42,539 R	73.4%	25.6%	74.2%	25.8%
AL	1948	121,968	74,076	PLUMLEY, CHARLES A.	47,767	READY, ROBERT W.	125	26,309 R	60.7%	39.2%	60.8%	39.2%
AL	1946	73,066	46,985	PLUMLEY, CHARLES A.	26,056	CALDBECK, MATTHEW J.	25	20,929 R	64.3%	35.7%	64.3%	35.7%

VERMONT

1990 GENERAL ELECTION

In addition to the county-by-county figures, data are presented for selected Vermont communities. Since not all jurisdictions of the state are listed in this tabulation, state-wide totals are shown only with the county-by-county statistics.

After publication of AMERICA VOTES 18, the state amended the returns for the 1988 vote for Governor and U.S. Senator. These amended returns are reflected in the Postwar Vote for Governor and Senator summary tables in the front section of the state chapter.

Governor   Other vote was 2,777 Libertarian (Atkinson); 1,389 Liberty Union (Gottlieb) and 395 scattered write-in.

Congress   An asterisk in the Congressional table indicates a candidate received votes from another party endorsing his/her candidacy. Other vote at-large was 117,522 Independent (Sanders); 1,965 Liberty Union (Diamondstone) and 1,116 scattered write-in. Bernard Sanders, the Independent candidate, received 56.0% of the total vote and won the election with a 34,584 plurality.

1990 PRIMARIES

SEPTEMBER 11 REPUBLICAN

Governor   38,881 Richard A. Snelling; 5,503 Richard F. Gottlieb; 485 scattered write-in.

Congress   Contested as follows:

AL.   27,339 Peter Smith; 17,444 Timothy Philbin; 957 scattered write-in.

SEPTEMBER 11 DEMOCRATIC

Governor   14,656 Peter Welch; 1,719 William Gwin; 550 scattered write-in.

Congress   Contested as follows:

AL   5,979 Dolores Sandoval; 5,716 Peter Diamondstone; 1,991 Bernard Sanders (write-in); 804 scattered write-in.

SEPTEMBER 11 LIBERTARIAN

Governor   David Atkinson, unopposed.

Congress   No candidate at-large.

VIRGINIA

GOVERNOR
L. Douglas Wilder (D). Elected 1989 to a four-year term.

SENATORS
Charles S. Robb (D). Elected 1988 to a six-year term.

John Warner (R). Re-elected 1990 to a six-year term. Previously elected 1984, 1978.

REPRESENTATIVES
1. Herbert H. Bateman (R)
2. Owen B. Pickett (D)
3. Thomas J. Bliley (R)
4. Norman Sisisky (D)
5. L. F. Payne (D)
6. James R. Olin (D)
7. D. French Slaughter (R)
8. James P. Moran (D)
9. Frederick C. Boucher (D)
10. Frank R. Wolf (R)

POSTWAR VOTE FOR PRESIDENT

Year	Total Vote	Republican Vote	Candidate	Democratic Vote	Candidate	Other Vote	Plurality	Total Vote Rep.	Dem.	Major Vote Rep.	Dem.
1988	2,191,609	1,309,162	Bush, George	859,799	Dukakis, Michael S.	22,648	449,363 R	59.7%	39.2%	60.4%	39.6%
1984	2,146,635	1,337,078	Reagan, Ronald	796,250	Mondale, Walter F.	13,307	540,828 R	62.3%	37.1%	62.7%	37.3%
1980	1,866,032	989,609	Reagan, Ronald	752,174	Carter, Jimmy	124,249	237,435 R	53.0%	40.3%	56.8%	43.2%
1976	1,697,094	836,554	Ford, Gerald R.	813,896	Carter, Jimmy	46,644	22,658 R	49.3%	48.0%	50.7%	49.3%
1972	1,457,019	988,493	Nixon, Richard M.	438,887	McGovern, George S.	29,639	549,606 R	67.8%	30.1%	69.3%	30.7%
1968 **	1,361,491	590,319	Nixon, Richard M.	442,387	Humphrey, Hubert H.	328,785	147,932 R	43.4%	32.5%	57.2%	42.8%
1964	1,042,267	481,334	Goldwater, Barry M.	558,038	Johnson, Lyndon B.	2,895	76,704 D	46.2%	53.5%	46.3%	53.7%
1960	771,449	404,521	Nixon, Richard M.	362,327	Kennedy, John F.	4,601	42,194 R	52.4%	47.0%	52.8%	47.2%
1956	697,978	386,459	Eisenhower, Dwight D.	267,760	Stevenson, Adlai E.	43,759	118,699 R	55.4%	38.4%	59.1%	40.9%
1952	619,689	349,037	Eisenhower, Dwight D.	268,677	Stevenson, Adlai E.	1,975	80,360 R	56.3%	43.4%	56.5%	43.5%
1948	419,256	172,070	Dewey, Thomas E.	200,786	Truman, Harry S.	46,400	28,716 D	41.0%	47.9%	46.1%	53.9%

In 1968 other vote was 321,833 American Independent (Wallace); 4,671 Socialist Labor; 1,680 Peace and Freedom and 601 Prohibition.

POSTWAR VOTE FOR GOVERNOR

Year	Total Vote	Republican Vote	Candidate	Democratic Vote	Candidate	Other Vote	Rep-Dem. Plurality	Total Vote Rep.	Dem.	Major Vote Rep.	Dem.
1989	1,789,078	890,195	Coleman, J. Marshall	896,936	Wilder, L. Douglas	1,947	6,741 D	49.8%	50.1%	49.8%	50.2%
1985	1,343,243	601,652	Durrette, Wyatt B.	741,438	Baliles, Gerald L.	153	139,786 D	44.8%	55.2%	44.8%	55.2%
1981	1,420,611	659,398	Coleman, J. Marshall	760,357	Robb, Charles S.	856	100,959 D	46.4%	53.5%	46.4%	53.6%
1977	1,250,940	699,302	Dalton, John	541,319	Howell, Henry	10,319	157,983 R	55.9%	43.3%	56.4%	43.6%
1973 **	1,035,495	525,075	Godwin, Mills E.	—		510,420	525,075 R	50.7%		100.0%	
1969	915,764	480,869	Holton, Linwood	415,695	Battle, William C.	19,200	65,174 R	52.5%	45.4%	53.6%	46.4%
1965	562,789	212,207	Holton, Linwood	269,526	Godwin, Mills E.	81,056	57,319 D	37.7%	47.9%	44.1%	55.9%
1961	394,490	142,567	Pearson, H. Clyde	251,861	Harrison, Albertis	62	109,294 D	36.1%	63.8%	36.1%	63.9%
1957	517,655	188,628	Dalton, Ted	326,921	Almond, J. Lindsay	2,106	138,293 D	36.4%	63.2%	36.6%	63.4%
1953	414,025	183,328	Dalton, Ted	226,998	Stanley, Thomas B.	3,699	43,670 D	44.3%	54.8%	44.7%	55.3%
1949	262,350	71,991	Johnson, Walter	184,772	Battle, John S.	5,587	112,781 D	27.4%	70.4%	28.0%	72.0%
1945	168,783	52,386	Landreth, S. Floyd	112,355	Tuck, William M.	4,042	59,969 D	31.0%	66.6%	31.8%	68.2%

In 1973 other vote was 510,103 Independent (Howell) and 317 scattered.

VIRGINIA

POSTWAR VOTE FOR SENATOR

Year	Total Vote	Republican Vote	Candidate	Democratic Vote	Candidate	Other Vote	Rep-Dem. Plurality	Total Vote Rep.	Dem.	Major Vote Rep.	Dem.
1990	1,083,690	876,782	Warner, John	—		206,908	876,782 R	80.9%		100.0%	
1988	2,068,897	593,652	Dawkins, Maurice A.	1,474,086	Robb, Charles S.	1,159	880,434 D	28.7%	71.2%	28.7%	71.3%
1984	2,007,487	1,406,194	Warner, John	601,142	Harrison, Edythe C.	151	805,052 R	70.0%	29.9%	70.1%	29.9%
1982	1,415,622	724,571	Trible, Paul	690,839	Davis, Richard	212	33,732 R	51.2%	48.8%	51.2%	48.8%
1978	1,222,256	613,232	Warner, John	608,511	Miller, Andrew P.	513	4,721 R	50.2%	49.8%	50.2%	49.8%
1976 **	1,557,500		—	596,009	Zumwalt, Elmo R.	961,491	596,009 D		38.3%		100.0%
1972	1,396,268	718,337	Scott, William L.	643,963	Spong, William B.	33,968	74,374 R	51.4%	46.1%	52.7%	47.3%
1970 **	946,751	145,031	Garland, Ray	295,057	Rawlings, George C.	506,663	150,026 D	15.3%	31.2%	33.0%	67.0%
1966	733,879	245,681	Ould, James P.	429,855	Spong, William B.	58,343	184,174 D	33.5%	58.6%	36.4%	63.6%
1966 S	729,839	272,804	Traylor, Lawrence M.	389,028	Byrd, Harry Flood, Jr.	68,007	116,224 D	37.4%	53.3%	41.2%	58.8%
1964	928,363	176,624	May, Richard A.	592,260	Byrd, Harry Flood	159,479	415,636 D	19.0%	63.8%	23.0%	77.0%
1960	622,820		—	506,169	Robertson, A. Willis	116,651	506,169 D		81.3%		100.0%
1958	457,640		—	317,221	Byrd, Harry Flood	140,419	317,221 D		69.3%		100.0%
1954	306,510		—	244,844	Robertson, A. Willis	61,666	244,844 D		79.9%		100.0%
1952	543,516		—	398,677	Byrd, Harry Flood	144,839	398,677 D		73.4%		100.0%
1948	386,178	118,546	Woods, Robert	253,865	Robertson, A. Willis	13,767	135,319 D	30.7%	65.7%	31.8%	68.2%
1946	252,863	77,005	Parsons, Lester S.	163,960	Byrd, Harry Flood	11,898	86,955 D	30.5%	64.8%	32.0%	68.0%
1946 S	248,962	72,253	Woods, Robert	169,680	Robertson, A. Willis	7,029	97,427 D	29.0%	68.2%	29.9%	70.1%

One each of the 1966 and 1946 elections was for a short term to fill a vacancy. In 1970 Harry Flood Byrd, Jr., the Independent candidate, polled 506,633 votes (53.5% of the total vote) and won the election with a 211,576 plurality. In 1976 Harry Flood Byrd, Jr., polled 890,778 votes as an Independent candidate (57.2% of the total vote) and won the election with a 294,769 plurality.

449

VIRGINIA

Districts Established June 12, 1981

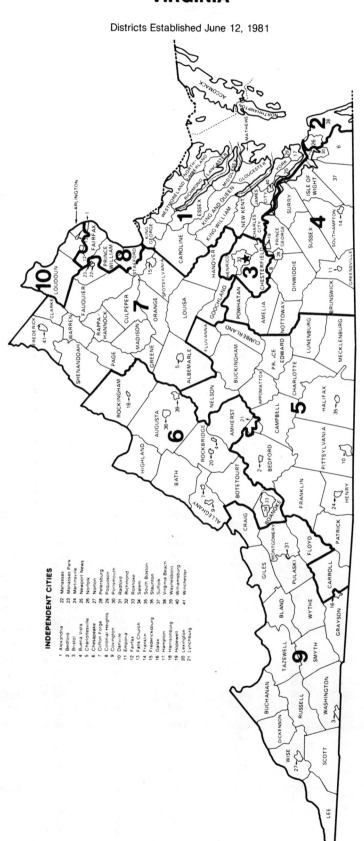

INDEPENDENT CITIES

1 Alexandria	22 Manassas
2 Bedford	23 Manassas Park
3 Bristol	24 Martinsville
4 Buena Vista	25 Newport News
5 Charlottesville	26 Norfolk
6 Chesapeake	27 Norton
7 Clifton Forge	28 Petersburg
8 Colonial Heights	29 Poquoson
9 Covington	30 Portsmouth
10 Danville	31 Radford
11 Emporia	32 Richmond
12 Fairfax	33 Roanoke
13 Falls Church	34 Salem
14 Franklin	35 South Boston
15 Fredericksburg	36 Staunton
16 Galax	37 Suffolk
17 Hampton	38 Virginia Beach
18 Harrisonburg	39 Waynesboro
19 Hopewell	40 Williamsburg
20 Lexington	41 Winchester
21 Lynchburg	

© ERC

VIRGINIA
GOVERNOR 1989

1990 Census Population	County	Total Vote	Republican	Democratic	Other	Rep.-Dem. Plurality	Rep. (Total Vote)	Dem. (Total Vote)	Rep. (Major Vote)	Dem. (Major Vote)
31,703	ACCOMACK	10,608	5,838	4,767	3	1,071 R	55.0%	44.9%	55.0%	45.0%
68,040	ALBEMARLE	20,776	9,998	10,743	35	745 D	48.1%	51.7%	48.2%	51.8%
13,176	ALLEGHANY	4,655	2,342	2,313		29 R	50.3%	49.7%	50.3%	49.7%
8,787	AMELIA	3,448	1,937	1,509	2	428 R	56.2%	43.8%	56.2%	43.8%
28,578	AMHERST	8,969	4,965	4,000	4	965 R	55.4%	44.6%	55.4%	44.6%
12,298	APPOMATTOX	4,849	2,528	2,321		207 R	52.1%	47.9%	52.1%	47.9%
170,936	ARLINGTON	53,212	17,452	35,716	44	18,264 D	32.8%	67.1%	32.8%	67.2%
54,677	AUGUSTA	14,664	10,146	4,502	16	5,644 R	69.2%	30.7%	69.3%	30.7%
4,799	BATH	1,672	900	770	2	130 R	53.8%	46.1%	53.9%	46.1%
45,656	BEDFORD COUNTY	13,972	8,094	5,871	7	2,223 R	57.9%	42.0%	58.0%	42.0%
6,514	BLAND	1,948	1,287	661		626 R	66.1%	33.9%	66.1%	33.9%
24,992	BOTETOURT	8,542	4,539	3,998	5	541 R	53.1%	46.8%	53.2%	46.8%
15,987	BRUNSWICK	5,674	2,493	3,181		688 D	43.9%	56.1%	43.9%	56.1%
31,333	BUCHANAN	9,553	3,875	5,678		1,803 D	40.6%	59.4%	40.6%	59.4%
12,873	BUCKINGHAM	4,531	2,515	2,014	2	501 R	55.5%	44.4%	55.5%	44.5%
47,572	CAMPBELL	15,658	9,611	6,043	4	3,568 R	61.4%	38.6%	61.4%	38.6%
19,217	CAROLINE	5,891	2,658	3,232	1	574 D	45.1%	54.9%	45.1%	54.9%
26,594	CARROLL	7,301	4,926	2,375		2,551 R	67.5%	32.5%	67.5%	32.5%
6,282	CHARLES CITY	2,605	554	2,050	1	1,496 D	21.3%	78.7%	21.3%	78.7%
11,688	CHARLOTTE	4,626	2,552	2,072	2	480 R	55.2%	44.8%	55.2%	44.8%
209,274	CHESTERFIELD	67,606	43,656	23,799	151	19,857 R	64.6%	35.2%	64.7%	35.3%
12,101	CLARKE	2,940	1,546	1,394		152 R	52.6%	47.4%	52.6%	47.4%
4,372	CRAIG	1,674	902	766	6	136 R	53.9%	45.8%	54.1%	45.9%
27,791	CULPEPER	6,902	4,230	2,670	2	1,560 R	61.3%	38.7%	61.3%	38.7%
7,825	CUMBERLAND	3,035	1,617	1,418		199 R	53.3%	46.7%	53.3%	46.7%
17,620	DICKENSON	5,673	2,131	3,536	6	1,405 D	37.6%	62.3%	37.6%	62.4%
20,960	DINWIDDIE	6,997	3,676	3,321		355 R	52.5%	47.5%	52.5%	47.5%
8,689	ESSEX	3,069	1,694	1,373	2	321 R	55.2%	44.7%	55.2%	44.8%
818,584	FAIRFAX COUNTY	227,711	99,957	127,236	518	27,279 D	43.9%	55.9%	44.0%	56.0%
48,741	FAUQUIER	12,249	6,700	5,545	4	1,155 R	54.7%	45.3%	54.7%	45.3%
12,005	FLOYD	3,954	2,387	1,566	1	821 R	60.4%	39.6%	60.4%	39.6%
12,429	FLUVANNA	3,621	2,063	1,554	4	509 R	57.0%	42.9%	57.0%	43.0%
39,549	FRANKLIN COUNTY	11,201	6,037	5,158	6	879 R	53.9%	46.0%	53.9%	46.1%
45,723	FREDERICK	10,330	6,581	3,746	3	2,835 R	63.7%	36.3%	63.7%	36.3%
16,366	GILES	5,038	2,468	2,568	2	100 D	49.0%	51.0%	49.0%	51.0%
30,131	GLOUCESTER	10,036	5,765	4,258	13	1,507 R	57.4%	42.4%	57.5%	42.5%
14,163	GOOCHLAND	5,567	3,092	2,473	2	619 R	55.5%	44.4%	55.6%	44.4%
16,278	GRAYSON	5,098	3,337	1,761		1,576 R	65.5%	34.5%	65.5%	34.5%
10,297	GREENE	2,589	1,726	863		863 R	66.7%	33.3%	66.7%	33.3%
8,853	GREENSVILLE	3,388	1,435	1,952	1	517 D	42.4%	57.6%	42.4%	57.6%
29,033	HALIFAX	9,769	5,205	4,562	2	643 R	53.3%	46.7%	53.3%	46.7%
63,306	HANOVER	23,975	16,552	7,391	32	9,161 R	69.0%	30.8%	69.1%	30.9%
217,881	HENRICO	80,042	46,947	32,939	156	14,008 R	58.7%	41.2%	58.8%	41.2%
56,942	HENRY	16,089	9,414	6,674	1	2,740 R	58.5%	41.5%	58.5%	41.5%
2,635	HIGHLAND	1,065	626	437	2	189 R	58.8%	41.0%	58.9%	41.1%
25,053	ISLE OF WIGHT	8,799	4,442	4,353	4	89 R	50.5%	49.5%	50.5%	49.5%
34,859	JAMES CITY	11,692	5,850	5,827	15	23 R	50.0%	49.8%	50.1%	49.9%
6,289	KING AND QUEEN	2,400	1,119	1,278	3	159 D	46.6%	53.3%	46.7%	53.3%
13,527	KING GEORGE	3,383	1,819	1,563	1	256 R	53.8%	46.2%	53.8%	46.2%
10,913	KING WILLIAM	4,061	2,265	1,794	2	471 R	55.8%	44.2%	55.8%	44.2%
10,896	LANCASTER	4,673	2,838	1,834		1,004 R	60.7%	39.2%	60.7%	39.3%
24,496	LEE	6,286	2,830	3,431	1	601 D	45.0%	54.6%	45.2%	54.8%
86,129	LOUDOUN	21,623	10,555	11,065	25	510 D	48.8%	51.2%	48.8%	51.2%
20,325	LOUISA	6,347	3,416	2,931	3	485 R	53.8%	46.2%	53.8%	46.2%
11,419	LUNENBURG	4,148	2,248	1,896		352 R	54.2%	45.7%	54.2%	45.8%
11,949	MADISON	3,570	2,121	1,448	4	673 R	59.4%	40.6%	59.4%	40.6%
8,348	MATHEWS	3,728	2,193	1,534	1	659 R	58.8%	41.1%	58.8%	41.2%
29,241	MECKLENBURG	8,663	5,373	3,287	1	2,086 R	62.0%	37.9%	62.0%	38.0%
8,653	MIDDLESEX	3,667	2,142	1,520	3	622 R	58.4%	41.5%	58.5%	41.5%
73,913	MONTGOMERY	17,634	8,513	9,121	5	608 D	48.3%	51.7%	48.3%	51.7%

VIRGINIA

GOVERNOR 1989

1990 Census Population	County	Total Vote	Republican	Democratic	Other	Rep.-Dem. Plurality	Percentage Total Vote Rep.	Dem.	Major Vote Rep.	Dem.
12,778	NELSON	4,311	1,961	2,341		380 D	45.5%	54.3%	45.6%	54.4%
10,445	NEW KENT	4,222	2,416	1,797	9	619 R	57.2%	42.6%	57.3%	42.7%
13,061	NORTHAMPTON	4,473	1,989	2,482	9	493 D	44.5%	55.5%	44.5%	55.5%
10,524	NORTHUMBERLAND	4,175	2,506	1,669	2	837 R	60.0%	40.0%	60.0%	40.0%
14,993	NOTTOWAY	5,100	2,768	2,331		437 R	54.3%	45.7%	54.3%	45.7%
21,421	ORANGE	5,935	3,468	2,465	1	1,003 R	58.4%	41.5%	58.5%	41.5%
21,690	PAGE	5,685	3,760	1,925	2	1,835 R	66.1%	33.9%	66.1%	33.9%
17,473	PATRICK	5,010	3,246	1,761		1,485 R	64.8%	35.1%	64.8%	35.2%
55,655	PITTSYLVANIA	16,967	10,616	6,349	3	4,267 R	62.6%	37.4%	62.6%	37.4%
15,328	POWHATAN	5,041	3,298	1,741	2	1,557 R	65.4%	34.5%	65.4%	34.6%
17,320	PRINCE EDWARD	5,555	2,732	2,822	2	90 D	49.2%	50.8%	49.2%	50.8%
27,394	PRINCE GEORGE	6,946	4,219	2,693	1	1,526 R	60.7%	38.8%	61.0%	39.0%
215,686	PRINCE WILLIAM	41,437	21,104	20,329	34	775 R	50.9%	49.1%	50.9%	49.1%
34,496	PULASKI	10,322	5,771	4,550	4	1,221 R	55.9%	44.1%	55.9%	44.1%
6,622	RAPPAHANNOCK	2,160	1,188	971	1	217 R	55.0%	45.0%	55.0%	45.0%
7,273	RICHMOND COUNTY	2,453	1,558	887	1	671 R	63.5%	36.2%	63.7%	36.3%
79,332	ROANOKE COUNTY	29,881	15,807	14,074	8	1,733 R	52.9%	47.1%	52.9%	47.1%
18,350	ROCKBRIDGE	5,051	2,713	2,314		399 R	53.7%	45.8%	54.0%	46.0%
57,482	ROCKINGHAM	14,473	10,019	4,452	24	5,567 R	69.2%	30.8%	69.2%	30.8%
28,667	RUSSELL	8,705	3,750	4,955	2	1,205 D	43.1%	56.9%	43.1%	56.9%
23,204	SCOTT	6,532	3,704	2,825		879 R	56.7%	43.2%	56.7%	43.3%
31,636	SHENANDOAH	9,580	6,186	3,390	3	2,796 R	64.6%	35.4%	64.6%	35.4%
32,370	SMYTH	8,995	5,438	3,557	4	1,881 R	60.5%	39.5%	60.5%	39.5%
17,550	SOUTHAMPTON	5,915	2,836	3,074		238 D	47.9%	52.0%	48.0%	52.0%
57,403	SPOTSYLVANIA	13,177	7,646	5,524	5	2,122 R	58.0%	41.9%	58.1%	41.9%
61,236	STAFFORD	14,340	8,565	5,775	7	2,790 R	59.7%	40.3%	59.7%	40.3%
6,145	SURRY	2,758	1,018	1,740		722 D	36.9%	63.1%	36.9%	63.1%
10,248	SUSSEX	3,815	1,561	2,251		690 D	40.9%	59.0%	40.9%	59.1%
45,960	TAZEWELL	11,170	5,831	5,338	3	493 R	52.2%	47.8%	52.2%	47.8%
26,142	WARREN	6,245	3,564	2,681	1	883 R	57.1%	42.9%	57.1%	42.9%
45,887	WASHINGTON	13,794	8,219	5,572		2,647 R	59.6%	40.4%	59.6%	40.4%
15,480	WESTMORELAND	4,522	2,322	2,197	3	125 R	51.3%	48.6%	51.4%	48.6%
39,573	WISE	11,136	4,495	6,641	3	2,146 D	40.4%	59.6%	40.4%	59.6%
25,466	WYTHE	7,800	4,970	2,817		2,153 R	63.7%	36.1%	63.8%	36.2%
42,422	YORK	13,284	7,283	6,001	13	1,282 R	54.8%	45.2%	54.8%	45.2%
	City									
111,183	ALEXANDRIA	33,021	10,493	22,451	77	11,958 D	31.8%	68.0%	31.9%	68.1%
6,073	BEDFORD CITY	1,998	1,035	961	2	74 R	51.8%	48.1%	51.9%	48.1%
18,426	BRISTOL	5,033	2,920	2,109	4	811 R	58.0%	41.9%	58.1%	41.9%
6,406	BUENA VISTA	1,698	823	869	6	46 D	48.5%	51.2%	48.6%	51.4%
40,341	CHARLOTTESVILLE	10,818	3,902	6,892	24	2,990 D	36.1%	63.7%	36.1%	63.9%
151,976	CHESAPEAKE	42,484	21,076	21,384	24	308 D	49.6%	50.3%	49.6%	50.4%
4,679	CLIFTON FORGE	1,588	676	912		236 D	42.6%	57.4%	42.6%	57.4%
16,064	COLONIAL HEIGHTS	6,523	4,954	1,568	1	3,386 R	75.9%	24.0%	76.0%	24.0%
6,991	COVINGTON	2,740	1,169	1,570	1	401 D	42.7%	57.3%	42.7%	57.3%
53,056	DANVILLE	17,169	10,223	6,944	2	3,279 R	59.5%	40.4%	59.6%	40.4%
5,306	EMPORIA	2,344	1,249	1,094	1	155 R	53.3%	46.7%	53.3%	46.7%
19,622	FAIRFAX CITY	6,431	3,027	3,398	6	371 D	47.1%	52.8%	47.1%	52.9%
9,578	FALLS CHURCH	4,149	1,530	2,617	2	1,087 D	36.9%	63.1%	36.9%	63.1%
7,864	FRANKLIN CITY	3,011	1,146	1,865		719 D	38.1%	61.9%	38.1%	61.9%
19,027	FREDERICKSBURG	4,839	2,321	2,515	3	194 D	48.0%	52.0%	48.0%	52.0%
6,670	GALAX	1,702	1,077	625		452 R	63.3%	36.7%	63.3%	36.7%
133,793	HAMPTON	38,608	15,489	23,097	22	7,608 D	40.1%	59.8%	40.1%	59.9%
30,707	HARRISONBURG	6,221	3,562	2,647	12	915 R	57.3%	42.5%	57.4%	42.6%
23,101	HOPEWELL	6,900	4,119	2,781		1,338 R	59.7%	40.3%	59.7%	40.3%
6,959	LEXINGTON	1,784	740	1,043	1	303 D	41.5%	58.5%	41.5%	58.5%
66,049	LYNCHBURG	20,991	10,927	10,060	4	867 R	52.1%	47.9%	52.1%	47.9%
27,957	MANASSAS	5,616	2,947	2,663	6	284 R	52.5%	47.4%	52.5%	47.5%
6,734	MANASSAS PARK	846	460	385	1	75 R	54.4%	45.5%	54.4%	45.6%
16,162	MARTINSVILLE	5,541	2,777	2,763	1	14 R	50.1%	49.9%	50.1%	49.9%
170,045	NEWPORT NEWS	46,581	21,261	25,284	36	4,023 D	45.6%	54.3%	45.7%	54.3%

VIRGINIA

GOVERNOR 1989

1990 Census Population	City	Total Vote	Republican	Democratic	Other	Rep.-Dem. Plurality	Percentage Total Vote Rep.	Dem.	Major Vote Rep.	Dem.
261,229	NORFOLK	57,291	19,385	37,844	62	18,459 D	33.8%	66.1%	33.9%	66.1%
4,247	NORTON	1,234	423	808	3	385 D	34.3%	65.5%	34.4%	65.6%
38,386	PETERSBURG	11,850	3,454	8,394	2	4,940 D	29.1%	70.8%	29.2%	70.8%
11,005	POQUOSON	3,981	2,626	1,353	2	1,273 R	66.0%	34.0%	66.0%	34.0%
103,907	PORTSMOUTH	32,284	12,281	19,998	5	7,717 D	38.0%	61.9%	38.0%	62.0%
15,940	RADFORD	4,075	1,980	2,092	3	112 D	48.6%	51.3%	48.6%	51.4%
203,056	RICHMOND CITY	72,819	23,239	49,513	67	26,274 D	31.9%	68.0%	31.9%	68.1%
96,397	ROANOKE CITY	28,095	11,483	16,590	22	5,107 D	40.9%	59.0%	40.9%	59.1%
23,756	SALEM	8,005	4,143	3,854	8	289 R	51.8%	48.1%	51.8%	48.2%
6,997	SOUTH BOSTON	2,430	1,441	987	2	454 R	59.3%	40.6%	59.3%	40.7%
24,461	STAUNTON	7,263	4,512	2,748	3	1,764 R	62.1%	37.8%	62.1%	37.9%
52,141	SUFFOLK	16,639	7,893	8,743	3	850 D	47.4%	52.5%	47.4%	52.6%
393,069	VIRGINIA BEACH	86,167	44,332	41,570	265	2,762 R	51.4%	48.2%	51.6%	48.4%
18,549	WAYNESBORO	5,744	3,637	2,102	5	1,535 R	63.3%	36.6%	63.4%	36.6%
11,530	WILLIAMSBURG	2,667	1,026	1,641		615 D	38.5%	61.5%	38.5%	61.5%
21,947	WINCHESTER	5,487	3,232	2,253	2	979 R	58.9%	41.1%	58.9%	41.1%
6,187,358	TOTAL	1,789,078	890,195	896,936	1,947	6,741 D	49.8%	50.1%	49.8%	50.2%

VIRGINIA

SENATOR 1990

1990 Census Population	County	Total Vote	Republican	Democratic	Other	Rep.-Dem. Plurality	Percentage Total Vote Rep.	Dem.	Major Vote Rep.	Dem.
31,703	ACCOMACK	6,917	5,344		1,573	5,344 R	77.3%		100.0%	
68,040	ALBEMARLE	14,426	11,415		3,011	11,415 R	79.1%		100.0%	
13,176	ALLEGHANY	2,189	1,925		264	1,925 R	87.9%		100.0%	
8,787	AMELIA	1,638	1,330		308	1,330 R	81.2%		100.0%	
28,578	AMHERST	4,998	3,997		1,001	3,997 R	80.0%		100.0%	
12,298	APPOMATTOX	2,018	1,700		318	1,700 R	84.2%		100.0%	
170,936	ARLINGTON	34,440	28,281		6,159	28,281 R	82.1%		100.0%	
54,677	AUGUSTA	8,032	6,672		1,360	6,672 R	83.1%		100.0%	
4,799	BATH	792	684		108	684 R	86.4%		100.0%	
45,656	BEDFORD COUNTY	7,764	6,590		1,174	6,590 R	84.9%		100.0%	
6,514	BLAND	1,272	1,080		192	1,080 R	84.9%		100.0%	
24,992	BOTETOURT	4,454	3,819		635	3,819 R	85.7%		100.0%	
15,987	BRUNSWICK	2,196	1,840		356	1,840 R	83.8%		100.0%	
31,333	BUCHANAN	2,475	2,023		452	2,023 R	81.7%		100.0%	
12,873	BUCKINGHAM	1,809	1,521		288	1,521 R	84.1%		100.0%	
47,572	CAMPBELL	6,969	5,939		1,030	5,939 R	85.2%		100.0%	
19,217	CAROLINE	3,163	1,909		1,254	1,909 R	60.4%		100.0%	
26,594	CARROLL	4,682	3,683		999	3,683 R	78.7%		100.0%	
6,282	CHARLES CITY	905	585		320	585 R	64.6%		100.0%	
11,688	CHARLOTTE	2,051	1,715		336	1,715 R	83.6%		100.0%	
209,274	CHESTERFIELD	40,192	31,861		8,331	31,861 R	79.3%		100.0%	
12,101	CLARKE	2,315	1,838		477	1,838 R	79.4%		100.0%	
4,372	CRAIG	1,012	782		230	782 R	77.3%		100.0%	
27,791	CULPEPER	4,898	4,199		699	4,199 R	85.7%		100.0%	
7,825	CUMBERLAND	1,046	934		112	934 R	89.3%		100.0%	
17,620	DICKENSON	2,280	1,482		798	1,482 R	65.0%		100.0%	
20,960	DINWIDDIE	3,055	2,297		758	2,297 R	75.2%		100.0%	
8,689	ESSEX	1,779	1,383		396	1,383 R	77.7%		100.0%	
818,584	FAIRFAX COUNTY	191,271	153,038		38,233	153,038 R	80.0%		100.0%	
48,741	FAUQUIER	9,571	8,114		1,457	8,114 R	84.8%		100.0%	
12,005	FLOYD	1,666	1,382		284	1,382 R	83.0%		100.0%	
12,429	FLUVANNA	1,864	1,483		381	1,483 R	79.6%		100.0%	
39,549	FRANKLIN COUNTY	6,469	5,316		1,153	5,316 R	82.2%		100.0%	
45,723	FREDERICK	9,123	7,752		1,371	7,752 R	85.0%		100.0%	
16,366	GILES	3,866	3,334		532	3,334 R	86.2%		100.0%	
30,131	GLOUCESTER	6,127	5,120		1,007	5,120 R	83.6%		100.0%	
14,163	GOOCHLAND	2,885	2,321		564	2,321 R	80.5%		100.0%	
16,278	GRAYSON	2,421	1,887		534	1,887 R	77.9%		100.0%	
10,297	GREENE	1,677	1,445		232	1,445 R	86.2%		100.0%	
8,853	GREENSVILLE	1,478	1,225		253	1,225 R	82.9%		100.0%	
29,033	HALIFAX	3,224	2,861		363	2,861 R	88.7%		100.0%	
63,306	HANOVER	14,765	11,802		2,963	11,802 R	79.9%		100.0%	
217,881	HENRICO	43,317	35,212		8,105	35,212 R	81.3%		100.0%	
56,942	HENRY	7,392	6,374		1,018	6,374 R	86.2%		100.0%	
2,635	HIGHLAND	623	471		152	471 R	75.6%		100.0%	
25,053	ISLE OF WIGHT	4,312	3,649		663	3,649 R	84.6%		100.0%	
34,859	JAMES CITY	7,897	6,457		1,440	6,457 R	81.8%		100.0%	
6,289	KING AND QUEEN	1,294	940		354	940 R	72.6%		100.0%	
13,527	KING GEORGE	2,522	1,822		700	1,822 R	72.2%		100.0%	
10,913	KING WILLIAM	2,308	1,791		517	1,791 R	77.6%		100.0%	
10,896	LANCASTER	2,896	2,491		405	2,491 R	86.0%		100.0%	
24,496	LEE	3,151	2,294		857	2,294 R	72.8%		100.0%	
86,129	LOUDOUN	15,840	13,427		2,413	13,427 R	84.8%		100.0%	
20,325	LOUISA	3,616	2,648		968	2,648 R	73.2%		100.0%	
11,419	LUNENBURG	1,761	1,574		187	1,574 R	89.4%		100.0%	
11,949	MADISON	2,371	2,030		341	2,030 R	85.6%		100.0%	
8,348	MATHEWS	2,405	2,089		316	2,089 R	86.9%		100.0%	
29,241	MECKLENBURG	3,969	3,589		380	3,589 R	90.4%		100.0%	
8,653	MIDDLESEX	2,246	1,893		353	1,893 R	84.3%		100.0%	
73,913	MONTGOMERY	10,124	7,857		2,267	7,857 R	77.6%		100.0%	

VIRGINIA

SENATOR 1990

1990 Census Population	County	Total Vote	Republican	Democratic	Other	Rep.-Dem. Plurality	Percentage Total Vote Rep.	Dem.	Major Vote Rep.	Dem.
12,778	NELSON	2,573	2,019		554	2,019 R	78.5%		100.0%	
10,445	NEW KENT	2,521	1,937		584	1,937 R	76.8%		100.0%	
13,061	NORTHAMPTON	2,541	2,059		482	2,059 R	81.0%		100.0%	
10,524	NORTHUMBERLAND	2,414	1,964		450	1,964 R	81.4%		100.0%	
14,993	NOTTOWAY	2,232	1,934		298	1,934 R	86.6%		100.0%	
21,421	ORANGE	3,749	3,165		584	3,165 R	84.4%		100.0%	
21,690	PAGE	4,447	3,423		1,024	3,423 R	77.0%		100.0%	
17,473	PATRICK	4,077	3,641		436	3,641 R	89.3%		100.0%	
55,655	PITTSYLVANIA	7,264	6,419		845	6,419 R	88.4%		100.0%	
15,328	POWHATAN	2,421	1,793		628	1,793 R	74.1%		100.0%	
17,320	PRINCE EDWARD	2,140	1,875		265	1,875 R	87.6%		100.0%	
27,394	PRINCE GEORGE	3,429	2,348		1,081	2,348 R	68.5%		100.0%	
215,686	PRINCE WILLIAM	32,878	26,661		6,217	26,661 R	81.1%		100.0%	
34,496	PULASKI	6,179	5,576		603	5,576 R	90.2%		100.0%	
6,622	RAPPAHANNOCK	1,683	1,295		388	1,295 R	76.9%		100.0%	
7,273	RICHMOND COUNTY	1,412	1,174		238	1,174 R	83.1%		100.0%	
79,332	ROANOKE COUNTY	30,296	25,845		4,451	25,845 R	85.3%		100.0%	
18,350	ROCKBRIDGE	2,699	2,345		354	2,345 R	86.9%		100.0%	
57,482	ROCKINGHAM	8,483	7,087		1,396	7,087 R	83.5%		100.0%	
28,667	RUSSELL	2,700	2,174		526	2,174 R	80.5%		100.0%	
23,204	SCOTT	2,963	2,416		547	2,416 R	81.5%		100.0%	
31,636	SHENANDOAH	7,828	6,382		1,446	6,382 R	81.5%		100.0%	
32,370	SMYTH	4,154	3,666		488	3,666 R	88.3%		100.0%	
17,550	SOUTHAMPTON	2,678	2,273		405	2,273 R	84.9%		100.0%	
57,403	SPOTSYLVANIA	10,605	8,105		2,500	8,105 R	76.4%		100.0%	
61,236	STAFFORD	10,630	8,096		2,534	8,096 R	76.2%		100.0%	
6,145	SURRY	1,292	1,054		238	1,054 R	81.6%		100.0%	
10,248	SUSSEX	1,557	1,379		178	1,379 R	88.6%		100.0%	
45,960	TAZEWELL	5,813	4,817		996	4,817 R	82.9%		100.0%	
26,142	WARREN	4,325	3,543		782	3,543 R	81.9%		100.0%	
45,887	WASHINGTON	5,579	4,877		702	4,877 R	87.4%		100.0%	
15,480	WESTMORELAND	2,541	2,012		529	2,012 R	79.2%		100.0%	
39,573	WISE	3,840	3,150		690	3,150 R	82.0%		100.0%	
25,466	WYTHE	3,403	3,049		354	3,049 R	89.6%		100.0%	
42,422	YORK	10,622	8,533		2,089	8,533 R	80.3%		100.0%	
	City									
111,183	ALEXANDRIA	25,734	19,835		5,899	19,835 R	77.1%		100.0%	
6,073	BEDFORD CITY	986	863		123	863 R	87.5%		100.0%	
18,426	BRISTOL	2,464	1,902		562	1,902 R	77.2%		100.0%	
6,406	BUENA VISTA	747	658		89	658 R	88.1%		100.0%	
40,341	CHARLOTTESVILLE	6,861	5,051		1,810	5,051 R	73.6%		100.0%	
151,976	CHESAPEAKE	18,856	14,548		4,308	14,548 R	77.2%		100.0%	
4,679	CLIFTON FORGE	726	645		81	645 R	88.8%		100.0%	
16,064	COLONIAL HEIGHTS	4,944	4,002		942	4,002 R	80.9%		100.0%	
6,991	COVINGTON	1,252	1,084		168	1,084 R	86.6%		100.0%	
53,056	DANVILLE	7,019	6,193		826	6,193 R	88.2%		100.0%	
5,306	EMPORIA	1,101	933		168	933 R	84.7%		100.0%	
19,622	FAIRFAX CITY	4,781	4,096		685	4,096 R	85.7%		100.0%	
9,578	FALLS CHURCH	2,805	2,174		631	2,174 R	77.5%		100.0%	
7,864	FRANKLIN CITY	1,393	1,181		212	1,181 R	84.8%		100.0%	
19,027	FREDERICKSBURG	3,136	2,411		725	2,411 R	76.9%		100.0%	
6,670	GALAX	899	757		142	757 R	84.2%		100.0%	
133,793	HAMPTON	22,120	17,821		4,299	17,821 R	80.6%		100.0%	
30,707	HARRISONBURG	3,514	2,994		520	2,994 R	85.2%		100.0%	
23,101	HOPEWELL	2,942	2,421		521	2,421 R	82.3%		100.0%	
6,959	LEXINGTON	894	788		106	788 R	88.1%		100.0%	
66,049	LYNCHBURG	9,448	8,273		1,175	8,273 R	87.6%		100.0%	
27,957	MANASSAS	4,359	3,456		903	3,456 R	79.3%		100.0%	
6,734	MANASSAS PARK	594	448		146	448 R	75.4%		100.0%	
16,162	MARTINSVILLE	2,331	2,059		272	2,059 R	88.3%		100.0%	
170,045	NEWPORT NEWS	31,815	26,311		5,504	26,311 R	82.7%		100.0%	

VIRGINIA

SENATOR 1990

1990 Census Population	City	Total Vote	Republican	Democratic	Other	Rep.-Dem. Plurality	Percentage Total Vote Rep.	Dem.	Major Vote Rep.	Dem.
261,229	NORFOLK	23,975	18,373		5,602	18,373 R	76.6%		100.0%	
4,247	NORTON	485	394		91	394 R	81.2%		100.0%	
38,386	PETERSBURG	5,368	3,878		1,490	3,878 R	72.2%		100.0%	
11,005	POQUOSON	3,175	2,625		550	2,625 R	82.7%		100.0%	
103,907	PORTSMOUTH	12,441	9,803		2,638	9,803 R	78.8%		100.0%	
15,940	RADFORD	1,760	1,433		327	1,433 R	81.4%		100.0%	
203,056	RICHMOND CITY	28,176	21,470		6,706	21,470 R	76.2%		100.0%	
96,397	ROANOKE CITY	22,142	18,233		3,909	18,233 R	82.3%		100.0%	
23,756	SALEM	6,829	5,812		1,017	5,812 R	85.1%		100.0%	
6,997	SOUTH BOSTON	950	806		144	806 R	84.8%		100.0%	
24,461	STAUNTON	3,481	2,960		521	2,960 R	85.0%		100.0%	
52,141	SUFFOLK	7,675	6,281		1,394	6,281 R	81.8%		100.0%	
393,069	VIRGINIA BEACH	47,986	37,249		10,737	37,249 R	77.6%		100.0%	
18,549	WAYNESBORO	3,202	2,733		469	2,733 R	85.4%		100.0%	
11,530	WILLIAMSBURG	1,627	1,321		306	1,321 R	81.2%		100.0%	
21,947	WINCHESTER	4,511	3,905		606	3,905 R	86.6%		100.0%	
6,187,358	TOTAL	1,083,690	876,782		206,908	876,782 R	80.9%		100.0%	

VIRGINIA

CONGRESS

CD	Year	Total Vote	Republican Vote	Republican Candidate	Democratic Vote	Democratic Candidate	Other Vote	Rep.-Dem. Plurality	Total Vote Rep.	Total Vote Dem.	Major Vote Rep.	Major Vote Dem.
1	1990	141,293	72,000	BATEMAN, HERBERT H.	69,194	FOX, ANDREW H.	99	2,806 R	51.0%	49.0%	51.0%	49.0%
1	1988	185,573	135,937	BATEMAN, HERBERT H.	49,614	ELLENSON, JAMES S.	22	86,323 R	73.3%	26.7%	73.3%	26.7%
1	1986	144,086	80,713	BATEMAN, HERBERT H.	63,364	SCOTT, ROBERT C.	9	17,349 R	56.0%	44.0%	56.0%	44.0%
1	1984	199,822	118,085	BATEMAN, HERBERT H.	79,577	MCGLENNON, JOHN J.	2,160	38,508 R	59.1%	39.8%	59.7%	40.3%
1	1982	142,802	76,926	BATEMAN, HERBERT H.	62,379	MCGLENNON, JOHN J.	3,497	14,547 R	53.9%	43.7%	55.2%	44.8%
2	1990	73,618			55,179	PICKETT, OWEN B.	18,439	55,179 D		75.0%		100.0%
2	1988	176,208	62,564	CURRY, JERRY R.	106,666	PICKETT, OWEN B.	6,978	44,102 D	35.5%	60.5%	37.0%	63.0%
2	1986	110,169	46,137	CANADA, A. J.	54,491	PICKETT, OWEN B.	9,541	8,354 D	41.9%	49.5%	45.8%	54.2%
2	1984	136,888	136,632	WHITEHURST, G. W.			256	136,632 R	99.8%		100.0%	
2	1982	78,205	78,108	WHITEHURST, G. W.			97	78,108 R	99.9%		100.0%	
3	1990	118,154	77,125	BLILEY, THOMAS J.	36,253	STARKE, JAMES A.	4,776	40,872 R	65.3%	30.7%	68.0%	32.0%
3	1988	187,898	187,354	BLILEY, THOMAS J.			544	187,354 R	99.7%		100.0%	
3	1986	111,179	74,525	BLILEY, THOMAS J.	32,961	POWELL, KENNETH E.	3,693	41,564 R	67.0%	29.6%	69.3%	30.7%
3	1984	198,567	169,987	BLILEY, THOMAS J.			28,580	169,987 R	85.6%		100.0%	
3	1982	156,891	92,928	BLILEY, THOMAS J.	63,946	WALDROP, JOHN A.	17	28,982 R	59.2%	40.8%	59.2%	40.8%
4	1990	90,731			71,051	SISISKY, NORMAN	19,680	71,051 D		78.3%		100.0%
4	1988	134,884			134,786	SISISKY, NORMAN	98	134,786 D		99.9%		100.0%
4	1986	64,835			64,699	SISISKY, NORMAN	136	64,699 D		99.8%		100.0%
4	1984	120,162			120,093	SISISKY, NORMAN	69	120,093 D		99.9%		100.0%
4	1982	148,406	67,708	DANIEL, ROBERT W.	80,695	SISISKY, NORMAN	3	12,987 D	45.6%	54.4%	45.6%	54.4%
5	1990	66,905			66,532	PAYNE, L. F.	373	66,532 D		99.4%		100.0%
5	1988	179,442	78,396	HAWKINS, CHARLES	97,242	PAYNE, L. F.	3,804	18,846 D	43.7%	54.2%	44.6%	55.4%
5	1986	89,653			73,085	DANIEL, W. C.	16,568	73,085 D		81.5%		100.0%
5	1984	117,778			117,738	DANIEL, W. C.	40	117,738 D		100.0%		100.0%
5	1982	88,324			88,293	DANIEL, W. C.	31	88,293 D		100.0%		100.0%
6	1990	112,377			92,968	OLIN, JAMES R.	19,409	92,968 D		82.7%		100.0%
6	1988	185,312	66,935	JUDD, CHARLES E.	118,369	OLIN, JAMES R.	8	51,434 D	36.1%	63.9%	36.1%	63.9%
6	1986	126,310	38,051	TRAYWICK, FLO N.	88,230	OLIN, JAMES R.	29	50,179 D	30.1%	69.9%	30.1%	69.9%
6	1984	196,560	91,344	GARLAND, RAY L	105,207	OLIN, JAMES R.	9	13,863 D	46.5%	53.5%	46.5%	53.5%
6	1982	137,140	66,537	MILLER, KEVIN G.	68,192	OLIN, JAMES R.	2,411	1,655 D	48.5%	49.7%	49.4%	50.6%
7	1990	140,620	81,688	SLAUGHTER, D. FRENCH	58,684	SMITH, DAVID M.	248	23,004 R	58.1%	41.7%	58.2%	41.8%
7	1988	137,476	136,988	SLAUGHTER, D. FRENCH			488	136,988 R	99.6%		100.0%	
7	1986	59,976	58,927	SLAUGHTER, D. FRENCH			1,049	58,927 R	98.3%		100.0%	
7	1984	193,156	109,110	SLAUGHTER, D. FRENCH	77,624	COSTELLO, LEWIS M.	6,422	31,486 R	56.5%	40.2%	58.4%	41.6%
7	1982	128,224	76,752	ROBINSON, J. KENNETH	46,514	DORRIER, LINDSAY G.	4,958	30,238 R	59.9%	36.3%	62.3%	37.7%
8	1990	171,121	76,367	PARRIS, STANFORD E.	88,475	MORAN, JAMES P.	6,279	12,108 D	44.6%	51.7%	46.3%	53.7%
8	1988	248,400	154,761	PARRIS, STANFORD E.	93,561	BRICKLEY, DAVID G.	78	61,200 R	62.3%	37.7%	62.3%	37.7%
8	1986	117,655	72,670	PARRIS, STANFORD E.	44,965	BOREN, JAMES H.	20	27,705 R	61.8%	38.2%	61.8%	38.2%
8	1984	224,091	125,015	PARRIS, STANFORD E.	97,250	SASLAW, RICHARD L.	1,826	27,765 R	55.8%	43.4%	56.2%	43.8%
8	1982	140,070	69,620	PARRIS, STANFORD E.	68,071	HARRIS, HERBERT E.	2,379	1,549 R	49.7%	48.6%	50.6%	49.4%
9	1990	69,230			67,215	BOUCHER, FREDERICK C.	2,015	67,215 D		97.1%		100.0%
9	1988	178,727	65,410	BROWN, JOHN C.	113,309	BOUCHER, FREDERICK C.	8	47,899 D	36.6%	63.4%	36.6%	63.4%
9	1986	60,466			59,864	BOUCHER, FREDERICK C.	602	59,864 D		99.0%		100.0%
9	1984	196,956	94,510	STAFFORD, C. JEFFERSON	102,446	BOUCHER, FREDERICK C.		7,936 D	48.0%	52.0%	48.0%	52.0%
9	1982	151,289	75,082	WAMPLER, WILLIAM C.	76,205	BOUCHER, FREDERICK C.	2	1,123 D	49.6%	50.4%	49.6%	50.4%

VIRGINIA

CONGRESS

CD	Year	Total Vote	Republican Vote	Republican Candidate	Democratic Vote	Democratic Candidate	Other Vote	Rep.-Dem. Plurality	Percentage Total Vote Rep.	Dem.	Major Vote Rep.	Dem.
10	1990	168,825	103,761	WOLF, FRANK R.	57,249	CANTER, N. MACKENZIE	7,815	46,512 R	61.5%	33.9%	64.4%	35.6%
10	1988	276,908	188,550	WOLF, FRANK R.	88,284	WEINBERG, ROBERT L.	74	100,266 R	68.1%	31.9%	68.1%	31.9%
10	1986	159,023	95,724	WOLF, FRANK R.	63,292	MILLIKEN, JOHN G.	7	32,432 R	60.2%	39.8%	60.2%	39.8%
10	1984	253,625	158,528	WOLF, FRANK R.	95,074	FLANNERY, JOHN P.	23	63,454 R	62.5%	37.5%	62.5%	37.5%
10	1982	164,035	86,506	WOLF, FRANK R.	75,361	LECHNER, IRA M.	2,168	11,145 R	52.7%	45.9%	53.4%	46.6%
10	1980	216,744	110,840	WOLF, FRANK R.	105,883	FISHER, JOSEPH L.	21	4,957 R	51.1%	48.9%	51.1%	48.9%
10	1978	132,882	61,981	WOLF, FRANK R.	70,892	FISHER, JOSEPH L.	9	8,911 D	46.6%	53.3%	46.6%	53.4%
10	1976	189,489	73,616	CALLAHAN, VINCENT F.	103,689	FISHER, JOSEPH L.	12,184	30,073 D	38.8%	54.7%	41.5%	58.5%
10	1974	125,304	56,649	BROYHILL, JOEL T.	67,184	FISHER, JOSEPH L.	1,471	10,535 D	45.2%	53.6%	45.7%	54.3%
10	1972	179,778	101,138	BROYHILL, JOEL T.	78,638	MILLER, HAROLD O.	2	22,500 R	56.3%	43.7%	56.3%	43.7%

VIRGINIA

Under Virginia's local government system a number of urban areas - 41 since 1977 - are organized as cities independent of county authority.

1989 GENERAL ELECTION

Governor   Other vote was scattered write-in. The data presented in the tabulation for Governor are for the recount. Original return figures were 897,139 Wilder (D) and 890,285 Coleman (R).

1990 GENERAL ELECTION

Senator   Other vote was 196,755 Independent (Spannaus) and 10,153 scattered write-in.

Congress   Other vote was 15,915 Independent (Broskie) and 2,524 scattered write-in in CD 2; 4,317 Independent (Simpson) and 459 scattered write-in in CD 3; 12,295 Independent (McReynolds), 7,102 Independent (Chandler) and 283 scattered write-in in CD 4; 18,148 Independent (Berg) and 1,261 scattered write-in in CD 6; 5,958 Independent (Murphy) and 321 scattered write-in in CD 8; 5,273 Independent (Minnich), 2,293 Independent (LaRouche) and 249 scattered write-in in CD 10; scattered write-in in all other CD's.

1989 PRIMARIES

JUNE 13 REPUBLICAN

Governor   147,941 J. Marshall Coleman; 141,120 Paul S. Trible; 112,826 Stanford E. Parris.

JUNE 13 DEMOCRATIC

Governor   L. Douglas Wilder, nominated by convention.

1990 PRIMARIES

JUNE 12 REPUBLICAN

Senator   John Warner, nominated by convention.

Congress   No candidate in CD's 2, 4, 5, 6 and 9. Candidates nominated by convention in all other CD's.

JUNE 12 DEMOCRATIC

Senator   No candidate.

Congress   Candidates nominated by convention in all CD's.

WASHINGTON

GOVERNOR
Booth Gardner (D). Re-elected 1988 to a four-year term. Previously elected 1984.

SENATORS
Brock Adams (D). Elected 1986 to a six-year term.

Slade Gorton (R). Elected 1988 to a six-year term. Previously elected 1980.

REPRESENTATIVES
1. John R. Miller (R)
2. Al Swift (D)
3. Jolene Unsoeld (D)
4. Sid Morrison (R)
5. Thomas S. Foley (D)
6. Norman D. Dicks (D)
7. Jim McDermott (D)
8. Rod Chandler (R)

POSTWAR VOTE FOR PRESIDENT

Year	Total Vote	Republican Vote	Candidate	Democratic Vote	Candidate	Other Vote	Plurality	Total Vote Rep.	Dem.	Major Vote Rep.	Dem.
1988	1,865,253	903,835	Bush, George	933,516	Dukakis, Michael S.	27,902	29,681 D	48.5%	50.0%	49.2%	50.8%
1984	1,883,910	1,051,670	Reagan, Ronald	807,352	Mondale, Walter F.	24,888	244,318 R	55.8%	42.9%	56.6%	43.4%
1980	1,742,394	865,244	Reagan, Ronald	650,193	Carter, Jimmy	226,957	215,051 R	49.7%	37.3%	57.1%	42.9%
1976	1,555,534	777,732	Ford, Gerald R.	717,323	Carter, Jimmy	60,479	60,409 R	50.0%	46.1%	52.0%	48.0%
1972	1,470,847	837,135	Nixon, Richard M.	568,334	McGovern, George S.	65,378	268,801 R	56.9%	38.6%	59.6%	40.4%
1968	1,304,281	588,510	Nixon, Richard M.	616,037	Humphrey, Hubert H.	99,734	27,527 D	45.1%	47.2%	48.9%	51.1%
1964	1,258,556	470,366	Goldwater, Barry M.	779,881	Johnson, Lyndon B.	8,309	309,515 D	37.4%	62.0%	37.6%	62.4%
1960	1,241,572	629,273	Nixon, Richard M.	599,298	Kennedy, John F.	13,001	29,975 R	50.7%	48.3%	51.2%	48.8%
1956	1,150,889	620,430	Eisenhower, Dwight D.	523,002	Stevenson, Adlai E.	7,457	97,428 R	53.9%	45.4%	54.3%	45.7%
1952	1,102,708	599,107	Eisenhower, Dwight D.	492,845	Stevenson, Adlai E.	10,756	106,262 R	54.3%	44.7%	54.9%	45.1%
1948	905,058	386,314	Dewey, Thomas E.	476,165	Truman, Harry S.	42,579	89,851 D	42.7%	52.6%	44.8%	55.2%

POSTWAR VOTE FOR GOVERNOR

Year	Total Vote	Republican Vote	Candidate	Democratic Vote	Candidate	Other Vote	Rep-Dem. Plurality	Total Vote Rep.	Dem.	Major Vote Rep.	Dem.
1988	1,874,929	708,481	Williams, Bob	1,166,448	Gardner, Booth		457,967 D	37.8%	62.2%	37.8%	62.2%
1984	1,888,987	881,994	Spellman, John D.	1,006,993	Gardner, Booth		124,999 D	46.7%	53.3%	46.7%	53.3%
1980	1,730,896	981,083	Spellman, John D.	749,813	McDermott, James A.		231,270 R	56.7%	43.3%	56.7%	43.3%
1976	1,546,382	687,039	Spellman, John D.	821,797	Ray, Dixy Lee	37,546	134,758 D	44.4%	53.1%	45.5%	54.5%
1972	1,472,542	747,825	Evans, Daniel J.	630,613	Rosellini, Albert D.	94,104	117,212 R	50.8%	42.8%	54.3%	45.7%
1968	1,265,355	692,378	Evans, Daniel J.	560,262	O'Connell, John J.	12,715	132,116 R	54.7%	44.3%	55.3%	44.7%
1964	1,250,274	697,256	Evans, Daniel J.	548,692	Rosellini, Albert D.	4,326	148,564 R	55.8%	43.9%	56.0%	44.0%
1960	1,215,748	594,122	Andrews, Lloyd J.	611,987	Rosellini, Albert D.	9,639	17,865 D	48.9%	50.3%	49.3%	50.7%
1956	1,128,977	508,041	Anderson, Emmett T.	616,773	Rosellini, Albert D.	4,163	108,732 D	45.0%	54.6%	45.2%	54.8%
1952	1,078,497	567,822	Langlie, Arthur B.	510,675	Mitchell, Hugh B.		57,147 R	52.6%	47.4%	52.6%	47.4%
1948	883,141	445,958	Langlie, Arthur B.	417,035	Wallgren, Mon C.	20,148	28,923 R	50.5%	47.2%	51.7%	48.3%

460

WASHINGTON

POSTWAR VOTE FOR SENATOR

Year	Total Vote	Republican Vote	Republican Candidate	Democratic Vote	Democratic Candidate	Other Vote	Rep-Dem. Plurality	Total Vote Rep.	Total Vote Dem.	Major Vote Rep.	Major Vote Dem.
1988	1,848,542	944,359	Gorton, Slade	904,183	Lowry, Mike		40,176 R	51.1%	48.9%	51.1%	48.9%
1986	1,337,367	650,931	Gorton, Slade	677,471	Adams, Brock	8,965	26,540 D	48.7%	50.7%	49.0%	51.0%
1983 S	1,213,307	672,326	Evans, Daniel J.	540,981	Lowry, Mike		131,345 R	55.4%	44.6%	55.4%	44.6%
1982	1,368,476	332,273	Jewett, Doug	943,655	Jackson, Henry M.	92,548	611,382 D	24.3%	69.0%	26.0%	74.0%
1980	1,728,369	936,317	Gorton, Slade	792,052	Magnuson, Warren G.		144,265 R	54.2%	45.8%	54.2%	45.8%
1976	1,491,111	361,546	Brown, George M.	1,071,219	Jackson, Henry M.	58,346	709,673 D	24.2%	71.8%	25.2%	74.8%
1974	1,007,847	363,626	Metcalf, Jack	611,811	Magnuson, Warren G.	32,410	248,185 D	36.1%	60.7%	37.3%	62.7%
1970	1,066,807	170,790	Elicker, Charles W.	879,385	Jackson, Henry M.	16,632	708,595 D	16.0%	82.4%	16.3%	83.7%
1968	1,236,063	435,894	Metcalf, Jack	796,183	Magnuson, Warren G.	3,986	360,289 D	35.3%	64.4%	35.4%	64.6%
1964	1,213,088	337,138	Andrews, Lloyd J.	875,950	Jackson, Henry M.		538,812 D	27.8%	72.2%	27.8%	72.2%
1962	943,229	446,204	Christensen, Richard G.	491,365	Magnuson, Warren G.	5,660	45,161 D	47.3%	52.1%	47.6%	52.4%
1958	886,822	278,271	Bantz, William B.	597,040	Jackson, Henry M.	11,511	318,769 D	31.4%	67.3%	31.8%	68.2%
1956	1,122,217	436,652	Langlie, Arthur B.	685,565	Magnuson, Warren G.		248,913 D	38.9%	61.1%	38.9%	61.1%
1952	1,058,735	460,884	Cain, Harry P.	595,288	Jackson, Henry M.	2,563	134,404 D	43.5%	56.2%	43.6%	56.4%
1950	744,783	342,464	Williams, Walter	397,719	Magnuson, Warren G.	4,600	55,255 D	46.0%	53.4%	46.3%	53.7%
1946	660,342	358,847	Cain, Harry P.	298,683	Mitchell, Hugh B.	2,812	60,164 R	54.3%	45.2%	54.6%	45.4%

The 1983 election was for a short term to fill a vacancy.

WASHINGTON

Districts Established March 29, 1983

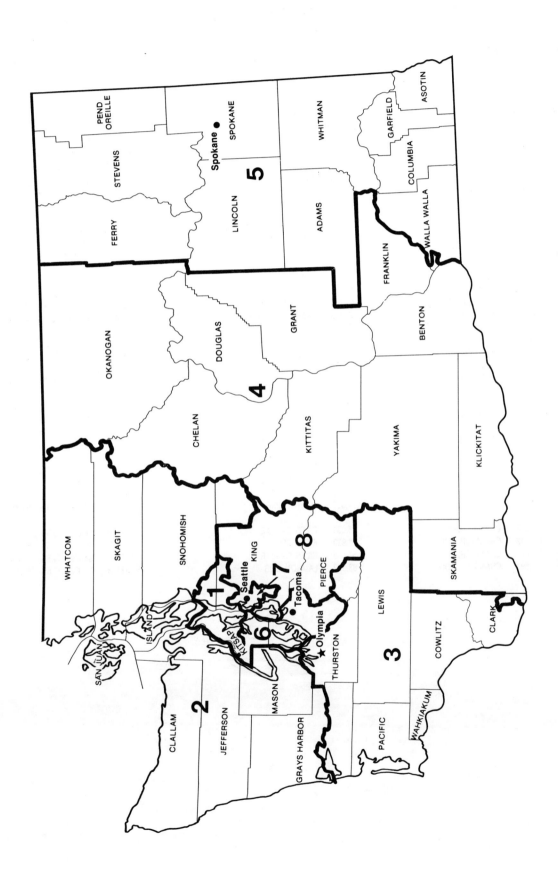

WASHINGTON

CONGRESS

CD	Year	Total Vote	Republican Vote	Republican Candidate	Democratic Vote	Democratic Candidate	Other Vote	Rep.-Dem. Plurality	Total Vote Rep.	Total Vote Dem.	Major Vote Rep.	Major Vote Dem.
1	1990	192,786	100,339	MILLER, JOHN R.	92,447	SULLIVAN, CYNTHIA		7,892 R	52.0%	48.0%	52.0%	48.0%
1	1988	274,911	152,265	MILLER, JOHN R.	122,646	LINDQUIST, REESE		29,619 R	55.4%	44.6%	55.4%	44.6%
1	1986	190,666	97,969	MILLER, JOHN R.	92,697	LINDQUIST, REESE		5,272 R	51.4%	48.6%	51.4%	48.6%
1	1984	262,927	147,926	MILLER, JOHN R.	115,001	EVANS, BROCK		32,925 R	56.3%	43.7%	56.3%	43.7%
2	1990	183,671	75,669	SMITH, DOUG	92,837	SWIFT, AL	15,165	17,168 D	41.2%	50.5%	44.9%	55.1%
2	1988	175,191			175,191	SWIFT, AL		175,191 D		100.0%		100.0%
2	1986	172,917	48,077	TALMAN, THOMAS S.	124,840	SWIFT, AL		76,763 D	27.8%	72.2%	27.8%	72.2%
2	1984	242,392	93,472	KLAUDER, JIM	142,065	SWIFT, AL	6,855	48,593 D	38.6%	58.6%	39.7%	60.3%
3	1990	177,914	82,269	WILLIAMS, BOB	95,645	UNSOELD, JOLENE		13,376 D	46.2%	53.8%	46.2%	53.8%
3	1988	218,206	108,794	WIGHT, BILL	109,412	UNSOELD, JOLENE		618 D	49.9%	50.1%	49.9%	50.1%
3	1986	156,050	41,275	ILLING, JOE	114,775	BONKER, DON		73,500 D	26.4%	73.6%	26.4%	73.6%
3	1984	211,651	61,219	ELDER, HERB	150,432	BONKER, DON		89,213 D	28.9%	71.1%	28.9%	71.1%
4	1990	150,786	106,545	MORRISON, SID	44,241	HOUGEN, OLE		62,304 R	70.7%	29.3%	70.7%	29.3%
4	1988	191,788	142,938	MORRISON, SID	48,850	GOLOB, J. RICHARD		94,088 R	74.5%	25.5%	74.5%	25.5%
4	1986	149,302	107,593	MORRISON, SID	41,709	GOEDECKE, ROBERT		65,884 R	72.1%	27.9%	72.1%	27.9%
4	1984	197,480	150,322	MORRISON, SID	47,158	EPPERSON, MARK		103,164 R	76.1%	23.9%	76.1%	23.9%
5	1990	160,199	49,965	DERBY, MARLYN A.	110,234	FOLEY, THOMAS S.		60,269 D	31.2%	68.8%	31.2%	68.8%
5	1988	210,311	49,657	DERBY, MARLYN A.	160,654	FOLEY, THOMAS S.		110,997 D	23.6%	76.4%	23.6%	76.4%
5	1986	162,911	41,179	WAKEFIELD, FLOYD L.	121,732	FOLEY, THOMAS S.		80,553 D	25.3%	74.7%	25.3%	74.7%
5	1984	222,426	67,438	HEBNER, JACK	154,988	FOLEY, THOMAS S.		87,550 D	30.3%	69.7%	30.3%	69.7%
6	1990	128,865	49,786	MUELLER, NORBERT	79,079	DICKS, NORMAN D.		29,293 D	38.6%	61.4%	38.6%	61.4%
6	1988	186,250	60,346	COOK, KEVIN P.	125,904	DICKS, NORMAN D.		65,558 D	32.4%	67.6%	32.4%	67.6%
6	1986	126,473	36,410	BRAATEN, KENNETH W.	90,063	DICKS, NORMAN D.		53,653 D	28.8%	71.2%	28.8%	71.2%
6	1984	188,041	60,721	LONERGAN, MIKE	124,367	DICKS, NORMAN D.	2,953	63,646 D	32.3%	66.1%	32.8%	67.2%
7	1990	147,642	35,511	PENBERTHY, LARRY	106,761	MCDERMOTT, JIM	5,370	71,250 D	24.1%	72.3%	25.0%	75.0%
7	1988	227,711	53,902	EDWARDS, ROBERT	173,809	MCDERMOTT, JIM		119,907 D	23.7%	76.3%	23.7%	76.3%
7	1986	171,148	46,831	MACDONALD, DON	124,317	LOWRY, MIKE		77,486 D	27.4%	72.6%	27.4%	72.6%
7	1984	247,846	71,576	DORSE, BOB	174,560	LOWRY, MIKE	1,710	102,984 D	28.9%	70.4%	29.1%	70.9%
8	1990	171,354	96,323	CHANDLER, ROD	75,031	GILES, DAVID E.		21,292 R	56.2%	43.8%	56.2%	43.8%
8	1988	246,862	174,942	CHANDLER, ROD	71,920	KEAN, JIM		103,022 R	70.9%	29.1%	70.9%	29.1%
8	1986	165,369	107,824	CHANDLER, ROD	57,545	GILES, DAVID E.		50,279 R	65.2%	34.8%	65.2%	34.8%
8	1984	235,270	146,891	CHANDLER, ROD	88,379	LAMSON, BOB		58,512 R	62.4%	37.6%	62.4%	37.6%

WASHINGTON

1990 GENERAL ELECTION

Congress   Other vote was Libertarian (McCord) in CD 2; Socialist Workers (Scherr) in CD 7.

1990 PRIMARIES

Washington's primaries are completely open, with all candidates for an office carried on the ballot together; thus a voter may vote for a Republican for Governor, a Democrat for Senator, and so on. In this so-called "jungle primary", nominations go to the highest party candidate, providing the winner receives a minimum of one percent of the total votes cast for the office. Independents qualify for a place on the General Election ballot by polling the same minimum requirement.

SEPTEMBER 18 REPUBLICAN

Congress

CD	1	41,976 John R. Miller; 2,759 Kerman Kermoade.
CD	2	25,382 Doug Smith (only Republican candidate).
CD	3	35,673 Bob Williams; 3,219 Gary L. Snell.
CD	4	71,057 Sid Morrison (only Republican candidate).
CD	5	1,390 Marlyn A. Derby (Republican write-in candidate) qualified.
CD	6	13,117 Norbert Mueller (only Republican candidate).
CD	7	12,681 Larry Penberthy (only Republican candidate).
CD	8	36,551 Rod Chandler; 6,700 Kenneth R. Thomasson.

SEPTEMBER 18 DEMOCRATIC

Congress

CD	1	27,410 Cynthia Sullivan; 8,339 Benny Teal.
CD	2	54,777 Al Swift; 3,288 L. J. Mansholt; 3,205 DeMilt Morse.
CD	3	48,891 Jolene Unsoeld; 5,644 Ned Norris.
CD	4	20,860 Ole Hougen (only Democratic candidate).
CD	5	73,007 Thomas S. Foley (only Democratic candidate).
CD	6	38,346 Norman D. Dicks; 14,772 Mike Collier.
CD	7	47,306 Jim McDermott; 3,909 Patrick Ruckert.
CD	8	19,461 David E. Giles (only Democratic candidate).

SEPTEMBER 18 MINOR PARTIES/INDEPENDENTS

Congress

CD	2	3,065 William L. McCord (only Libertarian candidate) qualified.
CD	7	1,125 Robbie Scherr (only Socialist Workers candidate) qualified.

WEST VIRGINIA

GOVERNOR
Gaston Caperton (D). Elected 1988 to a four-year term.

SENATORS
Robert C. Byrd (D). Re-elected 1988 to a six-year term. Previously elected 1982, 1976, 1970, 1964, 1958.

John D. Rockefeller (D). Re-elected 1990 to a six-year term. Previously elected 1984.

REPRESENTATIVES
1. Alan B. Mollohan (D)
2. Harley O. Staggers, Jr. (D)
3. Robert E. Wise (D)
4. Nick J. Rahall (D)

POSTWAR VOTE FOR PRESIDENT

Year	Total Vote	Republican Vote	Candidate	Democratic Vote	Candidate	Other Vote	Plurality	Total Vote Rep.	Total Vote Dem.	Major Vote Rep.	Major Vote Dem.
1988	653,311	310,065	Bush, George	341,016	Dukakis, Michael S.	2,230	30,951 D	47.5%	52.2%	47.6%	52.4%
1984	735,742	405,483	Reagan, Ronald	328,125	Mondale, Walter F.	2,134	77,358 R	55.1%	44.6%	55.3%	44.7%
1980	737,715	334,206	Reagan, Ronald	367,462	Carter, Jimmy	36,047	33,256 D	45.3%	49.8%	47.6%	52.4%
1976	750,964	314,760	Ford, Gerald R.	435,914	Carter, Jimmy	290	121,154 D	41.9%	58.0%	41.9%	58.1%
1972	762,399	484,964	Nixon, Richard M.	277,435	McGovern, George S.		207,529 R	63.6%	36.4%	63.6%	36.4%
1968	754,206	307,555	Nixon, Richard M.	374,091	Humphrey, Hubert H.	72,560	66,536 D	40.8%	49.6%	45.1%	54.9%
1964	792,040	253,953	Goldwater, Barry M.	538,087	Johnson, Lyndon B.		284,134 D	32.1%	67.9%	32.1%	67.9%
1960	837,781	395,995	Nixon, Richard M.	441,786	Kennedy, John F.		45,791 D	47.3%	52.7%	47.3%	52.7%
1956	830,831	449,297	Eisenhower, Dwight D.	381,534	Stevenson, Adlai E.		67,763 R	54.1%	45.9%	54.1%	45.9%
1952	873,548	419,970	Eisenhower, Dwight D.	453,578	Stevenson, Adlai E.		33,608 D	48.1%	51.9%	48.1%	51.9%
1948	748,750	316,251	Dewey, Thomas E.	429,188	Truman, Harry S.	3,311	112,937 D	42.2%	57.3%	42.4%	57.6%

POSTWAR VOTE FOR GOVERNOR

Year	Total Vote	Republican Vote	Candidate	Democratic Vote	Candidate	Other Vote	Rep-Dem. Plurality	Total Vote Rep.	Total Vote Dem.	Major Vote Rep.	Major Vote Dem.
1988	649,593	267,172	Moore, Arch A.	382,421	Caperton, Gaston		115,249 D	41.1%	58.9%	41.1%	58.9%
1984	741,502	394,937	Moore, Arch A.	346,565	See, Clyde M.		48,372 R	53.3%	4o.7%	53.3%	46.7%
1980	742,150	337,240	Moore, Arch A.	401,863	Rockefeller, John D.	3,047	64,623 D	45.4%	54.1%	45.6%	54.4%
1976	749,270	253,420	Underwood, Cecil H.	495,661	Rockefeller, John D.	189	242,241 D	33.8%	66.2%	33.8%	66.2%
1972	774,279	423,817	Moore, Arch A.	350,462	Rockefeller, John D.		73,355 R	54.7%	45.3%	54.7%	45.3%
1968	743,845	378,315	Moore, Arch A.	365,530	Sprouse, James M.		12,785 R	50.9%	49.1%	50.9%	49.1%
1964	788,582	355,559	Underwood, Cecil H.	433,023	Smith, Hulett C.		77,464 D	45.1%	54.9%	45.1%	54.9%
1960	827,420	380,665	Neely, Harold E.	446,755	Barron, W. W.		66,090 D	46.0%	54.0%	46.0%	54.0%
1956	817,623	440,502	Underwood, Cecil H.	377,121	Mollohan, Robert H.		63,381 R	53.9%	46.1%	53.9%	46.1%
1952	882,527	427,629	Holt, Rush D.	454,898	Marland, William C.		27,269 D	48.5%	51.5%	48.5%	51.5%
1948	768,061	329,309	Boreman, Herbert	438,752	Patteson, Okey L.		109,443 D	42.9%	57.1%	42.9%	57.1%

WEST VIRGINIA

POSTWAR VOTE FOR SENATOR

Year	Total Vote	Republican Vote	Republican Candidate	Democratic Vote	Democratic Candidate	Other Vote	Rep-Dem. Plurality	Total Vote Rep.	Total Vote Dem.	Major Vote Rep.	Major Vote Dem.
1990	404,305	128,071	Yoder, John	276,234	Rockefeller, John D.		148,163 D	31.7%	68.3%	31.7%	68.3%
1988	634,547	223,564	Wolfe, M. Jay	410,983	Byrd, Robert C.		187,419 D	35.2%	64.8%	35.2%	64.8%
1984	722,212	344,680	Raese, John R.	374,233	Rockefeller, John D.	3,299	29,553 D	47.7%	51.8%	47.9%	52.1%
1982	565,314	173,910	Benedict, Cleveland K.	387,170	Byrd, Robert C.	4,234	213,260 D	30.8%	68.5%	31.0%	69.0%
1978	493,351	244,317	Moore, Arch A.	249,034	Randolph, Jennings		4,717 D	49.5%	50.5%	49.5%	50.5%
1976	566,790		—	566,423	Byrd, Robert C.	367	566,423 D		99.9%		100.0%
1972	731,841	245,531	Leonard, Louise	486,310	Randolph, Jennings		240,779 D	33.5%	66.5%	33.5%	66.5%
1970	445,623	99,658	Dodson, Elmer H.	345,965	Byrd, Robert C.		246,307 D	22.4%	77.6%	22.4%	77.6%
1966	491,216	198,891	Love, Francis J.	292,325	Randolph, Jennings		93,434 D	40.5%	59.5%	40.5%	59.5%
1964	761,087	246,072	Benedict, Cooper P.	515,015	Byrd, Robert C.		268,943 D	32.3%	67.7%	32.3%	67.7%
1960	828,292	369,935	Underwood, Cecil H.	458,355	Randolph, Jennings	2	88,420 D	44.7%	55.3%	44.7%	55.3%
1958	644,917	263,172	Revercomb, Chapman	381,745	Byrd, Robert C.		118,573 D	40.8%	59.2%	40.8%	59.2%
1958 S	630,677	256,510	Hoblitzell, John D.	374,167	Randolph, Jennings		117,657 D	40.7%	59.3%	40.7%	59.3%
1956 S	805,174	432,123	Revercomb, Chapman	373,051	Marland, William C.		59,072 R	53.7%	46.3%	53.7%	46.3%
1954	593,329	268,066	Sweeney, Tom	325,263	Neely, Matthew M.		57,197 D	45.2%	54.8%	45.2%	54.8%
1952	876,573	406,554	Revercomb, Chapman	470,019	Kilgore, Harley M.		63,465 D	46.4%	53.6%	46.4%	53.6%
1948	763,888	328,534	Revercomb, Chapman	435,354	Neely, Matthew M.		106,820 D	43.0%	57.0%	43.0%	57.0%
1946	542,768	269,617	Sweeney, Tom	273,151	Kilgore, Harley M.		3,534 D	49.7%	50.3%	49.7%	50.3%

One of the 1958 elections and the 1956 election were for short terms to fill vacancies.

WEST VIRGINIA

Districts Established February 8, 1982

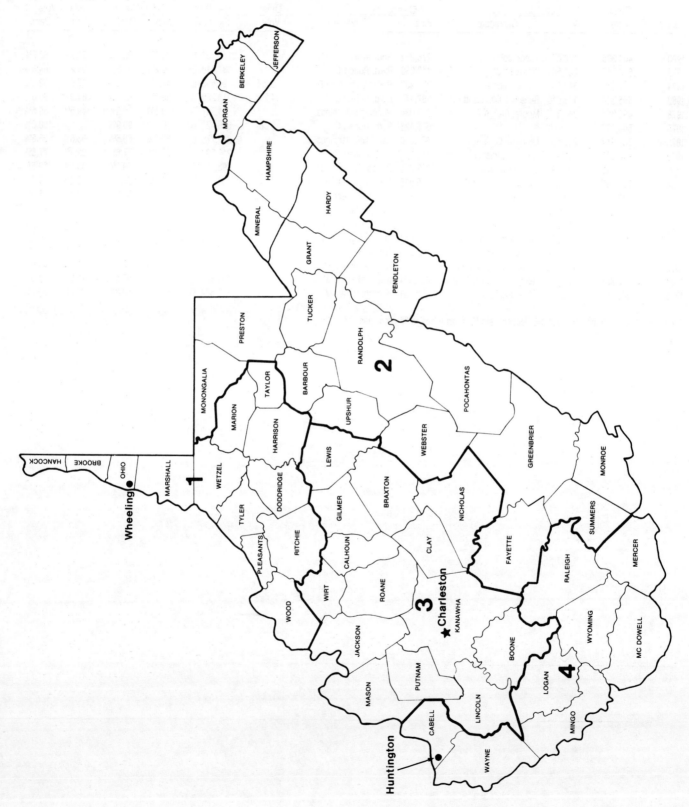

WEST VIRGINIA

SENATOR 1990

1990 Census Population	County	Total Vote	Republican	Democratic	Other	Rep.-Dem. Plurality	Percentage			
							Total Vote		Major Vote	
							Rep.	Dem.	Rep.	Dem.
15,699	BARBOUR	6,506	1,881	4,625		2,744 D	28.9%	71.1%	28.9%	71.1%
59,253	BERKELEY	10,620	5,044	5,576		532 D	47.5%	52.5%	47.5%	52.5%
25,870	BOONE	4,354	866	3,488		2,622 D	19.9%	80.1%	19.9%	80.1%
12,998	BRAXTON	3,124	791	2,333		1,542 D	25.3%	74.7%	25.3%	74.7%
26,992	BROOKE	5,877	1,230	4,647		3,417 D	20.9%	79.1%	20.9%	79.1%
96,827	CABELL	19,788	6,900	12,888		5,988 D	34.9%	65.1%	34.9%	65.1%
7,885	CALHOUN	2,718	836	1,882		1,046 D	30.8%	69.2%	30.8%	69.2%
9,983	CLAY	2,392	691	1,701		1,010 D	28.9%	71.1%	28.9%	71.1%
6,994	DODDRIDGE	1,971	1,016	955		61 R	51.5%	48.5%	51.5%	48.5%
47,952	FAYETTE	9,610	1,883	7,727		5,844 D	19.6%	80.4%	19.6%	80.4%
7,669	GILMER	2,091	619	1,472		853 D	29.6%	70.4%	29.6%	70.4%
10,428	GRANT	2,358	1,266	1,092		174 R	53.7%	46.3%	53.7%	46.3%
34,693	GREENBRIER	7,695	2,625	5,070		2,445 D	34.1%	65.9%	34.1%	65.9%
16,498	HAMPSHIRE	3,499	1,618	1,881		263 D	46.2%	53.8%	46.2%	53.8%
35,233	HANCOCK	9,015	2,105	6,910		4,805 D	23.3%	76.7%	23.3%	76.7%
10,977	HARDY	2,640	947	1,693		746 D	35.9%	64.1%	35.9%	64.1%
69,371	HARRISON	20,730	5,716	15,014		9,298 D	27.6%	72.4%	27.6%	72.4%
25,938	JACKSON	6,319	2,600	3,719		1,119 D	41.1%	58.9%	41.1%	58.9%
35,926	JEFFERSON	6,384	2,762	3,622		860 D	43.3%	56.7%	43.3%	56.7%
207,619	KANAWHA	45,053	16,117	28,936		12,819 D	35.8%	64.2%	35.8%	64.2%
17,223	LEWIS	4,733	1,463	3,270		1,807 D	30.9%	69.1%	30.9%	69.1%
21,382	LINCOLN	3,320	990	2,330		1,340 D	29.8%	70.2%	29.8%	70.2%
43,032	LOGAN	6,358	1,134	5,224		4,090 D	17.8%	82.2%	17.8%	82.2%
35,233	MCDOWELL	5,626	752	4,874		4,122 D	13.4%	86.6%	13.4%	86.6%
57,249	MARION	15,961	4,323	11,638		7,315 D	27.1%	72.9%	27.1%	72.9%
37,356	MARSHALL	9,293	2,568	6,725		4,157 D	27.6%	72.4%	27.6%	72.4%
25,178	MASON	7,992	2,467	5,525		3,058 D	30.9%	69.1%	30.9%	69.1%
64,980	MERCER	12,222	3,858	8,364		4,506 D	31.6%	68.4%	31.6%	68.4%
26,697	MINERAL	7,102	2,646	4,456		1,810 D	37.3%	62.7%	37.3%	62.7%
33,739	MINGO	5,246	808	4,438		3,630 D	15.4%	84.6%	15.4%	84.6%
75,509	MONONGALIA	17,365	4,651	12,714		8,063 D	26.8%	73.2%	26.8%	73.2%
12,406	MONROE	3,187	1,116	2,071		955 D	35.0%	65.0%	35.0%	65.0%
12,128	MORGAN	2,885	1,485	1,400		85 R	51.5%	48.5%	51.5%	48.5%
26,775	NICHOLAS	5,603	1,585	4,018		2,433 D	28.3%	71.7%	28.3%	71.7%
50,871	OHIO	12,410	3,193	9,217		6,024 D	25.7%	74.3%	25.7%	74.3%
8,054	PENDLETON	2,161	719	1,442		723 D	33.3%	66.7%	33.3%	66.7%
7,546	PLEASANTS	1,899	650	1,249		599 D	34.2%	65.8%	34.2%	65.8%
9,008	POCAHONTAS	2,892	914	1,978		1,064 D	31.6%	68.4%	31.6%	68.4%
29,037	PRESTON	6,830	2,513	4,317		1,804 D	36.8%	63.2%	36.8%	63.2%
42,835	PUTNAM	9,022	3,875	5,147		1,272 D	43.0%	57.0%	43.0%	57.0%
76,819	RALEIGH	14,902	3,885	11,017		7,132 D	26.1%	73.9%	26.1%	73.9%
27,803	RANDOLPH	7,110	2,040	5,070		3,030 D	28.7%	71.3%	28.7%	71.3%
10,233	RITCHIE	2,469	1,179	1,290		111 D	47.8%	52.2%	47.8%	52.2%
15,120	ROANE	3,881	1,728	2,153		425 D	44.5%	55.5%	44.5%	55.5%
14,204	SUMMERS	3,173	829	2,344		1,515 D	26.1%	73.9%	26.1%	73.9%
15,144	TAYLOR	4,077	1,297	2,780		1,483 D	31.8%	68.2%	31.8%	68.2%
7,728	TUCKER	2,364	626	1,738		1,112 D	26.5%	73.5%	26.5%	73.5%
9,796	TYLER	2,526	882	1,644		762 D	34.9%	65.1%	34.9%	65.1%
22,867	UPSHUR	5,483	2,009	3,474		1,465 D	36.6%	63.4%	36.6%	63.4%
41,636	WAYNE	8,269	2,578	5,691		3,113 D	31.2%	68.8%	31.2%	68.8%
10,729	WEBSTER	2,285	460	1,825		1,365 D	20.1%	79.9%	20.1%	79.9%
19,258	WETZEL	4,696	1,289	3,407		2,118 D	27.4%	72.6%	27.4%	72.6%
5,192	WIRT	1,301	449	852		403 D	34.5%	65.5%	34.5%	65.5%
86,915	WOOD	21,705	8,459	13,246		4,787 D	39.0%	61.0%	39.0%	61.0%
28,990	WYOMING	5,213	1,138	4,075		2,937 D	21.8%	78.2%	21.8%	78.2%
1,793,477	TOTAL	404,305	128,071	276,234		148,163 D	31.7%	68.3%	31.7%	68.3%

WEST VIRGINIA

CONGRESS

CD	Year	Total Vote	Republican Vote	Republican Candidate	Democratic Vote	Democratic Candidate	Other Vote	Rep.-Dem. Plurality	Total Vote Rep.	Total Vote Dem.	Major Vote Rep.	Major Vote Dem.
1	1990	108,506	35,657	TUCK, HOWARD	72,849	MOLLOHAN, ALAN B.		37,192 D	32.9%	67.1%	32.9%	67.1%
1	1988	159,988	40,732	TUCK, HOWARD	119,256	MOLLOHAN, ALAN B.		78,524 D	25.5%	74.5%	25.5%	74.5%
1	1986	90,715			90,715	MOLLOHAN, ALAN B.		90,715 D		100.0%		100.0%
1	1984	192,261	87,622	ALTMEYER, JAMES	104,639	MOLLOHAN, ALAN B.		17,017 D	45.6%	54.4%	45.6%	54.4%
1	1982	149,598	70,069	MCCUSKEY, JOHN F.	79,529	MOLLOHAN, ALAN B.		9,460 D	46.8%	53.2%	46.8%	53.2%
2	1990	113,882	50,708	LUCK, OLIVER	63,174	STAGGERS, HARLEY O., JR.		12,466 D	44.5%	55.5%	44.5%	55.5%
2	1988	118,356			118,356	STAGGERS, HARLEY O., JR.		118,356 D		100.0%		100.0%
2	1986	109,909	33,554	GOLDEN, MICHELE	76,355	STAGGERS, HARLEY O., JR.		42,801 D	30.5%	69.5%	30.5%	69.5%
2	1984	179,281	78,936	BENEDICT, CLEVELAND K.	100,345	STAGGERS, HARLEY O., JR.		21,409 D	44.0%	56.0%	44.0%	56.0%
2	1982	137,317	49,413	HINKLE, J. D.	87,904	STAGGERS, HARLEY O., JR.		38,491 D	36.0%	64.0%	36.0%	64.0%
3	1990	75,327			75,327	WISE, ROBERT E.		75,327 D		100.0%		100.0%
3	1988	161,670	41,478	HART, PAUL W.	120,192	WISE, ROBERT E.		78,714 D	25.7%	74.3%	25.7%	74.3%
3	1986	113,489	39,820	SHARP, TIM	73,669	WISE, ROBERT E.		33,849 D	35.1%	64.9%	35.1%	64.9%
3	1984	184,434	59,128	MILLER, MARGARET P.	125,306	WISE, ROBERT E.		66,178 D	32.1%	67.9%	32.1%	67.9%
3	1982	146,250	60,844	STATON, DAVID M.	84,619	WISE, ROBERT E.	787	23,775 D	41.6%	57.9%	41.8%	58.2%
4	1990	76,894	36,946	BREWSTER, MARIANNE R.	39,948	RAHALL, NICK J.		3,002 D	48.0%	52.0%	48.0%	52.0%
4	1988	128,565	49,753	BREWSTER, MARIANNE R.	78,812	RAHALL, NICK J.		29,059 D	38.7%	61.3%	38.7%	61.3%
4	1986	81,707	23,490	MILLER, MARTIN	58,217	RAHALL, NICK J.		34,727 D	28.7%	71.3%	28.7%	71.3%
4	1984	148,393	49,474	SHUMATE, JESS T.	98,919	RAHALL, NICK J.		49,445 D	33.3%	66.7%	33.3%	66.7%
4	1982	113,238	22,054	HARRIS, HOMER L.	91,184	RAHALL, NICK J.		69,130 D	19.5%	80.5%	19.5%	80.5%
4	1980	153,615	36,020	COVEY, WINTON G.	117,595	RAHALL, NICK J.		81,575 D	23.4%	76.6%	23.4%	76.6%
4	1978	70,035			70,035	RAHALL, NICK J.		70,035 D		100.0%		100.0%
4	1976	161,520	28,825	GOODMAN, E. S.	73,626	RAHALL, NICK J.	59,069	44,801 D	17.8%	45.6%	28.1%	71.9%
4	1974	66,420			66,420	HECHLER, KEN		66,420 D		100.0%		100.0%
4	1972	164,842	64,242	NEAL, JOE	100,600	HECHLER, KEN		36,358 D	39.0%	61.0%	39.0%	61.0%

WEST VIRGINIA

1990 GENERAL ELECTION

Senator

Congress

1990 PRIMARIES

MAY 8 REPUBLICAN

Senator   John Yoder, unopposed.

Congress   Unopposed in three CD's. No candidate in CD 3.

MAY 8 DEMOCRATIC

Senator   200,161 John D. Rockefeller; 21,669 Ken B. Thompson; 14,467 Paul Nuchims.

Congress   Unopposed in three CD's. Contested as follows:

   CD 4   37,581 Nick J. Rahall; 28,618 Ken Hechler.

WISCONSIN

GOVERNOR
Tommy G. Thompson (R). Re-elected 1990 to a four-year term. Previously elected 1986.

SENATORS
Robert W. Kasten (R). Re-elected 1986 to a six-year term. Previously elected 1980.

Herbert H. Kohl (D). Elected 1988 to a six-year term.

REPRESENTATIVES
1. Les Aspin (D)
2. Scott L. Klug (R)
3. Steven Gunderson (R)
4. Gerald D. Kleczka (D)
5. Jim Moody (D)
6. Thomas E. Petri (R)
7. David R. Obey (D)
8. Toby Roth (R)
9. F. James Sensenbrenner (R)

POSTWAR VOTE FOR PRESIDENT

Year	Total Vote	Republican Vote	Candidate	Democratic Vote	Candidate	Other Vote	Plurality	Total Vote Rep.	Dem.	Major Vote Rep.	Dem.
1988	2,191,608	1,047,499	Bush, George	1,126,794	Dukakis, Michael S.	17,315	79,295 D	47.8%	51.4%	48.2%	51.8%
1984	2,211,689	1,198,584	Reagan, Ronald	995,740	Mondale, Walter F.	17,365	202,844 R	54.2%	45.0%	54.6%	45.4%
1980	2,273,221	1,088,845	Reagan, Ronald	981,584	Carter, Jimmy	202,792	107,261 R	47.9%	43.2%	52.6%	47.4%
1976	2,104,175	1,004,987	Ford, Gerald R.	1,040,232	Carter, Jimmy	58,956	35,245 D	47.8%	49.4%	49.1%	50.9%
1972	1,852,890	989,430	Nixon, Richard M.	810,174	McGovern, George S.	53,286	179,256 R	53.4%	43.7%	55.0%	45.0%
1968	1,691,538	809,997	Nixon, Richard M.	748,804	Humphrey, Hubert H.	132,737	61,193 R	47.9%	44.3%	52.0%	48.0%
1964	1,691,815	638,495	Goldwater, Barry M.	1,050,424	Johnson, Lyndon B.	2,896	411,929 D	37.7%	62.1%	37.8%	62.2%
1960	1,729,082	895,175	Nixon, Richard M.	830,805	Kennedy, John F.	3,102	64,370 R	51.8%	48.0%	51.9%	48.1%
1956	1,550,558	954,844	Eisenhower, Dwight D.	586,768	Stevenson, Adlai E.	8,946	368,076 R	61.6%	37.8%	61.9%	38.1%
1952	1,607,370	979,744	Eisenhower, Dwight D.	622,175	Stevenson, Adlai E.	5,451	357,569 R	61.0%	38.7%	61.2%	38.8%
1948	1,276,800	590,959	Dewey, Thomas E.	647,310	Truman, Harry S.	38,531	56,351 D	46.3%	50.7%	47.7%	52.3%

WISCONSIN

POSTWAR VOTE FOR GOVERNOR

Year	Total Vote	Republican Vote	Candidate	Democratic Vote	Candidate	Other Vote	Rep-Dem. Plurality	Percentage Total Vote Rep.	Dem.	Major Vote Rep.	Dem.
1990	1,379,727	802,321	Thompson, Tommy G.	576,280	Loftus, Thomas	1,126	226,041 R	58.2%	41.8%	58.2%	41.8%
1986	1,526,960	805,090	Thompson, Tommy G.	705,578	Earl, Anthony S.	16,292	99,512 R	52.7%	46.2%	53.3%	46.7%
1982	1,580,344	662,838	Kohler, Terry J.	896,812	Earl, Anthony S.	20,694	233,974 D	41.9%	56.7%	42.5%	57.5%
1978	1,500,996	816,056	Dreyfus, Lee S.	673,813	Schreiber, Martin J.	11,127	142,243 R	54.4%	44.9%	54.8%	45.2%
1974	1,181,976	497,195	Dyke, William D.	628,639	Lucey, Patrick J.	56,142	131,444 D	42.1%	53.2%	44.2%	55.8%
1970 * *	1,343,160	602,617	Olson, Jack B.	728,403	Lucey, Patrick J.	12,140	125,786 D	44.9%	54.2%	45.3%	54.7%
1968	1,689,738	893,463	Knowles, Warren P.	791,100	LaFollette, Bronson C.	5,175	102,363 R	52.9%	46.8%	53.0%	47.0%
1966	1,170,173	626,041	Knowles, Warren P.	539,258	Lucey, Patrick J.	4,874	86,783 R	53.5%	46.1%	53.7%	46.3%
1964	1,694,887	856,779	Knowles, Warren P.	837,901	Reynolds, John W.	207	18,878 R	50.6%	49.4%	50.6%	49.4%
1962	1,265,900	625,536	Kuehn, Philip G.	637,491	Reynolds, John W.	2,873	11,955 D	49.4%	50.4%	49.5%	50.5%
1960	1,728,009	837,123	Kuehn, Philip G.	890,868	Nelson, Gaylord A.	18	53,745 D	48.4%	51.6%	48.4%	51.6%
1958	1,202,219	556,391	Thomson, Vernon W.	644,296	Nelson, Gaylord A.	1,532	87,905 D	46.3%	53.6%	46.3%	53.7%
1956	1,557,788	808,273	Thomson, Vernon W.	749,421	Proxmire, William	94	58,852 R	51.9%	48.1%	51.9%	48.1%
1954	1,158,666	596,158	Kohler, Walter J.	560,747	Proxmire, William	1,761	35,411 R	51.5%	48.4%	51.5%	48.5%
1952	1,615,214	1,009,171	Kohler, Walter J.	601,844	Proxmire, William	4,199	407,327 R	62.5%	37.3%	62.6%	37.4%
1950	1,138,148	605,649	Kohler, Walter J.	525,319	Thompson, Carl W.	7,180	80,330 R	53.2%	46.2%	53.6%	46.4%
1948	1,266,139	684,839	Rennebohm, Oscar	558,497	Thompson, Carl W.	22,803	126,342 R	54.1%	44.1%	55.1%	44.9%
1946	1,040,444	621,970	Goodland, Walter	406,499	Hoan, Daniel W.	11,975	215,471 R	59.8%	39.1%	60.5%	39.5%

The term of office of Wisconsin's Governor was increased from two to four years effective with the 1970 election.

POSTWAR VOTE FOR SENATOR

Year	Total Vote	Republican Vote	Candidate	Democratic Vote	Candidate	Other Vote	Rep-Dem. Plurality	Percentage Total Vote Rep.	Dem.	Major Vote Rep.	Dem.
1988	2,168,190	1,030,440	Engeleiter, Susan	1,128,625	Kohl, Herbert H.	9,125	98,185 D	47.5%	52.1%	47.7%	52.3%
1986	1,483,174	754,573	Kasten, Robert W.	702,963	Garvey, Edward R.	25,638	51,610 R	50.9%	47.4%	51.8%	48.2%
1982	1,544,981	527,355	McCallum, Scott	983,311	Proxmire, William	34,315	455,956 D	34.1%	63.6%	34.9%	65.1%
1980	2,204,202	1,106,311	Kasten, Robert W.	1,065,487	Nelson, Gaylord A.	32,404	40,824 R	50.2%	48.3%	50.9%	49.1%
1976	1,935,183	521,902	York, Stanley	1,396,970	Proxmire, William	16,311	875,068 D	27.0%	72.2%	27.2%	72.8%
1974	1,199,495	429,327	Petri, Thomas E.	740,700	Nelson, Gaylord A.	29,468	311,373 D	35.8%	61.8%	36.7%	63.3%
1970	1,338,967	381,297	Erickson, John E.	948,445	Proxmire, William	9,225	567,148 D	28.5%	70.8%	28.7%	71.3%
1968	1,654,861	633,910	Leonard, Jerris	1,020,931	Nelson, Gaylord A.	20	387,021 D	38.3%	61.7%	38.3%	61.7%
1964	1,673,776	780,116	Renk, Wilbur N.	892,013	Proxmire, William	1,647	111,897 D	46.6%	53.3%	46.7%	53.3%
1962	1,260,168	594,846	Wiley, Alexander	662,342	Nelson, Gaylord A.	2,980	67,496 D	47.2%	52.6%	47.3%	52.7%
1958	1,194,678	510,398	Steinle, Roland J.	682,440	Proxmire, William	1,840	172,042 D	42.7%	57.1%	42.8%	57.2%
1957 S	772,620	312,931	Kohler, Walter J.	435,985	Proxmire, William	23,704	123,054 D	40.5%	56.4%	41.8%	58.2%
1956	1,523,356	892,473	Wiley, Alexander	627,903	Maier, Henry W.	2,980	264,570 R	58.6%	41.2%	58.7%	41.3%
1952	1,605,228	870,444	McCarthy, Joseph R.	731,402	Fairchild, Thomas E.	3,382	139,042 R	54.2%	45.6%	54.3%	45.7%
1950	1,116,135	595,283	Wiley, Alexander	515,539	Fairchild, Thomas E.	5,313	79,744 R	53.3%	46.2%	53.6%	46.4%
1946	1,014,594	620,430	McCarthy, Joseph R.	378,772	McMurray, Howard J.	15,392	241,658 R	61.2%	37.3%	62.1%	37.9%

The 1957 election was held in August for a short term to fill a vacancy.

472

WISCONSIN

Districts Established March 31, 1982

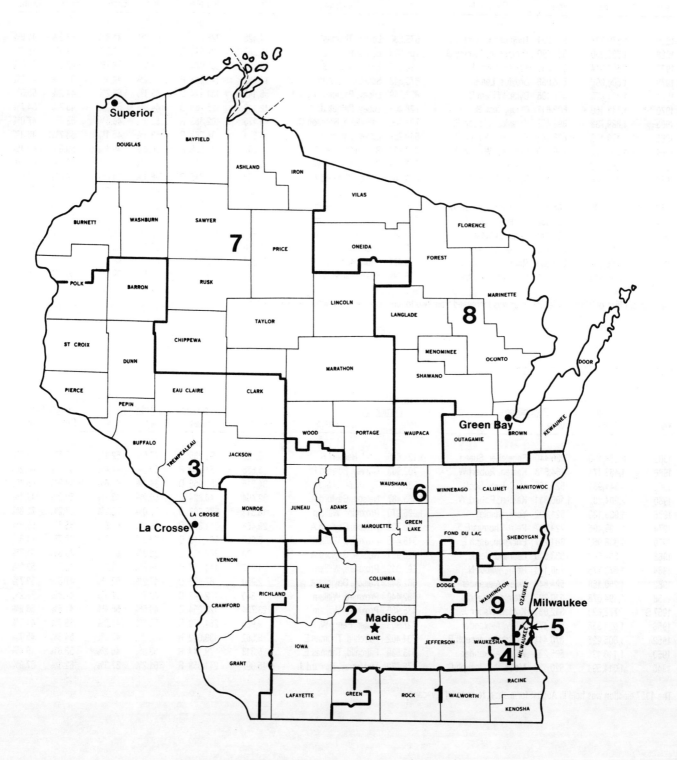

© ERC

WISCONSIN

GOVERNOR 1990

1990 Census Population	County	Total Vote	Republican	Democratic	Other	Rep.-Dem. Plurality	Percentage Total Vote Rep.	Dem.	Major Vote Rep.	Dem.
15,682	ADAMS	4,546	2,391	2,154	1	237 R	52.6%	47.4%	52.6%	47.4%
16,307	ASHLAND	5,154	3,066	2,087	1	979 R	59.5%	40.5%	59.5%	40.5%
40,750	BARRON	10,490	5,494	4,982	14	512 R	52.4%	47.5%	52.4%	47.6%
14,008	BAYFIELD	5,586	3,309	2,276	1	1,033 R	59.2%	40.7%	59.2%	40.8%
194,594	BROWN	61,718	35,561	26,143	14	9,418 R	57.6%	42.4%	57.6%	42.4%
13,584	BUFFALO	4,345	2,262	2,083		179 R	52.1%	47.9%	52.1%	47.9%
13,084	BURNETT	4,490	2,175	2,307	8	132 D	48.4%	51.4%	48.5%	51.5%
34,291	CALUMET	9,262	6,109	3,151	2	2,958 R	66.0%	34.0%	66.0%	34.0%
52,360	CHIPPEWA	14,499	7,954	6,542	3	1,412 R	54.9%	45.1%	54.9%	45.1%
31,647	CLARK	9,895	5,761	4,131	3	1,630 R	58.2%	41.7%	58.2%	41.8%
45,088	COLUMBIA	14,337	8,304	6,021	12	2,283 R	57.9%	42.0%	58.0%	42.0%
15,940	CRAWFORD	4,436	2,456	1,976	4	480 R	55.4%	44.5%	55.4%	44.6%
367,085	DANE	122,734	55,998	66,638	98	10,640 D	45.6%	54.3%	45.7%	54.3%
76,559	DODGE	19,176	12,325	6,842	9	5,483 R	64.3%	35.7%	64.3%	35.7%
25,690	DOOR	8,526	5,291	3,235		2,056 R	62.1%	37.9%	62.1%	37.9%
41,758	DOUGLAS	14,042	7,898	6,140	4	1,758 R	56.2%	43.7%	56.3%	43.7%
35,909	DUNN	9,527	4,613	4,900	14	287 D	48.4%	51.4%	48.5%	51.5%
85,183	EAU CLAIRE	27,580	14,864	12,711	5	2,153 R	53.9%	46.1%	53.9%	46.1%
4,590	FLORENCE	1,393	808	585		223 R	58.0%	42.0%	58.0%	42.0%
90,083	FOND DU LAC	24,042	16,043	7,992	7	8,051 R	66.7%	33.2%	66.7%	33.3%
8,776	FOREST	3,075	1,711	1,364		347 R	55.6%	44.4%	55.6%	44.4%
49,264	GRANT	10,920	6,782	4,131	7	2,651 R	62.1%	37.8%	62.1%	37.9%
30,339	GREEN	7,638	4,454	3,180	4	1,274 R	58.3%	41.6%	58.3%	41.7%
18,651	GREEN LAKE	4,938	3,412	1,526		1,886 R	69.1%	30.9%	69.1%	30.9%
20,150	IOWA	6,026	3,425	2,593	8	832 R	56.8%	43.0%	56.9%	43.1%
6,153	IRON	2,569	1,794	774	1	1,020 R	69.8%	30.1%	69.9%	30.1%
16,588	JACKSON	6,114	3,196	2,918		278 R	52.3%	47.7%	52.3%	47.7%
67,783	JEFFERSON	16,956	10,646	6,305	5	4,341 R	62.8%	37.2%	62.8%	37.2%
21,650	JUNEAU	7,404	5,244	2,158	2	3,086 R	70.8%	29.1%	70.8%	29.2%
128,181	KENOSHA	27,733	14,750	12,977	6	1,773 R	53.2%	46.8%	53.2%	46.8%
18,878	KEWAUNEE	7,227	4,140	3,087		1,053 R	57.3%	42.7%	57.3%	42.7%
97,904	LA CROSSE	30,956	16,790	14,164	2	2,626 R	54.2%	45.8%	54.2%	45.8%
16,076	LAFAYETTE	5,232	3,203	2,028	1	1,175 R	61.2%	38.8%	61.2%	38.8%
19,505	LANGLADE	5,982	3,637	2,341	4	1,296 R	60.8%	39.1%	60.8%	39.2%
26,993	LINCOLN	7,978	4,443	3,534	1	909 R	55.7%	44.3%	55.7%	44.3%
80,421	MANITOWOC	23,093	12,967	10,098	28	2,869 R	56.2%	43.7%	56.2%	43.8%
115,400	MARATHON	36,601	21,908	14,693		7,215 R	59.9%	40.1%	59.9%	40.1%
40,548	MARINETTE	12,812	7,524	5,286	2	2,238 R	58.7%	41.3%	58.7%	41.3%
12,321	MARQUETTE	3,775	2,245	1,526	4	719 R	59.5%	40.4%	59.5%	40.5%
3,890	MENOMINEE	934	390	544		154 D	41.8%	58.2%	41.8%	58.2%
959,275	MILWAUKEE	238,317	128,835	108,812	670	20,023 R	54.1%	45.7%	54.2%	45.8%
36,633	MONROE	8,738	5,189	3,546	3	1,643 R	59.4%	40.6%	59.4%	40.6%
30,226	OCONTO	9,272	5,441	3,831		1,610 R	58.7%	41.3%	58.7%	41.3%
31,679	ONEIDA	11,538	7,208	4,328	2	2,880 R	62.5%	37.5%	62.5%	37.5%
140,510	OUTAGAMIE	42,515	27,500	15,010	5	12,490 R	64.7%	35.3%	64.7%	35.3%
72,831	OZAUKEE	21,272	16,078	5,193	1	10,885 R	75.6%	24.4%	75.6%	24.4%
7,107	PEPIN	2,054	1,047	1,006	1	41 R	51.0%	49.0%	51.0%	49.0%
32,765	PIERCE	8,620	4,809	3,806	5	1,003 R	55.8%	44.2%	55.8%	44.2%
34,773	POLK	10,492	5,779	4,711	2	1,068 R	55.1%	44.9%	55.1%	44.9%
61,405	PORTAGE	15,495	7,976	7,514	5	462 R	51.5%	48.5%	51.5%	48.5%
15,600	PRICE	6,545	3,592	2,949	4	643 R	54.9%	45.1%	54.9%	45.1%
175,034	RACINE	47,561	29,318	18,243		11,075 R	61.6%	38.4%	61.6%	38.4%
17,521	RICHLAND	4,344	2,666	1,678		988 R	61.4%	38.6%	61.4%	38.6%
139,510	ROCK	36,233	19,979	16,231	23	3,748 R	55.1%	44.8%	55.2%	44.8%
15,079	RUSK	5,220	2,697	2,523		174 R	51.7%	48.3%	51.7%	48.3%
50,251	ST. CROIX	13,213	7,052	6,158	3	894 R	53.4%	46.6%	53.4%	46.6%
46,975	SAUK	13,655	8,191	5,458	6	2,733 R	60.0%	40.0%	60.0%	40.0%
14,181	SAWYER	4,291	2,530	1,757	4	773 R	59.0%	40.9%	59.0%	41.0%
37,157	SHAWANO	10,397	6,690	3,705	2	2,985 R	64.3%	35.6%	64.4%	35.6%
103,877	SHEBOYGAN	31,026	18,903	12,118	5	6,785 R	60.9%	39.1%	60.9%	39.1%

WISCONSIN

GOVERNOR 1990

1990 Census Population	County	Total Vote	Republican	Democratic	Other	Rep.-Dem. Plurality	Percentage Total Vote Rep.	Dem.	Major Vote Rep.	Dem.
18,901	TAYLOR	5,728	3,280	2,443	5	837 R	57.3%	42.7%	57.3%	42.7%
25,263	TREMPEALEAU	7,452	3,566	3,878	8	312 D	47.9%	52.0%	47.9%	52.1%
25,617	VERNON	7,377	3,945	3,426	6	519 R	53.5%	46.4%	53.5%	46.5%
17,707	VILAS	7,338	5,003	2,331	4	2,672 R	68.2%	31.8%	68.2%	31.8%
75,000	WALWORTH	18,387	11,937	6,447	3	5,490 R	64.9%	35.1%	64.9%	35.1%
13,772	WASHBURN	4,946	2,743	2,201	2	542 R	55.5%	44.5%	55.5%	44.5%
95,328	WASHINGTON	22,645	15,983	6,662		9,321 R	70.6%	29.4%	70.6%	29.4%
304,715	WAUKESHA	85,694	61,002	24,679	13	36,323 R	71.2%	28.8%	71.2%	28.8%
46,104	WAUPACA	10,856	7,227	3,619	10	3,608 R	66.6%	33.3%	66.6%	33.4%
19,385	WAUSHARA	5,198	3,300	1,896	2	1,404 R	63.5%	36.5%	63.5%	36.5%
140,320	WINNEBAGO	40,216	25,972	14,187	57	11,785 R	64.6%	35.3%	64.7%	35.3%
73,605	WOOD	19,351	11,540	7,811		3,729 R	59.6%	40.4%	59.6%	40.4%
4,891,769	TOTAL	1,379,727	802,321	576,280	1,126	226,041 R	58.2%	41.8%	58.2%	41.8%

WISCONSIN

CONGRESS

CD	Year	Total Vote	Republican Vote	Republican Candidate	Democratic Vote	Democratic Candidate	Other Vote	Rep.-Dem. Plurality	Total Vote Rep.	Total Vote Dem.	Major Vote Rep.	Major Vote Dem.
1	1990	94,539			93,961	ASPIN, LES	578	93,961 D		99.4%		100.0%
1	1988	208,176	49,620	WEAVER, BERNARD J.	158,552	ASPIN, LES	4	108,932 D	23.8%	76.2%	23.8%	76.2%
1	1986	143,139	34,495	PETERSON, IRIS	106,288	ASPIN, LES	2,356	71,793 D	24.1%	74.3%	24.5%	75.5%
1	1984	226,264	99,080	JANSSON, PETER N.	127,184	ASPIN, LES		28,104 D	43.8%	56.2%	43.8%	56.2%
1	1982	155,804	59,309	JANSSON, PETER N.	95,055	ASPIN, LES	1,440	35,746 D	38.1%	61.0%	38.4%	61.6%
2	1990	182,118	96,938	KLUG, SCOTT L.	85,156	KASTENMEIER, ROBERT	24	11,782 R	53.2%	46.8%	53.2%	46.8%
2	1988	258,977	107,457	HANEY, ANN J.	151,501	KASTENMEIER, ROBERT	19	44,044 D	41.5%	58.5%	41.5%	58.5%
2	1986	192,535	85,156	HANEY, ANN J.	106,919	KASTENMEIER, ROBERT	460	21,763 D	44.2%	55.5%	44.3%	55.7%
2	1984	251,357	91,345	WILEY, ALBERT E.	159,987	KASTENMEIER, ROBERT	25	68,642 D	36.3%	63.6%	36.3%	63.7%
2	1982	186,045	71,989	JOHNSON, JIM	112,677	KASTENMEIER, ROBERT	1,379	40,688 D	38.7%	60.6%	39.0%	61.0%
3	1990	154,935	94,509	GUNDERSON, STEVEN	60,409	ZIEGEWEID, JAMES L.	17	34,100 R	61.0%	39.0%	61.0%	39.0%
3	1988	230,467	157,513	GUNDERSON, STEVEN	72,935	KRUEGER, KARL E.	19	84,578 R	68.3%	31.6%	68.4%	31.6%
3	1986	162,869	104,393	GUNDERSON, STEVEN	58,445	MULDER, LELAND E.	31	45,948 R	64.1%	35.9%	64.1%	35.9%
3	1984	234,695	160,437	GUNDERSON, STEVEN	74,253	DAHL, CHARLES F.	5	86,184 R	68.4%	31.6%	68.4%	31.6%
3	1982	175,465	99,304	GUNDERSON, STEVEN	75,132	OFFNER, PAUL	1,029	24,172 R	56.6%	42.8%	56.9%	43.1%
4	1990	140,221	43,001	COOK, JOSEPH L.	96,981	KLECZKA, GERALD D.	239	53,980 D	30.7%	69.2%	30.7%	69.3%
4	1988	177,892			177,283	KLECZKA, GERALD D.	609	177,283 D		99.7%		100.0%
4	1986	120,803			120,354	KLECZKA, GERALD D.	449	120,354 D		99.6%		100.0%
4	1984	238,222	78,056	NOLAN, ROBERT V.	158,722	KLECZKA, GERALD D.	1,444	80,666 D	32.8%	66.6%	33.0%	67.0%
4	1982	137,024			129,557	ZABLOCKI, CLEMENT J.	7,467	129,557 D		94.6%		100.0%
5	1990	114,115	31,255	HAMMERSMITH, DONALDA A.	77,557	MOODY, JIM	5,303	46,302 D	27.4%	68.0%	28.7%	71.3%
5	1988	219,179	78,307	BARNHILL, HELEN I.	140,518	MOODY, JIM	354	62,211 D	35.7%	64.1%	35.8%	64.2%
5	1986	110,604			109,506	MOODY, JIM	1,098	109,506 D		99.0%		100.0%
5	1984	178,819			175,243	MOODY, JIM	3,576	175,243 D		98.0%		100.0%
5	1982	156,921	54,826	JOHNSTON, ROD K.	99,713	MOODY, JIM	2,382	44,887 D	34.9%	63.5%	35.5%	64.5%
6	1990	111,556	111,036	PETRI, THOMAS E.			520	111,036 R	99.5%		100.0%	
6	1988	223,495	165,923	PETRI, THOMAS E.	57,552	GARRETT, JOSEPH	20	108,371 R	74.2%	25.8%	74.2%	25.8%
6	1986	128,639	124,328	PETRI, THOMAS E.			4,311	124,328 R	96.6%		100.0%	
6	1984	224,546	170,271	PETRI, THOMAS E.	54,266	IAQUINTA, DAVID L.	9	116,005 R	75.8%	24.2%	75.8%	24.2%
6	1982	171,283	111,348	PETRI, THOMAS E.	59,922	LOEHR, GORDON E.	13	51,426 R	65.0%	35.0%	65.0%	35.0%
7	1990	161,041	60,961	MCEWEN, JOHN L.	100,069	OBEY, DAVID R.	11	39,108 D	37.9%	62.1%	37.9%	62.1%
7	1988	230,179	86,077	HERMENING, KEVIN J.	142,197	OBEY, DAVID R.	1,905	56,120 D	37.4%	61.8%	37.7%	62.3%
7	1986	171,712	63,408	HERMENING, KEVIN J.	106,700	OBEY, DAVID R.	1,604	43,292 D	36.9%	62.1%	37.3%	62.7%
7	1984	238,652	92,507	MICHAELSEN, MARK G.	146,131	OBEY, DAVID R.	14	53,624 D	38.8%	61.2%	38.8%	61.2%
7	1982	179,668	57,535	ZIMMERMANN, BERNARD A.	122,124	OBEY, DAVID R.	9	64,589 D	32.0%	68.0%	32.0%	68.0%
8	1990	179,142	95,902	ROTH, TOBY	83,199	VAN SISTINE, JEROME	41	12,703 R	53.5%	46.4%	53.5%	46.5%
8	1988	240,013	167,275	ROTH, TOBY	72,708	BARON, ROBERT A.	30	94,567 R	69.7%	30.3%	69.7%	30.3%
8	1986	175,432	118,162	ROTH, TOBY	57,265	WILLEMS, PAUL	5	60,897 R	67.4%	32.6%	67.4%	32.6%
8	1984	237,107	161,005	ROTH, TOBY	73,090	WILLEMS, PAUL	3,012	87,915 R	67.9%	30.8%	68.8%	31.2%
8	1982	177,152	101,379	ROTH, TOBY	74,436	CLUSEN, RUTH C.	1,337	26,943 R	57.2%	42.0%	57.7%	42.3%
9	1990	118,321	117,967	SENSENBRENNER, F. JAMES			354	117,967 R	99.7%		100.0%	
9	1988	247,104	185,093	SENSENBRENNER, F. JAMES	62,003	HICKEY, THOMAS J.	8	123,090 R	74.9%	25.1%	74.9%	25.1%
9	1986	177,408	138,766	SENSENBRENNER, F. JAMES	38,636	POPP, THOMAS G.	6	100,130 R	78.2%	21.8%	78.2%	21.8%
9	1984	245,716	180,247	SENSENBRENNER, F. JAMES	64,157	KRAUSE, JOHN	1,312	116,090 R	73.4%	26.1%	73.7%	26.3%
9	1982	111,570	111,503	SENSENBRENNER, F. JAMES			67	111,503 R	99.9%		100.0%	

WISCONSIN

1990 GENERAL ELECTION

Governor   Other vote was scattered write-in.

Congress   Other vote was 4,968 Independent (Stampley) and 335 scattered write-in in CD 5; scattered write-in in all other CD's.

1990 PRIMARIES

SEPTEMBER 11 REPUBLICAN

Governor   201,467 Tommy G. Thompson; 11,230 Bennett A. Masel; 4,665 Edmond Hou-Seye; 8 Willie G. Lovelace (write-in); 353 scattered write-in.

Congress   Unopposed in seven CD's. No candidate in CD 1. Contested as follows:

   CD 8   36,818 Toby Roth; 9,935 David J. Hemes; 3 scattered write-in.

SEPTEMBER 11 DEMOCRATIC

Governor   Thomas Loftus, unopposed.

Congress   Unopposed in four CD's. No candidate in CD's 6 and 9. Contested as follows:

   CD 1   16,781 Les Aspin; 2,706 Charles A. Olson; 4 scattered write-in.
   CD 4   19,725 Gerald D. Kleczka; 2,955 Daniel Slak; 1,664 Roman R. Blenski; 10 scattered write-in.
   CD 5   16,995 Jim Moody; 4,585 Peter Y. Taylor; 76 scattered write-in.

WYOMING

GOVERNOR
Mike Sullivan (D). Re-elected 1990 to a four-year term. Previously elected 1986.

SENATORS
Alan K. Simpson (R). Re-elected 1990 to a six-year term. Previously elected 1984, 1978.

Malcolm Wallop (R). Re-elected 1988 to a six-year term. Previously elected 1982, 1976.

REPRESENTATIVES
At-Large. Craig Thomas (R)

POSTWAR VOTE FOR PRESIDENT

		Republican		Democratic		Other		Percentage Total Vote		Major Vote	
Year	Total Vote	Vote	Candidate	Vote	Candidate	Vote	Plurality	Rep.	Dem.	Rep.	Dem.
1988	176,551	106,867	Bush, George	67,113	Dukakis, Michael S.	2,571	39,754 R	60.5%	38.0%	61.4%	38.6%
1984	188,968	133,241	Reagan, Ronald	53,370	Mondale, Walter F.	2,357	79,871 R	70.5%	28.2%	71.4%	28.6%
1980	176,713	110,700	Reagan, Ronald	49,427	Carter, Jimmy	16,586	61,273 R	62.6%	28.0%	69.1%	30.9%
1976	156,343	92,717	Ford, Gerald R.	62,239	Carter, Jimmy	1,387	30,478 R	59.3%	39.8%	59.8%	40.2%
1972	145,570	100,464	Nixon, Richard M.	44,358	McGovern, George S.	748	56,106 R	69.0%	30.5%	69.4%	30.6%
1968	127,205	70,927	Nixon, Richard M.	45,173	Humphrey, Hubert H.	11,105	25,754 R	55.8%	35.5%	61.1%	38.9%
1964	142,716	61,998	Goldwater, Barry M.	80,718	Johnson, Lyndon B.		18,720 D	43.4%	56.6%	43.4%	56.6%
1960	140,782	77,451	Nixon, Richard M.	63,331	Kennedy, John F.		14,120 R	55.0%	45.0%	55.0%	45.0%
1956	124,127	74,573	Eisenhower, Dwight D.	49,554	Stevenson, Adlai E.		25,019 R	60.1%	39.9%	60.1%	39.9%
1952	129,253	81,049	Eisenhower, Dwight D.	47,934	Stevenson, Adlai E.	270	33,115 R	62.7%	37.1%	62.8%	37.2%
1948	101,425	47,947	Dewey, Thomas E.	52,354	Truman, Harry S.	1,124	4,407 D	47.3%	51.6%	47.8%	52.2%

POSTWAR VOTE FOR GOVERNOR

		Republican		Democratic		Other	Rep-Dem.	Percentage Total Vote		Major Vote	
Year	Total Vote	Vote	Candidate	Vote	Candidate	Vote	Plurality	Rep.	Dem.	Rep.	Dem.
1990	160,109	55,471	Mead, Mary	104,638	Sullivan, Mike		49,167 D	34.6%	65.4%	34.6%	65.4%
1986	164,720	75,841	Simpson, Peter	88,879	Sullivan, Mike		13,038 D	46.0%	54.0%	46.0%	54.0%
1982	168,555	62,128	Morton, Warren A.	106,427	Herschler, Ed		44,299 D	36.9%	63.1%	36.9%	63.1%
1978	137,567	67,595	Ostlund, John C.	69,972	Herschler, Ed		2,377 D	49.1%	50.9%	49.1%	50.9%
1974	128,386	56,645	Jones, Dick	71,741	Herschler, Ed		15,096 D	44.1%	55.9%	44.1%	55.9%
1970	118,257	74,249	Hathaway, Stan	44,008	Rooney, John J.		30,241 R	62.8%	37.2%	62.8%	37.2%
1966	120,873	65,624	Hathaway, Stan	55,249	Wilkerson, Ernest		10,375 R	54.3%	45.7%	54.3%	45.7%
1962	119,268	64,970	Hansen, Clifford P.	54,298	Gage, Jack R.		10,672 R	54.5%	45.5%	54.5%	45.5%
1958	112,537	52,488	Simpson, Milward L.	55,070	Hickey, J. J.	4,979	2,582 D	46.6%	48.9%	48.8%	51.2%
1954	111,438	56,275	Simpson, Milward L.	55,163	Jack, William		1,112 R	50.5%	49.5%	50.5%	49.5%
1950	96,959	54,441	Barrett, Frank A.	42,518	McIntyre, John J.		11,923 R	56.1%	43.9%	56.1%	43.9%
1946	81,353	38,333	Wright, Earl	43,020	Hunt, Lester C.		4,687 D	47.1%	52.9%	47.1%	52.9%

WYOMING

POSTWAR VOTE FOR SENATOR

Year	Total Vote	Republican Vote	Republican Candidate	Democratic Vote	Democratic Candidate	Other Vote	Rep.-Dem. Plurality	Total Vote Rep.	Total Vote Dem.	Major Vote Rep.	Major Vote Dem.
1990	157,632	100,784	Simpson, Alan K.	56,848	Helling, Kathy		43,936 R	63.9%	36.1%	63.9%	36.1%
1988	180,964	91,143	Wallop, Malcolm	89,821	Vinich, John P.		1,322 R	50.4%	49.6%	50.4%	49.6%
1984	186,898	146,373	Simpson, Alan K.	40,525	Ryan, Victor A.		105,848 R	78.3%	21.7%	78.3%	21.7%
1982	167,191	94,725	Wallop, Malcolm	72,466	McDaniel, Rodger		22,259 R	56.7%	43.3%	56.7%	43.3%
1978	133,364	82,908	Simpson, Alan K.	50,456	Whitaker, Raymond B.		32,452 R	62.2%	37.8%	62.2%	37.8%
1976	155,368	84,810	Wallop, Malcolm	70,558	McGee, Gale		14,252 R	54.6%	45.4%	54.6%	45.4%
1972	142,067	101,314	Hansen, Clifford P.	40,753	Vinich, Mike		60,561 R	71.3%	28.7%	71.3%	28.7%
1970	120,486	53,279	Wold, John S.	67,207	McGee, Gale		13,928 D	44.2%	55.8%	44.2%	55.8%
1966	122,689	63,548	Hansen, Clifford P.	59,141	Roncalio, Teno		4,407 R	51.8%	48.2%	51.8%	48.2%
1964	141,670	65,185	Wold, John S.	76,485	McGee, Gale		11,300 D	46.0%	54.0%	46.0%	54.0%
1962 S	119,372	69,043	Simpson, Milward L.	50,329	Hickey, J. J.		18,714 R	57.8%	42.2%	57.8%	42.2%
1960	138,550	78,103	Thomson, E. Keith	60,447	Whitaker, Ray		17,656 R	56.4%	43.6%	56.4%	43.6%
1958	114,157	56,122	Barrett, Frank A.	58,035	McGee, Gale		1,913 D	49.2%	50.8%	49.2%	50.8%
1954	112,252	54,407	Harrison, William H.	57,845	O'Mahoney, Joseph C.		3,438 D	48.5%	51.5%	48.5%	51.5%
1952	130,097	67,176	Barrett, Frank A.	62,921	O'Mahoney, Joseph C.		4,255 R	51.6%	48.4%	51.6%	48.4%
1948	101,480	43,527	Robertson, Edward V.	57,953	Hunt, Lester C.		14,426 D	42.9%	57.1%	42.9%	57.1%
1946	81,557	35,714	Henderson, Harry B.	45,843	O'Mahoney, Joseph C.		10,129 D	43.8%	56.2%	43.8%	56.2%

The 1962 election was for a short term to fill a vacancy.

WYOMING

One At Large

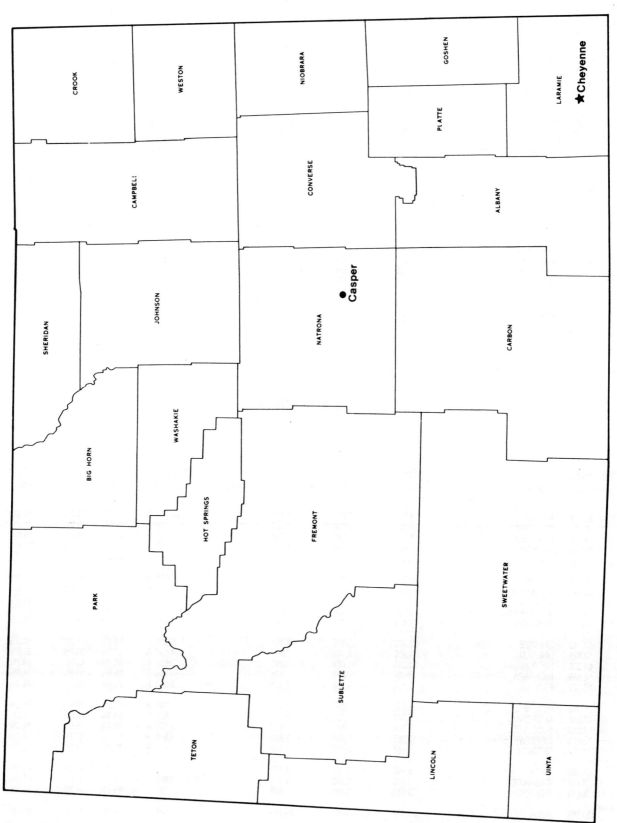

CROOK

WESTON

NIOBRARA

GOSHEN

LARAMIE

★Cheyenne

CAMPBELL

CONVERSE

PLATTE

ALBANY

SHERIDAN

JOHNSON

NATRONA

●Casper

CARBON

BIG HORN

WASHAKIE

HOT SPRINGS

FREMONT

SWEETWATER

PARK

SUBLETTE

TETON

LINCOLN

UINTA

WYOMING

GOVERNOR 1990

1990 Census Population	County	Total Vote	Republican	Democratic	Other	Rep.-Dem. Plurality	Total Vote Rep.	Dem.	Major Vote Rep.	Dem.
30,797	ALBANY	9,288	2,452	6,836		4,384 D	26.4%	73.6%	26.4%	73.6%
10,525	BIG HORN	4,146	1,506	2,640		1,134 D	36.3%	63.7%	36.3%	63.7%
29,370	CAMPBELL	8,399	4,155	4,244		89 D	49.5%	50.5%	49.5%	50.5%
16,659	CARBON	5,932	2,275	3,657		1,382 D	38.4%	61.6%	38.4%	61.6%
11,128	CONVERSE	3,884	1,358	2,526		1,168 D	35.0%	65.0%	35.0%	65.0%
5,294	CROOK	2,392	1,353	1,039		314 R	56.6%	43.4%	56.6%	43.4%
33,662	FREEMONT	11,627	3,724	7,903		4,179 D	32.0%	68.0%	32.0%	68.0%
12,373	GOSHEN	4,750	2,160	2,590		430 D	45.5%	54.5%	45.5%	54.5%
4,809	HOT SPRINGS	2,216	812	1,404		592 D	36.6%	63.4%	36.6%	63.4%
6,145	JOHNSON	2,650	1,233	1,417		184 D	46.5%	53.5%	46.5%	53.5%
73,142	LARAMIE	24,150	6,793	17,357		10,564 D	28.1%	71.9%	28.1%	71.9%
12,625	LINCOLN	4,756	2,129	2,627		498 D	44.8%	55.2%	44.8%	55.2%
61,226	NATRONA	21,557	5,512	16,045		10,533 D	25.6%	74.4%	25.6%	74.4%
2,499	NIOBRARA	1,203	584	619		35 D	48.5%	51.5%	48.5%	51.5%
23,178	PARK	8,465	2,814	5,651		2,837 D	33.2%	66.8%	33.2%	66.8%
8,145	PLATTE	3,689	1,244	2,445		1,201 D	33.7%	66.3%	33.7%	66.3%
23,562	SHERIDAN	9,448	3,601	5,847		2,246 D	38.1%	61.9%	38.1%	61.9%
4,843	SUBLETTE	2,232	1,035	1,197		162 D	46.4%	53.6%	46.4%	53.6%
38,823	SWEETWATER	12,183	3,541	8,642		5,101 D	29.1%	70.9%	29.1%	70.9%
11,172	TETON	5,614	2,204	3,410		1,206 D	39.3%	60.7%	39.3%	60.7%
18,705	UINTA	5,488	2,233	3,255		1,022 D	40.7%	59.3%	40.7%	59.3%
8,388	WASHAKIE	3,468	1,368	2,100		732 D	39.4%	60.6%	39.4%	60.6%
6,518	WESTON	2,572	1,385	1,187		198 R	53.8%	46.2%	53.8%	46.2%
453,588	TOTAL	160,109	55,471	104,638		49,167 D	34.6%	65.4%	34.6%	65.4%

WYOMING

SENATOR 1990

1990 Census Population	County	Total Vote	Republican	Democratic	Other	Rep.-Dem. Plurality	Total Vote Rep.	Dem.	Major Vote Rep.	Dem.
30,797	ALBANY	9,063	5,921	3,142		2,779 R	65.3%	34.7%	65.3%	34.7%
10,525	BIG HORN	4,130	2,934	1,196		1,738 R	71.0%	29.0%	71.0%	29.0%
29,370	CAMPBELL	8,299	5,696	2,603		3,093 R	68.6%	31.4%	68.6%	31.4%
16,659	CARBON	5,935	3,571	2,364		1,207 R	60.2%	39.8%	60.2%	39.8%
11,128	CONVERSE	3,877	2,482	1,395		1,087 R	64.0%	36.0%	64.0%	36.0%
5,294	CROOK	2,378	1,693	685		1,008 R	71.2%	28.8%	71.2%	28.8%
33,662	FREEMONT	11,327	7,072	4,255		2,817 R	62.4%	37.6%	62.4%	37.6%
12,373	GOSHEN	4,691	3,191	1,500		1,691 R	68.0%	32.0%	68.0%	32.0%
4,809	HOT SPRINGS	2,067	1,400	667		733 R	67.7%	32.3%	67.7%	32.3%
6,145	JOHNSON	2,440	1,834	606		1,228 R	75.2%	24.8%	75.2%	24.8%
73,142	LARAMIE	23,503	15,099	8,404		6,695 R	64.2%	35.8%	64.2%	35.8%
12,625	LINCOLN	4,690	3,143	1,547		1,596 R	67.0%	33.0%	67.0%	33.0%
61,226	NATRONA	21,255	12,054	9,201		2,853 R	56.7%	43.3%	56.7%	43.3%
2,499	NIOBRARA	1,199	821	378		443 R	68.5%	31.5%	68.5%	31.5%
23,178	PARK	8,579	6,555	2,024		4,531 R	76.4%	23.6%	76.4%	23.6%
8,145	PLATTE	3,661	2,205	1,456		749 R	60.2%	39.8%	60.2%	39.8%
23,562	SHERIDAN	9,360	5,525	3,835		1,690 R	59.0%	41.0%	59.0%	41.0%
4,843	SUBLETTE	2,206	1,641	565		1,076 R	74.4%	25.6%	74.4%	25.6%
38,823	SWEETWATER	12,085	6,562	5,523		1,039 R	54.3%	45.7%	54.3%	45.7%
11,172	TETON	5,466	3,947	1,519		2,428 R	72.2%	27.8%	72.2%	27.8%
18,705	UINTA	5,445	3,523	1,922		1,601 R	64.7%	35.3%	64.7%	35.3%
8,388	WASHAKIE	3,413	2,235	1,178		1,057 R	65.5%	34.5%	65.5%	34.5%
6,518	WESTON	2,563	1,680	883		797 R	65.5%	34.5%	65.5%	34.5%
453,588	TOTAL	157,632	100,784	56,848		43,936 R	63.9%	36.1%	63.9%	36.1%

WYOMING

CONGRESS

CD	Year	Total Vote	Republican Vote	Candidate	Democratic Vote	Candidate	Other Vote	Rep.-Dem. Plurality	Total Vote Rep.	Dem.	Major Vote Rep.	Dem.
AL	1990	158,055	87,078	THOMAS, CRAIG	70,977	MAXFIELD, PETE		16,101 R	55.1%	44.9%	55.1%	44.9%
AL	1988	177,651	118,350	CHENEY, RICHARD	56,527	SHARRATT, BRYAN	2,774	61,823 R	66.6%	31.8%	67.7%	32.3%
AL	1986	159,787	111,007	CHENEY, RICHARD	48,780	GILMORE, RICK		62,227 R	69.5%	30.5%	69.5%	30.5%
AL	1984	187,904	138,234	CHENEY, RICHARD	45,857	MCFADDEN, HUGH B.	3,813	92,377 R	73.6%	24.4%	75.1%	24.9%
AL	1982	159,277	113,236	CHENEY, RICHARD	46,041	HOMMEL, THEODORE H.		67,195 R	71.1%	28.9%	71.1%	28.9%
AL	1980	169,699	116,361	CHENEY, RICHARD	53,338	ROGERS, JIM		63,023 R	68.6%	31.4%	68.6%	31.4%
AL	1978	129,377	75,855	CHENEY, RICHARD	53,522	BAGLEY, BILL		22,333 R	58.6%	41.4%	58.6%	41.4%
AL	1976	151,868	66,147	HART, LARRY	85,721	RONCALIO, TENO		19,574 D	43.6%	56.4%	43.6%	56.4%
AL	1974	126,933	57,499	STROOCK, TOM	69,434	RONCALIO, TENO		11,935 D	45.3%	54.7%	45.3%	54.7%
AL	1972	146,299	70,667	KIDD, WILLIAM	75,632	RONCALIO, TENO		4,965 D	48.3%	51.7%	48.3%	51.7%
AL	1970	116,304	57,848	ROBERTS, HARRY	58,456	RONCALIO, TENO		608 D	49.7%	50.3%	49.7%	50.3%
AL	1968	123,313	77,363	WOLD, JOHN S.	45,950	LINFORD, VELMA		31,413 R	62.7%	37.3%	62.7%	37.3%
AL	1966	119,426	62,984	HARRISON, WILLIAM H.	56,442	CHRISTIAN, AL		6,542 R	52.7%	47.3%	52.7%	47.3%
AL	1964	139,175	68,482	HARRISON, WILLIAM H.	70,693	RONCALIO, TENO		2,211 D	49.2%	50.8%	49.2%	50.8%
AL	1962	116,474	71,489	HARRISON, WILLIAM H.	44,985	MANKUS, LOUIS A.		26,504 R	61.4%	38.6%	61.4%	38.6%
AL	1960	134,331	70,241	HARRISON, WILLIAM H.	64,090	ARMSTRONG, H. T		6,151 R	52.3%	47.7%	52.3%	47.7%
AL	1958	111,780	59,894	THOMSON, E. KEITH	51,886	WHITAKER, RAY		8,008 R	53.6%	46.4%	53.6%	46.4%
AL	1956	120,128	69,903	THOMSON, E. KEITH	50,225	O'CALLAGHAN, JERRY		19,678 R	58.2%	41.8%	58.2%	41.8%
AL	1954	108,771	61,111	THOMSON, E. KEITH	47,660	TULLY, SAM		13,451 R	56.2%	43.8%	56.2%	43.8%
AL	1952	126,720	76,161	HARRISON, WILLIAM H.	50,559	ROSE, ROBERT R.		25,602 R	60.1%	39.9%	60.1%	39.9%
AL	1950	93,348	50,865	HARRISON, WILLIAM H.	42,483	CLARK, JOHN B.		8,382 R	54.5%	45.5%	54.5%	45.5%
AL	1948	97,464	50,218	BARRETT, FRANK A.	47,246	FLANNERY, L. G.		2,972 R	51.5%	48.5%	51.5%	48.5%
AL	1946	79,438	44,482	BARRETT, FRANK A.	34,956	MCINTYRE, JOHN J.		9,526 R	56.0%	44.0%	56.0%	44.0%

WYOMING

1990 GENERAL ELECTION

Governor

Senator

Congress

1990 PRIMARIES

AUGUST 21 REPUBLICAN

Governor   51,160 Mary Mead; 24,916 Nyla Murphy.

Senator   69,142 Alan K. Simpson; 6,577 Nora M. Lewis; 6,201 Douglas W. Crook.

Congress   Unopposed at-large.

AUGUST 21 DEMOCRATIC

Governor   38,447 Mike Sullivan; 5,026 Ron Clingman.

Senator   12,103 Kathy Helling; 7,196 Howard O'Connor; 6,483 Al Hamburg; 4,455 Emmett Jones; 2,291 Dale Bulman; 1,983 Don C. Jolliffe.

Congress   Unopposed at-large.

DISTRICT OF COLUMBIA

GOVERNMENT
The District of Columbia is governed by a Mayor and City Council of thirteen.

MAYOR
Sharon Pratt Dixon (D). Elected 1990 to a four year term.

DELEGATE
Eleanor Holmes Norton (D)

POSTWAR VOTE FOR PRESIDENT

Year	Total Vote	Republican Vote	Candidate	Democratic Vote	Candidate	Other Vote	Plurality	Percentage Total Vote Rep.	Dem.	Major Vote Rep.	Dem.
1988	192,877	27,590	Bush, George	159,407	Dukakis, Michael S.	5,880	131,817 D	14.3%	82.6%	14.8%	85.2%
1984	211,288	29,009	Reagan, Ronald	180,408	Mondale, Walter F.	1,871	151,399 D	13.7%	85.4%	13.9%	86.1%
1980	175,237	23,545	Reagan, Ronald	131,113	Carter, Jimmy	20,579	107,568 D	13.4%	74.8%	15.2%	84.8%
1976	168,830	27,873	Ford, Gerald R.	137,818	Carter, Jimmy	3,139	109,945 D	16.5%	81.6%	16.8%	83.2%
1972	163,421	35,226	Nixon, Richard M.	127,627	McGovern, George S.	568	92,401 D	21.6%	78.1%	21.6%	78.4%
1968	170,578	31,012	Nixon, Richard M.	139,566	Humphrey, Hubert H.		108,554 D	18.2%	81.8%	18.2%	81.8%
1964	198,597	28,801	Goldwater, Barry M.	169,796	Johnson, Lyndon B.		140,995 D	14.5%	85.5%	14.5%	85.5%

Under the 23rd Amendment to the Constitution, the District of Columbia became entitled to choose Electors beginning with the 1964 election.

POSTWAR VOTE FOR MAYOR

Year	Total Vote	Republican Vote	Candidate	Democratic Vote	Candidate	Other Vote	Rep-Dem. Plurality	Percentage Total Vote Rep.	Dem.	Major Vote Rep.	Dem.
1990	169,066	19,764	Turner, Maurice T.	144,701	Dixon, Sharon Pratt	4,601	124,937 D	11.7%	85.6%	12.0%	88.0%
1986	131,802	43,676	Schwartz, Carol	80,666	Barry, Marion	7,460	36,990 D	33.1%	61.2%	35.1%	64.9%
1982	117,623	16,501	Lee, E. Brooke	95,007	Barry, Marion	6,115	78,506 D	14.0%	80.8%	14.8%	85.2%
1978	100,861	28,032	Fletcher, Arthur	69,888	Barry, Marion	2,941	41,856 D	27.8%	69.3%	28.6%	71.4%
1974	105,183	3,703	Champion, Jackson R.	84,676	Washington, Walter E.	16,804	80,973 D	3.5%	80.5%	4.2%	95.8%

DISTRICT OF COLUMBIA

POSTWAR VOTE FOR DELEGATE

Year	Total Vote	Republican Vote	Candidate	Democratic Vote	Candidate	Other Vote	Rep-Dem. Plurality	Percentage Total Vote Rep.	Dem.	Major Vote Rep.	Dem.
1990	159,627	41,999	Singleton, Harry M.	98,442	Norton, Eleanor Holmes	19,186	56,443 D	26.3%	61.7%	29.9%	70.1%
1988	170,933	22,936	Reed, William	121,817	Fauntroy, Walter E.	26,180	98,881 D	13.4%	71.3%	15.8%	84.2%
1986	126,855	17,643	King, Mary L. H.	101,604	Fauntroy, Walter E.	7,608	83,961 D	13.9%	80.1%	14.8%	85.2%
1984 * *	161,771	—		154,583	Fauntroy, Walter E.	7,188	154,583 D		95.6%		100.0%
1982	112,543	17,242	West, John	93,422	Fauntroy, Walter E.	1,879	76,180 D	15.3%	83.0%	15.6%	84.4%
1980	151,046	21,245	Roehr, Robert J.	112,339	Fauntroy, Walter E.	17,462	91,094 D	14.1%	74.4%	15.9%	84.1%
1978	96,306	11,677	Champion, Jackson R.	76,557	Fauntroy, Walter E.	8,072	64,880 D	12.1%	79.5%	13.2%	86.8%
1976	159,790	21,699	Hall, Daniel L.	123,464	Fauntroy, Walter E.	14,627	101,765 D	13.6%	77.3%	14.9%	85.1%
1974	104,014	9,166	Phillips, William R.	66,337	Fauntroy, Walter E.	28,511	57,171 D	8.8%	63.8%	12.1%	87.9%
1972	159,612	39,487	Chin-Lee, William	95,300	Fauntroy, Walter E.	24,825	55,813 D	24.7%	59.7%	29.3%	70.7%
1971 S	116,635	29,249	Nevius, John A.	68,166	Fauntroy, Walter E.	19,220	38,917 D	25.1%	58.4%	30.0%	70.0%

The 1971 election was held in March for a short term to the end of the 92nd Congress. In 1984 the Democratic candidate was also the nominee of the Republican and Statehood parties.

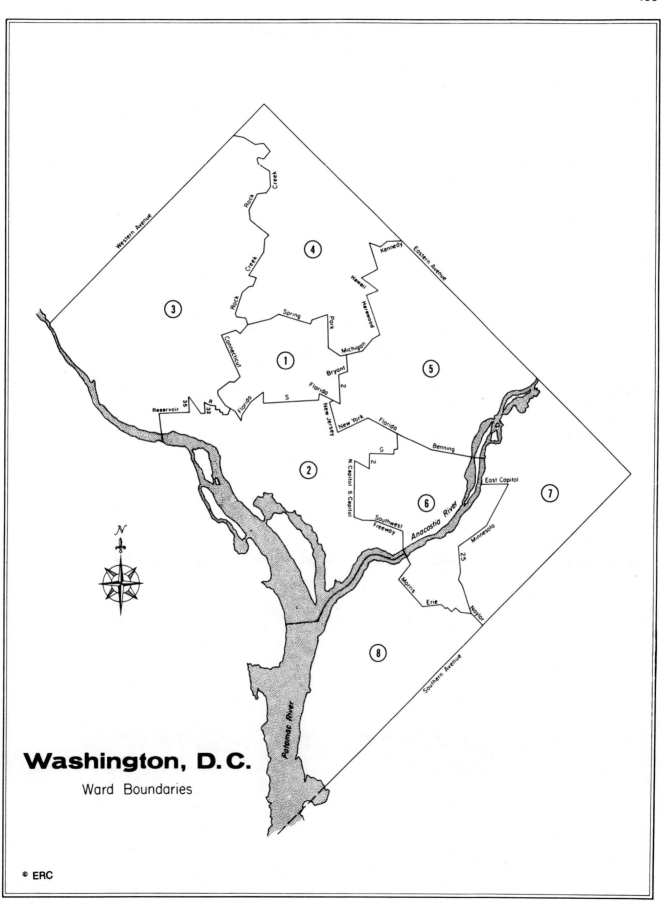

Washington, D.C.

Ward Boundaries

486

DISTRICT OF COLUMBIA

MAYOR 1990

1990 Census Population	Ward	Total Vote	Republican	Democratic	Other	Rep.-Dem. Plurality	Percentage Total Vote Rep.	Dem.	Major Vote Rep.	Dem.
	WARD 1	18,744	1,859	16,207	678	14,348 D	9.9%	86.5%	10.3%	89.7%
	WARD 2	19,564	2,663	16,215	686	13,552 D	13.6%	82.9%	14.1%	85.9%
	WARD 3	29,842	5,246	23,921	675	18,675 D	17.6%	80.2%	18.0%	82.0%
	WARD 4	26,699	2,652	23,393	654	20,741 D	9.9%	87.6%	10.2%	89.8%
	WARD 5	23,131	2,175	20,386	570	18,211 D	9.4%	88.1%	9.6%	90.4%
	WARD 6	20,808	2,194	18,053	561	15,859 D	10.5%	86.8%	10.8%	89.2%
	WARD 7	19,728	1,944	17,294	490	15,350 D	9.9%	87.7%	10.1%	89.9%
	WARD 8	10,550	1,031	9,232	287	8,201 D	9.8%	87.5%	10.0%	90.0%
606,900	TOTAL	169,066	19,764	144,701	4,601	124,937 D	11.7%	85.6%	12.0%	88.0%

DISTRICT OF COLUMBIA

DELEGATE 1990

1990 Census Population	Ward	Total Vote	Republican	Democratic	Other	Rep.-Dem. Plurality	Percentage Total Vote Rep.	Dem.	Major Vote Rep.	Dem.
	WARD 1	17,596	4,447	10,716	2,433	6,269 D	25.3%	60.9%	29.3%	70.7%
	WARD 2	18,432	7,090	9,110	2,232	2,020 D	38.5%	49.4%	43.8%	56.2%
	WARD 3	27,774	17,480	6,871	3,423	10,609 R	62.9%	24.7%	71.8%	28.2%
	WARD 4	25,374	3,499	19,005	2,870	15,506 D	13.8%	74.9%	15.5%	84.5%
	WARD 5	21,899	2,524	16,957	2,418	14,433 D	11.5%	77.4%	13.0%	87.0%
	WARD 6	19,700	4,747	12,546	2,407	7,799 D	24.1%	63.7%	27.5%	72.5%
	WARD 7	18,791	1,669	14,740	2,382	13,071 D	8.9%	78.4%	10.2%	89.8%
	WARD 8	10,033	536	8,479	1,018	7,943 D	5.3%	84.5%	5.9%	94.1%
	FEDERAL BALLOTS	28	7	18	3	11 D	25.0%	64.3%	28.0%	72.0%
606,900	TOTAL	159,627	41,999	98,442	19,186	56,443 D	26.3%	61.7%	29.9%	70.1%

DISTRICT OF COLUMBIA

1990 Population figures not available by wards for the District.

1990 GENERAL ELECTION

Mayor   Other vote was 1,163 Statehood (Frost); 980 Libertarian (Lord); 661 Independent (Cox); 325 Independent (Moore); 309 Independent (Brooks); 195 Independent (Carter); 187 Socialist Workers (Nahem); 142 Independent (Thorpe); 113 Independent (Faith) and 526 scattered write-in.

Delegate   Other vote was 8,156 Independent (Cure); 4,027 Statehood (Hunt); 3,334 Independent (Dabney) and 3,669 scattered write-in.

1990 PRIMARIES

SEPTEMBER 11 REPUBLICAN

Mayor   Maurice T. Turner, unopposed.

Delegate   4,107 Harry M. Singleton; 1,372 Jim Champagne; 487 Roffle M. Miller; 320 scattered write-in.

SEPTEMBER 11 DEMOCRATIC

Mayor   43,426 Sharon Pratt Dixon; 32,255 John Ray; 27,083 Charlene Drew Jarvis; 13,768 David A. Clarke; 9,261 Walter E. Fauntroy; 555 scattered write-in.

Delegate   48,352 Eleanor Holmes Norton; 40,695 Betty Ann Kane; 12,882 Sterling Tucker; 8,379 Joseph P. Yeldell; 7,717 Donald M. Temple; 2,233 B. L. Simmons; 1,425 George X. Cure; 786 scattered write-in.

SEPTEMBER 11 STATEHOOD

Mayor   Alvin C. Frost, unopposed.

Delegate   No candidate names appeared on the ballot; there were 252 write-in votes and Leon F. Hunt became the nominee by write-in votes.